# BIOLOGICAL ANTHROPOLOGY and PREHISTORY

## EXPLORING OUR HUMAN ANCESTRY

**Second Edition**

**Patricia C. Rice**
*West Virginia University*

**Norah Moloney**
*University College London*

PEARSON

Boston    New York    San Francisco
Mexico City    Montreal    Toronto    London    Madrid    Munich    Paris
Hong Kong    Singapore    Tokyo    Cape Town    Sydney

D0066601

*Senior Acquisitions Editor:* Dave Repetto
*Editorial Assistant:* Jack Cashman
*Marketing Manager:* Laura Lee Manley
*Production Supervisor:* Roberta Sherman
*Editorial Production Service:* Lifland et al., Bookmakers
*Composition Buyer:* Linda Cox
*Manufacturing Buyer:* Debbie Rossi
*Electronic Composition:* Modern Graphics, Inc.
*Interior Design:* Carol Somberg
*Photo Researcher:* Naomi Rudov
*Cover Administrator:* Linda Knowles

For related titles and support materials, visit our online catalog at www.ablongman.com.

Copyright © 2008 Pearson Education, Inc.

All rights reserved. No part of the material protected by this copyright notice may be reproduced or utilized in any form or by any means, electronic or mechanical, including photocopying, recording, or by any information storage and retrieval system, without written permission from the copyright owner.

To obtain permission(s) to use material from this work, please submit a written request to Allyn and Bacon, Permissions Department, 75 Arlington Street, Boston, MA 02116 or fax your request to 617-848-7320.

Between the time website information is gathered and then published, it is not unusual for some sites to have closed. Also, the transcription of URLs can result in typographical errors. The publisher would appreciate notification where these errors occur so that they may be corrected in subsequent editions.

ISBN-13: 978-0-205-51926-2

**Library of Congress Cataloging-in-Publication Data**

Rice, Patricia C.
   Biological anthropology and prehistory : exploring our human ancestry / Patricia C. Rice, Norah Moloney. –2nd ed.
      p. cm.
   Includes bibliographical references and index.
   ISBN 0-205-51926-1
   1. Human evolution. 2. Fossil hominids. 3. Paleoanthropology. I. Moloney, N. (Norah) II. Rice, Patricia C. Introduction to biological anthropology and prehistory. III. Title.

   GN281.R52 2008
   599.93'8—dc22

                                                             2007039882

Printed in the United States of America

10 9 8 7 6 5 4 3 2 1 RRD-OH 11 10 09 08 07

Credits appear on page 566, which constitutes an extension of the copyright page.

# About the Authors

**PAT RICE** grew up in Rochester, New York. Her broad education began with a degree in international studies at Ohio State University (OSU). Her interests then turned to anthropology. In graduate school at OSU, she continued her generalist focus by training in cultural and biological anthropology. She later studied archaeology at the Institute of Archaeology, now part of University College London, and participated in numerous excavations in England and France.

Her initial research interests were in European prehistoric art: Venus statuettes, bone art, and cave art. She has led a number of Smithsonian trips to Spain and France, with a focus on cave art.

More recently, she turned to writing about teaching anthropology. She has written a hands-on laboratory manual of archaeology exercises for undergraduates and has coedited three books on teaching anthropology. She is presently the coeditor of the biannual *Strategies in Teaching Anthropology*, of which five volumes have been published so far. In 1991 she and David McCurdy inaugurated the journal *General Anthropology*, sponsored by the General Anthropology Division of the American Anthropological Association (AAA). She writes a semi-annual column titled "Paleoanthropology," which provides synopses of the major fossil and artifact finds during the previous 6 months.

Pat is a past president of the General Anthropology Division of the AAA and presents annual teaching workshops at AAA meetings. In 1999 she won the AAA's Outstanding Teacher award. She has taught at Ohio State University, Pennsylvania State University, and West Virginia University, where she is an Eberly Teaching Professor.

**NORAH MOLONEY** originally trained in England as a school teacher but developed an interest in archaeology during extended trips throughout the world. She undertook undergraduate work at the School of Extension Studies, Harvard University, Boston, and continued her graduate studies, receiving an MA and a PhD in prehistoric archaeology, at the Institute of Archaeology, University College London, where she has taught since 1994. She also currently lectures in archaeology at Birkbeck College, University of London, and has taught other archaeology courses at London Metropolitan University, Oxford Brookes University, and at school venues for the nonspecialist public. Norah greatly enjoys working with students and the general public, whose participation and enthusiasm, she firmly believes, reinforce and stimulate her own understanding and knowledge of archaeology. Norah's research interests are directed primarily toward stone tool analysis, with a particular—although not exclusive—emphasis on the Paleolithic. She is also interested in the early human occupation of Europe, Asia, and the Americas. She has participated in archaeological fieldwork projects in France, Spain, Portugal, Turkey, Jordan, Kazakstan, and Armenia. She is currently working on a Middle Paleolithic project in Nagorno Karabagh (Armenia) and an Upper Paleolithic project in Spain. Her publications include papers and edited books.

# Brief Contents

Preface . . . . . . . . . . . . . . . . . . . . . . . . . . . . . . . . . . . . . . . . . .xxi

**1** Introduction to Anthropology . . . . . . . . . . . . . . . . . . . . . . . . . .1

**2** Theories and Methods in Studying Biological Anthropology . . . . . .15

**3** Principles of Biological Evolution . . . . . . . . . . . . . . . . . . . . . . .38

**4** Macroevolution: First Life to Mammals . . . . . . . . . . . . . . . . . .74

**5** Primates in Evolution . . . . . . . . . . . . . . . . . . . . . . . . . . . . .100

**6** Early Hominids in Africa: *Australopithecus* and
*Homo habilis* . . . . . . . . . . . . . . . . . . . . . . . . . . . . . . . . . .131

**7** Later Hominids: *Homo erectus* and *Homo sapiens* . . . . . . . . . .168

**8** The Archaeology of Early Human Societies: Theories
and Methods in Studying Prehistoric Archaeology . . . . . . . . . .207

**9** The Emergence of Culture in Early Hominid Societies
in the Old World . . . . . . . . . . . . . . . . . . . . . . . . . . . . . . . .230

**10** Later Hunter-Gatherers and Early Farming
Societies in the Old World . . . . . . . . . . . . . . . . . . . . . . . . . .268

**11** Early States in the Old World . . . . . . . . . . . . . . . . . . . . . . .307

**12** Later Hunter-Gatherers and Early Farming Societies
in the Americas . . . . . . . . . . . . . . . . . . . . . . . . . . . . . . . .346

**13** The Emergence of State Societies in the Americas . . . . . . . . . . .382

**14** Primates Today . . . . . . . . . . . . . . . . . . . . . . . . . . . . . . . .421

**15** Contemporary Humans . . . . . . . . . . . . . . . . . . . . . . . . . . . .460

**16** Conclusions: Who Are We? . . . . . . . . . . . . . . . . . . . . . . . . .501

Glossary . . . . . . . . . . . . . . . . . . . . . . . . . . . . . . . . . . . . . .513

References . . . . . . . . . . . . . . . . . . . . . . . . . . . . . . . . . . . . .525

Name Index . . . . . . . . . . . . . . . . . . . . . . . . . . . . . . . . . . . .550

Subject Index . . . . . . . . . . . . . . . . . . . . . . . . . . . . . . . . . . .556

Credits . . . . . . . . . . . . . . . . . . . . . . . . . . . . . . . . . . . . . . .566

# Contents

## Chapter **1** Introduction to Anthropology

*page* **1**

An overview of anthropology and the study of our human past considers the nature of humans and important features of the field itself.

- ■ **THE NATURE OF HUMANS AND ANTHROPOLOGY** 2
- ■ **ANTHROPOLOGY AND ITS SUBFIELDS** 2
  - How Anthropologists Do Their Work 7
  - Anthropology Is Holistic 8
  - Anthropological Ethics 10

- ■ **HIGHLIGHT 1.1: IN THE ALPS WITH THE ICEMAN** 4
- ■ **HIGHLIGHT 1.2: IN THE NEWS: THE AFRICAN BURIAL GROUND IN NEW YORK CITY** 12
- **CHAPTER SUMMARY** 14
- **KEY WORDS** 14

# Chapter 2

## Theories and Methods in Studying Biological Anthropology

**Bioanthropologists use the scientific method and various paradigms and techniques to reconstruct the human past and its changes through time.**

■ **THE SCIENTIFIC METHOD (TSM)** 16

■ **COMMON SENSE, SCIENCE, AND RELIGION** 19

■ **WHY EXPERTS DISAGREE** 21
Observation and Age, Sex, Experience, and Culture 21
Paradigms 23

■ **BIOLOGICAL EVIDENCE** 24
Preservation of Bone: Fossilization 25
Preservation of DNA 26

■ **FINDING BIOLOGICAL SITES AND FOSSILS** 28
Provenience Problems 29

■ **DATING BIOLOGICAL EVIDENCE** 30
Dating Fossils 31
Dating Molecules 31
Ice and Marine Cores: Do They Date Fossils? 33

■ **ANALYSIS OF BIOLOGICAL EVIDENCE** 34

■ **HIGHLIGHT 2.1: POMPEII** 27

**CHAPTER SUMMARY** 36

**KEY WORDS** 37

**SUGGESTED READING** 37

# Chapter 3

## Principles of Biological Evolution

*page* **38**

**Using the general principles of biological evolution (inheritance, mutations, and natural selection—that is, the modern synthesis), bioanthropologists reconstruct evolutionary events.**

■ **WHAT IS EVOLUTION?** 39
Early Ideas about Evolution 40
Eighteenth-Century Ideas 41
Nineteenth-Century Ideas 42
Modern Synthesis 42

■ **THE TEMPO OF EVOLUTION** 59

■ **THE CAUSES OF EVOLUTION** 60
Evolutionary Mutations 60
Evolutionary Selection 61
Gene Flow 66
Genetic Drift 66

■ **WHAT REALLY EVOLVES?** 68
The Species 68

The Genus and Subspecies 69
Speciation 70
Paleospecies and the ESC 71

■ **HIGHLIGHT 3.1: IN MENDEL'S GARDEN** 44

■ **HIGHLIGHT 3.2: IN THE NEWS: ICELAND AND THE HUMAN GENOME** 52

■ **HIGHLIGHT 3.3: IN THE GALAPAGOS ISLANDS WITH DARWIN AND HIS FINCHES** 62

**CHAPTER SUMMARY** 72

**KEY WORDS** 73

**SUGGESTED READING** 73

# Chapter 4

## Macroevolution: First Life to Mammals

Using scientific principles of contingency, common ancestry, and homology, experts reconstruct the macroevolutionary tree of life from first life through the first mammals.

- **PRINCIPLES OF RECONSTRUCTING MACROEVOLUTION AND COMMON ANCESTRAL GROUPS** 75

- **MACROEVOLUTION** 77
  Evolutionary Beginnings 78
  Archaeae, Prokaryotes, Eukaryotes, and Ediacara 82
  The Cambrian Explosion 83
  From "Fish" to Reptiles 85
  Reptiles: Evolution's First Amniotes 90
  Mammals in Evolution 92

- **MACROEVOLUTIONARY LESSONS** 96

- **HIGHLIGHT 4.1: IN THE FIELD AND THE MUSEUM WITH THE BURGESS SHALE** 86

- **HIGHLIGHT 4.2: THE END OF AN ERA: THE K/T MASS EXTINCTION** 94

**CHAPTER SUMMARY** 98

**KEY WORDS** 98

**SUGGESTED READING** 99

# Chapter 5

## Primates in Evolution

Using scientific principles of contingency, common ancestry, and homology, experts reconstruct the macroevolutionary tree from mammals through the last common ancestor (LCA) of modern humans and African apes.

■ **FROM MAMMALS TO PRIMATES** 101

■ **PRIMATE TAXONOMY** 101

■ **A BRIEF INTRODUCTION TO CONTEMPORARY PRIMATES** 103
Distribution and Ecology 104
Vital Statistics 105
Locomotion 105
Diet 106
Activity Patterns 106
Social Systems and
    Relations 106

■ **WHAT IS A PRIMATE, PAST AND PRESENT?** 107

■ **PRIMATE TRAITS** 108

■ **PRIMATE EVOLUTION** 110
Why Did Primates
    Evolve? 113
The Paleocene and
    Primatelike Mammals
    (65 to 55 myr ago) 114
Eocene Primates (55 to
    35 myr ago) 115
Oligocene Anthropoids
    (35 to 24 myr ago) 117
Miocene Hominoids (24 to
    6 myr ago) 120

■ **THE "MISSING LINK"** 122

■ **RECENT PRIMATE EVOLUTION: AFTER THE MAJOR SPLITS** 123

■ **THE LAST COMMON ANCESTOR (LCA)** 123

■ **POTENTIAL EARLY HOMINIDS: AN OVERVIEW OF THREE CANDIDATES** 124

■ **PRIMATE BEHAVIOR: RECONSTRUCTING ITS EVOLUTION BY STUDYING CONTEMPORARY PRIMATES** 125
Reconstructing Primate
    Behavior 126
The Evolution of Primate
    Behavior 127

■ **HIGHLIGHT 5.1: IN THE FAYUM DEPRESSION** 118

**CHAPTER SUMMARY** 129

**KEY WORDS** 129

**SUGGESTED READING** 130

*Chapter* **6** | Early Hominids in Africa:
*Australopithecus* and
*Homo habilis*                      *page* **131**

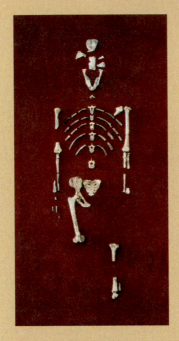

■ **WHAT IS A HOMINID?** 132

■ **HOMINID TRENDS** 133
Bipedalism 134
Why Bipedalism? 136
A Hominid Story 139
Brain Size
   and Complexity 139
Teeth and
   Dental Context 140
Reduction of Face
   and Jaws 140
Hairlessness 140

■ **TAXONOMY AND
NUMBER OF SPECIES
OF HOMINIDS** 140

■ **THE GENUS
*AUSTRALOPITHECUS*** 144
Australopithecine
   Taxonomy 145
Australopithecine Sites
   and Dates 146

Describing
   Australopithecines 146
What Happened to the
   Australopithecines? 160

■ **ENTER THE GENUS
*HOMO*** 160
*Homo habilis* 160

■ **HIGHLIGHT 6.1:
IN THE FIELD WITH
DON JOHANSON** 152

■ **HIGHLIGHT 6.2: IN
THE NEWS WITH THE
PILTDOWN FORGERY** 156

■ **HIGHLIGHT 6.3: PREY
OR PREDATORS?** 161

■ **HIGHLIGHT 6.4: THE
OTHER EVOLVING SEX** 164

**CHAPTER SUMMARY** 166

**KEY WORDS** 167

**SUGGESTED READING** 167

**Bipedalism defines
hominids. Bioenergetics
and thermoregulation best
explain the origin of
bipedalism. The
*Australopithecus* species
and *Homo habilis*
populations demonstrate
change in bipedalism as
well as other, later
evolutionary hominid
features.**

Chapter **7**

## Later Hominids: *Homo erectus* and *Homo sapiens*

*page* **168**

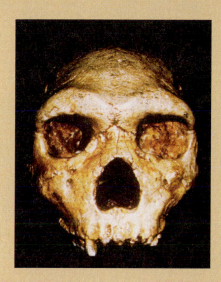

*Encephalization characterizes later hominid evolution. Homo erectus, archaic Homo sapiens, Neandertals, and AMH all show cranial changes as these populations spread out and populate the Old World.*

■ CHARACTERISTICS OF THE GENUS *HOMO* 169

■ *HOMO ERECTUS*: THE CONTROVERSY AND THE SPECIES 169
  African *Homo erectus* 175
  *Homo erectus* in Southeast Asia 175
  *Homo erectus* in China 178
  *Homo erectus* in Europe 179

■ FROM *HOMO ERECTUS* TO *HOMO SAPIENS* 180

■ EARLY ARCHAIC *HOMO SAPIENS* 181
  African Archaics 181
  Asian Archaics 182
  European Archaics 182

■ LATE ARCHAIC *HOMO SAPIENS* (NEANDERTALS) 183
  European Neandertals 187
  Middle Eastern Neandertals 187
  The Big Controversy: What Happened to the Neandertals? 187

■ ENTER ANATOMICALLY MODERN HUMANS (AMH) 191
  African AMH 195
  Middle Eastern AMH 195
  Asian and Australian AMH 195
  European AMH 196
  New World AMH 196
  Models of Evolving AMH 196

■ THE EVOLUTION OF SPEECH ABILITIES 202
  Communication, Language, Speech 202
  Evidence for Speech Abilities 203

■ HIGHLIGHT 7.1: IN AFRICA WITH NARIOKOTOME 176

■ HIGHLIGHT 7.2: IN THE NEWS WITH THE PORTUGESE KID 192

CHAPTER SUMMARY 205

KEY WORDS 206

SUGGESTED READING 206

*Chapter* **8**

# The Archaeology of Early Human Societies: Theories and Methods in Studying Prehistoric Archaeology

*page* **207**

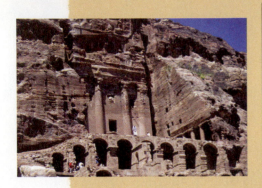

Archaeological evidence reveals much about prehistoric human societies. Finds must be analyzed and dated using reliable techniques— even so, all dates are provisional.

■ **WHAT IS ARCHAEOLOGY?** 208

■ **ARCHAEOLOGICAL EVIDENCE** 208
  Archaeological Sites and Context 208
  Preservation of Archaeological Data 210

■ **HOW ARCHAEOLOGISTS FIND EVIDENCE** 214
  Finding Sites 214
  Excavating Archaeological Sites 215

■ **ANALYSIS OF FINDS** 217
  Archaeological Theory and Interpretation 220

■ **DATING SITES AND ARTIFACTS** 221
  Relative Dating Techniques 222

Chronometric Dating 222
Other Dating Techniques 226
Summary of Dating Techniques 227

■ **HIGHLIGHT 8.1: IN THE NEWS AT OZETTE VILLAGE** 212

■ **HIGHLIGHT 8.2: A DAY IN THE FIELD** 218

**CHAPTER SUMMARY** 228

**KEY WORDS** 229

**SUGGESTED READING** 229

# Chapter 9

## The Emergence of Culture in Early Hominid Societies in the Old World

*page* **230**

Archaeological and anthropological studies reveal human cultural development between 2.6 million and 11,500 years ago. Changes in technology, social complexity, and symbolic behavior enabled humans to survive in diverse environments worldwide.

■ **THE ENVIRONMENTAL BACKGROUND** 233

■ **THE EVIDENCE: CLIMATE AND ARTIFACTS** 233

■ **EARLY HOMINID SOCIETY: THE LOWER PALEOLITHIC/EARLY STONE AGE** 235

Surviving in the Landscape 2.6 to 1.8 myr Ago 236

*Homo erectus*: Innovator and Adventurer 240

Stone Technology of *Homo erectus*: The Acheulian 241

Subsistence Strategies of *Homo erectus* and Early Archaic *Homo sapiens* 242

Fire 244

Structures 244

Burials and Symbolic Representations 245

■ **HUMAN ADAPTATIONS IN THE MIDDLE PALEOLITHIC/MIDDLE STONE AGE** 245

Technology 246

Subsistence Strategies 247

Habitation Areas and Organization of Space 248

Symbolism: Burials, Art, Ritual 249

■ **HUMANS ACROSS THE GLOBE: LIFE IN THE UPPER PALEOLITHIC/LATE STONE AGE** 251

Neandertals and Anatomically Modern Humans in the Landscape 251

Technological Complexity 253

Subsistence Practices 255

Habitation and Use of Space 258

Symbolism: Burial and Art 260

Upper Paleolithic/Late Stone Age Society 263

■ **HIGHLIGHT 9.1: IN TOUCH WITH STONE TOOLS** 238

■ **HIGHLIGHT 9.2: INTO AUSTRALIA AND THE PACIFIC** 256

■ **HIGHLIGHT 9.3: PALEOLITHIC IMAGERY IN EURASIA** 264

**CHAPTER SUMMARY** 266

**KEY WORDS** 267

**SUGGESTED READING** 267

# Chapter 10

## Later Hunter-Gatherers and Early Farming Societies in the Old World

*page* **268**

Rich Holocene resources underpinned population rise and increased sedentism among hunter-gatherers before the emergence of agriculture. The consequences of domestication are highlighted in case studies from the Middle East, Europe, China, and Africa.

■ **THE CHANGING CLIMATE OF THE LATE GLACIAL AND EARLY HOLOCENE** 270

■ **HUNTER-GATHERERS OF THE LATE GLACIAL AND EARLY HOLOCENE** 273

■ **SUBSISTENCE PRACTICES OF LATE GLACIAL AND EARLY HOLOCENE GROUPS** 273

How Did People Choose from Available Food Resources? 273

Animal and Fish Resources in the Natufian of the Middle East (14.5 to 11.5 kyr Ago) 274

Animal and Fish Resources in the Japanese Jomon (12.7 to 2.4 kyr Ago) 275

Animal and Fish Resources in the Scandinavian Mesolithic (10 to 6 kyr Ago) 276

Plant Resources and Later Hunter-Gatherer Groups 277

Later Hunter-Gatherer Technology 277

Pottery 279

Habitation and Use of Space 280

Symbolic Activities: Burials and Representational Imagery 281

Social Organization 281

■ **THE EMERGENCE OF FARMING IN OLD WORLD NEOLITHIC SOCIETIES** 282

Modeling the Causes of Farming 283

Evidence for Plant and Animal Domestication 284

Material Culture of Farming Groups 285

■ **FARMING IN THE MIDDLE EAST** 288

Houses at Jericho and Ain Ghazal 288

Ritual among Farming Communities in the Middle East 289

Long-Distance Contact 290

■ **AGRICULTURE IN EUROPE** 290

The LBK Phenomenon of Central Europe 291

Farming in Southern Scandinavia 295

■ **FARMING IN CHINA** 296

■ **PASTORALISM AND CULTIVATION IN AFRICA** 298

Nabta Playa 299

Sorghum, Millet, and African Rice 300

■ **SOCIAL COMPLEXITY AMONG FARMING COMMUNITIES** 300

Çatalhöyük: A Farming Village in Anatolia 300

Megalithic Monuments in Britain 303

■ **HIGHLIGHT 10.1: POTTERY AND ARCHAEOLOGY** 286

■ **HIGHLIGHT 10.2: GENES, LANGUAGES, AND FARMERS** 292

**CHAPTER SUMMARY** 305

**KEY WORDS** 306

**SUGGESTED READING** 306

# Chapter 11

## Early States in the Old World

*page* **307**

The study of Mesopotamia, Egypt, and the Indus, Shang, and Aksum states illustrates the underlying characteristics of early states. Although not traditional states, complex urban centers in Ethiopia and West Africa have state-like attributes.

■ **EARLY STATE SOCIETIES** 310

■ **MESOPOTAMIA** 312
Early Mesopotamian States 312
The Mesopotamian City 314
Craft Specialization 316
Trade and Exchange 316
Social Stratification 316

■ **THE EARLY EGYPTIAN STATE** 317
Birth of a State: Predynastic Egypt 318
The Early State: Egypt in the Early Dynastic and Old Kingdom 318
Craft Specialization 319
Trade and Exchange 319
King and Temple 320
The Age of Pyramids 320

■ **THE INDUS STATE** 323
Origins of the Indus State 323
Indus Cities 324
Craft Specialization 327
Trade and Exchange 327
Social Stratification 327
Ritual and Ruler 327

■ **THE SHANG STATE OF NORTHEAST CHINA** 328
Before Shang: The Erlitou State 328

The Early Shang State: Erligang Phase 329
Anyang: Capital of the Last Shang Dynasty 329
The Shang State Machine 334
Shang Bronzes 335
Trade and Exchange 335

■ **EARLY STATES AND URBAN COMPLEXITY IN EAST AND WEST AFRICA** 336
Early Ethiopian States 336
Jenné-jeno and Urban Complexity in the Middle Niger 339

■ **CONCLUDING COMMENTS ON EARLY STATES** 340

■ **HIGHLIGHT 11.1: THE EMERGENCE OF WRITING IN THE OLD WORLD** 330

■ **HIGHLIGHT 11.2: IN TEMPERATE EUROPE WITH THE CELTS** 342

**CHAPTER SUMMARY** 344

**KEY WORDS** 345

**SUGGESTED READING** 345

# Chapter 12

## Later Hunter-Gatherers and Early Farming Societies in the Americas

*page* **346**

Early human occupation of the Americas was patchy. Holocene resources underpinned regional diversity among Eastern Woodlands, Great Basin, Northwest Coast, and Southern California archaic cultures. Agricultural communities in Eastern and Southwestern North America developed distinct traditions.

■ **PEOPLING OF THE AMERICAS** 349
How Did the First Americans Get There? 349
Where Did They Come From? 351
When Did They Arrive in the Americas? 351
The Archaeological Evidence 352
Monte Verde Fits the Criteria 352
The Clovis Phenomenon 353

■ **HUNTING, FORAGING, AND FISHING IN THE HOLOCENE: ARCHAIC CULTURES** 356

■ **THE EASTERN WOODLANDS ARCHAIC** 357
Developing Technology 357
Settlement and Scheduling of Resources 358
Exchange Networks 358
Burial and Ceremony 359
Mound Building 360

■ **THE GREAT BASIN ARCHAIC** 360
Preservation in Caves 361
Bioarchaeological Studies in the Great Basin 364

■ **HUNTER-FORAGER-FISHER GROUPS OF THE NORTHWEST COAST** 364
Environmental Resources 365
Changing Technology 365
Settlements 366
Ritual, Status, and Warfare 366

■ **FORAGING, FISHING, AND HUNTING GROUPS OF SOUTHERN CALIFORNIA** 367
Marine Exploitation on the Channel Islands of Southern California 367
Mainland Subsistence Strategies 368
Emergence of Status 369

■ **THE DEVELOPMENT OF AGRICULTURE** 369

■ **AGRICULTURAL SOCIETIES IN EASTERN NORTH AMERICA** 372
Hopewell Agricultural Communities 372

■ **AGRICULTURAL SOCIETIES IN SOUTHWEST NORTH AMERICA** 374
Hohokam 374
Mogollon 376
Ancestral Pueblo (Anasazi) 378

■ **HIGHLIGHT 12.1: INVESTIGATING ANIMAL EXTINCTIONS** 354

■ **HIGHLIGHT 12.2: CAHOKIA, CROWN OF PREHISTORIC MISSISSIPPIAN CHIEFDOMS** 362

**CHAPTER SUMMARY** 380

**KEY WORDS** 381

**SUGGESTED READING** 381

*Chapter* **13**  **The Emergence
of State Societies
in the Americas**  *page* **382**

The earliest states and
empires in the Americas
arose in Mesoamerica and
South America. Olmec,
Teotihuacan, Maya, and
Aztec illustrate
Mesoamerican
developments; Moche,
Tiwanaku, Wari, and Inca
illustrate Andean
developments.

■ **EARLY MESOAMERICAN
STATES** 384
   Olmec 384
   The City of Teotihuacan 387
   The Maya 391

■ **EARLY STATES
IN SOUTH AMERICA** 398
   Moche 398
   Tiwanaku: State and
      Early Empire? 402
   Wari: State and
      Early Empire? 407

■ **EMPIRES OF THE
NEW WORLD** 408
   The Aztec Empire 409
   The Inca Empire 414

■ **CONCLUDING
COMMENTS ON
NEW WORLD STATES
AND EMPIRES** 418

■ **HIGHLIGHT 13.1:
CALENDARS AND WRITING
IN MESOAMERICA AND
SOUTH AMERICA** 392

■ **HIGHLIGHT 13.2:
IN THE FOOTSTEPS
OF ANCIENT
ANDEAN FARMERS** 404

**CHAPTER SUMMARY** 419

**KEY WORDS** 420

**SUGGESTED READING** 420

# Chapter 14

## Primates Today

The study of contemporary tarsiers, prosimians, Old World and New World monkeys, and apes gives insights into the evolution of the human lineage by allowing bioanthropologists to generate hypotheses about the LCA.

■ **PRIMATOLOGY: BIOLOGY, PSYCHOLOGY, AND BIOANTHROPOLOGY** 423
   A Brief History of Primatology 425
   In the Field, Lab, and Zoo 426
   Primate Taxonomy and Evolution Revisited 427
   Primate Cognition 427

■ **CASE STUDIES OF CONTEMPORARY PRIMATES** 429

■ **CONTEMPORARY TARSIERS** 429

■ **CONTEMPORARY PROSIMIANS** 431
   Sifakas 433

■ **CONTEMPORARY MONKEYS** 435
   Old World Monkeys 436
   New World Monkeys 438

■ **CONTEMPORARY APES** 440
   Gibbons and Siamangs (the Small Apes) 441
   The Large Apes 442

■ **ENDANGERED PRIMATES** 455

■ **HIGHLIGHT 14.1: CHECKING OUT CHIMPANZEE AND ORANGUTAN CULTURE** 444

■ **HIGHLIGHT 14.2: LANGUAGE ACQUISITION BY CHIMPANZEES AND BONOBOS** 450

■ **HIGHLIGHT 14.3: IN THE FIELD WITH THOSE SEXY BONOBOS** 456

**CHAPTER SUMMARY** 458

**KEY WORDS** 458

**SUGGESTED READING** 459

# Chapter 15

## Contemporary Humans    *page* **460**

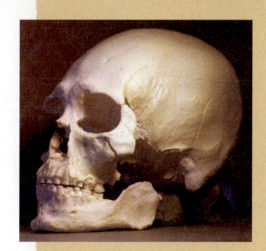

Humans reached anatomical modernity by 100,000 years ago and behavioral modernity by 50,000 years ago. Contemporary studies of humans have negated the concept of "biological races" and instead focus on human adaptations and forensic applications.

■ THE LAST 50 KYR IN THE OLD WORLD 462

■ NATIVE AMERICANS: FACTS AND CONTROVERSIES 462

■ CAUSES OF MICROEVOLUTION IN CONTEMPORARY HUMANS 469
Population Genetics 470

■ GENERAL TRENDS OF CONTEMPORARY HUMANS 471

■ HUMAN BIOLOGICAL VARIABILITY: THE SPECIES TODAY 473
How Do Humans Vary? 474
Why Do Humans Vary? 474
Group Variation: "Race" or Not? 479
*Homo sapiens* and Co-variation of Traits 480

■ A HISTORY OF "RACE" IN AMERICA: FROM BIOLOGY TO CULTURE 482
Intelligence and Racism 485

■ HUMAN ADAPTATIONS 486
Growth and Development, Health and Disease 487

■ APPLIED BIOLOGICAL ANTHROPOLOGY 488
Are Humans Naturally Violent? 488
DNA Fingerprinting and AIDS 488
Reconstructing Faces 489

■ FORENSIC ANTHROPOLOGY 493
Spitalfields: Verifying Knowledge 498

■ HIGHLIGHT 15.1: *HOMO FLORESIENSIS* 464

■ HIGHLIGHT 15.2: WE ARE WHAT WE WERE, OR ARE WE? 490

■ HIGHLIGHT 15.3: IN THE NEWS: IDENTIFICATION OF JOSEF MENGELE 494

CHAPTER SUMMARY 499

KEY WORDS 500

SUGGESTED READING 500

# Chapter 16

## Conclusions: Who Are We?

**Bioanthropologists and archaeologists find that biological and cultural change affected the human species in the same general time frame, but are different enough to be distinct, separate phenomena.**

■ **WHAT MADE HUMANS HUMAN?** 502

■ **BIOLOGICAL EVOLUTION AND CULTURE CHANGE: PARALLELS OR NOT?** 503

Biological Evolution: Co-variation? 503

Cultural Change: Co-variation? 504

Biological and Cultural Change: Comparing the Records 506

Conclusion: Different Processes 510

■ **THE FUTURE OF *HOMO SAPIENS*** 510

**GLOSSARY** 513

**REFERENCES** 525

**NAME INDEX** 550

**SUBJECT INDEX** 556

**CREDITS** 566

# Preface

The study of our human past is fascinating and exciting. What it is to be human is both biological (we are animals) and cultural (we use symbols in complex systems). In order to know how we got to be the way we are today biologically and culturally, we must study our human past relative to both culture and biology. Because the study of our human past falls in the discipline of anthropology, it is the domain of bioanthropologists and ar-

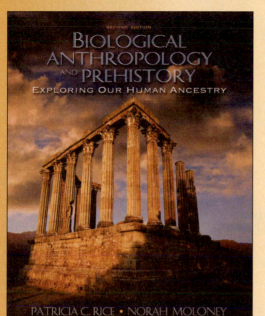

chaeologists. The term *paleoanthropology*—as used in its original sense— not only combines the study of our past biology and culture and the methods of bioanthropology and archaeology, but also studies the inter-relationships between our past culture and biology. This book will lead you and your students along the road of discovery of our human past.

Our human past is knowable. But, like all historical sciences, paleo-anthropology must grapple with many facts and many unknowns. We will discuss the knowns and hypothesize about the unknowns. When experts disagree about certain points in reconstructing the human past, we introduce the topic, discuss the disagreements, give evidence, and suggest how the disagreements might be alleviated. Instructors can "pick a position" or not. We emphasize paleoanthropology as a science and integrate theoretical and empirical findings.

Our aim in this book is to make the study of the human past under-standable to beginning anthropology students. It is more important to us that they understand the processes of change than whether they can memorize dozens of tongue-tying taxonomic terms. We discuss the human past in a population mode rather than describing fossils or arti-facts as isolated bits of bone or stone. We have intentionally taken the "lumper" perspective rather than the "splitter" perspective to enhance the understanding of what happened in the past and in an effort to "keep it simple." Being "lumpers," we use as few species names as nec-essary to explain the fossil material, for example. We always mention the alternative ty-pology and say why we will not be using it so that any student going on into advanced courses or reading the literature that uses the alternative taxonomy will not be lost.

## How This Book Is Organized

We have organized the book primarily by anthropological subdiscipline (archaeology and bioanthropology) and by chronology. We did so to emphasize the difference be-tween biological happenings and cultural happenings and to highlight the different methods used to understand and reconstruct past events. The introductory chapter provides a context for both biological anthropology and archaeology—the main topics of this book—by introducing the total discipline of anthropology and its four (or five) subfields in terms of what each is and how specialists in that area do their work. The chapter includes a section on the importance of holism and examples of why it is nec-essary to study both past and present and biology and culture in order to fully under-stand what it is to be human. Ethics is important to science, anthropology, and all of its subfields, and is covered in Chapter 1 as well. The next several chapters focus on the biological side of what it is to be human, with an introduction to biological anthropol-ogy and methods, theories, and dating of fossils and DNA (Chapter 2), followed by a chronologically based evolutionary tracing from first life to modern humans (Chapters 3 through 7). Then, the following chapters focus on the cultural side of what it is to be human, with an introduction to archaeological methods, theory, and techniques of dat-ing artifacts (Chapter 8), followed by a chronological tracing of the making of the first stone tools in the Old World through early civilizations (Chapters 9 through 11) and earliest migrations to the New World from hunting-gathering to civilizations (Chapters 12 and 13). Two chapters on contemporary primates and humans (Chapters 14 and 15) return the focus to biological anthropology, covering contemporary primates using a case study approach to prosimians, monkeys, and apes and considering contemporary humans as a biological species, asking about variability and whether "biological races" exist. The final chapter—Chapter 16, "Conclusions: Who Are We?"—asks whether biology and culture can be studied as a single unit.

We try, whenever possible, to give a global perspective of both human evolution and past cultures. We are limited to the Old World (Africa, Asia, and Europe) for human evolution. The examination of culture and its change through time, however, can be quite global. Of course, we cannot cover all prehistoric cultures worldwide or go into immense detail on those cultures we do cover. We hope that the chapters provide enough information to give a general overview of past human evolution and culture change and stimulate you to want to discover more.

# To the Student

The study of our human past is dynamic. Discoveries of new artifacts or fossils and interesting new interpretations or hypotheses about the human past are in the news on a regular basis; we have tried to pass on many of these recent developments to you. Undoubtedly, further discoveries will have occurred by the time you read this book. However, it is our hope that your interest will be sparked so that you, too, will enjoy the thrill each time you hear of a new find. Hopefully, by taking a course in paleoanthropology and reading this book, you will be able to put each new find into a broader context than just an announcement of a new bit of the distant past.

# Special Features

- Each chapter begins with an outline to give readers an overview of what lies ahead.

- Many of the chapters include a map of sites mentioned in the text and a chronological time line to help you situate your reading spatially and chronologically. We have tried to give general estimates of dates including many carbon 14 dates that have been calibrated using other dating methods.

**page 347**

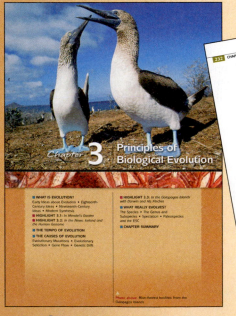

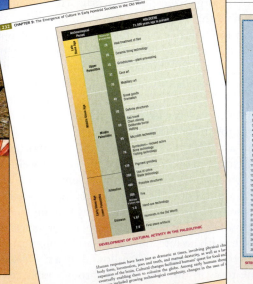

■ Within each chapter, full-color figures and photographs are used to illustrate key concepts and summarize information. Explanatory captions guide students through the illustrations, which make scientific and technical content easy to understand. Throughout the text, the beautifully rendered figures and carefully chosen photographs provide an excellent reference and study tool for students.

**page 133**

**page 320**

**page 437**

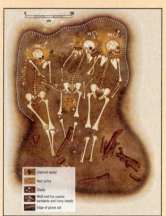

**page 496**

**page 416**

**page 26**

**page 278**

**page 262**

■ Each chapter concludes with an illustrated summary of major points covered in the chapter.

**pages 380–381**

■ Boldfaced key words throughout each chapter, highlighting the most important terms, are listed at the back of the chapter along with the page number where the term first appeared. All key words are defined in the margins within the chapter and in an alphabetized glossary at the back of the book as well.

■ Suggested readings for those interested in looking further into particular subjects are also provided at the end of each chapter.

# Boxed Features

Highlight boxes in each chapter show the relevance of current issues in bioanthropology and archaeology to today's world and present certain subjects in greater depth. Readers will learn more about Josef Mengele and how forensic anthropologists were able to identify his bones in "In the News: Identification of Josef Mengele" (Chapter 15). They will read about recent research on chimpanzee and orangutan culture in "Checking Out Chimpanzee and Orangutan Culture" (Chapter 14). They will read the latest analysis of the Iceman in "In the Alps with the Iceman" (Chapter 1). In "In the Fayum Depression" (Chapter 5), readers discover how more early primates have been found in one relatively small location in northern Egypt than in any other area of the world. Highlights in Chapters 9 and 10 inform readers of the potential information that archaeologists can get from stone tool and pottery analysis, while highlights in Chapters 11 and 13 address the development and use of writing in the Old and New Worlds. "Cahokia, Crown of Mississippian Chiefdoms" (Chapter 12) considers complex chiefdoms—an aspect of regional development that was contemporary with state societies.

**pages 118–119**

# Supplementary Materials

A wealth of supplementary materials is available to support your use of *Biological Anthropology and Prehistory: Exploring Our Human Ancestry.*

## Instructor's Manual and Test Bank

This **author-written supplement** includes learning objectives, lecture suggestions, discussion topics, in-class projects and research ideas, chapter summaries, and suggested readings. The Test Bank portion includes a wealth of multiple choice, true-false, short answer, and essay questions.

## Computerized Test Bank

This computerized version of the test bank is available with Tamarack's easy-to-use TestGen software, which lets you prepare tests for printing as well as for network and online testing. Full editing capability for Windows and Macintosh.

## AnthropologyExperience Web Site

AnthropologyExperience is an online destination designed to help students visualize how anthropologists conduct scientific and humanistic studies. Anthropology Experience addresses individual teaching and learning needs by providing multiple modes of visual media, which include videos, "in the news" articles, activities, pictures, graphs, tables, interactive timelines, a student resource center (including an interactive glossary, flashcards, and web links) and more!

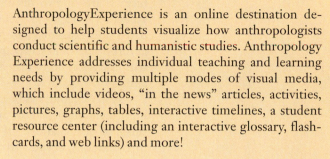

## Research Navigator™: Anthropology

Allyn & Bacon's new Research Navigator™ is the easiest way for students to start a research assignment or research paper. Complete with extensive help on the research process and three exclusive databases of credible and reliable source material (EBSCO's ContentSelect Academic Journal Database, *New York Times* Search by Subject Archive, and "Best of the Web" Link Library), Research Navigator™ helps students quickly and efficiently make the most of their research time. Research Navigator™ is *free* when packaged with any Allyn & Bacon textbook but requires an Access Code. Access Codes are value-packed with textbooks. Contact your local representative for more details.

## Recent Finds: Paleoanthropology

A six-month update of new fossil and artifact finds (and redates, updates, and interesting items in paleoanthropology) appears in each issue of the last 14 years of *General Anthropology*. This journal is published by the American Anthropological Association and is a perk of membership in the General Anthropology Division. Instructors and students can use an integrated list of new finds (a paragraph for each, plus the original publication source) as references for short or long term papers. They work well in assignments that focus on how a new find changes science's realm of knowledge. Write to Patricia Rice for that integrated resource at pat.rice@mail.wvu.edu.

## New to This Edition

The organization of the book has been changed so that biological anthropology and prehistory are in two distinct parts: Chapters 1–7 cover biological anthropology, and Chapters 8–13 cover archaeology. Discussions of theory and methods have been updated and expanded and placed in the appropriate chapters (Chapter 2 for biological anthropology and Chapter 8 for prehistory/archaeology). This new organization, along with the addition of many key words with their definitions placed in the page margins and in the expanded glossary, makes the book more accessible to students.

Every chapter has been thoroughly updated with discussions of new sites, new findings (including the three potential hominids found since the publication of the first edition), or new analyses. Of particular note is the addition of a new chapter (5, Primates in Evolution), devoted to the evolution of primates. It covers taxonomy, contemporary primates, primate traits, evolution, missing links, primates after the major splits to prosimians, monkeys, apes, the last common ancestor (LCA), potential early hominids *(Orrorin tugenensis, Sahelanthropus chadensis, and Ardipithecus ramidus)*, and the evolution of primate behavior.

## Acknowledgments

We started out writing a book that integrated the content of the classes we teach. Along the way, the book changed with the help of numerous people, perhaps our students more than any other group. The librarians at the Institute of Archaeology, University College London (UCL), particularly Robert Kirby and Katie Meheux, have been especially helpful in finding odd materials, and we are grateful for access to libraries in the UCL system, especially the Institute of Archaeology and Watson Science Library. Access to collections at the Smithsonian (Burgess Shale) and the Natural History Museum London (the Darwin finches at Tring) is greatly appreciated. Jennifer Jacobson at Allyn & Bacon had faith in our final product from the beginning and we thank her and Dave Repetto for their constant support and encouragement, and for pushing us when needed. Although it was sometimes difficult to coordinate the evaluative suggestions of the reviewers of the original manuscript and the first edition, we took each comment seriously and thank them for making this a better book. They include Pat Anderson, Western Illinois University; Joanna Casey, University of South Carolina; Joseph L. Chartkoff, Michigan State University; Joan Coltrain, University of Utah; James Delle, Kutztown University; Barbara G. Hornum, Drexel University; John Krigbaum, University of Florida; Randall McGuire, Binghamton University; Jack H. Prost, University of Illinois at Chicago; Patricia B. Richards, University of Wisconsin Milwaukee; Teryl Schessler, California State University, Fullerton; and Terance L. Winemiller, Louisiana State University. Finally, we have profited greatly by discussions with biologically minded colleagues, particularly Chris Stringer, John Relethford, Milford Wolpoff, Frank Harold, and Fred Smith; and with archaeologically minded colleagues, particularly Jim Aimers, Sue Colledge, Ignacio de la Torre, Dorian Fuller, Andrew Garrard, Elizabeth Graham, Ole Grön, Stuart Laidlaw, Roger Matthews, Kevin McDonald, Luisa Mengoni, Mary Ann Murray, Andrew Reid, Tobias Richter, Arlene Rosen, Steven Rosen, Jane Sidell, Bill Sillar, Ulrike Sommer, Dietrich Stout, Gudrun Sveinbjarndottir, and Michele Wollstoncroft. We also thank friends and family who have given us encouragement and moral support during the preparation of the book.

# Chapter 1 | Introduction to Anthropology

■ **THE NATURE OF HUMANS AND ANTHROPOLOGY**
■ **HIGHLIGHT 1.1:** *In the Alps with the Iceman*
■ **ANTHROPOLOGY AND ITS SUBFIELDS**
How Anthropologists Do Their Work • Anthropology Is Holistic • Anthropological Ethics

■ **HIGHLIGHT 1.2:** *In the News: The African Burial Ground in New York City*
■ **CHAPTER SUMMARY**

▲

**Photo above:** The Iceman, a 5,300-year-old man from the Alps

# The Nature of Humans and Anthropology

One day in 1991, in the area of the Alps where Austria borders Italy, two mountain climbers found the head and torso of a frozen body protruding from the ice. The climbers notified the local police. When the police came to the scene, however, they realized that this was not someone who had died within recent months—or even recent decades. They called scientists from the University of Innsbruck to investigate. The experts' verdict: The man had lain in the ice for more than 5,000 years.

This is how the famous Iceman was discovered. The extraordinary find made headlines around the world, and Highlight 1.1 (on pp. 4–5) tells more about what happened next. Beyond the general public, all anthropologists were excited about the news, because anthropology is the study of human beings, biologically and culturally, in the past and today. The Iceman was particularly important for bioanthropologists, who study humans biologically, and for archaeologists, who study human cultures in the past. Biological anthropologists wanted to know if the Iceman looked like modern people in the Alps because in the 5,300 years since his death, given 20 years per human generation, over 260 generations would have gone by and signs of evolution would be likely. They also wanted to sample his DNA to attempt to match it with that of modern people in the Alps. Would differences between the Iceman's DNA and that of modern people in the same area suggest that he was a traveler from elsewhere or that he was a local and evolutionary change caused the DNA to be modified over generations? Biological anthropologists also wanted to know how old the Iceman was and, in conjunction with his age, the state of his health when he died: Did he have arthritis, rickets, or other bone abnormalities? Did he have any healed broken bones? Archaeologists had just as many questions to ask: What was he wearing? Did he have any body decorations? Did he have tools with him, and if so, what kinds? Was there anything in his stomach or intestines that could tell us what he had eaten during his last 24 hours? The study of our human past and the relationship between bioanthropology and archaeology (biology and culture) will be the core theme of this book.

This chapter introduces anthropology as a whole, as well as its subfields and specializations, focusing primarily on bioanthropology and archaeology. It considers what it is that anthropologists do to find answers to their questions concerning humans. All anthropologists do certain things, but much of their work is specific to their particular subfield. Anthropology, because of its focus on one thing—human beings—is holistic, and often, it is mandatory to use more than one subfield to answer most questions. For example, why is it that 90 percent of northern Europeans are lactose tolerant while most East Asians suffer severe stomach disorders if they consume cow's milk? This biological question has a cultural answer. Why do African and many Middle Eastern populations have a high frequency of sickle cell anemia? This biological question also has a cultural answer. Why can humans and chimpanzees use sign language to communicate with each other but can't speak to each other? This cultural difference has a biological answer. To answer each of these questions, both culture and biology come together for analysis, and one subfield by itself is not sufficient.

Another factor that unites anthropology and its subfields is a concern for ethics. All anthropologists believe ethics to be of utmost importance in studying all aspects of being human, but each subfield has its own particular slant. This will be discussed as well.

**anthropology**
The science that investigates human culture and human biology in the past and present and that includes cultural anthropology, archaeology, linguistics, and biological anthropology.

# Anthropology and Its Subfields

In Greek *anthropos* means "human," and the suffix *ology* comes from the Greek word referring to the study or science of something. Hence, **anthropology** is the study or the science of human beings. Anthropologists, almost by definition, are very nosy critters.

## Figure 1.1

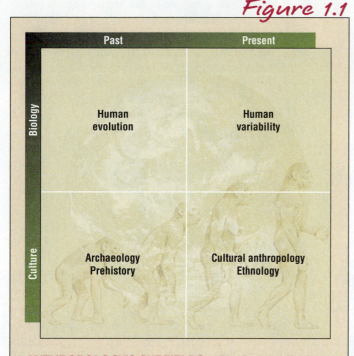

| | Past | Present |
|---|---|---|
| **Biology** | Human evolution | Human variability |
| **Culture** | Archaeology Prehistory | Cultural anthropology Ethnology |

**ANTHROPOLOGY'S SUBFIELDS.** The four subfields are divided by past versus present and by biology versus culture. Can you think of questions that might relate to humans both in the past and in the present or both culturally and biologically? How does this figure compare with the more traditional division of anthropology discussed in the main text?

The first anthropologist was probably a person who looked down the valley and saw people who looked, behaved, and talked differently, and then wondered why. Noting the differences makes you human; asking *why* makes you an anthropologist.

What it is to be human, and therefore how anthropologists study humans, can be divided into two parts in two different ways. First, because humans have a past and a present (and, we hope, a future), they can be studied both as a species with a past history and as a species that exists today. Additionally, because humans are both biological and cultural creatures, they can be studied biologically and culturally. If we diagram these components of what it means to be human, as shown in Figure 1.1, we use one way of defining the four basic subfields of anthropology: the study of our biological past (human evolution); the study of our biological present (human variability); the study of our cultural past (archaeology and prehistory); and the study of modern culture, including linguistics (cultural anthropology or ethnology). Alternatively, a more traditional scheme defines the four subfields of anthropology as biological (or physical) anthropology, cultural anthropology, linguistics, and archaeology. Let's look at the subdisciplines in that order.

**Biological anthropologists** study humans, both past and present, as a species of animal. These scientists are interchangeably called *bioanthropologists* or *physical anthropologists*. The latter name reflected the fact that these anthropologists were characterized as "great describers" of individuals and groups. By 1953, Sherwood Washburn, one of the first bioanthropologists who trained as an anthropologist first (most practicing biological anthropologists until the 1950s were trained as physicians, anatomists, or biologists), led the way in the use of hypothesis testing as the main methodology, not merely measuring bones with a caliper and measuring stick. The "New Physical Anthropology" launched at that time was a synthesis of evolutionary theory, genetics, and anatomy as well as human ecology and behavior; it also included the study of nonhuman primates. Such modern questions as "How do the Inuit cope with such a stressful cold climate?" and "Why did our ancestors evolve large brow ridges only to have them become smaller later on?" and "What can the study of pygmy lemurs tell us about humans?" became the norm rather than "What is the average cranial capacity of chimpanzees?"

Many biological anthropologists collect data about and analyze *Homo sapiens* (humans), just as other scientists would for *Canis familiaris* (dogs), in order to understand both human evolution and modern humans' biological status. They want to know the distribution of human fossil material and how to interpret fossil finds; they ask what were the steps in human evolution, whether the steps were smooth and continuous or quantum jumps, and *why* human evolution occurred as it did and when it did.

Many bioanthropologists focus on modern humans rather than on human evolution. Members of our species today have genetic differences that produce variations in their outer appearance. Bioanthropologists ask whether these differences vary together (covary) so as to form "races." If, for example, tall stature, light skin, and curly hair were always found together and in one geographic area, and short stature, dark skin, and straight hair were always found together and in another geographic area, covariation

**biological anthropologists**
Anthropologists who study humans as animals in the past (their evolution) and in the present (their modern form); also called bioanthropologists.

# Highlight 1.1

## In the Alps with the Iceman

IN 1991 TWO CLIMBERS discovered the frozen body of a man protruding from the Alpine ice just south of the Ötzal Valley, on the border of Austria and Italy. AMS (accelerator mass spectrometry) dating indicated that Ötzi (as people soon named the man), his clothes, and his equipment had been preserved in the ice for about 5,300 years. The find was important for four main reasons: (1) Ötzi is the oldest mummy in the world; (2) the body was that of an ordinary person, possibly a shepherd; (3) the ice preserved a range of items made of organic materials that rarely survive in the archaeological record; and (4) a mystery surrounds how and why Ötzi died—whether by murder or from natural causes. The find thus opened a window on elements of life in the distant past that we do not normally have. Ongoing studies of the Iceman show just how much we can learn from such finds, and new isotopic signatures from teeth and bones suggest he was born only about 60 km from where he died.

Apart from leather leggings, Ötzi appeared at first to be naked. However, fragments of clothing that lay beneath and near the body allowed archaeologists to reconstruct his wardrobe. He wore a leather loincloth over his leggings, both fastened by a leather belt. Beneath an outer cloak of plaited grass, Ötzi's inner garment was made of strips of fur sewn together. He had a fur cap that tied under his chin with leather straps, and socks of grass kept his feet warm inside leather shoes.

Ötzi's equipment included a longbow of unfinished yew, a skin quiver, 14 wooden arrows with flint heads, a copper axe bound in a wooden haft with leather strips, a fur backpack attached by grass cords to a wooden frame, two birchbark containers (of which one was apparently for carrying lighted

Also called Ötzi, the Iceman, found in 1991 on the Italian–Austrian border, is 5,300 years old, dating to the Neolithic. We do not know how or why he died.

embers), and flint tools and tinder in a leather waist pouch. Other items were a string sheath, netting and sinews, and some birch fungus that Ötzi may have carried for its medicinal properties.

Macro and micro examinations of the body itself have provided further enlightening information on Ötzi's life, health, and death. A man in his early 40s, Ötzi had many tattoos, possibly strategically placed to help relieve pain, perhaps from arthritis. His teeth show heavy wear, perhaps from chewing dried meat or softening leather. Periods of illness in the months before his death are indicated in Ötzi's fingernails, which show intervals of poor growth; X-rays show unhealed rib fractures. Examination of the contents of his colon revealed that he had eaten cereals and fruits in his last days, that he had drunk water from both lowland and upland locations, and that he had whipworm parasites that would have caused some discomfort. DNA analysis indicated genetic links with northern Europeans.

Originally researchers proposed that following some kind of attack, Ötzi had escaped to the mountains; there, exhausted and weak from his wounds (rib fractures), he sat down, fell asleep, and died from hypothermia—to be found more than 5,000 years later. Because pollen samples taken from ice around the body indicated autumn plants, Ötzi was thought to have died in that season.

More recent analysis has changed this original interpretation, however. Forensic studies have shown that at some time in the past the ice melted and the body moved in the meltwater before the ice reformed. This finding would account for the spread of clothing and possessions around the body. It now appears that ice pressure caused the rib fractures; also, pollen analysis of the gut content indicates spring to summer plant species, therefore casting doubt on the fall death scenario. Finally, more recent X-rays and CAT scans of the body have revealed a flint arrowhead embedded in Ötzi's left shoulder. It seems that he may have been attacked and may have bled to death from his wound rather than dying from exposure. (Some experts believe the arrow had nothing to do with his death.) Given that arrows are shot from some distance, hand-to-hand combat seems unlikely, and surely suicide can be ruled out. Someone seems to have shot him, but it could have been for any of a myriad of reasons. There is surely more news to come from Ötzi, but unfortunately, at this time, the board in charge of the Iceman in Bolzano will not allow additional invasive investigation because it would require another thawing.

*Sources*: Barfield, L. 1994. The Iceman reviewed. *Antiquity* 68:10–26.   Bortenschlager, S., and K. Oeggl, eds. 2000. *The Iceman and his natural environment*. New York: Springer.   Fowler, B. 2000. *Iceman*. New York: Random House   Spindler, K. 2001. *The man in the ice*. London: Orion.

turn back to your reading

would be present and would result in biologically distinct groups, or races. But because such traits do not covary, most bioanthropologists deny the existence of biological races. They recognize that there is a perception of races; but they maintain that perception is cultural, not biological, and that what people mean by *race* is closer to ethnicity. (See Chapter 15 for more on this issue.)

Humans do differ in various biological traits: Some people (and some groups) are tall, and some are short; some have long narrow noses, and some have short wide noses. These seemingly obvious differences are actually quite superficial, however—because humans today are about 99.8 percent the same in genetic composition (Enard et al. 2002; Pääbo 2003). Using genetic research (as well as other methodologies), bioanthropologists interested in modern humans study their variability in areas such as growth and development and the causes of certain diseases, among countless others.

**Cultural anthropologists** specialize in describing and explaining the cultures of modern people. Often a cultural anthropologist will spend years with people in another society, studying their behavior, cognition (knowledge and rules), and emotions. Once cultural anthropologists, or **ethnographers**, are satisfied that they can describe the culture of another group of people dispassionately and objectively, they write up the descriptions as **ethnographies**. Other cultural anthropologists are more interested in making comparisons and drawing larger-scale pictures of many societies; they may either incorporate many cultural descriptions into a study of a certain geographic area or extrapolate a particular subject from many ethnographies and write about it cross-culturally. For example, various kinds of kin groups or a particular kind of religion in highland New Guinea might be the topic of such an analysis. Finally, some cultural anthropologists have tried to put modern cultures together into a kind of megaculture, based on what all human groups in the world today have in common culturally. Universal cultural traits, such as "people in all cultures have kin groups" or "people in all cultures decorate their bodies," are the database for this compilation. Clearly, all cultures in the world today have a common cultural core, even if the details vary from place to place, but sometimes the cultural differences are emphasized to the detriment of the similar core.

Other social scientists describe and try to explain human society and culture, so what makes cultural anthropologists different? In the United States, sociologists specialize in Western society (their own), economists focus on Western economies (their own), political scientists focus on politics and power (either their own or the effect of power and politics in other countries on their own society). By contrast, cultural anthropologists are cross-cultural in their approach and try as objectively as possible to describe and explain other cultures as well as their own, either as an "insider" from the perspective of the "other" culture(s) (called the **emic perspective**) or dispassionately by comparing certain practices and beliefs in different cultures, including their own. When a cultural anthropologist studies a culture different from his or her own as an "outsider," he or she takes an **etic perspective**. Beyond the fact that other cultures are intrinsically interesting, the importance of cultural anthropologists' work is in validating statements from other social scientists (including psychologists) about certain phenomena being universal or "normal."

Some anthropologists specialize in **linguistics**—the study of the languages people use in other cultures. More precisely, these scientists are concerned with speech, or oral–aural (mouth–ear) human communication, and with speech communities. Linguistic specialists are interested in the origins of speech, the changes that take place in speech communities over thousands of years, which languages are similar to each other, and the roles of speech in ordinary conversation.

**Archaeologists** are cultural anthropologists in one sense, because the main concern of archaeology is people's culture. But because archaeologists study cultures in the past, they often have more in common with biological anthropologists than with cultural anthropologists. Their method of getting data is often exactly the same as that of bioanthropologists; that is, both use finely controlled excavation. Archaeologists may study

---

**cultural anthropologists**
Anthropologists who study the culture of contemporary humans anywhere in the world.

**ethnographers**
Anthropologists who study people in societies around the world, observing and talking with them in order to understand their cultures.

**ethnographies**
Written descriptions of anthropologists' observations of people's cultures.

**emic perspective**
An "insider" perspective on a particular culture, from the point of view of an anthropologist who acts as a member of the group being observed.

**etic perspective**
An "outsider" perspective on a particular culture, as for example, how an American anthropologist might view an Australian aboriginal group.

**linguistics**
The subfield of anthropology that studies modern human speech communities, the origins of speech and language, their changes through time, and their structure.

**archaeologists**
Anthropologists who study past cultures through the analysis of artifacts and their context.

anything from today's garbage to the splendors of a pharaoh's tomb to the bone, stone, and charcoal remains of a simple hunting camp abandoned hundreds of thousands of years ago. Prehistorians are archaeologists who study the prehistoric past; that is, the period before writing was fully developed. With no written material to rely on, and obviously with no on-the-spot informants to interview, prehistoric archaeologists use the animal, plant, and artifactual material recovered during excavations to describe how people lived in the past and to try to understand how, when, and why cultures changed through time. In contrast, historic archaeologists use historic (i.e., written) records as often as excavated materials. Sometimes, interestingly, what was written does not agree with what is excavated. Other subfields of archaeology include underwater archaeology, Egyptian archaeology, archaeobotany, zooarchaeology, archaeometallurgy, urban archaeology, and public archaeology. Each specialty uses somewhat different methods to acquire data about the past and often does research in different places.

**Applied anthropology** is often the neglected stepsister of the other subdisciplines of anthropology, but all anthropologists hope that eventually their research findings will help solve human problems. Biological anthropologists can point to their discovery of the connection between malaria and sickle-cell anemia as a way to begin eliminating malaria or to the design of modern buses, especially the steps, so that women who are shorter-legged than average can get up them. Additionally, bioanthropologists have played major roles in forensic cases as a result of their specialized knowledge of human skeletal anatomy and its modern variability. There is even the possibility of helping to solve worldwide problems if people would understand, as biological anthropologists do, that there are no such things as biological races, only cultural constructs. Cultural anthropologists can point to knowledge of the underlying causes of resentment and fear between neighboring tribes as a way of preventing local wars or of mediating between workers from different countries who have different cultures and languages but find themselves working in the same factory because of the European Union. Recently, an applied cultural anthropologist was instrumental in developing strategies for involving community groups in crime prevention activities. Applied cultural anthropologists can work wherever there are cultural problems to solve, at home or in foreign lands. Archaeologists can also point to research on raised fields in the Andes, a farming technique lost when the Spaniards imposed haciendas (plantations), as a way to help impoverished farmers increase potato production.

As you can tell from these descriptions, many anthropological issues do not belong to a single subdiscipline. To be human is a matter of both human biology *and* human culture. Additionally, the human condition today is contingent on—derives from—the human condition in the past. Many anthropologists are therefore quite multi-faceted within their discipline, sometimes combining cultural and biological research to study a particular human phenomenon or using the past to explain the present. Being a general anthropologist is often more difficult than being a specialist, because a generalist must master two or more subdisciplines.

**Paleoanthropology** is the term often used to describe a combined biological and cultural focus on humans in the past (Clark 2000; Clark and Howell 1966; Relethford 2001a). In reality, most paleoanthropologists specialize in either biological anthropology or archaeology; a few specialize in the interaction of some facet of both biology and culture.

# How Anthropologists Do Their Work

One factor that keeps anthropology a single, holistic, discipline is the fact that there are some similarities in how all anthropologists go about doing their work. Many anthropologists in each subfield travel to other countries to gather data: A bioanthropologist may travel to East Africa and become part of an international team excavating in Tanzania for fossils of human ancestors; an archaeologist may travel to Turkey to excavate a cave that holds ancient artifacts. A cultural anthropologist may spend two years in

**applied anthropology**
A fifth "subfield" of anthropology that uses what basic research has discovered about the human condition to attempt to solve contemporary human problems.

**paleoanthropology**
The scientific study of fossils and artifacts and the contexts in which they are found.

New Guinea in an attempt to figure out how trade works there in the absence of "money." And a linguist may travel to New Caledonia in the Pacific Ocean just to hear the language spoken by the local people before doing any analysis of that speech community. Traveling to exotic places is not required for anthropological work, but most anthropologists do it, and for some, the opportunity to travel and do research in faraway places is what attracted them to the field in the first place.

Other anthropological work is done in laboratories or libraries, depending on the nature of the research project. And, of course, many projects require multiple workplaces. For example, an archaeologist who excavates an unfamiliar artifact or a bioanthropologist who excavates a bone he or she does not recognize will go to an existing collection or library to see if the find really is new or is one of many such items. The archaeologist or bioanthropologist is likely to use the facilities of a research lab as well, because any new find has to be precisely measured, photographed, and compared with other seemingly similar artifacts or bones. Only then will the anthropologist feel ready to add to the field's accumulated knowledge via publication in a journal.

## Anthropology Is Holistic

**Holism** refers to the unified way of looking at human beings in both their past and their present and through their culture and biology. As the catchphrase suggests, "the whole is greater than the sum of its parts," meaning that by looking at many aspects of a particular subject one can get more insights than by looking at just one or two. Anthropology is, by definition, part past and part present; it is part biological and part cultural in its focus. Most anthropologists regard the exploration of the links between biology and culture and between the past and the present as vital, but there are also important differences between studying humans biologically and studying them culturally. For one, human biology is inherited through sexual reproduction of parents who produce offspring, whereas human culture is "inherited" through learning the proper way to behave, what to know, and how to feel from family members, friends, and others in individual societies. Because the modes of inheritance are different (sexual reproduction versus learning) archaeologists and bioanthropologists often have to take different approaches. There are other methodological differences as well. Cultural anthropologists study modern people whom they can see and with whom they can talk and interact. Paleoanthropologists cannot see or talk with the people they study, so in a sense paleoanthropology is removed a step farther from the people under study than is cultural anthropology. The methods the disciplines employ reflect these differences, with biological anthropologists and, to a lesser extent, archaeologists relying on the scientific method (described in detail in Chapter 2) as their main methodology, from constructing a research design and carrying out fieldwork to analyzing fossil materials or artifacts. Some archaeologists adhere strictly to the scientific method, but others often use written materials from early civilizations as well as mythology, depending on the time and location of the culture they are investigating. By contrast, cultural anthropologists often use a variety of techniques drawn from history and literature as well as from various sciences.

Because culture and biology, as well as the past and the present, have obvious ties to each other, let's consider some human characteristics that illustrate these links and that demonstrate the holistic nature of anthropology.

First, consider the simple act of walking. Walking has both a past and a present; humans have been bipedal for perhaps 5 million years (myr), and we still are. Walking is both biological and cultural. We are bipedal because we have genes that are responsible for the bones, muscles, tendons, nerves, and so forth that allow us to stand and walk upright (biology), but *how* we walk is cultural. People in different cultures and subcultures are all bipedal, but they differ in terms of how far off the ground they lift their feet or how much side-to-side or head movement they make when they walk (cultural).

**holism**

The idea that anthropologists must study the past as well as the present and biology as well as culture in order to fully understand what it means to be human.

Whether one must be kind to (or ignore) one's mother-in-law varies from group to group (cultural), but the knowledge one has about behaving correctly within one's group is housed in the human brain (biological). Speech is another example of a biocultural phenomenon, in that part of this human trait is biological and part is cultural.

Second, the **capacity for culture** has biologically evolved, again connecting culture and biology, the past with the present. For example, early ancestors of humans (called australopithecines) made tools (behavior) because they had knowledge of both the technique and the eventual use of the tools (cognition), and they probably "felt good" about making a sharp, effective tool (emotions). They had culture, defined here as the specific behavior, cognition, and emotions learned by particular groups of humans and passed down through generations. The culture was relatively simple, but in time tools were far better made because later generations had more knowledge about how to make them, and they still felt good about it. Eventually, humans made cars and planes because their brains had evolved to the point where they could do math and engineering, and, yes, they also felt good about these achievements. The evolution of the *capacity* for culture is obvious here. However, such a linear progression from prehistoric through historic times does not always occur. For example, the Roman Empire, with its long list of literary and scientific achievements, was followed by a stagnation in those cultural elements in the Dark Ages, and then by a Renaissance in the fourteenth century.

Third, the (cultural) capacity to speak has a biological base that evolved over time. Although scientists do not agree on what "piece of speech equipment" evolved first or in what form, the human tongue, larynx, and brain and the neurological connections among them allowed for human speech, have a biological basis, and changed (evolved) over time. As a result, humans speak thousands of different languages today, an ability usually viewed as cultural.

Now, let's look at two recent studies that show links between biology and culture and the past and the present.

The first study came about after workers at Stonehenge in southern England, when digging a trench for a water pipe, came across a grave that contained three adult men, a teenager, and three children. Since it was a burial site, the workers turned the materials over to an archaeologist for analysis. But when the archaeologist noted that all seven individuals had what appeared to be identical skull shapes, he turned to a bioanthropologist for aid in further analysis. Oxygen isotope ratios were obtained from the bones, and the experts concluded that all of the individuals were born in Wales some 4,000 years ago and had lived there until they were at least 6 years old. The famous blue stones at Stonehenge also came from Wales at about that same time. Is there a connection between the bodies (biological evidence) and Stonehenge (cultural materials) (Stone 2004)?

The second study illustrating how interrelated biology and culture are at times—though again, each has its unique mode of inheritance—involves lactose tolerance. It is easier to think of this as the ability to digest milk, mostly cow's milk. Children all over the world can digest milk until age 4; this is probably because of the importance of mother's milk when children are young. But the ability to digest any kind of milk after age 4 depends on a region of DNA that controls the activation of a single dominant gene on one regular (not sex) chromosome. The mutation that caused milk digestibility must have occurred after 9,000 years ago, when dairying first began. New research suggests that the mutation likely occurred more than once but the effect was the same on each population: European and Kenyan populations have different mutations but share the same level of lactose tolerance (Wade 2006). Because the mutation allowed those who had it to digest a high-quality food that is rich in calcium and phosphorus, the mutants survived and reproduced at a higher rate than those who were not lactose tolerant. And the gene spread rather quickly from one dairying group to another. It took almost 400 generations for that mutation to get to 90-percent tolerance, where it is today in northern Europe. Most Asian populations that did not have dairying are very high in the

**capacity for culture**
The inborn ability to do, to know, and to feel that is subject to the biological laws of inheritance and that allows humans to develop culture—that is, learned behavior, cognition, and emotions.

nontolerance gene (Stearns and Hoekstra 2005). Thus, biology (the gene for lactose tolerance) is linked to culture (dairying).

## Anthropological Ethics

While anthropological ethics is not a subfield of anthropology, it does demonstrate the holistic nature of anthropology as a discipline. No matter which subfield any anthropologist is most interested in, he or she is concerned with the issue of ethics. Indeed, there has been an increased focus on ethical issues in Western cultures in general in the past 25 years, as evidenced by scientists coping with life-sustaining technologies and their ramifications, lawyers faced with Watergate in the 1970s, and businesspeople and engineers confronted with bribery scandals in the 1980s. An International Society of Ethicists was set up in 1985, articles about ethics have increased in all kinds of professional journals, and centers have been set up to cope with ethical concerns (Turner 2005).

Some ethics questions are generic to the sciences. The AMA was the first professional group to pass a code of ethics in 1847; bioethical codes concerning experiments on humans were set up after the Nuremberg Code in 1947. The National Institute of Health established protections for humans involved in any research done under its auspices. And the Belmont Report, issued by the U.S. government in 1971, culminated in three principles: Do no harm, apply rules of justice fairly, and do not deprive anyone of freedom. Institutional Review Boards (IRBs) that review all nationally funded research (mostly in colleges and universities) use these codified federal rules. Additionally, in 1990 the U.S. government passed NAGPRA (Native American Graves Protection and Repatriation Act), which states that all cultural and skeletal remains of Native Americans found on tribal or federal land must be given to the living descendants of the tribe owning that land currently, the tribe occupying the land in previous time, or the tribe with the strongest demonstrated relationship. This applied even if the remains were museum pieces (Turner 2005).

Turning specifically to anthropology, anthropologists over the years have been accused of spying (in Thailand), giving information to the U.S. government (in Latin America), and falsifying data to make a point (in Venezuela), to name just a few incidents. Though in most cases, such accusations turned out to be false, they did push anthropologists into discussing the ethics of their own discipline and subfields, which resulted in the AAA (American Anthropological Association) Code of Ethics, approved in June 1998. (For the sake of brevity, other codes will not be discussed here.) The AAA's Code is general enough to be applied to all subfields of anthropology. The following highlights of this code are from sections on research and teaching.

### Specific to research:

- There are ethical obligations to the people and animals studied.
- Informed consent to do research must be gotten in advance of any research; this includes informing all individuals about possible problems and the impacts of the research.
- Anthropologists must not fabricate, deceive, knowingly misrepresent, or plagiarize any information.
- Anthropologists must not prevent the reporting of misconduct of others.
- Anthropologists must do all they can to give opportunities for others to follow them in the field.
- Anthropologists must disseminate the findings to sponsors and decision makers.

**Specific to teaching:**

- Anthropologists must not discriminate on the basis of sex, marital status, race, social class, political stance, disabilities, religion, ethnic background, national origin, sexual orientation, age, or any other criteria irrelevant to academic performance (Turner 2005).

Some ethical dos and don'ts are specific to anthropological subfields. For example, only cultural anthropologists could be accused of spying, as dead people and their artifacts couldn't be of interest to spies! Should contemporary people in South America be compensated fairly for giving drug companies information about local drugs they have used for generations that have resulted in billions of dollars of profits for those drug companies? There are also ethical issues pertinent to biological anthropology and archaeology that would not be of importance to cultural anthropologists. How does "treat fossil materials and artifacts with respect" translate into actual behavior? Does it mean reburial, as with Native American and Australian aboriginal remains? Does it mean consulting with modern representatives to decide which items can go on display in museums and which are too ritually important to expose to nonbelievers? Some biological anthropologists study nonhuman animals, particularly primates. How should these animals be treated? The Animal Welfare Act of 1985 set out rules for housing experimental animals (mice, monkeys) and what kinds of "pain and suffering are permitted." When in the field, bioanthropologists must be careful not to transmit human diseases to the animals they are studying.

Occasionally, ethical problems arise in anthropological work because there is a difference between what concerned people expect and what scientists believe they must do. This kind of situation arose with the discovery of over 400 graves of African Americans in New York City in 1991. (See Highlight 1.2, on pp. 12–13.) The professional excavation, led by an African American bioanthropologist, used standard archaeological techniques to remove the bone and artifact remains, yet some local African American citizens accused the investigators of not treating the burials with enough respect. The controversy was eventually resolved after those on both sides of the issue actually listened to instead of past each other.

# In the News: The African Burial Ground in New York City

HISTORIANS DOCUMENTING EVENTS in U.S. history have always had the luxury of written evidence, something archaeologists usually do not have. So the recovery of an unknown piece of American history that was all but forgotten, then accidentally rediscovered, excavated, and analyzed would be heralded by historians as an interesting event and might even be published in a history journal. But because that forgotten event was the burial of more than 400 African Americans between 1712 and 1794, representing the only concrete evidence of slavery in New York City, it became headlines.

The modern story began in 1990. That year the city of New York sold a parking lot two blocks from City Hall to the federal General Services Agency (GSA), which wanted to erect a building there to house an office of the U.S. Attorney General, a branch of the Environmental Protection Agency, and a district Internal Revenue Service office. Because the land was now U.S. Government property, an environmental impact study, including an archaeological assessment, was required before any work could begin. The company that was hired to do the assessment knew that the "Old Negroes' Burial Ground" had once been somewhere nearby, because it was marked on old maps; however, the company predicted that nothing would be found during its sampling.

This prediction was wrong. By the end of the summer of 1991, the assessors started finding human bones. A full excavation then began, financed by the GSA. At this point the local African

American community became concerned about the excavation and about what would happen to the bones and artifacts. Although there were some suggestions that the burials were not handled with proper respect, investigators used standard archaeological techniques in their systematic excavation for both bone and artifact materials. And although there were no coffin plates for identification, it was possible to keep the sets of bones together as units, because all of the 427 burials on the GSA property were in single coffins.

Why were the 427 African Americans buried where they were? What is their story? Back in 1626, when New York City was a Dutch colony (Nieuw Amsterdam), the Dutch East India Company sent its first shipment of African slaves to the New World to work the fields of the Dutch farmers. The Dutch colonists actually freed the slaves in 1644 and gave them small parcels of land to farm. However, when the British took over, they not only continued bringing in slaves but also made sure that the freed slaves lost their farmland. In time the slaves were working as dockhands, repairing city streets, and working in shipbuilding and construction. And in 1697 New York City adopted a kind of mortuary apartheid, declaring lower Manhattan churchyards off-limits to African Americans. Between 1712 and 1794, historians estimate between 10,000 and 20,000 poor people were buried in a five-acre plot now known as the African Burial Ground. Most of the people were descendants of original African slaves. On the eve of the American Revolution, New York City had more slaves than anywhere else in the New World except Charleston, South Carolina. Slaves were an important element in the building and functioning of colonial New York City. After 1794, however, no more slaves were interred in the Burial Ground. In 1795 the city filled the area with 20 feet of dirt. And though the cemetery appeared on maps, it was all but forgotten until the archaeological impact study began in 1990.

The next chapter in the story concerned not only the excavation, the excavators, and local citizens, but the mayor of New York, local congressional representatives, state senators, the press, the clergy, and academicians. After several years of contentious disagreement over how to handle the situation, Dr. Michael Blakey, an African American bioanthropologist, was appointed to be the scientific director of the project. Before and during the excavation, which ended in July 1992, Blakey, on behalf of Howard University and archaeological consultants, came up with a research proposal that both satisfied intellectual questions and benefited the African American community. The remains were turned over to him and are now in Washington, D.C., where African American researchers and students can study and interpret them.

The biological analyses of the Burial Ground remains are still ongoing; but preliminary findings suggest that approximately 93 percent of the 427 burials were African Americans; the other 7 percent appear to have been poor European Americans. Almost half of those buried (40 percent) were under 12 years of age, suggesting a child death rate twice that of the nonslave population of the time, and the general health picture shows high disease rates and poor nutrition. Two-thirds of the adults buried were male—which raises the question of where the females were buried, given that the sex ratio was presumably about 50:50. Little is known of the slaves' causes of death, though one rib cage contained a musket ball. Some diseases do not leave skeletal clues but are killers anyhow, and malnutrition can make people (especially children) vulnerable to conditions such as pneumonia and diarrhea.

Cultural evidence from the burials is quite meager, because the excavators found few artifacts. These were not the graves of rich people who wanted to be buried with a lot of material possessions to take to the next life. There were numerous shroud pins, and researchers found one glass bead and some cowrie shells—grave goods that were typical of West African burials. Interestingly, the cowrie shells may reflect the African practice of symbolizing "the passage in death across the sea and have been variously interpreted as a return to Africa or the afterlife" (Harrington, 36). The vast majority of burials lay with their faces turned toward the west, but the meaning of this is unknown.

The Burial Ground research design called for biological and archaeological assessments of the population to answer questions about biology, health, and culture (and cultural change) among the first generations of African Americans. On the biological side an inter-disciplinary team combines morphological, morphometric, and molecular genetic data to answer three basic research questions: (1) What were the origins of the individuals in the population? (2) What was the physical quality of life during the time the burial ground was used? (3) What can the site reveal about the transition from African to African American identities?

One of the reasons for involving African American scholars in the project was to ensure proper interpretation of artifacts that were either African or African American in origin. For example, when the excavators found a coffin with a heart-shaped pattern of nail heads on it, only an African specialist was able to interpret the pattern as symbolizing tying the past with the present in order to prepare for the future. It is fitting that the burials of the earliest African American generations are being interpreted by modern African American experts so that future generations of Americans can better understand the past.

Numerous anthropologists have been and continue to be involved in the African Burial Ground: The excavators used standard archaeological techniques; bioanthropologists are evaluating the demography, origins, and diseases of the population; and cultural anthropologists are attempting to explain how the meager burial goods reflect West African cultures. An important part of the ongoing project is public education. Volunteers conduct tours of the site, show slides, give lectures, and train teachers to explain this missing part of African American history. Additionally, a museum and memorial now stand near the excavation area. Many members of the local community are lobbying for final reburial of the site itself, which became a National Historic Landmark in February 1993. Funding by GSA will allow experts to produce a final report on the biology, archaeology, and history of the burials.

Sources: Anthropology Newsletter. 2003. Following the remains of enslaved Africans. November: 15–16. Harrington, S. P. 1993. Bones and bureaucrats. Archaeology 46 (2): 28–29. Harrington, S. P. 1999. Stories the bones will tell. Archaeology (September/October): 36–37. LaRoche, C. J., and M. L. Blakey. 1997. Seizing intellectual power: The dialogue at the New York African Burial Ground. Historical Archaeology 31 (3): 84–106. Perry, W., and M. L. Blakey. 1997. Archaeology as community service: The African Burial Ground project in New York City. North American Dialogue 2 (1).

turn back to your reading

Humans are biological organisms who also have cultures. Yet there is a very important difference between biology and culture in terms of how they are inherited; therefore, we will separate culture and biology in this book as we explore what happened in the human past. Because human ancestry in the form of bipedal (hominid) primates precedes any known cultural artifacts by more than 3 million years, it is logical to start with human biology and follow it with human culture.

Thus, Chapters 2 through 7 focus on bioanthropology, starting with Chapter 2's coverage of theories and methods that are vital to understanding evolution. Chapter 3 covers the principles of biological evolution, followed by Chapter 4's discussion of macroevolutionary steps from the earliest life on Earth to mammals. Chapter 5 follows with an introduction to primates in general and then their evolution. Chapters 6 and 7 focus on hominid (bipedal) human ancestors that appeared in the fossil record beginning about 5 myr ago and take us to our own species, *Homo sapiens*. Chapters 8 through 13 focus on human prehistory,

**page 3**

starting with theories and methods used to study past cultures and continuing with coverage of Old World and New World cultures. Chapters 14 and 15 return to biological anthropology, but this time the focus is on contemporary primates (prosimians, monkeys, and apes) and humans.

■ Paleoanthropology is the study of biological fossils (biological anthropology) and cultural remains (archaeology) of past peoples.

■ Many anthropologists do fieldwork, whether excavating fossils (biological anthropology), excavating artifacts (archaeology), or observing cultures different from their own (cultural anthropology).

■ Some anthropologists do research exclusively in laboratories or libraries; those who do fieldwork also use libraries to check on the validity of what they have recently excavated or observed.

■ Anthropology is holistic; it is necessary to study both past and present and both culture and biology in order to fully understand what it is to be human.

■ The capacity for culture involves both biological features (at the genetic or molecular level) and the resultant cultural traits.

■ The American Anthropological Association (AAA) adopted a Code of Ethics in 1998 that established rules for all anthropologists to follow in setting up their research, conducting it in the field, and writing it up. The AAA Code also protects students in classroom situations.

## KEY WORDS

anthropology, 2
applied anthropology, 7
archaeologists, 6
biological anthropologists, 3
capacity for culture, 9

cultural anthropologists, 6
emic perspective, 6
ethnographers, 6
ethnographies, 6
etic perspective, 6

holism, 8
linguistics, 6
paleoanthropology, 7

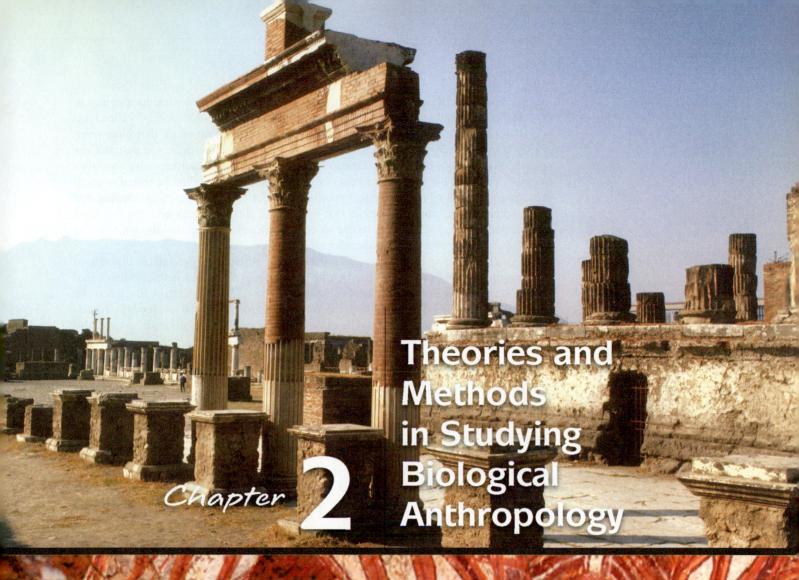

# Theories and Methods in Studying Biological Anthropology

*Chapter* **2**

■ **THE SCIENTIFIC METHOD (TSM)**

■ **COMMON SENSE, SCIENCE, AND RELIGION**

■ **WHY EXPERTS DISAGREE**
Observation and Age, Sex, Experience, and Culture • Paradigms

■ **BIOLOGICAL EVIDENCE**
Preservation of Bone: Fossilization • Preservation of DNA
■ **HIGHLIGHT 2.1:** *Pompeii*

■ **FINDING BIOLOGICAL SITES AND FOSSILS**
Provenience Problems

■ **DATING BIOLOGICAL EVIDENCE**
Dating Fossils • Dating Molecules • Ice and Marine Cores: Do They Date Fossils?

■ **ANALYSIS OF BIOLOGICAL EVIDENCE**

■ **CHAPTER SUMMARY**

▲
**Photo above:** The Roman city of Pompeii, destroyed in the volcanic eruption of Mount Vesuvius, Italy, in AD 79

All disciplines of science have to have a sound theoretical and methodological context. Without such a context, descriptions of likely biological happenings in the past would be superficial at best and attempts to understand why they happened would be daunting. This chapter lays out the basic framework that bioanthropologists use to study humans as a biological species, *Homo sapiens*, in the past and the present. For example, use of the scientific method constrains bioanthropologists either to gather data and use the data to generate hypotheses that can then be tested to see if they are supported or refuted *or* to hypothesize about some biological happening and then gather data to support or refute that hypothesis. Bioanthropologists are therefore constrained to using evidence to come to conclusions rather than wildly conjecturing some possible scenario and pontificating about it.

This chapter focuses on two major questions: (1) What is the general paradigm used by bioanthropologists to view "their world" of humans? (2) What is the evidence that they generate and use in order to make sense of that world? To answer the first question, we will begin with the bioanthropologist's foremost methodological framework, the scientific method. We will then assess the three world views of common sense, science, and religion in terms of both what each is and whether the three overlap, are totally separate, or a single entity. Next, we will consider why experts disagree on matters of human evolution even though they may have access to exactly the same data.

To answer the second major question, we will consider the nature of the evidence used by bioanthropologists to both reconstruct our human past and understand the present day status of our species, and then to explain why we were the way we were in the past and why we are the way we are now. What is biological evidence? How is it used?

Once we have set the theoretical parameters and described the evidence used to understand the biology of humans, past and present, we will be prepared to delve into the principles of biological evolution in Chapter 3 and reconstruct the likeliest scenario for the past 3.5 billion years of life in subsequent chapters.

# The Scientific Method (TSM)

**The scientific method (TSM)** is the center of what defines science. **Science** is a method of inquiry. Scientists believe that there is a knowable and orderly world out there and that past events can be explained if adequate observations or data are used correctly. That is, science goes beyond mere description or data gathering and attempts to explain things and happenings. It is a way of thinking about something that usually results in an activity, such as gathering data to test a hypothesis. But it is not always necessary to do experiments or use complex statistics; science does not necessarily involve bubbling retorts and white lab jackets. The only requirement is to think scientifically.

Thinking scientifically—applying the scientific method—begins with something interesting enough to investigate, some question worth answering. If there is a question, there are usually one or more possible answers to it. When the question is stated with a possible answer attached to it, it becomes a **hypothesis** (from the Greek meaning "foundation"), and stating a hypothesis is the first step in TSM. Where a hypothesis comes from is not important: its origins can be a dream, a flash of intuition, a casual comment from a colleague in a conversation, or something just read. What matters is that it can and must be tested for verification.

A hypothesis, then, is a good guess about something that is capable of being either supported or falsified; unless that good guess can possibly be found to be false, it cannot be a scientific hypothesis. In other words, there are some good guesses about interesting things that cannot be falsified, so they are not subject to TSM. The existence of the Tooth Fairy is an example; there is no way to gather appropriate evidence that would either falsify or support that existence. In contrast, "The sun will come up every day at the same time in the same place" may be simplistic, but it is a scientific hypothesis: It is a

**the scientific method (TSM)**
The method of doing science: generating hypotheses, collecting appropriate data, testing, and forming appropriate conclusions.

**science**
A way of learning about the world through observation and use of TSM.

**hypothesis**
An informed explanation of a set of observations that can be tested or falsified.

good guess about the sun, based on observations of what happened yesterday and the day before, and appropriate data can be collected to test it. Also, given that this three-part statement about how often, when, and where the sun rises is not necessarily true, the statement can be scientifically tested and falsified.

To test a hypothesis an investigator gathers information (data) and uses the data to judge the validity of the hypothesis. The data must, of course, be pertinent to the question asked. A question about the sun cannot be tested with data on the genetics of leaf-cutter ants. Data collection for the sunrise hypothesis might begin with the investigator's waking up before the expected hour of daybreak to see if the sun does rise. If it does, at least part of the hypothesis has been supported. To test the other parts, the investigator would have to check on the sunrise for many months to see if it came up at the same time and in the same place every day. After collecting and recording data on the sunrise question for a sufficient number of days, the investigator would conclude that the sun does come up every day, but not at the same time or at the same place on the horizon—unless the investigator were making observations on the equator. (And even at the equator, because of the axis of the Earth, there is an annual 15-minute variation of sunrises either side of 6:00 a.m.) If the observation spot were anywhere on the Arctic Circle, the sun would not come up at all for several weeks in mid-December.

A key point is that although hypotheses can be disproved (falsified), they cannot be proved. Two of the three parts of the sunrise hypothesis could be disproved anywhere in the world, and all three parts could be disproved at the Arctic Circle. Because all of the data pertinent to any subject are not usually known, it is better not to claim proof for any hypothesis—only support.

Because parents and teachers want young people to believe in the process of science, they often give the impression that hypotheses inevitably lead to truth and are proved. Articles about experiments that were not successful are seldom published in journals, re-inforcing the idea that hypotheses always somehow succeed. Elementary and high school teachers usually give students experiments that will work, again reinforcing this impression. But falsification is important too; it might be better if teachers sometimes left a chemical out of an experiment in order to help students understand that hypotheses have to be tested and can be falsified, or they are not science.

Many anthropological topics offer examples of the application of TSM. To take one interesting case, let's follow the topic of "Venus figurines" through the steps. Venus figurines are small female statuettes carved from bone, ivory, or stone of different kinds and dated to around 25 to 15 thousand years ago (kyr ago) in Europe and Asia. Researchers have found about 180 of these Upper Paleolithic figures from the Pyrenees north and east to Siberia. But what was their function? The traditional hypothesis was that the figurines represented female fertility. At the time the idea was proposed, it was a good guess, because many of the figures appeared to be pregnant. But a test of that hypothesis later showed it to be false. Because people in Europe 25 to 15 kyr ago were hunter-gatherers, the test compared Venus figurines to modern hunter-gatherers in age and pregnancy status. The study found a close correlation between the proportionate numbers of young, childbearing, and older females among the Venuses and the modern hunter-gatherers. As a result the researcher concluded that Venuses did not just represent fertility. There were too few figurines that looked pregnant and far too many that did not, or were not in the right age bracket to be pregnant. Additionally, not a single Venus statuette appeared to be delivering a baby and not a single one included a baby in the female's arms. If fertility were the function of the statuettes, it is reasonable to assume that these conditions would have been depicted at least once. These findings generated a new hypothesis: that the figures represented women, not just mothers. A further test using other data supported that hypothesis.

Is the new hypothesis about the function of Venus figurines the final word? No, because other Venus figurines or other ways to test the function hypothesis may be found. Science is self-correcting, and scientists engage in a constant stream of activities—generating hypotheses, collecting data, testing hypotheses against the data, and forming

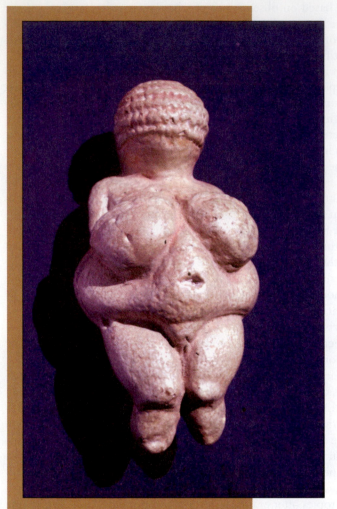

**A Venus figurine from Willendorf (Austria) dated to about 25 kyr ago and made from limestone. Like most Venus figurines, this one does not have traits of pregnancy and thus likely represents "women," not "mothers."**

**knowledge**
That which is probably correct given the data at hand but that may change as new data or new ways to interpret data are found.

**deductive reasoning**
The scientific process of hypothesizing, gathering data to test the hypothesis, and drawing appropriate conclusions.

conclusions (Rice 1981). Just because a particular expert endorses a particular hypothesis does not by itself bolster that hypothesis's validity. In the absence of evidence supporting a hypothesis, argument by authority is not appropriate.

Like hypotheses, "truth" cannot be proved, only disproved. Scientists may search for truth, but truth implies certainty, so they do not expect to find it. Lee Cronk (1999) suggests that scientists are asked to strike the following bargain: If they give up the goal of absolute knowledge and accept the permanent tentativeness of all scientific propositions, in exchange, science will give them a steadily improving understanding of the way things work. Thus, scientists are usually content with finding **knowledge**, defined as "a descriptive statement about something that is most probably correct, given the evidence currently available." Knowledge helps us make sense of the unknown. For example, all that humans currently know about sunrises constitutes knowledge. Scientists invite change in their ideas; it is scientifically healthy to be skeptical of any and all findings and to look continually for new evidence to refute, change, or bolster hypotheses.

There are variations on TSM beyond the steps we have outlined. For example, the order of steps can be changed. The sunrise hypothesis represents **deductive reasoning** in that the hypothesis preceded the gathering of data. The other way to do science, however, is to use **inductive reasoning**, as in the example of the Venus figurines, to gather all kinds of data relative to a particular topic with no preconceptions about the result. In inductive science the analysis of the data generates the hypothesis to be tested. For example, an investigator may want to know many things about sunrises and may proceed to collect data from numerous sources: information about time, place, periodicity, the brightness of the sun, the number of sunspots, and countless other aspects. After analyzing the data, the investigator may decide that the only patterned observations concern place, time, and periodicity. That conclusion can become the basis for a hypothesis to be tested with new data. And this is what usually happens in science: Investigators question a specific idea, gather data, and use the data to generate or to test a hypothesis; their conclusions then become new hypotheses to be tested. At any point in this chain, the hypothesis can be rejected—but falsification is knowledge too. This is what happened in the Venus figurines example.

Is anthropological research better done inductively or deductively? Some scientists argue that one way is better than the other. Some, for example, maintain that only deductive science yields strong findings that give confidence in their results; others agree with Sherlock Holmes, who in "A Scandal in Bohemia" (1891) said, "It is a capital mistake to theorize before one has data. Insensibly one begins to twist facts to suit theories, instead of theories to suit facts." Presumably this was the belief of Holmes's creator, Sir Arthur Conan Doyle, who was himself a physician/scientist. In fact, whether anthropological research is better done inductively or deductively depends on the nature of the question being asked. If the question has never been explored before, then gathering data first is the only way to begin (inductive method); if it is an ongoing question, a hypothesis can be generated based on previous work done on the topic, and then new data can be gathered

**inductive reasoning**
The branch of scientific discovery that starts by freely gathering data about some phenomenon worth investigating, then allowing the data to generate a hypothesis about that phenomenon.

**theory**
A hypothesis or a set of hypotheses that has been tested and retested and not found to be false, so confidence in its value is high.

(deductive method). Although the deductive method is better at disproving hypotheses, the inductive method enables scientists to acquire new knowledge (Pigliucci 2002).

What about theory? People use the word *theory* in at least three different ways. First, the adjective *theoretical* can refer to the conceptualization of some subject, as in "theoretical physics." Second, nonscientists sometimes use the word *theory* to refer to an abstract or conjectural idea. To scientists, however, a third meaning of *theory* is central: A **theory** is a hypothesis that investigators have tested and retested over many years using different methods. If the hypothesis has not been rejected after research has exhausted all known methods to refute it, then it may be elevated to the status of a theory. The validity of a theory is very high, although any theory can still be disproved—or at least modified—if even one test does not support it. Biological evolution is a good example here. English naturalist Charles Darwin (1809–1882) believed that natural selection was the main vehicle through which populations changed over time; when Darwin first proposed this idea in 1859, it was what we now call a hypothesis. Similarly, Austrian Gregor Mendel (1822–1884) believed that the inheritance of biological characteristics involved discrete units—what we now call genes. Mendel suggested hypotheses about heredity that seemed to explain his observations on experimental pea plants. Nearly 150 years later, Darwin's and Mendel's hypotheses have been exhaustively and independently tested and retested and occasionally modified. In the 1950s they were combined into what is now called the synthetic theory of evolution, or the modern synthesis (see Chapter 3). The modern synthesis is a true theory in the scientific sense, as it is composed of a series of hypotheses that have withstood extensive testing and is considered unlikely to be disproved.

Another way to look at hypotheses and theories is to think of them relative to the level of confidence they give. Confidence is grounded on the validated linkages of many levels of testing. On a scale of providing least to most confidence, hypotheses are at the low end because they are often found to be false. Sometimes theories are rejected as well; this happened with Jean Baptiste Lamarck's (1744–1829) theory of acquired characteristics, a theory that scientists believed for 200 years (see Chapter 3). In general, theories, such as atomic theory or quantum theory, give more confidence than hypotheses, even though they too can be falsified. Finally, at the high end of the confidence scale are scientific *laws*. The law of gravity is a good example of a physical law, but there are few laws in the biological arena. Mendel's two laws of inheritance have been modified since he postulated them in the mid-nineteenth century, but they are at least lawlike and give high confidence.

# Common Sense, Science, and Religion

We have defined science as a way to approach certain questions about the world. Other ways to approach questions are **common sense** and **religion**. Common sense, science, and religion are found in all societies, because humans are innately curious; and people in all societies use each of them to solve different kinds of problems. Common sense helps people answer a great many questions without having to invoke either science or religion. It is common sense to drink when you are thirsty and to avoid jumping into a river if it is filled with crocodiles. Neither religion nor science is better than common sense for answering questions like "Should I drink water" or "Should I jump in the river?" There are, however, many questions that science can answer better than either common sense or religion. And there are many questions that religion can answer better than common sense or science. For example, although questions about the ultimate source for the origin of the universe and the origin of life are better addressed by religion, questions about what happened in the known universe during the last 15 billion years (byr) are better addressed by science. Common sense can't begin to answer either

**common sense**
Based on past experience, common sense is used to solve certain problems.

**religion**
Framework of beliefs relating to supernatural or superhuman beings or forces that transcend the everyday material world.

kind of question. And questions concerning the meaning or purpose of life or how humans should behave are best addressed by religion.

The basic differences among common sense, science, and religion are clear if we think about individuals' attitudes toward discovering knowledge and enlightenment. If an individual believes that he or she can solve a problem by gathering data about the problem and using the data to come to a conclusion, then the individual's attitude is scientific. If an individual believes that divine intervention can solve a problem, then the person's attitude is religious. If an individual believes that he or she can solve a problem by thinking it through, that attitude relies on common sense. Science is based on the use of TSM, religious beliefs are based on faith, and common sense is based on individual experiences. But there is no intrinsic reason why any two of these approaches should be at odds—because, as we have noted, each has its own arena. Stephen Jay Gould (2001) said the same thing, though he left common sense out of his argument, when he said that science and religion reside in two "nonoverlapping Magisteria." Given that religion and science do not claim to be trying to answer the same questions, it is surprising that many people still believe they have to choose one over the other.

Cultural anthropologists point out that evolution belongs in the biology domain and religion belongs in the cultural domain. Remember that all cultures in the world have a feature that can be called religion. Cultural anthropologists often widen the scope of "religion" to include mythology and sometimes even magic because religion, magic, and myth are often indistinguishable to people in other cultures. A cross-cultural survey of one aspect of religion—beliefs about the creation of Earth, objects, and people—reveals certain similarities in all or most religions. Here are some examples: Across North Africa, from Algeria west to Timbuktu, people in different cultures believe that the first created object was a serpent, out of whose body the world and all life were made. In East Africa, the Bambara believe in a male/female duality of body and spirit, with females making the Earth and males making the Sky. Halfway around the world, in Borneo, the Dusun believe that in the beginning there was only a rock and water. The rock split to release a male and a female divinity who made Heaven and Earth and then started creating humans. They first made humans of stone, but the stones couldn't talk. So they tried again, this time making humans of wood, but the wood decayed. Their successful third attempt saw the divinities making humans from the earth of a termite mound! People in several Meso-American cultures believed in a divinity of male and female duality, and most North American Indians have a version of Mother Earth and Father Sky. Contrary to most cultures, Australian aborigines believe the Earth has always existed.

There are certain themes that show up in many, but not all, of the creation myths or beliefs: The Earth is often symbolized as an egg; there is a duality of the sexes, with males in charge of Sky or Heaven and women in charge of Earth; the Sky or Heaven is the special place for gods; serpents symbolize evil; and a supreme deity exists. The three main world religions (Christianity, Islam, and Judaism) fit very well with a cross-cultural perspective. People all over the world believe and want to believe; these beliefs are simply in a different arena from science.

In this context let's consider the question of why Americans don't believe in evolution. In a number of surveys on this question, Americans are usually at the bottom of the chart. When asked "Do you believe in evolution?" in 2006, more Americans than citizens of any other country except Turkey said no. In Japan, 96 percent of those polled by CBS said yes, but in the United States, only 40 percent said yes.

Why so many Americans do not believe in evolution is a fairly easy question to answer, at least on the surface. Jon Miller at Michigan State University, who headed the team doing the survey, suggests it is a combination of religious fundamentalism, bitter partisan politics (and its interrelationship with religion), and poor science education. For the rest of the world, evolution is not an issue. In this country, both Catholics and mainstream Protestants take the Biblical account of creation as only a metaphor and agree with scientists that the Earth must be much older than 6,000 years. But fundamentalist Protestants take the Bible literally and claim the Earth and humans are only 6,000 years old. Furthermore, a lack of a national U.S. curriculum for schools, something that is common in European countries, means that the teaching of evolution can be banned by any state (Hecht 2006).

*Creationism, creation science, intelligent design,* or any other term for the approach that attempts to explain all happenings and all things without using science has periodically been in the headlines from the Scopes trial in the mid-1920s to very recently. However, as explained above, there is no reason for any arguments between science and religion because they are indeed operating in different arenas. Religion is based on faith, and science is based on doubt (Tattersall 2002). If a scientist performs an experiment in hopes of finding support for a hypothesis, he or she will abandon that hypothesis if the experiment does not support it. But if a Christian's prayer goes unanswered, he or she will likely continue to pray because he or she has faith. Creationism or its variations is not scientific. First, it cannot be tested, and all science must be testable; second, creationism is not scientific because it cannot be found to be incorrect, and all science must be falsifiable. Third, creationism is not science because it can't change, and all of science is subject to change. Finally, science requires evidence, but faith does not.

# Why Experts Disagree

Before the 1930s, most disagreements between scientists in a given field were due to lack of understanding of some key element. For example, Darwin's contribution to the study of evolution was opposed because of a lack of understanding of genetics; once genetics and natural selection were joined, much of the disagreement disappeared. Even though all modern bioanthropologists claim they are scientists and use TSM, they often disagree about methodology, interpretation of data, and theoretical perspectives on big questions. Although individuals will often obtain the same results at a "low level," (e.g., each will get the exact same measurements on a series of skulls), they often interpret the results differently at a "medium level" (e.g., each will categorize the skulls differently, putting specific skulls into different categories), and each will end up using the same data to support totally different paradigms that guide his or her inquiries at the "highest, most abstract level" (the metaphysical or theoretical) (Clark and Lindly 1991). How can this happen?

## Observation and Age, Sex, Experience, and Culture

Thomas Kuhn, a leading philosopher of science, states that what people actually see depends on what they look at and what their "previous visual and conceptual experience has taught" them to see (1962, 111). In other words, what people "look at" is not necessarily what they "see," and scientists are no different from anyone else in that regard. Observation is not as finite as it might seem. What individuals see (and how that might differ from person to person) depends to some extent on age, sex, previous experience, and individual cultural milieu (Campbell and Rice 2008). Any one or a combination of these variables leads to at least some bias in the scientific arena. People of different ages are often interested in different aspects of a subject. Males and females often differ in their interests as well. Previous experience (often tied to age) can blind experts to particular lines of research because they know such lines were not possible to explore in the past. And a scientist's culture also casts a shadow over all aspects of the work.

Science as defined earlier does not occur in all other cultures, but such a definition of science is appropriate in Japan. However, one aspect of Japanese versus Western science can illustrate culture as a biasing agent. In the branch of science called primatology (see Chapter 14), which is basically the study of primates, there are two independent traditions: Western primatology and Japanese primatology. Western primatology goes back to 1929 when Robert Yerkes, a psychologist, began primate field work. Although primatologists from various Western countries have their differences in focus and interest, it is safe to say that Europeans and Americans have worked under the same tradition (paradigm) from that beginning. The Japanese tradition began in 1948 when J. Itani and S. Kawamura were observing semi-wild horses and came across a troop of Japanese macaques (Takasaki 2000). They stopped watching horses and began the first field observation of primates, literally in their own backyard. The Japanese tradition (paradigm) has been almost exclusively separate from the Western tradition ever since, and it is intrinsically tied to the powerful effect of Japanese culture in general. The Japanese focus on individuals and their role in their society, usually giving monkeys or apes personal names, and see no boundary of importance between humans and monkeys or apes. In contrast, Western primatologists separate "us" from "them" and concentrate on discovering "average" behaviors across all of a species.

Picture the following scenario: An American primatologist is in a semi-wooded area in Africa and sees a monkey on the ground. It is the first monkey he has seen, so he watches it for some time. Then he realizes there is another monkey nearby, so he watches it and its interaction with the first monkey, noting that the larger (first) monkey is sharing bits of food with the smaller (second one). He mentally notes that this might be a mother and child duo. He then notes a third monkey eating nearby, and little by little, he notices more and more monkeys that were partially hidden by foliage; they are interacting to varying degrees, and he notes all of this in his field notebook. Later in his tent that night, the investigator may conclude that he may be seeing an adult female monkey, then a mother/child duo, then a family, then a troop of monkeys. This is how his American culture has trained him to view multiple members of a single group—from individual to larger and larger groups. When this investigator sends in his report to his doctoral supervisor, he addresses it this way:

Professor's name

Department of Anthropology

Any State University

Any City

Any State, Zip Code, and US at the end

If the investigator is a Japanese doctoral student in the same circumstances, he will first note the large number of monkeys in front of him, some in full view, and some partially hidden behind foliage. He then notes that several are interacting with each other, and finally he notes and describes in great detail what each individual monkey is doing. When he writes up his report in his tent that night, he describes the troop, the family, the possible mother/child duo, and individual monkeys, in that order, from largest to smaller and smaller groups. When he sends his report to his doctoral supervisor, he addresses it this way:

Japan

A Prefecture

A City with Its Post Code

A Street Address

A University

A Department

Professor's name

The lesson to be learned here is that culture is an important variable that is sometimes missed when listing biases that affect what scientists observe and how they study a particular topic. In this case, American culture dictated that the investigator see individuals before groups, and Japanese culture just as surely dictated that the other investigator see the troop first, and then the individuals.

# Paradigms

An additional bias—due to intellectual tradition or paradigmatic differences—also can result in different conclusions by two individuals who have the same data, even if they are the same age and sex. In paleoanthropology (biological anthropology and archaeology), there are two major Western intellectual traditions that go back to the early twentieth century and continue today (and will probably continue way into the future, given the tenacity of their messianic-like supporters). The two **paradigms** are basically two different ways to view the particular features of the world that these scientists are investigating. In what is called the Old World tradition or paradigm (England and the continent), with its scientific roots in history, regionalism, geology, and paleontology, named groups of people are considered to be a cultural/biological/linguistic package. When change occurs to a group, adherents of this paradigm believe it does so rapidly, with one group replacing another, resulting in a good deal of **discontinuity**. By contrast, in the New World tradition or paradigm (the United States and Canada), with its much shorter historical roots, language, culture, and biology are considered to be separate units that may or may not be a single package found for any named group. When change occurs, adherents of this paradigm believe it is usually gradual and accumulative, resulting in **continuity**. When occasional change is rapid, it is assumed that a change in the environment is the cause (Campbell and Rice 2008; Clark 2001, 2002). Given these two paradigms, it seems obvious that one scientist, a male, aged 60, born in England and trained at a British university, and another scientist, an American male, aged 59, trained at a state university in the United States, may each take 30 measurements on a series of skulls and come up with very different reasons why those skulls differ in shape. Their intellectual traditions bias how they interpret what they see.

What might explain the differences in the intellectual traditions leading to the two paradigms, and why are the paradigms not apt to change in the near future? Geoffrey Clark (2001, 2002) and Lawrence Straus (2002) have suggested the following possibility: Europe's history is steeped in regionalism, language differences, and cultural clashes, a composite ingrained in the "lifelong experience and education of European prehistorians" (and bioanthropologists) (Straus 2002, 2). Europe has seen many conflicts on its soil, from world wars to internal wars, and has seen whole populations (that is, biological/linguistic/cultural packages) either exterminated or moved many miles away, with other populations moving into their physical space. Are thousands of years of European history thus reinforcing the concept of discontinuity? By contrast, Clark points to the fact that no world war has been fought on American soil. There was no large population displacement as the result of the Civil War, and immigration has been mostly diffuse, into cities and towns all across the country. In the New World continuity and "melting pots" are the norm. Does American history thus reinforce the idea of continuity? These two paradigms result in bias when experts are attempting to explain change in the human lineage: Were there mass extinctions with replacement of one species by another, or did an earlier species of humans evolve to a new version? (See Chapter 7.)

Unfortunately, differences of opinion often arise over fossil finds as well, biasing analyses. It seems that an expert sometimes judges fossil remains or findings solely on the basis of the fossil's being a rival to what he or she has found. This is particularly true when the fossil finds in question are potentially in the lineage leading to modern humans: "Mine is, your's isn't."

Finally, some experts believe in Ockham's razor, which suggests one should not make things more difficult or complex than they need to be in order to explain something, or in modern translation, "Keep it simple, stupid" (KISS). Other experts seem to get mired in detail.

Differences of interpretation play leading roles in this book. Instead of giving only one answer on controversial issues, the text will spell out the problem, indicate what evidence is used by each "side" and whether it has stood the test of time and hypothesis

**paradigm**
A way of looking at a broad subject, a world view—for example, science is a paradigm.

**discontinuity**
The interruption of one lineage or group by extinction or movement to another location, followed by establishment of a new population.

**continuity**
Change in a lineage that is gradual and accumulative, so that the lineage displays intermediate forms.

testing, and allow you to come to your own conclusion. We will concentrate on evidence and will not argue from our own authority, limited as all such opinion is.

# Biological Evidence

When studying humans in the past, biological anthropologists used to rely exclusively on fossils that were once live individuals. Now, however, although fossils remain the major source of evidence and constitute the framework for evolutionary schemes, bioanthropologists can also use molecular studies to both gauge relationships among species and attempt to date evolutionary happenings that cannot be dated by standard techniques. To sort out evolutionary happenings, bioanthropologists sometimes use pollen, animal bones, and sediments to reconstruct the environment that existed at the time of a specific happening and try to assess whether there is any causal relationship between the two. They also use oxygen isotope analyses of bones to determine migration routes of populations or to assess the kinds of food that were eaten, archaeological data to help reconstruct behavior, and X-rays and CT scans to look inside of fossils. But fossils of once-living beings remain their major source of information.

Technically **fossils** are any preserved remains of organic material from the past. Given the number of plants and animals that have ever been alive, fossilization is a rare event, as is clear from the fact that there are so few fossils. Although theoretically both animal bones and the woody parts of plants can fossilize, in reality plants do not fossilize nearly as often as animals, because they lack hard (bony) parts. Animals that lack bone do not readily fossilize either; as a result, animal fossils represent a biased sample relative to original numbers.

One very unusual kind of fossil is the flesh-and-skin fossil, such as the Iceman (see Highlight 1.1). He is over 5 kyr old and one of a kind. Several ritually prepared bodies of usually young women, which are assumed to be from an Inca ritual, have been found in the Andes Mountains, but they are only a few hundred years old. There are two other areas of the world where the preserved flesh of prehistoric humans has been found. The more famous of the two areas is in Northwestern Europe, where thousands of bog bodies have been found, some with hair, beards, skin, muscles, nails, and even fingerprints. Archaeologists are very interested in these bog bodies, mostly between 2,840 and 1,000 years old, but bioanthropologists are also interested in their potential pathologies. Surprisingly, of the several thousand individuals in the sample (more men than women), only six had signs of arthritis, and only a few showed dental evidence that suggested some years of less than adequate food intake. The other area where numerous prehistoric bodies with more than bone remaining have been found is in central Florida. About 7,000 years ago, Native American tribes there buried their dead under circumstances that preserved much of the brain tissue. The 160 recovered bodies were wrapped in grass mats, placed in "burial pools," and fastened to the bottom by stakes. Eventually peat filled in the ponds and sealed the burials, which were discovered in 1982, when modern housing units were to be built near Cape Canaveral. Although no hair, skin, or flesh was preserved, the remains of 90 brains were preserved. The bones suggest that many of the people lived to age 70.

Fossils provide evidence that bioanthropologists use in answering many kinds of questions—such as questions about how humans evolved, what early humans looked like, or what sorts of diseases and nutritional deficiencies past populations had. For example, because ridges or roughened areas on bone exist for muscle attachment, scientists often can infer the shape, size, and function of muscles from fossilized bones. Anthropologists can use bones to reconstruct faces and bodies and to describe what individuals from ancestral populations probably looked like. Finally, bones can offer clues about ancient lifestyles: Nutrition can affect stature, soft cereal diets can promote cavities, and general nutritional stress can result in dense concentration of bony material on the insides of long bones and cause porous bone on the upper surface of eye sockets (Rice 1998).

**fossils**
Remains of any ancient organism (plant or animal): bone, stains, casts, or molds.

Bioanthropologists who study modern populations of humans use various kinds of evidence, depending on its pertinence to their particular study. If, for example, a bioanthropologist wants to investigate the biological variability of a population, **anthropometry**—the measurement of particular parts of human bodies, faces, and dental traits—will supply evidence. Such a study might also involve comparing frequencies of blood types and other genetic traits. If a bioanthropologist wants to investigate the evolution of social behavior in early humans, analogies with modern primates and modern hunter-gatherers might generate hypotheses that could then be tested for clues to the social organization of ancestral groups.

Because fossils are such an important part of bioanthropological data, let us look at the process of fossilization in more detail.

## Preservation of Bone: Fossilization

Not all fossils are alike. Some are mineralized bone; some are casts or molds of once living plants or animals; and some are only imprints of previous life forms. For example, an insect can leave a fossilized impression after dying on a muddy surface that subsequently turned to stone. A stain may be all that is left of a human burial. The Laetoli footprints in Tanzania, preserved beneath the ash that fell from a volcanic eruption, are the fossilized evidence of 3.6-million-year-old behavior of early bipedal (two-footed) ancestors (White 1980). The La Brea tar pits in southern California date to 40 kyr ago when pools of tar came to the surface. When it rained, animals came to the pits to drink, became stuck, and died. The tar pits have yielded 660 species in an excellent state of preservation but only one human, dated at about 9 kyr ago (Thomson 2005).

Fossilization of bone is a source of much important information for the bioanthropologist. Animal soft tissues such as brain, muscle, hair, and skin tend to biodegrade quickly and survive as fossils only under rare circumstances. By contrast, bone, teeth, and shell decay more slowly and have a far better chance of becoming fossilized. For an organism to become fossilized, it has to be buried fairly quickly; if it is not, animals from bacteria to zebras will destroy the bone as well as the flesh or will stomp carcasses to dust. But if the organism lands in stagnant water (by perhaps rolling down a hill into a lake) or is covered by volcanic ash or mud, it will be safe from scavengers, and the depressed level of oxygen will inhibit decay. If the water contains minerals that infiltrate the pores and cell walls of the former organic matter, the bone can become a **true fossil**. Mineralization is a lengthy process and although many paleontologists maintain that only mineralized bones are true fossils, bioanthropologists who focus on more recent time periods normally consider any bone devoid of flesh a fossil. (Because much of the bone evidence of the human ancestry has not had the time or proper circumstances to become mineralized and because footprint images, bog people with flesh, and molds/casts are part of the evidence of our human past, we will consider any preserved remains of organic material as fossil evidence.) Once mineralized and covered in sediment or soil, bone—now a fossil—can remain for millions of years with little or no change. The longer bones have been fossilized in rock, however, the less likely they will survive, because rocks tend to be moved and "crunch up" what is in them.

Not all bones have an equal chance at becoming fossilized. Microorganisms are more active where it is warm, so cold climates act as a preserving agent, as happened with the Iceman. Moisture affects the amount and rate of fossilization as well, and the fact that early gorillas and chimpanzees have, with one recent exception, left no fossil remains is likely due to their living and dying in warm, moist tropical forests—the environment where fossilization is rarest. The age of an organism at death is also a factor in its potential fossilization: Infants and juveniles decay faster than older individuals with harder bones. Because teeth have a mineral content of 90 percent to begin with, they resist decay far longer than bone—and bone itself decays differentially, with larger bones such as skulls and mandibles (jawbones) becoming fossilized more frequently than smaller or thinner bones such as ribs or finger/toe bones. Even parts of bones have

**anthropometry**
Measurement of crania or other parts of bodies as a means of comparing populations.

**true fossil**
Ancient bone or tooth that has through time become mineralized.

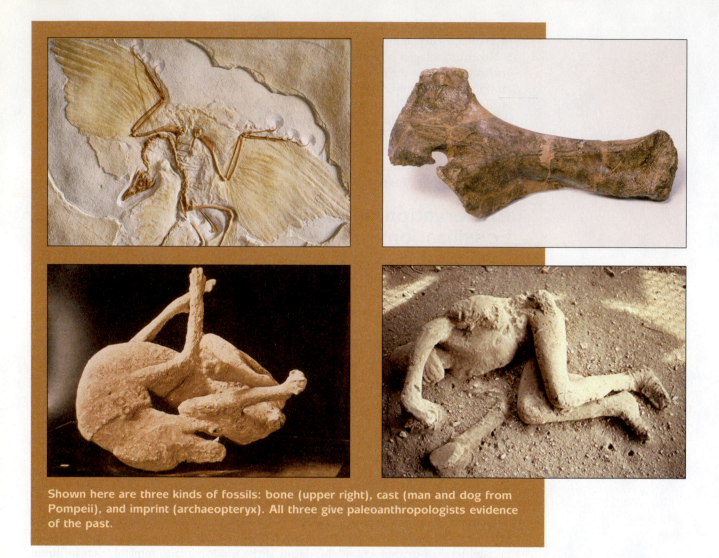

Shown here are three kinds of fossils: bone (upper right), cast (man and dog from Pompeii), and imprint (archaeopteryx). All three give paleoanthropologists evidence of the past.

different fossilization rates; the shafts of long bones resist decay longer than their ends. Also, ideal conditions for fossilization rarely occur naturally. Most lakes and streams do not contain enough minerals for complete fossilization, and many soils are too acidic for bones or teeth to survive long enough to become mineralized.

Because fossilization is such a rare event, often only a single bone or tooth must represent an entire individual. And often single individuals have to represent entire populations. Naming a new species on the basis of a single fragmentary specimen makes many investigators uncomfortable, and there have been surprises when additional fossils of the same or closely related specimens have surfaced. Yet in spite of the difficulties of dealing with fossils, they are the basic data that bioanthropologists use to describe and evaluate individuals and populations in the distant past. Highlight 2.1 focuses on one rare case of fossilization that resulted from the AD 79 eruption of Mount Vesuvius in present-day Italy, affecting the cities of Herculaneum and Pompeii.

## Preservation of DNA

**ancient DNA (aDNA)**
The nuclear or mitochondrial DNA, usually from bones or teeth, of formerly living organisms.

Although the technique of extracting **ancient DNA (aDNA)** from bones is still in its infancy, it is possible that aDNA analysis will eventually help to answer questions about relationships among individuals in particular cemeteries or tombs, relationships between entire populations, the sex of individuals (when skeletal material is poorly preserved), diseases of ancient people, and the dates when particular lineages branched off from ancestral populations. Ancient DNA can be preserved only if the bone (or tooth) contains

# Highlight 2.1

# Pompeii

ON AUGUST 24, AD 79, Mount Vesuvius near Rome erupted, and two nearby cities were affected differently. Herculaneum was not engulfed in the volcanic ash, though hundreds of people there died as a result of volcanic gases and mud. It appears that some tried to escape the event by going to the beach,

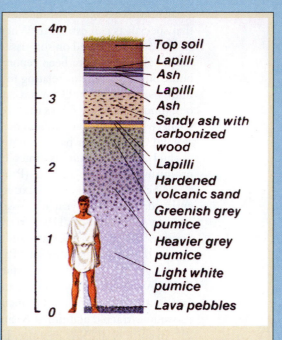

The fallout of pebbles, pumice, cinders, and ash formed a sequence of layers indicating the events of the volcanic eruption that destroyed Pompeii. A total of over 4 meters (13 feet) of rock and ash covered the city in places.

This map shows the locations of Mount Vesuvius, Pompeii, and Herculaneum. Although Herculaneum is 7 km (4.3 miles) and Pompeii is 10 km (6.2 miles) from the summit of the volcano, the wind blew most of the ash southward, leaving Herculaneum uncovered.

where they had boats in boat houses, but the pyroclastic surges with killer gases apparently overcame many. Excavators in 1982 found 40 bodies in the boat houses. The bones were often still articulated as they had been at the time of the deaths.

By contrast, Pompeii suffered a different series of cataclysmic events that night, resulting in another type of fossil for archaeologists to uncover. By the evening of the first day of the eruption, over 4 feet of ash covered the city and up to 9 feet by the next morning. Then came gases and fire. At least a thousand people died in the eruption (estimated to be 10 percent of the population), and their "remains" were excavated many years later. But these remains were not merely bones, as at Herculaneum. After an individual died by the gases or fire, the ash and pumice settled over the body, then rain washed the ash into cracks between the pumice rock, it all hardened, and the body was "cast." Flesh and clothing biodegraded,

but the bones and casts remained. Giuseppe Fiorelli, an early Pompeii excavator, in 1870, was the first to note hollow spaces in the ash and when he filled one with plaster of Paris and let it harden, a reasonable facsimile of the person as he or she looked when alive emerged. Animals, particularly dogs (pets), were also preserved in this way. So, not all fossils, used in the broad definition, are bones.

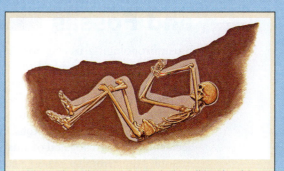

When Fiorelli located a "hole," he filled it with plaster and let it harden so that excavation around it would yield a casting that was a reasonable facsimile of the original body. Note the bones that remain in the cast.

*Sources*: Cooley, A. E. 2003. *Pompeii*. London: Gerald Duckworth.    Connolly, P. 1990. *Pompeii*. Oxford: Oxford University Press.

turn back to your reading

a calcium-based mineral called hydroxyapatite that protects aDNA from degrading so that specialists can extract it. When bone calcium degrades, aDNA is exposed to bacteria and fungi that feed on soft tissue, and it is soon gone (Sykes 2001). So far, a few spectacular successes have been reported, such as the extraction of DNA from Neandertal bone, but the problems relating to the survivability of aDNA molecules have limited the findings. As of now, aDNA has been recovered from human bones only up to 100 kyr old, though elephant bones that are 800 kyr old have yielded aDNA. Most aDNA analyses have been done on museum materials that by definition are detrimentally affected by storage. Researchers have recently noted that freshly excavated, nontreated and unwashed bones contain six times more DNA than museum samples; this discovery is promising for future analyses (Pruvost et al. 2007).

The first case of aDNA extraction occurred in 1980 when a group of Chinese scientists dated a 2,000-year-old fossil at the Hunan Medical School. This was followed in 1984 by extraction of aDNA from bones of a now-extinct quagga (a wild ass found in South Africa) to see if it was more closely related to horses or zebras (Hummel 2003).

In the early 1980s Svante Pääbo, a Swedish geneticist, compared DNA samples from Egyptian mummies to establish relationships among kings (pharaohs) (Fowler 2000). Almost 20 years later scientists removed aDNA from the right humerus (upper arm bone) of the original German Neandertal fossil. Since then researchers have successfully extracted additional Neandertal DNA samples (Relethford 2001a, 2001b).

In spite of aDNA's promise, however, very few samples are appropriate for extraction and analysis. Postdepositional chemicals can alter aDNA, and modern DNA can easily contaminate old samples. If a worker is extracting aDNA from the remains of an ancient, extinct animal (such as a mastodon) and the worker's DNA contaminates the sample, the differences between the DNA of the two species will be obvious. But if aDNA is from another hominid and is subsequently contaminated by a human worker, the contamination might not be picked up because the two kinds of DNA will show only relatively minor differences. The closer the evolutionary relationship between worker and sample, the more difficult it is to verify any conclusions. Finally, any aDNA extracted before 1995 is suspicious because scientists did not realize how susceptible it was to contamination (T. Brown 2001). Also, the technique is expensive.

Successful extraction is limited to bones found in dry and cold areas. Given these climatic restrictions, bioanthropologists are not likely to be able to extract aDNA from any African material.

# Finding Biological Sites and Fossils

Bioanthropologists usually formulate research designs before excavating. Often they have fossil material at hand (or in museum collections) and do not have to excavate. Viable hypotheses can be posed and tested by examining existing fossils in existing collections. Many theses and dissertations are formulated and completed in museum facilities without the investigators having to find new fossil material. Given the rarity of new fossils, this is fortuitous. Sometimes, however, bioanthropologists find fossils accidentally or are notified of amateurs' finds and generate hypotheses in hindsight. For example, the Gibraltar skull (Neandertal) appeared in 1848 when workers blasted out the north face of the famous rock; miners found the first australopithecine fossil in 1924; peat cutters discovered all of the hundreds of Iron Age bodies preserved in peat bogs in Europe; and mountain climbers discovered the famous Iceman. All of these were discoveries made by nonprofessionals.

Bioanthropologists often actively search the Earth's surface for fossils. Investigators seek out exposed geological layers that date to times when early humans or their ancestors were around and walk those areas, hoping to find fossils that have been exposed by

This 2,000-year-old man from Denmark, known as "Tolland Man," was found in a peat bog. Scientists believe that he probably died as a sacrificial victim or was killed as punishment rather than by accident.

the action of rain and wind. And sometimes Mother Nature rewards the patient walker. The Olduvai Gorge in Tanzania, East Africa, is an ideal geological setting for discovering human ancestors because an ancient river cut a canyon 92 m (300 feet) into the Earth and exposed layers that date to 2 million years (myr) ago. Both Olduvai Gorge and even older layers at Omo, Ethiopia, gained early reputations for yielding fossils of other animal species, so fossil hunters looking for remains of early humans have long concentrated on these two areas. Various Ethiopian sites are giving up fossils on a regular basis. Yet even though famed paleoanthropologists Mary and Louis Leakey chose the right place for fossil hunting, as subsequent finds attested, the Leakeys spent almost 30 years at Olduvai before finding a single human ancestor.

Once biological anthropologists find a potentially significant bone, they usually initiate a controlled excavation in hopes of finding more bones. Often such a project resembles an archaeological excavation. For example, in the 1990s anthropologists excavated the African Burial Ground in New York City with archaeological precision, but with the goal of finding both cultural and biological remains (see Highlight 1.2). Sometimes, however, excavating for fossils looks more like a treasure hunt than an excavation; this was the case in East Africa with an early potential human ancestor known as Nariokotome (Turkana Boy), as Highlight 7.1 describes.

## Provenience Problems

**Provenience** (or *provenance*) refers to the exact spot where a fossil (or an artifact) is discovered. By definition, provenience is three-dimensional, with two dimensions relating to the object's geographical north/south and east/west coordinates and the third relating to the depth of the object in the soil measured from some agreed upon spot called the datum point. When excavators find materials, they immediately measure the item(s) and plot them on maps, manually or by computer, photographing as needed. This is done so that

**provenience**
The three-dimensional location of artifacts in their matrix; also referred to as provenance.

**Alan Walker and Kamoya Kimeu, excavating at Nariokotome, are loosening surface soil in preparation for finding more of Nariokotome or "Turkana Boy," otherwise designated KNM-WT 15000.**

they can reconstruct the position of any item retrieved. Provenience maps often provide information about activities at the site, or lack thereof in the case of a burial. The relationship of a human bone to other seemingly associated human bones can reveal whether the individual was buried or just dumped. If a human bone appears at first glance to be isolated, a search begins for more bone material. (There are 206 bones in a human body, so there is potential to add to the initial find.) But many times, it appears that there is no pattern to the bones. And what if there is only one bone, or just a few? Scientists may or may not be able to conclude that the fossil material was a burial or had ever been articulated. If patternless, the bones are at least kept together as a single find.

Surface finds are particularly difficult to evaluate, and therefore to date satisfactorily. Even if an individual is purposely buried, or placed in a coffin or under a strong rock ledge and then covered with soil, the excavator still has a difficult assessment to make about provenience. What are called **postdepositional effects**—that is, any alterations or movements affecting bones (and artifacts) after they have been deposited—can change a fossil's ultimate position and affect any associational conclusions or dating. Geological disturbances, burrowing of small animals, falling boulders, and even an excavator's trowel can disturb it. If the bones are associated with burial goods, they can often provide a cultural date. But many bones in the human lineage predate the cultural custom of burials, so artifacts cannot help in dating those bones. And when bone cannot be directly dated, dating must rely on geological dates; but if the bone is found at the surface, even gross geological dating may be difficult.

# Dating Biological Evidence

Although dating fossilized bones and other evidence of human presence is as important to bioanthropologists as dating artifacts is to archaeologists, much of the detail about the dating techniques used in both disciplines will be left to Chapter 8. This section briefly discusses the dating techniques that are used exclusively for bioanthropological materials (fossils and molecules) and environmental events. Dating of fossils and dating of molecules complement each other: If molecular dating suggests that a species split into two lineages a million years ago and a number of fossils in each lineage can be dated, scientists can support the date of the splitting event and better trace the evolutionary happenings. Ice and marine cores are also important for dating biological events because they give evidence of past climatic changes, which may help discover causes of evolutionary happenings.

Bioanthropologists may suggest that correctly dating fossil material is more important than correctly dating artifact material because fossil materials are so much rarer than artifactual materials. The human body has only 206 bones to leave behind, whereas each hominid leaves thousands of bits of artifactual materials in a lifetime. Additionally, bones are much more fragile under depositional conditions than either flint or ceramics. And scientists would have to know the age of every bit of fossil material from museum collections or other archival facilities, most of which was found before any way to date it was known, as well as the age of all new fossil finds to scientifically order those

**postdepositional effects**
Alterations or movements that affect bones or artifacts after they have been deposited.

materials chronologically in even the simplest model of evolutionary events. That is, dating fossils is vital to any evolutionary reconstruction. So the first step after finding fossil materials is dating them so that they can be placed in their proper context. Only then can investigators minimally claim that "this species evolved from that one," "this species evolved before that one," or "this species is about 2 myr old."

Bioanthropologists know that they must regard every date as provisional. During their careers most researchers have seen specific fossils redated on more than one occasion or have relied on a particular dating technique only to find that technique rescinded later on. Just because dating of a recently discovered tooth was done carefully with the most expensive method available does not necessarily mean the tooth is correctly dated. Students, young scientists, and the public at large often do not understand the provisional status of all dates and accept as absolute truth the dates they read or hear about. As mentioned earlier in this chapter, scientists do not expect to achieve truth—they are happy with knowledge!

## Dating Fossils

Any fossil from an organism that died before about 40 kyr ago cannot be dated by using carbon 14 ($^{14}C$), but any fossil that is younger than 40 kyr old is within the time range for this technique. If a bioanthropologist finds material that he or she believes is older than 40 kyr, there are several other techniques that can be used. (Again, details about these techniques can be found in Chapter 8.) Bones found in stratified layers can be dated relative to one another by their locations, and sometimes by fluorine dating. Bones that are older than about 200 kyr and are found in association with volcanic ash can likely be dated by using potassium-argon (K-Ar). For materials between 200 and 40 kyr, neither the K-Ar nor the $^{14}C$ technique can be used; instead, more experimental and error-prone techniques such as thermoluminescence (TL), optically stimulated luminescence (OSL), electron spin resonance (ESR), uranium (U series), paleomagnetism, and acid racemization must be used.

## Dating Molecules

**Molecular dating** is unique among dating techniques, because it does not date artifacts, fossils, or even soil or rocks. Rather, it dates *events*—splits that occurred in evolving biological lineages, such as the split of monkeys and hominoids about 30 myr ago. The "molecular clock" is not a Big Ben that makes a mechanical click every minute for all of life's history. It is not the same for every organism or lineage (not universal); nor is it the same for every different DNA region of an organism (not global) (Klein and Takahata 2002).

Before the 1960s researchers had to base biological comparisons strictly on the morphology (outward form and structure) of individuals and species. When scientists realized that all organisms and species carry their evolutionary history in their DNA, however, the molecular comparison technique was born. The principle behind molecular comparisons is simple: Species of modern animals that are relatively more similar on the molecular level to each other than to other species share a more recent common ancestry with each other than with those less similar species. The greater the differences between species, the farther away their common ancestry. For example, experts compare the more than 250 species of primates on the molecular level by counting the similarities and differences among their amino acids, proteins, and/or nuclear or mitochondrial DNA (see Chapter 3). Scientists have used mitochondrial DNA (which is found outside of a cell's nucleus, in contrast to nuclear DNA) for decades because it has some advantages over nuclear DNA: far fewer base pairs and genes to compare, faster evolution, and many harmless mutations that can be used as genetic markers. By making molecular comparisons, scientists have attempted to sort out the evolutionary relationships among all primates. In general, this approach has confirmed relationships that primatologists and bioanthropologists had surmised from the fossil evidence (Goodman et al. 1998), and it has the advantage of filling in gaps when there is no fossil record.

**molecular dating**
The application of genetic analysis to estimate the sequence and timing of divergent evolutionary lineages.

Once molecular comparisons had helped establish the relative order of primate lineages, scientists' next step was to turn molecular comparisons into molecular dating by calculating the time when different primate groups split from each other. For example, in 1967, Allan Wilson and Vincent Sarich tried to assess the date of the last common ancestor of humans and apes using molecular comparison, the first such attempt with this brand new technique. They first had to accept the date, called a calibration date and based on the fossil record, of 30 myr ago for the splitting of the Old World monkey lineage and the human/ape lineage. They found by comparing the serum albumins of modern monkeys and humans/apes that the "genetic distance" between humans and African apes was one-sixth that between modern African apes and Old World monkeys. This implied that the African apes split from humans one-sixth of 30 myr ago, or about 5 myr ago. This dating is generally in accordance with the known fossil record (Jobling et al. 2004). When specialists compare the dates of branching events based solely on the fossil record with the dates based solely on molecular comparisons, the two records are usually in general agreement at least for primates (Chatterjee 2002). But for much earlier "events," the fossil record and molecular dates are far less often in agreement. For example, molecular dating puts chordate beginnings at 1 byr ago, but the first chordate fossils appear to be 520 myr old; the placental mammals are dated at 150 myr ago by molecular dates but at 90 myr ago by fossils (Kemp 1999). Other than for primates, a date obtained by molecular dating is almost always considerably earlier, sometimes twice as far back as the fossil record's date (Donoghue and Smith 2004). There will, however, never be total agreement because change in morphology resulting in fossil change over previous populations can often be large but the molecular change can be small if the mutation results in large effects.

Like other dating techniques, molecular dating has its problems and controversies (Pääbo 2003). One problem is the early assumption that mitochondrial DNA is inherited through females only. Recent evidence, however, suggests that up to 10 percent of all mitochondrial DNA may be the result of genetic transfer during the recombination phase of sex cell replication; that is, this DNA may be partially inherited from the male line (Kraytsberg et al. 2004). There is an additional potential problem with mitochondrial DNA. It appears to mutate faster than nuclear DNA (which resides on chromosomes in the nucleis of cells) because it has no way to repair itself the way nuclear DNA does. This means that studies of mitochondrial DNA and newer studies of nuclear DNA and the Y chromosome are not really comparable.

Another problem with molecular dating is the fact that generation time varies among species. A species with a 2-week generation time has far more opportunities for mutations than one with a 20-year generation time. Most molecular-based estimates do not take this into consideration, using the same formula for calculating time of divergence for all species.

Probably the biggest problem is the assumption that specific molecules, such as DNA, mutate at a constant rate. If all such molecules in all species mutated at a constant rate, then we could establish a global clock and date species' origins with great accuracy. Current evidence (Ciochon and Fleagle 2006; Goodman et al. 1983; Strauss 1999) suggests that no global clock exists; rather, mutations seem to occur at different rates in different lineages at different times. For example, mouse and rat genes appear to mutate two to three times faster than primate genes in general, and monkey genes mutate faster than human genes (Klein and Takahata 2002). In the long run, however, molecular mutation appears to be relatively uniform in its rate, because the slow and fast "glitches" even out over time. Local clocks within particular evolutionary lineages show some consistency, though there is a difference of opinion on this as well. Because eventually any clock has to be tied to "real" dates, scientists use an assumed common ancestor to date each particular event; but this approach is subject to error, as fossils do not necessarily date to the beginning of their lineage (M. Jones 2003). Finally, it is important to remember that molecular dates of divergence will always appear to be "far too early" relative to

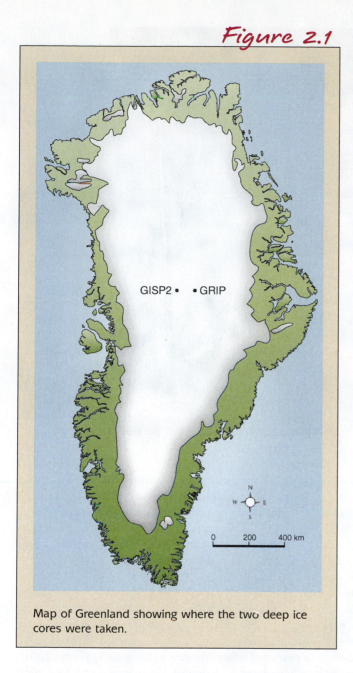

*Figure 2.1*

Map of Greenland showing where the two deep ice cores were taken.

fossil evidence; this is logical, because any genetic change would precede morphological change by a considerable amount of time (Stringer 2002a).

Because of the problems of molecular dating, it seems too early to side with the scientists who firmly believe in this technique. Most of the more fossil-oriented scientists feel that at this time the problems preclude having much confidence in using only molecular dates. But when the events being investigated occurred earlier than any existing fossilized remains, there is no other way to date those events (Donoghue and Smith 2004).

## Ice and Marine Cores: Do They Date Fossils?

The last 15 years have seen numerous press headlines stating that scientists have obtained **ice cores**, first from Greenland, which were 3,028 meters (9,901 feet) deep and represented the last 14.5 kyr of Earth's history, then others that went back to 100 kyr ago. (See Figure 2.1.) In 1998 the ice core data went back 123 kyr, then 420 kyr in East Antarctica. The most recent, the "great grand-daddy of ice cores" (also from East Antarctica), is purported to cover the last 740 kyr of Earth's history, recording all four major glaciations. The annual rings in the Greenland ice core are sharper than those in the latest Antarctic core, but the Antarctic core is considerably longer (Anderson et al. 2004). The two cores from opposite sides of the world will reinforce conclusions about past conditions over the entire globe. However, what does such work have to do with humans? After all, no humans lived in Greenland until a few hundred years ago, when some intrepid Inuits went there assumedly by boat from the mainland of Canada, followed by Vikings who did not stay very long. And no humans have ever lived in Antarctica.

Not to be confused with ice cores are marine cores. **Marine cores** are dug in ocean floors from special ships using special drills. What can marine cores tell us? The ratio of oxygen isotopes $^{18}O$ to $^{16}O$ in the microfossils (plankton and foraminifera) found in sediments represent differences in ocean temperature at the time the sediments were deposited. Study of marine cores has yielded climatic data back to 850 kyr ago, allowing a gross estimate of climatic change in five superstages called OIS 5 to 1 (Oxygen Isotope Stage 5 represents 150 kyr ago to the present). The data include the last glacial and interglacial cycles and show 24 oscillations from cold to warm to cold again. Again, what has this to do with humans? Are there fossils in these marine cores?

Both ice cores and marine cores are valuable to bioanthropologists, not because they contain any datable fossils but because they establish worldwide climatic changes that may be connected to evolutionary change. Many scientists believe at least some biological change is generated by climatic change, though how much is currently under debate (Prothero 2004). If, as Darwin suggested so many years ago, all species are adapted to their environments and there is variation within every species, it is logical that if the environment changes, say, from forests to grassy landscapes, those individu-

**ice cores**
Samples of ice used to date Earth's environmental changes up to 740 kyr ago.

**marine cores**
Samples obtained by passing a long tube from a ship down to the ocean floor and bringing up sediments that contain shells and pollen.

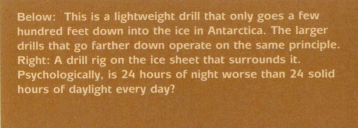

Below: This is a lightweight drill that only goes a few hundred feet down into the ice in Antarctica. The larger drills that go farther down operate on the same principle. Right: A drill rig on the ice sheet that surrounds it. Psychologically, is 24 hours of night worse than 24 solid hours of daylight every day?

als who can somehow adjust better and survive longer will outreproduce those who can't. If scientists find correlations between major biological events and major climatic changes, the likelihood of externally driven change will be strengthened. Although the ice cores have not been fully analyzed yet, one initial finding is that some climatic shifts occurred quickly over years or decades only, not millennia. Initial analysis also suggests that about 1.8 myr ago there was a global cooling with increased seasonality and a drying out of formerly tropical areas that became woodland and savanna (Lowe 2001).

Although neither kind of core has been fully analyzed as yet, some intriguing bits of information have come out. First, the microfossils from a deep marine core from the Atlantic Ocean match the newest Antarctic ice core in terms of general temperature fluctuations (McManus 2004). Additionally, some temperature oscillations are judged to have lasted for several thousands of years and others for just a few decades (Lowe 2001). This climatic variation may indeed have been a generator for at least some biological change in the human lineage.

# Analysis of Biological Evidence

Part of the challenge to biological anthropologists is to garner as much information about the human lineage as possible from a limited amount of fossil material supplemented by other available evidence. Bones, aDNA, and environmental clues from ice or marine cores are all isolated bits of evidence that do not stand alone. The bits of evidence must be organized into a meaningful data set and then added to (or substituted for) previous knowledge. This analysis of evidence is part of any research project.

If researchers find only a fragment of a fossil, it may never be possible to identify its species, age, or sex, and bioanthropologists feel uncomfortable analyzing very small amounts of material. Obviously, an entire skull is far easier to assess; an entire skeleton is worthy of a celebration; and a group of fossils representing an entire population, an exceedingly rare find, is a miraculous bonanza.

One aim of bioanthropologists is to trace the evolution of modern humans as far back in time as possible. In doing this work, researchers constantly ask why the human lineage evolved as it did. Because it is probable that populations often evolved in the course of adapting to new environmental pressures, it is vital that when bioanthropologists ask the "why" questions, they do so relative to changing climates. They must continually search for event correlations to support their hypotheses.

Biological anthropologists also compare fossil materials across different geographic areas but within the same general time span in order to gain knowledge about the range of variability of the evolving human lineage and to try to answer questions concerning how many ancestral species were co-existing at any one time.

Bioanthropologists who study modern populations analyze their data quite differently than do those who specialize in fossil remains of an evolving lineage: All present-day humans belong to a single species, so questions about how many human species there are now are not relevant. But knowledge about the range of variation that exists today within the single human species is important to scientists studying the present, as well as the past. Research on modern humans leads to information about growth, development, and adaptation. In studies of modern humans, biological anthropologists often draw on the expertise of other scientists, such as nutritionists, anatomists, environmentalists, medical doctors, or epidemiologists, as appropriate.

One of the newest branches of biological anthropology is human molecular genetics; bioanthropologists in this area of specialization use DNA evidence as an aid in their study of the human species. Most bioanthropologists (as well as most other scientists) realize that molecular genetics is not merely an end in itself but a tool that they can employ together with more established kinds of research in order to gain knowledge about a particular subject. In bioanthropology researchers use molecular genetics in combination with studies of fossil materials in order to understand human evolution. Although the findings from molecular genetics and fossil analysis are sometimes at odds, it is likely that the imperfect techniques in both areas will improve and the findings will become compatible (Chatterjee 2002).

Paleoanthropologists study people in the past by investigating their past biology and past culture. Humans are biological organisms who also have culture. Yet there is a very important difference between biology and culture in terms of how they are inherited. Because human ancestry in the form of bipedal (hominid) primates precedes any known cultural artifacts by more than 3 myr, it is logical to start with human biology and follow it when pertinent with human culture. Chapter 3 will focus on the principles of evolution. Chapter 4 will explore evolution from the beginning of life 3.5 byr ago to the evolution of mammals. Chapter 5 will focus on primates, first as they are today and then their evolution up to and including the first bipedal primates (hominids), about 6 myr ago. Chapter 6 will look at the early australopithecines, agreed to have been hominids, and Chapter 7 will continue the story of human evolution to *Homo erectus* and *Homo sapiens*.

■ Anthropology, the study of humans, has its biological and cultural specialties.

■ Paleoanthropology is the study of biological fossils (biological anthropology) and cultural remains (archaeology) of past peoples.

■ Paleoanthropological methodology uses the scientific method (TSM), a process of generating and testing hypotheses, to find knowledge about humans in the past.

**page 18**

■ Common sense, science, and religion are all quite different ways to answer certain questions people have about the world.

■ Experts disagree about the meaning of many fossils in the human lineage partly because of collective bias due to age, sex, experience, culture, and above all the intellectual paradigm the expert was raised in.

**page 30**

■ Bioanthropologists depend on fossil evidence for the study of the human past. Fossil evidence is rare, however, and inevitably biased because of differential preservation. Occasionally DNA is preserved.

■ Fossils come in many forms: bones, flesh and skin, brains, casts.

■ Ancient DNA (aDNA) is rare but often gives spectacular results.

■ Postdepositional effects may often alter the original deposition of fossils and we must carefully analyze the context.

■ Many dating techniques such as $^{14}$C and K-Ar are used to date biological and archaeological materials.

■ All dates assigned to finds are provisional, given the nature of science.

■ Molecular dating is relatively new and sometimes in conflict with fossil dates but it has provided approximate dates for evolutionary events and is important when there are no other dates.

■ Ice and marine cores don't date fossil materials because humans didn't live in areas where the cores are taken (ice, oceans), but they provide environmental proxies at specific times to use as context as animal life evolved.

## KEY WORDS

ancient DNA (aDNA), 26
anthropometry, 25
continuity, 23
common sense, 19
deductive reasoning, 18
discontinuity, 23
fossils, 24

hypothesis, 16
ice cores, 33
inductive reasoning, 19
knowledge, 18
marine cores, 33
molecular dating, 31
paradigms, 23

provenience, 29
postdepositional effects, 30
religion, 19
science, 16
theory, 19
the scientific method (TSM), 16
true fossil, 25

## SUGGESTED READING

Aitken, M. J. *Science-Based Dating in Archaeology*. New York: Longman, 1990. An excellent account of the major (and minor) dating techniques in easy-to-understand language. Covers relative as well as chronometric dating.

Connolly, P. *Pompeii*. Oxford: Oxford University Press, 1990. With lots of drawings and photos of what might have happened in AD 79 and of modern excavations, this book gives the personal touch to this disaster.

Cooley, A. E. *Pompeii*. London: Gerald Duckworth, 2003. A modern synthesis of the events at both Pompeii and Herculaneum, a complete history of the excavations, and the findings.

Feder, K. L. *Frauds, Myths, and Mysteries*. 4th ed. Boston: McGraw-Hill, 2002. A "fun" book filled with both archaeological and biological frauds and myths and including enigmas such as Piltdown Man (fraud), ancient astronauts (fraud), and Stonehenge (mystery).

Gould, S. J. *Rocks of Ages*. London: Jonathan Cape, 2001. Stephen Jay Gould firmly believes one can be both religious and a scientist, can believe in evolution as well as in religious teachings because each is in a different arena.

Taylor, R. F., and M. J. Aitken, eds. *Chronometric Dating in Archaeology*. New York: Plenum, 1997. Specialists in each of the major chronometric dating techniques explain their methods and provide excellent examples.

Walker, A., and P. Shipman. *The Wisdom of the Bones: In Search of Human Origins*. New York: Knopf, 1996. This narrative account of Alan Walker's excavations in Africa, primarily with Meave Leakey, captures the experience of being in the field and the excitement of finding a fossil as old and as complete as Nariokotome (Turkana Boy).

# Chapter 3

# 3 · Principles of Biological Evolution

■ **WHAT IS EVOLUTION?**
Early Ideas about Evolution • Eighteenth-Century Ideas • Nineteenth-Century Ideas • Modern Synthesis

■ **HIGHLIGHT 3.1:** *In Mendel's Garden*

■ **HIGHLIGHT 3.2:** *In the News: Iceland and the Human Genome*

■ **THE TEMPO OF EVOLUTION**

■ **THE CAUSES OF EVOLUTION**
Evolutionary Mutations • Evolutionary Selection • Gene Flow • Genetic Drift

■ **HIGHLIGHT 3.3:** *In the Galapagos Islands with Darwin and His Finches*

■ **WHAT REALLY EVOLVES?**
The Species • The Genus and Subspecies • Speciation • Paleospecies and the ESC

■ **CHAPTER SUMMARY**

▲
**Photo above:** Blue-footed boobies from the Galapagos Islands

**B**ecause humans belong to the animal kingdom, they can be studied in the same way as any species of animal. Humans are biologically unique in their combination of bipedal locomotion and large brains relative to body size; they are also unique in their ability to speak, in making and appreciating art, and in actively teaching their offspring all manner of things from survival skills to mother-in-law jokes. But as Robert Foley (1987) suggests, humans are not *the* unique species—they are "just another unique species." Because all forms of life today use a variant of the same DNA code, scientists are convinced that the differences between humans and viruses result from different amounts and sequences of DNA. Therefore, anthropologists can study humans using the same principles that scientists use in studying other animals. But because evolutionary biology is a historical science, "narrative hypotheses" must substitute for experiments to describe and explain evolutionary happenings and processes.

Studying humans biologically has inherent problems that studying most other animal species does not have. First, human generations are very long, averaging around 20 years, not 14 days as with fruit flies or 65 days as with guinea pigs. Some species, such as elephants, outdo humans in generation length, but these are rare. A second problem results from the fact that experimenters cannot control human matings the way they can control fruit fly, mouse, or guinea pig matings. Finally, the number of offspring produced by individual human couples is very small compared with the number produced by, say, rabbits or fish. It is therefore not surprising that Gregor Mendel established the principles of heredity using common peas, not humans, and that later scientists used guinea pigs and fruit flies to work out the details of modern genetics. The similarity in the DNA code from insects to humans allows scientists to move fairly freely among various animal species using the same biological principles, knowing that a principle discovered in one species is likely transferable to others.

Anthropologists study humans in groups rather than as individuals, and biological anthropologists are interested not only in how and why the human lineage evolved as it did from the past to the present, but also in the nature of modern human populations. In the descriptions and analyses of humans in subsequent chapters, it is the group that is the focus of inquiry, not the individual; and although this chapter focuses on the principles of evolution, these principles are valid for modern humans as well.

Before we look at the long "story of evolution" from the beginning of life to modern species, you need to understand the basic principles of evolution as they apply to any and all organisms and at any and all times. Because this book focuses on the human species, it will seem as though first life evolved directly to modern humans, but nothing could be further from the truth. In actuality, first life led to the millions of varied species of plants and animals that have ever lived, those that became extinct and those that survived to evolve to modern species. Evolution as a science (and as a paradigm for, or way to look at, life on Earth) has had a chronological history offering its own lessons to be learned. This chapter therefore begins with a look at what evolution is and then considers what early scientific thinkers believed about what we now call evolution. Those early ideas were not about change at all, but rather about fixation of particular kinds of plants and animals. Slowly, however, the geological events of Earth's past began to be discovered, and scientists came to realize that there was enough time for evolutionary happenings to have occurred. The mid-nineteenth century saw two pioneers—Gregor Mendel and Charles Darwin—begin the modern science of evolution, followed by a synthesis of many evolutionary hypotheses in the mid-twentieth century. The last half of the chapter focuses on how modern biology views evolution today, particularly in terms of the causes of evolution in the past and the present.

# What Is Evolution?

Biological evolution is both simple and complex. Charles Darwin defined evolution in 1859 as "descent with modification," with the word *descent* referring to time, and *modification* referring to change. A hundred and fifty years later, a good short definition of **evolution** is still "biological change through time." Fleshed out a bit, biological evolution is the process by which ancestral populations accumulate morphological and genetic changes to become more modern populations. Given this definition, biological evolution is fact, not hypothesis or theory, because change can often be observed.

For example, controlled experiments with fruit flies show the fact of evolution. If a fruit fly population is left alone in a cage with banana mush but no human manipulation, experimenters can compare two generations of fruit flies morphologically (in terms of outer appearance), inferring their genetics, for signs of change. Geneticists traditionally use fruit flies because some of their chromosomes are large and easily observed, and generation length is a mere two weeks. Variations in such observable traits as wing size (long, medium, short, or just nubbins) or eye color (red or white) can be counted for the first generation and recounted when the second generation takes its place, and simple proportions compared. The proportions will probably not be exactly the same. If the populations are numerically large, mutations or selection may alter the counts slightly; a single mutation, for example, can change wing size to nubbins in the mutated individual. If the populations are numerically small, chance will probably alter the counts. In any case, when a new population has changed biologically through time, it has, by definition, evolved. This change can be observed and measured. After five or six generations of fruit fly evolution, again with no human manipulation beyond feeding and removing dead flies, patterns of evolution can be established and causes hypothesized for the accumulated change. We will explore evolutionary causes later in this chapter.

Other lines of support, too, point to evolution as fact. First, the fossil record shows many different kinds of support for evolution. Scientists trace entire lineages by documenting succeedingly older and older fossils, demonstrating that change is occurring over time. Second, many cases of natural selection can be documented in nature. Such cases show how differential success in reproduction in a population results in differences in morphology and genetics in subsequent generations. Third, on the molecular level, humans are said to share 98.7 percent of both their structural genes and DNA with chimpanzees and bonobos. This argues strongly for a common ancestor of those three modern species in the not-too-distant past (Marks 2000a, 2000b). On the other hand, both humans and apes share a lot of their DNA with bananas as well (Marks 2000a)! The fact that *all life* is composed of the same amino acids points directly to an original common ancestor for living things that are as different today as bananas, chickens, and humans.

One line of evidence might be argued away, but the many different kinds of evidence argue that evolution is fact, and no successful alternative explanation for the fossil record and the molecular similarities has ever been found.

## Early Ideas about Evolution

Scholars have known for centuries that biological change occurs, but the scope and reasons for change were not known or appreciated until the nineteenth century. Unlike most classical philosophers, Anaximander, a sixth-century BC Greek, was one of the first classical thinkers to use a kind of evolutionary reasoning; he proposed that humans evolved from fish (Harris 1981). Two classical Greek philosophical tenets, however, were instrumental in keeping the idea of changing life forms from being accepted until the seventeenth century. Plato, like most scholars of his time, believed in **essentialism**, the notion that ideal types had been created in perfect form and had neither the ability nor the need to change. Aristotle proposed that these ideal types were arranged in a hierarchy of perfection, the "Great Chain of Being." As long as people regarded species as perfect and fixed, there could be no concept of change or evolution.

Two other obstacles stood in the way of acceptance of the idea of evolution. First, as long as the Catholic Church insisted on a literal reading of the Bible that claimed that God created individual species, there could be no acknowledgment of change. For centuries the Church exerted an enormous influence over scientists and scientific thinking,

**evolution**
Transformation of species of organic life over long periods of time.

**essentialism**
A belief of Greek philosophers that ideal types had been created in perfect form and so did not need to change.

with death as the punishment for contradicting its dogma. Second, for centuries there was a widespread belief among the scientific, clerical, and lay world that the Earth was not very old. Until a long existence for the planet was acknowledged, the concept of evolution could not take root.

As long as these obstacles remained, biological science consisted only of collections, descriptions, and classifications. During the seventeenth century, however, scientists began to seek explanations about the world by looking at the world itself instead of relying on philosophy or religion. Geologists began to ask "How old is the Earth?" instead of assuming the literal accuracy of Biblical stories, and they began to reconstruct the history of the Earth and its living creatures by studying the fossil record in its geological context. In time, people realized that both geological and biological records demonstrated the passage of enormous amounts of time, far beyond the mere 5,658 years (6,004 in the original) that Bishop Ussher proposed in 1654. Just as time constraining was the belief that the Flood had occurred in 2,349 BC, giving only a bit more than 4,000 years for the entire world of animals (including humans) to repopulate the globe from Mount Ararat in present-day Turkey.

## Eighteenth-Century Ideas

The Age of Exploration and discoveries of fossils and of stratified rock layers that ordered the fossils paved the way for new ways of thinking about life. As early eighteenth-century traders, missionaries, and explorers traveled around the world, they encountered peoples whose history seemed longer than the Bible would allow and plants and animals that were often very different from those at home. And if people looked different from one another on different continents, yet all came from the same ultimate source, Adam and Eve (which most people believed quite literally), then the existence of change was obvious. It was but one step for many scholars to consider all life as susceptible to change. Animal fossils, excavated in contexts that gave confidence in their great age, called into question the Great Chain of Being and its fixity. Fossils that were almost, but not quite, like modern populations also raised questions about fixity, particularly when they were of familiar animals, such as horses. And finding fossils of entire extinct animal lineages such as dinosaurs must have evoked wonder at first, and later the idea of extinction itself, which is the antithesis of fixity.

The Swedish botanist Carl von Linne (1707–1778), writing under the Latinized name of Linnaeus, standardized the rather haphazard early **taxonomy** (classification) into a scientifically based system. He classified each species, or group, as a member of a genus (plural *genera*) and added two more hierarchical levels, classes and orders. Each more inclusive level was based on more generalized traits. Two thousand years of classical thinking and knowledge, combined with considerable fieldwork by Linnaeus himself, formed the basis of modern taxonomy (Eckhardt 2000). Linnaeus's classification system has its inconsistencies, and scientists have learned a great deal more about taxonomic principles since the eighteenth century, but his system is so embedded in scientific communication that we continue to use it, warts and all. Although Linnaeus was a firm believer in the fixity of all species when he began his work, in the last edition of his famous *Scala Naturae* (1758), he began to weaken in his belief that all species were fixed and unchangeable. Linnaeus believed that fossils and the Bible could coexist.

Jean Baptiste Lamarck (1744–1829) is best remembered for his theory of **acquired characteristics**. Along with most scientists during the late eighteenth century, he believed that life changed, progressively, from simple to complex and from imperfect to perfect, all based on the needs and will of the organism. Although Lamarck never used giraffes as an example (Shanklin 1994), modern models use the giraffe's neck to explain these Lamarckian principles. For example: "In Africa, millions of years ago, there were animals that resembled modern okapis, long-legged herbivores with small heads and short necks. These early okapis survived because they ate tremendous amounts of leaves from bushes and short trees. But the environment cooled, the bushes disappeared, and

**taxonomy**
Scientific classification of groups based on evolutionary relationships.

**acquired characteristics**
Lamarck's eighteenth-century theory that traits acquired during the lifetime of parents (in body cells) could be inherited by their offspring.

leaves on trees were the only source of food. Browsing animals ate the lower-growing leaves, leaving more leaves higher up in the trees. The okapis, faced with a need to get food and a will to solve their problem, stretched their necks just enough to get to those elusive leaves. Neck-stretching okapis acquired slightly longer necks and were able to pass on this trait to their offspring, who then had slightly longer necks than their parents. This continued until the okapis eventually became giraffes with very long necks." End of story. In other words, Lamarck believed that a characteristic acquired during individual lifetimes, like a slightly longer neck gained through stretching, could be passed on to offspring. Given what little was known at that time about the causes of biological change, his idea was not ill founded, just incorrect.

## Nineteenth-Century Ideas

By the nineteenth century scholars believed that the Earth was considerably older than 6,000 years. Some suggested it was at least 75 kyr old. Geologists embraced the principle of **uniformitarianism**, the doctrine that the processes that form and change the Earth today are the same processes that were operating in the past. This principle replaced **catastrophism**, the doctrine that life on Earth was the result of many catastrophic events, each one wiping out the remains of the previous event and replacing older life with newly created life.

Two major nineteenth-century scientific thinkers, Charles Darwin and Gregor Mendel, were each surrounded by like-minded colleagues who were prepared to accept explanations for biological change. Charles Darwin (1809–1882), a member of the English upper middle class, discovered the principles of natural selection. Gregor Mendel (1822–1884), an Austrian monk working in the garden of a monastery in what is now the Czech Republic, discovered the principles of inheritance. The work of these two men, along with the development of the theory of mutations by the Dutch botanist Hugo de Vries (1848–1935), formed the three cornerstones that explain evolution: inheritance, natural selection, and mutations. The next section looks at these principles in the chronological order of their discovery, as each builds on knowledge of previous discoveries.

## Modern Synthesis

Although the basic principles of evolution were known by the beginning of the twentieth century, the details and the synthesis of inheritance, natural selection, and mutations have occupied the thinking and experimental world of many scientists for the last hundred years. The modern synthesis took place in two parts, the first a necessary precursor to the second. In the first round, R. A. Fisher (1890–1962), a British statistician and geneticist, J. B. S. Haldane (1892–1964), a British biologist, and Sewall Wright (1889–1988), an American statistician and geneticist, wrote technical papers that were vital to establishing evolutionary principles and theory. However, they were so technical that no one could read them! It took a second threesome—Russian-born geneticist Theodosius Dobzhansky (1900–1975), German-born ornithologist Ernst Mayr (1904–2005), and American paleontologist George Gaylord Simpson (1902–1984)—to expand the mathematical predictions and explain them so that they were understandable (Ridley 2004). These three population-minded biologists/geneticists gave us the modern synthesis in the mid-1950s.

Although the modern synthesis has had its critics, it did remove a good deal of "mythology" about evolution that was rampant in the first half of the twentieth century. The study of evolution also became far more field oriented as a result of these critics. For example, skeptics had a right to wonder if X-ray induced mutations on fruit flies in a laboratory were sufficient evidence of mutations as a major cause of evolutionary change.

**uniformitarianism**
Geological principle that states that the forces that cause the Earth to be the way it is today altered the Earth in the past as well.

**catastrophism**
Idea that the Earth went through a series of violent and sudden catastrophic destructions and subsequent creations with fossils in each layer bounded by these processes.

**heredity (inheritance)**
An individual's biological, genetic inheritance from both parents that is governed by principles (or laws) discovered by Gregor Mendel in the late nineteenth century.

**allele**
The alternative form of a gene (or DNA sequence) at a given locus.

## Mendel's Heredity

Before scientists could accept the causes of biological change, they had to understand the principles of **heredity,** or **inheritance**, and the reasons why populations are conservative, changing relatively little from one generation to the next. Mendelian inheritance is the first cornerstone of our modern understanding of evolution. Let's look at the context of Gregor Mendel's pioneering discovery of this major key to understanding what makes evolution work.

When Mendel was working in his monastery's garden, he was surrounded by fellow clergy who were also involved in scientific research, because monasteries were both scholarly and religious institutions at that time. In addition to theological training, Mendel had studied university-level math and botany; this scientific training was very pertinent to his eight years of experiments. (See Highlight 3.1, on pp. 44–45.)

Mendel chose to work with the common garden pea, contrasting seven pairs of highly visible traits. Figure 3.1 visually contrasts those traits: seed texture (round or wrinkled), seed interior color (yellow or green), seed coat color (gray or white), ripe pod shape (inflated or constricted), unripe pod color (green or yellow), flower position on stem (axial or terminal), and flower stem length (long or short). When there are two and only two forms of a gene for a particular trait, each is called an **allele**. (There are a few exceptions to this "two and only two" rule, such as the genes that determine AOB blood types.) For example, long and short are the alleles for the stem length gene. Mendel started with 70 true-breeding plants that showed the same singular form of each trait, generation after generation; for example, plants with long flower stems, when allowed to self-fertilize, produced only long flower stems every generation. In succeeding

*Figure 3.1*

**MENDEL'S SEVEN PEA PLANT TRAITS.** The seven traits Mendel used in his famous hybrid experiments are shown with their possible variations. What traits will the offspring show when a yellow, wrinkled pea is crossed with a green, round pea? What traits will the next generation show when those offspring plants are cross-pollinated?

*Source:* Adapted from Park (2003).

# Highlight 3.1

# In Mendel's Garden

GREGOR MENDEL (1822–1884) WROTE AN AR-TICLE in 1866 titled "Experiments in Plant Hybridization," not knowing that his work would eventually become the basis for understanding heredity. Farmers at the time knew how to hybridize plants and animals, but they did not understand the underlying principles of heredity. Mendel, a self-avowed plant hybridizer, discovered those principles from doing experiments on ordinary pea plants and outlined the principles in his 1866 article. He did not know that the principles he discovered were applicable to most of life, giving science a generalizing principle to equal that of Darwin's natural selection. It was 34 years later that three scientists independently rediscovered the principles Mendel outlined.

Mendel's choice of experimental plants was just plain good luck, because peas are normal sexually reproducing plants with the equivalent of sperm and ova that produce seeds. When Mendel later repeated his experiments on another plant, the hawkweed, the results were very different, and he might have deduced that each plant species was different in hybrid behavior. What he didn't know at the time was that hawkweed is an aberrant plant with respect to reproduction.

Born into a peasant farming family in 1822 in what was then Austria but is now the Czech Republic, Mendel learned about fruit tree and plant improvement during his childhood. He went into the priesthood because he knew he would not inherit the family farm and because it meant freedom from financial troubles in the outside world. In addition, in those days, monasteries were places of intellectual camaraderie, with priest–scientists as common as priest–philosophers. Both the monastery and the high school where Mendel taught biology had libraries with standard books on agriculture, horticulture, and botany, so to some extent he was a self-taught botanist. Before launching his experiments, he spent two years taking university-level courses on artificial pollination, physics, and math (including what we now call statistics). At that time plant hybridization as an aca-

The location of the garden in which Mendel conducted his famous hybrid pea experiments is indicated by an X on this depiction of the monastery. The monastery has been restored and made into a museum celebrating its famous former resident. Contrast this "laboratory" (the garden and a small inside room) with botanical laboratories today.
*Source*: Based on Orel, V. 1996. *Gregor Mendel, the first geneticist*. New York: Oxford University Press.

demic field focused on discovering the origins of particular species. People thought that one way to form new species would be through hybridizing two existing ones. Mendel's work with hybridization was in line with the interest in the origins of particular species. His finding of regularities of trait inheritance was an unexpected bonus.

Mendel's experiments began in 1856, three years before the publication of Darwin's *The Origin of Species*. He began with a small garden, where he ultimately planted almost 28,000 peas, and a greenhouse where he grew a few plants in each series of experiments to guard against insect pollination. Mendel's journals do not indicate precisely why he first planted peas, though some historians of science claim he was looking specifically for the range of traits that offspring of hybrids showed. Because his papers were burned after his death, we do not know much about his thinking at this time. After carefully counting the variations that occurred during seven generations and crossing thousands of plants using the chosen traits, he discovered that the "units of heredity" obeyed statistical laws. These numbers must have convinced him of the logic of the principles he deduced.

During eight years of experimenting, Mendel found some traits remained stable throughout (we would call them "fixed"), but that 14 traits showed alternative forms. He chose 7 of these traits for crossing and recrossing. (See Figure 3.1.) In his first experiment he crossed the two seed shape alleles, round and wrinkled. The shapes of the pea seeds in the next generation were uniformly round. But the next generation, of self-fertilized round-seeded hybrids, produced 5,474 round seeded peas and 1,850 wrinkled-seeded peas, or the now famous 3:1 ratio. Mendel referred to the round seeds as "dominating" and the wrinkled seeds as "recessive." He ran seven generations of experiments with each cross, crossed different traits (color, stem length, etc.), and combined traits and crosses. In each step he counted traits and reduced each to a ratio of dominant versus recessive.

Why did 34 years lapse between the time Mendel's paper was published and the rediscovery of his principles? Granted, the paper was in an obscure journal; but about 140 copies were exchanged with other local journals, and Mendel was cited 11 times during this period, suggesting his work was not totally unknown. Several factors seem to have caused the long delay. Mendel was a priest working alone in a monastery, not a professor of biology at some mainstream university. Most scientists come upon earth-shaking ideas not while reading journal articles, but rather in talking to fellow scientists. Mendel did not have this luxury. Also, although Mendel was able to duplicate the ratios and principles established for peas in four-o'-clocks (a flower), he was not able to duplicate them in other plant species; this may have made him wonder about possible generalizing principles established in the pea study. Several years after his pea work, Mendel was appointed head of his monastery, and he had no more time to do experiments. So, in essence, he stopped being a scientist. Some historians of science also point to the impact of Darwin's work after 1860 and suggest that there was no room in scientific circles for another "harebrained" radical theory. But perhaps most important is the fact that Mendel wrote the original paper for horticulturalists, and even those interested in heredity and generalizing principles saw his paper as being on plant hybridization. In other words, Mendel may have seen the generalizing principles, but others did not, perhaps because they were not looking for them in a paper on plant hybrids. His discoveries were not a revolution within a discipline, however, but the beginning of a new discipline—genetics. By 1900 three scientists working independently rediscovered the laws of heredity, discovered Mendel had worked out the laws 34 years earlier, and gave him credit for it. By then hybridization was no longer an interesting topic to study; heredity was.

The last half of the nineteenth century may have witnessed two harebrained theories, but once Hugo de Vries found that corn genes behaved the same way pea genes did, once Darwin's ideas were accepted as the molder of evolution, and once Thomas Hunt Morgan found that chromosomes in fruit flies behaved the same as chromosomes in peas, what can be called the "genetic theory of natural selection" became *the* generalizing principle of evolutionary studies.

*Sources*: Bowler, P. J. 1989. *The Mendelian revolution*. Baltimore: Johns Hopkins Press. Olby, R. 1985. *Origins of Mendelism*. 2nd ed. Chicago: University of Chicago Press. Orel, V. 1996. *Gregor Mendel, the first geneticist*. New York: Oxford University Press. Weiss, K. 2002. Goings on in Mendel's garden. *Evolutionary Anthropology* 11:40–44.

turn back to your reading

generations, Mendel hybridized the two alternative forms of each trait, then crossbred the hybrids back to the true-breeding parent. He carefully counted the number of plants that fell into each trait category and expressed them in ratios. Because he had no microscope to observe the genetic material directly and was not aware of the chemical realities of hereditary materials, he could only deduce principles of heredity by observing expressed traits in each generation. These deductions later became the principles of Mendelian inheritance. It was many years before any scientist could microscopically view chromosomes, genes, and DNA.

Mendel discovered four principles (sometimes called laws) that established the genetic basis of biological inheritance:

1. *The units of inheritance are discrete particles*, remaining discrete generation after generation; they do not result from blending of units from parents, nor will they blend in offspring, though they may look as if they do. In Mendel's day it was widely accepted that hereditary units from parents mixed so that offspring received an amalgam of traits: A tall male mating with a short female would produce medium-sized offspring; a light-skinned female mating with a dark-skinned male would produce offspring with medium-shaded skin. Mendel showed that although the theory of blending seemed logical, it was incorrect. For example, the inside seed color of peas occurs in two varieties, yellow and green; but no matter how many hybrids or back-crosses Mendel bred, they were never chartreuse. Mendel called these units of inheritance "factors"; today they are called **genes**.

2. *Individuals inherit one discrete unit, or gene, from each parent.* The units are located on paired **chromosomes**; the pairs separate during sex cell replication, and each chromosome lines up with the appropriate chromosome from the other parent during fertilization. Mendel called this the principle of **segregation** (see Figure 3.2). For example, the inside seed color trait is located on a particular spot on each of two paired chromosomes. After undergoing replication, the two paired chromosomes separate, each carrying one seed color gene. One of these chromosomes will then pair with the chromosome carrying the seed color gene from the other parent.

3. *The genes for different traits are inherited independently, as long as the genes are on different chromosomes.* In other words, according to the principle of **independent assortment**, whether a pea plant has a long or short stem has no effect on whether it has green or yellow seeds, because the genes for these two traits are located on different chromosomes.

4. *Individuals receive one gene from each parent for each trait, even though some genes may be recessive.* In the case of each of the seven pairs of genes in Mendel's pea experiments, one form (allele) often masked the form of the other in subsequent generations. This is the principle of **dominance and recessiveness**. Relative to the two possible pea seed colors, yellow and green, a plant's seeds will be green if it gets two green alleles from its parents, yellow if it gets two yellow alleles—and yellow if it gets an allele for each color. Why? Because yellow seed color is dominant over green. However, even if a plant with two different seed color alleles has yellow seeds, it may pass on some green alleles to its offspring in the next generation. The effects of recessive genes are often masked, but the alleles do not disappear.

Through experimentation Mendel found firm support for the principles he originally deduced. By the end of his experiments, he had used an estimated 28,000 pea plants, constantly hybridizing and back-crossing every combination of alleles. His meticulous observation and his mathematical skills were the backbone of his study; he could document each generation with ratios of trait occurrences.

In 1866 Mendel published his findings in a fairly obscure journal. Soon after, he became the head of his monastery and ceased doing scientific work. His findings were not known to the scientific world until the turn of the twentieth century, when three independent researchers rediscovered his principles. One of those researchers was Hugo de Vries, who is better known for his early work on mutations. Other important principles

**genes**
DNA sequences that code for specific proteins and functions.

**chromosomes**
Long strands of DNA sequences; the hereditary material in the cells' nuclei.

**segregation**
The process in which paired chromosomes separate into different cells during sex cell formation, resulting in sex cells that contain only one of the previously paired chromosomes.

**independent assortment**
A Mendelian principle that states that different traits are independently inherited from each other but that is applicable only to genes on different chromosomes.

**dominance and recessiveness**
The effects of alleles that either mask (dominance) or are masked (recessiveness) by the effects of other alleles in a heterozygous genotype.

*Figure 3.2*

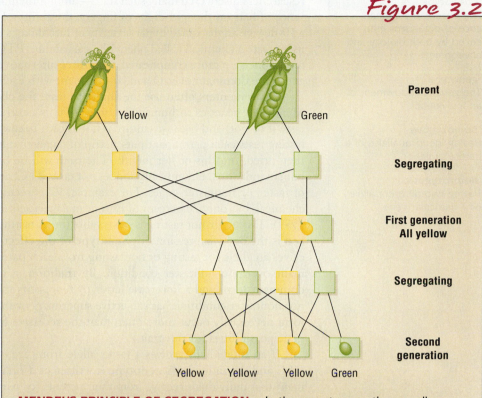

Parent

Yellow

Green

Segregating

First generation
All yellow

Segregating

Second
generation

Yellow   Yellow   Yellow   Green

**MENDEL'S PRINCIPLE OF SEGREGATION.**   In the parent generation, a yellow (dominant) pea plant is crossed with a green (recessive) plant. The sex cells each carry a color gene as they segregate. In the first generation, each pea plant has one of each color gene, but because yellow is dominant over green, all peas are yellow. When one of these heterozygous pea plants self-fertilizes, the color genes segregate into 50 percent green and 50 percent yellow. In the second generation, 25 percent of the peas will be homozygous yellow (and be yellow in color); 25 percent will be homozygous green (and be green in color); and 50 percent will be heterozygous and be yellow in color. This is the famous 3:1 ratio.

of genetics and inheritance soon followed Mendel's: In the late nineteenth century August Weisman (1834–1914) refuted Lamarckian theory by demonstrating that hereditary material is passed on to offspring only through sex cells (ova in females, sperm in males) and not through body/somatic cells; in 1911 the word *gene* was coined to refer to the outer manifestation of specific instructions, such as "genes for short wings"; scientists discovered that alleles carried on the same chromosomes are *linked*, or inherited by offspring as a unit; and the principles of inheritance were found to apply to humans as well as to peas (Grant 1991). And in 1953, with the discovery by James Watson (b. 1928) and Francis Crick (1916–2004) of the actual structure of the genetic material (DNA), modern genetics, not just the study of heredity, had been launched.

## From Peas to Humans

Once the principles of inheritance were established for all life forms, geneticists looked for simple Mendelian traits in humans that would be analogous to green versus yellow seed color in peas. They searched for traits that required the interaction of only two alleles for the trait's manifestation (one dominant or both codominant), that could be observed, and that would appear in the same ratios as Mendel's pea variations. Eventually

**phenotype**
The observable appearance of organisms influenced by both biology and environment.

**genotype**
The genetic endowment of an individual.

**homozygous**
Having identical alleles of a particular gene.

**heterozygous**
Having two different alleles of a particular gene.

researchers discovered many such traits—among them, for example, the presence or absence of hair on the mid-digits of fingers, the ability of the thumb to bend backward at a 50-degree angle (called hyperdexterity or hitchhiker's thumb), and the ability or inability to taste a chemical called phenylthiocarbamide (PTC). The familiar AOB blood system is one step more complicated, with three alternative alleles—A, O, and B—where A and B are dominant over O and co-dominant with each other.

Experimenters often use the ability to taste the chemical PTC to illustrate simple Mendelian genetics in humans because PTC is neutral (people don't care if they can taste it or not) and because culture is not known to mask or change the effect. In PTC-tasting tests each participant puts a strip of paper that has been soaked in the chemical, then dried, into his or her mouth. The taste will be bitter/salty or nonexistent. Every human individual either tastes or does not taste PTC, and groups differ in the frequency of taster or nontaster genes. For example, 97 percent of African Americans taste the chemical, but only 70 percent of European Americans are tasters (Allison and Blumberg 1959). Tasting or not tasting is observable (in its tasting sense), measurable (yes or no), and is the outer expression or **phenotype** of the effect of two alleles. Every human receives an allele for tasting or nontasting from each parent. The taster condition is dominant over the nontaster condition. By tradition, a capital letter *(T)* represents the dominant form and a lowercase letter *(t)* represents the recessive form. Neither taster nor nontaster condition has subjective superiority or inferiority, nor does the dominant form necessarily occur more often than the recessive form. (See Figure 3.3 for the genetic possibilities for this trait.)

If an individual receives a taster allele from each parent, the individual can taste PTC and the individual's **genotype** is written as *TT*. A genotype is the genetic endowment that individuals receive from their parents for particular traits. If an individual receives a nontaster allele from each parent, the individual cannot taste the chemical and the genotype is *tt*. In both cases, because the genotype is composed of the same form of the allele, the individual is considered **homozygous** for this condition. If the individual receives a taster allele from one parent and a nontaster allele from the other, the genotype is *Tt* and the individual is considered **heterozygous** for the condition. A person needs only one taster allele to be able to taste the chemical, so all heterozygotes are tasters.

For each simple Mendelian trait, the phenotype can be observed; the genotype of the recessive form (e.g., nontasting) is obvious, because each parent must contribute a recessive allele for the individual to be recessive; but because the effects of dominance mask the effects of recessive alleles, the genotype of the dominant form can be either homozygous (with each parent contributing one dominant allele) or heterozygous (with each parent contributing a different form of the allele, the effect of the recessive allele being masked or hidden). Mendel's principles work for humans as well as for peas.

Geneticists have found more than 4,000 of these simple Mendelian traits in humans. Some harmful genes are inherited as dominants, such as those producing achondroplasic dwarfism and brachydactyly (having very short fingers); some are inherited as recessives, such as

*Figure 3.3*

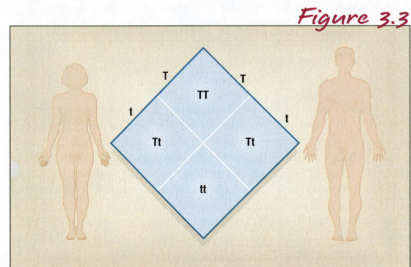

**PHENOTYPES AND GENOTYPES FOR THE TASTER ALLELE.**
PTC taster alleles are identified by *T* and nontaster alleles by *t*. Every individual human receives one allele from each parent during sexual reproduction. Note the four possibilities in this figure. Do you know what your genotype for tasting PTC is? Do you know what your parents' genotypes are? Try to figure out the possibilities if you know your genotype.

those producing cystic fibrosis and sickle-cell anemia. For the trait to be manifest, a person needs to inherit only one of the harmful genes if it is dominant, but two if it is recessive. Geneticists have also learned that the vast majority of traits are more complex than this. Very seldom does a gene make a trait by itself. Traits often result from the action of more than one set of alleles. Or the same set of alleles can affect two or more traits. Finally, environment can affect traits, as in the cases of certain childhood diseases and sunlight: Disease during an individual's growing years often results in shorter stature than genetically expected, and skin color can be darkened by the sun. Skin color, brain size, stature, and head shape are traits that have complex heredity. Some exceptions to Mendel's principles have been found as well. For example, as implied earlier, linked traits on the same chromosome usually are not subject to the principle of independent assortment.

## DNA, Genes, and Cells: From Atoms to Populations

Once the units and principles of inheritance were identified, scientists turned to studying genetic material at both the micro/molecular level (the gene/allele or smaller) and the macro/population level (the species or larger). Principles at both levels are now relatively well understood. Here we look at genetics at the molecular level. In Chapter 15 we'll briefly consider the population level of genetics, focusing on gene pools of modern human populations and how they change over a few generations.

A discussion of genetics can either start with atoms and end at populations (moving from smallest to largest units) or start with populations and end at atoms (largest to smallest units). The major steps from the smallest to the largest units in a linear genetic model are: atom to molecule (amino acid to protein or nucleic acid to DNA) to gene to chromosome to cell to individual body to population.

All substances are made up of atoms. The most common of the 116 kinds of atoms are the familiar carbon, hydrogen, oxygen, and nitrogen. Atoms join to become molecules, and the molecules common to living things are carbohydrates, lipids, proteins, and nucleic acids. Proteins are long chains of amino acids; in all of life on Earth, there are only 20 amino acids, but they differ in type, amount, and sequence for each species. Through a complex process of protein synthesis, humans become humans and chickens become chickens.

It is molecules of **DNA** that provide protein synthesis codes for all biological organisms. DNA exists in all plants and animals. Twenty-seven different kinds of ancient DNA were recently extracted from soil in Siberia and New Zealand, originating from plant roots and animal feces/urine deposits (Stokstad 2003). DNA directs protein synthesis within cells, and all cells in a species carry the same basic codes. For example, human skin, liver, and blood cells have the same basic DNA. It has been discovered that although the DNA sequence is the code that specifies which amino acids produce which proteins, messenger RNA (mRNA) provides the intermediate one-way transfer of that information. Because proteins are the major constituent of all body tissues, protein synthesis is vital to life. Proteins vary in function: Some form the structure of tissues, such as collagen in bone, while others form connective tissues. Hormones and enzymes are other kinds of proteins; hormones stimulate various kinds of cellular activity, and enzymes begin or enhance chemical reactions.

The **cells** of all living organisms can be called the basic units of life, because cells are the smallest units that perform all necessary life functions. It is in the nucleus of the cell that the units of inheritance reside. By using special microscopic techniques, scientists can see chromosomes in cell nuclei as long, narrow bodies with alternating light and dark bands (see Figure 3.4). Each species has a specific number of chromosomes in each cell; mammals, the taxonomic order to which humans belong, have between 40 and 80 chromosomes. Humans have 46, often referred to as 23 pairs because at replication they can be matched according to shape, size, and genetic material. After replication each pair moves apart, and one chromosome from each pair becomes part of a new cell.

**DNA**
Deoxyribonucleic acid; the double-stranded molecule that is found in the nuclei of cells and provides the genetic code for organisms.

**cells**
The smallest unit able to perform activities called life; all living organisms have one or more cells.

*Figure 3.4*

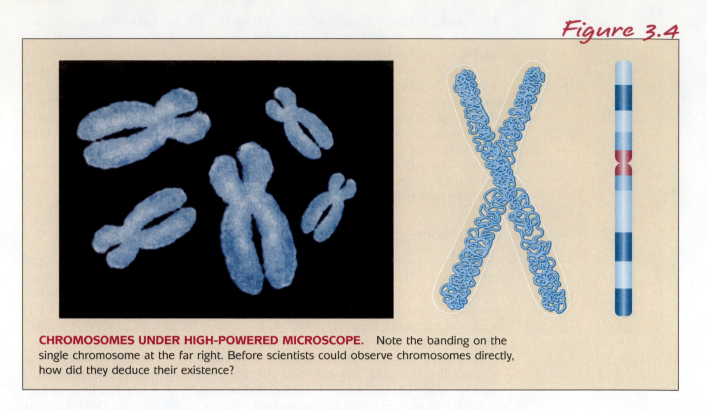

**CHROMOSOMES UNDER HIGH-POWERED MICROSCOPE.** Note the banding on the single chromosome at the far right. Before scientists could observe chromosomes directly, how did they deduce their existence?

DNA consists of very long strands, twisted around each other in a double helix shape. By contrast, an RNA molecule has only one helix. Figure 3.5 shows a simplified version of the famous Watson and Crick (1953a, 1953b) model of DNA. As the figure illustrates, the DNA strands are made of alternating sequences of phosphate and sugar units. Attached to each sugar is one of four bases: adenine (A), thymine (T), guanine (G), and cytosine (C). Biochemists had long known what DNA was made of, but in 1953 James Watson and Francis Crick figured out how the bases were connected to the sugar and phosphate units. Although their first attempt at modeling was totally wrong, they persevered until they lighted on the famous double helix. The two DNA strands are held together by chemical bonds that connect the bases: T bonds only with A, and G bonds only with C. When scientists speak of DNA sequences, they are referring to sequential arrangements of the four bases, such as AAGGTATCCAGACA. It is the order of the bases that gives DNA its specificity. It has been estimated that there are 3.2 billion base pairs in the human genetic code (Deloukas et al. 1998). There are 64 possible three-letter combinations of the four bases that provide the genetic code for the 20 amino acids needed for protein synthesis; CTT codes for glutamic acid, for example. This may sound like a very small amount of possible variation for all of life—but, by analogy, although the English language uses only 26 letters, a large dictionary contains a million words and a large library houses many millions of books (Relethford 2001a). The fact that there are only four kinds of bases in any DNA sequence (A, T, C, and G) means that the sequences of any two species can differ on average by no more than 25 percent. Human DNA and daffodil DNA are 35% identical, and human DNA and chimpanzee DNA are 98 percent identical, all because of common ancestry and the fact of only four bases (Marks 2000b). (See Highlight 3.2, on pp. 52–53, for a description of the Human Genome Project, the Iceland study, and the role of anthropologists in this venture.)

A gene is a segment of DNA on a chromosome; it gives certain instructions that will eventually be expressed as a trait in the individual who carries it and possibly in that individual's progeny. For example, the interaction of two alleles on a specific spot on the

*Figure 3.5*

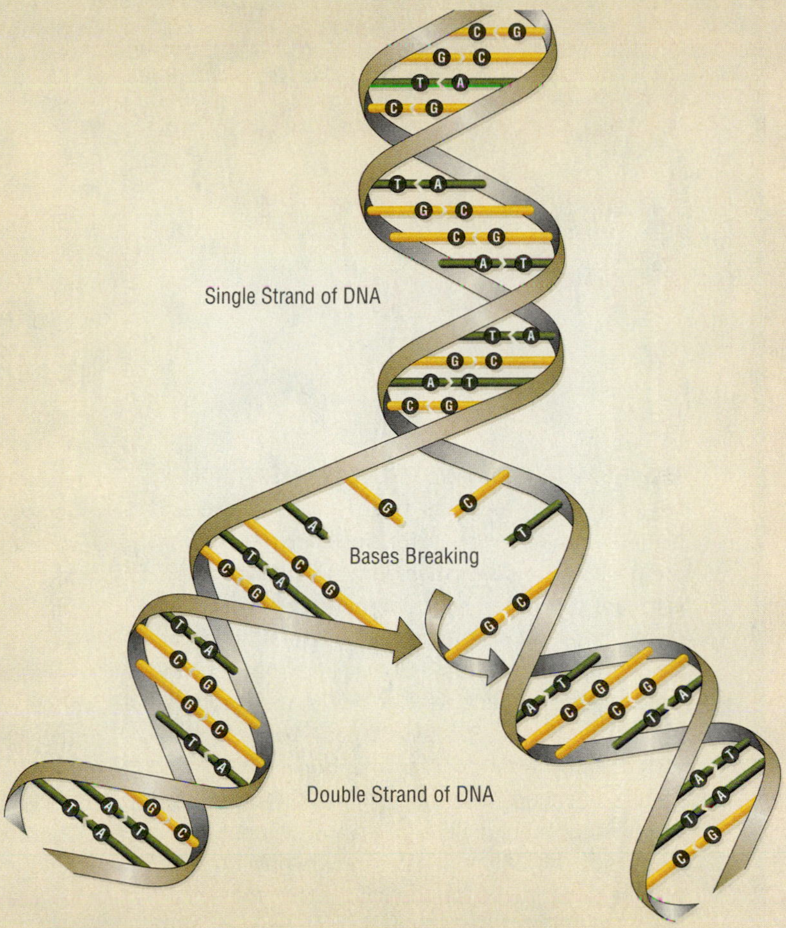

Single Strand of DNA

Bases Breaking

Double Strand of DNA

**SIMPLIFIED VERSION OF THE WATSON–CRICK MODEL OF DNA.** Intact bases are shown at the top, the double helix breaks in the middle, and each strand picks up nucleotides from the cell, forming two new strands at the bottom. This is how DNA replicates itself. Can you see why it is called a double helix?

*Source*: Adapted from Boyd and Silk (2006, 40).

ninth chromosome determines a person's blood type (Marks and Lyles 1994). The average number of genes on each human chromosome is about 1,500, but this number varies by the size of the chromosome and the density of the genetic material (Klein and Takahata 2002). Of the estimated 3.2 billion base pairs of the human genetic code only around 25,000 (an educated guess) are genes, giving instructions that will eventually be manifest (Wade 2003a). Genes are separated by long stretches of DNA with no role in coding proteins. The label *junk* was assigned to this noncoding part of DNA before its extent was known. Many now believe it has necessary functions, such as repairing or turning on genes. Researchers estimate that as much as 97 percent of nuclear DNA is noncoding, meaning that it is not building proteins and is not susceptible to natural selection (Groves 2001; M. Jones 2001; Klein and Takahata 2002). In humans each chromosome contains about a meter of DNA, tightly coiled upon itself many times; humans have 23 pairs of chromosomes, so every human cell is estimated to contain 46 meters of DNA (Margulis and Sagan 1997). When cells replicate themselves, which happens when

# Highlight 3.2

## In the News: Iceland and the Human Genome

THE HUMAN GENOME PROJECT (HGP) officially began in 1990 and has been a high-profile and high-interest enterprise ever since. Everything from the politics, the skirmishes between public and private labs, and the sheer magnitude of the project to the potential scientific results has attracted attention and controversy. But at least some of the waiting is over, because the first stage—sequencing the estimated 3.2 billion base pairs—is completed. Pithy phrases like "the book of life" and "nature's genetic instruction manual for making and maintaining human beings" and "a glimpse of an instruction book previously known only to God" were among those in the air in the summer of 2000 at the announcement of the project's "first stage conclusion." As of July 10, 2003, the first human chromosome—number 7—had been completely sequenced. Its 153 million base pairs represent 99.4 percent of the sequence. Researchers tackled this chromosome first because it is thought to be associated with various diseases.

From the beginning, there was a difference of opinion on whether the research should be public, funded mainly by the U.S. government but internationally supported and with results free for anyone to use, or private, funded by private enterprise and with the database restricted to those who paid for its use. The HGP is the public version. So far it has cost about $3 billion and involved 62 scientists from 13 labs all over the world, each sequencing a particular part of the genome. The private organization is Celera Genomics in Rockville, Maryland; it reportedly spent $330 million in private funding and used its own method of sequencing.

What is this project, and what does it mean to science and to the ordinary person? In simple terms, the human genome is a map of the genetic makeup of the human species. In every cell in every human body (except in the sex cells), there are 23 pairs of chromosomes, and on each chromosome there are genes that have certain functions, the genes being made up of thousands of base pairs. Though not every base pair is identical throughout the species (we each have our own unique genome), the sequencing of the genetic material is the same. The data came from 1,056 individuals in 52 world populations. Stage two will locate genes and determine their functions. Until this stage is completed, scientists do not know where one gene begins and then ends on a chromosome.

Rather than reinvent the wheel, once the genome is sequenced for humans, scientists will use the genomes from other species that have been completely sequenced so far—genomes for roundworms, fruit flies, mice, rats, mosquitoes, and several fish—as a start in determining gene function. (The chimpanzee genome is finalized, and the gorilla genome has begun to be sequenced.) To put it simplistically, the mouse genome can be laid next to the human genome, and where mouse functions are known for individual genes, scientists can hypothesize about parallel locations and functions in humans. Some genes have already been located and their functions identified.

Once scientists have located specific genes and ascertained their functions, stage three, applications using the new knowledge, can begin. Many people hope that the new knowledge will reinvent medicine, allow physicians to predict diseases, correct disease-carrying genes, and eventually eliminate diseases in individual patients, perhaps forever. Some diseases, such as sickle-cell anemia, can be explained by simple Mendelian genetics. Other conditions, such as Down syndrome, occur when there is an extra chromosome. Still other diseases are additive and need the interaction of many genes before they are manifest. These kinds of diseases are common, yet their causes have been elusive so far because scientists don't know where the genes are and which ones they are, much less how many are involved. Diabetes, heart disease, and some types of cancer are on the list. If a physician working with a geneticist who is a specialist in genome reading can identify genetic susceptibility to a particular disease in a patient, the physician can counsel the person about environmental factors (stress, overweight, lack of exercise, smoking, etc.) and perhaps forestall the onset of the disease. Or, a bit down the road, genetic replacement or removal of the faulty gene might be successful.

For some time to come, gene therapy will be exceedingly expensive, and this is where anthropological ethics will come into the picture. Think of the problems that would develop if everyone in the world survived until age 200. If only certain people could have gene therapy, who would they be? Who would make the decisions? Anthropologists also need to be involved in discussions about the ethics of making individual genomes public. If a physician has a patient's genome for consultation purposes, can insurance agencies and employers demand that information? Sequencing the human genome has resulted in so much complicated data that a new "index" to the "book of life"—called the HapMap—will allow geneticists and physicians to narrow down entry points. This strong biomedical focus is encouraging for the application of the results of the years of pure research.

One interesting and highly debated project involving the use of a database resulting from a genome project is under way in Iceland. In December 1999 an Icelandic company began to collect DNA from all 270,000 Icelandic citizens to link their genetic profiles with their health and family tree records; the parliament had approved the creation of the database the year before. The stated goal is to make predictions about diseases caused by faulty genes. Because Iceland's citizens are relatively homogeneous, being mostly descended from Scandinavian and Norse groups and having experienced little immigration over the years, Iceland is an excellent laboratory for studying genes.

But there is fear that the genetic information will not be used solely for the stated intention. Some argue that the safeguards protecting privacy are not adequate and that the database might be sold to pharmaceutical companies with the company that collected the data making a profit. At least 5 percent of citizens have asked that their data be excluded.

Iceland may be the first country to "go genetic" in terms of a biological database, but others may follow. Each country must decide whether the ethical problems are worth the potential rewards.

*Sources*: Billings, P. R. 1999. Iceland, blood and science. *American Scientist* (May–June): 199–200. Enserink, M. 2000. Start-up claims piece of Iceland's gene pie. *Science* 287:951. Hillier, L. W. 2003. The DNA sequence of chromosome 7. *Nature* 423: 157–164. Jones, S. 1994. *The language of genes*. New York: Doubleday. Wade, N. 2000. Now the hard part: Putting the genome to work. *New York Times* (June 27): D1–8. Wade, N. 2003. Once again, scientists say human genome is complete. *New York Times* (April 15).

turn back to your reading

organisms grow or cells replace themselves, the DNA strands unwind from each other by breaking at the bonds between the bases. Each strand replicates itself by picking up nucleotides (chemical compounds of salt, sugar, and bases) within the cell; normally the replication is exact, and whatever genetic material is on each strand is inherited as a unit.

During regular body cell replication, called **mitosis**, all 46 chromosomes come together at the equatorial plane of the cell (the analogy is with the equator on a globe) and replicate themselves, temporarily forming 92 chromosomes. The cell then divides into two, each daughter cell receiving a full complement of 46 chromosomes. It takes 30 to 90 minutes to complete this division. Cells are at rest most of the time, doing what they are supposed to do as muscle cells, skin cells, etc.

The process of replication differs in several ways between body cells and sex cells. In human sex cell replication, or **meiosis**, there are two cycles of cell division. In the first cycle, all 46 chromosomes line up at the equatorial plane and replicate themselves, again temporarily forming 92 chromosomes; the two sets of paired chromosomes then separate from each other and move to opposite sides of the nucleus, and the cell splits into two cells, each having 46 chromosomes. The second meiotic division separates newly paired chromosomes so that each newly formed sex cell (ovum or sperm cell) has 23 chromosomes. These will combine with the 23 from the other parent to form a zygote, a single cell from which a human being develops. That is, the zygote that results from fertilization has 23 pairs, or 46 chromosomes. If it were not for the second reduction division, a sperm and ovum would produce a zygote with 92 chromosomes. (See Figure 3.6.) Because of random assortment and segregation during this complex process, a zygote never has the same genotype as either parent. In fact, it has been estimated that the total number of possible genetic combinations from any human mating is in the trillions. The last important difference between body cells and sex cells is that although all body cells in each organism are identical (unless there have been body cell mutations), all sex cells are different from one another. Once a zygote is formed, however, it divides by mitosis over and over to produce the millions of cells in the individual's body.

Geneticists classify two basic types of genes: structural and regulatory (Jacob and Monod 1961). **Structural genes** give instructions that eventually are expressed in observable traits, such as protein-coding instructions for skin tissue. **Regulatory genes** function only to control some structural genes, governing the timing of certain events in an organism's life by turning on or blocking effects. For example, in human females, regulatory genes are responsible for triggering female sex cells (eggs) that were originally formed before birth. In males, regulatory genes trigger penis and testicle growth, the development of facial hair, and lowering of the voice. On the species level, many experts believe that much of the difference in structural genes between humans and chimpanzees or bonobos was caused by mutations on regulatory genes, particularly as they affect brain activity, at the time the last common ancestral group split into separate lineages (King and Wilson 1975; Pennisi 2002).

## Darwin's Natural Selection

After finding he had little talent and no taste for either medicine or the ministry, the 22-year-old Charles Darwin signed on as the gentleman naturalist on HMS *Beagle*, a ship that was exploring the coast of South America to establish longitude measurements. While on the 5-year voyage from 1831 to 1836, Darwin read books by the British economist Thomas Malthus (1766–1834) on the problems of overpopulation and Volume 1 of Charles Lyell's (1797–1875) *Principles of Geology* (1830) on uniformitarianism and the great age of the Earth. Apparently Lyell's Volume 2 arrived by mail boat when Darwin arrived in Montevideo (Gould 2002). The ideas of both Malthus and Lyell influenced Darwin's later biological observations and thinking, because at the time of the voyage, he believed in Lamarck's theory of acquired characteristics. The long voyage allowed Darwin to observe the variability that existed within many of the species he encountered, variability that became the anchor for his lifelong effort to explain evolution. In

**mitosis**
The process of replication followed by cell division by which a body cell produces two identical copies.

**meiosis**
The process of replication of sex cells by replication of chromosomes followed by two cycles of cell division so that each ovum or sperm has half of the parent's chromosomes.

**structural genes**
The genes that give instructions that eventually are expressed in observable traits.

**regulatory genes**
The genes that code for regulation of biological processes such as growth and development.

*Figure 3.6*

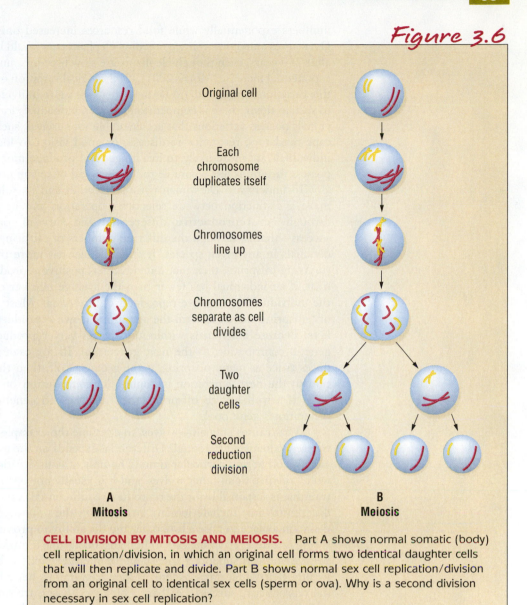

Original cell

Each chromosome duplicates itself

Chromosomes line up

Chromosomes separate as cell divides

Two daughter cells

Second reduction division

**A**
**Mitosis**

**B**
**Meiosis**

**CELL DIVISION BY MITOSIS AND MEIOSIS.**  Part A shows normal somatic (body) cell replication/division, in which an original cell forms two identical daughter cells that will then replicate and divide. Part B shows normal sex cell replication/division from an original cell to identical sex cells (sperm or ova). Why is a second division necessary in sex cell replication?

particular, he noted tortoise shape and size variability and finch beak size and shape variability on the Galapagos Islands, even if at the time he did not understand the significance of these phenomena. His findings can be summarized in the phrase identified with him, **natural selection**, the second cornerstone of our understanding of evolution. Natural selection is so straightforward and easy to understand that Thomas Huxley, a scientist and contemporary of Darwin, wrote that he felt "extremely stupid not to have thought of that" (Huxley 1901).

Darwin was hampered by a lack of knowledge that genetics, heritability, and mutations comprise the ultimate source of all variation (as well as by his belief in Lamarckian evolution and blending). He wrote about unusual traits never seen before, calling them "sports," but he did not understand their nature or importance. The thinking that led Darwin to his theory of natural selection went something like this: (1) All species are capable of producing more offspring than their food resources can sustain. (Here, he was obviously influenced by Malthus, who wrote that animals were able to increase their

**natural selection**
A mechanism for evolutionary change that favors survival and reproduction of some organisms over others because of certain biological traits.

numbers exponentially while food resources increased only additively.) For example, Darwin reasoned that a single breeding elephant pair would have 19 million descendants after 750 years, even though elephants are slow breeders, unless something stopped the exponential increase (Morris 2001). (2) Biological variation occurs within all species, and this variation is inherited. (3) Because there are more individuals born than there is food to sustain them, there is competition between individuals for sustenance. (4) Some individuals possess variations that are favorable for survival, such as additional speed to escape predators, resistance to disease, or good vision to locate food resources. These individuals are more likely to live longer and produce more offspring than those who possess variations less favorable to long life and offspring production.

To understand Darwinian natural selection and its role in evolution, we need to make a distinction between selection's operation and its effects. Selection operates through net **reproductive differential** and survival, or differential reproductive success—that is, through the differing numbers of offspring that survive among all individuals in any given species. If an individual has more than the average number of surviving offspring, then that individual has positive reproductive differential. By contrast, if an individual has fewer than the average number of surviving offspring, then the individual has negative reproductive differential. Most biologists use the criterion of "offspring surviving until the age of their own reproduction" to measure net numbers. Because individuals within any species vary reproductively, they differ in their genetic contribution to the next generation. If, for example, a particular wolf produces twice as many offspring as the average wolf, then that wolf's genetic contribution to the next generation is double the contribution of the reproductively average wolf. If a wolf has no offspring, then it makes no genetic contribution to the next generation's gene pool.

What causes animals—wolves, to continue the example—to have positive or negative reproductive differential? Differential depends on the total phenotype of each individual wolf at any particular time. The unit of consideration is each individual "total wolf," relative to all other wolves, and it is usually not possible to pick out one specific trait that is responsible for the reproductive differential. Factors in positive reproductive differential may include looking attractive to the opposite sex, being able to get and maintain a place to raise a brood, having the ability to produce twins instead of one offspring at a time, or, in the case of humans, being able to make people of the opposite sex believe you can support a spouse and numerous children by virtue of intelligence or wealth. Behavioral traits, as long as they are variable, heritable, and can affect differential reproductive success (i.e., have a biological base), are subject to natural selection as well. So a wolf who inherits the ability to be a better mother than other wolves will likely raise more of her cubs to maturity and thus will tend to pass on her talent for mothering. Traits that enhance reproductive success differ through time as circumstances change, however. Also, what favors reproductive differential may be very different from one species to another.

The effects of natural selection are often difficult to observe and/or measure. Darwin often wrote of **adaptation**, suggesting that in the long run, populations would become better adapted to their existing environments due to natural selection. He believed that the finches on the Galapagos Islands had beaks that varied relative to different island environments, and he argued that specific beak shapes were adaptations. He also pointed to the fact that many animals that live in cold climates have thick fur that makes them well adapted to that environment. If there are two wolves in northern Canada during a particularly cold winter, one with a thick pelt of fur and the other with a scraggly coat, the wolf with the thick fur will probably live longer and produce more offspring than the scraggly-coated wolf. In time, an entire population of thick-furred wolves that are better adapted to the cold Canadian winter will evolve. Theoretically, all traits that lead to better adaptation enhance survival and confer subsequent reproductive advantage. Some adaptations have clear benefits: Bats use echolocation to find insects, legs and feet evolved for walking, and eyes and ears evolved for seeing and hearing.

**reproductive differential**
An individual's success relative to others of the same species as measured by survival of offspring into adulthood.

**adaptation**
Successful interaction between a population and an environment resulting in greater behavioral or physiological fitness, which can be short-term and reversible or long-term and permanent.

These are, of course, the large-scale macroevolutionary adaptations that Darwin was attempting to explain. More recently, scientists have found that much small-scale micro-evolutionary change is neutral, showing no correlation to differential reproductive success (Stearns and Hoekstra 2005). In many cases it is not clear what is being adapted to or just how the adaptation is "better." Because natural selection acts on many traits at the same time, effects on some traits will often mask effects on others. Scientists can measure complexity by counting genes or traits, but it is subjective to claim that something is better just because it happened. And since more than 90 percent of all species that have ever lived have become extinct, natural selection does not always better adapt populations to existing environments.

Darwin believed in another kind of selection, **sexual selection**. A lion's mane, a peacock's tail, a human female's large breasts—all are expensive to develop and to carry around; but if the reproduction of that lion or peacock or human female is enhanced by having a bit more of that trait, perhaps members of the opposite sex will prefer that individual, the gaudy show as being a sign of good health and a worthy mate. In a recent experiment one scientist used swallows, cutting off the tails of one third of the males at mid-section. On another third of the swallows, he pasted the cut-off tail ends; thus, there were one-third long-tailed, one-third medium-tailed (normal), and one-third short-tailed male swallows in the experimental group. At breeding time the females preferred the long-tailed males. It has been said that natural selection adapts organisms for survival in their existing environment, but sexual selection adapts them to the needs of obtaining a mate and reproducing (Lewin and Foley 2004).

This relatively new idea about sexual selection is that females are selecting males (as sex partners) on the basis of their "good genes," as represented by morphological features such as long tail feathers or beak size that might translate as "good health." But one interesting experiment by Nancy Burley on the zebra finch suggests there is more to it than "good genes." In her experiment she made different colors of paper hats and fitted them on male birds. The female birds preferred mating with the red-hatted males. Paper hats would not occur naturally on male zebra finches so what females were selecting in this case was color, perhaps an aesthetic choice (Schultzhuitzen 2001).

Darwin was a populationist, principally because he observed so much variability in species. Although it is often difficult to know the range of variability in a species when there only a few specimens, Darwin's dictum was that scientists should think in terms of variable groups rather than of one example or one fossil somehow being *the* group. Darwin was also a holist, believing selection operated on whole or total individuals relative to others in the population. After about 1900 most scientists focused on the gene as the unit for selection, but in the mid-1970s science returned to the concept of the entire individual (Mayr 2000). To understand the impact of natural selection, however, you must keep in mind that although selection operates on individuals through reproductive differential, it is the population or species that evolves and adapts. The unit of selection is the individual, but the unit of evolution is the population.

Darwin wrote a short outline of his ideas in 1842, but he did not publish the full treatise until 1859. He apparently thought he had not collected enough data to support his hypothesis and had fears about addressing such a controversial issue. Indeed, his ideas were not met with universal delight—mainly because they did not include the notion of progress and they involved extinctions. Yet at least one other scientist, Alfred Russel Wallace, came to very similar conclusions about natural selection at approximately the same time as Darwin. In 1858 both men received credit for their work when their joint paper was read at the Linnaean Society of London (Desmond and Moore 1991).

Thomas Hunt Morgan (1866–1945), an American biologist, was initially critical of both natural selection and Mendelian inheritance. But after testing the mechanisms of both heredity and selection on fruit flies in his laboratory, he reversed his judgment and became a staunch proponent of modern evolutionary theory. It was Morgan who combined Mendel's and Darwin's famous laws in 1916 (Marks 2002).

**sexual selection**
A form of natural selection with an emphasis on the choosing of mating partners, often by some means of identifying "good genes."

Darwin's foremost contribution to our understanding of evolution was his explanation of how it works through natural selection, but he made additional contributions. He denied any notion of "progress," so beloved of previous scientists, instead focusing on trends. He also believed that evolution was branching or bushy. From Aristotle to Lamarck and beyond, scientists who believed in change (evolution) had thought of it as linear, a kind of "teleological march toward greater perfection" (Mayr 2000). Finally, Darwin rejected "typological thinking" in favor of population thinking, believing that it was the population that would show the effects of natural selection. He could observe that no two individuals were exactly alike in any population, but he saw that it was the population that evolved, not the individual. Finally, as a last word on Darwin, it is interesting that he used the word *evolution* only once in *The Origin of Species*, and it was the last word in the book.

The last of the three cornerstones of the science of evolution is the concept of mutations, the ultimate cause of change in hereditary materials.

## De Vries's Mutations

Mutations were discovered in 1886 when the Dutch botanist Hugo de Vries saw in evening primroses in an abandoned field traits that he knew he had never seen before. Darwin's "sports" became "mutations." Unfortunately, primroses are genetically odd, and what de Vries thought were mutations were just primrose irregularities. He was not seeing new species at all. Most of what scientists know about mutations they have learned either through experiments on laboratory animals or, in the case of humans, through funded research on medical abnormalities. The word *mutation* may bring to mind misshapen individuals or spontaneous abortions, but without mutations, evolution would not occur as it does. It has, however, been estimated that deleterious mutations are at least 100,000 times more frequent than beneficial ones simply because organisms are well adapted and any change is more apt to be deleterious than beneficial. Mutations should be thought of as the raw material of evolution because they are the only way new genetic material can be introduced into populations. Every biological trait that exists today in every species had its origin in a mutation somewhere in the species' evolutionary history. Without mutations, the first life would have been the only life on Earth; there might be more of it, but it would be the same today as when it began.

Most genetic material replicates itself exactly during cell replication. A **mutation** is any change that occurs in the genetic material when it is undergoing replication. Partial duplication, missing chromosomes, chromosomes with missing chunks, repeated sections, and broken chromosomes that are spliced onto others are all mutations; the effects of such chromosomal mutations are usually systemic and almost always fatal in humans, because in each case so many genes are involved. However, most mutations, including the nonfatal mutations that can become part of the evolutionary record, occur at the base pair level on the DNA and are analogous to one wrong note in an entire musical score. For example, a single instance of base C could mutate to base G. In relation to the entire number of replications, mutations are rare. Expert estimates of the mutation rate for humans vary from 1 to 4 to 200 in a single individual. Most mutations do not manifest in subsequent generations (Klein and Takahata 2002; McKee 2000). However, since males produce sex cells throughout their lifetimes, while females produce and store their sex cells before they are even born, males may contribute 50 times more mutations than females do and throughout their lifetimes. Most genetic change (good, bad, neutral) can therefore be laid at the feet of males (S. Jones 2003).

What causes mutations? Under laboratory conditions fruit fly genes can mutate when exposed to extreme heat or cold, X-rays, radioactivity, or chemicals. For ethical reasons scientists do not purposely cause mutations in humans, but human genes can mutate on their own when exposed to human-related factors such as cigarette smoking, chemical wastes in the air or water, chemicals added to foods and medicines, air pollution, or human-caused radioactivity. Mutations also can result from natural factors such

**mutation**
A mechanism for evolutionary change acting through random changes in the sex cells; the ultimate source of all genetic variation.

as cosmic radiation, radiation from under the Earth's crust, working with certain elements such as radium, increases in temperature, and the instability of DNA itself. Instability means that mutation patterns are unpredictable (Lowenstein 1992). Also, experiments on fruit flies have shown that radiation causes mutation rates to go up, yet fears that children of survivors of the atomic bombing of Japan would show increased expressions of radiation-caused mutations have not been borne out.

# The Tempo of Evolution

There are two prominent models of the tempo of evolution. Darwin's name is usually associated with the tempo of evolution called **phyletic gradualism**: the view that in general, evolutionary change occurs slowly and continuously over time. Darwin believed that natural selection operates on all variable traits, constantly favoring or rejecting one variation or another. He believed that this process results in species' changing slowly and, in his words, becoming better adapted. The other model of tempo is **punctuated equilibrium**, a concept once called saltation and repopularized in the 1970s by Stephen Jay Gould and Niles Eldredge (1977). According to the punctuated equilibrium view, the majority of evolutionary lineages show long periods of stasis, or little change, followed by short bursts, or punctuations, of evolutionary activity. (See Figure 3.7.) There are two reasons why punctuated equilibrium became popular again. First, the two scientists who supported it saw what they believed to be stasis and punctuation for the species in which they specialized: Eldridge saw 8 myr of no change in trilobites before they became extinct, and Gould found the same lack of slow and continuous change in snails (Morris 2001). Second, many scientists were bothered by the lack of transitional fossils between major groups of plants and animal. If the tempo of evolution were fast, that would explain why those fossils were missing. Even Darwin was conscious of the large gaps in the fossil record, but he believed, as many modern scientists do, that they were due to a lack of preservation or

**phyletic gradualism**
Darwin's idea of the tempo of evolution as being slow and gradual over long periods of time.

**punctuated equilibrium**
Model of macroevolutionary change in which long periods of little change are followed by short bursts of rapid change.

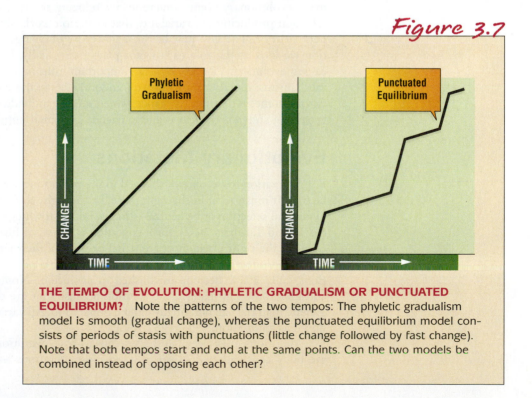

*Figure 3.7*

**THE TEMPO OF EVOLUTION: PHYLETIC GRADUALISM OR PUNCTUATED EQUILIBRIUM?** Note the patterns of the two tempos: The phyletic gradualism model is smooth (gradual change), whereas the punctuated equilibrium model consists of periods of stasis with punctuations (little change followed by fast change). Note that both tempos start and end at the same points. Can the two models be combined instead of opposing each other?

that the fossils just had not been found yet. This "absence of evidence" argument has been recently augmented by the fossil discovery of a number of transitional fossils, such as those of the earliest land animals.

An intensive and extensive look across the fossil record at different types of animals over a long amount of time does not point to only one tempo throughout time, place, or species. For example, certain molluses change only during speciation events but not at all during stasis, while rodents—and some other animals—change as much between as during speciation (Stearns and Hoekstra 2005). And in fact neither Darwin nor Gould and Eldredge claimed that *all* evolutionary events were in only one mode (Gingerich 1984). So what tempo is more common? Current evidence concludes that the general tempo is slow and continuous change for some lineages, and stasis and bursts for others. Michael Rosenzweig further suggests that "it depends on the scale at which it is measured" (1997, 1622). Both at a microevolutionary level over a small number of generations and from a very broad perspective of millions of years, species appear to show a pattern of slow and continuous change. At the speciation level, evolution often appears to occur in a punctuated equilibrium mode. Many paleoanthropologists are not convinced the tempo has always been in only one mode for the entire human lineage (Foley 1987), and one researcher even uses the term "rapid gradualism" (Dawkins 1994). Finally, many experts contend that given the nature of the fossil record and its preservation problems, evolution will always look punctuated whether it is or not (Ridley 2004).

# The Causes of Evolution

For almost 100 years scientists have understood that evolution is the result of the interaction of heredity (providing the continuity and consistency) and change (resulting in variability). Scientists have also identified the major causes or factors that interact to produce change over time: mutations, natural selection, gene flow, and genetic drift. (Whether to speak in terms of "causes," "factors," " forces," or "mechanisms" is a matter of choice.) Mutations and natural selection are responsible for the vast majority of macroevolutionary events, mutations introducing the new genetic material and natural selection producing the variability that evolution works on; but in the shorter run genetic drift or gene flow may be the major cause of change in some lineages. In this section we look at the role each factor plays individually, but it is their interaction that causes evolution. Chance plays an important role in evolution through several key mechanisms: mutations are chance (random) events; the exact combination of parental chromosomes is a matter of chance; which specific individuals meet to pass on gene flow is chance; and genetic drift is due to chance and small numbers (McKee 2000).

## Evolutionary Mutations

For a mutation to become established in the evolutionary record, three conditions must be met: It must occur in the right place, be the right size, and be operated on positively by natural selection or be neutral—that is, not bestow negative reproductive differential (Klein and Takahata 2002). Each condition is a kind of filter, as most mutations do not occur in the right place, most are lethal because of their size, and very few of them enhance reproductive differential. Thus, starting with a relatively large number of mutations, only a few become established in evolution. Nonetheless, mutations must be considered the raw material of evolution because they are the only known way that *new* genetic material can potentially enter a population. All variability was at one time introduced as a mutation.

Mutations must occur in the sex cells to have evolutionary significance. Most cells are body cells rather than sex cells, so most mutations occur during body cell replication and have no effect on evolution. Because there is no connection between body cell mutations and sex cells, there is no way for one to affect the other. Estimating mutation rates for humans is very difficult, but they occur in perhaps 5 percent of sex cell replications.

Large mutations, which are by definition lethal, have no chance to become evolutionary because they do not go beyond a single generation, whereas small mutations may accumulate small effects. Mutations that are systemic and cause change in developing organs often cause spontaneous abortions; mutations that cause early death also are considered lethal. It has been estimated that of the 20 percent of known conceptions in modern human females that end in spontaneous abortions, half of these outcomes are caused by sex cell mutations (Bogin 2001a). Such an estimate is probably low, however, because many spontaneous abortions occur early in pregnancy and are probably not noticed, reported, or counted.

## Evolutionary Selection

Only when mutations bestow positive reproductive differential on the individuals that initially carry them can the mutations be passed on to at least the next generation. Mutations that bestow negative reproductive differential on individuals who carry them (which is far more common) will disappear, usually in a generation or so. The action of positive selection on mutations is through individuals via their reproductive differential; but given time, the effect can change a population.

Specific small mutations that occurred originally in sex cells and conferred positive reproductive differential are all around us, given that all major biological change has taken place through this process. For example, a mutation that allowed an individual to see better in dim light than its conspecifics would likely allow that individual to feed longer, live longer, avoid predators better, and produce more offspring—who themselves could see better than their conspecifics in the next generation. In time the better-eyesight mutation would likely become fixed in the population. Even a recessive gene that began as a mutation can become all but fixed (0.997) after as few as 200 generations (Relethford 2001a). But again, most mutations neither bestow positive reproductive differential on an individual nor become established in successive generations. Most neutral mutations do not survive and even the seemingly advantageous ones merely have a somewhat better chance to survive (Klein and Takahata 2002). Mutations are not wish lists; they happen randomly. When particular mutations fortuitously occur, pass through the positive reproductive differential filter, and appear to be beneficial to a population, the population can be said to be better adapted to its environment. Not all traits in all species at any particular time are necessarily adaptive, however. Some may be linked to traits that are adaptive and may merely be "along for the ride"; these traits can be thought of as neutral, because if they were truly maladaptive, natural selection would eliminate them in subsequent generations.

One of Darwin's more important points about natural selection was that it operates on the variability found within any species. Establishing the fact of considerable variability within all species was one of the most difficult parts of his hypothesis to establish, but once it was accepted, it became a key part of natural selection. Two types of selection operate on the existing variability in a population long after the original variations evolve as mutations. In **directional selection**, the mean of a trait's variation moves in a constant direction, with succeeding generations showing short- or long-term directional change. For example, scientists observed and measured beak length in finches during drought years (1976–1977) in the Galapagos Islands (Grant 1986). Finch beak length increased during each generation, so it can be considered directional. Because beak length is showing existing variability, the change is directional selection—but perhaps of a short-term nature, given that drought is an abnormal condition in the Galapagos. (See Highlight 3.3 for a further description of

**directional selection**
A type of natural selection that moves the mean of a trait's variation in a population in a constant direction, with succeeding generations showing short- or long-term directional change in the trait.

# In the Galapagos Islands with Darwin and His Finches

IF YOU HAVE EVER HEARD OF the Galapagos Islands, you probably associate them with Charles Darwin and finches. Biology texts always report that Darwin, on his famous voyage on HMS *Beagle*, observed the variability of two types of animals he saw in the Galapagos when he was there in September and October of 1835—finches and giant tortoises. And supposedly the rest is biological history, because these observations resulted in Darwin's hypothesis that natural selection is a major actor in evolution. Unfortunately, this account is myth, not history. It is true that the *Beagle* and Darwin visited the Galapagos, but Darwin saw the finches (and tortoises) on only four of the islands; he collected (i.e., shot) specimens of only 9 of the 14 species; and he did not label them correctly by island. In his diary, written while on board, and in letters to friends, Darwin gave no indication that he understood the implications of variability at that point in his life; he didn't even mention the word *finch*. Indeed, he was still a Lamarckian until some time after he had returned and talked with other scientists in London about his observations. Perhaps these discussions sparked his formulation of his generalizing principle, the concept of natural selection. (Author's note: Given the unusual animal species in the Galapagos—blue-footed boobies, tiny penguins, albatrosses, giant tortoises, giant iguanas, and sea lions—it is surprising that Darwin collected and even remembered the finches. In a week's visit in 2002, I saw and counted a total of 12 finches. They were small, dark birds and totally without interest!)

When Darwin arrived in the Galapagos, he undoubtedly saw finches; he did collect about 100 specimens. Later he wrote of their variability relative to specific islands, but he thought they were all one species and all ate the same food—he never understood their variability or the importance of their beak shape differences. On the other hand, he never claimed to understand their variability or evolution. But the Galapagos were actually an excellent place to gain insights into natural selection, and perhaps Darwin intuited more than he put in writing. The Galapagos, by being isolated, showed

In the Galapagos Darwin focused on the rather small and drab finches (top) rather than on the flamboyant blue-footed booby (middle), though the tortoises (bottom) did catch his attention because of their size and age (up to 200 years old). Why do you suppose he focused on the finches?

the results of one likely migration of finches from the mainland, with secondary migrations to other islands. In their new homes the finches found themselves in different geographic areas that called upon parts of the variability that existed in the original migrating group. Darwin would not have seen such island specificity in rural England, because English finches interbred on their borders, keeping the species open and variable. The Galapagos were a unique laboratory for identifying the subtle and elusive effect of natural selection, that of adaptation.

Biologists now know a good deal more about finches and the Galapagos than any scientist did in the mid-nineteenth century. It is known, for example, that finches vary in color and body size as well as in the size and shape of their beaks, which are usually described in terms such as "sharp and pointed," "long and slender," "short and thick," "stout and straight," and so forth. Finches eat different kinds of foods, such as seeds, cactus spines, mangoes, twigs, leaves, insects inside trees, and ticks from tortoises. When you see a finch with a long slender beak poking into cactus spines and another finch with a short strong beak tearing apart bark to expose insects, it is tempting to hypothesize a direct correlation between beak shape and food taken. However, because no species of finch eats only one food, the relationship is considerably more complex. Nonetheless, beak size and shape are affected by food exploitation methods.

As Darwin did not correctly classify the finches, evolutionary studies had to wait until taxonomic and distribution problems were overcome before biologists could hypothesize about the birds' evolution. The modern model postulates three steps in finch evolution: (1) An initial group colonized one island from mainland South America, 600 miles away. DNA evidence suggests that this first group arrived about 2 to 3 myr ago. (2) When the carrying capacity of the original island was reached, finches dispersed to nearby islands and encountered different environmental circumstances, such as food resources. Beak mutations, acted on by natural selection, changed the population; this occurred on several different islands. (3) Reproductive isolation resulted in 14 species of finches in the Galapagos.

If these steps sound familiar, it is because scientists believe this is the normal way speciation occurs when geographic barriers (such as ocean and distance) effectively isolate populations. This finch speciation event may have taken only half a million years to complete.

Taking this research one step farther, Peter Grant, a contemporary American biologist, has studied the Galapagos finches for several decades, often with his biologist wife, Rosemary. Grant suggests that rainfall is the only important variable in Galapagos life. The amount of sunlight and the temperature do not change much from year to year, because the islands are on the equator. But rainfall can be quite variable, ranging from El Niño excess to normal to drought.

During five normal rainfall years, the Grants studied individual finches on Isla Genovesa, focusing on morphological and reproductive variability. A normal year has four wet and eight dry months. Finches breed only during the wet months and stop breeding when there are no more caterpillars or spiders for their fledglings. The Grants found that reproductive success was variable even in a normal

Galapagos climate extremes are visible in these photos. From the same vantage point, the photo on the left was taken in a drought year and the photo on the right in a normal year. What different kinds of food would be available or not available for birds and land animals under these two different circumstances?

(continues on the next page) ▶

year; 15 percent of the population produced no fledglings, leaving 85 percent to contribute to the next generation. The key to reproductive success during *normal* rainfall years was not morphological variation (body size, beak shape) but experience. Experienced birds (birds in their second or later year of laying eggs) already had mates from the previous year and started breeding early, thus producing multiple clutches. Inexperienced birds had to find mates; by the time they did, they were lagging behind the experienced birds in producing first clutches. Females chose their mates on the basis of courtship behavior, which is based more on experience and age than on genetics. The upshot of these factors was that, on average, experienced birds produced twice as many fledglings as inexperienced birds.

During *very wet* or *very dry* years, in contrast, body size and beak shape were more important in reproductive success than experience was. In very wet years the cacti were smothered and died, so long-beaked finches that fed on cactus spines did not produce as many offspring as wide-beaked finches that fed on insects. During the drought of 1976–1977, the Grants witnessed little food production at all, and no finches bred. Obviously, population declined, but survival rates varied, with survival depending on birds' ability to exploit difficult food resources. Only those who survived could become parents during the next breeding season. Large birds with strong beaks had a better chance of survival than small birds. The small seeds went first, to all sizes of birds with any beak shape; but when the small seeds were depleted, only large birds with wide beaks could exploit the large seeds. When the Grants compared the finches' average beak depth and size in the years before and after the drought, they saw an increase of 4 percent. Because there was no breeding during the drought year, this change was due to differential mortality. If either wet or dry conditions had continued over many years, beak traits would have changed directionally. Grant suggests that if 4 percent change per year had continued for as little as 46 years, it could have led to more speciation.

The Galapagos Islands were and continue to be a natural outdoor laboratory. One lesson to be learned is the value of variability. Although body size and beak shape were stable during normal rainfall years, beaks and body size changed after a single abnormal season. Because rainfall in the Galapagos is quite variable from year to year, survival of individual finch species depends on variability. That Darwin may have not used finches to formulate his theory of natural selection is really not very important; this lesson is.

Fernandina, a Galapagos island, is home to many unusual birds, land animals, and sea creatures.

*Sources*: Darwin, C. 1839/1989. *Voyage of the Beagle*, 267–291. New York: Penguin.    Desmond, A., and J. Moore. 1991. *Darwin*. New York: Viking Penguin.    Grant, P. R. 1986. *Ecology and evolution of Darwin's finches*. Princeton, NJ: Princeton University Press.    Grant, P. R., and R. Grant. 2002. Darwin's finches. *Science* 296:633–635.    Grant, R., and P. R. Grant. 1989. *Evolutionary dynamics of a natural population: The large cactus finch of the Galapagos*. Chicago: University of Chicago Press. Pryce-Jones, R. 2003. Interview (and personal observation) of Darwin's finches at Tring, Bird Depository of the Natural History Museum, London, June 23.    Rice, P. C. 2002. Tracing Darwin's footsteps: The Galapagos in 2002. *General Anthropology* 8 (2): 1–10.    Yoon, C. K. 2000. "Riches hidden in plain sight." *New York Times* (June 20): D1–4.

turn back to your reading

**stabilizing (balancing) selection**
A type of natural selection that holds the existing variability of a trait steady in a population generation after generation.

post-Darwinian observations on Galapagos Islands finches.) If we look at human evolution, increase in mean brain size over the past 2 myr and development of lactose tolerance in some populations are examples of long-term directional selection (Olson 2002). Although Darwin assumed directional selection to be a slow process, it has been seen to operate in less than 10 years on the wing length of wild North American fruit flies.

The other type of selection is called **stabilizing** or **balancing selection**. This form of selection stabilizes the existing variability of a trait in a population generation after generation. For example, one familiar species, the house cat, varies in hundreds of traits: size, color and texture of hair, whisker length, and tail length, to name a few. Although house cats vary in size, they are never as large as lions or as small as mice; stabilizing selection limits the size of cats to magnitudes within the range of the species' existing variability as long as no new mutations occur to change that range. Stabilizing selection would have been very familiar to Darwin, as it is constantly operating on the extremes of any trait's variability. If every variation of every biological trait of every species that ever existed is considered, the effect of stabilizing selection on species' variability is staggering.

## *An Example of Directional Selection*

It is fortuitous when we can observe natural selection operating directly on mutations, because the process normally occurs too slowly for us to see it. Nonetheless, scientists and others have observed and reported on more than 100 cases of natural selection occurring in nature. The peppered moth of Industrial Revolution fame in central England is the classic example of observed and noted directional selection on an initial mutation. Before the Industrial Revolution (particularly around Manchester), people often saw a certain species of moth resting on light-colored lichens on trees. (Lichens are symbiotic fungi and algae.) Because most of the moths also were light colored, they were camouflaged and not easy prey for birds. Roughly 1 percent of the moths were dark colored (a result of an initial mutation or mutations), but birds ate most of these uncamouflaged moths before they had a chance to reproduce. A small number of dark moths continued to appear during the pre–Industrial Revolution period, however, either because occasionally a dark moth avoided predation and reproduced or because mutations reoccurred on the color gene(s). After the Industrial Revolution began, chimney soot killed the lichens and exposed the dark-colored tree bark. Given the principles of natural selection, it is not surprising that the frequency of dark moths increased to 90 percent and the frequency of light moths decreased accordingly. Dark color became the camouflage color, and the light moths, now easily seen by birds on the dark tree bark, were picked off. After England passed the Clean Air Acts in 1956, pollution lessened considerably; the light-colored lichens returned to the trees; and the light-colored moths evolved back to their original high frequency (Grant 1991).

The moth on the right is well camouflaged; the moth on the left is not camouflaged and will likely be eaten by a bird. What happened to the dark moths after the industrial air pollution was cleaned up and the light-colored lichens returned?

Although the peppered moth is a well known and often cited example of natural selection, it occurred only after the Industrial Revolution, a human-caused event. Studies of melanin (dark pigment) developing in spiders as a result of industrial activity also indicate directional natural selection. A recent case of directional natural selection occurred without human interference, showing natural selection in operation in modern times. The "normal" color for pocket mice in Arizona is light, and, living on sandy surfaces, they are well camouflaged. Some pocket mice have mutated to a dark color, making them well disguised on nearby dark lava rocks (Yoon 2003).

The peppered moth example provides interesting insights. First, it indicates that directional selection works on the biological variability that exists within a species—in the moth, on its colors. It also demonstrates that the vehicle of selection is the relative reproductive differential or survival value of the two forms of moth color under two different environmental conditions. What was good under one set of conditions was bad under another. Finally, better adaptation to existing environments can be noted in this case. (Part of the research for this classic case has come under criticism recently, but it is difficult to get two different colored moths to sit on the same piece of bark and spread their wings at the same time for a photo opportunity!)

Mutations and natural selection form the causal core of evolution: Certain small, randomly occurring mutations in sex cells that bestow positive net reproductive differential on individuals are the major reason why ancestral populations change over time to become descendant populations.

## Gene Flow

Gene flow is of secondary importance in macroevolutionary change, but it is often of primary importance in microevolution. **Gene flow** is the movement of genes between populations through the sexual reproduction of organisms that do not normally interbreed. It can occur through true migration, when populations move into new areas and interbreed with existing populations, or through the exchange of genes on reproductive borders without significant migration, when interbreeding occurs between the two populations. In populations that inhabit areas of large extent, individuals are more likely to mate with those in close proximity than with individuals living far away. Often, natural geographic barriers such as rivers, mountain chains, or deserts exist between populations. These barriers limit random mating within the species and are one reason why subspecies can exist. But when members of populations interbreed after migration of one population into the breeding area of another or interbreed at their borders, the result is that genes flow from one population to another through offspring. Gene flow has three effects. First, it can spread beneficial mutations from one population to another. Second, it can prevent breeding isolation that would result in speciation by cladogenesis (splitting), a topic we'll discuss shortly. And third, it reduces the sometimes deleterious effects of inbreeding in small populations.

## Genetic Drift

Sewall Wright discovered in the 1920s that populations could change over time for a reason other than mutations, natural selection, or gene flow. He discovered that numerical size alone can cause populations to change via **genetic drift** in a single generation—and that the smaller the population size, the greater the possible effect. A population that numbers more than 10,000 (considered "infinite") is not susceptible to genetic drift because its large size ensures that each generation will be representative of its predecessor unless mutations, natural selection, or gene flow are causing change. A population that numbers fewer than 1,000 individuals can show up to 1 percent change due to chance alone in any two generations. But a population can show real change if the number is under 100 (up to 10 percent change per gene per generation), and even more if the number is under 10 (up to 60 percent change per

**gene flow**
A mechanism for evolutionary change resulting from movement of genes from one population to another through interbreeding, or exchange of genes between two populations, which introduces new genes and makes the populations more similar to each other.

**genetic drift**
A mechanism for evolutionary change resulting from random changes in gene frequencies from one generation to the next in small populations.

gene per generation). Obviously, the possible genetic drift effect increases as population size decreases. Another variable effect of gene drift is somewhat controversial, but there is some evidence that gene drift has a greater effect on neutral mutations and can "fix" them quickly (Klein and Takahata 2002).

Genetic drift gets its name from the fact that alleles can "drift" away or be lost. How does genetic drift work? Consider the nontaster gene in human groups. Until 10 kyr ago local human populations likely ranged between 50 and 25 individuals. In such groups up to 20 percent change per gene per generation is statistically possible. The change is totally random, because it is due to chance; so the change can be directional, with traits becoming fixed or totally lost, or gene frequencies can randomly increase and then decrease to end up where they began, or there may be no change at all. Figure 3.8 shows four computer simulations to show the effect of genetic drift on a very small population of 15 individuals; each simulation begins with an allele frequency of 50 percent for the nontaster gene. In one simulation the allele becomes fixed in the population after 10 generations; in another the allele is lost after 17 generations; and in another the frequency ends as it started 25 generations earlier. Statistical probabilities are just that—probabilities—and which path chance will take cannot be predicted. More than 99 percent of human groups have been (and some still are) susceptible to the effect of genetic drift, in which traits can become fixed or lost very quickly. Theoretically a small but extremely beneficial mutation could even cause speciation in relatively few generations (Relethford 2001a), although this idea is controversial.

*Figure 3.8*

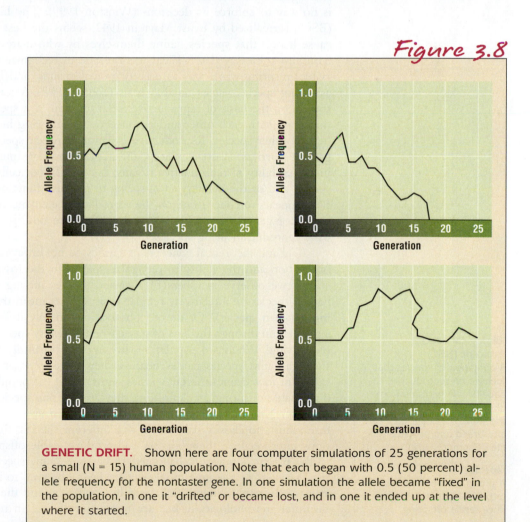

**GENETIC DRIFT.** Shown here are four computer simulations of 25 generations for a small (N = 15) human population. Note that each began with 0.5 (50 percent) allele frequency for the nontaster gene. In one simulation the allele became "fixed" in the population, in one it "drifted" or became lost, and in one it ended up at the level where it started.

# What Really Evolves?

The population or species evolves, not the individual or any higher taxonomic unit. The terms *species* and *population* are often used interchangeably, but although a species is a population, a population is not necessarily a species. By the definition of evolution, traits also can be said to evolve, as in the case of brain size or bipedalism—but always at the population level. At a micro level alleles evolve as well, because their proportions fluctuate in a population, whether directionally or more randomly, over time. This section considers the species level of evolution. Over a million and a half species have been formally named and described, but it is estimated there may be as many as 50 million species in existence today. Many of the undescribed groups live in the forest canopy where they are difficult to study; most are insects.

## The Species

There are certain concepts in the scientific literature that are particularly contentious: Cultural anthropologists argue over how to define culture, political scientists over the definition of democracy, and biologists over the best way to define "species," with over 22 definitions discovered in the literature as of 1997. The International Code of Zoological Nomenclature is the official body that accepts or denies new taxa, but there is no way to enforce its decisions (Winston 1999). The **biological species concept** (BSC), formalized by Ernst Mayr in 1942, seems the best definition to use here because it says that **species** define themselves by who mates with whom. The English naturalist John Ray (1627–1705) was the first to recognize that the ability to produce viable offspring was a way to classify animal groups, and Ray began the tradition of assigning species names on that basis (Young 1992). Most biologists define modern species on the basis of reproductive isolation; that is, a species consists of individuals that mate with each other and produce viable offspring but do not mate with members of other species. Reproductive isolation between species can be caused by geographic barriers, seasonal mating differences, lack of appropriate sexual attractants, incompatibility of reproductive organs, the inability of cells to fertilize and form offspring, and/or the inability of offspring to produce functional sex cells. Although the BSC appears to concentrate on the reproductive element, it does not ignore morphological or genetic similarities (Rennie 2002). The BSC is the best definition for sexually reproducing living species.

Real and theoretical concepts of species do not always coincide, however, and hybridization and the ability to recognize species in the fossil record remain problematic. If we observe members of a named species mating with members of another named species on a relatively regular basis, does it mean they are "hybridizing" (mating between species)? Or do our observations merely indicate that we are observing a population through the lens of stasis, when in reality species are always in the process of evolving? When two populations live in close proximity, human observers may give them different species names because they consider their morphological differences sufficient to warrant different species status; but if the populations interbreed and produce viable offspring, by definition, they are but one species. Modern baboons are an example. Numerous morphological differences in size, hair color, and behavior led taxonomists to classify baboons as five different species. But because baboon populations interbreed on their borders and produce viable offspring that often back-cross to the parent population, baboons are but one "superspecies," *Papio papio*. Similarly, two "species" of macaque monkeys have been observed to interbreed in Indonesia for at least 20 years (Bynum 2002), and humped zebu and the nonhumped nonzebu cattle differ morphologically but are totally interfertile in mixed herds in East Africa

**biological species concept (BSC)**
A definition of *species* that focuses on reproductive capabilities: Organisms from different populations are in the same species if they can interbreed and produce fertile offspring.

**species**
A group whose members interbreed naturally and produce fertile offspring.

Anubis and hamadryas baboons, two populations of baboons, are morphologically quite different, showing variations in size, color, length of muzzle, and other visible features. Yet the two populations interbreed on their borders, producing healthy and viable offspring. How do we know how much morphological difference has to exist before there can be no interbreeding of populations?

(M. Jones 2001). There are cases of true hybridization between species, but humans are almost always involved in the process: Donkeys and zebras do not mate normally but can be made to produce "zebronkeys" for sideshows, lions and tigers can be made to produce "ligers" and "tiglons," and mules (horse–donkey hybrids) can be created but are apparently always sterile. Although people love stories about hybridization between dogs and cats or between humans and gorillas, such interbreedings do not happen. Interestingly, however, many folk taxonomies match scientific ones quite well. One human group in New Guinea, for example, recognizes several hundred species of vertebrates and only four of them aren't found on Western scientists' lists of species (Ridley 2004).

George Gaylord Simpson, an American paleontologist who specialized in establishing the evolution of the horse, added the time dimension to Mayr's BSC in 1961 by defining species in evolution as "independently evolving lineages." He called his model the **evolving species concept (ESC)**. Simpson realized that it would always be problematic to identify individual species in evolving lineages and claimed there was no nonarbitrary way to divide up a continuum. Noting these difficulties, some experts have looked to major adaptive changes as clues to speciation and subsequent taxonomic delineation. Hominid bipedalism and primate arboreal life are examples of major adaptive changes. The premise underlying this approach is that such major changes would result in rapid morphological changes that could be noted in the fossil record. This approach does work for major changes but does not help with separating evolving lineages once the major change is fixed (Kimbel and Martin 1993).

## The Genus and Subspecies

Unlike the species, neither the genus nor the subspecies evolves. The **genus** is a taxonomic collection of species that has evolutionary significance only in the probability that all species assigned to a genus once had a common ancestor. Some species contain

**evolving species concept (ESC)**
A definition of *species* in evolution as "independently evolving lineages."

**genus**
Taxonomic groups of closely related species with similar adaptations.

**subspecies**
Groups within a species whose individuals share certain traits in higher frequencies with each other than with the species as a whole.

**speciation**
The origin of new species by change over time or splitting of a lineage.

**transformism (anagenesis)**
A mechanism of speciation in which one species changes over time as a whole unit to become a new species.

**chronospecies**
Ancestral and descendant species in the same lineage, where the former has transformed itself into the latter.

**subspecies**, groups whose individuals share certain characteristics and genes in higher frequencies with one another than with the species as a whole. In theory all members of a species should be able to interbreed and produce viable offspring; in actuality, however, sometimes they are unable to. Dogs are a good example. At one time probably all members of *Canis familiaris* could breed successfully, but humans using artificial selection have made large dogs larger and small dogs smaller. The result can be a physical mismatch, such as between a female Chihuahua and a male Saint Bernard. The concept of the subspecies is not at all universal; many species occupy small geographic areas where subgroups do not form.

## Speciation

When a species either changes over time and forms a new species or splits into two or more species, the process is referred to as **speciation**. In **transformism**, also called **anagenesis**, one species transforms itself as a whole unit into a new species over time. This time relationship between ancestral and descendant species makes them parts of a **chronospecies**. Through accumulated mutations, natural selection, and sufficient and periodic gene flow, the chronospecies becomes different enough in time from its ancestral condition that it is given a new taxonomic name. **Splitting**, also called **cladogenesis**, occurs when an effective isolating barrier, geographic, genetic, or behavioral, keeps members of two (or more) segments of a species from interbreeding. (See Figure 3.9.) Mutations that occur in one population have no way to spread to the other

*Figure 3.9*

**SPECIATION.** One species can speciate into two by splitting, or cladogenesis, as a result of some kind of isolating barrier between segments of the species. This figure depicts a geographic barrier. What would happen to the isolating barrier (the river) if the animals depicted could swim? What other isolating barriers could cause speciation by splitting?

**splitting (cladogenesis)**
A mechanism of speciation in which an effective isolating barrier (geographic, genetic, or behavioral) keeps two (or more) segments of a species from interbreeding long enough for mutations and natural selection to make the separated populations no longer able to interbreed and thus separate species.

**paleospecies**
Species that are extinct, though their descendant species may still exist.

population if gene flow is reduced to zero; and given that mutations are random, identical mutations are not likely to occur in both populations. Also, natural selection is likely to operate somewhat differently on each population, because each occupies a somewhat different environment. With or without genetic drift, the two populations in time will split—will become so different that even if the isolating barrier were removed, interbreeding could not occur.

The length of time it takes for speciation to occur by either transformism or splitting varies from species to species and from time to time. Theoretically, it takes only one important trait difference for a population to form a new species—a group incapable of mating back with the parent population (Wilson 1999). Although no one has ever seen speciation occur in nature, two American geneticists recently sorted two groups of fruit flies by their environmental preferences and bred each group separately for 35 generations. The resulting populations refused to interbreed (Rennie 2002). In nature, because most mutations do not affect reproduction directly, it is common for large land-based species to take half a million years or so to speciate. Predictably, a lineage that has high mutation rates, exists in differing environmental niches, and has numerous geographic barriers is likely to speciate more often and more rapidly than a lineage that has low mutation rates, exists in a homogeneous environment, and has no known geographic barriers.

## Paleospecies and the ESC

Most evolution experts use Simpson's ESC to define species. It is, of course, impossible to define **paleospecies**, extinct species, by reproduction criteria, because past breeding population boundaries are not known. So scientists use their knowledge of the range of variability in modern species and apply it to closely related past populations to try to identify where one species ends and a new one begins. If the basic question is "How much variation can there be within a past population for it to be considered a single species?" the answer is "the same kind and amount of difference as there is within a modern, closely related species" (Rose and Bown 1993). Many scientists use the 5 to 10 percent variability range as a kind of magic number for hominids. That is, if a group of recently discovered hominid fossils shows 5 percent variability in all comparable traits, it is plausible that there are two species; if that group shows 10 percent variability, it is probable that two species are present (Groves 1997). However, humans today show 12 percent variability in cranial capacity, so the rule is not ironclad (Henneberg 1997). It has been suggested that if a modern taxonomy specialist were to see the bones of all known 300 breeds (subspecies) of dogs, about 20 species (not subspecies or breeds) would be identified (McKee 2000). There continue to be numerous difficulties in using the ESC with paleospecies, yet there is no viable alternative. For example, if chronospecies could not be divided up, even stratomolites dating to 3.5 billion years ago would have to be *Homo sapiens*, because humans came from an unbroken line of life forms extending back to those stromatolites. Other difficulties in identifying paleospecies include small, biased samples and scientists' inability to know whether a given fossil represents "average" traits or whether it is from the beginning, middle, or end of its species' time (Foley 1991). Because scientists will always be able to arbitrarily divide up evolving lineages into taxonomic chunks, there will always be disagreements. And, unfortunately, the "observer effect" (or bias) is always present (Eckhardt 2000).

Before exploring the specifics of human evolution or the general lineage leading to humans, it is necessary to understand the principles that underlie evolution in general. Although most evolutionary knowledge is based on experiments with nonhuman animals, it is appropriate to use such knowledge to understand human evolution—because all animals share the basic stuff of life, the same amino acids. Once scientists understood the fundamentals of the three cornerstones of evolution—inheritance, natural selection, and mutations—they began looking for causes and seeking to answer *why* questions. There is still a lot to learn, however. Chapter 4 will focus on macroevolutionary happenings.

■ Humans are animals and can be studied the same way as any other species of animal. Biological anthropologists focus on populations of humans rather than on individuals.

■ Evolution is defined as biological change over time. Because change can be observed and measured, evolution is fact, not theory.

■ Early ideas about evolution began with Anaximander, a nontraditional sixth-century BC Greek thinker who suggested that humans evolved from fish.

■ Until the seventeenth century, mainstream thinking held that life was created in perfect form; thus, there was no need for change or possibility of change.

■ By the eighteenth century, travel had begun to enlighten scientists and the lay public. The Lamarckian theory of acquired characteristics was central to early explanations for biological variations and change.

■ Scientists in the mid- to late nineteenth century discovered the three cornerstones of evolutionary understanding: Darwin discovered the principles of natural selection, Mendel discovered the principles of inheritance (heredity), and de Vries named mutations as the ultimate source of variation. These understandings formed the basis for the modern synthesis.

■ The basic principles of Mendelian inheritance are as follows: Discrete particles are the units of inheritance; after sex cell replication, chromosomes separate, taking their genes with them (segregation); as long as traits are on different chromosomes, they will assort independently (independent assortment); and some alleles show dominance over and mask the effects of other alleles.

■ The principles of genetics are the same for all animal species. For each biological trait, there is a phenotype and genotype. For the more than 4,000 simple

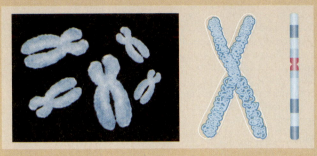

page 50

Mendelian traits in humans, individuals are either homozygous or heterozygous.

■ DNA provides codes for human traits by directing protein synthesis within cells. Genes are segments of DNA that occupy positions on chromosomes; they give particular instructions that are eventually expressed as traits.

■ Body cells replicate themselves and form new body cells; sex cells replicate themselves, then go through two reductions so that only half the genetic material from each parent is contributed to new organisms.

■ Natural selection operates through reproductive differential within species, resulting in differential genetic contributions by individuals to new generations. Many effects of natural selection are obviously adaptive; many are not.

■ The tempo of evolution has been described as either slow and gradual or fast but sporadic; it appears that the tempo is not always in one mode for all of life.

■ Evolution was and is caused by certain factors or mechanisms: mutations (the ultimate raw material of change), natural selection (through reproductive differ-

page 64

ential), gene flow, and genetic drift. Not all mutations are evolutionary, and natural selection eliminates most mutations that occur in sex cells. Gene flow keeps species from splitting and passes new genetic material throughout the species. Traits can be lost or fixed in small populations through genetic drift that is due to chance.

■ It is the species, not the genus or subspecies, that evolves; a species is self-defining.

■ Speciation can occur (new species can form) when existing populations transform themselves over time into a quite different species or split into two species. Extinct species are called paleospecies.

**page 70**

## KEY WORDS

acquired characteristics, 41
adaptation, 56
allele, 43
biological species concept
    (BSC), 68
catastrophism, 42
cells, 49
chromosomes, 46
chronospecies, 70
directional selection, 61
DNA, 49
dominance and recessiveness, 46
essentialism, 40
evolution, 40
evolving species concept (ESC), 69

gene flow, 66
genes, 46
genetic drift, 66
genotype, 48
genus, 69
heredity (inheritance), 43
heterozygous, 48
homozygous, 48
independent assortment, 46
meiosis, 54
mitosis, 54
mutation, 58
natural selection, 55
paleospecies, 71
phenotype, 48

phyletic gradualism, 59
punctuated equilibrium, 59
regulatory genes, 54
reproductive differential, 56
segregation, 46
sexual selection, 57
speciation, 70
species, 68
splitting (cladogenesis), 70
stabilizing (balancing) selection, 65
structural genes, 54
subspecies, 70
taxonomy, 41
transformism (anagenesis), 70
uniformitarianism, 42

## SUGGESTED READING

Cavalli-Sforza, L. L., P. Menozzi, and A. Piazza. *The History and Geography of Human Genes*. Princeton, NJ: Princeton University Press, 1994. An encyclopedic treatise on specific genes in global perspective; includes many computerized maps showing gene frequencies of certain traits.

Endler, J. A. *Natural Selection in the Wild*. Princeton, NJ: Princeton University Press, 1986. The author has scoured the literature for examples of natural selection in the wild, addressing over 100 such examples.

Grant, P. *Ecology and Evolution of Darwin's Finches*. Princeton, NJ: Princeton University Press, 1986. Armed with more than a hundred years of biological research and discoveries since Darwin's classic visit to the Galapagos Islands, Grant studied Darwin's finches in great detail, fortuitously being able to take advantage of a severe local drought and its rapid effects on finch beaks. Nicely illustrated, the book puts flesh on Darwin's more anecdotal study.

Marks, J. *Human Biodiversity: Genes, Race, and History*. New York: Aldine de Gruyter, 1995. A readable book that focuses on human genes and their relationship to modern humans as a population and as subpopulations ("races") and looks at how concepts of genes and "race" have changed over time.

Stearns, S. C. and R. F. Hoekstra. *Evolution: An Introduction*. 2nd ed. Oxford: Oxford University Press, 2005. An up-to-date and complete introduction to evolution from the perspective of two biologists.

# Chapter 4

# Macroevolution: First Life to Mammals

■ **PRINCIPLES OF RECONSTRUCTING MACROEVOLUTION AND COMMON ANCESTRAL GROUPS**

■ **MACROEVOLUTION**
Evolutionary Beginnings • Archaeae, Prokaryotes, Eukaryotes, and Ediacara • The Cambrian Explosion • From "Fish" to Reptiles • Reptiles: Evolution's First Amniotes • Mammals in Evolution

■ **HIGHLIGHT 4.1:** *In the Field and the Museum with the Burgess Shale*
■ **HIGHLIGHT 4.2:** *The End of an Era: The K/T Mass Extinction*

■ **MACROEVOLUTIONARY LESSONS**

■ **CHAPTER SUMMARY**

▲
**Photo above:** Stromatolites on an Australian beach

Stephen Jay Gould (1941–2002) perhaps the best-known contemporary historian of science, said that evolution need not have occurred as it did but could have occurred in millions of other ways (1987a, 1989). Over the almost 4 billion years (byr) of life on this planet (to the best of today's knowledge), there were countless opportunities for evolution to have gone in various directions; but the final result is that it did go in only one. The goal of evolution-minded scientists—primarily paleontologists, evolutionary biologists, and bioanthropologists—is to trace that evolutionary history. Scientists use different kinds of evidence—primarily fossils, supplemented by molecular data—to try to reconstruct the history of life on Earth. Although the evidence collected so far is sometimes conflicting, there has been only one history of life on Earth, and so the evidence will ultimately converge.

This chapter uses the principles of evolution developed in Chapter 3 as well as knowledge to date from fossil finds and dating techniques to reconstruct what happened from the earliest life to just before the appearance of primates, our taxonomic order. Again, because anthropology's main focus is on us—humans—this evolutionary reconstruction appears to run from first life to primates. However, every other existing animal order has its own evolutionary path. Because of the huge time frame, both relatively and actually, what is being discussed here is large-scale macroevolution. This chapter ends with a summary of macroevolutionary lessons from the last 3.5 byr that will hopefully further your understanding of the evolution of modern humans.

# Principles of Reconstructing Macroevolution and Common Ancestral Groups

**contingency**
The principle that states that in general, every population's genetics and morphology exist because the group evolved from a previous group.

**common ancestry**
The principle that states that if two groups evolved from the same earlier group, then they have common ancestry.

**common ancestral group**
The group from which any two existing sibling groups evolved.

**homology**
The principle that states that similarity is due to descent from a common ancestor.

**analogy**
Structures that are superficially similar and serve similar functions but have no necessary common evolutionary relationship.

**reconstruction**
Pulling together evidence from many sources to facilitate knowledge of what happened in particular lineages, such as the reconstruction of the human lineage.

No matter what life forms were like at any given moment in time, they were contingent on what happened previously. Future evolution is almost unpredictable, but past and present evolution is based firmly on what happened before. This is the principle of **contingency**. A silly example illustrates the principle of contingency: A species that is quadrupedal, has naked green skin, and lives in water would not have evolved over five generations from a flying, pink-furred, bipedal species. Contingency predicts that the species would have evolved from a quadrupedal, naked, greenish-yellow species that lived in water most of the time. The principle of contingency is the basis for the principles of **common ancestry** and **common ancestral groups**. These principles are quite logical: Two modern groups of animals that do not interbreed are by definition different species. If they are quite similar in anatomy, morphology, behavior, and genetics, it is probably because they inherited those similar traits from a common ancestral group in the not-too-distant past. This is the principle of **homology**. By contrast, the principle of **analogy** sees similarities between groups as due to similar evolutionary adaptations to similar environments; the famous example is of butterfly wings (insects) and bat wings (mammals), which show similar function but not common ancestry. But because homology, unlike analogy, is based on common ancestry, homology provides the principle scientists use for reconstructing common ancestral groups.

How does **reconstruction** of ancestral traits work? Hypothetically, we can reconstruct the traits of any ancestral group by comparing what the group passed on to its two (or more) daughter groups through inheritance. See Figure 4.1 for a visualization of this principle. Species A in the figure is the common ancestor, and the black dots within the group represent its biological traits (anatomical, morphological, behavioral, genetic). The two lines up to species B and C (the daughter species, which

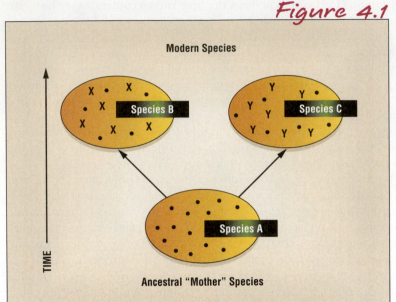

*Figure 4.1*

**Modern Species**

Species B

Species C

Species A

**TIME**

**Ancestral "Mother" Species**

**PRINCIPLE OF COMMON ANCESTRAL GROUPS USING HOMOLOGY AND CONTINGENCY.** Species A (the mother species) in time splits into species B and C, which are daughter species to A and sibling species to each other. The dots in species A represent the traits (anatomical, morphological, genetic, behavioral) common to the group. Through homology, the daughter species inherit most of these traits but evolve additional traits during the time after their split—traits represented by Xs in B and Ys in C. The traits shown as dots are inherited from the common ancestor and called ancestral traits, and the Xs and Ys in B and C are called derived traits. The traits of B and C are contingent on species A's traits. Why is the principle of analogy not used to reconstruct evolutionary events?

are sibling species to each other) represent evolution since the time when those two species split from species A. Species B and C share many traits with each other and with their mother species (A), because they inherited **ancestral traits** from A; those common traits are shown by the black dots. But each of the daughter groups also has evolved **derived traits** after splitting from the mother species; these traits are not apt to be the same for both groups, and are shown by Xs for B and Ys for C. Groups B and C may share the majority of their traits with each other and with species A. However, some traits have been lost between group A and groups B and C. The result is that scientists can reconstruct at least some aspects of the common ancestral group (A) by comparing the modern descendant groups. Fossil finds would reinforce the hypothetical reconstruction with direct evidence.

Please note that although much literature in the field uses terms such as *primitive* and *advanced*, these words are subjective and carry connotations of inferiority and superiority. We prefer to use *ancestral* (instead of "primitive") and *derived* (instead of "advanced"). These terms refer only to the time a trait or group evolved, avoiding subjective connotations. Ancestral traits are genetic traits inherited from earlier groups; derived traits are genetic traits that evolved after the common ancestral group split to two or more species.

The following scenario provides a more concrete example of the use of the principles of contingency, common ancestry, and homology; it also demonstrates which traits are ancestral and which are derived. Two modern species of rabbit in the state of Oregon are separated by a wide river. By definition, they do not interbreed. Investigator 1, a field biologist, studies the two modern species and makes up a list of anatomical, morphological, behavioral, and genetic traits for each; after comparing the trait lists, he concludes that the two species are 87 percent alike and 13 percent different. Why? Because they likely inherited 87 percent of their common ancestral group's traits some 20 thousand years (kyr) ago. These are the ancestral traits. The 13 percent difference is likely due to separate evolutionary trajectories during the last 20 kyr, when evolutionary pressures have been operating differently on each lineage. These are the derived traits. Investigator 1, can now hypothesize about the 20-kyr-old ancestral group, attributing to it the 87 percent of common traits possessed by the two modern species. Investigator 2, a paleontologist in this hypothetical scenario, can lay out 20-kyr-old rabbit fossils on a table, and both scientists can match the skeletal parts of a representative of each of the two modern groups with the skeletal parts of the fossils. If the modern skeletons and the fossil materials are 87 percent alike (allowing for variation because of age, sex, and individuality), the principles have been supported, at least for anatomical traits. This is a simplified hypothetical case, and some of the similar traits may be due to analogy; but the example shows the process of reconstructing past populations based on contingency, common ancestry, homology, and comparisons of modern populations. Additionally, the

**ancestral traits**
Traits that appear early in the evolution of a lineage; contrast with derived traits that appear after a particular split in that lineage.

**derived traits**
Traits that have changed from an ancestral state.

process allows scientists to separate ancestral traits from derived traits. Note that scientists will never be able to totally reconstruct an ancestral species based solely on a comparison of closely related modern species because each of the modern groups has lost a certain proportion of the ancestral traits over time. Only the traits shared by all of the modern groups can be identified as ancestral and then be used to reconstruct the common ancestral group.

What about traits that do not fossilize? For any species there are many morphological traits and entire categories of traits that would never fossilize. For rabbits examples include obvious traits such as ear length; the shape, color, and texture of the tail; and the color, texture, and length of the fur. Most of the entire category of behavior would not fossilize, yet at least some behavioral traits appear to be under genetic control and inherited biologically. For example, a rabbit raised in isolation would never see a conspecific hop; yet at a young age the rabbit would hop, not get up on its hind legs and walk bipedally. That is, this behavior has a biological, or genetic, base. Although the investigators in our hypothetical rabbit case could not make strong statements about nonfossilized traits in a now-extinct ancestral population, they could make hypotheses based on the commonalities of the modern descendants. If the two modern rabbit species had black coats and long floppy ears but had different colored tails, and if one tail was long and one short, the investigators could hypothesize that the ancestral rabbits were black, had long floppy ears, and had tails; the differences between the modern groups would prevent hypothesizing about tail variables. Note that none of these traits would have left fossil remains.

This chapter traces the major evolutionary steps from first life up to primates. The steps will be linear, in the sense that they form only the lineage eventually arriving at humans. Note that the tracing of evolutionary steps from the beginning of life to humans does not imply that humans are the pinnacle of evolution, somehow more evolved and "better" than any other species. Robert Foley (1987) reminds us that we are "just another unique" species, one of an estimated 1.8 million species that have ever existed on Earth. There are 1.8 million evolutionary stories to tell, but this book can trace the steps of only one. The steps will be macro in size—partly because the evidence needed to reconstruct a complete story from the beginning of life on Earth does not exist, but mainly because tracing evolution on a micro scale for even one life form's lineage would take every standing tree in the world to make the necessary paper. Four billion years is a very long time. In Gould's (1987b) words, it is "deep time."

# Macroevolution

Even though biological anthropology focuses on humans, a proper study of human evolution cannot begin with human beings. The word *human* is not a tight scientific term, and no two anthropologists are likely to agree on its definition in an evolutionary context or on the timing of the first evidence of humanness in the fossil record. Evolution-minded anthropologists would agree that humanness is based on a multitude of characteristics, so a chronological model would not show nonhumans on one side of a line and humans on the other. The taxonomically correct term for anatomically and behaviorally modern humans is *Homo sapiens*; anthropologists often use the terms **anatomically modern humans (AMH)** and **behaviorally modern humans (BMH)**. Because the species designation carries with it a suite of anatomical traits that identify the group, what is and what is not *Homo sapiens* should be easily identifiable in the fossil record; Chapter 7 will explore this topic. It is the evolution to *Homo sapiens*, not the study of *Homo sapiens*, that is the focus of this and the next two chapters.

But where does the evolution to modern humans begin? The most recent common ancestral group that would include the ancestors of *Homo sapiens* and its most recent sibling species has no generally agreed-upon name. Experts do not even agree whether only one sister group—chimpanzees/bonobos (*Pan*)—or two—chimpanzees/bonobos and gorillas (*Pan* and *Gorilla*)—share this last common ancestral group with humans (*Homo*).

**anatomically modern humans (AMH)**
Modern form of the human species that dates back 100 kyr or more.

**behaviorally modern humans (BMH)**
Although modern humans might have been anatomically modern and looked like modern humans before they acted like moderns being capable of the full complement of behavioral traits, this term refers to the whole complement of humanity and dates to perhaps 50 kyr ago.

For now, it is best to refer to this group as the **last common ancestor (LCA)**. For the ancestral group previous to the LCA—the group that includes the ancestors of *all* apes and humans, Eurasian and African—the established term is **hominoid**, or the Latinized Hominoidea, meaning "like hominids." The word **hominid** refers to the bipedal lineage that evolved from the LCA group and eventually became humans. But the hominoids evolved from the Anthropoidea, the ancestors of both modern monkeys and the hominoids. And this pattern continues back through time, with each ancestral group descending from still earlier ancestral groups. Where human evolution should start is arbitrary, so it is perhaps best to begin at the beginning. We can gain lessons about evolution in general by starting at the beginning instead of in the middle of the story.

The story begins with the origin of the universe, followed by the origin of the solar system, and then the origin of Earth. The appearance of first life on Earth was obviously a momentous happening because without it there would be nothing for subsequent happenings to be contingent upon. Early life eventually led to the origins of primates about 63 million years (myr) ago. The first 3.4 billion years (byr) of life's evolution hold a lot of lessons, even if our major interest is human evolution during the last few million years. Studying how life evolved allows you to practice thinking on a large scale, first in billions, then in millions of years, and practice using the principles of homology, contingency, common ancestry, and ancestral and derived traits. What happened to life in its first 3.4 byr versus what could have happened is fascinating as well.

Figure 4.2 is a macroevolutionary model. It is obviously anthropocentric, as is appropriate for paleoanthropology. Starting at the top and working downward, the model shows each common ancestor in the human lineage in very broad terms: "Where did this group come from? It evolved from group X." If we looked forward from the bottom of the model, from the earliest to the latest happenings, we would see the entire tree of life constantly branching, with the human lineage taking one and only one of innumerable possible paths.

Although macroevolution must be conceptualized on a very broad scale, most scientists believe it actually occurs through microevolution. Evolutionary scientists borrow an analogy from geology: Just as geologists anchor their study of past happenings on Earth on the principle of uniformitarianism, so too evolutionary biologists use the principles of evolution they observe today to infer biological happenings in the past. Scientists can actually observe only the microevolutionary level, so they must make inferences about macroevolution and back up their inferences by studying fossil materials. As we saw in Chapter 3, modern populations change over short periods of time through mutations, natural selection, gene flow, and genetic drift; so scientists assume that the same evolutionary mechanisms caused past populations to change as well. This principle of **bio-uniformitarianism** is basic to all evolutionary reconstructions and forms the basis for macroevolution (Grant and Grant 2002). In the 1950s, George Gaylord Simpson used the evolution of horses during the past 50 or so myr to exemplify macroevolution. Looking again at the same fossils Simpson studied, other investigators agree that speciation, diversification, adaptations, change rates, evolutionary trends, and extinctions show bio-uniformitarianism.

## Evolutionary Beginnings

Evidence for the origin of the universe is indirect and mathematical, as is evidence for the origin of the solar system and Earth. Astrophysicists put the origin of the universe between 15 and 11 byr ago, calling the event the Big Bang; they place the beginnings of the solar system at 4.7 byr ago and the origin of Earth at 4.6 byr ago. Scientists can't date the origin of Earth by dating its oldest rocks because those rocks have been drawn back into the interior. But assuming the entire solar system was formed at once, the oldest "outer space" rocks should approximate Earth's age. The oldest meteorite that has fallen to Earth dates to 4.6 byr ago, and Apollo astronauts brought back moon rocks dated to

**last common ancestor (LCA)**
The group that evolved into humans in one lineage and evolved into either chimpanzees and bonobos or chimpanzees, bonobos, and gorillas in the other lineage.

**hominoid**
Superfamily of anthropoids including apes and humans. Traits include no tail and a large brain to body ratio.

**hominid**
Humans and their bipedal ancestors since the time of divergence from the LCA of African apes and humans. The term *hominin* is preferred by some.

**bio-uniformitarianism**
Spin on the geological uniformitarian principle that the evolutionary mechanisms that cause modern species to change are the same as those that caused species to change in the past.

*Figure 4.2*

| Era | Epoch | Years Ago | Macrohappenings to Primates | Other Happenings |
|---|---|---|---|---|
| CENOZOIC | Eocene | | Humans | |
| CENOZOIC | Paleocene | 55M | Primates (63M) | Dinosaurs extinct (65M) |
| MESOZOIC | Cretaceous | 65M | Modern mammals (100M) | Horses, bats, whales (100M) |
| MESOZOIC | Jurassic | 145M | Early modern mammals (175M) Early mammals (190M) | Birds (190M) |
| MESOZOIC | Triassic | 210M | | |
| PALEOZOIC | Permian | 245M | Therapsids (MLR) (265M) | Permian extinction (250M) Dinosaurs (250M) |
| PALEOZOIC | Carboniferous | 290M | Reptiles (350M) Amphibians (365M) | |
| PALEOZOIC | Devonian | 360M | Lobe-finned fish (400M) | |
| PALEOZOIC | Silurian | 410M | Ray-finned fish (420M) | |
| PALEOZOIC | Ordovician | 440M | Jawed fish (440M) | |
| PALEOZOIC | Cambrian | 510M | First "fish" (505M) | Cambrian explosion (540–520M) |
| PROTEROZOIC | Precambrian | 570M | Ediacara (570M) | |
| PROTEROZOIC | Precambrian | | Plants/animals (1.3B) | |
| PROTEROZOIC | Precambrian | | Metacellular life (1.7B) | |
| PROTEROZOIC | Precambrian | | Eukaryotes (3B) | |
| PROTEROZOIC | Precambrian | | First life (3.8B) | |
| PROTEROZOIC | | 4.6B | | Origin of Earth (4.6B) |

**MACROEVOLUTIONARY MODEL: FROM FIRST LIFE TO PRIMATES.** Starting from the top, this chart shows macroevolutionary events going backward in time from primates to the dawn of life on Earth.

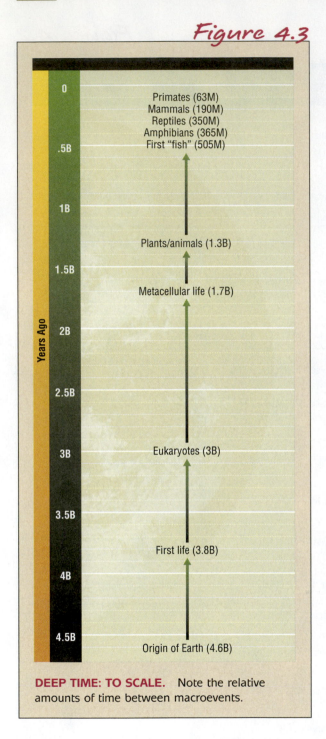

*Figure 4.3*

Primates (63M)
Mammals (190M)
Reptiles (350M)
Amphibians (365M)
First "fish" (505M)

Plants/animals (1.3B)

Metacellular life (1.7B)

Eukaryotes (3B)

First life (3.8B)

Origin of Earth (4.6B)

Years Ago

**DEEP TIME: TO SCALE.**   Note the relative amounts of time between macroevents.

**first life**

A hypothesized set of chemicals, genetics, and behaviors, but at minimum having a cell, living in water, and able to change.

4.53 byr ago (S. Jones 2000). To appreciate the huge amount of time envisioned here, picture a thousand of something—say a thousand beans. A thousand thousands equals one million beans in a pile. A thousand piles, each pile containing a million beans, equals a mountain of one billion beans. If each bean symbolizes a year, a little more than four and a half of those billion-bean mountains represent the hypothesized time for Earth's origin. This is deep time indeed. Figure 4.3 provides a visual representation of this large frame of time.

It is not known how or why **first life** occurred, though scientists and philosophers never run out of speculation on these issues. Scientists have been able to produce organic from inorganic compounds in laboratories for many years, showing that life can be formed out of nonlife—but, Dolly the cloned sheep notwithstanding, the ability to produce organic from inorganic compounds is not the same as producing life. Scientists cannot create even amino acids, much less entire organisms. Scientists can, however, make predictions, collect data, and test hypotheses concerning what the first living things were made of and what they were capable of doing. Because the first living things lacked hard parts and therefore were not likely to leave true fossils, scientists look for other kinds of evidence to identify what first life might have been like and when it existed.

One approach seems logical: to consider all of life today and predict what may have been necessary for first life. Biologists have concluded that all modern life forms have the capacity to evolve, a way to replicate/reproduce, grow, respond to environmental stimuli, and capture energy from the environment (Mayr 1997; Futuyma 2005). The extrapolation from modern life back to first life is complicated, however, by the fact that some scientists question the assumption that there was a single origin of life. In 1998 Carl Woese argued that there are three cell types that underlie modern life and they are so fundamentally different from each other that they must have evolved from different chemicals. This puts a damper on the "what first life needed" approach. Even if all of modern life did have one common origin, scientists sitting in their labs in the twenty-first century predicting what that first life would have needed know so little about the Earth's conditions at the time of that origin that they can only hypothesize about those necessities. However, most would agree that first life evolved on an Earth whose atmosphere contained methane gas, ammonia, carbon dioxide, and nitrogen, but no free oxygen. Laboratory experiments by Stanley Miller in 1953, using those components and water, heat, and fake lightning strikes, produced organic-like materials. Critics of these laboratory experiments have questioned whether Miller and his team could really know what the exact conditions of early Earth were, whether their spark was truly analogous to lightning, and how much of each assumed gas was part of early Earth conditions (Conway Morris 2003). However, scientists can only speculate about whether there was water, what the temperature was, and whether there were lightning strikes on Earth billions of years ago (Kardong 2005). Other scientists believe the physical conditions on Earth at that time were not far different from today and that the best place for first life to originate would have been in "sheltered, sunny lagoons around a strong volcanic island in high latitudes

Of all of the early evidence of bioactivity on Earth, these 3.5-byr-old stromatolites, or rocks of algae, from Australia are the surest evidence of early life. What does an early bit of life have to show in its "signature" to be acceptable to scientists?

where clays were forming in a freezing environment" (Cowen 2005, 9). Darwin suggested some warm pond filled with ammonia and salt! Scientists are still guessing. However, let's consider three scenarios about the emergence of first life, starting with one that is very likely, followed by one that is reasonable, and ending with one that is only theoretical.

First, William Schopf (1999) suggests that a kind of blue-green bacteria (called cyanobacteria), covered over by mud and silt that turned to stone, was preserved in stromatolites in western Australia, dating to 3.5 byr ago. Although these single-celled, non-nucleated organisms would have been simple relative to later organisms, they must have had precursors that were even simpler. The problem is that earlier evidence was likely obliterated by intense heat. Skeptics claim the stromatolites are not organic but artifacts of inorganic minerals and thus not life. Dated to the same time, 3.5 byr ago, are microscopic tubules found in rocks on sea floors off coastal South Africa that resemble tubules bored by modern microorganisms. Some scientists are skeptical about this.

A second scenario for life's origin takes us back to 3.85 byr ago and to western Greenland where geochemical evidence of early biotic activity in the form of carbonated inclusions in mineral grains has been found (Mojzis et al. 1996). Unfortunately, this kind of evidence is devoid of any information other than its presence, and even these "biosignatures" are controversial, with some skeptics suggesting that the layer in which the carbonated inclusions were found is volcanic and therefore nothing in it is organic in origin.

Finally, the third scenario is logical but purely hypothetical, based on the assumption of a common ancestor for all of modern life. The best estimate of the date of the last universal common ancestor of all life, affectionately called LUCA, is about 4 byr ago. This inferred LUCA would have had RNA and perhaps DNA, but not much else is known (Ridley 2000). Since LUCA was named in 1999, scientists have not had much luck reconstructing what it was like. It likely had the universal 60 genes common to all life today; however, since these 60 genes are probably not enough to sustain life, LUCA probably had other genes that did not survive to modern times (Whitfield 2004).

About the only certainty about earliest life is that it developed in water, but whether the water was salt or fresh, boiling hot or glacially cold, is controversial (Bada and Lazcano 2002). Also seemingly certain is the fact that the stromatolites from Australia and South Africa are the most concrete evidence of first life, and interestingly they continue as the most conspicuous fossils around for 300 myr (Cowen 2005). Although the details concerning what first life may have looked like or been capable of are purely speculative, all experts would agree that, at a minimum, it was a self-replicating molecule capable of change.

## Archaeae, Prokaryotes, Eukaryotes, and Ediacara

Carl Woese discovered what he called a "bizarre" class of microbes in 1998. This discovery led to a hypothesis of a three-domain life system: Archaeae, Eubacteria (including prokaryotes), and eukaryotes (Hamilton 2005). More recent research suggests bacteria evolved first, with eukaryotes and archaeae, which are more closely related to each other than either is to bacteria, evolving from bacteria at a later date (Pace 2006).

**Prokaryotes** (the name means "before nucleated life") replicated nonsexually (there were no males or females) by merely dividing in two. Blue-green bacteria and others that exist today trace their roots back to these nonnucleated, single-celled organisms. There are an estimated 60 different kinds of prokaryotes residing between your gums and any one of your teeth and more bacteria residing in your colon that there are humans on Earth (Klein and Takahata 2002).

The first **eukaryotes** (the name means "true nucleated life") evolved about 2.3 byr ago, some reproducing asexually and some sexually. Sexual reproduction by males and females allows for a lot more diversity than asexual reproduction, which is similar to cloning. On the molecular level, eukaryotes had complex mitochondrial DNA as well as nuclear DNA (Hamilton 2005). It has recently been proposed that billions of years ago, mitochondria were independent life forms but were then captured and incorporated by animal cells (Wade 2001). At least one scientist, Ernst Mayr (2001), suggests that the origin of the eukaryotes was the single most important event in the history of life because the sexual method of reproduction allowed three different kinds of life to evolve, each based on a different kind of "survival strategy": plants utilized photosynthesis (and there was apparently free oxygen by this time), fungi absorbed nutrients from the environment, and animals ingested energy by eating plants and each other (Eldredge 2004). Most eukaryotes are multicellular, though the earliest ones, the protists, were single-celled. Animals evolved from the multicellular eukaryotes, which had specialized organs, particularly sense organs, and a central nervous system and likely engaged in some kind of parental care (Southwood 2003).

Although early life was capable of changing (i.e., evolving), it took a billion years before even the simple single-celled organisms (prokaryotes) changed to more complex single-celled organisms with nuclei (eukaryotes).

Scientists now recognize five kingdoms of life: Fungi, protists (one-celled organisms), and bacteria originated early, and plants and animals later. Fossils of what are reported as the first animals were recently dated as 1.25 byr old—and the first reported plants have been dated at 1.3 byr ago (Svitil 1999). If the first plants and animals evolved at almost the same time, it strongly argues for two evolutionary lineages diverging from the same multicelled life—perhaps from fungi (Klein and Takahata 2002)—rather than one lineage evolving from the other. Because humans are animals, it is the evolution of the animal kingdom that will be the focus here, although plants will be mentioned when they are important to the evolution of animals. The traits and behaviors that distin-

**prokaryotes**
Literally, "before nucleated life"; non–sexually reproducing, single-celled, non–nucleated life forms, such as modern blue-green algae.

**eukaryotes**
Organisms that have a nucleus containing DNA in their cells.

guished the earliest animals from other kingdoms were food ingestion, the possession of nervous systems and sense organs, and the ability to move intentionally. Scientists have arrived at this characterization of the common ancestral group of all animals by comparing all modern animals, discovering what they have in common, and using homology to reconstruct that very ancient group.

Life on land is dated to 1.2 byr ago, as evidenced by fossils of bacteria or fungi found in Arizona (Horodyski and Knath 1994). Insects, the first land animals, do not appear until considerably later, giving plants a chance to be well established before insects invaded. The earliest plants were likely to have been leafless mosses, ferns, and horsetails, all of which still exist. These early plant types were as large as modern trees. Although there are no fossils of plants older than 400 myr, molecular dating puts plants on land by 700 myr ago (Southwood 2003).

Until recently only eight species of multicellular life were represented in the fossil record of the time between 1.7 byr ago and about 540 myr ago, a period of more than a billion years. This suggests there was a rather meager amount of evolutionary change in a fairly large amount of time. In the last few years, however, several exciting discoveries have given a far better look at this time period. Australia, Russia, Namibia, northern Europe, Newfoundland, and China have produced fossil material in the form of disc-shaped blobs of living matter, called the **Ediacara** (because they were originally found in the Ediacaran hills in southern Australia), to fill in the gap between 600 and 550 myr ago. They are the last probable common ancestor of modern multicellular life (Kerr 2000; Svitil 1999). For relatively early life, the Ediacara were surprisingly variable: Some resembled sponges with radial symmetry or with frondlike structure, some appeared to be large jellyfish, and others were similar to soft worms with bilateral symmetry and three layers of cells; all were flat and soft-bodied with no skeletal material, appendages, mouth, or internal organs (Futuyma 2005; Southwood 2003).

A controversial type of fossil, recently found in southwest China, has been called the transition to the Cambrian explosion (which we'll discuss next). These fossils have been characterized as tiny "oval blobs" and were found in 600-to-580-myr-old rocks. The life forms appeared to have bilateral symmetry as well as digestive tracts, mouths, pharynxes, guts, body cavities, three layers of body tissues (*endo*, *meso*, and *ecto*, or outside, middle, and inner), and "pits" in their outer surface that may have been sensory organs. Perhaps this discovery of a possible transitional animal is too good to be true; there are many skeptics (Stokstad 2004). On the other hand, some of the Ediacara show several of those features as well.

## The Cambrian Explosion

At the geological line separating the Precambrian from the Cambrian, geologists have identified a major event in the geological and evolutionary record. That major event resulted in what might be characterized as "life's body plans"; few of these forms had skeletons, so most of the fossils represent soft parts pressed in mud that hardened. There is no consensus as to why the event occurred; perhaps evolution speeded up because of unknown radiation, or perhaps evolution occurred normally but the evidence was obliterated by worldwide cataclysmic events.

Cambrian deposits occur in Wales (where they were first identified), Canada, the United States, China, Siberia, and Greenland, for a total of 40 deposits worldwide (Conway Morris 1998). The most recent formulation of a possible reason why the fauna of the Precambrian differed so much from the Cambrian points to the extinction of numerous animal species in two reef deposits dated at 542 myr ago, just as the Precambrian became the Cambrian. Noxious water may have been disgorged into the sea, causing those extinctions and triggering the Cambrian explosion at the same time (Kerr 2000). When numerous species become extinct, this usually opens up evolutionary niches. Regardless of the process, what is known as the **Cambrian explosion** lasted a mere 30 myr, from 550 to 520 myr ago (Conway Morris 2000; Kerr 2000). Thirty million years

**Ediacara**
Disc-shaped blobs of matter dated between 570 and 550 myr ago that are the probable common ancestor of modern multicellular life.

**Cambrian explosion**
The time (550 to 520 myr ago) when all animal phyla were then on Earth, living in watery environments. All subsequent life forms come from these early phyla.

may seem like a long period of time, but it represents less than 1 percent of the Earth's age (Ridley 2004).

The variable Ediacara, still living in water, continued into the Cambrian; some groups apparently became extinct, but some evolved into Cambrian life forms. Some scientists suggest that none of the Ediacara were ancestral to later life, becoming extinct at the end of the Precambrian (Brasier and Antcliffe 2004). Because the Ediacara had no mineralized hard parts and were at best "leathery," fossils are rare (Cowen 2005).

Stephen Jay Gould (1995, 2000) suggests that all animal evolution since the Cambrian explosion has been a series of variations on themes (animal phyla) that were already established by that time. Phyla are the highest category in a kingdom and are established on the basis of a grand *Bauplan* (body plan), a suite of traits that distinguish one large group of animals from another (Klein and Takahata 2002). Even the phylum to which humans belong—the vertebrates/chordates—makes an appearance at the beginning of the explosion. The Cambrian explosion was "announced" in the geological record with an abrupt appearance of skeletalized fossils. Animals with hard parts that left fossil remains may have evolved at that time because predators with powerful jaws and claws had evolved (Ridley 2006).

Not all of the Cambrian-era animals had skeletal hard parts; worms don't. However, this period marked the beginning of animals with hard parts, radically different kinds of animals. Luckily for paleontologists, a new kind of preservation began in this period, ranging from biomineralization to shell preservation to true skeletalization. Possibly sea water changed its chemistry or natural selection gave preference to animals that could protect themselves better from predators by having shells or skeletons (Mayr 2001).

The earliest Cambrian fossils are found in the **Chengjiang Formation** in China and are dated between 544 and 520 myr ago, with most around 525 myr ago. These fossils were first discovered in 1984, but only bits and pieces about them came out in the literature until 2004, when a full monograph was devoted to the entire faunal assemblage, all 13 phyla and 130 species. A major reason for the great variety at this site is that the area was at the edge of Gondwanaland, one of Earth's two major land masses, which had recently separated from Pangea at the time the fossils were living creatures. Originally the Chengjiang Formation was a shallow sea, and geological movements subsequently pushed it above sea level, where it dried out and then filled in with sediments. Since more of the earliest vertebrates/chordates, some measuring 6 cm (2½ inches) long, have been found here than anywhere else, the Chinese regard this formation as the "cradle of chordate evolution." Trilobites are the most common of the Cambrian animals found at Chengjiang, making up 60 percent of the collection and comprising literally hundreds of different species; their variable size, bilateral symmetry, external skeletons, and jointed legs like modern insects make them a revolutionary departure from earlier animals. Algae and bacteria represent about 30 percent of the collection, and starfish and sea urchins, molluscs, and double shelled bivalves that appear to be ancestral to modern octopus, mussels, and oysters, make up the remainder. The preservation is remarkably fine-grained. Scientists have identified muscle tissue, gills, intestines, and shells in the solidified mud.

It is the earliest vertebrates/chordates that interest anthropologists the most because they show the beginnings of backbones, which define the phylum Chordata of which humans are members. The earliest chordates found in the Chengjiang Formation in China are followed by those in the Burgess Shale.

The 5-cm (2-inch) specimens called *Pikaia* had no jaws or backbones and no true bony skeletons, but they showed vertebrate traits in their notochords (stiffening rods where modern vertebrates have backbones), dorsal fins, perhaps a mouth, and prerespiratory gills (Gould 2000; Xian-guang et al. 2004). They likely "swam" by undulating their flexible bodies from side to side just as modern fish do. They had what appear to be two tentacles (Conway Morris 1998).

Recently, Canadian excavators outside Kingston, Ontario, on what is now Lake Ontario, discovered in sandstone footprints of eight-legged (four pairs) animals dated between 500 and 480 myr ago. These were apparently small, segmented, shelled animals

**Chengjiang Formation**
Earliest Cambrian fossils found in China and dating between 544 and 520 myr ago.

Burgess Shale
The 525-myr-old deposits in the Canadian Rockies that contain all of the earliest phyla of animals including Chordates, the phyla to which humans belong.

(bugs) that perhaps were fleeing water-based predators or looking for dry places to reproduce. Nonetheless, they were able to come up on land for at least a certain amount of time (Broad 2002).

The first chordates discovered in the New World date to 525 myr ago and were found in the famous **Burgess Shale** in the Canadian Rockies. (See Highlight 4.1, on pp. 86–88, for a discussion of the Burgess Shale animals.) Because humans are vertebrates, it is this lineage of the evolutionary story that we will follow next; but it is humbling to note that all 35 phyla and all animals alive in the world today can trace their ancestry to the kinds of animal species that were on Earth more than half a billion years ago and that all evolution since then has been contingent on the kind of life that existed at that time.

## From "Fish" to Reptiles

It is in the fossil record of the Cambrian explosion that the first fishlike vertebrates appear, again in South China. The 3-cm (1¼-inch) fossils were jawless but had gills (Stokstad 2001). By about 505 myr ago, many of these "fish" are evident in the fossil record. (The use of "fish" with quote marks indicates that these early animals have some but not all of the specializations of modern fish, and particularly not the diagnostic traits.) These creatures show some specializations of fish: They were small in size (no more than 15 cm or 6 inches long), jawless, and rather motionless, merely sucking up food-laden water at the bottom of shallow seas, estuaries, and freshwater streams. They had true eyes, organs for smell, and skin. Their brains were divided into three parts: a hindbrain associated with hearing, balance, reflexive behavior, and control of autonomic functions such as breathing; a midbrain associated with vision; and a forebrain associated with the sense of smell (Relethford 2002). Thus, the chordate body plan with its ancestral traits began over half a billion years ago. All subsequent lineages and species, including humans, inherited this plan.

Fish with jaws appear in the fossil record about 440 myr ago. Some of these animals were as big as 6 to 9 meters (20 to 30 feet) long and were armored on their heads and fronts. Both types of fish, ray-finned and lobe-finned, had major roles to play in the evolution to humans. *Ray-finned fish* evolved directly out of bottom-feeding early fish; but because they had fins, they were more mobile and could move away from the ocean bottoms. Backbones were organs of locomotion as well as body structure, as backbone undulation displaced water and propelled the fish forward. *Lobe-finned fish* evolved from early ray-finned fish—and because the lobes were articulated by bone, muscle, and ligaments to the backbone, forming single locomotion units, they could be used as simple water-pushing appendages. Armed with air bladders (a kind of rudimentary lungs) and the ability to gulp oxygen outside of water, lobe-finned fish were able to spend at least small amounts of time on land (see Figure 4.4).

*Figure 4.4*

**LOBE-FINNED AND RAY-FINNED FISH.** Ray-finned fish (bottom) were in evidence by 440 myr ago; their modern descendants are the fish in contemporary rivers and oceans. Lobe-finned fish (top) evolved from ray-finned fish by 400 myr ago and had bones articulating between the lobes and the backbone, allowing the lobes be used in locomotion. Lobe-finned fish evolved to amphibians by 365 myr ago. What do amphibians have in common with modern humans?

# In the Field and the Museum with the Burgess Shale

STEVEN SPIELBERG SHOULD MAKE A MOVIE about the Burgess Shale. He could use stop-motion animation, with clay models of each Burgess animal reshaped manually for each movement. Yet the amazing features and astounding diversity of the animals found in the Burgess Shale would stagger even Spielberg's imagination. What makes this fauna so fascinating is that if the ancestry of every species of modern animal life could be traced back in time, all of the ancestors would meet in the Burgess Shale, as well as many additional animals that didn't survive to modern times.

As the story goes, back in 1909 Charles Walcott, a scientist (and later the director) at the Smithsonian Institution, was looking for trilobites in western Canada when one of the horses in his party stumbled on a rock. Walcott jumped from his horse and attempted to knock the rock off the trail with his hammer—and in the process he accidently split the rock open and discovered fossils of soft-bodied animals. Walcott wrote in his diary that he saw his first fossil in the shale on August 31. That was nearly the end of the 1909 expedition season, of course; but Walcott saw enough to become convinced of the find's importance, so he mounted full-scale expeditions from 1910 through 1913 and again in 1917; other museum and university groups, too, have subsequently carried out excavations. During the first several Walcott seasons, the workers split open tumbled rock and systematically excavated horizontal beds of shale. Picks, shovels, and even dynamite became tools of the trade.

The Burgess Shale was unique when it was discovered, because it gave up the first early Cambrian fossils found anywhere—fossils of soft-bodied creatures dating back to 525 myr ago, when life was pretty much confined to the ocean. Outcrops containing fossils like those in the Canadian shale have since been found at 40 sites, including locations in Utah, Greenland, Poland, and southern China. The reason why these same fossils are present in so many parts of the world is that 525 myr ago North America, Greenland, Europe, and Asia were all one large supercontinent located near the equator. Geologists have named that landmass Laurentia.

The Burgess Shale literally shows us what life was like in the Cambrian seas. Life on land was pretty stark at that time; the entire supercontinent looked like a desert, with a few scrubby plants but no land animals. What life there was existed in the seas that covered a large part of Earth.

Scientists have attempted to reconstruct the geological context for the Burgess fauna in order to determine why the animals' remains were so well preserved. The best reconstruction postulates an underwater cliff running along the edge of the continental shelf near the western edge of the landmass. At the base of this cliff (called Cathedra, meaning "chair," by geologists) were sediments that the Burgess animals lived in, lived on, and swam over. The animals that burrowed in the mud are called infauna. Others were epifauna on the top of the sediments; some were rooted to the sea floor, not moving much, and some (called strollers) walked or crawled across the mud on top of the sediments. Some animals, called nekton, could swim; some, called plankton, merely floated. Although there were no whales or fish in the Cambrian ocean, it was a busy place, nonetheless.

What caused these fauna to be preserved? Scientists speak of "the catastrophe" or "the event." The event may have been something as simple as a bad storm or a shift in sedimentary beds, or as cataclysmic as an earthquake. The initial event was probably violent enough to kill the animals, because some were deposited standing on their heads, as if there were no time to recover and realign themselves to their normal positions. Regardless of cause, scientists believe that a blanket of sediment and mud covered the entrapped animals, smothering them, and then moved them to a somewhat lower location. Here the mud settled, sediments solidified, animals were crushed, and eventually the mud became finely grained shale. There was little oxygen, so bacteria that cause decay did not survive, and animals' soft parts were well preserved. In time the entire area was uplifted to become part of the Rocky Mountains. Because 86 percent of the Burgess fauna are without fossilized skeletal parts, being soft-bodied animals that usually biodegrade, this collection gives scientists a far better picture of the actual Cambrian community than any other.

Based on a catalogue of 73,000 individuals on 30,000 slabs from British Columbia alone (of which the Smithsonian has 60,000), the Burgess fauna fall into several categories. Because scientists create a taxonomy of this kind not only to classify an existing population but also to trace evolutionary patterns, the cataloguers of the Burgess fossils based the classification on the similarities of particular groups to one another and to subsequent animal species up to modern times. The goal was to enable evolutionists to trace every lineage of animal back to 525 myr ago. On that basis, much of the Burgess fauna can be categorized as bacteria and algae, sponges, mollusks, worms, arthropods (including crabs, trilobites, scorpions, and spiders), sea lilies and sea cucumbers, and chordates. Arthropods are very common, representing almost 40 percent of the fauna, whereas there are only a few chordates. There are also a lot of animals that cannot be connected to modern animal groups because they did not evolve to modern status.

In total there appear to be about 170 species, 100 of them identified by Walcott. The species varied from very tiny algae to a 3-foot-long carnivorous animal called *Anomalocaris*. The most abundant animal (with 15,000 specimens represented) is called *Marrella*; though it was quite small (2.5 to 19 mm, or 1 to 7.5 inches), its head had two pairs of curved spines, one going back over the full length of its back, and two pairs of antennae, one with short segments down the length and the other ending in brushes (to sweep food into its mouth?), and it walked on 10 long, segmented paired limbs. *Marrella* is thought to be an arthropod that could have evolved to crabs, spiders, or trilobites. Equally bizarre (although we all have our favorites) is *Hallucigenia*. This animal was originally thought to be a worm. Then it became unclassified—hence its name—and then reclassified as a worm again. *Hallucigenia* fossils range from 0.5 to 3 cm long (0.25 to 1.25 inches), have long tubular bodies, and sport various paired appendages on both the sides/top and sides/bottom. When it was first reconstructed, *Hallucigenia* was pictured as walking on the stiff and pointed appendages with tentacles waving in the water; it has more recently been reconstructed as walking on flexible legs with spines extending from its upper surface for protection. Either way, it is a strange creature with no known lineage to follow. Unlike *Marrella* or *Hallucigenia*, a few of

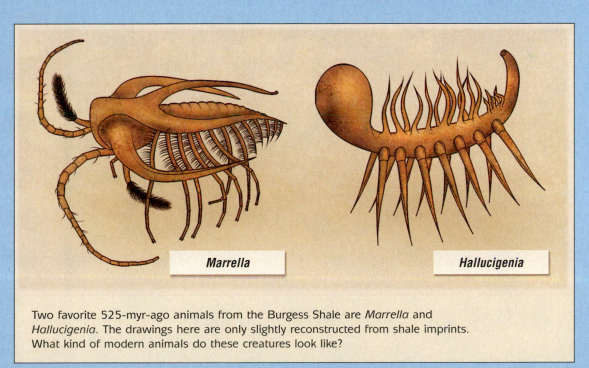

| Marrella | Hallucigenia |

Two favorite 525-myr-ago animals from the Burgess Shale are *Marrella* and *Hallucigenia*. The drawings here are only slightly reconstructed from shale imprints. What kind of modern animals do these creatures look like?

*(continues on the next page)* ▶

the animals actually look familiar, such as shelled animals.

In reconstructing the Burgess fauna, scientists work from a double imprint: Both the top and the bottom of the encased animal left imprints. Theoretically, when the shale is split into part and counterpart, the top and bottom surfaces of the animal are established. In reality, the animals were so squashed that the fossils originally yielded little three-dimensionality. But workers using high-precision drills or acids have managed to separate many layers in the squashed middles and have removed parts, sometimes uncovering other parts. Scientists often can reconstruct a flat and squashed imprint as a three-dimensional animal with confidence of being reasonably correct.

Work continues on the Burgess Shale in Canada, England, and the United States. Recently, a single specimen, which had originally been collected by Charles Walcott and whose relationship to modern animals had been a mystery for almost a century, was given an ancestral status. It is now believed to be related to early mollusks. Even after its reconstruction, it looks like "road kill," with a 4-cm-long parallel-sided body that is only 0.25 cm thick. Its two ends are blunt, and a unique feature is a strangely distinctive figure eight at the blunter end.

In order to appreciate the Burgess fauna, we need to fit them into a proper chronological context. Just previous to the Cambrian, some 570 to 550 myr ago, there was a group of animals called the Ediacara, mostly disc-shaped blobs of living matter. Given their nature, it is the Ediacara that hold the status of being the last probable common ancestor of all modern multicellular life. The Ediacara fauna fall into four categories, three of which are well known in Burgess fauna: jellyfish, worms, frondlike organisms, and a fourth group whose nature is unclear. The early Cambrian saw worms, mollusks, and shelled snails; then trilobites, early arthropods, and sponges. The Cambrian explosion produced many new kinds of animals. The rest is Burgess Shale history.

*Sources:* Briggs, D. 1994. *The fossils of the Burgess Shale*. Washington, DC: Smithsonian Institution. Conway Morris, S. 1993. Burgess Shale. In *Paleobiology: A synthesis*, eds. D. E. Briggs and P. Crowther. Oxford: Blackwell Scientific. Conway Morris, S. 1998. *The crucible of creation: The Burgess Shale and the rise of animals*. New York: Oxford University Press. Gould, S. J. 1989. *Wonderful life: The Burgess Shale and the nature of history*. New York: Norton. Kerr, R. A. 2000. Stretching the reign of early animals. *Science* 288:789. Xian-guang, H., et al. 2004. *The Cambrian fossils of Chengjiang, China: The flowering of early animal life*. Malden, MA: Blackwell Publishing. (See also this page on the website of the University of Calgary: http://www.geo.ucalgary.ca/~macrae/Burgess_Shale)

turn back to your reading

Lobe-finned fish were the first **tetrapods**. Taxonomically, a tetrapod is any four-limbed animal with digits on the end of the limbs, so the group includes all amphibians, reptiles, and mammals as well as the lobe-finned fish. (Tetrapods also have two eyes and one backbone, though they are variable in most other traits, such as size and lifespan.) But in an evolutionary sense, because lobe-finned fish are water animals, four-limbedness evolved before animals came out on land. The pectoral fins of lobe-finned fish, just under the skull area, have bones that are ancestral to humeri (upper arm bones); the pelvic fins near the tail have bones that are ancestral to femurs (thighbones). Each of these limbs ends in a "small radial fan" that can contain from five to eight digits, depending on the specific lobe-finned fish (Gee 2000). Four-limbedness apparently evolved before animals came out on land, and experts have questioned the function of extra limbs in water; perhaps they just made very good paddles and allowed their owners to escape prey, and survive longer than their nonlimbed cohorts, resulting in greater reproductive success. One thing is assured by evolutionary principles: Lobe-finned fish did not evolve four limbs to be efficient *later* on land.

Interestingly, the coelacanth, a modern lobe-finned fish that appears to be very similar to early lobe-finned fish and is occasionally caught in coastal African waters, has fin movement that is similar to the movement of most modern four-limbed creatures—the front fin on one side moves at the same time as the back fin on the other side, rather than in the way a rabbit locomotes, with its two front legs hopping at the same time (Southwood 2003). Humans "walk" this way as well, with each arm swinging forward as the opposite foot moves forward.

An intermediate fossil that spans fish and tetrapods was found recently in the most northeasterly part of Canada (near Greenland) on Ellesmere Island. This 9-foot-long transitional "fishapod" shows traits of both classes of animal. Its ancestral fish traits include scales and gills, and its derived traits include a trunk that allowed it to lift its head up and to flop its body out of water, showing that it could use land, perhaps to escape predators or get new food resources.

*Amphibians* evolved out of lobe-finned fish stock and were in evidence by 365 myr ago (Daeschler et al. 1994). Another "intermediate," a 2-foot-long fish/amphibian fossil, has recently been found in an ancient streambed in north central Pennsylvania and dated as 370 myr old, just 5 myr younger than the "fishapod." Its upper arm bone (humerus) suggests that at least some lobe-finned fish were not using those fins as paddles, but rather the fins were muscular enough to allow the creature to push its body up and lift its head above water, perhaps to breathe free air (Selim 2004). A recently discovered specimen in Scotland was 3 feet in length and although it showed paddlelike fins with digits, it was probably not walking (Carroll 2002). Fossils of other early amphibians have been found as far apart as Russia, Greenland, and the United States (Cowen 2005). The first true amphibians with four legs and feet were probably living in lagoons and hauling themselves up out of the water to gulp air and then going back down again. They probably ate fish in the water and insects on the shores (Southwood 2003). Some early amphibians were surprisingly large and looked more like modern crocodiles than any other modern animals.

Amphibians differ from fish in their ability to spend longer amounts of time out of water, returning to wet areas only to lay eggs. Another major change from lobe-finned fish to amphibians related to locomotion: Long bones with attached "radial fans" evolved to true "hinged" legs. The front (thoracic) fins of the lobe-finned fish evolved to become front legs with elbows flexing backward in amphibians; the back (pelvic) fins evolved into forward flexing knees. Joints at wrists and ankles made legs more efficient on land; eventually digits (fingers and toes) evolved at the ends of each limb. Additionally, amphibians evolved tougher, more leathery skin that became thick scales in reptiles (Cowen 2005). Amphibians were the first land-based animals of any size, and because early insects had evolved 75 myr earlier (440 myr ago), amphibians had good food resources on land (Browne 1995). Early plants that resemble modern mosses and horsetails formed miniature forests around fresh water estuaries and rivers, giving early

**tetrapod**
Technical name for the first lobe-finned fish, meaning four limbs with digits at their ends.

insects a land home. Insects (spiders, scorpions, mites) themselves became food resources for earliest amphibians (Attenborough 1981).

One branch of early amphibians evolved to modern amphibians, such as frogs, toads, and salamanders, and the other branch evolved into early *reptiles* by 350 myr ago.

# Reptiles: Evolution's First Amniotes

Reptiles differ from amphibians in several ways: They lay shelled eggs, so they are not tied to water at reproduction times, and their locomotion is more efficient. For most of their early evolution, reptiles slithered, dragging their bellies on the ground at slow speed. As Figure 4.5 suggests, later reptiles evolved legs that still emerged from the sides of their bodies but allowed the animals to lift their bellies off the ground—at least to some extent (Wilford 1994). The result was animals that could run faster, find more food, and escape from more predators.

Both amphibians and reptiles were and are cold-blooded, which simply means they have no internal temperature control but instead take on the temperature of their surroundings. Small amphibians and reptiles sit in the sun to warm up and sit in the shade to cool down, and large species simply take longer to change; the large species do not change their behavior to adjust body temperature as much as the small species do (Cowen 2005).

The first fossils of true reptiles were found in Scotland as was one of the earliest amphibians. You should not conclude from this fact that amphibians and reptiles were living and evolving in cold climates. What is now Scotland was actually located at the equator in the middle of Pangea, the single super continent on Earth at that time, and was therefore much warmer than now. Continental drift has moved Scotland further north during the past 350 myr. The anatomy of the first true reptile was so generalized that it could be ancestral to all later reptiles. It was relatively small and could have lived along river banks or under leaf litter on a forest floor; in either place, there would have been lots of insects for food resources.

*Figure 4.5*

**AMPHIBIAN AND REPTILIAN LOCOMOTION.**   The slithering locomotion of the amphibian (left) depends on legs that emerge from the sides of its body. The reptile (right) shows legs that still emerge from the sides of its body but allow the animal to lift its body off the ground. What would be the advantages of lifting over dragging?

Although reptiles lay fewer eggs than amphibians, they take care of their eggs and their offspring far better, so proportionally as many survive to become adults. Laying eggs on land has further ramifications. Fertilizing eggs out of water means the fertilization process is internal; that is, eggs are not laid by the female and then covered by sperm by a male. Eggs must also be large because they must hold enough food for the developing embryo to see it through the gestation period until it hatches.

One major macroevolutionary happening was the evolution of the **amniotes**. Reptiles were the first amniotes, the first vertebrates to evolve an internal membrane to enclose their embryos inside the eggs. This membrane first appeared in reptile eggs, continued in bird eggs, and changed to internal gestation in most mammals (Cowen 2005).

A larger midbrain and hindbrain suggest that reptiles depended more on vision and hearing for survival than their amphibian ancestors (Relethford 2002). Reptiles were so successful that they not only dominated the world in the form of dinosaurs but radiated in many directions, speciating into flying reptiles (pterodactyls), sea reptiles, and of course many land reptiles, large and small. And if success is measured by future evolutionary events, then reptiles were very successful, in view of the fact that they gave rise to both birds and mammals.

Another major happening in life's evolution acted as a kind of filter. About 250 myr ago, the **Permian extinction,** a global event, wiped out 95 percent of all animal species. Of the estimated 10 million species in existence at that time, only about 0.5 million survived (Eldredge 2004). The event may have been caused by a comet or asteroid that hit the Earth, causing ash and dust to become airborne into the atmosphere, blocking sunlight and preventing plants from photosynthesizing. Or the extinction might have resulted from a huge upswelling of carbonated water from the depths of the oceans, which could have produced a green-house effect and raised global temperatures. The latest hypothesis is that massive worldwide volcanic eruptions devastated most of life. The early mammals, perhaps because of their small size, high metabolic rates, and/or warm-bloodedness, were among those that made it though the Permian filter and survived, eventually taking over a large number of recently evacuated econiches (Browne 1996; Knoll et al. 1996; Stokstad 2001).

Dinosaurs were the dominant land animal from 230 to 65 myr ago; their ancestors, too, made it through the Permian filter. (Since the last dinosaurs became extinct before the first primates evolved, contrary to science fiction books and movies, humans and dinosaurs never lived at the same time.) During the 150 myr of dinosaurs' existence, there may have been over 1,000 species of them. In terms of thermal regulation, it may be best to think of large dinosaurs as neither cold-blooded nor warm-blooded, as any warmth they absorbed early in the day would probably have lasted them all day.

One recent hypothesis concerning the demise of the dinosaurs about 65 myr ago points to the possibility of an asteroid or comet's hitting the Earth, with subsequent cessation of photosynthesis. (There were 185 myr between the two possible asteroid/comet events, dated at 250 and 65 myr ago.) Large dinosaurs needed large food resources; the herbivorous dinosaurs might have died from lack of plant food and the carnivorous dinosaurs from lack of herbivores to eat. In contrast, even though not all dinosaurs were huge, all early mammals were quite small. It may be small size that proved to be fortuitous. The small mammals, with good eyesight and the ability to eat many different kinds of food, survived. Other explanations for the extinction of the dinosaurs often tie it to a slower global environmental change, from moist and warm to colder and drier. In another explanation, bioanthropologist Owen Lovejoy suggests that dinosaur extinction and the radiation of mammals were connected to mammals' evolving a better "reproductive strategy": smaller numbers of offspring but far better parental care. The outcome would have been more offspring in subsequent generations to outcompete the dinosaurs for space and similar resources, perhaps even eating their eggs (Johanson and Edey 1981). For whatever reason, the entire world changed its ecological balance, the dinosaurs lost out, and the less specialized mammals became their global successors,

**amniotes**
Vertebrates with internal membranes that enclose embryos inside of eggs; reptiles were the first to evolve this kind of egg.

**Permian extinction**
A global event probably caused by a comet or asteroid hitting the Earth that caused arboreal ash and dust and halted photosynthesis. Ninety-five percent of land species may have become extinct.

**placental mammals**
A member of the infraclass Eutheria that includes placentals.

**homeotherms**
Organisms that can maintain constant body temperature through physiological means.

**homodont**
Having teeth that are all the same in function, though they may differ in size.

**heterodont**
Having teeth that differ in type and function.

spreading out geographically and evolving into many different types. Birds as well as mammals evolved from reptiles, probably from feathered arboreal reptiles. Paleontologists now believe those ancestral reptiles had already evolved feathers while they were reptiles (Gee 2000). Birds, now counted at about 9,000 species, also survived the Permian filter perhaps again because of their small size. (See Highlight 4.2 for a global explanation for mass extinction.)

## Mammals in Evolution

Modern *mammals* differ from modern reptiles in many important ways. Some of those differences probably occurred early in the two classes' divergence, but it is hard to be certain, for traits such as newly evolved reproductive systems, the ability to breathe and locomote at the same time, and internal temperature control would not fossilize. Other mammal traits are unlikely to leave fossil remains: mammary glands for milk production, four-chambered hearts, genetically based behavior, and hair. Interestingly, some experts believe hair or fur did not evolve "from scratch," but rather from scales. Like hair, reptilian scales are produced by the interaction of the upper (epidermal) and under (dermal) layers of the skin.

Reproductively, early mammals inherited egg laying from their reptilian ancestors; the spiny anteater and the platypus still show that ancestral trait. The other two mammalian reproductive systems probably evolved later: Pouched marsupials evolved to modern kangaroos and opossum, and the **placental mammals** evolved into a much larger group of modern mammals, including humans. Placental mammals carry offspring internally and give birth to live offspring that are not capable of doing very much for some time.

Probably from the earliest days of mammalian evolution, mammals were **homeotherms** or warm-blooded (*homeo* = same; *therm* = temperature). Warm-bloodedness involves the ability of blood vessels to contract and expand as temperature needs change. Mammals have evolved additional traits that help keep their bodies within a range of temperature tolerance, including layers of fat under the skin, fur or hair for insulation, behaviors like shivering and panting, and sweat glands for cooling. Reptiles can't slither, walk, or run at the same time as they breathe because their chest area is either against or close to the ground and their lungs can't function if they are locomoting. Mammals, however, probably because of their erect stance and the positioning of their legs under rather than out the sides of their bodies, had the ability to both breathe and locomote at the same time (Cowen 2005).

Luckily, there was a further difference between reptiles and evolving mammals that did leave evidence: their teeth. Modern as well as ancestral reptiles have **homodont** teeth (*homo* = same; *dont* = teeth), meaning that all of their teeth are relatively similar in size, shape, and function and are replaced throughout the individual's life (see Figure 4.6). Reptile teeth are pointed and sharp-sided and are excellent for grasping prey before swallowing it whole. Modern and ancestral mammals, by contrast, have **heterodont** teeth (*hetero* = different): several kinds of teeth that differ in size, shape, and function and are lifelong once the permanent teeth are formed. Mammals have incisors, canines, premolars, and molars, each with a different dietary function ranging from slicing and cutting to grinding. Because teeth survive in the fossil record far better than any other skeletal material, mammalian evolution can be traced back to before 265 myr ago.

*Figure 4.6*

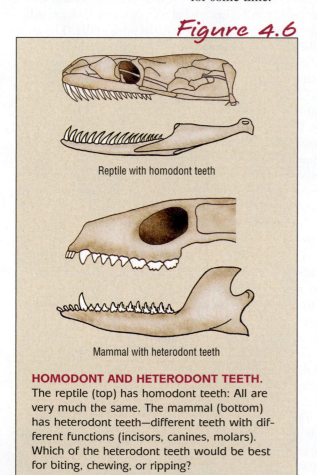

Reptile with homodont teeth

Mammal with heterodont teeth

**HOMODONT AND HETERODONT TEETH.**
The reptile (top) has homodont teeth: All are very much the same. The mammal (bottom) has heterodont teeth—different teeth with different functions (incisors, canines, molars). Which of the heterodont teeth would be best for biting, chewing, or ripping?

**therapsids**
An early group of mammal-like reptiles, ancestors of later mammals.

The mammalian brain also evolved over time. Modern mammals have enlarged forebrains that process sensory information and coordination and enable mammals to learn more about their environment, have better memories, and solve problems more efficiently than reptiles (Relethford 2002). Yet, in addition, built into mammals' brains are structures inherited from fish, amphibians, and reptiles, in turn.

Before true mammals evolved, perhaps 190 myr ago, a category of mammal-like reptiles, or **therapsids**, showed transitional status between the two classes. Early therapsids, dated to about 265 myr ago, were probably carnivorous and ranged from rat size to hippopotamus size. They had more reptilelike than mammal-like traits, but they had mammal-like heterodont teeth and may have been warm-blooded and covered with hair. Their limbs were not completely under their bodies, but there was sufficient room between their chests and the ground to allow them to evolve diaphragms and be able to eat, breathe, and locomote at the same time (Cowen 2005). By 190 myr ago, mammals had evolved true mammalian traits. These earliest true mammals, better called *shrewlike* mammals, were mouse size, probably nocturnal, and likely warm-blooded and probably had good senses of hearing and smell (Southwood 2003). Their legs were almost completely under their bodies. Further evolution and diversification produced *modern mammals* by 175 myr ago (Stokstad 2002). During this time, limbs evolved from their previous out-the-side projection to a position completely underneath the body, making mammals quite speedy as either predators or prey. (See Figure 4.7.) These earliest modern mammals were probably nocturnal and probably carnivorous, and they had well-developed senses of both smell and hearing. There are no indications that early modern

*Figure 4.7*

**MAMMALIAN LOCOMOTION.**    The mammal pictured here, a horse, differs from reptiles in locomotion because of the position of its legs, which emerge underneath its body rather than out its sides. What advantages might there be to this new form of locomotion?

# Highlight 4.2

# The End of an Era: The K/T Mass Extinction

THE ANSWER TO THE QUESTION of what generates biological change is ongoing. Is change ever, sometimes, or always generated by either external or internal causes? There is no consensus on this question, but hopefully there are open minds. When strong evidence appears to support one or the other type of generator, most scientists are happy to look in that direction. But when two possible generators for a single mega-change occur at the same time, the scenario becomes a mystery story. No one loves a good mystery story more than a scientist.

One mega-change that has two possible scenarios as to its cause is the K/T mass extinction. The mass extinction included the demise of dinosaurs, ammonites (shelled squid), sea mats, and fresh

water sharks to name a few; a total of 75 percent of Earth's animal species and 60 percent of the angiosperms became extinct in a geological moment of only a few thousand years. Geologists use this event to divide the Mesozoic era's last epoch—the Cretaceous—from the Cenozoic era's first epoch—the Tertiary—hence the Cretaceous/Tertiary boundary. Under the layer of rock referred to as the K/T boundary, which straddles the two eras, there are fossils of those dinosaurs and ammonites in large supply. Above that boundary, there are none, but there are fossils of lots of new kinds of animals, particularly mammals. When 75 percent of Earth's species became extinct, it created lots of empty econiches to be filled by the descendants of the survivors. The other four mass extinctions during Earth's existence as well as numerous smaller ones showed this pattern as well.

The change in the fossil record suggests something major likely happened at the boundary, but it did not affect all animals or plants nor was it random in its effects. The big animals, such as dinosaurs, seem to have been affected more, but some smaller ones, such as plankton, were also seriously affected. One thing is known for sure—the mass extinction was a global event as the same kind of boundary evidence exists all over the world.

And now for the million-dollar question: Why? Scientists are still generating many hypotheses to explain the change in the fossil record at the K/T boundary. A lot of these are on the crackpot side, but two hypotheses seem viable. Is one of the following the cause of the K/T mass extinction, or both, and if only one, which one?

Scenario 1: Since 1980, Walter and Luis Alvarez have hypothesized that a meteorite that was big enough to be called a small asteroid could have caused the K/T mass extinction. Their hypothesis was based not on finding the meteorite's impact zone, but rather on finding a rare metal called iridium in the K/T boundary layer in over 100 sites all over the world. This rare metal is common in meteorites. Twelve years after the Alvarezes made their hypothesis, a crater called Chicxulub was discovered in the northwest corner of the Yucatan Peninsula in Mexico. Melted rock underneath fill-in sediments in the crater was dated at exactly 65 myr ago, right in the middle of the K/T boundary. In addition to iridium in sites around the world, geologists could now point to shocked quartz crystals and tektites as evidence of a meteorite impact of huge

The K/T boundary between the Cretaceous and the Tertiary epochs is at the iridium band, which is the lighter layer at the top of the hammer's handle in this photo. This band is global evidence that a meteorite, which is typically rich in this metal, impacted Earth 65 myr ago.

Location of the Chicxulub crater in the Yucatan Peninsula (Mexico), where a meteorite impact about 65 myr ago may have caused 75 percent of the world's animal species to become extinct.

proportions. Evidence of a tsunami at the same time appears in Texas and up the east coast of the United States as if the meteorite impact sent one huge wave due north.

If this meteorite impact did occur, the effects would have been global. Due to a lack of sunlight, photosynthesis would have been shut down for weeks to years. Two major food sources depend on photosynthesis: plankton in the sea and leaves and grasses on land. The animals that depend on those bottom-of-the-food-chain items would have been hard put to find enough food to survive. Other possible effects might have included extensive wild fires and acid rain that was as strong as battery acid.

There is considerable evidence to support this hypothesis: The iridium, tektites, and shocked quartz crystals are not only evidence of a meteorite impact, but their distribution around the world with more of the bits of evidence closer to the impact site and fewer bits farther away—is consistent with the size (180 km, across) and location of Chicxulub. The species that would be most and least affected by a meteor impact were also as might be predicted, with the survivors being seeds and roots that could be dormant through the time of no sunshine, animals that could survive on the detritus caused by dead plants, and deep-dwelling, burrowing fish that could have survived by staying deep in the water.

For this scenario to be supported, both events—the meteorite impact and the mass extinction—would have to have occurred at the same time. A recent analysis of a new core taken from within the core, however, showed that the impact predates the K/T boundary and its extinction by 300 kyr. This strongly suggests that the impact alone could not have caused the mass extinction, but it may have been partly responsible.

Scenario 2: Continental drift has been pulling apart the African and Indian tectonic plates for millions of years, but about 65 myr ago, a huge volcano erupted between them, sending huge lava flows (like Kilauea in Hawaii) down its sides. This eruption could have also had global effects, with acid rain causing plants to die first and then the animals that required plants for food and then the animals that ate other animals. In addition, ozone depletion, a greenhouse effect, or a cooling effect could have followed.

Which scenario seems more likely to be the cause of the mass extinction? Scientists know meteorites have hit the Earth in the past, with major craters in Arizona and Canada. They have also observed volcanoes in action. The evidence for either scenario is mixed because the historical record does show both meteorite impacts and volcanic eruptions, but, though severe, none has been seen to cause even a single extinction. As Richard Cowen suggests, however, we may be seeing a "threshold effect; if the event is not big enough it will do nothing, but if it is big enough, it will do everything" (2005, 292). Although it is likely that one or the other, meteorite or volcano, could have been enough by itself to cause the mass extinction, the best bet is that both events were involved in the K/T mass extinction. Luckily, that 25 percent of species that made it through the disaster found lots of empty econiches and filled them quickly. Many of those niches were eventually filled with primates that evolved about 63 myr ago.

Sources: Cowen, R. 2005. History of life. 4th ed. Malden, MA: Blackwell. Keller, G., T. Addate, W. Stinnesbeck, et al. 2004. Chicxulub impact predicts the K/T boundary mass extinction. Proceedings of the National Academy of Sciences USA, March 14: 3753–3758. Schultzhuizen, M. 2000. Frogs, flies, and dandelions: Speciation—the evolution of new species. Oxford: Oxford University Press. Southwood, T. 2003. The story of life. Oxford: Oxford University Press.

turn back to your reading

**angiosperms**

Flower-bearing plants, the last plant category to evolve, about 75 myr ago.

**K/T mass extinction**

Extinction of 75 percent of Earth's animal species, including all dinosaurs, about 65 myr ago.

mammals were other than totally quadrupedal (four-footed) and terrestrial (ground-living), with all four legs the same length.

Early modern mammals already showed diversification into 19 taxonomic orders, most continuing into modern times, where there are an estimated 4,356 living species of mammals (Klein and Takahata 2002). Morphological evidence suggests placental and marsupial mammals diverged about 144 myr ago, and molecular evidence puts the split at 135 myr ago (Cifelli and Davis 2003; Goodman 1999). A fossil of what is purported to be the earliest placental mammal has recently been found in northeastern China and dated at 125 myr ago, a time when dinosaurs were still dominating the world. This is close to the estimated molecular dating of the split of placental and marsupial mammals, so perhaps it is at the "root" of placental mammals (Qiang et al. 2002). The small, shrew-sized mammal also shows some indications of being arboreal (tree-dwelling) with features that may indicate the first use of tree flowers, fruits, and nuts as food, since **angiosperms** are thought to have evolved by this time as well.

Rodents, bats, hoofed mammals, insectivores, carnivores, and primates were differentiated from each other about 100 myr ago; all survive today (Archibald 1996; Qiang 1999). At this point, scientists refer to the earliest differentiated forms as hooflike mammals, rodentlike mammals, and primatelike mammals, because each group is showing some specialization(s). There is no consensus, however, as to which mammal order evolved first or from what other group. Today, mammals range from elephants to bats to rats to whales to us. Mammals are carnivores, insectivores, and herbivores; they live in trees and on the ground, on rivers, in oceans; they walk, fly, and swim. Mammals are an extremely variable class of vertebrates, but the specifics of early mammal evolution are elusive as yet.

Modern mammals had evolved by about 100 myr ago; dinosaurs became extinct by 65 myr ago. The last epoch of the Mesozoic, when dinosaurs ruled the world, and the first epoch of the Cenozoic, when mammals took over, is called by geologists the K/T boundary (Cretaceous/Tertiary). Many animals changed from the Mesozoic to the Cenozoic but so did plants. After that geological boundary, all animals that survived the **K/T mass extinction** could take advantage of the full blossoming of the angiosperms, with their seeds, fruits, and flowers, all of which attracted insects (see Figure 4.8). Although flowering plants had their beginnings about 120 myr ago, it wasn't until after 65 myr ago that the burst of tree speciation was over.

# Macroevolutionary Lessons

Before we leave macroevolutionary events that occured from 3.5 byr ago to about 65 myr ago, or from the first life to the evolution of mammals, let's stop and consider what these events can tell us about evolution in general that is likely to apply to the rest of the evolutionary story, through primates and the more recent human lineage. In essence, these are "lessons to be learned."

One continuing theme of evolution is the change of habitat on Earth for animals and what this kind of change meant for evolving life: at first, only water was available, then land as soon as there was enough free oxygen; birds eventually evolved to "inhabit" the air; hence, sea, land, and air became occupied in that order. The number of species on Earth has increased from one (simplest life) to millions of species, regardless of five mass extinctions and many minor ones. Life has certainly become more complex over time, from single-celled organisms to chimpanzees and chickens. Complexity can be seen in major changes in locomotion, respiration, circulation, temperature control, and the five senses. Locomotion changed from movement constrained

*Figure 4.8*

Horsetail            Fern                        Gymnosperm                    Angiosperm

**MAJOR PLANT TYPES.**   The evolution of major plant types, always preceding major changes in animal types, is demonstrated by very early horsetail and fern, gymnosperm (plant with naked seeds), and angiosperm (plant with encased seeds, flowers, and fruits).

by an ocean habitat (undulation and using fins) to land locomotion from slithering to quadrupedal walking. Respiration changed from occurring directly through the walls of the body to occurring by gills, swim bladders, and lungs. Circulation changed from an open system, with blood flowing freely throughout the body, to a closed system that involves arteries and a heart as a big pump. Temperature control changed from very minimal (in "cold-blooded" creatures) to sophisticated use of sweating and hair and fur (in "warm-blooded" creatures). And the five senses changed; vision, hearing, touch, smell, and taste all became more complex (Langdon 2005).

A final theme concerns the causes of macroevolution and though scientists continue to argue over whether external causes (environmental change, asteroids, volcanoes) or intrinsic causes (mutations, natural selection, gene flow, genetic drift) are more common—and some scientists add chance to the mix as well—it is likely that a combination of all three causes underlies the "why did it happen" story of life.

All life has similarities at the molecular and chemical level. This is fortunate for the study of humans, given that scientists cannot ethically experiment with human subjects. Knowledge based on experiments with genetically simpler animals and drawn from the entire fossil record of the past 4 byr has allowed a myriad of scientists studying the lineages of particular animals to pull together a reasonably clear record of evolutionary events. This chapter focused on the specific lineage leading from first life to mammals. Chapter 5 will focus specifically on primates in evolution, setting the stage for the appearance of the first bipedal primates some 6 myr ago. Chapter 6 will pick up the account at the split of the last common ancestor with humans and will trace early hominid evolution.

- Reconstructions of evolutionary events are based on the principles of contingency (evolution depends on what was in place before), homology (most similarities between two contemporary populations are due to common ancestry), and analogy (some similarities occur because two contemporary populations evolve in similar environments). Bio-uniformitarianism is another principle scientists use in reconstructing evolutionary events.

- Ancestral traits are inherited from previous populations; derived traits evolve after a population has split into two populations.

- Tracing the evolution of humans back through time means beginning with the origins of the universe (15 to 11 byr ago), the solar system (4.7 byr ago), and Earth (4.6 byr ago).

- First life is currently dated to between 4.5 and 4 byr ago; it was simple and nonnucleated but could change.

- Prokaryotes (having cells without nuclei) preceded the first life forms having cells with nuclei, the Eukaryotes, which were muticellular and showed the beginnings of sense organs.

- The Ediacara, a group of early life forms arising 600 myr ago, continued the trend toward more complexity.

- The body plans of all modern animals, including the chordates/vertebrates, can trace their evolution back to the Cambrian explosion some 525 myr ago.

- Of the early fish to evolve, lobe-finned fish with appendages were one form. One branch evolved digits and became amphibians. One lineage of amphibians evolved to become reptiles.

page 90

- Reptiles have had a long existence on Earth. Early reptiles evolved into dinosaurs and eventually into two other lineages, birds and mammals.

- Early modern mammals were small but diversified into three reproductive types and 19 taxonomic orders.

- The steps in the macroevolutionary pathway to humans are: "fish" to amphibians to reptiles to mammals to earliest primates to humans.

page 93

## KEY WORDS

amniotes, 91
analogy, 75
anatomically modern humans
   (AMH), 77

ancestral traits, 76
angiosperms, 96
behaviorally modern humans
   (BMH), 77

bio-uniformitarianism, 78
Burgess Shale, 85
Cambrian explosion, 83
Chengjiang Formation, 84

common ancestral group, 75

common ancestry, 75

contingency, 75

derived traits, 76

Ediacara, 83

eukaryotes, 82

first life, 80

heterodont, 92

homeotherms, 92

hominid, 78

hominoid, 78

homodont, 92

homology, 75

K/T mass extinction, 96

last common ancestor (LCA), 78

Permian extinction, 91

placental mammals, 92

prokaryotes, 82

reconstruction, 75

tetrapods, 89

therapsids, 93

## SUGGESTED READING

Cowen, R. *History of Life*. 3rd ed. Malden, MA: Blackwell Science, 2000. This up-to-date encyclopedia of life on Earth is well illustrated and very readable. The index allows specific searches, or the work can be read in its entirety.

Gould, S. J. *Wonderful Life: The Burgess Shale and the Nature of History*. New York: Norton, 1989. This is the classic description of the Burgess Shale fossils (Cambrian explosion) in the Canadian Rockies. Photos and drawings expand the imagination back to more than 500 myr ago and explore the extraordinarily varied animal life at that time, which eventually gave rise to modern life.

Knoll, A. H. *Life on a Small Planet*. Princeton NJ: Princeton University Press, 2003. The author of this book has spent a good deal of his professional life searching out earliest life in "odd" places such as Siberia, Australia, and South Africa and offers a personalized account of those searches.

Southwood, T. *The Story of Life*. Oxford: Oxford University Press, 2003. This is an excellent composite of the evolution of life over the past 4 byr. It is well illustrated and fun to read.

Chapter **5** | # Primates in Evolution

■ **FROM MAMMALS TO PRIMATES**

■ **PRIMATE TAXONOMY**

■ **A BRIEF INTRODUCTION TO CONTEMPORARY PRIMATES**
Distribution and Ecology • Vital Statistics • Locomotion • Diet • Activity Patterns • Social Systems and Relations

■ **WHAT IS A PRIMATE, PAST AND PRESENT?**

■ **PRIMATE TRAITS**

■ **PRIMATE EVOLUTION**
Why Did Primates Evolve? • The Paleocene and Primatelike Mammals (65 to 55 myr ago) • Eocene Primates (55 to 35 myr ago) • Oligocene Anthropoids (35 to 24 myr ago) • Miocene Hominoids (24 to 6 myr ago)

■ **HIGHLIGHT 5.1:** *In the Fayum Depression*

■ **THE "MISSING LINK"**

■ **RECENT PRIMATE EVOLUTION: AFTER THE MAJOR SPLITS**

■ **THE LAST COMMON ANCESTOR (LCA)**

■ **POTENTIAL EARLY HOMINIDS: AN OVERVIEW OF THREE CANDIDATES**

■ **PRIMATE BEHAVIOR: RECONSTRUCTING ITS EVOLUTION BY STUDYING CONTEMPORARY PRIMATES**
Reconstructing Primate Behavior • The Evolution of Primate Behavior

■ **CHAPTER SUMMARY**

▲

**Photo above:** Black-and-white colobus monkeys in equatorial Africa are endangered because local people kill them for their beautiful pelts, which are worn as symbols of prestige.

When most people go to the zoo, they have two visits in mind: first to the big cats—the lions, leopards, and tigers—and second to "see the monkeys." Here "monkeys" means primates in general, including the prosimians, small apes, orangutans, chimpanzees, and gorillas as well as true monkeys. As we stand in front of their cages or look at them from outside their enclosures, we can't help but compare their outer appearance and behavior with our own. More so than the big cats or any other animal in or outside the zoo, the primates look a lot like us. And even more tantalizing, they behave a lot like us. Of course, this is for good reason—we humans are primates, too. All primates had a common ancestor some 63 myr ago but diverged into different lineages at that point, with many groups eventually becoming extinct and the successful ones evolving into modern times.

Before continuing the "story of evolution," it is necessary to introduce this order of mammals, the order that humans belong to, by discussing modern primates, their taxonomy and common names, their distribution and ecology, vital statistics, locomotion variability, diet, activity patterns, and social/political behavior. This background will allow you later in the chapter to more easily follow the evolution of lemurs, the split of Old and New World monkeys, and the divergence of gibbons from the rest of their early group. If you don't know what a lemur is, it is difficult to understand its evolution. By about 6 myr ago, all of the major splits in primate lineages had occurred, leaving the last common ancestral group of modern humans and their closest primate relatives. We will try to reconstruct that population that was neither ape nor human even though the fossil record is slim. The chapter ends with a description of the fossils that may represent human ancestry after the split with the last common ancestor.

## From Mammals to Primates

By 65 myr ago, the K/T mass extinction was over, and the survivors began to evolve into a multitude of new species. In the plant world, angiosperms dominated; in the animal world, mammals formed most of the new species. But of the three major types of plants, the angiosperms, with their flowers and encased seeds, filled in many of the empty econiches and the world changed: It became more colorful and had new scents. Angiosperms are particularly important to primate evolution because their seeds and flowers were food for early arboreal (tree-living) primates.

Mammals had differentiated into 19 orders before the beginning of the Cenozoic, and some generalized members of each order survived the K/T mass extinction, including pre-primates. Like the other orders of mammals, true primates emerged from a transitional group called **primatelike mammals**. Again, because humans are primates and not insectivores or whales, it is the evolution of the primate lineage that is the focus of this chapter.

## Primate Taxonomy

One way to introduce a discussion of the evolution of primates is via the taxonomy of modern primates. Taxonomy is a way to classify animals that appear to be closely related, so it can be used as a principle to model evolution of those animals as well.

Even taxonomists agree there is no such thing as a correct or perfect taxonomy for any order; rather, different taxonomies reflect honest differences of opinion on the importance of certain traits. In addition, some taxonomists emphasize morphology and some emphasize molecular comparisons; and some are "lumpers" (who see fewer differences among groups) whereas others are "splitters" (who see more differences among groups). (The taxonomy for humans, from kingdom to species, is given in Figure 5.1.) Because taxonomy is a tool for organizing thinking about modern plants and animals as

**primatelike mammals**
Early mammals that have some primate freatures but not enough to consider them "true primates."

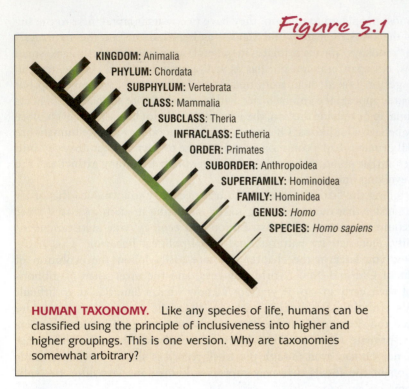

*Figure 5.1*

KINGDOM: Animalia
PHYLUM: Chordata
SUBPHYLUM: Vertebrata
CLASS: Mammalia
SUBCLASS: Theria
INFRACLASS: Eutheria
ORDER: Primates
SUBORDER: Anthropoidea
SUPERFAMILY: Hominoidea
FAMILY: Hominidea
GENUS: *Homo*
SPECIES: *Homo sapiens*

**HUMAN TAXONOMY.** Like any species of life, humans can be classified using the principle of inclusiveness into higher and higher groupings. This is one version. Why are taxonomies somewhat arbitrary?

well as for reconstructing evolutionary happenings rather than an end in itself, it does not matter that there is a lack of agreement. For example, some scientists see two suborders of primates; others see three, because they believe that one primate group does not fit the general picture of the other suborders but rather shows a unique set of traits. The traditional taxonomy of the order Primates sees two suborders, **prosimians**. (Prosimii) and **anthropoids** (Anthropoidea). But many experts have adopted a third suborder, because they believe that the **tarsiers** (Tarsioidea) show a unique set of traits not shared with the other two suborders: number of teeth, fusion of the tibia and fibula in the lower leg, the ability to jump many feet straight up as a result of having powerful limbs, and the ability to turn their heads almost 180 degrees (Napier and Napier 1985). Because of this unique set of features, we have adopted the three-suborder scheme. (See Figure 5.2 for a brief taxonomy of primates.) Among prosimians, the common names of major modern types are lemurs, indri, sifaka, and aye-ayes in Madagascar and lorises, pottos, and bush babies in Africa. There is but one family (with at least five species) of tarsiers, which lives on islands in Southeast Asia (Gursky 2007). For the suborder of anthropoids the major types are Old World and New World monkeys, Asian and African apes, and humans. It has been estimated by one expert that there are about 65 genera and 234 species of living primates as compared to 200 genera and 350 species of "known" extinct primates. Depending on how much splitting of modern species is done, there may be as many as 360 species of primates; also, a dozen or so new groups have been found in the last 20 years and given species designations (Groves 2004). To be consistent, we will use 250+ as the number of primate species, knowing that this is only an estimate. More than 5,000 primate species may have been around during the last 63 myr, but most did not leave descendants (Fleagle 2002).

New versions of primate taxonomy, some helpful and some not, have emerged recently based on comparative molecular studies rather than on new fossil finds. One new way to divide primates that is used by some scientists is to group those species that show a tooth comb (small pointed incisors in the lower jaw) and a complex of traits around their muzzle area, including a naked rhinarium (the patch of skin between the nose and upper lip) and a fold of skin that immobilizes the upper lip, into the suborder Strepsirhini. A second suborder, the Haplorhini, consists of those species that do not have a tooth comb, rhinarium, or immobilizing fold of skin (with the result that they have a mobile upper lip). This scheme places the tarsiers into the same suborder as monkeys, apes, and humans, whereas the traditional taxonomy puts them in the same suborder as lemurs and lorises, the prosimians. However, because tarsiers have several unique features and have shown these traits since they first appeared in the fossil record (Rose et al. 2006), we will consider them a separate suborder, for a total of three primate suborders.

A number of studies claim humans and chimpanzees are more closely related than either is to any other primate species, but different experts use different genotype comparisons and different results emerge. At this time claims for human "sharing" of DNA with chimpanzees vary from 91 to 99.4 percent (Wildman et al. 2003). The same experts who find close relations between humans and chimpanzees often suggest changing es-

**prosimians**
Members of the suborder Prosimii, which is likely ancestral to later primates and is characterized by small body size and frequently nocturnal adaptations, found today in Africa, Madagascar, and Southeast Asia.

**anthropoids**
Members of the suborder Anthropoidea, including monkeys, apes, and humans.

**tarsiers**
A major subdivision of the order Primates, considered a separate suborder by many experts, found today in Southeast Asia.

*Figure 5.2*

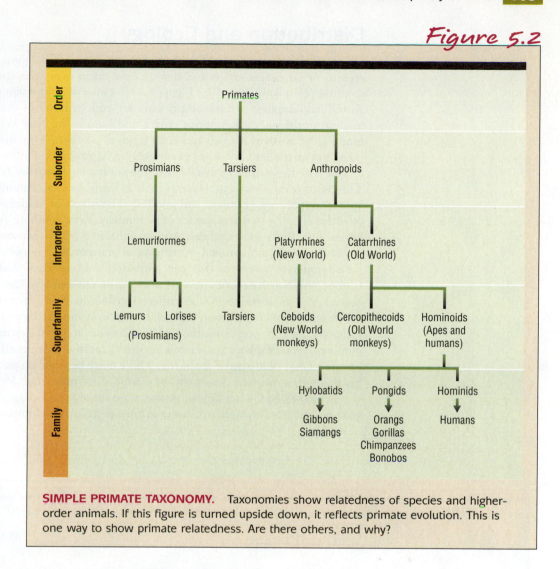

**SIMPLE PRIMATE TAXONOMY.** Taxonomies show relatedness of species and higher-order animals. If this figure is turned upside down, it reflects primate evolution. This is one way to show primate relatedness. Are there others, and why?

tablished taxonomy as well. Morris Goodman's team (Goodman et al. 2001) has recently proposed that chimpanzees, bonobos, and humans be combined into one taxonomic genus, *Homo*, with only species differences for the three groups. We do not find this lumping helpful in understanding human evolution; and, given the different molecular results leading to ambivalence over the relationships among gorillas, chimpanzees/ bonobos, and humans, it seems premature to change the traditional taxonomy. We will therefore continue to refer to *Pan troglodites* (chimpanzees), *Pan paniscus* (bonobos), and *Homo* (later humans) as different at the genus level.

# A Brief Introduction to Contemporary Primates

You are not likely to be familiar with all of the types of primates that exist today. We all know about chimpanzees and gorillas and monkeys, but fewer of us are familiar with the many species of prosimians, such as lemurs, lorises, and bush babies, much less aye-ayes. This section introduces modern primates using the three-suborder taxonomic scheme just introduced.

## Distribution and Ecology

In general, nonhuman primate distribution has decreased as human distribution has increased. That means, of course, that *we* have taken over *their* space—and the process continues on a daily basis. (See Figure 5.3 for a map of nonhuman primate distribution.) As the map implies, nonhuman primates are concentrated in the warmer areas of the modern world, in South America, Africa, and Asia. In the New World wild primates are found as far north as Mexico and as far south as northern Argentina. In Africa, with the exception of the Barbary "ape" (a monkey) in Morocco and a few small populations of monkeys in the southern Sahara desert, the nonhuman primates live south of the Sahara. The continental African inhabitants include many species of monkeys, prosimians, and apes (chimpanzees, bonobos, and gorillas). The island of Madagascar off the east coast of Africa is home to many species of prosimians. Even southern Arabia has a few monkey groups. India and Southeast Asia are inhabited by many monkey species as well as the smaller apes (gibbons and siamangs) and orangutans, and northern China and Japan have temperate monkeys that can withstand cold winters. Australia, New Guinea, Europe, and North America have no primates except humans. Contrasting modern nonhuman primate distribution with human distribution, which covers almost the complete globe, leads to the conclusion that nonhuman primates are basically warm-adapted animals. With some exceptions, the species distribution has not changed as much as sheer numbers have; monkeys are hunted for their beautiful pelts, gorillas for bushmeat, and lemurs so that Madagascar farmers can have more land for crops. Even so, Madagascar has the highest primate density in the world (Mittermier et al. 1999)

Ecologically, the nonhuman primates are variable and adaptable. Some live in jungles (marmosets, orangutans), some in forests (colobus, chimpanzees), some in semi-

*Figure 5.3*

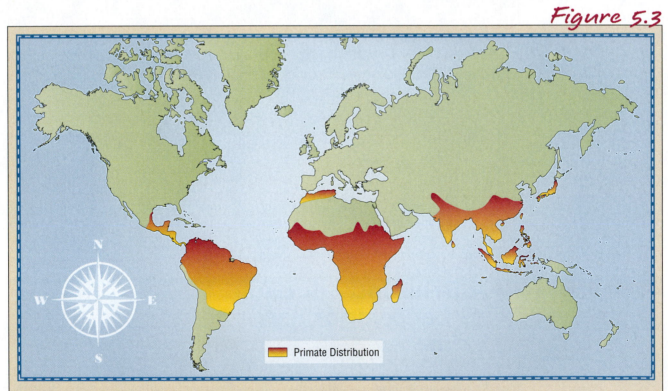

Primate Distribution

**MAP OF PRIMATE DISTRIBUTION.** This map shows the distribution of nonhuman primates as of mid-twentieth century. The overall distribution area of nonhuman primates is getting smaller.

scrub savannas (baboons), and some in true deserts (geladas). Some are at home around sacred temples, raiding gardens for food (langurs, rhesus macaques); some soak in hot springs (Japanese macaques). Finally, some live in zoos, where their environment is totally controlled. Some nonhuman primates do well in high altitudes, inhabiting parts of the Andes and Himalayas. The snub-nosed monkey in China lives in bamboo forests in areas up to 4,500 feet above sea level, where it snows and the temperature is below zero for several months of the year (Mittermier et al. 1999).

## Vital Statistics

Primates vary from huge to tiny, ranging from the 450-pound gorilla to the 25-gram mouse lemur that can fit into a human hand. These extremes are rare, however, and most primates are neither huge nor tiny. Some show considerable sexual dimorphism, such as gorillas (males are considerably larger than females), proboscis monkeys (males have huge pendulous noses and females have small turned-up noses), and some gibbons (males have pure black coats and females have pure blonde coats). In contrast, some species show equal-sized males and females, as do most lemurs. Some show little variability among members of the same age and sex group, whereas some differ considerably in individual traits.

Demographic reports are usually kept on animals in zoos, where dates of birth, death, first offspring, and likely paternity can be controlled. A general life pattern suggests an overall increase from prosimian to monkey to ape to human in gestation, parenting, age at first offspring, and life expectancy. For example, the average human life expectancy in Western nations is 78 years; that of capuchin monkeys is 50, chimpanzees 41, lemurs 40, gibbons 30, and macaques 25 (Fleagle 1988). Reproductive rates in primates vary from high (bush babies have four offspring yearly) to low (chimpanzees have five or six in their lifetime). There appears to be a relationship between number of offspring, body size, and relative brain size (Richard 1985). Most primates have only one offspring at a time, though tamarins and marmosets, and some prosimians, generally have twin births.

## Locomotion

Locomotion relates to diet, ecology, and size. All primates can do some combination of walking, running, bounding, climbing, clinging, leaping, brachiating (swinging from branch to branch in trees using the arms only), and hanging; but each species does one mode of locomotion well and habitually, several others fairly well, and the rest very poorly and far less often. For example, humans can do all of the noted locomotions but do not spend much time brachiating or leaping. Sifakas, on the other hand, leap and cling but do not walk on two legs for any length of time. Primatologists classify locomotion into seven general categories: (1) arboreal quadrupedalism (walking plantigrade with all four palms engaging the tree limb); (2) terrestrial quadrupedalism (walking plantigrade with all four palms on the ground); (3) leaping from tree trunk to tree trunk, then holding onto the tree trunk using strong hind legs; (4) hanging/suspensory under limbs and semibrachiating to change limbs; (5) brachiating; (6) terrestrial quadrupedalism with knuckle or fist walking (the term *knuckle walking* is actually not correct, as chimpanzees, bonobos, and gorillas walk with the middle portion of their fingers (phalanges) on the ground; orangutans are the only primates to walk quadrupedally with the outside of their wrists on the ground); and (7) terrestrial bipedalism. Arboreal quadrupeds such as colobus and capuchin monkeys have equal-length arms and legs and walk with their back legs flexed; they have grasping feet, long digits, and long tails for balance. Terrestrial quadrupeds such as baboons and macaques have similar-length arms and legs and short digits that plant them on flat ground. Their tails are usually short. Leapers such as indris and tarsiers have long and strong hind limbs. Suspensory primates such as orangutans and spider monkeys have short trunks and long arms and legs.

Brachiators such as gibbons and siamangs have long arms and short legs. And the only bipedal primates—humans—have long leg bones and relatively shorter arm bones.

## Diet

Each primate species' diet is related to the group's activity patterns, the physical size of individuals, the number of individuals that feed together, the availability of certain resources, and the group's adaptability. Given the variety of types of food available within any econiche (or in adjacent econiches), primates have a fairly large choice of plant foods: leaves, flowers, nectars, shoots, lichens, fungi, fruit, seeds, gums, and resins. Insects (termites, ants), invertebrates, and small vertebrates are also available. Some primates specialize in eating leaves (such as the African colobus monkey) and a few in insects (such as the tarsiers), but most are omnivorous to some extent. Except for a few prosimians and tarsiers, all primates are more plant than animal eaters. Perhaps the most distinctive diet is that of the aye-aye, a cat-sized prosimian on Madagascar. Aye-ayes are nocturnal and feed on "larvae puree." With their bat-shaped ears they listen to tree limbs for sounds of larval activity inside. When they hear the proper noises, they break open the limbs with their long, strong "toilet claws," mush up the larvae, and bring out the larvae puree for dinner! They have been seen to run from adult-sized bugs of the same larvae, however (Richard 1985).

## Activity Patterns

Activity patterns are related to diet. Most primates are **diurnal** (active during the day); only a few are **nocturnal** (active at night), among them owl monkeys, aye-ayes, bush babies, lorises, and tarsiers. Some are **cathemeral** (active at any time, day or night); among these are some Madagascar prosimians. Resting patterns vary from long siestas when it is warm to shorter but more frequent naps. Some primates seem to rest continually, but others appear always to be actively pursuing some bit of food or some female in estrus. This variability depends on how far primates have to travel for food and how scattered or focused it is; for example, seeds tend to be scattered and fruits tend to be concentrated.

## Social Systems and Relations

Primates are generally social animals. Why be social when it takes time and effort? Why not fend for yourself, feed yourself, and mate if the opportunity arises? Natural selection seems to be operating on primate sociality, and there are more reasons to be social than not (Fleagle 1988). First, social primates have more access to food, because as a group they can defend fruiting trees, locate and communicate about food, or flush out insects as they move through trees. Second, groups have better protection against predators: They can rely on the eyes and ears of all members, exchange warning calls, and gang up on a potential predator. Also, individual primates have more access to mates and mating if they are social. Finally, extra hands in social groups help with the care of offspring.

Most primates can't seem to get enough sociality, interacting constantly by grooming, mating, fighting, or just sitting side by side. The exceptions to primate sociality are scattered by continent and taxonomy but are somewhat related to activity patterns. In general, nocturnal primates are relatively unsocial; perhaps daylight helps animals identify and relate to conspecifics. But there are also diurnal exceptions, such as the orangutan in Southeast Asia. Orangutan females and their offspring feed in particular territories that usually overlap those of other similarly unsocial females. One male generally overlaps two to four females and "visits" each on occasion. Galagos and lorises, both nocturnal, have similar systems. Other primates are semisocial, in the sense that they stay close by one another; but they have so little interaction that their sociality appears to be loose at most.

**diurnal**
Active during the day.

**nocturnal**
Active at night.

**cathemeral**
Active both at night and during the day.

The size of primate social groups varies from 2 (in a monogamous gibbon system) to more than 200 (in some baboon troops). The type of unit has an effect on size: Monogamous units such as those of titis, De Brazzas, and gibbons by definition consist of one male and one female. One-male units, such as those in hamadryas baboons, and all-male units, as in langurs, are larger but never involve more than four to six adults. It is the multimale–multifemale units that are often quite large.

In general, female monkeys stay in their natal social units when they reach maturity; male monkeys tend to leave and join another unit as its one male, as a member of an all-male unit, or as a member of a multimale–multifemale unit. Adults in monogamous groups often force offspring of both sexes to leave at maturity. Apes are the opposite of monkeys: Among apes the females leave and the males stay in their natal units. In a few species (gorillas, red colobus, howlers), both sexes have been seen to move (Richard 1985). As long as one or both sexes leave, the population avoids inbreeding.

Who is in control in primate social systems? To some extent there is a correlation between social control and sexual dimorphism: Groups with equal-sized sexes usually are more egalitarian or even have females in charge. This is the situation with howlers, squirrel monkeys, and several Madagascar prosimians. In these species adult females dominate all males and younger female members of the group. In most of the other primate groups, however, males outrank females for access to food; and in some species, such as chimpanzees, males even attack and injure uncooperative females during breeding times.

Relations between adult individuals range from indifference to violence. Bonding between males is far more common than bonding between females. Relations between females and their offspring often last through the individuals' lifetime, even after offspring leave the natal group. Because the paternity of primate infants is not usually known, bonding between "fathers" and infants is rare. Male–female relations vary across the order; strong consortship relations last a week in some baboon groups, whereas other species show outright rape (orangutans) or other violence (chimpanzees). Among bonobos, females can gang up on a male.

# What Is a Primate, Past and Present?

**primate**
Any member of an order of mammals called Primates (which includes fossil and modern prosimians, tarsiers, monkeys, apes, and humans) that originally adapted to arboreal life, including the development of binocular vision and grasping hands.

**terrestrial**
Ground living.

**arboreal**
Tree living.

**generalized**
Adapted to a wide range of conditions or used in a general way.

**specialized**
Adapted to a narrow range of conditions or used in very specific ways.

Before we trace primate evolution, it is important to establish what a **primate** is and has been. Animals in the order Primates retained many generalized traits from their mammalian ancestors, whereas other orders lost those same traits over time, often evolving specialized traits in their place. For example, although primates retained the limb pattern of four appendages (two arms, two legs) and five digits on the end of each appendage, horses lost the five-digit trait and evolved a single hoof on each appendage. Horses do very well with hooves, because they have always been totally **terrestrial** (ground living); but primates retained the flexibility that goes with digited hands and feet, allowing them to be successful at both terrestrial and **arboreal** (tree living) life. Primates are therefore considered **generalized** as opposed to **specialized** animals. Animals can be generalized or specialized relative to each other or relative to particular traits. Humans, for example, are generalized relative to both horses and appendages.

As an order, primates theoretically can be diagnosed by a single trait. For a trait to be truly diagnostic, every member of the population must show the trait, but no other population can possess it. For example, the presence of large and pointed canines diagnoses the order Carnivora (carnivores), and hooves diagnose the two orders that include horses, deer, and bovines—because every carnivore has large and pointed canines and every horse, deer, and cow has hooves. The single diagnostic trait in hominids is the

**petrosal bulla**

A bone found in the middle ear that is usable as a diagnostic trait of primates.

**petrosal bulla**, a bone in the middle ear with no known function. All modern primates have this bone, and it has been found in fossils going back to the first true primates. No other mammalian order has this trait. At one time, tree shrews were regarded as primates, but once scientists discovered that they do not have this bone, their membership in the order was canceled (Klein 1999). Unfortunately, the petrosal bulla is a fragile bone that often does not survive in the fossil record. However, finding a petrosal bulla in modern primates as well as in fossil primates provides a link between the present and the past.

# Primate Traits

Many traits that are considered primate traits are found in most but not all primates, so none is usably diagnostic. It is a *set* of traits, some inherited from mammalian ancestors, but with the addition of the petrosal bulla, that identifies primates as an order and separates that order from all other mammalian orders. Many of these traits were in evidence at the beginning of the primate order and changed over time. Only by comparing all 250+ species of primates in existence today can bioanthropologists generate a list of morphological commonalities to use in tracing the evolution of the order. Such a comparative method is a standard approach in science, particularly when experimentation is not possible. A molecular comparison will eventually augment the list, but as of now only three primate genomes are completed, human, rhesus monkey, and chimpanzee. The gorilla's genome is to be sequenced next, leaving only 246+ species to go! For the present, a morphological comparison of primate traits must suffice. The following list presents 13 key primate traits and complexes of traits, based on the full morphological comparison. These traits form the basis for tracing primate evolution in the following section.

**1.** The position of the *foramen magnum* (the hole in the base of the skull through which the spinal cord passes) is not as high up on the back of the skull in primates as it is in, say, house cats. In the earliest primates the foramen magnum was located closer to the back than to the base of the skull; in certain lineages it later evolved to a position under the skull.

**2.** *Locomotion* is quite variable, ranging from the ancestral four-footed *(quadrupedal)* condition to two-footed *(bipedal)* locomotion to swinging from tree limb to tree limb *(brachiation)*, with many variations within those categories. Regardless of type, primates retain some degree of hind-limb domination, an ancestral trait (Martin 1990).

**3.** The *clavicle* (collarbone) allows arms to swing sideways and to remain out in front when arms cross over the body, and it supports the scapula (shoulder blade). Muscle attachment to these bones gives support for strong arms, whether the arms are used in locomotion or in lifting heavy objects.

**4.** *Vision* is vital to arboreal animals; most modern primates are arboreal, so early primates were probably arboreal as well. Most other mammalian orders are terrestrial and have only two-dimensional black-and-white vision. Primates move forward, backward, and sideways as well as up and down in trees. Overlapping binocular vision gives them three-dimensional depth perception that allows them to be aware of each branch and limb. Color vision, found in most primates, allows them to differentiate between food and nonfood and between predators and prey. **Postorbital bars**, which are bony extensions of both the frontal bone of the skull and the *zygomatic arch* (cheekbone), curve around the outside of the eye and support it from the side. In most primates a bone behind the eye, the *postorbital septum*, helps to anchor the eye socket (see Figure 5.4).

**postorbital bars**

A trait shown in the skulls of all fossil and modern primates and consisting of bony extensions of both the frontal bone and the zygomatic arch that curve around the outside of each eye and support it.

**5.** Primates inherited bilateral symmetry and an *appendage* package of four limbs with toes/fingers from their ancestors. Not only are primates able to flex their arms to a 90-

*Figure 5.4*

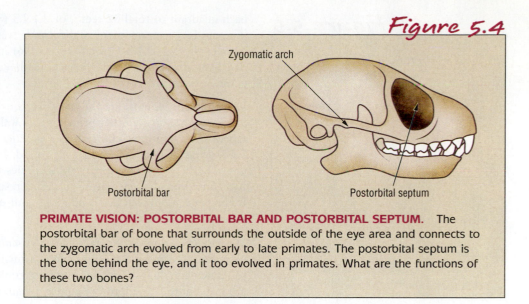

Zygomatic arch

Postorbital bar

Postorbital septum

**PRIMATE VISION: POSTORBITAL BAR AND POSTORBITAL SEPTUM.** The postorbital bar of bone that surrounds the outside of the eye area and connects to the zygomatic arch evolved from early to late primates. The postorbital septum is the bone behind the eye, and it too evolved in primates. What are the functions of these two bones?

degree angle at the wrist and to an even greater degree at the ankle, they can rotate their ulnas over their radii in their lower arms, making them extremely flexible. Too much flexibility may be a disadvantage in arboreal life, however, and the fact that the tibia and fibula in the lower legs do not rotate makes the back legs stable, helping to anchor primates on tree limbs.

6.  Most, though not all, primate species use their *hands* in locomotion; but all primates use their flexible hands to manipulate objects. All species have the power grip, although only humans have the true precision grip, in which fingers and thumbs work together to hold objects. Opposable thumbs are variable; all primates have mobile thumbs that can move toward the palm of the hand, but only humans have thumbs so opposable that they are able to touch each finger effortlessly. Primate *feet* are often as grasping as hands, and a grasping big toe is particularly important to arboreal life. Humans have lost the grasping big toe as well as all opposability of the big toe with other toes.

Together clavicles, eyes, arms and legs, and hands and feet constitute a very flexible package for successful arboreal life, from the shoulder down to the fingers and from the pelvis down to the grasping big toe. Equipped with such a package, an animal faces little risk of a fatal fall from high tree limbs.

7.  Whereas a good sense of *smell* is imperative for terrestrial life, in trees the sense of smell is less important than good vision. In trees predators and food can be on the same branch as the primate; it is usually faster to see than to smell an enemy. In addition, on the ground smells bounce off the ground toward the nose, but in trees smells dissipate very quickly. Accordingly, in most primate lineages both the snout and the areas of the brain that process olfactory information have become smaller.

8.  Primates have kept a generalized pattern of *dentition*, though the number of teeth has decreased from 44 in mammalian ancestors to fewer in modern species. Primates do not have flat molars like grazing horses or huge canines like lions; they do not have pointed molar cusps like insectivores or flat cusps like animals that crush and grind nuts. Instead, primates retained generalized incisors, canines, premolars, and molars. The **dental formula (DF)** indicates how many of each type of tooth there is in a mouth quadrant. Humans have two incisors, one canine, two premolars, and three molars in

**dental formula (DF)**
A shorthand way of indicating how many of each type of tooth—incisors, canines, premolars, and molars—are in a mouth quadrant; for humans the DF is 2.1.2.3.

*Figure 5.5*

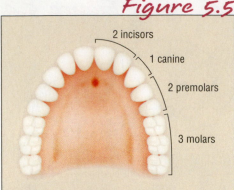

2 incisors

1 canine

2 premolars

3 molars

**DENTAL FORMULAE.** All mammals have heterodont teeth, characterized by specific tooth functions. In humans the dental formula (DF) is 2.1.2.3: two incisors, one canine, two premolars, and three molars in each quadrant of the mouth, as shown here. Can bioanthropologists classify primates on the basis of DFs?

each quadrant to total 32 teeth, or 2.1.2.3 (8 × 4 = 32); see Figure 5.5. The original mammalian dental formula was 3.1.4.3 (total teeth = 44). This evolved to 2.1.3.3 (total teeth = 36) in lemurs, lorises, and New World monkeys and to 2.1.2.3 (total teeth = 32) in Old World monkeys, apes, and humans.

9.  Although humans are the only primates that are constantly bipedal in locomotion, many other primates also walk on two legs for short distances. For example, chimpanzees practice bipedality when carrying food, as do gibbons when on the ground. It is a primate trait to sit in an *erect or semierect* position, even in species that never practice bipedality; some primates sleep sitting up. As a result of general erectness, the foramen magnum is located under the skull, at least to some extent, in all primates.

10.  Modern primates generally have five *nails* on each hand and foot; the exceptions are prosimians and tarsiers, which possess a "toilet claw" used to scratch and dig out insects from tree trunks. Although nails and claws are made of the same protein material, nails are flat and normally break off when they get long, whereas claws are curved at the sides and ends, are thick and strong, and do not break off. Primates also have ridged pads at the ends of their fingers and toes that enhance their sense of touch and allow them to manipulate tree limbs, food, and other objects. Fossil nails of course do not exist, but the shape of finger bones indicates the existence of nails or claws in ancestral groups (Martin 1990).

11.  Relative to other mammalian orders, primates have remained fairly general in their *diet*, most being omnivores. Although all primates have food preferences, their gut, stomach, and teeth allow them to ingest both plant and animal foods.

12.  Primate *brains*, relative to body size, are larger and more complex than those of other mammalian orders. The primate brain in general, and the forebrain in particular, allows primates to acquire, store, retrieve, and process large amounts of information. Additionally, primates have the ability to learn the majority of their behavioral traits rather than being genetically programmed for them.

13.  In contrast to patterns among many other orders of mammals, it is the norm for primates to take relatively good *care of their infants*. In general, primates are born unable to take care of themselves and must depend on parents and sometimes others for survival. General level and duration of caregiving are lowest in prosimians and increase successively in monkeys, apes, and humans. Because primates are essentially social animals, learning social skills is as important as learning motor skills, and a long period of growing up has advantages.

This combination of inherited ancestral mammalian traits and derived traits that evolved after primates first emerged forms a core of primate traits.

# Primate Evolution

Early primates are rare in the fossil record. One reason is that they were arboreal, and tree-living animals are never as common in the fossil record as their real numbers would predict. In addition, the prevailing wet and warm conditions during the time of early primate evolution were not conducive to fossilization. For these and other reasons, the primate fossil record is incomplete and biased. For many fossil populations there are no known modern representatives, and for some modern primates there are no direct links to specific fossil populations. At one time, when the number of fossil primate groups appeared to be the same as the number of modern primate groups, scientists were tempted to try to trace lineages from specific moderns back to specific fossil populations; but as soon as research had identified more fossil than modern types, it was obvious that modern primates were the successful ones and that many fossils represented lineages that became extinct.

In view of the fact that primates were arboreal during most of their evolution, using a tree analogy to model primate evolution is particularly appropriate. The trunk of the tree begins with the earliest primatelike mammals; continuing up the trunk we encounter limbs and then twigs. Places where limbs branch off the main trunk are analogous to major splits or divergences in the evolving primate order, such as suborders and superfamilies; places where twigs form are analogous to genus and speciation events. The tree continues to be anthropocentric rather than a general primate tree, because our goal here is a better understanding of human evolution. Figure 5.6 continues macroevolutionary happenings prior to the development of humans, with an emphasis on primate evolution.

As discussed in Chapter 2, molecular dating is relatively new and sometimes gives dates that disagree with those from more traditional dating methods. However, molecular comparisons not only date evolutionary events but sometimes date whole lineages when fossils are missing. Remember that the molecular dating of an event that marks the divergence of a lineage will always precede the dates for any fossils in that lineage. It takes a fairly long time before the new traits that led to a speciation event show up in the fossil record. The dating of primate events, those splits on the evolving primate tree, is primarily the work of Morris Goodman and his team at Wright State University. In 1998 they compared the sequences of part of a chromosome that in humans is chromosome 11 across 60 primate species, including all of the suborders and families; they then ordered the relationships of all primates to each other based on relative similarities. Taking a second step, they dated the splits of each major primate event as analogous to limbs on the primate tree and the splits of the smaller taxonomic units as twigs. As seen by the Goodman team, the dates of major divergences according to molecular dating are as follows.

- 63 myr ago—the last common ancestor (LCA) of all primates
- 58 myr ago—the split of the tarsiers from the other early primates
- 45 myr ago—the split of lorises/lemurs (prosimians) and Anthropoidea
- 40 myr ago—the divergence of monkeys from the Anthropoidea, followed by the split of Old World from New World monkeys
- 18 myr ago—the split of African and Asian large hominoids
- 17 myr ago—the split of the small Asian apes (gibbons and siamangs) from the evolving Asian hominoids
- 14 myr ago—the divergence of the orangutans from the evolving hominoids
- 8 myr ago—the split of gorillas from the evolving hominoids
- 6 myr ago—the split of chimpanzees/bonobos and "humans" from an LCA

Note that all of the splits on this list involve only the evolution of earlier to modern primates because molecular analysis can only be performed on modern species. Fossil evidence suggests that many lineages of primates did not survive to modern times, and it is not possible, therefore, to construct a complete tree based only on molecular comparisons.

Scientists use both fossil and molecular evidence to reconstruct the primate tree. Molecular evidence serves primarily to date each major primate branching event, and fossil evidence helps describe the common ancestral group before each branching event. The major thrust of the macroevolutionary tree is to describe the evolution of primate *populations* rather than to describe individual fossils. Because this model

*Figure 5.6*

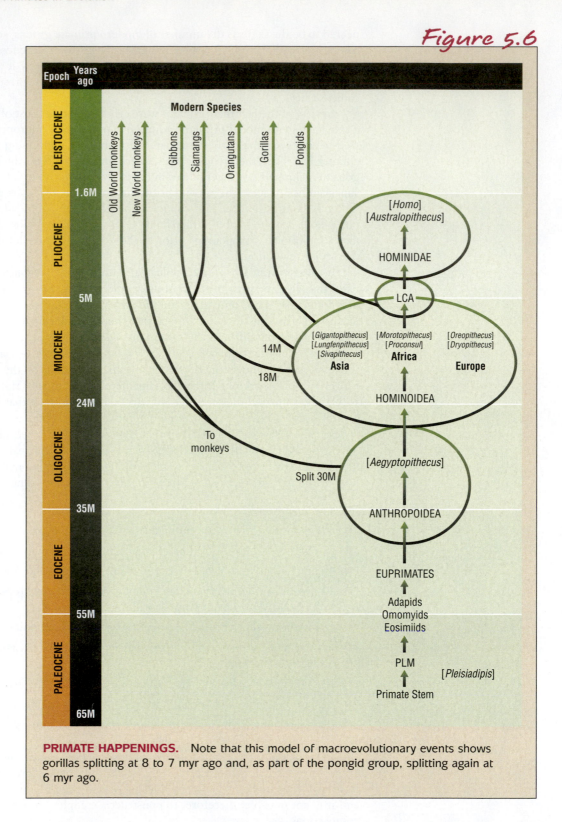

**PRIMATE HAPPENINGS.** Note that this model of macroevolutionary events shows gorillas splitting at 8 to 7 myr ago and, as part of the pongid group, splitting again at 6 myr ago.

emphasizes populations eventually leading to the human lineage, it may appear that only one group of primates was in existence at one time and that each group evolved into only one succeeding group. Nothing could be farther from evolutionary reality. The tree of life is a lush tree, filled with many limbs and twigs. Although the human lineage is the focus here, it is but one lineage. At any point during primate evolution, many limbs and an even larger number of twigs would have been in existence.

**arboreal hypothesis**
The idea that primate traits can be explained as resulting from mammalian ancestors that started living in trees and getting their food there.

# Why Did Primates Evolve?

Primates emerged at about the time of many other major Earth happenings. Europe and North America were still joined as a single land mass, so evolving early primates could walk between them (see Figure 5.7). Africa and the Eurasian continent were not connected at this time, and both South America and India were "floating islands," not connected to any other large land mass. The climate everywhere on Earth at this time was relatively warm and wet, and the angiosperms had diverged into many different plants, bushes, and trees, creating both a canopy high up and an understory near the ground. Both of these landscapes were new in the Cenozoic era, inviting new kinds of animals to evolve and adapt to the new econiches. Any animals that were arboreal would have had the advantage of protection in trees as well as access to new food sources in the form of nectar, insects, gums, fruits, and flowers (Bogin 2001a). Primates evolved such a large number of traits suitable for exploiting life in trees that primate evolution might well be thought of as arboreal evolution. The **arboreal hypothesis** suggests that primates descended from a population of terrestrial mammals that took to the trees and quickly evolved traits that adapted them arboreally: nails and tactile pads, flexible limbs, partially opposable thumbs, forward-facing eyes, stereoscopic vision and three-dimensional depth perception, good hand–eye coordination, and brains sufficiently complex to process necessary environmental information. The arboreal idea dates to Thomas Huxley in the late nineteenth century and was advocated until the 1980s. Although the hypothesis is based on logic, it does not answer the *why* question. Early primates likely took to the trees for protection at night, as all nonhuman primates do today, but what made them *habitually* arboreal? The answer to this question is probably linked to food getting.

In a variation of the arboreal hypothesis, Matt Cartmill (1974) suggests that primates evolved their traits while terrestrial as adaptations to insect eating. The ability to see and then catch flying and crawling insects would have been enhanced by stereoscopic, three-dimensional vision, as well as by grasping hands. Cartmill's idea has in turn come in for criticism on several grounds: Several species of modern prosimians eat insects on the ground; very few primates today have a diet that is primarily composed of insects; and modern insect-eating primates locate their prey by seeing, not hearing them, whereas at the time of original primates, vision was likely secondary to hearing. The *why* question had not yet been answered.

In a more modern hypothesis, Robert Sussman (1999) suggests that the earliest primates were

*Figure 5.7*

**THE CONTINENTS AT 65 MYR AND 35 MYR AGO.**   The drawing of the world at 65 myr ago (top) depicts the configuration of land masses at the time when primates are thought to have first evolved. The world at 35 myr ago (bottom) shows the configuration when monkeys evolved. What barriers to primate evolution existed because of the drift of continents away from one another?

*Source:* Adapted from Park (2003, 121).

omnivores feeding on small-sized plant and animal objects at the terminal branches of trees. He adds that this could not have happened before angiosperms reached their modern form and comprised stable climax forests. Birds using similar arboreal habitats radiated at this time as well. Sussman's hypothesis fits the data quite well, and it offers a likely answer to the *why* question: Primates became arboreal to take advantage of a newly formed ecological niche.

This section surveys primate evolutionary happenings within the framework of chronology. Note, however, that taxonomy "follows" chronology: First come primates, followed by the suborder Anthropoidea, the superfamily Hominoidea, and the family Hominidae. The focus is on populations, though individual fossils often must represent entire groups. To avoid confusion, when taxonomic terms are needed, we'll use the Latinized version, such as "Hominoidea"; but when we are talking about an ancestral population, we'll use the common term, such as "hominoids." And in keeping with the principles established in Chapter 3, we'll use the common name of a large group of animals only after its diagnostic specializations are in evidence, the same procedure followed with fish, amphibians, reptiles, and mammals. If reptiles are not reptiles until they show reptilian specializations, then, by the same principle, apes are not apes until they show ape specializations in the fossil record.

## The Paleocene and Primatelike Mammals (65 to 55 myr ago)

The Cenozoic era began about 65 myr ago and was characterized by the presence of modern animals. The first epoch, the Paleocene, was warm and wet, with North America and Eurasia connected as a single continent (see Figure 5.7). It is traditional to use the molecular date of 63 myr ago for the first primates (Goodman 1999; Goodman, Czelusniak et al. 2001; Goodman, Porter et al. 1998), though Robert Martin (2002) believes the common ancestor of all modern primates probably existed 80 myr ago. There are no true primate fossils older than about 55 myr. After the successful mammalian explosion, many groups evolved different trajectories, though most lineages became extinct. Paleocene fossils from Montana, Morocco, and Eurasia show a few primate traits each—but because each group shows mostly generalized mammal features, each is at best a primatelike mammal group. For example, these animals lacked postorbital bars, and their teeth were very unprimatelike, with incisors separated from molars by a large gap of bone. Figure 5.8 shows **Plesiadapis**, the most significant representative of these groups. The Plesiadapiformes varied from mouse size to cat size and had long snouts, small brains, and clawed digits. Their small brain cases were situated almost directly behind their faces, and their eye sockets were not fully enclosed in bone. They do not show a petrosal bulla. The conclusion is that although none of these primatelike mammals is a true primate, the variety of animals showing at least some primate traits indicates trends in a primate direction. That elusive first true primate, if it existed in the Paleocene, is yet to be discovered (Strier 2000).

Although there are no fossils of early primates from this early epoch, based on morphological comparisons of all living primate groups today and the earliest true primate fossils, the **primate stem group** can be predicted as showing the following traits (Martin 1990, 2002):

- arboreal quadrupedalism with fairly flexible hands and feet on four appendages
- generalized heterodont teeth
- good vision with semistereoscopic, three-dimensional depth perception
- a medium-sized snout and associated reliance on the sense of smell
- a clavicle
- periodic semierectness; foramen magnum halfway between back and bottom of skull

*Plesiadapis*
A primatelike mammal of about 50 myr ago that had a small brain, claws, and a large gap separating molars from incisors.

**primate stem group**
A hypothesized group of the earliest primates that was reconstructed from more modern primates.

*Figure 5.8*

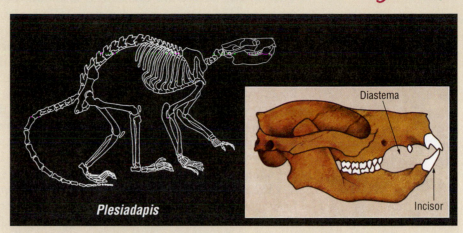

**PLESIADAPIS.**   Not regarded as a primate because its teeth show a huge diastema (gap) between incisors and molars, *Plesiadapis* is nonetheless among the preprimate mammals that existed in the Paleocene. The figure on the left is partially hypothesized. Are there any obvious primate features?

*Source*: Based on Fleagle (1988, 265).

- both claws and nails
- a basically insectivorous and frugivorous (fruit-eating) diet
- a brain large enough to process a certain amount of environmental information
- grasping feet with hind limbs dominating
- tails
- small size

New discoveries will test this prediction.

## Eocene Primates (55 to 35 myr ago)

The fossil record from the Eocene epoch includes animals with enough primate traits to be considered euprimates. By 55 to 50 myr ago, there were up to 67 primate genera in the still-joined North America and Eurasia (Simons and Rasmussen 1994). Although they varied in many characteristics, particularly in size, these genera had the following primate traits in common:

- petrosal bulla
- a postorbital bar around the eye; eyes facing almost forward
- large eye orbits, suggesting probable nocturnal activity
- no gap between incisors and molars
- snouts somewhat reduced from earlier forms
- brains larger than those of their mammalian ancestors, situated more over the face than totally behind it
- foramen magnum farther under rather than near the back of the skull
- long tails

Not all of the five known families of Eocene primates evolved to modern species; several became extinct early on, and several became extinct in the next epoch.

Several, however, evolved into lineages that eventually did become modern primates. The exact nature of this evolution is unknown. Eocene fossil primates are of three types: adapids, omomyids, and eosimiids. The *adapids* found in all four Old World continents, had four premolars, nails, grasping back feet with opposable toes, postorbital bars, and relatively forward-facing eyes (Napier and Napier 1985). These are all solid primate traits. Additionally, the adapids show the petrosal bulla that all modern primates have, and they had long, broad snouts that indicate a good sense of smell. Some were apparently diurnal and some nocturnal. All experts agree that, although adapids shared the aforementioned primate traits, there was considerable variability throughout the group (Rasmussen 2002). The *omomyids* were smaller, had a unique V-shaped jaw and fewer than four premolars, and were probably nocturnal. Recent work in China and Myanmar (Burma) has yielded a third type of Eocene primate, the *eosimiids*.

What is the evolutionary position, both before and after the Eocene, of these three types of primates? Because they share a large number of traits, it is likely they all evolved from a common ancestral group. Unfortunately, the fossil evidence for such a group is lacking. Given similarities between early adapids/omomyids and modern prosimians, some researchers have hypothesized that there is a general, if not a specific, link between the two Eocene primate types and the prosimian/tarsier lineage that branched from the primate stem perhaps before 50 myr ago (Goodman et al. 1998). Adapids might have evolved to become modern lemurs, and omomyids might have evolved to become modern tarsiers (Napier and Napier 1985). By the time of their first appearance in the fossil record some 45 myr ago, eosimiids show teeth, jaw, and anklebone traits that suggest they may be the earliest known members of the anthropoid suborder (Beard and Wang 2004; Beard et al. 1996; Gebo et al. 2000). It must be noted that these three early types of primates are only provisional candidates for evolution into the Oligocene (Culotta 1995).

If the Goodman team's molecular date of 58 myr ago for the divergence of the tarsiers is correct, Tarsiidae would be the first of the three suborders to show specializations and split off the primate stem group. A limited number of tarsier fossils from the early Eocene have been found in Europe, North America, and maybe Africa, as well as Asia. Mid-Eocene tarsier fossils are found only in Asia, and from then on, fossils of this group are quite rare (Gunnell and Rose 2002). Some experts have questioned that a lineage lasting from 40 myr ago (by fossils) or 58 myr ago (by molecular dating) to modern times could have changed so little, morphologically. Since tarsiers' teeth are the same now as in the Eocene and their body plan has not changed much either, it is likely that their diet stayed the same as well. Early fossils show that their eye orbits have always been large, so they are likely to have always been nocturnal (Rose et al. 2006). Modern tarsiers feed in the dense understory at night, and if their behavior has been the same for the past 40 myr, they would never have had much competition from any predators or from other species with similar food needs. The continuation of their ancient body plan may have occurred because they did not "need" to change to changing conditions.

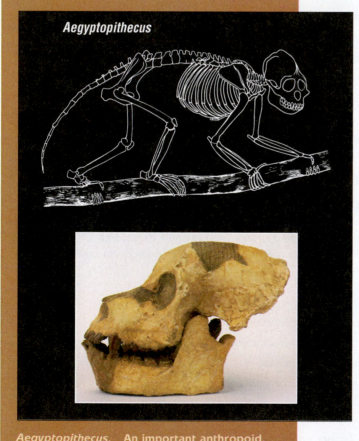

*Aegyptopithecus*

**Aegyptopithecus.** An important anthropoid, *Aegyptopithecus* was well adapted to life in the Fayum rain forest 34 myr ago. What kind of primate did *Aegyptopithecus* evolve from, and to which kind did it further evolve?

**Fayum Depression**
Area of present-day desert west of Cairo, Egypt, where many important early primate fossils were preserved.

**bilophodont**
Having two ridges of cusps with a low area between them; a diagnostic trait of the molars of monkeys.

# Oligocene Anthropoids (35 to 24 myr ago)

Although the detailed relationship between ancestral and modern prosimians is not known, the first split from the original primate population occurred before the end of the Eocene, and the lineage began to show prosimian specializations. At this point it is correct to refer to a prosimian lineage. The remaining group is the anthropoids—taxonomically the Anthropoidea, meaning "humanlike." The word *Anthropoidea* is both the taxonomic term for a collection of primate families and the name of an ancestral population that spanned 20 myr between about 50 and 30 myr ago (Goodman et al. 2001). This population was the common ancestral group that eventually evolved to become modern monkeys, apes, and humans. Although the first anthropoids can be provisionally traced to the late Eocene, anthropoids proliferated in types and became more numerous in the Oligocene. Although it is likely that Asian anthropoids migrated from Africa, new discoveries in Myanmar suggest that true anthropoids did not reach Asia until the end of the Oligocene (Ciochon and Grinnell 2002).

North America and Eurasia separated during the Oligocene, so primates could no longer move freely from one landmass to the other (refer to Figure 5.7). Most of the later anthropoid fossil material, including the well-preserved *Aegyptopithecus* crania and limb bones, was found in the **Fayum Depression** (Egypt), home of many early primate fossils. More than 100,000 fossils have been uncovered in the Fayum Depression, representing considerable variability among 17 anthropoid genera (Simons and Rasmussen 1994). (See Highlight 5.1, on pp. 118–119.) Fossil evidence complimented by morphological comparisons of modern Anthropoidea (monkeys, apes, and humans) characterizes Oligocene anthropoids as showing the following traits:

- small size and arboreal living patterns
- generalized slow-moving quadrupedalism, with more climbing and less leaping than their ancestors
- complete closure of the postorbital bone with fully enclosed eye sockets
- eyes rotated to the front; full binocular vision and good depth perception
- diurnal activity patterns
- teeth adapted to crushing and grinding, suggesting fewer insects and more plant foods
- reduced snouts and nasal areas and reduced sense of smell; no rhinarium (naked, moist nose)
- long tails
- flat nails on all fingers
- skulls more rounded than those of ancestors
- brains larger in relation to body size

Molecular evidence dates the split of the lineage leading to both Old and New World monkeys from the anthropoid lineage during the Oligocene, between 40 and 30 myr ago (Goodman 1999; Goodman, Czelusniak et al. 2001; Goodman, Porter et al. 1998; Schrago 2007). The fossil record of monkey specializations at this time is ambiguous, so 30 myr ago is a provisional date for this event (Martin 1990, 2002). The first fossil evidence of Old World monkeys consists of a group of 25-myr-old fossils from East Africa (mainly Uganda) called *Victoriapithecus* (Lewin and Foley 2004). Old World monkeys such as *Victoriapithecus* differ from earlier Anthropoidea and later apes by having evolved **bilophodont** molars; this literally means the teeth have two ridges of cusps with a "valley," or low area, between them (see Figure 5.9).

*Figure 5.9*

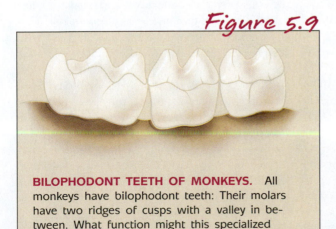

**BILOPHODONT TEETH OF MONKEYS.** All monkeys have bilophodont teeth: Their molars have two ridges of cusps with a valley in between. What function might this specialized molar form have?

# In the Fayum Depression

MORE EARLY PRIMATE FOSSILS have been found in one relatively small location of the Fayum Depression in northern Egypt than in any other area of the world. Given the principle of contingency, these early primates were our ancestors generally speaking, as well as the ancestors of modern monkeys and apes, and bioanthropologists rely on the Fayum primates as a window providing glimpses of what came next. Geologically, the Fayum formation covers the upper Eocene and the lower Oligocene, giving the primates early anthropoidean status.

The Fayum Depression today is about 50 miles from Cairo by car or camel. The area is part of the Sahara desert and offers no standing water, no oasis, no stands of trees, no grass. The fossil beds of early primates crop out in a series of bluffs and broad benches that rise from the shore of a large, below-sea-level lake bed.

Scientists have known of the Fayum's fossils since the 1870s, when a whale was found in an early context (though no real dates had been determined for any fossils at the time). Since then many international teams of paleontologists and primatologists have excavated the Fayum's vast sediments, including a British Museum team in 1900, major expeditions from the American Museum of Natural History, and teams from Yale and Duke Universities beginning in the 1960s.

The main formation measures some 340 m (1,130 feet) deep and has four distinct levels. In 1992–1993 workers found several skulls in the lowest level, about 0.40 m (18 inches) above the base of the formation. These finds came long after the other levels had been recognized, just because no one had investigated a hill fairly close to the base of the formation. These fossils, known as *Catopithecus*, are so small that many experts originally did not believe they could be the ancestors of later primates. A more recent excavation and report in 2005 on the oldest (base) level, dated at 37 myr ago, provided evidence of two distinct anthropoid species that their discoverers predict are the common ancestor of African anthropoids.

The second level is 100 m (330 feet) above the base and has yielded only one early primate fossil mandible, called *Oligopithecus*, dated at about 35 myr ago. The third level, about 170 m (558 feet) from the base, has produced two families of anthropoideans, each having several genera and species. The uppermost level, some 250 m (820 feet) from the base of the formation, continues to produce new species of the same two families and is well stocked with primate specimens.

The Fayum formation has been well dated, first by paleomagnetism, then by K-Ar from the basalt that caps the top of the formation, and third by fossil mammalian fauna that correlate well between the Fayum levels and other datable deposits. The cap at the top dates to 31 myr ago and the base to 37 myr ago, so the Fayum gives us a look at evolving early primates over the course of some 6 myr.

The Fayum Depression today does not resemble the home of our ancestors, who were tropical animals and adapted to wet climates. To gain an accurate environmental context for the evolution of these early primates, scientists must reconstruct the climate of the late Eocene and early Oligocene. Primatologist Adrian Kortlandt attempted such a reconstruction and suggested that the Fayum area was treeless, sparsely vegetated and arid to semi-arid. If Kortlandt's hypothesis were valid, it would be hard to make a case that any primates living in the Fayum region were arboreal: No trees equals no tree-living primates. Logically, however, terrestrialism seems unlikely—because using the contingency principle, primate evolutionists would have to explain the seemingly arboreal characteristics of the earliest primates and a shift to terrestrialism and then a shift back to arborealism after 37 myr ago.

Thomas Bown and his team of primatologists, geologists, and ecologists critiqued Kortlandt's assessment by evaluating each evidential bit. Their conclusions are that nearly all paleontologic, geologic, and environmental data show that the Fayum between 37 and 31 myr ago was coastal, tropical or semitropical, with seasonal rainfall varying from monsoonlike rains to relatively drier periods. Bown and his colleagues added that the Fayum had moist soils that could support large trees and a diverse forest environment. If so, then there were plenty of trees for early primates to live in, and the animals' arboreal traits are easily explained. The Bown team's evidence appears to be sound, as it is based on soil, pollen, and faunal evidence, all pointing to the same conclusion.

The environment of the Fayum is now believed to have been a tropical or semitropical rain forest with small flowing streams, ponds, large trees, and fernlike undergrowth—all providing a favorable context for arboreal primates and for small terrestrial mammals as well. The Fayum menagerie also included insectivores, bats, crocodiles, small herbivores, water birds, and minielephants.

Anatomical comparisons with modern primates allow paleoanthropologists to make inferences about the anatomy and behavior of the primates that preceded them. All Fayum primates appear to be both quadrupedal and arboreal. The earliest Fayum primates probably concentrated on an insect diet, supplemented by fruit; the primates in the upper two levels were primarily frugivorous, eating some insects and leaves. The data for the diet inferences come from a combination of known resources and the analysis of teeth. Most of the groups were diurnal (active by day), as evidenced by small eye orbits relative to body size (animals active at night need large orbits to gather enough light to see). The earliest primates in the formation probably marked their territory using olfactory glands as modern prosimians do, but later primates probably did not have moist noses or sensory apparatus for marking.

Now that we know that early primates evolved under tropical conditions and were arboreal, it will be much easier to continue to fill in the details of their evolutionary lineages.

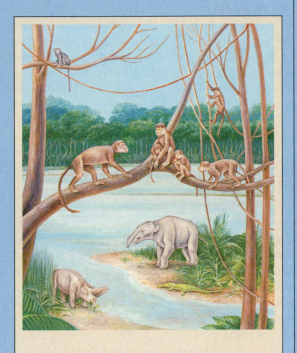

Primates and other mammals left fossils in the Fayum Depression in Egypt. Typical of the mammals in this wet forested area 37 to 31 myr ago were several of the animals shown here. Predict their diet.

*Sources*: Bown, T. M., M. J. Kraus, S. L. Wing, et al. 1982. The Fayum primate forest revisited. *Journal of Human Evolution* 11:603–632.  Fleagle, J. G. 1999. *Primate adaptation and evolution*. 2nd ed. San Diego, CA: Academic Press.  Jaeger, J. J. and L. Marivaux. Shaking the earliest branches of anthropoid primate evolution. 2005. *Science* 310: 244–245.  Kay, R. F., and E. L. Simons. 1980. The ecology of Oligocene African anthropoids. *International Journal of Primatology* 1:21–37. Rasmussen, D. T., T. M. Bown, and E. L. Simons. 1992. The Eocene–Oligocene transition in continental Africa. In *Eocene–Oligocene climatic and biotic Evolution*, eds. D. R. Prothero and W. A. Berggren, 548–564. Princeton, NJ: Princeton University Press.  Simons, E. S. The fossil record of human origins among the Anthropoidea. In *The Primate Fossil Record*, ed. W. Hartwig, 13–28. Cambridge: Cambridge University Press.

turn back to your reading

**ape**
Common term that includes small apes (gibbons and siamangs) and large apes (orangutans, gorillas, chimpanzees, and bonobos).

Early Old World monkeys were small, arboreal and terrestrial, quadrupedal fruit eaters that lived in open woodlands and showed moderately long snouts (Benefit and McCrossin 2002). These monkeys were relatively rare until about 9 myr ago (Jablonski 2002). At that point, both major types of Old World monkeys appear in the fossil record, the highly arboreal colobids (like the modern black-and-white colobus) and the more ground-living cercopithecids (like the modern baboons).

Given the separation of the Old and New World continents long before the time of the monkey divergence as well as molecular comparisons between the two groups, it appears that monkeys diverged but once from their anthropoid ancestors and that, shortly after they were established in Africa, one group rafted to the New World. Rafting can happen when oceanic storms rip portions of land or matted vegetation from their original anchorages and carry plants and/or animals from one place to another. The newly formed "islands" float freely, moved by ocean currents, to attach themselves to new landmasses. Rats and iguanas are known to have rafted great distances (Censky et al. 2002; Fleagle 1995; Hecht 2003), and early primates were not much bigger than rats. Africa and what is now South America were as close as 200 kilometers during the Oligocene. It would have taken only one pregnant female to populate an open continent; New World monkeys would have rapidly become successful and evolved to many different species.

## Miocene Hominoids (24 to 6 myr ago)

Once monkeys split from the anthropoids to form their own lineages, the primate group that was left is called the hominoids. (The taxonomic name, Hominoidea, means "hominidlike.") Some workers call this group "apes" at this point, but this book restricts the term **ape** to populations that evolved specialized and diagnostic apelike locomotor traits (Relethford 2002). During the Miocene hominoids remained generalized quadrupeds, likely *palmigrade* (walking with palms down). Locomotor specializations are not identifiable in the fossil record until much later.

At least 30 different genera of hominoids lived between 24 and 6 myr ago, all in the Old World. Because early Miocene hominoids have been found only in East Africa, it is likely they evolved from some East African anthropoid (Pilbeam 2002). Over time they became abundant, and eventually they migrated to Eurasia; Africa and Eurasia docked during the mid-Miocene, some 17 myr ago (Deacon and Deacon 1999). Based on fossil evidence and morphological comparisons with modern Hominoidea (apes and humans), the ancestral hominoid populations in the early and mid-Miocene periods showed the following traits (Begun 2002):

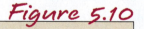

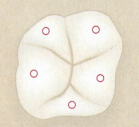

- variable size, from smaller than modern monkeys to larger than modern gorillas
- arboreal living patterns but with some inclination toward terrestrial life, probably in search of food
- posture more erect than that of previous primates
- unspecialized quadrupedal locomotion
- upper arms with considerable flexibility, such as the ability to lift arms up over heads
- fully extended forearm with swiveling elbow joints
- skulls more rounded than those of ancestors
- 2.1.2.3 dental formula; also Y-5 molar pattern, in which each molar has five raised cusps with "valleys" in between, forming a Y pattern (see Figure 5.10)
- no tails

**Y-5 MOLAR PATTERN.** The Y-5 pattern in the molars of apes and humans shows five cusps with low areas between them. Why would such a pattern have evolved?

- more complex and larger brains, leading to more complex behavior than shown by previous primates
- increased specialization of front teeth

Any one of several hominoid fossil populations might have been the common ancestral group that evolved to modern apes and humans: *Dryopithecus, Proconsul, Sivapithecus, Lungfenpithecus, Gigantopithecus, Oreopithecus,* or *Morotopithecus,* or some still undiscovered hominoid population. Even if none of these hominoids was ancestral to any modern ape or human group, their variability is instructive. Until the mid-1960s, researchers lumped mid-Miocene to late Miocene hominoids from Africa, Asia, and Europe into one big group and called them the Dryopithecines. But as workers found new fossils, they realized that the hominoids of this period were more variable than previously believed. Scientists now use Dryopithecines to refer only to European materials from 13 to 8 myr ago. Based on numerous crania, jaws, teeth, and limb bones, Dryopithecines can be described as medium-sized, fruit-eating hominoids with thin tooth enamel and without specialized locomotion.

*Proconsul* fossils all come from East Africa and date from 27 to 17 myr ago. They vary from the size of modern small monkeys to the size of gorillas, and they show some rather distinctive traits, such as a V-shaped dental arch. Like the other early hominoids, *Proconsul* species were generalized (probably arboreal) quadrupeds with equal-length limbs, had no tails, and ate leaves and fruit. Some experts feel that *Proconsul* was generalized enough and in the right place at the right time to be considered close to the last common ancestor (LCA) of all modern apes and humans (Begun 2002). Other experts believe the Dryopithecines show more similarities to African apes and humans than any other hominoid and deserve serious attention as a possible link to the LCA. However,

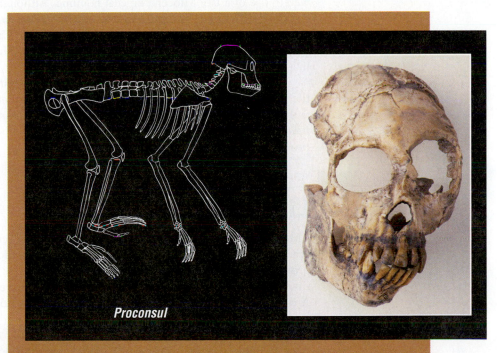

*Proconsul*

**Proconsul.** This reconstruction and photo depict the early African hominoid known as *Proconsul,* which showed generalized quadrupedal locomotion. What anatomical parts are associated with this kind of locomotion?

the Dryopithecines were European hominoids and the LCA was African, giving *Proconsul* more credibility at the present time.

*Sivapithecus*, a fairly large Asian hominoid, has been classified into six species that weighed 32 to 68 kilograms (70 to 150 pounds) and dated to between 14 and 7 myr ago. Because this genus shows several morphological similarities to modern orangutans, as well as shared continental proximity, until recently scientists believed *Sivapithecus* to be the best candidate for direct linkage to any modern ape. Both *Sivapithecus* and modern orangutans have oval eye orbits that are close together, a unique triangular nasal region, and the same shape and size of incisors. But *Lungfenpithecus*, a recent find from northern Thailand, is a more likely candidate as ancestral to orangutans. This 13.5-myr-old hominoid matches modern orangutans better in postcranial and dental traits; in addition, its location is closer to where modern orangutans are found (Chaimanee et al. 2003).

*Gigantopithecus*, an Asian hominoid restricted to India and China, is unique because of its potential large size and its apparent survival well beyond the rest of the Miocene hominoids. Based on teeth and mandibles (the only fossil evidence), *Gigantopithecus* may have been 2.8 m (9 feet) tall, though 1.8 m (6 feet) is more likely, and may have weighed perhaps 272 kilograms (600 pounds). The fossils of this group date from as early as 9 myr ago, and representatives of the group may have survived until 500 kyr ago (Ciochon et al. 1990; Relethford 2002). If the estimate of its size is accurate, *Gigantopithecus* was probably not in the lineage that eventually evolved to modern apes and humans.

Another new Miocene hominoid was found in Uganda in the 1990s and named *Morotopithecus* (Gebo et al. 1997). Because different techniques date this primate anywhere from 20.6 to 12.5 myr ago, the dating is not secure. But *Morotopithecus* may show tendencies toward brachiation (branch-swinging behavior), so if an early date holds, then it may be the first hominoid to show apelike specialization.

At one time experts thought that *Oreopithecus bamboli* bones from north-central Italy were those of a late Miocene bipedal hominid. Although the skull and teeth appear to be hominidlike, once the entire skeleton was extracted from a lignite matrix, the animal's arm bones turned out to be longer than its leg bones. Therefore, bipedalism was an unlikely mode of locomotion. Because this "swamp ape" shows a mosaic of traits, it is put in a family of its own; it likely did not evolve further.

Molecular evidence suggests that the Asian apes (gibbons and siamangs) split from the hominoid group between 22 myr and 18 myr ago and from each other between 8 and 6 myr ago; orangutans appear to have diverged about 14 myr ago. But at present no fossils that link those events to modern primates have been found, so the dates remain provisional (Goodman et al. 2001).

# The "Missing Link"

Although the term "missing link" is overused, if there were such an important undiscovered group, it would link hominoids to bipedal hominids in the time period from approximately 14 myr to 6 myr ago. Unfortunately, there simply are no fossils from the time spanning the hominoid/hominid transition. There are also no fossils of definite African apes (showing diagnostic locomotor specialization) from that time, though molecular dating puts gorilla beginnings at 8 myr ago (Ward 1997). Because molecular dating puts the small and large Asian apes (gibbons and orangutans) as splitting from the African hominoids before 14 myr ago, and because modern humans are more like modern African apes than any other animal group, it is Africa where scientists look for fossil evidence of any missing link—late Miocene hominoids that evolved to hominids by 6 myr ago. Such an undiscovered hominoid group, ancestral to African apes and humans, probably would have migrated from Eurasia, where hominoids were common in the late Miocene while still absent in Africa. At this time, their locomotion was probably generalized, and they were likely equally at home in the trees and on the ground. As David Begun (2002) suggests, "no known Miocene hominoid was either a biped or a knuckle-walker" (365), meaning none was specialized in locomotion.

# Recent Primate Evolution: After the Major Splits

Arboreal primates are generally rare in the fossil record because tree life does not promote fossilization as readily as terrestrial life; thus, the more recent primate fossil record is spottier than reality would predict. In the prosimian lineage, lemurs and lorises were probably a single evolving group until perhaps 20 myr ago, when they appear to have diverged. The oldest modern lemur is $^{14}$C dated at only 26 kyr ago, but its ancestral group probably rafted to Madagascar long before that as it has since evolved into 30 modern species. In the Old World monkey lineage, early baboon, mandrills, mangabeys, macaques, and modern baboons split between 8 and 6 myr ago, by molecular dating. For the ape lineage, as noted earlier, there are no fossils to support the molecular dating of a split between 14 and 6 myr ago. Fossil orangutans in southern China and Southeast Asia are less than 1 myr old. The first fossil reported to be in the chimpanzee lineage was recently found at a site in Kenya and dated to 545 kyr ago (McBrearty and Jablonski 2005), long after molecular dating suggests chimpanzees began their own lineage, separate from hominids. As the next section discusses, the term *last common ancestor (LCA)* is reserved for that yet unfound "missing link" that presumably lived in Africa and eventually evolved to the African ape and human lineages.

Hominoids apparently originated in the Miocene and showed an early period of adaptive radiation, through spreading into most of the Old World and by evolving into various types. Then, likely as a result of climate change (particularly heightened seasonality) during the Late Miocene, beginning 15 myr ago, their types and numbers appear to have diminished. Old World monkeys, by contrast, flourished during this period, probably as a result of higher breeding capacity and ability to exist on lower quality foods than hominoids (Hartwig 2007; Jablonski 2002).

# The Last Common Ancestor (LCA)

The idea of the last common ancestor (LCA) of modern apes and humans, a group technically called late hominoids and dated between 14 and 6 myr ago, has undergone a good deal of scrutiny in recent decades—scrutiny that has resulted in two polarized camps rather than a consensus (Rogers 1994). Because there is no fossil evidence for this hominoid group, one group of experts, the "bone camp," bases its evolutionary reconstruction on morphological comparisons of fossil groups that existed both before and after the elusive LCA. Anatomical evidence suggests that modern chimpanzees and gorillas are more like each other, bone for bone, than either is like modern humans (Andrews 1987).

The other group of experts, the "molecular camp," uses comparative genetics and notes that many regions in the human genome resemble chimpanzee and bonobo genomes more than they resemble that of any other modern hominoid. The molecular camp thus concludes that the LCA was ancestral only to chimpanzees, bonobos, and humans and that gorillas diverged a million years earlier, at 7 myr ago (Pääbo 2003; Wildman et al. 2003). Others suggest that the molecular evidence is ambiguous and that it is as likely that the LCA evolved a trichotomy (three-way division) of lineages leading to gorillas, chimpanzees/bonobos, and humans (Conroy 2002; Marks 1995b, 2002). Wendy Bailey (1993) analyzed the molecular research and reported that 13 studies found chimpanzees and humans genetically closest, with gorillas as the

**pongid**
A member of the family Pongidae, which includes gorillas, chimpanzees, and bonobos.

outgroup; 7 studies found chimpanzees and gorillas closest, with humans as the outgroup; and, perhaps most telling, 5 studies produced results too ambiguous to support any conclusions. She suggests it is too close to call. Nevertheless, although the evidence is inconclusive in terms of identifying the long-sought LCA, all experts agree that the ancestral group lived in Africa.

Until this issue is resolved, we take the position that the LCA between 14 and 6 myr ago was a generalized quadrupedal group at home both in the trees and on the ground—and that it split about 6 myr ago into an eventual **pongid** (chimpanzee/bonobo/gorilla) lineage and an eventual hominid (human) lineage, each subsequently evolving along its own pathway. As a result of this split, hominids became the bipedal lineage, and pongids became the brachiating, fist- or knuckle-walking lineage. Our choice of this interpretation is in keeping with our decision to offer the simplest explanation when there are viable alternatives (Lewin 2001).

An alternative scenario, favored by most molecular experts, sees the LCA as a group that included only the ancestors of humans, chimpanzees, and bonobos. According to this view gorillas diverged separately at 8 to 7 myr ago (Goodman 1999). This hypothesis would leave the LCA group in existence for only 1 myr, splitting to the pongid—without gorillas—and hominid lineages about 6 myr ago (Goodman 1999; Goodman et al. 1998). If this is the correct scenario, then two lineages evolved knuckle walking at different times: gorillas at 8 to 7 myr ago and chimpanzees/bonobos at 6 myr ago.

An alternative taxonomy that parallels this alternative LCA scenario began in 1988. In the alternative taxonomy modern humans and ancestral groups back to the LCA are called "hominins," and all African apes and humans and their ancestors back to their last hominoid ancestral group are called "hominids." For several reasons, we do not follow that terminology. First, the original use of "hominid" to refer specifically to bipedal hominoids goes back decades; it is confusing rather than enlightening to suddenly start using the word to refer to all African apes and humans regardless of locomotion specialization. The term *hominid* has always evoked specialized bipedism. Mode of locomotion is but one trait, but bipedalism appears to be such an overwhelmingly important trait in human evolution that many experts wish to preserve the "hominid equals bipedalism" exclusivity (Caspari 2002). Second, because all morphological and some genetic distance tests find gorillas and chimpanzees more closely related to each other than either is to humans, "the gorilla/chimpanzee/human trichotomy has not been resolved to the general satisfaction of qualified workers in the field" (Marks 2002, 275). Finally, it is easier for some experts to reconcile one rather than two knuckle-walking evolutionary events, though two such events are not impossible, given environmental similarities and contingency factors for the two pongid groups.

# Potential Early Hominids: An Overview of Three Candidates

Three recent fossil discoveries fall into the right time and place to be considered for the status of the first hominid. Unfortunately, they all share one flaw: None shows the diagnostic trait of bipedalism to everyone's satisfaction. Thus, these need to remain in a "candidate" or "potential" hominid category.

The first of the three candidates is called *Sahelanthropus tchadensis*. It was found in Chad in 2002 and has been relatively well dated at 7 to 6 myr old. A nearly complete cranium was found, indicating a small-sized brain. The fossil shows a mixture of earlier hominoid traits and a few traits that show up later in true bipedal hominids; however, until postcranial bones are found, the status of *Sahelanthropus tchadensis* as a hominid remains open. The location where it was found is perhaps the most interesting feature of this fossil because Chad is several hundred miles from where the first true bipeds have been discovered in the Great Rift Valley.

Another potential first hominid is called *Orrorin tugenensis*. This fossil was discovered in 2000 in Kenya and dated to between 6.2 and 5.6 myr ago. No cranial material was found, but the femur shows intriguing signs of bipedalism, although these are not definitive. Again, it remains only a candidate for hominid status.

The third potential first hominid probably makes the strongest case for bipedalism. Called *Ardipithecus ramidus*, the fossils discovered in Ethiopia have been dated at 5.8 myr ago. About five individuals represent this group. It is the location of the foramen magnum (a hole in the base of the skull that gives good evidence for bipedal locomotion) that indicates an upright posture. Whether this group was bipedal is not certain, but very likely. But whether it is in the lineage that gave rise to the group of populations called the australopithecines is, of course, unknown. There may have been more than one bipedal population in Africa at that time, and no direct ancestral/descendant relationships are established. Although every population in the past had ancestors, not every population necessarily left descendants.

There has been a good deal of publicity about these potential hominids and a good deal of conflict as well. Each of the discoverers claims to have found "the first hominid" and claims the others did not. Until new fossil evidence is discovered, each candidate remains a possible hominid only. The story of hominid evolution will be continued in the next chapter, starting with a more detailed definition of *hominid*.

# Primate Behavior: Reconstructing Its Evolution by Studying Contemporary Primates

This chapter so far has focused on the fossil record of evolving primates, using the anatomical traits that all modern primates have and individual primate fossils augmented by molecular dating to generate a model of primate evolution. Although there are gaps in the fossil record and some differences in interpretation, bioanthropologists are in agreement about the general evolution of primates during the last 63 myr. But, even if the fossil record were perfect, which it isn't, it goes only so far in reconstructing primate evolution. What about traits that leave no fossil clues, such as hair/fur and behavior? Hair/fur is likely an ancestral mammalian trait that continued throughout primate evolution. And some behavior can be inferred. For example, which foods were eaten can be inferred if a species' teeth are specialized and match foods known to have been available at that time and place; also, scratch marks on teeth can often show that hard seeds or nuts were eaten. Isotope analyses of bones can suggest large categories of food ingested (i.e., plants versus animals). And the type of locomotion a species employed can be inferred by observing fossilized long bones. But much behavior leaves no clues at all, direct or inferred. How can we know if the mothers in a particular primate species played with their infants or if any primates had lifelong pair bonds between single males and females? This section attempts to reconstruct the evolution of primate behavior. This topic is presented separately because the study of behavior uses techniques that are quite different from those used to study fossils.

By definition, all animals can intentionally move. Thus, all animals can be said to behave. For the last 200 years or so, scientists have fought the nature/nurture, biological determinism/cultural determinism war over the causes of behavior. As with so many ideas that involve two strong polar positions, the "truth" in this debate is somewhere in the middle and not at either end. That is, behavior is caused by both genes *and* learning. Because primates are animals, they behave; and because at least some behavior is under genetic control, genes are responsible, at least in part, for particular behavioral traits. In general, for any given species, scientists do not know which specific behaviors are under complete or even partial genetic control. Experiments with genetically simpler organisms such as fruit flies and rodents suggest there are few if any single genes that direct single behavioral traits. Rather, the genetic part of behavior involves multiple genes, some acting very subtly. Additionally, some genes may affect numerous behaviors, and some may be different for females and males. Add to these complications the fact that most behavior is also environmentally affected, and it makes discussing behavioral evolution a difficult task for scientists (Hrdy et al. 1994/1995). Ten or so years ago, when scientists inaugurated various genome projects, they hoped that they would eventually identify specific genes that were directly responsible for specific behaviors. Results from the already sequenced genomes of laboratory animals such as mice, voles, roundworms, and flies indicate about 30 genes that appear to have some effect on social behaviors related to bonding with the opposite sex and caregiving. But, even in laboratory animals, a gene does not cause a behavior. Environmental factors affect whether a particular gene will be manifest or not, and even in fruit flies, individual genes work differently in males or females (Wade 2005).

Even the decoding of the human genome will be of only minimal help in sorting out "behavioral genes"; it may locate some genes that have some effect on certain behaviors, but most of such effects are undoubtedly complicated by the multiplicity of genes involved in single behaviors, the pleiotropic effect of single genes on multiple behaviors, and the (very important) environment. Even if genetic causes of certain primate behaviors can be identified, there is a large gap between genes and action (behavior). The proximate (immediate) causes of behavior lie in the realm of hormones and physiological reactions to stimuli such as fear, sex, and hunger. At present scientists can study only the outer appearance of the behavior, not the string of causes from genes and/or environment to hormones and physiology. Scientists know that genes are involved in constructing brains that signal behaviors, and they also know that genes control some large patterns of behavior, but not individual behaviors in situations involving choices. Beyond this, they can only hypothesize.

Ant behavior is far easier to discuss than primate behavior, because ants rely on instinct for almost all of their behavioral repertoire. Outside stimuli trigger ant behavior through their genes; there is very little variability in ant behavior; and very little of ant behavior is learned. Ants don't think—at least not much—because they don't have much to think with. It is a different situation with primates (and many other animal groups), because their complex brains are much more flexible and allow for considerable thinking and problem solving. Therefore, primate behavior results from the interaction of genes and environment, of biology and learning, and saying what part of a behavioral trait is due to one factor or the other is beyond the ability of science at present. One thing seems clear: The principle of natural selection operates on behavior in the same way it operates on the color of a moth's wings. If any part of a behavioral trait is genetically based, the entire trait is subject to natural selection, because the sum of the individual (the phenotype) is the unit of selection. If a particular behavior is under some genetic control and in some way enhances reproductive differential and survival, the genetic part will be passed on and become part of the next generation's gene pool.

## Reconstructing Primate Behavior

Although fossilized bones can give clues to locomotion and fossilized teeth and plants can give clues to diet, the majority of behavior does not fossilize. Therefore, like any trait that does not fossilize, the reconstruction of 63 myr of primate behavior relies heavily on the *comparative method*. To reconstruct what the original primate stem group was like in its totality, in lieu of fossil evidence, scientists compare the anatomy, morphology, genetics, and behavior of all modern primates to come up with a catalogue of common traits. The premise is that modern groups share these traits because of inheritance from that primate stem group. This should be true of any shared biological trait, whether an anatomical trait, such as locomotion, or behavior. Of course, some common traits may not be evolutionary but may result from analogy. Experts differ in how they try to differentiate traits that are genetic and inherited, and therefore part of a lineage's evolution, from those that are not. One way is to restrict analysis to universals. In other words, if a behavioral trait is found in all 250+ modern primate species (i.e., is universal to the order), then it is likely the trait was inherited, is under genetic control, and is traceable back to the primate stem group. The alternatives are that the trait evolved 250+ times independently or that the primate stem group learned the trait 63 myr ago and all subsequent groups learned it in each generation or that there were 250+ parallel or analogous evolutions resulting in the same trait. Given the improbable nature of these alternatives, it is highly likely that universal similarities across species result from common inheritance. Therefore, once scientists can identify commonalities in behavior, one end of the thread tracing behavior throughout the primate lineage is anchored (Potts 1987).

Let's now look at primate behavioral evolution from 63 to 6 myr ago, from the primate stem group to the LCA. As just explained, this summary is a reconstruction based on the likelihood that similarities are due to inheritance.

## The Evolution of Primate Behavior

By comparing the behavior of all 250+ contemporary modern primate species, workers have found the following universal commonalities. Although the items on the list are basically behaviors inherited from mammalian ancestors and as such are rather mundane, they nevertheless provide a rudimentary behavioral picture of the primate stem group on which to build an evolutionary model of primate behavior through time:

- sleeping and resting, probably in trees
- eating; drinking freestanding water
- socializing within the group
- taking care of infants
- grooming self and others
- playing
- copulating
- locomoting quadrupedally in trees
- communicating

Any behavior that is universal to all contemporary primate species is bound to be very general—a very large behavioral category—because if it were more specific, it would no longer be universal. (An exception is the case of locomotion; not all primates today are arboreal quadrupeds, but fossil evidence supports this variety of locomotion for the earliest members of the order.) The comparative approach cannot provide behavioral details, but at least the chances are good that generalizing about behavior will not lead to huge mistakes. Variations on each general behavior evolved over time. Locomotion, for example, evolved to leaping and clinging in some lineages, knuckle walking in others, and bipedalism in yet another lineage; many lineages remained generalized quadrupeds. And learning must have played a big part in these behavioral complexes from the beginning.

A comparison of modern anthropoids (monkeys, apes, and humans) suggests that a division of labor by sex and age can be added to the list of anthropoid behaviors that was likely by Oligocene times. It is also likely that anthropoid groups were "compulsively social," that the residential core was female, and that males dispersed at adolescence. With related females as the core, there would have been female, but not male, bonds (Foley 1996).

A comparison of modern hominoids (apes and humans) suggests several behavioral additions or changes in the hominoid branch that split off in the Miocene era. Incest avoidance and technological behaviors were probably additional parts of the repertoire of Miocene hominoids. Socially, groups were probably stable but semiclosed (outsiders would have had trouble joining them); at adolescence females moved to other units but males stayed in their natal groups, forming alliances. Males may have had multiple sex partners (Foley 1996; Wrangham 1987).

This hypothesized model of primate behavior and its accumulative effect ends with the behavior of the LCA of contemporary humans and African apes. The common ancestral group between 14 and 6 myr ago likely showed the following additional behavioral traits (de Waal 1997; Foley 1996; Goodall 1965; Panger et al. 2003):

- arboreal quadrupedalism, with some terrestrial foraging
- good caregiving to offspring
- gestural and oral communication, but not speech
- play at all ages, but particularly in infancy and adolescence
- largely omnivorous diet, but dominated by plant foods; small game occasionally hunted and eaten
- copulation part of consort behavior and engaged in often
- grooming as a social activity, to reduce group friction
- multimale/multifemale social groups, with bonds between males
- departure of females from their natal group at adolescence while males remained
- technological behaviors, including building nightly nests in low areas of trees, using tools in various ways (perhaps rocks to crack nuts, sticks to dig tubers or to "fish" for termites, or rocks thrown at animals), and fashioning simple tools for short-term use
- considerable learning of flexible complex behavior
- food sharing between mothers and infants
- carrying of objects
- lifelong bonds with mothers
- male leaders and protectors

About 6 myr ago, the LCA group split either to chimpanzee/bonobo and human lineages or to gorilla/chimpanzee/bonobo and human lineages. Those earliest hominids, on their way to becoming humans, took an accumulated 30 or so behavioral complexes with them. So did chimpanzees. The evolution of hominid behavior is contingent upon this established pattern, and the saga will continue in subsequent chapters.

Since humans are primates, this chapter concentrated on this order of mammals, beginning with a brief description of modern primates. Primates evolved from some generalized mammal and have had their own evolution for the past 63 myr, separate from hoofed mammals, carnivorous mammals, rodents, etc.

■ Some mammals and angiosperms survived the K/T mass extinction and became the most common types of animals and plants after 65 myr ago. Primates evolved shortly thereafter, probably from some generalized, shrewlike mammal.

■ Primates are both a taxonomic category and a large group of past and present animals, unique in their combination of certain morphological traits.

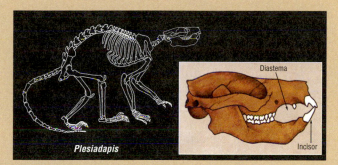

**Plesiadapis**

Diastema

Incisor

**page 115**

■ Primates are generalized animals that probably evolved specific traits early as adaptations to tree living: generalized quadrupedalism, good vision, flexible limbs, and brains that could sort out environmental information.

■ As a group, primates share certain traits, but only one—the petrosal bulla—is diagnostic of the order.

■ Earliest primates split into tarsier, prosimian, and anthropoidean lineages (the ancestral group to modern monkeys, apes, and humans) about 50 myr ago. Tarsiers and prosimians had their own evolution from then on, parting company with the more generalized anthropoids.

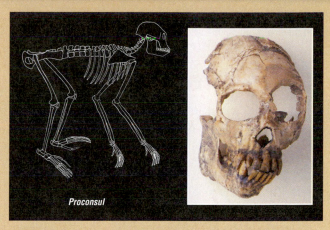

**Proconsul**

**page 121**

■ Anthropoidea split into monkey and hominoid lineages (the ancestral group that evolved to modern apes and humans) about 30 myr ago. Monkeys in the Old and New Worlds had their own evolution from then on, leaving hominoids as the more generalized group.

■ Many types of hominoids lived between 30 and 6 myr ago, with the Asian forms (ancestors of gibbons and orangutans) splitting off to form their own lineages perhaps 18 and 14 myr ago, leaving the LCA group between 14 and 6 myr ago.

■ A fossil gap between 14 and 6 myr ago is keeping the late Miocene evolution of hominoids a mystery at present.

■ About 6 myr ago, according to one view, the LCA group split into a chimpanzee/bonobo/gorilla lineage (pongids) and the lineage that includes modern humans (hominids).

■ According to an alternative view, gorillas split 8 to 7 myr ago, leaving the ancestors of chimpanzees/bonobos and humans as the LCA; then 6 myr ago the LCA split into the pongid and hominid lineages.

■ Using the comparative method plus the same principles used to reconstruct general macroevolution, scientists reconstruct the evolution of primate behavior noting likely changes over time.

## KEY WORDS

anthropoids 102
ape, 120
arboreal, 107

arboreal hypothesis, 113
bilophodont, 117
cathemeral, 106

dental formula (DF), 109
diurnal, 106
Fayum Depression, 117

generalized, 107
nocturnal, 106
petrosal bulla, 108
*Plesiadapis*, 114
pongid, 124

postorbital bars, 108
primate, 107
primate stem group, 114
primatelike mammals, 101
prosimians, 102

specialized, 107
tarsiers, 102
terrestrial, 107

## SUGGESTED READING

Campbell, C. J., A. Fuentes, K. MacKinnon et al. eds. 2007. *Primates in Perspective*. NY: Oxford University Press. Experts on each of the major primate groups as well as on many comparative primate topics (tool use, culture, cognition, etc) give a very comprehensive and current look at primates today.

de Waal, F. *Bonobo: The Forgotten Ape*. Berkeley. University of California Press, 1997. Bonobos are no longer regarded as small chimpanzees; their social organization is quite different from that of chimpanzees, and they appear to be less aggressive and more cooperative in the wild. On the other hand, unlike chimpanzees, bonobos have never been provisioned or studied for 40 years. Their sex life is particularly interesting.

Goodall, J. "Chimpanzees of the Gombe Stream Reserve." In *Primate Behavior*, ed. I. DeVote, 425–473. New York: Holt. Rinchart, & Winston, 1965. This is Goodall's science-based contribution to primate studies and is less anthropomorphic than her popular books. Because the article was written in 1965, there were only a few years of provisioning, so the research is regarded as a "wild" study.

Hartwig, W. (ed.). *The Primate Fossil Record*. Cambridge: Cambridge University Press, 2002. This is the "last word" on the evolution of primate suborders, superfamilies, and species, as known from the fossil record. All articles are written by specialists and presented in the same format, so this book provides an accessible guide to the comparative method in evolutionary primatology.

Martin, R. *Primate Origins and Evolution: A Phylogenetic Reconstruction*. Princeton, NJ: Princeton University Press, 1990. A chronologically based description of how and why primates evolved, written before the impact of molecular dating. The book emphasizes the early evolution of primates.

McGrew, W. *Chimpanzee Material Culture*. Cambridge: Cambridge University Press, 1992. The suggestion that humans are not alone in having culture has come a long way since McGrew first proposed the idea in 1992 in this book. He backs up his claim with carefully chosen examples, most from his own experience.

Walker, A., and P. Shipman. *The Ape in the Tree*. Cambridge, MA: Harvard University Press, 2005. Alan Walker has found as many *Proconsul* fossils as anyone and calls himself a "fossil hunter." Here, he describes, in anecdotal rather than purely scientific style, his discoveries in a way that puts the reader "into the picture."

# Early Hominids in Africa:
# *Australopithecus* and *Homo habilis*

*Chapter* **6**

■ **WHAT IS A HOMINID?**

■ **HOMINID TRENDS**
Bipedalism • Why Bipedalism? • A Hominid Story • Brain Size and Complexity • Teeth and Dental Context • Reduction of Face and Jaws • Hairlessness

■ **TAXONOMY AND NUMBER OF SPECIES OF HOMINIDS**

■ **THE GENUS *AUSTRALOPITHECUS***
Australopithecine Taxonomy • Australopithecine Sites and Dates • Describing Australopithecines • What Happened to the Australopithecines?

■ **HIGHLIGHT 6.1:** *In the Field with Don Johanson*
■ **HIGHLIGHT 6.2:** *In the News with the Piltdown Forgery*
■ **HIGHLIGHT 6.3:** *Prey or Predators?*

■ **ENTER THE GENUS *HOMO***
Homo habilis
■ **HIGHLIGHT 6.4:** *The Other Evolving Sex*

■ **CHAPTER SUMMARY**

▲
**Photo above:** The remains of one *A. afarensis*, the famous "Lucy"

The closer to the present the story of human evolution gets, the more interesting it becomes. Saying that humans have an ancestry in common with bacteria is likely to induce yawns or shrugs. Saying that humans have a common ancestry with all living monkeys might get some attention. But the question of whether Neandertals were or were not in the ancestry of modern humans sparks considerable interest. To whom are humans most closely related? Did humans really evolve from apes? What is it that makes humans different from apes? Just who are we? What does it mean to be human?

The most relevant question might be "What differentiates humans from apes?" Because there are observable, measurable, and objective biological traits that differentiate the two groups, theoretically scientists should be able to describe the last common ancestor (LCA) that split into the pongid and hominid lineages and then describe the evolution of the lineages. Molecular comparisons should reveal when the split happened.

The most obvious difference between modern apes and modern humans is locomotion. Humans are bipedal and apes are not. Some apes brachiate (swing on tree limbs), such as gibbons and siamangs; the rest are mostly quadrupedal, walking with their backs at an angle and their forelimb weight on either their knuckles or their fists (see Figure 6.1). The African apes give evidence of a previous evolutionary stage of semibrachiation in the form of having forelimbs longer than their hind limbs; they have become mostly terrestrial knuckle-walkers, probably as an adaptation to increases in size and weight. Chimpanzees and bonobos still do some brachiation; orangutans also brachiate when arboreal but walk on their fists when terrestrial. At the split, 6 myr ago, the African pongids began to specialize in knuckle walking and the earliest hominids began to specialize in bipedalism, both having evolved from the hypothesized LCA. That likely generalized quadrupedal LCA was perhaps equally adept in trees and on the ground. Unambiguous locomotor specialization shows up in neither fossil record before about 5 myr ago. Names such as "bipedal ape" or "ecological ape" or "intelligent ape" have been given to earliest hominid populations, but it would be just as appropriate to call the earliest pongid populations "knuckle-walking humans" or "dumb humans." Because the pongid lineage had its own evolutionary history after it branched from hominids, this chapter continues the story of evolution with the hominid lineage only.

## What Is a Hominid?

A proper definition of hominids must include past and present populations of the family Hominidae, beginning with the first hominids and continuing through modern humans. Most anthropologists use **bipedalism** as the single diagnostic trait to identify this lineage, believing that the trait has served well for this purpose ever since Johann Blumenbach proposed it in 1775 (Bramble 2002). This diagnostic approach is based not just on the single trait of bipedalism, but rather on all of what bipedalism implies. This change in locomotion was not only a new adaptation; it gave rise to a relatively new way of life that affected many morphological and behavioral traits and complexes. However, some anthropologists use dentition for identification in lieu of any anatomical locomotor clues or in combination with bipedal locomotion (Pilbeam 1968). Other traits are either not derived or not unique (Caspari 2002). So although it becomes increasingly difficult to identify definitive signs of bipedalism as ancestry gets closer to the split with pongids, if bipedalism is used as the single trait, diagnosing hominids is at least possible. If hominid status is defined by a multiplicity of traits, it becomes far more difficult. It is certainly possible that bipedalism evolved more than once in primates, complicating which groups were or were not in the lineage that led to modern humans.

**bipedalism**
Movement on two hind legs in a striding motion.

*Figure 6.1*

**MONKEY, APE, AND HUMAN LOCOMOTION.**　Locomotion is often a diagnostic trait of primates. Compare arms and legs for size, noting the differences among generalized quadrupeds (monkey on left), brachiators/knuckle-walkers (ape in middle), and bipeds (human on right). What types of arm and leg anatomy are needed for each type of locomotion?

*Source*: Based on Fleagle (1988).

In addition to locomotor differences, modern humans and, say, modern chimpanzees show a striking morphological contrast: A multitude of cosmetic differences between the two groups are expressed in every inch of bone and skin. Genetically, however, the two species are very similar. Some experts believe each of the genetic differences may have multiple functions, accounting for the wide morphological differences. For example, chimpanzees and humans have the same number of bones (206), but a comparison of their skeletons would show differences in the shape and size of every bone. It is important to remember that although the hominid and pongid groups inherited most of their common traits from the LCA, each lineage has had its own evolutionary trajectory for the past 6 myr, and each has added traits unique to itself (see Figure 6.2).

# Hominid Trends

Of all the traits identified with hominids, bipedalism occurred first, setting the stage for numerous associated derived traits and becoming, as we've noted, the diagnostic trait for most experts. Brain size and complexity, often cited as what makes humans unique,

*Figure 6.2*

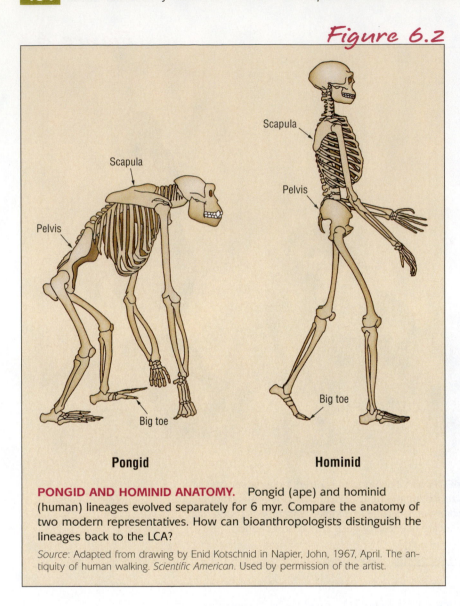

**Pongid**

**Hominid**

Scapula

Scapula

Pelvis

Pelvis

Big toe

Big toe

**PONGID AND HOMINID ANATOMY.** Pongid (ape) and hominid (human) lineages evolved separately for 6 myr. Compare the anatomy of two modern representatives. How can bioanthropologists distinguish the lineages back to the LCA?

*Source*: Adapted from drawing by Enid Kotschnid in Napier, John, 1967, April. The antiquity of human walking. *Scientific American*. Used by permission of the artist.

showed only minor changes from hominoid ancestry until long after bipedalism was established. Relative to body size, early hominids had brains no larger and probably no more complex than their hominoid ancestors or their early pongid cousins. Only later, and only as one hominid trend among many, did brains increase in size and complexity.

## Bipedalism

By all criteria, becoming bipedal was an evolutionary big deal in human history. Although hominids are not the only animals to be habitually bipedal (kangaroos and birds are other examples), they evolved bipedalism from an ancestor that probably was a generalized quadrupedal hominoid; all subsequent evolutionary change in hominid locomotion was contingent on that earlier generalized body plan. The fossil record suggests that **quadrupedalism** gave way to bipedalism in two stages—the first between 6 and 4.5 myr ago, when major anatomical changes took place, and the second between 3 and 2 myr ago, when modern limb proportions evolved. Although many anatomical traits changed rather drastically, no bones were added or subtracted; rather, changes to existing bones and muscles gradually added up to an efficient biped.

The most important question about bipedalism concerns why it evolved; but before addressing that question, let's look in some detail at *what* evolved. Picture a generalized quadruped that walks palmigrade standing next to a specialized brachiator/knuckle-walker and a specialized biped, as shown in Figure 6.1. The comparison is striking, because every inch of the body plan would have been affected when the generalized quadruped evolved into the two specialized locomotor lineages. The totality of walking on two feet is fairly complex. Imagine a slow-motion video of a human walking: If the biped stands motionless and begins to take a step, the weight of the body is shifted to the moving leg. When the foot of that leg hits the ground on its heel, the body weight has already shifted and the other leg now swings forward. As this occurs, the other foot pushes off and the body moves forward. Repeat, and the biped walks! But the process takes considerable balance and coordination, if not a lot of thinking about each move. Balance in bipeds results from straight legs; a vertebral curve; and the orientation of the pelvis that gives a low center of gravity over the hips, knees, and feet (Bramble 2002). So the transition to bipedalism would have involved basic changes in the position of the head on the spinal cord, the curvature of the spine, the shape of the pelvis, the proportions of the hind limbs versus the forelimbs, the length of the femur, and many details of the feet, right down to changes in big toes.

**quadrupedalism**
Movement with four limbs making contact with the ground or tree limbs and usually with the spine parallel to the ground.

1.   A quadrupedal primate carries its *head* high enough off the ground and its eyes forward enough to see most predators and locate food. The foramen magnum in quadrupedal primates is located halfway between the back of the skull and the middle of the base of the skull. A bipedal animal literally carries its head on top of its spinal column, so the foramen magnum is directly in the middle of the base of the skull. Because hominids evolved from hominoids, the foramen magnum had to evolve to a position in the middle of the base of the skull so that the skull (small though it was at the time) could sit directly on top of the spinal cord, which passes into it.

2.   A quadruped puts its *weight* relatively equally on all four limbs and walks efficiently with its backbone bowed upward or fairly straight from tail to neck. When bipedalism evolved, the body's center of gravity had to change. Additionally, in order to compensate for the constant pounding of feet and the weight of heavy skulls, the bipedal lineage evolved an *S-curved spine* that absorbs these stresses. The curve at the neck allows the skull to sit on the vertebral column through the foramen magnum, and the curve in the lower spine facilitates the orientation of the pelvic girdle. The two together allow for necessary flexibility when the biped is walking or running.

3.   The *pelvis* of quadrupeds is long and narrow; the pelvis of bipeds became basket-shaped, both to accommodate more musculature for hind limb locomotion and to support internal organs and the upper half of the body, which was no longer supported by forelimbs. The pelvis still had to allow females to carry fetuses internally.

4.   Quadrupedal animals have limbs of relatively equal proportions. Hominids evolved *long hind limbs* relative to forelimbs. One of the most obvious changes from hominoid to hominid anatomy is in the absolute length of the *femur*. Not only did the elongated femur make bipedal striding more efficient, but its longer length also allowed for greater muscle attachment—a necessity for constant walking on two legs. The angle at the knee, formed by the relative positions of the pelvis, knee, and ankle, changed. When a quadruped (such as a modern chimpanzee) stands, its knees are directly below the juncture of the pelvis and the femur heads, and the legs continue down to the ankle parallel to each other. By comparison, as shown in Figure 6.3, bipeds are knock-kneed, with the femur angled inward toward the midline of the body, the knees together, and the lower bones continuing straight to the ankle. This kind of alignment allows bipeds to walk in a relatively straight line instead of tottering from side to side with bent knees, as a quadruped does when walking bipedally.

5.   Finally, bipedalism required a redesign of the entire anatomy of the *foot* (but without the loss or addition of any bones). The divergent big toe, so vital in grasping tree limbs, would be a detriment to a smooth bipedal gait. Bipeds' feet evolved from grasping organs to flexible walking platforms; all their toes became shorter and lost flexibility, and the big toes lined up next to the other toes rather than continuing as foot thumbs.

All of these anatomical changes were needed for efficient bipedalism, but they certainly did not all evolve at exactly the same time; nor did total bipedalism occur overnight. Although it could be said jokingly that the last hominoid spent 51 percent of its time quadrupedally and 49 percent bipedally, whereas the first hominid spent 51 percent of its

*Figure 6.3*

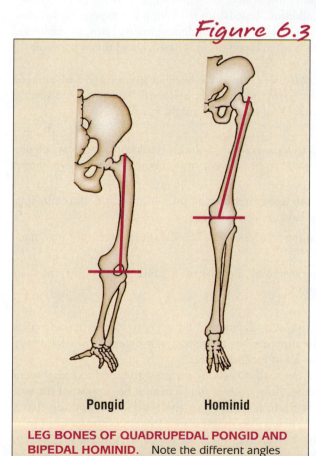

**Pongid          Hominid**

**LEG BONES OF QUADRUPEDAL PONGID AND BIPEDAL HOMINID.**   Note the different angles at the hip, knee, and ankle joints. How is each body plan beneficial to each type of primate?

*Source:* From Lewin, R. 1989. *Human evolution: An illustrated introduction.* 2nd ed. Boston: Blackwell, p. 67. Reprinted by permission of Blackwell Publishing.

time bipedally and 49 percent quadrupedally, both modes of locomotion probably were equally efficient for early hominids and continued to be exploited for several million years. Even after bipedalism became the dominant mode of locomotion for early hominids, fossilized foot bones and elongated arms relative to legs indicate that they still exploited trees, probably for food and as safe sleeping places. The term **facultative bipedalism** refers to transitional bipedalism—the pattern that prevailed when early hominids were as much at home in trees as on the ground but were bipedal when terrestrial. In contrast, **habitual bipedalism** is a totally bipedal locomotive pattern. But there are groups showing transitions between the two modes of locomotion as a facultative group did not evolve to a habitual group in a single generation.

## Why Bipedalism?

Why did bipedalism evolve? Why would a seemingly successful quadrupedal hominoid population have changed its means of locomotion so drastically? After all, bipedalism has numerous disadvantages relative to quadrupedalism. As one obvious disadvantage, bipedalism makes individuals more obvious to predators than quadrupedalism does; it also exposes to predators vulnerable parts of the body that quadrupeds can protect; it is not as fast as quadrupedal running; and it can cause considerably more hardship if an individual is injured. If a dog or any other quadruped injures its leg or paw, it can hop around on three legs until the wound has healed. If a biped injures its leg or foot, however, the result may be death. In addition, bipedalism is biologically expensive, because pumping blood up instead of horizontally to the brain defies gravity. Hips, lower backs, knees, and ankles all take extra strain when locomotion is bipedal, and this is particularly true for pregnant females.

In view of all this, it is clear that there must have been strong selective advantages for bipeds to have evolved from successful quadrupeds. Scientists have proposed several single-faceted hypotheses as to what these advantages might have been:

1. Bipedalism allowed hominids to look over large objects (rocks or grass) and see potential predators and/or possible food resources; this enabled them to live longer and reproduce more.

2. Bipedalism freed hominids from using their forelimbs in locomotion, thus allowing them to carry objects such as food and/or babies.

3. By freeing hominid forelimbs from locomotion, bipedalism allowed tool manufacturing and use.

4. Under certain ecological circumstances, bipedalism is more energy efficient than quadrupedalism for food getting.

**facultative bipedalism**
An early form of human bipedalism, probably used from 6 myr to 1.8 myr ago, that likely was accomplished with the knees bent and without a full stride.

**habitual bipedalism**
The modern form of human bipedalism that first appeared in the fossil record about 1.8 myr ago (*Homo erectus* times) and that is accomplished with straight legs and full strides.

Each of the first three hypotheses has serious faults; although each can be thought of as a result of bipedalism, none can be supported as the reason why bipedalism was initially advantageous enough to overcome all of its disadvantages.

The hypothesis about *looking* over tall objects to see predators or food may seem logical as an explanation of why bipedalism evolved, but it cannot be supported for several reasons. If the environment were heavily forested, there would be nothing that a hominid could actually look over by being 4 feet instead of 2 feet tall; if the environment were mixed scattered trees and short savanna grass, there would be nothing to see over. Only if the ground cover were thick tall grass would the ability to see over the grass be advantageous. But many monkeys and most apes are able to spend time on two legs periodically by standing, jumping, or tottering—so habitual bipedalism is not a prerequisite for seeing predators, prey, or food, even if there is thick tall grass. Finally, if environmental specialists are correct, the African environment during the time when bipedalism likely emerged was a mosaic of woods and open grasslands (see Figure 6.4).

*Figure 6.4*

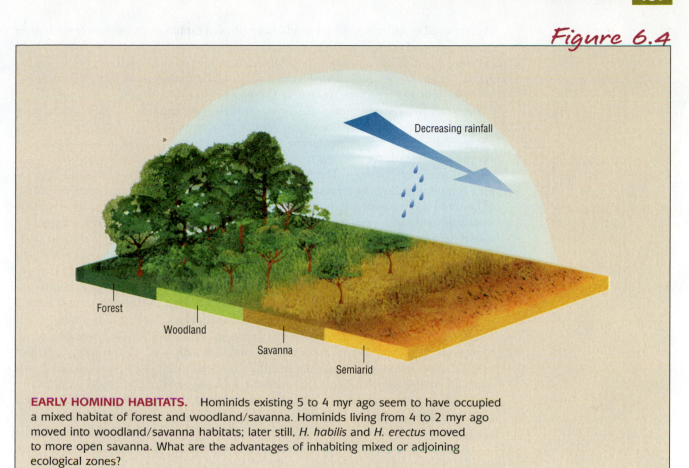

Decreasing rainfall

Forest

Woodland

Savanna

Semiarid

**EARLY HOMINID HABITATS.**   Hominids existing 5 to 4 myr ago seem to have occupied a mixed habitat of forest and woodland/savanna. Hominids living from 4 to 2 myr ago moved into woodland/savanna habitats; later still, *H. habilis* and *H. erectus* moved to more open savanna. What are the advantages of inhabiting mixed or adjoining ecological zones?

There were no visual impediments from quadrupedalism that would have made being bipedal advantageous (Tappan 2001).

The *carrying* hypothesis also lacks support. Modern quadrupedal primates usually eat food where they find it. Most food eaten by quadrupedal primates isn't worth carrying because the individual bits are so small that they would often be dropped. Nuts, berries, and so forth are all better eaten on the spot. Although quadrupedal primates may carry food in their mouths for short distances into trees so as to eat with more safety, long-distance carrying does not seem vital. Also, quadrupedal primates are less likely to drop their offspring than bipedal humans, because the infants of quadrupeds have grasping reflexes and cling to the fur on their mother's bellies. When bipeds drop their offspring, the infants can be severely injured, because they fall from a greater height. Carrying, therefore, does not translate into safer transportation (Hewes 1964).

The *tool manufacturing and use* hypothesis is attributed to Darwin and was upgraded by Sherwood Washburn in the 1960s, but it too can be dismissed for several reasons. First, tool use and manufacturing do not require bipedalism; rather, tool manufacturing requires hands that can manipulate raw materials. Besides, primates usually make tools sitting down, so locomotion is not involved. Additionally, the archaeological record shows that stone tool manufacturing did not begin until almost 2 myr after bipedalism was well established. It is very unlikely that bipedalism evolved to set hands free for tool making some 2 myr later.

In short, being able to look over objects, to carry objects or offspring, or to make and use tools can be considered an effect of bipedalism but is not likely a cause of it. Once bipedalism was established, hands could be used to manufacture and use tools and to carry food or offspring. And it would have allowed hominids to constantly see higher over the ground cover than their quadrupedal cousins. But because each of these possible functions of bipedalism was counterbalanced by the relative advantages of quadrupedalism, the cause of bipedalism is likely to be found elsewhere.

The fourth hypothesis, known as the **bioenergetics/thermoregulation model**, seems to answer the question of why bipedalism evolved reasonably well. It also meshes well with current knowledge about the African environment of the time. As a model, it has several necessary elements, including an environmental context that would favor a sweating, efficiently locomoting biped. It is assumed that Central or East Africa is the original home of hominids, because the first generally agreed-upon hominid remains were found there. Ecological reconstruction of Central and East Africa at the likely time of hominid evolution envisions major forests giving way to a mix of scattered deciduous woodland and semi-open savanna (Vignaud et al. 2002; Vrba 1995). Food resources would have been patchy in scattered woodland or open savanna (Foley 1987; Panger et al. 2003). Several million years later, hominids appear to have favored semi-open to open environments (refer to Figure 6.4).

In terms of bioenergetics, this fourth hypothesis argues that bipedalism is an energy-efficient means of locomotion under certain circumstances. Specifically, although quadrupedalism is twice as energy efficient as bipedalism at top running speed for short periods of time, bipedalism is energy efficient at slower speeds over longer periods of time (Foley 1992; Wheeler 1991b). And in the bioenergetics/thermoregulation model, endurance is more important than speed, and less heat is generated in the legs of bipedal than quadrupedal animals. Slower-walking animals with good eyesight, standing 4 feet tall, could see and exploit patchy food resources as they walked, whereas shorter but faster animals would run by the same resources. But for bipedal primates to be successful, they would have had to be able to walk many hours every day in search of the patchy resources: an unfinished haunch of antelope here, some underground melons there. If energy efficiency is defined as the amount of energy expended to complete a particular task, then bipedalism appears to be efficient under Africa's patchy resource ecology at the time the first hominids became bipedal.

The thermoregulation piece of this model relates to the time of activity. Given that large African carnivores were active in the early morning and in the mid- to late afternoon, the only safe time for hominids to search for food would have been when the carnivores were napping. Unfortunately, that meant the hottest time of the day—mid-morning to midafternoon. A generalized quadruped, such as a hominoid, would not have been successful at foraging for food in semi-open savanna or woodland during high sun time at the same time that intensive activity generated internal body heat, because the animal would not have had sufficient ways to cool off. Because modern apes as well as humans sweat, it is assumed that African hominoids also sweated—but not to the degree that humans do today, and probably not enough to avoid thermal stress. In contrast, a bipedal hominid that had evolved highly effective sweat glands and stood off the floor of the hot patchy woods or savanna, benefiting from some breeze, could survive this kind of thermal stress. Natural selection would have favored mutations that led to a more efficient sweating system, and this would explain why modern humans have the greatest sweating capacity of any animal species. The cost of water loss through sweating is relatively high, so hominids would have needed a constant source of water for replenishment. One estimate suggests that early bipeds living in mixed terrain would have needed to drink 1½ to 2½ liters of water a day. Perhaps this is why the majority of fossils of early bipeds have been found near ancient lakes and rivers. Another important point regarding thermoregulation is that bipeds expose only about one-third as much of their bodies to direct solar radiation as quadrupeds, thus being able to stay cooler (Foley 1987; Wheeler 1991a, 1991b, 1994). Although the time at which hominids became less hairy is not known, early hominids may have had less body hair than hominoids but as much head hair as modern apes and hominids, with the head hair acting as insulation for the brain. Reduced body hair would have meant more naked skin and thus more effective sweating.

**bioenergetics/ thermoregulation model**
The coupling of two ideas to explain the evolution of bipedalism: the energy efficiency of using two legs to walk slowly while looking for food and the reduction of thermal stress that resulted from being upright in the hot savanna (and being able to sweat).

If the bioenergetics/thermoregulation model is basically correct, the road to bipedalism was not an all-or-nothing evolutionary event. Mixed woodlands and lightly treed savannas suggest an ideal combination for mixed quadrupedal/arboreal and bipedal/terrestrial locomotion. Grasping feet and flexible arms would have allowed early hominids to quadrupedally exploit trees for food and as sleeping refuges and to bipedally exploit the more open savannas and areas among the trees for different food resources. Flexibility was advantageous in an environment that was not always wood-land *or* savanna but instead changed through time. And the most successful hominoid groups, those that evolved further, may have been those that were on the overlapping or adjacent edges of two econiches, where they could exploit food resources by means of two kinds of locomotion. Since 84 percent of chimpanzee bipedalism today occurs when they are feeding (reaching for fruits above their heads, for example), the LCA is likely to have been quite comfortable bipedally even if not truly committed to that form of locomotion (Bailey 1993).

## A Hominid Story

French paleontologist Yves Coppens (1994), elaborating on an idea by Adrian Kortlandt (Tattersall 2000a), provides a general and workable causation model for the split of the LCA into pongid and hominid lineages. The model combines features of the bioenerget-ics/thermoregulation model within an ecologic, geographic, and geologic context, and it is supported by most of the fossil evidence. Between 1960 and 1980 several teams exca-vated late Miocene beds in East Africa, looking for various missing links between homi-noids and hominids. Coppens plotted the distribution of the 200,000 excavated bones on a map and showed that all hominoid fossils that were older than 3 myr and had been found east of the Great Rift were hominids, without a single pongid bone. His model, which he appropriately titled "The East Side Story," sees LCA groups roaming through-out East Africa until 8 myr ago, followed by a tectonic crisis that produced the Great Rift Valley. The rift resulted in two distinct regions, each with a somewhat different climate and ground cover. The area west of the Rift remained humid and forested, and the west-ern branch of the LCA groups evolved to brachiating and then knuckle-walking pongids. Either gorillas had split off a million years earlier and the rest of the western branch con-tinued for another million years, eventually evolving to modern chimpanzees and bono-bos, or that western branch split to gorillas, chimpanzees, and bonobos by 6 myr ago. By contrast, the area east of the Rift became dryer, resulting in fewer trees and more open ground cover, and the eastern branch of the LCA groups evolved to bipedal hominids. It is a sobering comment on contingency to realize that if this model is correct, had it not been for the oceanic plate movements that created the Great Rift Valley, there would not have been a hominid lineage, just a continuation of forest hominoids.

If the recently discovered *Sahelanthropus tchadensis* from Chad in Central Africa proves to be hominid, the geographic/geologic part of this story will have to be modi-fied. The environmental context for bipedalism will not be affected, however, because most of Africa had a mixed cover of trees and savanna similar to that of East Africa at the time following the Great Rift (Vignaud et al. 2002).

Although most experts agree that bipedalism is the distinguishing characteristic of hominids, particularly for purposes of identification in the fossil record, other hominid traits evolved as well: brain size and complexity; size of teeth, face, and jaws; and hair-lessness. All of these traits had their beginnings during the first million years of hominidness. Fifty thousand human generations is more than enough for these major changes to have occurred (Cronin 1983). Let's consider those other hominid traits.

## Brain Size and Complexity

Brain cases do not normally fossilize, but researchers can measure brain sizes and re-construct some aspects of structure by making endocasts of the insides of fossil cra-nia. The meanings of the brain's convolution patterns, grooves, and enlarged areas or

## Figure 6.5

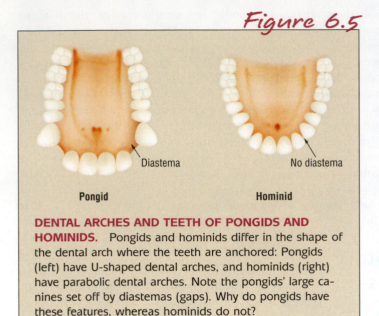

Diastema

No diastema

**Pongid**                 **Hominid**

**DENTAL ARCHES AND TEETH OF PONGIDS AND HOMINIDS.**   Pongids and hominids differ in the shape of the dental arch where the teeth are anchored: Pongids (left) have U-shaped dental arches, and hominids (right) have parabolic dental arches. Note the pongids' large canines set off by diastemas (gaps). Why do pongids have these features, whereas hominids do not?

**brain evolution**
An evolutionary step that followed bipedalism in later hominids and resulted in larger and more complex brains, allowing the development of problem-solving abilities and behavioral changes.

bumps are controversial, but early hominid brains exhibit more complex patterning than do the brains of hominoids, past or present. Over time hominid brain size increased dramatically, convolutions became far more internally folded, and grooves increased in number. The changes brought by **brain evolution** translated generally to superior problem-solving abilities in later hominids, as well as to greater ability to process information about the natural and social environment. Bigger and more complex brains also would have resulted in more effective ways to scavenge and, later, to hunt large game, along with greater ability to make efficient tools. The increased complexity probably also translated into better communication among members of local bands, including eventual language and speech.

## Teeth and Dental Context

Hominid dentition changed over time, though the pattern was established fairly early. Generally, the dental arch became parabolic rather than U-shaped, which is the ancestral hominoid shape (see Figure 6.5). Even the earliest hominids had fairly small canines and little to no accompanying diastema. Size of teeth is one aspect of change between evolutionary grades of hominids, especially in different areas of the mouth; for example, front teeth become larger and molar teeth become smaller.

## Reduction of Face and Jaws

Early hominids' faces and jaws were large relative to their crania, but the proportion decreased over time. This change was due more to skull size increase than to facial reduction. The relative placement of faces in relation to crania also changed, with crania moving from behind the face to a position on top; the increase in the forebrain was partially responsible. Jaws diminished in size as teeth became smaller.

## Hairlessness

Pliocene hominoids were likely covered with hair like modern apes, but hair on modern humans is restricted to only a few parts of the body, so the degree of hairiness had an evolutionary trajectory. It has been hypothesized that hair on hominid heads is important in heat conservation and cooling, protecting the brain from overheating or over-cooling. When reduction in body hair began is not known, but it is logical to argue that hominids lost their hairiness when they left Africa for areas of less sun. In less sunny regions a loss of body hair would have been a selective advantage, because less hair would have allowed more exposure to sunlight and thus higher production of vitamin D. If hair reduction did correlate with movement out of Africa, then it began between 2 and 1 myr ago.

# Taxonomy and Number of Species of Hominids

As already established, experts often disagree in assigning taxonomic status to populations and fossils because they have different paradigmatic biases as will be noted below. There is no perfect taxonomy and each must be thought of as a hypothesis to be tested.

Given evolutionary principles, the kind of animal that hominids are, and the amount of time that has elapsed since their first appearance around 6 myr ago, how many species can be predicted to have ever existed in the hominid lineage? Experts agree far more on the general "grades" and trends of hominids than on the number of predicted species or on predictions of the fossil record. Let's look at a grade scheme first. Grade schemes are based on general adaptations of groups that may or may not be separate species. Adaptations that are indicated by locomotion, diet, brain size, and body shape are typically reflected in the fossil record (Collard and Wood 1999). A chronologically ordered grade scheme places the australopithecines and *Homo habilis* in Grade 1, *Homo erectus* (or in another version, up to three species) in Grade 2, and Neandertals and anatomically modern humans (*Homo sapiens* or *Homo neandertalensis* and *Homo sapiens*) in Grade 3 (Collard 2002). (Subsequent chapters will discuss these populations/species.) Robert Foley (1999) put more flesh on similar categories by calling Grade 1 "Africa savanna bipedal hominids," Grade 2 "intelligent opportunists," and Grade 3 "technological colonizers." Although grades by definition are very general and not taxonomic in the traditional sense, most experts would find little fault with these grades or their membership.

Now let's turn to the more contentious issue of how many species there were in the human lineage. Currently, the number of identified hominid species ranges between 5 and 21, depending on the scheme. Glenn Conroy (2002) compared all mammals of the same body size as humans to predict the number of species in the human lineage. Robert Foley (1991) predicted the number of species on the basis of the length of time it would take a large land animal to both transform itself into a new species and diverge right after a successful change in body plan (in this case, bipedalism). Other experts have looked at the different morphology of fossils that appear to be in the human lineage and, using their knowledge of anatomy, have predicted when speciations occurred and then counted those instances. Though it may never be known for certain how many species comprise the human lineage, 5 is probably too few and 21 too many.

One reason for the lack of consensus on the number of hominid species is that experts differ in their approaches in terms of using phenetics or cladistics to work out taxonomic relationships and species evolution and in whether they are "lumpers" or "splitters." Let's look at these two sets of paradigms (see Figures 6.6 and 6.7).

Scientists use different paradigms, or models, to try to understand evolution, which can result in different species counts. Some experts, mostly lumpers, prefer a population model: They see populations of individuals as evolving through time, sometimes as a group and sometimes splitting to form new, separate lineages. Taxonomic classifications based on this approach, referred to as **phenetics**, result from the total overall biological similarity between various groups. In comparing species that appear to be closely related, this approach uses at least 100 characteristics—morphological, behavioral, anatomical—in a computer-assisted assessment of overall biological similarities between and among the groups being assessed. The phenetic approach assumes that some traits and complexes of traits are adaptationally and functionally more important than others and gives more weight to those. For example, phenetic taxonomies give more weight to the type of locomotion used than to the number of cusps on a molar tooth. Phenetic approaches have been criticized for being subjective because of this weighting.

The alternative approach, or paradigm, is called **cladistics**. Adherents of cladistics theoretically give all traits equal weight in identifying species, meaning that bipedalism would not be given more weight than the number of cusps on a molar. Additionally, only shared and derived traits of the species being analyzed are used to build taxonomies. Most splitters are cladists. Some bioanthropologists have suggested that cladistics works far better on bugs, of which there are thousands of species, than on hominids, of which there are perhaps 15. It is not surprising to find that the scientist who invented the cladistic approach in the early 1970s was an entomologist. Subsequently, fish biologists and paleontologists put cladistics to good use because of the sheer numbers of fossil fish species.

**phenetics**
A paradigm, or model, that stresses the overall similarities among organisms in forming biological classifications.

**cladistics**
A paradigm, or model, that stresses evolutionary relationships based only on a number of derived and shared traits as opposed to ancestral traits.

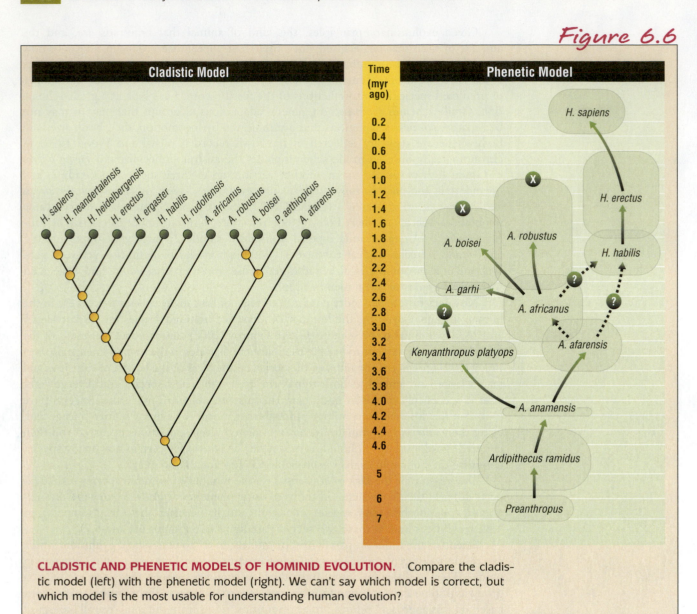

*Figure 6.6*

**CLADISTIC AND PHENETIC MODELS OF HOMINID EVOLUTION.** Compare the cladistic model (left) with the phenetic model (right). We can't say which model is correct, but which model is the most usable for understanding human evolution?

**modern taxa**
Species that evolved sometime in the past and that have contemporary descendents.

The main goal of cladistics is to predict the actual relationships between **modern taxa**, and it is probably better at this than phenetics because its users must be explicit about the morphological traits they use to model an evolutionary tree. However, cladistics has some disadvantages as well. First, it gives the erroneous impression that all changes occurred at the splits of a tree's branches and twigs, whereas changes actually accrue along the branches as well (Shipman 2002). Second, cladistics requires making some assumptions that cannot at present be substantiated, such as the assumption that derived traits evolved only once. If a trait such as a prehensile tail in New World monkeys evolved twice, it would confound the cladistic model (Trinkaus 1992). Third, since there can be a difference of opinion as to the selection of characteristics used, the cladistic approach is as subjective as the cladists accused pheneticists of being. And, although cladists claim that each characteristic is given equal weight in assigning relationships, it depends on whether the characteristics can be joined as complexes or not. For example, if 60 cranio-dental (skull/teeth) traits are used to establish relationships among a series

*Figure 6.7*

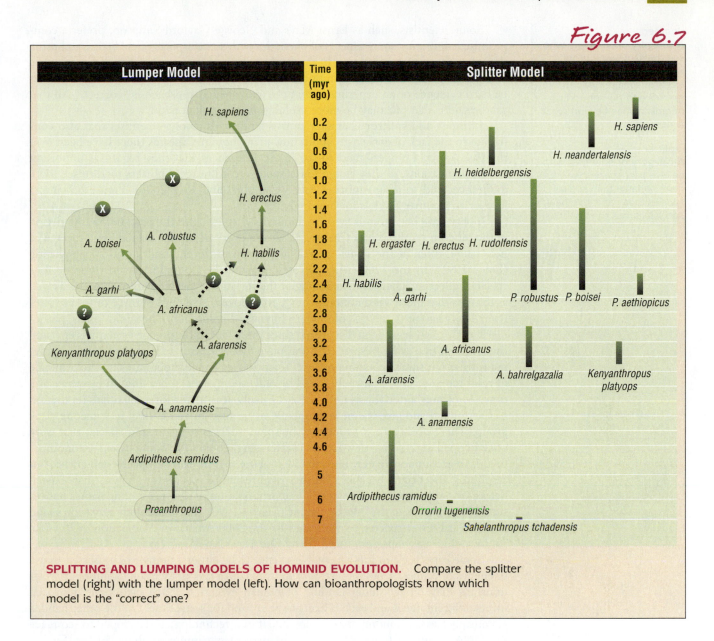

**SPLITTING AND LUMPING MODELS OF HOMINID EVOLUTION.** Compare the splitter model (right) with the lumper model (left). How can bioanthropologists know which model is the "correct" one?

of bovids, is each trait independent or part of some functional complex of traits that vary together? If all 60 of these traits are entered individually into the cladistic formula as 12 facial, 20 dental, 7 mandibular, 8 base-of-skull shape, and 13 cranial vault, the results could be quite different than if five functional complexes are entered: encephalization, mouth area protrusion, the angle of the base of the skull, chewing with molars, and biting with incisors. Even something as seemingly simple as determining the length of crania can be problematic; if 11 measurements are involved, is crania length 1 or 11 traits (Wesson 2005)? Until these kinds of problems are resolved, it is folly to claim that each trait is given equal weight (McHenry 2002). Two analyses by two different cladists can come to two different conclusions and end up with two different sets of relationships. Even two cladists using the same characteristics but different computer programs can end up with different results (Kimbel et al. 2004). Finally, cladistics does not take time into account at all, only relationships and their degree of differences (Walker and Shipman 2005). Ironically, if scientists applied cladistics to contemporary humans, they would conclude that there are at least six species, whereas of course there is but one.

**lumper**
A category of scientists who
see the same amount of
variability in past species as
exists in similar modern
species and do not add taxonomic names beyond what
is necessary.

**splitter**
A category of scientists who
believe past species were
more variable than similar
species today and give new
species names to new finds.

Some scientists, such as Ernst Mayr and George Gaylord Simpson, prefer a compromise, combining some aspects of phenetics with some aspects of cladistics, and using the strengths of each paradigm. In the final analysis, phenetics versus cladistics is only a debate about how to classify groups and only of real interest to a few. There will never be hard evidence or an experiment that can show which approach is "correct." All that can be said is that one may be more useful given the task at hand.

**Lumper** and **splitter** characterize two tendencies among scientists that also contribute to the lack of consensus about how many hominid species there have been over the past 6 myr. Lumpers tend to see fewer differences that they regard as important within populations, so they assign fewer species to a lineage. Splitters tend to see more differences and to assign more species (Campbell and Rice 2008). Figure 6.7 shows lumper and splitter models for hominid evolution.

There have been trends favoring lumping or splitting in the past; before the period of the modern synthesis (see Chapter 3), almost every newly discovered fossil received a new name, often at the genus as well as the species level, resulting in supersplitting (Foley 1991). In the 1980s Mayr severely pruned the hominid tree to three or four species, reflecting a new understanding of the variation expected within a species as well as the idea that there was a nonbranching, evolutionary sequence of three or four species from 4 myr ago until the rise of modern humans. Because more hominid fossils, particularly early ones, have been discovered since the 1980s, most modern scientists envision the hominid tree as far bushier than was once thought, with a number of species evolving further but some becoming extinct. Scientists also once thought, using the principle of resource exclusion, that there could be only one species of hominid in existence at a time. They now agree this is not the case. Finally, it is better for a scientist's reputation to find a fossil and give it a new taxonomic name than to add a fossil to someone else's group. Therefore, there is a tendency by some workers to again split species that were once lumped and to give new names to even single bones. To some extent taxonomists do this to accommodate new finds that do not seem to fit existing species categories, but resplitting also occurs because cladistics requires more species for analysis than existed before that approach was developed. The proliferation of new taxonomic names has resulted in confusion in the minds of many (Martin 1990). The pendulum may soon swing back toward fewer species, as witnessed by the 2000 American Association of Physical Anthropologists symposium titled "Read Our Lips: No More Taxa."

Some experts claim it is acceptable science to be either a lumper or a splitter, to use phenetics or cladistics, but unnecessary splitting and a lack of focus on evolutionary relationships may hinder understanding of human evolution. Each taxonomic approach meets different needs and each is likely to be around for some time. On the other hand, a genetically based taxonomy may be possible if new technology is developed to sequence the DNA of animal bones older than the present maximum of about 50 kyr. Such a methodology would put both phenetic and cladistic approaches on a historical shelf.

Taking direction from William of Ockham (ca. 1285–1349), the English philosopher who is credited with the principle of logic that says no more things should be presumed to exist than are absolutely necessary, this book uses a lumper model, employing geographical terms to differentiate populations when appropriate: The hominid tree will have only as many branches or twigs as are needed. We will mention other taxonomic schemes, however, because of the lack of consensus in the literature. Although the cladistic model has recently gained in popularity and has certain advantages, the phenetic approach is more compatible with our lumper tendencies and our population perspective.

# The Genus
# *Australopithecus*

The genus *Australopithecus* is regarded by all paleoanthropologists as being hominid because of the group's demonstrated bipedalism. As noted in Chapter 5, however, earlier bipedal hominids may have existed in the time period between 7 and 5 myr ago. The connection between any of those potential first hominids and the genus *Australopithecus* may be shown by the finds of *Ardipithecus ramidus* and, more recently, *Australopithecus anamensis* in the same geographic area in Ethiopia. The sites are only about an hour's walk from each other. It is perhaps too early to make a strong claim for this link, but the connection is not unlikely given the time, place, and morphology of both populations (White et al. 2006).

Before the first fossil of the group now called the **australopithecines** was discovered in 1925, human paleontologists knew that fossils demonstrating human ancestry did exist, but they were still searching for that special "missing link." Two fossil finds before 1925 had established the existence of prehumans: Neandertal bones in Germany in 1856 and *Pithecanthropus erectus* (now called *Homo erectus*) bones in Java in 1891. These two sets of fossils showed traits that were similar enough to modern humans to qualify them for inclusion in the human lineage. The skulls of *Homo erectus* were somewhat smaller than those of moderns and had a different shape, but *H. erectus* populations were fully bipedal and showed no signs of any immediate arboreal ancestry. Neandertals had an even larger cranial capacity than modern humans, a trait that irked many scientists at the time; but most Neandertals lacked chins and had sloping foreheads, making them less than totally modern looking. When the first australopithecine was discovered, however, its features were so different from anything considered to be in the human lineage at that time that almost all scientists regarded it with extreme skepticism. If the first australopithecine had been found before Neandertal or *Homo erectus*, it would likely have been dismissed as a freak. The fact that that first skull was of a child was an additional problem. Widespread acceptance for australopithecines' hominid status did not occur until more fossils, including the bones of adults, were found in the late 1930s.

Over the decades since 1925, science has come a long way toward accepting at least some australopithecines as early ancestors of modern humans. For example, scientists have learned more about the extent of species variability, so the range of traits accommodated in a related genus is now more stable. In addition, since the early 1960s, K-Ar dating has increased bioanthropologists' confidence in dating early materials. Finally, several thousand specimens that represent hundreds of individuals in the genus have been accumulated. According to an old saying in paleontology, "One skull is a mystery; 50 skulls are a population." But although all experts today agree that the australopithecines were hominids and that members of the genus were in some way ancestral to *Homo*, there is no consensus on how many *Australopithecus* species there were, what were the exact relationships among them, or which species did and which did not evolve into the genus *Homo*.

## Australopithecine Taxonomy

How many species of *Australopithecus* there were during the approximate 3-myr existence of the genus is unknowable. Even though early hominids were probably not as efficient at bipedalism as later hominids, speciation events could have been kept to a minimum during those 3 myr because the australopithecines were able to walk across rivers at shallow locations. In the coastal inland regions of eastern Africa, between the Cape of South Africa in the south and the Horn region in the north, there are 12 rivers that flow eastward to the Indian Ocean, but none is wide enough to form an effective geographic isolating barrier. However, one prediction about the number of species suggests four chronospecies and at least two cladogenic splits, to total six species at a minimum. Matching this prediction, most experts tally the following six species: *Australopithecus anamensis, A. afarensis, A. africanus, A. garhi, A. robustus,* and *A. boisei.* Other experts place the two robust species *A. robustus* and *A. boisei* in a separate genus, *Paranthropus,* and add an additional species, *P. aethiopicus,* to the list. We will adopt the lumper perspective—one genus and six species (see Figure 6.8). Keep in mind also that *Ardipithecus ramidus,* when fully described, may turn out to be more *Australopithicus*-like after all.

**australopithecines**
Collective name for the members of the genus *Australopithecus*, consisting of hominids that lived in Africa between about 4.2 and 1.2 myr ago and are characterized by bipedal locomotion, small brain size, large faces, and big teeth.

*Figure 6.8*

## Australopithecine Sites and Dates

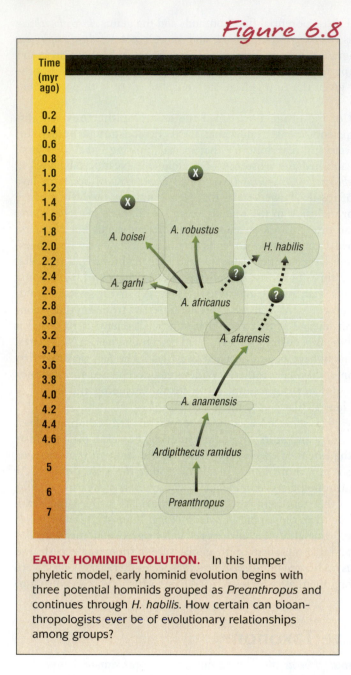

**EARLY HOMINID EVOLUTION.** In this lumper phyletic model, early hominid evolution begins with three potential hominids grouped as *Preanthropus* and continues through *H. habilis*. How certain can bioanthropologists ever be of evolutionary relationships among groups?

All australopithecine fossils have been found in Africa, and most are located either at sites east of the Rift Valley—Olduvai Gorge being the most famous—or in caves in South Africa. As shown in Figure 6.9, the Rift Valley runs from Ethiopia, south around Lake Turkana to Mozambique. A few outlier sites such as that in Chad have also yielded fossil remains. The australopithecine finds in Chad are particularly interesting, given the potential early hominid *(Sahelanthropus tchadensis)* that lived there some 7 to 6 myr ago (Brunet 2001; Brunet et al. 1995).

The reason most of the australopithecine sites cluster geographically is that early finds suggested where future excavations might be successful. This clustering may, however, bias thinking about where australopithecines lived. In the north, Don Johanson and his Ethiopian colleagues have excavated sites since the early 1970s in the Hadar region, once a former giant lake. Omo, in southern Ethiopia just north of Lake Turkana, is the location of many fossil finds excavated by American, French, and Kenyan teams in the 1960s and 1970s, though the original finds go back to 1911 (Coppens 1994). The beds at Omo have yielded fossils dated between 3.3 and 2.1 myr ago. Louis and Mary Leakey became world famous for their excavations at Olduvai Gorge. The gorge itself is only 25 kilometers (15½ miles) long, but the fault has exposed sediments and rock that are 100 meters (328 feet) thick. The Leakeys walked the eroded beds and, after many years of frustration, began to find important fossils in the late 1950s. Richard Leakey (their son), Meave Leakey (his wife), and Alan Walker have continued this fossil-finding success, making important discoveries in Kenya since the early 1990s. In South Africa Philip Tobias and other bioanthropologists have focused on numerous sites in limestone caves for fossil recovery.

If rocks contain sufficient potassium, workers can confidently date fossils associated with them using K-Ar dating. East Africa witnessed many volcanic eruptions during the time that australopithecines lived there and potassium-rich ash provided the basis for rock formation. It is particularly fortuitous when fossil material is sandwiched between two layers of datable ash. Also, because each geologic layer has a unique fossil and rock signature, it can be compared to others in different areas. Researchers have used this technique to date fossils in South Africa, an area where there were no volcanic eruptions, only breccia-filled limestone caves that could not be directly dated. By matching South African cave fauna to East African fauna embedded in K-Ar datable layers, workers can successfully date the South African fossils.

## Describing Australopithecines

No matter how much experts differ in their evaluation of australopithecines, they all agree that members of the genus share certain traits. Figure 6.10 presents a comparison of various australopithecine skulls and their derived traits. Although the australopithecines probably inherited many common traits from hominoid ancestors, the de-

*Figure 6.9*

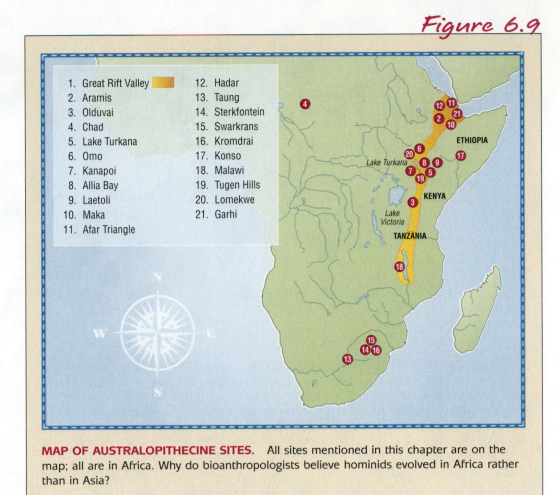

1. Great Rift Valley
2. Aramis
3. Olduvai
4. Chad
5. Lake Turkana
6. Omo
7. Kanapoi
8. Allia Bay
9. Laetoli
10. Maka
11. Afar Triangle
12. Hadar
13. Taung
14. Sterkfontein
15. Swarkrans
16. Kromdrai
17. Konso
18. Malawi
19. Tugen Hills
20. Lomekwe
21. Garhi

**MAP OF AUSTRALOPITHECINE SITES.**   All sites mentioned in this chapter are on the map; all are in Africa. Why do bioanthropologists believe hominids evolved in Africa rather than in Asia?

rived traits that evolved after the split from the LCA identify the genus. Listed below are shared australopithecine traits; ancestral traits include these:

- large degree of **sexual dimorphism** (males larger in size than females)
- moderate to large eyebrow ridges
- marked **postorbital constriction** with parietals (upper side walls of the skull) pinched in at the face
- flaring zygomatic arches that extend back beyond the ears
- large face relative to size of brain case
- relatively large and jutting jaw
- no chin
- premolars and molars large to very large, with thick enamel, but small canines
- life expectancy estimated at 44 years (Swisher et al. 2000)
- opposable thumbs

Derived traits include these:

- bipedal locomotion, essentially unchanged throughout the 3 myr of the genus (Tattersall 2000a)
- bowl-shaped pelvis

**sexual dimorphism**
The existence of differences between males and females of a species in stature, size, and other external morphological features.

**postorbital constriction**
Narrowness of the skull behind the eye orbits.

*Figure 6.10*

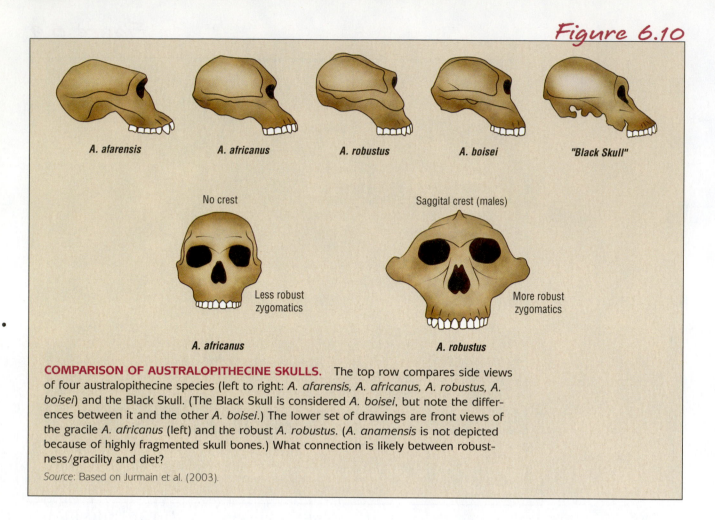

**A. afarensis**        **A. africanus**        **A. robustus**        **A. boisei**        **"Black Skull"**

No crest                                    Saggital crest (males)

Less robust zygomatics                                    More robust zygomatics

**A. africanus**                                    **A. robustus**

**COMPARISON OF AUSTRALOPITHECINE SKULLS.**   The top row compares side views of four australopithecine species (left to right: *A. afarensis, A. africanus, A. robustus, A. boisei*) and the Black Skull. (The Black Skull is considered *A. boisei*, but note the differences between it and the other *A. boisei*.) The lower set of drawings are front views of the gracile *A. africanus* (left) and the robust *A. robustus*. (*A. anamensis* is not depicted because of highly fragmented skull bones.) What connection is likely between robustness/gracility and diet?

*Source*: Based on Jurmain et al. (2003).

- cranial capacity somewhat larger than hominoid ancestors, averaging about 500cc
- bell-shaped occipital region (back of head) when viewed from the rear

Although the brains of australopithecines were only one-third the size of the brains of modern humans, they were three times the size of the brains of their Miocene hominoid ancestors, and their bodies were not much larger than those of the ancestors (Conroy 2005). Many bioanthropologists use the concept of encephalization quotient (EQ), which is the ratio between the brain size of an animal and the body mass expected for that animal. We will compare EQs throughout hominid evolution. For comparison purposes, the EQ for chimpanzees is 2.0 and that for modern humans is 5.8. The average EQ for all australopithecines, regardless of time or species, is 2.5. Australopithecines' average brain size increased from 400 to 500 cc between 4 and 2 myr years ago, again regardless of species designation. Though smaller than the later brain size increase of hominids, this 25-percent increase is still sizeable (Leonard 2002b).

The shared *Australopithecus* traits are found in all species, early and late, although not all of the traits are manifest to the same degree in each species. Additional traits diagnose particular species. Some experts refer to *A. robustus* and *A. boisei* as "robust" and all other species as "gracile," because the robust forms show skull crests and ridged bones for large muscle attachment and the graciles do not. Dean Falk and her team (2000) made endocasts of the brains of both gracile and robust australopithecines and found other differences: The robust individuals had small frontal and temporal lobes (like African apes) and the gracile individuals had larger frontal and temporal lobes (like *Homo sapiens*). In modern humans, frontal lobes are involved in planning and abstract thinking, so it is possible that the graciles had more of these cognitive abilities than the robusts. See Figure 6.11 for gracile and robust forms. We consider the species in chronological order of appearance, describing geographical location, dating range, sample size, distinctive traits, and likely evolutionary position. Table 6.1 offers comparative data on estimated date ranges, height, weight, and cranial capacity for five of the species.

## *Australopithecus anamensis*

The first ***Australopithecus anamensis*** fossil material (a mandible and a tooth) was found by Bryan Patterson at Kanapoi, Kenya, in 1965; Patterson estimated its age at about 5.5 myr old. In 1995 Meave Leakey and her colleagues began systematically excavating that site, and during the next four years the team found enough remains to justify naming and describing a new species, *A. anamensis*. The fossil materials from nearby Allia Bay are morphologically close enough to be classified within the same species. The two Kenya sites have yielded a total of 88 specimens to date: several maxillae (upper jaws) and six mandibles, more than 50 teeth, one portion of temporal bone, and important parts of the extremities. Ancestral hominoid traits of these specimens include a U-shaped dental arch, protruding canines, and a small diastema in the upper jaw. Unfortunately, no even reasonably complete skull has been found to date, so an estimate of the cranial capacity is not possible. The $^{40}Ar/^{39}Ar$ date for these finds is secure, with the fossil layer sandwiched between the lower bed dated at 4.17 myr ago and the upper bed dated at 4.07 myr ago (Leakey et al. 1995; Leakey et al. 1998; Ward et al. 1999). In 2006 Tim White and his team found and described a new cache of *A. anamensis* fossils several thousand miles north of the Kenya sites, at Aramis in Ethiopia. The age of 4.12 myr assigned to these fossils is within the dating range of the Kenya finds. The new fossils consist of 31 specimens belonging to at least 8 individuals (White et al. 2006). Since *A. anamensis* is found only in three sites in East Africa, it appears to be somewhat regional (Ward et al. 2001).

A. *anamensis* retains the most ancestral traits of the genus, though details of the tibia (lower leg) indicate the population was bipedal. Thus, *A. anamensis* is the first uncontested biped. What is still being argued is whether the species was only facultatively bipedal. The large tibia shows definite knee adaptations to bipedalism, and the angle of the femur at the knee is closer to that of bipedal than quadrupedal animals. Individual weight is estimated to be around 46 to 55 kg (100 to 125 pounds) (Andrews 1995); stature has not been estimated. *A. anamensis* is distinguished from other hominids by

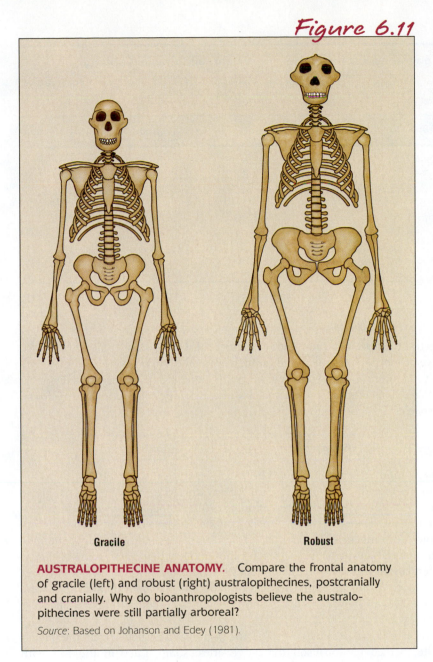

*Figure 6.11*

**Gracile**  **Robust**

**AUSTRALOPITHECINE ANATOMY.** Compare the frontal anatomy of gracile (left) and robust (right) australopithecines, postcranially and cranially. Why do bioanthropologists believe the australopithecines were still partially arboreal?

*Source*: Based on Johanson and Edey (1981).

***Australopithecus anamensis***
Hominid species that existed in East Africa between 4.2 and 4.1 myr ago and was bipedal but showed many ancestral hominoid features of skull and teeth.

## Table 6.1

### Australopithecine Species by Date, Geography, Estimated Height, Weight, and Cranial Capacity

The australopithecine date ranges given here are provisional, and estimated height and weight are averages for both sexes. What patterns emerge from these data?

|  | A. anamensis | A. afarensis | A. africanus | A. boisei | A. robustus |
|---|---|---|---|---|---|
| Date range in myr ago | 4.2–4.1 | 3.9–2.9 | 3.2–2.3 | 2.3–1.2 | 2.6–1.5 |
| Number of sites | 2 | 10 | 6 | 4 | 3 |
| Height (in cm) | Unknown | 105–151 | 115–138 | 113–137 | 110–132 |
| Average weight (in kg) | 50 | 42 | 36 | 37 | 37 |
| Cranial capacity range (in cc) | Unknown | 400–500 | 430–515 | 410–545 | 410–545 |
| Average cranial capacity (in cc) | Unknown | 440 | 460 | 520 | 520 |

dental traits, such as large molars with thick enamel and smaller canines, and the species may be ancestral to subsequent hominids (Leakey et al. 1995; Ward et al. 1999). Based on the relative proportions of molars and canines and analysis of microwear on the teeth, *A. anamensis* likely ate a lot of fruit, along with nuts, fish, and occasionally meat (Graslund 2005). This diet and pollen analysis of the soil in which fossils were found suggest the species lived in woodlands.

### Australopithecus afarensis

*Australopithecus afarensis* materials have been known since the early 1970s, and Don Johanson and his team have been successfully excavating sites in the Afar triangle in Ethiopia periodically ever since; the present tally is 300 fragments from 100 individuals at six sites. The Laetoli site in Tanzania, made famous by Mary Leakey's team's discovery of hominid footprints in 1978, has yielded similar fossils that are usually combined with the Afar materials into a single species. It is not unlikely that *A. afarensis* was a generalized descendant of *A. anamensis*. The sites of the *A. afarensis* finds show K-Ar dates ranging from 3.9 to 2.9 myr ago. During that time period *A. afarensis* populations were not static, as their fossils show definite directional changes in such features as mandibles and teeth (Lockwood et al. 2000).

The most famous *A. afarensis* fossil is the 3-myr-old "Lucy" from the Hadar (Ethiopia) site, named by Johanson for the Beatles' song "Lucy in the Sky with Diamonds." Some experts have questioned Lucy's sex, but most believe she was a fairly small female. The excavators found a total of 40 percent of her bones, and by using bilateral symmetry they were able to reconstruct most of her postcranial body. Since Lucy's discovery in 1974, excavators have uncovered 13 individuals at the site, including four infants. The fossils include a complete skull and mandible materials. Bioanthropologists estimate the stature of *A. afarensis* to be 1 to 1.5 m (5 feet to 5 feet 3 inches) and its weight to be 29 to 45 kg (70 to 108 pounds). (See Highlight 6.1, on pp. 152–153, for a description of Johanson's fieldwork.) In the 2000–2003 field sessions, "Lucy's baby," a 3.3-myr-old, remarkably complete fossil of a 3-year-old female, was found. The official name of the fossil is DIK-1, because it was found at Dikika, Ethiopia. Only the pelvis and parts of some limb bones are missing. The cranium has been excavated, but it will take several years to remove the postcranial bones from the cementlike matrix. Once totally excavated, this rare fossil of a child should reveal a lot about growth and development of this species (Almseged et al. 2006).

**Australopithecus afarensis**
Hominid species that existed in East Africa between 3.9 and 2.9 myr ago and that showed ancestral hominoid features in teeth and skull; Lucy is the most famous example.

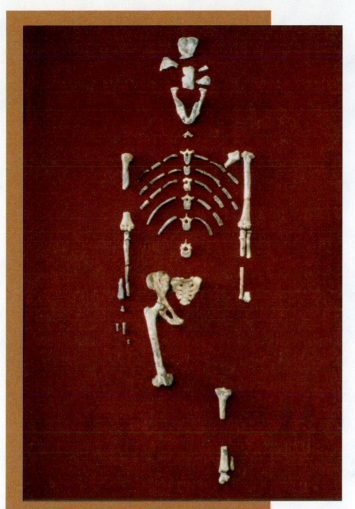

This is the skeleton of the famous *A. afarensis*, Lucy, as laid out on a table. What makes bioanthropologists believe she was at least partially arboreal?

An analysis of three anatomical complexes that reflect locomotion—the pelvis, arm and leg bones, and finger and toe bones—suggests that *A. afarensis* was bipedal but still capable of spending time arboreally. The basket-shaped pelvis was similar to the pelvis in modern humans, but the fingers and toes were curved, suggesting grasping. As further evidence of continued arboreal locomotion, the shoulder socket pointed upward, as in hominoids, rather than outward, as in later hominids; also, the arms were relatively long compared to the legs. That is, the upper limbs were in the same proportion to the torso as in modern humans, but the legs were not—suggesting that the arms were not really long, but the legs were short (Ward et al. 1999). The positions of the knees and hips also point to both bipedalism and climbing. Although the population was once thought to be less efficient at bipedalism than modern humans, one study of a hip bone concludes it was very much like modern humans (Lovejoy et al. 2002). Evaluations of energy efficiency suggest that Lucy and her family might have had to take more steps than moderns to keep to a certain speed, moving on flexed rather than straight legs, but that the gait would actually have taken less energy than the longer-legged gait of their descendants (Bramble 2002; Stern 2000).

Dental analysis shows that *A. afarensis* had fairly large and pointed canines that overlapped slightly, with a small accommodating diastema, and dental arches that were intermediate in shape between the likely U-shape of the LCA and the parabolic shape of later hominids (Rak 2000). Because the largest and the smallest individuals in the species have the same proportionately sized canines, there may have been considerable sexual dimorphism, with small Lucy-sized females and larger males. Some experts suggest *A. afarensis* was merely a variable species with no more sexual dimorphism than found for modern humans (Reno et al. 2003). Estimated cranial capacity varies between 400 and 500 cc, with an average of 440 cc (Kimbel et al. 1994). The EQ of *A. afarensis* is 2.2, at the lower end of the range for australopithecines.

The 75-foot Laetoli footprint trail provides additional details about bipedalism. When several hominids walked over a layer of freshly laid down volcanic ash that had been wetted by rain, they left footprints that subsequently hardened in the sun. Later, another ash flow filled in the footprints, sealing them. There is some disagreement about how many individuals are represented, but excavators uncovered 38 footprints in the trail of one hominid and 31 footprints in a trail that may be the remains of one hominid walking in the steps of another. The footprints confirm true bipedalism—because there were no palm, knuckle, or fist prints preserved in the sediment as would be predicted if hands had still been involved in locomotion. The footprints also indicate that the walkers were approximately 5 feet tall. The prints show feet that were very similar to those of modern humans, with well-developed arches and nondivergent big toes. These imprint fossils fit the model developed by the bone fossils fairly well, except that the imprints suggest less toe divergence and grasping than the bones indicated. By looking at the foot stroke and estimating speed and the stature

# In the Field with Don Johanson

BY HIS OWN ADMISSION, Don Johanson is lucky. Most bioanthropologists spend their lifetimes searching for fossil material and never find anything important. They are bound to find bits and pieces if they spend enough time at it, but most often the finds are isolated or meaningless. Don Johanson, the director of the Institute of Human Origins at Arizona State University, was lucky enough to be involved in two very important fossil events. Because the field conditions, the tempo of finding the fossils, and the species were very different, the two events are worth contrasting. The common denominators are the excavator and African fossils.

## FOSSIL-HUNTING CASE 1

Don Johanson did his graduate work at the University of Chicago with Clark Howell, a well-known but unlucky field excavator. Through Howell, Johanson got his feet wet as a fossil hunter, spending three years (1967–1970) at Howell's Omo Research Expedition site in Ethiopia. Here he learned the differences between pig, antelope, and hominid bones through on-the-spot experience. While at Omo, Johanson visited the French team working a few miles away and met a young geology doctoral student named Maurice Taieb; Taieb told him about the tremendous number of fossils being found at the site called Hadar, in the Afar region of northern Ethiopia. Taieb invited Johanson to visit the next year, and in 1973 the International Afar Research Expedition began in earnest with a small grant from the National Science Foundation. Taieb was the geologist, Yves Coppens the paleontologist, and Johanson the bioanthropologist.

Life in the field, at a site with no previous history of yielding hominid fossils, was high on expectations but low on creature comforts. The Afar triangle is 188 miles northeast of Ethiopia's capital, Addis Ababa—not the easiest place to outfit an expedition in the first place. From the beginning there were potential problems with warring tribes in the neighborhood, at least two military coups, and a great deal of political up-heaval on an almost daily basis. Getting permits to excavate and to remove fossils for further study (for a stated amount of time only, then to be returned) was very difficult. Out of the original grant money, the team had to purchase transportation, tents, and equipment as well as pay locals for cooking and other help. And then there was the weather: When dawn broke, it was 80 degrees, soaring to 110 by midday.

In the first year Johanson found several intriguing fossils that whetted his appetite. Taieb estimated the sediments the team was exploring to be about 3 myr old, a time period when fossil hominids existed only in the dreams of bioanthropologists. Johanson found three fossils that first year, but it was how they fit together that was tantalizing. The upper end of a tibia (lower leg), the lower end of a femur (upper leg) with half a condyle (the knob near the knee joint), and the other broken-off condyle all fit together. Not only was this the knee joint of a single individual, but also the angle was wrong for the small monkeylike creature Johanson initially thought the fossils belonged to. The bones of this fossil bent at an angle at the knee, just as in modern humans. Johanson had found evidence of bipedal locomotion dating back 3 myr, something there had been no evidence for previously. But that's all he found that first season.

Taieb was correct about the huge cache of fossils. Hadar is a perfect example of a place to let Mother Nature do the excavation. There would be no other way to excavate the area, given the sheer size of the landmass. Places like the Afar are excellent for searching for fossils on the surface, because the region is a former lake. Three myr ago, when the surrounding land surface was open woods and grasslands, bones were deposited in the lake, covered over by sediments, and fossilized. A fossil hunter today can walk a particular stretch of the desertlike hills, eyes constantly on the ground, and see nothing. But any rainfall (which is rare) is literally a gully washer, removing rock, pebbles, and soil and eroding out fossil materials. If that fossil hunter walks the same area right after a rain event, fossils may be there for the picking. Wait another week and they are covered by blowing sand and soil, or they have rolled down the slope and been crunched up by some roving animal. That's why fossil hunters have to be lucky.

As Johanson relates the story, in late December 1974 he and a young crew member had spent the morning fossil hunting and were walking back to their Land Rover to go back to camp. Johanson spied a piece of bone in a gully and said, "Bit of hominid." Right next to the bone was the back of a small skull; five minutes later the two had found a part of a femur, some vertebrae, and parts of a pelvis, ribs, and jaw. Because the material was so close together and apparently had no duplicates (no two right arms, for example), it dawned on Johanson that it might be the remains of a single individual. This by itself would have been remarkable, as materials this old are almost always bits and pieces of numerous individuals. When the investigators got back to camp, they laid out the bones and celebrated the new find. All through the night, as they whooped it up over their discovery, a tape of Beatles songs was playing over and over, and by morning the fossil had a name: "Lucy."

The next morning the entire team was down on their collective hands and knees doing a systematic excavation of the area near the original find, turning over every rock and pebble looking for more bone materials. In three weeks they found a total of more than 200 pieces, which they carefully pieced together to reassemble the fossilized remains of Lucy. There was no duplication of bones, so they knew they had a single individual. Lucy turned out to be no more than 3½ feet tall and probably weighed 90 pounds. Based on erupted wisdom teeth that had some wear, she was estimated to be 25 to 30 years old at death, which 3 myr ago was a reasonable life span. Given that there were no carnivore marks on her bones, the workers surmised that she probably lay down by the side of the lake and died. Johanson was able to remove the fossil materials from the country for a five-year study in the United States. After comparing the Lucy materials with every known fossil within a certain time range, he and colleagues decided that this hominid did not belong in the established taxonomic categories but deserved a species of its own, *Australopithecus afarensis*. In subsequent seasons excavators found a great deal more material, including 200 bones in 1975 that represented 13 individuals. In 1994 the discovery of most of a skull complemented the 80 percent that could be reconstructed from Lucy alone.

The Hadar story continues, although with a long hiatus in the middle. The first excavation round lasted from 1972 through 1976. Ethiopia then put a moratorium on all foreign research, and Johanson could not gain entry back into the country for many years. Instead he concentrated on obtaining as accurate a date as possible for the Hadar fossils. The date for Lucy turned out to be between 3.5 and 3 myr ago, a period not much different from the original estimate but validated by means of dating pure samples of basalt that lay at the base of the fossil-producing sediments. Johanson also began excavating a second site, in another African country, where again he was lucky.

## FOSSIL-HUNTING CASE 2

When Don Johanson learned in 1985 that the original Leakey camp at Olduvai was no longer being used, he and an international team began a new project, believing that Olduvai had not given up its last fossils. Life at Olduvai was very different from Hadar. The Olduvai camp had cottages, beds, and laundry service—but "terrible food." Johanson was quoted as saying, "this is supposed to be an expedition, not a vacation. In the Afar, we slept in tents, worked in hundred and ten degree heat and kept one eye out all the time for bandits. Here, the most threatening intruders we have to fear are some overenthusiastic tourists poking around the gate" (1989, 157).

During a foot survey workers discovered several pieces of hominid bone, and the entire team then went out on hands and knees, shoulder to shoulder, looking for more materials. This was the Dik Dik Hill excavation. But after weeks of systematic survey, including scalping the hill, bone materials only dribbled in and those bones that had been identified as hominid were pieced together. There was no moment of "Aha! I know what it is." The team painstakingly looked at every bone, compared the emerging fossil to everything known at that time, and concluded it was a female *Homo habilis*. In a move to link Lucy with the new find, Johanson gave the *H. habilis* the nickname "Lucy's baby." He spent two more seasons at Olduvai.

## FINALE

But Johanson's first love was Hadar, and in 1990 he went back. During the next three years, 53 new specimens were added to the inventory, including the first fairly complete adult skull. Several questions about *A. afarensis* have been answered: The material represents one species, not two, and Lucy and the other members of her species were committed bipeds who also spent time in the trees. The expedition continues.

Sources: Johanson, D. C., and M. A. Edey. 1981. *Lucy: The beginnings of humankind.* New York: Warner Books. Johanson, D. C., and J. Shreeve. 1989. *Lucy's child: The discovery of a human ancestor.* New York: Morrow. Kimbel, W. H., D. Johanson, and Y. Rak. 1994. The first skull and other new discoveries of *Australopithecus afarensis* at Hadar, Ethiopia. *Nature* 368:449–451.

turn back to your reading

of the imprinters, experts have concluded that the locomotion pattern was that of bipedal "strolling" (Schmid 2004).

A single partial mandible with molars, dated between 3.5 and 3 myr ago, was found in Chad in Central Africa in 1995 (Brunet et al. 1995). Most experts feel it shows enough similarities to *A. afarensis* to be included in that species; if correctly identified, it would considerably expand the geographic range of *A. afarensis*.

## Australopithecus garhi

Only one excavated fossil has been identified as representing the species ***Australopithecus garhi*** (meaning "surprise"). The fossil was found in Ethiopia in 1997, Ar/Ar dated to 2.5 myr ago, and described by its discoverer, Berhane Asfaw, and his colleagues (1999). The fossil likely represented a single individual and includes several fragments of cranium, allowing Asfaw to estimate the cranial capacity to be about 450 cc; a mandible with teeth that showed the hominid traits of larger molars, thick enamel, and small incisors; and parts of long bones. Unfortunately, the leg bone is not definitely associated with the cranial materials, so *A. garhi*'s position as a biped remains in some doubt (Culotta 1999). *A. garhi* differs in some dental features and cranial traits from similarly dated species. With only one individual representing the species and no range of dates, geography, or variability, it is difficult to be more than speculative about its evolutionary past or future. Although it is possible that *A. garhi* evolved to the genus *Homo*, there are better candidates for this evolutionary position.

## Australopithecus africanus

Chronologically, the last of the gracile australopithecines is ***Australopithecus africanus***, which ironically was the first australopithecine found. For 35 years *A. africanus* was the only known member of its genus, and for all scientists knew, it was the only species of that genus that ever existed. It was discovered in 1924 on a limestone plateau in South Africa at a site called Taung. Miners brought the skull, encased in rock, to Raymond Dart, an anatomist at the University of Witwatersrand. It took Dart 73 days to extract the skull from the limestone matrix, and four more years to separate the mandible from the skull. Dart published his findings in 1925 in *Nature*, describing his find as more "humanoid" in its crania, teeth, and mandible than "anthropoid." He believed that the Taung skull was a "missing link" between apes and humans, fulfilling a prediction made earlier by others (Dart 1925). However, his find and analysis were not met with general acceptance. In a subsequent issue the same year, *Nature* asked four leading experts to comment on this "man-ape." Their responses were properly cautious, and their consensus was that it was premature to express an opinion. Other criticisms came later: There was still skepticism about evolution in general, as the 1925 Scopes trial in the United States attested; no hominid had ever been found in Africa, and most scientists believed human ancestry was in Asia because of earlier hominid finds (then called *Pithecanthropus erectus*) in Java; the fraudulent Piltdown fossil was still regarded as *the* hominid model, with its large cranial capacity and apelike jaw (the very opposite of the Taung specimen); Taung was only one fossil; and finally, the fossil was of a child, and some experts argued that if it had been an adult, it would have looked very different. General acceptance of the *A. africanus* species as hominid took more than 20 years. (See Highlight 6.2, on pp. 156–157, for a discussion of the Piltdown hoax.)

The final acceptance of *A. africanus* resulted from the discovery of additional fossils. At least one scientist had supported Dart's find from the beginning: Robert Broom, a Scottish physician turned paleontologist. Broom moved to South Africa upon retirement and began looking for fossil material. He found his first *A. africanus* fossil at Sterkfontein, South Africa, in 1936, 11 years after the initial discovery at Taung. By 1949 limestone blasting had uncovered 30 individuals at five sites. Blasting may be hard on

**Australopithecus garhi**
A single hominid fossil, found in East Africa and dated to 2.5 myr ago, with large front and back teeth.

**Australopithecus africanus**
Hominid species whose fossils have been dated between 3.2 and 2.3 myr old and found mainly in South Africa; may be ancestral to *Homo*.

fossil material, but excavators found that, in concretelike limestone, blasting yielded more hominid bones than any other excavation method. The dating range given to the entire population of *A. africanus* is between 3.2 and 2.3 myr ago. Sterkfontein has been as well as four other sites with similar limestone matrices, including the prolific cave at Makapansgat, are still producing fossils. During the years when there was a boycott against South Africa's apartheid government, no analysis or publication of discoveries took place; new reports have since been emerging (Shreeve 1996). Several *A. africanus* fossils have also been found in Kenya and Ethiopia. The importance of these East African materials lies in their ability to be K-Ar dated and then cross-dated to the more prolific South African fossils.

At present more than 1,500 *A. africanus* fossils representing at least 400 individuals are known from Taung, Sterkfontein, and two other South African sites. A comparison suggests a picture of gracile hominids, their fairly smooth bones indicating lightly muscled bodies. Like its predecessors, but not its potential descendants, *A. africanus* was at home in both woodlands and partly wooded, bushy areas as opposed to open, grassy savannas. These hominids were not very different in size from the robust australopithecines and had similarly small brains, but they had smaller teeth in general, proportionately larger front than back teeth, a parabolic dental arch, and no diastema. Although their molars and canines were patterned like those of later hominids, they were somewhat larger and had thicker enamel. Showing their gracility and derived hominid traits, *A. africanus* individuals had skulls that were smooth with no crests, in contrast to some earlier australopithecines. Their faces jutted out a bit less as well. They had somewhat shorter arms and longer legs than earlier hominids. Their cranial capacity averaged 460 cc, and their EQ was 2.5. A study of their tooth wear suggests their mean age at death was 22 years. Although they were fully bipedal, they may have had somewhat mobile and divergent big toes, but the evidence is inconclusive.

One discovery from Sterkfontein was originally dated between 3.5 and 3.2 myr ago but has been redated to 2.2 myr ago (Walker et al. 2006). If this date is correct (and the fossil has been variously dated anywhere between 4.1 and 2.2 myr ago), the fossil is likely not in the direct lineage of later hominids. There are other hominids dated to that time that are far more similar to later hominids. This "distant cousin" does, however, help give scientists an idea of the bushiness of the australopithecine grade. Four foot bones of the individual were found in 1994 in a storage vault. Originally excavated in 1980, the individual had been given the nickname "Little Foot." Investigators returned to the excavation site in 1997 and uncovered the rest of the fossil, most of a complete skeleton, still embedded in limestone. Although "Little Foot" is still undergoing analysis and even the species is not yet identified (it could be either *A. afarensis* or *A. africanus*), preliminary results suggest that the foot retained a good deal of flexibility (Clarke and Tobias 1995; McKee 1996). The individual showed a heel that took considerable weight and short foot and hand bones like modern humans, but had grasping toes as well. If it is identified as *A. afarensis*, it will be the second of that species outside East Africa; and if it is *A. africanus*, it will extend the date of that species back a further 100 kyr and change ideas about habitual bipedalism.

Although most of the *A. africanus* materials are from South Africa, based on the dates for the South African and East African hominids and the dates and locations for earlier australopithecines, most experts agree that *A. africanus* probably evolved in East Africa from *A. afarensis* or a similar group and then migrated southward, unimpeded by any major physical barriers. The lack of fossils of any earlier South African hominids from which *A. africanus* could have evolved and the overall similarity in general body plan of *A. africanus* to *A. afarensis* lend support to this conclusion. Some experts place *A. africanus* in the lineage leading to *Homo* and eventually to modern humans, because it retained generalized and gracile traits. Others believe there are better candidates for this position and place *A. africanus* on the evolutionary path to the specialized australopithecines, along with *A. robustus* and *A. boisei*.

# Highlight 6.2

# In the News with the Piltdown Forgery

BECAUSE AMERICANS HAVE NEVER HAD a really old hominid fossil to claim for our very own, it may be hard for us to put ourselves in the shoes of the British, who occasionally see a glimmer of having "the first" or "the oldest" of something—only to have their primacy snatched away when some other country makes the same claim. There is a good deal of national pride on the part of nonscientists, not to mention the scientific snobbery that emerges at international meetings, over who has the biggest dinosaur or the oldest monkey or, most important, the first human. Germany has its Neandertals, France has its Cro-Magnons, and even Belgium has a famous skull called Spy; but as of the turn of the twentieth century, Britain had no famous fossils. The French, armed with both Neandertals and Cro-Magnons, even called the English paleoanthropologists "pebble collectors" (Blinderman 1986), pointing to their many artifacts but their lack of bones.

But in late November 1912, the *Manchester Guardian* broke the news that an old skull (but no face) and most of a half-mandible had been found at the Piltdown site in Sussex, in southern England. This ensured a packed house at the official announcement at the London Geological Society three weeks later. The discoverer, Charles Dawson, along with Arthur Smith Woodward, a zoologist from the Natural History Museum in London, presented the find. Dawson, an amateur geologist and a lawyer by trade, gave the geological context and described the artifacts; Woodward discussed the anatomical features of the fossils. The presenters cited extinct animal bones found in the same layer as evidence of antiquity, and they described tools to show that *Eoanthropus dawsonii*, or Piltdown Man, had tool-making ability.

For the next 40 years, Piltdown Man was a British icon. The skull at least looked more modern than other European fossils, with its high forehead and large capacity. The jaw had a very wide ramus (vertical portion "hinged" to the skull) and thick bone. The remains looked exactly like what two famous British scientists—Darwin and Huxley—had predicted: a transition between a modern ape (the primitive jaw) and a modern human (the large skull), or a true "missing link." Though the fossil's actual age was not known at that time (this was pre $^{14}$C days), experts thought it to be perhaps 500 kyr old.

During the next several years, additional finds propped up the initial Piltdown fossils. First, workers discovered a canine that looked just like the reconstruction made of it previously. Next, in 1915 Dawson found a second individual some two miles away with a brain case and molar tooth that were almost identical to those of the first find. Investigators also found additional artifacts. Although no more discoveries were made after 1915, for 40 years most British scientists continued to tout Piltdown's status as western Europe's earliest representative. Not everyone agreed.

Beginning in the early 1950s, however, even British scientists began to doubt Piltdown's age. Later experts began to suspect that the fossils had been purposely altered and planted in the Sussex beds. In November 1953 the *Bulletin of the British Museum (Natural History)* printed the official announcement that Piltdown Man was a hoax.

To the lay public, it was a crushing blow that England no longer had a claim to an important fossil. To scientists, the question was "Who perpetrated the fraud?" But the public feeling and the scientists' reactions are connected—because Piltdown should never have been believed to be a real fossil in the first place. In hindsight, we can see that the British scientists were unfortunately blinded to several oddities that should have been clues to the forgery:

- A diagnostic trait for modern humans, the chin, was missing and thus impossible to assess.
- The condyle that articulates the ramus of the mandible to the skull also was missing and later was found to have been purposely broken off. The condyle would have shown the mandible to belong to an ape.
- The original missing canine miraculously was excavated the year after an anatomist wondered about it.
- Dawson found a second individual that was almost identical to the first.

- No more fossils were found after Dawson died.
- The canine's wear pattern looked modern (like the skull) rather than "primitive" (like the jaw).
- No fossil is halfway between two existing modern populations (apes and humans).
- During the 40 years between the original find and 1950, other hominid fossils in Asia and particularly in Africa all showed the opposite trend: a relatively small cranial capacity combined with fairly modern human teeth, rather than the other way around.

Once there was suspicion, Kenneth Oakley of the Natural History Museum asked that the affair be reopened. Technicians ran eight chemical tests on the Piltdown skull, the mandible, and the associated animal bones. Every test showed that the skull was no older than 10,000 years and that the jaw was very modern. In addition, abrasions on the cranium and incisors could be seen with the naked eye (if people looked for them); some teeth were actually filed down; many bones were stained the same color; the tips of the molar roots were broken off (modern apes have long roots); and some of the Piltdown tools were made with metal. While drilling into the bone, Oakley reported that the skull and the mandible smelled different, one old and powdery, one new with a distinctive odor. Finally, the fauna that "verified" Piltdown Man's old age were found to have come from many different sources. As scientists discovered much later, the skull was probably from a grave less than 1,000 years old; the jaw came from a recently deceased orangutan, probably from the London Zoo.

There is no doubt that someone (or some people) went to a great deal of time and trouble to perpetrate this hoax. But who and why? It is now more than 90 years since the hoax and more than 50 years since it was uncovered, but we are no closer to knowing the truth than the day that question was first asked. There are at least 11 suspects, alone or in a conspiracy, including the original discoverer; both anatomists; a zoologist; a geologist; a priest; lesser figures at the Natural History Museum, including one Martin Hinton (whose trunk in storage at the museum was found to contain items that could have been involved in manufacturing a forgery); and even Arthur Conan Doyle, the author of the Sherlock Holmes books. But in each tentative indictment there is always something missing in terms of expertise, motive, access to the site, or needed materials. And all of the suspects are now long dead. If Dawson had the needed expertise, he would be the prime candidate: He was present at every find and actually discovered most of the important material himself; also, nothing further emerged after he died, though the search went on. But if Dawson did put together the very careful hoax, he was smart enough to play dumb and let the experts tell him what he had found.

The true lesson of the Piltdown hoax is that it was easy to pull off because people wanted to believe it. The perpetrator or perpetrators fooled some outstanding scientists—who wanted to believe that England had a place in human prehistory. We might say that even the British royal family wanted to believe in Piltdown, as three scientists who were closely involved were later knighted. A hoax of this size is not likely to occur again.

Sources: Blinderman, C. 1986. *The Piltdown inquest*. Buffalo, NY: Prometheus Press. Feder, K. 2002. *Frauds, myths, and mysteries*. 4th ed. Mountain View, CA: Mayfield. Spencer, F. 1990. *Piltdown: A scientific forgery*. New York: Oxford University Press. Weiner, J. S. 1980. *The Piltdown forgery*. New York: Dover.

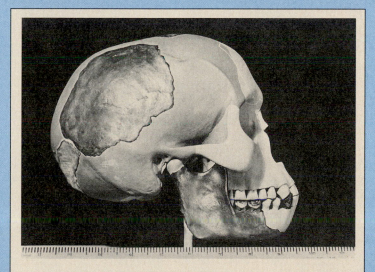

This is the reconstructed Piltdown skull; the actual skull lacked any chin area. Would modern experts have been fooled?

turn back to your reading

## *Australopithecus robustus* and *Australopithecus boisei*

When *A. africanus* was the only recognized early hominid, the evidence seemed to mandate a straight-line path of human evolution (i.e., one single evolving lineage). But the discoveries in 1938 and 1959 of two other sets of hominid fossils that appeared far more different from modern humans than was *A. africanus* called for a new way of thinking about the evolutionary process. ***Australopithecus robustus*** and ***Australopithecus boisei*** (sometimes given the genus name *Paranthropus*) are robust in overall cranial form. *A. robustus* remains were found in South Africa and *A. boisei* in East Africa. The two populations were separated by enough distance that they were likely different species, but they shared enough robust traits to separate both from the gracile populations (refer to Figure 6.11). The majority of these shared traits may be related to diet rather than being separate traits with individual explanations (Morell 1999). *A. robustus* and *A. boisei* faces would have appeared wide when viewed from the front, because their cheekbones flared outward, leaving a large amount of space between the zygomatic bone and the face for the passage of the temporalis muscle that connected the crest at the midline/top of the skull to the mandible. A second muscle, the masseter, runs from the back of the jaw to the forward part of the zygomatic arch; in these hominids it was used to open and close massive jaws to chew tough foods. It is likely that the robust versions evolved from an earlier gracile form such as *A. africanus* or *A. afarensis*. The diet-related large molars and small front teeth may have developed because of a change in the environment to a drier and hotter climate. Such a change could have led to food resources that were tougher to chew, such as hard-shelled seeds and nuts that were high in grit (which leaves evidence in the form of tooth wear) and fiber. The robust australopithecines show a specialization of eating primarily plant foods. The result was a face and jaw well suited as a chewing machine. Electron microscopic analysis supports an early view that these hominids ate small hard nuts and seeds, but bone strontium studies suggest that they were meat eaters as well. Given both clues, it is likely their diet included scavenged meat, greens, roots, fruits, seeds, tree pods, and berries—a well-balanced diet.

When Robert Broom first discovered *A. robustus* fossils in 1938, most experts disagreed with his designation, including them with *A. africanus* instead. Now, however, most workers give the fossils at least species status. *A. robustus* has been found at six South African sites, and the remains span 2.6 to 1.5 myr ago. The Swartkrans site alone has produced more than 100 individuals. The skulls are about the same size as those of *A. africanus* and range from 410 to 545 cc, with an average of about 520 cc; the EQ averages 2.9. Their most notable features are the large sagittal crest at the midline of the skull and very large jaws and molar teeth. Postcranial *A. robustus* fossil materials are rare. Several foot bones suggest divergent big toes, but the foramen magnum indicates bipedalism; perhaps grasping toes served in occasional arboreal forays. The postcranial fossils that have been found suggest a hominid about the same size as *A. africanus* (McKee 2000).

The first *A. boisei* fossil was found in 1959 by Mary Leakey at Olduvai Gorge. This was the first fossil dated by the K-Ar technique, setting the stage for all chronometric dating in Africa. In 1959 scientists didn't know much about species or genus variability, as the only australopithecine fossils known at that time were from South Africa; *A. boisei* was the first fossil hominid ever found in *East* Africa. It is no wonder that the Leakeys gave it not only a new species designation but also a new genus name, calling it *Zinjanthropus boisei* after their longtime benefactor Charles Boise. The initial find included an almost complete cranium and an upper jaw with dentition. Additional crania and mandibles subsequently added to the known variability of the population. The date is now placed between 2.3 and 1.2 myr ago.

In the 1990s investigators located nine *A. boisei* specimens at Konso, Ethiopia, including the first direct association of a mandible with a cranium (Suwa et al. 1997). This well-dated site is from the end of *A. boisei*'s spectrum, at about 1.4 myr ago. The morphology of the finds fits previously found specimens, with a cranial capacity of about 545 cc

*Australopithecus robustus*
Robust species of hominid that existed between 2.6 and 1.5 myr ago in South Africa.

*Australopithecus boisei*
Very robust hominid species that existed between 2.3 and 1.2 myr ago in East Africa.

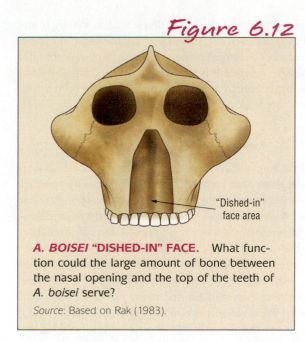

*Figure 6.12*

"Dished-in" face area

**A. BOISEI "DISHED-IN" FACE.** What function could the large amount of bone between the nasal opening and the top of the teeth of *A. boisei* serve?

*Source*: Based on Rak (1983).

and an EQ of 2.6; the excavators suggest that the cranium was of a relatively old man, because the sutures are almost fully fused. In general, *A. boisei* had even wider zygomatic arches and larger sagittal crests than *A. robustus*. It is distinctive in showing a very large dished-in face area—the midface between the nasal opening and the top of the teeth is very long and concave (see Figure 6.12).

Because both *A. robustus* and *A. boisei* coexisted with the genus *Homo*, neither species is regarded as being ancestral to modern humans.

### The Black Skull

Finally, one australopithecine cranium, discovered in 1985 at West Lake Turkana, Kenya, defies classification for many experts. There is a temptation to place this unique cranium in its own species, and some experts have done so, calling it *Australopithecus aethiopicus*. Because it is but one cranium with no associated postcranial materials, however, we tentatively place it in the *A. boisei* category—but with the note that it is "super *boisei*" in some of its traits. The fossil is colloquially called the **Black Skull** because of its dark color, the result of absorbing certain minerals when it was

**Black Skull**
Early australopithecine skull dated at 2.5 myr old and showing super-robust features; also called *A. aethiopicus*.

The Black Skull, called *A. aethiopicus* by some, is but a single cranium, so we prefer to lump it with the *A. boisei* group. Note the trait extremes. What function might they serve?

newly deposited. Relative to the other australopithecines, the Black Skull is a study in superlatives: It has the smallest cranial capacity (410 cc), the largest sagittal crest, the most prognathous face, the most dished-in face, the largest molars, and the largest zygomatic bones. Most of these traits are masticatory adaptations to a diet of seeds, nuts, and hard fruits. The Black Skull has been chronometrically dated at 2.5 myr ago, so it could possibly be the common ancestor of the two robust species of australopithecines (White 2002).

## What Happened to the Australopithecines?

Chapter 9 will explore possible tool making and tool use by australopithecines, as well as other aspects of their behavior and culture that archaeologists have been able to infer. Here we consider what happened to them in an evolutionary sense. It is easy to say that the australopithecines became extinct when the suite of traits that identify them disappeared at a particular point in time. To some extent they were preyed upon by predators such as leopards, but this was probably not the main cause of their disappearance. (See Highlight 6.3 for a predator/prey interaction involving an australopithecine.) What caused at least three seemingly successful species of late australopithecines to become extinct? Ecological evidence suggests that East and South Africa became cooler and drier once again, causing woodlands to decrease and savannas to increase (Vrba 1995). It is possible that new food resources—or the flexibility to choose additional food resources (Potts 1996)—may have allowed the newest hominids on the scene, early members of the genus *Homo*, to outcompete the late australopithecines. There is no direct evidence connecting any of the australopithecines with big game hunting for meat, though active scavenging was likely (Foley 2001). But new kinds of animals and plants were evolving as well, and if hunting even small game became important, the larger-brained members of the genus *Homo* could have processed environmental information more successfully and replaced the smaller-brained australopithecines on the African savanna. In any case, after about 1 myr ago, the genus *Homo* was the only member of the hominid family left (Potts 1996).

## Enter the Genus *Homo*

There is no consensus concerning the specific origins of the genus **Homo**. Most experts would put the choice between *A. afarensis* and *A. africanus* or a similar population; similarity in limb proportions between *A. africanus* and the first member of the *Homo* genus, *Homo habilis*, may give the nod to *A. africanus* (Berger 2002). The first evidence of the genus emerged in East Africa at roughly the same time as the robust australopithecines, about 2.3 myr ago. These evolutionary events may have been associated with drier climates, fewer trees, more savanna-like landscape, and more seasonality. Possibly the genus *Homo* evolved as an adaptation to these new conditions; or possibly the genus had already evolved, and the change in climate merely continued to shape its evolution. Some workers divide the early members of the genus into two species (*H. rudolfensis* and *H. habilis*), but analysis of the craniofacial variation among all *H. habilis* fossils does not support the idea of more than one species (Miller 2000). We will therefore refer to all early members of the genus as *H. habilis*.

### Homo habilis

The first specimen of the genus *Homo* was discovered in 1960 by Jonathan Leakey, son of Louis and Mary Leakey, at Olduvai Gorge. In 1964 Louis Leakey described the fossil, named it **Homo habilis** (meaning "handy" or "able" man), and assigned it a date of 1.75 myr ago. The announcement of *H. habilis* was met with skepticism by most workers, some calling it an "unnecessary creation"; and as long as only a single, highly

**Homo**
Genus of hominids having large brains and depending on culture to adapt.

**Homo habilis**
An early *Homo* species living in Africa 2.3 to 1.5 myr ago, showing brains half the size of moderns and ancestral features in the postcranial skeleton.

# Highlight 6.3

## Prey or Predators?

SOME TIME BEFORE THE DEBATE about whether East African hominids were hunters or scavengers began, Robert Brain had undertaken taphonomic studies of the formation process for early hominid cave sites in South Africa, such as those at Swartkrans, Sterkfontein, and Makapansgat (Brain

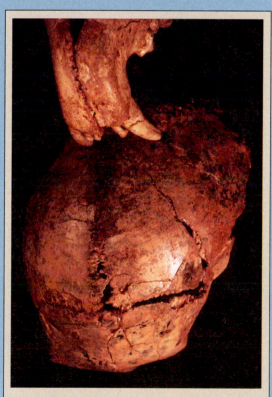

The two holes in the *A. robustus* skull found at Swartkrans (South Africa) exactly fit the canines of a leopard.

1981). *Taphonomy* is the study of what causes the formation of archaeological sites that bioanthropologists or archaeologists excavate: Do they find an animal bone and an artifact next to each other because one was used to cut the other, or did each exist at different times or places and perhaps roll down hills on two sides of a gully, ending up next to each other in a false association?

The cave assemblages that Brain looked at consisted of australopithecine bones as well as bones of other primates and nonprimate animals, including carnivores. Raymond Dart, who was responsible for putting the australopithecines on the fossil map, had previously assumed that the australopithecines were hunters. He believed they targeted their own species as well as others for food, using what he called an "osteodontokeratic tool kit" (tools made from animal bones, teeth, and horns). Brain studied cave formation and erosion, processes affecting animal bones in modern hunter-gatherer settlements, and carnivore and primate behavior. He concluded that the australopithecine bones in the cave sites in South Africa were probably the remains of carnivore meals. Brain suggested that large cats had been the predators, either dragging their prey into a cave to avoid scavengers or attacking groups of hominids and other primates as they slept inside caves. Evidence from Swartkrans—an australopithecine skull with two holes made by carnivore canine teeth—lends support to Brain's hypothesis.

At another site, Taung, where the first australopithecine skull was found, eagles were the agents of bone accumulation. The assemblage of skulls and bones of small animals displayed damage similar to what occurs when raptors take their prey.

Taphonomic studies have therefore demonstrated that the australopithecines in South Africa were prey rather than predators and that the parts of Dart's "osteodontokeratic tool kit" were likely the result of site formation processes rather than modifications by hominids.

*Sources*: Brain, C. K. 1981. *The hunter or the hunted? Introduction to African cave taphonomy.* Chicago: University of Chicago Press.   Dart, R. 1925. *Australopithecus africanus*: The man-ape of South Africa. *Nature* 115: 195–199.

turn back to your reading

fragmented mandible and several fragments of crania existed to represent what was heralded as the first fossil in the genus *Homo*, that skepticism continued. Only after investigators uncovered and described several more specimens did *H. habilis* gain general acceptance as a member of the same genus as modern humans. The fossil known as KNM-ER 1470 has been the most influential of the *H. habilis* finds; KNM stands for Kenya National Museum, ER stands for East Rudolf, and 1470 is the rounded-off number of the find at that site. This cranium has the largest cranial capacity of the habilines (see Figure 6.13). Until the discovery of the first *Homo* fossil, there was no strong evidence of multiple genera of hominids alive at the same time, but the earliest *H. habilis* finds were actually in the same levels as *A. boisei* materials. Thus, these discoveries put two genera in East Africa at the same time, changing the model of hominid evolution from lineal to bushy.

Other fossils have brought the habiline collection to at least five skulls, a mandible, arm and leg bones, teeth, and faces. Some cranial and postcranial materials probably belong to single individuals. In addition to Olduvai, four other East African sites—in Kenya, Ethiopia, and Malawi—and two sites in South Africa have yielded subsequent habiline materials. The dates for the *H. habilis* fossils range from 2.3 to 1.5 myr ago (Blumenschine et al. 2003; Walker 2002).

In general, although the habiline cranial materials are *Homo*-like, the postcranial materials are *Australopithecus*-like; but that kind of mosaic is expected in a new genus. From australopithecine ancestors *H. habilis* inherited short stature (still not much more than 137 cm, or 4 feet 6 inches), long arms relative to leg length, and likely climbing ability—yet the feet of these hominids are very humanlike and well adapted to bipedalism. Surprisingly, the arm-to-leg ratio is even more ancestral than in *A. afarensis*. Lucy's arm-to-leg ratio is 85 percent, and the ratio for modern humans ranges from 70 to 75 percent. By contrast, *H. habilis*'s arm-to-leg ratio is a whopping 95 percent, meaning that the arms would have hung almost to the knees. Other derived traits include flatter faces, somewhat smaller teeth and jaws, and smaller brow ridges than in *Australopithecus*. The larger brains of *H. habilis* were a derived trait as well, and it is their cranial capacity of 509 to 752 cc (average of 610 cc), a size increase of more than 20 percent, that most workers feel is sufficient to place them into the *Homo* genus. The environment was getting warmer and

*Figure 6.13*

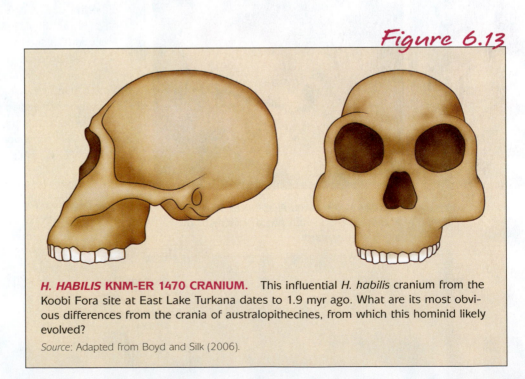

**H. HABILIS KNM-ER 1470 CRANIUM.** This influential *H. habilis* cranium from the Koobi Fora site at East Lake Turkana dates to 1.9 myr ago. What are its most obvious differences from the crania of australopithecines, from which this hominid likely evolved?

*Source:* Adapted from Boyd and Silk (2006).

*Homo habilis* **skull. Note the changes from the australopithecines: a rounder skull, smaller eyebrow ridges, and a flatter face with a less protruding jaw. What similarities to the australopithecines do you see?**

dryer during this time period, so natural selection would have favored larger brains if they made the habilines "smarter" in terms of finding food in more savanna-like terrain. The average EQ of *H. habilis* ranges from 2.5 to 3.1. Some experts see endocranial clues that suggest some ability to use speech, but this notion is controversial (Falk 2004). In any case, these hominids' larger cranial capacity probably did allow for more information processing than in australopithecines, perhaps giving them an advantage in food getting. Although their teeth were large by modern standards, they were reduced relative to australopithecines (Dunsworth and Walker 2002). (See Highlight 6.4, on pp. 164–165, for a look at likely male and female economic roles during early *Homo* days.)

In the late 1990s several workers questioned the taxonomic status of *H. habilis* again, this time suggesting that it did not meet criteria for the genus *Homo*, particularly in terms of cranial capacity. Their recommendation was to classify the species as *Australopithecus habilis* (Wood and Collard 1999).

# Highlight 6.4

## The Other Evolving Sex

PICTURE THIS: It is 2 myr ago, and we are looking at a hominid camp somewhere in East Africa. We see two males with pointed wooden spears walking swiftly away from the camp toward a small herd of antelope that just stopped to nibble grass half a mile away; we see another three males sitting around the hearth in the middle of the clearing, ripping meat off small haunches of cooked wildebeest with their teeth. Two of the males are fighting over possession of a particularly good piece. This is a typical picture of what we are led to believe life was like during late australopithecine or early *Homo* days: man the hunter, man the meat eater, man the aggressor. But where are the females in this picture? In this male-dominated scenario, at least females are good for sex and for producing new generations of little boy hunters. But where are they?

Until female anthropologists took a stand against male-only scenarios of evolution, terms such as "prehistoric man" and "early man" meant just that—males only. A 1968 collection of symposium papers (edited by Richard Lee and Irven DeVore) was titled *Man the Hunter*. Not only did this volume represent a compilation of what was generally believed about early human behavior at that time, but it also validated those views for the next decade or more. Of the 67 participants in the Man the Hunter symposium, only 4 were women; of the 29 articles in the volume, only 2 were by females.

The traditional view (including the view embodied in *Man the Hunter*) portrayed men as dominating women sexually and socially, hunting for large game, and bringing the food back to provision and protect the passive and defenseless women and children. This view also depicted males competing for females and being aggressive in their hunting behavior.

But there are numerous things wrong with this scenario, over and above the fact that females are playing almost no role. First, there is no strong evidence of big game hunting until *Homo erectus* days, and even then some experts are reluctant to put spears in the hands of human ancestors. In earlier hominid days evidence from butchered animal bones suggests that scavenging was the method for getting food, and either sex can scavenge. An examination of animal bones in early hominid sites shows that more often than not, human butchering marks are on top of carnivore marks. This suggests that carnivores brought down the animals and left their teeth marks on the bones, usually around the shafts of long bones. Hominids, finding those bones with meat still on them, cut the meat off using sharp stone tools. Hominid butchering marks are usually parallel to the shaft, not around it, and also appear at the ends of long bones, as if to disarticulate pieces for ease of transport. In addition, cross-sections of the two kinds of marks look different, carnivore teeth marks being shallow and U-shaped and hominid tool marks deep and V-shaped. The important point is that when both kinds of marks are on a single bone, if the hominid marks are *on top of* the carnivore marks, it strongly suggests scavenging, not hunting. Deciding which is on top is not as difficult as it might seem. A good analogy is to drive across soil that will leave a tire print (car or bicycle will do) and then drive over it again at a 90-degree angle; the second tire print will cut off part of the first print.

The other major thing wrong with a hunting-only scenario is that with only one exception, when modern foragers practice big game hunting, the big game is never the main food source: Gathered foods represent up to 80 percent of the food consumed by individuals and groups. The one exception is the Inuit (Eskimo) people, because there is a limited supply of plant food available during two short summer months. In modern foraging societies men may go out hunting singly or as a group, but more often than not they come home empty-handed. Females, by contrast, gather nuts, berries, and tubers; dig for small burrowing animals; collect insects; and so on, regardless of pregnancy or the need to carry a young baby, and regardless of their inability to run as fast or as far as men. Gathering takes patience, endurance, and knowledge of where resources are, and women exploit these predictable resources with ease.

Hunting is more exciting and dangerous than gathering; mushrooms aren't very exciting, they don't attack the mushroom picker, and the gatherer does not have to attack them with a spear. But the fact that a hunting way of life is more exciting does not mean it was the way of life of our early hominid ancestors. The evidence points to the contrary.

Reconstructing details of early hominid behavior requires some speculation, but speculation around facts is considerably preferable to romantic idealization of what the prehistoric past was like. With this in mind, what follows is a reconstruction of prehominid and hominid economic behavior—both male and female. How much of this behavior is genetically based and how much is learned is unknown. But because hominids evolved in Africa, gathering and then hunting must be looked at as specializations of the woodlands and savanna.

## PREHOMINIDS

Evidence from many primate studies under woodland and savanna conditions indicates that gathering is the basic food exploitation method. Although resources differ from fruits and nuts to leaves, insects, and tubers, the method of exploitation is to gather them. Nonhuman primate gathering differs from hominid gathering, however, in several ways: Nonhumans forage individually for themselves only; they eat the food when they find it; they do not usually use tools to get the food; they do not carry the food long distances; and they do not share with conspecifics. (The exception is sharing between mothers and infants.) These behaviors would have been typical of hominoids in East Africa before the split into the hominid and pongid lineages. Killing and consuming medium-sized animals occurs in most chimpanzee groups, but such meat never constitutes more than a rare source of food. The same was probably true in LCA groups.

## EARLY HOMINIDS

During early hominid days (6 to 2 myr ago), the basic economy consisted of the gathering of local resources by individuals. After collecting food, individuals carried it to a base camp and shared it with mates, offspring, and perhaps others in the group; there was delayed consumption (an interval between finding and eating food); and hominids used tools to procure and then process the food. For example, individuals dug tubers and roots with dig-ging sticks; knocked down fruits, nuts, and hives full of honey with sticks; cracked hard-shelled nuts; prodded small burrowing animals out of their holes with long sticks; and occasionally hunted and killed small mammals. Insects could be gathered at times as well. Once food was gathered, processing might include pounding with a rock. Males and females could and probably did do any of these jobs, sharing with each other and with their offspring. These activities would have been typical of the australopithecines and *Homo habilis*.

## LATER HOMINIDS

Whether the earliest *Homo erectus* males were big game hunters or not remains to be shown, but big game eventually became part of the economic picture. Even then, however, the basic economy did not change drastically: Females continued to collect the majority of the food eaten by themselves, their mates, and their offspring. It has been estimated that perhaps 1 percent of food in prehominid days was from animal sources (insects and monkeys) and that the proportion may have increased to 5 percent during the scrounging days of early hominids, increasing further to 15 or 20 percent in later hominid days. Hunting was probably never any higher than that in temperate or tropical areas where meat is lean, because humans who consume more than half of their calories in the form of lean meat die from protein poisoning.

Women in prehistory, then, were more than just baby makers or sex partners. They always had an important, sometimes vital, economic role.

*Sources*: Pringle, H. 1998. New women of the Ice Age. *Discover* (April): 62–69.  Tanner, N., and A. Zihlman. 1976. Women in evolution: Innovation and selection in human origins. *Signs* 1 (3).  Zihlman, A. 1997. The Paleolithic glass ceiling. In *Women in Human Evolution*, ed. L. D. Hager. New York: Routledge.

turn back to your reading

During the australopithecine and early *Homo* period, hominids lived and evolved exclusively in Africa. Earlier primate populations lived and evolved in Europe, Asia, and even the New World at certain times, but early hominid evolution was exclusively an African event. Bioanthropologists are able to trace early hominid evolution with some assurance of being correct. For the same time period, archaeologists point to the first hard evidence signaling the emergence of human culture in the form of artifacts—that is, tools. Oldowan tools made from volcanic rock, first found at the Gona site in Ethiopia, date before 2.5 myr ago. Although it is tempting to associate tool making with the genus *Homo* because of *Homo*'s larger brains, there are no fossil–artifact associations at this time. Chapter 9 will explore the question of who made the stone tools. Chapter 7 will continue the saga of human evolution, as hominids migrated out of Africa and hominid evolution began taking place on a scale far more global than previously.

■ Around 6 myr ago, some generalized quadrupedal population in Africa split into two lineages, perhaps as a result of tectonic forces that caused the Great Rift in East Africa and resultant climatic change.

■ Pongids (ancestors of modern apes) remained in the forested area west of the rift, whereas hominids (ancestors of modern humans) adapted to wooded and more open areas east of the rift.

**page 133**

■ Pongids evolved brachiation and later either fist or knuckle walking as locomotor specialties; hominids evolved bipedal specialization.

■ Early hominids are diagnosed by bipedal locomotion; later, brains became larger, teeth and jaws changed, and faces became smaller.

■ Bipedalism required a complete overhaul of anatomy from the foramen magnum in the skull down to platform feet and lined-up toes.

■ Of the various hypotheses explaining why bipedalism evolved, the bioenergeties/thermoregulation model best explains how bipeds could be successful in the mixed East African woods and savanna.

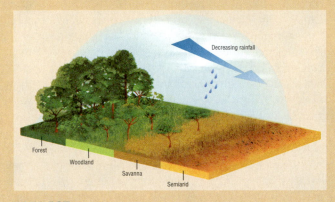

**page 137**

■ Taxonomically, two hominid genera are identified: *Australopithicus* and *Homo*.

■ The genus *Australopithecus* consists of gracile and robust forms, dates between about 4.2 and 1.2 myr ago, and is found exclusively in Africa.

■ The australopithecines share many traits, including habitual bipedalism, a small cranial capacity, large teeth, and no chins.

■ *A. anamensis* from Kenya, dated about 4.1 myr ago, is the earliest australopithecine, known from 78 specimens. *A. afarensis* and the famous "Lucy" fossil still have relatively longer arms than legs and are relatively small in both size and cranial capacities. *A. africanus* has been known since 1925 and represents the last of the gracile australopithecines, dating between 3.2 and 2.3 myr ago. *A. robustus* and *A. boisei* range from 3.2 to 1.2 myr ago; they have large saggital keels along the midline of their skulls, and very wide faces.

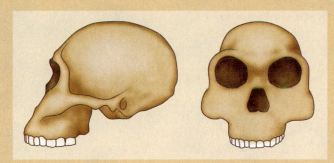

**page 162**

■ The genus *Homo* enters with *H. habilis*. Both the demise of the australopithecines and the rise of the genus *Homo* may have been due to a global cooling and drying with resultant change in food resources.

## KEY WORDS

australopithecines, 145
*Australopithecus afarensis*, 150
*Australopithecus africanus*, 154
*Australopithecus anamensis*, 149
*Australopithecus boisei*, 158
*Australopithecus garhi*, 154
*Australopithecus robustus*, 158
bioenergetics/thermoregulation
   model, 138
bipedalism, 132

Black Skull, 159
brain evolution, 140
cladistics, 141
facultative bipedalism, 136
habitual bipedalism, 136
*Homo*, 160
*Homo habilis*, 160
lumper, 144
modern taxa, 142
phenetics, 141

postorbital constriction, 147
quadrupedalism, 134
sexual dimorphism, 147
splitter, 144

## SUGGESTED READING

Dart, R. *Adventures with the Missing Link*. New York: Harper, 1959. This is an autobiography with an emphasis on finding, analyzing, and supporting the hominid status of the Taung child that Dart discovered in 1925.

Foley, R. *Another Unique Species: Patterns in Human Evolutionary Ecology*. New York: Wiley, 1987. Foley puts "us" in our place by showing that although we are one unique species, all other species are unique too. Although a bit dated, this book still gives some good insights into human evolution in the context of general evolution.

Johanson, D., and M. Edey. *Lucy: The Beginning of Humankind*. New York: Warner Books, 1981. A narrative account of Don Johanson's discovery of the famous "Lucy" fossil.

Reader, J. *Missing Links: The Hunt for Earliest Man*. Boston: Little, Brown, 1995. Another readable volume about hunting for and finding fossil materials. For those who love the adventure of finding fossils.

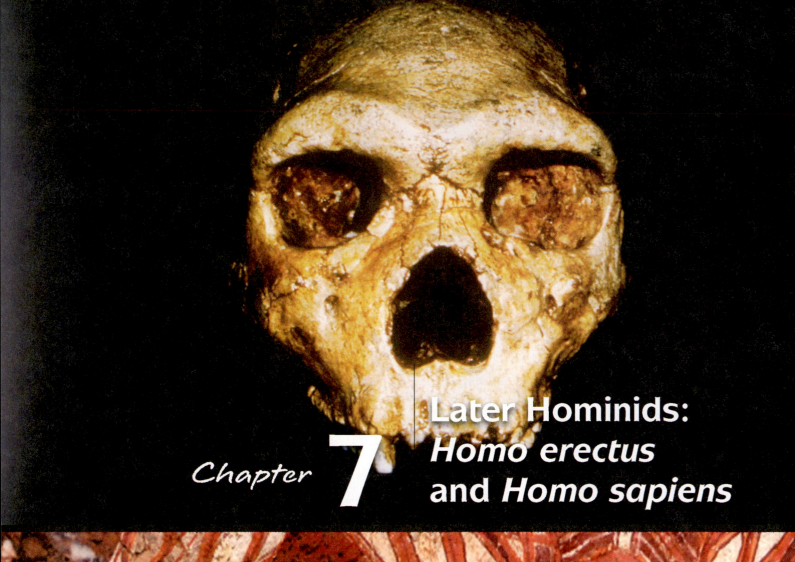

# Chapter 7

# Later Hominids: Homo erectus and Homo sapiens

■ **CHARACTERISTICS OF THE GENUS *HOMO***

■ ***HOMO ERECTUS*: THE CONTROVERSY AND THE SPECIES**
African *Homo erectus* • *Homo erectus* in Southeast Asia • *Homo erectus* in China • *Homo erectus* in Europe

■ **HIGHLIGHT 7.1:** *In Africa with Nariokotome*

■ **FROM *HOMO ERECTUS* TO *HOMO SAPIENS***

■ **EARLY ARCHAIC *HOMO SAPIENS***
African Archaics • Asian Archaics • European Archaics

■ **LATE ARCHAIC *HOMO SAPIENS* (NEANDERTALS)**

European Neandertals • Middle Eastern Neandertals • The Big Controversy: What Happened to the Neandertals?

■ **HIGHLIGHT 7.2:** *In the News with the Portugese Kid*

■ **ENTER ANATOMICALLY MODERN HUMANS (AMH)**
African AMH • Middle Eastern AMH • Asian and Australian AMH • European AMH • New World AMH • Models of Evolving AMH

■ **THE EVOLUTION OF SPEECH ABILITIES**
Communication, Language, Speech • Evidence for Speech Abilities

■ **CHAPTER SUMMARY**

▲
**Photo above:** The Petralona skull, a 300-kyr-old archaic *Homo sapiens* from Greece

Early hominid evolution is African evolution, from the first potential biped through the reorganization of the entire hominid body for effective and habitual bipedalism, and from the first australopithecine through the first species in the genus *Homo*. In contrast, later hominid evolution spread beyond Africa to the Middle East, Asia, and Europe. Early hominids are characterized by the bipedal lifestyle, but later hominids are characterized by encephalization (the reorganization and enlargement of the brain). From the neck down, other than modernization of limb proportions, relatively little changed in later hominids; but the cranium, face, and mandible have undergone considerable evolution during the last 2 myr.

Chapter 6 introduced *Homo habilis*, the first member of the genus. The habilines were all African hominids and appear to be the bridge between the genus *Australopithecus* and the rest of the genus *Homo*. This chapter first takes a closer look at what all members of the genus *Homo* have in common. This is followed by a continuing chronology, starting with the "intelligent opportunists," *Homo erectus*, who first ventured out of Africa, followed by our own species, *Homo sapiens*. The discussion of *H. sapiens* is divided chronologically into archaic *H. sapiens* (including Neandertal) and *Homo sapiens sapiens*, or anatomically modern humans (AMH). Finally, the topic of the evolution of speech abilities ends the chapter.

## Characteristics of the Genus *Homo*

The following derived cranial traits distinguish the genus *Homo* from *Australopithecus* (see the photo on p. 163). Because this set of traits defines the entire genus, for diagnostic purposes the traits must be present in both early and modern forms.

- a larger cranial capacity than *Australopithecus*
- less postorbital constriction
- more rounded crania
- absence of any crests
- absence of flaring zygomatic arches
- small facial skeleton relative to size of brain case
- absence of dish-shaped face
- less massive jaw
- smaller molars and premolars and smaller teeth than *Australopithecus*
- true parabolic-shaped dental arch

Traits such as taller stature, modern limb proportions, and much greater cranial capacity evolved after *H. habilis* and so do not define the entire genus.

## *Homo erectus*: The Controversy and the Species

*Homo habilis* was the first generally recognized species in the genus *Homo*, inhabiting East Africa between 2.5 and 1.8 myr ago, and some habiline population apparently evolved by transformism (anagenesis) to *Homo erectus* by 1.8 myr ago. Figure 7.1 diagrams the model of later hominid evolution used here. At least for now, experts accept this relatively direct evolutionary path because *H. habilis* was the only hominid population existing in East Africa before the first *H. erectus* evolved there some 1.8 myr ago.

*Homo erectus* is the taxonomic name traditionally given to the hominids that inhabited Eurasia as well as Africa between about 1.8 myr and approximately 400 kyr ago. *H. erectus* was the first hominid to leave Africa; all earlier hominids lived there. Very few Asian

**Homo erectus**
A species of *Homo* dated from 1.8 myr to approximately 400 kyr ago, first in Africa and then spreading to Asia and Europe.

*Figure 7.1*

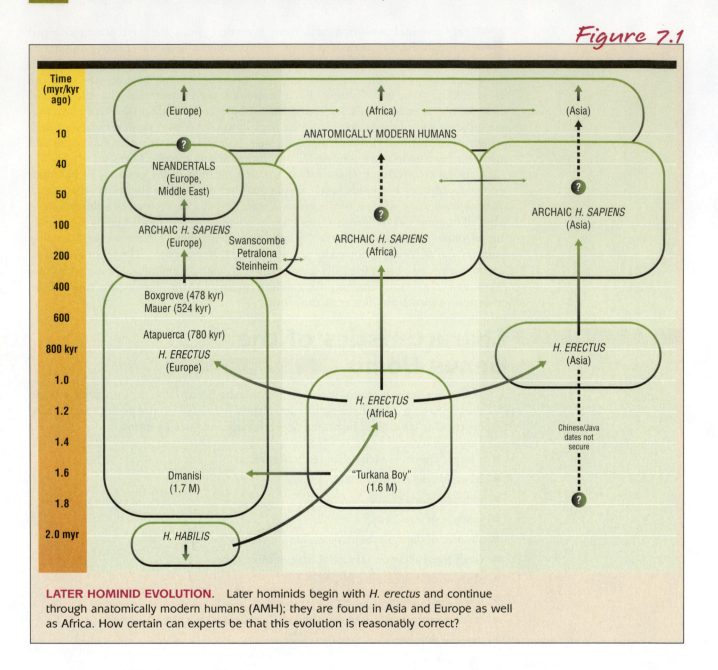

**LATER HOMINID EVOLUTION.**    Later hominids begin with *H. erectus* and continue through anatomically modern humans (AMH); they are found in Asia and Europe as well as Africa. How certain can experts be that this evolution is reasonably correct?

fossils have secure radiometric dates that are comparable to those for African fossils; ages assigned to most Asian fossils are based on faunal and paleomagnetic dating, complicating a global analysis of the species. It is likely, however, that migration out of Africa and then to the east began between 2 and 1 myr ago, followed by migration to the west between 1.5 and 1 myr ago (Manzi 2001).

There are three ways to approach the controversial status of this species, its taxonomy, and its populations:

1.  Milford Wolpoff (1996) suggests that *H. habilis* evolved directly into *H. sapiens*, with no "need" for *H. erectus* as an intermediate species.

2.  Fred Smith and his colleagues (1989) see *H. erectus* evolving in Africa and later migrating to Eurasia, with enough gene flow among many small populations to keep the species from splitting. Advocates of this "grade" approach do not ignore geographic distance but see the variability as being within the range of a single species.

3.   A third approach interprets the fossil evidence as variable enough to warrant species designations for each continent. Adherents of this view would retain the name *H. erectus* for East Asian fossils, because that name was first used in Asia. They propose *Homo ergaster* for African fossils and *Homo heidelbergensis* for European fossils. A new species, *Homo antecessor*, has been suggested for newly discovered Spanish fossils, but the term is not widely accepted (Arsuaga 2002; Stringer 2002a).

Figure 7.2 depicts these three approaches. Members of different schools of thought suggest from one to eight species for the genus *Homo*. To a large extent these different positions arise from a "super" lumper, lumper, or splitter perspective. It is not possible to state that one model is correct, but it is possible to decide which approach best helps us understand the last 2 myr of hominid evolution.

Fossils, and particularly artifacts attributed to *H. erectus*, are widely distributed in Africa, Europe, and Asia, as shown in Figure 7.3. There will always be more artifacts than fossils, however, for any hominid population. One reason lies in preservation bias: Flint tools do not biodegrade, but bone preserves only under exceptional circumstances (see Chapter 2). More importantly, a hominid has only one body to turn into a possible fossil, but an average hominid leaves thousands of artifact bits strewn behind in one lifetime. Therefore, artifacts are a better indicator of a population's distribution than fossils. And the widespread pattern of later hominid artifacts suggests that no group was likely totally isolated for a long period of time; groups probably interbred on their borders throughout the period of later hominids' existence (Eckhardt 2000).

These later hominids probably never migrated in the sense of purposefully moving to new territory. Rather, as populations expanded, certain groups within a band would

*Figure 7.2*

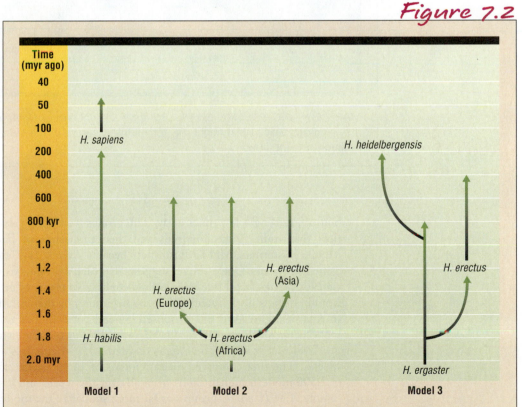

**HOMO ERECTUS: THREE POSSIBLE APPROACHES.**   Shown here are the "super-lumper" model of *Homo erectus* evolution (left), the lumper model we follow in this text (middle), and a splitter model (right). Which model best explains human evolution?

*Figure 7.3*

| | | |
|---|---|---|
| 1. Lake Turkana | 13. Kabwe | 25. Lagar Velho |
| 2. Olduvai | 14. Bodo | 26. Mladec |
| 3. Nariokotome | 15. Steinheim | 27. Klasies River |
| 4. Java (Solo River) | 16. Swanscombe | 28. Border Cave |
| 5. Zhoukoudian | 17. Petralona | 29. Omo Kibish |
| 6. Lantien | 18. Hadar | 30. Cro-Magnon |
| 7. Longgupo | 19. Gibraltar | 31. Niah |
| 8. Dmanisi | 20. Krapina | 32. Wadjak |
| 9. Ceprano | 21. Tabun/Kebara/Amud | 33. Lake Mungo |
| 10. Mauer | 22. Zafaraya | 34. Shanidar |
| 11. Boxgrove | 23. Vogelherd | 35. Herto |
| 12. Atapuerca | 24. Vindija | |

**MAP OF *HOMO ERECTUS* SITES.** Note the distribution of *Homo erectus* sites. Why are they semiclustered? What might the semidiffused nature of the sites tell us about species isolation or gene flow?

bud off, settling a few miles away. The groups were likely always in contact, with gene flow the result. With hundreds and then thousands of buddings, Africans became Middle Easterners, Middle Easterners became Asians, and later Middle Easterners became Europeans. One estimate suggests that such a process from East Africa to East Asia via North Africa and the Middle East could have taken as little as 25 kyr. K-Ar dating would not be able to detect either the beginning or the end of such a process, however (Eckhardt 2000). And this proposed general pattern does not exclude the probability that during this long period of time, many groups became extinct.

Two recent studies investigated whether *H. erectus* was a single species or several species. The first compared measurements of 16 *H. erectus* skulls to the measurements of 2,500 modern human skulls from all over the world and 8 skulls of a mixed hominid sample. The *H. erectus* group was far more similar to the modern individuals than to the mixed hominid species, suggesting on morphological grounds that *H. erectus* was a single species inhabiting a geographically variable area (Kramer 2002). A second study compared the two modern chimpanzee species to Asian and African *H. erectus* fossils.

This study concluded that the two chimpanzee species show far more variability than the Asian and African *Homo* populations and that *H. erectus* was one species (Williams and Hall 2005). Our position is that *H. erectus* was a single, variable species transitional between *H. habilis* and *H. sapiens* and that it migrated out of Africa via North Africa (and perhaps across the Straits of Gibraltar) and through the Middle East, and became established first in Asia and Southeast Asia and then in Europe. When necessary, this book includes a geographical term such as African, Asian, or European to identify specific *H. erectus* populations.

Regardless of time or geography, *H. erectus* populations shared certain traits. Important ancestral traits that are found in all specimens include heavy brow ridges that are continuous across the face, considerable postorbital constriction, sloping foreheads, football-shaped skulls, and conical-shaped rib cages. The following are the derived traits that evolved during the transformation and diagnose the species:

- smaller and more lightly constructed face and smaller teeth and reduced molar size compared to the australopithecines
- sagittal keel (depression and ridge across the midline of the skull) (see Figure 7.4)
- larger cranial capacity (30 percent larger than that of *H. habilis*) with a range from 700 to 1,250 cc and an average of 1,000 cc, increasing over time (though not continuously) and also varying by sex
- skull widest at the base when viewed from the back
- smaller and less flaring zygomatic arch than in *H. habilis*, with arch not extended beyond the ear
- flatter face with less general prognathism (jaw protuberance)
- alveolar prognathism (protuberance in mouth area only)
- taller stature than previous hominids
- less-sloping forehead
- pronounced occipital torus (bone that juts out on back of skull), probably for attachment of powerful neck muscles

*Figure 7.4*

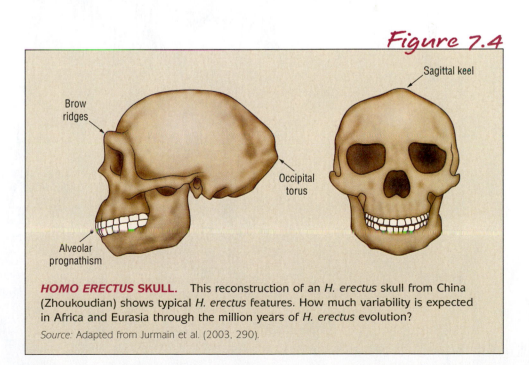

**HOMO ERECTUS SKULL.**  This reconstruction of an *H. erectus* skull from China (Zhoukoudian) shows typical *H. erectus* features. How much variability is expected in Africa and Eurasia through the million years of *H. erectus* evolution?
*Source:* Adapted from Jurmain et al. (2003, 290).

- projecting nose, as evidenced by the nasal aperture that projects forward and downward, perhaps as an adaptation to more temperate environments
- large eye orbits
- mandibular torus (thick bone at midline on inside of jawbone)
- thick long-bone shafts
- larger body size relative to body weight
- life expectancy estimated at 50 years (Swisher et al. 2000)
- modern proportions of legs and arms (Rightmire 1985) (see Figure 7.5)

The EQ for *H. erectus* as a genus ranges from 2.0 to 4.0, depending on the individual, the time, and the location.

*Figure 7.5*

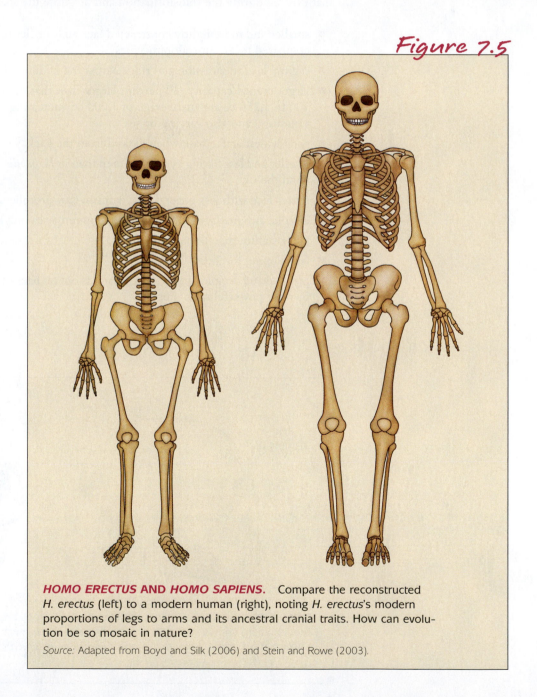

**HOMO ERECTUS AND HOMO SAPIENS.** Compare the reconstructed *H. erectus* (left) to a modern human (right), noting *H. erectus*'s modern proportions of legs to arms and its ancestral cranial traits. How can evolution be so mosaic in nature?

*Source:* Adapted from Boyd and Silk (2006) and Stein and Rowe (2003).

One problem that hampers the study of *H. erectus* relates to dating. Many *H. erectus* finds fall between the two reliable chronometric dating techniques, being too young for K-Ar and too old for $^{14}$C dating. Thus, researchers must use experimental dating techniques that support lower levels of confidence, as discussed in Chapter 8.

Why *H. erectus* migrated, whereas none of the australopithecines did, is not known. Shifts in worldwide sea levels may have been a factor in that they allowed movement out of Africa. Complex environmental conditions may have favored temperate dwellers with the social and intellectual nature of *H. erectus*. As Robert Foley (1987) reminds us, wolves, lions, leopards, hyenas, and hominids all reached Eurasia about the same time; all were large, carnivorous, social and, despite their origins in the African tropics, able to adapt to temperate environments. Additionally, it has been suggested that the possible carnivorous activities of *H. erectus* were connected to population expansion, because carnivores need large territories (Foley 2001; O'Connell et al. 2002; Walker and Shipman 1996).

We take a lumper perspective and refer to all *H. erectus* by one species name. This perspective assumes there was enough gene flow between adjacent groups that no group was totally isolated for long; nonetheless, all populations were not identical at any given time. What follows is a description of each of the continent-wide *H. erectus* populations, beginning with the first on the scene, in Africa, followed by the Southeast Asian and continental Asian populations, and then the the European population.

## African *Homo erectus*

The oldest *H. erectus* fossil materials showing the diagnostic derived traits come from the Lake Turkana site in Kenya and date between 1.8 and 1.78 myr ago. There are more than 100 individuals represented from Olduvai Gorge and Lake Turkana alone, and the inventory includes complete crania, many mandibles, and a representative assortment of postcranial bones. Some fossils from as far north as Ethiopia, as far west as Algeria, and as far south as South Africa have been given tentative *H. erectus* status. (See Highlight 7.1 for a description of one of the most complete fossils, nicknamed "Turkana Boy.")

Postcranial changes are not as dramatic as cranial changes in *H. erectus*, but two are worth noting. First, African *H. erectus* was the first hominid population to show limb proportions that are similar to those of modern humans; even *H. habilis* had long arms relative to legs. This finding suggests that *H. erectus* was a totally committed and habitual biped, with long strides and completely extended lower legs. Second, the body mass of *H. erectus* was 50 percent larger than that of *H. habilis*.

From the neck up, African *H. erectus* populations are distinctly different from *H. habilis*. First, the cranial capacity of *H. erectus* ranged between 750 and 1,250 cc, averaging 30 percent larger than that of habilines. The shape of the skull also changed, with a sagittal keel (a depression on either side of a small midline ridge) forming at the top of the skull. The width of the skull became largest at the base; and a less-sloping forehead evolved, as well as a pronounced torus (protuberance) at the back of the skull, large eye orbits, and a nasal opening that faced forward and downward.

East Africa was drier and warmer when *H. erectus* existed, with more open savanna than woodland. Sweating bipeds could successfully forage the savanna during the heat of the day, scavenging plant foods and grass-eating herbivores.

## *Homo erectus* in Southeast Asia

When Eugene Dubois found a skullcap, femur, and fragment of mandible at the Trinil site near the Solo River (Java) in 1891, he hailed his find as the "missing link" between apes and humans; his original name for the fossil, *Pithecanthropus erectus*, or "ape-man who walks erect," attested to his belief. At that time opinion was divided on whether humans evolved in Africa or Asia. Dubois was the first "adventurer" to search actively for

# In Africa with Nariokotome

SCIENTISTS JUDGE ONE ANOTHER'S WORK (and their own) on the basis of its methods of inquiry, including methods of gathering data. Methods that sound good in theory often do not work in practice. And sometimes scientists find their data by "dumb luck"—by stumbling across it.

One such piece of data in bioanthropology, and a very important discovery, is technically designated KNM WT 15000 and was found in August of 1984 on the west side of Lake Turkana, Kenya. The fossil is usually called by its nickname, "Turkana Boy"—because the investigators judged the hominid to have been a male (by virtue of the shape of the sciatic notch in his pelvis) who was about 11 years old at death. Turkana Boy has other designations: Nariokotome (pronounced nar-ee-oh-KO-tow-may) is the name of the site where he was found, and he fits the taxonomic category of *Homo erectus*. Before this discovery little was known of the postcranial skeleton of *H. erectus*. Now, although one fossil does not describe an entire species, matching existing pieces of postcrania with this almost complete fossil has allowed bioanthropologists to come to at least tentative conclusions about more than just the skull. The fossil has been well dated to 1.6 myr ago.

Turkana Boy was discovered when Richard Leakey and Alan Walker led a team doing a foot survey at Nariokotome. Nothing had been found in two weeks, and they were planning to move on to another spot if they were not successful soon. While Leakey and Walker were away in Nairobi doing administrative work, Kamoya Kimeu, the local head of the famous "hominid gang," found a piece of bone measuring about 2 inches by 1 inch. That was the original Turkana Boy find. The "hominid gang" of six was so named because of its tremendous success at finding hominid remains in East Africa; all six are members of the Wakamba tribe, and most are Kimeu's relatives. Kimeu describes his successful methodology as keeping his eyes on the ground and walking the same area over and over in different directions. Sunlight can high-light a sliver of bone that he might miss if walking in another direction; rain or blowing wind can move soil overnight to expose slightly different surfaces. But beyond methodology there is intuition. Most people are unable to articulate how they actively search for fossils in the most unlikely spots and find them. Almost anyone can excavate a bed designated by geologists as being of the right date, and such an excavation may be successful. But when an individual fossil is spread out over half a mile of rolling dry soil and the intuitive fossil hunter walks up an improbable ravine and finds a mandible, or looks under the roots of a small tree and finds a skull, or says "I'm gonna look over here again" knowing he or she has walked that area four times already but finds a fossil the fifth time around, that's fossil intuition.

On this particular occasion, Kimeu was in an improbable spot that had been well trampled by boys and their herds of cattle, but he saw and pulled up that bit of bone, looked at it, and knew immediately it was hominid because it was smooth inside. It turned out to be a piece of the frontal bone of a skull. The next day the "gang" searched for more bone bits on the surface but found nothing. A phone call to Nairobi alerted Leakey and Walker to the possibility of an important find, and they returned the following day. The closest thing to scientific methodology in this story is that the team then did a systematic survey and sieving of the entire area on hands and knees with "Olduvai picks," six-inch nails set in carved wooden handles. The workers used the picks to break up the top 2 inches of surface pebbles and sediment. After picking the area they put all of the loose soil in bowls and then ran it through a large sieve, removing potentially interesting pieces for further study. Bits and pieces of bone and tooth showed up until late September, after which nothing more was found. The National Geographic Society in Washington, D.C., a longtime financial supporter of the extended Leakey family, made the official announcement of the find.

Although the team had recovered most of Turkana Boy's bones (a total of over 150 pieces of bone and teeth), they anxiously looked forward to the second season (1985); during that season they succeeded in recovering all of the remaining teeth except one molar, as well as some additional bones. The team found a few bones in the third season, but only two pieces in the fourth season. In the fifth and last season, they found nothing, so the work stopped. Walker and Leakey calculated that during five seasons their team had turned and sieved 1,500 cubic meters of sediment by hand and had exposed 425 square meters of land surface; that's the equivalent of turning over a piece of land about 100 feet long by 45 feet wide. After assessing the bones (and gluing together some of the fragmented pieces), they calculated they had found 66 percent of the individual. Using the principle of bilateral symmetry, they reassembled the fossil and determined that the only missing bones were parts of long bones and most of the hand and foot bones.

Perhaps the most interesting findings about Turkana Boy are his likely stature and body proportions. If he had lived to adulthood, most experts believe he would have grown to be a six-footer. Although this stature measurement has been challenged, Turkana Boy was not unusual relative to the other five African *H. erectus* fossils that can be statured. With a range from 158 to 185 cm (5 feet 2 inches to 6 feet 1 inch) and averaging 170 cm (5 feet 6 inches), this population compares with the tallest 17 percent of modern human populations. Weight estimates put them into a middle weight category compared to moderns. Measuring Turkana Boy's arms and legs allowed Alan Walker and his zooarchaeologist wife, Pat Shipman, to calculate two ratios: the ratio between the lengths of the upper arm and the forearm, and the ratio between the lengths of the thigh and the lower leg. Individuals with high values in these ratios are said to be cold adapted by having extremities that conserve heat; individuals with low values are warm adapted, having extremities that dissipate heat. Turkana Boy turned out to be "supertropical," as are modern Africans in the same geographic area; geologists tell us the climate has not changed very much in the last 2 myr. Turkana Boy and his contemporaries were well adapted to their African environment. Using another test, Walker and Shipman concluded that Turkana Boy was superbly strong, running over the hot open savannas at a pretty good clip, sweating through the skin of his long, lean torso and extremities.

*Sources:* Walker, A., and R. Leakey, eds. 1993. *The Nariokotome Homo erectus skeleton.* Berlin: Springer.  Walker, A., and P. Shipman. 1996. *The wisdom of the bones: In search of human origins.* New York: Knopf.

turn back to your reading

fossils, and he was so convinced of an Asian origin that he purposely requested posting to the Dutch East Indian Army as a physician, serving on Java in what is now Indonesia. Dates for fossils were pure speculation then, but on the basis of comparative morphology, the Java materials were thought to be between 700 and 200 kyr old. Dubois's finds were not met with universal acclaim; as one story goes, he buried the bones under the floorboards of his house in the Netherlands and would not let anyone see them. Thirty years later he relented, still clinging to his belief that they constituted the missing link (White and Brown 1973).

Excavations between 1931 and 1993 at four other sites on Java added to the original materials, providing a total of 23 skulls and postcranial bones or teeth of more than 200 individuals (Baba et al. 2003). A general picture of the Java fossils, now classified as *H. erectus*, suggests the group had a somewhat differently shaped skull than the African group, with smaller brow ridges and a slightly smaller cranial capacity (in the 800 to 1,000 cc range).

K-Ar dates have resulted in controversy over the migration of African *H. erectus* into Asia. It was assumed until recently that about 1 myr ago African populations of *H. erectus* migrated north and then east, eventually reaching eastern China by about 700 kyr ago and Java by about 500 kyr ago. The K-Ar dates, however, put *H. erectus* populations on Java 1.8 to 1.6 myr ago (Swisher et al. 1994). But the first African *H. erectus* specimens have been given the same 1.8-myr date. So if both sets of dates are correct, migration out of Africa took place immediately after the evolution of *H. erectus* there and was fast and unidirectional (Dunsworth and Walker 2002). Alternatively, because the exact location of the original 1891 sites cannot be known with confidence (the samples were taken in the mid-1990s from the assumed original sites), the dating for the Java materials may not be correct (Gibbons 2001b; Lewin 1994).

Another dating controversy over Java *H. erectus* materials concerns the other end of the range. Electron spin resonance (ESR) and uranium (U-series) dating was performed on the enamel of bovid (ancestors of modern cows) teeth from museum collections and on newly excavated fauna from a late Java site. Assuming both the bovid and hominid bones were from the same layer, the surprising date the tests indicated—between 53 and 27 kyr ago—is considerably younger than any other estimate (Swisher et al. 1996). Many scholars remain skeptical, because the hominid fossils may not have been in the same level as the bovid teeth/bones. On the other hand, given Java's "outlier" geographic position, it is possible that there was a continuation of *H. erectus* there long after the other Asian groups evolved to *Homo sapiens* status or were replaced by more modern populations. (See Highlight 15.1.)

## *Homo erectus* in China

Chinese and Western investigators began excavations in China in the lower cave at Zhoukoudian (near Beijing) in 1927 and continued until the outbreak of World War II. The fossils they found were originally called *Sinanthropus pekinensis* ("ape-man from Peking") but are similar enough to the Java fossils to be subsumed in a single species. Of the original collection of 14 skullcaps (6 of which were relatively complete), several dozen cranial fragments, 15 mandible fragments, and more than 100 teeth (representing up to 45 individuals), all but 2 teeth were lost when the collection disappeared after workers packed it up for shipping to safety at the beginning of the war. Luckily, excellent casts and drawings had been made. From these researchers have identified male, female, and subadult specimens, providing a reasonably good view of the range of the population. The cranial capacity for the group ranges from 915 to 1,225 cc, with an average of 1,053 cc.

Dating Chinese materials has always been difficult. Until recently most experts assigned them to between 500 and 400 kyr ago (Stringer 2002a), but two new dates have potentially changed the timing for the first hominids in East Asia. The first new date is of tools dated by polarity and then K-Ar cross-dated in Africa to roughly 1.36 myr ago (Zhu et al. 2001). The second new date is a redate of an adult mandible found in

Longgupo cave. ESR coupled with paleomagnetism and paleofauna dating puts these finds as early as 1.9 myr ago, 100 kyr *before* the assumed ancestral population existed in Africa (Wanpo et al. 1995; Wood and Turner 1995). Obviously, the new dates may be incorrect, or there may be earlier unfound African *H. erectus* fossils, or Africa may not have been the homeland of all modern hominids. In view of the fact that two of the dating techniques gave dates that differ by 1 myr on the same material, it is likely that the 1.9-myr-ago date is incorrect.

At another site, Lantien, in central China, the fossil crania show thicker bones and a smaller cranial capacity (780 cc). These fossils' estimated age is between 800 and 730 kyr ago.

Chinese researchers have paleomagnetically dated two incisors attributed to *H. erectus* as early as 1.7 myr ago; these materials were found in 1965 in Yunnan Province, in southern China. However, the same materials were later dated at 600 to 500 kyr ago using another test and at 1.6 to 1.1 myr ago by ESR (Wu 2004). For materials from four other sites, using five different techniques, the dates range from 1.15 myr to 200 kyr ago (Liu et al. 2005). Again, dating of Chinese materials is difficult. However, the morphological traits for the group are relatively consistent, and sometimes morphology must serve as a way to date individual fossils.

The Chinese *H. erectus* population differs to some extent both from the African *H. erectus* population, from which it had presumably evolved several hundred thousand years previously and several thousand miles away, and from its nearer Southeast Asian (Java) cousins. The Chinese fossils also have a number of "purely Asian" similarities: shovel-shaped incisors (shaped like the edges of a shovel if it were pointed at you), low and flat upper facial areas, a unique trait of the sutures between the frontal bones, and nine other traits that are not unique but occur at a higher percentage than in any other *H. erectus* population (Wu 2004). The cranial capacity for these fossils ranges from 750 to 1,225 cc, with an average around 1,000 cc.

Paleoenvironmentalists have described China's climate during this time period as temperate. Thus, small animals such as hedgehogs, frogs, rabbits, and mice would have been available in large numbers for *H. erectus* to eat, as well as many unknown edible plants.

## *Homo erectus* in Europe

Some experts conclude there are no fossil materials in Europe attributable to the *H. erectus* grade and instead assign early *H. sapiens* status to all European remains. They also assign all artifact materials, many of which date earlier than any fossil material, to *H. sapiens*. Other experts assign a separate species designation and name, *H. heidelbergensis*, to the European fossils. Keeping to the lumper perspective, we will refer to fossils dated before about 400 kyr ago as European *H. erectus* (Dean and Delson 1995).

The earliest *H. erectus* materials in Europe are from Dmanisi, a site in the Caucasus Mountains in the Republic of Georgia (former USSR), well dated to between 1.8 and 1.7 myr ago by geomagnetism, radiometric dating of the basalt, and paleofauna. The original 1991 find was a single well-preserved mandible with thick bone, complete with 16 fairly small teeth (Gabunia and Vekua 1995; Lordkipanidze 1999). In 1997 investigators found two small crania (capacity under 800 cc), one with almost a complete face, and a foot bone; in 2002 four new and even smaller (600 cc) crania were found (Abrams 2003). The Dmanisi population contains skulls from individuals of both sexes and at least three adults, one young adult, and two adolescents, giving this group the variability that is helpful in establishing any hominid group's morphological range (deLumley et al. 2006). Some differences between the Dmanisi materials and African *H. erectus* would be expected, given the distance between them. Because of Dmanisi's pivotal location on the Eurasian border, and because workers located more than 1,000 African-looking tools along with the fossils, Giorgio Manzi—a paleoanthropologist from the University of Rome—has called the Dmanisi people "the missing link between Africa,

Europe, and Asia" (Balter and Gibbons 2000). When researchers compared the first Dmanisi skull to a *H. erectus* specimen from Africa, the two skulls were so similar that "they might have come from twins" (Shipman 2000, 492; see also Gabunia and Vekua 2001; Lontcho 2000). Because the Dmanisi skulls are somewhat smaller than other *H. erectus* skulls, however, some experts suggest *H. habilis* status; the original discoverer suggests they were merely small *H. erectus* (Wilford 2002). The early date of 1.7 myr for the Dmanisi fossils also gives support to an early migration for the East and Southeast Asia hominids.

Another early *H. erectus* fossil was found in 1974 at Ceprano, Italy, and K-Ar dated to about 700 kyr old. Although the cranium was incomplete, investigators have estimated the capacity at a fairly large 1,185 cc (Ascenzi et al. 1996; Ascenzi and Segre 2000). The Ceprano skull showed a low, receding forehead, no keel, large brow ridges, thick bones, and only moderate postorbital constriction. Because there are no other western European *H. erectus* crania, the capacity reflects a single estimate.

The most famous *H. erectus* material in western Europe is the Mauer mandible, named for the town near Heidelberg, Germany, where workers found the fossil in 1907. Mauer's original name was *Homo heidelbergensis*, the term now preferred by those who feel that the European fossils represent a species separate from the rest of the *H. erectus* grade. In the absence of any cranial material, it is difficult to assess the Mauer mandible's evolutionary position. The jawbone is massive, but it has surprisingly small teeth, given the thickness of the bone, and it shows no chin. The date is estimated to be 524 kyr ago (Arsuaga 2002).

A single tibia (lower leg bone) augmented by two incisors, probably representing three different individuals, may represent England's oldest hominids. The site of Boxgrove in southern England had produced hundreds of elegant hand axes for a decade before excavators discovered the tibia in late 1993. The tibia is missing its ends but is very thick and robust. Student volunteers subsequently uncovered the incisors. The Boxgrove fossils are well dated by paleofaunal materials to about 478 kyr ago (Arsuaga 2002; Roberts 1994; Roberts et al. 1994). Archaeological evidence in Britain suggests early *H. erectus* activity there perhaps as long as 1 myr ago, but no fossil material that old has been found and the archaeological materials are in a preliminary state of analysis. One interpretation is that the archaeological evidence may indicate a few initial forays by *H. erectus* groups into northwestern Europe, with no long-term occupation until 750 kyr ago (Billsborough 1999; Parfitt et al. 2005).

A potential species of *Homo*, found at the Gran Dolina site in Atapuerca, Spain, was named *H. antecessor* by its Spanish excavators and dated by biostratigraphy, paleomagnetism, and ESR to about 780 kyr old (Arsuaga 2002; Carbonell et al. 1995). The ongoing excavation has yielded 92 fragments of 6 individuals, some of whom are assessed as having been between 3 and 18 years old at death (White 2001). The Spanish excavators saw little African morphology in the Atapuerca material, so they gave it a new species name. The excavators also assert that some of the Gran Dolina fossils show traits that "foreshadow" links to moderns; other experts disagree.

# From *Homo erectus* to *Homo sapiens*

**Homo sapiens**
A species of *Homo* whose members are both anatomically and behaviorally modern.

Although most experts agree that some kind of *Homo erectus* evolved to some kind of **Homo sapiens**, unresolved questions remain as to which population(s) so evolved—and where, when, and by what process. Experts now generally agree on the set of traits that identify *H. erectus* as a grade and on the set of traits that identify the *H. sapiens* grade. If populations showing those traits could be accurately dated, it should not be difficult to conclude where, when, and how one population evolved into the other. Unfortunately, there are two problems. First, as mentioned earlier, fossil material between approximately 400 and 100 kyr old is too young for K-Ar and too old for $^{14}$C, so dating it is difficult. Second, because there are multiple traits that describe and identify each species, some being variations of ancestral traits, classification is sometimes contentious. Experts do not even agree about which traits are the most important.

Concentrating on morphological traits, a comparison of *H. erectus* with *H. sapiens* is presented in Figure 7.5. The traits used to identify *H. sapiens* must diagnose early as well as modern forms. Ancestral traits (assumedly from *H. erectus*) include modern limb proportions, efficient walking and running, relatively robust postcranial anatomy and bones, and relatively thick and often continuous brow ridges. Derived *H. sapiens* traits include:

- more rounded head with more vertical forehead than *H. erectus*
- larger brain, with varying cranial capacity, but at least 1,100 cc
- less postorbital constriction
- flatter and smaller face relative to cranium

Interpretation of early *H. sapiens* finds continues to be as much an art as a science, with experts interpreting the same fossil material in different ways. The first hint of *H. sapiens* traits may have emerged as early as 500 kyr ago or as late as 250 kyr ago. Although the evolution of *H. sapiens* can be thought of as a continual process from earlier to modern times, experts differ as to whether the species evolved as one lineage or as two increasingly separate lineages that led to two species, Neandertals and modern humans. In either case it is clear that earlier and later populations differed morphologically. We consider *H. sapiens* to be a single evolving lineage. We divide this lineage into chronological/geographical phases, referring to the populations as early archaic *H. sapiens*, later archaic *H. sapiens* (Neandertals), and *H. sapiens sapiens*, also known as anatomically modern humans (AMH).

# Early Archaic *Homo sapiens*

Early archaic remains of *Homo sapiens* have been found in Africa, Asia, and Europe. The dating is particularly difficult and therefore provisional for this entire group of fossils and the populations they represent. **Archaic *Homo sapiens*** by definition is transitional between *H. erectus* and full *H. sapiens* status, and early archaic populations show traits of each. The term *archaic Homo sapiens* is not technically correct but is so entrenched in the literature that it would be too difficult to try to change it. It is used for all of the hominids (and all in the genus *Homo*) that existed between *H. erectus* and anatomically modern humans.

## African Archaics

One candidate for earliest *H. sapiens* status is an almost complete cranium from Kenya's Lake Turkana region, yet unnamed but U-series dated between 300 and 270 kyr ago. In view of its cranial capacity of around 1,400 cc, the excavators feel the find is "nearly modern" (Brauer et al. 1997). Eight other archaic *H. sapiens* fossils represent populations in Africa: Kabwe (also known as Rhodesian Man or Broken Hill), Bodo, and six that are less complete. Excavators found Kabwe in the course of a mining operation in the mid-1920s in what is now Zambia. Based on faunal remains, the nearly complete skull is provisionally dated between 400 and 125 kyr ago. The skull fits the morphology of archaic *H. sapiens* by virtue of its 1,280-cc cranial capacity and its low sloping forehead, occipital torus, massive face, and brow ridges (see Figure 7.6). Kabwe has the largest brow ridges, continuous across the upper face, ever seen on a fossil hominid and also shows a slight keel, an ancestral feature from *H. erectus*. Bodo, an Ethiopian skull, has a very large face with the widest part at the top, thick brow ridges, and a cranial capacity of 1,250 cc.

**archaic *Homo sapiens***
Populations of the genus *Homo* that existed in Africa, Asia, and Europe from about 500 kyr ago and were transitional between *H. erectus* and full *H. sapiens* status.

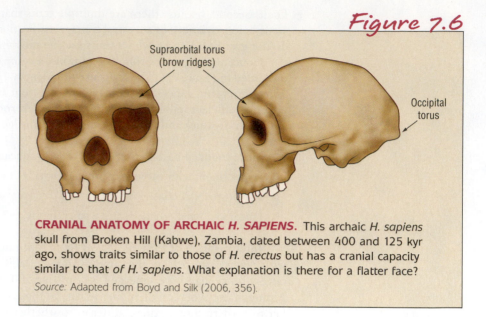

*Figure 7.6*

**CRANIAL ANATOMY OF *H. SAPIENS*.** This archaic *H. sapiens* skull from Broken Hill (Kabwe), Zambia, dated between 400 and 125 kyr ago, shows traits similar to those of *H. erectus* but has a cranial capacity similar to that *of H. sapiens*. What explanation is there for a flatter face?

*Source:* Adapted from Boyd and Silk (2006, 356).

## Asian Archaics

At least seven Chinese finds represent the populations of early archaic *H. sapiens* in Asia, dated between 300 and 200 kyr ago and showing cranial capacities ranging between 1,200 and 1,280 cc. In addition, all the skulls have large brow ridges and have retained the occipital torus.

One interesting fossil was of a single individual found at Jinniushan in northeastern China and dated to about 260 kyr ago. The cranial capacity is estimated to be about 1,300 cc, and the EQ is 4.5. It has been concluded that the fossil is a female, based on the pelvic bones, and a wide trunk and short limbs suggest she was well adapted to the cold climate in China at that time. This archaic female has been estimated to have been about 5 feet 6 inches (168 cm) tall and 175 pounds (79.5 kg) in weight (Rosenberg et al. 2000).

## European Archaics

European fossils of early archaic *H. sapiens* are relatively numerous, suggesting that populations roamed most of the continent. The fossils' mandibles are robust, and they have thick cranial bones, pronounced occipital toruses, and large brow ridges, all recalling *H. erectus* features. But they also show derived *H. sapiens* traits such as larger cranial capacity, ranging from 1,200 to 1,300 cc; more rounded occipital bones; flatter faces; larger parietals; and smaller teeth. Fossil crania from Steinheim (Germany) and Swanscombe (England) are good examples of northern European early archaics; the cranium from Petralona (Greece) shows some variation in archaics in

This archaic *H. sapiens* from Petralona, Greece, dates to perhaps 300 kyr ago. How much does it vary from the African specimen (Kabwe) in Figure 7.6?

Thirty-two individuals were found at the Pit of Bones site at Atapuerca in north-central Spain and dated at about 300 kyr ago. This "family portrait" represents the 32 hominids by age and sex. The artist's rendition of facial features is based on skull measurements and reconstructions. Did all 32 individuals live at the same time and constitute a single band?
*Source:* Mauricio Antón/Madrid Scientific Films. Used with permission.

southern Europe. Dating is difficult, but these archaics are judged to date from roughly 400 to 250 kyr ago (Stringer and Hublin 1999).

A second Spanish cave at Atapuerca has yielded a very different population from the older *H. erectus/antecessor* fossils half a mile away. The Sima de los Huesos (Pit of Bones) collection contains over 700 hominid bones, representing 32 individuals ranging from 4 to 35 years old and of both sexes, receiving the inevitable name "first family." This population is dated by ESR and U-series to about 300 kyr ago, and though variable, the population falls into the range of other European early archaics (Bermudez de Castro et al. 1997; Ferreras 1997). Some experts see resemblances to Neandertal in many of these early archaic fossils, particularly those from Steinheim and the Sima de los Huesos cave (Relethford 2001a).

## Late Archaic *Homo sapiens* (Neandertals)

**Neandertal**
A population of late archaic *Homo sapiens* that lived in Europe and the Middle East between about 150 and 28 kyr ago and are characterized by robust bodies and large cranial capacities.

We view Neandertals as a population of late archaic *H. sapiens*. The set of traits that diagnose these hominids appear to many experts to be similar enough to traits of both archaic and modern *H. sapiens* to include them in that species, but different enough to identify them with their own name: **Neandertal**. A number of molecular studies also support this classification (Note: There are two acceptable spellings of the name of these hominids: *Neandertal* and *Neanderthal*. But because the *h* is silent in German, the language of the name's origin, and the pronunciation is always with a silent *h*, *Neandertal* is the preferred spelling.)

Other experts, however, assign a separate species affiliation, *Homo neandertalensis*; this classification debate is one of hottest issues in paleoanthropology (Tattersall and Schwartz 1999). In fact, ever since the discovery of the first Neandertal, no population of hominids has caused as much disagreement. To some extent this controversy has to do with the fact that Neandertals are morphologically "strange" with their large brains, weak chins, and strong bodies. The negative public image began with the French anatomist Marcelin Boule's 1920 depiction of Neandertals as slouching, apelike beasts who walked on the outsides of their feet, using divergent big toes for balance; Boule had to admit that their cranial capacity was larger than that of modern humans, but he insisted that their brains were inferior to those of modern Frenchmen. The cartoon caricature of Neandertals as covered with hair, armed with clubs, wearing off-one-shoulder fur garments, dragging their mates into caves, and incapable of abstract thinking or speech was not far behind. There is still a great deal to understand about Neandertals, but it is now known that they were fully bipedal and did not walk on the outsides of their feet. Whether the Neandertal population had any place in the evolution of modern humans is still an unanswered question. But before we address that question, let's look at this interesting population in some detail.

Neandertal populations were restricted to a geographically circumscribed area: Europe (from Wales and Gibraltar in the west to Uzbekistan in the east) and the Middle East (from Israel to Iraq). There were no Neandertals in Africa or in Asia beyond Uzbekistan, though there were archaic *H. sapiens* populations there at the time. The group was also circumscribed in time: Some experts see Neandertal traits as far back as 350 kyr ago, and others believe they were a distinguishable population by 200 to 150 kyr ago (Stringer and McKie 1997). A bone in the inner ear area of all Neandertals called the "bony labyrinth" is found in early archaics such as those from Steinheim as well, suggesting possible origins from that archaic European population. Recently, some workers proposed an even earlier divergence based on molecular evidence and DNA "clocks." If the DNA clock is accurate, Neandertals and the lineage giving rise to anatomically modern humans (AMH) diverged 600 kyr ago, not later as the fossil evidence predicts (Arsuaga 2002; Marks 2002; Spoor et al. 2003). Although there are other scenarios, given their dates and distribution, Neandertals likely evolved in Europe and then some population(s) migrated to the Middle East, perhaps as a result of colder weather conditions further north.

The first identified Neandertal fossil, a skullcap, was found in a limestone quarry in the Neander Valley near Dusseldorf, Germany, in 1856. For over 150 years, its exact provenience was not known, as the limestone diggers merely tossed the skull over the edge of the front of the cave where they were digging. The skull's date will always be uncertain, because it is too old for $^{14}$C dating and there were no associated finds. Interestingly, in 1996 two German scientists deduced the location of the original dumped dirt and started excavating. Five years later, 86 more bone fragments had been found, some exactly fitting the original skull (Schmitz et al. 2002). Using comparisons and matching bones, the investigators deduced that at least three individuals came from the original Neander Valley site and could all have lived at the same time.

The first Neandertal skull ever found was at Gibraltar in 1848, but it went scientifically unnoticed for 16 years. Then the Neander Valley skullcap was discovered (Barton et al. 1999), followed by other early Neandertal fossils in Belgium and France between 1908 and 1909. The first Neandertal finds were attributed variously to a race of humans who lived in Europe before the Celts, then to a half-crazed man who happened to die in a shallow cave, to a Roman legionnaire on his way to France, and to a modern man with water on his brain. Obviously, there was no unanimity on what the early finds represented; there were few human fossils for context at that time, and only after additional fossils were found were they taken seriously. The total of Neandertal remains now exceeds 400 individuals, with both sexes and all ages well represented.

## Figure 7.7

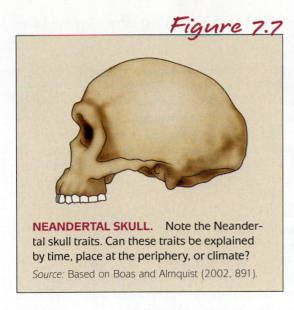

**NEANDERTAL SKULL.** Note the Neandertal skull traits. Can these traits be explained by time, place at the periphery, or climate?

*Source:* Based on Boas and Almquist (2002, 891).

## Figure 7.8

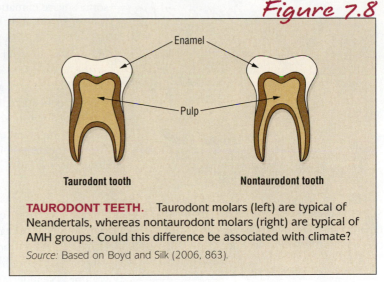

**TAURODONT TEETH.** Taurodont molars (left) are typical of Neandertals, whereas nontaurodont molars (right) are typical of AMH groups. Could this difference be associated with climate?

*Source:* Based on Boyd and Silk (2006, 863).

## Figure 7.9

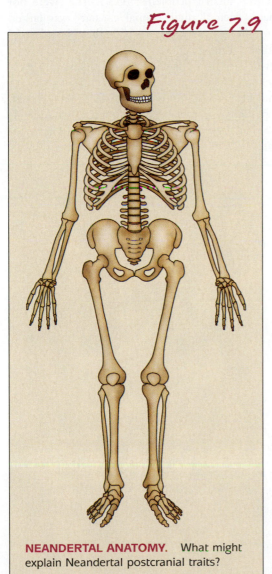

**NEANDERTAL ANATOMY.** What might explain Neandertal postcranial traits?

*Source:* Based on Tattersall (1999).

Although the Neandertal population did not evolve its identifiable characteristics all at once, it can be described as having the following distinctive morphological features, both ancestral and derived (Franciscus 2002; Frayer 1992a). Ancestral traits include the following:

- low sloping forehead, relative to AMH (see Figure 7.7)
- rounded and continuous brow ridge
- large and rugged mandible
- little or no chin
- relatively large incisors and relatively small molars
- taurodont molars (large pulp cavities and short roots) (see Figure 7.8)
- large, barrel-shaped rib cage (see Figure 7.9)
- long bones that are thick, somewhat curved, and rugged for muscle attachment

Derived traits include these:

- Shorter limbs than *H. erectus*
- large cranial capacity, ranging from 1,330 to 1,750 cc, averaging 1,520
- round eye orbits, like those of AMH
- occipital area of skull that comes to a "bun" (for attachment of neck muscles to counteract the pressure of the large face), resulting in an elongated skull
- large "pulled-out" face
- large and projecting nasal opening with likely large external nose
- retromolar space (space between last molar and ascending ramus of mandible) (see Figure 7.10)
- H-O (horizontal–oval) type of mandibular foramen (see Figure 7.11) in more than 50 percent of European fossils

One of the most distinctive Neandertal features is a "pulled-out" face with associated large nasal opening. Neandertals lived during

*Figure 7.10*

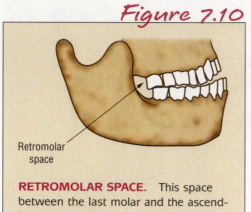

Retromolar space

**RETROMOLAR SPACE.** This space between the last molar and the ascending ramus is found only in European Neandertals and in AMH that replaced or interbred with Neandertals. What could its function be?

some severe climatic shifts, both long and short term. They lived during warm climates 150 to 125 kyr ago, then survived a cold phase between 90 and 80 kyr ago, followed by oscillating temperatures until 70 kyr ago, when cold climates returned and intensified until the demise of the population (van Andel and Tzedakis 1996). Neandertals' relatively short stature and barrel-shaped chest cavity likely evolved during the last cold stage, when being short and stocky could have helped in retaining body heat. Their large nasal openings probably allowed for the warming of air coming into nasal areas near the brain (Aiello 2000). It is likely that their large noses are related to temperatures, cold or warm. Retromolar space, a trait whose function is not understood, is found in at least 75 percent of European and Middle Eastern Neandertals (Franciscus and Trinkaus 1995).

The size of Neandertal crania is an embarrassment to those who want modern humans to be the tallest and the smartest and have the biggest brains. Although brain size does correlate loosely with problem solving (i.e., intelligence), complexity is apparently as important as volume. Neandertals were able to solve Neandertal problems just as modern humans can solve modern problems; Neandertals were not necessarily smarter than modern humans, even if their cranial capacity was larger. Because skull size also loosely correlates with body size, it is possible that Neandertals' larger body mass (not stature) explains their larger crania.

Postcranially, Neandertals show several features that distinguish them from both early archaics and modern humans. In general, they are more muscular and rugged, with slightly curved long bones. Although they averaged about 167 cm (5 feet 6 inches) tall, they had more body mass and weighed perhaps 30 percent more than modern individuals of equal height. The impression is that they had compact, powerful bodies that could conserve heat in cold environments and could endure great physical hardship.

*Figure 7.11*

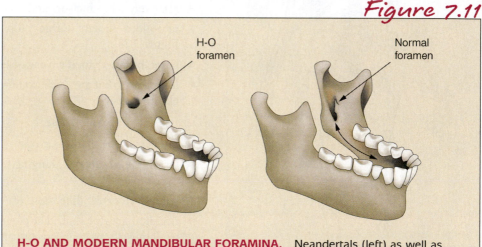

H-O foramen

Normal foramen

**H-O AND MODERN MANDIBULAR FORAMINA.** Neandertals (left) as well as many AMH that followed in Europe show the H-O (horizontal–oval) type of foramen (hole) in the jaw. As the label *H-O* indicates, a bar of bone covers the top of the *oval* hole and the long axis of the oval is oriented in a *horizontal* direction. Modern humans (right) show the non-H-O type. What function could the H-O mandibular foramen serve?

*Source:* From David W. Frayer, Milford H. Wolpoff, Alan G. Thorne, Fred H. Smith, and Geoffrey G. Pope, "Theories of Modern Human Origins: The Paleontological Test," *American Anthropologist,* Vol. 95, No. 1, p. 29. Copyright © 1993, American Anthropological Association. Used by permission. All rights reserved.

## European Neandertals

Neandertal fossils perhaps 120 kyr old and with the full complement of diagnostic traits were found at Krapina, Yugoslavia, where the remains of possibly 75 individuals were excavated (Trinkaus and Shipman 1992). Neandertals were the only hominids in Europe at that time. One European Neandertal trait is the H-O form of the mandibular foramen, a hole in the inside of the mandible that accommodates the mandibular nerve (refer to Figure 7.11). This feature occurs in more than 50 percent of European specimens. Neandertals continued to populate Europe until 28 kyr ago.

## Middle Eastern Neandertals

Neandertal remains in the Middle East (often referred to as Southwest Asia) have been found in about 20 burials at seven sites in Israel (including Kebara, Tabun, and Amud) and in Iraq (Shanidar) (Kaufman 2002). Experts believe that Neandertals "migrated" from eastern Europe in a southerly direction, perhaps during a warm interglacial period some 127 kyr ago. The Amud skull is the largest Neandertal skull from either Europe or the Middle East, coming in at a whopping 1,700 cc (Ronin 2003); Amud is also the tallest Neandertal at 178 cm (5 feet 10 inches). Generally, Middle Eastern Neandertals show less rugged features than European specimens; and though they are still recognizable as Neandertals, none shows the entire set of diagnostic traits. Stratigraphic and dating problems abound, and evidence is not conclusive as to whether Neandertals and AMH were in the region simultaneously or alternately (Kaufman 1999, 2002). Some fossils seem to show a combination of Neandertal and modern features, but this is a matter of interpretation; also, not all experts agree on which fossils show which traits. For example, the Amud fossil (perhaps 60 to 53 kyr old) has some Neandertal traits in the shape, length, and size of the skull. At the same time, however, Amud is tall and has small brow ridges, narrow zygomatic arches, a small mastoid, and even a small chin—all AMH traits. A specimen from Shanidar in Iraq, dated at 33 kyr ago, has similar features. No fossils with Neandertal traits less than 40 kyr old have been found in the Middle East.

## The Big Controversy: What Happened to the Neandertals?

Describing Neandertals and deciding from which population they likely evolved is relatively easy compared to the question of what happened to them. Claiming they became extinct at the time after which no fossils with Neandertal characteristics have been dated begs the question. Because there is no single diagnostic Neandertal trait, what happened to these hominids is subject to interpretation, and there is still much controversy (Clark 2002).

Based on 429 [14]C-dated sites in Europe that contain either Neandertal or AMH bones or artifacts, various scenarios interpret what might have happened to the Neandertals. Between about 250 and 40 kyr ago, the only hominids in Europe were Neandertals. They were the natives when early moderns started colonizing from the east some 40 kyr ago, perhaps coming through a corridor in the great North European Plain just north of the Danube River or by water along the Mediterranean coast. Neandertal sites dating from 40 to 30 kyr ago are found less and less often, with only two areas—France and the south and western parts of the Iberian Peninsula—showing Neandertal habitations until 32 kyr ago. Modern humans appeared in eastern Europe in only two areas by 43 kyr ago; but they moved westward, eventually colonizing all of Europe by 27,500 years ago (Bocquet-Appel and Demars 2000). An east-to-west movement of AMH mirrors an east-to-west and north-to-south decline of Neandertals.

Theoretically, there are at least three possible scenarios for the demise of the Neandertals:

1. Neandertals *evolved directly* into AMH in Europe and the Middle East, whereas archaic *H. sapiens* with somewhat different traits evolved separately to AMH in Asia and Africa.

2. Neandertals *were replaced* in Europe and the Middle East by AMH who migrated from Africa into Europe via the Middle East, with no intermating.

3. Neandertals *interbred* in Europe and/or the Middle East with AMH, who migrated from Africa into Europe via the Middle East; Neandertals then became extinct through biological and cultural absorption into the larger population.

An assessment of evidence that supports or does not support each scenario should evaluate the likelihood that one (or none) best answers the question of what happened to the Neandertals. Traditionally, scholars refer to Neandertal culture as the Middle Paleolithic and early AMH culture (at least in Europe) as the Upper Paleolithic.

## Direct Evolution Scenario

Loring Brace (1991) hypothesized that Neandertal populations as a whole *evolved directly* into AMH in Europe. Before chronometric dating, this was a viable hypothesis, but more finely tuned [14]C dating of fossil remains of both populations has shown up to 7,000 years of overlap. Many workers had believed that Neandertals always preceded AMH and thus had assumed that they literally became them in 10 or 20 kyr. Under this scenario that very Neandertal face would have faded once there were different foods, less strain on the jaws, and no longer a need for warming air in the nasal passage. The occipital torus would have disappeared once the large face became smaller. The barrel chest and muscular body would have become lighter once the lifestyle became less rugged. All of the Neandertal traits could have disappeared in a matter of a few hundred generations. But when two populations coexist for a considerable period of time, as these did, it is biologically impossible for one to evolve into the other. Thus, the direct evolution scenario has been rejected.

## Replacement Scenario

If invading AMH populations *replaced* Neandertals in Europe by any means (killing them, outsmarting them, outcompeting them for resources, coping better with rapid climatic change, outreproducing them, introducing an infectious disease for which Neandertals lacked immunity, or having better stone points for their spears), there should be some evidence of this replacement in the fossil and artifact record. To be called "replacement" any such process would have had to be fairly quick, with one population disappearing as the other established itself. Let's look at a series of predictions about how the replacement might have occurred and ask what evidence supports or undermines each. Of course, there would not necessarily be evidence for all of the predictions. But, if AMH replaced Neandertal, there should be evidence for one or more of the following:

■ One population killed the other. There is no evidence of this.

■ The replacing population was better able to extract foods or used different animal resources. Tool technology was more complex for AMH than for Neandertals, but the tools do not seem to have had more functional specificity (Clark 2002); that is, animal resources and hunting/butchering activities were no different for the two populations in either Europe or the Middle East (Adler et al. 2006; Marks et al. 2001; Speth and Tchernov 2001).

■ Superior speech abilities translated into better communication skills. Unfortunately, fossil evidence for speech is limited and controversial. (The last section of this chapter will examine the evolution of speech abilities.) Some experts believe Neandertals could not have talked as modern humans do, because their throat and tongue anatomy would not have allowed them to speak rapidly or to make enough different vowel sounds to constitute true speech. Others criticize these conclusions and suggest that other evidence shows that Neandertals had the ability to speak. "Jehn Fremlen," for example, countered a contention that Neandertals could not properly use the English vowels *a, i,* and *u* by providing this insightful message in "Neandertalese":

> … et seems emprebeble thet ther speech wes enedeqwete bekes ef the leck ef the three vewels seggested. The kemplexete ef speech depends en the kensenents, net en the vewels, es ken be seen frem the generel kemprehensebelete ef thes letter. (Fremlin 1975, 600)

Fremlin is suggesting that even if Neandertals could not use the same vowels that English speakers use, it is a moot point. After all, many modern languages do not have these vowels.

■ The last common ancestral population to both AMH and Neandertals (some early European archaic population) existed long enough ago—estimated by some to be 600 to 300 kyr ago—to have split into two lineages/species. Studies that compared the mitochondrial DNA of four Neandertals to that of contemporary humans concluded that the DNA was different enough to warrant separate species status, but many critics claim the data and findings can be interpreted in several different ways (Krings et al. 2000; Ovchinnikov et al. 2001; Relethford 2001b; Wong 1998). Comparisons of the DNA of various closely related species of modern primates give mixed signals, some analyses suggesting that Neandertals and AMH are different enough to be separate species and some suggesting they are not (Gibbons 2001a). One comparison of DNA between Neandertals and early AMH did not settle the issue, because the two early moderns from Italy were only 24 kyr old and the Neandertals were more than 40 kyr old—and perhaps much older (Caramelli et al. 2003). A proper comparison requires multiple samples from both populations, all of similar age in order to avoid the criticism that differences are due to mutations that occurred in the modern lineage since the demise of Neandertals (Gutierrez et al. 2000). An ideal comparison would be between 30-kyr-old Neandertals and AMH. The Max Planck Institute in Leipzig has recently instituted the Neanderthal Genome Project, an international collaboration of scientists for sequencing the entire genome by 2008 (Adler 2006). At this point, however, with genetic data yielding ambiguous results, perhaps morphological criteria could help in establishing the relationship between Neandertals and AMH. Unfortunately, however, experts disagree on most everything morphological as well as molecular, including what criteria are valid for assessment (Stringer 2002b).

■ AMH had a higher birthrate, a lower death rate, or a shorter gestation period than Neandertals (Stringer 1984), thus "outliving" them. Demographic modeling suggests that with only a 0.5-percent difference in mortality, Neandertal extinction could have occurred in 1,000 years (Eswaran 2002). Unfortunately, this remains an untested hypothesis.

■ Severe oscillations in temperature existed during the time of the Neandertal/AMH overlap, a period that included both the warmest and the coldest temperatures on record in Europe. These extremes happened in as little as 20 years, or a single individual's lifetime. It could be argued that Neandertal populations could not cope with the likely stresses (food, psychological) that would accompany such dramatic shifts but that modern humans could (Stringer 2000; Stringer and Davies 2001). Again, this hypothesis remains untested.

If AMH replaced Neandertals, there should be no evidence of biological or cultural mixing. Fossils should be of one type or another, not hybrids. If any sites show interstratification during the overlap period, tools should be of one or the other type, not combinations of techniques. Finally, there should be no Neandertal fossils found with Upper Paleolithic tools and no AMH fossils with Middle Paleolithic tools. As we'll discuss below, however, some fossils are interpreted as hybrids; there are several interstratified sites showing tool traits of both Middle and Upper Paleolithic traditions; and there are at least two cases of Neandertal fossils in association with Upper Paleolithic technology.

In summary, none of the predictions is fully supported.

## Interbreeding Scenario

If Neandertals and AMH *interbred* (a lot or a little), there should be evidence of that hybridization, both biologically and culturally. First, AMH and Neandertal populations would have to have lived at the same time for interbreeding to be possible. The latest Neandertal fossil is dated at 28 kyr ago from Gibraltar, and the earliest AMH fossil is dated at 32 kyr ago from Vogelherd, Germany. These dates suggest a 5-kyr overlap for the two populations. The latest Neandertal artifacts are dated at 30 kyr ago in both Croatia and Gibraltar, and the earliest AMH artifacts are dated at 43 kyr ago in Bulgaria. So the artifact overlap is 13 kyr (Klein 2000; Smith et al. 1999).

The 5- to 13-kyr overlap of the two populations means they *could* have interbred, not that they *did*; but if there were no overlap, they could not possibly have interbred. Some experts point out that the overlap occurs only when all of Europe is considered but does not occur in any one circumscribed geographic area or at any single site. For example, the recently discovered Neandertal fossil at Vindija, Croatia, dated at 32 kyr old, overlaps the earliest AMH fossil found at Vogelherd, Germany, by 1 or 2 kyr—but the two sites are geographically separated by several hundred kilometers. It may be that Neandertals remained in forested valleys and AMH stayed in unforested upland areas, exploiting different econiches and rarely encountering each other.

Is there biological evidence of interbreeding? Neandertal and early AMH fossils in Europe share up to 20 morphological traits that are absent in Middle Eastern and African fossils, suggesting at least some interbreeding in Europe (Frayer 1992a). For the mandibular foramen trait, 52.6 percent of European Neandertals show the H-O variation; 44 percent of early Upper Paleolithic fossils (representing AMH), 5 percent of late Upper Paleolithic fossils, 2 percent of fossils in the succeeding Mesolithic, and 1 percent of skeletal remains in medieval Hungary also show the trait (Frayer 1992a, 1992b). One possible conclusion is that post-Neandertal Europeans inherited the H-O foramen from Neandertals through at least some interbreeding. A second trait, the suprainiac fossa (a depression in the upper rear of the skull), is present in 96 percent of Neandertals, 39 percent of early AMH, 24 percent of late AMH and 2 percent of living European populations (Wolpoff 1999). Interbreeding could explain this distribution as well. Finally, retromolar space, found in 75 percent of European and Middle Eastern Neandertals, occurs in 60 percent of Middle Eastern AMH and in 6 to 30 percent of people in European AMH populations (Franciscus and Trinkaus 1995). A few individuals have the trait today. Again, was this due to interbreeding?

Although the idea of possible biological hybridization has many critics, it gained support in the late 1990s with the discovery of a burial in Portugal, [14]C dated at 24.5 kyr ago, of a 4-year-old boy who some experts believe shows both Neandertal and AMH features (Duarte et al. 1999; Holden 1999; Klein 2000; Kunzig 1999). At most, the boy is the result of hybridization some 100 generations earlier, in view of the fact that the last Neandertal in that area dates to no later than 28 kyr ago. Also, not all agree with the trait interpretations. Ian Tattersall suggests that the "Portuguese Kid" was "simply a chunky Gravettian child," meaning an early AMH, not the result of Neandertal and AMH interbreeding (1999, 7119); see Highlight 7.2 (on pp. 192–193). Other fossils from the chronological overlap are viewed by some experts as showing features of each population. The Mladec (Czech Republic) cranium, dated between 33 and 30 kyr ago, seems to combine Neandertal robustness with AMH features. Some workers have concluded that the variable degrees of both sets of traits in the Middle East offer evidence of interbreeding there as well as in Europe.

Culturally, mixtures of the two tool types—Middle and Upper Paleolithic—might indirectly imply interbreeding, because an exchange of tool recipes *could* lead to an exchange of genetic materials as well. The Vindija site, for example, shows an archaeology layer with a combination of Middle and Upper Paleolithic tool elements (Smith et al. 1999), and perhaps 20 similar transitional sites exist in eastern and central Europe (Clark 2002; Mellars 1999; Zilhao and d'Errico 2000). Experts disagree on what these finds might mean. Possible explanations might be observation and imitation, the invention of new tool technologies by both groups at the same time, or intermixing of the two populations.

Three or four sites may interstratify archaeologically (rather than showing Neandertals always preceding AMH): La Piage and Roc-de-Combe in France plus El Pendo in Spain (Rigaud 2000). This interstratification suggests that both the late Neandertals and the first AMH groups sometimes chose the same places to live, but the tools in specific layers suggest they did so at different times.

Speculations about whether Neandertals did or did not interbreed with AMH are inconclusive, because much of the evidence itself is contradictory. Perhaps the thinking about this question has been too narrow: If there were various Neandertal populations, each having a somewhat different gene pool and culture (for which there is evidence), and if more than one AMH population migrated into Europe or the Middle East, each having different ideas about meeting strangers, then the answer to the question of what happened to the Neandertals might emerge as more complex and varied than a single process. Not all Neandertals thought or behaved alike any more than all AMH did. Whether any interbreeding took place, and if so how much, probably depended on factors other than biological compatibility or pure geography—factors that differed across time and space. Some possibilities that might have affected interbreeding could have included cultural rules about who should or should not pair up with whom, proximity (the boy/girl-next-door effect), or periodic sex ratio disturbances that prompted changes in ideas of attractiveness. Most experts, even those who have argued for separate species status for Neandertal, agree that there was probably some, if limited, interbreeding (Relethford 2001a).

Regardless of why, the Neandertals as a population ceased to exist after about 28 kyr ago. Perhaps a combination of factors was responsible. For example, it was getting colder between 40 and 28 kyr ago, and the severe cold came from the north. AMH groups apparently came into Europe from the east; and if dates for late Neandertals and early AMH are correct in Spain and Portugal, Neandertals were alone in the southern part of the Iberian Peninsula while AMH was colonizing the northern part (d'Errico and Goñi 2003). If Neandertals could not adapt well to the cold and could not totally avoid AMH to the north, the stress caused by being in a pincer situation might have lowered their reproduction rate to the point where a less healthy population could no longer sustain itself. A few hardy individuals apparently held on in Iberia and perhaps in some protected areas of the Crimea and Caucasus, but eventually they too disappeared.

# Enter Anatomically Modern Humans (AMH)

The term *anatomically modern humans (AMH)*, which we've been using in our discussion of the Neandertals, is synonymous with the more formal taxonomic term *Homo sapiens sapiens* (refer to Chapter 4). It refers to hominid fossils that are morphologically enough

# In the News with the Portuguese Kid

DESPITE DNA EVIDENCE from three Neandertal fossils suggesting that Neandertals were too far away genetically from modern *Homo sapiens* to have interbred and thus to have had input into modern human ancestry, those who believe Neandertals did have a role in the evolution of modern humans got a shot in the arm from a find in Portugal in late 1998: the skeleton of a 4-year-old boy, dated as having lived 24.5 kyr ago and showing features of both Neandertal and AMH. This find is known as the "Portuguese Kid." Skeptics of the Neandertal DNA analyses have argued against the rapid and uncritical acceptance of molecular studies and their unquestioned use as final "proof" that Neandertals made no contribution to modern human evolution. These skeptics believe the finding of new evidence of interbreeding opens the door once again.

The little boy's skeleton was discovered in the Lapedo Valley, which is really a small, steep ravine, 85 miles north of Lisbon. Two archaeology scouts were checking out reports of prehistoric paintings in the vicinity. Like all good archaeologists they snooped around, and they spied a rock shelter across the narrow valley. They investigated the surface area and found charcoal, stone tools, animal bones, and two small bones stained with ochre. The ochre suggested human connections, so they took the bones to archaeological authorities. From then on the site was under the control of Portuguese archaeologists and bioanthropologists. A bulldozer had worked the area 6 years earlier, leaving only an 18-inch unbulldozed remnant along the length of the rock shelter wall. Although the bulldozer had damaged some of the find, it had excavated 6 to 9 feet of topsoil. It had uncovered many teeth and skull fragments as well as half of the boy's mandible; also ribs, vertebrae, pelvis,

long bones, and even rarely found foot and hand bones. The skull had been crushed into 100 pieces by the bulldozer and by postdepositional effects fairly soon after it was buried. The first things the excavators noticed were the "snowplow"-shaped chin and a pierced shell that lay near a vertebra, as if it had been worn as a pendant at the time of the burial. Both traits are normal for an Upper Paleolithic individual and burial. So the initial reaction was that this was the burial of a young human who was modern in both biology (AMH) and culture (Upper Paleolithic). An analysis of the teeth eruption pattern estimated the age at death to be about 4 years.

On closer examination of the body, however, the excavators found that there were some odd traits for a modern human—traits that appeared to be more like Neandertal characteristics. The evidence now points to a kind of mosaic of traits. As we've noted, similarity in form to either Neandertals or AMH does not necessarily equate with inheritance, because some traits can evolve by analogy; but a large number of similar traits leads to some confidence of common inheritance. Neandertal-like traits include body proportions that show "super-arctic" adaptation—short, strong arms and legs and a broad trunk—and shovel-shaped incisors. The femur length is outside the range of AMH but well within that of Neandertal children. Basic body shape patterns are said to be established by the fetal stage, so the proportions of this 4-year-old would not have changed during his lifetime. Additionally, the bones were robust, like Neandertal bones. Another Neandertal trait is what is called the symphereal retreat, which in simple terms means that the child's chin probably retreated behind his teeth rather than jutting forward of them. Anatomically modern traits include a definite pointed chin, small front teeth, and a narrow pelvis. The size of the mastoid process appears to be halfway between Neandertal and AMH sizes. Though manner of burial is a cultural phenomenon, this burial suggests AMH cultural affiliation. Modern humans in this part of the world buried their dead with grave goods and used red ochre, perhaps painting the body. The Portuguese Kid appears to have been wrapped in a shroud of leather that had been painted with red ochre, as there was red ochre in the sediments as well as covering his bones. A thin lens of charcoal directly under the body suggested that a ritual fire had been lit before the body was deposited over it. There were bones of red deer at the feet and head of the child; they were well preserved and showed no signs of being chewed by carnivores. These were probably grave goods, as they were directly associated with the burial. The excavators also found rabbit bones stained red, which may have been additional food offerings.

The mosaic of traits typical of two supposedly different populations became really interesting when the $^{14}$C dates came in—because the date of 24.5 kyr ago from the associated deer bone and charcoal samples was 3.5 kyr after the last Neandertal supposedly died in the Iberian Peninsula. The fossil of that last Neandertal was found recently in Gibraltar and $^{14}$C dated to 28 kyr ago.

As you would expect, different experts are interpreting this evidence differently. To those who believe Neandertal and AMH groups overlapped geographically and chronologically for 5 to 11 kyr, this is evidence of long-term interbreeding or long-term Neandertal trait residue. If the dates are correct, the Portuguese Kid can be interpreted as the result not of a one-time-only interbreeding event between a single Neandertal and a single AMH but of several thousand years of interbreeding on some kind of scale. If there had been but a single mating event several thousand years previously, the Neandertal contribution would have been diluted to zero by sheer numbers of generations of AMH influence. And, although the Portuguese Kid is the latest fossil with claimed mixed status, it is not the first. The Vindija finds in Croatia show a slight chin and small eyebrow ridges along with Neandertal-like robustness. Croatian archaeologists claim there are Upper Paleolithic tools in the same level as the fossil materials.

Other experts are unconvinced by these points, however. They do not believe Neandertal and AMH interbred, and they put forth several reasons: biological incompatibility, different econiches, xenophobia, and the inability to communicate. They suggest that the limb proportions may be distorted because of the age of the child. Ian Tattersall and Jeffrey Schwartz are quoted as saying that the Portuguese Kid is most likely "a chunky Gravettian child" (Wong, 102). And human paleontologist Chris Stringer says that "when I look at the morphology of these people [Vindija], I see robustness, I don't see Neandertal" (Wong, 100).

Comparing the DNA of a 40-kyr-ago Neandertal and a 40-kyr-ago European AMH with the Portuguese Kid might be productive. Unfortunately, the fragile bones have undergone so much chemical weathering that it is not likely that enough DNA can be extracted for analysis.

*Sources:* Duarte, C., J. Mauricio, P. B. Pettitt, et al. 1999. The early Upper Paleolithic human skeleton from the Abrigo don Lagar Velho (Portugal) and modern human emergence in Iberia. *Proceedings of the National Academy of Sciences USA* 96 (13): 7604–7609. Kunzig, R. 1999. Learning to love Neanderthals. *Discover* (August): 68–75. Norris, S. 1999. Family secrets. *New Scientist* (June 19). Wong, K. 2000. Who were the Neandertals? *Scientific American* (April): 99–107. Zilhao, J. 2000. The fate of Neandertals. *Archaeology* (July–August): 24–31. Zilhao, J., and E. Trinkaus, eds. 2002. *Portrait of the artist as a child: The Gravettian human skeleton from the Abrigo do Lagar Velho and its archaeological content.* Lisbon: Trabalhos de Arqueologia 22.

turn back to your reading

like modern humans to fall within the range of human variability today. Derived traits for AMH include:

- rounded head with large cranial capacity, ranging from 1,200 to 1,700 cc and averaging 1,350 cc
- high forehead and bulging parietals (the largest width of the skull at the top)
- round occipital bone at back of skull
- small, somewhat flat, narrow face
- small eye sockets
- relatively small (or nonexistent) brow ridges, always divided in the middle
- small nasal opening and likely small external nose
- pronounced chin with one or two bony "points"
- small teeth
- light postcranial skeleton and smooth thin-walled long bones

Four obvious differences that distinguish AMH from archaics are high foreheads, rounded skulls, chins, and the extent to which the face is "tucked under" the brain case rather than "sticking out" in front of it. A comparison of face placement relative to brain case is shown in Figure 7.12 for australopithecines, *H. erectus*, and AMH. Although Neandertals had a larger cranial capacity than AMH, their crania differed in shape. The biggest difference is in the frontal area, where high foreheads and bulging parietals make modern heads look more like basketballs than footballs. Modern faces are relatively flat and small. But it is the presence of a chin that is often used to diagnose AMH, because no previous population in the human lineage had "real" chins. A chinlike area shows up on some Neandertals, but as many experts suggest, this may be a result of hybridization with AMH; no early Neandertal shows a chin. The external chin may act as a brace to reduce stress during chewing, and speaking is probably easier with the brace on the outside.

Dates for early AMH are again contentious, because neither K-Ar nor [14]C can be used. Yet models of where, when, and by what process AMH evolved demand accurate dates. Because early AMH are found all over the Old World (unlike the geographically circumscribed Neandertals), the following subsections discuss these populations by continent and chronology. All dates remain provisional, however.

*Figure 7.12*

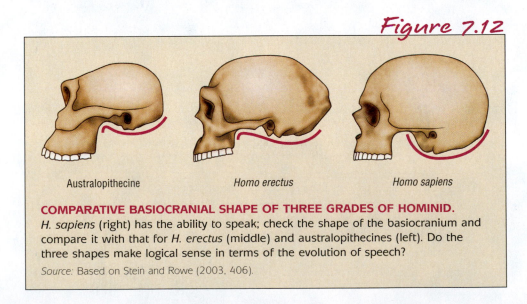

Australopithecine        *Homo erectus*        *Homo sapiens*

**COMPARATIVE BASIOCRANIAL SHAPE OF THREE GRADES OF HOMINID.**
*H. sapiens* (right) has the ability to speak; check the shape of the basiocranium and compare it with that for *H. erectus* (middle) and australopithecines (left). Do the three shapes make logical sense in terms of the evolution of speech?

*Source:* Based on Stein and Rowe (2003, 406).

## African AMH

Neandertals were roaming over Europe and the Middle East by 150 kyr ago, but African fossils from Ethiopia to the Cape of Good Hope with the same approximate date look more like modern humans than Neandertals do, though they are not quite modern. Scholars have assigned early AMH status to fossil material from four African sites, but only one of the sites is without problems. The South African Klasies River Mouth fossils have been dated to perhaps 120 kyr ago (Stringer 2002a), but the fossil material is so extremely fragmentary that a cranial capacity cannot be assigned. Because only one of the four Klasies River Mouth mandibles shows a definite chin, neither of the two usual criteria—large cranial capacity or presence of a chin—validates AMH status. The Border Cave cranium from northern South Africa shows AMH features in its small face and high and rounded cranium; but its provenience and therefore its date are troublesome because they are unverifiable, the skull having been found by local fertilizer diggers. Material at Omo Kibish, Ethiopia, may or may not be an early example of AMH, because two fossils were found in the same layer, one showing archaic and one showing modern features. One of them is likely an intrusive burial, but which one is unknown. As a result, the dating is questionable.

In June 2003 Tim White and his team announced that they had found three "near modern" crania while working at Herto in the Afar triangle (Ethiopia) in 1997. They called the Herto finds *Homo sapiens idaltu; idaltu* means "elder" in the Afar language. The date of 160 kyr ago is relatively secure: There was only one datable cranium, but the layer it was found in was dated by $^{40}Ar/^{39}Ar$. The other two crania were surface finds. The layer on top of the datable cranium could not be dated because of contamination and so had to be cross-dated with a layer at another site. The date of this layer at 154 kyr ago is logical, however. There is no mandible, so no "chinness" can be assessed; but the cranial capacity of the fossils is large enough at 1,450 cc to qualify the crania as "almost" AMH (White et al. 2003).

## Middle Eastern AMH

Two sites in Israel, the Skhul and Qafzeh caves on Mount Carmel, contain reportedly early AMH fossils, and three other sites in the same area contain reportedly Neandertal fossils (Shea 2003). Some scholars assign some of these fossils to mixed status, and not all agree on which fossils belong in which category. Current, but controversial, dating puts AMH in the Middle East between 128 and 71 kyr ago, averaging about 100 kyr ago.

## Asian and Australian AMH

There is a complete fossil gap in mainland Asia until about 35 kyr in China and perhaps 33 kyr ago in Mongolia. AMH groups may have been in Indonesia by 40 kyr ago. The upper cave at Zhoukoudian, China, has yielded several modern skulls dated between 18 and 10 kyr ago that show considerable variability. Several early fossils in Southeast Asia meet the trait criteria of AMH as well. The modern skull from Niah cave, Borneo, dates to the upper limit of $^{14}C$ dating—just over 41 kyr ago. The skull shows the expected set of traits, such as a high forehead and rounded cranium, and is said to resemble the skulls of modern populations in New Guinea. The earliest fossils from New Guinea have been $^{14}C$ dated to just over 9 kyr ago. The Wadjak skulls from Java are modern but show some ancestral traits, such as large brow ridges, big teeth, and short, slanted foreheads. The Wadjak hominids appear to be in the morphological range of modern Australian aborigines (Wolpoff 1996). The oldest Australian material, probably male, is a fossil found in 1974 at Lake Mungo in southern Australia. Originally dated at almost 25 kyr ago, the Lake Mungo material was redated surprisingly early, to about 62 kyr ago (Thorne and Curnoe 2000), then re-redated to less than 40 kyr ago (Bowler and Magle 2000). Four labs have since concluded that the material is 40 kyr old; thus, given the inland location of Lake Mungo, the ancestors of the aborigines arrived perhaps 50 kyr ago, rapidly spreading across the island, which lacked any other hominid populations or predators (Mellars 2006b; Young 2003). These first Australians must have had boat- or raft-building abilities far earlier than previously thought.

## European AMH

The first AMH fossils found in Europe were excavated by railroad workers at Les Eyzies, France, in 1868. Because the men found these fossils at the base of Cro-Magnon hill, both the fossils and a hotel later built on the site are called by that name; in fact "Cro-Magnon" became synonymous with AMH in Europe. The Les Eyzies finds were dated at 28 kyr old, but Upper Paleolithic artifacts excavated subsequently in Bulgaria date to 43 kyr ago and a mandible with teeth found in Romania dates to 36 kyr ago, putting AMH in eastern Europe by about 40 kyr ago. Experts have hypothesized that AMH came to Europe from Africa via Asia from the east, penetrating open woodlands in eastern Europe, then continuing to migrate further west, killing, avoiding, or interbreeding with established Neandertals.

The European AMH fossils show small faces, high foreheads, prominent chins, fairly large brow ridges, and cranial capacities reaching 1,590 cc. They range from 162.3 to 167.6 cm (5 feet 4 inches to 5 feet 6 inches) tall, and many are quite robust. The horizontal–oval (H-O) type of mandibular foramen occurs in 44 percent of the early AMH fossils, practically disappearing by 10 kyr ago (Frayer et al. 1993; Wolpoff and Caspari 1997).

## New World AMH

The earliest Native American fossil material is later in time than the populations being discussed in this chapter. Therefore, we will introduce the first New World populations in the appropriate time frame, in Chapter 15.

## Models of Evolving AMH

It may be too simplistic to reduce ideas about the identity, origins, timing, and evolutionary background of the first modern human populations to two opposing models, or hypotheses. The reality is, however, that beginning in the mid-1980s ideas began to crystallize around two models that pointedly address these ideas. Both models have very strong proponents; some personality clashes have resulted, and at times evidence has taken a back seat to unsubstantiated opinions. Here, we present each model in its original form and outline the supporting evidence used by the model's proponents. Then we will offer a critique of the two models and will ask if either fits the available evidence. Two newer models will then be described. Because there is no way of knowing for certain what happened 200 to 100 kyr ago, it is evidence that must dominate any assessment, and the likelihood that one model is correct must rest on evaluation of the evidence, not on any argument from authority. Although it is possible that neither of the older hypotheses is correct, given their nature, it is certain that both cannot be correct.

### Multiregional (MR) Model

Before the mid-1980s most experts believed that the most recent evolutionary event in the human lineage was the transformism of archaic *H. sapiens* to modern humans. Because fossils of both populations existed on every Old World continent (except Antarctica), it seemed logical to believe that this evolution was a worldwide event, with sufficient gene flow or migration to transform archaic *H. sapiens* (including Neandertals) into AMH.

After being named the **multiregional (MR) model** this hypothesis acquired regional details. Milford Wolpoff, the leading proponent of this basically American model, points to certain similarities among all East Asian fossils, from *H. erectus* to archaic *H. sapiens* to modern Chinese populations. Examples include nonprotruding zygomatic arches; flat, vertical faces; arched eyebrow ridges; 90 percent shovel-shaped incisors (as opposed to 15 percent in Europeans and African Americans), and small teeth. Multiregional proponents also point to similarities in Southeast Asia between hominids from *H. erectus* to archaic *H. sapiens*—some 700 kyr of fossils—and onward to contemporary Australian aborigines. These include thick cranial bones; continuous eyebrow ridges; large, projecting faces; and very large molars and premolars. Note that the similarities are lineal within but different between regions. These regional traits are small in number relative to the number of traits that are similar for the entire evolving species. Multiregionalists believe that certain mutations occurred in particular geographic areas and were positively selected for, adapting regional populations to their particular environment. The resultant changes would remain local; other mutations that adapted the species globally would be passed on through gene flow to other populations and eventually throughout the species. Multiregionalists believe there was enough gene flow and/or migration to keep the species from splitting yet not so much as to eliminate regional variations (Templeton 1996; Thorne and Wolpoff 1981, 1992; Wolpoff et al. 2001).

To demonstrate worldwide applicability, multiregionalists have looked for regional variations in Europe and Africa as well. Several European traits, such as large noses, large molars, and the H-O mandibular foramen in both European Neandertals and earliest AMH, do seem to continue over time and are not found elsewhere (Wolpoff et al. 1994; Wilford 2003). Evidence for African regionalism is not as forthcoming. In keeping with their continuity model, advocates of the MR model propose that transitional or hybrid groups existed in various parts of the world.

Multiregionalists do not state when they believe archaic *H. sapiens* evolved to AMH status, because transformism over a large geographic area is an uneven process that takes considerable time. They suggest that by 100 kyr ago, archaic *H. sapiens* was on its way to evolving to AMH throughout the Old World (Templeton 1997; Wolpoff and Caspari 1997).

## Recent African Origin (RAO) Model

The **recent African origin (RAO) model** of AMH evolution has a more precise date for its inception: In 1984 English human paleontologist Chris Stringer introduced the hypothesis in its modern form. The RAO model had earlier precursors in the mid-1960s, but Stringer put the time, place, and process together for the first time. Stringer wrote his doctoral dissertation on Neandertals, but he dismissed the possibility of Neandertals' being ancestors of modern humans and began questioning whether archaic populations in all parts of the world had equal ancestor input into AMH. When he learned of reported early dates for African and Middle Eastern AMH fossils, Stringer countered the MR model by suggesting that "it is necessary to look to Africa for the origin of the earliest modern humans" (1984, 7). The RAO model of AMH evolution also has been called the "replacement model," the "Eve" hypothesis, and **Out of Africa–2 (OOA-2)** (*H. erectus* being Out of Africa–1).

The original RAO model suggested that AMH evolved from a small, somewhat isolated, archaic *H. sapiens* population of an estimated 10,000 individuals somewhere in East or Southeast Africa before 100 kyr ago. The model sees certain mutations occurring in this population that resulted in a new species, incapable of interbreeding with other populations. This first AMH population spread out in Africa, replacing all other groups, presumably because its mutations and adaptations made it reproductively more successful than the populations it replaced. In time this new species migrated out of Africa and replaced all existing Asian and European populations.

**multiregional (MR) model**
The hypothesis that after the dispersion of *Homo erectus* anatomically modern humans evolved as a single species throughout the Old World by means of gene flow between populations and/or migration.

**recent African origin (RAO) model**
The hypothesis that holds that anatomically modern humans evolved in Africa before 100 kyr ago and then spread out to Asia and Europe after 100 kyr ago, replacing all existing populations; also called OOA-2.

**out of Africa–2 (OOA–2)**
Another name for the RAO model of the evolution of anatomically modern humans.

Recently, Chris Stringer and Peter Andrews (2005) suggested three possible routes from Africa to Europe: via the Middle East, over islands in the Mediterranean, or across North Africa and then to Gibraltar. However, there may not have been a continuous land bridge across the Mediterranean at that time, so the Middle Eastern route seems most likely.

Under this model no other population contributed genes to what eventually became contemporary humans. The hypothesis predicts that fossils of transitional groups will not be found outside of Africa; only fossils of original inhabitants followed by those of the very different-looking African newcomers who replaced them (Pääbo 2003; C. Stringer, personal communication 2002; Stringer and Andrews 1988).

Luigi Cavalli-Sforza (2000) points out that there is likely a considerable passage of time between the mutation(s) that would have caused the speciation and the period when the hypothesized population would have begun to replace other populations and leave Africa. He suggests that the genetic change(s) and speciation occurred at 150 kyr ago and the migration/replacement by 50 kyr ago.

## Critiquing the Two Models

The preceding subsections described the original, rather extreme, versions of the two models of AMH evolution. Over time compromises or changes have occurred, with the proponents of each model taking several steps toward a more common ground. RAO proponents now maintain that they never said that there could be *no* gene flow, only that it was negligible (Brauer 2001). And multiregionalists concede that transformism to AMH status probably began in Africa. The criticisms that have been pointed at both models are a good lesson in science's ability to be self-correcting. In science no answer to a question is finite, and all questions are subject to constant reevaluation.

Multiregionalists point to evidence in Asia and Europe as demonstrating regionalism. Marta Lahr, an RAO advocate, criticizes the lack of regional continuity in traits in general, pointing to continuity in only 11 of 30, or 37 percent, of the traits used in the analysis (1996). MR supporters counterclaim that only some continuity in traits is needed, not 100 percent. Another statistically analyzed comparative study resulted in support for multiregionalism. Andrew Kramer (2002) compared 16 mandibular traits of the Java *H. erectus* specimens to traits in modern Kenyans and modern Australian aborigines. Close results between *H. erectus* jaws and those of modern Kenyans would support the RAO hypothesis; close results between the *H. erectus* jaws and those of modern Australian aborigines would support MR. There were nine statistically significant differences between the *H. erectus* jaws and Kenyans' jaws, but only three between *H. erectus* jaws and those of Australian aborigines. Kramer therefore concluded that his comparison supported MR, not RAO. He warns, however, that the sample was small.

Multiregionalists predict the existence of transitional populations through hominid times. A fossil dated at "about 1 million years ago" was found in northeastern Africa and was reported to show a mixture of *H. erectus* and *H. sapiens* traits. The *H. erectus* traits include a small cranial capacity (800 cc), skull width that is greatest at the bottom, and large brow ridges. *H. sapiens* traits include a substantially vertical forehead and no sagittal keel (Abbate et al. 1998). More recently workers found a new skull dated at 1 myr ago at Bouri, Ethiopia. The excavators report that it shares key features with later African fossils as well as with Asian fossils, potentially linking them into a single interbreeding species (Asfaw et al. 2002).

Multiregionalists suggest that continuity is as important as regionalism, meaning that there should be no breaks in either fossils or artifacts that would suggest an African migration. This seems to be the case in Asia and on the Indian subcontinent, where a study of all skeletal and dental specimens found no African features in any prehistoric or modern people in Pakistan, India, or Sri Lanka. Because there are only gradual changes through time in this part of Asia, the conclusion supports continuity. Given the high frequency of shovel-shaped incisors in both fossil and modern populations in China, if there had been an African invasion that totally replaced those populations, shovel-shaped incisors would have had to re-evolve—not a likely event. There are no abrupt changes in artifacts, either, as would be expected if replacement had occurred (Kennedy 2001).

Direct evidence of gene flow (or of its absence) is not likely to be found, and its results are difficult to demonstrate. But if the behavior of moderns is any predictor, when groups of strangers met in the past, in some cases they probably ran away from each other because their cultural beliefs fostered stranger avoidance. In other cases the groups probably joined for a period of time, and gene exchange would have been likely. Constant fusion and fission would have resulted in temporary groups that were geographically not very far apart; maintained periodic contact; and exchanged members, fire when it was needed, and genes.

Turning to the RAO (or OOA–2) model, two years after the modern version of this model was announced, Rebecca Cann, Allan Wilson, and Mark Stoneking (1987) published their now-famous research that used mitochondrial DNA to date the LCA of all modern humans. They chose to use mitochondrial rather than nuclear DNA because the former has only 16,569 base pairs and only 37 genes. Molecular dating was brand new in 1987, but their finding—that AMH evolved in Africa 200 kyr ago—supported Stringer's RAO hypothesis. Because mitochondrial DNA was believed to be inherited only in the maternal line, the popular press unfortunately claimed there was a common ancestress of all modern humans, "Eve." Over the next decade, critics questioned the 1987 molecular research on grounds of methodological errors, incorrect use of computer programs, small sample size and an inappropriate sample, and flaws in calculating mutation rates (Swisher et al. 2000). For example, 18 of the 25 "African" females were African-American females; because there has been considerable flow of European genes into the African-American population over the past several hundred years, these 18 individuals were "inappropriate" as being representative of African populations. Another criticism suggests that mitochondrial DNA comprises less than 1 percent of the total genetic structure of humans. What would the other more than 99 percent of the genome show? The date for the last common ancestor of modern humans was based on the assumption that humans and chimpanzees diverged 5 to 4 myr ago. That date is now regarded as too late, and the entire molecular clock is in some doubt (Stearns and Hockstra 2005). Retests, using a larger and more appropriate sample, better computer programs, and a more realistic range of mutation rates, have been consistent enough to convince many experts that most, if not all, recent human origins are in Africa (Ingman et al. 2000).

Not all genetic studies have agreed with a "deep rooted," totally African source for AMH. For example, some studies of nuclear rather than mitochondrial DNA have shown options other than total African ancestry. As one critic concludes, "the genetic evidence is inconsistent, contradictory, and confusing" (Billsborough 1999). However, dating methods, fossil morphology, and molecular evidence also seem inconsistent, contradictory, and confusing at this point! Some studies show a small amount of Asian genetic input through migration or population explosion (Templeton 2002).

The RAO model rests on accurate dating of early modern fossils—because for the model to be logical, AMH must be shown to have existed first in Africa, then in the Middle East, then Eurasia. But dating of fossils throughout this period remains problematic, except for the reasonably well-dated Herto cranium from Ethiopia.

One criticism of the RAO model is its inability to satisfactorily explain the reason(s) for replacement. It seems biologically prudent to assume that if a population is well adapted to its environment, there must be important reasons why another population— from elsewhere—could be reproductively more successful and replace the original group in its own environment. But what might those reasons be? RAO proponents suggest that AMH might have possessed more efficient speech, better technology (such as better projectiles), the ability to deal with particular diseases, the ability to cope with rapid and extreme environmental shifts in a single lifetime, differential fertility, and/or simply wider social networks to use in times of stress (Stringer and McKie 1997).

## Other Models: Assimilation Model and Diffusion Wave

Compromises between contending models do not receive as much attention in the press (or from colleagues) as do confrontations. Nevertheless, the **assimilation model** may eventually replace the competing MR and RAO models, because it explains more of the data. Fred Smith and Eric Trinkaus (Smith 1992, 1994; Smith et al. 1989) suggest that Africa was the original source of moderns but that there was enough systematic interbreeding (gene flow) with archaics as the Africans spread out to keep the evolving group a single species, and enough natural selection to keep some regional patterns as well. Additionally, Smith and Trinkaus suggest that genes moved through gene flow on population borders rather than through wholesale migrations of groups. A study using mitochondrial DNA, Y chromosome DNA, and nuclear DNA concludes that Africa played a dominant role in the most recent evolution, perhaps as much as 90 percent, but that both reoccurring gene flow and population expansion resulting in interbreeding occurred as well (Templeton 2002).

In a new, creative hypothesis that builds on the assimilation model, V. Eswaran, an Indian who is a mechanical engineer by training, and two American bioanthropologists (Eswaran 2002; Eswaran, Harpending, and Rogers 2005) have suggested in some detail *how* the transition to anatomical modernism could have occurred. They call this process a **diffusion wave**. Their hypothesis assumes that AMH ancestry had its roots in Africa, yet at least some interbreeding/hybridization occurred between archaic *H. sapiens* and AMH. Assuming a new population of AMH evolved in East Africa and began a slow, wavelike spread northward and then out of Africa, first to the east to Asia and then to the west to Europe, in small random movements, hybridization with the locals and natural selection could have resulted in the evolution and success of the modern genotype, a "character change" rather than a speciation event. AMH would have hybridized with archaic *H. sapiens* only on the frontier and little by little spread throughout the Old World.

Eswaran calculates that a diffusion wave from Ethiopia (Herto provided the first almost modern *H. sapiens* dated at 160 kyr ago) could have reached both Southeast Asia and Eastern Europe in 4,000 generations, or 80 kyr. The transition from archaic to modern occurred essentially on that wave front, a narrow hybrid zone moving geographically and altering local populations. This same process could also have occurred between Neandertals and AMH in Europe between 45 and 25 kyr ago. Eswaran suggests that since the wave would have produced hybrids in only a narrow zone and for only a short time, fossil hybrids would be rare, as is the case. If interbreeding took place only on the wave front, that would also explain why there were no large changes in artifacts during this time period. By contrast, large-scale migrations or replacements would likely have resulted in discernible artifact discontinuities in the archaeological record, which have not been observed.

The idea of a diffusion wave is a compelling hypothesis that seems to avoid the extremes of both the MR and RAO models and allows for all of the known evolutionary causes (mutations, natural selection, gene flow, and genetic drift) to have operated.

## Which Model Best Fits the Evidence?

Whenever there are several fairly clear ways to look at a problem, in this case the evolution of AMH, it is fortunate if the evidence is as clear as the models. In this case, how-

---

**assimilation model**
A "compromise" model that explains the origin of anatomically modern humans as evolving in Africa and then spreading out to other Old World continents and interbreeding with native populations of archaic *Homo sapiens*.

**diffusion wave**
A hypothesis about how anatomically modern humans arose throughout the Old World, which suggests that an original population evolved in East Africa and expanded as a wave of migrants, interbreeding on its borders with local archaic *Homo sapiens* populations.

ever, it is not. Leaders on both sides of the MR versus RAO debate have stepped away somewhat from their original polar positions, and at times it appears both sides are using old labels but making similar arguments. Multiregionalists agree that Africans today show more genetic variability than people in other continents and that this variability may be linked to a longer evolution in Africa—though some counter that it is larger population size in Africa that causes Africa's greater DNA variability (Relethford 2001a; Relethford and Harpending 1995). For their side, RAO advocates suggest that there may have been a limited amount of interbreeding between AMH and the archaics they replaced—but that it was negligible.

Looking at all of the evidence, molecular and fossil, we believe the assimilation model, along with the diffusion wave, answers more questions about the evolution of of AMH than either of the original models. The current best scenario sees AMH ancestors arising somewhere in sub-Saharan Africa beginning between 150 and 100 kyr ago and dispersing north into the Middle East via the Horn of Africa perhaps 75 to 50 kyr ago; one branch then moved east along the coast of India, interbreeding on the moving wave front all the way to Southeast Asia, northern Asia, and Australia (Macaulay et al. 2005; Mellars 2006). The other branch moved out of Africa via the Middle East and moved north and then west, interbreeding with the archaic *H. sapiens* populations on the moving wave front in Eastern Europe beginning about 40 kyr ago. (See Figure 7.13.) These are the same moderns who replaced or interbred with Neandertals, so the combination of assimilation model and diffusion wave is consistent with the evidence of the demise of Neandertals as well. Time will tell if this scenario is supported by new fossil finds.

*Figure 7.13*

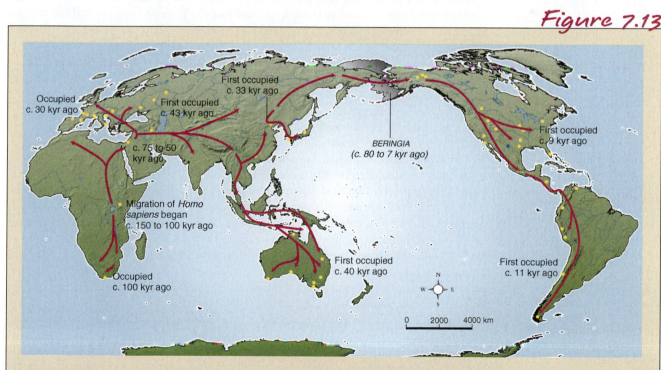

**PEOPLING THE WORLD WITH ANATOMICALLY MODERN HUMANS.** The fossil and molecular evidence point to an initial evolution of AMH in East Africa. The new version of *H. sapiens* migrated south and then north to the Middle East, east to Asia and Australia, and west to Europe. Eventually, AMH migrated across the Bering Strait and populated the New World. All dates are provisional. Do the migration paths and dates appear to be logical?

# The Evolution of Speech Abilities

Speech is one of the hallmarks of humanity because only humans can speak, and therefore it is worthy of special note. There is very little direct evidence indicating when speech abilities evolved, because speech mechanisms generally do not fossilize. If speech abilities had been addressed where the topic might fit chronologically, it would have cropped up in many different parts of the last two chapters. But because there is so much interpretation and difference of opinion on the evolution of speech abilities, it seems appropriate to cover the topic in this separate section.

## Communication, Language, Speech

English speakers sometimes use the words *speech* and *language* interchangeably. But although the words are related, they are not identical, and it is speech and the biological ability to speak that we focus on here, not language. Both language and speech are parts of a more encompassing phenomenon, **communication**. Communication is the giving and/or taking of information about something. It need not be two-way, or be intentional, or use a specific vehicle, or be between conspecifics, or have a direct biological basis. For example, a dog can urinate on a water hydrant, but the hydrant is not taking information even if the dog is giving it. If a woman stands at a bus stop with her coat collar turned up and a frown on her face, she will unintentionally communicate to every passerby that she is cold and impatient with her situation. If the woman speaks to the dog and the dog then wags its tail to her, the two of them are communicating to each other though they are not of the same species. And one human can merely nod at another and communicate a message. **Language** is a specific kind of communication: It is structured (it has rules), symbolic (one thing stands for another, such as a wave of the hand symbolizing "hello"), and complex (it is not a simple set of symbols). There are many kinds of language, such as speech, computer language, sign language, and bee language. **Speech** is vocal, or oral/aural (i.e., mouth-to-ear), language, uttered thought that is used by most humans. Language is in the brain; speech involves the language in the brain being transformed into sounds by the structures of the vocal tract (Tattersall 2002).

In evolutionary sequence, speech is contingent on language, and language is contingent on communication. But *when* did speech abilities evolve? One of the few aspects of speech evolution that experts agree on is that because of its complexity, speech did not evolve all at once. Although the spoken language used by modern people is learned and therefore cultural, the ability to speak is biological—subject to evolutionary forces and anatomically very complex. Speech apparatus involves the brain (cerebral factor); the throat, tongue, jaw, and lips (vocal factors); and the neurological connectors between the two. Many areas of the brain are involved, including Broca's area, which controls the muscles for sound production, and Wernicke's area, which controls the understanding of sound.

No primate species except humans can speak, and a comparison of human speech apparatus with comparable anatomical areas in other primates indicates why: Nonhuman primates have some of the needed cerebral and vocal factors, but not the proper neurological connectors between them. Given that chimpanzees cannot speak, it is clear that the critical biological bases for speech evolved after hominids split from the LCA; speech ability is a derived trait of hominids. Chimpanzees can be taught to use some aspects of human language (although there is controversy even over this) but cannot be taught to speak.

**communication**
The transmission of information from one individual to another by sensory means.

**language**
A type of communication that is complex, symbolic, and structured, but not necessarily oral (speech); examples are sign language, computer language, and bee language.

**speech**
The vocal, or oral/aural, version of language used by most humans.

*Figure 7.14*

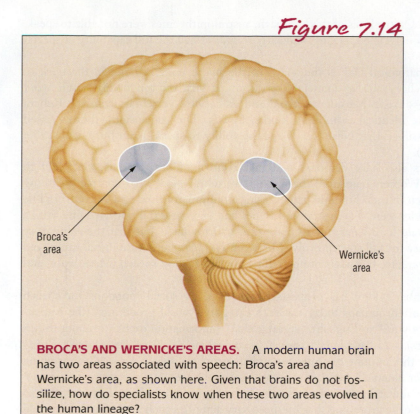

Broca's
area

Wernicke's
area

**BROCA'S AND WERNICKE'S AREAS.**   A modern human brain has two areas associated with speech: Broca's area and Wernicke's area, as shown here. Given that brains do not fossilize, how do specialists know when these two areas evolved in the human lineage?

# Evidence for Speech Abilities

Although speaking and having the ability to speak are potentially different things, it is not unreasonable to assume that if evidence exists that populations had the ability to speak, then they did. Direct evidence for the ability to speak includes endocranial markings on the inside of the skull, openings in the side of the skull for the passage of nerves that control movement of the tongue, the shape of the hyoid bone in the throat, and anatomical clues for breathing control. Is this evidence in logical evolutionary order?

Broca's area (sound production) and Wernicke's area (sound comprehension) are located in the brain, the former on the left side of the frontal lobe and the latter on the upper part of the temporal lobe (see Figure 7.14). Modern skulls give evidence of these areas as endocranial "bumps"—marks on the inside of the skull bone. Whether bumps appear on the insides of fossil skulls is controversial. Matt Cartmill (1998a) suggests that fossilized bumps are not perceptible, because the brain and the cranial bone do not fit tightly together. Philip Tobias (1998) disagrees, suggesting that *A. africanus* shows small "bulbosities" in the Broca's area portion of the endocrania and that *H. habilis* shows bumps in both areas. The two speech areas appear to be modern in shape by *H. erectus* times (Wynn 1998).

Cartmill has analyzed the hypoglossal canal, a hole in the side of the cranium through which the hypoglossal nerve passes on its way to the back of the mouth, where it controls tongue movement. His analysis of the canal's shape and size concludes that australopithecines had small, oval canals, suggesting they did not have control over their tongues needed for true speech; *H. erectus* canals are midway between those of australopithecines and *H. sapiens*, suggesting they were able to use their tongues in speechlike movement; and archaic *H. sapiens* and AMH had large, round canals and could wag their tongues a good deal (Cartmill 1998a; Kay et al. 1998). Another study, however, claims there is no correlation between the size of the fossil canals and the size of the nerve. Additionally, this study finds that nonhuman primates and three australopithecine species have canals as large as those of modern humans (DeGusta et al. 1999). Although hypoglossal canal size may no longer predict speech capabilities, shape (round or oval) may still provide evolutionary clues.

The shape of the basiocranium (the base of the cranium; see Figure 7.12) may also provide clues for speech ability. In modern humans a curved basiocranium correlates with a low larynx that is capable of making the specific speech sounds humans make today. In contrast, in modern apes a straight basiocranium correlates with a high larynx—and apes are seemingly unable to make the sounds necessary to speak. Because the larynx is soft tissue and does not fossilize, researchers substitute the shape of the base of the cranium for the position of the larynx for purposes of hypothesizing about speech evolution. If the correlation is valid, hominids with straight basiocrania would have been incapable of speech, but the beginning of curved basiocrania would indicate evolving speech abilities. On the basis of this approach, australopithecines were not able to speak, *H. erectus* was doing some speaking, and early *H. sapiens* had the full capability of speech (Laitman 1985).

Another anatomical clue is the shape of the hyoid bone, a bone in the neck of animals that anchors muscles connected to the jaw, larynx, and tongue. Although hyoid bones rarely fossilize, a Neandertal hyoid and its cervical vertebrae from the Kebara site in Israel are identical to modern human hyoids. The conclusion—though based on only one fossil—is that Neandertals had the ability to speak (Arensburg et al. 1990; Kaufman 1999).

Researchers also have demonstrated that control of breathing is connected to speech ability. Workers compared the thoracic vertebral canals that control breathing needed in speech in each hominid group, using nonhuman primates as a control. The study's conclusions were that australopithecines and *H. erectus* did not have fine breath control and would have been able to make only short sounds, but that the respiratory control necessary for full speech evolved between *H. erectus* and Neandertal times, and that all *H. sapiens* have had adequate breathing control for full speech (MacLarnon and Hewett 1999).

Robin Dunbar (1996) has proposed three basically social functions for speech based on how often humans today use each category: "vocal grooming" (the equivalent of "how are you?" in English), "social gossip" (information exchange about things and conspecifics), and "symbolic" speech (technical or religious discussions). Using calculations of the amount of time nonhuman primates spend physically grooming one another (for assumed social control and maintenance) and the estimated size of social groups, Dunbar hypothesized that early hominids would have had to spend so much time physically grooming that life-necessary activities such as getting food would suffer. He therefore suggests that early hominids substituted vocal grooming for physical grooming to serve the same function. Eventually, he proposes, the ability to do vocal grooming evolved to social gossip and then to symbolic language. These sound-based communications would have had the advantage of being broadcast rather than one-on-one; also, groups could accomplish other chores while talking. Based on estimates of social group size, Dunbar suggests that the australopithecines were limited to vocal grooming; *H. erectus* populations added social gossiping (perhaps exchanging information about hunting, for example); and archaic *H. sapiens* groups were also discussing religion, magic, and technical matters.

Various evidence, then, allows a summary of the evolution of speech abilities. As modern apes cannot speak, the LCA group was a non-speaking population that probably used gestures and several dozen different sounds in communication, but with no sound combinations. As in communication among modern chimpanzees, each sound would have represented one idea (Goodall 1965). It is proposed that australopithecines had some rudimentary speech and used "vocal grooming" as a substitute for physical grooming; by *H. erectus* times, speech probably also functioned to maintain group cohesion through social gossip about individuals and events. Beginning with archaic *H. sapiens*, true speech abilities had evolved, and populations were capable of discussing technical and religious matters. Although this scenario is very provisional, evidence of many kinds agrees, so there is a logic to the conclusions.

This chapter focused on the evolution of later hominids, beginning with *Homo erectus* and ending with modern humans. *H. erectus* culturally falls into the late phase of the Lower Paleolithic, where hand axes in Europe and Africa predominate. Neandertals are culturally assigned to the Middle Paleolithic. The Upper Paleolithic in Europe and Asia and the late Stone Age in Africa saw biologically modern humans, new kinds of tool resources and types, and true art. These cultural phases will be fully explored in Chapter 9.

■ *H. erectus* evolved in Africa by 1.8 myr ago and migrated to Eurasia. *H. erectus* shows a suite of derived traits that identify the species throughout the Old World. *H. erectus* was completely bipedal, with modern limb proportions. The cranium began to enlarge during this grade.

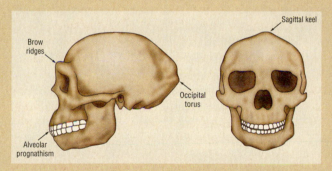

**page 173**

■ *H. erectus* evolved to *H. sapiens* grade between 400 and 100 kyr ago, but exactly when, where, and through what process is controversial.

■ Early archaic *H. sapiens* shows a set of derived traits that identify the population. Most evolutionary changes were in the cranium.

■ Neandertals (late archaic *H. sapiens*) lived in Europe and the Middle East from about 150 to 30 kyr ago, evolving a set of traits that differentiate them from other archaics.

■ Fossil and artifact overlap of Neandertals and AMH in Europe and the Middle East can be interpreted as replacement or interbreeding, but both populations did cohabit Europe for 5 to 13 kyr and the Middle East for up to 60 kyr.

■ What happened to the Neandertals is controversial; they did not evolve directly into AMH, but they could have either been replaced by or interbred with moderns.

**page 183**

The set of traits that identify Neandertals disappeared in the Middle East by 40 kyr ago and in Europe by 28 kyr ago; the youngest Neandertal fossil was discovered at Gibraltar.

■ AMH are found on all Old World continents (except Antarctica), showing an identifiable suite of traits that include enlarged crania and chins.

■ The two original contending models for the origins of AMH are debated: recent African origin (RAO) and multiregionalism (MR). Evidence can be interpreted to support either model; at present which (if either) is correct is unknown.

■ Two newer models to explain the origins of modern humans account for more of the known facts: The assimilation model hypothesizes the origins of AMH in East Africa, a spread of the population into the rest of the world, and interbreeding with local populations of archaic *H. sapiens*. The diffusion wave adds a process to the assimilation model by suggesting that AMH interbred with local populations only at the wave front as AMH spread out.

■ Human speech abilities evolved over time: Australopithecines likely did not speak but used gestures and numerous sounds; *H. erectus* likely used rudimentary speech to discuss events and people, *H. sapiens* likely used speech to discuss technological and religious matters.

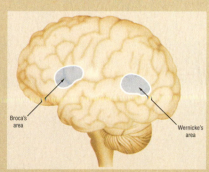

**page 203**

## KEY WORDS

archaic *Homo sapiens*, 181
assimilation model, 200
communication, 202
diffusion wave, 200
*Homo erectus*, 169

*Homo sapiens*, 180
language, 202
multiregional (MR) model, 197
Neandertal, 183
Out of Africa–2 (OOA-2), 197

recent African origin (RAO)
   model, 197
speech, 202

## SUGGESTED READING

Relethford, J. *Genetics and the Search for Modern Human Origins*. New York: Wiley-Liss, 2001. The author attempts to bring genetics and fossils together in analyzing the two models of emerging modern humans, concluding that AMH came "mostly from Africa."

Stringer, C. B., and P. Andrews. "Genetic and Fossil Evidence for the Origin of Modern Humans." *Science* 239 (1988): 1263–1268. Based on his Ph.D. dissertation work, this is the first formal description of Chris Stringer's RAO (recent African origin) hypothesis.

Stringer, C. B., and C. Gamble. *In Search of the Neandertals: Solving the Puzzle of Human Origins*. New York: Thames & Hudson, 1993. An excellent assessment of Neandertal evidence (to the date of writing) written by a biological anthropologist and an archaeologist who believe the Neandertals were a species separate from modern humans.

Thorne, A. G., and M. H. Wolpoff. "The Multiregional Evolution of Humans." *Scientific American* 266 (1992): 76–83. The original statement of Thorne and Wolpoff, architects of the multiregional hypothesis, giving evidence for regional evolution in East and Southeast Asia.

Trinkaus, E., and P. Shipman. *The Neandertals: Changing the Image of Mankind*. New York: Knopf, 1993. A readable account of the Neandertals' evolution and place in the human lineage by two experts who believe there was at least some interbreeding between Neandertals and European AMH.

Walker, A., and P. Shipman. *Wisdom of the Bones: In Search of Human Origins*. New York: Knopf, 1996. Although the book focuses on the entire African fossil evidence of human evolution, the chapters on *Homo erectus*, and particularly on Nariokotome (Turkana Boy), include personal accounts by Alan Walker, who discovered most of the Nariokotome fossil.

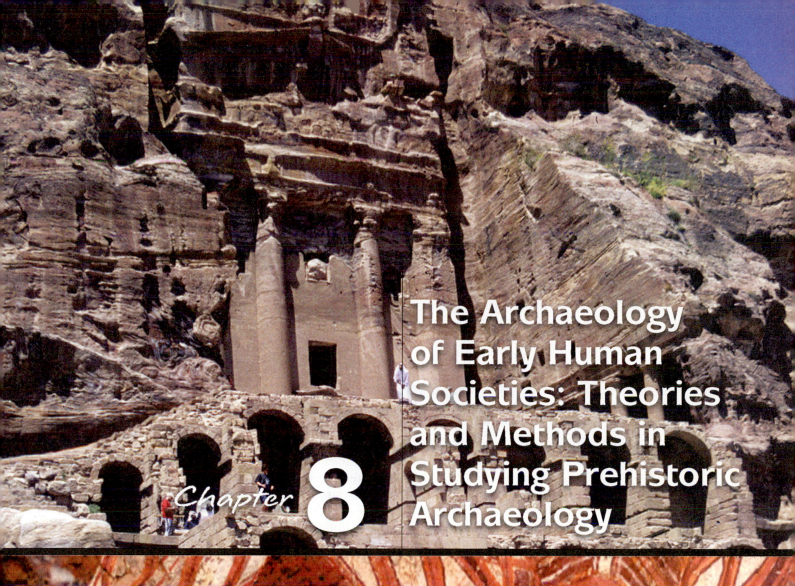

# Chapter 8

# The Archaeology of Early Human Societies: Theories and Methods in Studying Prehistoric Archaeology

■ **WHAT IS ARCHAEOLOGY?**

■ **ARCHAEOLOGICAL EVIDENCE**
Archaeological Sites and Context • Preservation of Archaeological Data

■ **HIGHLIGHT 8.1:** *In the News at Ozette Village*

■ **HOW ARCHAEOLOGISTS FIND EVIDENCE**
Finding Sites • Excavating Archaeological Sites

■ **HIGHLIGHT 8.2:** *A Day in the Field*

■ **ANALYSIS OF FINDS**
Archaeological Theory and Interpretation

■ **DATING SITES AND ARTIFACTS**
Relative Dating Techniques • Chronometric Dating • Other Dating Techniques • Summary of Dating Techniques

■ **CHAPTER SUMMARY**

▲ **Photo above:** 2,400-year-old Nabataean rock-cut temple at Petra, Jordan

# What Is Archaeology?

Prehistory is the period before writing became the common medium to convey historical information about past societies. The aim of prehistoric archaeology is to describe the life of our ancestors and to explain it as well as possible so that we may begin to understand their social and cultural behavior. To achieve this, archaeologists use data revealed through excavation to describe people and cultural events in the past and to test explanatory hypotheses. The subject is therefore by necessity multi-disciplinary, encompassing a broad range of methods and techniques from other disciplines, including botany, zoology, environmental sciences, chemistry, anatomy, genetics, linguistics, art history, and cultural anthropology. Archaeologists tend to specialize in a particular field, for example: archaeobotany, zooarchaeology, geoarchaeology, archaeometallurgy, underwater archaeology, or ceramic and lithic analysis. They may also have a preference for a particular period or region, or both, for example: Paleolithic, Archaic, ancient Egypt, classical, or historical. In this chapter we look more closely at how archaeologists work.

# Archaeological Evidence

Some archaeological sites themselves constitute valuable evidence. Certain famous sites have been visible since their construction; examples are the Great Wall of China, Pompeii, Stonehenge, and the Great Serpent Mound in Ohio. The human constructions at such places not only provide tangible links to the past but also link us to previous generations that have been awed by them. Ancient **artifacts** (portable objects made and used by humans in the past), on display in modern museums, also yield information. Museums usually display items discovered through legitimate excavation; unfortunately, however, destructive illegal looting of sites also takes place, and looted objects often find their way into the black market in antiquities. Museum displays include familiar artifacts such as pottery vessels (generally found as broken pieces and reconstructed), flint spear points and arrowheads, bronze daggers, or jewelry made from various materials.

Other types of archaeological evidence, as important but not necessarily as glamorous, are very difficult or impossible to remove from archaeological sites without destroying them. **Features**—elements such as walls, pits, postholes, and blackened areas of former **hearths** (fireplaces)—hold vital information about human activity in the past. Features can be thought of as "nonportable artifacts." **Ecofacts** are culturally relevant but nonartifactual elements such as animal bones, plant remains, charcoal, fish and insect remains, soils, and sediments. By analyzing ecofacts, scientists can reconstruct both human diets and the environment in which people lived.

## Archaeological Sites and Context

An archaeological site is a place where artifacts, ecofacts, and features exist, either separately or in some form of association. A site may consist of a few arrowheads around a bison skeleton, a single structure and its contents, a group of buildings, or a large city such as ancient Babylon, Teotihuacan, or Petra. Researchers may study individual sites separately, or they may investigate grouped sites or larger entities—a single house in a hamlet, all houses in the hamlet, or numerous similar hamlets in a geographical area.

It is tempting to describe archaeologists as glorified treasure hunters, especially when occasional spectacular finds grab the headlines. The crucial difference between archaeologists and treasure hunters is in the way they treat their finds: For archaeologists **context** is a critical element of the search. Context comprises matrix, provenience, and association, and together these factors provide invaluable information about excavators' finds. **Matrix** is the material surrounding the objects. Usually this is some type of sediment or

**artifacts**
Portable objects made and used by humans in the past, including pots, spearpoints and arrowheads, and jewelry.

**features**
Nonportable artifacts such as walls, pits, postholes, and hearths.

**hearths**
Ancient campfires.

**ecofacts**
Culturally relevant nonartifactual finds, such as animal bones, plant remains, charcoal, and soils, that archaeologists can analyze to reconstruct past human diets and environments.

**context**
The immediate setting where artifacts or fossils are found, comprising matrix, provenience, and association.

**matrix**
The material, such as soil or sediment, surrounding archaeological finds.

This rock-cut temple is located at Petra, Jordan, a city hewn out of rock about 2,400 years ago by an Arab tribe known as the Nabataeans. What does Petra tell us about the Nabataeans?

**provenience**
The three-dimensional location of an object in the matrix.

**association**
A meaningful relationship between objects within the matrix, which may indicate their function.

**cultural transformation processes**
Human actions that cause changes in the archaeological record at a site.

**natural transformation processes**
Natural phenomena that cause changes in the archaeological record at a site.

soil that may relate to the period of site occupation. Or the material may have been deliberately deposited; for example, mounds of earth, built to cover tombs, are a feature of 5,000-year-old barrow burials in Europe. **Provenience** is the exact horizontal and vertical (three-dimensional) location of an object within its matrix. Recording the provenience is crucial because it enables archaeologists to determine the nature of any **association** between remains within the matrix. True associations between objects often indicate the function of an object, as in the case of hearth stones and burned bones (Drewett 1999).

Context must be understood before investigators can interpret the meaning of a find. A series of postholes may indicate a structure, perhaps a hut. The materials found within this structure may indicate its function, perhaps as a dwelling place. The artifacts inside may relate to activities that took place there: Loom weights could indicate weaving, flint bits could indicate flint knapping (chipping), and animal bones could be the remains of food.

It is important to realize that sites revealed by excavation are rarely exactly as they were when they were occupied in the past. Many processes can affect, change, or transform the patterning of materials (Schiffer 1987). If archaeologists hope to understand cultural activities that occurred in the past, they must determine how the artifacts, ecofacts, and features got to be where they were found. But this process is not as straightforward as it may sound—because changes take place both while a site is occupied and after it is abandoned. Every living context is constantly changing. For example, people may recycle objects; they may remelt a metal object and recast it as something different, or reuse wooden house beams in later buildings. People generally dump everyday items when they are worn out, but they guard precious items to pass on to successive generations. They take valuable items such as metals and jewelry with them when changing locations, but usually leave easily made or heavy objects behind. Subsequent newcomers at an abandoned site may clean it and scavenge materials from it to build new dwellings on the same spot. Finally, farmers or modern builders churn up the earth and everything in it. These transformations to a site are the result of human and therefore cultural actions, which are called **cultural transformation processes**.

Nature, too, plays a part in making life more difficult for the archaeologist. **Natural transformation processes** such as wind, ice, frost, and meandering rivers can cause erosion, movement, and mixing of sediments and materials. For example, people occupied Copan, an important Maya settlement in Honduras, for about 2,000 years before abandoning it. When the site was discovered, a change in the course of the Copan River had eroded away part of the site (Sharer and Ashmore 2003).

Large animals can trample artifacts and break up fragile pieces; smaller burrowing animals can cause dramatic movements of soils and sediments and their archaeological contents. The roots of dense vegetation are destructive and can even break up buried stone monuments. Chemical and bacterial processes, though less visible, also have the potential to change the nature of sites. Acids may affect the structure of metals, causing them to rust or decompose; in many cases only a stain in the soil remains as testament to the metal object that once was there. Bacterial action often causes organic objects to decay rapidly, leaving nothing but discolored soil (Drewett 1999).

## Preservation of Archaeological Data

Fortunately, transformation processes do not destroy all evidence of the past. Although they may alter the original patterning of sites, they do not always totally destroy the patterns. So what survives? Inorganic material survives almost everywhere. Pottery and flint are the most common finds on most sites—not because they were the only materials used in the past but because, on the whole, they survive well. Organic materials such as wood, skin, hair, fabrics, and food are much more fragile and survive only under special conditions, if at all. Certain conditions, usually environmental, have a strong effect on what is preserved or destroyed: freezing, waterlogging, dry or arid conditions, charring, and natural disasters.

- *Freezing.* Just as the freezer section of a refrigerator keeps food for an indefinite period, natural frozen conditions present in some parts of the globe preserve organic materials—sometimes for many millennia. A superb example of preservation by freezing is the well-preserved body of the Iceman (refer to Highlight 1.1).
- *Waterlogging.* Preservation of organic material may occur in wet environments because the absence of oxygen can prevent bacterial decay. Although seasonal waterlogging is bad for preservation because objects are exposed to oxygen for part of the year, permanent year-round waterlogging can provide excellent preservation of organic objects. Wet conditions have preserved bog bodies and ancient wooden trackways in Swiss lake villages and in other areas of northern Europe and North America (Coles and Coles 1986, 1989). Florida has many waterlogged sites, including the 7,000-year-old Windover burial site (Purdy 1992). The dead, and frequently their grave goods, were wrapped in textiles and placed in the bottom of a pond. Excavators at this site have recovered the remains of 168 individuals, many still retaining soft tissue. Among other organic materials preserved at Windover were wooden handles and pointed stakes; tightly woven textiles made from plant materials (bags, hoods, blankets, and clothing); cordage; baskets; and at least 31 food and medicinal plants.

This 2,000-year-old man from Denmark, known as "Tolland Man," was found in a peat bog. Scientists believe that he probably died as a sacrificial victim or was killed as punishment rather than by accident. What conditions aided the preservation of the body?

Tons of volcanic ash and pumice from the volcanic eruption of Mount Vesuvius almost 2,000 years ago buried the Roman city of Pompeii, but in doing so preserved it. In what ways are Pompeii and Ozette village similar?

- *Dry or arid conditions*. Rapid desiccation preserves organic material where dry, arid conditions are present, for example, in Egypt, areas of North America, and coastal regions of South America. The dry conditions of Danger Cave in Utah protected a wealth of organic materials in the deeply stratified, 11-kyr-old sequence of the cave (Jennings 1957). Excavation uncovered fragments of vegetable fiber string, rope, netting, and baskets that reveal 14 different techniques of basket making; scraps of skillfully worked buckskin and hide; wooden bows, arrows, and spear-throwers (atlatls); animal coprolites (feces); and even lumps of chewed desert bulrush fiber.

- *Charring*. Charring provides much information about food in the past. In 1983 archaeologists found a 7,000-year-old hoard of 1,400,000 charred lentil seeds on the floor of a house at Yiftah'el, a Neolithic (early farming period) site in Israel (Garfinkel et al. 1988), indicating the early cultivation of lentils in the Near East. At other sites charred grains are embedded in pottery; probably the grains stuck to the damp clay surface of the pot as it was placed on the ground to dry and subsequently charred during the firing process.

- *Natural disasters*. Natural disasters such as mud slides, volcanic eruptions, and fierce storms can bury sites rapidly, causing devastation. Nevertheless, such calamities prove helpful to archaeologists, because in some cases the rapidity of a disaster preserves much of a site. This happened at Akrotiri on Santorini (a Greek island) 3,500 years ago, at Pompeii almost 2,000 years ago, and at the Native American village of Ozette in Washington state about 500 years ago (see Highlight 8.1, on pp. 212–213).

# In the News at Ozette Village

OZETTE VILLAGE IN WASHINGTON STATE, situated on the Pacific coast on the westernmost tip of the continental United States, could be called "America's Pompeii." Like the Roman city of Pompeii in Italy, Ozette Village was buried in a rapidly occurring event that blanketed and preserved the site; many of the material remains that normally biodegrade were preserved; and archaeologists have been able to study the residents' material culture and to make inferences about their economy, social organization, and religion. But there are differences as well. Pompeii was covered by volcanic ash from an eruption of Mount Vesuvius in AD 79, whereas Ozette was covered by a mud slide in AD 1500. Pompeii was considerably larger, with at least seven temples, three theaters, and hundreds of individual houses; Ozette Village contained no ritual buildings and probably only a dozen houses. Additionally, Pompeii's remains are molds of people, animals, and artifacts; in contrast, Ozette has actual preserved artifacts. A final difference is that a large number of Pompeii's people, perhaps 2,000 of them, were unable to escape Mount Vesuvius's eruption and were buried under the ash. At Ozette, however, there was apparently enough warning that all humans were safely out of the village when the mud slide occurred.

Before the mud slide 500 years ago, Ozette was a major whaling village inhabited by Northwest Coast people (see Chapter 12). The settlement faced out to sea, from which the majority of the villagers' livelihood came. In addition to hunting whales, the villagers fished—mainly for halibut and cod—and occasionally hunted fur seals, porpoise, dolphin, sea lion, and land-based deer and elk. Although excavators at Ozette found no boats, ocean canoeing, reef fishing, and shellfish collecting were likely. The investigators recovered only two projectile points, and the bows used to shoot them were very small, adding to the picture of true ocean resource procurement.

In addition to artifacts connected to food procurement, the excavations unearthed three cedar-planked longhouses that contained some artifacts from early historic contact with traders (china, glassware, coins) as well as a surprising trove of organic materials, such as perfectly preserved twisted cedar rope, cedar mats, planks, and baskets. The total number of organic materials is staggering: The 42,000 artifacts included baskets, mats, hats, tumplines, loom uprights, fishhooks, harpoons, tool handles, chisels, wedges, fragments of boxes, and bowls. Even a single braid of human hair was found in a hardwood bowl!

As reconstructed, the split-cedar houses were quite large, ranging from 60 to 70 feet (18 to 21 m) by 35 feet (11 m), each with several hearths. Raised platforms along the walls were likely used for sleeping and storage. Each house contained different kinds of shells (from shellfish), giving the impression that each household exploited a different shell bed and owned or controlled different stretches of beach. This suggests economic specialization. A computer map of the site shows that one longhouse was of higher status than the other two. The higher-status house was closer to the ocean and larger; an estimated 28,000 board feet of cedar went into its construction, versus 18,000 for the lower-status houses. This house had the highest proportion of decorated shell artifacts and had more salmon, halibut, and whale bones. Woven cedar hats were also found in the high-status house. Additionally, most of the seal-hunting gear was found here, suggesting that high-status males specialized in seal hunting. And surprisingly, the higher-status house was kept neater than the other two houses. Ethnographic parallels with modern descendants of the Ozette people support each of these deductions.

The tale of how the artifacts were excavated and preserved began in 1967, when Washington State University archaeologist Richard Daugherty and his students began excavating a trench inland from the sea. A comparison of the area with photos taken in the 1890s had suggested that there were once houses there. After digging down through four previous beach layers, the team found shells, bones, and patterning that suggested housing. But, as often happens at archaeological sites, the investigators uncovered these finds at the very end of the season. Daugherty and his group could not reopen the site for several years because of previous commitments. But in 1970 a ferocious storm cut up the beach, exposing numerous artifacts. The local Native Americans—the Makah, who are descendants of the Ozette villagers and live in the area—remembered Daugherty's earlier work and asked him to return to finish the excavation before more of their heritage was destroyed. Daugherty reopened the site in 1970, and the excavation continued for eight years.

To preserve the fragile artifacts and to help excavate a wet and slippery site, Daugherty employed a high-pressure hose, using water pumped from the ocean to separate the artifacts from their mud matrix. Uncovered artifacts were immediately preserved in polyethylene glycol. "Hands and knees" excavation would not have worked well and could have damaged fragile artifacts such as mats.

Today, many of the Ozette artifacts are housed in the new Makah Cultural and Research Center at Neah Bay, not far from the original village and excavation. The Makah worked with the archaeologists, both assisting with the excavation as volunteers and helping interpret the artifacts. Although the material culture and deductions can-

not paint a complete picture of Ozette Village life, Makah elders have told the archaeologists that there may have been six chiefs in Ozette, each ranked relative to each other; that commoners could never rise to chief rank; that the villagers had two-week potlatches (ceremonial feasts featuring the distribution of gifts) just as other Northwest Coast people did; and that the bits of art on boxes were probably used in potlatching. Today the roots of Makah culture are better preserved in the Tribal Museum than they were in the mud.

*Sources*: Ames, K. M., and H. D. Maschner. 1999. *Peoples of the Northwest Coast: Their archaeology and prehistory*. New York: Thames & Hudson.    Kirk, R., and R. Daugherty. 1978. *Exploring Washington archaeology*. Seattle: University of Washington Press.    Pascua, M. P. 1991. Ozette: A Makah village in 1491. *National Geographic* (October): 38–53.

The Pacific Ocean site of Ozette Village, in Washington State, shown here in an artist's reconstruction, was occupied until AD 1500 by ancestors of the modern Makah Indians. Why are most of the artifacts of the material culture made of wood?

*Source:* Painting by R. Schlect in Pascua, M. Parker. 1991. Ozette: A Makah village in 1491. *National Geographic* 180 (4): 38–53.

turn back to your reading

# How Archaeologists Find Evidence

Once archaeologists decide on a research project, how do they find evidence? The research design sets the parameters of the project and normally includes the hypothesis to be tested. Many research projects do not include excavation and finding artifacts but rather involve using existing data to investigate an idea that has not been previously studied. If testing the hypothesis will require excavation, however, then selecting sites to obtain the necessary data is often an archaeologist's first move. Once artifacts have been found, they must be dated; after that the researcher analyzes the finds in an attempt to determine their meaning and to decide whether they change previous knowledge. Publication of the research results ensures that new knowledge is disseminated to others.

## Finding Sites

Construction and development can be instrumental in uncovering sites, particularly in urban areas; such was the case in 1978 when electricians digging in Mexico City discovered the Great Temple of the Aztecs at Tenochtitlan (Matos Moctezuma 1988). However, construction and development also have the potential to destroy. The greatest salvage project ever undertaken preceded the construction of Egypt's Aswan Dam in the 1960s. Construction of the dam caused much of the rich heritage of Upper Egypt and northern Sudan to be submerged in the rising waters of the resulting artificial Lake Nasser. Before that happened, archaeologists and other specialists undertook intensive survey and recording of sites and their contents. In the process they discovered many previously unknown sites. Some sites, such as the temple of Abu Simbel, were physically moved so that they would remain above the water line (Save-Soderberg 1987).

More often, however, archaeologists, employ a range of techniques to actively look for sites. In this quest they utilize many kinds of resources. Written evidence, in the form of stories or records, can be extremely useful for historic periods. Heinrich Schliemann discovered Troy by following clues in Homer's *Iliad* and *Odyssey*, which recounted the siege of Troy and Odysseus's wanderings. Similarly, Helge Ingstad (1985) studied Viking sagas and subsequently found Viking settlements on Newfoundland.

Maps play an important part in all aspects of archaeological research, and finding sites is no exception. Old maps may show features that are no longer visible or that have not been closely examined. For example, irregularities in field or woodlot boundaries, roads, or paths may be of archaeological interest, because people may have created them deliberately in order to avoid an ancient structure such as a fortress or temple.

Because archaeological sites are fairly rare and are usually buried, searching for them can seem like looking for the proverbial needle in a haystack. Therefore, archaeologists employ strategic approaches to use their time effectively. A study of geology and geomorphology can indicate areas suitable for particular exploitation. Areas with good farming soils or with good raw materials such as flint or building stone may have attracted human groups in the past. The most common way to find sites is through **survey**. In *ground survey* people walk over an area, scanning the ground for artifacts or for something that looks out of place such as ash or different-colored soil. The surveyed area is usually divided into sections, often determined statistically. The chances of finding anything increase when the ground is clear after plowing or when heavy rains or winds have caused surface erosion. Such disturbances may bring buried artifacts to the surface. Researchers plot finds on a map and check for spatial patterns, such as areas where finds are dense, which could indicate that there is something of interest below the ground.

**Remote sensing techniques** such as aerial photography, radar mapping, and satellite imagery can help archaeologists to find sites or, when they know the location of a site, to determine what lies underground without disturbing the surface. Buried walls, ditches, and roads disturb subsurface soils, resulting in *crop and soil marks* that are visible

**survey**
The most common way to locate archaeological sites or finds without excavation.

**remote sensing techniques**
Survey techniques, such as aerial photography, radar mapping, and satellite imagery, used to find archaeological sites buried underground without disturbing the surface.

from the air. Crops flourish in deep, nutrient-rich soil, and those growing over buried ditches and pits receive greater moisture and nutrients than those growing over buried walls or roads. The result: stronger growth for the former and more stunted growth for the latter. From the air the richer, denser growth appears darker. Plowing, on the other hand, brings buried soils to the surface. Soils from old ditches, earthworks, and banks tend to contain organic matter; when brought to the surface, they appear darker than the surrounding area. Conversely, soils over roads and walls will appear lighter. The low angle of the rising and setting sun may cause long-buried earthworks or mounds to cast *shadows* that are visible from the air (Riley 1987). Finally, *satellite imagery* and *radar mapping* can enable researchers to trace large-scale features such as the remains of irrigation canals in ancient Mesopotamia or Maya field systems and settlements in the Mexican Yucatan (Renfrew and Bahn 2000).

Among the least complex of archaeologists' **subsurface survey techniques** is simply to thump the ground with a rod and listen for reverberations that may indicate the presence of solid or hollow features beneath the surface. Another inexpensive technique is the use of an *auger* or *borer* that functions somewhat like a giant corkscrew, bringing samples of soil (and anything in it) to the surface. More sophisticated noninvasive detection methods include electrical resistivity, ground-penetrating radar, and magnetometers (Clark 1990). An *electrical resistivity* meter measures and records soil resistance to the passage of electric current through the ground. Water conducts electricity, whereas rocks do not; an electrical current passes more easily through the relatively moist soil of buried pits and ditches than through subsurface walls or roads. Variation in resistivity patterns can be seen in a computer printout. In a somewhat similar manner, *ground-penetrating radar* directs electrical or magnetic waves through the ground and reflects back differences in subsurface features. *Magnetometers* measure different amounts of magnetism in buried objects such as iron tools, hearths, kilns, and pottery. Simple *metal detectors* also help investigators locate metal objects that are buried slightly below the surface.

Survey techniques provide a range of interconnecting spatial data that can provide a picture of the archaeological potential of an area. Making sense of the information can be daunting. **Geographic Information Systems (GIS)** has become one of the most useful tools in recent archaeological research. It is a sophisticated software that links databases and maps; data can be collected, stored, manipulated, retrieved, and presented in visual form (Lock and Harris 1992). The program can combine separate sets of data using overlays to show relationships relevant to the research questions being posed.

# Excavating Archaeological Sites

Pre-excavation surveys are virtually nondestructive and can provide considerable information about archaeological sites, such as types of sites and activities that took place there; in fact, surveys often suffice to fulfill the requirements of projects. If more information is needed, then excavation may be necessary.

Ideally, an archaeologist sets up a **research design** for an excavation before the first trowel goes into the ground. The research design should cover everything the archaeologist intends to do throughout the investigation, from formulating the particular questions to be investigated to publishing the results. It should include plans for data acquisition, processing, analysis, and interpretation. However, it is not always possible to create—or to adhere to—a complete research design. If a researcher discovers a site by accident, for example, he or she will modify the research design to fit the find.

Excavation destroys sites. Therefore, it is essential to record every step in detail. Only with good excavation and recording techniques can sites and their contents be reassembled in the laboratory. Teams now rarely excavate sites entirely; they usually leave part of any site for future archaeologists. The principle here is that future investigators may have different research questions—as well as more sophisticated techniques that may enable them to discover information unobtainable by today's methods. Excavation is expensive, and project directors usually plan a project in minute detail;

**subsurface survey techniques**
Survey techniques, such as thumping the ground with a rod, using an auger or bore, or measuring electrical resistivity or magnetism, that determine what lies below the surface at a potential archaeological site.

**Geographic Information Systems (GIS)**
Software that links databases and maps to show relationships relevant to research questions.

**research design**
A carefully formulated and systematic plan for executing an archaeological excavation from formulating the research question(s) through publication of the results.

they work for months before any excavation starts in order to secure funding, obtain permits, and find staff.

No matter what kind of excavation an archaeologist chooses as likely to be the most productive, the principle of **stratigraphy** is fundamental. Stratigraphy is the charting of the sequence of strata (layers) of deposits that have accumulated over time. Theoretically, each stratum in a sequence is deposited before the one covering it and after the one on which it rests. Consequently, each level (and anything within it) is older than the levels above it and younger than those below it (Harris 1979). A stratigraphic section—a slice through strata, like a slice of layer cake—can consist of geological (natural) layers or archaeological (cultural) layers, or a mixture of the two (see Figure 8.1). An ideal stratigraphic section would have distinct, almost parallel, layers. However, life is not always that easy. Numerous factors, including site transformation processes discussed earlier, may disturb neat stratigraphic layers; examples include geological movement or erosion, burrowing animal activity, and human burial pits, storage pits, or house foundation trenches. Consequently, site stratigraphy has to be very carefully assessed throughout the excavation.

**stratigraphy**

The charting of the sequence of strata (layers) of deposits that have accumulated over time at a site; can be used to assign relative dates to objects in different layers.

*Figure 8.1*

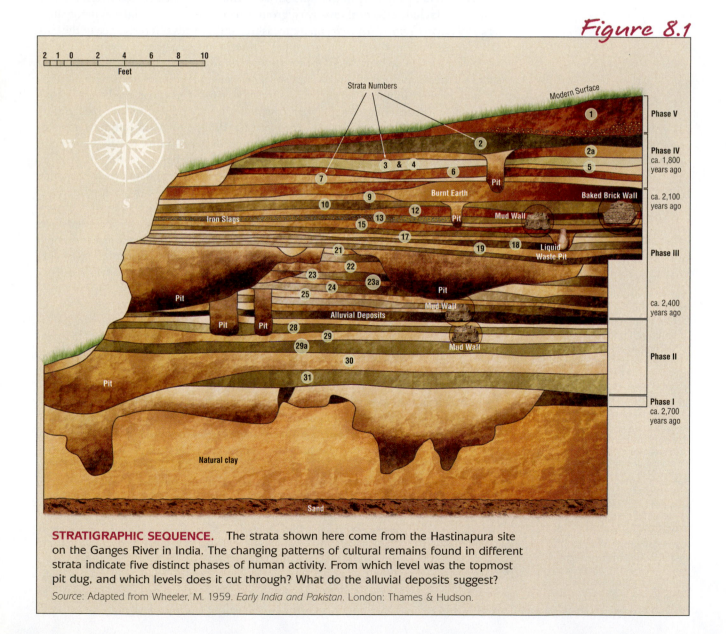

**STRATIGRAPHIC SEQUENCE.**   The strata shown here come from the Hastinapura site on the Ganges River in India. The changing patterns of cultural remains found in different strata indicate five distinct phases of human activity. From which level was the topmost pit dug, and which levels does it cut through? What do the alluvial deposits suggest?

*Source:* Adapted from Wheeler, M. 1959. *Early India and Pakistan.* London: Thames & Hudson.

Methods of excavation differ according to the questions being researched, the country in which the work is taking place, the amount of time and money available, the nature and depth of the deposits and the sediments in which they lie, and the whim of the excavator (Barker 1995). There are also differences between types of sites. Large urban sites produce enormous amounts of soil, artifacts, and features; in contrast, at the oldest sites there are few features or artifacts, and excavators must carefully examine virtually each grain of soil.

Excavations may be horizontal or vertical. Horizontal excavations expose large areas and often reveal spatial relationships between contemporaneous artifacts, ecofacts, and features. Vertical excavations cut into the deposits, reveal stratification, and show change through time.

*Test pits* are the most basic and least expensive form of excavation. Test pits penetrate vertically into deposits, and by using them investigators can obtain information on the stratigraphic history of the site as well as sampling what the site has to offer (Drewett 1999). Often employed in survey, test pits usually precede more extensive excavation. However, they lack horizontal breadth. *Trenches* are essentially test pits with one side extended in the horizontal plane; archaeologists use trenches to investigate features such as burial mounds or earthen platforms. In *open area excavation* workers peel off each layer of the site, carefully record everything, and remove the artifacts and ecofacts. Regardless of the particular strategy, investigators usually separate sites into grid squares for mapping and recording purposes and set up a datum point or marker as the central reference point from which all mapping will be done.

However careful an excavator is, fragments of material are always missed. Sieving the excavated soil helps to offset the bias toward larger finds. On very old or small sites, it is normal for workers at least to *dry sieve* the soil (i.e., put all the soil through a 10-mm or ¼-inch mesh). On large sites this would be impossible, so workers normally sieve samples of soil. Plant and other small, fragile remains can be retrieved with the aid of water through wet sieving and flotation. *Wet sieving* is a manual process in which the investigator places a sample of soil in a sieve and immerses it in water. *Flotation* is a mechanical process in which a constant flow of water causes light materials to spill over the edge of the container into a series of nesting sieves. In all sieving, soil passes through the sieve, leaving the archaeological raw evidence. Flotation has been critical in the recovery of small seeds. Additionally, during excavation, specialists remove samples of pollen, soil, and charcoal for environmental analysis at an off-site laboratory.

Once investigators have excavated a surface, they remove the exposed material. But before anything can be removed, all uncovered items must be carefully recorded and plotted on maps. Specially prepared recording sheets help standardize the procedures and provide a complete record of the context of finds. After doing the recording, workers carefully lift the material, number it, and place it in bags or containers to be taken to the field laboratory. In the past, field lab workers usually cleaned the artifacts; today, however, the trend is to avoid extensive cleaning in order to prevent potential loss of information. For example, pots may contain food residue that can be examined later. At the field lab, team members label each numbered piece and make an inventory of all finds. Analysis can begin before an excavation is concluded—but the final analysis always awaits the last trowel of soil, which always holds the potential to reveal one last piece of information.

Highlight 8.2 (on p. 218) gives a look at the reality of working on a dig.

# Analysis of Finds

Modern archaeology is a multi-disciplinary subject: It requires the skills of specialists from a wide range of disciplines covering both the sciences and the arts. Investigators may consult specialists before, during, and after excavation; and specialists' contributions

# Highlight 8.2

## A Day in the Field

BEING ON A DIG IS FUN; it is a stimulating experience, both socially and archaeologically. But it is hard work. When diggers return home at the end of the season, they are exhausted, but nevertheless happy and fulfilled.

Numerous factors affect excavation schedules, including the country in which the excavation takes place, local climate, geographical features, the type of site, research objectives, available funding, size of the project, and number of diggers. Excavators work between 8 and 10 hours a day, excavating on site as well as processing finds. On-site tasks include digging, recording, planning, and dry sieving. If there is water nearby, then wet sieving and flotation may also occur on site. Off-site tasks, which often take place at the dig house (or base camp), include washing, labeling, sorting, recording, and photographing finds, as well as helping specialists with flotation, wet sieving, or initial analysis.

In hot, arid regions, such as the Middle East and parts of East Africa, where midday temperatures can be unbearable, the day starts early. The team rises and breakfasts before sunrise in order to arrive at the site in time to take advantage of the cooler morning hours. During the hottest part of the day, the group returns to the dig house for lunch and rest. Later in the afternoon postexcavation work goes on in the dig house lab for a further 2 or 3 hours. Then dinner, after which it is time to relax, although the finds have a way of seducing some people back to the lab.

The number of daylight hours affects excavation schedules. In equatorial regions darkness comes at around 6 p.m., so excavation work has to stop by about 5 or 5:30 p.m. In cooler places, such as Iceland, for example, heat and light are not problems; summer evenings are wonderfully long, with mild temperatures. However, windy or rainy spells are common in Iceland and can make life uncomfortable.

In intertidal zones by the coast or along tidal rivers, excavation is possible only when tides are low. Consequently, excavators need to plan around predicted tides. Furthermore, some sites may only appear when the tide is very low, perhaps twice a year, and if that time falls in the middle of the night, excavation is impossible. Sometimes excavators may have an hour or less in which to work before the tide again covers the area. Planning fieldwork in an intertidal zone requires careful risk assessments to ensure that excavators are not stranded. Working in tidal zones is fine in the summertime, but it can be miserable on cold winter days, and, of course, it is a muddy process.

Daily transport is necessary when the dig house is at a distance from the site. In places where roads are poor or nonexistent, the daily ride can be long and bone rattling. Cave sites are often accessible only on foot, requiring a strenuous daily hike up steep slopes. The effort of hiking to a cave site can be exacerbated when there is a lot of equipment to carry. On the other hand, those working on an urban site may go to the site by public transport.

Accommodation can vary from the luxurious (e.g., hotels) to the basic (camping) and encompass anything in between (e.g., mattresses on schoolroom floors, cold water, outhouses). Depending on the region, it can be necessary to take precautions against mosquitoes and other biting and potentially poisonous insects, scorpions, rodents, wild dogs, hyenas, jackals, snakes, and other animals. If the dig house is in a village or town, there may be cafes, often with Internet access, and bars in which to relax with local people. In fact, local people are often involved in excavation work or in running the base camp. Many other local people are interested in learning about the excavation. Indeed most excavations make arrangements for site visits by the public; sometimes a day is set aside for visitors, and sometimes members of the team give site tours. Very large, well-known sites have visitor centers nearby.

Organizers of an excavation have to take numerous factors into consideration so that the most can be gained out of an expensive venture. But, given the potential knowledge gained through excavation, it is well worth the effort, and a most rewarding experience for excavators.

turn back to your reading

increasingly enable researchers to obtain more information about sites, their contents, and their settings. Additionally, **experimental archaeology** and **ethnoarchaeology** (observation of existing societies from an archaeological perspective) often aid in interpretation. This section focuses on some of the key disciplines and methods on which researchers draw in analyzing various types of finds.

First, it is crucial to reconstruct the environment of a past time period in order to understand how people and their culture adapted to and exploited it. *Geology* and *geomorphology* provide information on changing land formations in past millennia. Scientists reconstruct global climates by drilling cores deep into sediments below the sea and checking them for the ratio of cold-adapted to warm-adapted microorganisms (called foraminifera) to determine past ice ages and interglacial periods. Ice cores from Greenland and Antarctica provide finely tuned evidence on the Earth's changing temperatures. The study of soils helps to determine what has happened to a landscape, such as forest clearance prior to cereal planting or animal grazing or intensive exploitation that led to nutrient-poor soils, and eventual agricultural disaster.

*Palynologists* analyze microscopic pollen grains, from which they derive information on tree and ground cover and on temperature and rainfall (Figure 8.2). The identification of plant materials collected from sites, usually in the form of charred remains, determines the extent to which human groups chose to use some species rather than others that were also available in the environment. For example, craftspeople may have chosen to burn a certain kind of wood because it burned slowly or with particular intensity, both of which would be useful in firing pottery or smelting metal (Shimada and Merkel 1991). In addition to helping with environmental reconstruction, *archaeobotany* provides information on the importance (or unimportance) of plant food in human diets—and possibly data on other uses of plants, such as for medicine.

Because animal bones are preserved more frequently than plants, they are usually more prominent in archaeological sites. Humans have long used animals for a variety of purposes, but particularly for food, clothing, shelter, and traction. Early groups may also have kept animals as pets or items of prestige. *Zooarchaeologists* are interested in the species, age, and sex of animal remains. They also want to know about animal use, hunting, and butchering patterns (as appropriate) and even season of death. Additionally, beetles and land mollusks can provide valuable information on small changes in environment and climate, because many of these creatures are habitat specific (Davis 2002).

Artifacts yield information in many ways. Analysis from a technological perspective focuses on the materials used, techniques of manufacture, and the degree of skill represented. Stylistic analysis can indicate cultural preferences as well as changes over time and across space. Functional analysis may be macroscopic, such as examination of cooking marks on a pot, or microscopic, such as study of residues within the pot; discard patterns may indicate the final use of a piece. Researchers can address questions of trade and exchange and the mechanisms affecting them by sourcing (determining the original sources of) either the raw materials used in artifact manufacture or the artifacts themselves. Because trade may bring wealth to those who control it, artifacts made elsewhere may be evidence of wealth and social inequality. Trade and contact also facilitate the exchange of ideas, which may be evident in the production of local products in nonlocal styles.

Archaeologists look for spatial patterns of artifacts, ecofacts, and features on sites to see if they suggest patterns of organization. For example, on large urban sites, there may be workshops or artisan areas, living areas, shops, temples, palaces, or rubbish dumps.

It is important to remember that although archaeological evidence can provide much information about the past, surviving remnants are usually only a fraction of what was once there. Also, there are certain aspects of past behaviors that are impossible to understand fully, particularly the belief systems of societies that did not use writing.

**experimental archaeology**
The use of experiments to develop hypotheses about or interpret particular human activities or processes in the past.

**ethnoarchaeology**
The study of traditional activities in existing societies from an archaeological perspective in order to develop hypotheses about past societies.

*Figure 8.2*

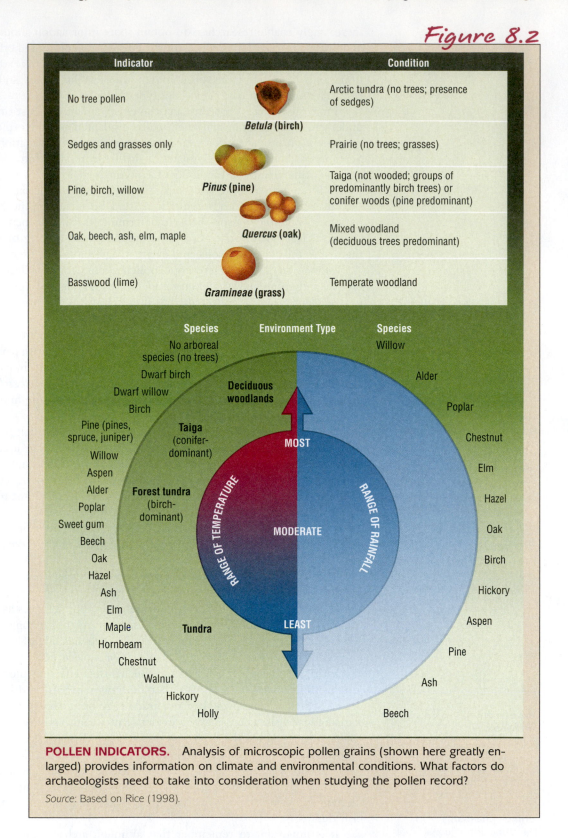

**POLLEN INDICATORS.** Analysis of microscopic pollen grains (shown here greatly enlarged) provides information on climate and environmental conditions. What factors do archaeologists need to take into consideration when studying the pollen record?

*Source:* Based on Rice (1998).

# Archaeological Theory and Interpretation

Archaeologists and paleoanthropologists study the physical and cultural remains of the past to better understand our human ancestors and their way of life. Excavation and context provide the raw data, but interpretation of that data is essential for understanding.

**cultural historical approach**

The traditional descriptive approach to interpretation of archaeological evidence whose main focus was establishing chronological sequences of cultural groups and thus developing culture histories; similarities between cultures (as shown by similarities in artifacts) were seen as arising primarily through migration of peoples or diffusion of ideas.

**processual archaeology**

A theoretical approach to interpreting archaeological evidence that promoted a problem-oriented, scientific type of archaeological research, seeking explanations rather than just descriptions; it was known as *new archaeology* when it was first developed.

**postprocessual archaeology**

An approach that developed as a reaction against the rigid scientific approach of processual archaeology and that stresses the individual and the interactions between humans and their groups, their material culture, their landscape, and their symbolic world.

Approaches to understanding the archaeological record have changed over the past 150 years. Until the early 1950s archaeologists looked for similarities in data in order to distinguish cultures that they identified with particular people in specific regions. The main focus was establishing chronological sequences of cultural groups and thus developing culture histories. In this descriptive **cultural historical approach**, scholars interpreted similarities between cultures (as shown by similarities in artifacts) as arising primarily through migration of peoples or diffusion of ideas (Binford 1968a; Johnson 2000). The late 1950s and early 1960s, however, saw a reaction against this traditional descriptive approach. Advocates of the new approach, known as **processual archaeology**, were interested in the processes of change and sought explanations rather than mere descriptions. They saw any given culture as a system with various subsystems (such as technical, subsistence, and environmental subsystems); by definition, change in one part of the system would affect the rest of the system. Processual archaeologists promoted a scientific approach: They conducted problem-oriented archaeological research, formulating hypotheses and testing those hypotheses through the use of scientific techniques in excavation and analysis. The results allowed researchers to make generalizations about the archaeological problems addressed (Binford 1968a; Renfrew and Bahn 2000).

Although a problem-oriented, scientific approach is now a fundamental element of archaeological research, criticisms of processual archaeology have arisen since the early 1980s. The resulting range of theoretical approaches to and perspectives on the interpretation of the archaeological record are collectively referred to as **postprocessual archaeology**. Advocates argue that the individual has been lost in the generalizations resulting from the rigid scientific approach of processual archaeology. Individuals—men, women, young, old—played an active role in all past cultures, not only adhering to societal rules but also manipulating and modifying those rules. At times manipulation and modification could have caused substantial changes to a culture; or they may have had minor effects that were absorbed into group traditions and passed on. People's interactions with each other, with their material culture, and with the landscape around them were both mundane, serving daily needs, and symbolic, serving ideological needs. Although archaeologists aim to be unbiased in their interpretations, it is clear that all humans are products of their culture, background, and experiences, which influence the way they perceive the world. Postprocessual theorists argue that just as there are different philosophies and different political agendas in the world, there are also various interpretations of the past (Dobres and Robb 2000; Hodder 1991, 2003; Johnson 2000; Shennan 2004).

# Dating Sites and Artifacts

Often the first question archaeologists or bioanthropologists ask about an artifact or bone is "How old is this?" For some projects it is not necessary to know an object's age in calendar years; however, researchers must establish the relative order of fossils or artifacts in order to make sense of changes occurring in the human past. Other kinds of projects need precise dates in calendar years. For example, a sudden change in a group's pottery style may have occurred as the result of an invasion of foreign settlers, whereas gradual change may indicate long-term development within a stable group.

By tradition, paleoanthropologists use abbreviations for time designations. In this text we use "byr" (billion years), "myr" (million years), and "kyr" (thousand years), adding "ago" or "old" as appropriate. When something is less than 10,000 (10 kyr) old, we will use the full numeral.

Dating techniques have come a long way since the first half of the twentieth century. Before the 1950s the only ways scientists could date artifacts or fossils were by identifying the stratigraphic layers in which they were located; by comparing fossil features or styles or types of artifacts; or by relying on historians, who could supply dates for the past 5,000 years. Beginning in the 1950s, however, scientific advances ushered in new, highly technical methods of determining the age of archaeological and biological remains—among them isotopic, chemical, and molecular dating. The post-1950 dating methods may seem more "scientific" than the previous reliance on stratigraphic dating, yet each of the more modern methods has its own set of assumptions and limitations. Although many of the problems with these techniques have been resolved, some of the techniques remain experimental and some show a lack of internal consistency. Archaeologists and bioanthropologists have learned that **cross-dating**—using as many different appropriate techniques as possible, including stratigraphy—is the only way to have confidence in dates assigned to objects. As many experts have said, "One date is no date."

Biological anthropologists use techniques that date fossil material between about 6 myr and 25 kyr ago. Archaeologists, by contrast, have nothing to date (no human artifacts) before 2.6 myr ago but a great deal to date thereafter. In view of the time spans they study, biological anthropologists rely mostly on K-Ar (potassium–argon) dating or its $^{40}Ar/^{39}Ar$ variation. In contrast, because most archaeological sites are younger than 40 kyr old, archaeologists rely primarily on $^{14}C$ (carbon14) dating or its AMS (accelerator mass spectrometry) variation. Neither technique is unique to one subdiscipline, however. In addition, both archaeologists and bioanthropologists use molecular techniques to date biological (fossil) or cultural (burial) materials. Let's look more closely at all these approaches.

## Relative Dating Techniques

Researchers use **relative dating** to order fossils or artifacts in a sequence—to identify which items are older, younger, or approximately the same age as one another. Because relative dating does not establish calendar dates, a relative chronology enables specialists to make statements about changes over time but not about how long it took for those changes to occur. Relative dating techniques include stratigraphy; biostratigraphy; fluorine, uranium, and nitrogen (FUN) dating; and typological sequencing. *Stratigraphic dating* orders artifacts according to the layer in which they are found. *Biostratigraphy* is based on the principle that particular combinations of certain fossil animals and plants, as found in soil or sediment, will covary from site to site. If excavators find similar combinations and proportions of animal and plant remains in certain layers of soil in two geographically close-by areas, they can assume that the layers are the same age; and if the investigators can date one layer by some other technique, then they can regard the other as being of the same date. *FUN dating* measures the amount of fluorine, uranium, or nitrogen found in teeth and bones. This form of relative dating is known more for the few special fossils it has dated—or falsified, such as the infamous fraudulent Piltdown Man (Highlight 6.2)—than for large numbers of samples dated. *Typological sequencing* capitalizes on the fact that many artifacts share characteristics, particularly shape or style of decoration. Because these characteristics usually change through time in the same way that whims of fashion do, types may serve as relative chronological markers. Typology often works well on a regional basis; for example, ceramic types in the American Southwest are good indicators of different time periods. Archaeologists often use typology to supplement other dating methods.

## Chronometric Dating

The word *chronometric* means "measuring time" (*chronos* means "time" and *metron* means "measure"). **Chronometric dating** techniques were once called "absolute"; but the term *absolute* connotes truth and certainty, whereas chronometric techniques provide knowledge, not truth. Although chronometric techniques do not provide calendar dates with total accuracy, they are able to specify ranges of dates that give researchers confidence at a medium to high level, depending on the specific technique.

The major chronometric dating techniques are potassium–argon (K-Ar), carbon 14 ($^{14}C$), dendrochronology, thermoluminesence (TL) and optically stimulated lumines-

**cross-dating**
Use of several appropriate dating techniques to improve confidence in the dates assigned to objects.

**relative dating**
A comparative method of dating that orders fossils or artifacts in a chronological sequence from older to younger but does not establish calendar dates.

**chronometric dating**
A method of dating fossils and artifacts that specifies ranges of dates at a medium to high level of confidence.

cence (OSL), and electron spin resonance (ESR). Other dating methods also can be used under special circumstances. Sometimes investigators focus on dating an object itself; sometimes they date only the surrounding matrix or associated materials, such as rocks or sediments. Two general constraints on chronometric dating are that (1) most samples are susceptible to contamination that would make dates inaccurate, and (2) most techniques are based on assumptions about the constancy of the isotopic clock. Individual techniques have additional limitations. For example, Greenland ice cores have shown datable layers of compacted ice and snow that appear to have been deposited annually as far back as 110 kyr ago; but because few fossils or artifacts are apt to be found in Greenland, ice cores are more useful to calibrate [14]C and to serve as proxy climate indicators than to date individual items.

Figure 8.3 provides a visual summary of the range of dates covered by the major chronometric techniques. Note that theoretically all time periods during the last 6 myr are datable and that in many cases two or more techniques cover the same time period. Not all techniques can be used on all fossils or artifacts, however, and techniques vary in the level of confidence they support. Because of their high degree of use and general internal consistency, we will discuss K-Ar, [14]C, and dendrochronology dating in some detail.

## Potassium–Argon (K-Ar) Dating

Most of the Earth's elements are stable and do not change into other elements; 20 elements, however, are radioactive, meaning that they are unstable and can change into other elements under certain circumstances. When an element occurs in more than one form, the different forms are called isotopes. There are four elements that not only are radioactive and isotopic but also occur in large enough quantities to be useful in dating early materials. Of these, radioactive potassium (K), with its nonradioactive product (Ar), has been used most often; interestingly, scientists have used the K-Ar pair to date lunar as well as Earth rocks. Unfortunately, potassium exists

*Figure 8.3*

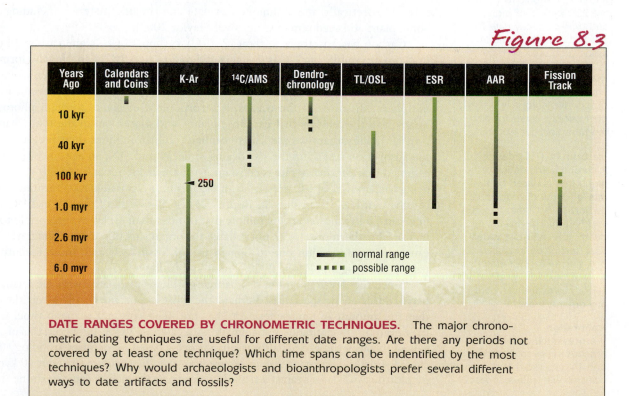

**DATE RANGES COVERED BY CHRONOMETRIC TECHNIQUES.**   The major chronometric dating techniques are useful for different date ranges. Are there any periods not covered by at least one technique? Which time spans can be indentified by the most techniques? Why would archaeologists and bioanthropologists prefer several different ways to date artifacts and fossils?

only in igneous (volcanic) and metamorphic (formed in the Earth's core) rocks and not in sedimentary rocks (formed by hardening of soil and mud), so dating based on it is somewhat limited in applicability.

The principle behind **K-Ar dating** is that the radioactive isotope of potassium in rocks decays into argon (a gas) under intense heating—for example, during a volcanic eruption. It is assumed that the rate of decay from potassium to argon is constant. Therefore, the ratio between the radioactive potassium and the nonradioactive argon can indicate the date when the rock was formed. Scientists can thus indirectly date fossils and artifacts found in association with the rock—though with caution unless the association is certain.

K-Ar dating was first used in 1959 on the Olduvai Gorge materials, but experts soon realized that the technique was plagued with potential contamination; for example, bits of volcanic ash can be redeposited through stream action and can become mixed with materials that are older or younger (Walter 1997). The $^{40}Ar/^{39}Ar$ technique, which uses two isotopes of argon and is also known as the single-crystal laser fusion technique, eliminates this contamination problem by dating single grains of material. The **half-life** for potassium–argon is 1.3 byr (billion years). This means that after 1.3 byr half of the original potassium in a rock sample will have decayed; after another 1.3 byr half of the remaining potassium will have decayed, and so on. As the half life is so long, K-Ar dating is suitable for dating very early materials. Theoretically, K-Ar should date everything between the formation of the universe and 250 kyr ago (Tattersall 2000b). The technique's internal consistency is quite high, meaning that numerous samples from the same material and site give comparable dates. But its usability depends on an unambiguous association of volcanic material and a fossil or artifact.

## Carbon 14 ($^{14}C$) Dating

Discovered by the American Willard Libby in the late 1940s, **carbon 14 ($^{14}C$) dating** is the most widely used dating technique in archaeology because its range of effectiveness (up to 40 kyr and potentially 70 kyr) covers so much of what archaeologists want to date. Theoretically, the technique can date any organic material, including charcoal, bone, plant and seed remains, and shell (Taylor 2002).

Carbon has 3 isotopes: carbon 12, ($^{12}C$), carbon 13 ($^{13}C$), and carbon 14 ($^{14}C$); the first two are stable, but $^{14}C$ is unstable and radioactive. $^{14}C$ is continually formed in the upper atmosphere through the interaction of cosmic ray neutrons with nitrogen. It then combines with oxygen to form carbon dioxide ($CO_2$), which disperses evenly into the atmosphere, dissolves in the oceans, is incorporated in plants through photosynthesis, passes into the animals that eat those plants, and moves on up the food chain. In this way, all living organisms absorb atmospheric $^{14}C$ throughout their lifetimes. At death, the absorption stops and the $^{14}C$ begins to decay into $^{14}N$, an isotope of nitrogen. It is assumed that this decay rate is constant, with a half-life set at 5,568±30 years. By measuring the amount of $^{14}C$ present in an organism, it is possible to determine the amount of time that has passed since its death. Because almost all of the original $^{14}C$ will decay in about 70 kyr, however, any sample that is older than 40 kyr is susceptible to contamination. Furthermore, $^{14}C$ is not reliable for organisms that existed since AD 1500, because of contamination due to human use of fossil fuels and, more recently, nuclear testing (Ludwig and Renne 2000; Taylor and Aitken 1997).

Since the development of $^{14}C$ dating, problems associated with the technique have been addressed by specialists. Perhaps the most important problem was the discovery that the amount of atmospheric $^{14}C$ has not been constant through time; thus, years measured by $^{14}C$ dating do not coincide with calendar years. However, this problem was solved through the use of **calibration**, a process based on dendrochronology (to be discussed shortly). Tree-ring sequences are known to be accurate to about 10 kyr ago, and by plotting $^{14}C$ dates against a tree-ring sequence, specialists can determine the correct

---

**K-Ar dating**

A chronometric dating technique that uses the ratio between radioactive potassium (K) and nonradioactive argon (Ar) to date igneous and metamorphic rocks that are 250 kyr old or more, and thus indirectly date fossils and artifacts found in association with such rocks.

**half-life**

The time it takes for half of a radioactive isotope in a sample to decay; varies for different radioactive isotopes.

**carbon 14 ($^{14}C$) dating**

A chronometric dating technique that is based on the rate of decay of radioactive carbon 14 ($^{14}C$) into nitrogen 14 ($^{14}N$) that begins at death; it is the most widely used technique in archaeology, has a range of effectiveness over the past 40 kyr or more, and can date any organic material.

**calibration**

A process that uses dendrochronology to correct carbon 14 dates so that they coincide with calendar dates.

calendar date. Use of corals and ice cores in addition to tree rings has allowed calibration of $^{14}$C dates back to 24 kyr ago (Bard 2001), and scientists hope to calibrate even earlier. An additional hurdle that plagued early users of $^{14}$C dating was the need for fairly large samples. A refinement called AMS (accelerator mass spectrometry) requires as little as 1 mg of carbon. Because samples can be small, AMS often allows experts to date what they actually want to date, such as a single seed or a pinpoint-sized bit of pigment used in a cave painting. Although many problems concerning the reliability of $^{14}$C dating have been eliminated and internal consistency is now relatively high, some of the dates given in the early literature must be considered historical as opposed to scientific knowledge.

## Dendrochronology

**Dendrochronology** is properly named, as *dendron* is Greek for "tree" and *chronology* comes from the words meaning "telling time." Dendrochronology relies on the annual rings that numerous tree species form. The rings are caused by periods of winter dormancy followed by spurts of growth in the spring and summer that turn into a single ring representing the year. Given that one ring equals one year, counting tree rings is paleoanthropology's most finely tuned (to a single year and sometimes to a single season) and most accurate dating technique. Unfortunately, however, it seldom dates what scientists want dated, because the current limit of tree-ring counting is 11,494 years ago at best—and zero at worst, when there are no trees with rings to count (Schweingruber 1993). Also, trees that have year-round growth do not produce annual rings, so only temperate areas of the world have trees with suitable rings. In addition, given Earth's environmental variation, master chronologies must be set up for every region to reflect local variability. So far only central Europe, Ireland, and the American Southwest have complete master chronologies.

Despite these temporal and geographical limitations, dendrochronology has not only calibrated $^{14}$C dates but also been used as a dating technique in its own right. If an ancient building has wood in its construction, such as the beams that hold up roofs in the American Southwest, and if that wood has been at least partially preserved, archaeologists can determine the exact year when the trees were cut. Of course, a single beam in a house might have been made from old wood and so might give a misleading date. But if every beam in a house dates from the same year, then the beams probably were cut to build the house and thus can provide an accurate construction date. Once researchers have dated a house, they can assume that everything associated with it is about the same age.

## Thermoluminescence (TL), Optically Stimulated Luminescence (OSL), and Electron Spin Resonance (ESR)

**Thermoluminescence (TL) dating, optically stimulated luminescence (OSL) dating,** and **electron spin resonance (ESR) dating** are techniques based on the accumulation rather than the decay of radioactivity (Aitken 1990; Taylor & Aitken 1997; Wagner 1998). Researchers use TL to date burned materials such as pottery, burned flint, and stone; OSL to date wind- and water-borne sediments; and ESR to date tooth enamel and speleothems (calcite deposits such as stalactites and stalagmites). Sediments and anything buried in them are exposed to natural radiation. This causes energy in the form of excited electrons to become trapped in the lattice structure of crystalline materials. The number of trapped electrons increases through time as a result of this exposure to radiation, but their energy is released in the form of light when the material is heated (in the case of TL) or exposed to light (OSL); the emission of light is called thermoluminescence or luminescence. The amount of light given off can be measured by a photomultiplier. In the case of ESR, the electrons' energy is not emitted as light but

---

**dendrochronology**
A chronometric dating technique involving the counting of tree rings, based on the fact that trees in temperate climates accumulate one growth ring a year; can date wood objects back to about 11 kyr ago.

**thermoluminescence (TL) dating**
A chronometric dating technique that is based on the accumulation of radioactivity rather than its decay and is used on burned materials such as pottery.

**optically stimulated luminescence (OSL) dating**
A chronometric dating technique that is based on the accumulation of radioactivity rather than its decay and is used on wind- and water-borne sediments.

**electron spin resonance (ESR) dating**
A chronometric dating technique that is based on the accumulation of radioactivity rather than its decay and is used to date tooth enamel and calcite deposits.

measured by the amount of electromagnetic power they absorb when exposed to a high-frequency magnetic field. In general, these radioactivity-accumulation techniques are generally less accurate than K-Ar or $^{14}$C dating. Used with caution, however, they are helpful in dating fossils and artifacts that fall between the effective ranges of K-Ar and $^{14}$C; that is, between 250, or possibly 500, and 40 kyr ago.

## Other Dating Techniques

**Obsidian hydration dating** works on the principle that freshly cut surfaces on obsidian (a volcanic glass), such as a freshly knapped facet of an obsidian tool, will begin to absorb water from soil or air. The penetration rate can be measured microscopically. The technique is obviously exclusive to obsidian artifacts, and it is necessary for the specialist to know the temperature at which the obsidian absorbed the water—a variable that is not easy to control (Friedman et al. 1997).

**Fission track dating** works well for ash deposits (tephra) resulting from volcanic action. As volcanic eruptions can cover hundreds of square miles, ash deposits may be used as stratigraphic markers over large areas and thus help correlate ages. The method is based on the spontaneous splitting, or fission, of the isotope uranium-238. The fragments that result from fission leave microscopic tracks on the mineral structure of the rock. When the rock is heated, these tracks anneal and disappear. Heating (volcanic eruption) therefore sets the clock to zero, after which fission and track formation begin again (Aitken 1990). The number of tracks in an ash sample can be counted, and an age deduced. Fission track dating is best for materials older than 300 kyr and has been used successfully to date volcanic deposits in Olduvai Gorge to about 2 myr ago.

**Amino acid racemization (AAR)** can be used to date shells, bones, and teeth, although most success has been with shells. Proteins present in all living organisms are composed of amino acids, which occur naturally in two configurations that are often chemically identical but are mirror images of each other. These configurations are known as left-handed (L) and right-handed (D) forms. Dating is based on the slow change (racemization) from L amino acids to D amino acids that commences on death; the ratio of D amino acids to L amino acids indicates the age of the material. The technique is useful because it requires very small amounts of material and is less complicated to carry out than many other techniques. However, accuracy is affected by temperature in that rates of racemization increase with temperature increase. Consequently, the ancient temperature of the area where the material was formed needs to be taken into account. Rates of racemization also vary with taxa, and so the same or similar species need to be compared. The age range covered runs from 1,000 years to 1 myr or more (Hare et al. 1997; Johnson and Miller 1997).

## *Calendars and Coins*

With the advent of writing more than 5,000 years ago came written accounts of past societies that included chronological lists of rulers, the lengths of their reigns, and events that occurred under different regimes. If researchers can link such lists to modern calendars, they can potentially establish "good" dates. However, these lists must be used with caution, as they are not always reliable; for example, written records sometimes deliberately exaggerate or omit certain reigns. True calendar systems, such as those developed in Mesoamerica (see Chapter 13), provide accurate dates. Coins, too, provide a date of minting, although they do not necessarily date the archaeological context in which the coins are found. As coins often are saved and often stay in circulation for an indefinite period, they provide a date only in the context of an archaeological deposit.

---

**obsidian hydration dating**
A dating technique based on measurement of the extent of absorption of water into an obsidian artifact through its exposed surfaces.

**fission track dating**
A dating technique for volcanic ash deposits that is based on the spontaneous splitting, or fission, of the isotope uranium-238, which leaves microscopic tracks on the mineral structure of the rocks.

**amino acid racemization (AAR)**
A dating technique that can be used on shells, bones, and teeth and is based on the slow change (racemization) from L amino acids to D amino acids that commences on the death of an organism.

## Table 8.1

### Chronometric Dating Techniques

All dating techniques, relative and chronometric, have positive and negative features. Some date the object to be dated and some only the surrounding matrix. What are the advantages and disadvantages of dating the surrounding matrix and not the object?

| Technique | Age Range | Materials Used | Level of Confidence | Limitations |
|-----------|-----------|----------------|---------------------|-------------|
| K-Ar | 6 myr to 250 kyr ago | Rocks with volcanic potassium | High | Not all rocks contain potassium; high standard deviation |
| $^{14}$C | 40 kyr ago to AD 1500 | Organic material: charcoal, bone, shell | High | Contamination of samples; statistical probability only; need for large samples |
| AMS | 40 kyr ago to AD 1500 | Same as for $^{14}$C | High | Contamination easy |
| Dendrochronology | 11,494 years ago to present | Dead trees | High | Limited geographic and temporal range |
| TL/OSL | 100 kyr to 20 kyr ago | Sand, pottery, burned flint | Moderate | Assumptions are questionable, results inconsistent |
| ESR | 1 myr to 1,000 years ago | Speleothems; bone, shell, teeth | Moderate | Assumptions are questionable, results inconsistent |
| Obsidian hydration | 100 kyr to 200 years ago | Obsidian | Moderate | Hydration rate is variable |
| Fission track | 2+ myr to 300 kyr ago | Volcanic ash (tephra) | Moderate | Limited geographic range |
| AAR | 100 kyr to 1,000 years ago | Bone, shell, teeth | Moderate | Racemization rate is variable |

## Summary of Dating Techniques

Some dating techniques are by definition tried and true: Stratigraphy and dendrochronology are based on such straightforward principles that using them is hardly more than common sense. Other techniques require making certain assumptions but, like K-Ar and $^{14}$C dating, have been used long and often enough that scientists have high confidence in them. Still other techniques are either problematic or experimental (or both), and it will take time and concentrated effort to bring them up to the same level of reliability. Table 8.1 summarizes the major dating techniques, covering the materials they date, the range of years they cover, the confidence level they afford, and their limitations.

Archaeology is the multi-disciplinary study of the human past through its physical and cultural remains.

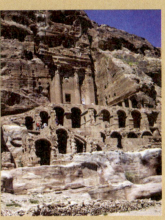

**page 209**

Archaeologists analyze data (facts or evidence) to describe people and cultural events in the past and to test explanatory hypotheses. This chapter introduced the methods and techniques that archaeologists employ in their quest to understand the past. The information presented in Chapters 9 through 13 is the result of applying this archaeological methodology.

■ Archaeological evidence includes artifacts (portable objects made and used by people); features (nonportable artifacts such as walls and pits); and ecofacts (nonartifactual elements such as plant remains or animal bones that are culturally relevant).

■ An understanding of context is important for archaeological interpretation. Context includes the matrix surrounding archaeological remains, the provenience (exact location) of each object, and the association between materials within the matrix.

■ Natural and cultural processes affect archaeological sites, so they rarely survive as they were in the past. Organic materials are preserved only under rare conditions—when they are waterlogged, frozen, arid, or charred. Consequently, evidence more often consists of nonorganic materials such as flint, metals, and ceramics.

■ Before undertaking an archaeological project, a researcher must set up a research design that covers all stages of investigation from the formulation of questions through data collection, analysis, and publication of results.

■ Archaeologists often discover sites and artifacts by foot survey. Aerial photography and subsurface survey can reveal sites hidden beneath the surface. Geographic Information Systems (GIS) software is used increasingly for the detection and analysis of sites.

■ Methods of excavation differ by the questions asked, the country in which the excavation takes place, the amount of time and money available, and the nature and depth of the archaeological deposits. Test pits are small vertical excavations that penetrate the deposits; trenches are test pits extended in a horizontal plane. Open area excavation reveals deposits at a site layer by layer.

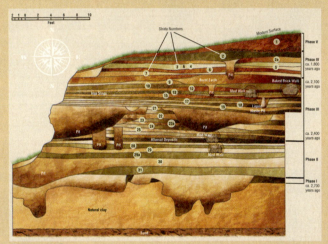

**page 216**

■ Archaeological excavation is destructive, so it must be done under controlled conditions. Detailed records, including site maps, must be kept throughout.

■ Because analysis of artifacts always takes place within the context of their environments, reconstructing environments always precedes analysis. Analysis of artifacts provides knowledge about the technological, social, and symbolic aspects of the culture under investigation.

■ Modern archaeologists are more interested in the process of culture change and in explanations of past cultures than in mere descriptions.

■ Dating artifacts places them in a temporal context. Relative dating techniques such as stratigraphy order objects as being older, younger, or the same age as one another. Chronometric dating provides dates in calendar years. Potassium–argon and carbon 14 dating and dendrochronology give high degrees of confidence; other chronometric methods have individual problems, creating less confidence in the results.

## KEY WORDS

amino acid racemization (AAR), 226
artifacts, 208
association, 209
calibration, 224
carbon 14 ($^{14}$C) dating, 224
chronometric dating, 222
context, 208
cross-dating, 222
cultural historical approach, 221
cultural transformation processes, 209
dendrochronology, 225
ecofacts, 208

electron spin resonance (ESR) dating, 225
ethnoarcheology, 219
experimental archaeology, 219
features, 208
fission track dating, 226
Geographic Information Systems (GIS), 215
half-life, 224
hearths, 208
K-Ar dating, 224
matrix, 208
natural transformation processes, 209

obsidian hydration dating, 226
optically stimulated luminescence (OSL) dating, 225
postprocessual archaeology, 221
processual archaeology, 221
provenience, 209
relative dating, 222
remote sensing techniques, 214
research design, 215
stratigraphy, 216
subsurface survey techniques, 215
survey, 214
thermoluminescence (TL) dating, 225

## SUGGESTED READING

Aitken, M. J. *Science-Based Dating in Archaeology*. New York: Longman, 1990. An excellent account of the major (and minor) dating techniques in easy-to-understand language. Covers relative as well as chronometric dating.

Drewett, P. *Field Archaeology: An Introduction*. London: UCL Press, 1999. Written by a British archaeologist but with worldwide application, this book encompasses all phases and types of field archaeology.

Feder, K. L. *Frauds, Myths, and Mysteries*. 4th ed. Boston: McGraw-Hill, 2002. A fun book filled with both archaeological and biological frauds and myths, including Piltdown Man (fraud), ancient astronauts (fraud), and Stonehenge (mystery).

Hester, T. R., H. J. Shafer, and K. L. Feder. *Field Methods in Archaeology*. 7th ed. Mountain View, CA: Mayfield, 1997. An updated edition of a classic book with an emphasis on New World archaeology.

Sutton, M. Q, and R. M. Yohe, II. 2006. *Archaeology: The Science of the Human Past*. Boston: Pearson/Allyn & Bacon. This book explains archaeology clearly and provides up-to-date coverage of the standard archaeological topics.

Taylor, R. E., and M. J. Aitken, eds. *Chronometric Dating in Archaeology*. New York: Plenum, 1997. Specialists in each of the major chronometric dating techniques explain their methods and provide excellent examples.

Chapter

# 9

# The Emergence of Culture in Early Hominid Societies in the Old World

■ THE ENVIRONMENTAL BACKGROUND

■ THE EVIDENCE: CLIMATE AND ARTIFACTS

■ EARLY HOMINID SOCIETY: THE LOWER PALEOLITHIC/EARLY STONE AGE
Surviving in the Landscape 2.6 to 1.8 myr Ago • *Homo erectus*: Innovator and Adventurer • Stone Technology of *Homo erectus*: The Acheulian • Subsistence Strategies of *Homo erectus* and Early Archaic *Homo sapiens* • Fire • Structures • Burials and Symbolic Representations

■ HIGHLIGHT 9.1: *In Touch with Stone Tools*

■ HUMAN ADAPTATIONS IN THE MIDDLE PALEOLITHIC/MIDDLE STONE AGE
Technology • Subsistence Strategies • Habitation Areas and Organization of Space • Symbolism: Burials, Art, Ritual

■ HUMANS ACROSS THE GLOBE: LIFE IN THE UPPER PALEOLITHIC/LATE STONE AGE
Neandertals and Anatomically Modern Humans in the Landscape • Technological Complexity • Subsistence Practices • Habitation and Use of Space • Symbolism: Burial and Art • Upper Paleolithic/Late Stone Age Society

■ HIGHLIGHT 9.2: *Into Australia and the Pacific*

■ HIGHLIGHT 9.3: *Paleolithic Imagery in Eurasia*

▲

**Photo above:** A sample of the 32-kyr-old rock art at Chauvet Cave in France—aurochs (wild cattle) and wild horses

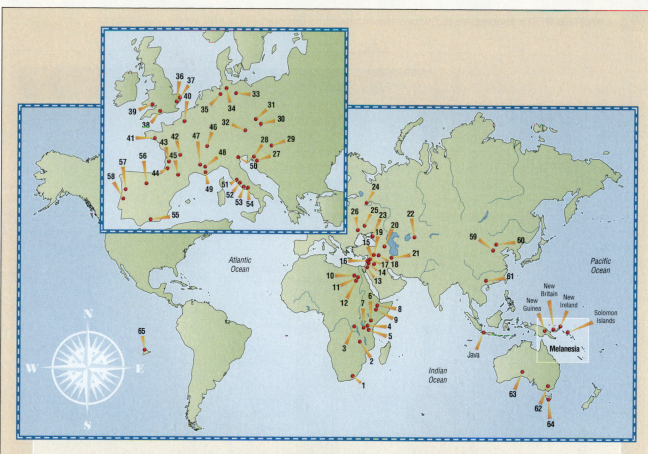

## SITES MENTIONED IN THE CHAPTER

1. Blombos Cave, South Africa
2. Mumbwa and Twin Rivers, Zambia
3. Katanda, Congo
4. Olduvai, Tanzania
5. Laetoli, Tanzania
6. Chesowanja, Kenya
7. Lokalelei, Kenya
8. Gona, Ethiopia
9. Bouri, Ethiopia
10. Taramsa Hill, Egypt
11. Nazlet Khater, Egypt
12. Wadi Kubbaniya, Egypt
13. Kebara Cave, Israel
14. Ubeidiya, Israel
15. Ohalo II, Israel
16. Qafzeh, Skhul, Tabun Caves, Israel
17. Gesher Benot Ya'aqov, Israel
18. Umm el Tlel, Syria
19. Douara Cave, Syria
20. Dmanisi, Georgia
21. Shanidar Cave, Iraq
22. Teshik-Tash, Uzbekistan

23. Mesmaiskaya Cave, Russia
24. Sungir, Russia
25. Mezhirich, Ukraine
26. Molodova, Ukraine
27. Vindija Cave, Croatia
28. Krapina Cave, Croatia
29. Vértessöllös, Hungary
30. Pavlov, Czech Republic
31. Dolní Vestonice, Czech Republic
32. Bocksteinchmiede, Germany
33. Bilzingsleben, Germany
34. Schöningen, Germany
35. Gönnersdorf, Germany
36. Beeches Pit, England
37. Pakefield, England
38. Boxgrove, Egland
39. Paviland Cave, Wales
40. Pincevent, France
41. Menez-Dregan, France
42. Lascaux Cave, France
43. Les Pradelles, France
44. Saint-Germain-la-Rivière, France

45. Aurignac Cave, France
46. Solutré, France
47. Chauvet Cave, France
48. Moula-Guercy, France
49. Terra Amata, France
50. Monte Poggiolo, Italy
51. Grotta Guattari, Italy
52. Grotta Breuil, Italy
53. Grotta di San Agostino, Italy
54. Grotta dei Moscerini, Italy
55. Fuent Nueve 3, Barranco León, Spain
56. Atapuerca, Spain
57. Coa Valley, Portugal
58. Vilas Ruivas, Portugal
59. Zhoukoudian Cave, China
60. Majuangou, China
61. Bose Basin, China
62. Lake Mungo, Australia
63. Koonalda Cave, Australia
64. Tasmania, Australia
65. Easter Island

Chapter 6 and 7 discussed the physical development of early and later hominids—australopithecines, *Homo habilis*, *Homo erectus*, Neandertals and Archaic *Homo sapiens*, and anatomically modern humans (AMH). This chapter considers developments in human culture from its earliest manifestation some 2.6 myr to ago about 12 kyr ago. Humans are highly adaptable. Over the past 2.6 myr, they have successfully confronted numerous, and sometimes dramatic, changes in climate and environment.

| Archaeological Period | | | HOLOCENE 11,500 years ago to present |
|---|---|---|---|
| Late Stone Age | | **Thousands of years ago** 20 | Heat treatment of flint |
| Middle Stone Age | Upper Paleolithic | 26 | Ceramic firing technology |
| | | 30 | Grindstones—plant processing |
| | | 32 | Cave art |
| | | 35 | Mobiliary art |
| | Middle Paleolithic | 40 | Grave goods / Cremation |
| | | 50 | Definite structures |
| | | 60 | Sea travel / Chert mining / Deliberate burial / Hafting |
| | | 65 | Microlith technology |
| | | 70 | Symbolism—incised ochre / Bone technology / Fishing technology |
| | | 120 | Pigment grinding |
| Early Stone Age / Lower Paleolithic | Acheulian | 200 | Use of ochre / Blade technology |
| | | 400 | Possible structures |
| | | 500 | Fire |
| | | **Millions of years ago** 1.6 | Hand-axe technology |
| | Oldowan | 1.8? | Hominids in the Old World |
| | | 2.6 | First stone artifacts |

**DEVELOPMENT OF CULTURAL ACTIVITY IN THE PALEOLITHIC**

Human responses have been just as dramatic at times, involving physical changes in body form, locomotion, jaws and teeth, and manual dexterity, as well as a large-scale expansion of the brain. Cultural changes facilitated humans' quest for food and shelter, eventually enabling them to colonize the globe. Among early humans these cultural changes included growing technological complexity, changes in the uses of space and resources, and eventually a rise in symbolic behavior. By reconstructing these developments, we can gain glimpses into the minds of our distant ancestors. In order to reconstruct their lives, however, we must first understand the physical world in which they lived and the archaeological evidence of their activities.

# The Environmental Background

**Beringia**
The landmass joining Alaska and Siberia that was exposed during glacial periods because the levels of the Bering Strait and Chukchi Sea dropped as their water was taken up in ice.

About 2.3 myr ago, a series of alternating cold/glacial and warm/interglacial periods began. Such changes reflect variation in the amount of solar energy reaching Earth, which in turn results from changes in the orbit, tilt, and spin of the planet. Plate tectonic movement, changes in ocean currents, and volcanic activity also affect the Earth's climate. During glacial periods much of the Earth's water was concentrated in ice sheets that covered large areas of northern Europe, Asia, and North America. At periods of maximum cold, sea levels dropped about 125 m (410 feet) below today's levels, exposing continental shelves and joining some areas that were separated by water in interglacial times. For example, a "land bridge" called **Beringia** joined Alaska to Siberia across what is now the Bering Straits; England was connected to continental Europe, and Indonesia and the Southeast Asian mainland were linked (Lowe and Walker 1997; Mulvaney and Kamminga 1999). One of the main lines of evidence indicating climatic fluctuations comes from deep ocean sediments (marine cores) that contain microscopic marine organisms whose skeletons reflect warm and cold periods (see Figure 9.1).

When considering past glacial environments, we must keep in mind that there are no modern analogs to help us fully understand the nature of those environments, particularly in the Earth's middle latitudes. During the coldest periods, worldwide average temperatures would have been significantly colder than today, with bitterly cold winters and cool summers. Close to the glacial front, tree cover diminished, giving way to arctic tundra landscapes. Here, beneath surface sediments that froze during the winter and thawed in the short summers, lay permanently frozen ground known as permafrost. Further away from the glacial front, cold steppe grasslands developed. In southerly areas, such as parts of Africa and Australia, increasing aridity caused the expansion of desert and savanna. Interglacial periods, in contrast, brought a rise in sea levels and regeneration of forests (Deacon and Deacon 1999; Lowe and Walker 1997). Punctuating the long glacial and interglacial periods were shorter warmer or cooler phases known as stadials and interstadials. These interludes sometimes occurred within a few decades—that is, within individual or group memory (Bell and Walker 1992; Davies et al. 2000).

Changes in climate and vegetation caused changes in animal populations. During glacial periods herds of cold-loving, seasonally migratory herbivores, such as woolly mammoth, woolly rhinoceros, musk ox, steppe bison, reindeer, and wild horse roamed the plains of the northern continents. Southern Africa was home to large grazing animals such as the giant Cape buffalo and giant hartebeest. In interglacial periods northern regions' large mammals were replaced by hippopotamus, woodland rhinoceros, forest elephant, forest bison, fallow deer, and red deer; bush and woodland browsers replaced grazers in South Africa (Davis 2002).

Humans, too, formed part of these glacial and interglacial landscapes—and increasingly so after about 1.7 myr ago, when groups began to colonize the Northern Hemisphere. In order to survive, human populations had to adapt to changes around them.

# The Evidence: Climate and Artifacts

Archaeologists use many lines of evidence to determine climate change. Among important sources of information are geomorphological data (evidence of glacial land forms, sea-level rise and fall, the formation of river terraces); lithological clues (sediments,

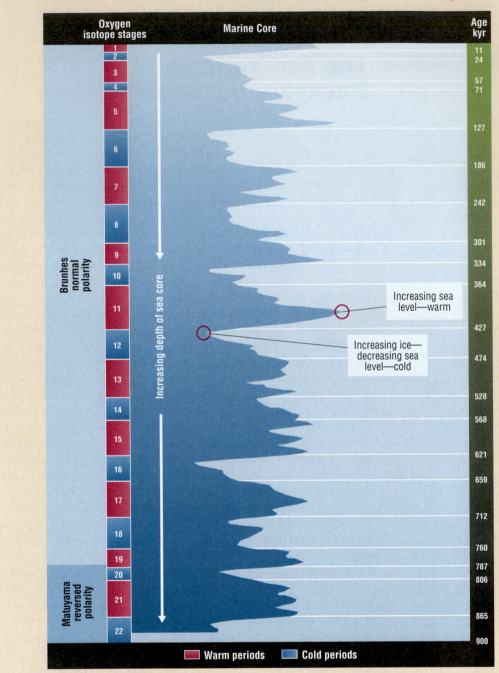

**MARINE CORE SHOWING CHANGES IN TEMPERATURE THROUGH TIME.** Temperature changes in ocean waters affect the ratio of the isotopes oxygen 18 ($^{18}O$) and oxygen 16 ($^{16}O$), which is reflected in the calcium carbonate shells of foraminifera (microscopic marine organisms) in ocean sediments. The study of cores drilled from the ocean bed has enabled scientists to track numerous glacial and interglacial periods over the past 900 kyr. The numbers assigned to oxygen isotope stages correlate with particular periods, even numbers referring to cold stages and odd numbers to warm stages. Dating is by $^{14}C$ for the most recent 50 kyr or so; earlier dates were determined by paleomagnetism (changes in the Earth's magnetic field).

*Source*: Adapted from Klein, R. G., Archaeology and the evolution of human behaviour. *Evolutionary Anthropology*, Vol. 9, No. 1, 2000, pp. 17–36. Reprinted with permission of Wiley-Liss, Inc, a subsidiary of John Wiley & Sons, Inc.

**Pleistocene**

A geological period of glacial and interglacial cycles that began 2.3 myr ago.

**Paleolithic**

The archaeological term used in most of Eurasia for the period between the arrival of the first hominids in the Old World outside Africa, about 1.7 myr ago, and the end of the last Ice Age, about 10 kyr ago.

**Stone Age**

The period between the emergence of culture in sub-Saharan Africa, about 2.6 myr ago, and the beginning of farming, about 2,000 years ago.

including the foraminifera record of marine cores); and biological traces (pollen, phytoliths, plant macrofossils, beetles and insects, fossil rodents, land and marine mollusks, and large fossil mammals) (Lowe and Walker 1997; Rapp and Hill 1998).

The period of glacial and interglacial cycles beginning 2.3 myr ago is referred to in geological terms as the **Pleistocene**. In archaeological and human terms it is called the **Paleolithic** in most of the Old World, and in particular Eurasia, and the **Stone Age** in sub-Saharan Africa. It is further subdivided into three stages, respectively termed in Eurasia and sub-Saharan Africa as the Lower Paleolithic or Early Stone Age (ending about 250 kyr ago), the Middle Paleolithic or Middle Stone Age (ending roughly between 40 and 30 kyr ago), and the Upper Paleolithic or Late Stone Age (ending between 13 and 10 kyr ago, and later in sub-Saharan Africa). At present the Earth is in an interglacial period, the Holocene. The first hominids appeared during the Miocene and the Pliocene, periods immediately preceding the Pleistocene (see Chapter 6).

Until about 10 kyr ago, people everywhere lived in small, mobile groups. They foraged for plant foods and shell fish; hunted animals or scavenged animal carcasses; and, in some areas, caught and killed fish and birds. Such a lifestyle did not lend itself to the formation of permanent settlements, and the material culture associated with mobile groups is limited. People on the move simply cannot carry much with them; artifacts made from organic materials seldom survive for thousands of years; semipermanent settlements leave few traces, and over hundreds of millennia the forces of nature tend to destroy most of the traces that do remain. The record of early human societies, therefore, is biased by what archaeologists have managed to recover. For earlier periods this means primarily stone artifacts and animal bones. In later periods bone, antler, and ivory artifacts appear, together with evidence of increasing complexity in settlement organization, burials, and symbolic representation.

# Early Hominid Society: The Lower Paleolithic/ Early Stone Age

East and South Africa are rich in early hominid locales. Geological activity over millions of years has dramatically changed the landscape of the East African Rift region. Lakes and depressions filled with water-derived sediments and volcanic ash were later cut through by rivers or eroded by heavy rains and winds. River cutting, erosion, and geological faulting reveal deeply buried evidence of past human cultures (Gowlett 1992). Extensive mining and quarrying activities in South Africa led to the discovery of early sites there (Deacon and Deacon 1999).

**Gona**

Ethiopian site with the earliest evidence of hominid activity (2.6 myr ago).

**cores**

Stone blocks from which flakes have been removed.

**flakes**

Fragments of stone that are removed from a block of stone (core) and used as tools.

Accumulations of deliberately manufactured stone tools, sometimes in association with broken bones, form the first evidence for hominid activity, 2.6 myr ago at **Gona** Ethiopia, and 2.34 myr ago at Lokalalei, Kenya. At these sites early hominids produced flakes from a range of volcanic rocks; indeed, the tools from Gona indicate that their makers often chose to work with trachyte (a fine-grained rock with good knapping qualities) in preference to other rocks. Nor was tool manufacture a hit-and-miss affair or the fortuitous result of bashing two stones together; at both Gona and Lokalalei, the **cores** from which **flakes** were struck reveal a well-developed understanding of knapping technology (Roche et al. 1999; Semaw et al. 1997).

Investigators did not find stone tools at Bouri, a 2.5-myr-old lakeside site in Ethiopia; but they found fossil animal bones with distinctive cut marks made by stone tools and indicative of defleshing, breaking, disarticulating, and filleting. As there would have been few available stone resources near that site, hominids must have carried the tools with them as they moved around the landscape, saving them for later use (de Heinzelin et al. 1999).

Archaeologists use the term **Oldowan technology,** or **Mode 1 technology,** to describe the suite of cores, flakes, and waste from the earliest stone working, because the first (although not the oldest) of these artifacts were found at **Olduvai Gorge** in Tanzania. The finds from Gona and Lokalalei demonstrate that early hominids had mastered Oldowan technology more than 500 kyr earlier than formerly believed.

Although the earliest stone tools may appear rather crude to most people, they reveal much about the conceptual and cognitive development of early hominids. The stone technology of 2.5 myr ago indicates manual dexterity and development of hand–eye coordination; an understanding of the basics of stone fracture mechanics; an understanding of the qualities of different types of stones; knowledge of the landscape and where to find sources of stone; and a developing concept of forward planning and the need for tools. Tool use gave early hominids access to a wider range of food sources that provided an increase in energy needed to sustain brain growth (Ambrose 2001; Schick and Toth 1993; Stout 2005; see also Highlight 9.1, on pp. 238–239).

Evidence for the deliberate manufacture of bone tools is not as compelling as that for stone tools. However, researchers who studied bone fragments from the earliest levels at Swartkrans Cave in South Africa determined that the ends of some long bone fragments were smooth and displayed striations caused by use. At first specialists believed these wear patterns were the result of hominids using pointed bones to dig for underground tubers; more recent study shows they were used to dig for termites (Backwell and d'Errico 2001; Brain 1989). Furthermore, hominids deliberately chose either horn cores or long, straight, heavily weathered bone fragments, within a size range from 13 to 19 cm (5 to 7.5 inches) long. They knew exactly what would serve their purposes.

Who were the toolmakers? Early sites are on the edges of ancient lakes and rivers and in delta regions, particularly in the East African Rift Valley and to a lesser extent in limestone caves in South Africa. Both areas are also rich in fossils of australopithecines and *H. habilis*. At one time experts thought that *H. habilis* was the first maker of tools (hence the name, which means "handy man"), but it seems increasingly likely that at least some australopithecine hominids were also tool makers.

## Surviving in the Landscape 2.6 to 1.8 myr Ago

Olduvai Gorge was a good place to live between 2.5 and 1 myr ago; its rich habitat attracted both animals and hominids to its lake shores and stream edges (see Figure 9.2). Debates have long raged over the interpretation of different patterns of bones and stone artifacts at early sites. Some experts viewed sites where excavators found stone tools close to the remains of a single large animal or a few smaller animals as butchery or kill places. These theorists saw sites with a dense covering of stones and bones as camplike areas or home bases to which people returned regularly. They considered material at other sites near water sources to be the result of movement by water and therefore not indicative of a single event.

Traditional interpretations held that butchery and home base sites were the result of deliberate hominid action: Early, small-brained hominids hunted animals and brought meat back to their home base to share with the rest of their "family" in a very humanlike pattern (Isaac 1978; Leakey 1971). But it was not long before experts (including some of the original excavators) began to question such interpretations. Were the accumulations as deliberate as they might appear, or could other forces have affected the archaeological patterning? Researchers designed a series of projects aimed at (1) recognizing and determining the origins (natural and human) of fracture patterns on stone, (2) differentiating between marks on bones made by stone tools and by carnivores' teeth, (3) identifying those parts of a carcass carnivores prefer and where tooth marks rather than cut marks should occur if carnivores work on carcasses before hominids, (4) identifying the agents (human, animal, or environmental) of bone accumulation and dispersal, (5) pinpointing locations of stone sources and other resources in the landscape, and (6) reconstructing past environments (Binford 1983; Dominguez-Rodrigo and Pickering

**Oldowan technology (Mode 1 technology)**
The earliest stone-working tradition in Africa; named after Olduvai Gorge, Tanzania, where many early—but not the oldest—stone tools have been found.

**Olduvai Gorge**
Area in Tanzania that is rich in Early Stone Age sites.

*Figure 9.2*

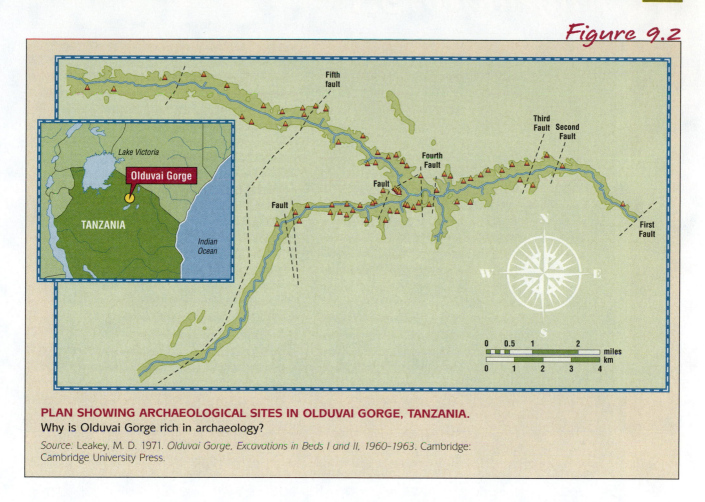

**PLAN SHOWING ARCHAEOLOGICAL SITES IN OLDUVAI GORGE, TANZANIA.**
Why is Olduvai Gorge rich in archaeology?

*Source:* Leakey, M. D. 1971. *Olduvai Gorge, Excavations in Beds I and II, 1960–1963.* Cambridge: Cambridge University Press.

2003; Dominguez-Rodrigo and Barba 2006; Isaac 1984; Schick and Toth 1993). Such detailed study of the processes affecting the formation of archaeological sites is known as **taphonomy**.

Experts remain divided in their views on the hunting and scavenging abilities of early hominids. Hominids may have scavenged meat from large animals but perhaps hunted small animals. Nor is there consensus about the home base hypothesis, although some experts have proposed that hominids regularly returned to particular areas to eat, sleep, and socialize. However, few, if any, of the early sites reflect a single past human activity. Rather, the sites have been formed and affected through time by the activities of a variety of agents, including hominids, carnivores, raptors (birds of prey), winds, and floods—all of which are now identifiable.

Some time before the East African hunting/scavenging debate, Charles Brain had undertaken taphonomic studies of the formation processes affecting early hominid cave sites in South Africa such as Swartkrans, Sterkfontein, and Makapansgat. The cave assemblages consisted of australopithecine bones as well as bones of other primates and animals, including carnivores. Earlier, Raymond Dart had assumed that the australopithecenes were the hunters; he thought they had targeted their own species among other prey, using an "osteodontokeratic tool kit" (that is, tools made from animal bones, teeth, and horns). Brain studied cave formation and erosion, made ethnoarchaeological observations of processes affecting animal bones in modern-day traditional settlements, and observed carnivore and primate behavior. He concluded that the australopithecine bones were probably the remains of carnivore meals. Brain suggested that large cats had been the perpetrators, either dragging their prey into a tree to avoid the pressures of

**taphonomy**
Study of the processes affecting the formation of archaeological sites.

# Highlight 9.1

# In Touch with Stone Tools

ABOUT 2.5 MYR AGO, our hominid ancestors in East Africa were well enough aware of the sharpness of freshly broken rocks that they began to break them intentionally. These broken fragments of rock constitute the earliest evidence of hominid material culture. Through time humans produced a diverse array of stone tools, using a variety of complex manufacturing techniques. It was because of the ubiquity of stone artifact discoveries that scholars coined the term *Paleolithic*, or *Old Stone Age* (*paleo* means "old" and *lithic* means "stone"). The advent of metals, in particular iron in the last few thousand years, presaged the decline of stone tools.

As stone is almost indestructible, stone tools have endured at most prehistoric sites and are an important source of information about past human behavior. Indeed, they are often the only evidence available. Fortunately, lithic studies have advanced to such a degree as to dramatically increase the potential information obtainable from stone artifacts. The study of the raw material (stone), manufacturing processes, types and uses of artifacts produced, and the social contexts of tool manufacture and use are important avenues of research for the modern lithic analyst.

The type and form (pebble, outcrop, block) of stone can indicate preference for a particular rock, perhaps for its fracture qualities or its suitability for a special task. Geological sourcing indicates whether the rock was available near the site or not. Tools made of nonlocal stone indicate knowledge of resources in the landscape, transport, and—in later periods—possible trade connections and the various implications of trade. The relative abundance or rarity of stone may have affected discard and "curation" patterns; that is, hominids may have maintained and held onto nonlocal tools more carefully than local tools.

Stone tools can be made in a variety of ways, and different techniques and procedures leave traces that the trained analyst can identify. Under exceptional conditions at some sites, investigators can refit flakes and pieces removed during the manufacturing process, somewhat like assembling a puzzle. Experimental reproduction by expert knappers (stoneworkers) helps clarify different stages of the manufacturing process. Refitting and experimentation help lithic analysts discover the choices and decisions made by prehistoric knappers, the mistakes they made, and their subsequent reactions—such as correcting a fault or discarding the piece.

Stone tools come in a range of shapes. A knapper may have deliberately designed a tool to fulfill a particular function, or the hardness, grain, or purity of the stone may have governed the tool's shape. In addition, tool manufacture and style usually follow group traditions and thus reflect cultural influences. Because changes in material culture reveal changing traditions, stone tools can sometimes serve as chronological markers.

Microwear (also called use wear) of stone tools can be analyzed by various means and often can tell how the tools were used and on what type of material. Procedures available today can identify blood residues and fatty tissues on stone, and DNA analysis may pinpoint the animal species.

The spatial location of stone tools and debris (waste) may indicate areas of human activity and sometimes may offer clues about what kind of people (experts, beginners) were active in a particular area. Refitting pieces between areas can suggest movement within the site; for example, such refits can show that people dumped waste from a manufacturing area in another area.

In sum, lithic analysis can tell us how, why, where, and perhaps under what conditions a tool was made. It can reveal something about the social and symbolic context within which Stone Age hominids made and used their tools, and it can provide a glimpse into the minds and cognitive processes of the toolmakers themselves.

*Sources:* Loy, T. H. 1993. The artifact as site: An example of biomolecular analysis of organic residues on prehistoric tools. *World Archaeology* 25 (1): 44–63. Moloney, N., and M. Shott. 2003. *Lithics at the millennium.* London: University College London. Rosen, S. A. 1997. *Lithics after the Stone Age.* Walnut Creek, CA: Altamira Press. Schick, K., and N. Toth. 1993. *Making silent stones speak.* London: Weidenfeld & Nicolson. Semaw, S., et al. 1997. 2.5 million-year-old stone tools from Gona, Ethiopia. *Nature* 385:333–336.

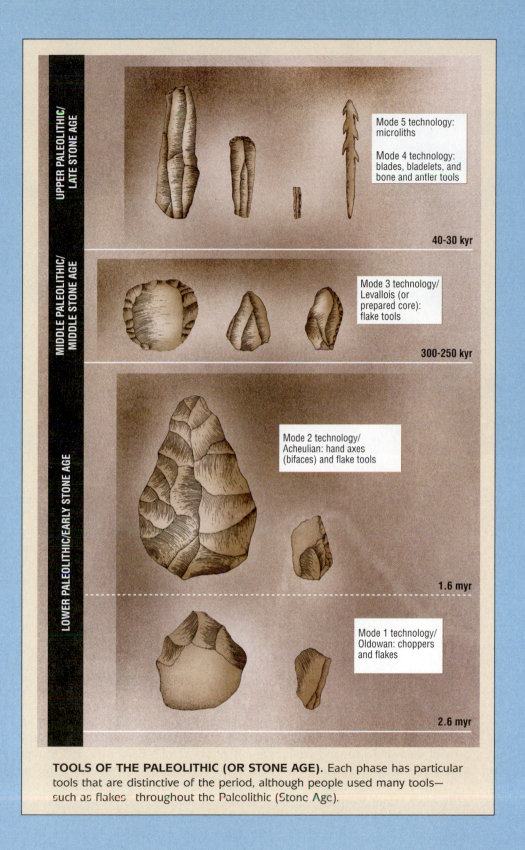

**UPPER PALEOLITHIC/ LATE STONE AGE**

Mode 5 technology: microliths

Mode 4 technology: blades, bladelets, and bone and antler tools

40-30 kyr

**MIDDLE PALEOLITHIC/ MIDDLE STONE AGE**

Mode 3 technology/ Levallois (or prepared core): flake tools

300-250 kyr

**LOWER PALEOLITHIC/EARLY STONE AGE**

Mode 2 technology/ Acheulian: hand axes (bifaces) and flake tools

1.6 myr

Mode 1 technology/ Oldowan: choppers and flakes

2.6 myr

**TOOLS OF THE PALEOLITHIC (OR STONE AGE).** Each phase has particular tools that are distinctive of the period, although people used many tools—such as flakes throughout the Paleolithic (Stone Age).

turn back to your reading

Olduvai Gorge, Tanzania, is rich in paleontological and archaeological sites spanning 2 myr. Why have so many sites been found here?

other scavengers or attacking groups of hominids and other primates as they slept inside caves. Evidence from Swartkrans—an australopithecine skull with two holes made by carnivore canine teeth (see Highlight 6.3)—lends some support to Brain's hypothesis (Brain 1981; Deacon and Deacon 1999). Eagles were the agents of bone accumulation at the Taung site, where investigation of the bone remains, including the first australopithecine skull ever found, revealed an assemblage of small animals whose skulls and bones displayed damage similar to that which occurs when raptors take their prey (Berger and Clarke 1995). Taphonomic studies, therefore, have demonstrated that australopithecines were prey rather than predators, and that Dart's "osteodontokeratic tool kit" was the result of site formation processes rather than hominid activity.

## *Homo erectus*: Innovator and Adventurer

Paleontological and archaeological evidence indicates that *Homo erectus* was present in Africa for at least a million years after the species first evolved about 1.8 myr ago. Some *H. erectus* groups moved out of Africa, however, perhaps shortly after 1.8 myr ago, as witnessed by fossils and artifacts found in the Middle East, Asia, and Europe. These groups may have traveled across the present land bridge between Egypt and the Middle East, or they may have walked at periods of low sea level from Ethiopia to southern Arabia or from Morocco to Spain. The best and earliest evidence so far points to the use of the first route. At **Dmanisi**, Georgia, researchers have securely dated *H. erectus* fossil materials found in association with stone tools and animal bones to 1.7 myr ago (Gabunia et al. 2000). Ubeidiya, a lakeside site in the Jordan Valley of Israel with 60 archaeological levels rich in stone tools, has dates between 1.4 and 1 myr ago (Bar-Yosef 1994). Other investigators have proposed dates of 1.8 to 1.6 myr ago for sites in Java or 1 myr and more for sites in China, although many such claims are contested (Schick and Zhuan 1993). However, at the lakeside Majuangou site in northeastern China, excavators uncovered stone tools associated with broken animal bones in four levels dated be-

**Dmanisi**
Lower Palaeolithic site in Georgia with the earliest *H. erectus* fossils and artifacts in Europe (1.7 myr old).

tween 1.66 and 1.3 myr ago. As most of the tools were fashioned from nonlocal rocks, people must have carried rocks to the site. Later animal trampling has hidden any cut marks on the bones, but it has not destroyed marks made as people broke the bones with a stone hammer to get at the marrow (Zhu et al. 2004). Stone artifacts in deposits dated to approximately 840 to 700 kyr ago have been found on the Indonesian Island of Flores. Given that island-hopping sea voyages would always have been necessary to reach Flores, these dates, if correct, would indicate the earliest evidence of water transport and would imply seacraft construction (Morwood et al. 1999). Southern Europe appears to have been colonized by at least 780 kyr ago, or possibly more than 1 myr ago, as suggested by skeletal evidence and relics of material culture from Monte Poggiolo in Italy, **Atapuerca sites** in northern Spain, and Barranco León and Fuente Nueva 3 in southern Spain (Carbonell and Rodríguez 2006; Oms et al. 2000; Peretto 2006). Severe climatic conditions in northwest Europe were a deterrent to a continuous human presence in the region; excavations at Pakefield in England show that hominids had reached the western edge of Europe by 700 kyr ago, but forays into what is now England were sporadic (Parfitt 2005). After 500 kyr ago, the number of sites increased, indicating that early settlers were able to live in the harsh climatic conditions of northwest Europe.

## Stone Technology of *Homo erectus*: The Acheulian

From about 1.6 myr ago, *H. erectus* groups in Africa introduced changes in their stone technology. The typical tool of the Early Stone Age is the **hand axe**: a pebble or large flake that hominids worked bifacially, removing flakes from both sides of the stone. Other large tools associated with *H. erectus* include cleavers (similar to hand axes but with a straight sharp edge at one end) and picks (with a triangular or quadrangular tip and a more globular base). A series of **flake tools,** flakes with one or more edges modified by retouch, also form part of the tool kit, as do unretouched flakes with extremely sharp edges. The term **Mode 2 technology** is used to distinguish this suite of stone artifacts, associated with *H. erectus* and later groups of archaic *H. sapiens*, from the earlier Mode 1 technology. Assemblages with hand axes are also often called **Acheulian** after the French site of St. Acheul, where the first (though not the oldest) hand axes were found.

Hand axe technology lasted for over 1 myr, until about 200 kyr ago, but manufacturing techniques developed through time: Knappers employed hard (stone) and soft (bone and antler) hammerstones to refine large flakes and pebbles into a range of standardized and generally symmetrical shapes. Hand axes are not chance outcomes of flaking but often appear to be deliberately fashioned into specific forms. Different forms may not always indicate cultural choice, however. For example, the original shape and type of stone may influence final form; repeated reuse and resharpening of a hand axe may alter its outline; some hand axes, too, may have served as cores to produce flakes (McPherron 2000; Moloney 1996; White 1994). Nevertheless, the numerous well-made, finely finished pieces in standardized shapes support the idea that the toolmakers, at least at times, had a preconceived shape in mind. This transference of preconceived ideas into practice demonstrates a leap in the mental capabilities of *H. erectus.*

Although hand axes are present in quantity at many sites in the Old World, they are rare in Southeast Asia. The lack of good rock sources or the fact that heavy forests hid such sources may have inhibited their manufacture in that region. However, bamboo (which is abundant and can be given razor-sharp edges) would have served equally well. Given the early dates for human presence in Java, it may be that groups had left Africa before the invention of hand axe technology and, because of the relative isolation of the region, continued to use simpler technology (Ambrose 2001; Swisher et al. 1994). However, hand axes from the Bose Basin in South China demonstrate knowledge and use of bifacial technology about 800 kyr ago, at the same time as African and Middle Eastern hominids were making hand axes (Yamei et al. 2000). Various hypotheses attribute the absence of hand axes at some early European sites to differences among cultural groups, a lack of suitable local stone, or differing environmental conditions (Gamble 1999).

---

**Atapuerca sites**
A series of sites in northern Spain that date from between 1 myr and 300 kyr ago.

**hand axe**
A pebble or large flake that hominids worked bifacially, removing flakes from both sides of the stone, to make a tool that is typical of the Lower Paleolithic/Early Stone Age; also called a *biface*.

**flake tools**
Flakes with one or more edges modified by retouch that were part of the tool kit from the time of *H. erectus* groups 1.6 myr ago in Africa and throughout the Paleolithic/Stone Age.

**Mode 2 technology**
Stone-working technique used by *H. erectus* and later groups of archaic *H. sapiens* to make hand axes.

**Acheulian**
A tool tradition, originating in Africa but later found in Europe and parts of Asia, in which hand axes are common; named after the St. Acheul site in France, where the first (though not the oldest) hand axes were found.

A selection of hand axes (also called bifaces) from East Africa and western Europe. Made from flint, quartz, basalt, and phonolite, these tools are between about 800 kyr and 200 kyr old. What can they tell us about the hominids who made and used them?

Hand axes were clearly useful tools, but their exact uses remain enigmatic. The "paleolithic Swiss Army Knife" was essentially a multi-purpose tool. It was efficient at butchery, skinning, cutting, and scraping; it was good for digging and woodworking; it even could serve as a missile if aimed discus-style to stun an animal (O'Brien 1981). Most experts see animal butchery as hand axes' main use—an interpretation supported by microwear analysis (refer to Highlight 9.1). Additionally, experiments have shown that it is easier to butcher a large animal with a hand axe than with a flake (Jones 1980). Hand axes that are very large or particularly well made, more so than required to accomplish a butchery task (at least to the modern mind), may have had some symbolic meaning to their makers. Or, as one proposal suggests, they may have been made by males to attract females (Kohn and Mithen 1999).

## Subsistence Strategies of *Homo erectus* and Early Archaic *Homo sapiens*

The archaeological evidence of subsistence activities greatly increases after 500 kyr ago, but it is biased toward animal bones. Although plant foods must have played an important part in the diet of *H. erectus* and early archaic *H. sapiens*, they have been preserved only in rare cases. One such case is at Zhoukoudian, near Beijing, China, a cave site with a stratigraphic sequence spanning a period from 500 to 250 kyr ago. Excavations uncovered thousands of hackberries along with quartz artifacts, animal bones, and bone that may have been burned. Hyena bones found in some layers indicate that hyenas as well as humans were responsible for some of the bone accumulation (Schick and Zhuan 1993). Excavations at Gesher Benot Ya'aqov, Israel (a site dated to about 790 kyr), revealed remains of nuts, seeds, and fruits along with pitted stones that the excavators claim were used to crack nuts (Goren-Inbar et al. 2002).

Animals were important food sources too—especially in northern regions during the winter, when plant availability would have been limited. Vast herds of herbivores grazing on the steppe tundra landscapes of glacial periods would have provided a potentially rich food supply. Humans probably exploited natural deaths of animals; they also may well have utilized frozen animal carcasses by thawing the meat over a fire, something other animals could not do (Gamble 1999).

There is evidence for deliberate hunting during the Acheulian period. At the 500-kyr-old site of Boxgrove, England, cut marks on large mammal bones indicate careful butchery practices. The variety and locations of marks suggest that humans cut through muscle attachments to get large chunks of meat, cut through tendons and ligaments to disarticulate bones, scraped bones, and finally smashed the bones to get at nourishing marrow. Furthermore, carnivore marks overlying butchery marks on some bones show that hominids had first access to the meat. Microwear studies on a sample of the hundreds of hand axes from the site gave further evidence of meat processing (Roberts and Parfitt 1999). Although a small, round hole on a horse scapula at Boxgrove may be a spear wound, no spears were found at the site, possibly because of preservation conditions. However, several wooden javelins (throwing spears) were discovered at Schöningen, a 400-kyr-old site in Germany, in association with animal bones and stone artifacts; a wooden spear tip from Clacton in England is of a similar date (Barton 1997; Thieme 1997). If the Boxgrove evidence indicates (as its excavators claim) preplanning and hunting rather than mere scavenging of chance kills, then big game hunting may have been part of the general cultural repertoire of *H. erectus*.

Evidence from Atapuerca, Spain, is suggestive of cannibalistic practices. Excavators working on the TD6 level (dated to about 800 kyr ago) of Gran Dolina found human and animal bones mixed together. Close scrutiny of the bones showed that groups at the site had processed and discarded human bodies in exactly the same manner as animal carcasses: Butchery marks on human bones indicate skinning, meat removal, and marrow extraction, but there is no evidence of ritual treatment. Researchers have ruled out starvation scenarios, as pollen analysis reveals temperate conditions and a food-rich habitat; these findings are supported by the range of animal species found in the TD6 level. Consequently, it appears from the assemblage at Gran Dolina that the

From Boxgrove, England: a scanning electron photograph of a stone tool cutmark on a rhinoceros bone fragment overlain by carnivore gnawing. What does the sequence of marks imply?

Gnawing by carnivore

Stone tool cutmark

A 400-kyr-old wooden spear found at Schöningen, Germany. The Schöningen spears were crafted with one end weighted and the opposite end tapered, making them good throwing weapons. What information do the spears provide about early hominids?

humans at this site ate other humans as part of their diet (Fernandez-Jalvo et al. 1999).

## Fire

The control of fire is a useful skill: Fire provides heat (particularly necessary in northern regions) and light, keeps predators away, and is essential for cooking. Only after humans had achieved control of fire could they exploit plant foods that require cooking to eliminate toxins and facilitate digestion (Stahl 1984). Fire also can be used to shape wood and heat flint, facilitating modification of both materials. Ash, charcoal, soil baked by fire, burned food remains, burned flints, and rings of stones around hearths are indicators of human fire use. The challenge for archaeologists lies in determining whether a given fire was deliberately started or resulted from natural causes, such as lightning or the spontaneous combustion of organic material. In addition, mineral discoloration of bones, stones, and sediments can mimic burning (James 1989).

It is possible that hominids were exploiting fire more than 1 myr ago in East and South Africa: At Chesowanja, Kenya, patches of burnt clay associated with stone artifacts and animal bones may indicate the use of fires, as may burnt bones recovered from Swartkrans, South Africa. However, some researchers believe that the fires at Chesowanja and Swartkrans may have had natural origins (Gowlett 1992; Rolland 2004). Gesher Benot Ya'aqov in Israel provides more convincing evidence for hominids' use of fire 900 kyr ago. Excavations at this waterlogged site revealed burnt seeds, wood, and flints (heat causes crazing and cracking of flint). As the burnt material was found in localized areas and the flints occurred in clusters that the excavators interpret as being around hearths (campfires), the deliberate use of fire is likely (Goren-Inbar et al. 2004).

After about 500 kyr ago, unequivocal evidence for deliberate and repeated use of fire is widespread. For example, concentrations of burnt flints and associations of bones with slightly depressed areas of burnt sediments suggestive of hearths occurred in several levels at Beeches Pit in England. Similar patterning is evident at other European sites, such as Bilzingsleben and Schöningen in Germany, Terra Amata and Menez-Dregan in France, and Vértesszöllös in Hungary (de Lumley 2006; Gowlett 2006).

The lack of very early evidence for the use of fire may not necessarily indicate the absence of such use. Clearly fire would have been essential in northern areas, but erosional forces and the movement of massive ice sheets obliterated many early sites in those areas. Nevertheless, the lack of evidence for fire use in those early sites that have survived suggests that only later hominids were able to deliberately control and use fire.

## Structures

There is no good evidence for structures in the Lower Paleolithic/ESA. At DK, one of the oldest sites at Olduvai, searchers found an accumulation of stone artifacts and bones near a semicircle of basalt stones that they saw as the base of a windbreak (Leakey 1971).

The evidence is inconclusive, however; the circle is on a basalt lava flow, and the blocks may have been broken and rearranged by tree roots, coincidentally forming a circle.

Excavators at Terra Amata, a 500-kyr-old site in southern France, believed they had found evidence of huts in the form of the oval clustering of stones and bones, the location of some larger stone blocks, and a centrally placed hearth. The excavators felt that these objects were virtually in situ—that is, positioned as they had been when the site was occupied—and must have been circumscribed by some kind of structure. However, later study and refitting of artifacts showed that the materials had diffused through stratigraphic levels, calling into question the idea of structures (Villa 1983). A more hopeful case might be the lakeside site of Bilzingsleben, Germany, which dates to about 350 kyr ago, where three circular patterns of large stones and bones, each surrounding a central empty space, have been interpreted as weights to secure tentlike structures. Hearths and activity areas were located in front of the circles, and a large oval paving of small bones and stones was in a nearby activity area (Bosinski 2006; Mania 1995). However, empty circular spaces also could indicate the presence of ancient trees, and patterning on the site might represent the debris left by multiple short visits. Consequently, the validity of the structures' interpretation remains in question (Gamble 1999).

## Burials and Symbolic Representations

No clear evidence exists for deliberate burials during the Lower Paleolithic/ESA. At Sima de los Huesos (Pit of Bones) in Atapuerca (a later site than the TD6 level mentioned previously and dating from about 300 kyr ago), excavations in an underground cave system revealed the remains of 32 humans along with carnivore bones and a few bear bones. A quartzite hand axe was recovered in 1998. Many of the human bones display carnivore gnawing as well as the effects of postdepositional trampling. The members of the Atapuerca research team agree that hominids were responsible for the bone accumulation, but there is controversy over the level of deliberate action. Some researchers believe that the bodies were originally left outside the cave and were carried into it by carnivores or mud slides; others suggest that people took the bodies into the cave through an ancient entrance that has long since disappeared (Andrews and Fernandez-Jalvo 1997; Arsuaga et al. 1997; Carbonell et al. 2003). The crucial difference between the two proposals is that the latter infers special treatment by early hominids for others in their group.

Although some claims have been made for symbolic representations on rocks or bones during the Lower Paleolithic, at present there is no credible evidence for this type of activity.

## Human Adaptations in the Middle Paleolithic/ Middle Stone Age

**Middle Paleolithic**
The archaeological term commonly used in Eurasia for part of the Paleolithic period outside sub-Saharan Africa, from about 250 kyr to 35 kyr ago.

**Middle Stone Age (MSA)**
The archaeological term for part of the Stone Age in sub-Saharan Africa, from about 250 kyr to 22 kyr ago.

The European and Asian **Middle Paleolithic** and its African counterpart, the **Middle Stone Age (MSA)**, began about 250 kyr ago and ended about 35 kyr ago in Europe and 22 kyr ago in sub-Saharan Africa. This is the period associated with Neandertals and archaic *H. sapiens* in Eurasia and with archaic and anatomically modern humans (AMH) in Africa (Chapter 7). Differences in stone technology distinguish early Middle Paleolithic/MSA sites from their Acheulian predecessors, and more evidence of cultural complexity becomes apparent beginning about 130 kyr ago. Increasing numbers of rock shelters, cave sites, and open-air sites in a range of habitats indicate growing human populations, some of which ventured into the harsh environments of the southern areas of eastern Europe. Some rock shelters and cave sites have long stratigraphic sequences of occupation; open-air sites can be affected by erosion, however, so most of these have disappeared.

# Technology

The Middle Paleolithic/MSA is characterized by its stone artifacts. People of the period made flake tools in fairly standardized forms, using manufacturing techniques that were more complex than those of the Lower Paleolithic and are classified as **Mode 3 technology**. The **Levallois technique**, or **prepared core technique**, required skillfull preparation of a stone block to produce flakes of a predetermined shape and size. Toolmakers mastered Levallois technology in Eurasia and Africa, where Levallois products are common in many lithic assemblages of the period. There was a wider range of flake tools than in the Acheulian; and hand axes, when present, were often smaller and less ubiquitous than in previous periods. Tool types such as blades and microlithic pieces, often considered to be indicative of later periods, are more common in the Middle Paleolithic/MSA than was once thought (McBrearty and Brooks 2000). Middle Paleolithic people at Umm el Tlel, Syria, extended the complexity of tool manufacture by heating bitumen to a sticky consistency to glue flint tools onto handles (Boëda et al. 1996). Investigators at Middle Paleolithic sites in the Crimea discovered that a range of stone tools showed wood residues and wear patterns caused by hafting, probably as people made projectiles or spears (Hardy et al. 2001). At Taramsa Hill sites in Egypt, groups dug pits and trenches in order to exploit subsurface chert cobbles, testing the stones for flaws before choosing the most suitable ones to work. Hundreds of primarily unretouched flakes (including Levallois pieces), cores, and tested cobbles littered the area—and these were probably a fraction of the products that must have been taken away to other sites in the region and beyond. Dating indicates that the Taramsa chert quarries were exploited for about 130 kyr, from 180 kyr to 50 kyr ago (Vermeersch and Paulissen 1997; Vermeersch et al. 1998).

**Mode 3 technology**
A stone-working technique that includes the Levallois (prepared core) technique and is characteristic of the Middle Paleolithic/Middle Stone Age.

**Levallois technique (prepared core technique)**
A stone-working technique in which the knapper (stone worker) prepares a stone block (core) to produce flakes of a predetermined shape and size; characteristic of the Middle Paleolithic/Middle Stone Age.

Levallois core and flake. Skillful preparation of the core (left) results in a flake of a predetermined shape (right). The negative scars of flake preparation and the flake are visible on the core. With which hominid species is the Levallois technique primarily associated?

Middle Paleolithic/MSA people undoubtedly made and used bone and wood tools, but these artifacts rarely survive. Barbed and unbarbed bone points found at Katanda, Congo, and bone tools from Blombos Cave, South Africa, demonstrate skilled working perhaps 80 to 70 kyr ago. Harpoon technology does not appear in Europe until about 14 kyr ago.

In order to study Middle Paleolithic tools, archaeologists give the items names such as *scrapers*, *points*, *denticulates*, and *notches*. In the 1950s the French archaeologist François Bordes developed a classification scheme of 63 different tool types based on his observations of Middle Paleolithic tools from southwest France. Bordes grouped the tools into categories based on the percentage of particular types in each assemblage, and he proposed that the groups represented culturally distinct tribes that lived in the region but had little contact with one another over tens of thousands of years (Bordes 1961). Other researchers have challenged Bordes's interpretations in a debate that has lasted ever since the mid-1960s. Alternative interpretations suggest that (1) tool variability may reflect different tasks (e.g., butchery, plant processing, maintenance) for which specific tools are required (Binford and Binford 1966); (2) frequent resharpening of a dulled tool edge eventually changes the original edge shape so that the tool when found may not be the same "type" as the original (Dibble 1984); (3) the type and source of stone (local or nonlocal) can affect manufacture and preservation of a tool (Dibble and Rolland 1992); and (4) variability may result from cultural change through time, not differences between and groups (Mellars 1996). Clearly, no one of these causal explanations (and more have been proposed) can explain stone tool variability. It probably reflects a complex combination of factors that may differ across time and space.

## Subsistence Strategies

Neandertals were meat eaters par excellence, as demonstrated by isotope analysis of bone collagen that reveals dietary composition (Richards et al. 2000). Neandertals and early modern humans scavenged carcasses at times, but good evidence points to a greater reliance on deliberate hunting and targeting of particular animals in terms of species and age. For example, reindeer were the focus of Neandertal hunting about 70 kyr ago at Les Pradelles, France, where their bones form 90 percent of the animal bone assemblage (Costamago et al. 2006). Bison, sheep, and goats were the main meat source at Mezmaiskaya Cave in Russia between about 60 kyr and 40 kyr ago (Skinner et al. 2005), while the Neandertal occupants of Kebara Cave in Israel hunted not only small gazelles but also the more dangerous adult aurochs (wild cattle) and wild boar (Speth and Tchernov 1998). Successful hunting tactics require that people know where to find living or dead animals and that they prepare in advance to exploit particular situations. Mary Stiner (1994) examined faunal assemblages from Grotta Guattari and Grotta dei Moscerini (110 to 50 kyr ago) and from Grotta di San Agostino and Grotta Breuil (55 to 35 kyr ago). Heads of old animals dominated the Guattari and Moscerini assemblages—a pattern reminiscent of predator scavenging behavior, as seen with hyenas that transport heads and hooves back to their caves. As there was little evidence for hyena activity at the sites, Stiner concludes that the animal remains resulted from Neandertal scavenging. A different pattern of animal remains was revealed at the more recent San Agostino and Breuil sites, however. There, the presence of almost entire carcasses of adult deer suggested that humans had hunted the animals and transported them back to the caves. Stiner interprets the earlier sites as indicating periods of food shortage: Heads are not particularly good packages of meat but retain final vestiges of animal fat to be exploited as a last resort. She further supports her argument for food stress by noting signs of the exploitation of mollusks and tortoises (small food packages) in the caves; people ate whatever they could find. In contrast, the later sites indicate ambush strategies that enabled people to capture animals in their prime. Some researchers have questioned Stiner's interpretation on the grounds that her evidence for scavenging may result from bias in her sampling; these researchers propose that Neandertals hunted regularly (Marean 1999;

Villa et al. 2005). As far as hunting is concerned, it is clear that ambush techniques cannot be employed successfully unless a group is well organized and hunters cooperate with one another, factors clearly evident in the Middle Paleolithic.

Richard Klein believes that the faunal evidence from South African cave sites shows that between 120 and 30 kyr ago, early modern human groups hunted eland antelopes, probably by driving them over a cliff edge. MSA hunters rarely attacked more dangerous species, such as Cape buffalo and bushpig, and when they did so, they concentrated on weaker young or old animals rather than on adults in their prime (Klein 1989b). People also exploited tortoises and shellfish, the latter extensively at times as indicated by huge shell middens, but good evidence for fishing and fowling does not appear until the Late Stone Age (LSA). The domination of Cape buffalo and bushpig bones in LSA assemblages suggests to Klein that MSA people had neither the strategies nor the technology to hunt the more dangerous land animals or to exploit all available marine resources. Nevertheless, it is clear that early modern groups in sub-Saharan Africa and Neandertals in Eurasia understood the landscape in which they lived and had both the social organization and the strategic approaches to enable them to hunt effectively despite the potential limits of their technology (Milo 1998).

As always, plant remains from the Middle Paleolithic/MSA are scarce. Hackberries and wild plum pits were found in the Middle Paleolithic levels of Douara Cave, Syria, however; and wild peas were found by hearths at Kebara Cave in Israel. Underground geophytes (such as bulbs, roots, and tubers) were an important plant food for MSA and LSA groups and have survived in a few South African sites where conditions promoted preservation. As geophytes flourish after the ground has been burned, MSA people may have deliberately set fire to geophyte patches to promote growth (Deacon and Deacon 1999). Archeobotanists have had greater success in finding evidence of plants since they started employing recovery techniques that target micro plant remains. These techniques may show that Middle Paleolithic/MSA people ate more veggies than we give them credit for (Hardy et al. 2001).

## Habitation Areas and Organization of Space

There is much more variability in Middle Paleolithic/MSA cave and open-air sites than in those of previous periods, but there are still few signs of structures or coverings to indicate huts or shelters. The best contender for structures in Eurasia is at Molodova, Ukraine, where rings of mammoth bones have been interpreted as windbreaks and are associated with stone tools, other animal bones, and hearths. However, the effect of natural processes may have caused some of the patterning (Klein 1999). Indications of postholes have been revealed at late coastal sites in North Africa and in the Sahara (McBrearty and Brooks 2000). Investigators at Mumbwa Cave in Zambia unearthed three semi-circular features with postholes; the excavators interpreted these as windbreaks delimiting a semi-circular spread of lithic waste, bone, ash, and burned earth and dated the site to 100 kyr or older (Barham 2000). Undoubtedly most shelters, particularly open-air structures, have disappeared with time. Nevertheless, there are well-preserved sites with well-defined knapping and butchery areas from which lithics can be refitted, and where evidence of structures ought to be visible if structures did exist. No such evidence has been found.

Analysis of Middle Paleolithic/MSA sites indicates a relatively unstructured use of habitation space. At many sites habitation space consists of two areas: a living zone around hearths and a dump area. Although the use of fire is clearly evident from ash layers at many locations, hearths delineated by stones—as at Vilas Ruivas, Portugal, and Mumbwa, Zambia—are rare (Barham 2000; Stringer and Gamble 1993). Many circular and oval hearths (not defined by stones) in 60- to 48-kyr levels at Kebara may have served different purposes: cooking and eating (bones around the hearth) and lighting (bone-free zone). The Kebarans dumped bone and lithic rubbish along one wall of the cave (Bar-Yosef et al. 1992).

# Symbolism: Burials, Art, Ritual

Paul Mellars (1996, 369) defines **symbolism** as any "object, sign, gesture or vocal expression which in some way refers to or represents something beyond itself." Today we use symbols continuously in our interactions with others: Our material culture and the way in which we use it (e.g., the clothes we wear, our homes, our interests, our religion, the people we associate with, and the way we speak) express aspects of our identity and the groups with which we identify. The nature and extent (if any) of symbolic activities in the Middle Paleolithic/MSA is hotly debated. Sally McBrearty and Alison Brooks (2000, 492) propose a number of "archaeological signatures" that signify symbolic behavior, among them are pigment use, incised artifacts, body decoration, burials with grave goods and ochre, regional artifact styles, and representations. The evidence is limited, in sharp contrast to what appears in the following period. Yet it is reasonable to see the beginnings of symbolism in the use of color, personal ornaments, and burials.

Lumps of color pigments, particularly ochre (a mineral producing ranges of red and yellow colors), charcoal, and black manganese dioxide, often showing use-wear patterns, have been found at many Middle Paleolithic/MSA sites. Grinding stones with signs of ochre at some African sites indicate ochre processing. Color pigments were exploited 200 kyr ago, and possibly even as far back as 400 kyr at the Twin Rivers site in Zambia, where evidence indicates substantial collecting and processing of iron and manganese minerals (Barham 2002). The mere presence of color pigments and evidence of their processing does not necessarily imply symbolic meaning; ochre may be used in hide processing or hafting, as medicine, or to keep odors at bay. Ochre use as medicine or air freshener is not evident in the early archaeological record. Given that organic materials disintegrate, hide processing is difficult to determine, although wear on ochre-tipped bone tools at Blombos Cave is consistent with their use to pierce soft materials (Henshilwood et al. 2001). Experimental work and ethnographic observation supports archaeological evidence that ochre was used in hafting; the location of ochre stains on stone tools at a number of Middle Paleolithic/MSA sites indicates the use of tools for both processing ochre and hafting purposes (Hovers et al. 1997, 2003; McBrearty and Brooks 2000; Wadley et al. 2004). There is no doubt about the authenticity of two pieces of ochre with geometric engravings from levels dated to 70 kyr ago at **Blombos Cave**, South Africa. At Blombos Cave workers also recovered more than 8,000 pieces of ochre, some scraped to produce powder and others in the form of ochre crayons (Henshilwood

**symbolism**
Use of an object, sign, gesture, or expression to represent something beyond itself.

**Blombos Cave**
A Middle Stone Age site in South Africa where engravings on ochre that may indicate use of symbolism were found.

Engraved ochre artifact from 70-kyr-old MSA levels at Blombos Cave, South Africa. What are the implications of this artifact concerning the development of symbolism?

et al. 2001, 2002). Although people may have used ochre for body paint, such evidence would not remain in the archaeological record.

Researchers have proposed that various incised bones and stones indicate symbolic actions. The case for symbolism is tenuous, however, because the incisions do not follow any pattern. Indeed, some could have been caused by butchery, and others may be the result of natural abrasion (Chase and Dibble 1987; Copeland and Moloney 2003). Nevertheless, pendants made from a swan vertebra and a wolf foot bone with clearly perforated holes surfaced at Bocksteinschmiede, Germany (Bednarik 1992); pierced animal teeth and shells have been found at a number of sites from France to sub-Saharan Africa (d'Errico et al. 2003; Vanhaeren et al. 2006); and workers have recovered bone pendants, drilled quartzite flakes, ostrich eggshell beads, and signs of bead working at MSA sites (McBrearty and Brooks 2000).

Lithic MSA assemblages in Africa include a range of pointed types that vary stylistically between areas and may indicate regional groups that would identify with particular point types (McBrearty and Brooks 2000). Such regional differences are less apparent in the European lithic assemblages from the Middle Paleolithic.

The deliberate burial of a corpse, in contrast to the discard of a body, suggests care for the dead and perhaps a belief in life after death. The deposition of grave goods with the burial is clearly a symbolic gesture demonstrating respect for the dead person. There is some evidence for intentional burials in deliberately dug pits in the Middle Paleolithic. For example, excavators found bodies in pits at the Kebara, Tabun, Qafzeh, and Skhul cave sites in Israel and at several sites in southwest France. In one burial at Qafzeh, a child lay at the feet of a young woman; in another an adolescent held deer antlers. The mandible of a wild boar accompanied one of the burials at nearby Skhul (Vandermeersch 2006). The Qafzeh and Skhul burials were of AMH; the other burials are Neandertal. Claims for grave goods arouse more scepticism (Chase and Dibble 1987; Mellars 1996). At Shanidar Cave, Iraq, investigators found eight Neandertal skeletons; four of them had died under rock falls, but the others seemed to be deliberate burials. Samples taken from soil around a male burial included flower pollen, which the pollen analyst interpreted as resulting from flowers placed with the burial. Counterarguments suggest that the pollen could have blown into the cave, been tracked in on excavators' shoes, or been brought in by rodents. Most common among the rodent remains in the cave were those of the Persian jird, a gerbil-like rodent that nests in caves and stores vast quantities of flower seeds, particularly the species identified in the pollen sample (Sommer 1999). Similarly, the stones and bones found in some other burials may not have been deliberate deposits. For example, at Teshik-Tash, Uzbekistan, some researchers made claims for the deliberate placement of goat horns—but goats are the most common animal found on the site, so their horns may have been incorporated naturally into the burial.

A practice of placing bodies in particular caches may explain sites where investigators have found partial remains of many individuals but have discerned no preparation of grave cuts, as seen at Krapina, Croatia (Pettitt 2002). If the cache hypothesis is valid, then, as Paul Pettitt points out, these locales may have been of particular significance.

Many claims for cannibalism have turned out to be baseless. For example, although some of the bones at Krapina and Vindija Cave, Croatia, have cut marks that suggest post-mortem defleshing (a mortuary practice evident in later periods), there is no indication that people had smashed the bones to extract marrow, an activity suggestive of cannibalistic practices (White 2001). However, cannibalism is clearly indicated in the 120- to 100-kyr-old levels at Moula-Guercy, France. At Moula-Guercy the remains of six Neandertals show patterns of exploitation identical to those of red deer remains in the same levels: defleshing, disarticulation, marrow extraction, and discard (Defleur et al. 1999).

The question as to whether symbolism was used before 40 kyr ago has an emotional dimension and has yet to be resolved to everyone's satisfaction. It is clear that something was happening at that time that was not essential for day-to-day living. True, people may have been doodling or experimenting; but just because the evidence is not as prolific as in the Upper Paleolithic/Late Stone Age (LSA), there is no reason to dismiss it out of hand. Indeed, as Robert Bednarik (1992) points out, the same types of questionable evidence dismissed for earlier periods may be acceptable in later contexts—because symbolic activity is clearly evident in the Upper Paleolithic/LSA.

# Humans across the Globe: Life in the Upper Paleolithic/ Late Stone Age

The final 40 kyr of the last Ice Age is known as the **Upper Paleolithic** in Eurasia and the **Late Stone Age (LSA)** in sub-Saharan Africa. The transition from MSA to LSA occurred later in southern Africa, at about 22 kyr ago. This period, as we saw in Chapter 7, brought the distinctive changes in behavior patterns associated with modern humans. At the beginning of the period, in Europe at least, two kinds of humans coexisted: Neandertals and anatomically modern humans (AMH). By 27 kyr ago, however, the last Neandertals in Europe had disappeared and only modern humans remained.

Evidence of behavioral changes includes increasingly diverse stone tool production; an increasing use of bone, antler, and ivory tools; more extensive networks of long-distance contacts; organized, cooperative hunting and targeting of specific animals; the construction of semi-permanent dwellings; and systematic use of space (see Table 9.1). Notable changes of a symbolic nature include the attention paid to the dead, the proliferation of personal ornaments (suggesting a developing sense of self and group identity), and the appearance of highly creative symbolic traditions. Furthermore, a heightened sense of inquisitiveness led groups to move out of familiar areas into the relative unknown and to colonize all areas of the world, except the Arctic, remote islands in the Pacific, and the Antarctic, by 10 kyr ago. The changes in the Upper Paleolithic were rapid by Paleolithic standards, occurring within 30 kyr, in contrast to the 200 kyr or so of the previous period. Some researchers believe that the rate and extent of change during the "Upper Paleolithic revolution" can be explained only by the appearance of fully fledged language—that is, of speech.

## Neandertals and Anatomically Modern Humans in the Landscape

One of the most controversial topics in paleoanthropology today centers on the crucial period linking the Middle and Upper Paleolithic, particularly in Eurasia. In that area the earliest phase of the Upper Paleolithic, the **Aurignacian** (after the French site of l'Aurignac), is characterized by new types of stone tools but also consistently includes bone and ivory tools, pendants, and representational art. Many researchers claim that this suite of artifacts is similar from Israel to Spain, although the similarities in the Israeli material are tenuous (Clark 2002). Human remains, when found in Aurignacian sites, are always anatomically modern. Aurignacian industries seem to appear abruptly in the archaeological record; they have no antecedents in, and indeed often replace, earlier local industries. In general, Aurignacian sites are older in eastern and southeastern Europe than in western Europe, suggesting movement of populations from the east (Mellars 1996). Perhaps these AMH groups settled first along coasts and rivers and later moved into other areas (Davies 2001).

Neandertals were still around when modern humans moved into Europe, and archaeological evidence shows that the two populations lived in close proximity for an extended period before the Neandertals disappeared from the scene. In France, as Chapter 7 described, the material culture (termed the Chatelperronian) associated with the last

**Upper Paleolithic**
The archaeological term commonly used in Eurasia for part of the Paleolithic period outside sub-Saharan Africa, from about 40 kyr to 11.5 kyr ago.

**Late Stone Age (LSA)**
The archaeological term for the later part of the Stone Age in sub-Saharan Africa, from about 22 kyr to 2,000 years ago.

**Aurignacian**
The earliest period of the Upper Paleolithic in Europe, which lasted from about 35 kyr to 28 kyr ago and is named after the French site of l'Aurignac.

*Table 9.1*

## Characteristics of Upper Paleolithic/Late Stone Age, Middle Stone Age, and Middle Paleolithic Cultures

| | Upper Paleolithic/Late Stone Age | Middle Stone Age | Middle Paleolithic |
|---|---|---|---|
| *Technology* | Blades, microliths, hafting, composite tools, specialized tools<br><br>Standardization of tool types<br><br>Geographic and chronological variation in tool types and styles<br><br>Bone, antler, and ivory working | Levallois technique; blades in many assemblages; microliths at 60–70 kyr; hafting and composite tools<br><br>Regional styles evident in stone points<br><br>Some bone harpoons and bone points | Levallois technique; some blades; hafting<br><br>Some bone points in the Chatelperronian (MP/UP transition) period |
| *Economic and Social Organization* | Systematic hunting, selection of particular species (including dangerous animals), primary access to kills<br><br>Intensification of use of aquatic resources; fowling, fishing<br><br>Intensification of use of plant resources<br><br>Population increase, more and larger sites<br><br>Structured organization of sites (e.g., pits, huts, well defined hearths)<br><br>Long-distance exchange of stone and "exotic" items such as amber; wider kin networks | Selection of prey species; dangerous animals hunted at times; primary access to carcasses indicated<br><br>Mollusk collection, fishing at Blombos, Katanda, and Nile sites; seals captured in southern Africa<br><br>Geophytes exploited and possibly managed<br><br>Increase in sites over ESA<br><br>Structured organization limited<br><br>Use of nonlocal stone | Selection of prey species; primary access to carcasses<br><br>Mollusk collection<br><br>Plant remains include berries, fruits, and peas<br><br>Increase in sites over LP<br><br>Structured organization limited<br><br>Some long-distance exchange of stone in central and eastern Europe |
| *Symbolic Behavior* | Representational art; personal ornaments<br><br>Widespread use of ochre<br><br>Burial with grave goods | Perforated shell, bone, and stone ornaments; ostrich eggshell fragments; incised and notched bones<br><br>Ochre at many sites; incised ochre at Blombos | Infrequent perforated shells; bone beads and simple line incisions on bone, ivory, and stone at the end of the period<br><br>Use of ochre<br><br>Burials, limited grave goods |
| *Ecology* | Occupation of a wide geographic range of environments: tropical lowlands, islands, northern Europe, northern Asia, Australia, and Americas<br><br>Varied diet | Occupation of most of Africa, including arid areas and tropical forest<br><br>Varied diet | Expansion into harsh environments of southern parts of eastern Europe<br><br>High meat intake in Eurasian Neandertal populations |

*Sources:* Based on Clark (2002), Henshilwood and Marean (2003), and McBrearty and Brooks (2000).

Neandertal groups overlaps that of the earliest modern humans (the Aurignacian) (see Table 9.2). As Chapter 7 discussed, the heated debates relating to the Middle/Upper Paleolithic transitional period relate primarily to the replacement of Neandertals by modern humans as opposed to the coexistence and interbreeding of the two groups. Some researchers claim that archaeological evidence for the spread of Aurignacian industries supports genetic evidence indicating differences between Neandertal and modern genes; this argument strengthens the replacement hypothesis. Others reject this notion and propose that differences in technology, subsistence, and art do not suddenly appear in Europe with the Aurignacian. Rather, they are a continuation of development that began in the Middle Paleolithic and therefore cannot have been introduced by

## Table 9.2

| The Upper Paleolithic Cultural Sequence in France and Northern Spain | |
|---|---|
| *Dates* | *Terminology* |
| 18–10 kyr ago | Magdalenian |
| 21–18 kyr ago | Solutrean |
| 29–21 kyr ago | Gravettian |
| 35–28 kyr ago | Aurignacian or Early Upper Paleolithic |
| <32 kyr ago | Chatelperronian or Late Middle Paleolithic |

modern humans (Clark 2002). Sally McBrearty and Alison Brooks (2000) propose that the "new" behaviors have their roots in the African MSA—and consequently that there was no "revolution" at 40 kyr ago (see Table 9.1). Geoff Clark (2002) further suggests that attributes associated with modern human cultural behavior (such as symbolic behavior) developed slowly and did not become a hallmark of the Upper Paleolithic repertoire until about 20 kyr *after* the transitional period. He suggests that it is improper to ascribe developments covering thousands of kilometers and lasting tens of thousands of years to cultural "traditions," and he criticizes many prehistorians for doing just that. No doubt, debates on the emergence of modern humans and the fate of the Neandertals will continue for some time.

## Technological Complexity

In many areas of the world, and particularly in Europe, the linchpin of stone tool manufacture in the Upper Paleolithic was the production of long, narrow, parallel-sided **blades** struck from cores of siliceous stone such as flint. Good blades may appear simple to make, but in fact they require complex techniques of core preparation and blade extraction. The glory of the blade core was that from one carefully prepared nodule of flint, a toolmaker could produce dozens of standardized pieces; these in turn could be modified into a myriad of more specific designs for specific functions. Consequently, Upper Paleolithic tools include various types of points, scrapers, piercers, engravers, knives, and spear barbs. Many tools were hafted onto bone or antler handles. Blade production also is an economical way to exploit flint, as it produces more cutting edge per volume of stone than flake production.

Blades are not the hallmark of the period throughout the world, however. In South Africa, for instance, much smaller **microliths** (flakes and blades) of the LSA foreshadow similar types found in Europe many thousands of years later during the Mesolithic (Deacon 1989). In parts of Southeast Asia, assemblages were often a mixture of flakes, blades, and bladelets (Chen and Olsen 1990); the Australian tool kit consisted of simple cores and flakes. Cultural traditions may have accounted for the variation, although in places raw material restrictions may have limited the use of certain techniques. Some writers have suggested that tool types change according to the animals hunted, but people successfully hunted large herbivores in southern Africa and Eurasia using different tool kits.

In addition to utilizing flint, Upper Paleolithic/LSA people also turned their attention to other raw materials: From the earliest part of the period, artisans fashioned bone, antler, and ivory into standardized tools and ornaments. In Eurasia, for example, researchers have found pieces such as piercers, chisels, picks, points, spears, harpoons, and eyed needles. It is highly likely that the diversity in technology and products seen for flint and bone also was manifested in wood but that the wooden artifacts have not survived. Tool types are often regionally specific, perhaps indicating an emerging sense of ethnic identity. Because Upper Paleolithic/LSA types of tools changed relatively rapidly

**blades**
Long, narrow, parallel-sided stone tools that were struck from cores of siliceous stone such as flint; the hallmark of the Upper Paleolithic in Europe, although also found in earlier periods.

**microliths**
Small stone flakes or blades, characteristic of the Late Stone Age in South Africa and the early Holocene in Eurasia.

**Chatelperronian**
The last Middle Paleolithic period associated with Neandertal material culture in France and Spain.

**Gravettian**
A period of the Upper Paleolithic in France and Spain between 29 and 21 kyr ago.

**Solutrean**
A period of the Upper Paleolithic in France and Spain from about 21 kyr to 18 kyr ago, characterized by very finely worked leaf-shaped flint points.

**Magdalenian**
The final period in the Upper Paleolithic in France and Spain from 18 kyr to 10 kyr ago.

and are associated with developments in other aspects of material culture, such as burials and art, they can serve as general chronological markers, identified by regional terms to signify different periods. For example, in France and Spain, the last Middle Paleolithic period associated with Neandertal material culture is known as the **Chatelperronian**. The earliest Upper Paleolithic period, associated with anatomically modern humans, is, as we have seen, termed the Aurignacian. It is followed by the **Gravettian** and **Solutrean** periods. The **Magdalenian** is the final period of the Ice Age (refer to Table 9.2).

The technological complexity of the Upper Paleolithic tool kit suggests different levels of ability among toolmakers. Undoubtedly, everyone could make the basic tools needed for everyday use; but some pieces could have been made only by specialists. For example, during the Solutrean period artisans produced leaf-shaped flint points, some so thin that the flint is almost transparent. In order to make the finest points, knappers heated their flint and worked it using pressure flaking, knowing that both techniques gave them greater control over manufacture (Bordes 1968).

Several levels of knapping skills are visible at the late Magdalenian site of Pincevent, near Paris (Audouze 1987; Karlin 1992). As Pincevent was in situ, that is, nothing had disturbed the archaeological deposits since the departure of the last Paleolithic occupants, most blades could be refitted onto the cores from which they had been removed 12 kyr ago (see Figure 9.3). The best knappers exploited the finest flint and worked

*Figure 9.3*

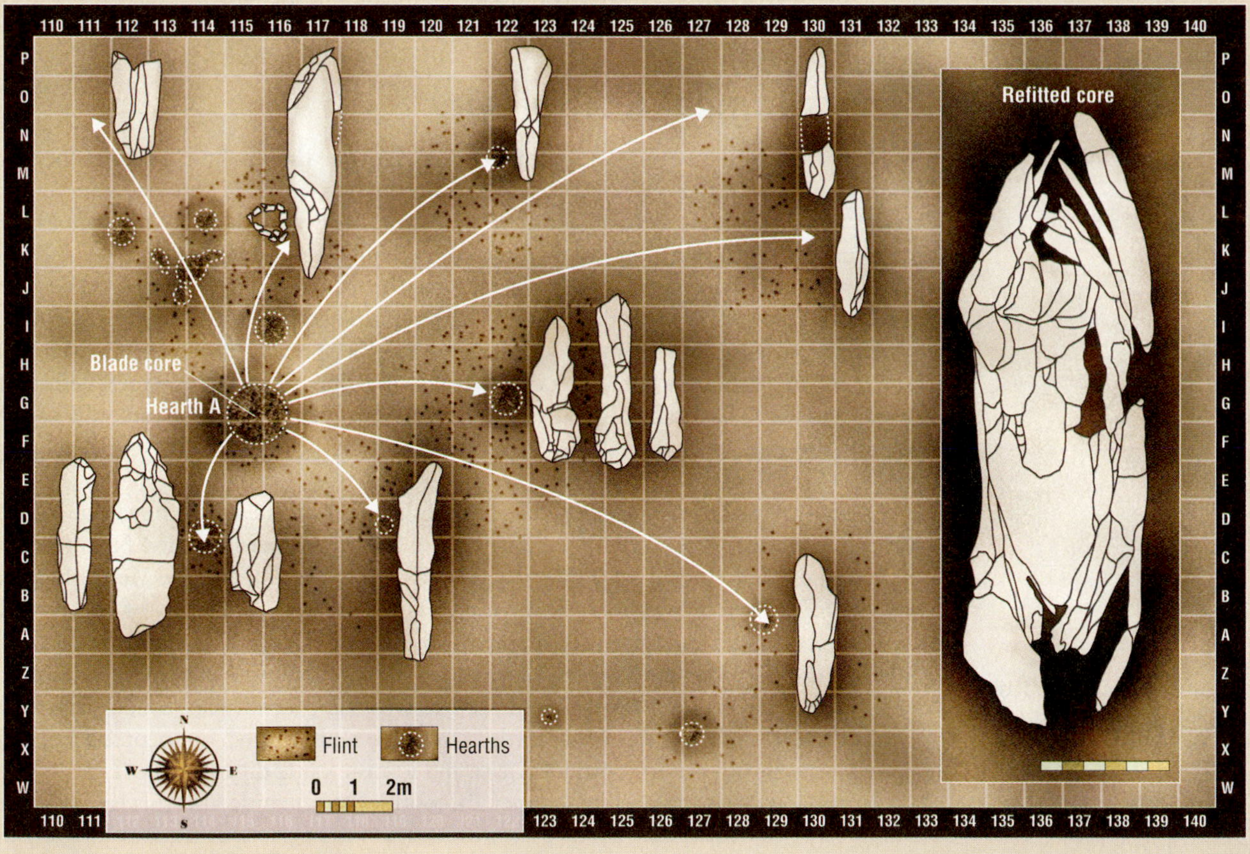

**BLADES AT PINCEVENT, FRANCE.** Blades found in different areas of this Upper Paleolithic site were refitted onto a core at hearth A. Why is refitting an important facet of archaeological research?

*Source:* Adapted from drawing by Dr. Pierre Bodu, Laboratoire d'Ethnologie Préhistorique, Paris, France. Used with permission.

blade cores with exact precision to produce long, standardized blades. The cores and blades indicate that the knappers knew exactly what procedures to follow and, more importantly, made no mistakes. Many of these top-quality blades were found in different parts of the camp; some appear to have been kept as a reserve, and people took others away when they left camp (as shown by refitted but incomplete blade cores that indicate missing blades). Average knappers were less careful and made many mistakes, which can be seen on the cores. These toolmakers produced blades that were shorter but still useful for domestic purposes. There also seems to be evidence of work by apprentices or children—whose cores showed many mistakes and very low levels of skill.

Bone, antler, and ivory require special knowledge to work. For example, it is easier to work antler when it is wet, so presoaking may have been common practice. To make points and harpoons, workers often used strips of antler that had been removed by the "groove and splinter" technique. A worker would etch two long parallel grooves into the antler with a burin (a chisel-edged blade), join the grooves at each end, then pry the splinter out. The long splinter could then be transformed into such tools as smooth and barbed points, eyed needles, and awls.

Upper Paleolithic/LSA sites yield much greater evidence than those of the preceding period for tool manufacture using nonlocal or exotic raw materials, some from sources hundreds of kilometers distant. Some groups exploited underground sources of stone: Researchers at Nazlet Khater 4 in the Nile Valley found evidence of extensive chert mining in the form of surface trenches, mine shafts, and underground galleries. Miners used gazelle and hartebeest horns as picks, and pick marks remain on gallery walls. Carbon 14 dates for many hearths in the mines indicate that the chert was exploited between 35 and 30 kyr ago (Vermeersch et al. 1990). People mined flint, too, at Koonalda Cave, beneath the Nullabor Plain in southern Australia (see Highlight 9.2, on pp. 256–257).

## Subsistence Practices

Animal and plant resources available to humans at any given time depend on the climate and environment. The Upper Paleolithic/LSA covers the final part of the last Ice Age—a time when glaciers spread over much of the northern latitudes. The coldest period—the last glacial maximum—was between 25 kyr and 18 kyr ago. Advancing ice led to vast tundra and grassland plains across the middle latitudes from northern and eastern Europe to Siberia, and to increasing aridity and desertification in many areas of Africa and Australia. In some regions, however, microenvironments offered respite to human populations. For example, in parts of Eurasia the plains were dissected by deep valleys in which tree cover was greater, plant growth better, and resources more easily accessible. These river valleys probably afforded animal and plant habitats when climatic conditions were at their worst.

The Eurasian plains attracted herds of migratory gregarious herbivores: woolly mammoth, woolly rhinoceros, reindeer, horse, bison, and musk ox. The remains of carnivores such as lions, hyenas, and bears have been found on sites, but not in great quantities; most likely, humans and large carnivores avoided each other as much as possible (Klein 1999).

Hunters' knowledge about animal behavior and the organization of hunts ensured a fairly predictable food supply. Technological developments also aided hunting: The various points, spears, and harpoons all served their deadly purposes. In addition, the Upper Paleolithic saw the invention of the spear-thrower, or atlatl, which effectively extended the range of the hunter's arm, adding force and accuracy and consequently greater impact and penetration.

Besides serving as food, animals provided raw materials for shelter, clothing, tool and ornament manufacture, and—when required—fuel. Human groups often targeted a particular animal, so one or two species dominate many faunal assemblages. It is clear that hunts were carefully planned and often focused on migration routes. At Pincevent, for example, 98 percent of the faunal assemblage consists of reindeer bones. The site is in

# Highlight 9.2

## Into Australia and the Pacific

THE UNFOLDING STORY of the antiquity of human occupation in the Pacific, and in Australia in particular, is closely tied to the development of carbon 14 ($^{14}$C), thermoluminescence (TL), and electron spin resonance (ESR) dating. In the 1950s scholars believed that Australia had not been colonized before 5 kyr ago. Today dates from sites throughout the continent show that humans were well established in Australia by 40 to 30 kyr ago and that early occupation must have occurred some thousands of years earlier, possibly between 50 and 45 kyr ago. The original colonizers were anatomically modern humans.

The Pacific is dotted with islands. Because of the sheer distance between many islands, researchers long believed that colonization must have occurred very recently. They were wrong. People colonized some islands around the periphery of the Pacific surprisingly early: 33 kyr ago for New Britain and New Ireland in the Bismark Archipelago, and 30 kyr ago for the Solomon Islands. About 4,000 years ago, the more remote islands of Melanesia saw the arrival of people who used Lapita ware, a distinctive type of decorated pottery that has been found throughout Melanesia. The first settlers reached Hawaii and Easter Island about 1,500 years ago, and New Zealand about 1,100 years ago.

One reason why researchers are interested in finding out when humans first arrived in Australia and the Pacific is the fact that colonization required sea travel—sometimes between landmasses that were beyond the visible horizon. Southeast Asia and Australia are good examples. At peak glacial periods some landmasses were joined; for example, New Guinea connected with Australia, and Tasmania with the Australian mainland. However, deep-sea channels have always separated many islands of Southeast Asia, so these islands can be reached only by sea voyages, some as long as 100 km (62 miles).

The simple rafts used by aborigines today and the dugouts noted by the first Europeans in Australia would not have survived long on the open sea. Prehistoric voyagers may well have used bamboo craft; bamboo is abundant in Southeast Asia and has a silica outer covering that acts as a waterproofing agent. With such a craft, helped by monsoon winds, the journey to Australia could take as little as a week to 10 days. The later Polynesians had double-hulled canoes capable of ocean travel to the remote islands of the Pacific. Polynesians navigated by the stars and ocean and took their own plants and animals with them in preparation for life on new islands.

The resources of coastal Australia would have been familiar to people from islands in Southeast Asia. Further inland, encounters with large animals such as flightless birds, large wombats, and giant kangaroos (all now extinct) would have been new but not necessarily alarming experiences. As there were few carnivores in Australia, the large, often slow-moving animals may not have feared the newcomers in the landscape and thus were easy targets for human predators.

Lake Mungo, in the Willandra Lakes system, lies more than 2,700 km (1,680 miles) south of northern Australia, where the first Australians would have landed. Today the Willandra Lakes area is dry, remote country, but during interglacial periods in the past it was a land of lakes teeming with fish. People exploited the resource-rich area for thousands of years, camping around hearths sheltered by dunes on the eastern side of Lake Mungo. They fished, collected mussels and emu eggs, and hunted a variety of land animals and birds: rat kangaroo, wallaby, wombat, and native cat, the remains of which have been found around the many hearths in the area. Burials at Lake Mungo include a cremation (the earliest in the world) and an inhumation. Recent redating of both burials gave results of about 40 kyr—indicating that the cremation and the inhumation were contemporaneous.

During glacial periods the ice-covered mountains of Tasmania were about 1,000 km (620 miles) from the Antarctic ice sheet. Although the Tasmanian highlands might seem to have been a cold, inhospitable, uninviting area in which to live, the grassland plains were rich in food resources that attracted people for thousands of years. Between 35 and 14 kyr ago, the limestone caves along the island's rivers were home to groups of people. The settlers collected emu eggs and hunted birds and kangaroo, but their prime targets were the thousands of red-necked wallabies that grazed the plains.

Although it is clear that the life of the first Australians was just as complex as that of their contemporaries elsewhere in the Old World, their stone tool assemblage was simple—unlike the blade industries elsewhere in Eurasia and Africa, but similar to the assemblages found in Southeast Asia. However, this simplicity masks an underlying complexity. For example, in Tasmania, a volcanic, meteoric glass has been found in sites up to 75 km (47 miles) from its source. Between 24 and 14 kyr ago miners exploited galleries of flint that extended deep inside Koonalda Cave beneath the Nullabor Plain in southwestern Australia.

In addition, researchers have found ground axes with grooves to facilitate hafting, and grinding stones used to grind ochre and possibly plant foods, in Australia, New Guinea, and Southeast Asia. These form some of the earliest evidence in the world for grinding technology, which becomes a hallmark of the later farming periods around the globe.

Australia has a long, rich tradition of symbolic representation. At the earliest sites excavators have found ochre, either in lumps or sprinkled on burials. Wall paintings, etchings, and engravings are perhaps as old as those found in Europe and include hand stencils, geometric engraving, and paintings. The rock shelters of Arnhem Land, in northern Australia, are particularly rich in paintings—among them representations of animals that became extinct after the last Ice Age. In contrast to European cave art, these paintings often depict humans, sometimes wearing ornaments and headdresses, in scenes that seem to reflect everyday life, such as dancing or hunting kangaroos. However, such scenes may postdate European cave art.

Present-day Australian aborigines create art evoking the "Dreamtime" when mythical beings brought life to the land. It would seem that modern aboriginal painters continue a tradition that has its roots in the Ice Age and binds them to their ancestral past.

Exposed land surfaces of Southeast Asia and Australia during peak glacial periods. What routes might have led to Australia?

*Sources*: Bowler, J. M., H. Johnston, J. M. Olley, et al. 2003. New ages for human occupation and climatic change at Lake Mungo, Australia. *Nature*, 421:837–840.  Flood, J. 1995. *Archaeology of the Dreamtime: The story of prehistoric Australia and its people*. Sydney, Australia: Angus & Robertson.  Gamble, C. 1993. *Timewalkers: The prehistory of global colonization*. Stroud, UK: Alan Sutton.  Mulvany, J., and J. Kamminga. 1999. *Prehistory of Australia*. Washington, DC: Smithsonian Institution Press.  O'Connell, J. F., and J. Allen. 1998. When did humans first arrive in Greater Australia and why is it important to know? *Evolutionary Anthropology* 6 (4): 132–146.  O'Connell, J. F., and J. Allen. 2004. Dating the colonization of Sahul (Pleistocene Australia–New Guinea): A review of recent research. *Journal of Archaeological Science* 31:865–853.  Thorne, A., and R. Raymond. 1989. *Man on the rim*. Sydney, Australia: Angus & Robertson.

turn back to your reading

a valley near the confluence of the Seine and Yonne rivers where, 12 kyr ago, hunters gathered for a few weeks in the fall to target reindeer herds migrating to winter grazing lands. All parts of the reindeer skeletons were recovered at Pincevent, indicating that the hunters carried whole animals to the camp for butchering and processing (Audouze 1987).

LSA hunters in South Africa targeted the dangerous Cape buffalo and bushpig more often than the docile eland that MSA hunters had favored, although the latter had hunted dangerous species too. The bones of fish and flying seabirds are common at LSA sites, indicating fishing and fowling (Klein 1989b). Richard Klein suggests that the stone and bone tool kits found at coastal LSA sites were developed to aid fishing and fowling; it would have been safer to hunt the dangerous land animals with bow and arrow, but bows rarely survive in the archaeological record. The many small stone microliths, however, would have made good arrow tips.

Plant foods, too, were available and exploited, although the evidence is limited because of preservation problems. Although animal remains are important, particularly in the more northerly areas, plant gathering would have been responsible for a significant part of the diet in all environments. For example, the Wadi Kubbaniya sites on the Nile (north of Aswan) were occupied repeatedly by small groups during the last glacial maximum. The locale by water enabled these groups to survive successfully for many months on a diet based on catfish and plant foods (Close and Wendorf 1990). People caught thousands of catfish during their summer spawning and may have dried or smoked some in order to store them for consumption later in the year. Groups moved away as yearly floodwaters inundated the area, then returned as the waters retreated to exploit a variety of late autumn and winter plant foods, including tubers. Grinding stones found at Wadi Kubbaniya provide supporting evidence of plant exploitation; in particular, the stones show the importance of tubers, which people would have had to grind and cook to remove toxins.

Ohalo II, a waterlogged site on the shore of Lake Galilee in Israel, has provided archaeologists with a wealth of information on plant exploitation 23 kyr ago. Excavations revealed the charred remains of six oval brush huts, grass bedding, hearths, flint and bone tools, various bones (animal, bird, and fish), plant remains, groundstone net sinkers, a grinding stone, fragments of cord, hundreds of shell beads originating from the Mediterranean, and a human burial. Seeds of wild cereal grasses, among them wild emmer wheat and wild barley, formed the bulk of the 90,000 pieces of plant remains that also included a range of nut species, olives, fruits, and berries. Cereal grains associated with a grinding stone indicate processing occurred, a time-consuming and laborious activity needed to prepare seeds for cooking and consumption. The inhabitants at Ohalo II exploited a wide range of resources around the site that may have enabled them to have lived there on an almost permanent basis (Nadel et al. 2004; Weiss et al. 2004).

## Habitation and Use of Space

There is clear evidence for structures and highly organized use of space in the cold winters of northern latitudes in the Upper Paleolithic. People in much of western Europe made use of caves and rock shelters when they were available, often adding stone walls or animal skins as extra protection against the cold. In the harsh open landscape of the east European plain, communities built sturdy dwellings from the most abundant suitable raw material at hand: mammoth bone. Excavators have uncovered numerous mammoth-bone dwellings that endured under meters of loess (wind-borne glacial sediments). The structures were usually round and semi-subterranean. People probably windproofed them by stuffing loess, turf, and small bones into cracks between the larger structural bones and covering the shelters with hides. They may have roofed these dwellings with wood.

Five such dwellings at **Mezhirich**, Ukraine, date to between 18 kyr and 15 kyr ago. Dwelling I was constructed of 21,000 kg (46,300 pounds) of bones and had a foundation of 25 mammoth skulls driven into the ground, on top of which the builders had set 95

**Mezhirich**
Upper Paleolithic site in the Ukraine with mammoth bone houses dated to between 18 kyr and 15 kyr ago.

mammoth mandibles in a herringbone pattern (Gladkih et al. 1984). Flanking the entrance were two inverted mammoth tusks. Because of limited sources of wood, Mezhirich dwellers burned mammoth bones in hearths located both inside and outside the huts. Pits dug into permafrost outside the dwellings served as virtual freezers for food storage (see Figure 9.4). Stone and bone work and cooking activities took place inside the dwellings. A bone needle found in one hut shows that people were sewing—probably making clothes. Excavators recovered the remains of 49 mammoths at Mezhirich; some may have been actively hunted, but different weathering patterns indicate that people also collected bones from mammoth carcasses in the landscape (Bosinski 1990). Other animals such as arctic foxes and wolves were hunted too, but possibly for their warm pelts rather than their meat. Mammoth bones decorated in red ochre, jewelry of ivory, shell, and animal teeth, and bone, ivory, and amber figurines found at Mezhirich and other similar sites testify to the use of symbolism by groups living on the east European steppe.

Mammoth-bone dwellings clearly took planning and cooperation to build and probably were home to large groups for up to nine months of the year. At other times

*Figure 9.4*

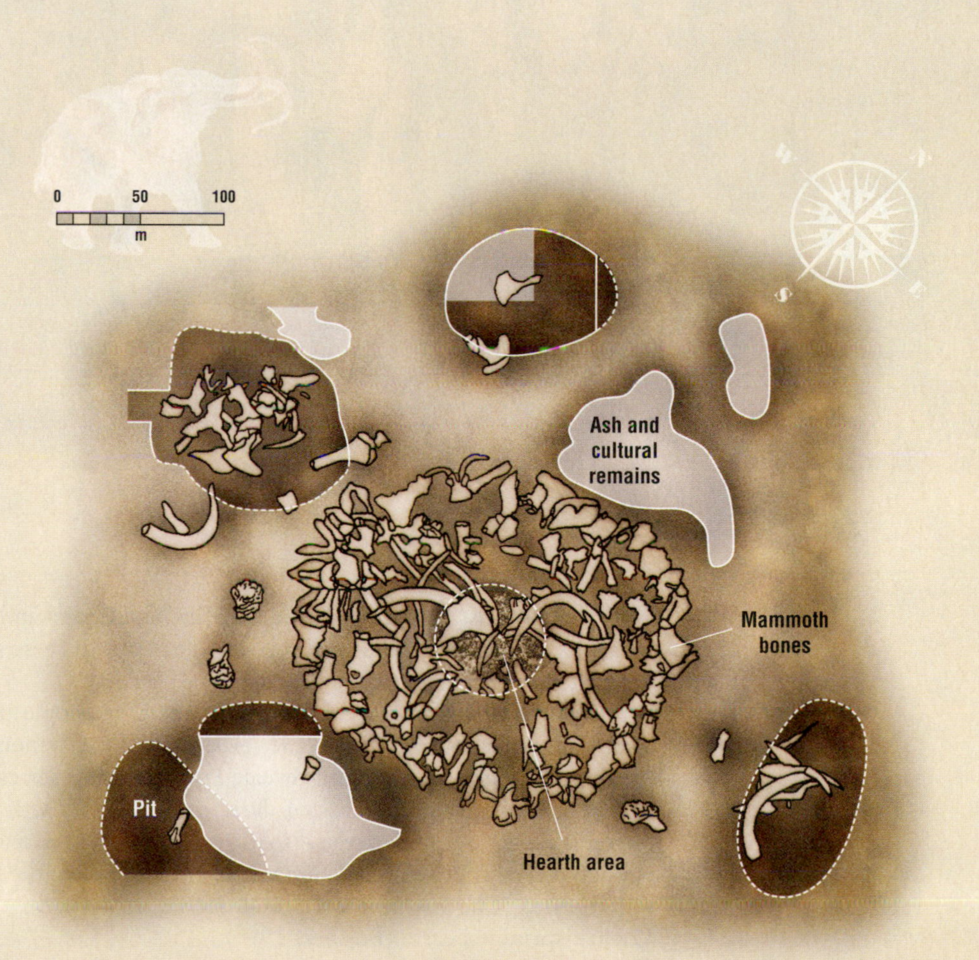

**PLAN OF ONE OF THE MAMMOTH-BONE STRUCTURES AT MEZHIRICH.** What can you say about the use of space in and around this dwelling?

*Source:* Adapted from Soffer, O., et al. 1997. Cultural stratigraphy at Mezhirich, an Upper Palaeolithic site in Ukraine with multiple occupations. *Antiquity* 71:48–62.

**Excavation of an Upper Paleolithic mammoth-bone dwelling at Mezhirich, Ukraine. What can this structure tell us about the people who lived at Mezhirich?**

the groups must have moved around. Flint, shells, and amber from sources as far as 800 km (500 miles) away have been recovered at some of these sites, indicating long-distance contacts or exchange.

It is evident from elsewhere in Europe that people used easily found materials to construct dwellings. For example, excavations at Gönnersdorf, a site on the Rhine in Germany that is 12.6 kyr old, revealed evidence of a series of huts—circular patterns of postholes and round patches of dark, organic-rich earth surrounding a larger central area. The excavators suggested that the huts would have consisted of circles of wooden posts, probably covered by horsehides, as horses were the most common animal species at the site. The hut builders paved the floors by laying large slabs of local stone on ochre-sprinkled earth (Bosinski 1990).

## Symbolism: Burial and Art

From about 35 kyr ago, there is ample evidence for a range of artistic representation, personal decoration, and ritual. There is some indication of such behaviors in the Middle Paleolithic/MSA, but claims for an explosion of creative and symbolic behaviors in the Upper Paleolithic/LSA are well founded. This subsection looks at burial and art; the next will consider religious or magical rituals.

## Burials

Beginning about 30 kyr ago, intentional burials occurred with much greater frequency than in previous periods, although they do not represent all members of society. Upper Paleolithic burials of modern humans are found throughout the Old World. They are primarily inhumations (burial in the ground), but at **Lake Mungo**, Australia, researchers uncovered a cremation dating to 40 kyr ago (Bowler et al. 2003). In Europe burials often followed similar rituals: slightly flexed bodies; presence of ochre; the dead dressed in clothes decorated with ivory beads, pierced animal teeth, and shells. Grave goods included spears; knives; other ivory, antler, bone, or flint tools; and sometimes figurines. A grave might hold a single individual or a small group of two or more. Some of the burials were deliberately covered by rocks, soil, or tree branches. Communities invested a considerable amount of time and effort in burials, particularly those that were rich in grave goods. For example, it could take up to 45 minutes to produce a single pierced ivory bead, and it must have been equally time-consuming to pierce an animal tooth (Bahn and Vertut 1988). Such finds in graves range from a few to thousands.

The largest number of burials for the Upper Paleolithic has been found at Dolní Vestonice in the Czech Republic, where investigators have recovered at least 35, dating from 30 to 25 kyr ago. A triple burial of a young woman buried between two young men is particularly interesting. The three bodies had been buried at the same time. As shown in Figure 9.5, the corpses had been placed in extended positions and the skulls and surrounding soil sprinkled with ochre. Pierced arctic fox and wolf teeth and small beads of mammoth ivory found on the male skulls perhaps were the remains of elaborate hats. The grave had been covered with wood; then the wood had been set on fire but extinguished before it had burned completely. Soil had then been scattered over the grave (Klima 1988; Svoboda et al. 1996). Studies of the teeth, jaws, and crania show many similarities among the three bodies, so they may have been related (Alt et al. 1997).

At Sungir, 200 km (125 miles) northeast of Moscow, excavators unearthed at least six burials dating to about 22 kyr ago. Two were exceptionally rich: a single grave of a man and a double grave of two children (a boy and girl), who were laid head to head and flanked by carefully carved ivory spears more than 2.4 m (8 feet) long. The graves had been dug into the permafrost, the bodies placed on their backs with their arms crossed and then covered with ochre. The excavators recovered almost 15,000 mammoth ivory beads from the two graves, along with pierced animal teeth, ivory bracelets and rings, and a variety of bone, ivory, and flint tools (Bosinski 1990).

Many graves are simpler than these rich burials, however. And researchers have found few graves in the Middle East or South Africa for this period. One hypothesis is that the simplicity of burial practices in the Middle East may have been due to small group size and a highly mobile lifestyle, particularly between 22 and 13 kyr ago (Gilead 1995).

The extent and nature of burial practices and the deposition of grave goods in the Upper Paleolithic suggest respect for, and perhaps the status of, the individuals buried and possibly a belief in an afterlife. Whether they also indicate feelings of grief and perhaps a sense of loss remains enigmatic.

## Creative Imagery/Art

The magnificence of human artistic creativity in the Upper Paleolithic period is renowned. Indeed, scholars often speak of a "creative explosion" when describing the brilliant artistic traditions that emerged after about 35 kyr ago. People exploited a variety of techniques and materials: Carving, engraving, modeling, and painting on stone, bone, antler, ivory, and clay as well as on rock walls, such as on the walls of **Chauvet Cave** in

**Lake Mungo**
Upper Paleolithic site in southeastern Australia where a cremation was found that dates to 40 kyr ago.

**Chauvet Cave**
The earliest Upper Paleolithic painted cave site in France.

*Figure 9.5*

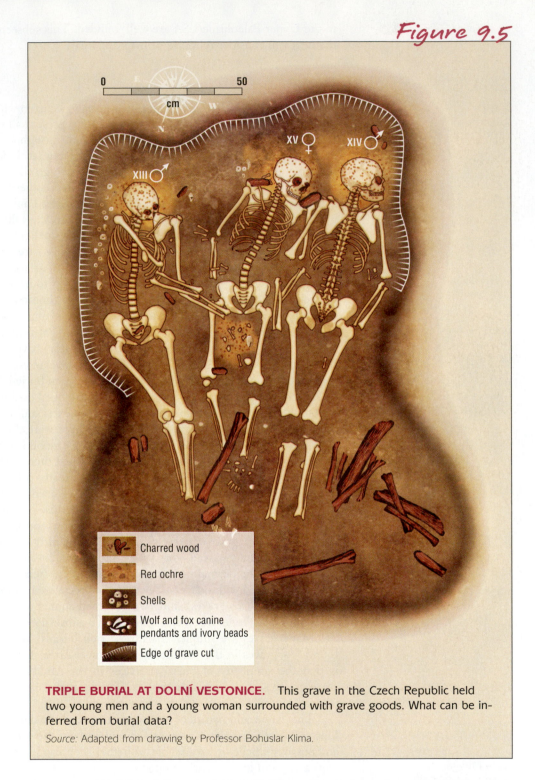

| | |
|---|---|
| | Charred wood |
| | Red ochre |
| | Shells |
| | Wolf and fox canine pendants and ivory beads |
| | Edge of grave cut |

**TRIPLE BURIAL AT DOLNÍ VESTONICE.** This grave in the Czech Republic held two young men and a young woman surrounded with grave goods. What can be inferred from burial data?

*Source:* Adapted from drawing by Professor Bohuslar Klima.

France (see Highlight 9.3, on pp. 264–265). The evidence shows the range of skills people employed to create artistic images as well as their ability to present complex symbolic messages in many different forms and media (Mellars 1994).

## Religion and Magic

Paleoanthropologists will never know for certain what ideological belief systems underpinned Upper Paleolithic groups living in Eurasia. However, they can make reasonable hypotheses and test them against the symbolic evidence. Evidence from both **mobiliary art** (portable items) and **parietal art** (cave or rock paintings) suggests concern with animals, particularly those that were food sources (Rice and Paterson 1985, 1986). In an attempt to flesh out this relationship, some scholars point to modern hunter-gatherer groups that perform rituals to promote hunting success. Could similar rituals have been performed at some prehistoric sites—where, in addition to portraying animals, people stuffed fragments of bone, antler, animal teeth, shells, and flint chips into cracks in cave walls (Clottes 1999)? It is tempting to interpret the few images of part human/part animal beings as representing shamans who conducted ritual ceremonies, and to hypothesize that the presumed movement of the animals painted on cave walls in the flickering Paleolithic lamplight was the focus of those ceremonies. Noting that shamans of modern hunter-gatherer groups often fall into trance states and experience visions, David Lewis-Williams (1997, 2002) proposes that cave wall paintings depict similar visions and that Upper Paleolithic shamans mediated between the world in which people lived and the spirit world that lay behind cave walls. Shamans may well have played a pivotal role in most aspects of Upper Paleolithic/LSA society, and their possession of ritual knowledge may have afforded them special status, as seen in burial practices (Soffer 1985). However, shamanism is not universal to hunter-gatherers today; so it cannot be cited as unequivocal evidence that such beliefs and practices existed in the past.

Belief in supernatural powers may also be reflected in mobiliary art. People may have carried pierced items or figurines as good-luck amulets; they may have considered Venus figurines to be fertility symbols and kept them to ensure survival and continuation of the group. Special treatment of the dead implies ceremony and may represent a measure of respect—and possibly an effort to help the deceased pass into ancestral realms of the afterlife.

## Upper Paleolithic/Late Stone Age Society

Upper Paleolithic/LSA people were well adapted to the environmental conditions of the last Ice Age. They fashioned tools to suit a diverse range of domestic, hunting, and artistic purposes. They showed a high degree of organization in cooperatively hunting and processing animals, constructing dwellings, and making extensive long-distance contacts. Differences in tool styles as well as in mobiliary and parietal art may have been symbolic of ethnic affiliation and kinship networks. Alliances between groups would have been essential for survival in Ice Age conditions and may have been cemented through long-distance exchange networks. Most cave art sites in Europe are in areas of great ecological diversity, an important survival factor during the coldest periods of the Ice Age. Researchers have suggested that groups may have aggregated occasionally at the largest cave art sites, perhaps to celebrate puberty rituals or initiation rites, to find partners, or to consolidate kinship ties (Mellars 1994)—mutual obligations that could provide help in times of stress.

Although scholars generally regard Paleolithic society as egalitarian, the rich burials and exotic items found at some sites may indicate differences in status and rank. For example, the burial of a young adult female, surrounded by large stone slabs, at Saint-Germaine-la-Rivière in France suggests an element of inequality within a group 15 kyr ago. Among the grave goods were 70 pierced red deer canines, primarily from young stags, many with incised decoration. The teeth originated from 66 animals but, as there were few red deer bones among the faunal remains at the site, may have taken years to collect and were likely exotic, valuable items (Vanhaeren and d'Errico 2005). Adults can acquire rank during life, but the child burials at Sungir (for example) suggest inherited rank, as the children were too young to have acquired the rank necessary to merit such rich grave goods. These two examples indicate that females and children, as well as males, may have had privileged positions in Upper Paleolithic society.

**mobiliary art**
Artwork that is portable, usually applied to Paleolithic and Stone Age art.

**parietal art**
Rock wall and cave paintings.

# Paleolithic Imagery in Eurasia

PALEOLITHIC IMAGERY CAN BE DIVIDED into two broad categories: mobiliary art (portable artworks) and parietal art (works on rock or cave walls). Mobiliary art has been found from South Africa to Siberia and from Europe to Australia. It has an unequal distribution in Eurasia, being particularly abundant in central and eastern Europe and rare in some other regions. In contrast, most of the parietal art in Eurasia consists of works on cave walls and rock faces in southern France and northern (Cantabrian) Spain. Although there are cave sites in central Europe, researchers have found no cave art there. Some French and Spanish sites are vast, multi-chambered caves covered with hundreds of images; in France the walls of Chauvet Cave hold more than 300 paintings and engravings either in isolation or in groups of 50, and Lascaux Cave has 600 paintings and about 1,500 engravings. Smaller sites have far fewer images.

Symbolic representation does not form a consistent part of human behavior until the Upper Paleolithic. The earliest mobiliary art in Eurasia dates to between 35 and 30 kyr ago; rock and cave art is younger, although Chauvet Cave may date to 32 kyr ago.

Scholars use both direct and indirect techniques to date artwork. Location, stratigraphy, and association with other artifacts help to date portable objects. Rock and cave art is more problematic; sometimes indirect dating on the basis of style is the only method available. It is sometimes possible to distinguish among superimpositions of figures to clarify different phases of work; at Altamira, Spain, researchers have identified five different phases, although only a few years may have separated each phase from the next. Pieces of cave wall that have fallen onto Paleolithic deposits are dated by their association with the deposits. Today's increasingly sophisticated methods allow specialists to date pigments used in painting; for example, at Chauvet pinprick-sized samples were dated by the AMS (ac- celerator mass spectrometer) version of $^{14}$C dating. However, problems of sample contamination continue to plague absolute dating techniques and raise questions as to the antiquity of sites such as Chauvet.

## MOBILIARY ART

Eurasian mobiliary art includes jewelry, engraved stone, bone, antler, and ivory. People of the Upper Paleolithic used teeth, shells, bone, and fossils perforated with stone drills as pendants or strung them together and sewed them on clothing. Deliberate choice of material is evident; selected shell species have been found hundreds of kilometers from their original source. For example, seashells at Mezin, Ukraine, came from 600–800 km (375–500 miles) away. There also is evidence of manufacturing processes; for example, at the Paviland Cave bead workshop in Wales, investigators found pieces of ivory and ivory rods from which beads were made, along with a mammoth skull and tusks.

Using stone tools, specialists carved intricate figurines out of bone, antler, and ivory. They also made carvings on spear throwers, often depicting animals in flight or licking their flanks. And they molded clay: Fragments of more than 700 baked clay figurines at Dolní Vestonice and Pavlov, Czech Republic, date to 28 to 24 kyr ago—the earliest ceramics in the world. The figurines may have been deliberately fired at low temperatures so as to explode during firing.

Female Venus figurines have been found throughout Eurasia. Many have exaggerated features, particularly buttocks, bellies, and breasts, and less clearly defined arms, legs, and faces. Others are much more stylized, uncannily modern in line. Hairstyles are sometimes clearly visible; other marks suggest traces of clothing and/or tattoos. Researchers originally believed that Venus figurines were symbols of fertility (hence the name). Subsequent study found that the figurines represented females in many age groups, not simply childbearing women. Some experts have argued that female figurines emphasize the importance of women within Paleolithic society, perhaps as the main food providers, as symbols of fertility, or both.

## PARIETAL ART

European parietal art primarily features images of animals that were important to the Upper Paleolithic economy: horses, bison, aurochs (wild cattle), red deer, ibex, mammoths, and reindeer. More dangerous animals such as lions, bears, wolves, and hyena appear less often. Images of fish, insects, and reptiles are even rarer. About 5 percent of images represent humans, occasionally depicted as part human, part animal. Handprints (stencils), dots, zigzag lines, geometric signs, and other lines form part of the artistic repertoire—but the artists never painted Ice Age landscapes. People left their mark on cave floors too, in the form of footprints, but perhaps less deliberately than on walls.

Techniques of parietal art in Europe included painting, engraving, and sculpting. Artists often incorporated bulges and curves in the rock face into the imagery; for example, as the belly or hump of an animal. Formerly scholars believed that most European cave artists worked deep inside caves. However, we now know that rock faces at and close to cave or rock shelter entrances were equally important, though many works in such locations may have been destroyed by weathering. For example, investigators have discovered a wealth of rock engravings, some of which appear to be Paleolithic, in the Coa Valley in Portugal. Nevertheless, much surviving art is deep within caves. These areas were often difficult and dangerous to access. Furthermore, people would have painted and viewed the images by the flickering light of stone lamps, which would have created an illusion of animal movement.

The paintings are not the opportunistic results of artistic dabbling for fun. Theorists have proposed several interpretations, primarily based on ethnographic observations of hunter-gatherer groups, to explain Upper Paleolithic imagery. Given the importance of hunting, the paintings may have served as hunting magic or as aids to teach the young about hunting. Given the importance of group solidarity in harsh environments, artworks may be totemic symbols of ethnic groups. Alternatively, paintings may represent the mental images seen by shamans in contact with the spirit world through trance. A structuralist approach sees Paleolithic imagery as representing binary oppositions intrinsic in societies—oppositions such as male versus female, dark versus light, danger versus safety. The true meaning of Paleolithic imagery may incorporate all, some, or none of these interpretations and other proposals that undoubtedly will emerge. It will always remain enigmatic.

Sources: Bahn, P., and J. Vertut. 1988. *Images of the Ice Age*. Leicester, UK: Winward. Clottes, J. 1999. Twenty thousand years of Paleolithic cave art in southern France. *Proceedings of the British Academy* 99:161–175. Lewis-Williams, J. D. 1991. Wrestling with analogy: A methodological dilemma in Upper Paleolithic art research. *Proceedings of the Prehistoric Society* 57 (part 1): 149–162. Mellars, P. A. 1996. *The Neanderthal legacy: An archaeological perspective from western Europe*. Princeton, NJ: Princeton University Press. Pettitt, P., and P. Bahn. 2003. Current problems in dating Palaeolithic cave art: Candamo and Chauvet. *Antiquity* 77 (295): 134–141. Rice, P. 1981. Prehistoric Venuses: Symbols of motherhood or womanhood? *Journal of Anthropological Research* 37 (4): 402–404. Soffer, O., P. Vandiver, B. Klíma, and J. Svoboda. 1993. The pyrotechnology of performance art: Moravian Venuses and wolverines. In *Before Lascaux: The complex record of the Upper Paleolithic*, eds. H. Knecht, A. Pike-Tay, and R. White, 259–275. Boca Raton, FL: CRC Press.

Painted panel in Chauvet Cave, France. Can Upper Paleolithic painting be described as "art for art's sake"?

turn back to your reading

This chapter covers the emergence of culture from 2.6 myr to 11.5 kyr ago, a period in which all hominids from australopithecines to modern humans played a part. (The physical aspects of hominids are covered in Chapter 6 and 7.) At times more than one species inhabited the landscape concurrently, but by 26 kyr ago only one species remained: modern humans.

■ A series of glacial and interglacial cycles began about 2.3 myr ago and caused changes in temperature, landscape, environment, and animal and plant resources. Climatic change was sometimes gradual and other times rapid. Humans adapted and developed under these conditions.

■ The earliest cultural sites, found in the Rift Valley of East Africa, are between 2.6 and 1.9 myr old. They are associated with *Homo habilis* and australopithecines. Hominids lived by collecting plant foods and generally scavenging for meat. However, the patterning of stone tools and bones found at many sites is not always the result of hominid activity but may have been affected by other animals and natural forces.

**page 240**

■ *Homo erectus* populations arose in Africa, but groups moved northward into Eurasia and the Middle East; there they adapted to different, often much colder, environments. They could control fire and acquired meat by hunting and scavenging. The stone tool technology of *H. erectus* groups shows their ability to conceive and produce particular shapes, and hand axes are the hallmark of their stone traditions. There is no clear evidence for structures, burials, or symbolic expression in this period (1.8 myr to about 250 kyr ago).

■ The hominids of the Middle Paleolithic/Middle Stone Age (MSA), from about 250 to 30 kyr ago, were Neandertals and archaic *Homo sapiens* in Eurasia and anatomically modern humans (AMH) in Africa. These groups lived in a range of environments in caves, rock shelters, and open-air sites. Anatomically modern humans were well established in Australia by 40 kyr ago, having reached Australian shores by boat many millennia earlier.

■ Eurasian Middle Paleolithic stone tool assemblages consist predominantly of flake tools, characterized in many areas by Levallois, or prepared core, technology. There are few bone tools. Groups hunted animals, sometimes targeting particular species, but also scavenged carcasses. They gathered plant foods and collected shellfish. There is little evidence for structures or for the organization of living areas at Middle Paleolithic/MSA sites.

**page 249**

■ Use of symbolism may have first begun in the Middle Paleolithic/MSA. Deliberate burial of the dead begins to occur, although it is not common; there is no convincing evidence for grave goods. Ochre is present at many sites, though never as painting on walls. A few incised stones, bones, blocks of ochre, and perforated pendants have been recovered.

■ The Upper Paleolithic/Late Stone Age (LSA), 40 kyr to 11.5 kyr ago (or later in Africa), coincides with the latter part of the last Ice Age. By about 11.5 kyr ago, anatomically modern humans had colonized all areas of the globe except the Arctic, remote Pacific islands, and Antarctica.

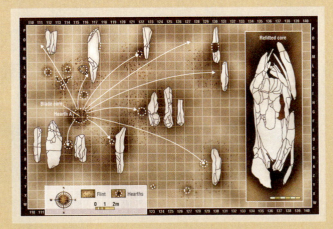

**page 254**

■ Upper Paleolithic/LSA tool kits included many different stone, bone, and antler tools manufactured primarily to meet specific needs. Stone technology in many areas emphasized the production of blades from which a range of other tools could be made. Groups generally targeted particular species of animals and often set up camps along animal migration routes. They also exploited coastal and riverine resources. And they consumed plant foods, processing some of these to remove toxins through washing and grinding on stone mortars.

■ Evidence of structures (such as mammoth-bone dwellings) with interior and exterior hearths and storage facilities indicate periods of reduced mobility.

■ Symbolism played an important role in Upper Paleolithic/LSA society. Burials, personal ornaments, and cave wall and rock art suggest a sense of personal and group identity. Symbolism may have played a role in the maintenance of extended kinship networks.

## KEY WORDS

Acheulian, 241
Aurignacian, 251
Atapuerca sites, 241
Beringia, 233
blades, 253
Blombos Cave, 249
Chatelperronian, 254
Chauvet Cave, 261
cores, 235
Dmanisi, 240
flakes, 235
flake tools, 241
Gona, 235

Gravettian, 254
hand axe, 241
Lake Mungo, 261
Late Stone Age (LSA), 251
Levallois technique (prepared core technique), 246
Magdalenian, 254
Mezhirich, 258
microliths, 253
Middle Paleolithic, 245
Middle Stone Age (MSA), 245
mobiliary art, 263
Mode 2 technology, 241

Mode 3 technology, 246
Oldowan technology (Mode 1 technology), 236
Old Stone Age, 247
Olduvai Gorge, 236
Paleolithic, 235
parietal art, 263
Pleistocene, 235
Solutrean, 254
Stone Age, 235
symbolism, 249
taphonomy, 237
Upper Paleolithic, 251

## SUGGESTED READING

Bahn, P., and J. Vertut. *Journey through the Ice Age*. London: Orion, 1997. This well-illustrated survey of European Paleolithic cave and portable artworks addresses past and present explanations of the art. Written in easy-to-read yet informative style.

Deacon, H. J., and J. Deacon. *Human Beginnings in South Africa*. Walnut Creek, CA: Altamira Press, 1999. With long experience in the Stone Age archaeology of South Africa, the authors have produced a valuable account of the period from the earliest hominids to the introduction of domestic animals. They include a discussion on present-day hunter-gatherer groups and their links with people of the LSA.

Klein, R. *The Human Career: Human Biological and Cultural Origins*. 2nd ed. Chicago: University of Chicago Press, 1999. Klein covers biological evolution and culture change in some detail and sets these developments within a geological and environmental context. The archaeology includes many geographically wide-ranging case studies demonstrating similarities and differences in behavioral adaptation around the globe. Klein provides explanations of competing interpretations of the data.

Mulvaney, J., and J. Kamminga. *Prehistory of Australia*. Washington, DC: Smithsonian Institution, 1995. Australia is a continent of varied environments and resources that its aboriginal inhabitants successfully exploited for millennia. Dramatic discoveries and new dating techniques have given a greater time depth to Australian prehistory. The authors' account ranges from the earliest arrival, more than 40 kyr ago, to European contact in the seventeenth century and later.

Scarre, C. (Ed.). *The Human Past: World Prehistory and the Development of Human Societies*. New York: Thames and Hudson, 2005. This book provides a highly informed and well balanced summary of world prehistory. Each chapter, written by a specialist, covers a general time period and region. An excellent supplement for students who wish to know more about a particular period.

Schick, K., and N. Toth. *Making Silent Stones Speak*. London: Weidenfeld & Nicolson, 1993. This book focuses on the Early Stone Age in Africa, where the two authors undertook much of their original research. It covers primarily the problems of understanding very early hominid evolution and the range of approaches researchers adopt to interpret evidence from sites.

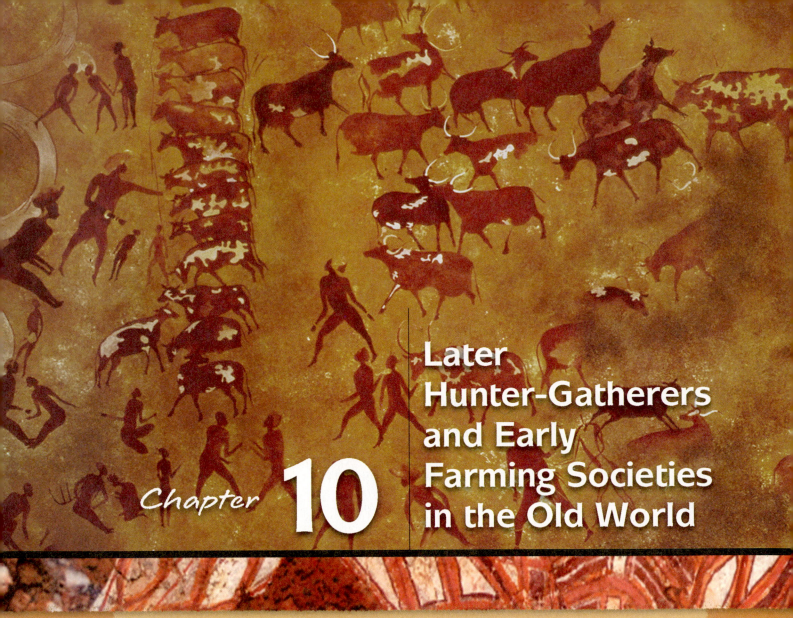

# Later Hunter-Gatherers and Early Farming Societies in the Old World

## Chapter 10

■ **THE CHANGING CLIMATE OF THE LATE GLACIAL AND EARLY HOLOCENE**

■ **HUNTER-GATHERERS OF THE LATE GLACIAL AND EARLY HOLOCENE**

■ **SUBSISTENCE PRACTICES OF LATE GLACIAL AND EARLY HOLOCENE GROUPS**
How Did People Choose from Available Food Resources? • Animal and Fish Resources in the Natufian of the Middle East (14.5 to 11.5 kyr Ago) • Animal and Fish Resources in the Japanese Jomon (12.7 to 2.4 kyr Ago) • Animal and Fish Resources in the Scandinavian Mesolithic (10 to 6 kyr Ago) • Plant Resources and Later Hunter-Gatherer Groups • Later Hunter-Gatherer Technology • Pottery • Habitation and Use of Space • Symbolic Activities: Burials and Representational Imagery • Social Organization

■ **THE EMERGENCE OF FARMING IN OLD WORLD NEOLITHIC SOCIETIES**
Modeling the Causes of Farming • Evidence for Plant and Animal Domestication • Material Culture of Farming Groups

■ **HIGHLIGHT 10.1:** *Pottery and Archaeology*

■ **FARMING IN THE MIDDLE EAST**
Houses at Jericho and Ain Ghazal • Ritual among Farming Communities in the Middle East • Long-Distance Contact

■ **AGRICULTURE IN EUROPE**
The LBK Phenomenon of Central Europe • Farming in Southern Scandinavia

■ **HIGHLIGHT 10.2:** *Genes, Languages, and Farmers*

■ **FARMING IN CHINA**

■ **PASTORALISM AND CULTIVATION IN AFRICA**
Nabta Playa • Sorghum, Millet, and African Rice

■ **SOCIAL COMPLEXITY AMONG FARMING COMMUNITIES**
Çatalhöyük: A Farming Village in Anatolia • Megalithic Monuments in Britain

▲

**Photo above:** A 5,000- to 6,000-year-old cave painting of cattle pastoralists at Tassili n'Ajjer, Algeria

**SITES MENTIONED IN THE CHAPTER**

Map legend:

1. Peiligang
2. Bashidang
3. Pengtoushan
4. Shangshan
5. Hemudu
6. Laoguantai
7. Mawaki
8. Ikawazu
9. Sweet Track
10. Stonehenge
11. Grimes Graves
12. South Street
13. Windmill Hill
14. Flomborn
15. Schwetzingen
16. Talheim
17. Ringkloster
18. Skateholm
19. Nabta Playa
20. Tassili
21. Jenné-jeno
22. Catalhöyük
23. Abu Hureyra
24. Ain Mallaha
25. el Wad
26. Ain Ghazal
27. Jericho

| Years ago | Temperature | Middle East | Southeast Europe | Central Europe | Northwest Europe | China | Japan | Southeast Asia | Africa |
|---|---|---|---|---|---|---|---|---|---|
| 2,200 | Warming | State societies | State societies | Urbanization | Neolithic | State societies | Neolithic Farming | Neolithic | State societies |
| 3,000 | | | | | | | | | |
| 4,000 | | | | Neolithic | | | | | Neolithic Pastoralism |
| 5,000 | | | Neolithic | | | | | | |
| 6,000 | | | | | | Neolithic | | | |
| 7,000 | | Neolithic | | Mesolithic | | | Jomon | | |
| 8,000 | | | Mesolithic | | Mesolithic | | | | |
| 9,000 | | | | | | | | | |
| 10,000 | | | | | | | | Paleolithic Hoabinian | |
| 11,000 | | | | | | | | | |
| 12,000 | Younger Dryas, Cold | Natufian | | | | | | | |
| 13,000 | | | | | | | | | |
| 14,000 | Warming Moist | | Paleolithic | Paleolithic | Paleolithic | Paleolithic | | | Late Stone Age |
| 15,000 | | | | | | | Paleolithic | | |
| 16,000 | Older Dryas, Cold | Epipaleolithic | | | | | | | |
| 17,000 | | | | | | | | | |
| 18,000 | | | | | | | | | |
| | Last Glacial Maximum | | | | | | | | |

**CULTURAL SEQUENCE DISCUSSED IN THE CHAPTER**

**Younger Dryas**
Period between 12,900 and 11,500 years ago during which the warming trend at the end of the Ice Age was reversed and a substantial drop in temperatures caused changes in environmental conditions, to which humans had to adapt.

**interglacial period**
A period between glacial periods, or ice ages, when temperatures rise and the extent of ice sheets decreases.

**Holocene**
The present interglacial period, which began 11,500 years ago.

The glacial advance of the last Ice Age reached its peak between about 25,000 and 18,000 years ago. Thereafter temperatures began to rise, slowly at first, then rapidly, with an increase in rainfall between 15,000 and 13,500 years ago—only to plunge once more about 12,900 years ago. The world was gripped by a cold period, termed the **Younger Dryas**, that prompted renewed advances of ice sheets and a further 1,300 years of frigid temperatures. About 11,500 years ago warmer and wetter conditions returned, heralding the present **interglacial period**, the **Holocene** (Bar-Yosef 2002; Roberts 1998). Rising temperatures caused dramatic changes in the global environment and topography, although the timing of the changes varied worldwide. Late glacial and early Holocene hunter-gatherers exploited the new conditions remarkably well; so well, in fact, that many groups eventually changed their way of life: They became settled farmers (see Figure 10.1).

# The Changing Climate of the Late Glacial and Early Holocene

As ice sheets began to melt, sea levels rose, drowning large areas of former coastlines and severing links between many landmasses. For example, Britain was separated from continental Europe by about 8,000 years ago, and Alaska from Siberia by about 7,000 years ago. The rise in sea level was not a smooth process; instead, the seas advanced to much higher levels and retreated to lower levels than today before stabilizing at current levels. The increase in water volume reduced coastlines and also flooded former river valleys, causing the formation of numerous inland lakes.

Although coastal land was lost to rising sea levels, land formerly covered by glaciers was exposed. The weight of glaciers, which often were more than 1.6 km (1 mile) thick, had been so great in some areas—parts of Scandinavia and Scotland, for example—that it had depressed the land surface beneath it, a consequence balanced by a rise in land in other areas. Glacial melting reversed the balance, but to such an extent in southern Scandinavia that land formerly dry is now submerged, and archeological sites on that land are now below sea level.

Environmental change succeeded climatic change (see Figure 10.2). Steppe tundra landscapes and open grasslands diminished, to be replaced by initially open, but later dense forests of more temperate species. In Eurasia large, cold-loving animals moved north (for example, bison, reindeer, and horse). Many eventually became extinct (for example, woolly mammoth and woolly rhinoceros) and were replaced by smaller woodland species (for example, red and roe deer, ibex, and aurochs). In South Africa small browsing animals replaced large grassland herbivores, which moved inland from the coast. Seas and inland lakes abounded in marine and freshwater resources for human consumption (sea mammals, fish, waterfowl, and mollusks). In places as widely separated as Japan, South Africa, and northwest Europe, large **shell middens** formed, indicating intensive exploitation of shellfish. Changes in vegetation resulted

**shell middens**
Mounds formed through the accumulation of shells (mainly of mollusks), indicating intensive exploitation of shellfish.

*Figure 10.1*

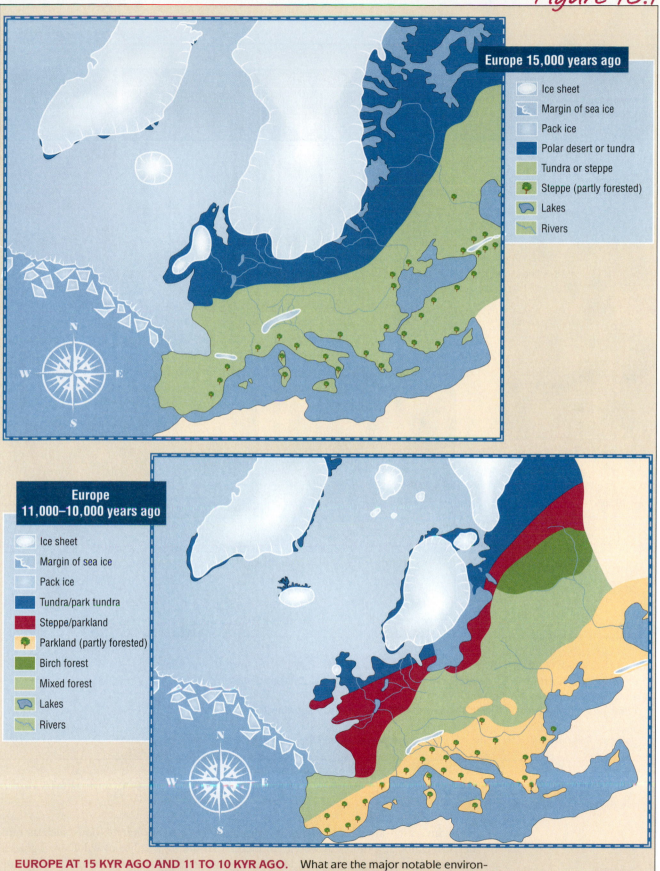

**Europe 15,000 years ago**

- Ice sheet
- Margin of sea ice
- Pack ice
- Polar desert or tundra
- Tundra or steppe
- Steppe (partly forested)
- Lakes
- Rivers

**Europe 11,000–10,000 years ago**

- Ice sheet
- Margin of sea ice
- Pack ice
- Tundra/park tundra
- Steppe/parkland
- Parkland (partly forested)
- Birch forest
- Mixed forest
- Lakes
- Rivers

**EUROPE AT 15 KYR AGO AND 11 TO 10 KYR AGO.** What are the major notable environmental changes shown on these maps, and what effects might these changes have on human groups?

*Source:* Adapted from Andersen, B. G., and H. W. Borns Jr. 1994. *The Ice Age world.* New York: Oxford University Press.

*Figure 10.2*

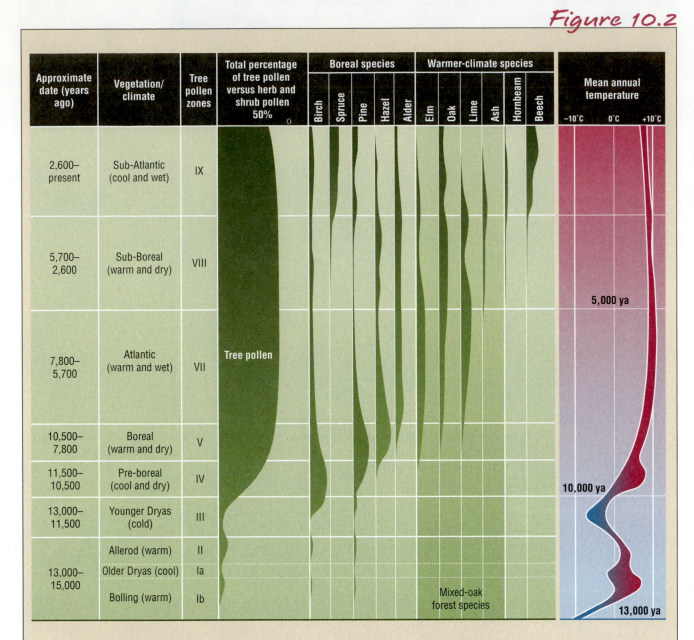

**POLLEN AND TEMPERATURE CHANGES IN SOUTHERN SCANDINAVIA.** Shown here are southern Scandinavian vegetation and inferred climate at different periods from 15,000 years ago to the present. Which tree species are the earliest Holocene colonizers? What patterns emerge between the pollen and temperature diagrams?

*Source*: Adapted from Andersen, B. G., and H. W. Borns Jr. 1994. *The Ice Age world*. New York: Oxford University Press. Reprinted by permission of Universitetsforlaget (Scandinavian University Press), Oslo.

in an increased abundance and wider distribution of edible plant foods such as nuts, berries, fruits, and tubers as well as an increase in the availability of wild cereal grasses, particularly in parts of the Middle East (present-day Lebanon, Israel, Jordan, and Syria) and parts of Africa.

**Natufian**
The period from the final stages of the last Ice Age, when people lived by hunting and gathering, to the beginning of settled farming in the Middle East; the same period is called the Mesolithic in Europe, the Hoabinian in Southeast Asia, the Jomon in Japan, and the Archaic in the Americas and is part of the Late Stone Age in sub-Saharan Africa.

**Mesolithic**
The period from the final stages of the last Ice Age, when people lived by hunting and gathering, to the beginning of settled farming in Europe.

**Hoabinian**
The period from the final stages of the last Ice Age, when people lived by hunting and gathering, to the beginning of settled farming in Southeast Asia.

**Jomon**
The period from the final stages of the last Ice Age, when people lived by hunting and gathering, to the beginning of settled farming in Japan.

**Archaic**
The period from the final stages of the last Ice Age, when people lived by hunting and gathering, to the beginning of settled farming in the Americas.

**Late Stone Age (LSA)**
The later part of the Stone Age in sub-Saharan Africa, from about 22 kyr to 2,000 years ago, characterized by the dominance of hunter-gatherers.

**Neolithic**
The New Stone Age, the period characterized by the emergence of farming cultures.

# Hunter-Gatherers of the Late Glacial and Early Holocene

In archaeological terms, the early Holocene—the period from the final stages of the last Ice Age to the beginning of settled farming—is known as the **Natufian** in the Middle East, the **Mesolithic** in Europe, the **Hoabinian** in mainland Southeast Asia, the **Jomon** in Japan, the **Archaic** in the Americas, and is part of the **Late Stone Age (LSA)** in sub-Saharan Africa. The late glacial and early Holocene world was inhabited by mobile hunters, fishers, and gatherers. These human groups developed successful adaptive strategies to exploit the wide range of dietary resources available to them. With such a broad-spectrum diet (Flannery 1969), many groups became increasingly sedentary, and social organization became more complex, culminating in some areas in the eventual adoption of farming that heralded the **Neolithic** period. The transition to the Neolithic was not a synchronous worldwide event, however; it occurred from about 11,000 to 9,500 years ago in the Middle East, possibly 9,000 years ago in China, 6,000 years ago in northwest Europe, 4,000 years ago in Africa, about 2,300 years ago in Japan, and between 6,000 and 4,000 years ago in the Americas or perhaps even earlier (Imamura 1996; Piperno and Stothert 2003; Smith 1995).

There is no modern equivalent of the late glacial/early Holocene environment or of the people who inhabited it. The few hunter-gatherer groups in existence today follow diverse lifestyles but in environments that are currently of little interest to the wider world. Although these populations have become marginalized, they do not live in isolation; they are in contact with settled societies and experience the effects of global politics and a global economy. For this and other reasons, anthropologists cannot directly relate ethnographic knowledge to the archaeological record of the past. Nevertheless, they can set up and test archaeological models based on observations of modern hunter-gatherer behavior (Bettinger 2001; Kelly 1995). Several models suggest a dichotomy between two broad types of hunter-gatherer subsistence systems based on differences in degrees of group mobility or sedentism, methods of food collection and storage, and pressure on resources. Such differences, in turn, affect group demography, social organization, technology, and ideology. Well-known models of this dichotomy include Lewis Binford's (1980) "foragers/collectors" and James Woodburn's (1980) "immediate/delayed returns," as shown in Table 10.1. These models reveal how variation in social complexity can be detected through material remains, and they are therefore potentially useful when studying past hunter-gatherer societies (Keeley 1991).

# Subsistence Practices of Late Glacial and Early Holocene Groups

In this section we consider late glacial and early Holocene hunting, fishing, and gathering practices in different geographic areas; then we look at technological, cultural, and social developments among hunter-gatherer peoples of the period.

## How Did People Choose from Available Food Resources?

Food remains recovered from archaeological sites reflect those resources that people chose to exploit from a range of possible alternatives in the surrounding landscape. Archeologists use theoretical models to help them understand why hunter-gatherers

## Table 10.1

### Models of Hunter-Gatherer Systems and Archaeological Correlates

Material remains seem to substantiate theoretical models of different hunter-gatherer societies. What potential problems might be associated with these archaeological correlates?

| Foragers/Immediate Return Systems | Archaeological Correlates |
|---|---|
| Food consumed shortly after collection; no storage technology needed | Low archaeological visibility<br>Animal bones with cut marks and deliberate breakage marks |
| Tools easily replaceable, rapidly (but skillfully) made, and portable. No pottery. | Scatters of tools across landscape |
| Seasonal food pattern strategies exploiting resources<br>Highly mobile<br>Group size varies; large and small campsites | Predominantly small-scale sites around the landscape with scatters of stone tools and/or animal bones, hearths; no signs of permanent structures |
| Egalitarian | Few differences in burials and grave goods |
| **Collectors/Delayed Return Systems** | **Archaeological Correlates** |
| Food procurement logistically organized<br>Time invested in tool and food production<br>Food storage and processing equipment | Larger base camps with evidence of range of activities: food preparation, cooking, tool production and repair; composite tools, storage pits; also smaller hunting/special-purpose camps |
| Management of wild resources | Pollen diagrams indicating light-loving trees and shrubs |
| Possibly semi-sedentary | Evidence for structures, evidence for reoccupation of site, accumulation of waste |
| Non-egalitarian | Special burials for certain individuals |

*Sources*: Adapted from Binford (1980) and Woodburn (1980).

chose some food resources over others and to assess the efficiency of past foraging practices. **Optimal foraging theory** is one such model. It assumes that foragers target resources that give the greatest returns in energy (most calories) for the least amount of effort spent in obtaining them. You might think that people would automatically target those resources that are locally available and abundant. However, if these foods require extensive processing before they can be eaten (as, for example, small seeded grasses do), they may be less cost-effective than others that are more easily processed and provide similar energy returns, but take longer to walk to because they are further away. By considering the available resources, archeologists predict which foods were desirable.

Ethnographic studies show that predictions based on optimal foraging theory may work in certain cases but not in others. Many factors may affect the choice of foods, including available technology, season, ritual (for example, food taboos), trade, gender, or just momentary whim (Kelly 1995; Shennan 2002). However, models such as this one are useful as they force archaeologists to continually question their results and to look for alternative answers to their questions.

**optimal foraging theory**
Theoretical model used to assess the efficiency of foraging practices used by hunter-gatherers; it assumes that foragers target resources that give the greatest returns in energy (most calories) for the least amount of effort spent in obtaining them.

# Animal and Fish Resources in the Natufian of the Middle East (14.5 to 11.5 kyr Ago)

The western region of the Middle East, often called the Levant, consists of several ecotones, or transitional areas between different ecological communities. A narrow coastal plain gives way to two inland mountain ranges separated by the Rift Valley, which leads to an increasingly arid interior and eventual desert. The Mediterranean coastal zone is rich in resources that diminish with distance from the coast.

In the Natufian period (14,500 to 11,500 years ago) animal resources in the Levant included aurochs (wild cow), fallow and roe deer, wild boar, ibex (wild goat), and gazelle. The waters of the Levantine Mediterranean coast were poor fishing grounds, but inland lakes provided good sources of freshwater fish; this is evident from the thousands of fish vertebrae at Ain Mallaha, a site near ancient Lake Hula (Bar-Yosef 2002).

The importance of gazelle is particularly well documented at Abu Hureyra, near the Euphrates River in Syria. The occupation sequence at Abu Hureyra spans 4,500 years, from 12,000 to 7,500 years ago. During much of this period, groups hunted gazelle by driving them into specially constructed enclosures now called "desert kites" (because they look like kites from the air). Eighty percent of animal bones from the early levels at Abu Hureyra were gazelle; other hunted animals included wild sheep, wild cattle, fallow deer, onager (wild ass), hare, and fox. Zooarchaeologists have determined that the gazelle assemblage included animals of all ages, indicating the mass killing of whole herds. By comparing the ages of young gazelles with their known season of birth, researchers have found that hunting occurred in early summer, the time of gazelle migrations (Legge and Rowley-Conwy 2000). Gazelle hunting was so successful that it continued long after people had begun to cultivate their own cereals; later, however, it was abandoned, possibly because of depletion of gazelle herds. Similarly, onager, hare, and fox may have been overhunted early in the Abu Hureyra sequence, as suggested by their declining numbers in the bone assemblages.

## Animal and Fish Resources in the Japanese Jomon (12.7 to 2.4 kyr Ago)

Japan is a long (more than 3,000 km or 1,864 miles) and relatively narrow group of islands with a varied geography of inland mountains, valleys, alluvial plains, rivers, and an extensive indented coastline. There are substantial differences in altitude, between the interior mountains and the coast, and in temperature—Hokkaido in the north is subarctic and Okinawa in the south is subtropical (Takahashi et al. 1997).

Groups in the Japanese Jomon (12,700 to 2,400 years ago) exploited a wide range of land animals, particularly deer and wild boar, and marine mammals including dolphins, seals, and sharks. Riverine, coastal, and deep-sea fishing was important, and the kind of fish caught varied according to season and area and through time. Specialists can determine directly what foods people ate by analyzing carbon, nitrogen, and strontium isotopes in human bone and teeth (see Table 10.2 for a summary of these techniques). People in coastal Hokkaido depended primarily on marine resources; but those in more southerly coastal areas enjoyed a mixed diet of plants, meat, and marine resources (Minagawa and Akazawa 1992). Although there were fewer species of fish in northern Japan than in the south, salmon should have been present in great numbers between September and early December, as happens today. At present, the small number of salmon bones researchers have recovered from Jomon sites does not indicate extensive salmon exploitation; however, it is possible that the scarcity of bones is due to preservation bias or to the way Jomon groups processed fish (Matsui 1996). A wider range of species was available south of Hokkaido because of warmer waters and the migratory habits of species such as tuna and bonita (Habu 1996).

A partial excavation of the Mawaki site (dated to about 5,000 years ago) on the coast of the Japan Sea revealed 19 species of fish from coastal and deep-sea habitats. Mackerel, skipjack tuna, and sardines predominated, but there were bones from a few sharks, bluefin tuna, and marine mammals such as whale and dolphin. Dolphin fishing was a spring and summer activity; Jomon fishermen probably drove dolphins into nets and speared them. Nets rot, of course, but excavators recovered grooved stones that they interpreted as net weights. Mawaki groups probably used dolphin fat for food and fuel—and perhaps as insect repellent, as has been documented ethnographically. With bows and arrows, and possibly aided by dogs, they hunted deer, wild boar (mainly in fall and

## Table 10.2

### Tracking Dietary Patterns through Stable Isotope and Elemental Analyses

Elements such as carbon, hydrogen, nitrogen, oxygen, calcium, and strontium are present in living organisms. Elements can have different forms, depending on the number of neutrons in the nuclei of their atoms; these forms are called isotopes. Stable isotopes do not change over time. The food we eat leaves chemical signatures in our bodies. Stable isotope analyses, particularly of carbon, nitrogen, and strontium isotopes, can help identify these chemical signatures in bone collagen and teeth; strontium elemental analysis distinguishes between plant and meat intake. These analyses allow archaeologists to identify dietary patterns of the past.

| Carbon isotopes | Nitrogen isotopes | Strontium isotopes |
|---|---|---|
| During photosynthesis, plants absorb the carbon isotope $^{13}C$ from the atmosphere. The manner in which photosynthesis occurs varies among types of plants and affects the uptake of $^{13}C$. Depending on the amount of $^{13}C$ taken up, plants fall into three groups: C3, C4, and CAM. Most plant foods we eat fall into the C3 and C4 categories. C3 plants include trees, shrubs, temperate grasses, and tubers; C4 plants include tropical and savanna grasses, maize, sorghum, millet, and sugar cane. (Marine plants form a separate group, as the amount of $^{13}C$ they contain lies between the values for C3 and C4 plants.) CAM plants are succulents. The isotope content of plants passes along the food chain, fixing in the bone collagen and teeth of animals and humans. | Plants take up nitrogen from the soil and the air. In general, marine, lake, and river plants have higher amounts of the nitrogen isotope $^{15}N$ than terrestrial plants. As these values pass along the food chain, it is possible to distinguish between terrestrial- and marine-based diets. Additionally, terrestrial animals retain higher levels of $^{15}N$ than terrestrial plants, so it is possible to distinguish between a vegetarian diet and a meat-based diet. | Strontium intake occurs when bedrock nutrients pass through the soil and groundwater to plants and then up the food chain to humans. The strontium isotopic ratio in teeth occurs during tooth formation and remains stable throughout life, but in bones it changes every decade or two. Therefore, a difference between the strontium ratios of an individual's teeth and bones could reflect movement from one area to another. Strontium elemental analysis (of bone apatite) distinguishes among herbivores, carnivores, and omnivores: Herbivores retain more strontium than carnivores; omnivores lie somewhere between them. |

*Sources:* Adapted from Larsen (1997), Pearsall (2000), and Schoeninger (1995).

winter), wolves, and otters. However, animals were clearly of lesser importance in their diet than marine resources (Hiraguchi 1992).

## Animal and Fish Resources in the Scandinavian Mesolithic (10 to 6 kyr Ago)

Human occupation of both coastal and inland areas in Scandinavia occurred during the Mesolithic. Most large sites are located around coastlines or on inlets, estuaries, lakes, or rivers; others have been wonderfully preserved in inland bogs. Fluctuating sea levels have drowned some sites, and land uplift has left some sites many meters above present-day sea level.

Hunters of the Scandinavian Mesolithic (10,000 to 6,000 years ago) exploited a variety of large and small animals but targeted primarily red deer, roe deer, and wild pig. Arrowheads embedded in animal bones, together with remains of traps and pits, provide direct evidence of hunting techniques (Larsson 1990). Domesticated dogs, whose bones have been found on sites, may have aided hunting. Marine and freshwater resources also became an important part of people's diet. People occasionally caught porpoises, dolphins, seals, and whales to obtain blubber and oil as well as meat (Andersen 1995). They used traps, nets, and hooks and lines to catch a range of smaller fish, targeting in partic-

Nuts were a staple element of the diet of early Holocene hunter-gatherers everywhere. Why were they such an important food?

ular vast shoals of seasonally migratory species when those were available. Huge shell mounds along Scandinavian coastlines testify to intensive shellfish collecting; shellfish were probably a secondary dietary resource, but crucial at times of the year when other foods were limited. The few bird bones recovered from sites suggest that fowling, too, was a secondary food source.

## Plant Resources and Later Hunter-Gatherer Groups

In addition to rich animal resources, the peoples of the late glacial and early Holocene had access to equally rich plant resources: edible nuts, berries, tubers, grasses, and fruits. Protein-rich nuts were particularly important, as groups could store them for later consumption. Hazelnuts were available everywhere in northern Europe during the Mesolithic, complemented by acorns and chestnuts. Jomon sites in Japan present a similar scenario with an emphasis on chestnuts, walnuts, and acorns, and to a lesser extent, herbaceous plants (Takahashi et al. 1997). Natufians in the Levant exploited a variety of plant foods, among them wild lentils, almonds, pistachios, pears, broad beans, and, crucially, a wide range of edible wild cereal grains, including barley, einkorn wheat, and rye (Garrard 1999). Plant remains usually degrade rapidly unless they are charred, water-logged, or desiccated; therefore, they are much less apparent archaeologically than animal bones. However, they are of fundamental importance in human nutrition, and researchers have demonstrated their use through chemical analysis of human bone. For example, strontium–calcium ratios of Natufian bones from Galilee sites in Israel indicate a reliance on plant foods (Valla 1999).

## Later Hunter-Gatherer Technology

All later hunter-gatherer groups adapted their technology to fully exploit changing dietary resources. As shown in Figure 10.3, people continued to chip stone into a variety of forms—particularly into **microliths**, made by snapping blades into small segments. Microlithic technology was not invented in the late glacial period. Its use is evident in many late Upper Paleolithic sites, particularly in the Middle East during the Epipaleolithic period that preceded the Natufian. Microliths formed parts of composite tools as arrowheads, barbs on spears, and points for hunting. People attached small blade segments to wooden or bone hafts to form cutting tools; in the Middle East people made sickles by setting microliths side by side in wood or antler handles. These tools often acquired a distinctive gloss from cutting through silica-rich cereal stems, reeds, and rushes (used for thatching). Groups used larger tools such as axes and adzes to clear woodland and for other heavy-duty activities.

**microliths**
Small stone flakes that were made by snapping blades into small segments and that formed parts of composite tools.

*Figure 10.3*

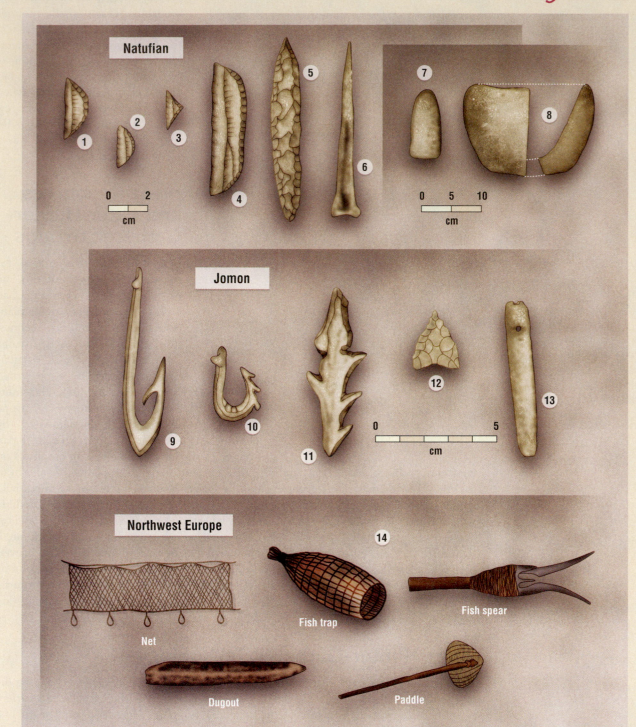

**EARLY HOLOCENE TECHNOLOGY.** Natufian: Items 1 through 3 are flint microliths; 4, sickle blade; 5, flint pick; 6, bone point; 7, basalt pestle; 8, limestone mortar. Jomon: Items 9 and 10 are bone fishhooks; 11, antler harpoon; 12, stone arrowhead; 13, bone needle or net shuttle. Northwest Europe: Items labeled 14 are fishing tools from the late Mesolithic of Denmark. How can you account for such a diversity of tool types?

*Sources*: Based on Aikens and Higuchi (1982), Andersen (1995), Bar-Yosef (2002), and Matsui (1998).

Neolithic ground-stone axes from Scandinavia and Ireland. Many thousands of ground-stone axes have been found in western Europe, although the wooden hafts in which they would have been inserted are missing. Why? Why is this type of Neolithic artifact so common?

Hunter-gatherer artisans laboriously ground tough rock, such as basalt, into bowls, mortars, pestles, and axes, as needed. Ground-stone production is time-consuming; it often takes days of continuous work to abrade a stone surface into a shape. Researchers have found early mortars at some late Upper Paleolithic sites, where they were used to process plant food and grind minerals such as ochre. But ground-stone production increased in the early Holocene, reflecting increased processing of plant foods. Stones with small indentations from the constant cracking of nuts have been found on Jomon sites.

People continued to work bone, antler, and ivory; they produced a range of fishing and hunting tools (hooks, spears, barbed points, harpoons), as well as digging, hide-working, and basketry tools. They made nets, developed complex fish and animal traps, and devised methods of food storage (such as pits and baskets). They also developed water transport, essential for marine-based economies, as indicated by finds of dugout canoes and paddles (Aikens and Higuchi 1982; Andersen 1995; Barnes 1999).

Modern hunter-gatherer groups modify their landscape to encourage plant growth and attract animals. Their ancestors did likewise. Pollen evidence in northern Europe indicates partial forest clearance by fire (Zvelebil 1994), while similar evidence from many Jomon sites indicates an increase in chestnut trees and a decrease in other types of trees. The abundance of chestnut remains and chestnut charcoal on Jomon sites and DNA analysis of those remains support deliberate management of chestnut forests. Chestnut trees not only were an important source of food, but were also used for buildings and fuel (Matsui and Kanehara 2006).

## Pottery

There is a general tendency to associate the first appearance of pottery with settled farming societies. This is often the case, but there are exceptions. Jomon groups were the first people to make pottery vessels, and they made them amazingly early—about 16,000 years ago. They used these vessels as containers, for storage, to transport goods, for burials, and for ritual ceremonies (Habu and Hall 1999). A sequence of changing pottery styles and decoration covers the entire Jomon period and serves as an accurate dating tool, verified by $^{14}$C dating, stratigraphy, and tephrachronology (sequencing of volcanic ash eruptions). Jomon pottery is distinctive for the cord-marked patterning that decorates many vessels; indeed, this patterning gave its name to the period: The word *Jomon* means "cord pattern" (Kobayashi 2004).

Mesolithic groups in Scandinavia imported pottery from their southern farming neighbors about 7,000 years ago. In southwest Asia pottery emerged a few hundred years earlier, but only in settled farming communities, not in Natufian hunter-gatherer contexts.

## Habitation and Use of Space

Archaeologists have found more evidence of habitation sites for the late glacial and early Holocene than for the preceding Upper Paleolithic. Structures are more substantial in the Middle East than in northern Europe, where wood and brush were the usual building materials. The Natufians planned their dwellings carefully, building oval or semi-circular, semi-subterranean structures supported by stone walls with bark and brush super structures. Excavations of the earliest phase of Ain Mallaha, a Natufian hamlet, uncovered houses, each about 25 m² (269 ft²) aligned along a slope, their stone walls still standing as much as 1 m (3 feet) high. One wall was partly covered with crushed limestone and painted red. Evidence from one house revealed domestic activities occurring around two interior hearths: There were tools and flint waste (from the manufacture and repair of tools), mortars and pestles (food or pigment processing), and food remains. A third hearth seems to have been used solely for heat and light (Valla 1995).

In areas where wood was the primary construction material, all that often remains of Mesolithic dwellings are postholes indicating the shapes of the former structures: circular, oval, trapezoidal, or rectangular. Scandinavian groups sometimes insulated the floors of semi-subterranean houses with birchbark and brush. Large houses were probably winter dwellings, or base camps; smaller houses may have been for seasonal, short-term use (Mithen 1994).

Thatched pit houses—single-family, circular dwellings with a sunken floor and an internal stone-lined fireplace—characterize Jomon settlements, although in the early period caves and rock shelters also served as shelters. Wooden posts supported the walls and the roof of pit houses. Small settlements consisted of a few pit houses, but large settlements usually comprised pit houses and storage pits set in a semi-circle around a central open plaza area. In the plaza were pit burials and raised structures, the latter deduced from posthole marks in the earth. It is possible that these raised structures were for storage. Some Jomon sites have a dwelling much larger than the norm, which researchers suggest may be a communal center. Survey and excavation have revealed as many as 600 pit dwellings on Jomon sites, but these numbers do not always reflect dense occupation; rather they may result from successive phases of construction, use, and abandonment over hundreds of years (Kobayashi 2004; Takahashi et al. 1997).

In all areas during the Holocene, larger sites formed base camps around which groups often established smaller, temporary special-task camps. Storage facilities (pits) at large base camps, such as those at large Jomon settlements, ensured confidence in food supplies that would support longer periods of occupation. Early Natufian sites have few pits, but people could have used baskets for above-ground storage. Groups stayed in smaller camps on a seasonal basis as they exploited particular resources to take back to the main settlement. For example, hunters went to Ringkloster in southern Scandinavia in winter and spring to get skins and furs and to hunt aurochs and wild pigs to take back to the main settlement (Rowley-Conwy 1999).

The question of whether later hunter-gatherers had year-round, permanent settlements is contentious. In all the areas discussed here, there are large settlements with some evidence of substantial house structures, heavy tools such as mortars, storage facilities, cemeteries, and deep occupational deposits. Some researchers believe that such patterning of remains indicates permanent residence (Kobayashi 2004; Pearson 2006; Price 1991). Others who disagree use ethnographic evidence of non-portable tools and substantial houses in modern hunter-gatherer contexts, where mobility remains part of life (Boyd 2006). Archaeologically, there is evidence for rebuilding of houses and reuse of sites that suggests movement away from and return to settlements on a regular basis

(Bar-Yosef 2002). Perhaps the answer to this question depends on how much time (three months, a year, or more) is considered as indicating permanent residence.

## Symbolic Activities: Burials and Representational Imagery

Cemeteries associated with settlements become common in the early Holocene. Variations in mortuary practices occur in all areas and include individual and multiple burials, inhumation (burial in the ground) of bodies, cremation, boat burial (Schulting 1998), secondary burial, movement of bones, and skull removal. Natufians also buried their dead beneath deserted houses or in stone-lined pits that they occasionally marked with a stone (Valla 1995). Researchers have found Jomon burials in caves, pits, and abandoned pit dwellings. Sometimes stone markers indicate Jomon burials, and in the late Jomon period stone circles and earthen banks enclose graves (Kobayashi 2004; Takahashi et al. 1997).

Grave goods included jewelry, tools, beads, shells, and clothing decoration. In Scandinavia grave goods might differ according to sex: Excavators have found axes and knives with males and decorative items with females (Larsson 1990). In both Scandinavia and the Middle East, dogs have been found in human burials, perhaps indicating dogs' importance in hunting and the special relationship that had developed between humans and dogs (Larsson 1995; Valla 1995). Excavations at the Skateholm cemeteries in southern Sweden uncovered dog burials accompanied with grave goods and a sprinkling of ochre, but without a human burial (Schulting 1998). The presence of postholes around some human burial pits at Skateholm suggests a mortuary structure; food remains (animal bones) mixed in the grave fill beneath this structure may well be the remains of a mortuary meal (Larsson 1995).

In northern Europe, artistic representations became less common in the early Holocene than they were in the Upper Paleolithic; they differ in form and likely function, and they are concentrated in different regions. Mesolithic art includes rock carvings and paintings, decorated bone and antler tools, painted wooden paddles, amber carvings and figurines, carved limestone and sandstone blocks, and fine rock carvings. Geometric and abstract designs are much more common than representations of animals (Larsson 1990). Natufian art is much richer than art in the Paleolithic period; it consists of decorated bone, stone, and shell ornaments, carved tool hafts, engraved limestone blocks, and figurines. Representations of animals and humans are common (Bar-Yosef 1995; Valla 1995). In Japan ceramic female figurines and stone rods from the middle Jomon (4,800 to 4,000 years ago) suggest a preoccupation with fertility. The Jomon pottery from this period is so highly ornate and well made that it may have been used for ritual or ceremonial purposes (Imamura 1996).

## Social Organization

Evidence of social organization comes from many late glacial and early Holocene discoveries. Finds in the Middle East, Japan, and Scandinavia indicate that some groups successfully adapted to changing environmental conditions and seemed to thrive. Although it was necessary to travel around the landscape to exploit seasonally available food resources (as seen in specialized small sites), some groups settled in one place for increasingly longer periods of time (as shown by larger base camps and hamlets). A system of scheduling food resources, together with the use of preservation and storage facilities, made semi-permanent settlements possible. This pattern is apparent in different parts of the Old World.

Semi-sedentary groups exploit a more restricted geographic range than highly mobile groups—a range that is crucial to subsistence and is considered tribal territory. Differences in tool kits, jewelry, and burial practices in all areas may indicate distinct group identities, possibly associated with tribal territories. Mortuary treatment suggests a concern for the dead; perhaps this was the beginning of ancestor ideology, which lays claim to tribal lands. Although people understood their landscape in terms of settlement areas and the scheduling of resources, they also saw it as imbued with symbolic meaning, as do present-day hunter-gatherer groups (Zvelebil 2003). Researchers have suggested that large settlements could have been central places where groups' daily and ceremonial activities occurred, and that as such they would have been sacred places (Larsson 2003). Particular points in the landscape may also have been considered sacred, such as rock art sites; other sacred places may have been constructed of organic materials and may no longer be visible. For example, a huge posthole by a grave in Skateholm (in Sweden) and similar holes of Mesolithic origin near Stonehenge (in England) once held massive logs, perhaps totemic symbols uniting groups with their daily and ideological world.

Later hunter-gatherer groups did not live in isolation. Contact with others through either trade or exchange is evident in the movement of nonlocal marine shells, greenstone, and malachite in the Middle East; amber in northern Europe; and in the introduction of pottery from nearby farming communities of central Europe. Jade, amber, obsidian, asphalt, and pottery moved among Jomon groups—and Jomon groups also may have had contact with Chinese and Korean groups, as suggested by finds of stone jewelry from China and pottery from Korea on Jomon sites. Japanese obsidian has been found on Siberian sites.

It is clear that rich resources underpinned the growing social complexity that is evident in late glacial and early Holocene groups, many of which were collectors with delayed return subsistence patterns (Binford 1980; Woodburn 1980; refer to Table 10.1). Investment in food acquisition, processing, and storage technology supported a semi-sedentary lifestyle, which in turn promoted an increase in population. Burial practices, body decoration, and items originating from distant areas suggest that some people in society were accorded special treatment—a sign of status and power. And these status distinctions among people were mirrored by the ranking of settlements, as the larger settlements with their associated cemeteries became the focal point for tribal groups. Contact and exchange between groups provided desired goods and marriage partners and strengthened kinship ties. However, evidence of violence, in the form of arrowheads embedded in human bones, suggests aggressive and lethal confrontations as well. Violence may have resulted from competition for resources and from territorial clashes between tribes. It may have been directed against encroaching farmers, whose needs to tame the land automatically led to possession and exclusion of hunters and gatherers from land that was once theirs.

An increase in complexity could be and was reversed; gatherers could and did return to a highly mobile lifestyle as circumstances dictated. The late Natufian period coincided with the onset of the Younger Dryas about 12,900 years ago, a period of falling temperatures and consequent changes in environmental conditions. Settlement patterns changed, sites became smaller, group sizes decreased, and there were fewer burials with grave goods and signs of status (Bar-Yosef 2002). Natufian groups adapted to their new circumstances initially by returning to a foraging lifestyle and later by settling and farming their lands.

# The Emergence of Farming in Old World Neolithic Societies

For more than 4 myr, our human ancestors had lived by gathering, fishing, hunting, and scavenging. Then, between 11,000 and 9,000 years ago, innovations in food procurement strategies developed by late Natufian groups brought dramatic and lasting consequences: people began to deliberately cultivate cereal crops and to take control of particular species of animals. They became farmers, which ushered in the Neolithic period.

The development of farming had such far-reaching influences that Gordon Childe (1981) saw it as revolutionary, calling it the Neolithic Revolution. Why was agriculture so successful, and what were the consequences?

- Farming consistently yielded more food from smaller tracts of land than did hunting and gathering.
- Farmers produced surplus food to store for later consumption or to fulfill trade and social obligations.
- Hardy domesticated crops underpinned settlements in a range of environments.
- People built more substantial housing and developed technology to meet their farming and living needs.
- Population size grew, as shown archaeologically in a rise in settlement numbers.
- Eventually full-time craft specialists met communities' demands for daily and luxury goods.
- Farming led to the appearance of social differentiation and stratification, the development of hierarchies, the rise of complex societies, and thus the emergence of the first great civilizations.

This success story has a negative side, however. Farming is demanding, time-consuming work: Cereals need to be planted, tended, harvested, and stored, and animals need to be cared for, protected, milked, and fed when necessary. Neolithic diets were high in starch and nutritionally less diverse than hunter-gatherer diets. Occasional crop failure caused famine and starvation in farming communities; people who were tied to their land could not move elsewhere in search of food. People who lived in permanent settlements also were more vulnerable to disease caused by unsanitary conditions and refuse-loving pests (Cohen 1989; Larsen 2006). Finally, overuse and development of land leads to environmental degradation.

## Modeling the Causes of Farming

If life was so good for early Holocene hunters and gatherers, why did some people turn to farming? Models proposed to explain the transition cover natural and cultural reasons and range from hypotheses proposing a single, global cause to ideas about multi-causal, regionally driven motives.

In 1956 Gordon Childe hypothesized that a severe drought at the end of the Pleistocene drove people and animals to fertile oases where they subsequently began to farm (Childe 1981). However, there is no evidence for large-scale aridity at the end of the Pleistocene. In 1960 Robert Braidwood suggested that farming was a natural development in areas where the wild progenitors of domesticated species naturally occurred. In a 1968 article Lewis Binford (1968b) proposed that the expansion of wild grasses in the warmer conditions of the late Pleistocene led to population increase and pressure that caused groups to split from parent settlements and move on. Then, as landscapes began to fill, people began to farm to meet their dietary needs. Kent Flannery (1969, 1973) supported Binford's hypothesis but suggested that agriculture began not in zones of optimal wild grasses but rather in marginal areas where people were forced to grow food. However, no early farming sites have been found in marginal areas to support Flannery's argument. Whereas Binford and Flannery saw agricultural origins as multi-causal, occurring within an interlocking natural and human system, Mark Cohen (1977) believed global population growth to be the prime mover.

Other models consider cultural factors as prime motivators. Barbara Bender suggested in 1978 that status promoted agricultural growth: People needed surplus food to exchange for status objects. In similar fashion, Brian Hayden (1992) proposed a scenario

*Figure 10.4*

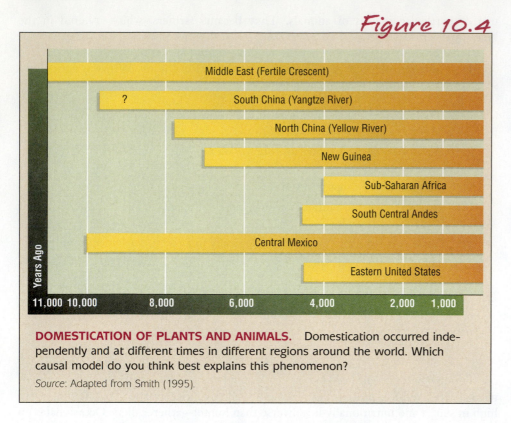

**DOMESTICATION OF PLANTS AND ANIMALS.**   Domestication occurred independently and at different times in different regions around the world. Which causal model do you think best explains this phenomenon?

*Source*: Adapted from Smith (1995).

of competitive feasting through which chiefs gained status and power, and for which food was an essential requirement. Although both factors may well have played a part in food intensification, they are generally considered as unlikely to have been underlying primary causes of the origins of agriculture.

The key to farming is human domestication of living things. **Domestication** has been defined as "the human creation of a new form of plant or animal—one that is identifiably different from its wild ancestors and extant wild relatives" (Smith 1995, 18). When humans deliberately affect the growth of certain wild plant and animal species, within a few generations phenotypic (visually apparent) and genetic changes will occur in these wild species as they adapt to different life cycles. The changes are such that eventually the evolved species will be unable to live without human aid.

There are 7 to 10 centers, or core areas, of domestication in the world (see Figure 10.4). Bruce Smith notes similarities in the patterns of development of plant domestication in the Middle East, China, Africa, and Central and South America that might provide clues to answer the "why" question (Smith 1995). Domestication first occurred in well-watered areas where wild species were present in abundance and were exploited by the local hunter-gatherer groups. The presence of a constant source of food allowed people to settle on a more permanent basis and to experiment with food production. In all areas there is evidence of increasing population and, shortly before the first domesticates appear, a dramatic change in climate. Most experts agree that population increase and climate were catalysts for domestication. However, a rich resource base that enabled settlements to grow would also have had social consequences, in relation to control of land and resources, as we've discussed. Domestication did not appear suddenly in the core areas but was a slow, step-by-step process. It resulted from a combination of factors rather than from a single factor.

## Evidence for Plant and Animal Domestication

Cereals (mainly wheat and barley), sheep, goats, pigs, and cattle formed the early farming package in the Middle East and Europe. The African package consisted of millet, sorghum, African rice, cattle, and goats; Chinese domestication was based on rice and millet, pigs, water buffalo, and chickens. New Guinea domesticates were banana, taro, and sugar cane (Neuman 2003). Domesticated mammals not only provide meat but also can be exploited for their milk, which can be turned into a range of dairy foods; for their wool, which can be made into cloth; and for dung, which can be used primarily for fuel but also for building. People have exploited both wild and domesticated animal hides, bones, and horns for clothing, shelter, tools, and a range of other artifacts. Indeed, all parts of an animal are potentially of use—for example, stomachs can be used as water

**domestication**

Phenotypic and genetic changes in plants or animals that are the result of human intervention and that make the evolved species unable to live without human aid.

containers and sinew has been used as a type of cord. Larger animals can pull plows, making agricultural activities more efficient; they can be harnessed to carts to carry people and goods from one destination to another; and they can be mounted or harnessed to chariots to make more effective war machines.

Direct evidence for plant and animal domestication is occasionally present in the form of the plants and animals themselves. Unlike their wild counterparts, domesticated cereals have large seeds within light seed coats and are attached to the stalk by a tough rachis (the stem between the seed and the stalk) that breaks only when harvested. However, plants are fragile and are preserved only under special conditions. Most plant remains are recovered through flotation techniques or as charred remains, but they also survive as imprints in pottery.

Indirect evidence for domestication comes from the technology used in plant processing, such as grinding tools, sickles, and storage pits. Also cereal foods leave signatures on human teeth and bone (refer to Table 10.2). For example, early agricultural communities in prehistoric Georgia (in the United States) had a higher incidence of caries than preagricultural communities, a fact interpreted as the result of the adoption of maize (corn) agriculture (Larsen 1984). Isotopic bone analysis of Mesolithic and early Neolithic communities in Portugal showed a change from a marine and terrestrial diet in Mesolithic times to a Neolithic diet dominated by land animals and plants; the excavators interpreted this shift as showing a transition from hunting and fishing to farming (Lubell et al. 1994). The microscopic study of tools and vessels for indications of processing wear and tear or food residues can provide further evidence for the use of domesticated plants as food. Researchers interpret the origin of such residues according to the context of the site. However, remember that hunter-gatherer groups also used mortars and pestles to process food, so food-preparation artifacts on their own do not necessarily imply farming.

Other kinds of indirect evidence also can offer clues to domestication: Pollen analyses will reveal cereal pollen, the presence of weeds associated with cultivation, and evidence of forest clearance, which often preceded planting. Plow marks discovered beneath the surface of a burial mound at South Street, Avebury, England, showed clearly that the soil had been systematically disturbed, probably in preparation for sowing (Whittle 1999).

The remains of domesticated animals show morphological and size differences. Domesticated animals tend to be smaller than their wild counterparts; horns and tusks may change shape; hair tends to be shorter. Sex and age profiles among animal bone assemblages can indicate domestication by revealing culling patterns. For example, assemblages dominated by female animals may indicate a dairy herd with a few males kept for breeding, whereas assemblages of prime-age adults of both sexes suggest meat priorities. Zooarchaeologists also consider profiles of animal species that change over time. For example, gazelles were the primary source of meat for people at Abu Hureyra in Syria for more than 3,000 years, roughly from 12,000 to 9,000 years ago. Later, however, domestic sheep and goats, and to a lesser extent cattle, dominate the assemblages. These profiles demonstrate a change in food acquisition strategies from exploitation of wild sources to reliance on domesticated ones (Moore et al. 2000).

## Material Culture of Farming Groups

Changes in material culture accompanied the changes in food production among early farming groups. The most common artifact found on sites since Neolithic times is the potshard. Early pottery making did not require complex technology: Households could produce vessels themselves to meet their everyday needs. Pottery mass production involving wheels and molds came later. (For more information about pottery, see Highlight 10.1, on pp. 286–287.)

Stone continued to play a crucial role as a tool component, particularly in sickle blades for harvesting and in ground-stone axes for forest clearance. Miners dug shafts with antler picks and animal shoulder blades to reach the best underground flint. Groups

# Pottery and Archaeology

GIVEN THE FACT THAT POTTERY is so breakable, how does it happen that archaeologists rely quite heavily on pottery for information about life in the past 10,000 years? The answer lies in the composition of clay. When moist and of the right consistency, clay can be shaped into a range of forms. If it remains damp, it will eventually break down and disintegrate—but heating transforms clay into a durable material that, even if broken, generally does not disintegrate and can last for thousands of years.

Clay is versatile. In addition to using clay to make countless types of containers for hot or cold liquids or food, artisans have transformed it into statues and figurines, beads and other items of jewelry, hunting and fishing equipment such as clay pellets and fishing-net weights, weaving equipment such as spindle whorls and loom weights, smoking pipes, water pipes, and even coffins. In many areas clay is an important building material for items such as bricks and roof tiles; in some of those same areas it was also the earliest medium for writing. Clay is truly a multi-functional material. Consequently pottery shards (fragments) are the most common artifact on most archaeological sites less than 10,000 years old (the time at which pottery developed in many areas of the Old World, although the earliest Jomon pottery from Japan may be 6,000 years older). Pottery analysis helps archaeologists answer questions concerning the manufacture, distribution, and function of goods, settlement organization, cultural expression, and dating.

Pottery production involves a series of steps that are often distinguishable in the archaeological record: digging clay, preparing it, shaping the vessel or object, applying prefiring treatments, drying, firing, and applying postfiring treatments. Pottery is made from a range of clays, most of which people have to process—either to remove particles that will hamper manufacture or to add materials (known as temper or filler) to improve the quality and performance. Tempers include crushed rock, flint, sand, ground shell, ground pottery shards, and organic materials such as dung, grass, and seed husks.

Once a vessel has been shaped by hand or on a wheel, it is placed to dry before being heated in an open bonfire or kiln. Before firing the vessel, the potter may use a wet cloth, a pebble, a paddle, or other device to smooth the surface of the vessel (called burnishing) or may add a coat of thin clay (called a slip). Both techniques improve the quality of the surface and add a decorative sheen. The firing process is a delicate procedure, because pots may break if the heat is not well controlled. The potter can cause changes in surface color by controlling the amount of oxygen entering the kiln: Adding extra oxygen gives a reddish-brown tinge, whereas blocking oxygen turns a vessel gray or black. Potters employ a variety of materials and techniques to decorate pots, among them painting or glazing, adding metals, incising damp clay, or applying strips of clay to the vessel. Crucial to archaeology is the fact that it is potentially possible to determine all stages in pottery manufacture, including variation in heating temperatures.

The chief use of pottery has always been in the form of receptacles related to food storage, preparation, and transport. Storage jars may be large or small and may contain hot or cold liquids or solids for short or long periods. Preparation of food includes mixing, stirring, and cooking activities. And transport may occur over short distances, as in the serving of food, or in long-distance trade. Vessels with particular attributes meet the requirements for different functions. For example, containers with small openings are suitable receptacles for storing and serving liquids; it is easier to eat cereals from a plate or bowl than from a bottle; thick, sturdy containers can withstand long-distance transport; round cooking vessels conduct heat more efficiently than sharply angled vessels.

Archaeologists have various ways of determining the original function of a piece of pottery. The clay's physical properties and the manufacturing methods can produce pots suited to particular functions, as can surface treatments (slips, glazes, handles). Vessel shape may offer clues—as may the context in which shards were found, such as a burial or a cooking area. Fires often leave soot marks on pots; wear marks on inner surfaces may result from stirring, pounding, or scraping actions. Too much heat can char and so preserve contents, or microscopic food residues trapped within the vessel walls may be revealed through chemical analysis.

By identifying the physical and chemical properties of clay and temper through petrographic analysis and a battery of scientific techniques, investigators often can pinpoint the origins of the materials. Once analysts have compared these

Variation in decoration on traditional Spanish pottery distinguishes regional styles from one another. Why might anthropologists and archaeologists find such styles useful?

riage rites; it may have been designated for use by females or males or by adults or children. It is clearly difficult to identify such particular uses in the archaeological record, however. Ethnographic studies provide insights into perceptions of pottery in traditional societies; these insights help archaeologists interpret ancient material, and they suggest models of pottery production, distribution, and use. But although ethnographic studies open up avenues for thought, they do not give direct answers to archaeological questions.

Before the advent of $^{14}$C dating, researchers used changing pottery forms and styles to determine relative chronological order for archaeological assemblages. Attributes of pottery (style, shape, size, decoration) change over time, as do present-day fashions—so when various attributes are plotted, a chronologically significant pattern of emerging, increasing, and declining use can emerge. Seriation, as this technique is known, can validate stratigraphic relationships, and vice versa. Organic materials such as seeds are sometimes trapped in pots, allowing $^{14}$C dating. Shards themselves may be directly dated by thermoluminescence (see Chapter 8).

Although based on what may appear to many to be the lowly shard, pottery studies have become increasingly sophisticated and address a much wider range of topics than covered here. As it is now possible to get blood from a stone (see Chapter 9), so it is possible to get milk from a potshard.

sources with the final location of the pottery, they may consider possibility of trade. Of course, clay may have originated in one place and temper somewhere else; manufacture may have occurred in a third area, and the finished vessel may have been widely distributed. Researchers plot the location of pottery types on distribution maps and use the maps to track the movement of goods from sources of production, where more of a type may be found, to areas of consumption. In historic periods potters often left their marks on their goods, making their movements easier to track.

Many styles of pottery decoration are distinctive to particular groups and express group identity. Decoration and vessel shape also may indicate specific activities. For example, a vessel may have been made for ceremonial drinking, burial rites, or mar-

*Sources*: Barley, N. 1994. *Smashing pots: Feats of clay from Africa*. London: British Museum. Orton, C., P. Tyers, and A. Vince. 1993. *Pottery in archaeology*. Cambridge: Cambridge University Press. Rice, Patricia. 1998. *Doing archaeology: A hands-on laboratory manual*. Mountain View, CA: Mayfield. Rice, Prudence. 1987. *Pottery analysis: A sourcebook*. Chicago: University of Chicago Press. Rye, O. S. 1981. *Pottery technology: Principles and reconstruction*. Washington, DC: Taraxacum.

turn back to your reading

quarried good sources of stone and flint, roughly shaping axes at quarry sites before trading them on. Indeed, some axes have been found hundreds of miles from their source. Some fine, highly polished axes would have been useless as woodworking tools and must have had special significance, perhaps as status or alliance markers or votive offerings. For example, a jadeite axe of Alpine origin was found beneath the Sweet Track, a 6,000-year-old trackway across marshland in southern England (Coles and Coles 1986).

**Jericho**
Tell site in the Jordan Valley in what is now Palestine that has evidence of the transition from hunter-gatherer groups to farming groups; known for its monumental stone walls and tower and for the ritual burial of plastered human skulls and plaster statues of humans.

**Ain Ghazal**
Neolithic village site in what is now Jordan that is known for ritual burials of plaster-covered human skulls and large plaster statues of humans.

**tell**
An artificial mound formed through repeated occupation of the same site over thousands of years by people who built mud-brick houses on top of earlier structures; called a *tepe* in Iran and a *höyük* in Turkey.

# Farming in the Middle East

The earliest farming communities in the Middle East developed along the Fertile Crescent. This famous crescent-shaped area extends for about 2,000 km (1,250 miles); beginning at the Negev in southern Israel, it runs north along the Mediterranean coast before curving southeast along the Zagros Mountains of Turkey and Iran. After the Natufian period, there is clear evidence of permanent villages and increasing settlement complexity. We will look at two representative sites: **Jericho** in the Jordan Valley (10,500 to 9,000 years ago) and **Ain Ghazal** (9,000 to 7,000 years ago), a much larger site than Jericho, covering 30 hectares (74 acres) on the banks of the Wadi Zarqa in Jordan (Rollefson et al. 1992).

Jericho is a **tell** site—a large artificial mound formed through repeated occupation over thousands of years by people who lived in mud-brick houses, building on top of the broken and disintegrating mud bricks of earlier structures. The archaeological sequence at Jericho includes 25 levels of farming settlements, beneath which lie Natufian settlements (Smith 1995). The millennia of settlement formed a tell that today is 20 m (66 feet) high, 320 m (1,050 feet) long and 140 m (460 feet) wide. At both Jericho and Ain Ghazal, a gradual increase in domesticated species and a decrease in wild species are clearly evident from Natufian through Neolithic periods. In addition to physical remains of plants and animals, indirect evidence of agriculture includes sickle blades, grinding stones, storage pits, and houses indicating permanent settlement.

## Houses at Jericho and Ain Ghazal

Tell es-Sultan, better known as ancient Jericho, in Palestine, as it was in 1957. Its crater-like appearance is the result of numerous excavations over the past 150 years. A tell is a höyük in Turkey and a tepe in Iran. Why are there so many tells in the Middle East?

Early farming groups modified and changed their houses through time. The early houses at Jericho had one or two rooms and were round; later these were replaced by rectangular structures, a pattern seen in many of the early farming settlements in the area (Bar-Yosef 1995). House construction and modification were more elaborate at Ain Ghazal, where people dug terraces into the riverbank to create flat areas on which to build. Whereas at Jericho construction was of mud brick set on a stone base, builders at Ain Ghazal made houses out of stone. At both sites people covered house floors with lime plaster, often colored with red ochre, on which they sometimes placed round or square rush mats (seen as impressions on floors) (Kenyon 1957). The earliest structures at Ain Ghazal consisted of large rooms, but over time occupants divided the larger rooms with

**ideology**
Belief systems of a group.

stone walls (some still standing as high as 1.5 m, or 5 feet) or built further additions; indeed, one of the later houses seems to have been a two-story building (Rollefson et al. 1992). Roofs were probably flat and, to judge from the Jericho evidence, made of a lattice of reeds and mud; the reeds have vanished, but their imprint appears in lumps of collapsed mud roofing recovered from house floors. Charred remains recovered from a small room at Ain Ghazal suggest a storage function for that room and for other, similar small rooms at both sites.

The inhabitants of Jericho built a spectacular series of high stone walls (up to 3.6 m, or 12 feet) and ditches around part of their village. Furthermore, inside the earliest wall built, they constructed a stone tower almost 10 m (33 feet) high with an interior staircase of 22 dressed stone slabs. Archaeologists originally interpreted the wall as a defensive barrier, but a more recent interpretation suggests that the villagers may have built it to protect against flooding from nearby rivers (Bar-Yosef 1986).

## Ritual among Farming Communities in the Middle East

The manufacture of mud bricks and lime plaster, the transport and dressing of large stones, and the layout and maintenance of structures in the earliest farming period show an organization of labor that implies permanent ties to the land. **Ideology** strengthened such ties. Ritual among early farming communities in the Middle East relates to ancestors and fertility. People regularly placed their dead beneath house floors or under courtyards. The practice of skull removal, first witnessed in Natufian levels, increased with the separate burial of skulls and bodies. Several adult skulls at Jericho and Ain Ghazal, and indeed at many other sites in the area, were covered with plaster, colored, and given cowrie shell eyes (Bar-Yosef 1995). The Ain Ghazal skulls are intriguing: When excavators found them, little of their original plaster modeling remained, but the excavators found no plaster in the burial pit to indicate that deterioration had occurred after burial. Therefore, the skulls must have been in the same condition when buried as when excavated. Perhaps groups displayed and worshipped the plastered skulls of ancestors for some time, so the skulls had begun to deteriorate before being buried (Rollefson et al. 1992). Not all community members received such treatment, however, as some complete bodies were found in rubbish pits, where they had apparently been dumped. Later farming groups changed burial practices, abandoning the tradition of skull burial for the burial of complete bodies.

An ancestor cult is further suggested by the large, lime plaster statues of humans that investigators recovered from Jericho and especially from Ain Ghazal. At Ain Ghazal villagers had deliberately buried in a pit more than 20 statues—some complete with arms and legs, others just torsos. Some statues are almost 1 m

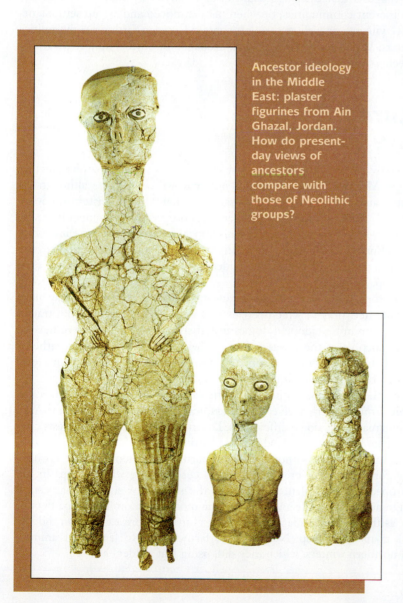

Ancestor ideology in the Middle East: plaster figurines from Ain Ghazal, Jordan. How do present-day views of ancestors compare with those of Neolithic groups?

(3 feet) tall, retain traces of ochre, and have eyes outlined in black. As with the Ain Ghazal skulls, these statues may have been displayed before burial, as many of their feet show slight damage that did not occur after burial (Tubb 2001–2002). Smaller human and animal figurines made of clay, limestone, chalk, and plaster also surfaced at Ain Ghazal, some perhaps worshipped during fertility or other ceremonies (Rollefson 1997).

At many sites certain rooms contain features such as altars, wall niches, or large stone slab arrangements not found in domestic structures. These rooms appear to have been shrines or temples; such spaces clearly played an important role in early farming community ritual, as they would continue to do for thousands of years.

## Long-Distance Contact

Many of the items at Jericho originated from other areas in the Fertile Crescent: Excavating teams have found greenstone from northern Syria; shells from the Mediterranean and the Red Sea; salt, tar, and sulfur from the Dead Sea area; turquoise from the Sinai Peninsula; and obsidian from as far away as Turkey. Long-distance contact was important to community members as a means of obtaining status items. Ofer Bar-Yosef (1995) suggests that exchange could have occurred through marriages between people of different communities, or when people moved and set up settlements outside their native villages, as well as through contact between farming communities and hunter-gatherers. Whatever the mechanism, exchange of objects indicates a transfer of ideas and technology as well.

## Agriculture in Europe

Farming spread westward from the Middle East by land and sea to Anatolia (ancient Turkey) and Europe. Most early domesticates do not grow wild in Europe, although the wild range for cattle and pigs was far greater than for other Middle Eastern domesticates. Additionally, $^{14}$C dates for farming settlements get progressively younger from the Fertile Crescent westward. Two main mechanisms appear to account for the introduction of farming into Europe: colonization by immigrants who brought their mode of living with them, and adoption of the farming idea by local Mesolithic groups. (See Highlight 10.2, on pp. 292–294.)

In southern Europe, around the Mediterranean, the idea of farming may have spread through trade networks in which cereals and animals were among the traded goods. Mesolithic communities adopted domesticated species when they were needed (Bogucki 1996). In such cases there was continuity with the former hunter-gatherer lifestyle. The material culture remained similar through time, but with accruing evidence of new domesticated species not previously present in the area.

Central and northern Europe do not enjoy the same climate as the Middle East. Instead, Mesolithic groups experienced cold winters, warm summers, more rain than in the Middle East, and marked seasonal differences. During the Neolithic vast forests covered the region, so people had to clear land before planting. The soils were different too, though fertile and easy to work without ploughs. Farmers adapted the new farming practices to these conditions. For example, whereas cereals were winter crops in the Middle East, European farmers planted cereals in the spring for summer harvesting (Bogucki 1996). Domesticated cattle and pigs became more common in Europe than in the Middle East, as these species adapted to colder climates more easily than did the Fertile Crescent's goats and sheep. Nevertheless, farmers had to feed their animals through the cold northern winters, which they did, using leaf fodder.

# The LBK Phenomenon of Central Europe

The **Linearbandkeramik (LBK)**, or Linear Pottery, culture—so called because of its members' distinctive pottery designs—provides a good example of rapid colonization by Neolithic farmers. Between 6,500 and 6,000 years ago, LBK groups moved westward across central Europe settling along fertile river valleys, as shown in Figure 10.5. Archaeologists have documented thousands of LBK sites from present-day Ukraine to eastern France, all remarkably similar in their farmsteads and material culture. LBK settlers brought with them wheat, barley, peas, lentils, poppy, flax, cattle, sheep, goats, and a few pigs, as well as their pottery. They built long, wide timber houses (often 40 m by 6 m, or 130 feet by 20 feet), distinguishable today by rows of postholes and the burned daub (clay or mud) with impressions of wattle (branches and sticks) from which they were made. In their time **wattle-and-daub** LBK longhouses would have been the largest buildings in the world (Bogucki 2000; 2003).

Because there are so few Mesolithic sites and so many LBK sites in central Europe, it appears that LBK groups colonized virgin territory. The land was heavily forested, however, and they had to clear it in order to farm. The relatively sudden appearance of new types of standardized settlement, distinctive pottery, domestic animals, and cereals indicates that LBK people arrived with the farming package. Furthermore, skeletal remains show physical differences between Mesolithic and Neolithic people in the area.

**Linearbandkeramik (LBK)**
The first farming culture of Europe; its name means Linear Pottery and reflects the distinctive pottery designs of members of the group.

**wattle-and-daub**
A building technique in which clay or mud is used to cover a superstructure made of interwoven wooden poles and sticks.

*Figure 10.5*

Highland      Linear Pottery Culture

**MOVEMENT OF LBK FARMING GROUPS ACROSS EUROPE, AS INDICATED BY REMAINS OF WOOD AND CLAY LONGHOUSES FOUND ALONG RIVER VALLEYS.**
What would have been the advantages and disadvantages of settling along river valleys?

*Sources*: Based on Bogucki, P. 1996. The spread of farming in Europe. *American Scientist* 84 (3): 242–253. Whittle, A. 1994. First farmers. In B. Cunliffe (ed.), *The Oxford illustrated prehistory of Europe*, 167–201. New York: Oxford University Press.

# Highlight 10.2

# Genes, Languages, and Farmers

FARMING, NOT AN INDIGENOUS EUROPEAN INVENTION, traces its origin to the Middle East. The concept of domestication reached Europe partly through the physical migration of small farming groups that brought with them their way of food production and partly by adoption of all or part of the farming package by indigenous hunter-gatherers. Luca Cavalli-Sforza believes that the migration of farmers is visible in the genetic makeup of present-day populations. He suggests that early farmers would have moved initially into regions of Europe that were little populated by local hunter-gatherers. As a result, the genetic makeup of people in those regions today would be similar to that present in the areas where farming first appeared—that is, the Middle East and Anatolia (Turkey). However, the consequence of farming groups' moving into increasingly distant regions of Europe would be a greater genetic variation compared with the source area. In the 1990s Cavalli-Sforza tested this hypothesis by surveying 39 different genes from European populations and subjecting the resulting data to a principal components analysis, a procedure that highlights variation in gene frequency among populations. The outcome was as predicted, and the resulting map of gene variation from the Middle East across Europe correlates well with $^{14}$C dates indicating increasingly more recent dates for farming communities from the southeast to the northwest.

Cavalli-Sforza proposed that the main perpetrators of genetic variation were Neolithic farmers such as the Linearbandkeramik (LBK) groups, who appear to have moved rapidly across Europe. Later migrations—one possibly associated with pastoralists from southern Russia, another indicating Greek expansion from about 3,000 to 2,500 years ago— as well as the indigenous Mesolithic and Upper Paleolithic populations also have left their genetic mark on Europe.

More recent analyses of mitochondrial DNA (mtDNA, passed through the female line) and Y chromosomes (passed through the male line) contradict Cavalli-Sforza's conclusions. Both indicate a much greater contribution from Upper Paleolithic than from Neolithic genes in modern European populations. Further analysis of mitochondrial DNA in modern European women shows almost no inheritance from Neolithic groups, suggesting that the genetic composition of Neolithic farmers has been greatly diluted with genes from other groups.

Together, the genetic evidence and the archaeological evidence clearly show that the arrival of farming in Europe was not a simple matter of either diffusion of farming groups into Europe or adoption of the farming package by indigenous hunter-gatherer groups. Instead, it was a complex and regionally variable process.

## LANGUAGE AND FARMERS

The number of spoken languages in the world is diminishing; the 6,500 languages spoken today are fewer than in the past, and the prognosis for the future is a continuing decline. Scholars group present-day languages into larger language families based on similarities in grammar and vocabulary. As most European languages are part of the Indo-European language family, it is natural to question the origin and spread of Indo-European languages. Cavalli-Sforza believes that there is a connection between genetics and language and that this connection shows up in the archaeological record of the movement of early farming groups. It is possible that early Neolithic migrants introduced to European groups not only farming but also their language—the proto-Indo-European language.

Research, however, shows that various political, social, and economic factors may affect language spread:

- Languages may change or alter through divergence, in which dialects in remote areas gradually change to form a new language.
- Conversely, contemporaneous languages may exchange words and grammar and eventually converge to form a new language.
- An increase in trade may give rise to a "lingua franca," or trade language, that allows trading partners to understand each other; as the trade language becomes increasingly common, it may replace other languages.
- Conquering powers may impose their language on groups, as occurred with Latin in the Roman Empire.
- The introduction of immigrants with a new technology that promotes population growth may result in the spread of the immigrants' language.

■ Language also may be influenced by the movement of individuals (e.g., marriage outside the group).

It is difficult to postulate exactly how an Indo-European language spread in the Neolithic period. Marek Zvelebil believes that over thousands of years small groups of farmers colonized southeast and central Europe, bringing their farming techniques and their language with them. Mesolithic groups elsewhere in Europe adopted the idea of farming through contact with the colonists. A common language, suggests Zvelebil, would facilitate communication as farming spread; the language would be that of those who introduced the new technology—the migrant farmers. Thus, in time the Indo-European language became the means of communication. Furthermore, new technology brings prestige, and adopting the new language would increase a group's prestige.

Although the process by which Indo-European languages spread is not established, the expansion of Bantu languages is a good example of language spread associated with the diffusion of new technology—in this case, farming and iron production. Today more than 2 million people throughout a vast area of Africa speak upwards of 450 Bantu dialects, which are fairly easily understood between groups. The first archaeological evidence of agriculture, herding, settled villages, ironworking, and often pottery in East, South, and West Africa appears at sites associated with Bantu ironworking and farming groups. Because these elements appear in the archaeological record at the same time, and because there is no prior evidence for them in those areas, researchers conclude that they were introduced as a package by newcomers. It appears that these features may have originated earlier, farther north, possibly in Cameroon and eastern Nigeria about 4,000 years ago, and then spread as a package as people moved in search of land. Supporting the idea of movement from the north are not only [14]C dates but also genetic evidence of present-day Bantu speakers and statistical analysis of Bantu languages. For example, Clare Holden took 92 basic Bantu terms and subjected them to a maximum parsimony analysis; this technique produced language trees (similar to phylogenetic evolutionary trees) that show the spread of, and changes in, Bantu languages.

Correlating language with genes may be possible for more recent periods (4,000 to 3,000 years ago), as has been demonstrated in the Bantu case, where genetic variation coincides well with language groups. It is much more speculative for the prehistoric period, however, because languages change more rapidly than genes. It is also clear that similarity in aspects of material culture does not necessarily indicate similarity in all aspects of group

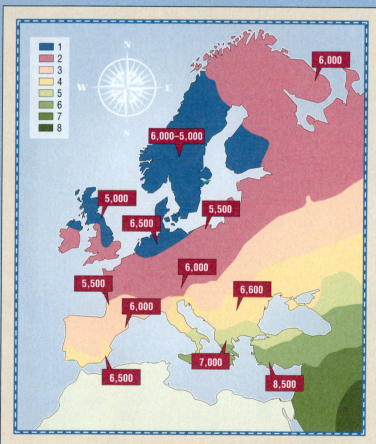

Mapped here are genetic groupings that Luca Cavalli-Sforza claims reflect migration of early farming groups into Europe. An approximate date (given as the number of years ago) indicates the arrival of the earliest groups in each region. How do you account for the early dates around southern Europe?

*Sources: Adapted from Cavalli-Sforza, L.L., and F. Cavalli-Sforza. 1995. The great human diasporas: The history of diversity and evolution. Reading, MA. Addison-Wesley. Dates adapted from Gkiasta, Russell, Shennan, and Steele (2003).*

(continues on the next page) ▶

life. However, research into language, genetics, and populations is active and promises exciting discoveries.

*Sources*: Bentley, R. A., L. Chikhi, and T. Price. 2003. The Neolithic transition in Europe: Comparing broad scale genetic and local scale isotopic evidence. *Antiquity* 77 (295): 63–66. Cavalli-Sforza, L. L. 1996. The spread of agriculture and nomadic pastoralism: Insights from genetics, linguistics and archaeology. In *The origin and spread of agriculture and pastoralism in Eurasia*, ed. D. Harris. London: UCL Press.   Cavalli-Sforza, L. L., and F. Cavalli-Sforza, 1995. *The great human diasporas: The history of diversity and evolution*. Reading, MA: Addison-Wesley.   Chikhi, L., R. Nichols, G. Barbujani, and M. Beaumont. 2002. Y genetic data support the Neolithic demic diffusion model. *Proceedings of the National Academy of Sciences* 99 (17): 11008–11013.   Diamond, J., and P. Bellwood. 2003. Farmers and their languages. *Science* 300: 597–602.   Haak, W., P. Forster, B. Bramanti, et al. 2005. First European farmers in 7,500-year-old Neolithic sites. *Science* 310: 1016–1018.   Holden, C. 2002. Bantu language trees reflect the spread of farming across sub-Saharan Africa: A maximum-parsimony analysis. *Proceedings of the Royal Society of London* 269: 793–799.   Phillipson, D. W. 1993. *African archaeology*. Cambridge: Cambridge University Press.   Renfrew, C. 2002. Genetics and language in contemporary archaeology. In *Archaeology: The widening debate*, eds. B. Cunliffe, W. Davies, and C. Renfrew. Oxford: British Academy.   Renfrew, C., and P. Bahn. 2000. *Archaeology: Theories, methods and practice*. 3rd ed. London: Thames & Hudson. Richards, M., V. Macauley, E. Hickey, et al. 2000. Tracing European founder lineages in Near Eastern mtDNA. *American Journal of Human Genetics* 67: 1251–1276.   Richards, M., V. Macauley, and H-J. Baudelt. 2002. Analyzing genetic data in a model-based framework: Inferences about European prehistory. In *Examining the farming/language dispersal hypothesis*, eds. P. Bellwood and C. Renfrew, pp. 459–466. Cambridge: McDonald Institute for Archaeological Research.   Robb, J. 1993. A social prehistory of European languages. *Antiquity* 67: 747–760.   Semino, O., G. Passarino, P. Oefner, et al. 2000. The genetic legacy of Paleolithic *Homo sapiens* in extant Europeans: A Y chromosome perspective. *Science* 290: 1155–1159. Zvelebil, M. 2002. Demography and dispersal of early farming populations at the Mesolithic-Neolithic transition: Linguistic and genetic implications. In *Examining the farming/language dispersal hypothesis*, eds. P. Bellwood and C. Renfrew, pp. 379–394. Cambridge: McDonald Institute for Archaeological Research.

turn back to your reading

However, there is some evidence for interaction between the groups; for example, archaeological finds in the middle Rhine Valley in Germany suggest that the earliest LBK immigrant settlers and local Mesolithic groups may have traded stone tools and pottery with each other. Over time Mesolithic sites declined. Most experts believe that indigenous hunter-gatherer groups either adopted the LBK package or abandoned the area, although such a scenario might be too simplistic (Price et al. 1995, 2001).

Strontium analysis can shed light on the question of whether people were migrants or natives (refer to Table 10.2). Researchers have applied strontium analysis to samples from two LBK cemeteries, Flomborn and Schwetzingen in the upper Rhine Valley, Germany. Results from Flomborn indicated male and female migrants. Archaeological evidence from grave goods recovered at Flomborn included spondylus (prickly oyster) shell artifacts, the first of that particular shell species found in the Rhine Valley; the shells' origin in southeast Europe suggests migration from that area. The Schwetzingen strontium analysis indicated young females had migrated from a nearby rather than a distant region. They could have come from a Mesolithic group and entered the farming community through marriage, or they could have been born nearby into another settled farming group and subsequently married into the Schwetzingen group. The beginning of farming in central Europe may not have been a simple process of colonization or adoption but a more intricate combination of both (Price et al. 2001).

Ditch earthworks enclose many settlements on the northern periphery of the LBK area. Some were fortifications against attacks from other LBK groups; however, some earthworks were composed of a series of discontinuous ditches, clearly not defensive, and their purpose is unknown. Violence between LBK groups was a fact of life; for example, at Talheim, in Baden Wutemburg, Germany, excavators found the bodies of 34 men, women, and children who had died as a result of violent attack and had been dumped in a pit. Specialists who studied the bone and skull fractures determined that they were the result of blows from stone adzes typical of those associated with LBK groups. Adzes are normally woodworking tools, but obviously also make powerful weapons (Bogucki 2000; Scarre 2005a).

LBK people buried their dead in cemeteries along with grave goods such as flint, pottery, adzes, and spondylus shell ornaments. Some of these goods originated from distant sources, indicating either long-distance exchange networks or, as mentioned earlier, incoming migrants.

## Farming in Southern Scandinavia

Life was good for Mesolithic groups: The sea was a constant source of food, and the land provided plants in abundance and meat from land animals. There was no good reason for Scandinavian groups to follow in the steps of their southern neighbors and take up farming. And they didn't: Ertebölle (late Mesolithic) groups continued their hunting–gathering–fishing way of life. However, they had contact with farming groups and, by 6,500 years ago, had begun to selectively incorporate into their own culture items from the farming culture, such as pottery, bone combs and rings, and antler axes. A further 500 years passed before the full farming package appeared throughout southern Scandinavia; even then domesticates were still not the primary form of subsistence, as wild plants and animals continued to dominate in the diet. Furthermore, there is no evidence for widespread forest clearance for cultivation. It was only in the later Neolithic, about 5,300 years ago, some 1,200 years after Neolithic artifacts first appeared on Mesolithic sites and more than 1,000 years after farming had begun in central Europe, that the farming way of life took hold in Scandinavia (Price 2003; Price et al. 2001).

The suite of artifacts and cultural traditions that heralded the adoption of farming in southern Scandinavia included domesticated plants and animals, polished stone axes, new types of pottery, new burial traditions for the elite (i.e., monumental **long barrow** tombs), and caching of special deposits such as amber or copper. This farming package is

**long barrow**
A long earthen burial mound widely constucted in northwestern Europe during the Neolithic.

**Funnel Beaker culture**
A farming group that orginated in what is now Poland and may have influenced the adoption of farming by southern Scandinavian Mesolithic groups; the name reflects the group's distinctive pottery.

associated with the **Funnel Beaker culture** (named after its distinctive pottery) that originated in what is now Poland. Although it is tempting to think that colonists introduced farming into southern Scandinavia, there is a good case for the adoption of farming by indigenous Mesolithic groups. The slow increase in farming and the ephemeral presence of domestication in the early Neolithic are not suggestive of incoming colonists. Furthermore, Mesolithic types of pottery, flint tools, and non-elite burial traditions continued at many Neolithic sites. And skeletal evidence shows no indication of newcomers but rather continuity of the former Mesolithic population. Neolithic occupation is stratified above Mesolithic levels at some coastal sites, although later Neolithic groups focused primarily on inland areas, settling near sources of fresh water and good grazing land. Carbon and nitrogen isotope analyses show interesting differences in diet that appear to reflect changing subsistence patterns: Mixed consumption of marine and terrestrial foods in the Mesolithic changed to a purely terrestrial diet in the Neolithic (Richards et al. 2003). This change, however, may not have been as rapid or total as many researchers believe. Some isotopic analyses show that Neolithic groups continued to exploit both terrestrial and marine sources for a long time. Given the richness of Scandinavian coastal resources, this would not be surprising. More analyses and refining of the isotopic method should help clarify the pattern (Lidén et al. 2004; Milner et al. 2004).

It is difficult to determine why Mesolithic populations in Scandinavia adopted farming. There was no shortage of food and no sudden increase in population; no dramatic climatic factors would have affected food resources. Why, then, would these people give up an easy life? Douglas Price (2000, 2003) believes that the good life may have been the catalyst. Abundance and trade gave rise to a nascent elite and subsequent competition among some Mesolithic groups, and people turned to farming to produce the surplus required to pay for their increasing demand for status goods. Farming may have had nothing to do with subsistence but rather may have reflected changing social organization.

# Farming in China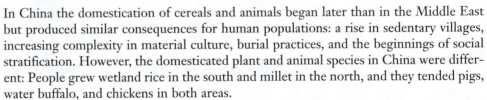

In China the domestication of cereals and animals began later than in the Middle East but produced similar consequences for human populations: a rise in sedentary villages, increasing complexity in material culture, burial practices, and the beginnings of social stratification. However, the domesticated plant and animal species in China were different: People grew wetland rice in the south and millet in the north, and they tended pigs, water buffalo, and chickens in both areas.

Hunter-gatherer groups exploited a range of wild rice species that flourished in subtropical South Asia. Excavations at cave and terrace sites in the middle Yangzi valley revealed rice husks and **phytoliths** (microscopic particles of silica from plant cells), from levels dating between 14,000 and 9,000 years ago, although it is difficult to determine if the rice was deliberately cultivated (Toyama 2002; Underhill 1997). Recent excavations at Shangshan in the lower Yangzi valley uncovered a sedentary village site that dates to 10,000 years ago. As well as posthole evidence for wooden pile dwellings (raised houses set on wooden posts), artifacts included flaked and ground stone tools, mortars and pestles, and pottery tempered with charred plant remains, among them rice husks. Specialists studying the morphology (shape) of the rice husks believe them to be in the initial stages of domestication (Jiang and Liu 2006).

Archaeologists recovered quantities of rice from waterlogged deposits at sites of the Pengtoushan and Bashidang culture (8,900 and 7,500 years ago) in the middle Yangzi valley. At present archaeobotanists are not sure whether the rice at Pengtoushan sites was domesticated (Crawford 2006). Some suggest that the groups must have been cultivating rice, as the evidence from these sites indicates stable village life: a range of house types, including pile dwellings, rice-tempered pottery, polished stone axes, burials and storage pits. Phytolith and other microscopic analyses show the Bashidang rice to be at an early stage of domestication (Higham and Lu 1998; Underhill and Habu 2005). At Bashidang

**phytoliths**
Microscopic particles of silica that are present in many plant cells, preserve well, and can be diagnostic of plant types.

**Hemudu (or Ho-Mo-Tu)**
Neolithic wetland site in China with excellent preservation of domesticated and wild plants and evidence of sophisticated woodworking skills.

there were semi-subterranean and ground-level dwellings as well as wooden pile structures surrounded by ditches. Artifacts included a range of bone, wood, and bamboo tools, among them wooden spades and pestles. Domesticated animals included deer, ox, and pigs. However, early rice cultivators continued to include wild resources in their diet. The expansion of rice cultivation from 8,000 to 7,500 years ago underpinned the rise of village communities similar to those of Pengtoushan and Bashidang along the Yangzi River.

Laoguantai and Peiligang cultures consisted of early Neolithic communities of millet farmers who settled along the plains of the Yellow River in northeast China by at least 8,200 years ago. These groups lived in villages of round houses, stored grain in pits, fired pottery in kilns, and buried their dead with grave goods of pottery, axes, hoes, sickles, and mortars and pestles. Their domesticated animals included pigs, chickens, water buffalo, sheep, and dogs. However, they also continued to exploit wild plant and animal resources (Smith 1995; Underhill 1997).

**Hemudu** (also named **Ho-Mo-Tu**), on the edge of swampland south of Shanghai, is an agricultural village whose people exploited a range of domesticated and wild species between about 7,000 and 6,000 years ago. The wetland setting preserved much organic material. In the lowest of four stratigraphic layers, excavators discovered wooden houses as much as 23 m (75 feet) long and almost 7 m (23 feet) wide, each with an outside veranda. Raised above the swamp on wooden piles, the houses are testimony to the skill of Hemudu carpenters—in particular, to their use of mortise-and-tenon joints. Excavators recovered about 120 tons of domesticated rice remains from thick deposits beneath the houses, as well as gourds, water chestnuts, and lotus root (Higham 1996). Domesticated animals included pigs, water buffalo (probably used as draft animals), and dogs. Among the wild animals were elephant, deer, turtles, and bear, many small mammals, birds, waterfowl, and a variety of fish. Such rich wild and domestic resources ensured a varied diet for the Hemudu villagers.

Excavators also recovered a wealth of artifacts at Hemudu. There were stone artifacts; wooden paddles, spindle whorls, handles, and lacquered objects; bone arrowheads, needles, weaving shuttles, and whistles; spades made from animal scapulae, with surface wear polish indicating use in soft mud; and rice-tempered pottery (Chang 1986; Higham 1996). A sampling of these artifacts can be seen in Figure 10.6.

*Figure 10.6*

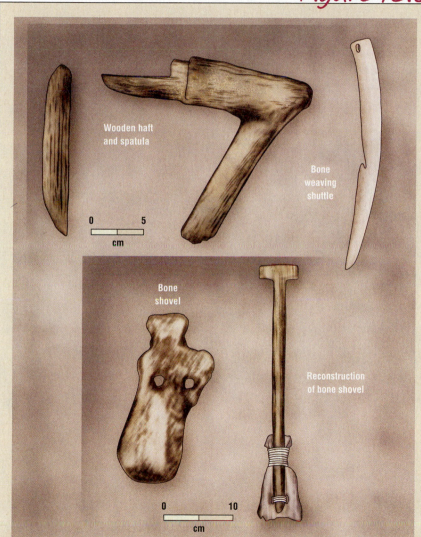

Wooden haft and spatula

0   5
cm

Bone weaving shuttle

Bone shovel

Reconstruction of bone shovel

0   10
cm

**WOODEN AND BONE ARTIFACTS FROM HEMUDU, CHINA.** Shown here are a wooden spatula and haft, a bone weaving shuttle, a bone shovel, and a reconstruction of a bone shovel on a wooden haft (wooden hafts were also recovered from Hemudu). How much potential information can these artifacts provide on Neolithic life?

*Source*: Adapted from Chang (1986).

The invention of pottery in China, as in Japan but in contrast to the Middle East, preceded agriculture—and may have happened more than 12,000 years ago. As had occurred in the Middle East, Chinese hunter-gatherer groups had exploited a range of wild resources and had used ground-stone technology long before they began to cultivate plants. They also may have domesticated plants other than rice and millet, such as taro and soybean; evidence for these may be found if researchers systematically employ plant recovery techniques such as flotation. There also may be yet undiscovered areas where the independent development of domesticated animals occurred. Future excavations in China will undoubtedly fill some of the gaps in our knowledge.

# Pastoralism and Cultivation in Africa

**pastoralism**
An economy in which food production is based on animal husbandry.

**Pastoralism**, or herding of cattle or other animals, so important in many areas of modern Africa, may have a 9,000-year history. Researchers long believed that African cattle were introduced from western Asia; however, more recent research proposes that African groups domesticated indigenous wild species of cattle. Originally based on archaeological evidence, these claims have gained credibility from genetic evidence that

Cave painting of cattle pastoralists at Tassili n'Ajjer, Algeria, that may be between 5,000 and 6,000 years old. Domestication of indigenous cattle may predate the painting by thousands of years. Why are cattle important to nomadic pastoralists?

suggests separate areas of domestication for European, African, and Indian cattle (MacDonald 2000).

The agricultural package that appeared along the Nile Valley about 6,500 years ago was a combination of sheep, goats, cattle, barley, and wheat (Smith 1995). Experts generally agree that all of these elements except the cattle were introduced from the Middle East. In the rest of Africa, the pattern differs from findings in other areas of the world in that some domesticated animals, cattle in particular, preceded the appearance of domesticated plants—often by thousands of years.

Claims for early cattle herding come from the eastern Sahara in Egypt. It is difficult to imagine that anything could survive under the arid conditions of the present-day Sahara, particularly grazing animals. Yet the environment in the early Holocene was less arid than it is today, because an increase in moisture had replaced the hyperaridity of the late Pleistocene. Summer rains formed **playas**, or shallow seasonal ponds, and temporary streams; for a short period each year, grasses and shrubs flourished in these areas. Such conditions attracted humans and animals as early as 9,500 years ago. Apart from three further periods of hyperaridity, archaeological evidence indicates the increasing presence of human groups around small and large playas for the following 4,000 years of the Neolithic period (Wendorf and Schild 1994).

## Nabta Playa

The **Nabta Playa** sites in Egypt provide good evidence of Neolithic pastoralists who took their animals into the playas after the summer rains and moved elsewhere for the dry season. It is unclear whether the earliest bones at these sites are of domestic cattle or not. Arguments in favor of domestic cattle are based on the ecological behavior of animals found in faunal assemblages (hare, gazelle, and cattle) and on human dietary practices. Hare and gazelle are dry-adapted animals needing little water, but cattle need water daily and cannot survive in the wild without permanent sources of water. Therefore, the argument goes, herders must have driven cattle to drink at desert playas where dry-adapted animals also congregated. Early Neolithic sites have few cattle bones, a finding that makes sense if herders kept cattle for their milk and blood rather than for their meat—as is done by many present-day African cattle herding groups (Wendorf and Schild 1994, 1998).

The number of settlements at Nabta Playa increased through time, eventually forming small villages of oval houses, sometimes partially semi-subterranean, constructed of wattle-and-daub walls (as shown by imprints in clay) on a base of stone slabs. Many houses had their own storage pits; indeed, large storage pits are characteristic of most sites in the later period in the area. Both deep and shallow wells occur at all but the earliest Neolithic sites, but about 8,000 years ago people began to dig large walk-in wells, presumably to provide easier access to water for their cattle. The artifact assemblage includes stone tools, grinding stones, and a few pieces of pottery made from local clays (Wendorf and Schild 1994). The Nabta Playa groups exploited a variety of wild plants that included millet and sorghum. Analysis of some sorghum grains indicates that people may have begun initial experiments with cultivation, deliberately planting grains that were still morphologically wild (Haaland 1995).

Archaeological evidence indicates increasing complexity among groups at Nabta Playa after 7,500 years ago. A few very large sites with deep **midden** deposits suggest repeated, intensive occupation. A megalithic complex is associated with one such site (E-75-8) at Nabta Playa. It includes an alignment of nine **megaliths**, (large stones), a stone circle, and several stone-covered mounds that contained cattle burials. The exact purpose of the site is unknown. It may have been a place where people gathered for social activities, such as trade and the formation of alliances, or a ceremonial center used for ritual purposes associated with cattle. Such rituals may have included feasts of cow meat, given the large numbers of cattle bones found at the site (Wendorf et al. 1996).

**playas**
Shallow ponds that result from seasonal rains in arid and semi-arid areas and around which grasses and shrubs grow for a short period each year.

**Nabta Playa**
Series of sites in Egypt with evidence for Neolithic pastoralism and an early megalithic complex.

**midden**
Mound formed through the accumulation of people's refuse.

**megalith**
A large stone set up as a monument.

## Sorghum, Millet, and African Rice

Increased rainfall during the early Neolithic not only made cattle pastoralism possible in the Sahara but also promoted a particularly resource-rich environment in the Sahel grassland region. Today the Sahel lies south of the Sahara, but at the time the grasslands extended into what is now the Sahara. The late domestication of cereals in the Sahel is probably due to the presence of abundant wild cereals in the area. The main indigenous African crops are sorghum, millet, and African rice, but the timing of their first use as crops is currently unclear (Smith 1995). As we've seen, Africans may have experimented with sorghum cultivation as early as 8,000 years ago. The earliest secure date for sorghum domestication is about 4,000 years ago in the Sudan–Chad area (northeast Africa); from there it spread to other areas in Africa. Domesticated sorghum dating to about 4,000 years ago has been found in southern Arabia and India, but it is not native to those regions and may have arrived originally as an item of trade from Africa. Two scenarios seem plausible. One hypothesis is that sorghum was domesticated outside of its African homeland and then reintroduced. Alternatively, perhaps sorghum was domesticated earlier in Africa, although such evidence is currently lacking (Harlan 1993). Domesticated pearl millet appeared about 3,000 years ago in West Africa; the first evidence of domesticated African rice dates from AD 200 at the site of Jenné-jeno in West Africa.

# Social Complexity among Farming Communities

Early farming communities in many parts of the Old World clearly showed an increase in social and economic complexity. Considerable organization of people must have been necessary for the construction of mud-brick or timber houses, and particularly for the building of stone structures such as the Jericho walls and tower. Long-distance contacts enabled people to obtain exotic goods and to enhance their prestige. At the same time, community members had to invest time and effort in the practical aspects of cultivation and animal tending or herding. Ethnographic evidence suggests that farming increased workloads for women, as their additional duties probably included tending, harvesting, processing, grinding, and cooking the crops. Given that population size increases with sedentism, women in farming societies would have had to perform these daily domestic tasks in addition to rearing more children (Harlan 1993). So although hunter-gatherers may not necessarily have had an easy life, the arrival of farming did not automatically bring security and leisure time.

Ceremony and ritual played an increasingly important role in farming communities. Two examples serve to illustrate this change in worldview: the site of Çatalhöyük in Turkey and the monumental architecture in Neolithic Britain.

## Çatalhöyük: A Farming Village in Anatolia

The two large mounds (**höyüks**) of **Çatalhöyük** (also spelled **Çatal Hüyük** or **Çatal Höyök**) rise above the Konya Plain in south central Turkey—the region called **Anatolia** in ancient times. These are not natural formations but the debris of thousands of years of human occupation, from the early Holocene to about 1,500 years ago. Beginning about 9,000 years ago, Neolithic groups lived in the area for at least 1,000 years (Hodder and Cessford 2004). James Mellaart and his team first excavated Çatalhöyük in the 1960s. A second series of excavations, directed by Ian Hodder, has been ongoing since the early 1990s. Differences in excavation techniques and advances in scientific approaches have enabled present-day researchers to verify some earlier interpretations, to suggest changes to others, and to reveal new information about Neolithic communities.

---

**höyük**
A large Neolithic mound in what is now Turkey (known elsewhere as a *tell* or a *tepe*).

**Çatalhöyük (or Çatal Hüyük or Çatal Höyök)**
Neolithic farming village in what is now Turkey, known for the inhabitants' emphasis on symbolic representation.

**Anatolia**
Region that is now Turkey.

## 1960s Excavations

The 1960s excavations revealed a farming village of rectangular mud-brick houses built around courtyards without any visible intervening streets or alleyways, as seen in Figure 10.7. There were no doorways to the exterior; access was via an opening in the flat roof and down a wooden ladder into the interior. Houses comprised two rooms. One room had a hearth and oven and was the center of domestic activities; the second often appeared to be of a more ritual nature, with painted murals and raised platforms along two walls, beneath which people had buried their dead. Layers of plaster covered house floors, platforms, and walls (Mellaart 1967, 1975).

Mellaart suggested that Çatalhöyük farmers not only grew wheat and barley and a variety of legumes but also collected wild nuts and other fruits. The predominance of cattle over sheep, evident in the faunal assemblages from the early excavations, suggested a reliance on cattle (believed to be domestic) rather than on sheep (believed to be wild) (Mellaart 1975).

Çatalhöyük is best known for the elaborate decoration in many houses, and Mellaart termed these houses "shrines." Murals, often repeatedly plastered over and repainted, depicted scenes of cattle and deer hunting, vultures, and headless corpses. Other murals

*Figure 10.7*

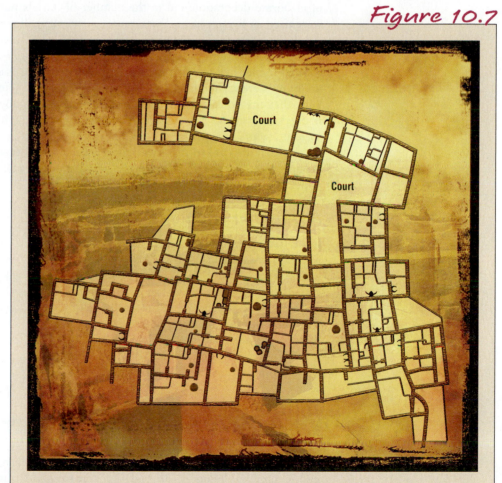

**A SECTION OF THE TIGHTLY KNIT VILLAGE OF ÇATALHÖYÜK.**  What can we infer about the people who lived at Çatalhöyük from the layout of the village?

*Source*: Mellaart, J. 1967. *Catal Hüyük: A Neolithic town in Anatolia.* London: Thames & Hudson. Reprinted by permission of James Mellaart.

featured nonrepresentational geometric designs. Statuary included human and animal figures, plastered animal horns, and cattle horns set in benches, some with associated food offerings. Mellaart interpreted the iconography as representing an ideology centered around goddesses, gods, and a cult associated with bulls.

A range of well-made obsidian (volcanic glass) artifacts—including daggers, blades, and mirrors—indicated sophisticated technological expertise. Advanced workmanship also was evident in bone tools, baskets, leather bags, wooden and pottery containers, copper beads, and woven cloth. Indeed, given that most people in the community were buried in a shroud, textile production must have been an important industry. Mellaart suggested that Çatalhöyük became rich through its control of trade over a wide area and gained importance not only as a trade center but also as a spiritual center (Mellaart 1967, 1975).

## Recent Excavations

Ian Hodder's recent excavations at Çatalhöyük have revealed the same types of Neolithic buildings and artifacts as were found in the 1960s. Houses are consistently similar to each other in plan and with regard to the activities undertaken within them. Çatalhöyük residents kept their houses remarkably clean and repeatedly covered walls, floor, and platforms with lime plaster. Larger buildings (Mellaart's "shrines") differ in the amount of elaborate decoration and in the number of burials under their platforms, but they were used as living places. Furthermore, several smaller houses appear to be grouped around one "shrine." Recent excavations have also found what might be alleyways or refuse dumps separating some blocks of buildings (Hodder 2005; Hodder and Matthews 1998). Hodder believes that the small groups of houses associated with the larger house might indicate related families. He and Craig Cessford (Hodder and Cessford 2004) believe that the consistent location and layout of Çatalhöyük houses—which often remained the same for hundreds of years—served to teach villagers the social rules of their society. People did specific activities in strictly defined areas of the house—a repetitive pattern that also linked them with their ancestors and created a social memory of their group. It was, suggest Hodder and Cessford, a way of maintaining order among a large population living in a densely packed area.

## A Question of Cattle

Cattle are important symbolic images in Çatalhöyük. However, they are less important for their meat than Mellaart believed. Modern techniques of fine-sieving deposits, which allow researchers to recover smaller bones, reveal greater exploitation of sheep and goats than of cattle (Martin 2000–2001). Furthermore, the domestic status of cattle at Çatalhöyük is unclear, but the small size of sheep bones appears to indicate that they were domesticated. Patterns of fracture and processing of sheep and goat bones indicate their use as meat, but finds of large cattle joints, often in articulation, suggest large-scale feasting—perhaps a further indication of the ritual importance of cattle shown by the wall decorations and installations.

## Where Were the Crops Grown?

Researchers formally assumed that Çatalhöyük farmers grew crops in fields around their village. However, recent geomorphological studies indicate that the village was on low-lying land and was surrounded by marshland that became even wetter during spring flooding; definitely not a good environment for agriculture. Phytolith analysis can distinguish between cereals grown on wet land and those grown on dry land; analysis of wheat phytoliths from Çatalhöyük indicates that most grew on dry land. Çatalhöyük farmers, then, must have grown wheat in fields some distance from the village, perhaps as much as 10 km (6 miles) away, where there was suitable agricultural land.

What strategy drove the people of this Neolithic community to set up their homes in the middle of marshland, where they would have had to travel so far to grow their crops? The location was likely of practical and symbolic importance. In the semi-arid environment of the Konya Plain, the site had to be close to water. Analysis of wood charcoal indicates the seasonal exploitation of the marsh, woodland, steppe, and hills for fuel, animal fodder, and wild foods (Asouti and Fairburn 2002). Wild cattle, so important in Çatalhöyük iconography, would have roamed the area around the site. Ian Hodder (2006) proposes that the extensive clay quarry pits found near the site also may have been an attraction: They provided a local abundant source of good clays for house construction, pottery, figurines, wall reliefs, and other clay artifacts. Furthermore, the quarry pits gave villagers a ready source of lime-rich clays for the vast amounts of plaster they used to maintain and decorate their buildings. At Çatalhöyük, it seems, practical daily life was imbued with symbolic meaning that united villagers in their present and through the memory of their shared past.

# Megalithic Monuments in Britain

Megalithic structures, rather than community settlements, characterize the early farming period in Britain. Yet these prehistoric stone monuments were as much a part of the domestication package as were plants and animals. Megaliths were emblems of an ideology that united farming societies at a local level and far beyond; they formed a link between ancestors and farming groups of the time. Such structures had a constant presence in the landscape. They were visible to people living in or passing through the area—and even when they were not immediately visible, groups would have known where they were. Monuments went through repeated modifications over hundreds of years as succeeding prehistoric groups changed their layouts, probably to conform with changing ideological and social beliefs.

Neolithic groups in Britain buried some of their dead beneath stone cairns or under long barrows or mounds of earth, which covered stone and wooden burial chambers. These people rarely buried complete bodies; instead, they used chambers as ossuaries in which they placed bones from several individuals, often moving bones around to make room for later burials. Evidence indicates that sometimes groups left bodies to deflesh in the open (a process called excarnation) before later burial (Whittle 1999). From the evidence of pig and cattle bones found in front of some mounds, mortuary feasting must have been part of the burial ritual.

## *Circular Symbolism*

For thousands of years farming groups in Britain circumscribed areas of land with circular monuments of earth, wood, and stone. The earliest constructions consisted of a series of discontinuous ditches flanked by small banks of earth dug from the ditches; each ditch and bank were separated from the next set by a causeway, giving rise to the term **causewayed enclosures**. Enclosures constructed on the chalklands of southern England would have been highly visible landmarks in the green landscape, as their banks would have been covered with white chalk rubble dug from encircling ditches. Windmill Hill near Avebury, one of the largest enclosures, has three sets of ditches and banks, the outer circle being about 350 m (1,150 feet) in diameter; the entire area covers an estimated 9.6 hectares (almost 24 acres). Although people disposed of their trash in the ditches of Windmill Hill, there also is evidence of deliberate, structured deposits of items including animal and human bones (Malone 1989). Over the millennia causewayed enclosures served many purposes: They functioned as marketplaces where people met at certain times of the year, as settlement areas, as places for excarnation of bodies, and as sites of other ritual and ceremonial activities.

The theme of circularity continued after the decline of causewayed enclosures with the emergence of a new form of monument: **henges**, or circular banks and ditches with two to four entrances and with internal settings of wood or stone. Except at the entranceways, henges fully enclosed the area within their bounds. **Stonehenge** is the most famous but least typical of Britain's henge monuments. The construction and

**causewayed enclosures**
Early Neolithic monumental constructions in Britain consisting of a series of discontinuous ditches flanked by small banks of earth and forming a circular enclosure; each ditch and bank were separated from the next set by a causeway.

**henges**
Late Neolithic monumental constructions in Britain consisting of a circular enclosure formed by banks and ditches with two to four entrances and internal settings of wood or stone.

**Stonehenge**
Complex megalithic henge monument in Britain.

modification of Stonehenge spanned 1,500 years, beginning about 5,000 years ago. Over this time groups removed wooden settings within the circle and replaced them with large upright settings of gigantic sarsen (cemented sandstone) stones and smaller bluestone elements. Transportation of the stones to Stonehenge constituted a phenomenal undertaking: The bluestones originated in Wales, more than 322 km (200 miles) away, although the sarsen stones were available a few miles from the site. Once the stones had arrived at Stonehenge, people had to shape them with stone hammers so that the lintels (horizontal crosspieces) fitted onto the standing stones rather like pieces of a jigsaw puzzle.

Stonehenge was not alone in the landscape, nor are such monuments rare in Britain. Both the natural world and the humanly modified landscape were sacred (Whittle 1997). The use of circular structures through hundreds of years reinforced memories of the past; the megalithic monuments were places of the dead as well as the living (Parker Pearson and Ramilisonina 1998). The ceremonies, feasting, and rituals that took place inside and outside the monuments strengthened ties between farming communities and ancestors. Many monuments incorporated astronomical features emphasizing the rising and setting sun and especially the winter and summer solstices, which must have signified a sense of seasons' passing and returning.

Causewayed enclosures and henges differ in the degree to which they enclose space. Causewayed enclosures do not restrict movement into or around the monument, whereas the layout of henges suggests control over access to the interior (Harding 1998). Henges appear to set an interior/exterior boundary: The ritual occurring *inside* the henge would have been witnessed by most of the community from *outside* the encircling ditch. The people inside the henge could experience views of the monument and surrounding focal points in the landscape from which outside onlookers had been excluded. However, a common ideology united the society.

Monumental architecture is not a phenomenon restricted to the British Isles but was a feature of Neolithic cultures in many other areas in Europe and elsewhere; examples include the Jericho tower and the Nabta Playa megalithic complex. The building of such massive monuments required an enormous investment of labor, however—and the Neolithic population in Britain does not appear to have been extremely large. Although construction of causewayed enclosures and henges may have taken place at quieter times of the farming year, it must have been as much a part of life as breathing, eating, and sleeping. The monuments are not haphazard constructions. They required detailed technical planning and subsequent organization of the workforce, the workers' tools, and the workers' sustenance over the course of the project. Organization on such a scale indicates the controlling hand of people in power.

The patterning at Stonehenge reflects the circular theme of Neolithic communities in Britain. A project to preserve the site by removing nearby roads and increasing grassland areas around the site is now in progress. How important is the conservation of prehistoric sites such as Stonehenge? What potential problems do conservators face?

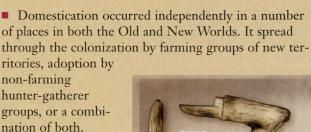

When the early Holocene began, anatomically and behaviorally modern humans were the only hominid species on the planet. The rich terrestrial, marine, and riverine resources of the late glacial and early Holocene provided groups of hunters, gatherers, and fishers with relatively secure food supplies; this allowed them to set up semipermanent bases from which to exploit their environment. In time people began to manipulate and eventually to control the growth of wild cereal plants and certain animals; they began to farm. Within a few thousand years farming hamlets and villages spread throughout much of the Old World. Increasing complexity is evident in technology, settlements, social organization, long-distance contacts, burial practices, and belief systems.

■ The onset of the present interglacial period, the Holocene, at about 11,500 years ago saw changes in global environment and geography caused by rising temperatures, reduction in glaciers, and rise in sea levels.

■ Hunter-gatherer economies continued to be based on hunting, gathering, and fishing. Nuts were an important resource everywhere. Natufian populations in the Middle East exploited stands of wild cereals.

■ Technology reflected a change in subsistence patterns with an emphasis on microliths, axes, fishing gear, and ground-stone processing tools.

■ Settlement patterns indicate longer periods of occupation at base camps and short-term use of smaller special purpose camps. The first cemeteries to appear show a range of burial practices and grave goods.

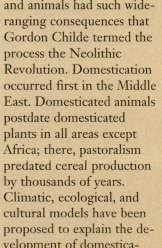

■ Domestication of plants and animals had such wide-ranging consequences that Gordon Childe termed the process the Neolithic Revolution. Domestication occurred first in the Middle East. Domesticated animals postdate domesticated plants in all areas except Africa; there, pastoralism predated cereal production by thousands of years. Climatic, ecological, and cultural models have been proposed to explain the development of domestication and of settled

page 289

communities. A number of factors, rather than a single prime mover, probably motivated the emergence of farming.

■ Domestication occurred independently in a number of places in both the Old and New Worlds. It spread through the colonization by farming groups of new territories, adoption by non-farming hunter-gatherer groups, or a combination of both.

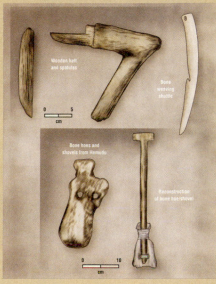
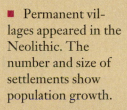
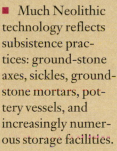

■ Permanent villages appeared in the Neolithic. The number and size of settlements show population growth.

■ Much Neolithic technology reflects subsistence practices: ground-stone axes, sickles, ground-stone mortars, pottery vessels, and increasingly numerous storage facilities.

page 297

■ Evidence of contact and trade between communities, much of it involving prestige items, suggests the beginnings of stratification in societies.

■ New ideologies are evident in varied burial practices, large and small figurines, murals, and large stone and earth monuments. The symbolism at Çatalhöyük suggests that ritual was a significant part of life in the community.

■ The Neolithic in Britain is known more from its megalithic monuments than from farming settlements. Structures such as Stonehenge suggest an ideology that reinforced ties between Neolithic farmers and their ancestors.

page 301

## KEY WORDS

Ain Ghazal, 288
Anatolia, 300
Archaic, 273
Çatalhöyük (or Çatal Hüyük or Çatal Höyök), 300
causewayed enclosures, 303
domestication, 284
Funnel Beaker culture, 296
Hemudu (or Ho-Mo-Tu), 297
henges, 303
Hoabinian, 273
Holocene, 269

höyük, 300
ideology, 289
interglacial, 269
Jericho, 288
Jomon, 273
Late Stone Age (LSA), 273
Linearbandkeramik (LBK), 291
long barrow, 295
megalith, 299
Mesolithic, 273
microliths, 277
midden, 299

Nabta Playa, 299
Natufian, 273
Neolithic, 273
optimal foraging theory, 274
pastoralism, 299
phytoliths, 296
playas, 299
shell middens, 272
Stonehenge, 303
tell, 288
wattle-and-daub, 291
Younger Dryas, 269

## SUGGESTED READINGS

Davis, S. J. *The Archaeology of Animals*. London: B. T. Batsford, 1995. This clearly written introduction to zoo-archaeology is well illustrated and includes many relevant case studies.

Levy, T. E. (ed). *The Archaeology of Society in the Holy Land*. New York: Facts on File, 1995. This is a multi-authored volume covering prehistoric and historic periods. The three chapters on the Natufian and Neolithic periods in the Middle East provide a good overview in a well-organized and accessible format.

Mithen, S. "The Mesolithic Age." In *The Oxford Illustrated Prehistory of Europe*, ed. B. Cunliffe, pp.79–135. Oxford: Oxford University Press, 1994. Because this article discusses the Mesolithic in Europe in general, it provides a wider context in which to place the Scandinavian Mesolithic.

Price, T. D., ed. *Europe's First Farmers*. Cambridge: Cambridge University Press, 2001. Region-by-region coverage of farming in Europe, with a good introduction and summary. A useful volume to consult for a particular area.

Price, T. D., and A. B. Gebauer, eds. *Last Hunters First Farmers*. Santa Fe, NM: School of American Research Press, 1995. This useful multi-author volume covers theoretical issues as well as presenting particular case

studies of the Old and New World, including rice cultivation in Southeast Asia.

Scarre, C., ed. *The Human Past: World Prehistory and the Development of Human Societies*. New York: Thames and Hudson, 2005. This book provides a highly informed and well-balanced summary of world prehistory. Each chapter, written by a specialist, covers a general time period and region. An excellent supplement for students who wish to know more about a particular period.

Smith, B. D. *The Emergence of Agriculture*. New York: Scientific American Library, 1995. Smith covers plant and animal domestication worldwide, and the beautiful maps, drawings, and photographs complement the text superbly. If you read only one book on this topic, this should be the one.

Takahashi, R., T. Toizumi, and K. Yasushi. "Archaeological Studies of Japan: Current Studies of the Jomon Archaeology." *Archaeological Studies of Japan: Current Studies of the Jomon Archaeology*, eds. R. Takahashi, T. Toizumi, and K. Yasushi, pp.105–137. Tokyo: Japanese Archaeological Association, 1997. An English-language overview of the Jomon period. The article is structured under subheadings that allow easy access to areas of interest (e.g., fishing, mortuary practice, exchange).

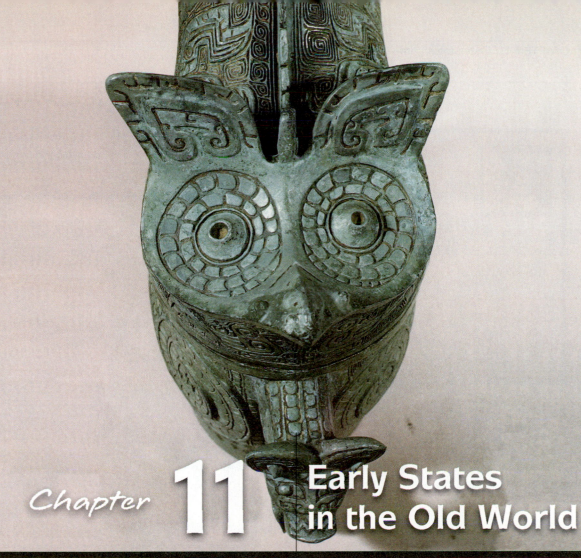

# Chapter 11 Early States in the Old World

■ **EARLY STATE SOCIETIES**

■ **MESOPOTAMIA**
Early Mesopotamian States •
The Mesopotamian City • Craft
Specialization • Trade and Exchange •
Social Stratification

■ **THE EARLY EGYPTIAN STATE**
Birth of a State: Predynastic Egypt • The Early
State: Egypt in the Early Dynastic and Old
Kingdom • Craft Specialization • Trade and
Exchange • King and Temple • The Age of
Pyramids

■ **THE INDUS STATE**
Origins of the Indus State • Indus
Cities • Craft Specialization • Trade and
Exchange • Social Stratification • Ritual
and Ruler

■ **THE SHANG STATE OF NORTHEAST
CHINA**
Before Shang: The Erlitou State • The Early
Shang State: Erligang Phase • Anyang:
Capital of the Last Shang Dynasty • The
Shang State Machine • Shang
Bronzes • Trade and Exchange

■ **HIGHLIGHT 11.1:** *The Emergence of Writing
in the Old World*

■ **EARLY STATES AND URBAN
COMPLEXITY IN EAST AND WEST AFRICA**
Early Ethiopian States • Jenné-jeno and
Urban Complexity in the Middle Niger

■ **CONCLUDING COMMENTS
ON EARLY STATES**

■ **HIGHLIGHT 11.2:** *In Temperate Europe with
the Celts*

▲
**Photo above:** Owl-shaped bronze vessel from
the Shang Dynasty, China

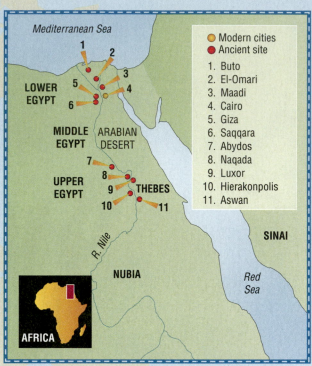

Modern cities
Ancient site

1. Buto
2. El-Omari
3. Maadi
4. Cairo
5. Giza
6. Saqqara
7. Abydos
8. Naqada
9. Luxor
10. Hierakonpolis
11. Aswan

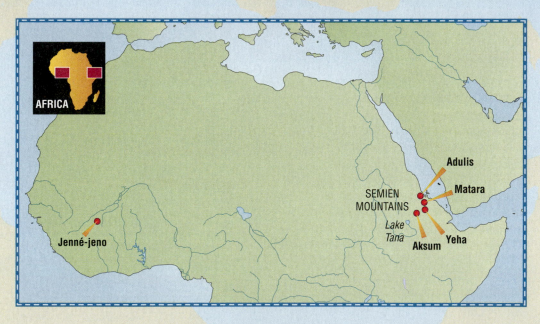

**SITES MENTIONED IN THE CHAPTER**

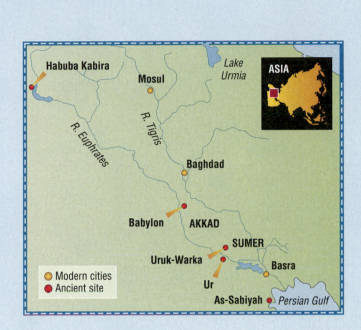

Habuba Kabira
Mosul
Lake Urmia
R. Euphrates
R. Tigris
ASIA
Baghdad
Babylon
AKKAD
SUMER
Uruk-Warka
Basra
Ur
As-Sabiyah
Persian Gulf

○ Modern cities
● Ancient site

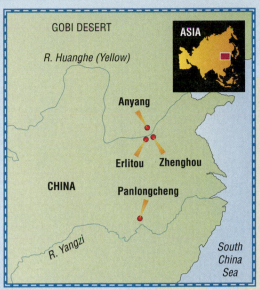

GOBI DESERT
R. Huanghe (Yellow)
ASIA
Anyang
Erlitou
Zhenghou
CHINA
Panlongcheng
R. Yangzi
South China Sea

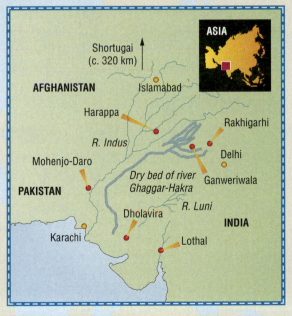

Shortugai
(c. 320 km)
AFGHANISTAN
Islamabad
Harappa
Rakhigarhi
R. Indus
Delhi
Mohenjo-Daro
Dry bed of river
Ghaggar-Hakra
Ganweriwala
PAKISTAN
R. Luni
Dholavira
INDIA
Karachi
Lothal

N
W    E
S

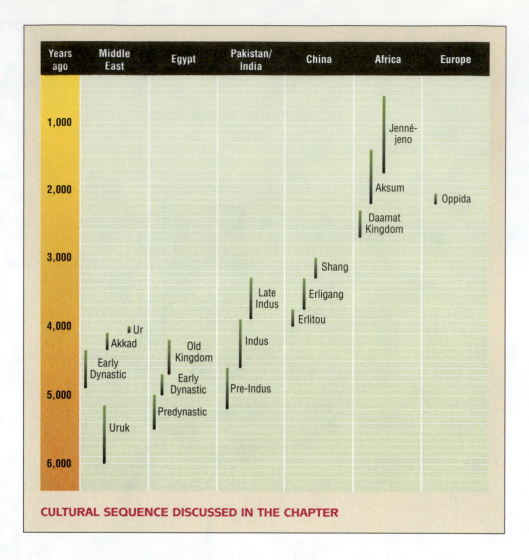

| Years ago | Middle East | Egypt | Pakistan/India | China | Africa | Europe |
|---|---|---|---|---|---|---|
| 1,000 | | | | | Jenné-jeno | |
| 2,000 | | | | | Aksum / Daamat Kingdom | Oppida |
| 3,000 | | | | Shang | | |
| 4,000 | Ur / Akkad / Early Dynastic | Old Kingdom | Late Indus / Indus | Erligang / Erlitou | | |
| 5,000 | Uruk | Early Dynastic / Predynastic | Pre-Indus | | | |
| 6,000 | | | | | | |

**CULTURAL SEQUENCE DISCUSSED IN THE CHAPTER**

# Early State Societies

The emergence of state societies radically and rapidly transformed the ancient world, because states exerted considerable political, economic, social, and ideological control over cities and surrounding hinterlands. Before we delve into the complexities of early states, we must clarify the term **state** (in some regions, it is synonymous with *city*). In 1950 Gordon Childe, one of the most influential archaeologists of the twentieth century, proposed a set of criteria he believed characterized state societies (Childe 1950). Childe's criteria have since been modified and expanded but remain essentially valid, although they are not all necessarily true of every state:

**1.** States have areas of high population density: larger settlements that include both domestic and nondomestic structures. Settlement patterns often involve a hierarchy—large city surrounded by smaller villages and hamlets between which goods and services are interchanged (Trigger 1993).

**2.** Division of labor occurs, including the emergence of full-time specialists who do not produce their own food but receive food from state storehouses. Specialization is archaeologically evident in the artifacts produced as well as in remains of workshop areas, in written records, and in communities' architecture and workers' living quarters.

**state**
A political structure that is socially and economically stratified under the leadership of a strong central authority whose power is generally legitimized by an army and often strengthened by an ideology; key characteristics include high population density, hierarchical settlement pattern, monumental architecture, and full-time specialists.

**3.** The state receives taxes in the form of goods and labor. These tributes are documented in written records and are visible in evidence of city grain storage areas, state-controlled projects such as monument building, and conscription into military service.

**4.** Monumental architectural projects such as temples, palaces, or irrigation systems reinforce and symbolize the organization and controlling power of the state. Such labor-intensive construction requires the harnessing of large populations (Scarre and Fagan 2003).

**5.** State societies are socially and economically stratified. A ruling elite, not necessarily related through kinship, derives power from centralized control of surpluses. Evidence of social stratification includes elite burials accompanied by rich grave goods, differences in house structure, inscriptions on monuments, and written records.

**6.** Record keeping is essential to control the complexity of state activities and to increase output (Baines and Yoffee 1998). The earliest Old World states had writing and recording systems; the Inca of Peru did not have writing as we know it but kept records using a system of knotted cords called the **quipu**.

**7.** State development promotes advances in sciences such as mathematics and astronomy. Scientific principles are evident in the engineering and construction of monumental structures as well as in detailed accounting and recording systems.

**8.** Long-distance trade expands to meet the state's increasing demand for nonlocal goods and materials. Archaeological evidence of trade consists of artifacts and/or materials originating from nonlocal sources. Records and letters discussing trade and exchange indicate the extent of trade as well as the existence of colonies beyond state frontiers. Trading relations may be peaceful or not; either way, states affect communities with which they are in contact, whether through material goods or through the transfer of ideas (Scarre and Fagan 2003).

**9.** People unite under a state ideology with a pantheon of gods, often including the state ruler. Temples, statuary, and ritual objects indicate the importance of the state ideology, and the promulgation of myth often reinforces the ideology.

**10.** A state army controls populations and undertakes military campaigns—a pattern clearly evident in most early states.

Childe's criteria make it relatively easy to identify cities and states archaeologically on the basis of their geographic extent, population size, and centralized organization. Evidence such as written records, **stelae** (inscribed stone slabs or pillars), statuary, and pictorial depictions can help researchers map the extent of state territory beyond city limits. A more vexing problem arises, however, in attempting to explain *why* states develop. Early proposals stressed location on fertile floodplains; the idea was that the development of irrigation agriculture and production of surplus food led to population growth and increasing social and political complexity. Other hypotheses suggested trade, warfare, or the importance of cultic centers as possible catalysts for the emergence of states. Models conceived during the 1960s proposed multiple, rather than single, causes for state development. Important among these was the systems model. Systems thinkers view states as large cultural systems incorporating numerous subsystems (e.g., subsistence, trade, technology, ideology, social organization) that interact with one another and are controlled by individuals and institutions. All, in turn, are part of a wider ecological system. A disruption occurring in one part of the system (e.g., technological innovation, warfare, flood) affects other parts of the system and results in change (e.g., expansion or reduction of the state) or adaptation to maintain the status quo (Flannery 1972). Recent social theories of state development stress the importance of individuals, aggressive "alpha males" as Kent Flannery calls them (Flannery 1999, 14): Powerful rulers, priests, or elites might supervise food production and distribution, organize trade and manipulate ideology, or rebels might usurp leaders (Scarre and Fagan 2003). In

**quipu**
Inca recording system consisting of cords knotted in various ways.

**stelae**
Inscribed stone slabs or pillars that commemorate important events or serve as territorial markers, tomb markers, or votive markers; the singular form is *stela*.

short, although there may be similarities behind the rise of states, there are also differences; each state is unique. There is no universal answer to the question of why states developed. Instead, there are many, varied answers—some of which may be combinations of those offered here, and some perhaps yet to be discovered. Furthermore, the development into a state is not an inevitable outcome for all small-scale societies. Many small communities of farmers and hunter-gatherers continued their way of life separate from the control of early states (Scarre 2005b).

The first four sections of this chapter will examine the earliest state societies in the Old World (in chronological order): Sumer in Mesopotamia (ancient Iraq), Egypt, Indus (Pakistan and India), and the Shang of China. The Mesopotamian, Egyptian, and Indus states overlap in time; the Shang is contemporary with the later phase of Egyptian and Mesopotamian states. The period of these states witnessed the beginning of written records, which researchers can use to complement and expand on archaeological evidence. The final sections of the chapter will look at the Aksumite state of ancient Ethiopia (East Africa), the "city" of Jenné-jeno in present-day Mali (West Africa), and Highlight 11.2 discusses the oppida (towns) of temperate Europe. Although these are much later developments, they are among the earliest complex urban societies in their respective regions.

# Mesopotamia

**Mesopotamia**
The region between the Euphrates and Tigris rivers that today encompasses most of Iraq and parts of Syria; location of the earliest cities and states in the world.

**Sumer**
Area in southern Mesopotamia where the first states emerged.

**Akkad**
Area in the northern part of southern Mesopotamia whose ruler, Sargon, first unified Mesopotamia by conquering the city-states of Sumeria about 4,350 years ago.

**Uruk period**
Period between 5,500 and 5,000 years ago that saw the emergence of state societies in Mesopotamia.

**hierarchical settlement pattern**
A pattern of differentially sized settlements (large urban center, villages, and hamlets) distributed across a region.

**Ubaid period**
Period that preceded the Uruk period in Mesopotamia and spanned the transition from Neolithic cultures to state societies.

Ancient **Mesopotamia** was the area between the Iranian mountains and the deserts of Arabia and Syria; today this region encompasses most of Iraq and parts of Syria. The name *Mesopotamia* comes from the Greek word meaning "land between the rivers," describing its location between the Euphrates and Tigris Rivers. As Africa is called the "cradle of humanity," so Mesopotamia is called the "cradle of civilization," because its southern regions of **Sumer** and **Akkad** were home to the world's earliest cities and states. Irrigation channels diverted waters from the Euphrates and Tigris across arid alluvial plains, converting them into fertile agricultural regions that could produce enough food to support large populations. Not only was the construction of such irrigation channels essential for cultivation, but their maintenance was also crucial to prevent the onset of salinization and the return of desert conditions (Butzer 1995). City granaries were repositories of surplus grain, which municipalities used in trade and as payment for labor. The construction and maintenance of irrigation channels, the building of monumental structures, the control and redistribution of goods—all these activities required considerable administrative organization to be successful (Postgate 1994).

## Early Mesopotamian States

Cities, states, and writing appear at about the same time in Mesopotamia—about 5,500 to 5,000 years ago, or during the **Uruk period** (named after the Sumerian site of Uruk-Warka). The period saw (1) the emergence of a **hierarchical settlement pattern** of city, villages, and hamlets on Mesopotamian alluvial plains; (2) increased bureaucratic control; (3) social stratification; (4) technological innovations; (5) extensive trade networks; (6) the emergence of leaders; (7) warfare; and (8) writing.

Cities of the Uruk period emerged from a tradition based on the earlier **Ubaid period**, which spanned the transition from Neolithic to state societies in Mesopotamia, between 7,900 and 6,200 years ago. During the Ubaid, prototypes of later, typical Mesopotamian temple compounds appeared for the first time; for example, excavation of the temple complex at Eridu exposed a series of temples, each constructed over an earlier temple but larger and grander than the previous structure—and the smallest and earliest building was an Ubaid temple. Excavations have revealed similar types of structures in other areas of Mesopotamia, suggesting a cultural and ideological homogeneity throughout much of Mesopotamia from the Ubaid onward and demonstrating the pivotal role of the temple in the development of states in Mesopotamia (Matthews 2003,

**Uruk-Warka**
Largest city in Mesopotamia and in the world about 5,000 years ago.

**cylinder seal**
A cylindrical, bead-like object used in the ancient Near East to produce a type of signature; usually made of stone and incised with designs or scenes that transferred as impressions onto wet clay as the seal was rolled over it.

2005). Evidence from late Ubaid sites indicates the presence of specialist workers, storage areas, and long-distance trade associated with temple compounds; the widespread occurrence of distinctive Ubaid pottery further suggests contact between areas. Recent excavations at As-Sabiyah in Kuwait provide supporting evidence for maritime contact with Arabia between 7,500 and 7,000 years ago. In addition to Ubaid pottery, excavators discovered a model of a reed boat, a disc with a painted depiction of a sailing boat, and numerous fragments of bitumen (a waterproofing material) with reed impressions and/or encrustations of barnacles (Carter 2006).

## The City-State of Uruk-Warka

Between 6,200 and 5,500 years ago, a number of large settlements dotted the plains of southern Mesopotamia. However, in the subsequent 500 years many settlements in the northern area of that region disappeared as people abandoned them and moved further south to settle around the city of **Uruk-Warka**. The city covered about 2.5 km² (1 square mile) and may have housed more than 20,000 people within its 9-km (6-mile) encircling wall. At that time Uruk-Warka was the largest city not only in Mesopotamia but in the world. Two large compounds dominated the urban center, and indeed all smaller settlements in the surrounding rural hinterland. The Eanna complex, the public and economic core of the city, covered a 300-m² (3,229-square-foot) area and was surrounded by its own wall; the highly decorated Anu temple complex formed the religious center. Both compounds represented substantial investments of labor and time—perhaps five years with 1,500 people working 10-hour days to build the Anu temple alone (Matthews 2003; Nissen 2001). In addition to domestic housing, there is evidence of craft specialization (including carnelian, flint, metals, and mass-produced pottery), gardens, and open spaces.

Excavations at Uruk-Warka revealed thousands of **cylinder seals** and writing tablets, some of which show a ruler or king in distinctive dress. Various renderings show the leader as a warrior, hunter, lawgiver, or conductor of rituals or depict him reviewing captives paraded before him by his soldiers. Most seals and tablets, however, are administrative, indicating tight control over production and redistribution of goods such as metals, textiles, grain, wool, and food given to workers. Exotic (nonlocal) items in the form of precious metals, semiprecious stones, and alabaster bowls, found in administrative buildings, imply exchange/trade outside the core area. Indeed, Uruk-Warka appears to have had its own trading colonies in regions beyond its borders, an interpretation suggested by sites that have architecture, pottery, seals, and an administrative structure similar to those in Uruk-Warka (Algaze 2001; Matthews 2003).

Uruk-Warka was a typical Sumerian city-state in southern Mesopotamia, in that tight control of its surrounding hinterland emanated from the center. But it was only one of many such independent walled states that characterized early Mesopotamia. These city-states varied in population and geographic extent but shared similar cultural traits and traded with one another (Trigger 2003). However, they also vied constantly for overall dominance in power struggles that

This 36.6-cm (14.4-inch) copper head of an Akkadian ruler was originally believed to be Sargon of Akkad but probably represents his grandson Naram Sim. What information does this portrait provide about Akkadian rulers?

often led to open aggression. In Mesopotamia's early dynastic period, people abandoned their hamlets and villages, depopulating the countryside in favor of the cities; possibly the migrants hoped to find a better life with better living conditions, or possibly they sought to avoid dangerous isolation during periods of intercity warfare. Although based in the city, farmers continued to tend their fields outside the city walls (Pollock 1999).

About 4,350 years ago Sargon of Akkad (the northern part of southern Mesopotamia) conquered the city-states of Sumeria, bringing unity to southern Mesopotamia for the first time. Despite the new ruling structure, there was much continuity from previous periods in ideology, architecture, and settlement patterns. But a major change was the legitimization of kingship through military conquests rather than through divine authority, as seen in iconographic depictions and royal inscriptions. In another change the Akkadian language replaced the Sumerian for written documents. After a relatively short rule, however, the Akkadian dynasty collapsed. A period of unrest then brought independent city-states back into ascendancy until the Ur III dynasty unified them once again (Pollock 1999).

## The Mesopotamian City

Cities and smaller settlements, usually surrounded by walls, tended to be sited along the waterways of Mesopotamia, the highways of their time; and some cities built harbors on the river edge. River clay provided building material in abundance—mud-bricks that dried quickly in the hot sun or were baked in kilns. People used kiln-baked mud-bricks sparingly, as their production would have been an expensive undertaking in the arid, tree-poor landscape of Mesopotamia. Mud-brick houses were built around courtyards

Excavations of the ziggurat at Ur were undertaken in the 1920s and 1930s under the direction of British archaeologist Sir Leonard Woolley. Some archaeologists believe that there was a temple on top of the ziggurat. What can we infer about the social organization of Ur society on the basis of the Ur ziggurat?

**Ur**

A major Mesopotamian city on the Euphrates River famed for its ziggurat, temples, urban neighborhoods, and cemetery.

**ziggurat**

A temple complex on raised, steplike platforms that dominated most Mesopotamian cities.

and had flat roofs where people would dry goods or sleep during hot summer evenings, much as happens in the region today (Crawford 1992). The Sumerian trading post of Habuba Kabira, on the banks of the Euphrates River in Syria, was surrounded on three sides by a large wall with two well-defended entrances. A main road paved with pottery shards ran through the town and divided it into separate areas, some of which may have served different functions. The town boasted a garden or orchard area as well as domestic dwellings, and it was dominated by a temple complex. The city of **Ur** (4,100 years ago) covered 100 hectares (247 acres); it had one harbor on the Euphrates and a second harbor on a large canal, both incorporated within an outer defensive city wall. Inside the city, a further wall surrounded a complex of temples, palaces, and the great ziggurat. The rest of the city was divided into neighborhoods of streets and lanes lined with large and small houses, small shops, and in one area a school (Crawford 1992).

Each Mesopotamian city had a temple or temples dedicated to its patron deity. Temples were often erected on the foundations of earlier temples or set on platforms, and eventually the **ziggurat** style developed: a tradition of building steplike structures with temples at the top. Although heavily eroded today, the ziggurat of Ur, made from approximately 7 million baked and sun-dried mud-bricks, still rises majestically above the Mesopotamian plain (Sauvage 1998) (Figure 11.1). To create such a structure the city leaders had to have bricks made and transported, supervise construction, pay laborers for their work, and maintain detailed records throughout the project. Although people saw temples as the home of the gods, these structures also had other functions, including serving as storage and administrative areas and as domestic quarters for priests and their servants (Pollock 1999).

As with temples, palaces served multiple functions: They housed the private apartments of the king and his family, domestic living quarters, ceremonial areas, administrative areas, craft workrooms, and storage areas (Crawford 1992). The monumental temple and palace architecture reinforced the powers and the prestige of the gods (and

*Figure 11.1*

**THE ZIGGURAT OF UR.**   This artist's rendition shows the form the ziggurat may have taken as it towered above the Mesopotamian plain. What effect would such a building have had on the citizens of Ur and beyond?

*Source*: Adapted from Wooley (1939).

therefore the temple priests) and rulers. Texts indicate the wide range of community activities controlled by palaces and temples. For example, the priests and rulers owned large tracts of agricultural land and supervised the cultivation and distribution of its produce; they owned herds of domestic animals and controlled irrigation schemes and fishing rights. And they controlled the manufacture and exchange of textiles and products made from leather, wood, metal, and stone (Postgate 1994).

## Craft Specialization

In the cities of Mesopotamia, some crafts were produced in domestic households; others were manufactured, under strict control, in palace and temple workshops. One Ur III craft archive lists the specialists working for the temple: wood and ivory workers, goldsmiths and silversmiths, stoneworkers, carpenters, leather workers, rope makers, and workers in reed. Women and girls worked in palace and temple workshops producing wool and flax textiles, many destined for export; indeed, one record mentions 600 tons of wool (Postgate 1994). Skilled metalworkers produced exquisite objects in copper, bronze, silver, and gold that are often found in rich burials (for example, in the royal burials at Ur, as we'll see shortly); metal shops also mass-produced blades for agricultural tools and a variety of axes, daggers, spears, and arrows (Crawford 1992). Although households made their own domestic pottery, the development of the fast pottery wheel and molds brought mass-produced pottery as well. Temple and palace officials kept records of products made, tools issued and returned, and workers—their age and sex; the responsibilities they held; and the payment they received, mainly in the form of food, wool, cloth, and oil (Postgate 1994).

## Trade and Exchange

The early city-states developed extensive trading networks to supply needed raw materials not found in southern Mesopotamia. Traders transported goods along the major rivers, overland along caravan routes, and by sea up the Persian Gulf coast (Crawford 1992). Imported goods included lead, silver, copper, timber, stone, and obsidian from Anatolia (modern Turkey); lapis lazuli from Afghanistan; semiprecious stones and chlorite bowls from Iran; and slaves to work for the state. Exported goods included textiles and grain. Sumerian city-states established trading links with the Indus Valley, Bahrain, and Oman. Indus seals and weights found in Mesopotamia and Bahrain testify to the extent of trading transactions, many of which were recorded on Sumerian **cuneiform** tablets. Texts also indicate the establishment of Sumerian trading colonies beyond the realms of Sumeria (Matthews 2005; Postgate 1994).

## Social Stratification

The king was at the pinnacle of society in a Mesopotamian state, particularly when invested with divine status. Social stratification is clearly evident from professional lists and titles set out in rank order, as well as from detailed accounts of rates of pay (Nissen 2001). Stratification is also evident in burial practices—in particular in the 1,850 burials, spanning the early dynastic to Ur periods, excavated at Ur. The Ur cemetery is famous for its 16 early dynastic royal burials. However, the variety in grave goods shows that this was a burial ground for lesser mortals, too; though not for young children, who were interred beneath house floors (Crawford 1992). The royal burials (perhaps kings, queens, priests, and priestesses) were in brick-built burial chambers that also held human sacrifices; sacrificial oxen with their chariots; and offerings of bread, dates, fish, vegetables, pig, sheep, and goat. Royal remains wore clothes made of fine cloth decorated with gold, semiprecious stones, and shell, and were accompanied by other goods originating from distant sources. Poorer people were generally wrapped in matting or placed in coffins. Grave goods such as military weapons or woodworking tools might in-

**cuneiform**
The earliest form of writing developed by the Sumerians, a system of signs produced with a stylus that left wedge-shaped imprints on clay (the term derives from *cuneus*, Latin for "wedge").

dicate profession in life, although no graves had goods indicating agricultural workers—the bulk of the population. Texts show that ordinary people received barley, beer, and fish to nourish them in the afterlife. A few of the 1,850 graves were partial cremations, perhaps reflecting a burial practice for people with beliefs different from those of the rest of the occupants of the cemetery. Whether the dead were rich or poor, however, the culture's belief in a life after death is evident.

# The Early Egyptian State

It can be argued that the emergence and success of the ancient Egyptian state owes much to the rise and fall of waters of the Nile River and the general ecological similarity found along most of the river's length (Wenke 1999). Rising in the highlands of central and eastern Africa, the White Nile, Blue Nile, and Atbara Rivers flow northward until their waters merge in northern Sudan to form the Nile. The single river continues its passage through Upper Egypt (southern Egypt), then branches out across its delta in Lower Egypt (northern Egypt) before flowing into the Mediterranean. Each year heavy rains in the Nile's feeder rivers increase the river's volume, causing it to flood its banks and cover adjacent lands with rich deposits of fertile silts. People have long channeled and saved the floodwaters to further irrigate land as needed. Salinization was not a problem for the ancient Egyptians, as it was for their Mesopotamian neighbors, as the Nile floodwaters flushed the salts that were part of their load into the sea (Butzer 1995).

The ancient Egyptians began planting each year as the floodwaters subsided. Usually the resulting harvests were enough to feed the populace and provide a large surplus, all in a land that does not have enough rainfall to allow rain-fed agriculture. The ancient Nile provided other sources of food: the shoals of fish that filled its waters and the varied wildfowl that nested in its attractive habitats. Domestic cattle, sheep, goats, and pigs added to the food sources available in the Egyptian landscape. However, the desert and its potential for danger began where the floodwaters ended. The Egyptians understood this well: They named the desert the Red Land and called the fertile agricultural strip, with its covering of mud and silts, the Black Land.

The 1,200-km (750-mile) course of the Nile between the Mediterranean coast and Aswan permitted easy access through Egypt. The river was ancient Egypt's main highway, with watercraft transporting people, goods, and massive blocks of stone for monumental building projects. Towns and villages grew up near the river, whereas temples were often constructed on the edge of the desert and connected to the river by canals (Brewer and Teeter 1999). Unlike Mesopotamian cities, which were always closely associated with temple complexes, early Egyptian cities evolved around administrative centers and palace complexes. However, most of the population lived in rural communities (Bard 2000).

Egypt was rich in natural resources. The bedrock is mostly sandstone and limestone; but outcrops of other building and sculpting stones—such as granite, diorite, quartzite, and alabaster—occur in regions close to the river, making these materials easy to transport. Copper, semiprecious stones such as turquoise and amethyst, and malachite (used for cosmetics and paint) were available in the eastern desert. Natron (used for ritual purposes) came from the western desert. Most highly prized, perhaps, were the gold deposits in southern Egypt and in the desert of Egypt's southerly neighbor, Nubia (Manley 1996).

The ecological similarity and ease of transport that characterized the lands along the Nile underpinned the development and maintenance of a highly organized and centralized Egyptian state system. We next look more closely at how this system grew and at how the Egyptian state exploited its rich resources—both to support the governmental and pharaonic machine and to carry on trade with neighbors to the north and south (Manley 1996).

# Birth of a State: Predynastic Egypt

Between 5,500 and 5,000 years ago, numerous thriving independent towns flourished in Upper (southern) Egypt and in the northern delta region. Archaeological excavations indicate the emergence of social stratification at the sites of Naqada, Hierakonpolis, and Abydos in Upper Egypt. For example, investigations at Hierakonpolis have revealed a temple area, a palace complex, grain storage areas, workshops for pottery manufacture, stoneworking, bead production, and other specialized crafts. Through time, differences in social status become apparent in the rise of mortuary cultic practices; in elite cemeteries that differ from those of the general populace in location, architecture, and richness of grave goods; and in evidence of long-distance exchange. The earliest **hieroglyphic** inscriptions occur in a burial chamber at Abydos, and the earliest painted tomb is at Hierakonpolis. The wall friezes at Hierakonpolis depict hunting scenes; victory in warfare; and, significantly, a male figure holding a mace and overpowering enemies in one scene and killing and taming lions in another, actions later seen as symbols of kingship (Bard 2000; Seidlmayer 1998).

At the same time, Nile delta settlements such as Buto, Maadi, and El-Omari show signs of increasing wealth. Distinctive pottery and other artifacts from Palestine and the Middle East found at these sites indicate established trade links; for example, at Buto, a coastal town and probably an important port, finds of clay cones similar to those decorating Uruk temples imply links with Mesopotamia (Wenke 1999).

Until about 5,000 years ago, Upper and Lower Egypt had distinct artifact styles. Eventually, however, southern elements supplanted northern ones—a transition clearly seen in the disappearance of Lower Egyptian pottery styles and their replacement by Upper Egyptian styles. The increase in settlement size, evidence of social stratification, and similarity of pottery and architectural styles throughout Egypt likely indicate unification of the country and emergence of the Egyptian state. Traditionally, scholars have often seen unification as consisting of the conquest of Upper Egypt by King Narmer (also called Menes). A ceremonial flat stone, called the **Narmer palette**, found at Hierakonpolis, depicts the king defeating opponents; he wears the red crown of Lower Egypt on one face of the palette and the white crown of Upper Egypt on the reverse (Figure 11.2). Most Egyptian archaeologists today, however, feel that unification involved a more complex mix of acculturation and competition for power between chiefdoms. The process may have involved initial alliances between, or unification of, some groups, perhaps into small kingdoms, before the eventual unification and formation of the Egyptian state (Hassan 1997; Wenke 1991, 1999).

# The Early State: Egypt in the Early Dynastic and Old Kingdom

The Early Dynastic and Old Kingdom period in Egypt lasted from about 5,000 to 4,200 years ago. During those centuries the distinctive elements of the Egyptian state—settlement patterns, administration, architecture, writing, ideology, craft specialization, and trade—became securely established under the rule of a hereditary line of kings (the dynasty) who had divine status (Wenke 1999). It was a highly centralized state, organized from the capital at Memphis by a hierarchical bureaucracy of ministers. Chief among these was the king's principal advisor, or vizier, who was the most powerful individual after the king. In the early dynasties, the king's relatives held many ministerial posts, but in time high-ranking civil servants replaced royal ministers. Ministers' titles, conferred on them by the king, indicate a range of governmental departments that included the treasury, construction, granaries, archives, and army. Egypt was divided into provinces or regions each with its own governor. Provincial administration followed the same pattern as that of central state organization at Memphis, but on a more restricted scale and always under the strict control of state ministers (Brewer and Teeter 1999). Taxes, paid in grain or labor, enabled the state to undertake monumental building projects, organ-

**hieroglyphic**
The ancient Egyptian pictographic script in which signs could represent objects or sounds; used for inscriptions on monuments and literary texts.

**Narmer palette**
A carved flat stone that is traditionally believed to depict the unification of Egypt by King Narmer.

*Figure 11.2*

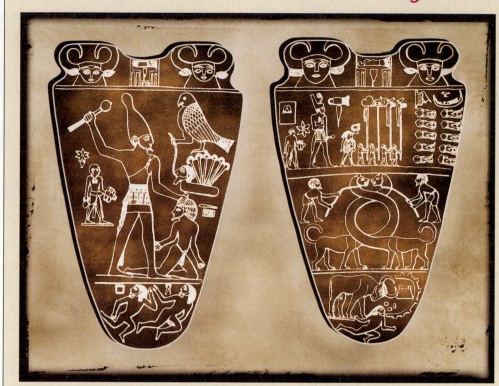

**THE NARMER PALETTE.** Carved from slate, this palette shows the king wearing the white crown of Upper Egypt (left) and the red crown of Lower Egypt (right). What do you think was the purpose of the Narmer palette?

ize military campaigns, and feed state workers. Scribes recorded everything meticulously; for example, harvest size, herd size, goods produced, building supplies, tools given to workers, and military campaigns. These records are on papyrus in **hieratic**, a cursive form of ancient Egyptian writing.

## Craft Specialization

The skill of ancient Egyptian artisans is legendary. Weaving and pottery were female activities; other crafts were male domains. These included carpentry; stone vessel and sculpture manufacture; metalwork; jewelry production; and bone, flint, and ivory work. Craft traditions often passed down through a family. Most specialists, like the metal workers shown in Figure 11.3, worked for royal or temple workshops producing items for prestige and ritual use. Tomb models show teamwork suggestive of assembly-line production; such teamwork is particularly evident in tomb construction. It is possible that a large state such as Egypt, with its network of skilled artisans, provided more opportunity for specialists to develop their skills than would a smaller city-state (Trigger 1993).

## Trade and Exchange

Although Egypt was rich in mineral resources, the state also needed to acquire nonlocal commodities through peaceful—or aggressive—trade. Good-quality timber was one such commodity; pine and cedar came from Syria and Lebanon, and Nubia provided ebony. Nubia also supplied Egypt with silks, ivory, and exotic animal skins, and Nubia's

**hieratic**
A cursive form of ancient Egyptian writing, written with pen and ink and used for everyday purposes.

*Figure 11.3*

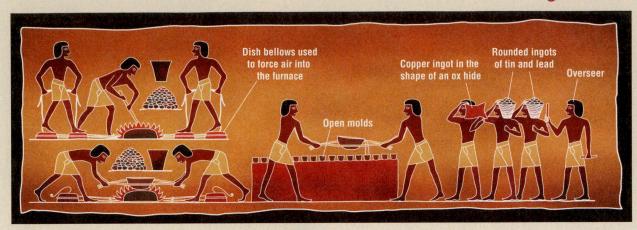

Dish bellows used to force air into the furnace

Copper ingot in the shape of an ox hide

Rounded ingots of tin and lead

Overseer

Open molds

**METALWORKING IN ANCIENT EGYPT.** The tomb paintings shown here depict workers transporting copper ingots and melting and casting metal in molds. Why are tomb paintings an important source of information about ancient Egypt?

rich gold resources attracted Egyptian attention and military presence (Manley 1996). Turquoise came from the Sinai, obsidian from Anatolia, and lapis lazuli from Afghanistan. To its own copper reserves Egypt added copper sources from Sinai and farther away. Goods arrived via overland transport by animal caravans and by boat along the Nile and the Red Sea. Egypt's military might protected or enforced trade links; for example, texts record campaigns against Bedouins in southern Israel, Libyan raiders around the western oases of Egypt, and Nubian tribes (Kessler 1998).

## King and Temple

Ancient Egyptians saw the king as both human and divine. Egyptian myths, texts, inscriptions, and paintings show kings in various roles. The king's duty in his governmental role was to oversee the smooth running of the country. In his divine status, he mediated between his people and the gods to ensure that harmony would prevail over chaos in life. He was associated with many gods, in particular Horus, Seth, Osiris, and the sun god Re. The ancient Egyptians carefully attended to the needs of the pantheon of gods that permeated all aspects of Egyptian life and death, believing that the gods in turn would protect the populace from calamities, such as Nile droughts. Priests, working on the king's behalf, provided statues of the deities with food and drink; dressed and purified them regularly; and, during festivals, paraded the statues to allow the people to show their devotion and request favors. The general public had limited access to large temples and ceremonies, but people had their own smaller shrines in the countryside and in their houses (Brewer and Teeter 1999).

## The Age of Pyramids

The royal cemeteries at Abydos were the final resting place for the first kings of Egypt, between 5,150 and 4,890 years ago. The king was buried in a **mastaba** (a large, rectangular, underground tomb made of mud-brick and stone). Surrounding the royal chamber were many smaller rooms where priests placed grave goods and food offerings to accompany the king on his journey to the afterworld. For a short period between 5,050 and 4,890 years ago, some of the king's retainers were sacrificed and buried in the ad-

**mastaba**
A large, rectangular underground tomb made of mud-brick and stone in ancient Egypt.

The mortuary complex of Djoser at Saqqara was the first monumental structure of worked stone in the world. Compare the monumental architecture of Egypt with that of other states discussed in this chapter.

joining chambers, presumably to help their royal master on his underworld journey. A superstructure of mud-bricks probably covered the entire complex (Brewer and Teeter 1999; Malek 2000; Manley 1996).

From about 4,890 years ago, Saqqara (and later Memphis) became the focus for royal burials, and the era of pyramid building began. Conceived by the king's architect and vizier, Imhotep, the step pyramid of King Djoser, built about 4,600 years ago, was the first monumental stone construction in the world. Although the pyramid started as a three-step mastaba, its final form was of six stepped levels rising more than 60 m (200 feet), faced with limestone on the exterior, and with a burial chamber lined with granite blocks transported from Aswan, 934 km (580 miles) south of Giza. A wall 1.6 km (1 mile) long surrounded the pyramid and its adjoining complex of smaller ritual temples (Stadelmann 1998).

The great pyramid of Khufu (also known as Cheops) at Giza is the largest and most perfect pyramid. Rising to a height of almost 130 m (430 feet) and made of 2,300,000 stone blocks ranging in size from 2.5 to 15 tons, the pyramid may have taken as long as 20 years to build. Corridors and passages lead to interior chambers and the burial crypt. Researchers have concluded that small shafts emanating from chambers, once interpreted as ventilation shafts or stellar observatories, were never open to the exterior; the shafts may have been designed as ritual passages through which the king's spirit could fly on its heavenly route. A complex of temples surrounded the pyramid, and a causeway 810 m (2,660 feet) long connected it to the king's mortuary temple (Brewer and Teeter 1999, Stadelmann 1998).

The construction of pyramids demonstrates the prowess of Egyptian architects and engineers as well as the skills of stone and other craft workers involved in the process. In addition to the permanent corps of specialist workers, ancient texts indicate that the state conscripted unskilled laborers for short periods of time—an estimated 25,000 to 30,000 people each three months for a staggering total of over 100,000 workers per year (Lehner 1997). Towns grew up near the construction area to house workers and officials. Recent excavations undertaken by the Giza Plateau Mapping Project (GPMP) revealed a town near the Giza pyramids (Lehner 2002). The settlement spreads over 9 hectares (22 acres) and includes two large areas of houses where skilled workers and their families lived (named Eastern Town and Western Town on Figure 11.4); an administrative and storage building; many bakeries and craft workshops; and four blocks (galleries) about 35 m (115 feet) long, each composed of a number of long, narrow, rectangular buildings. Spaced at regular intervals along the inside of these buildings and extending toward a small, central dividing wall are low, single-bed-sized platforms. Mark Lehner and his colleagues believe these to be the unskilled laborers' quarters (Lehner 2002; Murray 2004–2005).

*Figure 11.4*

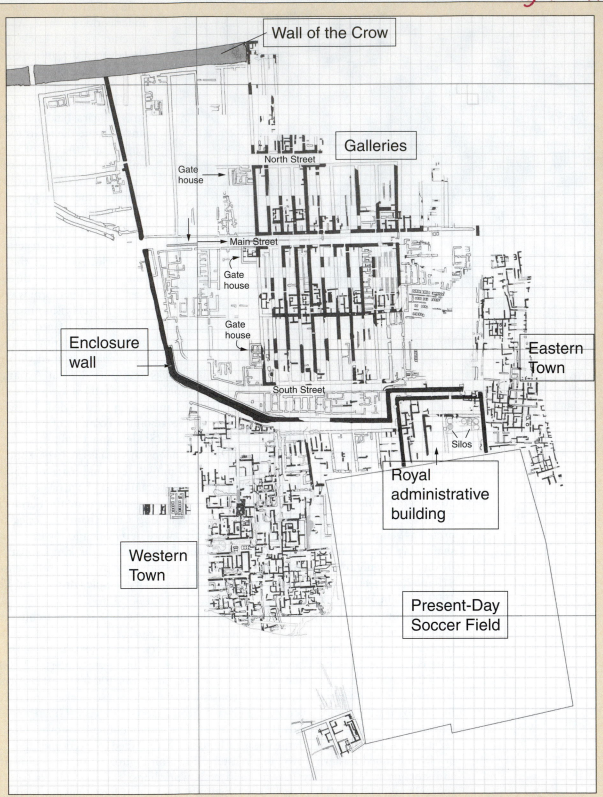

**PLAN OF THE PYRAMID WORKERS' TOWN AT GIZA.** The site extends over 9 hectares (22 acres). How does the town reflect ancient Egyptian social organization?

*Source:* From drawing by Mark Lehner. Used with permission.

Mary Ann Murray, the archaeobotanist on the GPMP project, recovered charred seeds of emmer wheat and barley, the former used to make bread in town bakeries and the latter used to make beer, the standard drink of ancient Egyptians. The workers' diet also included fruit, vegetables, meat, and fish. However, excavators found evidence of a greater range of food in the domestic area than in the unskilled laborers' quarters; skilled workers had a better diet.

The practicalities of pyramid construction remain a mystery, as no ancient texts describe the building process. Bones of the pyramid builders, recovered from the workers' cemetery at Giza, provide a glimpse of the hardships they suffered: fractures, heavy wear and tear on joints, and injuries caused by crushing (El Mahdy 2003; Hawass 1997).

Pyramid building must have been part of Egyptian life, much like the agricultural cycle. The effort invested suggests that many in the populace shared strong beliefs in the king's divine status and in the afterlife. These beliefs were not universal, however, because all tombs were later plundered.

# The Indus State

The first state organization in South Asia emerged along the Indus and the ancient Ghaggar-Hakra Rivers about 4,600 years ago. Known as the **Indus** (after the river) or **Harappan** (after Harappa, the first Indus city to be discovered), the state controlled an area of almost 805,000 km² (310,000 square miles), more than twice the size of either Egypt or Mesopotamia, and remained powerful for 700 years (Kenoyer 1998). The power of the Indus state extended beyond the core river regions of its largest cities, from Afghanistan in the north to the coasts of Pakistan and southern India (Mughal 1991). The state was based on river-fed agriculture and pastoralism. It supported large populations, including specialized artisans, and it had thriving long-distance trade connections; a writing system; and large, well-planned cities with monumental architecture, as well as smaller settlements. However, although more than 1,500 Indus settlements have been discovered, far less is known about the Indus state than about either Mesopotamia or Egypt—for the simple but crucial reason that the Indus script has not been deciphered. Furthermore, there is no convincing evidence for large temples or for palaces and kings as seen in Mesopotamia and Egypt. Most of what is known about the ancient Indus world has emerged through archaeological excavation and analysis.

Melting snows of the Himalayas and summer monsoon rains caused the ancient Indus and Ghaggar-Hakra rivers and their tributaries to swell and breach their banks, covering the valley plains with fertile alluvial sediments that supported good, generally reliable harvests. The rivers also provided good transport routes between settlements and cities, as well as access to areas rich in raw material resources (Kenoyer 1998). But high river floods could have disastrous consequences to settlements, too. Indus architects dealt with this risk by constructing massive, high mud-brick platforms on top of which they built their cities.

## Origins of the Indus State

The Indus state emerged from a long period of growth and development of agricultural communities in the region. An increase of sites occurred over a wide geographic area between 5,200 and 4,600 years ago, indicating rising population numbers. Archaeological investigation has revealed a widespread similarity of cultural traits among groups, for example: pottery styles, craft work, formal settlement planning with mud-brick architecture, and trade networks. The end of this pre-state period is marked by the abandonment of numerous sites, many of which show signs of large-scale burning. However, there is no evidence to suggest that the burning was the result of warfare (Coningham 2005). Gregory Possehl (2002) thinks people may have destroyed their settlements deliberately,

**Indus (or Harappan)**
The first state society in South Asia, which emerged about 4,600 years ago in what is now India and Pakistan.

**Mohenjo-Daro**
The largest of the cities of the Indus state.

**Harappa**
A major city of the Indus state.

in a symbolic break with their past, prior to beginning a new way of life. Most sites were never reoccupied, and many of the later Indus sites were founded on virgin territory. Nevertheless, evidence of pre-Indus occupation has been found in the lower levels of some Indus sites, for example, Harappa.

Within the 100 years or so, characteristics evolved that were typically Indus: development in technology, craft specialization, baked and mud-brick architecture, town planning, methods of water management, the introduction of writing, a system of weights and measures, long-distance trade, and the development of maritime technology (Kenoyer 1998). It is clear that features of the Indus state developed in the pre-Indus phase, but the transition between the two periods is not yet well understood. This situation may improve as archaeologists focus on the problem.

## Indus Cities

Five large Indus cities have been discovered: Mohenjo-Daro, Harappa, Rakhigarhi, Ganweriwala, and Dholavira. The largest and best known are **Mohenjo-Daro** (about 202 hectares, or 500 acres), and **Harappa** (150 hectares, or 370 acres). These major cities were considerable distances from one another. For example, Mohenjo-Daro was 570 km (354 miles) from Harappa; the unexcavated city of Ganweriwala was about halfway between the two; and distances of 300 km (186 miles) separated most cities. Each city was surrounded by agricultural land and would likely have controlled goods passing through its area.

The layout of the large cities indicates planning. Often built on large mud-brick platforms or mounds surrounded by massive mud-brick retaining walls, the cities enjoyed some safety from floods. Usually one mound rises above the rest of the city. For example, the highest mound at Mohenjo-Daro (see Figure 11.5) rises 12 m (39 feet) above the surrounding plain, whereas the lowest area is buried beneath 7 m (23 feet) of alluvial silt (Jansen 1991). Because of the clusters of monumental buildings on the high mounds at Mohenjo-Daro and Harappa, scholars initially interpreted them as fortified citadels, a deliberate part of city planning. Later researchers have questioned this interpretation, noting that the walls did not serve defensive purposes but provided protection against floods. In addition, the monumental structures on a high mound were forceful symbols of power (Dales 1991; Possehl 2002).

The Great Bath in the citadel complex at Mohenjo-Daro is unique among Indus buildings. A rectangular tank measuring 12 by 7 by 2.4 m (39 by 23 by 8 feet), made of kiln-baked mud bricks waterproofed by a lining of bitumen, it is surrounded on three sides by a pillared veranda and smaller bath rooms. Bathers entered the bath via steps at each end of the structure. Water probably entered the tank from a side room and drained out through a drain on one side of the tank (Jansen 1991). The exceptional prowess of the Indus architects is also evident in other grandiose buildings on the citadels at Mohenjo-Daro and Harappa, such as the large pillared building at each site. Archaeologists once interpreted these pillared structures as granaries but no longer see them as such, because corroborating evidence (grain) is

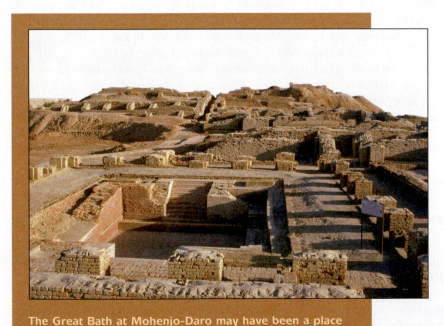

The Great Bath at Mohenjo-Daro may have been a place where water rituals took place. Why might Indus groups view water with reverence?

absent. Possibly the buildings were the equivalent of large city halls (Kenoyer 1998) or places for communal rituals (Maisels 1999).

Major streets in Mohenjo-Daro and Harappa were oriented east–west and north–south, although smaller streets and lanes were often at more irregular angles. Although there is evidence for living areas, workshops, and open spaces on the higher mounds, the major living and industrial hubs of Indus cities were on the lower mounds: Excavations of those mounds have revealed housing complexes, workshops, open spaces (probably market areas), and also monumental buildings. One of Mohenjo-Daro's

*Figure 11.5*

**CITADEL AT MOHENJO-DARO.** The citadel area with its monumental buildings dominates the city. How could the citadel area have had an impact on the citizens of Mohenjo-Daro?

*Sources*: Based on Possehl (2002) and Wheeler, M. 1966. *Civilizations of the Indus Valley and beyond*, 14, 22. London: Thames & Hudson.

neighborhoods covered 28 blocks and included 90 house compounds separated by wide streets (the widest about 10 m or 33 feet) and narrow lanes (see Figure 11.6). Larger houses were built around a central courtyard with outside walls backing onto streets, thus increasing the privacy of inhabitants. Such houses contained many rooms of varying sizes and may have combined workshop and living areas within a single compound. Still other units appear to be single-room tenement-type dwellings (Kenoyer 1998).

Each Indus city had a system of wells, cisterns, and reservoirs to hold water; well-maintained drainage systems within houses; and an extensive network of street drains. Some of these drains functioned as conduits for rainwater, and others channeled waste to the edge of the settlement. Many houses had their own toilets, often large jars or sump pots inserted into the floor, sometimes connected to a drain (Kenoyer 1998).

The building blocks of Indus architects were standardized sun-dried or baked mud-bricks made from the ever abundant river clay. In many cities all water-related structures (including drains), were made of baked mud-bricks, as were some of the large buildings. However, wood and dressed stone were used in some construction; for example, Dholavira is distinctive for its dressed stone walls, gates, pillars, and drains (Patel 1997).

*Figure 11.6*

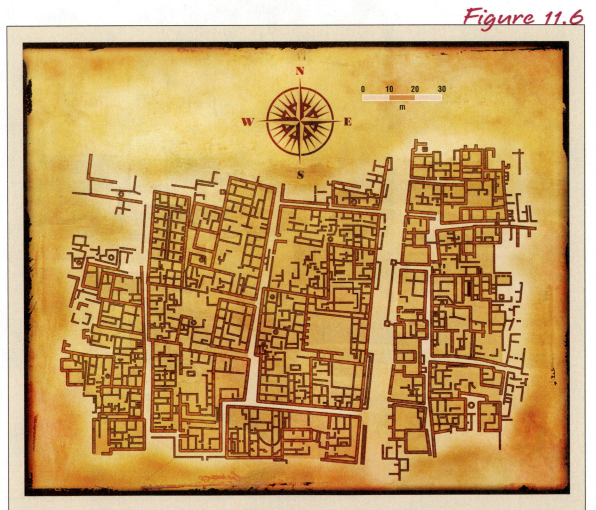

**PLAN OF PART OF A RESIDENTIAL AREA OF MOHENJO-DARO.** Careful city layout is evident in other Indus cities as well. What factors did Mohenjo-Daro architects need to consider when planning residential areas?

*Sources*: Based on Possehl (2002) and Wheeler, M. 1966. *Civilizations of the Indus Valley and beyond*, 14, 22. London: Thames & Hudson.

## Craft Specialization

The wide range of objects as well as the various workshop areas found at many Indus cities indicate the technical skill of Indus craft specialists: potters, bead makers, metal-smiths, jewelers, stoneworkers, weavers, basket makers, bangle makers, seal makers, and stone tool specialists, among others. Most people produced their own domestic pottery, made baskets, and wove cloth; processes like metallurgy and stone bangle production, however, required specialist knowledge. There are some regional differences—for example, in local pottery styles and construction materials. Nevertheless, throughout the large geographical area controlled by the Indus state, a high degree of standardization is evident in building techniques, in brick making, in the system of weights and measures, and also in settlement patterns.

## Trade and Exchange

The Indus state had wide-ranging trade networks connected by sea, river, and overland routes. Imports included copper from Baluchistan in the west and Rajasthan in the east; carnelian and agate from Gujarat; shells from coastal areas; and lapis lazuli from Baluchistan and Afghanistan, where a distant Indus colony, **Shortugai**, has been identi-fied. Mesopotamian texts refer to Indus merchants: Scripts mention Indus traders sup-plying ivory, gold, carnelian, hardwoods, rare animals, and slaves; an inscription by Sargon of Akkad mentions ships from the Indus, Bahrain, and Oman at Akkadian har-bors. In addition, Gulf seals found at Indus sites, and Indus seals found on Gulf sites, suggest trade between the two areas. Indus seals and typical Indus chalcedony beads found at Mesopotamian sites support textual evidence. Indus artifacts have also been found at sites in Oman; the Indus state set up trading posts, some of which have been identified, not only in Oman, but along the Arabian coast (Dales 1991). It is likely that part of the Indus import trade via Arabia was in perishable goods—camels, dates, and African cereals such as millet and sorghum (Tosi 1991). As the evidence shows, the Indus state had a thriving trading network through which it successfully accessed the materi-als and goods it required from nearby and more distant locales.

## Social Stratification

Although not as clearly defined as in Mesopotamia and Egypt, potential aspects of so-cial stratification are indicated in the Indus state. The population consisted overwhelm-ingly of rural farming and herding groups but also included artisans, architects, merchants, scribes, bureaucrats, and rulers. At the lowest level of society were slaves, mentioned in Mesopotamian texts as items of trade. Stratification is evident in house types and sizes: Some were large and had multiple rooms, whereas others had one room. Objects made of exotic materials, whose manufacture required complex technology, also suggest differences in status: For example, ornaments in semi-precious stones, metal work, and fine pottery are found in some houses, but not in all. Furthermore, the walls with gateways that surrounded monumental buildings may have served to restrict access to selected groups.

## Ritual and Ruler

Knowledge of the Indus state is limited, and this is particularly true in the sphere of rit-ual, religion, and rulers. Large temples—and clear signs of small temples, gods, or priests—are absent from the Indus region. Certain depictions on stone seals, such as a seated male reminiscent of the Hindu god Siva and water buffalo, may be of ritual sig-nificance. Although female figurines with large breasts and hips may have been fertility goddesses, they appear at larger sites but rarely elsewhere in the Indus region, contrary to what one might expect of a regionwide ideology (Dales 1991). Water was clearly an

**Shortugai**
Indus colony in Afghanistan.

important element of the Indus culture: The Great Bath at Mohenjo-Daro, other buildings related to water storage (such as the reservoir at Lothal), waterproof platforms connected with drains, and extensive city drainage systems suggest an emphasis on ritual cleansing.

The rulers of the Indus state also are shrouded in mystery. Unlike Mesopotamia, with its palaces and inscriptions, its statues and seals of rulers, and its displays of wealth and prestige, the Indus geographic area has yielded up no such indicators. It seems unlikely that a hereditary monarchy ruled the Indus state. Monumental buildings in the large cities must have been seats of political and administrative power, but there is little to clarify the mechanisms and people behind this power. A few broken statues found at Mohenjo-Daro may be images of leaders or ancestors; researchers have dubbed the most famous of these the "priest king," a name that nicely emphasizes the dilemma regarding rituals and leaders in the Indus state. Gregory Possehl (2002) proposes that a council of leaders ruled the Indus, rather than a single figurehead. Mark Kenoyer (1998), who has studied the Indus for many years, argues that the square seals with animal motifs and writing found at various sites indicate different ruling clans: Each animal (for example, elephant, humped bull, rhinoceros, water buffalo, or goat) could represent a clan totem, above which is the ruler's name.

Descriptions and interpretations of the Indus state in the early twentieth century emphasized homogeneity and an almost rigid standardization over a vast geographic area that suggested tight bureaucratic control. Such a picture was based on early excavations at the two largest sites in the Indus state: Mohenjo-Daro and Harappa. More recent excavations of other sites support some overall regional similarities but also indicate regional differences. It is possible that the Indus consisted of a number of city-states that functioned through alliances with each other. Just how the mechanics of such cooperation worked is unknown. Unlike other early states, the Indus state shows no indication of a standing army or warfare; nor do Indus seals depict scenes of fighting. Mark Kenoyer (1998) suggests that aggression manifested itself in other ways—for example, puppeteers may have used masks, such as those found at Mohenjo-Daro and Harappa, to act out scenes of aggression. In present-day Pakistan and India, puppets are a medium for transmitting myths and legends. In sum, knowledge of the Indus state has increased enormously, but much remains to be learned; perhaps the breakthrough will come when the script has been deciphered.

# The Shang State of Northeast China

The **Shang** is one of several regional states, varying in size and importance, that emerged almost 4,000 years ago during the Chinese Bronze Age. Interaction among these states' urban centers was vital to facilitate exchange of raw materials and products, but it was not always peaceful. Some scholars have suggested that state societies in China emerged from increasing, often aggressive, competition between chiefdom groups in search of power (Liu 1996). Although the Shang is not the first Chinese state, it is the first Chinese dynasty for which there are documentary records (see Highlight 11.1, on pp. 330–333). Written evidence supplemented by archaeological evidence provides more information about the Shang than about any other contemporaneous urban society in East Asia. Before discussing the Shang state, however, we need to consider briefly an earlier state—the **Erlitou.**

## Before Shang: The Erlitou State

Between 3,800 and 3,500 years ago, features associated with a state society were evident in the Erlitou culture: increasing population, social stratification, hierarchical settlement patterns, centralized control, monumental construction, elaborate ritual practices, craft

**Shang**
Early regional state that emerged almost 4,000 years ago in China.

**Erlitou**
An early state in China that preceded the Shang state.

specialization, and long-distance contacts. Excavations at the capital, Erlitou (from which the state gets its name), revealed a site extending over an area of about 1.5 by 2.5 km (1 by 1.5 miles), which may have had a population of up to 30,000 at its peak. There were numerous enclosed compounds in the palace/temple complex; all structures were on raised platform foundations consisting of thin layers of pounded earth—a common method of construction in this and subsequent periods. Outside the complex were specialist bone and pottery workshops, non-elite housing, and burial sites. Of particular note is a large bronze foundry that revealed remains of extensive bronze production—but of objects destined primarily for ritual purposes, rather than for domestic use (Liu 1996, 2004; Liu and Chen 2003, 2006).

The Erlitou core area, in the alluvial plain of the Yilou basin, southwest of the Huanghe (Yellow) River was rich in agricultural resources, but the inhabitants had to look further afield for resources such as copper, lead, tin, kaolin clay (to make fine pottery), salt, and timber. This need spurred state expansion and the development of Erlitou sites in more distant areas, probably set up by colonists.

## The Early Shang State: Erligang Phase

Between about 3,500 and 3,400 years ago, the **Erligang** phase of the Shang state emerged, characterized by the production of cast bronze on a scale never previously seen and of a uniform style over a wide area. Erligang sites vary from large fortified cities to smaller walled towns to simple settlements.

Erligang cities were political, ritual, and economic centers. Zhengzhou, the capital city, covered 25 km² (9.7 square miles). A massive, pounded earth wall enclosed the city centre, an area of 3 km² (1.1 square miles). The base of the wall was between 20 and 30 m (66 and 98 feet) thick, and parts of it still reach a height between 5 and 9 m (16 and 30 feet). A second, massive outer wall, the remains of which stretch 5 km (3 miles), may have surrounded the city and its suburbs (Liu and Chen 2003; Thorpe 2006).

Within the city center excavations revealed the remains of more than 20 large buildings set on pounded earth foundations; these were most likely temples and palaces. Ritual activity is suggested by pits that contained human and animal sacrifices. Among the workshops outside the enclosure walls were several bronze foundries, a pottery production area, and a bone workshop. Excavators have unearthed burials with bronze vessels, but Zhengzhou's richest burials remain to be found. Construction work in the last 40 years revealed three pits, which contained huge bronze vessels, some weighing between 50 and 86 kg (110 and 190 lbs); these must have been made for people of great status, possibly rulers (Liu and Chen 2003; Thorpe 2006).

Robert Thorpe (2006) believes that the Erligang elite gained power through control of the technologies required for the production of prestige goods. Pounded earth construction requires the organization and supervision of a substantial labor force. Like the preceding Erlitou state, the Erligang had to go beyond the core area to obtain exotic resources, and this may have stimulated expansion—through a combination of military conquest, migration, colonization, alliance formation, marriage, and trade.

## Anyang: Capital of the Last Shang Dynasty

The Shang territorial domain centered on the rich, fertile alluvial lands of the Huanghe (Yellow) River valley in northeast China, but its cultural influence extended over a much wider area (Barnes 1999).

Much of our knowledge about the Shang state derives from more than 50 years of archaeological excavation at **Anyang**, capital of the last dynasty of Shang kings (3,200 to 3,027 years ago) (Chang 1980). (Although the importance of Anyang cannot be denied, interpretations of the Shang state that are based primarily on this one major site may possibly be biased.) The city consisted of a royal, administrative, and ceremonial

**Erligang**
An early phase of the Shang state.

**Anyang**
Last capital of the Shang dynasty of China.

# The Emergence of Writing in the Old World

WRITING IS A RELATIVELY RECENT HUMAN AC-TIVITY. Writing first developed between 5,500 and 5,000 years ago in Sumeria, Elam (in southwest Iran), and Egypt. It appeared a few hundred years later in the Indus realm and perhaps 1,500 years later in Shang China.

## DEVELOPMENT OF WRITING IN SUMERIA

The rise of cities with their concomitant need to control production and trade stimulated the development of writing. The Sumerians "wrote" on wet clay that hardened in the hot sun. The earliest of their clay writing tablets, recovered by the thousands from pre-5,000-year-old levels of the Eanna temple complex in Uruk-Warka, are primarily economic records. Such written records had their roots in Mesopotamian Neolithic systems of counting and recording on geometric-shaped clay tokens that date to 8,000 or possibly 10,000 years ago. Specialists believe that tokens represented goods (1 token = 1 item) and that perforated tokens could have been strung together to indicate transactions of multiple items. In time, tokens with incised lines and grooves appeared. Then, about 5,500 years ago, a system emerged in which people placed tokens inside a *bulla*, or clay ball, that they closed and stamped with one or more seals. Subsequently, people began to impress or incise token shapes on the outside surface of the bulla. Scholars suggest that tokens inside the bulla probably tallied with shapes on the outside, thus serving as a security device for the transported goods; however, X-rays of intact bullae show that this did not always occur. Shortly before the appearance of writing, rectangular clay numerical tablets with surface impressions of tokenlike shapes replaced the cumbersome bullae. Some numerical tablets have a further stamp seal of authorization: The tablet not only recorded the number of goods but also identified a person of authority associated with the goods.

The use of cylinder seals roughly coincided with the emergence of writing tablets and generally superseded use of the stamp seal. A cylinder seal was a stone cylinder with designs carved on its outside surface; rolling the seal over soft clay left an imprint of the design on the clay. Such sealings, applied to a range of containers such as jars and boxes and even to doors, ensured security of the goods within as well as identifying the person who used the seal. Seal designs tend to show agricultural, religious, or warlike themes, perhaps reflecting the preoccupations of people at the time.

The earliest writing was primarily pictographic; that is, each sign represented a particular object. An important development occurred when signs could represent either objects or the sounds of the names of the objects. For example, the sign for *sun* could indicate the sun, or could mean "son," or could be used to form *sun day*; this is known as the rebus principle. Thus, people could combine sounds to build words and incorporate more complex grammar. From the onset of writing, a range of written documents appear: small tags that were probably attached to containers denoting ownership; larger tablets with numerical notation and a few signs, probably indicating the number and a list of goods; and tablets with lists of information. The latter tablets are the most common and differ from the others in that their surface is divided into columns to allow multiple entries on a single tablet.

Sumerian scribes used a reed stylus (pen), triangular at one end and pointed at the other, that left wedge-shaped marks in the wet clay. As information increased, the signs became more abstract and linear, gradually taking on the form known as cuneiform (*cuneus* = wedge in Latin). Cuneiform lasted for more than 3,000 years and was the written form for many different languages. It served a range of purposes, among them recording religious, political, and literary documents as well as lists and letters.

## ANCIENT EGYPTIAN WRITING

Because the earliest evidence for Egyptian writing slightly postdates Sumerian, some scholars believe that the development of cuneiform influenced Egyptian writing and therefore that writing was not an indigenous Egyptian invention. However, it is necessary to consider the material on which texts were written: Sumerians wrote on clay, a material that, when hardened, can last thousands of years; Egyptians wrote on papyrus and wood, organic

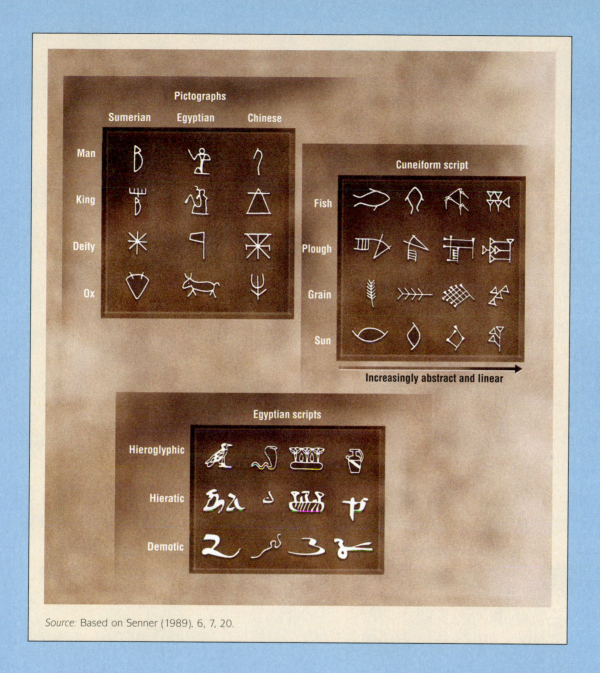

*Source:* Based on Senner (1989), 6, 7, 20.

materials that are prone to decay. Although the earliest Egyptian writing comes from a tomb at Abydos dating to approximately 5,150 years ago, marks or inscriptions on pottery are common during the preceding 400 years. Furthermore, hieroglyphic writing appears suddenly, with no indication of any apparent developmental stages; it is distinct from cuneiform and, if influenced by cuneiform, may be influenced in concept rather than in form.

The ancient Egyptians considered writing and words to be a gift of the gods—indeed, the word *hieroglyph* literally means "holy sign." Hieroglyphic writing is similar to Sumerian in that both are pictographic, both forms worked on the rebus princi-

ple, and both were in use for more than 3,000 years; but whereas Sumerian changed to simpler forms, hieroglyphic always remained pictographic. However, the Egyptians used two other forms of script: hieratic and demotic. Hieratic, a cursive script, developed at roughly the same time as hieroglyphic and was written with pen and ink on papyrus, leather, wood, and ostraca (pottery shards and fragments of limestone). Hieroglyphs were used primarily for religious inscriptions on monuments, inscriptions that were meant to last. In contrast, hieratic was the script for everyday purposes. Demotic, a simplified form of hieratic, appeared about 2,700 years ago, replacing hieratic for everyday use. At that point hieratic, in turn, became the

*(continues on the next page)* ▶

script for religious writing, and hieroglyphs continued in use for monumental inscriptions. As with hieratic, scribes wrote demotic primarily on papyrus
and ostraca, and more rarely as inscriptions on
stone. The Rosetta Stone is a rare instance of an inscription in demotic, Greek, and hieroglyphs—a
combination that helped scholars decipher hieroglyphics. Given the visibility of hieroglyphic writing
preserved in stone, it would be easy to conclude
that Egyptian writing was primarily religious in content. But such a belief would be mistaken: Ancient
Egyptian documents include king lists, accounts of
historic events, moral codes, medicinal and scientific books, and writings on magic as well as on literary and religious topics.

### THE INDUS SCRIPT

The earliest Indus seals were retrieved from
Harappan levels dating to 4,600 years ago. Pottery
with painted and inscribed symbols, some similar
to characters on seals, also has been recovered
from levels some 200 years older. The Indus script
is present on more than 3,700 objects recovered
mainly from Harappa and Mohenjo-Daro, but also
from about 60 other sites in the Indus Valley and
Arabia. Most Indus writing consists of short inscriptions on small stone stamp seals, although researchers have found a larger wooden board inlaid
with gypsum characters at the coastal site of
Dholavira. Between 400 and 450 different signs
have been distinguished—but, as yet, the Indus
script has defied decipherment.

### EARLY WRITING IN CHINA

Writing in China developed about 3,500 years ago,
during the Shang period, and is clearly recognizable
as Chinese in its similarity to present-day Chinese
characters. As with Sumeria and Egypt, the use of
signs and symbols on pottery, stone (jade), and turtle shells can be traced to the Neolithic period in
China. Knowledge of the Shang script comes from
inscriptions primarily on animal bones and turtle
shells and to a lesser extent on bronzes and pottery.
However, most writing would have been on perishable materials such as wood, bamboo, and silk.
David Keightley believes that scribes probably kept
notes about divination rituals on perishable materials and later transcribed them to oracle bones and
bronze vessels. It is known that scribes at the Shang
court used brush and ink to record important events
on strips of wood or bamboo that they then tied into
books called *ts'e*. The books no longer exist, but
Shang inscriptions include the Chinese character
*ts'e*, a pictogram of slips of wood tied with string.

Oracle bones are animal bones (primarily shoulder blades, or scapulae) and turtle shells. The
Shang used oracle bones in divination
rituals in which people consulted their
ancestors about a range of topics. The
diviner would heat the bone or shell
and then "read" the cracks that would
appear. The questions posed and the
replies received were recorded on the
cracked surfaces. Excavators have
found more than 100,000 oracle bones
relating to the Shang state; the bones
provide crucial information on the
state's geographical, military, and political organization, but unfortunately little
relating to economic matters. Economic
records probably were written on perishable materials.

### SCRIBES

Although writing was of crucial importance to rulers of early states in the Old
World, few people were literate; literacy
was the domain of scribes. Texts indicate that it was not easy to master the
art of writing and reading. In

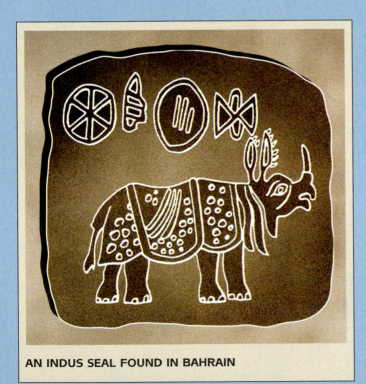

**AN INDUS SEAL FOUND IN BAHRAIN**

methods included hours of copying exercises, dictation, rote learning, and group recitation. Students who made mistakes, were lazy, misbehaved, arrived late at school, or committed some other misdemeanor received harsh punishment. Nevertheless, the tough early training preceded sweet rewards for scribal graduates in later life. For scribes, particularly those who worked at royal courts, must have been powerful people.

*Sources:* Brewer, D. J., and E. Teeter. 1999. *Egypt and the Egyptians*. Cambridge: Cambridge University Press.   Chang, K. 1980. *Shang civilization*. New Haven, CT: Yale University Press. Chang, K. 1986. *The archaeology of ancient China*. New Haven, CT: Yale University Press.   Crawford, H. 1992. *Sumer and the Sumerians*. Cambridge: Cambridge University Press.   David, R. 2000. *The experience of ancient Egypt*. London: Routledge. Gaur, A. 2000. *Literacy and the politics of writing*. Bristol: Intellect.   Keightley, D. 2006. Marks and labels: Early writing in Neolithic and Shang China. In *Archaeology of Asia*, ed. M. T. Stark, pp. 177–201. Malden, MA: Blackwell Publishing. Kenoyer, J. M. 1998. *Ancient cities of the Indus civilization*. Karachi: Oxford University Press/American Institute of Pakistan Studies. Nissen, H., P. Damerow, and R. Englund. 1993. *Archaic bookkeeping: Early writing and techniques of the economic administration in the ancient Near East*. Chicago/London: University of Chicago Press. Pollock, S. 1999. *Ancient Mesopotamia*. Cambridge: Cambridge University Press.   Wimmer, S. 1998. Hieroglyphs: Writing and literature. In *Egypt: The world of the pharaohs*, eds. R. Schulz and M. Seidel, pp. 34–46. Cologne: Könemann.   Xueqin, L., G. Harbottle, J. Zhang, and C. Wang. 2003. The earliest writing? Sign use in the seventh millennium BC at Jiahu, Henan Province, China. *Antiquity* 77:31–44.

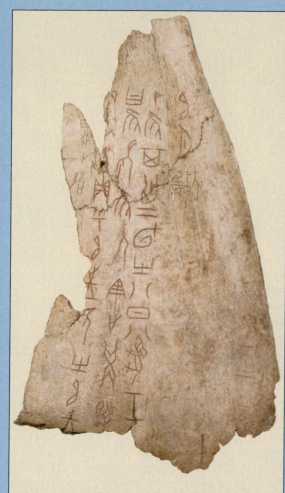

This Shang oracle bone is an inscribed ox shoulder blade. How reliable are written records?

Mesopotamia and ancient Egypt, scribes learned their trade through years of hard and often painful study in scribal schools. Training began early—at age 5 to 7 in Mesopotamia and at about 10 in Egypt—and continued into adulthood. Teaching

turn back to your reading

complex and a series of cemetery, industrial, and habitation areas covering about 30 km² (11.6 square miles) (Bagley 1999).

The palace, temple, and ceremonial area formed the core of the Anyang complex, although there was no surrounding enclosure wall. Excavations revealed three areas with more than 50 large buildings whose wattle-and-daub (wood and mud) superstructures were set on pounded earth platforms. Burials, found in two areas within the complex, included horse chariot inhumations. Several semi-subterranean pit houses served as servant areas, workshops, and storage areas; large, deep storage bins contained grain, bronze weapons, **oracle bones**, and pottery (Chang 1986).

Anyang's royal cemetery was located north of the main complex. Here excavations revealed 11 huge graves, thought to be those of the Shang rulers, and more than 1,000 smaller graves. Construction of the elaborate royal graves indicates colossal organization and investment of labor. Each of these cruciform (cross-shaped) graves consisted of a central deep pit accessed by four long ramps. Accompanying funerary goods included spectacular bronze vessels, jades, shells, pottery, and chariots. In addition, human and animal sacrifices formed an important part of Shang mortuary ritual. Most royal tombs were robbed in antiquity, but the unplundered tomb of Fu Hao, a Shang queen, provides a window into royal wealth in much the same manner as that of the young minor Egyptian king Tutankhamun. Much smaller than many of the other royal tombs, Fu Hao's tomb included 16 human sacrifices; six dogs; 1,600 kg (3,527 pounds) of bronzes, more than 750 jades, hundreds of bone artifacts, semi-precious stones, fine pottery, ivory, and more than 6,000 cowrie shells (a form of currency) (Zhenxiang 1996). The numerous smaller graves within the cemetery show a variety of Shang burial rituals. These included single and multiple burials; complete bodies with pottery and bronze grave goods; and headless bodies or just skulls, usually without accompanying grave goods (Chang 1986).

## The Shang State Machine

At the center of the Shang state was the king, who ruled supreme with the aid of a hierarchical structure of aristocratic, governmental, and military officials. The royal capital was surrounded by a number of smaller walled towns, which the king granted to kin members in return for services and donations that were in fact taxes of grain and other goods. No one owned land privately. Oracle bones document the king's concern with harvest yields; this was a valid concern, as yields would affect the amount of grain the royal regime received in taxes (Chang 1980). The walled towns of the aristocracy, with their ceremonial centers, temples, palaces, and tombs, might be seen as microcosms of the capital, showing that the aristocracy could amass their own wealth. Although local lords were loyal to the king, they sometimes waged war with one another (Scarre and Fagan 2003).

Artisans, peasants, and slaves formed the numerically greater, as well as socially lower, classes of Shang hierarchy. Oracle bone inscriptions indicate a variety of skilled occupations, some of which appear to have had their own special insignia; such skilled artisans may have enjoyed more privileges than peasant farmers. For example, excavations at Anyang revealed a bronze workshop built on pounded earth, a form of construction associated with higher-status buildings and their occupants. Given the importance of bronze in Shang rituals, the workshop construction may indicate a high status for bronze workers in the society.

The military played an important role in Shang state structure. The king, as head of the army, appointed relatives to lead military regiments. The armed forces consisted of small companies and larger regiments of foot soldiers, archers, and charioteers (the latter only in the late Shang period). Oracles bones refer to extensive military campaigns involving from 3,000 to 13,000 troops who fought with bow and arrow, halberd (a long battle-axe), and small knife. In time of warfare an influx of conscripts, provided by provincial aristocrats as part of their duty to the king, swelled the numbers of the standing army (Chang 1980; Roberts 1996). The army not only served the king's expansion-

**oracle bones**
Animal bones (usually scapulae) and turtle shells used in the Shang state in divination rituals; when the bone or carapace was heated, cracks appeared that a diviner "read."

ist and defensive needs but also helped the king exert control over his subjects.

## Shang Bronzes

Shang artifacts are the product of gifted specialists; particularly renowned are their exceptional works in bronze and jade. Artisans also produced sophisticated engraved and glazed pottery, made from carefully selected and mixed clays, and counted laquer working among their skills (Chang 1980). Chinese bronze technology occurred much later than in western Asia (Roberts 1996); Shang bronzes became a major industry in response to the demand for food and wine vessels for use in rituals (Rawson 1996). The scale of bronze working is evident in the size of one Anyang foundry; it covered an area roughly equivalent to 10,000 m² (1 hectare). Large and small bronze vessels were cast from clay molds, rather than being hammered from sheet bronze, as was the tradition in western Asia. Bronze objects often required vast amounts of metal, so their conspicuous use by Shang elite for ritual offerings stresses the importance of both bronze and ritual in Shang society.

## Trade and Exchange

Archaeologists have found few Shang economic records dealing with trade. This lack of records does not necessarily indicate poor accounting, however; instead, it suggests that officials probably recorded transactions on perishable materials. Movement of goods was primarily in favor of the king. According to Anyang oracle bones, such goods included grain, wild game, domesticated animals, industrial products, and services. The king, in return, sent gifts to aristocrats in provincial towns and provided supplies to maintain the army (Chang 1980).

Despite the absence of written records, scholars deduce indirect evidence of trade or movement of goods by sourcing raw materials used in the manufacture of prestige objects. Copper and tin mines have been found 100 to 400 km (60 to 250 miles) from Anyang, although it is not known if these were Shang mines or if the ore was traded (Chang 1980). Primary ore preparation and smelting at the mines produced bars of ore that were transported to the cities (Rawson 1996); city foundries then further refined and cast the metals. Cowrie shell strings, prized by the Shang, consisted of two types of marine shells—one of east coast Chinese origin, the other a nonnative species. The trading mechanism for these shells is unclear. Highly prized, too, were turtle shells, particularly those found in southern regions. Oracle bone inscriptions indicate that officials introduced most carapaces to Anyang. The sources of jade nearest to Anyang are about 375 km (230 miles) away, suggesting that some form of trading or tribute mechanism probably accounted for jade's presence in the city (Chang 1980). Chariots were a western Asian product, although it is not known whether the Shang adopted the idea or acquired actual chariots. In any event, it is clear that the Shang state must have had wide-ranging contacts with groups outside its immediate domain.

Chinese cultural traditions that developed and prospered during the 500 years of Shang power did not disappear with the Shang state's demise but were embraced and promoted by the succeeding Chou and the later great states of China.

Bronzes such as this owl-shaped vessel were important in Shang society. Why?

# Early States and Urban Complexity in East and West Africa

East and West Africa are regions of varied geography, topography, and geology; they possess resources that are abundant but unevenly distributed. However, resources are transportable, and many items (such as animals, plants, salt, copper, and iron) were objects of local and long-distance trade and exchange networks. Archaeological evidence indicates that between 3,000 and 2,000 years ago, these regions saw an increase in population numbers and permanent settlements. Differences in settlement size show that some sites became larger than others and had specialist work areas. Clear indications of social stratification, too, exist in certain regions, such as the state of **Aksum** in highland Ethiopia. Such differentiation is not as clear in other areas, such as the inland Niger delta. There is no doubt about the rise of urban complexity in the region, however. At one time researchers believed that the emergence of states in East and West Africa was a direct result of the arrival of Arab traders, but more recent investigation has shown this interpretation to be wrong. State development was an indigenous process—probably fueled by power, control over resources, and trade—rather than the result of influences from states outside Africa (Connah 2001). In this section, we look at urban complexity in the highlands of Ethiopia and in the inland Niger delta in West Africa.

## Early Ethiopian States

The Ethiopian high plateau ranges in altitude from less than 1,800 m (6,000 feet) to more than 2,400 m (8,000 feet) and lies within mountain ranges that soar to 4,200 m (13,780 feet). Blessed by a good climate, the plateau supports a diverse range of vegetation, as can be seen today in the variety of crops, vegetables, and fruits that flourish in fertile agricultural soils, along with grazing for herds of cattle, sheep, and goats. Under such circumstances, the Ethiopian pre-Aksumite and Aksumite states enjoyed a reasonably secure subsistence base. Elephant ivory, rhinoceros horn, hippopotamus teeth, and lion and leopard skins were some of the trade goods provided by wild animals of the African interior; mineral resources included highly valuable gold and iron ore as well as silver, lead, and tin. Furthermore, building stone and timber were readily available. It is not surprising that the state of Aksum was the center of an extensive trade network system between interior Africa and Egypt, the Mediterranean, southern Arabia, the Persian Gulf, India, and Sri Lanka. The Red Sea was the highway link to interior Africa, the Mediterranean, and beyond (Connah 2001).

### The Pre-Aksumite Kingdom of Daamat

For many years scholars believed that Aksum, which emerged about 2,000 years ago, was the first state in East Africa. However, investigations have revealed pre-Aksumite complexity, including a monarchy, writing, iron and bronze working, sophisticated architecture, temples, palaces, rock-cut tombs, and evidence of an elite class. According to written inscriptions, the Kingdom of Daamat flourished between approximately 2,700 and 2,300 years ago. More than 90 pre-Aksumite sites have been discovered, many in the northern Ethiopian highlands; the largest of these, and the probable state capital, was Yeha, itself surrounded by smaller sites (Munro-Hay 1993). Trade networks with Egypt and South Arabia, particularly the Kingdom of Saba, were important for the exchange of goods and the introduction of new ideas. Indeed, south Arabian influences are evident in aspects of Daamat religion, royal titles, inscriptions, and architecture, and continue in the monumental architectural style of the later Aksumite state (Bard and Fattovich 2001; Phillipson 1998).

**Aksum**
Early state that emerged in highland Ethiopia about 2,000 years ago.

## The Aksumite State

The Aksumite state of 2,000 years ago was characterized by urban centers, a hierarchical settlement pattern, a system of writing, coinage, monumental architecture, specialization in building techniques, extensive internal and external trade networks, and control over a wide region, including part of the Red Sea coast. Information about the Aksumite state comes from archaeology; from classical writings such as those of Pliny the Younger, Ptolemy, and early Islamic writers; and from trade manuals, inscriptions and representations on coins, and inscriptions on stone (often propaganda, such as accounts of military actions). Inscriptions are in Ge'ez (old Ethiopian), Sabaean (south Arabian), and sometimes Greek (Connah 2001).

## Urban Centers of the Aksumite State

According to Ptolemy, Aksum was a flourishing city. Archaeological investigations indicate three monumental, multi-story, multi-roomed palaces or elite buildings set on large stepped platforms made of stone masonry that supported superstructures of wood, mud, and rubble. Smaller stone platforms may have been bases for royal thrones set under canopies supported by four stone pillars. The palaces were probably administrative centers as well as royal living quarters. Lower-ranking members of society lived in smaller stone structures within the city and in smaller settlements around it (Connah 2001).

Aksum is justly famous for its more than 140 stone stelae (standing stones), which probably served as tomb markers for the underground tombs with which they are associated. Some stelae are tall, thin, and carved to depict multi-story buildings; others are smaller and plain (Figure 11.7). The tallest stela still standing today is a block of carved granite 21 m (69 feet) high; but an even larger carved stela, 33 m (108 feet) high and weighing 517 tons, lies broken where it fell as it was being raised. While stelae are found throughout the Aksumite region, the largest and most elaborate are in the ancient capital.

Matara (in present-day Eritrea) was a large urban center strategically located between the capital, Aksum, and the Aksumite Red Sea port of Adulis. Excavations at Matara have supported its importance, revealing several levels of elite and ordinary buildings, tombs, and churches—a hierarchical structure that is reminiscent of the capital and Adulis. Although Matara was not the capital, artifacts recovered from the city suggest the presence of wealthy individuals (Phillipson 1998).

## External Trade

Trade was a source of wealth and power. Aksum had trading connections with the eastern Mediterranean, Egypt, Arabia, and South Asia, exporting African goods such as ivory, gold, emeralds, rhino horn, aromatic substances, live animals and slaves. Imports included metals, metal goods, glass, ceramics, clothing, wine, and spices, all primarily for the elite market. Adulis, the cosmopolitan hub of the Aksumite trading network system, was a relatively short distance from the capital; from Aksum trade routes led north into Egypt and south into the African interior. Aksum was the first African state to mint its own gold, silver, and bronze coins; the coins have been found with imported items on all well-excavated Aksumite sites.

## Social System of the Aksumite State

Inscriptions with kings' names, coins depicting a crowned king, monumental palaces, tombs, and imported goods indicate that the Aksumite state was headed by a king, probably with the support of elite officials and retainers. Although it does not appear that the king had special advisors, written sources mention names of regional governors. Monumental buildings symbolized the power and prestige of the ruling body. Temples and grave markers (stelae) show the importance of religion in the lives of

*Figure 11.7*

**STELA 3 AT AKSUM.** Made from a block of granite, this carved stela is 21 m (69 feet) high with about 3 m (10 feet) below ground; the design represents a nine-story building. What skills did the construction of such stelae require?

*Source:* Adapted from Connah (2001).

Aksumite peoples and serve as symbols of divine approval of the state machinery (Phillipson 1998). From pre-Aksumite and early Aksumite times, belief systems centered on a polytheistic pantheon. Following Aksum's fourth-century adoption of Christianity and construction of churches, the king, believed to be a descendent of Solomon, had semi-divine status. The presence of specialist workers is indicated by such evidence as stone quarries, building techniques, stelae, and finely made metal items. However, the bulk of the population consisted of peasants, and in later periods slaves (slavery predated colonial times by hundreds of years) who produced Aksum's food supply and provided labor for monumental building (Phillipson 1998).

During its florescence, the Aksumite state was powerful, controlling resources and trade routes and flexing its military might when needed. Surveys have revealed many more sites than have been excavated: small sites, towns, temples, stone quarries, stelae, workshops, tombs—a hierarchical settlement pattern typical of what might be expected in a state system. The apparent lack of defensive town walls suggests a stable state (Munro-Hay 1993). The state heartland lay in the Aksum–Yeha region, probably because the fertile lands of the high plateau could support a burgeoning population of elites, specialists, and ordinary workers (Connah 2001). Ultimately, however, the continual exploitation and clearance of the land for cultivation, building materials, and fuel probably caused the onset of erosion followed by a deterioration in soil cover. Environmental degradation may have precipitated the decline of the Aksumite state in the seventh century, a decline that was further accelerated when the Arabs gained control of the Red Sea trade routes in the same century.

## Jenné-jeno and Urban Complexity in the Middle Niger

Early West African cities differ from other cities discussed in this chapter in their apparent lack of monumental architecture, writing, and social stratification. Yet although they were "cities without citadels" (McIntosh and McIntosh 1993), they were undeniably complex urban societies. As with the Aksumite state, a reliable subsistence base and strategic location within a wide trade network system underpinned the emergence of West African cities.

The savanna of West Africa, a region of grasslands, woodlands, and shrubs, is sandwiched between tropical rain forests to the south and the Sahara desert to the north. It encompasses a variety of environmental zones rich in resources. Two to three thousand years ago, savanna resources included sorghum, millet, rice, yams, vegetable oils, domestic cows, sheep and goats (and their products), wild animals (and their products, including ivory), fish, wild plants (used for basketry and matting), iron ore, alluvial gold, rocks for grindstones, clay (for pottery and bricks), and slaves (Connah 2001). The uneven distribution of these resources caused extensive trade networks to develop. Historic sources document trade from West Africa to North Africa that passed through present-day Jenné (established in the fifteenth century) and Timbuktu; a return traffic brought glass, North African pottery, and salt to West Africa. The ancient city of **Jenné-jeno** lay about 3 km (almost 2 miles) southeast of today's Jenné and was as well placed on the trade route as its successor (McIntosh and McIntosh 1993). It is a good example of the many complex urban societies in West Africa at the time.

### The Ancient City of Jenné-jeno

Located near a former small river in what is now Mali, on the inland Niger delta, Jenné-jeno is a mound 8 m (26 feet) high. Excavations from 1977 to 1981 revealed three phases of growth between 1,750 and 600 years ago. The city grew from 25 hectares (62 acres) in the initial phase to 33 hectares (82 acres) by 1,200 years ago. Together with the contemporary adjacent site of Hambarketolo, linked to Jenné-jeno by a causeway, the urban area covered 42 hectares (104 acres) by AD 800 (McIntosh and McIntosh 1993). At its height Jenné-jeno was an intricate web of alleyways running between compounds of dense round and square houses built of a mixture of matting, wattle, and mud. A mud-brick wall, 2 km (1 mile) long and almost 3.6 m (12 feet) wide at its base, enclosed the city. Estimates of population range from 7,000 to 13,000; if we include the 25 smaller sites surrounding Jenné-jeno as part of the city complex, however, the population could have been as great as 27,000.

**Jenné-jeno**
Ancient city in West Africa.

The remains of mud-brick buildings, iron and slag, clay figurines, copper artifacts, grinding stones, pottery shards, and bricks from the mud-brick wall cover the entire area of Jenné-jeno. Eleven locations sampled during excavation revealed craft workshop, residential, burial, and refuse areas. From the earliest occupation of Jenné-jeno, specialists worked iron, making tools, ornaments, and jewelry. As the closest deposits of iron ore are at least 50 km (31 miles) away, people must have transported either iron ore or partially worked iron to the city. Fragments of crucibles and moulds also testify to copper and bronze working. Specialist potters produced finely made and decorated thin-walled pottery (McIntosh and McIntosh 1993).

### Jenné-jeno Trade Network System

A hierarchical pattern of settlements lies within a 25-km (16-mile) radius of Jenné-jeno, the largest and most powerful site in the region. Susan and Roderick McIntosh, who have worked in this region for many years, believe that the settlement hierarchy around Jenné-jeno is part of a regional trade network system. Local trade may have exchanged food products such as rice and fish, and perhaps other goods such as gold, for copper, iron ore, salt, and other goods. The city's riverside location provided easy access to river transport, the best way of moving goods through difficult terrain; its fertile alluvial plains and the relatively nearby deposits of iron ore may have been key factors in the growth of the community as a trade center (McIntosh and McIntosh 1993).

### Social Stratification at Jenné-jeno

Between 1,700 and 1,200 years ago, the increasing number and hierarchical nature of settlement sites in the region around Jenné-jeno, the increasing size of Jenné-jeno itself, and the homogeneity of material culture over a wide area suggest that the city was at the center of a statelike polity (Connah 2001). A state center implies a social complexity and stratification that in other states (such as Aksum) involves a controlling hierarchy. As we've seen throughout this chapter, monumental buildings, inscriptions, and grave goods are evidence of social stratification. At present such evidence is missing from Jenné-jeno—although very little of the site has been excavated, and perhaps indications of differential wealth may lie hidden in unexcavated areas. Nevertheless, construction of the massive city wall implies an organizing power. Indeed, the wall itself may have constituted a symbol of power and prestige in addition to fulfilling other functions, whether for defense or protection against seasonal flooding. Elsewhere in West Africa tombs and grave goods from both before and after the Jenné-jeno period indicate differences in social status and burial rites (Connah 2001). Perhaps at Jenné-jeno smaller groups such as craft guilds or trading associations may have shared authority (McIntosh and McIntosh 1993). Further excavation should provide more information on social organization.

# Concluding Comments on Early States

Let's step back and look at the state societies we have considered in the light of the perceived hallmarks of early states listed at the beginning of this chapter: increased populations, craft specialization, imposition of taxes, monumental building projects, social stratification, record keeping, development of the sciences, trade networks, a state ideology, and armies. Of this list, population growth, craft specialization, and trade are evident in all areas. Long-distance trade was important for access to commodities not locally available; craft specialists produced items for local consumption and for the trade market, most of which was in response to elite demand. Craft specialization and trade were not new developments in early states, but the extent and control of both indicate an increase in bureaucracy not present in preceding communities.

Some form of recording would have been essential for the smooth performance of the state machine, and written records are clearly evident in Sumeria, Egypt, and Aksum. Shang writing on oracle bones served divination purposes, but it is likely that records about matters of state were written on perishable materials. The Indus is enigmatic; there is evidence for writing, but it is limited and undeciphered. Jenné-jeno and the oppida (towns) of temperate Europe (see Highlight 11.2, on pp. 342–343) appear to have functioned without a system of writing, although the Celts were acquainted with Greek and Latin script. Alternative systems of keeping records must have operated within the Indus, Jenné-jeno, and the oppida, however, given the importance of trade networks within these states.

Except at Jenné-jeno and European oppida, there is clear evidence that all the early states harnessed labor for monumental building projects. The wall around Jenné-jeno, the ramparts around European oppida, and posthole remains of larger buildings within the oppida also might be considered examples of a type of monumentality, albeit on a different scale. In itself the presence (or indications) of monumental structures gives evidence of advancing mathematical and engineering skills.

The apparent lack of social stratification at Jenné-jeno is intriguing and may indicate alternative forms of authority, perhaps in the hands of small corporate groups such as craft guilds or trading groups. Likewise, although social stratification was a factor in the Indus state, power may have rested in the hands of a council of leaders rather than a supreme king. Different forms of leadership might explain the absence of a military component in the Indus and Jenné-jeno: Perhaps military force was unnecessary in both areas, if power was not under a central control but shared among corporate groups.

Whether recorded or not, it would seem inevitable that taxes in preindustrial, premonetary societies would have been paid in kind—for example, through agricultural production, state building projects, or military conscription. Where written records are missing, however, it is impossible to know the extent of tribute exacted by the ruling authority.

Only at Jenné-jeno, and to a lesser extent the Indus, are clear signs of a unifying ideology lacking. In the Indus evidence points to a prominent role of water that might indicate the importance of ritual bathing. But although the few godlike figurines found on Indus sites may represent a belief system, the state lacks the visual pantheon of Sumeria or Egypt. However, visibility is a key factor affecting understanding of the past. Archaeological evidence is biased by what is preserved; the archaeological record usually lacks those elements of a society that were expressed through organic materials.

In conclusion, early state societies shared many similar attributes, but the ways in which they approached state organization differed. The reasons for their differences rest in the details. There is clearly no single recipe for the emergence of early states; each is unique, and that is what makes them so interesting.

# Highlight 11.2

# In Temperate Europe with the Celts

THE EMERGENCE OF COMPLEX CELTIC URBAN SOCIETIES in temperate Europe (Europe north of the Alps) occurred during the later Iron Age, between 2,200 and 2,050 years ago, at a time when Rome, established as an empire, was expanding its hegemony. European urbanism did not suddenly emerge; Celtic chieftains had had trading links with the Greek, Etruscan, and Roman worlds for 300 years or more. The early signs of European urbanism appear at sites located on strategically favorable points along trade routes. In pre-Roman times the Celts' imports from the Mediterranean had included Greek and Etruscan artifacts, in particular drinking and feasting vessels and wine amphorae. The Celts buried their powerful chiefs in wooden chambers and provided sumptuous grave goods to accompany them to the afterworld: four-wheeled wagons; horse trappings; swords; and gold and bronze objects, including heavy gold *torcs* (that chiefs wore around their neck) and bracelets. Loyal followers then covered the burial chamber under a large mound of earth. Excavation at Vix in Burgundy, France, uncovered a wagon burial with luxury goods, some from the Greek and Etruscan world—including an intricately decorated bronze wine vessel 1.6 m (5 feet 5 inches) high, the largest of its type known. Another intriguing aspect of the Vix burial is that the body was female; apparently women, as well as men, could achieve power and prestige.

Contact between the Roman world and Celtic Europe grew about 2,200 years ago, fueled by Rome's need for European commodities such as metals, iron agricultural tools, hides, furs, and slaves and by the Celts' desire for prestige goods. In response to the Roman market, industrialization in Europe increased and was organized within walled towns that Julius Caesar named *oppida*—the Latin for "towns" (singular, *oppidum*).

1.6 meters
5 feet, 5 inches

This bronze wine vessel from a female burial in Vix, France, is the largest of its type discovered so far. What might such a vessel suggest about Celtic society?

## OPPIDA

Oppida were centers of tribal territories, usually established in strategic defensive locations on trade routes or near raw material sources. The largest oppida (500 hectares, or 1,200 acres in size) were densely populated manufacturing, administrative, and trade centers; others were smaller in size and population. The town layouts of oppida differed from that evident in classical Greek, Mesopotamian, and Egyptian cities in the absence of monumental buildings and central temple complexes, although Caesar does refer to "marketplaces" and "senates." Town planning is evident in the careful layout of streets in some oppida, and in the separation of zones according to function.

Oppida served a variety of functions: protection of goods and people, collection of tribute, distribution of food and goods, organization of industrial production, and supervision of regional and long-distance trade networks. Trade with the Roman world was important, perhaps primarily for luxury goods. But regional trade was extensive and important too, as is evident in the presence of non-local raw materials, exotic objects, and foreign coinage at all sites. Oppida were often, though not always, the focus of a hierarchical settlement pattern of villages, farms, and small rectangular enclosures that may have been cult places or elite estates. The settlement pattern reflected the stratification of Celtic society among nobles, druids (priests), common people, and slaves.

## THE OPPIDUM OF MANCHING

Manching, the most extensively excavated oppidum, was located at the confluence of the Danube and Paar rivers in Germany. As this was a strategic point in the east–west land routes, Manching must have controlled trade routes. Ramparts extended 2.5 km (1.6 miles) around its perimeter, enclosing an area of almost 350 hectares (900 acres), but having several gates large enough to allow the passage of wheeled carts as well as pedestrians. The center of Manching was densely packed with small and large wooden houses, pits, and enclosures and included industrial areas for the production of pottery, coinage, iron, bronze, glass, textiles, and bone and wooden items. Elite palisaded enclosures were set in the less densely populated town periphery.

The extent of industrial activity evident in Manching is not unusual for oppida; all oppida produced iron tools to meet specialist demand and improve agricultural production. Indeed, Manching's smiths produced more than 200 different types of iron tools. Iron production and pottery manufacture at Manching illustrate the role of regional trade; oppida manufactured goods from imported raw materials for local, regional, and long-distance redistribution.

## CELTIC IDEOLOGY

Much of what scholars know about Celtic belief systems comes from Roman iconography and sources. These sources indicate that Celtic religion, with its polytheistic pantheon, was part of daily life and that religious practices were controlled by powerful and respected druids (priests). Rituals included intentionally damaging weapons and jewelry and then discarding them into watery graves in springs and rivers; in addition the bogs of northern Europe were the final resting place for human sacrifices. Ditch and bank enclosures, found within and around oppida, served not only as domestic trash dumps but also as places for the long-term accumulation of ritual deposits.

Celtic societies were nonliterate, although acquainted with writing through contact with the Mediterranean world. They have left no written account of themselves but are described and discussed by outsiders from Rome and Greece. Such texts, together with archaeology, show a distinct Celtic identity in temperate Europe by 2,000 years ago.

*Sources*: Collis, J. 1997. *The European Iron Age*. London/New York: Routledge. Kristiansen, K. 1998. *Europe before history*. Cambridge: Cambridge University Press. Wells, P. S. 1990. Iron Age temperate Europe: Some current research issues. *Journal of World Prehistory* 4 (4): 437–476. Wells, P. S. 2000. *Beyond Celts, Germans and Scythians: Archaeology and identity in Iron Age Europe*. London: Duckworth.

turn back to your reading

■ Characteristics of early states include some or all of the following criteria: high population, craft specializations, taxation, monumental building, social stratification, record keeping, development of the sciences, trade, a state ideology, and a military presence.

**page 313**

■ The earliest states in the Old World emerged in Mesopotamia and Egypt between about 5,500 and 5,000 years ago and in the Indus Valley about 4,600 years ago.

■ Sumer and Akkad in southern Mesopotamia were the locations of a number of small independent city-states, periodically united into larger polities through aggression by one of them. Uruk-Warka was the largest city of its time. Power rested in large religious and administrative complexes that dominated the city center. Cylinder seals and cuneiform writing on tablets indicate tight state control over the production and distribution of food and goods. These early city-states developed extensive trading networks with other states in Anatolia, Egypt, Arabia, Pakistan, and India.

■ The ecological similarity of the landscape and the ease of transport along the Nile were important in the formation of a single Egyptian state, ruled by an hereditary line of kings who had divine status. Ancient Egypt was a highly centralized state organized from the capital at Memphis. Taxes, paid in grain or labor, enabled the state to undertake monumental building projects, military campaigns, specialized craft production, and feeding of state workers. Scribes kept detailed records of everything under state control. Pyramids, built as burial mausoleums for the king and nobles, testify to the might and organization of the Egyptian state.

**page 320**

■ The Indus state of southern Asia was much larger than any other early state. The state had well-planned cities with monumental architecture, thriving long-distance trading networks, a writing system, specialist workers, and farming groups. The standardization evident throughout the region suggests a central authority, but there is no evidence of a single ruler. Until the Indus script has been deciphered, the bureaucratic system of the Indus state will remain a mystery.

■ Although the Shang state was not the earliest of Chinese states, it is currently the best understood, thanks to excavations at the last royal capital at Anyang. The Shang is also the first Chinese dynasty for which there are documentary records, in the form of oracle bones and inscriptions on bronzes. Shang kings were supreme rulers aided by aristocratic officials and a strong military machine. Shang artisans are renowned for their bronze and jade artifacts; bronze production was a major industry as a result of large-scale demand for ritual vessels by the elite. Many Shang rulers are believed to be buried in elaborate tombs in the royal cemetery near Anyang.

**page 333**

■ Information about the Aksumite state of ancient Ethiopia comes from archaeology and a range of written records. The state emerged a little more than 2,000 years ago and was ruled by kings supported by elite officials. Aksum gained power through control of a wide trade network linking Africa with the Mediterranean and Asia. It is famed for its extraordinarily tall, carved stone stelae that probably were tomb markers and indicate the important role of religion. The people adopted Christianity about 1,600 years ago.

■ Jenné-jeno, in the middle Niger, like many other urban centers of that time in West Africa, appears to be a city rather than a state, but it gained importance because of its strategic location on trade routes.

■ The oppida of temperate Europe were independent complex urban centers, similar in many respects to city-states but without monumental buildings and temple complexes. Ruled by Celtic chiefs, oppida were centers of production and traded regionally and throughout the Roman market. Celtic societies were nonliterate, although they had contact with writing through the Mediterranean world. Archaeology and the writings of Greeks and Romans provide information on the Celts.

## KEY WORDS

Akkad, 312
Aksum, 336
Anyang, 329
cuneiform, 316
cylinder seal, 313
Erligang, 329
Erlitou, 328
Harappa, 324
hierarchical settlement
    pattern, 312

hieratic, 319
hieroglyphic, 318
Indus (or Harappan), 323
Jenné-jeno, 339
mastaba, 320
Mesopotamia, 312
Mohenjo-Daro, 324
Narmer palette, 318
oracle bones, 334
quipu, 311

Shang, 328
Shortugai, 327
state, 310
stelae, 311
Sumer, 312
Ubaid period, 312
Ur, 315
Uruk period, 312
Uruk-Warka, 313
ziggurat, 315

## SUGGESTED READING

Brewer, D. J., and E. Teeter. *Egypt and the Egyptians*. Cambridge: Cambridge University Press, 1999. The choice of good books on ancient Egypt is endless. Many coffee-table books offer wonderful color photographs but may be short on content. With line drawings, plans, and black-and-white photographs, this book covers aspects of ancient Egyptian life in thematic rather than chronological order.

Chang, K. *The Archaeology of Ancient China*. New Haven, CT: Yale University Press, 1986. Covers in some detail the archaeology of the Paleolithic, Neolithic, and early state periods in China. The many location maps help situate the reader, and the numerous drawings of artifacts and site plans show the diversity of material culture in China.

Connah, G. *African Civilizations: An Archaeological Perspective*. Cambridge: Cambridge University Press, 2001. This well-written book examines the rise of urbanism in seven regions of Africa. For easy reference each chapter is organized under separate topics such as subsistence, technology, social system, ideology, and trade.

Kenoyer, J. M. *Ancient Cities of the Indus Valley Civilization*. Karachi/New York/Delhi: Oxford University Press, 1998. Aimed at the general public, this book is comprehensive in its coverage of the origins and mechanisms of the Indus civilization. Lavishly illustrated with photographs, drawings, and maps.

Postgate, J. N. *Early Mesopotamia: Society and Economy at the Dawn of History*. New York: Routledge, 1994. A comprehensive account of early Mesopotamia with plenty of maps, drawings, plans, and black-and-white photographs. The book is well structured, clearly written, and easily accessible for reference purposes. *Ancient Mesopotamia* by Susan Pollock (Cambridge: Cambridge University Press, 1999) also is useful and highlights lives of the ordinary people.

Scarre, C., ed. *The Human Past: World Prehistory and the Development of Human Societies*. New York: Thames & Hudson, 2005. This book provides a highly informed and well-balanced summary of world prehistory. Each chapter, written by a specialist, covers a general time period and region. An excellent supplement for students who wish to know more about a particular period.

Scarre, C., and B. M. Fagan. *Ancient Civilizations*. New York: Longman, 2003. Places the study of early civilization and state in a theoretical context. A good introduction to Mesopotamia, Egypt, and the Indus and Shang states. The book also covers New World civilizations; the Aegean, Greek, and Roman worlds; and states in Southeast Asia.

Chapter **12**

# Later Hunter-Gatherers and Early Farming Societies in the Americas

■ **PEOPLING OF THE AMERICAS**
How Did the First Americans Get There? • Where Did They Come From? • When Did They Arrive in the Americas? • The Archaeological Evidence • Monte Verde Fits the Criteria • The Clovis Phenomenon

■ **HIGHLIGHT 12.1:** *Investigating Animal Extinctions*

■ **HUNTING, FORAGING, AND FISHING IN THE HOLOCENE: ARCHAIC CULTURES**

■ **THE EASTERN WOODLANDS ARCHAIC**
Developing Technology • Settlement and Scheduling of Resources • Exchange Networks • Burial and Ceremony • Mound Building

■ **HIGHLIGHT 12.2:** *Cahokia, Crown of Prehistoric Mississippian Chiefdoms*

■ **THE GREAT BASIN ARCHAIC**
Preservation in Caves • Bioarchaeological Studies in the Great Basin

■ **HUNTER-FORAGER-FISHER GROUPS OF THE NORTHWEST COAST**
Environmental Resources • Changing Technology • Settlements • Ritual, Status, and Warfare

■ **FORAGING, FISHING, AND HUNTING GROUPS OF SOUTHERN CALIFORNIA**
Marine Exploitation on the Channel Islands of Southern California • Mainland Subsistence Strategies • Emergence of Status

■ **THE DEVELOPMENT OF AGRICULTURE**

■ **AGRICULTURAL SOCIETIES IN EASTERN NORTH AMERICA**
Hopewell Agricultural Communities

■ **AGRICULTURAL SOCIETIES IN SOUTHWEST NORTH AMERICA**
Hohokam • Mogollon • Ancestral Pueblo (Anasazi)

▲

**Photo above:** Sixteenth-century illustration of maize harvesting in Inca times

1. Bluefish Caves
2. Paul Mason
3. Namu
4. Marmes
5. Hogup Cave
6. Lovelock Cave
7. Hidden Cave
8. Clovis
9. Windover
10. Chaco Canyon
11. Bear Village
12. Snaketown
13. Shelltown and Hind Site
14. Anzick
15. Colby
16. Koster
17. Cahokia
18. Mound City
19. Turner Farm
20. Meadowcroft
21. Cactus Hill
22. Indian Knoll
23. Black Earth
24. Poverty Point
25. L'Anse Amour
26. Tehuacán (San Marcos)
27. Oaxaca (Guilá Naquitz)
28. San Andrés

**SITES MENTIONED IN THE CHAPTER**

The lands of North and South America are physically and environmentally diverse: There are high and moderate mountain ranges; vast expanses of flat savanna grasslands; coniferous, deciduous, and tropical forests; arid deserts; marshlands and swamps; large river systems; and coastal plains. Such variety provides habitats for an equally diverse array of animal and plant species. In postglacial times people in North America hunted large mammals such as caribou, elk, bison, deer, and antelope along with a host of smaller mammals. South America's native large animals are limited to camelids (ruminants such as llamas and vicuña); like its northern neighbor, however, South America is rich in small mammals, some of which (such as the capybara) are large enough to provide a family with meat for a week. Both continents boast a rich array of bird species and marine and riverine resources as well as a range of edible grasses, tubers, plants, and nuts (Gibbon 1998). The subsistence strategies of the Americas' early inhabitants, therefore, differed according to environmental conditions and potential resources—and these differences generated a variety of culturally rich traditions.

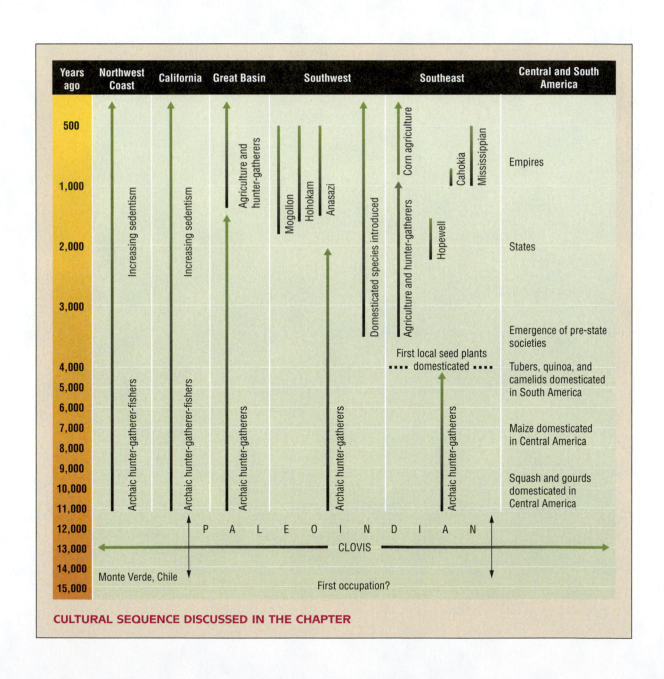

**CULTURAL SEQUENCE DISCUSSED IN THE CHAPTER**

This chapter opens with a look at the how, where, and when of the first human colonization of the Americas. Then we turn to hunter-gatherer groups in various regions. Finally, we will consider agricultural and subsistence traditions in different areas of the New World.

# Peopling of the Americas

The first peopling of the Americas was a relatively recent event. Most scholars believe that it probably occurred between 30 and 15 kyr ago, but the actual date of the first arrivals is a highly contentious issue—as are the identity of the first Americans, the place(s) they came from, and the means by which they got to and traveled through the Americas. In this minefield of often acrimonious debate, one undisputed fact is that the first Americans were modern humans (see Chapter 15 for a discussion of biological aspects of modern humans). Lacking written records, researchers have striven to assemble the prehistory of the Americas through such diverse disciplines as archaeology, geology, ecology, linguistics, paleontology, molecular biology, and anthropology among others. Let's review what they have learned.

## How Did the First Americans Get There?

It is generally agreed that the first Americans came from Siberia, either across the exposed landmass of **Beringia** (now the Bering Strait, a body of water 90 km [55 miles] wide that separates Alaska and Siberia) or along the Pacific coast. A third suggestion proposes arrival on the east coast after journeys from Spain following the North Atlantic ice front that connected Western Europe and North America (Stanford and Bradley 2002). The Beringia theory is widely accepted, although the coastal route is gaining momentum; the Atlantic crossing concept is widely rejected (Straus 2000). Today the bed of the Bering Strait lies under 37 m (120 feet) of water. During ice ages, when sea levels dropped by as much as 100 m (330 feet), the Bering Strait was a steppe tundra landscape almost 1,500 km (1,000 miles) long that extended into an ice-free area of Alaska between the Brooks and Alaskan mountain ranges (see Figure 12.1) (Dumont 1987). Although poor in tree cover, this landscape supported grazing animals such as woolly mammoth, musk ox, bison, horse, and wild sheep. It is likely that humans crossed Beringia in pursuit of game. Once across Beringia, groups wishing to move south through the interior had to contend with the Laurentide and Cordilleran ice sheets, which covered eastern and western regions of North America. During maximum glaciation the ice sheets met near the present-day border of British Columbia and Alberta. During slightly warmer periods the ice masses retreated slightly, opening up an **ice-free corridor** 25 to 100 km (15 to 62 miles) wide through which animals and people could pass onto the plains of southern Alberta. However, some geologists believe that even during warmer periods environmental conditions in the ice-free corridor would have been too cold and wet to allow passage of animals and people (Dillehay 2000).

Beringia was exposed several times between 70 kyr ago and 11.5 kyr ago, when it was last inundated. Theoretically, people could have crossed it at any of those times. Dates for the earliest sites in the Americas suggest a later rather than earlier crossing, however. It seems most likely that the crossing occurred at some time either before 21 kyr or after 14 kyr ago—before or after the Laurentide and Cordilleran ice sheets had reached their maximum extent, and when hypothetical passage through them was possible (Meltzer 1993). If the earliest settlers used the land bridge route, then we might expect to find the earliest New World sites in Alaska. But although there is evidence for humans in northern Eurasia between 40 and 28 kyr ago, no sites in Alaska have been securely dated earlier than 14 kyr ago (Hoffecker and Elias 2003).

**Beringia**
The landmass between Alaska and Siberia that was exposed during glacial periods, when the levels of the Bering Strait and Chukchi Sea dropped as their waters were taken up in ice.

**ice-free corridor**
The possible land route from Alaska southward into Alberta that was exposed when the two major ice sheets in North America (Cordilleran and Laurentide) began to retreat.

*Figure 12.1*

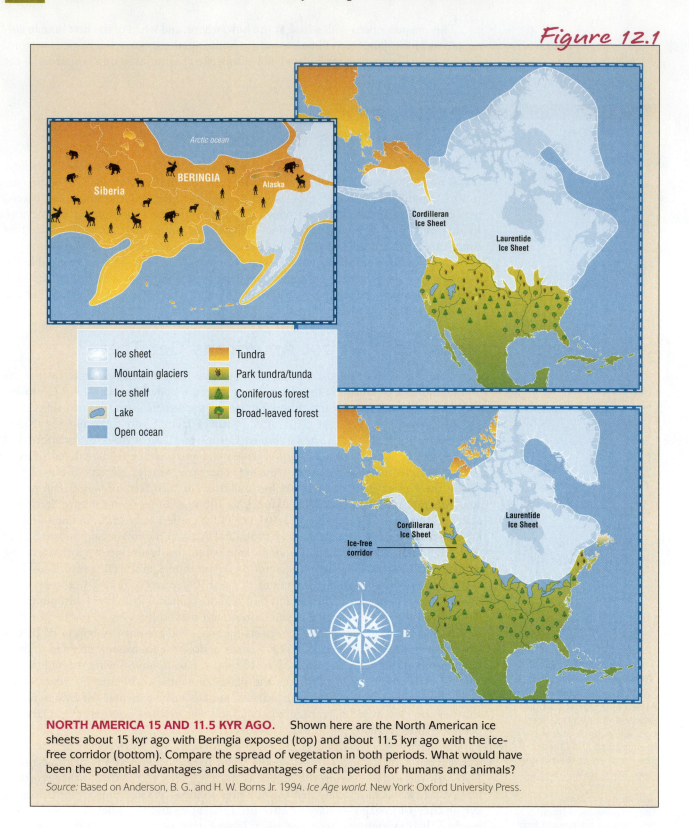

**NORTH AMERICA 15 AND 11.5 KYR AGO.**    Shown here are the North American ice sheets about 15 kyr ago with Beringia exposed (top) and about 11.5 kyr ago with the ice-free corridor (bottom). Compare the spread of vegetation in both periods. What would have been the potential advantages and disadvantages of each period for humans and animals?

*Source:* Based on Anderson, B. G., and H. W. Borns Jr. 1994. *Ice Age world*. New York: Oxford University Press.

All in all, the Beringia/southern ice-free corridor route would seem to be arduous to say the least. A coastal route seems rather more attractive—because even though the northwest coast, too, was affected by glaciers, deglaciation along the continental shelf and offshore islands had occurred by about 17 kyr ago, at least 3 kyr earlier than inland. Theoretically, then, travel southward along the coast would have been possible earlier than travel by way of the ice-free corridor (Dixson 2000). Groups were familiar with sea travel, because people had used their navigational skills to reach Australia many thousands of years before. Furthermore, **Upper Paleolithic** sites in Japan provide indirect evidence for the use of boats; obsidian found on sites near Tokyo originated from an island more than 170 km (106 miles) off the Japanese coast (Bonnichsen and Schneider 1999). In addition, the extended coastlines of glacial times with their alluvial plains, deltas, and wetlands would have been rich in resources that were easy to exploit with simple tool kits (Dillehay 2000; Dixson 2000).

Unfortunately, sites of early coastal travelers have long since disappeared beneath the rising sea levels of postglacial millennia; until such early coastal sites are found, archaeologists can only theorize about a coastal route into the Americas. It's important to remember that the peopling of the Americas was not a single event. Different groups could have used coastal routes, land routes, or a combination of both (along the coast and inland along rivers) at different propitious times.

## Where Did They Come From?

Dental and molecular evidence suggests that the first colonists came from northeast Asia, thus supporting both the Beringia and Pacific coastal hypotheses. Christy Turner studied 200,000 human teeth recovered from about 20 prehistoric sites and maintains that native Americans have certain dental traits in common with native populations in north China, Mongolia, and eastern Siberia but different from populations in Southeast Asia and Europe. Studies of mitochondrial DNA (mtDNA) also support a Mongolian connection (Fiedel 1999a; Turner 1985).

## When Did They Arrive in the Americas?

The question of when people entered the Americas is perhaps the most hotly debated issue in **Paleoindian** studies. The debate centers on two competing models: (1) late entry/Clovis first and (2) early entry (Bonnichsen and Schneider 1999). **Clovis** sites (a tradition indicated by distinctive fluted projectile points) dating from about 13.2 kyr ago have been found and accepted throughout North and Central America and claimed in areas of South America. The sites cluster tightly within a few hundred years of one another, suggesting rapid movement throughout the two continents of peoples using a similar technology. According to model 1, there should be antecedents to Clovis **fluted points** north of the ice-free corridor—that is, in Alaska. But there are no fluted points in either Siberia or Alaska. Also, if Clovis groups entered from the north, then sites in South America should be younger than those in North America. However, sites with fluted points in South America are more or less contemporaneous with Clovis sites further north. Furthermore, many researchers reject the claim that early fluted points in South America are associated with Clovis peoples; these researchers propose that the points simply indicate local adaptations to environmental changes (Bonnichsen and Schneider 1999).

On the basis of a human presence in northern Eurasia by 40 to 28 kyr ago, model 2 advocates propose arrival in the Americas by about the same time. This early entry model assumes a Pacific coastal route, for which evidence would now be underwater. DNA specialists believe that it would have taken 15 to 25 kyr for the diversity of mitochondrial DNA seen in present-day Native Americans to develop (Bonnichsen and Schneider 1999).

Linguistic studies seem to support both models. Today indigenous American peoples speak more than 600 native languages. In the past there were more. Put simply, linguists look for similarities among languages to identify larger language groups that may originate from a common ancestor. Linguists do not agree on the number of language families in the Americas, however. Joseph Greenberg (1996) proposes three major families that indicate three migrations: **Amerind**, **Na-Dene Athabaskan**, and **Eskimo-Aleut**. According to Greenberg the earliest group, the Amerind, would have been

---

**Upper Paleolithic**
Term used in the Old World outside of Africa for the period between about 40 kyr and 11.5 kyr.

**Paleoindian**
Term denoting the earliest hunter-gatherer groups in the Americas before about 11 kyr ago.

**Clovis**
Groups associated with a distinctive type of fluted projectile points, which are the first undisputed evidence of widespread occupation of North and Central America.

**fluted points**
Projectile points produced with a stone-working technique that thins the base to assist hafting.

**Amerind**
One of the major language families associated with the early occupation of the Americas.

**Na-Dene Athabaskan**
One of the major language families associated with the early occupation of the Americas.

**Eskimo-Aleut**
One of the major language families associated with the early occupation of the Americas.

contemporaneous with Clovis groups. However, most other linguists disagree with Greenberg, some proposing that the present-day diversity in native languages would require 35 kyr to develop (Fagan 2000; Meltzer 1993).

## The Archaeological Evidence

Claims for early sites from Alaska to Tierra del Fuego are plagued with problems. For example, an association between stone tools and Pleistocene animal bones in Bluefish Caves in the northern Yukon, dated to about 14 kyr ago, is unsure. Also, burrowing animals may have caused mixing of sediments at Cactus Hill in southeast Virginia, so stone tools apparently found in an 18-kyr-old level may have come from a younger level. And radiocarbon dates from Taima Taima in Venezuela may have been contaminated by old carbon from coal in the area (Fiedel 2000).

In light of such difficulties and ensuing controversies, David Meltzer (1993) proposed that validation of the authenticity and antiquity of each site should rest on three criteria: (1) clear evidence of human presence (such as artifacts or bones); (2) stratigraphic position in undisturbed geological deposits; and (3) radiometric dates. Clovis sites from about 13.2 kyr ago have consistently met these criteria. In general, however, most claims for earlier sites do not meet all the criteria. A further problem is that although many archaeologists will accept a given piece of proposed evidence, others will reject that same evidence. Consequently, the literature is littered with claims and counterclaims.

Arguments surrounding the excavations at **Meadowcroft Rockshelter** in Pennsylvania demonstrate the difficulties in getting acceptance for pre-Clovis dates for a site. Meadowcroft is a deeply stratified site with more than 50 consistent dates ranging from 19 to 11 kyr ago. Twelve dates are older than 12.8 kyr ago, and six of these came from deposits with associated human artifacts. All dates since 12.8 kyr ago have been accepted, but the older dates have been challenged. The challengers point to claimed contamination of the radiocarbon samples; and they argue that the deposits' fauna and flora lack the glacial signatures they should have, given that glacial ice would have been 153 km (95 miles) away. Over the years the excavators have undertaken studies to answer questions and have taken more radiocarbon dates. For example, micromorphological analysis of sediments indicates no contamination that would affect radiocarbon samples (Goldberg and Arpin 1999); furthermore, no reason can be found to explain the claimed presence of contamination in the lower levels but not in the upper ones. Environmental studies suggest a protected refugium (area of unaltered climate with little impact from glaciation), thus explaining the lack of glacial tree species (Adovasio et al. 1999). Some archaeologists still reject the early dates, but many now accept the antiquity of Meadowcroft Rockshelter.

## Monte Verde Fits the Criteria

For many archaeologists **Monte Verde**, located between the Andean highlands and the Pacific coast of southern Chile, has compelling evidence for early occupation at 14 kyr ago or slightly earlier (Dillehay 1999; Fiedel 2000). The riverside site and its organic content were preserved by peat. Excavation revealed the wooden foundations of two structures; some fragments of **mastodon** hides (perhaps remains of an outer covering); clay-lined hearths; cooking pits; mastodon, camelid, and small animal bones; a range of plant remains; and wooden and stone tools. The diversity of plant material, originating from different environmental zones between the coast and the highlands, highlights the importance of plant food in the occupants' diet. In addition, excavators recovered plant-processing tools: wooden mortars, digging sticks, and grinding stones. Meat was not a primary food source but an addition to the plant-based diet. The paleobotanical remains from Monte Verde also included medicinal species, indicating an understanding of the healing properties of particular plants (Dillehay 1999; Dillehay and Rossen 2002).

**Meadowcroft Rockshelter**
Deeply stratified site in Pennsylvania that may be one of the earliest occupied sites in the Americas.

**Monte Verde**
Well-dated site in Chile that may be the oldest Paleoindian site in the Americas.

**mastodon**
Extinct relative of mammoth and elephant.

People questioned the validity of Monte Verde for many years. Finally, in 1997 a team of specialists, including skeptics, visited the site and studied the artifacts and other remains. They concluded that the evidence strongly supported the authenticity of the site (Meltzer et al. 1997), although a few doubters remain (Fiedel 1999b; Roosevelt 2000). If people were in Chile by 14 kyr ago, then they must have entered the north much earlier. Yet despite intensive search, earlier northern sites remain elusive.

## The Clovis Phenomenon

Clovis sites with their distinctive fluted spear points form the first undisputed evidence of widespread human occupation of much of North and Central America. Clovis finds span about 400 years, beginning about 13.2 kyr ago (Fiedel 2002). Incidentally, the name *Clovis* comes from a site near the town of Clovis, New Mexico, where the first Clovis points were found in the 1930s. Spectacular animal kill sites in the central plains and in the North American Southwest gave Clovis groups their reputation as big game hunters who specialized in mammoth and bison hunting, (see Highlight 12.1, on pp. 354–355). In reality, the reputation for big game hunting may be an exaggeration, as only 14 mass kill sites have been found; furthermore evidence at some Clovis sites indicates that the people hunted smaller animals and collected plants and berries, suggesting a more broad-based subsistence economy (Fiedel 1992; Grayson and Meltzer 2003).

Skilled toolmakers, Clovis groups chose high-quality siliceous stone such as chalcedony, jasper, or flint for their tools. Careful choice of stone is evident in the distance between find spots of tools and stone quarry sources—a distance often greater than 300 km (180 miles) (Meltzer 2002). Stout, lanceolate-shaped Clovis points have a base that is often smoothed through grinding and further thinned by the removal of flakes upward from the base (fluting), which facilitates hafting (Meltzer 1993). Replication experiments show that Clovis point manufacture was time-consuming but that the end product was deadly sharp. Also, when a point became dull, it could be resharpened by the removal of small flakes around the edge. When hafted to a lance, Clovis points formed effective hunting spears that could penetrate thick hides, causing extensive wounding, so that one or two experienced hunters might conceivably bring down a mammoth (Frison 1999). Clovis groups made relatively few bone, antler, and ivory tools.

Clovis stone points have been found in association with, and sometimes embedded in, the carcasses of as many as 13 mammoths per kill site. Kill sites tend to be in areas of ancient ponds or streams; animals may have been driven in or ambushed as they floundered in the mud (Fiedel 1992), although it would have been difficult to

These Clovis spear points made of various kinds of stone (andesite, chert, quartzite, and rhyolite) were found in association with animal kill sites in Arizona. What does the range of stone types imply about Clovis technology?

# Investigating Animal Extinctions

BY 10 KYR AGO MORE THAN 35 GENERA OF MEGAFAUNA in North and South America had become extinct—among them mastodon, mammoth, native American horse, saber-toothed cat, giant beaver, giant ground sloth, giant armadillo, and camel. The majority of these mammals were herbivores, although a few carnivores disappeared; some bird species also became extinct, but few small or marine mammals were affected. What could explain this die-off?

Such large-scale extinctions had not happened during previous interglacial periods in the Americas, so a change in temperature (and therefore environment) cannot have been wholly responsible. Perhaps significantly, during previous interglacial periods there had been no humans in the Americas. Humans' aggressive hunting techniques would have been particularly effective against animals that were not used to the dangers the new settlers posed. Further, many extinctions seem to coincide with the spread of Clovis groups. With all this in mind, some experts have proposed a scenario of mass overkill resulting in animal extinction and have seen Clovis hunters as the prime perpetrators of the deed.

Researchers who oppose the overkill scenario argue that although it may account for the loss of some animal species, it does not account for all. The bones of only a few species have been found at kill sites; of these mammoth, mastodon, horse, and camel disappeared, whereas bison and buffalo also were hunted but did not become extinct. In addition, there are no known kill sites of other extinct species such as the giant sloth or giant armadillo. Therefore, an alternative scenario is that changing climate and environment played a major role. The rise in temperature in the Holocene reduced the diversity of plant communities; the former mixed grasslands of the Pleistocene, on which megafauna flourished, gave way to Holocene grasslands of fewer plant species. This change must have caused stress in some mammals such as mammoth and ground sloth, whose digestive systems required diversity; in contrast, ruminants such

Saber-toothed cat

Great North American short-faced bear

Woolly mammoth

Ground sloth

Lion-like cat

American mastodon

Some of the extinct North American mammals.

as bison could continue to thrive. Change in environment also may have triggered a change in habitat for smaller species, which would then have been in competition with the megafauna. A reduction in carcasses would have had a drastic effect on scavenging carnivores and raptor birds, causing these species in turn to die out.

A chicken-and-egg scenario has been proposed by Gary Haynes. Haynes suggests that mammoth and mastodon would have been preferred targets for hunters because of the massive return in meat, which could be stored if necessary. These animals were easy for humans to track, because they left highly visible trails of footprints, trampled grassland, and dung signatures. As preferred habitats dwindled in size and number, hunters could predict the areas to which their prey would head. And by refining hunting techniques, hunters gained greater chances of success.

Animal maturation and gestation rates may have played a part, because large animals generally take longer to mature and longer to reproduce than smaller animals. If American megafauna were affected by other factors, including environmental stress and hunting, then the big animals may not have had enough time to reproduce.

Refinements in $^{14}$C dating have now further complicated the picture by showing that some extinctions occurred before 12 kyr ago—that is, before the end of the Pleistocene. So at this point it seems that probably no single factor was the sole cause for animal extinction. A combination of events (and not necessarily those mentioned here) that occurred at the same time, with for some species the addition of aggressive human hunters, may finally have taken their toll. It is important to remember, too, that many causes for extinction, such as diseases, may not be archaeologically visible.

*Sources:* Davis, S. J. 1995. *The archaeology of animals.* London: B. T. Batsford.    Dillehay, T. D. 2000. *The settlement of the Americas.* New York: Basic Books.    Grayson, D. K. 1991. Late Pleistocene mammalian extinctions in North America: Taxonomy, chronology, and explanations. *Journal of World Prehistory* 5 (3): 193–231.    Grayson, D. K. 2001. The archaeological record of human impacts on animal populations. *Journal of World Prehistory* 15 (1): 1–68.    Grayson, D. K., and D. J. Meltzer. 2003. A requiem for North American overkill. *Journal of Archaeological Science* 30:585–593.    Haynes, G. 2002a. The catastrophic extinction of North American mammoths and mastodons. *World Archaeology* 33 (3): 391–416.    Haynes, G. 2002b. *The early settlement of North America: The Clovis era.* Cambridge/New York: Cambridge University Press.    Martin, P. 1984. Prehistoric overkill: The global model. In *Quaternary extinctions: A prehistoric revolution,* eds. P. Martin and R. Klein, pp. 354–403. Tucson: University of Arizona Press.

turn back to your reading

**ochre**
Mineral pigment that has color ranges of reds and yellows.

butcher a mired mammoth, let alone remove it from a bog (Frison 1999). Such large animals provided skins for clothing and shelter and enough food to see a group through weeks, if not months. With that in mind, researchers have proposed that sites with multiple mammoths may represent repeated butchery events over some period of time rather than a single mass kill. Furthermore, fall hunts would have provided groups with enough food for the winter months if the meat could be stored (Stanford 1999). Indeed, piles of carcasses at some kill sites may have been placed over caches of meat, then covered with mud or grass, dampened, and left to freeze. Such a scenario has been suggested for the Colby site in the northwest plains, where a mammoth skull topped a pile of bones that covered a partial animal skeleton (Frison 1999).

Although most Clovis sites are small, a few large campsites have been found. At these sites the evidence points to a range of activities: tool making, hide processing, bone carving, and woodworking. Debris is often found scattered around hearths where people may have gathered together to work and eat (Fiedel 1992).

Little is known about the belief systems of Clovis groups. Excavators have uncovered a few caches of stone tools and bone artifacts, often covered with **ochre**. Given the similarity between the contents of these collections and the inclusion of particularly fine specimens, some archaeologists argue that they were deliberate deposits for purposes other than mere caching for future use (Frison 1999). However, David Meltzer (2002) suggests that stone caches simply served practical purposes—as known alternative sources of stone for those occasions when groups could not find good stone. There is very little evidence of Clovis art; investigators have found a few engraved stones and possibly bones, but nothing similar to the artwork of the European Upper Paleolithic. The only known clear Clovis burial site, at Anzick in Montana, was of two children covered with red ochre and buried with stone and bone artifacts (Fiedel 1992).

Specialists agree that Clovis groups spread rapidly. Meltzer (2002) suggests that rapid movement of small, mobile groups was essential for survival in an unfamiliar landscape. People had to learn about resources in the territories through which they passed, and highly mobile people traveling in small groups would have greater chances of survival if food became scarce. Secure sources of stone in caches could have been useful to such groups. The lack of burials and artwork may further support this scenario. And the geographically wide similarity in tool kits implies both rapid movement and open social networks among groups to facilitate exchange of information. The tools themselves, Meltzer theorizes, may have been symbolic markers unifying groups. Meltzer further posits that differences in tool kits in post-Clovis times indicate the emergence of different groups living with accumulated knowledge of resources in familiar landscapes.

# Hunting, Foraging, and Fishing in the Holocene: Archaic Cultures

The rise in temperatures in the postglacial period of the **Holocene**, as we saw in Chapter 10, brought about environmental changes that caused human populations around the world to alter their subsistence patterns significantly. After about 10 kyr ago, when much of the ice had retreated to the polar regions, there was a spreading northward of warmer-adapted vegetation. Tundra conditions appeared in newly deglaciated areas; spruce and pine forests, followed by birch and alder, replaced former tundra areas; and deciduous forests replaced fir forests. In the New World large areas of grasslands and lakes dried up in western North America, and tropical forests replaced grasslands in Amazonia (Fiedel 1992; Snow 1996).

Animal extinctions (see Highlight 12.1) left gaps in the subsistence base on which many human groups and their predecessors had relied for millennia. However, the changing environment of the Holocene was rich in other resources: smaller game in the

**Holocene**
The present interglacial geological period that began 11,500 years ago.

**Archaic**
The period from the early Holocene to the beginning of farming in the Americas, during which hunting, foraging, and fishing cultures were predominant.

forests; fresh- and saltwater fish; shellfish; sea mammals and waterfowl; and a variety of edible fruits, nuts, and grasses. In addition, many of these resources (e.g., salmon runs or acorn harvests) could be found at particular places or at particular times of the year, or both. Groups developed technologies that enabled them to successfully exploit new habitats; among these technologies were manipulation of the environment (e.g., forest clearance to attract animals) and the planting of wild foods. The relative security of resource availability, combined with the requisite processing and storage technology, allowed people to schedule their movements and therefore to settle for longer periods in one place. In time, population numbers slowly rose (Snow 1996).

Throughout the Americas the general pattern of subsistence strategies was predominantly broad-spectrum exploitation of resources. Resources varied between regions, however. As a result, exploitation strategies also varied, giving rise to regional diversity—for example, diversity in settlement patterns and artifact styles. Long-distance contact between groups developed, probably in order to maintain or develop alliances through the exchange of gifts rather than to trade for essential goods. It is likely that groups within defined territories spoke distinct languages, the protolanguages of more recent Native American tongues (Snow 1996).

The term **Archaic** is used to distinguish between these hunting, foraging, and fishing communities and subsequent settled, farming communities. The Archaic cannot be neatly sandwiched between calendar dates, as resources in some areas (e.g., the northwest coast of North America) were so abundant that the adoption of farming was unnecessary and thus long delayed. It would be impossible to cover here the details of Archaic cultures throughout the Americas, so the next sections discuss four North American regions: the Eastern Woodlands, the Great Basin, the Northwest Coast, and Southern California.

# The Eastern Woodlands Archaic

The hickory, beech, and other deciduous woodlands of eastern North America were rich in resources that included deer, raccoon, opossum, turkey, nuts, and acorns. Archaic groups exploiting river valleys added fish, waterfowl, turtles, mussels, and edible seeds to their diet. After about 6,000 years ago, when rising sea levels had stabilized, people in the **Eastern Woodlands** targeted coastal resources and seasonal fish runs more intensively. The extensive exploitation of riverine and marine shellfish is evident in the many shell middens that date to the Archaic (about 9,500 to 2,200 years ago).

## Developing Technology

**Eastern Woodlands**
The region of eastern North America, rich in resources that underpinned a flourishing Archaic lifestyle.

**mano**
Term used in the Americas, synonymous with pestle or handstone; used in conjunction with a metate to grind substances, particularly seeds.

**metate**
Term used in the Americas, synonymous with mortar; the stone slab on which substances are placed for grinding with a mano.

People of the Eastern Woodlands developed a range of tools to help them fully exploit the wide array of resources. In addition to flaked stone tools, people manufactured polished stone tools such as axes, adzes (for woodworking), and stone mortars and pestles (known also as **manos** and **metates**) for grinding and pounding seeds (Snow 1996). Such tools take time to make and can often be very heavy; mortars, for example, would not have been moved far. The Archaic saw the earliest exploitation of native copper in the New World as groups around Lake Superior began to hammer it to form spearheads, knives, harpoons, and awls.

Fishing gear increased and became more complex. Inland and coastal fishing kits included bone hooks, barbed fish points, toggling harpoons (whose points detach from the shaft when embedded in the flesh), fiber nets, and net sinkers (to secure nets in water). People devised fish traps such as a line of tightly packed wooden poles stuck into mudflats that trapped fish as the tide went out. Boat technology developed for transport and fishing purposes; for example, swordfish bones at the Turner Farm shell midden site in Maine indicate deep-sea fishing that would have required sturdy watercraft (large dugout canoes) and spears (Fagan 2000).

Excavations at Koster, Illinois, began in 1969 and continued until 1979. What factors do investigators need to consider when undertaking a large excavation such as that at Koster?

Many foods require special processing before they are edible. For example, acorns need to be leached of harmful toxins; seeds must be ground; and certain foods, such as skunk cabbage, require extensive boiling. Before the invention of pottery, people heated water by dropping small hot pebbles or baked clay balls into bark, skin, or waterproof basket containers; contact with water caused cracking of the stone or clay surface, thus providing indirect evidence for the boiling of food (Snow 1996). Sometime after 4,000 years ago, groups began to use pottery containers that allowed them to cook food over open fires. Pots were also suitable storage containers. Methods for drying food, in particular for drying fish taken in fish runs, would also have been important.

Unless preserved under special conditions (e.g., dessicated, waterlogged, frozen, or charred) plant-based artifacts and technology are poorly represented in the archaeological record. Archaeologists thus felt as though they had hit the jackpot when they excavated the wetland burial site of Windover in Florida. As well as 168 burials, excavations revealed a wealth of organic artifacts, among them wooden tools, plant fiber cordage, and woven bags, hoods, blankets, and clothing that displayed a range of weaving methods (Purdy 1992). Windover provides a glimpse of what is missing from other Archaic sites.

## Settlement and Scheduling of Resources

An increase in the number and size of Eastern Woodlands sites after about 8,500 years ago indicates a growing population that often stayed almost permanently at, or returned regularly to, the same place. In these sites there is evidence of dwelling structures, storage facilities (permitting occupation during times when fresh food might be scarce), accumulation of waste, and burials. People could schedule their food acquisition activities from such sites. The **Koster** site in Illinois has a long stratigraphic sequence spanning the Archaic period. The site was reoccupied many times and grew from a camp of 0.3 hectares (almost 0.75 acre) about 8,500 years ago to a village of 2 hectares (5 acres) between 5,900 and 4,800 years ago. Koster people hunted deer and small animals, fished and collected shellfish, and in time caught waterfowl and turkeys. They also exploited rich harvests of nuts, in particular, pecan and hickory when in season; and from the earliest period they exploited seeds, which became an increasingly important part of their diet. By about 7,600 years ago the settlement took on a more permanent aspect with rectangular houses made of wood and clay. By 5,900 years ago houses large enough to accommodate an extended family were partially dug into the ground (Fiedel 1992; Struever and Holton 1979).

## Exchange Networks

As Eastern Woodlands populations grew, territorial demarcations restricted people's ability to move at will around the landscape in search of materials or commodities. As a result, extensive **exchange networks** developed to move goods rather than people.

**Koster**
A site in Illinois with a long stratigraphic sequence that spans the Archaic period of the North American Eastern Woodlands.

**exchange networks**
Mechanisms by which goods are transferred between people, whether between two individuals or by means of a system of redistribution by a central authority or a currency-based market economy.

This aerial view shows the Archaic site at Poverty Point, Louisiana. What features make Poverty Point visible from the air? Why?

Desired goods included copper from Lake Superior; seashells from the Gulf and Atlantic coasts; galena from the Appalachians, the Ozarks, and the upper Mississippi valley; jasper from eastern Pennsylvania; and chalcedony and black slate from Canada (Fagan 2000). Some Archaic sites may have gained importance because of their strategic position along exchange routes. An example is **Poverty Point**, Louisiana (3,500 to 2,700 years ago, now a World Heritage Site). The central village layout at Poverty Point shows an elliptical pattern of six rows of segmented raised earthen banks around a central area of 15 hectares (37 acres). Several other large and small mounds, including two enormous bird-shaped mounds, form part of the complex. Material evidence indicates domestic residences at the site, but it is unclear whether people lived there on a permanent basis or not. The entire Poverty Point site covers more than 3 km² (1.2 square miles). Excavations at the site revealed vast amounts of stone and minerals imported from the Southeast and Midwest, among them chert, slate, soapstone, hematite, magnetite, galena, and copper. Some of these materials originated as far away as 2,250 km (1,400 miles). Although worked and partially worked artifacts were counted among the imports, most stone arrived in unmodified form, and local workers chose particular stones to make specific tools. The unanswered question is what the Poverty Point people exchanged for these minerals. No Poverty Point artifacts have been found in the source regions of the imported stone. Furthermore, it is unlikely that Poverty Point groups exported pelts, food, or other organic items, as these were reasonably common throughout the Eastern Woodlands (Gibson 1994, 1996). It is tempting to see Poverty Point as the center of a chiefdom that received tribute from those under its domain. Kenneth Sassaman (2005) does not think so. He suggests that groups in the area and beyond were independent, but shared a common belief system centered on Poverty Point. Thus, the range of raw materials at the site is perhaps the result of gifts donated to the sacred center by pilgrims.

## Burial and Ceremony

Throughout the Archaic, evidence points to increasing social and technological complexity among Eastern Woodlands groups, which is reflected in burial and ritual activities. Cemeteries serve to reinforce group identity and may indicate territorial claims to the land where ancestors lie. The earliest burial construction in this region occurs at L'Anse Amour, Labrador. There, 7,600 years ago, a 12-year-old child was placed in a pit accompanied by grave goods that included a walrus tusk, an antler toggling harpoon (used to hunt seals and marine mammals), a pestle, a bone whistle, bone points, and stone projectile points. Mourners then covered the burial pit with a mound of earth and stones (Fagan 2000; Fiedel 1992).

Burial customs and grave goods vary with regions: Females and males may have particular items related to gender or not; some goods may reflect differences in status or not. For example, at the **Black Earth** site in southern Illinois, carefully controlled excavations of levels dating from about 6,000 to 5,000 years ago revealed at least 154

**Poverty Point**
Archaic center in Louisiana that displays many large earthworks and is located in a strategic position on exchange routes.

**Black Earth**
Archaic site in southern Illinois where differences in burial practices reflect differences in status and age- and sex-related tasks.

**Indian Knoll**
Archaic site in Kentucky where grave goods indicate differences associated with status and sex-related tasks.

**mound building**
Construction of large earthen structures, often associated with burials, by Archaic and early farming communities in the American Midwest and Southeast.

**chiefdom**
Hierarchical society usually under the control of a hereditary chief.

**Cahokia**
Center of a powerful Mississippian chiefdom in the Mississippi River Valley.

**Mississippian**
Term for a group of chiefdoms in eastern North America between about 1,150 and 400 years ago, associated with large mound complexes.

burials. Differences in burial practices were apparent: In general, people younger than 35 were buried with their bodies in an extended position, whereas the bodies of older adults were flexed. Twenty-seven percent of burials included grave goods, a fact that may indicate special treatment of a few individuals; indeed, grave goods were associated mainly with the extended (younger age group) burials. Males had a greater range of utilitarian, ornamental, and ceremonial items than females. Utilitarian items suggest sex- and age-related tasks: male food procurement activities, female food-processing activities. The lack of utilitarian artifacts in children's graves suggests that children had no particular duties to fulfill. Although children did not have ornamental artifacts, decorated pins associated with a few juvenile burials imply that the deceased possessed a level of prestige during life (Jefferies and Lynch 1983).

About one-third of the 1,100 burials recovered from **Indian Knoll**, Kentucky, a site dating to about 4,000 years ago, contained grave goods. Some indicated differences in status or work-related activities: axes, woodworking tools, fishhooks, and projectile points found mainly in male graves suggest male procurement tasks; nut-cracking stones, bone beads, and pestles in female graves suggest processing tasks. A few graves contained items from distant sources, among them copper from Lake Superior and shells from the Atlantic and Gulf of Mexico coasts. Found in both male and female graves were artifacts associated with shamans, such as rattles and medicine bags (Fiedel 1992).

Death in the Archaic was not always peaceful. Bodies with wounds or arrows show that aggression and warfare was present, perhaps linked to the need to protect the resources of a tribal territory from outsiders.

## Mound Building

The Eastern Woodlands region is famous for its many impressive prehistoric mounds. **Mound building** is not uniquely associated with the great **chiefdom** societies of later periods, such as those at **Cahokia**, capital of a powerful **Mississippian** chiefdom located near present-day St. Louis (see Highlight 12.2, on pp. 362–363); it began during the Archaic. More than 60 mound groups have been identified in the southeast region, most in Louisiana but some also in Florida. There may be 2 to 10 mounds (or more) in a group, and mounds range from 1.5 m (5 feet) to more than 7 m (23 feet) in height. The earliest are perhaps 6,000 years old or more. Most mounds are near major rivers, estuaries, or wetland areas; the rich resources of these areas may have enabled people to stay more permanently in one place, and the ready food supply meant that people had more time for activities such as mound building (Russo 1996). The purpose of mound building is not readily apparent. Most mounds contain neither burials nor artifacts. The larger mounds would have required great organization, although the smaller mounds could have been built by a few people over a year. Jon Gibson (1996) believes mounds served several functions: Perhaps they served as territorial markers, legitimizing a group's ties to the land while at the same time reinforcing the group's identity; perhaps they stood as reminders of the special ritual nature of a place within a group's belief system; or perhaps they were centers for ritual and civic ceremonial activities.

## The Great Basin Archaic

The Great Basin region includes present-day Utah, Nevada, and parts of neighboring states. The area is topographically and environmentally diverse, with mountains, valleys, deserts, and rich marshland environments. Such diversity in habitat afforded varied food resources for Archaic groups to exploit—fish, waterfowl, roots, tubers, seeds, grasses, small mammals, bighorn sheep, bison, and antelope. Average rainfall is sparse over much of the area, although higher in the mountains; however, yearly rainfall is unreliable and might have caused fluctuations in the food supply that affected prehistoric food acquisi-

**Hogup Cave**
Archaic site near the Great Salt Lake, in which the dry conditions preserved an extensive range of organic materials.

tion strategies (Fagan 2000). Sites found in a range of topographic locations indicate that Great Basin populations adopted a mobile lifestyle in their quest for food.

## Preservation in Caves

Archaic groups regularly took shelter in caves, and preservation in caves can offer us clues about prehistoric life that are not available elsewhere. Excavations of cave sites in the arid Great Basin have revealed a rich array of organic materials, among them hide, fur, sinew, grasses, seeds, wood, bark, feathers, and human coprolites (fossilized feces) (Aitkens and Madsen 1986). Such finds of organic materials are rare but significant, because they add details about past lifestyles that researchers usually cannot glean from excavations. Evidence from **Hogup Cave**, near the Great Salt Lake, provided extensive information on plant and animal exploitation between 8,400 and 3,200 years ago. Hogup individuals extensively exploited the abundant stands of pickleweed along the lake margins and processed the seeds on milling slabs, leaving the chaff on the cave floor. Direct evidence of pickleweed consumption came from pollen in human coprolites. People exploited plants for industrial purposes, producing fiber sandals and hemp baskets, cordage, and nets. Although they hunted bison, antelope, sheep, and deer, they targeted smaller animals such as rabbits, hares, and rodents more intensively than the larger mammals. Fragments of netting suggest a rabbit-hunting technique similar to the rabbit drives documented in later Native American groups. The marsh habitats were home to a range of bird species that added variety to the diet. Animals provided more than meat for the occupants of Hogup Cave: The people there fashioned bone awls and needles, hide thongs and pouches, and rabbit-fur blankets or capes (Aikens 1983; Aikens and Madsen 1986).

A 1912 photograph of artifacts at the entrance to Lovelock Cave, Nevada. Why is the preservation of organic artifacts important?

# Cahokia, Crown of Prehistoric Mississippian Chiefdoms

CAHOKIA WAS A POLITICAL AND CEREMONIAL CENTER under the leadership of powerful Mississippian chiefs and their kin-related elite between 1,000 and 800 years ago. Located in the fertile floodplain region of the Mississippi River valley, near present-day St. Louis, Cahokia was a complex of 123 earthen mounds, plazas, and dense habitation areas that extended over an area of 13 km$^2$ (5 square miles). A further series of mounds linked central Cahokia to two nearby large mound complexes: those of the East St. Louis groups. The core area controlled and likely received tribute from a hinterland of smaller towns and individual settlements within a limited radius of the center. However, it did not have a statelike bureaucratic system to govern distant groups.

With an estimated population of between 10,000 and 16,000 people in the eleventh century, Cahokia was not only the largest of the many chiefdom societies in the United States at the time, but also the largest settlement in North America. The power of its leaders is evident in their ability to mobilize, organize, and control the huge labor force needed for mound building, which required moving millions of tons of sediment.

Cahokia's fame was widespread, as can be seen in the Cahokian artifacts made from exotic materials originating from distant areas, as well as in Cahokian objects (and copies of them) found on sites well beyond the chiefdom's territory.

At 30 meters (almost 100 feet) high, Monks Mound at the center of Cahokia dominated the landscape. Surrounded on three sides by huge plazas, including the 19-hectare (47-acre) Great Plaza, it was the political and ritual focus of the city. Its size, prominent location, and visibility (from up to 20 km, or 12 miles, away) made Monks Mound a potent symbol of the religious and political power of Cahokia's leaders. A palisade of about 20,000 logs surrounded the core area. Probably defensive in nature, the palisade also served to restrict access (for all except the elite) to the interior. This central area comprised elite dwellings, elite burials, and ceremonial structures. Most of Cahokia's population lived around and outside the center in neighborhoods of family compounds set around smaller plazas. Compounds included wood and thatch living quarters, storage buildings, and areas for processing and cooking food. Each neighborhood had its own round sweat lodge, meeting house, granaries, and storage buildings. Differences in house sizes suggest differences in status among the population.

Many of Cahokia's mounds have disappeared beneath developers' bulldozers and farmers' tractors. However, investigations of those that remain show that they fall into three groups: (1) platform mounds that once held residential and religious buildings, (2) conical mounds, some of which served as burial places; and (3) ridge-top, mortuary mounds.

Burial mounds cover the graves of elite personages (some of whom must have been Cahokia's chiefs), mass burials, and sacrificial burials. Mound 72 was the resting place for more than 260 people, some carefully buried and some not. One pit contained the bodies of two males associated with a cloak of 20,000 shell beads; in another burial excavators found 36,000 shell beads and a group of 19 females. Grave goods recovered from various burials included hundreds of unused arrowheads—made of stone from different geological sources—and sheets of mica and copper. A burial of 53 women associated with the bodies of four males who had had their heads and hands cut off suggests human sacrifice, an interpretation supported by the discovery of 39 bodies of men and women, whose wounds clearly showed that they had been executed. Timothy Pauketat proposes that public executions might have taken place in front of thousands of people in the Great Plaza, near which Mound 72 is located.

Mounds set around central plazas are characteristic of the chiefdoms of the Mississippian culture. Cahokia is unique, however, in its five large circles of wooden posts, called woodhenges because of their similarity to henges in Britain (see Chapter 10). Researchers identified these circles by stains in the soil where the posts had been, the wood having long rotted away. Interpretations of the circles vary: They may have been structures for tracking celestial movements, surveying aids for town planning, sacred ceremonial areas, or areas of restricted access used to legitimize a chief's powers.

From Cahokia's location close to the confluence of the Mississippi and Missouri Rivers, its chiefs controlled one of the main waterways of the Southeast and had contact with both nearby and distant regions. The exotic Cahokian artifacts found beyond the Cahokian realm may indicate an exchange system designed to cement alliances between chiefs; those artifacts would have been desired status symbols indicating association with a powerful chiefdom.

About 800 years ago, Cahokia declined rapidly, and people left the city. Numerous factors may have contributed to this decline: Overexploitation of local woodland for building and agriculture may have caused soil erosion and subsequent clogging of water sources, leading to flooding and crop failures; climatic cooling from the beginning of the thirteenth century also may have caused flooding and crop failures; contagious diseases arising from dense living conditions could have decimated the population; a predominantly maize diet could have led to malnutrition; factional fighting between competing elites may have undermined the ruling authority. Whatever the causes, by about 600 years ago, the once mighty town had been abandoned and the power of Cahokia was part of the past. However, Cahokia's greatness has again gained recognition, and it is now a designated World Heritage Site.

*Sources:* Anderson, D. G. 1997. The role of Cahokia in the evolution of southeastern Mississippian society. In *Cahokia: Domination and ideology in the Mississippian world,* eds. T. R. Pauketat and T. E. Emerson, pp. 248–268. Lincoln/London: University of Nebraska Press. Demel, S. J., and R. L. Hall. 1998. The Mississippian town plan and cultural landscape of Cahokia, Illinois. In *Mississippian towns and sacred places: Searching for an architectural grammar,* eds. R. B. Lewis and C. Stout, pp. 200–226. Tuscaloosa/London: University of Alabama Press. Iseminger, W. R. 1996. Mighty Cahokia. *Archaeology* (May–June): 33–36. Pauketat, T. R., and T. E. Emerson. 1997. Introduction: Domination and ideology in the Mississippian world. In *Cahokia: Domination and ideology in the Mississippian world,* eds. T. R. Pauketat and T. E. Emerson, pp. 1–29. Lincoln/London: University of Nebraska Press. Pauketat, T. R., and N. H. Lopinot. 1997. Cahokian population dynamics. In *Cahokia: Domination and ideology in the Mississippian world,* eds. T. R. Pauketat and T. E. Emerson, pp. 103–123. Lincoln/London: University of Nebraska Press. Pauketat, T. R. 2004. *Ancient Cahokia and the Mississippians.* New York: Cambridge University Press. Pauketat, T. R. 2005. The forgotten history of the Mississippians. In *North American archaeology,* eds. T. E. Pauketat and D. DiPaolo Loren, pp. 187–211. Malden MA: Blackwell.

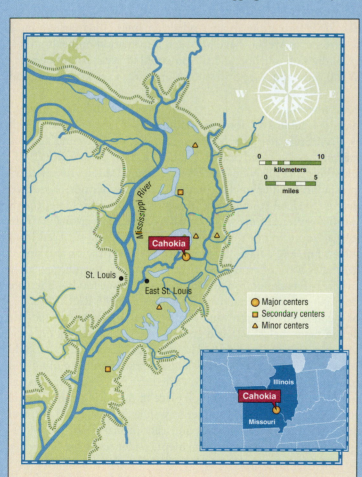

**MISSISSIPPIAN CHIEFDOMS.** Mapped here are the locations of chiefdoms of the Mississippi River valley at the time of Cahokia's ascendency. What factors underpinned Cahokia's success?

*Source:* Based on Anderson, D. G. 1997. The role of Cahokia in the evolution of southeastern Mississippian society. In *Cahokia: Domination and ideology in the Mississippian world,* ed. T. R. Pauketat and T. E. Emerson, 248–268. Lincoln: University of Nebraska Press.

turn back to your reading

**bioarchaeology**
The study of human remains in the archaeological record to determine factors such as diet, health, and demographics in past populations.

**enamel hypoplasia**
Defects in tooth enamel caused by periods of stress, usually due to shortages of food, during formation of the enamel.

Some caves and rockshelters in the Great Basin served as caches rather than as living space. Sites such as Lovelock Cave (4,500 to 1,500 years ago) and Hidden Cave (5,000 to 810 years ago) in the western Basin (Nevada) produced little evidence—such as lithic debitage (waste) or hearths—that would indicate daily domestic activities. Instead, the caves had numerous pits that were used occasionally for human burials, but primarily to store equipment such as baskets, nets, fur blankets, moccasins, bark clothing, pipes, duck decoys, fishhooks, and traps for use during groups' seasonal visits to the area. David Hurst Thomas (1985) believes that the small entrance, dark interior, and dust of Hidden Cave made it unlikely as a residence but good for storage and as shelter from searing summer temperatures. Survey and excavation have revealed residential camps around lakes and permanent water, and at these locations excavators have uncovered house sites and evidence of everyday occupational debris. Shells from the Pacific coast and obsidian from 22 different sources show that Great Basin people did not live in isolation but maintained contact with other groups through exchange networks (Elston 1986).

## Bioarchaeological Studies in the Great Basin

Because the Great Basin's wetlands and marshes are rich in resources, archaeologists have searched these areas for information about Archaic peoples. Bioarchaeological studies of human skeletons from the Archaic have provided information on health, diet, skeletal wear and tear, sexual division of labor, and the potential for year-round occupation between 4,000 and 2,500 years ago. The Stillwater Marsh area sites provide a good case study.

One technique of **bioarchaeology**, stable isotope analysis of human bone collagen, is a direct indicator of diet (see Table 10.2 for information on isotope analysis). Such analysis indicates that people at Stillwater Marsh ate a mixed diet of plants and animals suggestive of both marshland and upland environments (Larsen and Kelly 1995; Schoeninger 1999). Despite this generally good diet, however, dental studies revealed evidence of **enamel hypoplasia** (arrested enamel formation) implying periods of stunted growth when food was scarce. Skeletal studies show a robust people who had a tough lifestyle. Both men and women suffered from osteoarthritis of the back, probably from carrying heavy loads; men had more robust thighbones than women and suffered from osteoarthritis of the shoulder, hip, and ankle. The evidence of osteoarthritis and sexual dimorphism indicates that males were often on the move over rough terrain, probably hunting bighorn sheep, whereas females collected and processed plant foods—a female activity noted in the ethnographic record (Larsen and Hutchinson 1999; Ruff 1999).

In sum, the results of the bioarchaeological studies at Stillwater Marsh show people who had a tough lifestyle but nevertheless enjoyed general good health based on a diversified diet, much of it from marshland resources (Hemphill and Larsen 1999). Could groups have resided permanently in the area? Archaeologists know from the contents of human coprolites found at Lovelock Cave that people visited the cave at all seasons except winter. It is likely that male hunting activities took place in the spring and autumn, that marshland areas could be exploited in the summer as well as in spring and fall, and that winter was the time to settle in winter houses and rely primarily on stored resources. Thus, although people may not have had permanent residences in the Stillwater Marsh area, they may have spent a good part of each year there when conditions permitted. Such a scenario might also apply to groups that congregated around other Great Basin wetland areas for much of the year.

# Hunter-Forager-Fisher Groups of the Northwest Coast

The Northwest Coast region stretches from Oregon to Alaska, covering a coastal area about 1,800 km (1,118 miles) long (Ames 2003). At European contact in the late eighteenth century, groups in this region were essentially leading a hunting, foraging, and fishing way of life. (See Highlight 8.1 about 500-year-old Ozette Village in Washington state, which was preserved by a mud slide.) Nevertheless, many groups also were living in large, permanent villages as part of societies that were hierarchically ranked—a form of social organization that normally occurs in settled agricultural communities. The development of such a complex organization was due to the rich resources available to these groups. Similar complexity developed in other equally rich environments farther south in California, too. Although the Northwest Coast was the domain of different cultural groups, the following discussion addresses general similarities between them during the period from 12,000 to 1,500 years ago.

## Environmental Resources

The mild, wet climate of the Northwest Coast promotes the growth of dense forests, whose plants and trees were sources of food, medicine, tools, and building materials to Archaic groups in the area. Plant foods included rhizomes, roots, bulbs, berries, and nuts. In the later prehistoric period, people used red cedar to build houses and canoes, to create smaller artifacts such as boxes, and to produce distinctive Northwest Coast art. The forests were home to varied prey: elk, deer, bears, mountain sheep and goats, beavers, carnivores, and rodents. The marine environment along the coast offered a wide range of fish (up to 20 species of fish have been recovered from single sites), vast communities of shellfish, and sea mammals such as otters, seals, porpoises, and whales. The Frazer and Columbia Rivers are two of the many rivers with major runs of salmon, trout, and smelt. Patterns of subsistence reflected specific habitats; for example, where salmon populations were low, people exploited coastal and inland resources, but in salmon-rich areas that fish increasingly became the dominant food species. This coastal and riverine pattern of exploitation is evident from 8,000 years ago and must reflect subsistence patterns from preceding periods, although evidence from earlier years has been lost in the rising seas and the increasing forest cover of the early Holocene (Matson and Coupland 1995). Although groups may have targeted specific species such as salmon, they also broadened their dietary intake with a range of other foods. For example, about 7,000 years ago at Namu, on the British Columbian coast, people exploited salmon in the fall and herring in the late winter to early spring; they added shellfish to their diet by about 6,000 years ago. Throughout the region, large shell middens dating to about 6,000 years ago indicate an increase in the gathering of shellfish (Ames and Maschner 1999; Cannon 2002).

An Athapaskan fish-drying structure from the historic period in Alaska (about 1915). What forms of technology and social organization enabled prehistoric people to exploit fish runs long before the advent of mechanization?

## Changing Technology

Stone tools are the major source of direct information on early Holocene technology of the Northwest Coast. Two major regional traditions of stoneworking are apparent: Assemblages dominated by microblades and microliths are more commonly found in the northern areas, and assemblages dominated by points are common in central and southern areas. There is no evidence for specialized tool kits, but the flexibility of microblades made it possible to use them as hafted tools for hunting and fishing. Bone, antler, and wooden tools formed part of the tool kit in all areas but are rarely preserved. In addition to making chipped-stone points, knives, and scrapers, people used polished stone, shell, and antler to craft blades for adzes, chisels, and other woodworking tools. Ground-stone axes were efficient at felling trees, and there were bone and antler wedges for splitting wood. Slate spearhead points and a variety of barbed bone harpoons made effective tools for spearing fish and hunting sea mammals. It is likely, too, that fishing groups used nets and basket traps (Ames 2003; Ames and Maschner 1999). Given the importance of marine food resources, people must have used boats for fishing for coastal and deep sea fish and for transport along the coast and inland. Methods of storing food such as roasting, smoking, or sun or wind drying (lost to the archaeological record) would have been essential for groups to survive the long winters. Similarly, clothing and bedding also would have been essential to survival on the Northwest Coast but are rare finds.

## Settlements

The diversity of resources in the Northwest enabled groups to remain in one place permanently—or at least for longer periods than did Archaic groups in most other regions. The earliest Northwest Coast dwellings date to about 6,000 years ago. These semi-subterranean pit houses were found in the interior regions; similar shelters may have been in use in coastal areas but have not been preserved (Ames and Maschner 1999). Thick waste deposits indicate that pit houses were used year after year, although they probably were not year-round dwellings but rather winter settlements. Aubrey Cannon (2002) proposes that evidence for fall and winter fishing of salmon and herring at Namu indicates a winter settlement, although evidence for structures is lacking. The presence of burials and cemeteries are often indicators of longer-term settlement; the earliest preserved burials on the Northwest Coast are at Namu and date to about 5,400 years ago, and the earliest cemeteries are slightly later, at about 5,000 years ago. By 4,000 years ago cemeteries span lengthy time periods indicating stability in group settlement (Ames 2005).

The first village on the Northwest Coast dates to about 3,000 years ago; excavators uncovered it at the **Paul Mason** site near Prince Rupert, British Columbia, Canada. Ten large multi-family rectangular houses, each 8 to 11 m (26 to 36 feet) long and 5 to 6 m (16 to 20 feet) wide, were set in two rows, one behind the other. In each house raised earthen platforms that may have been used as beds flanked a narrow, sunken floor that extended along the center. Hearths were set in the sunken floor, and evidence of postholes indicates that logs served as roof supports (Matson and Coupland 1995). Cooperation between members of large households led to increased food production, craft specialization, settlement stability, and wealth that smaller groups could not achieve (Ames 2003).

## Ritual, Status, and Warfare

A study of the burial practices of Archaic people on the Northwest Coast indicates a change through time from egalitarian to **ranked societies.** Early Holocene groups were egalitarian, but different aspects of burial practices (inhumation or cremation, midden burial, and types of grave goods) hint at changing perceptions of individuals. About 11,500 years ago groups placed bone and stone tools and marine shell beads with some burials at Marmes in Washington State; many of the artifacts would have been time-consuming to make, and the shells had probably been acquired through trade. Starting about 6,000 years ago, **labrets** (lip ornaments) became status symbols; labrets leave distinctive wear patterns on teeth, so both labrets and tooth wear are indicators of the practice (Ames and Maschner 1999). As noted earlier, the first known cemeteries date to about 5,000 years ago; these burial grounds may represent markers of particular social groups (Ames 2003).

Through time, population numbers increased and groups along the Northwest Coast became increasingly sedentary, a lifestyle made possible by the intensive exploita-

**Paul Mason**
Archaic Northwest Coast village with large rectangular, multi-family houses.

**ranked societies**
Hierarchical societies in which people do not have equal access to status and prestige.

**labrets**
Lip ornaments used by Northwest Coast people as a sign of status.

tion of a few normally reliable resources that could be stored after processing. The manufacture of tools to meet specific exploitation needs had the added effect of producing specialized craftspeople. Sites in which organic artifacts have been preserved allow more glimpses of the range of technology among later Northwest Coast groups (refer to Highlight 8.1). Fragments of baskets show that different production techniques were used by contemporaneous groups; these variations may indicate cultural preferences rather than functional differences. Carefully made watertight wooden boxes were used for storage and cooking. Other organic finds include bark clothing and fragments of cordage (Ames and Maschner 1999). The emergence of hierarchies, the desire for prestige goods, and the growth of populations may well have promoted conflict situations.

Warfare rears its ugly head on the Northwest Coast beginning about 6,000 years ago, as is apparent from burials. Excavations at Namu revealed a skeleton with a point embedded in its spine. Other indications of violence include skull fractures caused by clubs (stone and bone clubs have been recovered from sites and burials), parry fractures on arms from defending against a blow, and decapitation (Ames and Maschner 1999). Evidence of warfare increases after about 4,000 years ago. Perhaps people fought to protect territories and resources, or perhaps to gain items of status; for example, the purpose of decapitation could have been the acquisition of trophy heads (Matson and Coupland 1995).

# Foraging, Fishing, and Hunting Groups of Southern California

It has been estimated that when the Spanish first arrived in California in the sixteenth century, they encountered a native population of more than 300,000 people, many of whom were members of hierarchically organized communities living in large permanent villages. Hierarchy and permanence were not based on farming, an association anthropologists traditionally make. As with the Northwest Coast, the rich resources available in the California area allowed people to continue hunting, gathering, and fishing—a lifestyle that is theoretically Archaic, albeit highly complex. Abundance was not spread uniformly however but occurred in numerous microenvironments with different resources (Chartkoff 1998). Oak grasslands provided acorns, seeds, and small mammals and birds. Larger mammals roamed the redwood forests. Coastal California was exceptionally rich in marine resources such as shellfish and deep-sea fish as well as the great food potential offered by whale migrations (Fagan 2000). Diversified environments gave rise to diversified subsistence strategies. From about 8,000 years ago, early Archaic groups had broad-based subsistence strategies linked to the exploitation of seasonally available resources. Although generally plentiful, food supplies could be affected by natural events, such as changes in climate and the **El Niño** phenomenon. Population growth probably also affected food resources. Through time, dependence on acorns increased in some areas on the mainland, perhaps reflecting a decline in other resources as a result of overexploitation.

## Marine Exploitation on the Channel Islands of Southern California

Excavations of large shell midden sites on the Channel Islands of southern California provide a window on marine exploitation by Archaic inhabitants. Abalone shells dominate low stratigraphic levels but are replaced by mussels at higher levels (later periods), probably as a result of overexploitation of abalone rather than a change of ancient groups' shellfish preference (Kehoe 1992). Midden deposits also consist of fish and sea mammal bones, including bones of dolphins, seals, porpoises, and whales. The predominance of

**El Niño**
Cyclical climatic event that lowers temperatures in the Pacific ocean along coastal South America, causing a reduction in marine life and heavy rainfall that can lead to extensive flooding.

female and juvenile seal bones in the earlier deposits suggests that hunters targeted breeding grounds, where they would find it relatively easy to kill their prey. People could have killed whales when they found them stranded on the beach. Hunting dolphins and porpoises in the open sea is a more complex matter, for which many experts believe that harpoons and fast boats are necessary. Given the ease of clubbing seals as opposed to the perceived difficulty of hunting open-sea mammals, seal bones should dominate the bone assemblages in middens. But, after about 6,000 years ago bone remains from sites on Santa Catalina, Santa Cruz, and San Clemente islands show that people increasingly targeted dolphins, although excavators have not found evidence of complex hunting gear. One hypothesis is that groups simply may have surrounded dolphins and disoriented them by making noises, before driving them toward the coast, where other community members could kill them with stone knives. Such tactics would not require sophisticated boats or weapons (Glassow 2005; Porcasi and Fujita 2000). Jim Cassidy and his coworkers (2004) propose that people on the Channel Islands may have had the technology to make seafaring boats. Simple tools found at the Eel Point site on San Clemente Island included stone drills, wedges, and tar-stained pebbles (tar is used for waterproofing). Cassidy and his team point out that those components are similar to tools used by historic Chumash groups to make sturdy plank boats.

Dolphins provide more meat than seals and, if they are relatively easy to catch, provide a stable food resource for people. Whale bone–roofed houses on San Clemente that date between 5,000 and 4,000 years ago as well as earlier evidence of hearths, activity areas, and possible structures suggest that people lived on the island on a permanent or semi-permanent basis because they had reliable food resources. Nevertheless, faunal and mollusk evidence from the Channel Islands indicates that groups may have overexploited some species at times. Midden deposits at the Eel Point site show a gap in occupation between 8,000 and 6,000 years ago, which implies a depletion of sea mammal stocks due to hunting. Developments in fishing technology indicate an increased reliance on fishing, particularly after about 1,000 years ago (Porcasi et al. 2000).

## Mainland Subsistence Strategies

On the mainland, people collected seeds and ground them into flour with manos and metates. They caught freshwater fish using spears or lines, collected mussels, and hunted deer and small animals. After about 5,000 years ago, a change from a more to a less varied diet becomes apparent: Evidence of acorn processing, in the form of larger, heavier manos and metates, increases substantially. Acorn processing requires a heavy investment of time and labor (collecting, soaking, boiling, and drying) to remove the acorn's toxins and make them edible. However, acorns are nutritious, harvests are fairly reliable, and the nuts can be stored. The increase in acorn exploitation, replacing a former reliance on seeds, was likely a sign of growing population numbers and a decrease in other resources: Sheer hunger led people to invest time in acorn processing (Basgall 1987). Groups' mobility between the interior and coast, seen in the early Archaic, also decreased. People settled in villages from which men made hunting and fishing forays while women undertook ever-increasing processing activities (Jones 1996).

This photograph taken by Edward Curtis in the early twentieth century shows baskets, winnowing trays, and a seed beater used by historic Pomo Indians of northern California to collect seeds, acorns, and other nuts. Are baskets purely functional?

**ascribed status**
Status that is inherited rather than achieved through a person's efforts.

# Emergence of Status

Differences in status are clearly evident in burials in the southern California coastal region from about 4,000 years ago. Specifically, grave goods, especially items from distant places, are present in some but not all graves. Furthermore, grave goods accompanying the burials of young people indicate **ascribed status**—that is, status inherited from kin, rather than achieved through one's own efforts (Jennings 1989).

Obsidian, shell, and steatite (soapstone) artifacts found elsewhere than these materials' source areas indicate movement of these objects. Such movement may not always have been the product of trade and exchange systems, however. In the early Archaic, when mobility was higher, movement of goods could have occurred as people traveled on a seasonal circuit (Chartkoff 1998). By the later Archaic there is much more evidence for the movement of goods; trade and exchange may have played greater roles by this time, perhaps reflecting people's desire for status items.

Looking back at the Archaic as a whole, we can see that Archaic groups in the Americas adapted to the changing environment of the Holocene by exploiting a broad spectrum of resources, scheduling food acquisition and storage, and developing technologies to carry out these activities effectively and efficiently. The predictability and abundance of certain faunal and floral species allowed some groups to remain for longer periods in one place. People's competence in food acquisition and storage underpinned an increasing social complexity, as can be seen in settlement size and layout, long-distance exchange networks, ideology and ritual, and the emergence of a nascent hierarchy.

# The Development of Agriculture

The peoples of the Americas domesticated a profusion of native plants, among them maize (corn), various species of beans and squash, potato, sweet potato, manioc, tomato, chili pepper, avocado, sunflower, amaranth, many species of *chenopodium* (seed plants), pineapple, papaya, and cocoa. Nonfood domesticated plants include tobacco, coca, cotton, and container gourds. Many of these plants are now staple foods worldwide; others are used as flavorings, as stimulants, or for industrial purposes. In contrast to the great variety of plants, few native animals were domesticated: camelids (alpaca and llama) and guinea pigs, both in South America, plus turkeys. Given the topographic and environmental diversity of the Americas, it is not surprising that **domestication** occurred independently in at least three separate areas of the continent—in Central America, in the South American Andes, and in eastern North America. Some plants were domesticated independently in more than one area; for example, species of *chenopodium* and squash were domesticated in all three areas, beans in Central and South America, and gourds in Central America and eastern North America (Smith 1995).

When Europeans first encountered Native Americans in the fifteenth century, the staples of the American diet in many areas were maize, squash, and beans. This triad of domesticates is nutritionally healthy, as together the foods provide calories, carbohydrates, protein, and essential amino acids. Furthermore, maize and beans are good growing partners, because maize removes nitrogen from the soil but beans replenish it (Fagan 2000).

Some of the earliest evidence of domesticated plants in the Americas has come from dry caves in the semi-arid regions of the Tehuacan and Oaxaca valleys in Mexico. AMS (accelerator mass spectrometry) dating of maize cobs from Guilá Naquitz Cave in Oaxaca produced a date of 6,250 years ago—some 700 years older than cobs recovered from San Marcos Cave, Tehuacan, formerly the oldest known domesticated maize (Piperno and Flannery 2001). However, pollen evidence from the San Andrés site near the Gulf coast of Tabasco potentially pushes initial maize domestication back a further

**domestication**
Physical and genetic changes in plants and animals that are the result of human intervention.

**Many foods that are common in today's world were originally domesticated in the Americas. In what ways would these foods have changed life for Old World peoples after the fifteenth century?**

**teosinte**
Wild ancestor of maize.

**phytoliths**
Microscopic silica particles that are present in many plant cells, preserve well, and may be diagnostic of plant types.

**Tehuacan caves**
Caves in the Tehuacan Valley of Mexico that have long occupation sequences and that together document the gradual adoption of farming.

**quinoa**
Grain crop that grows in highland South America.

**camelid**
Family of animals that includes domestic llamas, alpacas, and wild vicuñas.

1,000 years (Pope et al. 2001). As **teosinte**, the wild ancestor of maize, does not grow near these areas, domesticated maize must have been introduced at an earlier period from elsewhere; possibly it came from the Balsas River valley, some 250 km (155 miles) from Tehuacan, where stands of wild teosinte grow today. From its Mexican heartland domesticated maize spread north and south into the rest of the Americas.

Maize was not the earliest domesticate in Central America, however. Analysis of **phytoliths** (hard silica particles in plants) has revealed the presence of domesticated squash and gourds in sites in southwestern Ecuador between 10,000 and 9,000 years ago (Piperno and Flannery 2001; Piperno and Stothert 2003). Phytolith and pollen analyses are proving extremely useful for charting the emergence of plant production in tropical lowlands, areas where plant remains are rarely preserved. Such analyses show that the adoption of cultivated species occurred at about the same time in highland and lowland areas.

The long stratigraphic sequence of the **Tehuacan caves** documents the presence of hunter-gatherer groups in the valley from about 12,500 years ago, the groups' gradual adoption of domesticated plants, and the establishment of permanent hamlets about 3,500 years ago. The archaeological evidence (small campsites, botanical remains, tools) shows that groups did not drastically change their hunting-gathering way of life when they first began to cultivate domesticated plants. Rather, the domesticated species began as additions to their dietary base and only slowly increased in importance as a food source. As we will see, this pattern recurs elsewhere in the Americas (McClung de Tapia 1992).

Elevation, climate, and environment vary widely in different parts of the Andean region. On the west the land rises from an arid coastal strip, through river valley environments, forest scrub, temperate forests, and high cold grasslands (the altiplano), to permanently snowcapped mountain peaks. On the east the upper grasslands give way to lower tropical forests. Numerous microenvironments exist within these three main ecological areas (Pacific coast, mountain zone, and eastern slopes), and different plants and animals are adapted to each. **Quinoa**, potato, other tubers, and **camelids** are found in the high altitudes; maize, legumes, beans, and chiles in the middle altitudes; and root crops, maize, beans, squash, amaranth, chilis, guava, coca, and cacao in the lower levels (see Figure 12.2). People could therefore exploit the produce of different but accessible microhabitats.

Quinoa, potatoes, camelids, and guinea pigs seem to have been domesticated in the Andes between 5,000 and 4,000 years ago. The earliest evidence of domesticated quinoa and camelids has been found in caves in the Lake Junin Basin of Peru. Archaeologists deduce herding of camelids from the increasing number of young camelid bones (reaching up to 50 percent of all camelid bones) found in older archaeological levels; that is, they base conclusions about herding on the premise that younger animals are more likely to die of natural causes in wild herds than in protected domestic herds. Chemical analysis of soil samples taken from a restricted area (defined by postholes) at the site of Asana near Lake Titicaca indicates animal presence, and the fenced area has been interpreted as a corral (Smith 1995).

As elsewhere, people in the Andean highlands added domesticated plants to the wild foods they collected. Agriculture took hold more slowly along the coast and was for some time secondary in importance to the rich coastal and marine resources. For exam-

*Figure 12.2*

**MAIZE HARVESTING IN INCA TIMES.** In the sixteenth century Felipe Guaman de Ayala, a native Quechua speaker, made drawings such as this one of Inca workers in Peru. What information does the illustration provide on Inca agricultural techniques?

*Source:* Guaman Poma de Ayala, F. 1615. *La nueva cronica y buen gobierno*, trans. L. Bustors Galvez, 1956. Lima: Editorial Cultura, Dirección de Cultura, Arqueolia e Historia del Ministerio de Educacion Pública de Perú. Courtesy of The Granger Collection, New York.

ple, at Pampa, an early permanent village site in the Ancón-Chillón region of the central Peruvian coast, villagers exploited wild tubers and rhizomes but also cultivated various types of domesticated squash, beans, and peppers and grew cotton for fishing nets and textiles. Nevertheless, marine resources continued to be an important part of the community's subsistence economy (Fiedel 1992).

The rest of this chapter concentrates on the development of agricultural communities in two areas of North America: eastern North America and the American Southwest.

# Agricultural Societies in Eastern North America

Eastern North America, bounded by grasslands to the west and coastlands to the south and east, was and to some extent still is a vast area of deciduous forests transected by numerous rivers. Differences in temperature from south to north, particularly in the number of frost-free days per year, affect the growing season; and in past millennia these differences influenced the extent to which people took up farming—if they took it up at all. It was in the central, riverine region of this area that the first domesticates appeared: varieties of *chenopodium*, marsh elder, sunflower, and squash. As oily and starchy seed crops, these plants in their wild forms comprised a nutritious part of hunter-gatherer diets that could be stored for consumption during the winter months. Domesticated between approximately 4,000 and 3,500 years ago, *chenopodium* (goosefoot), marsh elder, squash, and sunflower were not taken up as important dietary components for more than 1,000 years; rather, they were added to the hunter-gatherer diet of wild foods and animals. They became a major source of food between about 2,200 and 1,100 years ago. Domesticated maize (corn), introduced into the Northeast (probably from Mexico via the Southwest) about 1,800 years ago, played a minor dietary role for another 600 years before it became the major domesticate sometime between 1,200 and 900 years ago (Cordell and Smith 1996).

The development of agriculture in the central northeastern region coincides with a rise in mortuary complexity, the construction of large earthworks and ceremonial mounds, production of well-made artifacts, and expansion of long-distance networks. Ranked societies and large ceremonial centers appeared once maize had become an accepted dietary staple.

## Hopewell Agricultural Communities

The **Hopewell**—the name derives from the Hopewell mound site in Ohio—culture flourished between approximately 2,200 and 1,600 years ago in the central riverine area of eastern North America, although its influence extended well beyond that core area. Although similarities in material culture and way of life indicate contact and exchange between groups, there is no evidence to suggest that the Hopewell culture consisted of a single political entity ruled by a powerful chief. It is more likely that smaller groups, with the same basic belief system, maintained contact with each other through the exchange of goods, primarily to cement alliances and increase personal status. In the past investigation centered on the highly visible burial mounds and large earthworks characteristic of the period, to the detriment of settlement sites. That bias is gradually changing.

Hopewell groups cultivated seed crops in small gardens but also continued to hunt, fish, and gather foods. They lived in small hamlets along the edges of tributary river valleys and in larger settlements (but not necessarily villages) with associated burial mounds along main river valleys. In the Lower Illinois River valley, complexes of village and mortuary mounds occur at regular intervals of 15 to 20 km (9 to 12 miles), close to areas where tributary rivers join the main branch (Cordell and Smith 1996). The archaeological traces of these simple settlements consist of the remains of postholes indicating small circular or oval structures, refuse dumps, food storage pits (distinguished from refuse pits by size), earth ovens (deep pits with fire-cracked rocks), and hearths. Other indications of Hopewell settlements include patterns of postholes that may indicate drying racks, fences, windbreaks, or open shelters. Excavators have found larger refuse dumps on slopes near settlements (Smith 1992).

**Hopewell**
Early farming culture of the central riverine area of eastern North America; known for mound building.

## Mound Building

Both regional variation and social disparity among Hopewell groups are evident in mortuary traditions and large earthwork structures. Ceremonial mound sites are distributed evenly throughout the main Hopewell area; however, the largest and richest mounds are in the Ohio Valley. For example, Hopewell itself comprises 38 mounds inside a rectangular earthwork enclosure that encompasses a 45-hectare (110-acre) area; at Mound City, 24 mounds lie within a 5.25 hectare (13-acre) area. An Ohio mound averages about 9 m (30 feet) high and 100 feet (30 m) across and would have taken about 200,000 hours to construct (Fagan 2000).

Hopewell groups usually buried their dead in log crypts (tombs) or in charnel house structures erected above ground. In the first stage of the burial rite, bodies were left to deflesh, a process that could take many months to complete. Mourners then buried the defleshed skeletons in extended or flexed positions, or they made bone bundles and placed them elsewhere in the crypt. Cremations took place in charnel houses. When a crypt or charnel house was full, people sealed the crypt or burned the charnel house and then covered it with a mound of earth (Dancey 2005).

Geometric earthwork enclosures are further evidence of large-scale group labor. They can be massive, enclosing areas greater than 12 hectares (30 acres), and some consist of multiple associated earthworks. Some of these structures are near burial mounds, but not all. Hopewell earthworks likely had a ritual function and formed part of a wider symbolic landscape (Bernardini 2004). Burial mounds and earthworks indicate communal labor on a large, extended scale. The construction of such monuments must have been an important event in the lives of Hopewell farmers, reinforcing group ideology and identity.

## Long-Distance Contact

Grave goods are an important source of information on Hopewell crafts, the artisans who made them, and the extent of long-distance trade networks. Transport of goods and movement of people were relatively easy along the extensive river system of the Eastern Woodlands. Hopewell communities traded for obsidian from Wyoming, meteoric iron from Kansas, shell from the Gulf of Mexico, mica from North Carolina, native copper from the Great Lakes, and silver from northeastern Ontario. From these materials artisans made superbly crafted objects—among them copper ear spools, birds, and breast plates; pan pipes; stone platform pipes; effigy pipes; mica mirrors; mica and copper cut-out forms; and pottery figurines and containers (Cordell and Smith 1996). Manufacturing debris found in structures near mortuary areas clearly indicates the production of status items to be deposited with the deceased (Smith 1992). Hopewell artifacts found in regions far outside the Hopewell core area are further evidence of long-distance exchange.

Hopewell influence, but not domination, reached many groups in the Southeast. Mounds, earthworks, similarities in mortuary traditions, and the presence of Hopewell artifacts all combine to suggest shared ideologies and political ties. The exchange of valuable objects and the tradition of rich burials indicate a prestige economy in which ostentatious display and disposal served to emphasize the status of tribal chiefs. It is possible that the exchange of elite goods was accompanied by an exchange of ritual information restricted to the elite few, thus

This copper bird is from the Hopewell culture. How, and from where, did Hopewell groups obtain raw materials for artifact manufacture?

enhancing their status (Gibson 1994). Indeed the Hopewell tradition was the genesis of the later great chiefdoms of the Mississippian culture (refer to Highlight 12.2).

# Agricultural Societies in Southwest North America

The southwestern area of North America is geographically very diverse, comprising mountains, mesas, valleys, and deserts and ranging in altitude from about sea level to more than 4,000 m (13,000 feet). The Southwest has a semi-arid to arid climate and unpredictable rainfall. Its rivers are difficult to navigate, it has no coastline, and it is not rich in mineral resources (Cordell and Smith 1996). It is not surprising that hunting-gathering populations were small. What *is* surprising is that the region witnessed a considerable increase in population (increases in both the number and the size of settlements) between 1,300 and 900 years ago. In that period there were more people living in the area than at any time previously (Plog 1997). Why? Partial explanations probably include the gradual adoption and spread of domesticated crops as well as the strategies groups devised to maximize and guard their crops—storage, **irrigation**, and the development of crop strains suited to the climate (Cordell and Smith 1996).

Corn, beans, and squash were introduced into the American Southwest from Mexico between 3,500 and 1,800 years ago. Cotton, sieva beans, and pigweed arrived later, as did tobacco and agave. The first crops southwestern people began cultivating were corn and squash. A few hundred years after cultivation began, people started making pottery; this allowed them to process their food more efficiently and nutritiously (for example, by boiling dried seeds) and to store food more successfully. Besides serving as food, plants were used for textile and basketry production and for medicinal and ceremonial purposes. Groups in the northern part of the region domesticated turkeys for both food and feathers (Cordell and Smith 1996). As was the case in all areas of the Americas, the domesticated species were a dietary addition, supplementing hunted and gathered produce.

Although there were numerous different cultural groups in the Southwest, scholars recognize three cultures as the most influential: Mogollon, Hohokam and Ancestral Pueblo (Anasazi). Each of these cultures had its own distinctive aspects; at the same time, many types of artifacts are common to the whole area. Among these are turquoise and shell jewelry, clay human figurines, clay pipes, baskets, and leather and basketry bags. Other shared traits include house patterns that developed from semi-subterranean or pit houses in the earlier periods to above-ground housing in later times. Each culture had its own individual and beautiful ceramic traditions, and archaeologists use these designs as guides to chronology.

## Hohokam

The **Hohokam** (whose name means "those who have gone") culture was centered in the Sonoran Desert area of southern Arizona around the Gila, Salt, and Santa Cruz Rivers, all of which had year-round water during Hohokam times. Rain falls only during two short rainy seasons but can be intense and cause flooding. Groups who lived along the main river valleys devised irrigation systems, channeling the river waters into a vast system of major, minor, and feeder canals to water their crops. Those who lived farther away from rivers relied solely on rainfall, floodwaters, and rain runoff (Reid and Whittlesey 1997; Snow 1976). Hohokam canal construction and maintenance must have required an enormous input of labor and extensive organization, although the nature of this organization is unknown. The location of the larger settlements along canal systems would have allowed control over canals and facilitated contact between settlements (Bayman 2001; Reid and Whittlesey 1997).

**irrigation**
Supplying water artificially to promote crop growth.

**Hohokam**
Early farming culture of the Sonoran desert of southern Arizona.

A Hohokam red-on-buff pottery vessel is shown on the left, and a Mogollon pottery vessel is shown on the right. How can you account for the similarities in Hohokam and Mogollon culture?

## Hohokam Settlements

Hohokam villages consisted of small clusters of square houses built in shallow pits. The houses were made of wattle and daub (wood/branches and mud or clay, called **jacal** in the Southwest) and were set around a small courtyard. In larger settlements, groups of courtyard clusters surrounded a central plaza. Researchers have estimated that each courtyard cluster housed about 16 to 20 people—perhaps an extended family. Associated with the house groups were trash mounds shaped and covered with **caliche** (a plaster of calcium carbonate), work areas, and burials. About 850 years ago Hohokam people began to build above-ground single-story adobe dwellings of multiple rooms clustered within compound walls. Later some villages even included large multi-storied house complexes (Reid and Whittlesey 1997).

## Ceremony and Burial

Until about 900 years ago, Hohokam people usually cremated their dead and buried them in pottery jars in pits. Larger settlements had cemeteries, but in the smaller villages burials were placed between houses. A change in burial practice occurred about 850 years ago, after which many groups adopted inhumation rather than cremation. Graves associated with rich grave goods have been found in larger settlements (Cordell and Smith 1996).

About 1,300 years ago Hohokam groups began to build large, slightly oval **ball courts** with floors sloping toward the center that suggest adoption of a Mexican ritual ball game (although no one knows how this was played). Some sites have one ball court, some have more, and some have none. Ball courts were the foci of ceremonial rituals and may also have been places where trade and exchange activities took place. About 850 years ago, construction of ball courts declined, and groups began to concentrate on platform mounds—another Mexican influence. Made of trash, earth, and rubble, covered with caliche and often surrounded by cobble or adobe walls or palisades, these mounds were built in larger settlements, as well as at regular intervals along rivers, where they probably served the needs of smaller, dispersed communities. Rituals associated with ball courts and platform mounds likely united Hohokam communities under a single ideology. However, whereas everyone may have participated in ball court ceremonials, access to rituals associated with the enclosed platforms mounds may have been restricted to a privileged few. Larger villages with ball courts and platform mounds probably enjoyed greater status

**jacal**
Term used in the North American Southwest for wattle and daub, a building technique in which mud or clay covers a superstructure of interwoven wooden poles and sticks.

**caliche**
Plaster of calcium carbonate, or calcite (limestone, marble, or chalk).

**ball court**
Rectangular court with sloping sides in which a Mesoamerican ball game was played.

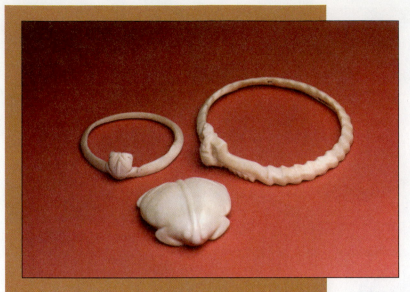

**Hohokam marine shell bracelets. In what ways might groups in the past have perceived shell bracelets as more than just decorative jewelry?**

than others; for example, **Snaketown**, home to between 300 and 600 people, boasted several platform mounds, plazas and two ball courts, one of which was large enough to hold 500 spectators (Plog 1997).

### Hohokam Trade

Characteristic Hohokam crafts include red-on-buff or red-on-brown decorated pottery, marine shell and turquoise ornaments, obsidian and chert projectile points, copper bells, carved stone bowls, and fired clay figurines. Artisans produced objects for local consumption and for exchange over a wide area. Some sites were well placed on trade routes, so merchants could control outgoing and incoming goods moving to and from California and Mexico. Between 1,200 and 1,100 years ago, marine shell ornaments—particularly bracelets—were widespread throughout the Hohokam area. The standardization in bracelet size and manufacturing technique suggests specialized manufacturing areas, and the **Shelltown and Hind** sites corroborate this supposition. Excavators at these sites recovered shell debris, dust, unfinished ornaments, and shell-working tools, but few finished shell ornaments. Most of the shell species recovered were from the Gulf of California and would have been acquired through trade. As the Shelltown and Hind sites are in a marginal area for agriculture, local shell artisans may have traded shell items for food (Howard 1993).

Hohokam traders would have been exposed to the ideas of other cultures that were different from their own. Such transfer of ideas may explain the Mexican influence seen in the ball courts and platform mounds. Hohokam sites also have provided evidence of growing social stratification over time: richer grave goods, larger settlements with significant amounts of prestige goods, and restricted access to ritual ceremonies. Differential living patterns suggest a distinction between elites and non-elites: A few villagers lived on platform mounds, some lived within platform mound enclosures, but most lived outside the enclosures. Many characteristic artifacts had ritual significance, were likely symbols of group identity, could have served as badges of office, and would have been symbols of status and power. Their acquisition and display probably served to emphasize differences between people (Bayman 2002; Hegmon 2005).

## Mogollon

**Mogollon** groups lived in a vast area covering parts of what are now central and southern New Mexico, east central Arizona, western Texas, and northern Mexico. The area is predominantly mountainous, with deep canyons and alpine meadows, but also includes desert. The Mogollon mountains gave rise to the name of the culture. The environment differs from that in the neighboring Hohokam regions; it is wetter, colder, and more wooded along the Mogollon Rim and Plateau, but its southern region is desert (Plog 1997).

### Subsistence, Settlement, and Ceremony

Between 1,800 and 1,400 years ago, early Mogollon settlements consisted of small villages of round pit houses. The people sited these communities on hilltops and ridges, perhaps for defense against raiding parties. Larger houses with hearths were probably

**Snaketown**
Large Hohokam settlement in Arizona with several platform mounds and two ball courts.

**Shelltown and Hind**
Hohokam sites specializing in the manufacture of shell ornaments.

**Mogollon**
Early farming culture in east central Arizona, southern New Mexico, western Texas, and northern Mexico, regions that are mainly mountainous but that also contain desert.

**pueblos**
Villages of apartment-style adobe or masonry structures with blocks of contiguous rooms set around a plaza; characteristic of early farming communities of the American Southwest.

**kivas**
Subterranean or semi-subterranean ceremonial rooms used by Ancestral Pueblo (Anasazi) and Mogollon groups in the American Southwest.

**Ancestral Pueblo (Anazasi)**
Farming groups of the American Southwest known for stone pueblo construction and cliff dwellings.

dwellings; smaller structures without hearths but with grinding equipment may have been storage rooms or food-processing areas. Cooking activities also occurred around hearths outside houses (Reid 1989). These early settlements overlook agricultural land, so groups may have been cultivating garden plots, although they continued to live primarily by hunting and gathering.

Later, people moved to valley floors. Mogollon sites located near streams suggest an increased interest in cultivation as a supplement to hunting and gathering activities (Cordell and Smith 1996). Houses changed form from round pit houses to rectangular pit houses with a sloping entrance ramp (see Figure 12.3). These later dwellings had fewer storage pits, perhaps because people had begun to use pottery vessels for storage (Cordell 1997). Finally, between 900 and 600 years ago, the Mogollon replaced pit houses with **pueblos**: surface masonry structures of blocks of contiguous rooms, ranging from a few up to 50 rooms, set around a plaza (LeBlanc 1989).

Before 900 years ago, **kivas** (ceremonial structures) played an important role in Mogollon ritual life. Larger villages had their own large, rectangular Great Kivas; smaller, dispersed villages shared small round kivas that were accessible to several settlements and would have been a mechanism to unite groups (Reid and Whittlesey 1997). In contrast to Hohokam groups, the Mogollon practised inhumation, burying their dead in shallow pits beneath house floors or in trash middens (Plog 1997).

## Mogollon and Ancestral Pueblo (Anasazi)

The masonry building methods, changing pottery styles, and features of burial practices in Mogollon areas between about 1,050 and 850 years ago appear to indicate the influence of **Ancestral Pueblo (Anasazi)**. Contact with Ancestral Pueblo people may have occurred through trade or may have come about as people moved throughout the Southwest. Evidence from the Bear Village site in Forestdale Valley, Arizona, indicates

*Figure 12.3*

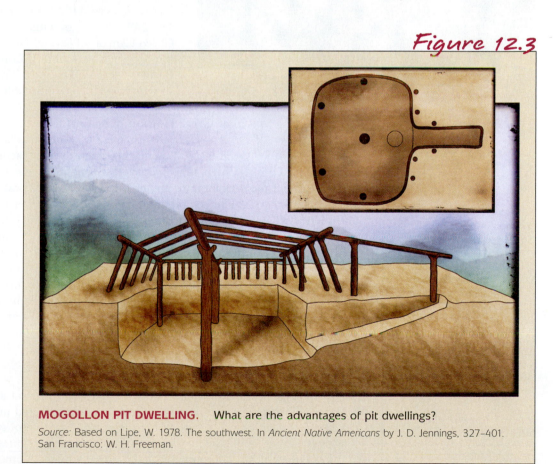

**MOGOLLON PIT DWELLING.**    What are the advantages of pit dwellings?

*Source:* Based on Lipe, W. 1978. The southwest. In *Ancient Native Americans* by J. D. Jennings, 327–401. San Francisco: W. H. Freeman.

This aerial view shows Chaco Canyon with Pueblo Bonito at the bottom. How can we account for the success of the Chaco system?

**Chaco Canyon**
Location in present-day New Mexico where, between 1,100 and 850 years ago, several Ancestral Pueblo (Anasazi) pueblos developed and gained wide influence.

**Pueblo Bonito**
The largest Anasazi Great House in Chaco Canyon.

**Great Houses**
Multi-storied constructions with hundreds of connecting rooms set in a semi-circle around a plaza; an architectural feature of Anasazi groups.

the presence of people with differing cultural practices: Burials show various patterns of cranial deformation, some exhibiting Mogollon patterns, others Anasazi, and one showing no deformation at all. Cranial deformation resulted from the practice of carrying babies tightly bound in cradle boards. As cradleboard styles varied according to cultural group, patterns of cranial deformation may indicate different types of cradle boards, and hence different groups (Reid and Whittlesey 1997).

## Ancestral Pueblo (Anasazi)

The Anasazi (meaning "the old ones") area is north of the Hohokam, in the Four Corners region, where New Mexico, Colorado, Arizona, and Utah meet. The most famous of Anasazi settlements are those in **Chaco Canyon**, New Mexico. The Chaco system covered about 53,000 km² (20,460 square miles), where over a period of about 600 years Anasazi settlements prospered and grew.

### Anasazi Pueblo Construction

Between 1,500 and 1,250 years ago, single-story, above-ground adobe and sandstone houses with connecting rooms replaced the pit houses found in the earliest Anasazi settlements. The period between 980 and 860 years ago witnessed the development in Chaco Canyon of several large, well-planned pueblo centers, such as **Pueblo Bonito**, Peñasco Blanco, Pueblo Alto, and Una Vida. These multi-storied constructions, each consisting of hundreds of connecting rooms set in a semi-circle around a plaza, are often referred to as **Great Houses**. In its final form, Pueblo Bonito, the largest center, covered an area of 0.8 hectares (almost 2 acres) and had about 700 connecting rooms, some reaching four or five stories high. Outer rooms that benefited from sunlight may have been living areas, but the dark inner rooms appear to have been storage and corn-processing areas (Lekson 2005). The complex also had several subterranean small kivas and two Great Kivas. Anasazi groups built 14 carefully planned Great Houses along a 16-km (10-mile) stretch of the Chaco Canyon floor, using hundreds of tons of carefully worked sandstone blocks cut from the canyon walls and hundreds of thousands of wood beams for roofing and flooring. Given that there is little local wood, the Chaco Canyon builders had to carry an estimated 250,000 pine timbers into the canyon from some considerable distance (Cordell 1997). Tree ring dating shows that hundreds of small villages located along the canyon were contemporaneous with the Great Houses. These smaller settlements were probably the source of labor for Great House construction.

### The Chaco Road System

The planned landscape of mounds, plazas, and roads around and beyond the Great Houses indicates their significance in the Chacoan world and provides additional evidence of engineering skills, particularly the roads. A system of straight roads, some as long as 100 km (62 miles) connected Chaco Canyon with colonies located as far away as 160 km (100 miles). The purpose of these roads remains enigmatic. There was no wheeled traffic at that time; furthermore, in order to keep roads perfectly straight, Anasazi builders cut steps into rock or built ramps to take roads over higher elevations. In places, roads do not seem to go anywhere but end abruptly after a few miles. Whereas some roads would have been useful for transport, researchers believe that others likely had ritual significance (Plog 1997).

## Anasazi Subsistence and Trade

Chacoans cultivated corn, beans, and squash on their naturally dry land by building ditches and dams to divert water runoff from heavy summer rains onto the canyon floor. There they laid out large agricultural plots and subdivided them into smaller garden plots. Chacoans raised domestic turkeys, but they also relied on wild animals—in particular deer, rabbits, gophers, and birds—to supplement their diet (Plog 1997).

The Anasazi traded widely, and the Chacoan communities may have benefited from their strategic location on southwestern trade routes. In the tenth century Chaco Canyon was an important player in the turquoise trade: Workshops and artifacts throughout the canyon testify to local manufacture involving turquoise that Chacoans acquired from sources 200 km (124 miles) to the east (Lekson 2005). Luxury goods found in the Great House sites included cylindrical vases; copper bells; macaw skeletons; human effigy vessels; wood, shell, and basketry items inlaid with mica and turquoise; and pottery incense burners (Cordell 1997).

## Chacoan Society

Construction of Great Houses and roads, as well as the setting up and maintenance of irrigation systems, required a massive labor force to undertake long hours of arduous work. Considerable organization was needed to supervise such enormous undertakings and to control and feed the labor force. The reins of power, then, had to lie in the hands of forceful members of society, most likely those who lived in the Great Houses. A number of factors suggest that Great Houses were hubs of political and social power: The limited number of rooms with hearths indicating domestic usage suggest relatively few residents; activities in most rooms relate to storage and corn processing; the kivas were ritual centers; rich burials, containing rare exotics, are found only in Great Houses; skeletal study indicates that the people buried in Great Houses enjoyed better health than those elsewhere in the Canyon. Great Houses may have been palace-like structures for the Chacoan elite, who themselves may have been ruled by those who lived at Pueblo Bonito, given its size and the richness of its contents (Lekson 2005).

The complex and organized Anasazi society at Chaco Canyon flourished during a period when dendrochronological records indicate the climate was moist, favorable for raising food resources. It was a time of relative peace, in contrast to the preceding period when raiding and violence were part of life. Nevertheless, violent acts occurred. Although the Anasazi clearly buried most people with care, a few burials differ from the usual pattern—they contain a jumble of bones that show signs of violence, mutilation, and dismemberment. Some anthropologists interpret this evidence as the result of cannibalism (Billman et al. 2000; Marlar et al. 2000; Turner and Turner 1999). Others believe that it represents a form of ritual killing. Such violent acts, whether cannibalistic or not, may have served political purposes: Group executions could have been condoned by Anasazi leaders who used them as a mechanism of social control (Lekson 2002; White 2001).

## Abandoning of Chaco Canyon Settlements

Between about 830 and 730 years ago Chaco settlements declined rapidly. Construction stopped, populations decreased, and people moved out of the area. The society's decline and the dispersal of Anasazi groups seem to have coincided with a 50-year drought that would have had drastic effects in an area with so little moisture at the best of times. The drought may have spurred groups to leave Chaco Canyon.

# Chapter Summary

This chapter has covered the initial colonization of the Americas by modern human groups. The colonizing groups successfully adapted to and mastered new environments. Initially they subsisted through hunting, gathering, and fishing; later, in most areas, they augmented these strategies with farming. The period sees an increase in social, ideological, and technological complexity.

■ People moved into the Americas between 30 and 15 kyr ago, traveling either across Beringia to Alaska and then southward, or by boat along the coastline. At 14 kyr old, Monte Verde in Chile is the oldest securely dated site in the Americas.

■ By 13 kyr ago Clovis groups, with their distinctive projectile points, had spread through North America and into parts of South America.

page 359

page 353

■ Archaic groups developed a range of technologies to exploit the variety of plant, animal, and marine resources that emerged in the Holocene. Different groups' varied settlement patterns, subsistence strategies, and material cultures reflect diverse regional environments. Four important regions were the Eastern Woodlands, the Great Basin, the Northwest Coast, and Southern California.

■ Given the predictability of certain food sources, Archaic groups scheduled their food acquisition strategies so that some sites were occupied almost permanently.

■ Extensive trade networks developed to overcome territorial boundaries and essentially provided items for an incipient elite.

■ Ceremonial practices increased during the Archaic, as seen in burials, some with grave goods indicating differences in status.

■ At the time of first European contact groups on the Northwest Coast and in California were ranked societies living in permanent settlements but not reliant on agriculture.

■ Plant and animal domestication occurred independently in Mexico, the South American Andes and eastern North America. The great variety of domesticated plant species contrasts with the small number of domesticated animal species.

■ In the Eastern Woodlands, the development of seed crops evident at Hopewell sites coincides with a rise in mortuary complexity, large earthworks, and extensive long-distance trade networks, along which the products of skilled craftspeople moved to supply the needs of burgeoning elites. Ranked societies and large ceremonial centers of the Mississippian chiefdom appear with the adoption of corn as a staple some 3,000 years after local seed crops had been domesticated.

page 377

■ Domesticated corn was introduced to the American Southwest from Mexico. Groups employed a range of irrigation techniques to cultivate crops in the semi-arid to arid climate of the region.

■ Although Hohokam, Mogollon, and Anasazi are distinct cultures, there are similarities in aspects of material culture. All three peoples created individual and beautiful ceramic traditions. Ball courts and platform mounds united Hohokam groups under a single ideology. Kivas were ceremonial locales for the Mogollon and Anasazi.

■ Chaco Canyon was the site of numerous large Anasazi pueblos and small settlements, and Chacoan roads connected many outlying settlements.

## KEY WORDS

Amerind, 351
Ancestral Pueblo (Anazasi), 377
Archaic, 357
ascribed status, 369
ball court, 375
Beringia, 349
bioarchaeology, 364
Black Earth, 359
Cahokia, 360
caliche, 375
camelid, 370
Chaco Canyon, 378
chiefdom, 360
Clovis, 351
domestication, 369
Eastern Woodlands, 357
El Niño, 367
enamel hypoplasia, 364
Eskimo-Aleut, 351

exchange networks, 358
fluted points, 351
Great Houses, 378
Hogup Cave, 361
Hohokam, 374
Holocene, 356
Hopewell, 372
ice-free corridor, 349
Indian Knoll, 360
irrigation, 374
jacal, 375
kivas, 377
Koster, 358
labrets, 366
mano, 357
mastodon, 352
Meadowcroft Rockshelter, 352
metate, 357
Mississippian, 360

Mogollon, 376
Monte Verde, 352
mound building, 360
Na-Dene Athabaskan, 351
ochre, 356
Paleoindian, 351
Paul Mason, 366
phytoliths, 370
Poverty Point, 359
Pueblo Bonito, 378
pueblos, 377
quinoa, 370
ranked societies, 366
Shelltown and Hind, 376
Shaketown, 376
Tehuacan caves, 370
teosinte, 370
Upper Paleolithic, 351

## SUGGESTED READING

Ames, K. M., and H. D. Maschner. *Peoples of the Northwest Coast: Their Archaeology and Prehistory*. London: Thames & Hudson, 1999. Comprehensive and well illustrated. Initial chapters provide a chronological account giving a clear general background; chapters on selected topics follow. Good to dip into.

Bonnichsen, R., and K. L. Turnmire, eds. *Ice Age People of North America: Environments, Origins, and Adaptations*. Corvallis: Oregon State University Press, 1999. An excellent series of case studies focusing on regional topics.

Cordell, L., and B. D. Smith. "Indigenous Farmers." In *The Cambridge History of the Native Peoples of the Americas*, vol. 1, *North America*, eds. B. C. Trigger and W. E. Washburn, pp. 201–206. Cambridge: Cambridge University Press, 1996. A comprehensive discussion of agricultural groups in eastern North America and the Southwest; allows for comparison within and between areas.

Dillehay, T. D. *The Settlement of the Americas*. New York: Basic Books, 2000. A clear summary of the earliest occupation throughout the Americas, with an emphasis on South American material.

Fagan, B. *Ancient North America: The Archaeology of a Continent*. 4th ed. New York: Thames & Hudson, 2005. This book addresses in detail the periods covered in this chapter and examines regions and periods not discussed here.

Pauketat, T. R., and T. E. Emerson, eds. *Cahokia: Domination and Ideology in the Mississippian World*. Lincoln/London: University of Nebraska Press, 1997. A series of articles that cover a range of topics and together provide a complete picture of Cahokia.

Smith, B. D. *The Emergence of Agriculture*. New York: Scientific American Library, 1995. Essential reading on agriculture in both Old and New Worlds, with an excellent section on agriculture in the Americas.

Snow, D. R. "The First Americans and Differentiation of Hunter-Gatherer Cultures." In *The Cambridge History of the Native Peoples of the Americas*, vol. 1, *North America*, eds. B. C. Trigger and W. E. Washburn, pp. 125–199. Cambridge: Cambridge University Press, 1996. This article covers all the Archaic cultures of North America, but the section on the Eastern Woodlands is particularly detailed, with subheadings that enable rapid access to particular topics.

# Chapter 13

# The Emergence of State Societies in the Americas

■ **EARLY MESOAMERICAN STATES**
Olmec • The City of Teotihuacan • The Maya

■ **HIGHLIGHT 13.1:** *Calendars and Writing in Mesoamerica and South America*

■ **EARLY STATES IN SOUTH AMERICA**
Moche • Tiwanaku: State and Early Empire? • Wari: State and Early Empire?

■ **HIGHLIGHT 13.2:** *In the Footsteps of Ancient Andean farmers*

■ **EMPIRES OF THE NEW WORLD**
The Aztec Empire • The Inca Empire

■ **CONCLUDING COMMENTS ON NEW WORLD STATES AND EMPIRES**

▲
**Photo above:** Street of the Dead at Teotihuacan, Mexico

From about 4,000 years ago, as we saw in Chapter 12, New World trade networks became more extensive in response to the growing demand for prestige goods. Hand in hand with material exchange went an exchange of ideas, both practical (for example, technology associated with food production) and ideological. Changes that took place within some groups resulted in an increase in wealth, status, and control for those in power.

North America remained a mosaic of chiefdoms—some, such as Cahokia, wielding considerable power—until European colonization. Prestate chiefdoms were kin-based structures in which a hereditary chief ruled over a hierarchically ranked society. The chief, with the aid of kin-related nobles, organized his chiefdom and oversaw the acquisition, production, and redistribution of goods, food, and resources. At times there were numerous autonomous chiefdoms across the landscape; some became powerful

1. Teotihuacan
2. Mexico City Tenochtitlan
3. Tlatilco
4. Tlapacoya
5. San Lorenzo
6. La Venta
7. Palenque
8. El Mirador
9. Calakmul
10. Nabke
11. Uaxactun
12. Tikal
13. Caracol
14. Quirigua
15. Copan
16. Kaminaljuyu
17. Quito
18. Pampa Grande
19. Sipán
20. Cerro Blanco
21. Chavín de Huántar
22. El Paraíso
23. Lima
24. Wari
25. Machu Picchu
26. Cuzco
27. Pikillaqta
28. Nevado Ampato
29. Cerro Mejia
30. Cerro Baúl
31. Omo Complex
32. Tiwanaku

**SITES MENTIONED IN THE CHAPTER**

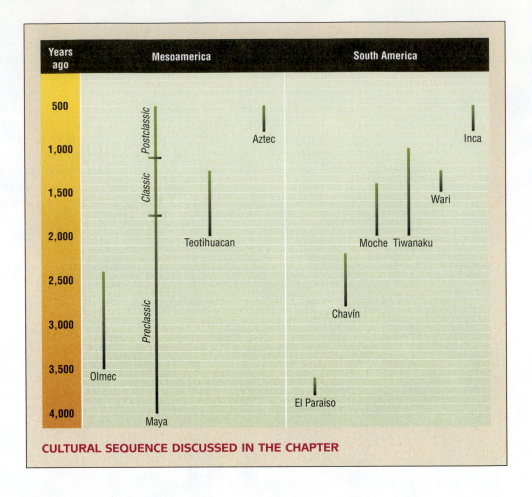

CULTURAL SEQUENCE DISCUSSED IN THE CHAPTER

**Mesoamerica**
A culture area that included much of present-day Central America, in which different ethnic groups shared similar belief systems and some cultural traits.

and were able to exact resources and goods from others. However, even complex chiefdoms lacked the bureaucratic machine and standing army needed to control distant areas (Scarre and Fagan 2003).

In contrast, state societies and empires developed in **Mesoamerica** (much of present-day Central America) and in South America. Evolving from a base of villages and towns, over time these states became increasingly complex in social, economic, and ceremonial spheres. This chapter explores early Mesoamerican states, early South American states, and the great Aztec and Inca Empires.

# Early Mesoamerican States

The term *Mesoamerica* relates to a culture area in which a variety of different ethnic groups shared similar belief systems and certain cultural traits—among them the use of cacao to make chocolate, a rubber ball game, complex calendars, stepped pyramid structures, and human sacrifice. The geographical borders of Mesoamerica did not coincide with present-day Central America, as is often assumed, but fluctuated through time. When the Spanish arrived in 1519, Mesoamerica included central and southern Mexico, Belize, Guatemala, and parts of Honduras and El Salvador (Pye and Clark 2000).

## Olmec

**Olmec**
One of the complex societies of Mexico that preceded Mesoamerican states; was composed of different groups that showed similar cultural attributes.

The **Olmec** (approximately 3,500 to 2,400 years ago) is the best known of the complex societies that preceded the emergence of Mesoamerican states. The word *Olmec* does not signify a particular ethnic group but identifies what were probably different ethnic

**celt**
A type of axe.

**San Lorenzo**
The earliest large Olmec urban and ceremonial center with monumental architecture, located in the Mexican Gulf coast region.

groups with similar cultural attributes. Typical Olmec attributes included symbolic town planning, monumental stone sculptures, polished greenstone axes (**celts**), incised pottery, terracotta figurines, ritual areas, and a characteristic art style (Clark and Pye 2000). The Olmec heartland was in the tropical lowlands of Veracruz and Tabasco in Mexico; both areas had fertile soils for agriculture, in addition to ample wild resources, to feed growing populations. Indeed, the agricultural potential of the region may have been a factor that stimulated the emergence of societal complexity (Sabloff 1997). At one time scholars generally interpreted Olmec-type traits observed in areas well beyond the core region as evidence of contact with and/or influence by Olmec groups. These interpretations underpinned claims for an Olmec state with hierarchical settlement patterns, a controlling hierarchical elite, and long-distance trade networks. Such models sometimes see the Olmec state as the prime influence, or "mother culture," leading to all later Mesoamerican states. An alternative interpretation places less emphasis on the impact of the Olmec, seeing it as one among several contemporary complex cultures whose elites exchanged goods and ideas, leading to the independent development of many features termed "Olmec" (Clark and Pye 2000; Diehl and Coe 1996). Much of what we know about the Olmec has emerged since the early 1980s from regional surveys, mapping projects, environmental studies, and excavation of small sites as well as large areas such as San Lorenzo and La Venta.

## San Lorenzo: An Early Olmec Center

Spread over an area of 690 hectares (1,700 acres) and strategically located on a plateau overlooking the Coatzacoalcos River, the Olmec center at **San Lorenzo** was a prominent landmark in its surrounding landscape and the dominant center in the Gulf lowlands between 3,200 and 2,900 years ago. Formerly, researchers believed that the plateau was an artificial construction and thus viewed it as the earliest evidence for monumental structures in Mesoamerica. Later excavation and survey demonstrated the role of erosional processes rather than human action as the agent of platform formation (Cyphers 1997). Nevertheless, successive phases of occupation artificially increased the height of the plateau (similar to tell formation in the Middle East).

San Lorenzo rulers and their kin lived in palaces and elite residences on the plateau summit; commoners lived in smaller wattle-and-daub houses on terraces constructed around the sides of the plateau. Besides exploiting local stone, sand, clay, wood, and earth for building materials, Olmec architects imported basalt from the Tuxtla mountains some 60 km (37 miles) away. Given the distance and the difficulty of transporting stone, basalt was a luxury commodity for elite use. For example, the "Red Palace" (named after its red hematite-stained floors) had basalt columns, benches, aqueducts, and sculptures, including 10 massive basalt heads (some weighing more than 25 tons) believed to be portraits of San Lorenzo rulers (Cyphers 1997; Diehl and Coe 1996).

This massive head in basalt may portray an Olmec ruler. What is the significance of stone sculptures such as this?

As items of value, basalt and other stones were carefully conserved. Craft workshops located near palaces included basalt workshops and sculpture recycling areas where disused monuments were a source of grinding stones, plates, and lids. The size and siting of these workshops imply industrial-scale production under elite control (Cyphers 1996).

San Lorenzo enjoyed wide-ranging trade networks with other areas of Mesoamerica. The city obtained obsidian (volcanic glass) and kaolin clay (fine white clay for the production of elegant pottery) from the Mexican highlands, jade from Guatemala, magnetite (a black mineral used for mirrors) from the Valley of Oaxaca in southern Mexico, probably cacao from the Pacific coast, and textiles and **quetzal** feathers (feathers from a brilliant tropical bird) from other areas (Sharer 1994). Trade items could be transported with relative ease to and from San Lorenzo along the extensive river systems of the region. Archeologists believe that given San Lorenzo's strategic position, those who governed it were probably able to control the movement of goods and therefore to increase their prestige and power; at the same time, exchange networks promoted the transfer of ideas and strengthened political and religious ties.

### La Venta: A Later Olmec Capital and Ceremonial Center

Following the decline of San Lorenzo about 2,900 years ago, possibly because of tectonic activity in the area, **La Venta** became the largest and most important Olmec center of the Gulf coast. Located on a rise above the Rio Palma in Tabasco and surrounded by wetlands, La Venta benefited from the rich resources provided by four ecosystems within its range: marsh, mangrove swamp, tropical forest, and ocean (González Lauck 1996). Good supplies of food and building materials, in addition to maize cultivated on river levees, underpinned a rise in population numbers and an increase in social complexity. La Venta, estimated to cover more than 200 hectares (494 acres), was the pinnacle of a hierarchical settlement pattern of occupation sites built on platforms, some larger and more elaborate than others, surrounding a major center.

Modern development has destroyed much of La Venta, but the surviving remnants indicate a symmetrically planned center of earthen mounds, platforms, plazas, and monumental ceremonial and administrative buildings. Surface survey and excavation revealed large residential areas within and beyond the center. Rising to a height of 30 m (100 feet), a Great Pyramid, or Great Mound, dominated the area. Monumental sculptures stood at the southern and eastern part of the mound, some carved with faces of mythical or supernatural beings. Numerous polished greenstone celts found by the mound were probably votive deposits (González Lauck 1996).

The ceremonial complex at La Venta, located north of the Great Mound, was one of numerous stepped platform mounds, plazas, and courts constructed over a 400-year period. Excavation revealed greenstone celts, magnetite and ilmenite (a black mineral) mirrors, jade figurines, mosaic pavements of serpentine, and massive pits filled with serpentine blocks hidden from public view beneath the complex (Diehl and Coe 1996). As at San Lorenzo, basalt continued to be of special significance at La Venta: Huge basalt columns are a consistent feature of the site. Excavators also found burials within the ceremonial complex, including those of young people, all accompanied by rich grave goods (González Lauck 1996).

### Olmec Ideology

Ideological beliefs united groups in the culture area of the Olmec, and researchers have learned much about these beliefs from the iconography and symbolism of Olmec sculptures, pottery, greenstone objects, and wooden effigies, as well as from the contexts in which these items were placed. Large and small sculptures were often placed in tableaux settings that may have recorded Olmec myths or historical events or represented specific ceremonial activities (Diehl 2000). Water played a particularly significant role in Olmec ideology, as indicated by finds from the spring area of El Manatí, 20 km (12

**quetzal**
A Central American bird whose colored feathers were prized by Mesoamerican artisans.

**La Venta**
Large Olmec urban and ceremonial center with monumental architecture that succeeded the earliest Olmec center, San Lorenzo.

miles) from San Lorenzo. Here, between 3,600 and 3,000 years ago, people placed offerings of greenstone celts, wooden busts, rubber balls, animals, plants, and the bones of infants. When unearthed by the excavators, a few offerings retained traces of red paint; others still had parts of their original leaf wrappings (Ortiz and Rodríguez 2000). The presence of rubber balls at El Manatí provides the earliest evidence of the ball game that in subsequent periods formed a pan-Mesoamerican characteristic. Olmec iconography portrays a variety of fantastic creatures combining features of tropical animals and humans, a theme also common in later Mesoamerican cultures. In addition, increasing representation of maize motifs and symbolism, seen from La Venta times onward, indicates the growing importance of maize in the Olmec diet. Such motifs also are present in Maya and Aztec iconography, as are representations of quetzal plumage (Taube 2000). Certain Olmec artifacts such as mirrors, spoons, and awls, some of which are depicted in art, may have been used in ritual activity; for example, in **bloodletting** and in the use of hallucinogenic substances (Diehl 2000). Representations of Olmec ideology in a variety of media have led some researchers to propose that Olmec rulers played a shamanistic role in rituals, similar to the ceremonial roles of Maya and Aztec rulers.

## State or Chiefdom?

Was there an Olmec state? Debate on this question continues. The carefully planned layouts at San Lorenzo and La Venta, together with monumental building, resident specialists, long-distance networks, representations of rulers, settlement hierarchy, and ranked societies, may represent city status. However, there is no evidence of a formal army, administrative officials, taxation, or warfare—all of which are important traits of state systems, as discussed in Chapter 11 (Serra Puche et al. 1996). San Lorenzo and La Venta appear to have been contemporaneous with other Mesoamerican urban centers, such as Tlatilco and Tlapacoya in the Basin of Mexico. Both of the latter sites have evidence of hierarchical settlement patterns, ranked societies, rich burials, platform mound construction, iconography that includes pan-Mesoamerican themes, and grave goods that indicate long-distance exchange networks ranging throughout Mexico. Tlatilco and Tlapacoya were regional centers in control of surrounding areas that interacted with other regions, including the Olmec (Neiderberger 2000). Contact among these centers facilitated the exchange of goods and ideas, which may explain the development of similarities in iconography. Although Olmec influence is apparent in aspects of later Maya sculpture, many motifs of Mesoamerican iconography, once believed to have originated in the Olmec region, are thought by many experts to have developed in various areas—not to reflect domination by an Olmec state. Such an interpretation is not universally accepted; some experts see the Olmec as the foundation of Mesoamerican civilizations (Blomster et al. 2005; Neff et al. 2006; Sharer et al. 2006). Future studies should help to resolve the debate.

## The City of Teotihuacan

Some 1,600 years ago **Teotihuacan** (near today's Mexico City) was one of the largest cities in the world, with an estimated population of between 120,000 and 200,000 people. In 1962 Rene Millon mapped the area, using aerial photography and ground survey (see Figure 13.1), and revealed a city extending over 20 km² (8 square miles). From its inception Teotihuacan had been carefully planned on a grid whose main axes were the **Street of the Dead**, a 5-km (3-mile) north–south avenue, and an equally long east–west avenue (Cowgill 1997). Millon's mapping program and excavation uncovered a city with 600 pyramidlike religious and administrative structures, many located along or near the Street of the Dead; among them were the Pyramids of the Sun, Moon, and Feathered Serpent and the Ciudadela (Citadel) complex. There were also workshop areas, marketplaces, and more than 2,000 walled apartment compounds, each large enough to house between 60 and 100 people. Apart from the craft specialist compounds, there were no

**bloodletting**
A ritual practiced in many Mesoamerican cultures in which people deliberately pierced parts of their bodies in order to draw blood.

**Teotihuacan**
One of the largest cities in the world some 1,600 years ago, located near present-day Mexico City; its influence extended into distant areas of Mesoamerica.

**Street of the Dead**
A 5-km (3-mile) long avenue, lined with large pyramidlike structures, that bisected the city of Teotihuacan.

*Figure 13.1*

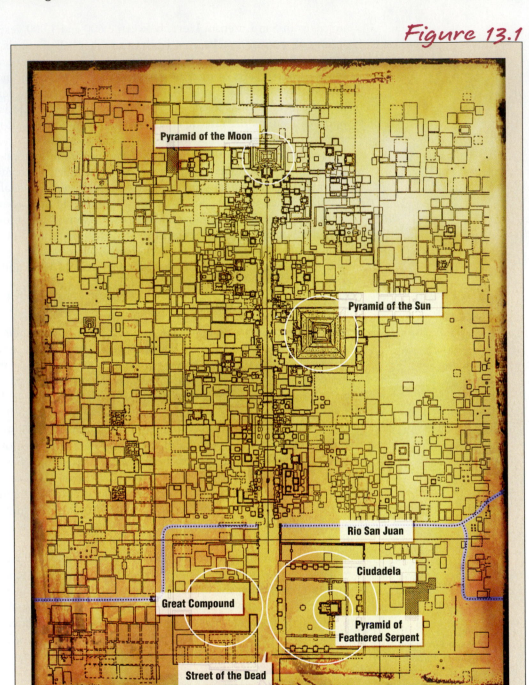

**PLAN OF THE CENTRAL AREA OF TEOTIHUACAN.** What factors needed to be considered in the planning of such a large city?

*Source:* Adapted from Millon, R. 1973. *Urbanization at Teotihuacan, Mexico,* Vol. 1, Pt. 1. Austin: University of Texas Press. Copyright © 1973 by René Millon. Adapted by permission of René Millon.

distinctive neighborhoods, or barrios, except for two areas inhabited by groups from Oaxaca and the Gulf lowlands—as indicated by artifacts, architectural features, and burials that were not in the Teotihuacan style and also by bone and tooth isotopic analysis (see the section on Teotihuacan foreign contacts). Archaeological research has shown that an increase in population within Teotihuacan coincided with a decrease of sites in the surrounding country. One hypothesis proposes that this happened because a powerful Teotihuacan ruling authority forced people to move into the city to meet its labor requirements and to free up potential agricultural land around the city (Sabloff 1997).

Several factors may account for Teotihuacan's power. The city was strategically placed on trade routes to the east and south, and it controlled nearby sources of gray and green obsidian. With the aid of irrigation, the surrounding land provided a rich agricultural base to support a large population. Furthermore, offerings discovered in a cave beneath the Pyramid of the Sun suggest a religious element that may have been present from the birth of the city (Sabloff 1997). Teotihuacan, then, was an important religious, as well as economic, center and a place of pilgrimage.

## Ceremony and Ritual

Ritual and ceremony played a vital role in all Mesoamerican cities. Teotihuacan was no exception. Both the sheer number of buildings and their size—for example, the Pyramid of the Sun rises to a height of 60 m (almost 200 feet) and measures more than 213 m (700 feet) on each side—highlight their importance; religion must have been a unifying force for Teotihuacan society. The extent of monumental structures also emphasizes the great control over resources and labor that the ruling authority wielded. Major ceremonies took place at the large pyramid structures; for example, more than 200 human sacrifices were made during the construction of the Feathered Serpent pyramid, and human sacrifices also took place at other pyramids (Manzanilla 2002). Many Teotihuacan deities were later worshipped by the Aztecs, among them Tlaloc (the Rain God), the Feathered Serpent, the Sun God, and the Moon Goddess (Coe 1994). Various other deities were the focus of beliefs at the household level (Cowgill 1997).

Some burials were beneath room or patio floors, perhaps reflecting an ancestor cult. Different burial practices give evidence of the multi-ethnic composition of Teotihuacan's

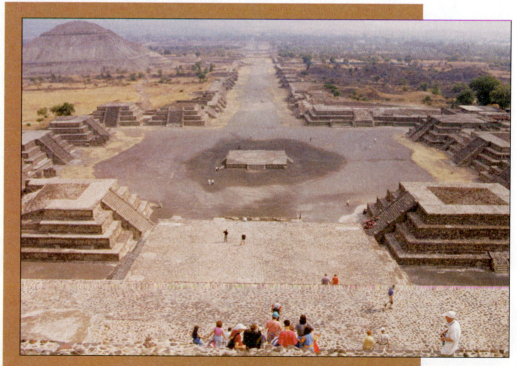

Street of the Dead, Teotihuacan. Compare Teotihuacan with Tikal and Copan, discussed in the next section.

population: The native population of Teotihuacan often buried their dead in a flexed position in pits or cremated them, whereas foreign inhabitants appear to have followed their own particular cultural traditions, although sometimes including Teotihuacan articles as grave goods (Manzanilla 2002).

## Craft Specialization

Millon's survey revealed both state-controlled craft workshops and the production of goods on a household basis. Imports were primarily in the form of raw materials to be worked by Teotihuacan's artisans. Craftspeople hewed large statues of stone; made masks of jade, basalt, greenstone, and andesite with inlaid eyes of obsidian or shell; and produced shell and stone beads and fine feather items. Workers in hundreds of obsidian workshops manufactured blades, arrowheads, points, and small figurines. Two local sources of obsidian were available to them; one quarry provided a poorer-quality material that served for everyday use, whereas the other quarry supplied a high-quality green obsidian that was used to manufacture elite items that have been found throughout Mesoamerica. Most obsidian waste was found near the Pyramid of the Moon, suggesting state control of obsidian workshops. Specialists who worked on monumental structures included masons, plasterers, and carpenters. Households made their own domestic pottery, but the manufacture of fine pottery and ritual items, such as censers (incense burners), was probably state controlled (Manzanilla 1999, 2001).

## Teotihuacan Foreign Contacts

The size, layout, and—by inference—power of Teotihuacan must have made the city one of the wonders of the Mesoamerican world. Its influence reached well beyond the Valley of Mexico, as is clear from the fact that other contemporary Mesoamerican cities adopted or imported Teotihuacan architectural features, artifacts, and symbolism. Nevertheless, Teotihuacan's influence was patchy, being slight in some areas and stronger in others. The mechanism of the city's impact is uncertain; some Mesoamerican specialists argue that Teotihuacan exercised control through military domination, citing as an example the Maya center of **Kaminaljuyu** in Guatemala, where buildings, pottery, and artifacts reflect a strong Teotihuanacan influence. The Mexican superpower was keen to ensure access to trade, which might have led it to use force against Kaminaljuyu, a key center along the Maya highland trade routes. However, interaction between Teotihuacan and other states may have been peaceful in nature. The city may have engaged in contacts for economic or political reasons (for example, to forge alliances through marriage). Or the spread of religion may have been a motive, as various Maya states adopted aspects of Teotihuacan ideology and incorporated them into their own symbolism. For example, warfare, which must have been a crucial element of the state's power, is clearly evident in Teotihuacan symbolism; George Cowgill (1997, 2003) suggests that the Maya adopted Teotihuacan war deities and symbolism to enhance their own war skills and conquests.

Oxygen and strontium **isotope analyses** support evidence of foreign inhabitants at Teotihuacan. The isotopic composition of water varies according to local geology and environment. The water people drink and the food they eat leaves an isotopic signature in teeth and bones. The signature in teeth forms during tooth growth and is permanent, but that in bone changes during life. Isotopic analysis, therefore, can indicate where a person lived and/or moved while young and where he or she died. Oxygen isotope analyses of a sample of the 200 mostly male sacrificial victims found in the Feathered Serpent pyramid revealed nonnative Teotihuacanos. As the men were dressed as soldiers, the implication is that recruits to Teotihuacan's army included foreigners. Isotope results indicated that other victims were short-term residents of the city before their deaths, perhaps visiting merchants or priests. Furthermore, variation in dental modification showed men from the Valley of Oaxaca and Maya areas. Isotopic analysis of a

**Kaminaljuyu**
A Maya center in present-day Guatemala, where buildings and artifacts suggest possible Teotihuacan domination.

**isotope analyses**
Measurements of ratios of stable isotopes of carbon, nitrogen, and strontium to determine past dietary patterns and population movements.

sample of burials from one of the neighborhoods inhabited by Oaxacans indicates movement into Teotihuacan from highland and lowand areas of Mexico throughout the period of the city's preeminence (White et al. 2002, 2004).

### Ruling Authority

Several large compounds, including the Ciudadela complex, differ in shape and size from the other compounds and may have served as palaces or administrative centers, or both. The size of Teotihuacan, the number of craft specialists, the flourishing economy, and the obvious importance of religion and ceremony all indicate governance by a ruling body of secular and religious leaders. The Teotihuacan state had developed a system of signs that were adequate for record keeping, although less well developed than Maya writing. However, signs were rarely used on statues, artifacts, or public buildings or to name individual people. Furthermore, no statues glorify rulers. George Cowgill (1997) suggests that in Teotihuacan individuality was less important than communal activity. Perhaps the massive stepped pyramids were sufficient to emphasize the power of the ruling authority, and perhaps that ruling authority was corporate in nature, with governance occurring through a system of power sharing.

Although Teotihuacan's power eventually diminished, it was revered by subsequent states. Indeed, the Aztecs gave it the name *Teotihuacan*, meaning "the place of the gods," believing the city to be the place where the gods created the world. Interestingly, the architecture of some buildings in the sacred precinct of the Aztec capital, Tenochtitlan (which we'll consider later in this chapter), was Teotihuacan in style and must have been imbued with symbolism for the Aztecs (Kowalski 1999).

## The Maya

The **Maya** culture area covers the Yucatan Peninsula, parts of the Mexican states of Tabasco and Chiapas, Guatemala, Belize, El Salvador, and western Honduras. In this diverse region of volcanic highlands, western limestone lowlands, tropical forest, and coastal plains, many large city-states arose (Harrison 1999). These centers shared key cultural characteristics. Among them were mathematics, including the concept of zero; writing and calendrical systems (see Highlight 13.1, on pp. 392–394); the knowledge and use of astronomy; stepped temple pyramids; stone monuments carved with dynastic information; bas-reliefs; wall paintings; and polychrome (multi-colored) pottery (Coe 1993). Limestone, stucco, and plaster were common building materials. At larger cities raised causeways provided links between the city core and its periphery. Although Maya city-states were culturally similar in many ways, they never united politically but vied constantly for power and dominance over one another. As a result, shifting political alliances and warfare were always part of Maya life (Henderson 1997). Today four million descendants of the Maya speak one or another of 28 surviving Maya languages (Sharer 1996).

### Environmental Background

Maya culture developed against a richly varied environmental backdrop. Temperatures range from tropical in the plains and lowlands to cooler in the highlands. In arid areas the Maya collected water in wells, reservoirs, and canals. Volcanic and alluvial soils were fertile and could be intensively farmed; poorer soils required more effort. The highlands were rich in mineral resources for local use as well as for trade items—greenstone, serpentine, obsidian, and volcanic rocks—and were home to valuable trees, wild animals, and birds, including the quetzal bird with its highly prized feathers (Sharer 1996). The highlands were also, however, an area of active volcanoes and earthquakes, which destroyed communities in ancient Mesoamerica just as they have done in more recent times. The limestone underlying much of the lowlands was a source of building material, lime for limestone plaster, and chert (a silica-rich stone used for tool making).

**Maya**
Mesoamerican culture that encompassed numerous city-states, known for its pyramidal architecture, stelae, and writing.

# Calendars and Writing in Mesoamerica and South America

IN THE OLD WORLD, writing and recording slowly developed over millennia and eventually became the present-day systems with which we are familiar. This was not the case in the New World. Although the earliest evidence of ancient Mesoamerican recording is about 1,700 years old, its origins are probably much older. By the seventeenth century, although Maya people spoke a number of distinct languages, they no longer understood the ancient Maya glyphs that comprised writing. The Spanish conquerors had banned the use of glyphs and burned most Maya books. Today specialists who have deciphered Maya writing have begun to teach it to the Maya people.

## CALENDRICAL SYSTEMS

Astronomers of ancient Mesoamerica and South America saw the passing of time as cyclical—and its recording as crucial to agricultural success and ritual life. They based their calendrical systems on movements of the sun, the moon, certain planets, and star constellations. The ancient peoples of the Americas timed their agricultural and ritual activities primarily according to lunar and solar activity.

The Mesoamerican peoples followed various calendrical systems, the most important being a 260-day ritual calendar and a 365-day solar calendar, which combined to form a 52-year calendar cycle. In addition to these, they had other cycles of important days. The 260-day ritual calendar involved 20 day names along with a numbering system from 1 to 13, so the 14th day saw a return to number 1. The cycle was complete after each number and day had coincided, which took 260 days. The solar calendar consisted of 18 months of 20 days and one month of 5 days. It took 52 years for all associations of days and counts on both the ritual and solar calendars to coincide, forming the calendar round. As scholars have been able to correlate the Gregorian and Mesoamerican calendars, we can date Maya and Aztec events accurately.

Modern texts often portray the Mesoamerican calendrical system as a series of interlocking wheels: The 13-day numerical wheel interlocks with the 20-day name wheel of the ritual calendar, which in turn interlocks with the 365-day solar calendar, which in turn interlocks with the 52-year calendar round. The Aztecs feared the end of a 52-year cycle as they believed that the world would end at the conclusion of a cycle. On the eve of a new cycle, the people of Tenochtitlan would go to the hills outside the city and welcome the dawn joyously.

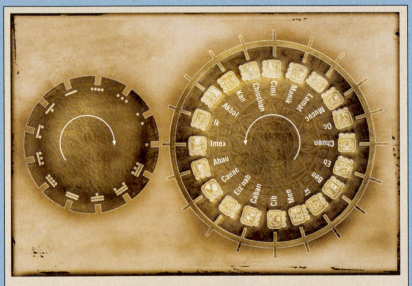

**THE 260-DAY MAYA RITUAL CALENDAR.** In this schematic illustration, the glyphs on the right indicate the 20 separate day names. The numbering system from 1 to 13 is on the left. In what ways do the Mesoamerican and present-day Western views of time differ? Are there any similarities between the two?

*Source:* Based on Coe, M. D. 1987. *The Maya.* London: Thames & Hudson.

Less is known about the Inca calendars. The Inca used two calendars based on cycles of the sun and moon. However, such cycles did not coincide naturally, as a lunar month is shorter than a solar one; researchers are not sure how the Inca solved this problem. Spanish chroniclers indicate that ceremonies and rituals were linked to the lunar calendar.

## WRITING IN MESOAMERICA

Several Mesoamerican cultures used writing systems; two important examples are the Maya and Aztec systems.

Maya writing was partly phonetic, part logosyllabic (a sign means a word), and partly pictographic. It was the only Mesoamerican script that provided a written form of a spoken language (Maya). Aztec writing was predominantly pictographic but included a limited number of glyphs, or symbols, to convey ideas. The Aztec system served as a type of prompt; those who "read" were able to recount the full story of the events and people portrayed. Nonnative speakers could understand many of the Aztec pictograms, whereas reading Maya was a skill restricted to those with specialist training, such as scribes and nobles.

Maya and Aztec books, or codices (singular codex), include ritual manuals, narratives of historical events, administrative and tribute accounts, and maps. They were made of long strips of lime-coated bark paper, folded accordian style and written on on both sides. At some Aztec sites archaeologists have recovered paper-making tools that suggest specialist production areas. Although bark paper was the main medium used for books, the Aztecs occasionally wrote on deer hide or cloth.

## INCA RECORDING

The Incas did not have a system of writing as we know it in the Western world. They administered their empire through the use of quipu—different lengths of colored cotton and wool string, spun and twisted in different ways, having varied combinations of knots. Trained experts called quipumayocs formed and read the cords. The information encoded in the colors, textures, lengths, and knots has not been deciphered but may have been analogous to mathematical or musical notation. Although a few of the early Spanish chroniclers likened the quipu system to writing, most did not see it as such. Furthermore, the small number of depictions of quipus in Spanish texts indicate that the Spanish had little interest in them. As a result, Inca quipus were not destroyed to the extent that the Mesoamerican codices were.

Writing is not the only medium through which information can be disseminated, of course. Some scholars of Inca life have suggested that different types and patterns of symbols on textiles may have had political, ethnic, and religious significance that specialists could "read." Such symbols also may occur on keros (Inca ritual cups). Textiles and keros were both important items in the Inca world and were given as gifts—particularly to elites in areas that had accepted Inca rule, where they were later displayed on ceremonial occasions. It may be that they served to evoke significant historical events.

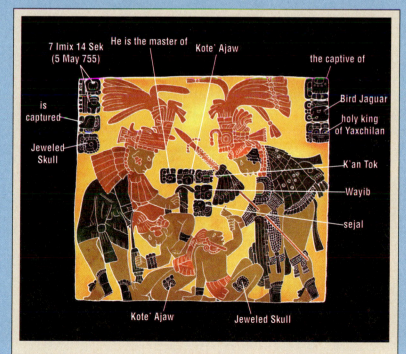

**MAYA GLYPHS.** These glyphs appear on Lintel 8 at Yaxchilan, Mexico. Can you decipher the message? Check your success below.

*Source:* Based on Coe, M. D., and M. Van Stone. 2001. *Reading the Maya glyphs,* 92, 171. London: Thames & Hudson.

Message: "Bird Jaguar IV, the king of Yaxchilan, and his *sejal* [provincial war leader] K'an Tok Wayib, captured Jewelled Skull and Kote' Ajaw on 7 Imix 14 Sek [5 May 755]."

*(continues on the next page)* ▶

## Highlight 13.1 *(continued)*

*Sources:* Bauer, B. S., and D. S. Dearborn. 1995. *Astronomy and empire in the ancient Andes.* Austin: University of Texas Press.    Coe, M. D., and J. Kerr. 1997. *The art of the Maya scribe.* London: Thames & Hudson.    Cummins, T. 1994. Representation in the sixteenth century and the colonial image of the Inca. In *Writing without words: Alternative literacies in Mesoamerica and the Andes,* eds. E. Hill Boone and W. D. Mignolo, pp. 188–219. Durham/London: Duke University Press.    Hill Boone, E. 1994. Introduction: Writing and recording knowledge. In *Writing without words: Alternative literacies in Mesoamerica and the Andes,* eds. E. Hill Boone and W. D. Mignolo, pp. 3–27. Durham/London: Duke University Press. Robinson, A. 1995. *The story of writing.* London: Thames & Hudson.    Sharer, R. J. 1994. *The ancient Maya.* 5th ed. Stanford, CA: Stanford University Press.    Smith, M. E. 2003. *The Aztecs.* 2nd ed. Malden, MA/Oxford: Blackwell.

**THE INCA QUIPU RECORDING SYSTEM.** In this sixteenth-century drawing, an Inca quipumayoc uses quipu to keep an account of produce stored in state warehouses.

*Source:* Guaman Poma de Ayala, F. 1615. *La nueva cronica y buen gobierno,* trans. L. Bustors Galvez, 1956. Lima: Editorial Cultura, Direction de Cultura, Arqueolia e Historia del Ministerio de Educatión Pública de Perú. Courtesy of the Granger Collection, New York.

turn back to your reading

Lowland forests provided materials for clothing, housing, medicines, and wild plants; also, the forests were home to the jaguar, an important symbol of power for the Maya.

## Sources of Information

Mayan inscriptions on monuments give names and genealogies of rulers as well as dates of their reigns and of particular ritual occasions, warfare, or visits by foreign dignitaries. Carvings, paintings, and figurines show scenes of Maya life, clothing fashions, personal and ritual adornments, captives taken and sacrificed, and rituals such as bloodletting by men and women. But although written inscriptions and representational art help augment the archaeological evidence, they need to be judged carefully, because they functioned as propaganda to further the agendas of rulers (Jones 1991). The only reliable clues to the life of the ordinary people are those that emerge through archaeological evidence.

Most aspects of state societies were present in the Preclassic Maya period (between about 4,000 and 1,750 years ago). Centers such as El Mirador and Nabke in Guatemala, for example, show monumental architecture, large populations, trade connections, and signs of social stratification. However, complex states developed more fully during the Classic Maya period (between about 1,750 and 1,100 years ago). At that time clear social stratification, full-time craft specialists, centralized government, defined territory, monumental architecture, state ideology, settlement hierarchy, long-distance trade, writing and notation, and military power are evident. The power of the ruler was legitimized by links to deities as well as by carefully recorded dynastic succession (Sharer 1994).

## Maya Cities

Complexes of palaces, temples, public buildings, elite houses, and ball courts arranged around large open plazas were the focal points of Maya cities. City layout symbolically represented Maya cosmology, thus enhancing the sanctity of the city. Monumental buildings rose pyramidlike in a series of masonry-faced stepped platforms topped by one or more stone structures, accessed by steep staircases. Surfaces were covered with limestone plaster, decorated with stone and plaster sculptures, and painted. Drainage systems and reservoirs collected water runoff. Craft specialists may have had their own section of the suburbs and lived in larger houses than farmers. Farmers lived beyond the city core in thatched wattle-and-daub houses built on raised earthen platforms (Sharer 1996).

The Classic period saw the emergence of numerous city-states in the Maya culture area, among them Tikal, Calakmul, Caracol, Copan, and Palenque, each identified by its particular emblem in the form of a **glyph** (symbolic figure or character). Dominated by these were numerous increasingly smaller cities and villages. The constant striving for dominance among cities ensured that changing alliances and conflict remained endemic in Maya life (Coe 1993). The following subsections consider two of the city-states, Tikal and Copan.

*Tikal.*    **Tikal**, in the tropical forests of Guatemala, is one of the largest (though not the earliest) of Maya cities. Inscriptions on **stelae** trace a Tikal dynasty of 39 rulers, many of whose named tombs have been found at the city. At the time of its collapse 1,100 years ago, Tikal covered 65 km² (25 square miles) and had more than 3,000 visible structures, with many others hidden beneath forest growth. At its pinnacle, about 1,200 years ago, Tikal's population may have reached 100,000 or more (Harrison 1999).

The Great Plaza at Tikal with its complexes of monumental buildings—some constructed on top of earlier structures—was the focal center of Tikal. The temples, as at other Maya sites, emphasize the importance of religion and ritual in Maya life. For example, carvings and paintings often depict scenes of nobles deliberately piercing parts of their body with stingray spines to draw blood. The Maya also practised human sacrifice—often by decapitation—of war victims, losers of the ritual ball game, male

**glyph**
A symbol used in Mesoamerican writing that can indicate a concept, a word, a sound, or a mixture of these elements.

**Tikal**
One of the largest of Maya cities, located in the tropical forests of present-day Guatemala.

**stelae**
Stone slabs with inscriptions and pictures that commemorate important events, such as wars or accession to the throne, or serve as territorial markers, tomb markers, or votive markers.

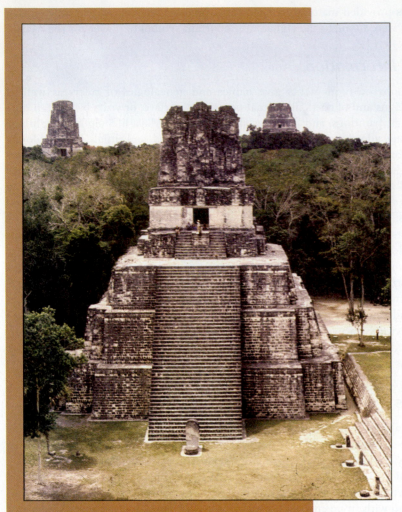

**Tikal's temples tower above the tropical forest of Guatemala. How do forest environments affect archaeological investigations?**

and female retainers or relatives of a deceased person of rank, and sometimes children. Bloodletting and human sacrifice took place to commemorate special events, such as the accession or death of a king, the auspicious setting of a planetary constellation, or a high-status burial (Schele and Freidel 1990; Sharer 1994).

Like many great cities, Tikal enjoyed a strategic geographic position with easy access to major river systems and overland trade routes. Along these highways obsidian, jade, prized quetzal feathers, cacao, shells, and agricultural produce moved between the Caribbean coast, the Gulf of Mexico, and central Mexico. Consequently, Tikal was in contact with other important centers such as Copan, Teotihuacan, and highland Kaminaljuyu (Harrison 1999).

At Tikal, as throughout the Maya world, warfare was a means by which rulers expanded power, levied tribute, and took captives for sacrifice ceremonies; more importantly, war brought prestige to the ruler. The sacrifice of high-ranking captives, in particular the enemy ruler, greatly increased the victor's prestige while causing widespread despair among the defeated populace. Because many cities and towns vied with Tikal for power and control of trade routes, alliances were made and broken regularly. A stela at Caracol records that city's alliance with Calakmul and defeat of Tikal 1,438 years ago. For the next 130 years the people of Tikal left no inscriptions—until the city defeated Caracol and later successfully defeated the regional capital of Calakmul (Harrison 1999).

*Copan.* **Copan** was the most important Maya city in the lowlands of Honduras. Evocative drawings done by Frederick Catherwood in 1839 depict ruins emerging from forest cover. Today, after more than 100 years of intensive study, researchers have uncovered much more of the city, although parts have been lost forever. In past centuries erosion by the Copan river cut a long, deep section of the Copan Acropolis (central building complex), revealing a substantial sequence of building construction. Further tunnel excavations into the section have helped to unravel architectural development through time.

Preservation at Copan is poorer than at most Maya cities. Copan's architects used local volcanic **tuff** (consolidated volcanic ash) for the construction of the city's large stone buildings, sculptures, altars, and floors, and large structures and floors were coated with lime plaster as a protection against the effects of rainwater. Unfortunately, if not maintained regularly, the lime plaster and the mud mortar used in Copan are easily destroyed by lush vegetation, rain, and earthquakes. Such was the fate of Copan's structures once the city had been abandoned; as a result, much of the city consists of thousands of fragments of buildings and sculpture. The massive task of rebuilding these ruins is slowly being undertaken by multidisciplinary teams of archaeologists, **epigraphers** (scholars of ancient inscriptions), art historians, artists, and architects (Fash 1991).

**Copan**
An important Mesoamerican Maya city located in the lowlands of Honduras.

**tuff**
Consolidated volcanic ash.

**epigrapher**
Someone who studies ancient inscriptions.

Around 1840, Frederick Catherwood drew these Maya stelae at Copan, Honduras. What role did stelae play for the Maya? Why are they of interest to present-day researchers?

The core area of Copan covers 12 hectares (30 acres) and includes large stepped platform buildings and numerous stelae and altars set around plazas. Buildings in the Acropolis grew in height over time as 16 successive rulers emphasized their dynastic legitimacy by building over the structures of their predecessors (Martin and Grube 2000). Copan's dynastic lineage is inscribed on stelae and on the steps of what is known as the **Hieroglyphic Stairway**, 21 m (69 feet) high, whose more than 2,200 individual glyphs form the longest Maya inscription (Sharer 1996).

Peasant farmers settled throughout the 13-km (8-mile) Copan Valley. Although there is evidence of dense occupation, population numbers at Copan (25,000), restricted by the size of the valley, never reached those of Tikal (Henderson 1997).

Copan was at its most powerful during the seventh and eighth centuries AD, under the reigns of Smoke Imix and his successor, 18 Rabbit. Both rulers oversaw intensive construction in the Copan Valley as well as the core area. At this time Copan also controlled the nearby city of Quirigua and, through Quirigua, the greenstone trade route (Sharer 1994). Copan's great flowering came to a halt when the ruler of Quirigua captured and killed 18 Rabbit (an event inscribed on a stela at Quirigua). As Quirigua became independent of Copan's dominance, Copan declined, losing control of agricultural lands and trade routes (Martin and Grube 2000; Sharer 1994).

Another possible factor in Copan's eventual decline was the very success of the city. That is, population growth eventually exceeded the carrying capacity of the Copan Valley, despite intensive agricultural practices. People stripped the valley sides of trees for building materials and fuel, causing subsequent soil erosion. Burials from the eighth century onward indicate nutritional stress in the form of increased child mortality. As hardship increased, people began to leave the valley whose rulers could no longer support them (Fash 1991; Martin and Grube 2000).

**Hieroglyphic Stairway**
Stairway of a temple in Copan that has more than 2,200 glyphs on its steps, which comprise the longest Maya inscription.

# Early States in South America

*Figure 13.2*

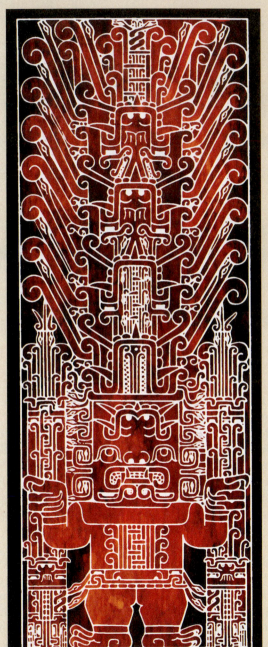

**THE STAFF DEITY MOTIF OF CHAVÍN AT HUÁNTAR.** This deity motif recurs constantly in Andean prehistory. What other factors do prehistoric Andean states share? What purposes do they serve?

*Source:* Based on Moseley (2001, 169).

At 8,000 km (almost 5,000 miles) long, the Andes mountain chain dominates the western edge of South America, separating, by only a few hundred kilometers, the arid western coast from tropical jungles inland. This narrow geographic region has many micro-habitats: rich coastal fishing grounds; warm inland valleys and high mountain slopes, where irrigation supports cultivation of a range of crops; high grasslands (puna) for herds of llama and alpaca; and tropical forests that provide exotic birds and animals. In addition to food resources, the region is rich in mineral resources. Such variety gave rise to an array of cultures.

The earliest complex ritual centers in South America emerged on the west coast of the continent about 4,500 years ago. They are contemporary with the pyramids of Egypt and the ziggurats of Mesopotamia, and they precede Olmec constructions by 1,000 years (von Hagen and Morris 1998). About 3,800 years ago **El Paraíso**, a large coastal site near Lima, was a complex of stone platform mounds, buildings, and domestic structures covering 50 hectares (124 acres). Littoral (shoreline) resources formed the dietary mainstay, supplemented by agricultural produce and wild foods. El Paraíso people grew cotton from which they wove simple textiles. Fortunately, the arid environment has preserved some of these fabrics, providing the New World's earliest evidence for cloth—a commodity that was to continue in importance in the Andean region.

The Andean highlands also saw the rise of complex centers from an early period. The cult center of **Chavín de Huántar** comprises a U-shaped stone-stepped temple with many interior corridors, rooms, stairways, and stone water conduits and airways, built about 3,000 years ago. Distinctive Chavín motifs (a mixture of humans, jungle animals, and mythical creatures) within the complex, seen in Figure 13.2, occur throughout much of the Andean region, suggesting the adoption or inclusion of the Chavín cult over a wide area (von Hagen and Morris 1998).

Centers such as El Paraíso and Chavín de Huántar were antecedents of the many powerful states that arose in the Andean region, three of which we discuss here: the north coast Moche state (1,900 to 1,250 years ago) and the highland Tiwanaku (1,900 to 1,000 years ago) and Wari states. The latter two are often considered to be early forms of empire preceding the Inca empire.

## Moche

**Moche** (pronounced "mochay") rule lasted for about 700 years from 1,900 years ago. At the state's peak period, the style and religious iconography that define the Moche culture extended for about 550 km (342 miles) in northern Peru, spanning at least eleven river valleys and a range of ecological zones from tropical forests to temperate regions, each with a variety of re-

**El Paraíso**
Early complex center in coastal Peru.

**Chavín de Huántar**
Early complex site in the highlands of Peru, many of whose distinctive symbolic motifs occur in cultures throughout the Andean region.

**Moche**
Early state in what is now northern Peru that flourished for about 700 years, from 1,900 to 1,250 years ago; known for its characteristic architecture, symbolic iconography, and skilled craft specialists.

**guano**
Bird excrement that provides excellent fertilizer for crops.

**Cerro Blanco**
Largest of the Moche ceremonial, administrative, and residential centers in Peru, dominated by two pyramids.

**Huaca del Sol and Huaca de la Luna**
Monumental mud-brick pyramid complexes at the Moche center of Cerro Blanco.

**El Niño**
Cyclical climatic event that lowers temperatures in the Pacific ocean along coastal South America, causing a reduction in marine life and heavy rainfall that can lead to extensive flooding.

**anthropomorphic**
Having human attributes.

**mit'a**
Payment of taxes through labor; characteristic of the Inca, but also used in pre-Inca states.

sources. Moche settlements were situated primarily on river valley floodplains; there the people exploited rich agricultural land, which they irrigated by harnessing inland mountain water runoff. In addition to tapping the bounty of coastal resources, Moche groups exploited offshore islands for their rich deposits of **guano** (bird droppings), renowned as an excellent fertilizer that could substantially increase crop yields (Donnan 2004; Shimada 1999).

There are two regions of Moche influence: a larger southern area from the Chicama River valley southward, and a smaller northern area from the Jequetepeque valley north. Researchers formerly believed that the Moche represented a large, centralized state that was ruled from the "capital" at **Cerro Blanco** in the Moche River valley. Excavations, however, indicated that Moche presence in the area is not always culturally homogeneous: Objects, rather than sites, show Moche characteristics. Consequently, an alternative interpretation proposes that instead of a single Moche state, there were independent principalities with their own rulers, but shared religious iconography and political alliances united these entities (Pillsbury 2001).

## Moche Urbanism at Cerro Blanco and Pampa Grande

Cerro Blanco, located 6 km (3.7 miles) inland in the Moche valley, is the largest of Moche centers. It is dominated by two massive mud-brick terraced platform structures, **Huaca del Sol and Huaca de la Luna** (Pyramid of the Sun and Pyramid of the Moon), separated by a residential plaza 550 m (about 1,800 feet) across. Although episodes of flooding, torrential rains from **El Niño**, erosional processes, and looting have robbed these stepped platforms of their former glory, they still remain an impressive testimony to Moche power. Moche laborers constructed Huaca del Sol and Huaca de la Luna in multiple phases. In the process they added platforms, structures, and plazas that Moche artisans decorated with polychrome murals of **anthropomorphic** representations. It was necessary, too, to do regular repairs on structures damaged by El Niño rains. Experts have estimated that more than 140 million mold-made mud-bricks went into the construction of Huaca del Sol, the largest platform mound in the Andes (von Hagen and Morris 1998). The more than 100 distinct identity marks on the bricks may indicate collective participation in construction by groups from different communities; perhaps labor was a way to fulfill a state tax duty, a practice known as **mit'a** in later Inca times (Moseley 2001; Wilson 1999). Elite burials and occupational debris at Huaca del Sol suggest that the structure served a multi-functional use as elite residence, civic center, and ceremonial area. Activities at Huaca de la Luna appear to have been related to religion and ceremony (Wilson 1999).

The densely packed residential area between Huaca del Sol and Huaca de la Luna could have housed a population of an estimated 10,000 people (von Hagen and Morris 1998). The city of Cerro Blanco was well planned; there were water conduits, plazas, and walled compounds of houses and workshops linked to Huaca de la Luna by a warren of narrow streets (Chapdelaine 2001). Elite and middle-class groups occupied the central area—excavation there has revealed nonutilitarian objects and differences in house size and burials. Furthermore, the lack of agricultural implements in the area shows that the occupants did not produce their own food but may have obtained it from smaller agricultural settlements in the valley, where farmers and their families lived and worked.

## Craft Specialization

Moche specialists were superb metallurgists, potters, and weavers, but their output also included items made from gourds, wood, shells, precious stones, and feathers. Some craft work required such skill and was so uniform over the Moche domain that it must have been produced by full-time specialists under the control of elite groups. Excavation at Pampa Grande, a large Moche center is the Lambayeque valley in the northern part of the Moche realm, revealed craft workshops for the production of cotton textiles, metals, shell work, ceramic, and **chicha** (maize beer). Small raised platforms that provided a view over workshop areas may have been used by supervisors to monitor production. Workers received food and *chicha* that was prepared in small rooms near the workshops (Shimada 2001). Products were kept in the numerous storage areas at Pampa Grande and at Cerro Blanco until they were needed or were transported to other areas.

Textiles were important in the Andes: They were used to cover walls; to wrap mummies; and to make nets, bags, hats, and clothes (Wilson 1999).

Although the Moche people did not have a writing system, they left us a comprehensive view of their natural and supernatural worlds in their mold-made and handcrafted pottery. Portrait vases of distinctly different faces must be true likenesses of Moche leaders; indeed, some vases show particular men at different stages of their lives (Donnan 2004). Pottery workshops often produced particular types of pots that were subsequently dispersed throughout Moche territory. Other workshops produced a variety of goods including spindle whorls, crucibles, and tuyeres (nozzles for bellows in smelting furnaces).

Moche metallurgical products included tools and weapons as well as elite items of decoration. The grave goods accompanying the fabulously rich and unlooted tombs at **Sipán** in the Lambayeque valley aptly reflect the skill of Moche metalworkers. Bracelets, necklaces, ear and nose ornaments, bells, and masks were among the artifacts of gold, silver, gilded copper, and bronze. To make these items craftspeople employed a range of techniques, among them hammering, molding, casting, soldering, and welding (Alva and Donnan 1993).

## Warfare and Ritual

Until recently, the traditional view of the Moche state saw it engaging in territorial expansion and control of river valleys primarily through military aggression. Researchers formerly believed—and some still maintain—that once a valley had been conquered, the Moche introduced large-scale irrigation schemes and set up provincial capitals with stepped platform buildings, residential areas and workshops similar to those at Cerro Blanco but on a smaller scale (Shimada 1999). According to this model, iconographic imagery on platform murals and pottery represented state propaganda. Such images included scenes of Moche warriors triumphant in battle, killing and torturing prisoners, and people offering tribute (Wilson 1999).

However, further study of Moche iconography, particularly on pottery, has caused many researchers to alter their interpretation of the Moche state. Battle scenes on pottery show warriors in one-on-one combat rather than warring armies. Combatants' clothing, headgear, clubs, and shields are mostly characteristic of Moche warriors rather than foreigners; indeed, there are very few representations of foreign warriors. The iconographic evidence, therefore, does not appear to support large-scale warfare between opposing armies but may depict ritualized combat between individual warriors (Bourget 2001).

At Cerro Blanco, the excavation of more than 70 skeletons at a plaza east of the main mound of Huaca de la Luna has provided compelling evidence in favor of ritual one-on-one combat and sacrifice among the Moche elite. The bodies were all male, aged between 15 and 39 years old, and in good physical health. Most bodies had been mutilated, disarticulated, and scattered over the surface of the excavated area. Bones displayed old, healed fractures but also fresh wounds such as skull fractures and broken ribs, indicating violent contact (Verano 2001). Near the bodies were fragments of broken, unfired portrait vases decorated with faces in the same way as on portrait vases of Moche leaders (Donnan 2004). Researchers suggest that the combined evidence gives the impression of a warrior cult of Moche elite who voluntarily participated in individual combat.

Iconographic representation also indicates events following combat: Defeated warriors were taken prisoner, stripped naked, tied around the neck with a rope, and paraded

**chicha**
Beer made from maize.

**Sipán**
Rich, unlooted tombs of Moche individuals of high status.

before the lord of the area. They were then sacrificed, and their blood was caught in a goblet and drunk by the warrior priest (who may have been the lord) (see Figure 13.3). Marks on the skeletons found near Huaca de la Luna indicate the tools used to kill the victims: crescent-shaped copper knives (similar to those depicted in the iconography) and clubs. One club retrieved at the site tested positive for human blood (Bourget 2001).

The remarkable discovery of 12 tombs at Sipán in the Lambayeque valley further filled in the picture. Three tombs were those of high-status individuals, as indicated by their regalia, a wealth of rich goods, the inclusion of human and animal sacrifices, and other funerary trappings (Alva and Donnan 1993). The burial context of the individuals correlates with pottery depictions of the sacrifice ceremony; together, these clues indicate that two bodies were lords of the sacrifice ceremony and that a third was the attending priest. High-status female burials found in other areas of the Moche realm correlate with a priestess figure depicted in iconographic scenes (Bourget 2001). Portrait pots also indicate that some lords ended up as sacrificial victims themselves. Christopher Donnan's long-term study of Moche ceramics has revealed a series of portraits depicting the same individuals at different periods of their lives; in some cases the final portrait shows the individual as a prisoner, naked and bound, presumably about to be sacrificed. Rather than meant to degrade the victim, Donnan believes that the final portrait would have been made to commemorate and honor a brave warrior (Donnan 2001, 2004).

Warrior combat and sacrifice were part of Moche rituals for generations. The stratigraphic positions of the bodies at Huaca de la Luna indicate at least five different combat events. In addition, the Sipán burials are not contemporaneous, suggesting a lasting tradition. Evidence of sacrifice and ritual at numerous Moche centers emphasizes the belief system that united independent and possibly competing Moche principalities.

## Figure 13.3

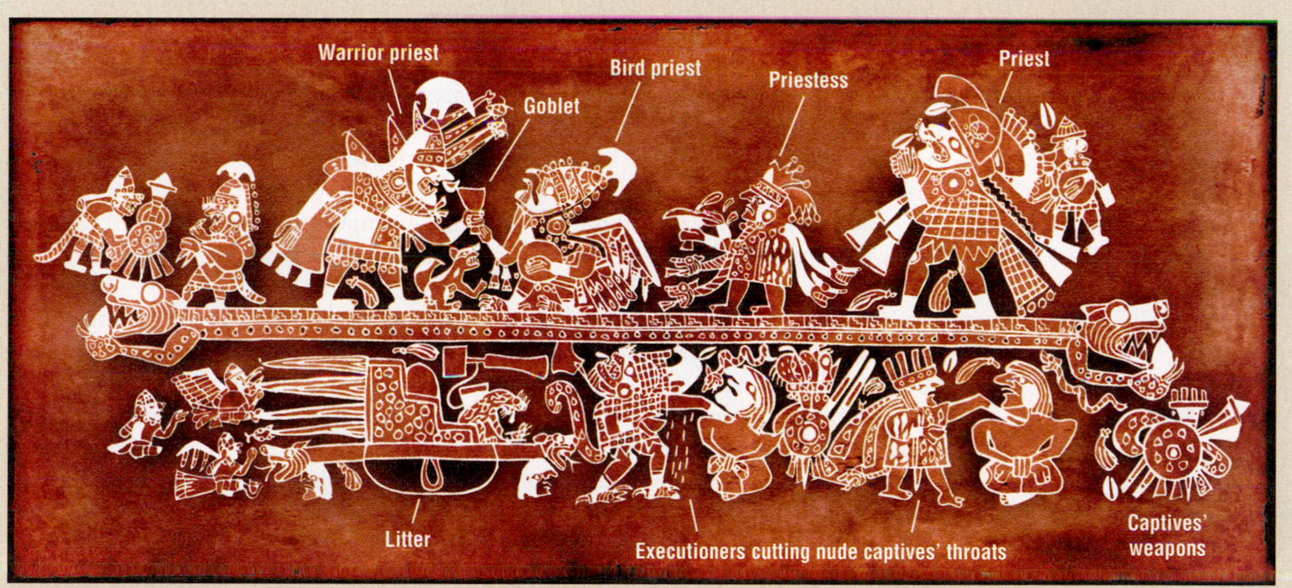

**MOCHE SACRIFICE CEREMONY.**   Pottery vessels depict the sequence of events of human sacrifice among the Moche warrior elite. How has this ceremony been verified archaeologically?

*Source:* Adapted from drawing by Donna McLelland. In Donnan, C. B., and D. McClelland. 1999. *Moche fineline painting*, 131. Los Angeles: Fowler Museum of Cultural History, University of California. Used by permission of the artist.

# Tiwanaku: State and Early Empire?

Located in the Bolivian **altiplano** at 4,000 m (13,123 feet) above sea level, **Tiwanaku** was the highest urban center in the Americas. The city was also an important pilgrimage center, situated as it was in the sacred landscape of Lake Titicaca, surrounded by the snow-capped Andes. The first appearance of monumental construction at Tiwanaku, nearly 2,000 years ago, heralded the city's emergence as an important ritual and political center. By about 1,500 years ago, it was the state capital and was home to some 20,000 to 40,000 people, whose numbers swelled periodically during times of mass pilgrimage. Within the following few hundred years, the power of Tiwanaku had extended to the Bolivian lowlands, southern Peru, and northern Chile (Kolata 1993). In the view of some Andean specialists, control of regions beyond the Tiwanaku heartland turned the Tiwanaku state into an early empire.

## Tiwanaku Ceremonial Center and Secular City

Tiwanaku covered an area of 6 km² (2.3 square miles). The massive stone buildings of the ceremonial center typify Tiwanaku architecture: temples, palaces, sunken stone plazas, monumental stone gateways, and stelae carved with Tiwanaku iconography, all of which combined to symbolize the power of the state. Some structures would have been brightly painted or perhaps covered with textiles (Kolata 1993). Two large artificial stepped mounds, the **Akapana** and Pumapunku complexes, dominated the northern and southern areas of the ritual center; large open areas in the city accommodated the populace at public ceremonies. The ceremonial precinct was laid out on a grid with its main buildings aligned to the cardinal points, perhaps to emphasize the perceived sacred nature of the surrounding landscape. A moat separated the ritual center from the rest of the city, a separation that Tiwanakans may have intended to symbolize the sacred island shrines of Lake Titicaca and the islands of the Sun and Moon (von Hagen and Morris 1998).

The Akapana complex of temples and palaces is the largest and most impressive structure at Tiwanaku, rising through six stone-faced terraces of earth, clay, and gravel to a height of 17 m (56 feet). At its summit lies a sunken court of stone blocks. Visible from the top of the Akapana are the snow-capped peaks of the Andes and the waters of Lake Titicaca, both ideologically important features linked to creation mythology (Kolata 1993). Thus, this view would have been not fortuitous but rather a preplanned outcome of construction. A system of subterranean and surface drains carried water, accumulated in the sunken court during torrential downpours, down through the Akapana to the Tiwanaku River and subsequently to Lake Titicaca, thus linking the center with the lake.

The ritual nature of the Akapana is further indicated by a series of offerings, among them burials of humans and llamas. Study of one such offering revealed that most human skeletons were either headless or missing body parts, and that the amputations had occurred after death rather than being the cause of death. The burials included ceramics decorated with images of human heads, representative of real trophies taken in battle and ritual sacrifice—a practice of many Andean societies, including most likely the elite of Tiwanaku (Kolata 1993).

Several other monuments, skillfully faced with dressed stone, graced the core ceremonial center of the Akapana. One of these, the Semi-subterranean Temple, is a sunken court of sandstone blocks in which numerous stelae and sculptures surround the Bennett stela, a sculpture 7 m (23 feet) high that was carved from a single block of red sandstone. The Kalasasaya, a 120 by 130 m (394 by 426 feet) slightly elevated walled enclosure with a sunken court, has in its northwest corner the intricately carved Gateway of the Sun, hewn from massive blocks of andesite (an igneous rock). Geological sourcing has revealed that much of the stone originated some distance from Tiwanaku; for example, the temple builders transported andesite across Lake Titicaca and quarried sandstone some 10 km (6 miles) from Tiwanaku (von Hagen and Morris 1998).

**altiplano**
High plateau of southern Peru and Bolivia.

**Tiwanaku**
Pre-Inca state that was contemporaneous with Wari, had its capital in the Lake Titicaca area of the Andean highlands, and was known for its monumental architecture; some experts give it early empire status.

**Akapana**
The largest complex of monumental buildings in Tiwanaku, in the Bolivian altiplano.

**raised fields**
Artificially raised blocks of land intersected by canals and used for cultivation of crops.

Priests likely resided in the temples, and palaces within the core ceremonial area housed Tiwanaku rulers. Lesser elites and commoners lived outside the ceremonial center in wattle-and-daub houses, although differences in house construction and contents indicate different status levels. For example, some houses were of a sturdier build than others; had drainage systems, wells, and storage pits; and contained artifacts of metal, semiprecious stone, engraved llama bone, and fine ceramics that indicate differences in wealth and status between groups. Agricultural workers lived in hamlets and villages that dotted the countryside beyond the core area (von Hagen and Morris 1998).

## Craft Working

Manufacturing waste found in workshops at the edge of the city of Tiwanaku indicates the working of basalt, lapis lazuli, turquoise, and other semiprecious stones as well as the production of plain and fine ceramics. At times artisans lived in these workplaces, as suggested by the presence of domestic waste. Craft production was not confined to workshops but was also a household activity undertaken by both elite and commoner groups; work done in households included weaving, bone carving, basalt and obsidian working, and gold and silver manufacture (Kolata 1993).

Detail of the Gateway God on the Gateway of the Sun, Tiwanaku. What were the symbolic and political roles of the massive stone architecture of Tiwanaku?

## Economic Basis of Tiwanaku Power

The economic foundations of Tiwanaku power rested on the rich fishing resources of Lake Titicaca, extensive llama and alpaca herds that grazed the high puna (plateau) grasses, and the intensive cultivation of tubers and grains in the surrounding altiplano through a system of **raised fields** and complex hydraulic technologies (see Highlight 13.2, on pp. 404–405). Yields from altiplano cultivation and camelid herding together provided ample food, wool, and transport resources to meet the needs of the Tiwanaku populace. Survey has revealed almost 150 km² (58 square miles) of raised fields around Tiwanaku that could have yielded enough potatoes each year to feed a population of 250,000 (Kolata 2001). However, although there are some large platform mounds in the agricultural area, evidence of permanent settlements is lacking. Researchers have interpreted the platform mounds as administration centers that supervised agricultural activities for the state and have suggested that farm laborers may have done the work as a form of paying state taxes.

State expansion saw the establishment of Tiwanaku colonies at lower elevations, around Lake Titicaca and beyond, for the cultivation of maize and coca—not to feed the populace but probably to fulfill the needs of ritual hospitality, an important feature of Andean states. Ritual hospitality underpinned the formation and maintenance of good relationships between groups. Furthermore, given that maize and coca could be stored and used as gifts and items of trade between the elite, the desire for them may have spurred Tiwanaku expansion (Kolata 1996).

## Expansion: From Early State to Empire?

The Tiwanaku state expanded its influence through a mixture of military conquest, colonization, and reciprocal trade relations with elite groups in other areas (Kolata 1993). Initially the state took control of

# In the Footsteps of Ancient Andean Farmers

THE MODERN AYMARA PEOPLES of the altiplano, a plateau area around Lake Titicaca, are very much at the mercy of the elements with regard to crop harvests. The altiplano is a cold, windy, often bleak area that experiences great variation between day time and nighttime temperatures; devastating frosts often wipe out Aymara farmers' crops. How, then, could the ancient state of Tiwanaku have fed its capital city with a population of 20,000 to 40,000 people?

The answer lies in Tiwanaku's system of raised-field agriculture. Archaeological survey and aerial photography have revealed a vast network of long-abandoned raised fields around Lake Titicaca. These were rectangular platforms 5 to 10 m (16 to 33 feet) wide and up to 200 m (656 feet) long or even longer, built on a base of cobbles, overlain by layers of gravels and clay, and topped with freshly dug aerated earth. Channels, or canals, between the platforms carried water from local sources. The water absorbed solar heat during the day, then slowly released the warmth around and through the mounds at night, offering protection against frost action. Furthermore, the plants, animals, and other organisms that colonized the water channels provided natural fertilizer. High crop yields resulted in such a nutrient-rich and protective environment. Evidence indicates that Andean farmers had developed raised-field technology before Tiwanaku's

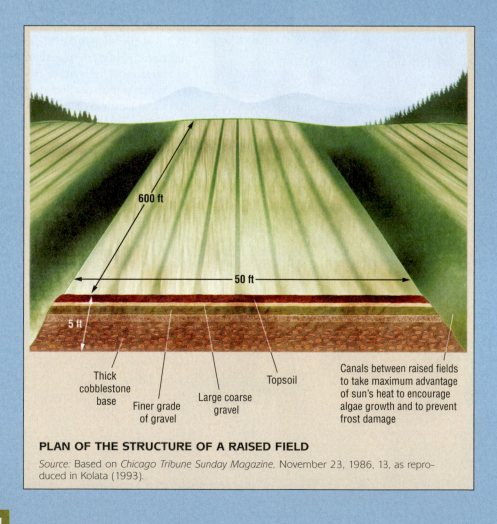

600 ft

50 ft

5 ft

Thick cobblestone base

Finer grade of gravel

Large coarse gravel

Topsoil

Canals between raised fields to take maximum advantage of sun's heat to encourage algae growth and to prevent frost damage

**PLAN OF THE STRUCTURE OF A RAISED FIELD**

*Source:* Based on *Chicago Tribune Sunday Magazine,* November 23, 1986, 13, as reproduced in Kolata (1993).

rise to power. However, intensification of the system was directed by the state.

The people of the altiplano had long abandoned the raised-field system of agriculture when Alan Kolata and colleagues proposed an experimental reconstruction in the 1980s. Kolata had noticed that the Aymara farmers did not enjoy the agricultural success of their Tiwanaku forebears. In fact, life was much more precarious in the 1980s than it had been 1,500 years earlier. Under Kolata's supervision farmers revived some of the ancient raised fields and planted a variety of crops, including the traditional potato and quinoa. Shortly before harvest a bitter frost wasted 70 to 90 percent of the traditionally grown crops—but caused minimal damage to the raised-field crops.

Further experimentation appeared to show that raised-field agriculture can provide yields up to seven times higher than the traditional Aymara system of agriculture. Nevertheless, there are potential problems that may limit the systematic use of raised fields: crop rotation and fallow periods, which may affect crop yields, are necessary to regenerate soil fertility and keep crop parasites at bay. Furthermore, construction of raised fields is immensely labor intensive, and farmers cannot devote the time that would be needed for large-scale implementation as that would detract from other subsistence activities. This ancient technology may provide only an alternative to dryland farming although just how much it could influence crop yield over time remains to be determined.

*Sources:* Bandy, M. S. 2005. Energetic efficiency and political expediency in Titicaca Basin raised field agriculture. *Journal of Anthropological Archaeology* 24:271–296. Janusek, J. W., and A. Kolata. 2004. Top-down or bottom-up; rural settlement and raised field agriculture in the Lake Titicaca Basin, Bolivia. *Journal of Anthropological Archaeology* 23: 404–430. Kolata, A. 1986. The agricultural foundations of the Tiwanaku state: A view from the heartland. *American Antiquity* 51 (4): 748–762. Kolata, A. 1993. *The Tiwanaku: Portrait of an Andean civilization*. Cambridge, MA/Oxford: Blackwell. Kolata, A. 1996. *Valley of the spirits: A journey into the lost realm of the Aymara*. New York: Wiley. Sánchez de Lozada, D., P. Bareye, R. F. Lucey, et al. 2006. Potential limitations for potato yields in raised soil field systems near Lake Titicaca. *Scientia Agricola* (Piracicaba, Brazil) 63 (5): 444–452.

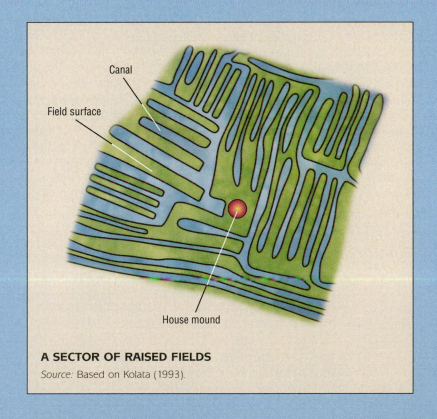

Canal

Field surface

House mound

**A SECTOR OF RAISED FIELDS**

*Source:* Based on Kolata (1993).

turn back to your reading

the Titicaca basin to enlarge its agricultural domain; it placed officials in smaller Tiwanaku administrative centers around Lake Titicaca to administer agricultural lands. An emphasis on state ideology reinforced colonial control: Temples at local centers were smaller-scale copies of those at Tiwanaku; the **Gateway God**, a deity linked with natural forces, was depicted on sculptures and carvings in the state capital and throughout the Tiwanaku area of influence; many rituals were associated with the agricultural cycle. Such a shared ideology served to unify dispersed groups while promoting the state policy of increasing agricultural output.

It is clear that the state used force when the occasion demanded it. Archaeologists have found numerous broken stelae from distant areas at Tiwanaku itself; they deduce that when Tiwanaku armies overpowered opponents, they ritually demonstrated their superiority by taking the sacred symbolic stelae of conquered groups back to the capital city. To help maintain peace, however, Tiwanaku absorbed local gods into the state cult and erected their statues among the Tiwanaku deities. Furthermore, alliance with a rich and powerful state such as Tiwanaku had benefits, among them the protection it offered against other potentially aggressive states and the value of its technological expertise in irrigation techniques (Kolata 2001).

Tiwanaku colonies have been found in southern Peru and northern Chile. Irrigation systems were set up to exploit the agricultural potential of the Moquegua River valley, about 300 km (186 miles) southwest of Tiwanaku. In this region hierarchical settlement patterns similar to those around the Tiwanaku heartland are evident, and civic and domestic structures, artifacts, and ideology reflect state influence. Furthermore, skeletal evidence indicates genetic links with Tiwanaku peoples of the altiplano (Blom et al. 1998). However, the study of **cranial deformation** shows that the mechanism of colonization may have been more complex than people from Tiwanaku simply moving from the highlands to the lowlands. Cranial deformation was common practice in the prehistoric Andes, and different styles of deformation served as group identity markers. Tiwanaku and Moquegua styles differ. But whereas archaeological and genetic evidence indicates Tiwanaku influence in the Moquegua Valley, cranial deformation evidence is solely Moqueguan. In contrast, both deformation styles were present at Tiwanaku. What does this mean? It seems that some people from the Moquegua Valley moved to the Tiwanaku area, but that perhaps no native Tiwanaku people remained permanently in the Moquegua Valley. Perhaps, too, the Moquegua people maintained their particular style in order to reinforce their group identity at a time of powerful Tiwanaku influence (Blom 2005).

Llama caravans carried raw materials, produce, and goods from Tiwanaku colonies to the capital, returning with such items as fine textiles and pottery. However, Tiwanaku objects found at some sites in northern Chile and northwestern Argentina indicate patterns of interaction different from that evident in Tiwanaku colonies—interaction consisting of long-distance trade in cult objects rather than colonial domination. Tiwanaku artifacts in these areas, found only in rich tombs, are primarily textiles, ritual drinking cups, feather items and other articles connected with ritual and ideology. Furthermore, the assemblages of artifacts vary from site to site, suggesting selective acquisition according to the needs and beliefs of each region (Kolata 1993).

## Politics and Ideology

As in many early states, the Tiwanaku leaders used ideology both to motivate people to work and to control and regulate that work. The image of the Gateway God, depicted on the Gateway of the Sun at Tiwanaku itself, appears on public monuments in all areas under Tiwanaku control. The Gateway God was associated with elements governing crop production; as such, the deity was seen as having some control over growth and may even have represented an agrarian calendar. The Gateway God also was portrayed on items associated with the ruling elite, such as architecture and textiles. This iconography imputed to the elite a divine status that legitimized their power as protectors of produce (Kolata 1993, 2001).

**Gateway God**
An important Tiwanaku diety.

**cranial deformation**
The practice of changing the shape of a human head through gradual application of force, for example, through head binding.

# Wari: State and Early Empire?

Also in the Andean highlands was a third early South American state, **Wari**. Between about 1,500 and 1,000 years ago, the Wari state, much like its contemporary power, Tiwanaku, controlled regions well beyond its immediate borders. For the most part, however, the political domains of these two superpowers of the Andes did not overlap, except in a small area near the south coast they were politically independent. Wari's control extended across the Andean highlands from Cuzco to northern Peru, whereas Tiwanaku controlled areas south of Lake Titicaca (von Hagen and Morris 1998). Although Wari influence extended over a much wider area than that of Tiwanaku, Wari has been overshadowed archaeologically by its fellow state, quite simply because for hundreds of years archaeologists were unaware of it.

Located at an altitude of more than 2,800 m (9,000 feet) in the southern highlands near Ayacucho, the Wari capital (called Wari or Huari) covers an area of more than 15.5 km$^2$ (6 square miles) and may have housed up to 70,000 people (Morell 2002). Wari architecture differs greatly from that at Tiwanaku but is equally distinctive. The grid layout of the city comprises a series of large rectangular compounds enclosed by high, thick, white-plastered walls, which can be 150 to 300 m (490 to 985 feet) long. Inside each compound is a series of open patio courtyards surrounded by narrow, conjoined, multi-storied rooms with small doorways. Underground water conduits ensured water supplies for domestic and ritual needs. Remains of hearths and food debris found inside some of the ground-floor rooms indicate domestic activities. Other rooms appear to have been workshops for making pottery, jewelry, and stone tools; and the many bowls and cups recovered from a few rooms imply ritual drinking and feasting activities. Rooms on upper floors may have served as storage areas. The regularity of courtyard compounds is a defining characteristic of Wari architecture at all sites. When associated with Wari pottery, this architectural pattern is a clear indicator of Wari presence outside the state's heartland (Moseley 2001; Schreiber 1992).

As at Tiwanaku, ritual was an important factor of Wari life. Large and small D-shaped structures in the capital and at provincial sites had religious significance. Megalithic buildings associated with mortuary practices were uncovered in the Cheqo Wasi compound at Wari, where excavation revealed semi-subterranean burial chambers constructed of massive, shaped stone blocks. In addition, the presence of the skulls and bones of more than 100 people, some stained in red, gives further evidence of the ritual nature of Cheqo Wasi. Grave goods included a range of pottery, mortars and grinders, stone figures, and metal and bone tools, as well as luxury items such as spondylus shell artifacts. (Benavides 1991; Isbell and Vranich 2004).

## Terraces and Irrigation

Wari engineers introduced systems for terracing and irrigating hillsides that the Inca later adopted and expanded. Although labor-intensive to construct, these innovations enabled the people to cultivate steep slopes. Specialists developed new strains of maize that flourished on high slopes, complementing traditional maize production in valley basins. Terrace and irrigation technology not only increased food production but also provided food security at times when shortages might have been expected, such as periods of drought (Moseley 2001). Furthermore, maize assured a constant supply of beer for Wari rituals and feasting.

## Wari Expansion

As the Wari state expanded, its administrators set up provincial centers connected by road systems (a precursor to the network of Inca roads) throughout the Wari domain. Wari bureaucrats likely oversaw the construction of terracing and irrigation arrangements as well as changes in settlement and subsistence patterns in the area. All provincial towns have characteristic Wari structures, town plans, and ceramics. **Pikillaqta**, in

**Wari**
Pre-Inca Andean state that was contemporaneous with Tiwanaku and developed systems of terracing, irrigation, and roads later adopted by the Inca; possibly an empire.

**Pikillaqta**
The largest provincial center of the Wari state in the Cuzco Valley of Peru.

**Cerro Baúl**
The only Wari settlement located in Tiwanaku territory.

the Lucre Basin of the Cuzco Valley, 250 km (155 miles) from Wari, is the largest of the Wari provincial centers and may have been an administrative and ceremonial center controlling the southern highlands of the Wari sphere. The site, covering 2 km² (almost 1 square mile), was planned on a rectangular grid and divided into sectors surrounded by high white-plastered walls. In the main block of the largest sector, there are more than 700 small conjoining rooms with few windows and doors opening onto the exterior, suggestive of strict control over access. Formerly, researchers believed these rooms were for storage, but further excavations revealed evidence of domestic and ritual activities. The rooms may have housed soldiers or state laborers; or they could have served as resting places for the bodies of dead ancestors when ancestor worship rituals occurred. Indeed, ritual and ceremony are associated with many structures at Pikillaqta (McEwan 1991, 2005).

### Wari and Tiwanaku in the Moquegua Valley

The Moquegua River valley in southern Peru is the only region in which Wari and Tiwanaku presence overlapped. More than 30 Tiwanaku sites, distinguished by distinctive Tiwanaku pottery and monumental architecture and spanning a period of more than 300 years, have been located in the valley (Moseley et al. 1991). The **Cerro Baúl** complex, the only Wari settlement in the area, may have functioned as the southern boundary of the Wari state. It is impressive by virtue of its location—600 m (1,970 feet) above the valley floor on the summits and high slopes of three mountains: Cerro Baúl, Cerro Mejia, and Cerro Petroglifo. Cerro Baúl itself was the monumental and ceremonial center of the settlement, with residential areas for elites and craft specialists. People of lesser rank lived on Mejia and Petroglifo. Massive walls blocked access to the settlement from the valley floor and lower slopes. Engineers constructed systems of terracing and irrigating that enabled Wari colonists to exploit upland areas not previously farmed by Tiwanaku colonists. The nature of contact between the two groups in the valley is unclear, although the monumental walls around the Wari settlement suggest defense (Schrieber 1992). The irrigation canals on the higher slopes would have restricted the water supply to valley fields, particularly in times of drought, and consequently would have caused tension between the two groups. When water was plentiful, then Wari and Tiwanaku elites may have shared diplomatic ritual feasts with *chicha* drinking (Williams and Nash 2002).

The Tiwanaku and Wari states expanded beyond their immediate centers, exercised control over distant areas, and influenced economic production and exchange throughout areas under their control. In addition, subject regions adopted Tiwanaku and Wari ideological beliefs, whether through conviction or as a result of judicious strategy. Given such aspects of power, Tiwanaku and Wari might be thought of as incipient empires, although they never achieved the power and size of the Inca empire. The next section considers the two great empires that did develop in the the Americas: the Aztecs and the Incas.

# Empires of the New World

**Aztec**
Mesoamerican empire centered in the Valley of Mexico, with its capital at Tenochtitlan; conquered by the Spanish in the sixteenth century.

Archaeologists specializing in the Aztec and Inca empires have a source of information not available in previous periods: recorded histories, in the form of eyewitness accounts from Spanish soldiers and missionaries. The **Aztec** people had a form of writing and kept **codices**, or records in bark-paper books folded in accordion fashion. The Incas never had a writing system but used a recording system based on **quipu**, or knotted cords, that has not yet been deciphered. Fortunately, a few Spanish friars, dedicated to converting the Aztecs and Incas to Christianity, spent a lifetime interviewing indigenous peoples about their customs, beliefs, and myths. And in the centuries following the

Spanish conquest, the Aztecs recorded their own histories and customs in their native languages as well as in Spanish. Together with Spanish colonial administrative documents, such sources augment the archaeological evidence. It is important to bear in mind that Spanish documents offer a biased account, in that they view Aztec and Inca life from a Spanish worldview and in light of Spanish interests. Furthermore, Aztec and Inca sources may have had their own agendas. Nevertheless, these chronicles provide a crucial window on the two great empires of the New World.

# The Aztec Empire

In February 1978 electricity workers, digging in the center of Mexico City, discovered a large carved stone statue of Coyolxauhqui, the Aztec moon goddess. This was an important find in itself, but even more important was the discovery of its location: the **Great Temple**, the most sacred Aztec temple known to have been constructed in the center of **Tenochtitlan**, the Aztec capital. Excavations between 1978 and 1997 revealed the Great Temple and its contents, which substantially increased existing knowledge of the Aztecs.

Known by their contemporaries as the Mexica, the Aztecs were not natives of the Valley of Mexico. They claimed Aztlan, a mythical region in the north, as their place of origin. They had moved south and by about AD 1325 had settled on an artificial island reclaimed from the swamplands at Lake Texcoco (Matos Moctezuma 1988). Through judicious alliances between their city, Tenochtitlan, and other city-states in the Valley of Mexico, and through military aggression, the Aztecs gradually grew in power. By the time the Spanish arrived in 1519 the Aztecs had built an **empire** covering an area of about 200,000 km² (77,225 square miles), including the lands of more than 500 city-states between the Gulf of Mexico and the Pacific, and extending along the southwest coast to Guatemala (Graham 1992; Webster and Evans 2005).

## Tenochtitlan: The Aztec Capital

Tenochtitlan, the capital of the Aztec empire, was one of the largest cities in the world in its day. The Spaniards' awe when they first saw it is conveyed by the words of Bernal Díaz, one of Cortes's soldiers: ". . . we were astounded. These great towns and *cues* [temples] and buildings rising from the water, all made of stone, seemed like an enchanted vision. . . . Indeed, some of our soldiers asked whether it was not all a dream . . . and [I] thought that no land like it would ever be discovered in the whole world" (Díaz 1963, 214–215). The city was divided into four main areas laid out on a grid around the huge walled ceremonial Central Plaza of temples, shrines, and ball court (see Figure 13.4). Outside the Central Plaza lay the rulers' palaces; administrative buildings; craft workshops; flower, herb, and vegetable gardens; a zoo with jaguars, foxes, and snakes; and an aviary with exotic birds (Matos Moctezuma 1988). Four major causeways linked Tenochtitlan with the mainland, and roads and canals crisscrossed the city.

An estimated population of 200,000 lived in Tenochtitlan. An additional 400,000 lived in areas surrounding the city, so—judging from the number of settlements in the Valley of Mexico (revealed through archaeological survey and excavation)—the population of greater Tenochtitlan may have risen to a million or more people (Smith 1996). The fertile land of the Valley of Mexico was intensely cultivated, and terracing of less fertile hill slopes improved their agricultural yields. As a result, peasants could provide enough food for themselves and the tribute required by the state, in addition to surplus to be sent to market. On the southern fringes of Tenochtitlan people reclaimed swamps by building up rectangular blocks of land with silts, reeds, and vegetation from the lake. Shored by fences and trees and separated from other plots by canals, these raised plots (called **chinampas**) were enriched by their organic composition and were thus productive year round. Waterways facilitated the transport of produce to market. Systems of water control consisting of dikes, ditches, and aqueducts ensured an ample supply of fresh water in the city, enabling Tenochtitlan to flourish.

**codices**
Maya or Aztec books of glyphs and pictures usually drawn on bark paper coated with lime but sometimes drawn on animal skins; singular is *codex*.

**quipu**
Inca recording system, not yet deciphered, in which information is encoded in strips of colored cotton and wool strings, spun, twisted, and knotted in different ways.

**Great Temple**
The religious center of the Aztec world, located in the capital, Tenochtitlan.

**Tenochtitlan**
Capital of the Aztec empire, beneath present-day Mexico City.

**empire**
An extensive territory that is under the rule of a single, powerful state.

**chinampas**
Raised plots reclaimed from swamps to form fertile blocks of land where year-round cultivation was possible.

Figure 13.4

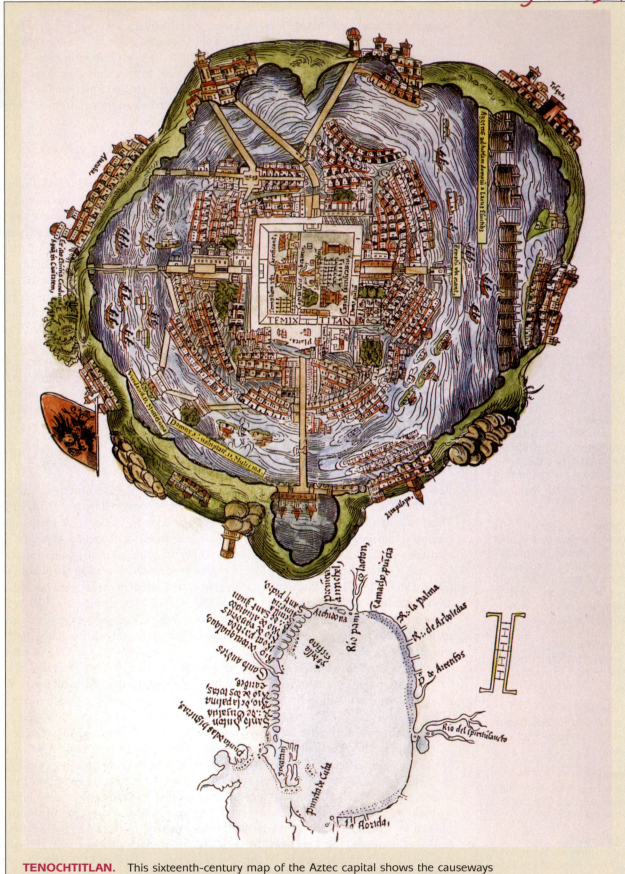

**TENOCHTITLAN.**   This sixteenth-century map of the Aztec capital shows the causeways linking the city to the surrounding land. In what ways can old maps help archaeologists?

*Source:* The Granger Collection, New York.

## Tlatelolco Market

Most Aztec settlements had a market; but the market at **Tlatelolco**, a sister city attached to Tenochtitlan, surpassed all other markets in the empire and was a further source of wonder to the Spanish. Thousands of people thronged the massive market plaza to shop for everything from everyday items to luxury goods from all corners of the empire. In general, Aztec markets were not state controlled; the main traders were professional merchants (**Pochteca**) who traveled throughout the country in search of luxury goods required by the king and nobles. Regional merchants (Tlanecuilo) dealt mainly in food produce. The Tlatelolco market was orderly; judges monitored trading to ensure good practice. Cacao beans from the tropical lowlands were the usual form of currency for small transactions, but buyers used standard lengths of cotton cloth for larger exchanges (Smith 1996, 2003). Bernal Díaz recorded that the Spaniards ". . . were astounded at the great number of people and the quantities of merchandise, and at the orderliness and good arrangements that prevailed, for we had never seen such a thing before" (Díaz 1963, 232).

Tenochtitlan and Tlatelolco were not typical of Aztec cities or markets; they attracted much more description than other cities precisely because they were unusual. Whereas a few cities had estimated populations of 10,000 to 30,000, most, although capitals of smaller city-states, were not much more than towns, each with its own palace and temple (Smith and Hodge 1994). Markets varied in size and frequency, some selling a range of goods and others specializing in particular types of goods. For example, the market of Acolman in the Basin of Mexico specialized in dogs (Blanton 1996).

## Aztec Society

Strict **social stratification** characterized Aztec society. The king was a supreme secular and religious ruler. Below him were an upper class of nobles, a middle class of merchants and specialist craftspeople, and a lower class of free commoners, serfs, and slaves (Graham 1992). Rules governing the use of particular types of clothing, housing, food, and goods distinguished the upper classes from the rest of society. For example, nobles could wear decorated cotton garments, drink chocolate, and participate in the ball game; commoners were restricted to garments of maguey (agave) fibers and could neither drink chocolate nor play in the ritual ball game. The king's advisors and administrators wielded considerable authority and power and received gifts of land from the king. Less prestigious nobles served many functions—they might be tribute collectors, ambassadors, priests, teachers, or officials, for example (Smith and Berdan 1996). Nobles maintained their status and cemented relationships through strategic networking and gift giving.

The Pochteca were professional merchants, members of guilds. These men undertook long-distance trade missions inside and beyond the bounds of the empire and monitored the Tlatelolco market as well as other markets in the Valley of Mexico. Pochteca merchants could gain wealth and status as they traded in a range of exotic items desired by the nobility: gold, jade, jadeite, necklaces, earspools, animal furs and skins, and slaves (Graham 1992). Specialist workers who manufactured luxury goods were also organized in guilds and, like Pochteca members, could improve their status through their craft skills.

Below the professional groups were commoners, serfs, and slaves, who paid tribute in goods, labor, and war service (Smith 1996, 2003). Most were farmers or others who provided service for the upper classes. They were organized into *calpolli*—groups of families who lived in the same city neighborhood, where they farmed a *chinampa* block, or in small settlements in the countryside. Both city and rural groups worked for noble overlords. Commoners could achieve upward mobility through distinguished war service or by entering the priesthood. People became slaves through debt or punishment, but slavery was not inherited.

**Tlatelolco**
City that was adjacent to Tenochtitlan and in which the largest and most diverse market of the Aztec empire was based.

**Pochteca**
Professional merchants who traveled throughout the Aztec empire for the king, simultaneously monitoring political activity.

**social stratification**
A characteristic of a society in which people do not have equal access to resources, wealth, prestige, or power.

## Administration of the Empire

Driving Aztec expansion were the state's needs for tribute and for victims to use in ritual sacrifice. Although the presence of Aztec soldiers in conquered areas was minimal, knowledge of Aztec power was often enough to prevent uprisings. The empire controlled distant states through indirect rather than direct rule. Rulers of conquered city-states usually maintained their position but had to pay tribute. Tax officials from Tenochtitlan collected the tribute—primarily in the form of luxury goods that the Aztecs used to underwrite military campaigns and foreign trade, as gifts to cement social and political ties, as burial deposits, and for ritual ceremonies (see Figure 13.5) (Smith and Berdan 1996). Tribute included goods such as cacao, honey, cotton, building wood, military uniforms, headdresses, textiles, pottery, jewelry, semiprecious stone, gold, exotic animals and birds, animal skins, and marine shells. Through time the empire also began to demand agricultural supplies to feed the increasing population in the Aztec heartland. The amount of tribute exacted was often enormous, causing real hardship among communities and an inevitable rise in antagonism toward the conquerors. Pochteca merchants, who also acted as spies for the Aztec king, alerted the ruler to signs of unrest (Matos Moctezuma 1988; Smith 1996, 2003).

There were other powerful states in Mesoamerica that successfully resisted Aztec domination. The Aztecs saw these states as enemies because of their potential ability to disrupt trade and tribute. The empire's strategy in such cases, which worked successfully, was to require city-states that had submitted to Aztec control and that were located near enemy borders to patrol and control the border regions. In return, these client city-states did not have to pay tribute but received gifts from the Aztecs (Smith 1996).

## Aztec Ritual

The Spanish witnessed human sacrifices taking place on the Great Temple at Tenochtitlan; their accounts of the procedure, including the ripping out of victims' pulsating hearts, make for chilling reading. Such practice is shocking to us today, as it was to the sixteenth-century Spanish invaders (although they did not object to burning heretics at the stake). Yet, as this chapter has shown, Aztec human sacrifice was part of a long and sacred tradition in ancient Mesoamerica. The Aztecs linked human sacrifice to the Aztec deities, who had sacrificed themselves to create the world. Human sacrifice and bloodletting were essential to give praise to the deities, and thus to allow life to continue. Sacrifice had a divine purpose. Everyone practiced autosacrifice (bloodletting) at special moments during life by piercing their ears with maguey thorns. At times people, in particular priests, pierced other body parts; they might also enlarge the piercing by pulling a reed through the hole. Indeed, priests practiced autosacrifice on a nightly basis. The Aztecs saw the victims of human sacrifice as entering the realm of deities. Preparation for the sacrificial event might take as long as a year, during which the chosen victim received special treatment, lived well, and was treated with great deference. However, the Aztecs also practiced human sacrifice on a mass scale as a symbol of Aztec power, a propaganda tool (Smith 1996, 2003).

The Great Temple at Tenotchtitlan was the last of at least seven temples erected at different times on the same spot. Glyphs carved in stones have enabled archaeologists to date some of the Temple's construction phases. Two parallel sets of steps led up to shrines of Huitzilopochtli, the God of War and Blood, and Tlaloc, the God of Rain and Fertility, in front of which sacrifices took place. Discovered during excavations were cremations and sacrifices as well as an altar with rows of carved stone skulls, on which human skulls would probably have been displayed. Excavations revealed more than 6,000 offerings, most coming from tribute-paying areas; some were the work of Aztec artisans, and some came from earlier cultures, such as a 2,000-year-old Olmec greenstone mask. Excavators found statues of Tlaloc but none of Huitzilopochtli—because, as Spanish chroniclers indicate, statues to Huitzilopochtli were usually made of dough

*Figure 13.5*

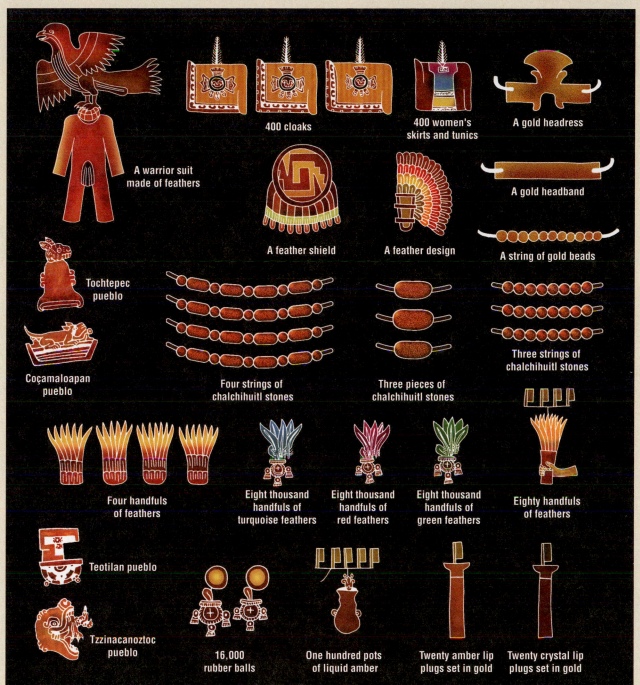

400 cloaks

400 women's skirts and tunics

A gold headress

A warrior suit made of feathers

A feather shield

A feather design

A gold headband

A string of gold beads

Tochtepec pueblo

Coçamaloapan pueblo

Four strings of chalchihuitl stones

Three pieces of chalchihuitl stones

Three strings of chalchihuitl stones

Four handfuls of feathers

Eight thousand handfuls of turquoise feathers

Eight thousand handfuls of red feathers

Eight thousand handfuls of green feathers

Eighty handfuls of feathers

Teotilan pueblo

Tzzinacanoztoc pueblo

16,000 rubber balls

One hundred pots of liquid amber

Twenty amber lip plugs set in gold

Twenty crystal lip plugs set in gold

**AZTEC TRIBUTE ACCOUNT.** This sixteenth-century codex records part of the tribute the Aztecs exacted from towns in Tochtepec province. Towns sent tribute to Tenochtitlan on a yearly basis, except for *mantas*, which were required twice a year. Considering the effort needed to fulfill tribute requirements, what might have been the effects on the tribute-paying towns?

*Source:* Based on Berdan, F., and P. Anewalt. 1997. *The essential Codex Mendoza*. Berkeley: University of California Press.

and seeds. These do not preserve and so are lost to the archaeological record (Matos Moctezuma 1988).

The Great Temple was the religious center of the Aztec world. Scholars have suggested that each part of the temple and its contents were imbued with symbolic meaning and represented Aztec mythology, religion, empire building, economy, and other aspects of Aztec life. As a sacred monument that the Aztec populace could "read," the Great Temple also served to unite the empire (Matos Moctezuma 1999).

# The Inca Empire

Although the status of Tiwanaku and Wari as early empires in South America may be debatable, there is no doubt about the **Inca** empire. When the Spanish arrived in Peru in 1532, they encountered the largest empire of the New World, a realm covering more than 1,800,000 km² (about 700,000 square miles), which included much of present-day Ecuador, all of Peru and Bolivia, and parts of Argentina and Chile (Wilson 1999). **Tawantinsuyu** ("The Four Parts Together"), the Inca name for their domain, was an empire of more than 10 million people. A highly organized state machine ruled without the aid of a formal writing system, although *quipu*, a system of knotted cords, served for record keeping (D'Altroy 2002). As with the Aztecs in Mesoamerica, Spanish records have provided a more detailed picture of life under the Inca system than was available for any previous state in South America.

## Cuzco: The Inca Capital

**Cuzco** was the political, economic, and ritual center of the Inca world. It was a city of monumental stone temples, plazas, and palaces and houses for Inca royalty and the Inca elite. The capital city had two main sections: a central core of royal palaces and religious complexes, and outer suburbs that were home to lesser Inca elites and lords of conquered provinces. Straight but narrow roads, many paved with stone, divided the city into unevenly sized blocks. Rulers (both living and dead) and nobles had country residences in the agriculturally rich zone that extended almost 60 km (40 miles) beyond the city in the Urubamba River valley (D'Altroy 2002).

The Cuzco city plan was in the shape of a puma whose head was the massive fortress of Saqsawaman, overlooking the city. The distinctive Inca stone architecture of Saqsawaman suggests that it may have served ritual as well as military purposes: The fortress was built of gigantic stone blocks, some of which people had hauled from nearby quarries, others from a quarry 35 km (22 miles) away (Wilson 1999).

The central Awkaypata plaza, which today lies beneath modern Cuzco's Plaza de Armas, was surrounded by monumental buildings and had a system of underground water channels. Great walls of dressed stone masonry, so carefully shaped that blocks fitted tightly and securely together without any mortar, enclosed royal and religious buildings. Awkaypata was the ceremonial theater of Cuzco, where on special occasions the mummies of past rulers were displayed and feted (Wilson 1999).

Spanish accounts record the splendor and richness of the city. The focal point of religious buildings must have been the Qorikancha, or Golden Temple—today the location of the Santo Domingo monastery, which is still partly surrounded by remains of the original outer Inca wall. The Qorikancha complex was a place of gold, silver, and precious stones. Its walls were covered with gold plate and its rooms contained sumptuous images of deities; in its famed garden were life-sized representations of plants, birds, animals, and people, all made in precious metals. The Spanish invaders rapidly dismantled and removed the temple's riches, including 700 gold plates, each about 0.5 m (1.6 feet) long and weighing 2 kg (4.4 pounds) (D'Altroy 2002). Much about the Inca capital remains unknown as it was destroyed by Spanish construction, fires, and earthquake damage.

**Inca**
The empire that controlled much of western South America in the fifteenth century, up to the Spanish conquest.

**Tawantinsuyu**
The name the Inca used for their empire, meaning "The Four Parts Together."

**Cuzco**
The political, economic, and ritual center of the Inca empire.

## The Inca Road System

The extraordinary prowess of Inca engineering is evident in the Inca road system, which emanated from Cuzco to all corners of the empire. Road construction was not an Inca innovation; as with most Inca technology, however, the Inca improved on earlier development, in this case the Wari road system. The Inca network of 25,000 km (15,500 miles) of roads traversed mountains, valleys, and coastal regions, facilitating swift movement of goods, military units, and couriers. Large roads were paved in stone, and walls, wooden posts, or stone markers often indicated their trajectory. Smaller roads were dirt, sand, or grass tracks. A drainage system prevented roads from getting waterlogged; stone bridges or floating reeds allowed travel across marshy areas, and spectacular rope suspension bridges up to 45 m (150 feet) long hung across deep chasms (D'Altroy 2002; von Hagen and Morris 1998).

Inca stone wall at Saqsawaman, near Cuzco. Consider the work required to quarry, transport, and work the stone blocks and then to build the walls. Can you cite any parallels elsewhere in the ancient world?

Hundreds of *tampu*, small roadside buildings at regular intervals along the roads, provided rest houses. These were particularly useful for state couriers and facilitated the rapid transfer of messages from courier to courier. Spanish chroniclers noted that the couriers could cover 240 km (150 miles) in a day and could transmit messages from Cuzco to Quito in a week—faster than the Spanish themselves could travel. Travelers rested and goods were stored at large administrative centers situated about four or five days' travel apart (Wilson 1999). This impressive system enabled the rulers to keep abreast of events throughout the empire. Furthermore, the road system served as a propaganda tool; together with other monumental structures and technological developments, it emphasized Inca might and power.

## Conquest, Integration, and Organization

The Inca expanded their empire by means of both diplomacy and conquest. Each of the four main regions of the empire consisted of smaller regions whose borders often coincided with the territorial boundaries of conquered groups. The Inca emperor headed not only the state but also the state religion and the imperial army. He had a close group of advisors in Cuzco to whom provincial governors were accountable. In general, lords of conquered areas continued as local rulers, but Inca nobles held the most important government positions. Once the Inca had conquered an area, they set in place their own style of architecture and material culture in large centers but tolerated rural traditions. They typically moved a quarter to a third of a newly conquered population to a different region; and often they moved entire loyal communities to newly conquered areas or regions of potential trouble (a process known as *mitmaqkuna*). Resettlement helped prevent rebellions and relocated specialists to areas where the state required their services (D'Altroy 2002; Wilson 1999).

One of the main duties of provincial officials was to conduct the regular census of births, deaths, and marriages in order to control and organize the tax duties that people paid through compulsory labor (called *mit'a*). The Inca employed *mit'a* labor to build and maintain roads and bridges, to farm and tend camelid herds, and to work in mines, in the military, and in textile production. Inca officials supervised the exploitation of

An example of Inca terraces at Pisac between Cuzco and Machu Picchu. Was terrace technology an Inca invention?

copper, gold, and tin—materials used only for state purposes—in mines throughout the realm. Textiles were highly prized for day-to-day needs as well as for presentation as gifts on special occasions and in diplomacy (a tradition that preceded Inca times). Indeed, Spanish chroniclers noted the extraordinary quality of Inca textiles, declaring that they surpassed those made in Spain. Large centers had specialist textile production compounds where women, chosen from throughout the empire, lived their lives weaving for the ruler (D'Altroy 2002; Morris and von Hagen 1993; von Hagen and Morris 1998).

## Agriculture and Pastoralism

Maize and camelids were important parts of Inca life and ritual. Maize was a status item—particularly maize beer, or *chicha*, of which enormous amounts were stored in special containers and drunk at ceremonies. In order to put as much land as possible under maize agriculture, the Inca built stone-faced terraces on slopes and developed a system of irrigation canals; both of these are still visible today. Camelid herders raised vast herds of animals for transport, wool, leather, and especially sacrifice. Numerous camelid corrals found around Cuzco testify to the importance of these animals for the state machine (Rostworowski and Morris 1998).

## State Warehouses

Spanish sources describe the great range of food and produce stored in the thousands of state warehouses, called *qollqa*, throughout the Inca empire. Warehouses stood along the road network, in large administrative centers, in Inca towns, and around state farms. "These storehouses were always kept full," said one account. "There was a large amount of maize, quinoa, . . . dried potatoes, beans, and other vegetables; ample amounts of dried meat from llamas, deer, and vicuñas; different kinds of clothing made from wool, cotton, and feathers; shoes. . . , arms . . . to supply the soldiers when they moved from one place to another, and a large amount of all other things that were sent from throughout the kingdom as tribute to the king . . ." (Cobo 1979, 221–222). Well-built storehouses in the highlands kept organic goods cool during the heat of the day and protected them from night frosts. Produce, used to feed state workers and to fulfill the needs of Inca hospitality, was tightly controlled by state officials who kept records on *quipu*. And as with the road network, the state warehouse system also served as a propaganda tool by demonstrating the power of the Inca (Morris and von Hagen 1993).

## Inca Ideology

**Inti**
The Inca sun god.

The Inca worshipped numerous gods, the most important of which were Wiraqocha, the Creator God, and above all **Inti**, the Sun God. Inca rulers claimed descent from Inti,

**Machu Picchu**
Inca town in the Andean mountains above the Urubamba Valley, near Cuzco.

thus appropriating divine authority for their power. All major centers had sun temples where ceremonies dedicated to Inti took place on a regular basis to ensure agricultural productivity and the well-being of the empire. Gold was the color of the Sun God, silver that of his wife, the Moon Goddess. Points in the natural landscape such as mountains, caves, rivers, streams, or rocks held religious significance for the Inca and were the focus of ritual activity. The Inca also observed the night sky, giving names to stars, constellations, and the dark patterns between stars in the Milky Way (Bauer and Dearborn 1995). However, comets and eclipses were poorly understood and a cause of fear.

Life under the Inca, as in earlier Andean societies, was inseparable from ritual and ceremony. Rituals to honor deities took place throughout the agricultural cycle for a multitude of reasons—among them the well-being of emperors both living and dead, the success of the empire and its people, and victory in military campaigns. Sacrifice formed an important element of ritual; and although at times the Inca sacrificed humans, they more commonly sacrificed prime camelids and the finest goods, both in vast quantities. Adult and child sacrifice occurred on particularly solemn occasions, such as the accession or death of a ruler. Sites at high altitudes were part of the Inca sacred landscape and were sanctified through sacrifice, sometimes of children. Such sites are important archaeologically, as the extreme cold acts as a preserving agent. For example, the bodies of two young girls and a boy were discovered at Nevado Ampato in Peru, a shrine almost 6,300 m (20,670 feet) above sea level. Dressed in rich textiles, the victims had taken a cocktail of *chicha* and coca leaves before death and had been buried with small statuettes, coca leaves, and maize (D'Altroy 2002).

## Machu Picchu

Mention of "the Inca" is more likely to evoke images of **Machu Picchu** than any other Inca achievement. In a spectacular setting 100 m (330 feet) above the Urubamba River and surrounded by mountain peaks, Machu Picchu is the most famous of Inca sites. Present-day tourists still follow the Inca road that linked the town with smaller surrounding settlements. Machu Picchu is a good example of a carefully planned Inca

The Inca settlement at Machu Picchu. How do you imagine the people of Machu Picchu perceived their world?

town with a plaza, temples, residences, and stone water channels and cisterns; it could have housed a population of up to 1,000 people. Produce grown on terraces around the town would have met the needs of its residents but could not have produced a surplus destined for the storehouses and redistribution center at Cuzco. Thus, Machu Picchu was not a community of farmers. It may have been a royal residence (D'Altroy 2002), although the location, quality of construction, and difficulty of access suggest that it was imbued with symbolic significance. In any event, the function of Machu Picchu, which remains elusive, appears to have been more than residential (D'Altroy 2002; Morris and von Hagen 1993). Today Machu Picchu is a UNESCO world heritage site, but its conservation is threatened by the vast numbers of tourists who visit the site yearly. The situation is being closely monitored by UNESCO to ensure that the site is not destroyed.

# Concluding Comments on New World States and Empires

The states and empires we have explored in this chapter share similarities with one another and with states in the Old World (discussed in Chapter 11); large populations, craft specialization, record keeping (inferred for those states without a formal system of writing or recording), levying of taxes, monumental architechture, trade networks, social stratification, the development of sciences, a state ideology, and, in the case of the Aztec and Inca empires and possibly of some of their predecessors, a state army. The size of the Aztec and Inca empires surpassed that of all earlier states in the region, as did their degree of centralized control and organization of the populace. Ideology was clearly a powerful mechanism of political and social control in ancient Mesoamerica and South America. Although the defeat of both Aztecs and Incas was due partly to superior Spanish weapons and different approaches to combat, it was also due to aid given the Spanish by discontented native groups; and, in the case of the Inca, probably to the chaos that followed the breakdown of native organization once centralized leadership had been removed. Within a short time the Spanish invaders had looted the Aztec and Inca empires, spread diseases that killed millions of the native population, and brought the surviving peoples under subjugation.

This chapter covered the development of early states in Mesoamerica and South America. Increasing social, economic, political, and ideological complexity culminated in the rise of the Aztec and Inca empires.

■ The earliest states in Mesoamerica and South America evolved from chiefdom societies governing villages and towns in which growing complexity in social, economic, and ceremonial spheres is evident.

■ The Olmec consisted of different groups sharing similar cultural attributes. Evidence of social stratification, long-distance trade, hierarchical settlement patterns, and monumental buildings exists at San Lorenzo and La Venta, but there remains debate over whether these were capitals of an Olmec state, given that there is no evidence of administration officials, armies, or warfare.

page 385

■ Teotihuacan was one of the largest cities in the ancient world. It was a carefully planned city with a ceremonial and administrative central core, workshop areas, marketplaces, and more than 2,000 apartment compounds. Although Teotihuacan's influence was widespread among its contemporaneous states and in later empires in Mesoamerica, the nature of its leadership remains uncertain.

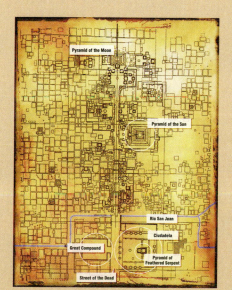

■ Maya city-states show clear evidence of stratification, fulltime craft specialists, centralized government, defined territory, monumental architecture, state ideology, settlement hierarchy, long-distance trade, writing and notation, and military power. Inscriptions on stone record Maya dynasties and indicate the constant vying for power among Maya polities.

page 388

■ The Moche area of northern Peru may have included many independent principalities, each with its own ruler, that were united by shared religious iconography and political alliances. Artistic production was highly skilled, particularly in metalwork, pottery, and textiles. Moche iconography, burials, and skeletal evidence reveal the importance of ritual warrior combat and sacrifice.

■ Tiwanaku, the highest urban center in the Americas, was the capital of the Tiwanaku state that developed around Lake Titicaca. In time Tiwanaku influence expanded through a mixture of military conquest, colonization, and reciprocal trade relations, perhaps presaging the emergence of empire.

■ Wari was contemporaneous with Tiwanaku; like Tiwanaku, the Wari state expanded beyond its immediate borders, setting up provincial centers that were standardized in layout, suggesting a strong controlling authority. The Wari state established a road system linking its provincial centers and developed the *quipu* recording system, both later adopted by the Incas.

■ Spanish chronicles provide an extra source of information on the Aztecs and the Incas. Aztec writings also cover that empire's history; but there is no equivalent for the Incas, who did not have a system of writing.

■ The Aztec empire controlled many, but not all, of the city-states in Mesoamerica through a system of indirect governance. Local rulers continued to rule but had to pay tribute to the Aztec capital, Tenochtitlan. The extent and quantity of tribute goods in Tenochtitlan, as well as the city itself, amazed the Spanish conquerors, but the common practice of human sacrifice appalled them. Human sacrifice was seen by the Aztecs as a divine requirement, but it was also a symbol of Aztec power.

■ The Inca empire was the largest empire in the

page 416

Americas. The Inca built provincial centers, rest houses, warehouses, and an extensive network of roads that allowed swift movement of goods, soldiers, and couriers throughout the empire. Inca accountants used *quipu* to keep detailed records for the central authority. Spanish narratives record the splendor and richness of Cuzco, the Inca capital, the like of which they had never witnessed. As with Tenochtitlan, the Spanish removed most of Cuzco's wonders as booty.

## KEY WORDS

Akapana, 402
altiplano, 402
anthropomorphic, 399
Aztec, 408
bloodletting, 387
celt, 385
Cerro Baúl, 408
Cerro Blanco, 399
Chavín de Huántar, 398
chicha, 400
chinampas, 409
codices, 408
Copan, 396
cranial deformation, 406
Cuzco, 414
El Niño, 399
El Paraíso, 398
empire, 409
epigrapher, 396

Gateway God, 406
glyph, 395
Great Temple, 409
guano, 399
Hieroglyphic Stairway, 397
Huaca del Sol and Huaca de la
    Luna, 399
Inca, 414
Inti, 416
isotope analyses, 390
Kaminaljuyu, 390
La Venta, 386
Machu Picchu, 417
Maya, 391
Mesoamerica, 384
mit'a, 399
Moche, 398
Olmec, 384
Pikillaqta, 407

Pochteca, 411
quetzal, 386
quipu, 408
raised fields, 403
San Lorenzo, 385
Sipán, 400
social stratification, 411
stelae, 395
Street of the Dead, 387
Tawantinsuyu, 414
Tenochtitlan, 409
Teotihuacan, 387
Tikal, 395
Tiwanaku, 402
Tlatelolco, 411
tuff, 396
Wari, 407

## SUGGESTED READING

Benson, E. P., and B. de la Fuente, eds. *Olmec of Ancient Mexico*. New York: Abrams, 1996. This series of papers covers the Olmec world in some detail and includes beautiful photographs of Olmec artifacts.

Cowgill, G. L. "State and Society at Teotihuacan, Mexico." *Annual Review of Anthropology* 26 (1997): 129–161. Cowgill reviews the literature on Teotihuacan and provides a good synopsis of the state.

D'Altroy, T. N. *The Incas*. Malden, MA: Blackwell, 2002. D'Altroy combines Spanish chronicles and archaeology to provide a well-researched and highly readable synthesis of the Incas.

Pillsbury, J., ed. *Moche Art and Archaeology in Ancient Peru*. Washington, DC: National Gallery of Art/Yale University Press, 2001. An excellent compilation of papers offering exciting information on Moche ideology and society.

Scarre, C., ed. *The Human Past: World Prehistory and the Development of Human Societies*. New York: Thames & Hudson, (2005.) This book provides a highly informed and well-balanced summary of world prehistory. Each chapter, written by a specialist, covers a general period and region. An excellent supplement for those who want to know more about a particular period.

Sharer, R. J. *The Ancient Maya*. 5th ed. Stanford, CA: Stanford University Press, 1994. A comprehensive, well-written account of Maya society and an excellent, readable introduction to Maya studies.

Smith, M. E. *The Aztecs*. Malden, MA/Oxford: Blackwell, 2003. This extremely readable introduction to the Aztecs has chapters organized under specific topics to give the reader easy access to particular aspects of Aztec life.

von Hagen, A., and C. Morris. *Cities of the Ancient Andes*. London: Thames & Hudson, 1998. A well-illustrated introductory volume that provides an outline of the Andean environment and the emergence of cities, states, and empires.

Chapter **14** Primates Today

■ **PRIMATOLOGY: BIOLOGY, PSYCHOLOGY, AND BIOANTHROPOLOGY**
A Brief History of Primatology • In the Field, Lab, and Zoo • Primate Taxonomy and Evolution Revisited • Primate Cognition

■ **CASE STUDIES OF CONTEMPORARY PRIMATES**

■ **CONTEMPORARY TARSIERS**

■ **CONTEMPORARY PROSIMIANS**
Sifakas

■ **CONTEMPORARY MONKEYS**
Old World Monkeys • New World Monkeys

■ **CONTEMPORARY APES**
Gibbons and Siamangs (the Small Apes) • The Large Apes

■ **HIGHLIGHT 14.1:** *Checking Out Chimpanzee and Orangutan Culture*

■ **HIGHLIGHT 14.2:** *Chimpanzee Language Acquisition*

■ **HIGHLIGHT 14.3:** *In the Field with Those Sexy Bonobos*

■ **ENDANGERED PRIMATES**

■ **CHAPTER SUMMARY**

▲
**Photo above:** A New World monkey (capuchin) at home in a tree

Chapter 5 focused on the evolution of primates from the primate stem group, hypothesized to have existed some 63 myr ago, to the last split in the primate tree, between pongids and hominids, at 7 to 6 myr ago. It was necessary to introduce the order Primates before discussing the evolution of primates. That brief introduction discussed primates' global distribution (see Figure 5.3), ecological context, vital statistics, locomotion (from vertical leaping to quadrupedalism), variable diets, activity patterns (ranging from diurnal to nocturnal), social organization (from pairs to huge groups), and political organization (from single-level local groups to three levels). The major lesson from that discussion is that primates vary considerably by taxonomy, location, anatomy, morphology, and behavior. Because primates inhabit every type of tropical environment, including rainforest, woodland, shrubbed savanna, and semi-desert, and temperate and subalpine areas as well, they show considerable variation in all aspects of their lives, including the food they eat, the reproductive strategies they engage in, and many other basic behaviors.

This chapter uses case studies to focus on contemporary primates and show how studying them aids understanding of humans and human evolution. (It's necessary to keep in mind that we share a common ancestry only 6 myr ago with chimpanzees and bonobos and perhaps gorillas.) Each case study section will give you a glimpse of a day in the life of a group of primates by discussing the geographic distribution, ecology, diet, social organization, and general, everyday behaviors of that group. First, however, you'll learn about the field of primatology and review primate taxonomy and evolution; then a section explores primate cognition.

The term **contemporary primates** refers to living groups of primates, including humans. In this chapter, however, for convenience that term or the term *primates* often excludes humans and refers only to nonhuman primates.

There is an obvious evolutionary link between contemporary humans and other contemporary primates: They all share a common ancestry. Because humans today are a single species, experts cannot compare multiple modern hominid species for insights into the biological forces that were involved in human evolution, much less map out the major steps. But because of the link between humans and all other primates, bioanthropologists often use contemporary nonhuman primate anatomy, physiology, genetics, and behavior to help explain causation, process, function, and evolution in humans (Hinde 1986). The comparative method is used for any study of primates, whether the researchers' interest is in anatomy or behavior. Bioanthropologists also study primates for insights into what it is that makes humans different. Are we really so different from our closest primate "cousins"—chimpanzees, bonobos, and possibly gorillas? We may share more than 99 percent of our genes with these other species, but any comparison of anatomy, morphology, or behavior shows there is a lot that differentiates "us" from "them." One of the aims of bioanthropologists is to show the ways in which each primate species is unique. But as anthropologists, they put the focus on humans.

It was common until the 1980s for a single species of primate to be used as a model for hominid or human evolution. Researchers once used baboons in this way because baboons' environment today is similar to what scientists assume to have been the early hominid environment; and chimpanzees or bonobos are still sometimes used, because they had a common ancestry with hominids until 6 myr ago. Other than generating hypotheses to be tested against universal primate traits or the fossil/environmental record, however, such single-species models are now regarded as questionable at best (Potts 1987). So, a word of warning: No matter how tempting it may be to draw parallels, no contemporary primate species can directly represent any human evolutionary stage, because nonhuman primates have had just as long an independent evolution as humans. On the optimistic side, the study of any or all contemporary primates can generate hypotheses about human evolution. This is the strength of primate studies.

**Nonhuman primates** may be human "cousins," but they are collateral, not ancestral/descendant relatives. Given that 250,000 generations have passed since humans

**contemporary primates**
All primate groups living today, including humans.

**nonhuman primates**
All primates, contemporary or fossil, that are not hominids; includes prosimians, tarsiers, monkeys, and apes.

*Figure 14.1*

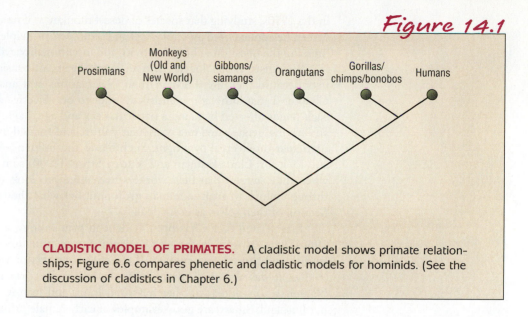

Prosimians  Monkeys (Old and New World)  Gibbons/siamangs  Orangutans  Gorillas/chimps/bonobos  Humans

**CLADISTIC MODEL OF PRIMATES.**   A cladistic model shows primate relationships; Figure 6.6 compares phenetic and cladistic models for hominids. (See the discussion of cladistics in Chapter 6.)

shared a common ancestor with any other species, instead of first or even third cousins, other primates would be 250,000th "cousins" to humans at the closest. See Figure 14.1 for a primate cladogram that shows the relationships among the groups. (Cladistics was defined in Chapter 6.)

# Primatology: Biology, Psychology, and Bioanthropology

**Primatology**, or the study of primates, is not exclusively the domain of biological anthropologists. Many **biologists** focus on primate species just as on any other species of animal: In theory, studying Japanese macaques is no different from studying Japanese quail. Biologists describe, compare, and trace the evolution of any species by observing its morphological, genetic, and behavioral traits as well as the environmental context in which it lives today. **Psychologists** also study primates, focusing on how they learn as well as on other cognitive traits. Biological anthropologists compare the various kinds of primate traits to understand human evolution and modern human variation. The differences among biologists, psychologists, and biological anthropologists are often blurred; each discipline brings different questions and insights into play, and there are many areas in which primatologists from two or more disciplines cooperate to investigate problems. Often other scientists, such as medical doctors, become involved in primate research—for example, on projects related to HIV in Africa.

At one time it could be said that bioanthropologists focused on "what" questions (what is a primate; what is unique to humans), psychologists asked "how" questions (how do individual monkeys differ; how do apes recognize themselves in mirrors), and biologists asked "why" questions (why are there connections between particular social structures and particular ecologies; why doesn't sexual dimorphism correlate with monogamy). But the process, function, and evolutionary aspects of primatology are now so interwoven that it is often hard to tell which field or lab worker has been trained in which discipline (McGrew 2001). Sometimes scientists are trained in one field but take on the perspective of another under particular circumstances. Robin Dunbar, for example, is a psychologist by training but did a lengthy study of the Ethiopian gelada "baboon"

**primatology**
The scientific study of any or all of the 250+ species of contemporary primates.

**biologists**
Scientists who study primates the same way they study any group or species of animal and who are interested in the animals' evolution and their modern morphology, genetics, and behavior.

**psychologists**
Scientists who study primate cognition and who are interested in how primates learn and in the similarities and differences between human and primate cognitive abilities.

in the 1970s, studying that species of desert monkey as if he were a biologist. Later in his career, he applied both psychological and biological principles to human evolution by addressing the question of how creativity and intentionality evolved.

Biologists, psychologists, and anthropologists all consider themselves to be scientists because they use TSM in their observations and analyses. But remember from Chapter 2 that although scientists attempt to be objective and unbiased in their work, each one is affected by being a particular sex and age, having had different experiences, and having been reared in a particular culture and trained in a specific field and under a particular intellectual paradigm. Such biases can influence what primatologists look at and look for. Linda Fedigan and Shirley Strum (2000) sum up the effects of our biases when they suggest that field workers may intend to look at primates as a kind of lens through which to analyze human evolution, but what they end up seeing is often a reflection of themselves as individuals.

Bias related to sex has been evident in primatology, as in many fields. Before the 1960s, women were in the extreme minority in primatology, among those doing the studies and those being studied. If a female investigator was directly involved in field studies, it was almost always as an appendage to her primatologist husband. Prudence Napier (who worked with her husband, John) and Jeanne Altmann (who worked with her husband, Stuart) are good examples of early female primatologists who stood "in the shadow" of their husbands. Jane Goodall was an exception, but even she began her study of chimpanzees only after Louis Leakey paved her way. Leakey was also largely responsible for getting Dian Fossey and Birute Galdikas established for their early work on gorillas and orangutans. It was just not typical for females to do independent field work before the 1960s. And regarding the subjects of that field research, there was sex-based bias as well: 50 percent of the animals in each population were usually being ignored in favor of studying the big adult males. Eventually the male primatologists admitted they were biased toward observing males because they didn't believe females were doing anything very important (except having offspring). Today, both male and female primatologists study both sexes of the species they are interested in.

The cultural background of the primatologist and the school he or she was trained in also have an impact on what is studied and how. Chapter 2 mentioned that Japanese primatologists engage mainly in description, claiming not to have enough information to be able to analyze their findings. The Japanese primatological journal *Primates* is almost completely descriptive, whereas other primatological journals include both descriptions and comparative or analytical studies. It is recognized that there is a cultural, paradigmatic difference between Japanese and Western researchers that affects what they study and how they study it.

Some primatologists are interested exclusively in the study of primate behavior, or observable outward conduct. Neither the cognition of nonhuman primates (what they know) nor their emotions can be studied easily, so behavior becomes the default. Primates have thought processes (cognition in the human sense), but it is exceedingly difficult to know what they are. Also primates show emotional states, and observers can often see what stimulus provoked a given response, but the exact nature of the emotions is not known. Many of the similarities between human and nonhuman primate emotional states are so remarkable that it is sometimes impossible not to anthropomorphize. As Jane Goodall suggested after studying chimpanzees for 30 years, "chimpanzees experience emotions similar to those which in ourselves we label pleasure, joy, sorrow, anger, boredom, and so on" (1990, 16). Sue Savage-Rumbaugh, who trained a bonobo named Kanzi for more than 15 years, beginning when Kanzi was six months old, would agree that bonobos exhibit considerable humanlike cognition as well as humanlike emotions (Savage-Rumbaugh et al. 1998). It is best to couch any description of what looks like the same emotion in terms that clearly stipulate the degree of anthropomorphism and cognition being used, however. For example, it's appropriate to say that "the monkey behaved *as if* it knew the snake was poisonous," not "the monkey screamed in terror *because* it knew the snake was poisonous." Anthropologists can ask fellow humans about what they know, about their attitudes and values (their cognition), and about their feelings (emotions); scientifically, however, they can do no more than *observe* the *behavior* of non-human primates. Scientists can observe and describe behavior relatively objectively (to the extent that they avoid bias) and can quantify and compare primate behavior, and, given that the biological basis of behavior evolves, they can reconstruct the evolution of primate behavior.

The focus of this book is humans, so primates are of importance here mainly because their study is applicable to humans. Bioanthropologists applaud the biological and psychological study of primates—but unless knowledge about primates can be applied to humans, it isn't anthropological. Thus, the main purpose of this chapter's discussion is to provide insights into human evolution and the nature of our unique species.

## A Brief History of Primatology

Robert Yerkes is usually cited as the founder of primatology, though he was a psychologist who studied primates only in zoos and labs in the 1920s and 1930s. If defined as the study of primates in general, primatology has a long history. Aristotle was interested in and mentioned monkeys, probably because he saw some that had been brought to Europe by early travelers. Marco Polo described "small, strange, manlike creatures" after his return to Italy from the Far East and was probably referring to gibbons. In the eighteenth century Linnaeus combined monkeys and apes with humans into a single order (though he included bats and sloths as well) (Ankel-Simons 2000). Many nineteenth-century amateurs studied primates in their backyards, for example, baboons in South Africa, and though books on primates were published, none was written by a professional scientist until the late 1920s.

Before 1950, only six field studies of primates had been undertaken: three by professional scientists (all psychologists) and three by amateurs. One of the more interesting early studies was that of R. L. Garner, an amateur American zoologist who spent 112 days in a cage in Gabon waiting for chimpanzees and gorillas to walk by! The first professional field observer was Ray Carpenter, an American psychologist, who studied howler monkeys in Panama in 1934. Four years later, Carpenter studied gibbons in Thailand for a short period of time and then stocked an island near Puerto Rico with about 500 rhesus monkeys transplanted from India. His study sites in Panama and Puerto Rico remain ongoing research centers, providing valuable multi-generational data. On the other side of the Atlantic Ocean, Sir Solly Zuckerman, a physician and anatomist, studied hamadryas baboons almost exclusively at the London Zoo (with nine days of observation in the wild) in the 1920s and 1930s. His conclusions about the baboons were almost totally incorrect; the crowded zoo conditions likely made them behave differently from wild hamadryas. Zuckerman had numerous conflicts with Carpenter over the relative value of zoo and field studies (Sussman 2000).

The intellectual climate changed after 1950, which spurred both biologists and bioanthropologists to join with psychologists in studying primates; the disagreements of Carpenter and Zuckerman pushed many of these scientists into the field rather than zoos. Once the Piltdown man with his "big" brain was shown to be a fake, even small-brained primates, such as prosimians and monkeys, became acceptable to study. Also, in 1960 advocates of the new anthropology proclaimed that humans evolved from Old World primates, opening the doors to studying all primates. Funded by the National Science Foundation and other organizations, hundreds of bioanthropologists, biologists, and psychologists began to study baboons in Africa, langurs in India, and lemurs in Madagascar, among others. Studies of other primates, many in-depth studies that took several years and many shorter studies, followed, all in the Western tradition.

The Japanese school of primatology began in 1948 when two ecologists spotted some Japanese macaques while they were doing field observations of wild horses. The Japanese Monkey Center was established in 1956, and the journal *Primates* was published in Japanese a year later and in English two years later.

**field studies**
Studies that observe primates or other animals in their natural habitat with a minimum of human interference.

**zoo studies**
Studies of primates or other animals that reside in captivity in order to supplement findings from the field or observe behavior not seen in the wild.

In addition to emphasizing description rather than explanation, Japanese primatologists are more willing to be anthropomorphic in interpreting behavior than Westerners are, and they train young students by sending them out in the field without preconceptions of how the primate they are to study should behave or even how to collect data (Dolhinow and Fuentes 2000).

Japanese primatologists have gone beyond studying monkeys in their own backyard and have studied gorillas, langurs, chimpanzees, bonobos, orangutans, and lemurs, among others. The Japanese tend to regard long-term studies lasting 20 to 30 years as vital to understanding primate populations. The Western and Japanese traditions have different, but complementary, research goals (Asquith 2000).

## In the Field, Lab, and Zoo

Primatologists work in the field under natural conditions, in zoos, and in laboratories, depending on the nature of their research.

**Field studies** were popular and well funded by government granting agencies, universities, and private foundations from the 1950s through the 1970s, and many primate species were well studied for the first time during that period. Not all 250+ species have been studied in their natural habitats, because some are difficult to observe; even so, more than 100 solid field studies have been published and can be used for comparative purposes. Investigators continue to find new primate species periodically, mostly in the high canopy of South American jungles. Two new species of arboreal titi monkeys were named in Brazil in the summer of 2002, and three new species of mouse lemur were discovered in 2000 on Madagascar. All of the modern apes and Old World monkeys have been well studied, and most of the prosimians and larger New World monkeys as well. At a few field stations primates have been studied since the late 1930s with a minimum of human interference, as is the case with the howlers and the transplanted rhesus monkeys first studied by Ray Carpenter. Jane Goodall's chimpanzee study at Gombe, Tanzania, began in 1960 and is another long-term primarily behavioral study. Other long-term chimpanzee studies at Mahale (Tanzania), the Budongo Forest (Uganda), and Kibale (Uganda) in East Africa and in Congo and the Taï Forest (Ivory Coast) in West Africa total several hundred years of chimpanzee watching. Field studies vary in the amount of human interference they involve, from none to a lot. Because any interference has the ability to change behavior, field workers must make trade-offs. Observing totally natural behavior means staying concealed; getting closer to the study subjects means taking the chance of affecting behavior. Unfortunately, current funding is usually limited to small-scale projects focusing on one sex or age group and one morphological trait or behavior.

Dian Fossey is shown here with mountain gorillas. Note how close she is sitting to these seemingly dangerous animals. Would her proximity to the animals affect their behavior?

**Zoo studies** have advantages and disadvantages. Obviously, the subjects cannot run away, cannot turn and attack (unless the investigator is in the cage with the primate), can be easily viewed, and are available at the convenience of the investigator. Zoo studies can often supply details to supplement initial findings in the field and can often add a range of behavior not observed in the wild. On the other hand, the mere fact of human presence may change the behavior of any animal species. Also, because the animals are provisioned, they do not spend time finding food and often become inactive because of boredom or exhibit aberrant behavior. They are not living in their natural habitat.

**Laboratory studies** are less expensive than field studies, but confinement can affect the animals. Some very specific studies have been extremely fruitful, such as the classic 1962 study of rhesus macaques and socialization in which Harry Harlow experimentally demonstrated that artificial "mothers" covered with terry cloth were more attractive to very young monkeys than those that dispensed milk but were bare metal. And Richard Wrangham studied two captive groups of chimpanzees under laboratory conditions, carefully recording their "pant-hoot" sound patterns to see if individuals learned the proper sounds after joining the group (Vogel 1999). Experiments that need careful monitoring or attention to some fine detail are best done under laboratory conditions; but again, both confinement and human presence may affect behavior.

## Primate Taxonomy and Evolution Revisited

Chapter 5 introduced a primate taxonomy (refer to Figure 5.2) and considered primate evolution in some detail. There are newer taxonomic schemes, but we are adhering to the traditional taxonomy, with one change, because of lack of consensus on newer classifications. To review, the order Primates consists of three suborders: the Prosimii, the Tarsioidea, and the Anthropoidea. Primates likely evolved from some generalized mammalian group by 63 myr ago. The prosimian lineage was the first to split from the more generalized early primates, by 60 myr ago. Old and New World monkeys split from the more generalized primate group about 30 myr ago and Asian apes about 14 myr ago. The last common ancestral group included the ancestors of all African apes and humans. Either gorillas split off at 8 myr ago, leaving the hominoid ancestors of chimpanzees, bonobos, and humans, or the ancestors of all African apes and humans were in a single evolutionary lineage until 6 myr ago, when three separate lineages evolved. The chronology of evolution reviewed here is reflected in the order of the chapter's case studies of groups of contemporary primates.

## Primate Cognition

Before turning to case studies of specific primate groups, let's look at the cognitive abilities of contemporary primates. This section discusses what cognition is, where cognitive abilities "reside," how anthropologists study them, whether such abilities follow an evolutionary track, and what cognitive similarities and differences primates show.

Anthropologists define human cognition as the shared and learned knowledge that people have in different cultures; human cognition thus differs from one culture to another. It involves shared knowledge about how to make a living, how to get along with your in-laws, what ancestors to worship, and such mental constructs as rules, beliefs, and values. Cognition is what generates human behavior. Anthropologists discover what the rules, beliefs, values, and knowledge in a specific culture are by asking local informants. They can observe only the results of cognition, but talking about the rules helps connect them with the resultant behavior.

But what about cognition in dogs or monkeys? Do dogs or monkeys know things? Of course, but how do we know this? By observing what they do. Can we talk with them about what they know? Of course not, and this is what makes studies of cognition in nonhumans so difficult. Often researchers overinterpret the behavior they observe, anthropomorphize about what they observe, or are totally puzzled by certain behaviors.

For the most part, it is comparative psychologists who try to understand nonhuman cognition. These psychologists are in general agreement about what questions to ask and what kinds of experiments to perform to try to get answers to those questions, but

**laboratory studies**
Studies of primates or other animals conducted in research facilities and often involving experimentation that must be tightly controlled and requires monitoring.

they are not always in agreement about interpreting their observations. What is merely imitation to one psychologist is problem solving to another.

Since African apes are the primates that are most similar genetically to humans, most experimental work on cognitive abilities has been done with chimpanzees. Baboons and capuchin monkeys are sometimes used in studies about the specific cognitive abilities of monkeys. Very little is known about the cognitive abilities of prosimians, colobines, or the smaller apes. Therefore, researchers must be careful about making sweeping evolutionary statements about all 250+ species of primates. They must also be careful about comparing results from studies of primates involving different contexts: Chimpanzees raised in a forest environment by their conspecifics behave differently from those raised under zoo conditions or reared by humans. Their behavior is not only different, but how they use their likely species-specific cognitive abilities differs as well (Tomasello and Call 1997).

Cognitive abilities arise mainly in the neocortex—the "thinking" part of the brain. This cognitive base can be traced throughout the primate lineage by looking at fossil endocrania as well as contemporary crania. In general, there is an increase in the size of the neocortex from prosimians to monkeys to apes to humans, so different cognitive abilities can be expected in these groups. Primate brains appear to be different both quantitatively (size) and qualitatively (which parts are larger or organized differently). As one example, the frontal cortex or frontal lobe in humans is considerably larger than in any other primate. There are dozens of other brain differences; thus, humans have unique cognitive abilities (Rilling 2006).

Comparative psychologists have done thousands of experiments; let's look at a few of these studies to compare certain cognitive abilities in primates: the ability to recognize self, the ability to perceive intentionality on the part of others, the ability to deceive, the ability to be altruistic and collaborate with conspecifics, and the ability to plan ahead.

In 1977, George Gallup experimented with many animal species to try to discover which ones have the ability to recognize self. To do this, he marked individuals under anesthesia with colored dye on parts of their bodies they could not normally see, then released them into a room with a mirror. Only apes looked in the mirror, saw the dye spots, and rubbed them or tried to remove them, thus showing that they recognized the image in the mirror as "self." Experiments with fish, birds, other mammals, and other primates showed they did not recognize themselves. Self-recognition implies self-knowledge and knowledge about others.

The ability to perceive intentionality on the part of others is another cognitive ability that has been well studied by comparative psychologists. Many anecdotes from the field were followed by controlled laboratory experiments. Deception is a form of intentionality; that is, telling lies is an intentional act. Not only do apes and monkeys appear to intentionally deceive conspecifics (and humans), so do cats and dogs; however, only apes have been shown to distinguish between malevolent and benign intentions (Byrne 1996).

In contrast to the cognitive ability to intentionally deceive is the ability to be altruistic and collaborate with others. Chimpanzees are well known to cooperatively hunt and kill monkeys and conspecifics, but is this the extent of their collaboration? A recent laboratory experiment shows that human-raised chimpanzees behaved altruistically, with no reward for themselves (Warneken and Tomasello 2006). Information on other species is still only anecdotal: For example, vervet monkeys emit three different calls when they perceive three different kinds of danger (snakes, eagles, and leopards) and only do so when they are with a group, even though calling might draw attention to themselves while warning others. Orangutans appear to cooperate toward a common goal at least occasionally. Capuchin monkeys do not (Boesch 2003). Whether prosimians or other monkeys cooperate for others' benefit is not known.

Evidence for the ability to plan ahead is difficult to establish because human investigators may overinterpret what they observe. But experiments suggest that bonobos, chimpanzees, and orangutans do plan ahead but that monkeys do not.

Related to cognitive abilities is personality. Many have wondered whether primates other than humans have personalities. The answer is yes. Individuality in nonhumans has only been studied seriously in the last 30 years, perhaps because humans wanted to be unique in this dimension. Individuality becomes personality when specific traits can be described and ascribed to different members of a species. One index of personality uses 12 descriptors, such as friendly, assertive, cautious, and jealous. A study based on this index of 59 baboons and chimpanzees in British zoos concluded that individuals not only had personalities but fell into personality types, just as humans do. The investigators defined Personality A and Personality B on the basis of their objective findings (Murray 2002).

How does the current, rather limited knowledge of primate cognition reflect the evolutionary perspective? Given the differences in the size of the brain and its organization across primate species, cognitive differences are logically expected. The cognitive ability to recognize self underlies intentionality and deception, and the abilities to cooperate and plan ahead depend to some extent on the ability to use one's imagination. Thus, there does appear to be some evolutionary pattern to these cognitive abilities. Does any cognitive ability separate humans from all other primates? Chimpanzees deceive, imitate, predict other's intentions, plan ahead, and even use imagination at times. We humans have all of these cognitive abilities and use them more fully, especially our ability to imagine what is not reality.

# Case Studies of Contemporary Primates

Every one of the 250+ species of contemporary primates is interesting to bioanthropologists in itself, but, in addition, each offers a glimpse of "what might have been" at some point during the 63 myr of primate evolution. For example, all primates have had to survive predator pressure, particularly in Africa, and observing contemporary primates reveals what they do (behaviorally) or how they have evolved (biologically) to cope with predators. Size is one major way to cope: either be so big that predators will look elsewhere for dinner or be so small that predators can't find you or look elsewhere for a bigger bit of food. Other ways to cope with predators are to be nocturnal, live in very large groups, move slowly so that predators don't notice you, have multiple offspring several times a year to keep your population numbers ahead of predation, and share infant care responsibilities with many other adults to help ensure the survival of your young. The primate lineage went through size changes, and many primates were or still are nocturnal. Many primates do live in large groups, lorises are very slow movers, and some primates have multiple births and several birthing seasons every year. Thus, observing contemporary primates' morphology and behavior gives many insights into the course of primate evolution.

In the following sections, each of the major taxonomic groups of primates is briefly surveyed and one species is documented in more detail, to gain insights into human evolution. Not all of the groups have the same extent of coverage because not all have been studied in the same depth. It is much easier to spend a year or two observing terrestrial anubis baboons in the Amboseli National Park in Kenya than trying to observe a species of monkey that stays in the top of the tree canopy in the jungle in Brazil and never comes to the ground. As a result, we know a lot about baboons, but precious little about those small and elusive Brazilian monkeys.

# Contemporary Tarsiers

Tarsiers (genus *Tarsius*) are something of an enigma: They share common ancestral traits with both prosimians and anthropoids, but they also show unique derived traits. Therefore, we place them in their own suborder. The Tarsioidea appear to have split from the early primate stem group about 58 myr ago, suggesting a long and successful evolution. The ancestral tarsiers share the following traits with prosimians:

- arboreal quadrupedalism
- huge eyes
- large mobile ears
- use of olfactory marking
- grooming claw and tooth comb

With the anthropoids, tarsiers share these ancestral traits:

- a dry nose (no rhinarium)
- eye sockets that are at least partially encased in bone
- lack of a membrane that anchors the upper lip

**We see tarsiers as a separate suborder, distinct from both prosimians and anthropoideans. Using the list in the text, what morphological traits can you identify in the tarsier shown here?**

Unique to tarsiers and likely derived are the following traits (Bearder 1986; Doyle and Martin 1974; Simons 1995):

- enlarged ankle bone and bone at back of foot (tarsals)
- an exclusively faunal diet of insects, lizards, and occasionally other vertebrates
- two toilet claws—not one—on each hind foot
- 34 teeth with a unique dental formula, having "lost" an incisor in the jaw but retaining it in the upper mouth; no other primate has asymmetrical numbers of incisors
- conical incisors
- fusion of the two bones in the lower leg, giving them the ability to jump as high as five meters (16 feet) almost straight up in the air
- like owls, the ability to turn their heads almost 180 degrees (Doyle and Martin 1974)

Tarsiers are found today only in the rainforests of Sulawesi (former Celebes), Sumatra, Borneo, and the Philippines, all islands near Southeast Asia. Depending on who is making the comparisons, there are between four and seven species. How tarsiers got to these islands is unknown; in mainland Southeast Asia, where they probably evolved, only one possible fossil molar, dated to the middle of the Miocene, has been found (Coven 2002).

The five or so species of tarsiers are similar in general traits but differ in numerous morphological details—and, surprisingly, in chromosome numbers, which range from 40 to 86 (Gursky 2002). Though classified as "nocturnal," tarsiers actually forage at twilight, rest during the middle of the night, forage again before dawn, and rest in dense undergrowth during the daytime (Doyle and Martin 1974). They use their sense of hearing more than their sense of sight to locate insect prey; this behavior is likely connected to their activity cycle. Their locomotion is technically called *saltatory*; this means that when arboreal, they leap from tree limb to tree limb and when terrestrial, hop to the next tree trunk. Their huge leaps are remarkable for an animal the size of a rat.

Socially, tarsiers form pair bonds: Each unit consists of a male, a female, and their offspring. Whether there are social units larger than the pair-bonded units is yet to be established. Courtship involves chasing, displaying, and vocalizing before the bond is confirmed, but even in mating there is little physical contact between the involved individuals (Bearder 1986). Although mothers "park" their infants in trees while they feed, they are not negligent, as they are always nearby. "Parking" behavior is necessary, because tarsier infants weigh one-third of their adult weight at birth and grow fast. Mothers are optimizing their feeding time by parking the infants instead of carrying them (Gursky 2002).

Tarsiers urine mark and gland mark; although such marking appears to be related to territoriality, its true function is unknown. They occasionally fight "invaders." Because tarsiers are not known to have any predators, they are endangered only by human-related activities such as timbering and clearing for cultivation. Their specialized diet will not allow them to move to less disturbed areas, and they do not do well under zoo conditions. In some places in the wild where yearly censuses have been taken for extended periods, they have disappeared (Gursky 2003).

The study of tarsiers does not generate much in the way of hypotheses about human evolution but does provide data on species variability. If, as suggested here, tarsiers are a long-term success story in evolution, beginning with one Southeast Asia population in early primate times and ending with one contemporary group some 60 myr later, that long-lived single lineage is perhaps tarsiers' most important contribution to our understanding of human evolution.

# Contemporary Prosimians

Prosimians have had their own evolutionary trajectory since about 60 myr ago, though specific prosimian lineages are not apparent in the fossil record until millions of years later and the genera that eventually gave rise to the contemporary species are not in evidence until about 10 myr ago. In addition to sharing basic primate traits (see Chapter 5), with few exceptions contemporary prosimians show additional derived traits, evolved after their split with the Anthropoidea. Because of the variability within the suborder, some experts suggest that the term *prosimian* be used only as a folk taxonomy to refer to any small-brained primate that is not a tarsier or a monkey; these taxonomists prefer to group lemurs and lorises into a taxonomic unit at the semi-order level (called Strepsirhini, meaning "with wet noses") and all other primates in another such unit (called Haplorhini, meaning "with dry noses"). This scheme groups tarsiers with humans, apes, and monkeys (Groves 1998). But most experts see enough similarities to continue to regard prosimians as an evolutionary and taxonomic unit; we follow this scheme. All modern prosimians share the following traits (Falk 2000; Napier and Napier 1985):

- unfused suture on top of head and unfused midline in lower jaw
- stereoscopic vision with eyes slightly to the sides of the face
- postorbital bar, but not fully enclosed bony eye socket
- partially prehensile hands and feet with big toes separated from the other toes
- long muzzles with moist, hairless noses like dogs (rhinarium)
- good sense of smell (with large olfactory lobes in the brain) and medium-sized snout
- tactile whiskers on their eyebrows and in the muzzle area, like cats
- large, mobile external ears

- toilet claws on the second digits of their feet, but otherwise all flat nails
- 36 to 32 teeth, with a tooth comb formed by four long, thin incisors in lower jaw
- scent glands in the genital region and on the backs of wrists used to mark territory
- immobile upper lips that reduce facial gestures and make them appear expressionless
- breeding seasons and multiple births
- two-chambered uterus

Other nonshared prosimian traits demonstrate evolutionary happenings since the time when lineages diverged from an early prosimian stock. For example, 75 percent of contemporary prosimian species are nocturnal and have large eyes to gather light for night vision. Prosimians as a group vary in weight from 56.7 g (2 ounces) to 4.1 kg (9 pounds), in locomotion from terrestrial quadrupedalism to leaping and clinging, and in dental formulae.

Geographically, modern prosimians can be found on Madagascar (32 species) and in Africa (14 species) and Asia (8 species). The Madagascar prosimians are particularly interesting. Madagascar was an island long before primates evolved, having split from the African continent some 165 myr ago and now lying 250 miles offshore; so the only viable answer to how the earliest prosimians got there from the mainland is through a chance rafting event. The Zambezi River runs due east in Africa, reaching the Indian Ocean exactly where the island of Madagascar is today. Annual flood waters bring uprooted trees to the ocean, and these would have been perfect boats for prosimian ancestors. DNA analysis suggests that the earliest prosimians were similar to very small modern dwarf lemurs that hibernate for a month annually. If those earliest prosimians also hibernated, a small group of them could have safely rafted inside a tree trunk to Madagascar (Kappeler 2000). Rats and iguanas are known to raft long distances, and a parallel study on Madagascar carnivores shows they all evolved from a single group that must have rafted from Africa as well (Censky et al. 2002; Hecht 2003). From DNA evidence it appears that all contemporary Madagascar prosimians evolved from a single ancestor and in time evolved independent lineages as different as the large sifaka and the unique aye-aye. The Madagascar prosimians were successful partly because there were no large predators and no food competitors, at least not until humans arrived 2,000 years ago. Humans drove at least 15 species to extinction very quickly (Miller and Treves 2007). Contemporary prosimians are in danger of extinction, however, because of logging and the demands of Madagascar farmers for more tillable land.

There are over 15 species of lemur on the island, the ring-tailed being the best known. Lemurs show the typical prosimian traits of a good sense of smell but only moderately developed stereoscopic vision, and they use genital and wrist olfactory glands to mark their territories. Lemurs are either quite small or quite large: The larger lemurs are terrestrial quadrupeds. The small ones weigh about 2 ounces, are nocturnal and solitary, and eat a variety of food, mostly gums and saps. The large ones weigh up to 9 pounds, are diurnal, live in large social units, and eat flowers, leaves, and insects. The differences between the two contemporary types suggest that each lies at an extreme of the size spectrum as a result of different survival strategies, whereas middle-sized groups were unsuccessful and became extinct.

The sifaka and indri are lesser-known Madagascar prosimians. They are large diurnal leapers and clingers; they spend most of their time in trees, grasping trunks with very strong hind legs and springing off to land on the trunk of another tree. They feed on leaves and fruit. The aye-aye is a most elusive prosimian; it is nocturnal, eats mainly insects, and has a mixed set of claws and nails. Because of its scurrying activity pattern, it was originally thought to be a large rat. The aye-aye is on the verge of extinction.

African prosimians are smaller in size than most of the Madagascar groups; small size is common among species that are preyed on yet must compete with other

Modern prosimians include the aye-aye (left) and the ring-tailed lemur (right). Using the list of traits in the text, what morphological traits can you identify in these two photos?

species for food. Galagos and bush babies are confined at present to South Africa. They are nocturnal, lead relatively solitary lives, are quadrupedal runners, and eat fruit, tree gum, and insects. They mark their territory using urine.

Finally, there are two or three species of prosimians in South Asia: the slender loris in India and Sri Lanka and the slow loris in Southeast Asia. These animals represent a likely case of incomplete speciation. That is, although the Indian and Sri Lankan lorises are morphologically different, they will reproduce in captivity, though with lowered reproductive viability (Groves 1998). All lorises are nocturnal, have dental combs, and have grooming claws on their second toes. Their diet is variable.

## Sifakas

Sifakas (*Propithecus verreauxi*) are the focus of the case study to exemplify contemporary prosimians because sifakas are very large, standing more than a meter (3 feet) tall, and because they have an unusual mode of locomotion—clinging and leaping. From a vertical clinging position, sifakas leap as much as 30 feet in a curved trajectory, landing feet first on another trunk as shown in Figure 14.2. This behavior appears to be an evolutionary adaptation to their forested environment, because the original Madagascar prosimians were small and apparently quadrupedal. Sifakas are almost exclusively arboreal, but unlike arboreal monkeys they spend most of their day "just sitting." They wake at dawn, move a few meters, eat available fruits and leaves (their diet is approximately 65 percent fruit, 25 percent leaves, and 10 percent flowers), lie back on a tree limb exposing their stomachs and absorbing sunlight, turn over and "do" their back sides, self-groom with their foot toilet claw to clean and scratch their ears, urinate and defecate, take a 3-hour siesta (sitting), travel a few more meters to their afternoon feeding spot,

*Figure 14.2*

**SIFAKA LEAP.** Sifakas are leapers and clingers. As shown here, they cling to a tree trunk with the large, strong muscles of their back legs, then push off from that position, turn around in midair, and land (without breaking anything) on another tree trunk. Can you imagine yourself doing this without breaking something—branch or bone?

feed on leaves and fruits again, settle in for the night, and go to sleep at sundown (Jolly 1966; Richard 1978). Sifakas do not have a very active lifestyle.

Sifakas live in stable troops that average five adults and two subadults, but there is surprisingly little social interaction. Normally the troop members feed in the same trees but engage in little contact or signaling; when sitting as a group, they sit as if they were the cars of a toy train, one behind the other. Occasionally individuals groom each other; young sifakas may play-wrestle for short periods of time. The troop is basically a foraging unit, and several troops make up "neighborhoods" whose basic function is to set the limits of reproduction. Male and female sifakas have similar ranks, with only estrus females or those carrying infants enjoying any additional rank in the form of feeding priority. Any sifaka can initiate movement, as there are no leaders. Male–female relations appear by human standards to be relatively loose; there is no pair-bonding, multiple sex partners are the rule, and proximity appears to be the main factor determining choice of partners (Brockman 1999).

There are occasional "battles" between sifaka troops, though scent marking appears to function to keep aggression to a low level. Both males and females anal–genital mark by rubbing tree limbs and scent mark by rubbing their throat glands three or four times against vertical surfaces. Other troop members note this marking and scent mark the same spot. Males also urine mark by spreading their knees and waddling up a vertical tree, leaving urine drops as they move; other males in the troop smell and do the same marking. Other troops occasionally attempt to "invade" a troop's territory, leaping, staring, and growling at the local inhabitants; but the residents usually bunch together, hop toward the invaders, and force them with their own stares and growls to withdraw.

Anthropologists do not expect to find many applications to humans from research on prosimians, because humans and prosimians have not had common ancestry for 60 myr—although the large size and specialized locomotion of certain prosimians do match hominid evolution patterns. And although Allison Jolly (1966) and Allison Richard (1978) observed and described scent marking and sniffing by sifakas and assumed that marking likely functioned to keep the peace between troops, there is little confidence in the meaning behind such behavior. Does scent marking transmit information about sex, sexual receptivity of females, or emotions, or does it merely relay an individual's anxiety (Doyle and Martin 1974)?

# Contemporary Monkeys

Molecular dating puts the split of Old and New World monkeys from the Anthropoidea at 30 myr ago and from each other at 25 myr ago. Major branches of each lineage evolved about 6 myr ago, but contemporary species go back only 3 myr. All monkeys, no matter what kind or where they live share the following traits:

- postorbital bars that are almost completely enclosed in bone
- bilophodont molar teeth (two ridges of raised enamel separated by a low area between them; see Figure 14.3)
- quadrupedalism
- external tails
- large brains relative to those of prosimians
- reliance on vision as primary sense
- color vision and diurnal activity (except for the owl monkey, *Aotus*, which is nocturnal)
- one-chambered uterus, unlike prosimians' two-chambered uterus
- larger-sized newborns than prosimians have

In view of the fact that anthropoid groups existed in both the Old and New Worlds before 30 myr ago, it is possible that each monkey group evolved from its own anthropoid group. But there is a gap in the New World fossil record of more than 16 myr for which there are no primate fossils. It is therefore more prudent to hypothesize that monkeys split only once from African anthropoids. Once established in Africa, monkeys could have rafted on vegetation mats and populated the New World. Of course, the idea that rafting was the vehicle for monkey transportation is only half of the hypothetical scenario; the second half requires that monkeys form an evolving lineage once on dry land in the New World. Geologists tell us that 25 myr ago, South America and Africa were closer to each other than they are now. Even so, because no competent observer had fully documented an over-water dispersal of any animal group, rafting and colonization were strictly hypothetical until the 1990s. In 1995, however, 15 green iguanas were seen on the beaches of Anguilla, a Caribbean island, where they had never been seen before. A mat of logs and uprooted trees on the beach appeared to be the raft. Today the population is flourishing, so both ends of this dispersal by rafting are documented—the iguanas rafted safely 300 km (480 miles) to Anguilla from Guadalupe, their ancestral home, and established themselves as a population in the new setting. In a similar manner, a pregnant African monkey or a group of both sexes could have rafted in three weeks from Africa to South America (Censky et al. 2002).

## Figure 14.3

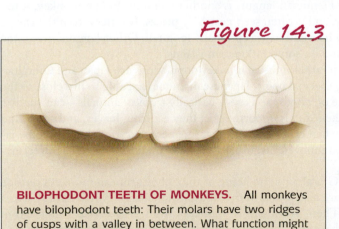

**BILOPHODONT TEETH OF MONKEYS.** All monkeys have bilophodont teeth: Their molars have two ridges of cusps with a valley in between. What function might this specialized molar form have?

# Old World Monkeys

**Old World monkeys** are taxonomically called Catarrhini and did not evolve to modern species status until about 3 myr ago, but there is fossil evidence for major lineages by about 6 myr ago (Burton 1995; Eckhardt 2000). There may be as many as 60 species of extinct Old World monkeys; there are 116 living species. Taxonomically, they are separated, primarily on the basis of diet, into two subfamilies: the cercopithecines (with 66 species) and the colobines (with 50 species). All Old World monkeys share the following derived traits:

- catarrhine nose (nostrils separated by a narrow nasal septum and nostril openings pointed downward)
- three premolars
- well-developed opposable thumbs
- ischial callosities (areas of hair-free, toughened skin on the buttocks) that act as sitting pads while the monkeys sleep in a tree notch in an upright position

Cercopithecines eat almost anything, depending on where they live, but the colobines are almost exclusively leaf eaters.

Familiar African cercopithecine monkeys include the widespread vervets, the savanna patas, and the forest-living guenons. There are 20 species of macaques in North Africa, India, China, Southeast Asia, and Japan, and there are baboons (including true baboons, mandrills, drills, and geladas) in Africa. A new species called the Arunachal macaque was announced in 2004; it lives in the Himalayan mountains, which accounts for its not being previously identified. The familiar colobines include black-and-white and red colobus monkeys in Africa, langurs in India, leaf monkeys in Southeast Asia, and so-called odd-nosed monkeys in China and Borneo.

Some Old World monkey species are arboreal and some are terrestrial. Arboreal monkeys such as mangabeys and colobus monkeys eat food from their treed environment, mangabeys specializing in fruits and seeds and colobus monkeys in leaves. The terrestrial Old World monkeys, such as baboons, patas, and mandrills, occasionally outnumber humans in their regions. All terrestrial monkeys eat fruits, seeds, grass, and leaves. They are often pests when invading buildings, fields, and gardens for food, and they can be provoked into aggression.

The Indian rhesus macaque is well known in medical research as well as to farmers and visitors to holy places in India. Macaques have kept their flexible quadrupedal bodies and have become highly "domestic," adapting to life in cities and climbing with ease to the tops of buildings and monuments and into second-story windows. The gray langur (sometimes called the Hanuman langur) is another common Indian monkey; it too is terrestrial, eats anything, and is often seen near holy places. It differs from the rhesus in its long and glossy gray hair and its exceptionally long tail. Other langurs live in the forests of Southeast Asia and on some Indonesian islands.

Finally, two places with rather unusual monkey populations are Japan and Gibraltar. By making use of steaming thermal pools, Japanese macaques are able to live close to the apparent northern extreme of where monkeys—basically tropical animals—can survive. As with other macaques, their diet is opportunistic; they eat fruit, leaves, and seeds, and they raid cultivated fields when crops are ripening. Japanese macaques have become famous for their documented innovations, usually termed "traditions," such as sweet potato washing.

The famous Rock of Gibraltar is the home of the only European monkeys outside of zoos. (These monkeys are also found in the Atlas Mountains of North Africa, across the Straits of Gibraltar.) There are fossils of monkeys from as late as 2.5 myr ago in Europe, so it is possible that the Gibraltar monkeys are a remnant population on that continent; but it is more likely they were reintroduced from across the Mediterranean in Roman times. One of the more interesting features of this almost tail-less monkey is

**Old World monkeys**
Species of monkeys, some arboreal and some terrestrial, that are found in Africa and Asia; their nostrils point downward and are separated by a narrow nasal septum.

Old World Monkeys include the black-and-white colobus (right) and langur (left). Colobus monkeys (Africa) are mostly arboreal, and langurs (South and Southeast Asia) are mostly terrestrial. Using the trait list in the text, can you identify the derived morphological traits?

that males take care of infants from the time they are born and return them to their mothers only for feeding (Burton 1995).

## Hamadryas Baboons

Though many researchers claim there are five species of baboons, more and more experts agree that there is but one species with five subspecies that are morphologically somewhat different but that breed on their population borders, forming hybrid zones. All baboons breed indiscriminately in captivity. In the wild the five groups fit the definition of subspecies by being both geographically and biologically distinctive. They live in different areas, and they differ morphologically in size, muzzle details, and fur coloration, among other traits. Furthermore, these traits co-vary—that is, all of the baboons with yellow hair are quite small and have black muzzles (South Africa); all of the baboons that are reddish in color are of medium size and have naked, long, straight muzzles (West Africa); all of the baboons that are olive in color are large and their noses overhang their mouths (East Africa). The other two groups of baboons also show a co-variation of traits. This co-variation pattern means there are no yellow baboons with overhanging noses or olive baboons with black muzzles. A recent genetic analysis agrees with this taxonomic lumping and suggests that based on molecular dating all baboons evolved from a single group in South Africa some 1.8 myr ago (Newman et al. 2004). One of the five subspecies of baboons (*Papio papio hamadryas*) is discussed in detail here because its complex sociopolitical system appears akin to the human system.

Hamadryas baboons are sometimes called "the desert baboon" due to their distribution in the arid bush of Ethiopia and surrounding nations (Kummer 1968; Zinner et al. 2001). These baboons are favorites in zoos because the males look fierce with their huge canines and mantles of pilo-erecting hair around their shoulders. Anthropologists find them particularly interesting, too, because their social organization of several levels is uniquely complex. There are one-male units (the male "herding" his females), "clans," and troops. Entire troops of up to 750 animals sleep as a single unit on one large sleeping ledge on a vertical rock face up to 15 m (50 feet) high; there are no tall trees in the desert for sleeping (Kummer 1968). These monkeys follow a daily routine beginning at sunrise, when they leave their sleeping ledges to go topside and sun themselves for as long as several hours, dozing, engaging in mutual grooming, chasing one another, copulating, and playing. After some false starts, the troop climbs down from the cliff and moves as a unit for 30 to 60 minutes toward an eating area. Troops have been known to travel as far as 19 km (12 miles) to eat, but normally the trek is much shorter. Once at a feeding spot, the baboons spread out as one-male units to forage on grass seeds, flowers, and even locusts during their swarming season. After a midday rest hamadryas baboons often look for water in drinking holes in river beds and begin to wander back to their sleeping rocks, eating seeds they discover on the way. Topside of the sleeping ledges, they again engage in play activity, copulate, and mutually groom. At dusk they climb down to the sleeping ledges and sleep.

Socially, the one-male units are composed of an adult male, one or more unrelated females that were "adopted" when they were adolescent and presexual, and one to several offspring. Unlike females in most monkey species, the females in a hamadryas unit do not grow up together and are not related. A variation on the one-male unit is called a "two-male team," in which a subadult male regularly leads or follows the unit. Sexual activity is normally a perk of the main male. Females do find ways to solicit and copulate with males other than their "leader," but males do not solicit females in units other than their own. Most of the social behavior is within the one-male unit. Although all females are in such units, about 25 percent of males at any given time are "loners," which accounts for the multiple-female demography. The young adopted females begin to follow and groom "their" male and become sexually active 2 or 3 years later. When senior males become injured or too old to herd their females, other leader males or solitary adult males take over the females—partly because females do not bond when they are members of the same unit and do not simply "disappear" when their male becomes elderly (Swedell 2000). Clans are more inclusive social units made up of several one-male units. The males in clans tend to resemble one another morphologically, so researchers believe they are likely to be patrilineally related; this is not yet confirmed, however (Abegglen 1984). Troops consist of groups of clans that sleep together on a ledge, but they are not stable units, as one-male units and clans join different troops on occasion.

Male hamadryas baboons seldom fight with each other, and when they do, it is mostly with sham bites and cuffing; generally one animal flees rather than turning the encounter into a real fight. What wounds are visible are in nonfatal areas such as legs and hands (Kummer 1968).

It is in the complexity of sociopolitical organization that hamadryas baboons take on anthropological interest. Most primates show but one or two levels of organization; three levels is a human trait. Hamadryas baboons' three-tiered system of one-male units, clans, and troops initially sound like human families, clans, and tribes. Other baboon subspecies (*Papio anubis*, for example) are matrilocal, meaning that females remain in their mother's social unit. Perhaps the hamadryas pattern is ecologically related, with resource depletion resulting in a need for cooperation for maximum food exploitation. Predator pressure is minimal, and the formation of troops negates what little threat exists. By contrast, perhaps female common residence in other baboon subspecies is due to more ample resources and less need for related male cooperation. If ecology is at the root of social organization differences among baboons, it would indicate that the differences are noninherited and nonbiological and thus could change as quickly as the environment.

## New World Monkeys

**New World monkeys**
Species of monkeys, mostly highly arboreal, that are found in Central and South America; their nostrils point straight ahead.

Taxonomically, **New World monkeys** are called Platyrrhini, a name based on their nose shape. All New World monkeys share the following derived traits, which apparently evolved after the split with Old World monkeys some 30 to 25 myr ago:

- platyrrhine nose (flat with nostrils separated by a wide septum and pointed straight ahead)

- small body size, with the largest about 4.5 kg (10 pounds) and the smallest 84.5 g (3 ounces)
- three premolars, whereas the other Anthropoidea have two
- arboreality (no New World monkey spends the majority of its time on the ground and some never come to the ground)
- no external swelling of females during ovulation
- no cheek pouches for food storage

New World monkeys belong to four families, including the Callithricidae and the Cebidae. The small Callithricidae include marmosets and tamarins, which are almost totally arboreal. These monkeys have 30 teeth (only two molars per quadrant), usually twin births, and claws instead of nails on all but their big toes; their tails are not prehensile. Most Cebidae, such as the familiar capuchin (organ-grinder) and squirrel monkeys, are much larger. Squirrel monkeys occupy much of the South American rainforest (and numerous "monkey jungle" establishments), come to the ground for short periods of time, and eat fruits and insects. Howler, titi, saki, woolly, and spider monkeys make up the rest of the Cebidae family. These monkeys show nails on all digits; have 36 teeth (3 molars per quadrant); and, with one exception, have prehensile tails that they can use as a fifth limb in locomotion. Their tails even have "fingerprints" on the ends! Researchers have discovered that white-faced and brown capuchins demonstrate "traditions" of food washing and nut cracking that are close to "culture" in chimpanzees and humans (Perry and Manson 2003).

Shown are members of two medium-sized, mostly arboreal New World monkeys: squirrel monkey (top) and capuchin (bottom). What derived traits can you observe? Compare these New World monkeys to Old World monkeys.

### Howler Monkeys

Howler monkeys (genus *Alouetta*) are large Cebidae that are found in the middle to upper regions of tall trees ranging from southern Mexico through most of Central and South America and as far south as northern Argentina. There are six species of howlers. Their folk name comes from the fact that the males, particularly, use their enlarged hyoid and laryngial sacs to "howl" first thing each morning and at certain other times; this vocalizing tends to aid in intertroop spacing and helps keep aggression low. The diet of howler monkeys, regardless of species or geographic location, consists entirely of leaves, fruits, and flowers of trees and vines, with leaves being the main source of protein and fruit the main source of energy. Within certain areas there may be as many as 135 different species of trees, with at least some producing young sprouts at every season. Howlers use a minimal amount of energy during their daily routine; they spend about 4 hours feeding, from 15 to 16 hours resting or sleeping, and no more than 3 hours traveling in search of food (Milton 1980).

Howlers are the largest of the New World monkeys, weighing up to 10 kg (22 pounds). In spite of their relatively large size, they are almost completely arboreal, walking quadrupedally on branches and even crossing from one tree to another by walking, not jumping. Their prehensile tails come in handy when they are tree feeding: They can suspend their weight from them, freeing all four limbs for feeding.

Socially, howlers live in closed troops that have overlapping home ranges, each with a membership that ranges from 7 to 18, usually including more adult females than males and several immatures (Estrada et al. 2002; Milton 1980). Both male and female howlers leave their natal groups before they are sexually mature, thus reducing the risk of inbreeding (Kinzey 1997). There is some ranking among males, with only the dominant male doing the mating. Within its territory a howler troop travels 300 to 600 meters (or yards) a day, which is a relatively small core area. Howlers travel only to get food; they find mates within the troop, and they sleep wherever it is convenient at the end of the day. The leaves are succulent enough that they get enough water through leaf eating (Crockett and Eisenberg 1986).

One of the more interesting traits of howlers is the fact that although troops' feeding ranges overlap extensively, agonistic behavior between adjacent troops is practically nonexistent. Most primate species show the opposite pattern. It is tempting to suggest that the important variable in aggressive behavior is food resources: Howlers have ample food available, whereas baboons—among whom intertroop male aggression is high—have scarcer resources. But the reason for low agonistic behaviors among howlers is likely to be considerably more complex than simple food resources. Howlers know where neighboring troops are located by their "dawn choruses," which would not be needed if food resources were the only important variable. Nonetheless, howlers manage to eat well without risky competition from other groups. Hypotheses might be generated concerning the possible connections among food, environment, and social organization among early hominids. For example, assuming early hominids lived in both semiopen savannas and woods, was there more competition for resources in savannas or in woods? Can agonistic behavior be predicted for areas where there are poor resources?

# Contemporary Apes

The reputation of contemporary apes has had its ups and downs. Not long ago, as portrayed in the original *King Kong* movie, gorillas were seen as nasty killers, carrying human women off to rape them. Indonesian natives ran from orangutans. But after Jane Goodall, Dian Fossey, and Biruté Galdikas wrote their popular books in the 1970s and 1980s, the aggressive, cannibalistic chimpanzee, gorilla, or orangutan (choose one) could also be sharing, altruistic, and good at mothering. Some modern researchers stress either the violent or the peaceful side of apes' nature (though some give an even balance), but in reality, apes are primates and, like humans, are violent under certain circumstances but more often peaceful (Corbey 2005).

In the taxonomy we are using, modern apes are divided into four families: Hylobatidae (siamangs and gibbons), Pongidae (orangutans), Gorillidae (gorilla), and Panidae (chimpanzees and bonobos). [In one new scheme, proposed by Wildman and colleagues (2003), chimpanzees and bonobos are grouped with humans.] All modern apes share certain derived traits:

- 2.1.2.3 dental formula
- Y-5 molar pattern with rounded cusps
- absence of tails
- the ability to raise their arms above their heads, as a consequence of their flexible shoulders
- large brains relative to body size
- diurnal activity

Humans also share all of these traits, but two important diagnostic traits differentiate apes and humans: locomotor specializations and the size and shape of their cra-

**small apes**
Common name for the smaller apes found in Southeast Asia: gibbons and siamangs.

nia. Modern apes either are primarily brachiators or are fist- or knuckle-walking quadrupeds that show vestiges of ancestral brachiation in their elongated forearms and narrow pelvises. And although modern apes have brains that are large relative to their body size, there is considerable variation in brain size, and none is relatively as large as the human brain.

Violence among apes (and among humans, for that matter) has been a focus of both scientific and popular literature, with all but bonobos being cited as violent. The observed violence follows species-specific patterns, but it is interesting that the patterns differ: Female orangutans are raped but there are no orangutan infant killings; female chimpanzees are battered and raped and sometimes their infants are killed; female gorillas are not battered or raped but most mothers have had at least one infant killed. Of course, humans batter, rape, and kill as well (Wrangham 1996). But, again, violence and aggression among apes are relatively rare events.

## Gibbons and Siamangs (the Small Apes)

Gibbons and siamangs are sometimes called the "lesser apes," but the term **small apes** is more appropriate. Today the nine species of small apes live only in Southeast Asia. Both gibbons and siamangs are almost exclusively arboreal brachiators, with much longer forelimbs than hind limbs. They use their hooklike hands and swinging arm-over-arm locomotion to travel from one fruiting tree to the next. When they walk on the ground, which is rare, they teeter bipedally with their arms over their heads as if for balance. They are very popular in zoos because of their acrobatic talents. Molecular dating indicates that small apes, large apes, and humans split from their last common ancestor (a hominoid) by about 18 myr ago (Wildman et al. 2003).

Siamangs (*Symphylangus* with one species) are larger than gibbons and weigh an average of 25 pounds (11.36 kg). They are found in China, Vietnam, Cambodia, the Malay peninsula, and Sumatra. Until recently, they were considered to be "just another species" of gibbon, but their larger size and avoidance of gibbons (the gibbon species interbreed on borders) have given them taxonomic status at the genus level. Unfortunately, they have not been well studied. Siamangs are expert brachiators and live in small family groups, defending their ranges with noisy shouts.

Gibbons (*Hylobates*), the better-studied small apes, are much smaller and more slender than siamangs, with long arms, hands, and feet. Because all populations interbreed on the borders of their range, gibbons should be considered a "superspecies." Interestingly, gibbons are the only apes that do not make nightly nests, perhaps because their small size precludes that necessity. Almost 80 percent of their diet comes from fruit, and the remaining 20 percent from leaves, buds, and flowers (Reynolds 1967). Socially, gibbons pair for life and live in family units consisting of one adult male, one adult female, and typically one juvenile and one infant. Although family units sleep in the middle of their approximately 50-acre territories and males vocalize their location by morning hoots, they do meet other family units on mutual borders where they feed. When this happens, there

Gibbons (shown here) and siamangs, the smallest apes, live in Southeast Asia. Their most obvious trait is brachiating. Note their long arms relative to their legs. How would they walk on the ground?

is a good deal of branch waving and chasing as well as vocalization until one group retreats (MacKinnon 1974).

Both gibbons and siamangs appear to be extremely well adapted to their forested environment, but this is why they are endangered. As populations of farmers increase, forests decrease through deforestation for farms. Siamangs and gibbons are so specialized to forest life that most conservationists believe they cannot adapt to any other ecological niche.

Given that modern humans pair-bond and have strong family units, gibbons might appear to be excellent candidates for hypotheses about how these social complexes came about in the hominid lineage. However, there are substantial differences between the social complexes. Gibbons pair-bond for life, and only two adults are involved. In contrast, humans often pair-bond several times during their lifetimes, and most human societies allow plural marriages (pair bonds) at the same time. What is perhaps more important is the strength of the bonds that exist within each family unit of gibbons.

## The Large Apes

Orangutans, gorillas, chimpanzees, and bonobos are often called the "great apes," but we prefer to use the term **large apes**. These animals are primarily terrestrial, have a variable diet, have longer front than back legs, and are tail-less. Based on molecular evidence, orangutans appear to have split from the lineage that eventually evolved to African apes and humans about 14 myr ago, and perhaps gorillas split between 7 and 6 myr ago.

### *Orangutans*

Orangutans *(Pongo pygmaeus)*, sometimes called "red apes" because of their long red-brown hair, are found today only in Southeast Asia. The population in Sumatra has a different facial configuration from that in Borneo, probably as a result of early dispersion throughout the area and subsequent establishment on two large islands. Orangutans on both islands share certain traits, and members of the two populations will interbreed in captivity. A recent study by Carel van Schaik and his team (van Schaik 2004), however, claims that one group—the so-called swamp orangutans of Northwest Sumatra—is quite different from the other orangutans. We will first describe the other orangutans, returning to this unusual group later.

Orangutans are vegetarian and fairly slow moving; when they walk terrestrially, the sides of their fists rest on the ground, an apparent variation on knuckle-walking. Their forelimbs are 40 percent longer than their hind limbs. In spite of their large size, which in males is up to 91 kg (200 pounds), orangutans spend much more time in trees than on the ground, walking on tree limbs in larger trees and rocking branches until they are close enough to walk to a new tree. Because these apes spend 60 percent of their day napping, observers find it easy to follow and observe them. After a day's foraging on more than 100 different species of fruit (54 percent of the diet), leaves (30 percent), flowers (12 percent), and vines and bark (14 percent), orangutans build nests for the night in the last tree visited (MacKinnon 1974; Parker and McKinnon 2005).

Unlike the other apes, and in very unprimatelike fashion, orangutans do not form stable male–female groups even during the mating season. From one perspective, mothers and infants are the basic social unit and males are loners. From another perspective, a single male occupies the territory of several females and their offspring, a "scattered harem." This male defends the territory by bellowing loud calls as he wanders around it; there are numerous younger males with no established territory or females. A recent study of younger males shows that during their "development spurt," they have twice the normal level of hormones. This may be why they often mate with females in estrus on older males' territories. It appears to human observers that these females do not choose to mate with the young males, biting them and emitting loud sounds only heard in this particular context. Because even young males are almost twice the size of females,

**large apes**
Common name for the bigger apes: orangutans (Asia) and gorillas, chimpanzees, and bonobos (Africa).

they usually succeed in mating, however. Humans have called this activity "rape" because it involves unwilling females and forceful males. It must be noted that, unlike human females, no female orangutans have been seen to be physically injured as a result of "rape." In general orangutans are relatively unsocial, with males in the company of females and infants only during mating seasons (Naggioncalda and Sapolsky 2002).

Like early hominids, orangutans show considerable sexual dimorphism; males weigh about twice as much as females. Is this degree of sexual dimorphism connected to these primates' "loner male" pattern, in which female–infant social units have little interaction with males? Is it connected to females being "raped" by subadult males? Why do male orangutans fight more among themselves when females are in estrus (Maple 1980)? Or is males' loner behavior due to patchy food resources? Hominids are thought to have had an environment with patchy resources during their early bipedal stage and also to have shown sexual dimorphism. Could the third element, the lone male, be inferred? Finally, observers in some (though not all) geographic areas have seen orangutans engaged in 24 behaviors, mostly connected to food acquisition, tool use, or social groupings, that, as in chimpanzees, show similarities to human culture (Peters 2001; van Schaik et al. 2003). (Highlight 14.1, on pp. 444–446, explores cultural behaviors of chimpanzees and orangutans.)

The unique group of orangutans in Northwest Sumatra live in a very different environment from that of other orangutans, which is probably why they differ in so many ways. Carel van Schaik and his team studied the orangutans in the Suaq swamp from 1994 to 1999 under miserable conditions. This group of orangutans had not been studied before simply because their swamp is not at all conducive to the study of any arboreal animal. The team was constantly in water and fighting every flying bug imaginable. Van Schaik and his team found this group to be very sociable and to use a variety of tools, both traits that are in contrast to other orangutans. Figs are a favorite food, and the swamp orangutans spend time together in fruiting fig trees, sharing this delicacy. They also forage for ants and termites in dead branches and even bite the soft dead wood away to get to the inner larvae and pupae. They use sticks to get to honey and to remove sharp seeds from the edible soft parts of certain fruits. This group of orangutans is considerably more social than any others, with males and females spending time together without the occurrence of rape (van Schaik 2004).

Unfortunately, orangutans are the most endangered of the apes. Deforestation, poaching by natives for bushmeat, and capture and sale to zoos and the pet trade all threaten their populations (Nadler et al. 1990). Because the females give birth only every 8 to 12 years, increasing the numbers of existing populations will be a slow process, if it happens at all. Very little orangutan territory is under any governmental protection, so their continued existence in the wild is highly uncertain. Even the establishment of halfway houses for rescued pet orangutans has not worked well, and such facilities will never work if there is no rainforest for the orangutans to return to. Carel van Schaik (2004) has estimated there were about 315,000 orangutans in Borneo and Sumatra in 1900 but less than 50,000 by 2000, or only about 15 percent of the estimated earlier population. There is an obvious connection to the fact that the human population increased from 37 million to 220 million in the same 100 years. Not only did human numbers increase dramatically, but the timber industry has removed about 50 percent of the forests that are the orangutans' habitat. The December 2004 tsunami that devastated so much of Southeast Asia had an impact on the orangutans in Sumatra as well. Many died as a direct result of the killer wave (how many is not known), and the damage to food resources on the island will affect the animals for years to come.

## Gorillas

Gorillas (*Gorilla gorilla*) are the largest living ape species. Until the 1960s gorillas had an undeserved reputation as being aggressive and dangerous, but that reputation was based on human fear: Unless provoked, gorillas flee from humans. Only one type of gorilla,

# Checking Out Chimpanzee and Orangutan Culture

FIRST IT WAS TOOLS, then it was language, and now it looks as if chimpanzees and orangutans (and possibly, as we have noted, capuchin monkeys) have culture. But let's not get too excited and think there are no differences between them and us (other than that they have more hair and we wear clothes). Chimpanzee tools are no more complex than a stick (and orangutan tools are just as simple), whereas humans have built space ships to travel to the moon; chimpanzees can be taught to use sign language and simplified computer boards (orangutans have not been taught language), but they cannot speak; and although chimpanzees and orangutans may have culture, it is chimpanzee or orangutan culture, not human culture.

Whether nonhuman primates have culture or not boils down to a matter of definitions and the intellectual paradigms of scientists.

## DEFINITIONS

You can take your favorite definition of culture (and there are many) and see if chimpanzees or orangutans fit that definition, or you can observe these primates and see if what they do fits a human-derived definition of culture. Either way, it is the definition that is important. Anthropologists are notorious for the number of definitions they have put forth for the concept of culture; no two anthropologists define it the same way. Why? Because culture is a complex construct, not a concrete object such as, say, a flint tool. Most anthropologists would agree that there are two different approaches to what culture is, the behavioral and the cognitive. The behavioral approach focuses on variations of learned group *behavior*. In this view cul-

ture is not genetic but is learned; it is observable behavior, and it pertains to groups, not individuals; it varies from one population (or society) to another, and the transmission is generational. The cognitive approach focuses on *cognition*, or what goes on in people's heads; it emphasizes what groups of people know, value, and believe in; it concerns symbols and meaning. The basic difference between the two approaches is their primary focus, but the approaches agree that human culture is variable among populations, learned (not genetic), customary for particular groups, and transmitted generationally. Most anthropologists combine the two approaches and define human culture as what humans do (behavior), what they know (cognition), and how they feel (emotion).

Anthropologists have little insight into what other primates know or value; sometimes their vocalizations seem to provide clues to their emotions, but such interpretations may be wrong. One thing anthropologists do well is observe. Objective observation of behavior is the only means of learning about primates. When group behavior varies between populations, is learned, and is transmitted to subsequent generations, most anthropologists would conclude that the group has culture.

But what if the group is not a human group? What if the members are chimpanzees or orangutans? Can anthropologists still attribute culture to them? What if the members were viewed as humans who cannot talk? Won't they still have culture, as long as they meet the other requirements? Would it be scientific (or "fair") to impose the necessity of speech so humans can keep culture to themselves? Is it fair to move the goal posts so humans can win the game?

## INTELLECTUAL PARADIGMS

Although all scientists realize that a certain amount of bias is present in fieldwork (sometimes nicely called the "observer effect"), it surprised some Western scientists to realize that Japanese primatologists were the first to recognize "traditions" or "incipient culture" in nonhuman primates because of the Buddhist religion. Western-trained scientists, steeped in a Darwinian worldview and seeing all species as separate entities, were reluctant to attribute human qualities such as culture or individuality to nonhuman primates. Japanese primatologists have attributed such traits to their own macaques and to the chimpanzees they study in Africa because the Buddhist tradition sees a continuity between nonhuman primates and humans. The Japanese do not see a sharp divide between monkeys and humans, as Westerners do. It is no wonder the Japanese primatologists saw what Western-trained scientists did not. The famous example of sweet potato washing among one group of Japanese macaques was the first "tradition" noted: One macaque named Imo, which means "sweet potato" in Japanese, "invented" washing sweet potatoes in the ocean (the act removed sand and added a bit of salt), and in time most of rest of the troop observed and learned the behavior. Later these macaques began to wash wheat and then began to eat fish. Sixty years later the monkeys are still being provisioned, but sweet potatoes are now bought at the market already washed. Since the monkeys still dip them in the ocean, it is assumed that they do so for the salt flavor.

Other animals have certain group variations in behavior that appear to be learned as well: Some songbirds have dialects in their songs; vervet monkeys have been seen dipping acacia pods into pools of water in a tree, soaking them, and eating them. As single learned behaviors, however, these actions were not considered cultural.

In a refreshing, methodologically sound examination of chimpanzee behavior and its variations, Andrew Whiten and eight colleagues have concluded that chimpanzees have culture. This conclusion is based on their collective work over many field seasons in Africa. After looking through the literature on chimpanzees in natural or provisioned conditions in Africa during the last 40 years, Whiten came up with a list of 65 behavioral traits that he thought might fit the cultural bill, but he did not know how variable these traits were throughout chimpanzees' geographical distribution. The behaviors included those related to tool use, grooming, courtship, and food acquisition. The directors of seven well-established chimpanzee field stations (stations with 10 to 40 years of observations, two in West Africa and five in East Africa) coded those 65 behaviors in terms of frequency, stating whether each behavior was customary, frequent, rare, or absent. They also could comment if there was a likely environmental explanation or if the behavioral trait and its frequency was unknown. Of the 65 traits, 39 were present among the members of at least two of the seven observed groups, learned and behaviorally variable. If only one group showed a particular behavioral trait, it could have been genetically caused and inherited.

Ant dipping is a good example of variability on the theme of "food" acquisition. In the Taï forest (Ivory Coast in West Africa), chimps use sticks about 30 cm long, dip them about 12 times a minute into ant holes, remove them with an average of 15 ants on them, and use their lips to sweep the ants into their mouths. (They can take 180 ants per minute.) By contrast, the chimpanzees at Gombe (Tanzania in East Africa) use much longer sticks, dip them about 2.6 times per minute, and scoop the ants off with their other hand, flicking them into their open mouths. (They average 760 ants per minute.) Most of the chimps in both populations have learned the behavior by imitating members of their group. No Gombe chimp uses the Taï system, or vice versa.

Other potential cultural behaviors include grooming hand clasps, nut cracking, and the use of large leaves as seats. In four groups both grooming partners simultaneously extend an arm over their head and clasp the partner's hand; with the free hand they then mutually groom armpits. It looks like chimpanzee high fives. Nut cracking is habitual in two populations and absent in five. In the Taï forest observers have seen chimps crack nuts with stones for five hours at a time without stopping; 200 kilometers (125 miles) away, no such behavior has been seen, even though nuts and proper stones for cracking are available. At three sites it is common for chimpanzees to use large leaves to sit on, whereas at four sites leaf use has not been observed.

After Whiten and his colleagues had analyzed all 39 behavioral traits, it was clear not only that there was variability in many, but that there were different patterns of that variability. One group was high in several traits but low in others, whereas their neighbors were high in the behaviors the first group was low in. These kinds of patterns make each group unique in its behavioral complex, mirroring exactly what occurs in human cultures. Since publication of Whiten's results in 1999, another behavioral trait has been added to the list; "social scratching" was found at two of the sites, but each showed subtle variation. This brings the total, to date, to 40 traits that may indicate culture.

Chimpanzee modes of cultural transmission include invention (doing something never done before) and emulative/imitative social learning of behavior. But when closely observed by humans over a long period of time, chimpanzees turn out to be quite creative. Christophe Boesch watched his Taï forest group for four years and saw seven brand-new cultural behaviors, or two a year on average. Humans have an additional mode of transmission: We learn at least some of our culture by having it taught to us. Teaching involves active participation on the part of the facilitator, and teaching—whether it succeeds or not—is intentional. A schoolteacher intends to teach skills of some sort to students, and parents intend to instill notions of

*(continues on the next page)* ▶

ethics and proper etiquette in their children. Very few acts of intentional teaching have been documented in nonhuman primates, but this apparent rarity is complicated by the fact that determining intentionality through observation is extremely difficult. And, of course, cultural teaching is facilitated by use of language and speech. Humans not only transmit cultural information over great stretches of time and space but also transmit certain kinds of information that chimpanzees cannot. Humans can tell their offspring why they may flirt with certain cousins but must stay clear of other cousins; humans can talk about ancestors and gods. Chimpanzees cannot do this, so their cultural repertoire will always be relatively limited.

Shared meaning, a human cultural cognitive trait, also can be seen in chimpanzees, though it is only weakly developed. For example, when three groups of chimpanzees do the same behavior but the chimpanzees that observe it in each group react differently, the varied reactions are likely to be due to different meanings attached to the behavior.

Finally, once human culture got started, it took off; the cumulative richness of human cultures has no parallel in the chimpanzee lineage. This near-exponential growth of culture appears to be human only and is likely one of the reasons why we are us and chimpanzees are chimpanzees.

Following the example of the Whiten team with chimpanzees, Carel van Schaik recently led an "orangutans have culture too" team and found 24 behaviors at six orangutan sites, with some groups showing some behaviors, but not all. As with chimpanzees, the largest category of behaviors involved food acquisition variations.

Once the hubbub dies down over the idea of chimps and orangutans having culture, anthropologists should be able to use the exchange of views and the comparative data to inquire further into the origin of human culture, something that is very speculative at present. All anthropologists, whether they are on the culture-is-behavior or the culture-is-cognition side of the fence, and whether or not they think that chimpanzees have "at least some" rudiments of culture, agree that we share an LCA with chimpanzees, bonobos, and perhaps gorillas. Knowing what these primates do now and the extent of their cognition will be invaluable to the inquiry into the biological basis of human culture.

*Sources:* Boesch, C. 2003. Is culture a golden barrier between human and chimpanzee? *Evolutionary Anthropology* 12:82–91.  Boesch, C., and H. Boesch. 2000. *Chimpanzees of the Taï forest: Behavioral ecology and evolution*. Oxford: Oxford University Press.  Boesch, C., and M. Tomasello. 1998. Chimpanzee and human cultures. *Cultural Anthropology* 39 (5): 591–614.  Janson, C. H., and E. A. Smith. 2003. The evolution of culture: New perspectives and evidence. *Evolutionary Anthropology* 12:57–60.  Matsuzawa, T., ed. 2001. *Primate origins of human cognition and behavior*. New York: Springer.  McGrew, W. C. 1998a. Culture in non-human primates? *Annual Review of Anthropology* 27: 301–328.  McGrew, W. C. 1998b. Behavioral diversity in population of free-ranging chimpanzees in Africa: Is it culture? *Human Evolution* 13 (3–4): 209–220.  McGrew, W. 1992. *Chimpanzee material culture*. Cambridge: Cambridge University Press.  van Schaik, C. P., M. Ancrenaz, G. Bogen, et al. 2003. Orangutan cultures and the evolution of material culture. *Science* 299:103–105.  Whiten, A., J. Goodall, W. C. McGrew, et al. 1999. Cultures in chimpanzees. *Nature* 399:682–685.

turn back to your reading

the mountain gorilla of Dian Fossey's long-term project, has been well studied, and unfortunately the mountain type represents only 1 percent of gorillas (McGrew 2001). Lowland gorillas, which live in West Africa as well as in two locations in East Africa, represent the other 99 percent but have not been well studied. Therefore, most of what scientists think they know about gorillas is based on one small mountain group. And comparison of the mountain and the lowland gorilla groups suggests they differ in food resources and in behavior.

The three groups appear to be only subspecies, even though they live in noncontiguous areas and differ in morphology and diet. The most obvious gorilla trait is size: Males weigh up to 273 kg (600 pounds) and average 160 kg (350 pounds); by contrast, females average 70 kg (155 pounds). Because of their size, gorillas seldom climb trees but are mostly terrestrial knuckle-walkers. Well-developed muscles and strong joints allow their hands to handle the stress of their large bulk pressing on small knuckles while walking.

Gorilla diet is generally leaves (up to 85 percent), tree pith, vines, and fruit. It varies from a more frugivorous (fruit) diet in the west to a mostly leaf diet in the east (Doran and McNeilage 1998). Western lowland gorillas also eat leaves, bark, insects, and even algae from ponds. They seldom travel more than a kilometer (0.62 mile) in a day while foraging. Because leaves are such a low-energy food, gorillas spend most of their day foraging; some researchers nickname them "primate cows" (Stanford 1999).

Gorilla social units usually consist of one silver-backed adult male, one or more black-backed adult males, and numerous females and their young; the average is eight animals per unit (Parnell 2002). The silver-backed male does most of the breeding but not all. Most females (72 percent) stay in their natal group, but the dominant silverback comes from another group. Once established, he does not wander; but the subadult males eventually leave and wander from troop to troop or remain loners. If a silverback dies, the females are taken over by an adult male who has no females. Although the social units are stable, the tenure of a silverback is on the order of only five years. Play activity is not common and usually is restricted to youngsters.

Gorilla males are seldom aggressive. They do not usually fight over food, because it is abundant and, for the mountain gorilla, undifferentiated. Among western lowland gorillas, there is some fighting over food: These gorillas' food resources are patchier, and preferred food such as fruit is not always available (Doran and McNeilage 1998).

It is in connection with food differentiation and aggression that we may hypothesize gorilla analogies with humans. A comparison of western lowland and eastern mountain gorillas suggests that western gorillas are more aggressive, have patchier and higher-energy foods (fruit), show somewhat more tolerance among males, are somewhat smaller in size, and have smaller social groups than the mountain gorilla. Do the social behaviors correlate with ecological conditions? If so, and if enough environmental details are known, can anthropologists use this information to hypothesize about social units of early hominids?

Gorillas are in danger of extinction. Their physical size is not a successful defense against humans, diseases, and an occasional leopard attack. The parts of East and Central Africa that are home to many gorillas are currently under war conditions, so gorillas are killed for meat for soldiers, shot accidentally, and see their home territories constantly changing for the worse. It has been estimated that the Ebola virus has killed a third of the world's lowland gorillas in the past decade.

## Chimpanzees

Scientists know more about the genetics of modern chimpanzees than about the genetics of any other primate, because of the many molecular studies that compare humans to chimpanzees. The most publicized finding is that humans and chimpanzees share 91 to 99.4 percent of their genes (Wildman et al. 2003). Eighteen of the 23 pairs of

*Figure 14.4*

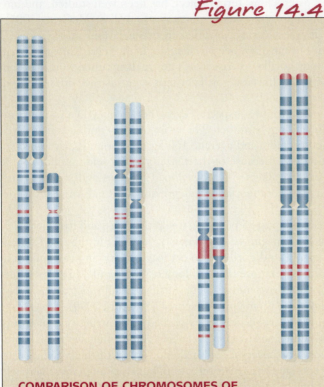

**COMPARISON OF CHROMOSOMES OF CHIMPANZEES AND HUMANS.**   Shown here are four different chromosomes of humans and chimpanzees. Human chromosomes are shown on the right of each pair and chimpanzee chromosomes on the left. Note the similarities and differences for each pair. With such great genetic similarity, why do humans look so different from chimpanzees?

*Source:* From Yunis, J. J., J. R. Sawyer, and K. Dunham. 1980. The striking resemblance of high-resolution G-banded chromosomes of man and chimpanzee. *Science* 208:1145–1149. Reprinted with permission from AAAS.

chromosomes that the two species have in common are virtually identical. (See Figure 14.4.) Perhaps only 50 genes differ (Enard et al. 2002). Some experts predict that the majority of these gene differences are in regulatory genes that turn certain other genes on and off and regulate their functions. In a first step toward compiling the chimpanzee genome, Asao Fujiyama and his team compared 77,461 chimpanzee chromosome end sequences to the publicly available human genome, finding some large areas of difference (Fujiyama et al. 2002). Because molecular analyses are ambivalent in their findings, the fact that the chimpanzee genome has been drafted at least is encouraging for evolutionary studies (Cyranoski 2002). Regardless of whether or not 99.4 percent is the correct figure, we do share considerable genetic material with chimpanzees and bonobos. This should be expected because we have shared over 99 percent of our ancestry with them. But it does not mean that "chimpanzees are us." Humans may have the same number of bones as chimpanzees (we have the same anatomical body plan as all mammals) and share a lot of genes, but a comparison of morphology and behavior shows striking differences: Chimpanzees are covered with hair, and we aren't; they have longer arms than legs, and we show the reverse pattern; we talk, and they don't. (Highlight 14.2, on pp. 450–451, considers language acquisition by chimpanzees.) There are also other differences. The following descriptions of chimpanzees and bonobos characterize them as unique species, not as humans in fur coats.

Chimpanzees *(Pan troglodytes)* are the best-known ape, primarily through the research and popular writings of Jane Goodall and her team at the Gombe Stream Reserve in Tanzania. Goodall has been studying chimpanzees since the early 1960s. Her findings, together with long-term observations by other workers in other areas, have shown that there is enough variation in learned behavior among chimpanzee groups for many experts to conclude that chimpanzees have culture. (Refer to Highlight 14.1.)

The five subspecies of chimpanzees live only in Africa; they are found in the Taï forest (Ivory Coast) in West Africa, in Congo, and in Tanzania and Uganda in East Africa—a total distance farther than from New York City to Los Angeles. No matter where they are found, chimpanzees share many traits, both morphological and behavioral. They are knuckle-walking quadrupeds while on the ground, but they do climb trees in play, while seeking fruits, to hunt red colobus monkeys, and to make and sleep in nightly nests. They can walk bipedally for short distances while carrying food, tottering from side to side. In the wild chimpanzees spend 6 to 7 hours a day feeding; fruits, leaves, and small to medium-sized animals make up their diet. Chimpanzees' life expectancy is 41 years versus humans' 76 (in 2002). Female chimps emigrate from their natal troops to another band at about age 11 and have their first birth at 13.

Socially, chimpanzees have a "fission–fusion" type of social organization. That is, groups ranging from 20 to 100 individuals loosely form a "community," the largest social unit; but the membership is fluid and constantly changing, and groups fission off and then fuse together. The community's makeup at any one time is the result of individuals' mutual attraction, friendship, and inclination, with relatives often but not necessarily belonging to the same group. Within the large, loosely structured group, there are no subgroups other than mothers with their offspring (Stanford 1999). There are no pair bonds between particular females and males, and indeed male–female sexual relations are promiscuous (Pusey 2001). Females spend about half of each day alone with their offspring in a core feeding area of about 2 square kilometers; males spend only about 18 percent of their time alone, the rest in the company of other males. What bonding there is, shown by mutual grooming and support during the few times of crisis, occurs between males. In spite of the fact that males stay in their natal group through life and are thus related, male groupings are based more on age and status than on kinship (Jones 2003). Females, who come from outside and are strangers to one another, almost never bond and appear indifferent to one another. There is a loose dominance hierarchy, but in Goodall's (1988) view it is not important. Males rank over females and older over younger, but such rankings are apparent only when humans purposely experiment with food rewards. This is probably because there is ordinarily little to have rank over: Food and sex are not in short supply (Stanford 1999).

Chimpanzees are relatively nonaggressive within and between groups, with the exceptions noted below, and with other species, hunting being a relatively rare event. Researchers noted no aggression in chimpanzees before 1970; since then, the picture has changed. Perhaps additional years of observation have turned up behavior that observers simply missed before, or perhaps something triggered aggressive behavior after 1970. It is always possible that a mutation causing a predisposition to aggression occurred and spread quickly through the species. If some factor triggered new behaviors, however, it is more likely that the factor was human-related. Researchers' provisioning of the chimpanzees at Gombe in order to view them more easily may have been that cause (Power 1991, 1995). Goodall herself observed 284 agonistic encounters, noting that 66 percent were due to banana provisioning (1988). Various kinds and levels of male chimp aggression have been seen since 1970, from mild fighting (resulting in minor injuries such as a slashed ankle), to killing fellow adult males on respective borders, to infanticide and the eating of chimpanzee infants. And at Uganda's Kibale National Park, observers have reported six cases of male chimpanzees' using sticks to severely beat females (Lindon 2002; Stanford 2001a). In the life of most chimpanzees, however, these behaviors are not everyday happenings.

Violence by chimpanzees may not occur on a daily basis, but it does occur between individuals (males batter females when they won't cooperative sexually; males fight other males for access to certain females) and between groups. Both of these phenomena have attracted considerable attention because of their similarity to human behavior. Some of the group-against-group violence appears to be due to spontaneous encounters with bordering groups, and other instances appear to be "planned" in some way. The most extreme group-against-group violence occurred at Gombe when one group eventually killed off another entire group over a 3-year period (Wrangham et al. 2006). It has been calculated that male chimpanzees live an average of 10 years less than females in the wild and in zoos, primarily because of their fighting in both contexts (deWaal 2001).

Chimpanzees have been known to use tools since Portugese missionaries described that behavior in the sixteenth century in Sierra Leone, but such tool use was not widely known among scientists or the public until the 1960s, when Goodall discovered Gombe chimpanzees "termiting." Termiting involves making a tool by breaking a twig to a certain length and stripping it of leaves so it can be stuck in termite nest holes. From the termite's perspective, when its nest is invaded by a stick, its reaction is to cling to the stick; when a chimpanzee pulls the stick out of the nest, a dozen or so tasty termite morsels are attached to be wiped off with the lips or the arm into the mouth. Since Goodall's initial report, observers have witnessed both tool making and use in the behavioral repertoire of all chimpanzee groups. Types of tool use include throwing sticks and stones at intruders, including humans, fake leopards, and snakes; using leaves as napkins to sponge up water from crotches of trees or as "leaf clippings," whose function is unknown; using twigs to fish for termites and ants; and using stones to bash numerous species of hard-shelled nuts on permanent stone anvils (McGrew 1998a, 1998b; Parker and McKinney 2005). (Refer to Highlight 14.1.)

# Highlight 14.2

## Language Acquisition by Chimpanzees and Bonobos

ONE ASPECT OF CHIMPANZEE INTELLIGENCE that has grabbed headlines for decades is language acquisition. That chimpanzees, like all primates, communicate with conspecifics (and with other species, too) is not under scrutiny. Nor is the inability of chimpanzees or gorillas to speak: Apes cannot speak, or else they would, given that for decades anthropologists, biologists, and psycholo-gists have offered countless rewards to encourage them to speak. Scientists in the 1940s to 1960s were much impressed with what chimpanzees could do and were certain that if they could figure out a way to get chimpanzees to talk, the chimpanzees would communicate their thoughts directly to their human trainers. Alas, the most trainers got out of chimpanzees in terms of speech were three or four "words." Speech is not possible for nonhuman primates, because their larynxes are high and they cannot completely close off their nasal and oral cavities as humans can.

But is language acquisition, that complex structural and symbolic communication system associated with humans, within the capabilities of chimpanzees, bonobos, or gorillas? Emily Schultz has defined language as "the system of arbitrary symbols we use to encode our experience of the world, which may imply spoken or written or signal media." Substitute "chimpanzees and gorillas" for "we" and "their" for "our," and the question becomes: Do chimpanzees and gorillas use language? Note that the definition does not require speech. Just as important, even if some primates can be *taught* language, if they do not use it in the wild, is it appropri-

Kanzi, a bonobo, has been trained to use symbols and a sign board to communicate with his human teachers. What would Kanzi do if he saw something he wanted to communicate about but there was no symbol on his board?

ate to conclude that they have language abilities? Or is it more correct to conclude that they have the ability to acquire language and leave it at that?

In a famous series of experiments, researchers have taught chimpanzees, bonobos, and gorillas how to use sign language or to use symbols for common things like food and people on computer keyboards (and later to use the same symbols on folding boards that could be transported outside of labs). Such efforts continue, their goal being to establish whether nonhuman primates have language acquisition abilities. Experts have argued for decades on both sides of the issue. Some say that nonhumans lack the ability to acquire language—that they are only taking cues from trainers and "aping" trainers' signals so as to get rewards. Others claim that large apes do have language capabilities, because they comprehend symbols (up to 250 spoken words, geometric symbols, or signs) and use proper grammar and syntax that gives meaning to word order. For example, chimpanzees demonstrate their understanding of the difference between "put the orange into the pot" and "put the pot into the oranges" or "dog bite snake" and "snake bite dog" (syntax) by doing each activity when asked (using stuffed animals for the dog-and-snake scenarios). Experimental chimpanzees and bonobos can accomplish these linguistic feats at the same level as a 2½-year-old human child; additionally, at least one bonobo (Kanzi) has a word vocabulary larger than a child of that age. A relatively recent approach looks at the brain itself, par-

ticularly at the planum temporale (PT), a bit of brain lying in the auditory association cortex that attaches meanings to sounds. The majority of autopsied chimpanzees that died natural deaths in zoos show the same form of PT as humans. If chimpanzees and bonobos show language acquisition skills and use language with the same brain structures as humans, it is hard to deny that they have at least language acquisition potential.

Could gestures have been the basis of human language, with sounds added later? Living apes use many gestures when communicating to one another; humans use many gestures with their hands and heads to emphasize certain points when they speak; and it has been hypothesized that the visual–gesture means of communication preceded and evolved into the vocal–auditory (speech) mode.

*Sources:* Begley, S. 1998. Aping human language. *Newsweek* (January 19): 56–58.  Stanford, C. 2001. *Significant others: The ape-human continuum and the quest for human nature.* New York: Basic Books.  Ingold, T. 1994. Relations between visual-gestural and vocal-auditory modalities of communication. In *Language, tools, and cognition,* ed. K. R. Gibson and T. Ingold, pp. 35–42. Cambridge: Cambridge University Press.  Savage-Rumbaugh, S. 1998. *Apes, language, and the human mind.* Oxford: Oxford University Press. Schultz, E. 2002. Discourse and politics: Development in linguistic anthropology since the 1970s. *General Anthropology* 8 (2): 1–7.

turn back to your reading

Chimpanzees also use tools for purposes not related to obtaining food: sticks to help groom, leaves to clean themselves, sticks to protect their feet and rumps while feeding in thorny areas, and leaves as umbrellas. Finally, one chimpanzee was observed using a stick to dig out a rotten tooth from another chimpanzee. How common this particular behavior may be has not been established (Parker and McKinney 2005).

In spite of the different kinds of tools made and used by chimpanzees, there appear to be limits to the new tool techniques they can learn, even when a preferred food is the reward. In a 10-year experiment, Kathy Schick has been attempting to teach Kanzi, the famous bonobo who can use hundreds of different computer icons to communicate with his trainers, how to make simple flint tools. Humans made such tools by percussing one rock on another to get chips of various sorts. But after 10 years Kanzi only learned how to throw the rocks on the cement floor of his cage and use the resultant chips to cut the cord holding his banana reward (de la Torre 2004).

All chimpanzee groups that have been well studied have been known to hunt to some degree. Hunting varies by sex, however, as well as by the species of the prey hunted, the methods used, and the sharing of the spoils. Females sometimes hunt, but far less than males. Interestingly, females termite and ant dip three times more often than males. Is this analogous to human females' collecting small-sized food units? Though not every male in every group has been seen to hunt, it is likely that hunting is in the repertoire of virtually every male at some time during his life. Observers have documented 35 different prey species that together make up about 3 percent of chimpanzees' diet (Stanford 2001a). Chimpanzees hunt numerous species of monkeys, as well as immature warthogs and impalas, but red colobus (monkeys) are the most hunted prey species. At Gombe and Kibale groups of chimpanzees take as many as seven colobus in a single hunting event, and researchers have calculated that chimpanzees hunt, kill, and consume an average of 10 to 20 percent of the colobus population each year (Walls and Mitani 2002). Normally, infants are the target; often chimps snatch a baby colobus from its mother's arms, leaving the mother untouched unless she tries to rescue her infant—in which case she too will probably be killed and eaten (Stanford 1999, 2001a). Hunting does not seem to be planned, but once a group of chimpanzees encounters a prey animal, one or all members attack the animal. At Gombe there is only limited cooperation among the hunters, and most of the carcass is consumed by the hunter, other males who also took part in the hunting event, certain relatives, and estrus females. At Taï there is much more cooperation among the hunters, and almost any chimpanzee can beg for and receive bits of meat (Boesch and Boesch 2000). A recent observation of 22 cases of chimpanzees biting the tips of sticks and using them like spears to jab into holes in trees and pull out bushbabies (small prosimians) and then eat them reminds us again of the similarities between chimpanzee and human hunting behavior. Interestingly, most of the hunters in this case were female (Gibbons 2007).

Because chimpanzees (and bonobos) and humans had a common ancestral group only 6 myr ago, it is not surprising that chimps and humans share so many similarities in DNA, anatomy, morphology, and behavior. And the list keeps growing. Interesting similarities such as the ability to lie and deceive have come to light. Although bioanthropologists sometimes overanalyze behaviors with anthropomorphic overtones, it is hard to deny intentional deceit on the part of a male who presents his enlarged penis to a female, then uses his hands to cover it when the dominant male walks by (Dickinson 1988). It is natural, therefore, for comparisons between humans and chimpanzees to generate numerous hypotheses about common ancestors and human evolution. Comparisons in the areas of intelligence, language ability, and culture have resulted in a better understanding of both that elusive LCA and early hominid behavior. Additionally, some anthropologists have focused on chimpanzees' hunting to generate hypotheses about the active scavenging of early hominids. Although all primatologists note that chimpanzees hunt, some have suggested that hunting was the key to human intelligence. Craig Stanford (1999, 2001a), who extensively studied chimpanzee hunting and meat consumption at Gombe for 4 years, calculates that on average chimpanzees consume the same amount of meat that modern human foragers consume during lean months. Early hominid hunting may not have been very different from this chimpanzee behavioral pattern.

Stanford (2001a) also hypothesizes that the sharing of meat is at the root of human brain expansion. He notes that chimpanzees (and early hominids, by analogy) need good memory to recall with whom they share meat and with whom they form alliances—and that memory is dependent on brain size. Hominid brain size did not increase dramatically for several million years, and big game hunting did not occur until several million years after the split, but both could have had precursors in earlier times.

Finally, a number of psychologists have attempted to teach chimpanzees how to use language. Speech (oral language) is tied specifically to the human vocal apparatus. But language need not be oral, and sign language and using lexigrams are within the cognitive abilities of Washoe, Kanzi, and other chimpanzees and bonobos. This is the focus of Highlight 14.2.

## Bonobos

Bonobos (*Pan paniscus*) were the last ape population to be identified by scientists—in the 1920s—and are relatively uncommon. Western scientists did not know very much about bonobos until recently because the early studies were done by Japanese scientists and published only in Japanese. Formerly, bonobos were referred to as "skinny" chimpanzees. They are now given separate species status. They do not interbreed with chimpanzees in the wild, having split 2.5 to 2 myr ago, but will interbreed in captivity (Eckhardt 2000; Stanford 1998). Bonobos live only in a small area of Africa, south of the Zaire River, with the river forming a speciation barrier with chimpanzees. Two long-term sites in central Congo, Klomako and Wamba, have provided good observations of bonobos; the apes were provisioned with sugar cane at Wamba. Although bonobos share many general morphological traits with chimpanzees, they differ in their slightly smaller average size and leaner build, smaller heads, and straighter stance when bipedal. They can remain bipedal longer than other apes because their knees can lock in place; other apes have to bend their knees when bipedal. Bonobos have flatter faces and higher foreheads than chimpanzees, and their hair is parted neatly in the middle (de Waal 2001). Bonobos appear to be as capable as chimpanzees at acquiring language skills. (See Highlight 14.2.) Like chimpanzees, they eat fruit and other plants, but they neither hunt nor eat animal food to any noticeable extent. They also differ in their less frequent use of tools and in their social organization. They live in large fission–fusion "communities" ranging from 25 to 75 individuals, and females often take the dominant role at least in feeding situations. Although females leave their natal group and are therefore originally strangers to one another, they nonetheless form bonds, and males do not (de Waal 1997; Stanford 1999). Male bonobos are somewhat larger in size than females, so there is the potential for male aggression toward females (or other males). But, although adult males in a group do not seem overly fond of one another, female–female and female–male bonding seems to keep the peace. If a male bonobo tries to intimidate or attack a female, several females will band together and mob him. One primatologist saw a female bonobo bite off the penis of a male when he would not stop annoying her with sexual invitations (Dunbar 2005). It is possible that female bonobos have been able to become dominant because of ecological reasons, while female chimpanzees have not. The Congo area where bonobos live is like a never-ending buffet, with huge food supplies, and females do not have to go far to forage. They therefore have time to spend together bonding. By contrast, female chimpanzees have to forage most of the day in patchy areas to find enough food.

Among the large apes orangutans (top left) are Asian; gorillas (top right), chimpanzees (bottom left), and bonobos (bottom right) are African. Note their morphological traits. Do chimpanzees and bonobos look the most alike? Do chimpanzees and bonobos look more like humans than gorillas do? What does this tell you about morphological comparisons?

Unlike chimpanzees, bonobos have never been seen to practice lethal aggression: no infanticide, no cannibalism, no intergroup warfare (de Waal 2001). Bonobos are the only large ape species that does not engage in individual or group violence. They don't fight among themselves, use sexual coercion, kill infants, or compete for rank. They occasionally capture a monkey and play with it! When they meet other groups of bonobos, they socialize and engage in sexual activities. They are the "odd" ape in this regard, but the question is, why aren't they violent? Some experts suggest bonobos have as much genetic predisposition toward violence as other apes, but the circumstances that cause such behavior in other apes have not arisen in bonobos' case. For example, there is some seasonal food resource pressure on chimpanzees, but food is readily available year-round for bonobos, and this may explain some of the differences in the behavior of the two species (Stumpf 2007). Others suggest that bonobos "lost their violence genes" several million years ago, after they split with chimpanzees (Wrangham 1999).

Perhaps the most interesting trait, to humans, that bonobos show is their zeal in sexual matters: As Highlight 14.3 (on pp. 456–457) describes, bonobos not only appear to enjoy sex for its own sake but also use it to solve a lot of daily problems.

Bonobos today live where they did 2.5 myr ago; at the time of their split, it was the chimpanzees that moved. Therefore, it is possible that the modern bonobo group is more like the LCA than modern chimpanzees are—assuming chimpanzees had to change and adapt to new environmental conditions. If so, the LCA group might be characterized as having had a female-dominated social system, with sex serving political as well as social functions, and a society devoid of warfare (de Waal 1997).

Bonobos are threatened with extinction. There are only about 100 of them in zoos, so zoo breeding programs are not apt to save them. In the wild poachers continue to kill them for bushmeat. In Africa, more and more villagers and townsfolk consider primates as suitable bushmeat so the market is there. One 2000 estimate of the bonobo population in the Congo was between 10,000 and 50,000 individuals. But a nine-month survey done in 2003 in the only area where bonobos are officially protected failed to sight a single bonobo, and the team heard only one bonobo vocalization in the entire time (Graham-Rowe 2004). This is crisis indeed.

# Endangered Primates

It has been estimated that 195 of the 250+ primate species are under threat of extinction. Some terrestrial primates, like baboons and rhesus macaques, are sufficiently numerous and gregarious to be in no danger (and the rhesus macaques are somewhat protected by religious beliefs). But as more and more forests in Madagascar and jungles in South America are cleared for farming, there is less and less tree canopy for primates and their food. The resource in short supply is trees more than food. Two entire families of primates and both small and large apes are in the "most endangered" category, with close to a dozen other species "severely threatened" (Kottak 2008; Strier 2007). A study of gorillas and chimpanzees in Gabon and Congo (areas that contain 80 percent of the world's wild individuals) shows that these species declined more than 50 percent between 1983 and 2000 because of living in war zones, being hunted for live animal trade, commercial hunting (for bushmeat), being eaten by miners who are mining tantalum for cell phones, loss of territory (from mechanized logging), and disease (Ebola) (Walsh 2003). It has been estimated by the United Nations' Great Apes Survival Project (GRASP) that by 2030 only 10 percent of the habitat used by African apes will remain and less than 1 percent for Asian orangutans. Other dire predictions claim orangutans will become extinct in Sumatra in 5 years and bonobos in 10 years. On paper, all countries have laws to protect apes, but they are obviously not working. One wonders how much money would have to be thrown at the problem to fix it.

# In the Field with Those Sexy Bonobos

IN MOST PRIMATE SPECIES sexual activities appear to function strictly for procreation purposes; sex is limited in duration and is basically hardwired, or under genetic control. Females come into estrus periodically, and males both observe the enlarged pink areas in female anal regions and smell female excreted hormones—and members of each gender do their part without learning to do it and whether they want to or not. With only a few exceptions, sexual intercourse takes place only during the times when females are fertile.

One of the few exceptions to this pattern—sex as procreation only and only during fertile periods—is humans, who engage in sex often and without regard to state of receptivity (human females do not show signs of being fertile and as far as is known, human males do not notice female hormones). So it is interesting to both specialists and the lay public that another species of primate, the bonobo, engages in sexual activity often, without regard to the state of female receptivity, and seemingly enjoys it. Additionally, like humans, bonobos use sex for purposes other than reproduction.

In the zoo and in the lab as well as in the wild, bonobo sex takes place not merely between adult males and adult females, but in every possible age group and sexual category: male–female, female–female, male–male, and adolescent–adult of all categories. Bonobos also engage in sex in every position imaginable: Males and females use both frontal and rear positions; females rub each other frontally, one lifting the other off the ground and clinging to her as they rub; males do rump-to-rump rubbing. However although males mutually rub penises, they do no anal penetration. Males even do "penis fencing," by hanging from branches facing each other and rubbing their erect penises as if they were engaging in sword play! Both sexes engage in oral sex with males, and both sexes masturbate. But there is no ejaculation of semen except during male–female sex.

Although chimpanzees appear to be interested in sex and watch others perform it, they do not attempt to get involved. Bonobos do. If an adult male thrusts his penis at a young male, the young male jumps on him and starts rubbing.

Yes, but do they enjoy it? Frans de Waal, who has probably seen more bonobo sexual activity than any other human, says yes. The evidence: Their heart rates increase; the females have rapid uterine contractions; and both sexes give "pleasure grins," squeals, and screams. How often do they do it? In zoos, where bonobos' sexual activity can be closely monitored, it averages every 90 minutes, day in, day out. In contrast, chimpanzees have sex every seven hours on average (and only seldom is it other than male–female); human sexual activity is difficult to monitor, but in no society is it 16 times a day! How long does bonobo sexual activity last? Only 13 seconds in zoos and 15 seconds in the wild. When observers compare zoo-living bonobos with wild chimpanzees, bonobos get the sex award without question; but if both species are observed either in the wild or in zoos, the levels of sexual activity are somewhat more equal. Given age spans, menstrual cycles, and length of pregnancies, chimpanzee females are receptive only 5 percent of their lives, but bonobo females are receptive 50 percent of their lives.

What is the function of bonobo sexuality, other than the obvious procreative one? De Waal calculates that 75 percent of all sexual encounters have nothing to do with reproduction. Given the stimuli noted for sexual activity, de Waal and others have hypothesized that bonobos use sex as a substitute for power competition and aggression as well as in normal day-to-day socialization. Sex also substitutes for communication under certain circumstances. For example, when food arrives in the zoo, all males as a group get erections and engage in a bit of a sex orgy before settling down to eat. In the wild, when a group finds a fig tree loaded with their favorite fruit, they engage in 1 to 5 minutes of indiscriminate sex. Bonobos appear to use sex to overcome and reduce social tensions within the group and to keep aggression with other groups to a minimum. Within the troop, males probably substitute rubbing for rivalries, as males are allowed to hang out with females and even engage in sex with them after rubbing the male rival. When strange males encounter each other, they scream, go bipedally erect, but soon touch genitals and then embrace. (It is interesting to contemplate the idea of the world's political leaders adopting this behavior before sitting down at the conference table to discuss mutual problems.) Females appear to use sex to get food; estrus females solicit males who are hoarding food and steal the provender while still engaged in sexual intercourse.

Are bonobos a good model in regard to sexual activities among early hominids? Although some will use the similarities between modern human and bonobo sexuality as analogous, the resemblances are probably not homologous. Bonobos live in lush forests where females pair-bond and are somewhat dominant over males; in contrast, early hominids lived in more open woods and semi-savanna environments where female dominance was not likely. This kind of sexuality was probably not found in the LCA either.

*Sources*: de Waal, F. B. 1997. *Bonobo: The forgotten ape*. Berkeley: University of California Press. Susman, R. L. 1984. *The pygmy chimpanzee: Evolutionary biology and behavior*. New York: Plenum.

turn back to your reading

Contemporary primates are instructive to anthropologists because knowledge about them can be used to form hypotheses regarding human evolution, that elusive LCA, and the behavior of early hominids.

■ No contemporary primate species can be used as a direct representation of any past species.

■ Primatology is the field that studies nonhuman primates, and within the field psychologists, biologists, and bioanthropologists ask somewhat different questions.

page 434

social organization; howler monkeys (New World) are nonaggressive. Both of these findings suggest hypotheses about human evolution.

■ Primatologists study their subjects in the field, in zoos, and in laboratories, depending on the nature of the project.

■ Because the focus of this book is on humans, applications of primate studies to humans are at the forefront of the discussion, which uses a case study approach.

page 430

■ Modern tarsiers differ from prosimians and are found only in Southeast Asia and Indonesia.

■ Modern prosimians share a considerable number of general derived traits plus those they evolved after they split to separate lineages.

■ Old and New World monkeys share many general derived traits plus those they evolved after they split. Hamadryas baboons (Old World) have three levels of

page 437

■ Apes include gibbons and siamangs (small apes) and orangutans, gorillas, chimpanzees, and bonobos (large apes). Each has a set of ancestral traits as well as traits that have evolved since the lineages split. Chimpanzees and bonobos share many "intelligence" traits with humans, and both species can be taught rudiments of language. No nonhuman primate can speak.

■ Many primates are endangered because of small numbers and encroachment by human activities.

## KEY WORDS

biologists, 423
contemporary primates, 422
field studies, 426
laboratory studies, 427

large apes, 442
New World monkeys, 438
nonhuman primates, 422
Old World monkeys, 436

primatology, 423
psychologists, 423
small apes, 441
zoo studies, 426

## SUGGESTED READING

Campbell, C. J., A. Fuentes, K. C. MacKinnon, M. Panger, and S. K. Bearder, eds. *Primates in Perspective*. New York: Oxford University Press, 2007. This recent publication covers reproduction, ecology, behavior, and intelligence in all primates, including tarsiers, prosimians, monkeys, and apes. Chapters are written by species experts.

de Waal, F. *Bonobo: The Forgotten Ape*. Berkeley: University of California Press, 1997. This is the main source for information on bonobos, with excellent photos of them in the wild. The book goes into great detail on bonobos' sex lives and how they use sex politically and socially.

Goodall, J. *In the Shadow of Man*. Boston: Houghton Mifflin, 1988. This book describes chimpanzee behaviors during the years before Goodall began provisioning at Gombe.

MacKinnon, J. R. *In Search of the Red Ape*. New York: Holt, Rinehart, & Winston, 1974. MacKinnon weaves an adventure story of the world of the orangutans in Borneo, "taking you there" as he follows the orangutans through the forest day after day.

Matsuzawa, T., ed. *Primate Origins of Human Cognition and Behavior*. New York: Springer, 2001. Japanese primatologists have specialized in studying Japanese macaques and chimpanzees and are particularly strong in their studies of chimpanzee culture, Japanese macaques' tool use, and additional cognitive aspects of primate behavior. This collection, in English, summarizes much of this work.

McGrew, W. *The Cultured Chimpanzee: Reflections on Cultural Primatology*. Cambridge: Cambridge University Press, 2004. McGrew was the first anthropologist to suggest that chimpanzees had culture after he discovered a learned behavioral trait in a chimpanzee colony that did not exist in the colony he had been studying. It has been an uphill battle to convince the rest of the discipline. In this book, he reflects on the growing evidence of the phenomenon.

Wrangham, R., ed. *Chimpanzee Cultures*. Cambridge, MA: Harvard University Press, 1994. In the early 1990s William McGrew first began to popularize the idea that chimpanzees had culture. This book brings together discussions by numerous experts in the field of primatology on various aspects of chimpanzee culture, from tools to language acquisition.

# Chapter 15 | Contemporary Humans

- ■ **THE LAST 50 KYR IN THE OLD WORLD**
- ■ **HIGHLIGHT 15.1:** *Homo floresiensis*

- ■ **NATIVE AMERICANS: FACTS AND CONTROVERSIES**

- ■ **CAUSES OF MICROEVOLUTION IN CONTEMPORARY HUMANS**
  Population Genetics

- ■ **GENERAL TRENDS OF CONTEMPORARY HUMANS**

- ■ **HUMAN BIOLOGICAL VARIABILITY: THE SPECIES TODAY**
  How Do Humans Vary? • Why Do Humans Vary? • Group Variation: "Race" or Not? • *Homo sapiens* and Co-variation of Traits

- ■ **A HISTORY OF "RACE" IN AMERICA: FROM BIOLOGY TO CULTURE**
  Intelligence and Racism

- ■ **HUMAN ADAPTATIONS**
  Growth and Development, Health and Disease
- ■ **HIGHLIGHT 15.2:** *We Are What We Were, or Are We?*

- ■ **APPLIED BIOLOGICAL ANTHROPOLOGY**
  Are Humans Naturally Violent? • DNA Fingerprinting and AIDS • Reconstructing Faces

- ■ **FORENSIC ANTHROPOLOGY**
  Spitalfields: Verifying Knowledge

- ■ **HIGHLIGHT 15.3:** *In the News: Identification of Josef Mengele*

- ■ **CHAPTER SUMMARY**

**Photo above:** Kennewick Man

The term *modern humans* is not scientifically precise and has different meanings for different people: For some the term is synonymous with "bipedally walking hominids"; for others the term refers exclusively to people who are alive today; for others it refers to all ancestral forms that show the ability to do what contemporary humans do. This chapter uses the term **modern humans** in an evolutionary sense to refer to those hominids whose fossilized anatomy suggests they would fall within the range of people living today and who leave evidence that they were able to do what people living today are able to do. In behavioral terms, this usually refers to the ability to do and have art, ritual, religion, science, and speech, behaviors not attributable to the LCA. Again, only the genetic parts of behavior are evolutionary. We will use the term **contemporary humans** when we refer to human populations in existence today or in the very recent past.

Chapter 7 introduced the terms *anatomically modern humans* (AMH) and *behaviorally modern humans* (BMH), detailing the traits of AMH. The term BMH is used for hominids showing behavioral capabilities similar to those of contemporary humans. Being behaviorally modern does not mean taking taxis and using cell phones. It means having the *ability* to do what all humans living now can do. Until recently, the definition of BMH was based on a list that compared those behaviors absent in the Middle Paleolithic to those present in the Upper Paleolithic. This has a decidedly Eurocentric bias. Today, experts attempt to define modern behavior as

> behavior that is mediated by socially constructed patterns of symbolic thinking, action, and communication that allow for material and information exchange and cultural continuity between and across generations and contemporaneous communities (Henshilwood and Marean 2003, 645).

Such behavior might include—but is not limited to—language/speech and art, and it might initially be found in Africa, Asia, or Europe. Once "modernity" is defined, anthropologists can look for its evidence in the artifact record.

As established earlier, behavior is the result of the interaction of both genes and learning—both biology and culture. By Neandertal times all of the main categories of human behavior were in evidence except art/aesthetics; the category of culture called "teaching" also lacks hard evidence, but it is difficult to believe that parents were not purposely teaching their children how to hunt or do other tasks.

For populations to be modern in an evolutionary sense, they must be both AMH and BMH. AMH traits appeared in the fossil record before many critical BMH traits. Most experts date AMH to at least 100 kyr ago. Sally McBrearty and Alison Brooks (2000) have argued for some early behavioral advances in Africa at the same time as anatomical modernity, pointing to bone tools and blade technology at 90 kyr ago; but unambiguous evidence of art, ritual, and religion do not appear until about 40 kyr ago. Fifty thousand years ago seems an appropriate date to suggest the beginnings of truly modern humans, although further evidence will probably alter that date. Because all people alive today are anatomically and behaviorally modern, this chapter is the anthropology of us.

Like Chapter 14 on contemporary nonhuman primates, one purpose of this chapter on humans is to find patterns that might help in understanding human evolution. The phrase "we are what we were" means that analyzing contemporary humans may help anthropologists generate hypotheses about humans in the past that they can test against the fossil, archaeological, and environmental records.

The first sections of this chapter look at humans living during the last 50 kyr in the Old World and at Native Americans. Then, several sections focus on contemporary moderns. These sections discuss microevolution, general trends of contemporary humans, human biological variability between groups, the notion of "race," and human adaptations. The chapter ends with discussions of applied bioanthropology and forensic anthropology.

**modern humans**
Humans from between 100 and 50 kyr ago through modern times who are both AMH and BMH.

**contemporary humans**
Humans that are alive today; contemporary humans are all modern humans, but some modern humans are not contemporary.

# The Last 50 kyr in the Old World

As we saw in Chapter 7, anatomically modern humans (AMH) very likely evolved first in Africa and spread into the rest of the Old World, either replacing or interbreeding with hominids already in place. (Much later, humans arrived in the New World.) Evidence for moderns exists in Europe, Asia, and Australia before 40 kyr ago. The continents and some of the larger islands, such as New Guinea, were populated earlier than Japan, Tasmania, or the Oceanic islands (Bowler et al. 2003; Gillespie 2002). Biological anthropologists, molecular scientists, archaeologists, and linguists often combine efforts to reconstruct these migrations. For example, Easter Island has always been a favorite of anthropologists; and evidence from both DNA and oral traditions, together with evidence of material culture, biological comparisons, and linguistics, reaffirms Polynesian ancestry for Easter Islanders (Hagelberg et al. 1994). Linguists, archaeologists, and biological anthropologists are helping to work out the details of how Europe became populated with modern humans: Was it *people* who moved from east to west, bringing their genes as well as Neolithic farming, beginning about 8,000 years ago? Or did the *idea* for farming diffuse in a westerly direction without any large-scale human migration (which would have resulted in a rapid change in the biological gene pool)? Studies suggest that the majority of modern European mitochondrial DNA was established by the Upper Paleolithic, with less than 20 percent of the DNA coming from Middle Eastern farmers during the Neolithic (Cavalli-Sforza 2001; Renfrew 2000; Richards 2003; Richards, Macauley, et al. 2000; Wade 2003b). This biological evidence suggests that although some farmers did migrate westward, Europeans became farmers mainly through stimulus diffusion from neighbors. In other words, only the idea was borrowed, resulting in gene change similar to what would be expected through unidirectional gene flow.

In 2004 bioanthropologists were amazed to learn that there perhaps was a species of humans other than *Homo sapiens* on Earth after 50 kyr ago. The remarkable *Homo floresiensis* is discussed in Highlight 15.1 (on pp. 464–467).

# Native Americans: Facts and Controversies

Anthropologists—including cultural anthropologists, linguists, archaeologists, and bioanthropologists—have long been interested in studying **Native Americans** (or American Indians). Some Europeans questioned whether Native Americans were humans, but after a few interbreedings produced human offspring, the Pope declared they had souls so were human. Europeans and then European Americans nevertheless treated them about as badly as the British treated native Tasmanians and Australians. The Native Americans lost their land, their populations decreased drastically due to disease for which they had no immunity, and their social lives were disrupted and often destroyed. They continued to suffer as a population and were all but forgotten by most Americans until the 1970s, when having Native American ancestry became acceptable.

A Spanish cleric named Fray José de Acosta first suggested in 1590 that Native Americans walked across a land bridge from Asia to Alaska at the Bering Strait; and with few exceptions, this idea has dominated subsequent hypotheses about where these peoples came from. There have been alternative suggestions—such as the idea that Native Americans were one of the Lost Tribes of Israel or that they were closely related to French Solutrean people—but all credible evidence points to Asia as the home of Native Americans, though which part of Asia is not resolved. Some experts side with the old idea of Northest Asia as the homeland of all Native Americans, while others point to closer anatomical similarities to people in south Asia or some part of the Pacific Rim (Dillehay 2003). Evidence to support Asia as the homeland is particularly strong in comparative biology, both at the morphological level (body build, skin color, eye color, hair

**Native Americans**
The descendants of the wave(s) of humans who left Asia via a land bridge at the Bering Strait to inhabit the New World beginning between 25 and 15 kyr ago.

form and color, sparseness of face and body hair, height of cheekbones, and shovel-shaped incisors) and at the molecular level (genetic profiles and presence of certain blood antigens). Comparative linguistics also points to Asian ancestry, as does recent archaeological evidence. DNA studies comparing modern Asians and modern Native Americans suggest that the Lake Baikal area of east central Asia might have been the last ancestral home. These studies indicate that a single migration of Asians to the New World may have occurred, but it did so before the time when Asians evolved the morphological traits of modern Asians (Fiedel 2002).

Although the "where" and "who" questions about Native Americans' origins seem to be reasonably well answered, and perhaps the "how" and "why" as well (walking across the land bridge while following game), the "when" question continues to stymy experts. De Acosta suggested that the migration took place 2,000 years before his time (so 2,400 years ago). Early archaeologists suggested 5,000 years ago, but this idea was based on pure speculation (Fiedel 2000). In the 1920s spear points were found embedded in bones of bison that had been killed on the high plains. Thirty years later the bones were $^{14}$C dated; the results gave an average date of 10,780 years ago—and, by good association, for the spear tips, called **Clovis points**, as well. More recently experts have revised this $^{14}$C date to reflect new understanding of "wiggles, jumps, and plateaus" in such dates; this revision yielded a range for the Clovis tradition from 13.2 to 12.8 kyr ago, a window of only 400 years (Fiedel 2000, 2002). Some archaeologists believe that Clovis people were the first New World population and see no reason to postulate the migration of Native Americans before 15 kyr ago. But some specialists question whether there was enough time for groups to move from Alaska to the high plains in only 2,000 years; others point to the many deposits of artifacts that appear to be stratigraphically below Clovis finds, artifacts that are much simpler and lack flutes. Such **pre-Clovis artifacts** range from Wisconsin, Pennsylvania, and Virginia to Chile (Waters and Stafford 2007). If substantiated, the earlier artifacts suggest an earlier colonization of the New World. However, all potential pre-Clovis finds are problematic except for the materials at Monte Verde (Chile) and Wisconsin; the problems range from unconfirmed dates due to contamination or inconsistent stratigraphy to identification of stones as tools (Fiedel 2000; Roosevelt 2000). Five skulls from central Mexico (found in the storeroom of the National Museum of Anthropology in Mexico City) have been provisionally $^{14}$C dated as 13 kyr old (Svitil 2003). If substantiated, these not only are the oldest bones in the New World but also suggest a pre-Clovis date. Mexico is a considerable distance from Alaska.

If the dates for an ice-free corridor from Alaska through western Canada are correct, then dates for Monte Verde and other sites and fossils are perhaps most consistent with a date between 25 and 11 kyr ago for the migration to Alaska. It would need to be closer to 25 than 11 kyr ago for there to be enough time for people to migrate to South America by 14 kyr ago.

The issue of when the first Native American set foot on New World soil is only part of the question; the other part asks whether there was a single migrating event or more than one wave of migration. As mentioned earlier, some DNA evidence points to a single migration from the middle of Siberia. Other biological (and linguistic) evidence, however, suggests that there were as many as four waves, separated by thousands of years, each bringing a new kind of Asian group with a different gene pool (Brace and Nelson 1999). A related question asks what route or routes the migrants took. The two major possibilities are (1) the inland route south, through an ice-free corridor that geologists suggest was closed between 21 and 14 kyr ago, and (2) the coastal route along the Pacific Ocean, with groups using simple boats to island-hop. As for the pre-Clovis/Solutrean hypothesis, which would have Europeans colonizing the New World before the Vikings or Columbus, there is no genetic or linguistic evidence to support it. Even archaeological evidence is lacking, as there is a 6,000-year void between the end of the Solutrean in France and the first Clovis tools on the high plains (Fiedel 2000). So we will not discuss this hypothesis further.

**Clovis points**
The fluted projectile points made between about 13.2 and 12.8 kyr ago in North America.

**pre-Clovis artifacts**
Tools found in the Americas that predate Clovis points.

# Homo floresiensis

LIKE ALL SCIENTISTS, ANTHROPOLOGISTS are well known for their disagreements, both public and private—at professional meetings, in the hallways, on paper or in person, friendly or vicious. But the controversy over a single find in Indonesia, announced on October 28, 2004, has been a three-ring circus. The find was a 3-foot-tall hominid, the now famous, or infamous, "Hobbit," whose technical name, at least for now, is *Homo floresiensis*.

## SOME FACTS

Archaeologist Michael Morwood (University of New England, New South Wales, Australia) excavated a site in central Flores, an island in the eastern part of Indonesia, in 1998 and dated stone tools (but no bones) to 840 kyr ago. Because of the dating, Morwood attributed the tools to *Homo erectus*. Since this was not fantastic news, it was hardly covered by any media. Indonesian archaeologists had been excavating a cave site called Liang Bua in western Flores intermittently since the 1970s, depending on funding availability, but they concentrated on the upper layers in the cave. In July 2001,

Morwood and his team discovered the bones of a pygmy elephant and some stone tools. The first hominid material, an isolated tooth, was unearthed at the end of the third season in 2003, and a week later, the Indonesian team found the first of the hominid bone materials, called LB1 (Liang Bua 1). Since then, more hominid bones were excavated, for a total of nine individuals.

Peter Brown (University of New England, New South Wales, Australia) is the lead bioanthropologist on the Liang Bua project. He claims the bones are very fragile and not yet fossilized. The LB1 find includes cranium, mandible, right leg, left pelvis, partial left leg, hand bones, feet bones, vertebrae, sacrum, scapula, clavicles, and some ribs. The arms were missing. The skull was very small, first assessed at 380 cc but now put at 417 cc. The skull shows no keeling, a trait of the Asian *Homo erectus* skulls. Some experts believe LB1 is female; some think it is male.

The bipedal adult hominid stood about 3 feet tall. Modern traits include the shape of the braincase, the thickness of the bone, hands and feet, small teeth, and a narrow nose. Its small brain case, lack of chin, and wide pelvis are not like modern *Homo sapiens*. Some American bioanthropologists, led by Dean Falk, were allowed to do endocasts and reconstructions based on CT scans that they then compared to apes, two australopithecines, *H. erectus*, *H. sapiens*, a modern human pygmy, and a microcephalic modern human—all hominids (except the apes) that the Flores find might resemble. They came to no definite conclusion because the hominid resembles the australo-

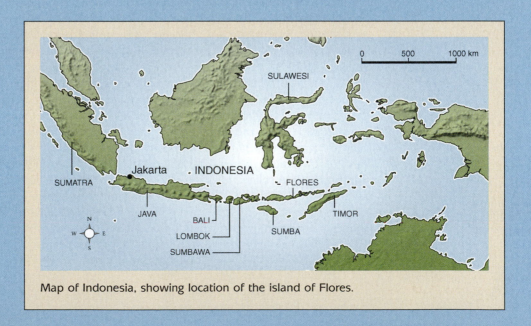

Map of Indonesia, showing location of the island of Flores.

Excavations in the cave of Liang Bua, where the remains of *Homo floresiensis* were found.

pithecines in one set of measurements and *H. erectus* in another.

Michael Morwood is the lead archaeologist on the project. He reports that most of the bones of the 26 pygmy elephants found were juveniles, suggesting selective hunting of the less dangerous animals. Some were adults, however. Some of the bones had butchery marks and were charred, and several circular clusters of burned stone appear to be hearths, so the hominids were likely cooking in the cave. Only 32 stone tools were found in the same layer as the bones, but thousands of simple flakes were found in other sections of the cave. The tools apparently look very much like those excavated in central Flores and dated to 840 kyr ago, which were originally attributed to *H. erectus*. In addition, a set of more complex tools was uncovered that included points, perforators, blades, awls, and even microliths that might have been hafted on wooden staves as spear points.

Teuku Jacob (Gadjah Mada University) demanded that the bones be turned over to him. After three months, he returned them, but the Morwood-Brown team claims some of the bones were seriously damaged in transit or in Jacob's lab,

a claim Jacob denies, countering that the bones were intact when they left his lab. While he had the materials in his possession, he sent off a 1-gram sample to the Max Planck Institute in Germany, a lab well known for its DNA analysis.

## ON DATING

The dating of the find was apparently in the hands of the archaeology team, as it is discussed in the archaeology report in *Nature*. The following techniques were listed as having been used in the dating: $^{14}C$ (AMS), luminescence (IRSL), ESR, and U-series. The dates range between 38,000 and 6,800 years ago for the original find. Overlaying layers were dated by calibrated $^{14}C$ dating of "associated charcoal"; luminescence (IRSL) dated sediment samples alongside and above the fossil, giving a date between 14,200 and 6,800 years ago. TL emission dates for two quartz samples were 38 kyr and 35 kyr old; a U-series was run on flowstone overlying the premolar, giving it a date of 37.7 kyr ago. First, note that none of these techniques dated the bone itself. The investigators give the date of 18,000 years ago for the Flores hominid, although only associated charcoal and sediments

*(continues on the next page)* ▶

were dated. If the fossil is the age suggested, the bone itself could have been dated by $^{14}$C. The investigators contend the dates are "consistent."

The big mystery is, how can an adult hominid dated as 18,000 years old be only three feet tall and have a brain the size of a grapefruit at about 400 cc, but make and use fairly sophisticated tools? An adult hominid from that period in Indonesia should be 5 feet 8 inches tall and have a brain size of 1,350 cc. This is, of course, the meat of the controversy, as the Flores find is like nothing ever seen before.

## SOME INTERPRETATIONS

One interpretation of the hominids' ancestry and taxonomic status says that they evolved from *H. erectus* some 250 kyr ago and evolved their shortness in isolation after they got to Flores. There is an "island rule" that suggests that if a population is isolated, there are no big predators, and food resources are limited, populations will become smaller in size. Animals larger than rabbits tend to shrink on islands. Both the elephants and the hominids could have gotten smaller on Flores. Animals smaller than rabbits tend to get larger on islands and indeed there are giant rats on Flores. The finding of a very small *H. erectus* in Kenya and the small crania of the Dmanisi hominids suggest that *H. erectus* had small size in its biorepertoire. On the other hand, neither the Kenya nor Dmanisi hominids were from populations on islands.

Other interpretations concerning ancestry are these:

- The hominids evolved from *H. sapiens* between 55 and 35 kyr ago after reaching AMH status on mainland Asia. Their short stature is due to microcephaly or some other pathology.
- The hominids are late australopithecines and are the first of that species found outside of Africa.
- The hominids are *H. habilis* and are the first of that species found outside of Africa.

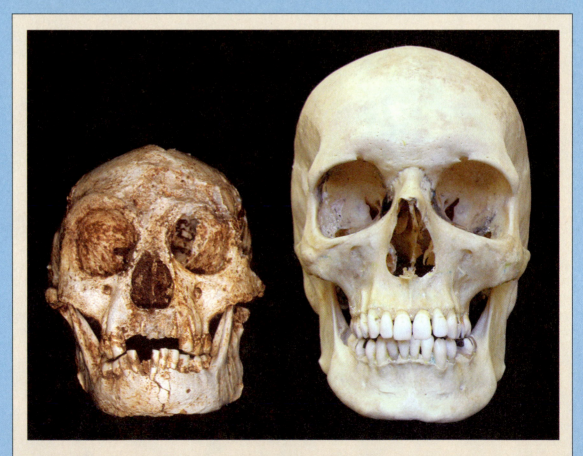

A comparison of the Flores skull (left) with a modern human skull (right) shows most of the difference is in cranial capacity.

It's also possible there is some other correct interpretation.

Based on the their tool kit, the hominids were culturally and intellectually comparable to modern humans in cognitive complexity. Dean Falk's team looked at the frontal lobes and concluded they were consistent with capabilities for higher cognitive processing.

## CONCLUSIONS

There is no doubt that the Flores hominid is the find of the decade, at least, but until many questions have been answered, it is premature to say much. One thing that is clear is that we will be hearing much more about this fossil find. Although planned work for 2006 had to be postponed because the Indonesian government would not issue excavation permits to the two Australian scientists, permission was granted in January 2007 for excavation for the summer of 2007, and work was expected to resume at that time.

*Sources:* Anonymous. 2004. The littlest human. *Science* 306:2013.   Balter, M. 2005. Skeptics question whether Flores hominid is a new species. *Science* 306:1116.   Brown, P., M. J. Sutikna, M. Morwood, et al. 2004. A new small-bodied hominid from the Late Pleistocene of Flores, Indonesia. *Nature* 431:1055–1061.   Culotta, E. 2005. Battle erupts over the "Hobbit" bones. *Science* 307:1179.   Culotta, E. 2005. Discoverers charge damage to "Hobbit" specimens. *Science* 307:1848–1849.   Dalton, R. 2004. Little lady of Flores focuses a rethink of human evolution. *Nature* 431:1029.   Falk, D. 2005. The brain of LB1, *Homo floresiensis. Science* 308:242–245. Lahr, M., and R. Foley 2004. Human evolution writ small. *Nature* 431:1043–1044.   Morwood, M., R. P. Soejono, R. G. Roberts, et al. 2004. Archaeology and age of a new Hominin from Flores in Eastern Indonesia. *Nature* 431:1087–1091.   Wong, K. 2005. The littlest human. *Scientific American* 292 (2): 40–49.

turn back to your reading

**Buhl Woman**
North American female found in Idaho in 1989, dated to 11 kyr ago and reburied under NAGPRA.

**Kennewick Man**
Male found in 1996 in the state of Washington and dated to 7,880 years ago; originally thought to be Native American and thus subject to reburial under NAGPRA but having morphology closer to that of Polynesians than of modern Native Americans.

This section on Native Americans concentrates on biological evidence, as early artifactual evidence was covered in Chapter 12. Figure 15.1 maps early New World sites. The oldest Native American remains (other than, possibly, the five Mexican museum skulls) belong to **Buhl Woman**, found in Idaho in 1989 and dated to 12,825 years ago. Buhl Woman's skeletal remains were reburied in 1991 under the Native American Grave Protection and Repatriation Act of 1990 (NAGPRA) and are not available for study.

**Kennewick Man**, a fossil found in 1996 in the state of Washington, is controversial. On the one hand, because the 350 bone fragments that make up the find, representing 90 percent of the man's skeleton, have been redated to 7,880 years ago (Taylor et al. 2001), the remains are subject to reburial under NAGPRA; on the other hand, because of their age, the bones are vital to biological anthropologists who seek answers to questions concerning early Americans. Initial observations of the skeletal material, done before the bones were "sealed," suggest that Kennewick Man was about 1.77 m (5 feet 10 inches) tall and weighed around 73 k (160 pounds), was between 35 and 45 years of age at death, was likely buried, and ate a lot of fish during his lifetime, as would be expected on the Pacific coast. He had suffered several blows to his head and ribs during his life and showed healed shoulder and elbow injuries. A spear point lodged in his hip probably did not kill him. The cause of his death is still unknown (Lemonick and Dorfman 2006).

The initial observations suggest that Kennewick Man looked more like modern Polynesians than like modern Asians. Although the decision to rebury Kennewick or scientifically study his bones could have ended up in the Supreme Court, in February 2004, the U.S. Court of Appeals for the Ninth Circuit upheld the decision of the district court that NAGPRA does not apply to Kennewick because the remains are "not Native

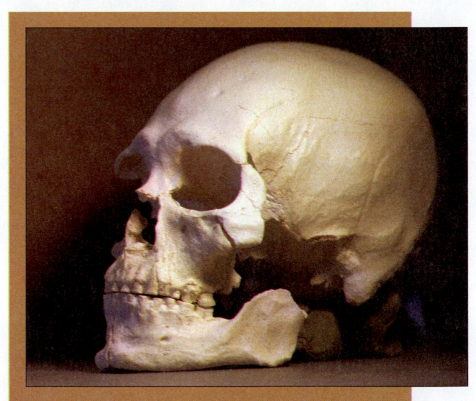

Kennewick Man, a 7,880-year-old early American from the state of Washington, is the object of much controversy. Native Americans and NAGPRA proponents argue for his reburial, but scientists urge further study first. Which side are you on?

*Figure 15.1*

**EARLY NATIVE AMERICAN SITES.** All New World sites mentioned in this chapter, as well as several other important early sites, are on the map. Does the clustering of the sites indicate any pattern?

American remains within the meaning of NAGPRA" (Saunders 2004, 1). In December 2005 scientists were given the opportunity to study the bones but have not yet presented any findings. Before the bones were sealed, three labs attempted to extract DNA from them to compare with DNA from other similarly dated human bones for potential clues regarding the closest affinity, but no DNA could be extracted. Hopefully, new attempts to extract DNA, this time from teeth, will be successful.

A more recent find from the Pacific coast area and the same time period as Kennewick Man also looks like neither modern Asians nor modern Native Americans, as does a skeleton from the Spirit Cave, Nevada, site (Taylor 2000). Because the morphological features of contemporary Asians did not evolve until after 7,000 years ago (Fiedel 2000, 2002), it is not surprising that these early Native Americans did not look like either contemporary Asian or contemporary Native American populations. Any population leaving Asia before 7,000 years ago would not show traits that had not yet evolved! Three Zhoukoudian (China) fossils dated at about 10,000 years ago do not show contemporary Chinese features either—because, again, those features had not yet evolved. A genetic marker called Lineage X, discovered in the 1990s, shows an ancient link between early Eurasians and Native Americans. Contemporary Europeans and Native Americans have the marker, but not contemporary Asians (Morell 1998). Again, this fits the hypothesis that the original migrants to the New World had somewhat different biological traits than contemporary Asians have. Furthermore, the five early skulls found in the Mexican museum are long and narrow, a trait that is also unlike contemporary Native Americans.

# Causes of Microevolution in Contemporary Humans

Human evolution over only a few generations is called **microevolution**, a much smaller-scale version of macroevolution. All four causes of macroevolution—mutations, natural selection, gene flow, and genetic drift—cause generations of humans to differ, but in addition, there are three other potential causes of change: non-random mating, unequal numbers of breeding males and females, and birth control. None of these three has strong enough effects to be important in macroevolution.

**microevolution**
The process of change over only a few generations of a population, which can often be measured and explained.

Random mating theoretically means every person has equal opportunity to mate with every other individual of the opposite sex in specific populations, but this does not happen; humans practice **non-random mating**. "Interracial" and interreligious matings and marriages are frowned on in many cultures, as is severe age differences between mates. The incest taboo between parents and children and between brothers and sisters is universal. Most populations have relatively equal numbers of males and females, but if for some reason, the gender ratio goes to 60/40 in either direction, that alone can cause change between generations. **Birth control** is like genetic drift on a micro scale. If a human couple limits its number of offspring to only two, much of the parental genome will not be manifest in the next generation.

Another factor in microevolution is the **founder effect**. If a part of a population decides or is forced to migrate, it takes only its portion of the collective gene pool with it to found a new population. The migrating group also leaves the gene pool of the original population somewhat different just because part of that population left; this is referred to as the **stay-at-home effect**. Genes and traits can be lost because migrants tend to be entire families. In modern times Tristan de Cunhans in the Atlantic Ocean, the Amish of Pennsylvania, and the Dutch settlers in South Africa have all experienced the founder effect.

## Population Genetics

Specialists who focus on microevolutionary studies and use a good deal of mathematical modeling are population geneticists. They want to know first how much genetic change there is from generation to generation and what caused it. Population genetics originated in the late 1920s and 1930s when mathematically minded Sir Ronald Fisher and Sewall Wright combined Darwin's natural selection with Mendel's genetics in order to make predictions about gene/allele frequencies in a small number of successive generations.

Population genetics is firmly anchored in work done 30 years earlier by an American agriculturalist named William Castle, a British mathematician named Godfrey Hardy, and a German physician named Wilhelm Weinberg. What has subsequently come to be known as the Hardy-Weinberg law was published in 1908. Castle's name was dropped even though he published his version of the law 3 years earlier; he offered no mathematical support for his version apparently because he thought it was too obvious to need it. The Hardy-Weinberg law allows population geneticists to predict causes of change between any two generations. It is based on a simple statement:

A population will *not* change from one generation to the next in its frequencies of (1) phenotype (outer appearance or manifestation of some trait) (2) genotype (percentage of each possible gene combination for the homozygous and heterozygous conditions in the population; and (3) gene frequency (percentage of each gene involved in the trait found in the gene pool of the total population)
IF
there are no mutations,
natural selection is not affecting the numbers of offspring that individuals have,
there is no gene flow from other populations,
the population in question is infinite in size.

Subsequent to this original statement of the Hardy-Weinberg law, the following stipulations were added: The population does not have to be infinite in size since there is no such thing, but it must be large enough to rule out gene drift as a cause of change; eventually, 10,000 individuals was agreed on as the minimum size. In addition, random mating must be practiced, there must be fairly even numbers of males and females in the population, and the population must not practice birth control. If a population fulfills all of these requirements, then there will be no change in the phenotype, genotype, or gene frequency between any two generations. Note that this is an if/then statement, and like most such statements, the "if" part is almost never fulfilled. In this case, since the

**non-random mating**
The practice whereby humans do not have an equal opportunity to mate with any other human because of incest taboos and cultural restrictions or choices.

**birth control**
Practice that can change gene frequencies between any two generations just because the small number of offspring do not represent the total genome of the parents.

**founder effect**
When a human group leaves its original population, it does not necessarily take a representative sample of that population's overall gene pool with it, so the next generations of the migrating group will have a different gene pool.

**stay-at-home effect**
When small groups leave to become "founders" elsewhere, the loss of their genetic material affects the next generations in the population left behind.

seven conditions in the "if" part are the known causes of evolution and since change in gene frequency is evolution, the Hardy-Weinberg law simply says there will be genetic equilibrium (no change at all) only if all seven conditions are met. And, of course, they never are. Evolution is always occurring, and there are always reasons why. Genetic equilibrium is hypothetical, but the Hardy-Weinberg law does allow population geneticists to do two things: first, to make predictions about what will happen in the next generation in the gene pool of a population that meets most of the requirements, and second, to look at the gene frequency in a population for any two generations and attempt to explain why the frequency changed.

Making predictions about what would happen to a population if cause X, Y, or Z were or were not operating or about what might have caused a change observed in a gene frequency over two succeeding generations in a population is complex, highly mathematical, and beyond the scope of this book. And because of the long generation time of humans and ethical constraints about doing experiments on them, most population genetics work has been done under laboratory conditions using fast-reproducing fruit flies. The results of the work done by population geneticists is used extensively by biomedical practitioners, particularly in genetic counseling. Population geneticists advise doctors who can advise patients of their risks (Lewis 2005).

For pure rather than applied research, being able to predict either from a cause to a result or from data to a cause is worthwhile. Sewall Wright's classic "Modes of Immediate Change" (1948) allows population geneticists to both (1) predict from causes to results and (2) analyze data to establish causes. In what Wright called the deterministic mode, recurring mutations, systematic selection, and consistent gene flow will all show the same effect over a number of generations. In Wright's stochastic mode, genetic drift will show large but totally random changes or none at all—random means just that. In his third mode, called unique events, a large population should show slow and continuous change (due to one or more causes), but then a large change between two specific generations, with subsequent generations showing the same pattern as before. The unique event obviously occurs between the two specific generations showing the large change. Wright suggests the founder effect is likely to be the only major such event for human populations.

The descriptions of Hardy and Weinberg's and Wright's contributions to population genetics are very simplistic and use no mathematical modeling. Since their initial mathematical support for natural selection and genetics, other scientists have found their mathematical modeling to be substantially correct, and the final mapping of the human genome will allow the mathematically minded population geneticists of the future to do real counts, not estimates.

# General Trends of Contemporary Humans

Regardless of details of colonization and migration, all contemporary humans are members of a single species, *Homo sapiens*. That is, all modern humans are potentially able to breed and produce fertile offspring. For example, England and Australia are as far away from each other as any two countries on Earth, but matings between British colonials and Australian aborigines showed no lowered fertility. This biological fact has been true far longer than written records.

During the last 50 kyr, there have been a few morphological trends that characterize the entire species. First, moderns, although they do not have larger cranial capacities than Neandertals, do have larger crania than non-Neandertal archaics from Africa and Asia. Contemporary cranial capacity averages 1,350 cc, having decreased somewhat in the last 10 kyr (Henneberg 1988). Second, stature during the past 2 myr has shown no overall trend: Nariokotome and other African *Homo erectus* populations were quite tall; Neandertals averaged only 167 cm (5 feet 6 inches); early AMH were fairly tall, but the average stature of moderns has decreased since then. Stature averages for different populations are perhaps more informative than a single average for all contemporary humans; some populations average 183 cm (6 feet) and some 147 cm (4 feet 10 inches). Third, teeth and faces are somewhat smaller in contemporary humans than in previous populations, and skeletal ruggedness has decreased as well. Finally, humans have probably become less hairy than in the past, with evidence pointing to the decline in hairiness occurring well before 50 kyr ago.

There are interesting differences between contemporary males and females that likely existed in the past as well, given that sexual dimorphism in stature—though variable through time—is documented to earliest hominid days. Today, there are 105 males born for every 100 females; by age 16 the ratio is 103 males to 100 females; and by age 70 there are twice as many females alive as males. At age 100, nine times more females are alive than males. Part of this discrepancy and trend seems to be biological, with males making fewer antibodies than females and thus less able to fight infections and cancers. Another part is cultural: Males have more accidents and are more likely to kill each other (Jones 1994, 2001).

Sex differences exist in the brain as well, though the effects are small. Females perform better on tests of verbal skills, reading comprehension, essay writing, and understanding nonverbal body language. Males are better at perception and manipulation of spatial relationships, map reading, maze tracing, mathematics, and musical composition. This means that, although there are males that are outstanding at writing and speaking and there are females that are outstanding at solving mathematical puzzles and composing music, the average performances of all males and all females fall into these two categories (Falk 2004).

Despite the major advances of the 1990s, geneticists are not able to trace DNA records in Africa beyond the last 10 kyr, because DNA preservation requires a dry and cool climate (Panger et al. 2003). For this reason, bioanthropologists studying general human trends must be satisfied with skeletal data.

Probably the most frightening trend in contemporary humans is their tendency to breed. When Thomas Malthus warned of potential disastrous overpopulation in 1798, there were only 1 billion people in the world. Today there are 6 billion, and the number is still growing. The number itself isn't the issue, of course, but what it does to people in terms of overcrowding, poverty, aggression, wars, and disease, and to the Earth in terms of pollution and use of nonrenewable resources. Malthus suggested people use "restraint"—delay marriage and abstain from sex. We don't seem to be doing that. The biggest cause of overpopulation, however, is cultural—good prenatal and health care. Social animals such as lions and elephants that do not have doctors or hospitals raise only 12 to 18 percent of their offspring to adulthood; chimpanzees raise 36 percent of their offspring to adulthood; and people in the industrial West, with hospitals and neonatal clinics, raise 95 percent of their offspring to adulthood. Modern hunter-gatherers raise 60 percent of their offspring to adulthood, and it is likely that this was the norm for humans until recently (Bogin 2001a).

Contributing to population growth is another trend in the West, a change in life expectancy—for the better. Until the 1930s, infant and child death rates put the average life expectancy at a fairly low level. The life expectancy in the United States has risen slowly but steadily from 63.3 years in 1943 to 77.6 years in 2003. American women now have a life expectancy of over 80 years. Japan has the longest life expectancy, at 82 years, and six other countries top the 80-year mark.

J. E. Cohen (2004), a demographic expert, gives a picture of widespread population changes in the last few years and future trends. It took only 13 years for the world population of 5 billion to increase by 1 billion people. In the Western world, from 2000 on, old people will outnumber young people, and urban populations will outnumber rural. Cohen predicts these trends will continue: more people (up to 9 billion by 2050), more urbanism, and aging populations. He further predicts that most of the population increase will be in economically strapped countries like India, Pakistan, Nigeria, and Uganda. He also predicts that some populations will decrease: in Germany, Italy, Japan, and the Russian Federation.

# Human Biological Variability: The Species Today

"No two people are exactly alike (except identical twins)" is a statement we have all heard since third grade. It has been estimated, however, that humans are 99.8 percent genetically identical, with only 0.02 percent of genes accounting for all biological group, sex, and individual differences (Coughlan 2000; Pääbo 2003). (See Figure 15.2.) Humans are genetically less variable than any species of great apes, including chimpanzees—which have four times more genetic variability (Templeton 1998). It has been suggested that humans have substituted cultural diversity for biological variability.

*Figure 15.2*

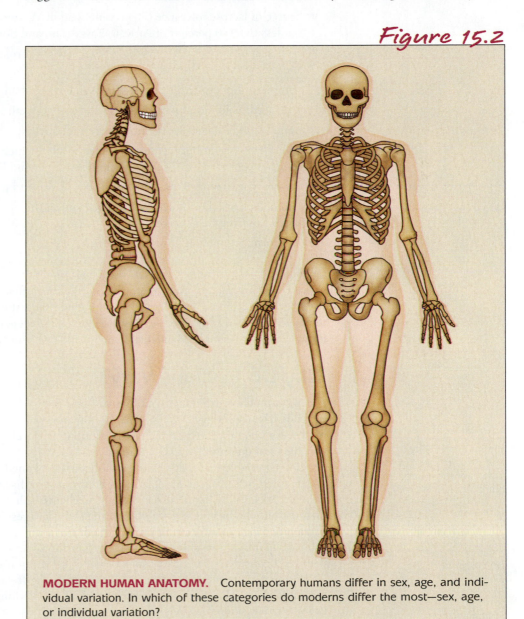

**MODERN HUMAN ANATOMY.**   Contemporary humans differ in sex, age, and individual variation. In which of these categories do moderns differ the most—sex, age, or individual variation?

# How Do Humans Vary?

Within the world population of more than 6 billion people, humans differ from one another biologically, but only in minor ways. Morphologically, some people are tall and some are short; some have brown eyes and some have blue eyes; and so forth. Genetically, some people have two genes for tasting phenylthiocarbamide (PTC) and some have none; some have one sickle-cell gene, some have two, and some have none; and so forth. Sometimes variability is stronger within than between groups. For example, on average, the Dutch are tall and the Mbuti are short; but the range of stature within either the Dutch or the Mbuti population is larger than the difference between the average statures of most populations. A small sample of morphologically variable traits among contemporary humans includes the following:

- degree of facial prognathism, from flat to jutting forward in general or specifically in the mouth area (alveolar prognathism)
- degree of lactose tolerance (70 percent of adult Western Europeans can digest milk but less than 30 percent of African, East Asian, and Southeast Asian adults can)
- nose shape that correlates with climate (low and broad with hot and humid; high and narrow with cold and dry)
- number of bones, with some people having more than 206 (Mays 1998)
- stature (the biological part of the trait), from very tall to very short
- weight (the biological part), from heavy to light
- body shape (using Bergmann's and Allen's Rules, which are discussed shortly), from short and compact with short extremities to long and linear with long extremities
- earwax type, from yellow, sticky, and fatty to dry and not fatty
- skin color (based on the amount of melanin in the epidermis or upper layer of the skin), from very dark to very light
- hair form, from straight to woolly

Genetic traits that vary across the species include the genes responsible for the above traits and many more. More than 1,500 genes that control blood factors alone have been identified. Physiological traits include such things as metabolic rates, hormone activity, and growth rates. Sickle-cell anemia is regarded as a physiological trait, though it follows simple Mendelian genetics and has a morphological manifestation.

# Why Do Humans Vary?

Although much of **human variability** can be described and measured, explaining the variability is not always easy. In general, human variability is the product of the same mechanisms as those that drive macroevolution but develops specifically in response to variable local environmental conditions.

Some variable traits can be reasonably well explained, because a mutation can be documented or the agent of selection is known; those that cannot be explained are due either to selection with unknown causes or to chance—that is, to genetic drift. Scientists disagree on whether most variability in the short run results from natural selection or from pure chance. Among those variable traits that can be reasonably explained are skin color, body build, nose shape, and sickle-cell anemia. Let's look at each of these in turn; then we'll consider some other traits for which selection mechanisms are less clear.

**Skin color** is one of the few variable traits that correlates fairly well with environmental features. When the average skin color of populations is plotted on a world map, it is clear that skin color falls along north–south **clines**, or gradients, with the darkest skin color usually near the equator and the lightest closer to the poles (see Figure 15.3). Although this is generally true in the Old World, particularly in Africa and Australia,

**human variability**
The study of clinal manifestations of those modern human traits that vary.

**skin color**
The human trait often used by non-anthropologists to define and classify "biological races"; does not co-vary with most other traits.

**clines**
Systematic gradations in some trait (phenotype) over large geographical areas.

*Figure 15.3*

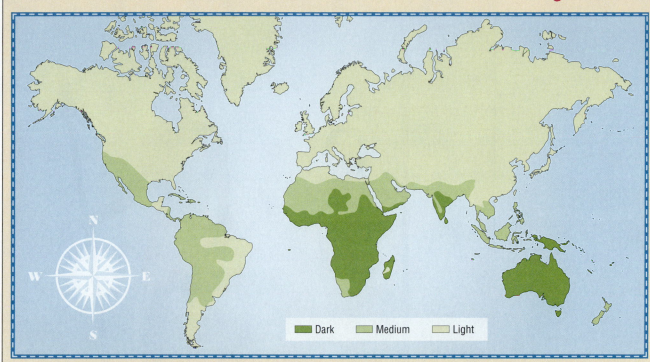

**DISTRIBUTION OF SKIN COLOR IN THE OLD WORLD.**   This map averages skin color under three general descriptions: dark, medium, and light. Note the geographic patterning. Is the pattern merely general, or does it prevail without exception? Why are light-colored skins found where they are?

*Source:* Based on Biasutti (1967).

people have not lived in the New World long enough for the effect to show. Gloger's Rule suggests there is a tendency for more heavily pigmented populations to be located near the equator. The explanation for this observation seems fairly straightforward: People who live near the equator are adapted to the high amount of ultraviolet radiation produced by intensive year-round sun rays by having a large number of melanin cells, and the result is darker skin that protects against skin cancer (Jablonski and Chaplin 2000). Several lines of evidence support this hypothesis. Populations who live near the poles do not need as much sun protection but do need to be able to synthesize enough vitamin D from the weak sunlight to allow calcium absorption, which in turn prevents rickets and promotes strong bones. Light skin with few melanin cells allows vitamin D synthesis. (Vitamin D is found in some foods, such as seafood and dairy products, but in very small amounts.) Further support comes from the fact that in high-sun areas people with light skins get three times more skin cancer than dark-skinned people do. Also, far more light-skinned people get skin cancer in high-sun areas than in low-sun areas. Finally, dark-skinned people are more susceptible to rickets in areas of low sun than are light-skinned people. The correlations appear to indicate causation.

**Body build** is another human trait that can be explained environmentally (see Figure 15.4). One hundred and fifty years ago, Carl Bergmann, a German physiologist who was interested in the relationships among body mass, surface area, and heat production in warm-blooded animals, discovered the principle now called Bergmann's Rule. He observed that populations of a species that live in the coldest areas of the species' range tend to have short, compact bodies. Such bodies have less surface area relative to

**body build**

The shape of the human body as measured by the ratio between extremities and body core.

*Figure 15.4*

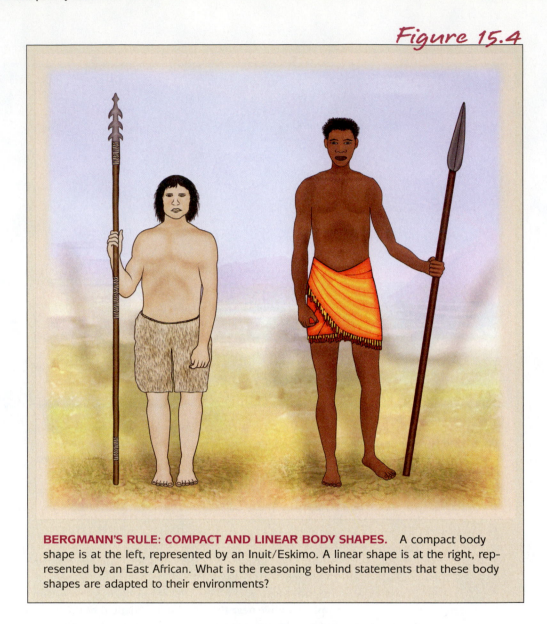

**BERGMANN'S RULE: COMPACT AND LINEAR BODY SHAPES.** A compact body shape is at the left, represented by an Inuit/Eskimo. A linear shape is at the right, represented by an East African. What is the reasoning behind statements that these body shapes are adapted to their environments?

mass than more linear bodies, thereby conserving heat. By contrast, populations that live in the warmest areas of a species' range tend to have long, linear bodies that absorb less heat, particularly at times when the sun is high, and that dissipate heat through sweating, particularly in the morning and late afternoon.

Related to Bergmann's Rule is Allen's Rule, which is based on similar laws of physics: People who live in hot areas have elongated arms and legs that afford more skin surface for sweating and cooling. Human populations living in cold areas tend to have short arms and legs, smaller surface area, and therefore more heat retention.

The rules that govern body shape have apparently been operating on humans as well as on other animals for a considerable period of time, though confirmation of the rules for humans did not come until the 1950s. Alan Walker and Pat Shipman (1996) found Nariokotome, the 1.6-myr-old *H. erectus* from East Africa, to have a long, linear body, just as would be expected for a modern 12-year-old African living in the same area under the same environmental conditions. Using the same indices to assess arm and leg proportions, Walker and Shipman measured a complete Neandertal fossil as well, and found it to be "superarctic" in proportions. In both cases the body shape of the represented populations seems well adapted to their environment.

**Nose shape**, as indexed by Thompson's Rule, also appears to be environmentally adaptive, as it correlates with humidity and, secondarily, with heat. Long and narrow noses occur in areas of low humidity such as deserts and mountains, and shorter and wider noses are found in more humid areas. Populations in the cool East African highlands tend to have longer noses than their neighbors in the hotter and more humid lowlands. Apparently, colder and drier air needs more surface area inside the nose to make it the right temperature and humidity before it gets near the brain (Beall and Steegman 2000).

Scientists also know a lot about **sickle-cell anemia**, mainly because in certain populations it affects up to 20 percent of individuals and causes many deaths every year. Red blood cells that have sickle shapes cannot carry sufficient oxygen to nourish body tissues; as a result, individuals who have the anemia experience fatigue, retarded physical development, increased infections and miscarriages, and severe pain. Sickle-cell anemia is inherited genetically and normally affects people while they are still young, so in most cases those who are affected die before the age of reproduction.

Common sense suggests that sickle-cell anemia should not exist, because people who have it usually die before they can pass it on to any offspring. But two factors promote its continuance. First, the sickle-cell gene is recessive, meaning that individuals who have it must have inherited a gene from each parent and be homozygous for the condition (refer to Chapter 3). If an individual has two non–sickle-cell genes, the disease will not be manifest in the individual and he or she cannot pass on sickle-cell genes to offspring. If an individual has one sickle-cell gene and one non–sickle-cell allele, the disease will not be manifest, and that individual will be immune to certain kinds of malaria—but the individual can pass on a sickle-cell gene to 50 percent of his or her offspring. Therefore, those who have "hidden recessives" and do not manifest the disease keep the gene in the population by passing it on to half of their offspring.

The second factor is the relationship between sickle-cell anemia and malaria, a disease carried by mosquitoes. The malaria immunity conferred by the sickle-cell gene was discovered many years ago when the global distributions of the two diseases turned out to be very similar, mostly in Africa and around the Mediterranean Sea in Italy, Greece, and Spain; see Figure 15.5. (Note that contrary to a familiar factoid, sickle-cell anemia is not solely a disease of dark-skinned Africans, as it affects lighter-skinned neighbors across the Mediterranean as well.) Because malaria also causes death and natural immunity to it lasts an individual's lifetime (including the reproductive years), heterozygotes have neither sickle-cell anemia nor malaria. But passing one sickle-cell allele on to approximately half of offspring keeps the allele in those populations where malaria is common. If malaria is ever eradicated, the sickle-cell gene will become so infrequent that chances of an individual's inheriting two such genes will be very low.

Sickle-cell anemia has its cultural connections as well. It wasn't until people cleared their lands to plant food crops that there were standing pools of mosquito-ridden water to play host to malaria. Also, in countries with high levels of medical care, a certain percentage of children with two sickle-cell genes do not die and sometimes reproduce, thus increasing the frequency of the allele.

Several other human traits may also result from selection processes. Could natural selection operate on blood types—the familiar A, B, O, and AB? That is, might people with a particular blood type have an advantage over those with different blood types? Several correlations between blood types and certain diseases argue for such selection. For example, people with A blood have higher-than-expected frequencies of bronchial pneumonia, smallpox, typhoid, pernicious anemia, and stomach cancers; people with O blood have more than their share of malaria, bubonic plague, and duodenal and stomach ulcers but are less susceptible to syphilis (Ridley 1999). Those with B blood have some protection against infantile diarrhea, which under certain conditions can be lethal. Most of these diseases can shorten life and thus play a potential role in natural selection.

Stature variability is only partially explainable at present, and many anomalies remain to be worked out. In mammal species in general, as we've discussed, shorter populations live in colder areas, probably because it is advantageous to conserve heat; taller populations generally live in warmer areas where they can dissipate heat. But although

**nose shape**
The external conformation of the nose, which appears to correlate with climate; populations in cool areas have long, narrow noses, and populations in hot, humid areas have short, wide noses.

**sickle-cell anemia**
A genetic disease that occurs in individuals homozygous for the recessive allele that causes immunity to malaria.

*Figure 15.5*

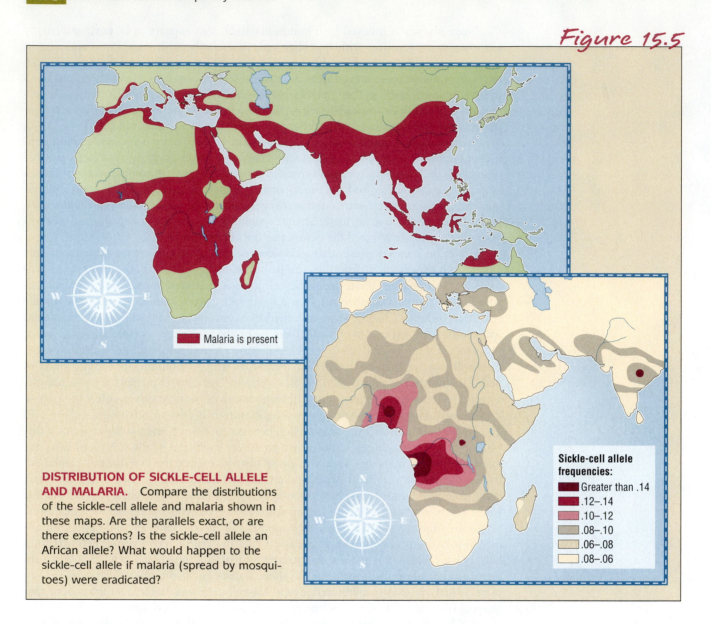

Malaria is present

**Sickle-cell allele frequencies:**
- Greater than .14
- .12–.14
- .10–.12
- .08–.10
- .06–.08
- .08–.06

**DISTRIBUTION OF SICKLE-CELL ALLELE AND MALARIA.** Compare the distributions of the sickle-cell allele and malaria shown in these maps. Are the parallels exact, or are there exceptions? Is the sickle-cell allele an African allele? What would happen to the sickle-cell allele if malaria (spread by mosquitoes) were eradicated?

Eskimos (Inuit) fit the short/cold category and upper Nile River–dwelling people fit the tall/warm category, Mbuti pygmies are short and live in a warm climate—and the Dutch, who on average are the tallest people in the world, live in a relatively cold climate. Culture and environment are important variables as well. First, there is a positive relationship between stature and reproductive success in males (females may prefer taller partners), but not in females. Second, children who suffer acute stress early in life are taller than those who do not, independent of other genetic and environmental variables (Grey and Wolfe 2002).

Other traits, too, are incompletely explained. Some types of hair form may have evolved and been positively selected because they offer insulation for the head from the sun (Lieberman and Rice 1997); face size, which is correlated with tooth size, may have become reduced after humans in some areas adopted cooking (Brace 1996). But no one has been able to explain why there are fat folds on eyelids among some Asian populations; or why some populations have thin lips and some have thick lips; or why the men in some populations go bald at a young age; or why some populations have very wrinkled skins, whereas their neighbors show few wrinkles even into old age. Variations in these traits may be due to sexual selection (one sex chooses mates according to some cultural standard of attractiveness) or to random genetic drift.

## Group Variation: "Race" or Not?

Because biological anthropologists study groups of modern humans from a biological perspective, an appropriate question to ask is this: Do humans form distinct geographic and biological groups? If the subject were baboons *(Papio papio)*, we would call such groups subspecies; if the subject were dogs *(Canis familiaris)*, we would call such groups breeds. It might be instructive to look further at baboons and dogs relative to subgroups. Baboons appear to form distinct biological and geographic groups; the groups interbreed successfully on their borders, producing viable offspring (see Figure 15.6). One subspecies, the anubis, or olive, baboon, is morphologically homogeneous in dozens of traits and, most important, looks different from other subspecies. Its neighbor, the homogeneous hamadryas baboon, is very different from the anubis in such traits as size, color,

*Figure 15.6*

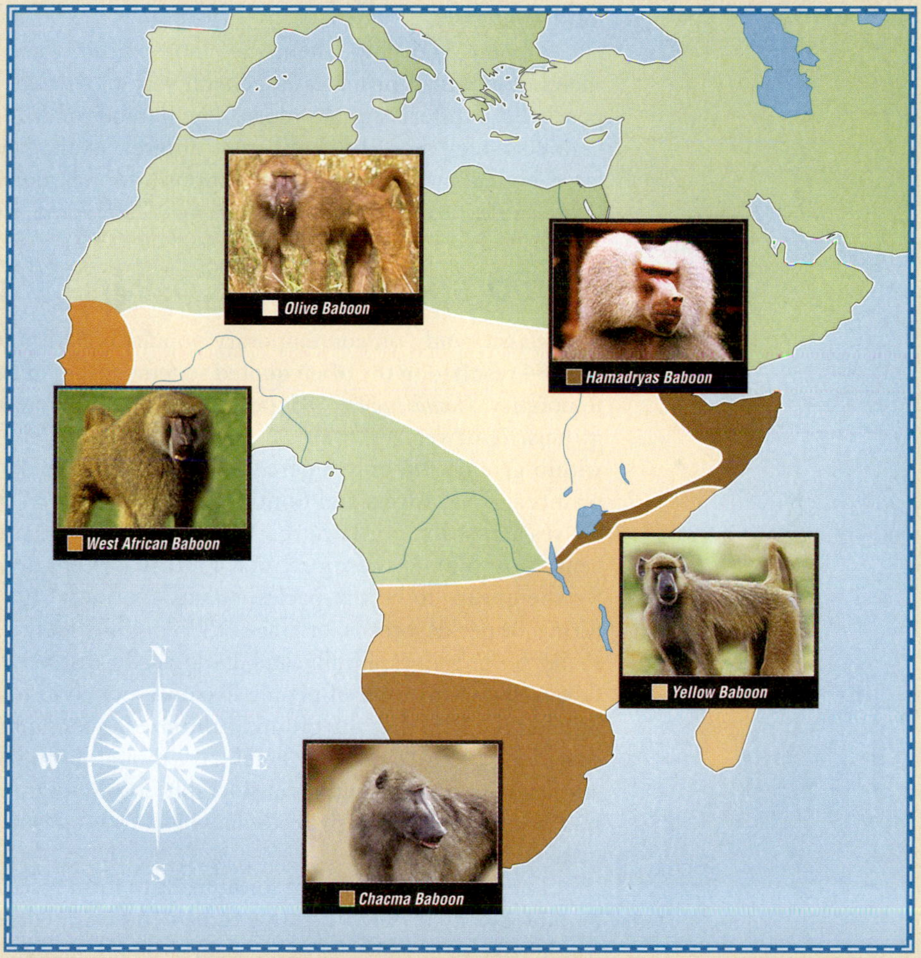

- Olive Baboon
- Hamadryas Baboon
- West African Baboon
- Yellow Baboon
- Chacma Baboon

**DISTRIBUTION OF BABOONS IN AFRICA.**    Baboons should be thought of as a single "superspecies" with five subspecies; the subspecies can interbreed and produce fertile offspring. Are baboons like humans in terms of subspecies? Why or why not?

*Source:* Adapted from *Primates in Nature* by Alison F. Richard. Copyright © 1985 by W. H. Freeman and Company. Used with permission.

sexual and social behavior, and length of fur. Similarly, the hamadryas baboon's neighbor, the yellow baboon, is internally homogeneous but differs from the other groups. Baboon groups also differ genetically. What makes each of the five baboon groups biologically distinct is their **co-variation of traits**: the fact that some traits that each group possesses vary together, or are concordant. This means that every baboon with long hair, for example, also possesses the entire suite of traits of that group, traits that are not shared with the other four subspecies. This exclusionary principle results in biologically distinct units. The hybrids on the borders demonstrate traits of both subspecies, but hybrids make up only a very small proportion of the total baboon population. Because each group inhabits an exclusive geographic range rather than being intermixed in a large area, baboon subspecies can be said to be geographically distinct as well.

Baboons are a result of natural forces; dogs are not. Humans have bred dogs (by artificial selection) for thousands of years, most recently in order to produce biologically different breeds. Great Danes are characterized by their size, color, hair length, length of muzzle, and countless other traits, and they are not only morphologically but also genetically different from Chihuahuas. Each breed shows a unique package of trait variations. As with baboons, that package co-varies, making each dog breed biologically distinctive from all other breeds in the species. But because humans take their dogs with them, different breeds do not form geographically distinct populations. And there are a lot of mongrels.

Baboons and dogs, then, vary more within their species than humans do within theirs; nonhuman primates in general vary more than humans, and humans have purposely bred differences into dogs. The number of differences among humans is considerably smaller than the number of differences that identify subspecies in most other large-bodied mammals. So on traditional grounds alone, humans do not vary enough to be divisible into sharp biological groups (Templeton 1998).

## *Homo sapiens* and Co-variation of Traits

The classic study on contemporary populations of humans that Richard Lewontin did in 1984 resulted in the often quoted statement that of the little variability shown by contemporary *Homo sapiens*, 85 percent is within groups and only 15 percent between groups. A newer study on 52 populations claims the genetic diversity is 94 percent within groups and only 6 percent between groups. By comparison, populations of elephants in East Africa and South Africa can differ by as much as 40 percent, and gray wolves across the northern reaches of North America and Europe can differ by 75 percent. Most biologists estimate that 15 to 30 percent difference between groups is needed for the groups to be subspecies, breeds, or "races" (Olson 2002b). For *Homo sapiens* to form subspecies, breeds, or "races" (biologically identical terms), the groups would have to be both geographically and biologically distinct, like baboons (Cartmill 1998b). Given that all manner of people live on every continent and in most cities, it would be difficult to claim that any group of any size is geographically distinct. This has been true since long before cities ever emerged—though in the last two hundred years, ships and airplanes have contributed considerably to the migration of groups and individuals to new homes far from their birthplaces and to the resultant mix of people from different original homelands.

The second requirement for humans to form "races" would be that each group must be biologically distinct. For this to be demonstrated, the traits used to identify "races" would have to co-vary. As we've seen, although modern humans are 99.8 percent genetically identical, they do vary in many traits, including body build, stature, weight, skin color, nose shape, hair color, hair form, blood type, the sickle-cell gene, the ability to taste PTC, and the absence or presence of hair on the phalanges of their fingers (called mid-digital hair). In principle, if traits did co-vary, then, to use a hypothetical example, tall people would always be heavy, have light skin and dark straight hair, taste PTC, and have hairy fingers, to name just seven traits. If tall people always showed those traits,

**co-variation of traits**
The fact that certain traits in a group or population always vary together, or are concordant.

then the conclusion would be that they form a distinct biological group. This would be meaningless, however, unless there were another group of humans who always were short and lightweight, had dark skin and light and curly hair, and neither tasted PTC nor had mid-digital hair. Given this exclusionary requirement, the question is, do the traits scientists or laypeople use to classify people into "races" co-vary, thus identifying distinct biological groups? Or are the traits biologically discordant?

Several examples will show that with few exceptions, biological traits do not co-vary. The exceptions include height and weight, because in general tall people weigh more than short people. Shoe size is also concordant with height and weight, because big people have bigger feet than small people. Another example of co-variation concerns coloration in eyes, skin, and hair. Although the genetics of these traits is complex, they are all affected by what can be called "master color genes." Just as we can generally predict the size of people's feet by knowing their height, we can often predict hair color by knowing skin color. But these concordant or co-varying traits are the exception; most traits do not follow this pattern (Lieberman and Rice 1997).

For example, as we've discussed, the distribution of skin color is related to distance from the equator, sunlight, and vitamin D. Stature is not as well understood, but its distribution is known. Do these two traits vary together? Suppose we simplify skin color variations to three categories (dark, medium, and light) and assign stature to three categories (short, medium, and tall). If we plot the known distributions of these traits on a map, there is no correlation between the variations; this means the traits do not co-vary. (See Figure 15.7, and compare it to Figure 15.3.) That is, people with any skin color

*Figure 15.7*

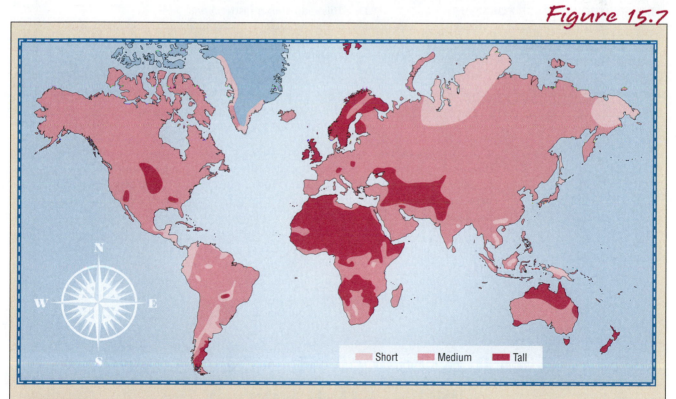

**DISTRIBUTION OF STATURE IN THE OLD WORLD.**  This map shows stature averages under three broad descriptions: tall, medium, and short. Compare this map with the map in Figure 15.3. Do the traits co-vary? Does tall stature correlate with any of the three skin colors? Why or why not?

*Source:* Based on Biasutti (1967).

*Figure 15.8*

**DISTRIBUTION OF HAIR FORM IN THE OLD WORLD.** This map shows distributions of average hair form in three general categories: curly/woolly, wavy, and straight. Compare this map with the maps in Figure 15.3 and 15.7. Do any of the three traits co-vary? For example, is straight hair always found in short people with medium-colored skin? Look at all combinations of the three traits and see if any of the traits co-vary. If they don't, there is no such thing as a biological race.

*Source:* Based on Biasutti (1967).

come in tall, medium, or short stature. Add a third trait, such as hair form, and the picture of co-variance gets even muddier (see Figure 15.8). Hair form variations, reduced to three categories (curly/woolly, wavy, and straight), can be plotted on a map and compared to skin color and stature. If we do this, it becomes clear that people with any hair form variation can have any stature or skin color variation. For example, using the tall variety of stature as the constant, Polynesians have medium skin color and wavy hair; East Africans have dark skin and woolly hair; and the Dutch have light skin and straight hair. And there are examples of every other combination as well, leading to a single conclusion: Human traits are not biologically exclusionary and do not co-vary. Thus, groups of humans are not biologically distinct, and the second requirement for "races" is also not fulfilled. Is it any wonder that biological anthropologists have concluded there is no such thing as a "biological race"?

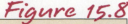

# A History of "Race" in America: From Biology to Culture

**"biological race"**
A geographically constrained group that shares a set of biological/genetic traits that no other group of the species has in its entirety; nonexistent in humans.

Although it is not possible to put an exact date on when the concept of **"biological race"** came into common use, a review of the literature suggests that the concept did not exist until the seventeenth century. Egyptians wrote of neighbors (and themselves) as being red, yellow, white, or black, but no one knows what the Egyptians meant by this other than a simple morphological observation. Herodotus (484–425 BC), the "father of history," saw cultural but apparently not biological differences between the groups he came in contact with (Brace 2005). Two world travelers in the thirteenth and fourteenth centuries, Marco Polo, who journeyed to China and back via Southeast Asia, and Ibn Battuta, a medieval Arabic geographer who traveled to Timbuktu and Europe, never mentioned any group variation of the people they met in their long and geographically widespread travels. Although some might argue that, traveling as they did on horseback and on foot, there would have been little variation to notice from one day to the next. But surely as they reflected on their travels, differences among the people they saw would have come to mind—if such differences had been important at that time. Apparently, different skin colors, nose forms, or other morphological features were not important then. Only when such differences became associated with the distribution of wealth and power did they become important.

Many believe the word *race* comes from a fourteenth-century Spanish word, *raza*, meaning "a kind of something." By the middle of the nineteenth century, the word was used as synonymous with the general term "variety." It was Linnaeus who first articulated the association of variety and biology; in 1738 he included humans in his famous *Scala Naturae*, claiming there were four biological varieties of humans. Expanding on Linnaeus's concept of four "biological races" were J. F. Blumenbach (1752–1840) in Germany, who proposed five "races," and G. de Buffon (1707–1788) in France who proposed six. In the first half of the twentieth century, Germans perceived Jews and Gypsies as distinct "races," and the English have often thought of the French and the Irish as "racially" distinct from themselves (Brace 2000). Even in the early days of classifications, however, experts did not agree on how many "biological races" there were, much less what constituted them. And this lack of agreement did not improve. In 1946 E. A. Hooton proposed three primary and 21 "subraces"; in 1950 Carlton Coon proposed six primary "biological races," and in 1965 Stanley Garn proposed nine primary and 32 local "biological races." Interestingly, whenever theorists gave groups hierarchical rankings, the "race" of the classifier always ranked at the top.

Before the seventeenth century, people's self-identification came from kinship, occupation, and religion. Americans learned ideas about social hierarchy from their European heritage, and in colonial America biological differences became the rationalization for brutal treatment of both Native Americans and African slaves. Although many Americans probably believed there were good biological reasons for such actions, it was wealth, power, opportunity, and privilege that lay behind land displacement and slavery. After the Civil War slavery ended, but "biological race" became the primary source of American social identity. No longer were kinship, religion, education, occupation, language, or geographic location of prime importance in giving groups and individuals a sense of who they were; "biological race" was (Smedley 1998).

By the 1950s genetics began to contribute to the study of modern populations. But the biological basis for "race" became even murkier, at that point, because genetic data did not support the concept of distinct biological groups any more than morphological data. Biologists introduced the concept of the *cline*, a gradation in measurable traits, to document patterns and then to explain individual trait variability. As often happens in biology, the concept had to be demonstrated for other species before it could be applied to humans. Field studies on many species, including mice, birds, and frogs, showed that individual traits did not co-vary, on the contrary, the studies established that such traits vary randomly within species (Brace 1996). These findings led Frank Livingstone to make the famous statement that "there are no [biological] races, only clines" (1964, 47).

By the 1990s, however, biological anthropologists were no longer using the term *cline*, and textbooks began to state there was no such thing as a "biological race." Folk beliefs that "races" do exist continue in most cultures today, but these beliefs are cultural constructs, not biological reality. They belong to the study of culture, not biology, and to the disciplines of sociology and cultural anthropology. As Jonathan Marks puts it, people can still believe in "races," but they cannot use biology to support those beliefs (1995a).

In most contemporary Western societies, if you ask anyone to name some "races" and to say what traits define a given "race," you will probably hear about skin colors and ethnic, religious, and even linguistic groups; the defining traits will probably include a conglomerate of biology (characteristics such as skin color, hair form, stature), culture (food preferences, learned mannerisms, music choices), religion (Buddhism, Judaism, Islam), and even language. The contemporary use of the word "race," then, is a far cry from biologically distinct groups. **Ethnicity** is probably close to what most people mean when they refer to "race" today, but trying to get billions of people to talk about "ethnicity" would be impossible. The word *ethnic*, once relatively neutral, even became charged with negative connotations when the word *cleansing* was added to it and it became a euphemism for mass expulsion or genocide. Perhaps, at some psychological level, people need to identify with a group that is based not on kin, occupation, or religion but on perceived ethnicity. Such identification is not necessarily bad if it fosters group cohesion and pride, but it is destructive when used as a basis for dividing "us" against "them."

A sample of findings clearly demonstrates that the concept of "race" in Western society is a cultural construct:

■ Different world cultures in the past and present have counted and named different numbers of "races." Most Americans are comfortable with a three-"race" system (Asian, black, white); Brazilians classify dozens of "races"; and Anglo Australians classify four races, because they feel a need to categorize their own aboriginal population and do not see them fitting into the three-"race" system.

■ Some anthropologists in the heyday of classifications divided Europe into dozens of "races" but seldom classified African populations into more than one or two groups, despite the fact that African populations differ in morphology and genetics far more than European populations.

■ The U.S. government currently requests individuals applying for federal jobs to fill in their "ethnic group" affiliation (it was once called "race") and lists five choices that are a mix of language, culture, and biology: The word *Hispanic* connotes Spain and its language; the words *African American*, *Asian American*, and *Native American* connote geographic locations combined with a bit of biology and culture; the word *white* is a color!

■ Since the 1960s Americans have used the terms *Negro*, *Black*, *Afro-American*, and *African American*—to refer to the same population. The label has changed from a "racial" term, to a color, to an ethnic group in 40 years.

■ The 1960 U.S. census was the first time Americans were allowed to self classify their ethnicity. In that year, 0.5 million people officially classified themselves as Native Americans. By 1980, 1.4 million claimed that status, and in 2000, 4 million did so. Since the Native American population didn't increase by eight-fold in two generations, those growing numbers must reflect cultural decisions, not biological reality (Olson 2002b).

■ In Japan a group of people called Burakumin are morphologically (biologically) indistinguishable from other Japanese, but a cultural myth contends that they are biologically different. The Japanese consider themselves a "biological race" distinct from Chinese and Koreans (Bogin 2001b), but all three populations are very similar at the genetic level (Cavalli-Sforza 2001).

■ In the United States the "race" designation written on a birth certificate is not necessarily what is written on the person's death certificate. This finding suggests that individuals can change their "race" during their lifetime—a cultural, not a biological, change.

■ Inhabitants of the subcontinent of India have darkly pigmented skin like many Africans, show European-like facial features and hair form, and live in Asia.

■ The French think of themselves as a single people (except for recent immigrants), but at the time of the Celts, between the fifth and third centuries BC, there were 74 dif-

**ethnicity**
An individual's cultural affiliation and ancestry.

ferent tribes within France's modern borders, followed by Romans, Franks, Anglo Saxons, and Vikings, all with somewhat different biological profiles. The French are as mongrelized biologically as the citizens of most countries, united only by a modern common language, and of course language is a cultural factor (Olson 2002b).

■ Finally, in 1987, a secretary in the state of Virginia sued her employer claiming she was discriminated against because she was black. She lost on grounds that she had red hair and thus must be white. She next worked for a black employer and sued him claiming she was discriminated against because she was white. She lost on grounds that she had gone to a black school (Jones 1994).

Although biological anthropologists question the biological distinctiveness of human groups, and sociologists study the social ramifications of modern beliefs about "race," all scientists must concern themselves with the issue of racism. **Racism** by definition has three parts: (1) Racism assumes *groups* can inherit biological traits that include intelligence and behavior; (2) racism assesses individuals on the basis of perceived group characteristics; and (3) racism assumes some groups are superior to other groups in those traits. Racism is used to legitimize the unequal distribution of wealth, power, and prestige within the societies in which it exists.

## Intelligence and Racism

Probably the most common myth about "races" and one of the worst forms of racism is the idea that some "races" are more intelligent than others. No one assumes that all individuals are equally smart, but some people believe that generalized statements about intelligence (however defined) can be applied to different "races." In fact, several seemingly reputable scientists have put their stamp of approval on studies showing that certain "races" are more intelligent than others. Given that there is no such thing as a "biological race," let us assume that by "race" these scientists mean ethnicity, with bits of biology, culture, and even language or religion involved. The definition of **intelligence** is problematic, but we will use the term here in the sense of "success in problem solving." Although defining "human intelligence" in terms of how well humans solve human problems is fine in principle, different groups have different problems to solve. Therefore, equating intelligence—problem solving—with the result of one test that was devised to test problem solving in one group of people is not scientifically valid.

**IQ** (intelligence quotient) tests were devised to test the problem-solving ability of middle- and upper-class Europeans and Americans. As written tests, with time constraints, to be done individually, IQ tests were valid for the groups they were intended to test, because middle- and upper-class students are used to writing, having time constraints, and working individually. And IQ tests can identify learning disabilites and do predict success in mainstream schools designed and run by middle-class educators. As more than one critic has quipped: "IQ scores measure the ability to take IQ tests." They measure performance (on the test), not ability. Interestingly, IQ tests do not do well at predicting success later in life, even for middle- and upper-class individuals.

But any person whose cultural background includes the importance of group rather than individual decision making, or who sees no reason for time constraints, or who does not expect to go to college (where the results of such tests are important), or who believes the results of the test will be used against him or her, is not going to successfully complete an IQ test. Problem solving is a culturally constrained activity. For example, imagine putting a Mensa member, the winner of the last international *Jeopardy* contest, and a Nobel-prize winner in literature with three Australian aborigines on an island with limited resources where the problem to solve is basic survival. Who would be the best at problem solving under these conditions?

As far as is known now, there is no group of humans in the world today that is more intelligent than any other, in spite of the fact that a lot of people have been looking for

**racism**
A policy or attitude that unfairly generalizes real or perceived characteristics of some group to every member of that group.

**intelligence**
The ability to solve problems of concern to the species.

**IQ**
Intelligence quotient; the score on a standardized psychological test designed by North American and Western European psychologists to measure problem-solving ability in North American and Western European middle-class and upper-class students.

evidence for such a difference for a long time. The reverse is true as well: There is no group that is less intelligent than any other. Again, this says nothing about individual differences in problem-solving ability, only group differences.

# Human Adaptations

When applied to humans, the term *adaptation* has several meanings. In one sense, adaptation is synonymous with evolution: Darwin believed that evolution resulted in individuals and groups that were better adapted to their environment and equated the entire process of evolution with the process of adaptation. In this sense adaptation is genetic, with new genes substituting for others through mutations or through gene reshuffling; the specific skin color, body build, or stature that a human population has can be considered long-term adaptations to specific environmental conditions.

Other meanings of adaptation are not as genetically finite. For example, human metabolic rates change as seasons change, rising at the beginning of winter to produce more body heat and declining in the spring to produce less heat. This kind of adaptation is temporary and reversible—and local, because metabolic changes can occur only in areas that have seasonality (Bogin 1998). Adaptation to extremes of heat, cold, or altitude are physiologically possible because the human body is flexible and can adjust to living in a range of environments. But this kind of adaptation is reversible as well, because individuals can leave one environment and do well in another. Only the ability to adjust is biologically inherited.

Acclimation is a variation of adaptation, but it is a short-term physiological change that occurs right after exposure to environmental stress, such as sweating when hot and shivering when cold. Physiological reactions are biological. Acclimatization is also physiological but takes days to months to manifest, as with an increase in lung expansion at high altitudes (Relethford 2005). Relative to extreme temperature, populations in hot climates show vasodilation when the temperature exceeds 26.7°C (80°F), and capillaries in the skin bring heat from inside the body to the skin surface. One good way to cope with heat stress is to sweat, and under extreme conditions, humans can sweat 10 to 12 liters an hour (Frisancho 1993). Populations living in extremely cold regions show vasoconstriction when the temperature is below 0°C (32°F): Subcutaneous blood vessels constrict and limit the flow of warm blood. This decreases the skin temperature and reduces heat loss. Not every human is climatically affected the same way; tolerance depends on sex, age, and size. Groups vary as well, and Australian aborigines, South African Ju/'Huansi, Acalufs (Tierra del Fuego), Lapps (Finland), and Inuit (Alaska) are able to cope with cold temperatures far better than Europeans. Populations with West African ancestry fair poorly in cold tests, with frostbite—a biological response to the inability of the body to cope with extreme cold—occurring far more often in such groups than in European or Asian populations (Beall and Steegman 2000).

The Spaniards noticed and described the differing effects of high altitude on themselves and Native American populations when they conquered Peru. Although living at high altitudes includes coping with increased solar radiation, low humidity, high winds, cold climate, and rough terrain, it is hypoxia, or lack of oxygen, that affects all human organs. Hypoxia puts a strain on the heart, decreases eyesight, impairs memory and learning, and results in muscular weakness and weight loss. The bodies of people who live above 3,000 m (9,846 feet) adapt to the stress of high altitude by increasing lung volume, physiologically increasing oxygen in the blood, and increasing the diffusion of oxygen from blood to tissues. People going from low to high altitudes can adjust biologically in a moderate period of time, but until they do, they are likely to experience symptoms such as nausea, fatigue, and vomiting (Beall and Steegman 2000).

Anthropologists often speak of cultural adjustments as "adaptations," as when people use culture to adapt to an existing environment by wearing the appropriate amount of clothing and building appropriate housing. But this kind of adaptation is neither biological nor inherited.

# Growth and Development, Health and Disease

Human infants are born almost totally helpless and remain highly dependent until about age 7, yet they grow in size and develop coping abilities. Bioanthropologists study these patterns of growth and development, often comparing the patterns to those of other species. They have found, for example, that chimpanzees have faster and less prolonged growth periods than humans do. The long periods of slow growth from weaning to the beginning of the adolescent growth spurt in humans might allow energy to be used for brain activities.

Rather than simply using chronological age, anthropologists identify five stages of human growth: birth and post-natal (approximately up to 1 year), infancy (1–3 years), childhood (4–7 years), juvenile (8–12 years), adolescence (13–17 years), adulthood (18–50) and senescence (over 50). The age ranges are approximate. For example, the juvenile stage begins when individuals are no longer dependent on their caregivers, but this developmental milestone varies from culture to culture and also by individual. And, of course, life is continuous, not chopped up into arbitrary stages. Each stage builds on previous ones, with developing cognitive powers allowing for new activities, especially learning about the adult roles individuals will eventually take on. Additionally, individuals learn the social behaviors necessary to survive until adulthood, attract a mate, and reproduce. The juvenile learning stage is particularly long in highly social animals such as wolves and primates.

Average stature has increased in European and North American humans since records have been kept, and in Japanese people since the Second World War. But this increase is likely due to better nutrition (more protein in the diet) than to any genetic change. All groups that have immigrated to Western Europe or North America have shown are increase in average stature due to better nutrition (Bogin 2001a).

The growth and development of the brain has been the specific target of many developmental psychologists, who test children for various mental milestones, such as acquiring a "theory of mind." Anthropologists focus on biological brain development cross-culturally. For example, in all human populations today, nearly adult brain size is reached at age 7 but the last spurt of brain growth occurs simultaneously with the adolescent growth spurt in the body in general. The brain growth is mostly in the frontal and parietal lobe areas where "higher" brain functions such as decision making reside.

Finally, human females are unique among animals in having menopause, which occurs when women run out of the 400 or so eggs their ovaries stored in the fifth month of gestation. Menopause occurs at about age 50 in all groups. Women then live an average of 20 to 30 years after they no longer are able to reproduce, and again this is not found elsewhere in the animal world (Bogin 2003). Some primates do show a decline of estrus with age, but not a complete stop. For women and men, senescence, a process of non-growth, is a natural part of the aging process in which individuals decline in their abilities to adapt to new stresses. Age of onset and extent of decline are extremely variable, even within cultures.

Many bioanthropologists are involved in research on health and disease. Anthropologists with cross-cultural interests and training can help in research projects focusing on particular diseases, for example, investigating whether some populations are more likely to get a certain disease and why. Or, if a new drug is thought to be helpful in treating a particular disease, is it as effective in every population? Bioanthropologists do genetic counseling because they have researched the probabilities of certain inherited diseases becoming manifest given known genetic combinations. Some bioanthropologists have been involved in paleopathological investigations to determine the origins and history of certain diseases, usually those that leave clues in bone. They are interested in whether those diseases are increasing or decreasing among populations. And, recently, anthropologists have attempted to help modern humans eat better. Highlight 15.2 (on pp. 490–492) focuses on nutrition and the Paleolithic lifestyle.

# Applied Biological Anthropology

Applied sciences use knowledge gained from research to attempt to solve human problems. Just as engineers use concepts from math, physics, chemistry, and other sciences to try to find ways to cut down on pollution and make better roads, bioanthropologists use knowledge about modern human variability to attempt to solve contemporary problems that are biological in nature. This section considers a few ways biological anthropologists apply this knowledge—to debunk myths such as "humans are violent by nature because they are really super-apes," to identify murderers or rapists via DNA fingerprinting, and to reconstruct faces from skulls for identification or for historical reasons. The next section will examine the science of forensic anthropology.

## Are Humans Naturally Violent?

Based primarily on the work of Jane Goodall at the Gombe Stream Reserve, a few researchers view humans as if they were grown-up apes without fur coats and attribute many modern human traits to ape ancestry—including "natural" violence. This is bad science for several reasons. Although comparing chimpanzees, bonobos, and humans to deduce behaviors in the LCA group is acceptable science, most of the behaviors of that group remain unknown (see Chapter 5). Scientists do know that chimpanzees at Gombe became aggressive primarily when they learned that aggression was the key to success in competition for food. In 1965 Goodall began to provision her chimpanzees with bananas (an introduced food) in order to get close enough to observe them easily and take photos. She reported that the majority of the aggressive acts she observed were due to competition over the provisioned bananas (Sussman 1997). In 1991 Margaret Power did a literature search and found that it was only after banana provisioning that observers at Gombe reported aggressive behavior; in addition, she noted that at other field stations, where there was no provisioning, chimpanzees were not aggressive (Power 1991, 1995). So much for chimpanzee aggression being "natural" and genetic. Additionally, bonobos are apparently related to humans just as closely as chimpanzees are, and bonobos have never been observed behaving in an aggressive manner. Thus, those who wish to claim that humans are naturally violent will have to do it without attributing violence to genetic inheritance from a common ancestor.

## DNA Fingerprinting and AIDS

DNA analysis has applications to pure bioanthropological research. Once the base-pair sequences have been worked out for humans, chimpanzees, and eventually other contemporary apes, researchers can use comparisons to try to answer questions such as how and why humans differ from those other primates and whether the split from the LCA was a trichotomy (gorillas, chimpanzees/bonobos, and humans; see Chapter 5) or involved only humans diverging from chimpanzees and bonobos.

The first archaeological DNA to be analyzed was from the liver of an ancient Chinese corpse. Next came studies of DNA from an extinct horselike animal called a quagga, from Egyptian mummies, and from brains from the Windover, Florida, site. Then scientists analyzed DNA from human remains in cemeteries, from human feces and urine, from leaves and plants, and from a famous mammoth dated to between 50 and 40 kyr ago (Jones 2001; Mays 1998).

DNA analysis is already playing a part in forensic cases, identifying accused rapists through their semen or accused murderers through bits of skin under their victims' fingernails, and in paternity cases. DNA fingerprinting is based on the widely accepted estimate that the same chromosome randomly chosen from any two unrelated humans will differ at a frequency of 1 in 300 base pairs; sequencing a 15,000 base-pair segment is enough to answer with 99.9 percent probability of being correct the question of whether the two humans in a paternity case were related or whether skin found under the nails of a murder victim was the same as that of a suspect (Krawczak and Schmidke 1998).

DNA analysis is also sometimes used to determine kinship and ancestry. From 1975 to 1983, between 9,000 and 15,000 people in Argentina were killed during the so-called "Dirty War." The children of the victims were kept by prison authorities or sold. DNA fingerprinting has allowed experts to match (to 99.8 percent probability) at least 63 of the 250 orphaned children to their grandparents without the availability of the intervening generation. And in a well-publicized case in the United States, the Y chromosome marker of one of the children of Sally Hemmings (a slave who was owned by Thomas Jefferson) matched that of President Jefferson.

Another applied use of DNA analysis involves the origin of HIV (human immunodeficiency virus), which causes acquired immunodeficiency syndrome, or AIDS. Ever since AIDS was discovered in 1983, scientists have been actively searching for its origin, both to seek a possible cure and to understand the potential evolution of other AIDS-like diseases. DNA analysis of the types of HIV in humans and in suspected African chimpanzee hosts points to one subspecies of chimpanzee as the virus's origin. When ape hunting for bushmeat became big business, hunters slaughtered chimpanzees without taking proper precautions, and the HIV virus moved from chimpanzee to human (Weiss and Wrangham 1999).

DNA analysis is currently helping investigators solve paleoanthropological mysteries as well. For example, scientists argued for years about whether Europeans brought tuberculosis to Native Americans. DNA analysis of material from mummies dating to before European contact has shown that TB was already in North America before that event (Jones 2001).

## Reconstructing Faces

The art and science of facial reconstruction on ancient skulls has been less widely practiced than DNA fingerprinting, because it is more arbitrary and speculative: It depends to some degree on the instincts of the sculptor. Some clues to a face's structure are fairly secure, such as the zygomatic arch/cheekbones—high or low—and the height of the forehead. But many traits that would identify a specific individual, such as lips and ears, do not leave clues on skeletal remains. In an attempt to validate facial reconstruction, scientists have performed several blind analyses based on known persons. In each case the sculptor based a reconstruction only on a skull; the scientists then compared the results to photographs of the individual. Outcomes were mixed (Prag and Neave 1997).

The process of reconstructing is standard: The specialist puts the bones together and fills in anything that is missing, using the principles of bilateral symmetry. The sculptor then makes a mold and uses seventeen standard markers to place pegs to represent different thicknesses of the soft parts of the face and skull—more for cheek areas, less for skull bones, with adjustments for sex, assessed age, and ancestry. Using clay strips, the sculptor builds up the muscles of the face, reconstructs the nose according to a formula for width and length based on the width of the nasal opening, and makes educated guesses on lip, ear, and nose cartilage details.

In cases of missing persons, authorities report a success rate of 50 to 60 percent in identifying remains when a face reconstruction is distributed by posters, TV newscasts, or newspapers and people are asked if they "know this person." Modern technology can create reconstructions using skulls and CT scans hooked to computers. The success rate is about the same as the rate with manual replicas, and the work can be done in far less time (Prag and Neave 1997).

A story that reveals a lot about the validity of facial reconstruction concerns an attempt by the German State Police to identify a 3-year-old skull found in a forest. The police knew the sex, age, and some pathological details but still could not identify the

# We Are What We Were, or Are We?

HUMANS LIVE MODERN LIFESTYLES but with Stone Age bodies. For at least 5 million years, bipedal hominids have foraged for food, their bodies adapting by natural selection to existing environmental conditions. For example, their hearts beat faster at high activity levels, as in chasing down large animals; their digestive and vascular systems are adapted to low-fat, high-fiber, high-plant diets. Beginning only 10,000 years ago (a drop in the chronobucket), domestication of plants and animals began; 6,000 years ago, people began living in urban environments. Today we sit in front of our TV and computer screens, munching Big Macs, drinking beer, and smoking cigarettes—whereas our bodies are adapted for strenuous activity, high-fiber low-fat diets, and no substance abuse. It's no wonder that we suffer from "chronic diseases of civilization." Anthropologists can tell the world exactly what went wrong, when, and how to fix it. They are trying to get the message across to nutritionists, physicians, and anyone else who will listen. Alarm bells are ringing!

Before 10,000 years ago, our ancestors' lifestyle was based on foraging. Using fossils, artifacts, and ethnoparallels with modern foragers, anthropologists can reconstruct that lifestyle with reasonable accuracy. Human genes have not changed very much during the past 10,000 years, but our culture has changed drastically and fast. Bones of ancestral foragers suggest that before farming began, people were fairly tall, probably because of a diet high in protein from wild plants and animals. This supposition is confirmed by studies of strontium/calcium ratios in bones of individuals who lived right before and right after farming first began. Also, fossils tell us that our ancestors were quite muscular, because their bones show hefty rough areas for muscle attachment. Healthwise, these early foragers had good teeth, with only 2 percent cavities in contrast to 70 percent among modern populations.

Ethnoparallels with more than 50 modern forager groups recreate early forager diets—artifacts cannot be used to do this because most food residue biodegrades. Early forager diets were varied, not dependent on a single type of food; the amount of animal versus plant food varied from 90 percent meat in very cold climates to 15 percent in desert areas, but on average 65 percent plant and 35 percent meat resources were the typical diet. Wild animals contain about one-seventh as much fat as domestic animals, so meat was very lean. People ate no dairy products or processed grains, and they ate honey, not processed sugar. Their fiber intake was high, as was their intake of calcium and potassium, and their sodium intake was low. Because they likely consumed fewer calories than moderns, they were not obese. Just think of liquids: Early foragers drank only water, not calorie-ridden drinks such as beer, colas, or "sport" beverages.

Ethnoparallels also give an idea of early forager health, providing clues that bones and artifacts cannot. Mainly because they had diets low in saturated fat, early foragers had little coronary heart disease and low incidences of most cancers (breast, uterus, prostate, colon). And because they did not smoke, drink alcohol, or do drugs, they did not suffer lung cancer, have liver damage, or kill themselves in highway accidents. Of course, average life expectancy before medicinal drugs and professional care was considerably lower than it is today. Conditions such as heart disease, cancer, and vascular disease generally are illnesses of older people, and most early foragers did not live long enough to manifest them. Though the average life expectancy of foragers was only 30 to 40 years, however, many lived well beyond this, as evidenced by fossil materials. And those foragers who did live to a ripe old age did not show signs of those "lifestyle diseases" even in later life. In contrast, young people in modern industrialized societies show incipient symptoms of most of them.

Foragers did die, of course, but from injuries, childbirth, bone disease, and noninfectious diseases. They suffered from lice, pinworms, yaws, sleeping sickness, and perhaps malaria, some of which would have been lethal; they were infected through insect bites and eating contaminated flesh. They probably got hurt in skirmishes over hunting territory and over females, and they probably endured infections from deep wounds and fractures. Some local herb use and splints/bandaging may have been possible, and families must have supported those who survived accidents and wounds, but deaths did result from these factors. There may have been some infectious diseases as well; but because foragers lived in small, widely dispersed, and nomadic populations, the effects were minimal—without a lot of people to infect, microorganisms that caused illnesses died.

Overall, the level of physical exercise of early foragers was considerably higher than that of the modern couch potato: Nomadic groups were constantly moving from place to place, and when men hunted, their heart rates increased intermittently, a healthy adaptation to a foraging lifestyle.

And then things began to change. About 10,000 years ago—first in the Middle East, but not much later in East and South Asia, Africa, Mexico, and the Andes highlands—people began to domesticate plants and animals. Diets changed drastically, activity patterns changed, and eventually the brewing of beer and wine began. People's health changed accordingly. First, many early farming populations relied on a main food crop (wheat, barley, rice, or corn). Though they probably had many creative recipes for that one type of food, the variety was low, producing vitamin and/or protein deficiencies and diseases; an example was pellagra, caused by too exclusive a reliance on corn. Grains for gruels and breads resulted in mouths filled with starch, good breeding grounds for tooth decay–causing bacteria. In addition, teeth became worn down from chewing improperly ground grain (and chewing grinding-stone fragments as well). The results were drastically increased rates of tooth decay, tooth loss, abscesses, and sometimes ensuing death.

Farming demanded a sedentary lifestyle, and this too affected health in several ways. First, when people began to farm, more mouths could be fed. This change led to larger populations concentrated in small areas. Infectious diseases now had lots of people living in close quarters to spread among. Community water supplies often became contaminated, and sanitary conditions were often poor, so new parasitic diseases such as intestinal flukes resulted from contact with human feces. Other infectious diseases spread through larger groups, including smallpox, measles, mumps, chicken pox, and the bubonic plague, all of which can be fatal. Animals brought diseases that could be transmitted to humans as well: anthrax, typhus, malaria, and yellow fever. Food stored in large quantities under unsanitary conditions could result in mass food poisonings, and disease-spreading rats loved living in large granaries. Even irrigation was a health hazard, because canals carried schistosomiasis.

As a result of farming, people became shorter (from eating less protein), suffered nutritional stress when crops failed, and had higher infant mortality. There were more humans, but their living conditions hardly improved.

During the past two centuries, many health measures have improved. We now have drugs such as antibiotics and professional health care providers and institutions. In 2002 the average life expectancy at birth was 76 years. In spite of increased average life spans, however, the quality of those additional 30 years is not what it should be. Many diseases that killed people under foraging and early farming conditions have been eliminated or are no longer life-threatening; polio has been dramatically reduced, and smallpox has been eradicated. But because of modern diets, activity levels, and smoking, drinking, and drugging, our health has not increased to the same degree as our life spans. Instead, for earlier infectious diseases we have substituted chronic "diseases of civilization," which are responsible for up to 75 percent of deaths in Western nations. Although these illnesses affect older more often than younger people, they develop at all ages. Modern humans living under "civilized" conditions have strokes, peripheral vascular diseases, adult-onset diabetes, hypertension (high blood pressure), emphysema, cirrhosis, many types of cancer, and obesity, all of which start with bad habits when people are young. "Civilized diseases" are lifestyle related. And they are under our control, if we choose to take advice.

Many modern diets contain far too much fat, far too little fiber, far too many calories, and too few micronutrients such as beta carotene (vitamin A) and selenium. Many modern humans do not have daily activity patterns that burn calories and strengthen their hearts. And many modern people smoke, drink to excess, and take drugs that affect their health sooner or later. Almost all of the diseases of civilization are strongly affected by diet, exercise, smoking, alcohol, and drugs; in other words, they are greatly affected by environment. Epidemiologists suggest that it is theoretically possible to reduce every type of cancer by 70 to 90 percent, which is the estimated environmental portion of cancer's causes. Their advice for lowering the odds of any cancer is to restrict dietary fat, increase fiber, consume a wide variety of fruits and vegetables, avoid obesity, consume food with high amounts of vitamins C and A (beta carotene), not smoke, and consume alcohol moderately if at all. Age is not the primary variable here; lifestyle is.

*(continues on the next page)* ▶

New factors now affect human health, too: Diseases can spread as fast as airplanes can carry them; new diseases mutate and are spread because there are 6 billion of us; many germs are mutating faster than scientists can invent new antibiotics to cure them; prostitution and promiscuity—male and female—spread sexual diseases. Industrial wastes, pesticides, polluted water, and polluted air affect us all; the depleted ozone layer may yet do us in. People living in high-density urban areas worry about the possibility of devastating epidemics that might spread too quickly to avoid. The Centers for Disease Control has listed 22 new diseases that have emerged since the 1980s, including Legionnaires' disease, Ebola, Lyme disease, hepatitis C, mad cow disease, SARS, and HIV; TB has mutated to new strains, and bacteria and viruses in food are causing many deaths. Because doctors prescribe antibiotics inappropriately, hospitals have become the source of drug-resistant strains of bacteria that can infect hundreds of patients at a time. Farmers supplement animal feed with antibiotics as a matter of routine.

The statement "We are what we were" is only partially correct. We have stayed "what we were" biologically, but culturally we have become a threat to our own selves. Anthropologists may have a lot of the answers here, but unfortunately even some of them eat too much steak, are overweight, and drink to excess.

*Sources:* Armelagos, G. J. 1998. The viral superhighway. *The Sciences* (January–February): 24–29. Armelagos, G. J., K. Barnes, and J. Lin. 1996. Disease in human evolution: The re-emergence of infectious disease in the third epidemiological transition. *AnthroNotes.* Eaton, S. B., and M. Konner. 1985. Ancient genes and modern health. *Anthroquest.* Eaton, S. B., M. Konner, and M. Shostak. 1988. "Stone Agers in the fast lane: Chronic degenerative diseases in evolutionary perspective. *American Journal of Medicine* 84 (4): 739–749.

turn back to your reading

individual. As it happened, an international conference on facial reconstruction was being held in Belgium that year, and the German government offered to pay the conference fee of any expert who would attempt a facial reconstruction from the skull. Twenty-one experts agreed, and working independently, each did a reconstruction. They came up with 21 quite different-looking faces. Why? Although reconstructions are based on averages, much artistic license occurs with lips, hair, and the like. And because most of us know our relatives and friends because of their individuality, not their "averageness," it is not likely that any of the 21 reconstructions would match a particular person (Mackenzie 2006).

# Forensic Anthropology

The word *forensic* means "legal or court related." Although cultural anthropologists and archaeologists are sometimes asked to bring their expertise to bear on court cases, it is biological anthropologists who are most closely associated with courts and legal matters. DNA fingerprinting, discussed above, is one technique used in the field of **forensic anthropology**. Before DNA and other molecular aids, bones (including teeth) were the only source of evidence for the forensic anthropologist. Even the bones of an individual can be problematic in terms of identification unless police have some idea who the person is likely to be; even if DNA can be extracted, the police will not know whom to contact for DNA comparison. Still, analyzing bones can help narrow the field of potential relatives. Bones will be the focus of this discussion.

Although forensic sciences began in the eighteenth century, physical anthropologists were not involved until relatively recently (Hunter et al. 1996). Since the early 1990s, however, they have assisted medical examiners in identifying remains in many situations. Well-known examples include the Branch Davidian compound in Waco, Texas; missing American soldiers in Southeast Asia; and members of the Russian imperial family, the Romanovs, who were executed in 1918 (Maples 1995). In the case of the Romanov family, Prince Philip, Duke of Edinburgh, donated mitochondrial DNA to compare with the remains of what researchers believed to be the czarina and her three children, because Prince Philip and the czarina shared that DNA through a common maternal relative (Harren and King 2002). The body of Nazi physician Josef Mengele was also identified by means of modern forensic anthropology (see Highlight 15.3, on pp. 494–496).

Unfortunately, forensic anthropologists must often become involved in tragic situations, helping to identify victims of mass accidents (train and plane crashes, cemetery floodings, bombings) or to identify victims in human rights investigations, as in Argentina in the late 1970s and early 1980s. In Croatia in 1991, searchers found 2,000 bodies in a mass grave, the likely result of the siege of a town by Serbian troops. Using 263 blood samples taken from probable relatives of the victims, forensics experts identified 44 of the bodies. Forensic anthropologists were also involved in identifying victims of the September 11, 2001, World Trade Center tragedy.

Because biological anthropologists are knowledgeable about both modern and ancestral populations, they have the natural combination of skills to identify bones within the context of living populations. Not all human bones can be identified, of course. For example, identification can be impossible when preservation is poor, when a missing person is not reported, when people do not wish to be identified, or when homeless people die with no identification. In many cases identifying skeletal material is not necessary; but to resolve cases of foul play, or to provide disaster survivors with closure, or to discharge legal claims or obligations of estates, identification of remains can be important.

Forensic anthropologists want to answer five questions, all related to the skeletal material of people who cannot be identified by normal means:

1. Are the remains human? Some untrained persons confuse human and dog bones.

2. If human, do the remains indicate one individual or many?

**forensic anthropology**
Application of skeletal and DNA identification techniques to solve legal problems.

# In the News: Identification of Josef Mengele

SOME BIOLOGICAL ANTHROPOLOGISTS specialize in the identification of skeletal material; and some try to help police, lawyers, and special committees or commissions match missing people with existing bones. Although most forensic, or legal, cases are local and stay local, some categories of missing people are extremely large—national or international in scope—and require a great deal of communication between law officers in different areas and between police and the public. If the police and courts of law become involved, identification cases are forensic. From time to time, however, identification cases are important only for historic knowledge. The bones of Amelia Earhart or Hitler, for example, would be simply of historical interest.

Some matchings make headlines when skeletal material is suspected to have been someone famous. On the assumption that the stories of Adolph Hitler's having been cremated are not true, journalists and others have searched for Hitler's skeletal remains since 1945. For some reason, finding his bones is important to some people. The reverse occurs as well: Occasionally bones turn up and are thought to be those of a famous person, and forensic anthropologists begin attempts at matching, sometimes under a good deal of pressure to come to the "right" conclusions. An example comes from the famous (and at times infamous) Tower of London, which has been in continuous use for almost a thousand years. Given the fortress's huge size and many uses, various human bones have been uncovered from time to time. When the bones of two adolescents (by their size) were found in 1674, the assumption was that they were the remains of "the two princes" who had been incarcerated in the Tower after the death of their father, the king, in 1483 and never seen again. Modern analysis is difficult, because the only paintings of the boys glamorized their features and no dental or medical records existed at that time. The result is that the identification of the Tower bones remains inconclusive. Several suspects for the princes' imprisonment and murder have been mentioned, but that is another part of the mystery that probably will never be solved.

Perhaps the most famous case of a match between both skeletal remains and DNA and a well-known person in recent history is that of Josef Mengele, the so-called Nazi Angel of Death. Mengele was a camp physician at the Auschwitz concentration camp in Poland. He is said to have personally selected 400,000 prisoners to die in gas chambers and to have conducted medical experiments with twins and dwarfs in an effort to create a blue-eyed, blond-haired race. U.S. troops arrested Mengele but then freed him before learning of his role at Auschwitz, and he therefore escaped trial and sentencing for his war crimes. He fled to South America, where he lived in Argentina, Paraguay, and finally Brazil. Various sightings prompted a novel and movie *(The Boys from Brazil)* about a fictionalized Mengele.

In February 1979 in Brazil, a man who went by the name of Wolfgang Gerhard accidentally drowned and was buried in a São Paulo cemetery. When it was suspected in 1985 that the man who drowned might have been Mengele, the corpse was exhumed and the matching attempt began. Because the remains were largely skeletonized, it became the work of skeletal biologists/forensic anthropologists in Brazil, the United States, and Germany, under a request from the Brazilian government, to try to answer the identity question.

The first step was to find all records about Mengele that the investigators could use to match the person with the skeleton. Often mismatches come to light quickly (stature, unusual teeth patterning, anatomical anomaly) and no further work is needed. As Mengele had been in hiding since 1945, however, there were no records of him since that date. The only existing dental records dated from 1937–1938; three fillings in molars did match, but that fact was insufficient to be more than suggestive. But the records from an SS medical examination report in 1938 gave certain physical features, listed in the table under "SS Report."

|  | SS Report | Cadaver |
|---|---|---|
| Born (age) | March 26, 1911 (68 years) | 60–74 years |
| Height | 174 cm (5′ 8″) | 174 cm (average measurement) |
| Weight | 77 kg (170 pounds) | |
| Cranial circumference | 57 cm | 54 cm |
| Cranial form | Brachycephalic | |
| Body type | Athletic | |

The SS report, two photographs taken at age 27, and one piece of anecdotal evidence—plus the skeleton—were the extent of the physical evidence. While a camp doctor at Auschwitz, Mengele supposedly had a motorcycle accident, injuring his right leg; witnesses reported this, as did Mengele's diary entries and letters. If the remains were Mengele, he would have died at age 68, and the formula used to assess stature should have concluded he was 5 feet 8 inches tall. At age 27 Mengele weighed 170 pounds and was assessed as having an athletic physique. If the cranium was measured correctly in 1938 (and there is reason to believe it was not), his cranium measurement was 57 cm and his head shape relatively broad and short (brachycephalic) as opposed to long and narrow (dolichocephalic). Age can alter weight and physique, which are difficult to assess on the basis of skeletal remains even in young persons. But stature, cranial circumference, and head shape should not change much through adulthood. This is what the team had to go on.

## BONE MATCHINGS

The team measured various parts of the skeleton of the buried individual, as shown in the table above under "Cadaver." The skull had been broken, but there were no missing pieces and it was put together with no problems. They then interpreted their findings.

- *Sex:* Mengele was male, so the team needed to determine only the sex of the cadaver. The skull measurements were clearly male, with 9 of the 11 measurements falling into the male but not the female range, with a 5 percent margin of error. The bones of the legs and arms were clearly male.
- *Stature:* Because the body was assumed to be that of a European male, the investigators applied a formula for that group to the measured length of the long bones. Using only the left leg yielded an estimated stature of 175 cm; using the right leg (which might have been traumatized in the motorcycle accident) gave 173 cm; the average is 174 cm, exactly the same as Mengele's reported stature.
- *Aging:* Observation of the bone structure of the femur and humerus gave an estimate of 60 to 74 years of age.
- *Cranial circumference:* Here a discrepancy exists between the cadaver and Mengele's SS report. But Mengele probably made the measurement himself and might have added a few centimeters to accommodate the steel helmet for which the measurement was taken. Or he might have taken the measurement using an incorrect plane. Or it may be the measurement was larger because he was measuring a skull plus flesh and hair, rather than just the bony skull.
- *Anatomical anomalies:* There were traces of an old fracture line on the right side of the pelvis, attributable to his alleged motorcycle accident. There were no other anomalies.

The conclusions about the bone matchings were that sex, age, stature, and one anatomical anomaly clearly matched. The cranial circumference measurement did not, but is easily explainable.

## PHOTO COMPARISON

Two photographs of a 27-year-old Mengele exist, one front and one side view. Several photos of the alleged Mengele at age 65 were used for comparisons. A special photo made from the originals of both the 27-year-old and the 65-year-old was superimposed over a photo of the skull. There was complete conformity in the proportions of the head, face, eyes, nose, and mouth in both photos. The investigators concluded that the photographs matched the skeletal remains perfectly. As the head of the team reported, "By virtue of the clear evidence of all the findings taken together there is no room for doubts that the exhumed skeletal parts are the remains of the corpse of Josef Mengele" (Helmer, 1632).

*(continues on the next page)* ▶

## DNA TESTING

If the bone evidence were not enough, a more recent DNA test confirmed the skeletal evidence. In an unusual paternity test, technicians compared the DNA of Mengele's wife (the mother of his son), the DNA of his son, and DNA from the skeletal materials identified as Mengele. The report stated that "the results were consistent with the deceased having been the father of Mengele's son" (Watson, 320). That is, the remains were Mengele. The chance that another person could possess DNA consistent with Mengele's son's particular parentage is estimated at 1 in 1,800.

Although not all of the forensic investigators in the Mengele case were biological anthropologists, all skeletal biologists specializing in human remains use the same methods as forensic anthropologists. The identification of the bones of Josef Mengele may have been the case of the twentieth century, but there are still missing famous people: Butch Cassidy and the Sundance Kid, Amelia Earhart, Jimmy Hoffa, and, yes, even Adolph Hitler.

*Sources:* Helmer, R. P. 1987. Identification of the cadaver remains of Josef Mengele. *Journal of Forensic Sciences* 32 (1): 1622–1644.   Kernan, M. 2000. Bone specialist on call. *Smithsonian* (April): 16–17.   Stirland, A. 1999. *Human bones in archaeology.* Buckinghamshire, UK: Shire Publications.   Watson, N. 1998. The analysis of body fluids. In *Crime scene to court: The essentials of forensic science,* ed. P. White, pp. 289–325. Cambridge: Royal Society of Chemistry.

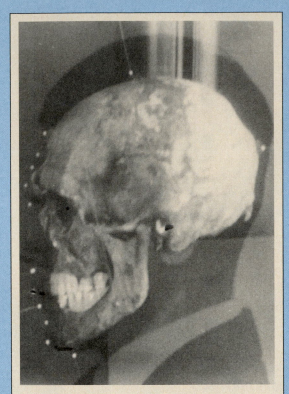

Compare the two pieces of superimposed evidence—the skull of the man thought to be Josef Mengele and the photo of Mengele. Can you see where the matches are and why the experts concluded that the exhumed body was that of Mengele?

turn back to your reading

3.  What is the biological profile of the person: sex, age, ethnicity or ancestry, height, physique, handedness, unusual anomalies or pathologies? Anthropologists spend a good amount of time on this particular question.

4.  Did the person die a natural death, or was there a crime involved? This is the main interest of police; similarly, lawyers may be interested in matching a missing (rich) person with bones.

5.  In the case of a crime, when did the person die? Was the person transported? And what was the probable mode of death (shooting, stabbing, being hit with a blunt instrument, etc.)? These context questions can help police solve crimes.

Of all of the questions listed, the one about biological profile is foremost to forensic anthropologists. Through their knowledge of anatomical differences and changes through life in contemporary males and females, their ability to reconstruct stature from long bones based on standard formulae and to estimate body physique based on ridges for muscle attachment, and their skill in pinpointing unusual anatomical features and even analyzing ethnic/ancestral differences, forensic anthropologists attempt to narrow down the possibilities. They cannot say, "This is Mary Jones"—but they hope to be able to say, "These are the remains of a 20- to 25-year-old female of European ancestry who was between 5 foot 8 and 5 foot 10 and of slight build, who died of natural causes between 6 and 8 months ago." Then police can attempt to match missing persons with the description. These descriptions and uses vary, depending on the case.

How do forensic anthropologists deduce an individual's sex from skeletal material? In general, crania, mandibles, and pelvises provide enough clues to separate males from females. As Figure 15.9 shows, a male skull generally has prominent eyebrow ridges, two bumps on the lower forehead, large mastoid processes, long zygomatic (cheek) bones extending to or beyond the ear holes, strong ridges on the base of the skull, wide and sharply angled rami (the mandible, or jawbone, parts that ascend toward the skull), and a square chin with two bumps. A male pelvis usually is relatively long and narrow, has a less-than-90-degree sciatic notch where the two parts of the

*Figure 15.9*

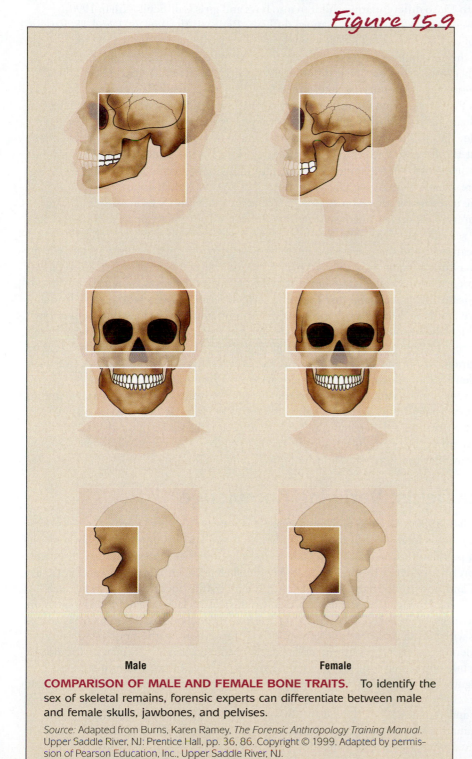

Male                 Female

**COMPARISON OF MALE AND FEMALE BONE TRAITS.**   To identify the sex of skeletal remains, forensic experts can differentiate between male and female skulls, jawbones, and pelvises.

*Source:* Adapted from Burns, Karen Ramey, *The Forensic Anthropology Training Manual.* Upper Saddle River, NJ: Prentice Hall, pp. 36, 86. Copyright © 1999. Adapted by permission of Pearson Education, Inc., Upper Saddle River, NJ.

pelvis join, and is generally more V-shaped (Mays 1998). In contrast, a female skull probably will show smooth brow ridges, no bumps on the forehead, small mastoid processes, zygomatic bones that do not extend beyond the ear holes, weak ridges on the base of the skull, narrow and less angled rami, and a rounded or pointed chin. Female pelvises have wider angles where the two parts of the pelvis join and are more bowl-shaped, because of their function as birth canals. The sciatic notch is wide and shallow. If both the pelvis and the skull of unknown remains are available, the success rate for identifying sex is 98 percent; if only the pelvis is available, the rate drops to 96 percent; if only the skull is available, it is only 92 percent (Mays 1998). Unfortunately, sex differences do not fully develop until age 12 to 15, so differentiating children into boys and girls is difficult (Killan 1990).

Assessing age from bones is more difficult. Between the ages of 1 and 15, various kinds of teeth erupt at predictable times; after age 21, all teeth are fully formed. The fusion of the ends of long bones (epiphyseal fusion) can be used to age children and adolescents, because fusion occurs at different ages. Girls are always a year or two ahead of boys, however, so sex must be determined first. Bones and teeth degenerate after age 21 at rates that vary depending on diet, lifestyle, and dental care, so without knowledge of an individual's habits, it is difficult to incorporate these variables in the assessment. Other possible clues to the age of skeletal remains include the joint where the two pubic bones meet at the front (pubic symphysis), suture closings on the skull, rib end shape, tooth wear, bony growth in the spine, and bone pitting. After analyzing all available clues, experts are usually able to give a likely age spread of 4 years. When done by an experienced forensic investigator, this estimate can be 97 percent accurate (Steadman 2003).

Forensic experts estimate stature by using certain formulae, once they have determined sex and ethnicity. For example, if an investigator assesses an individual as a European male and then measures the humerus, the formula will indicate stature within a range of error (standard deviation) of about 4 inches.

Forensic anthropologists claim that police want information on ancestry (though the police call it "race") and that they can fairly accurately assess where an individual's ancestry originated based on bone remains. Among additional clues that help narrow down identity are obvious pathologies such as old bone fractures or the effects of osteoarthritis or bone infections. Even habitual tasks or recreations, such as kneeling to grind grain, scrubbing floors, or playing tennis, can alter bones. And handedness can help identify individuals, as 11 to 15 percent of Americans are left-handed.

Forensic anthropology may sound romantic and adventurous, but it is a challenging field. It can be ethically and personally difficult to identify victims of mass genocide or an airplane crash. Also, becoming a board-certified forensic anthropologist is a long and arduous process. As of 2002 there were only 64 board-certified diplomates of the American Board of Forensic Anthropology (Kennedy 2003).

## Spitalfields: Verifying Knowledge

In the late 1980s, forensic anthropologists had a rare chance to verify their assumptions about skeletal identification by studying more than 1,000 interments of a single human population from a crypt in Christ Church, Spitalfields, near London, England. The interments dated from 1729 to 1857; the skeletal material was in excellent condition; and, most important, brass plates on many coffins identified the individuals by sex and age (giving names and birth/death dates). The lack of identifying plates on many coffins, however, reduced the database to 387 individuals. Blind analysis of remains, with the investigator not knowing the information on the brass plate, successfully identified sex in 98 percent of cases. As predicted, age assessments were not as successful, but patterns of error emerged that will help future forensic studies: The investigators consistently underaged older people and consistently overaged younger people. Stature, estimated by formula, showed sexual dimorphism; males averaged 5 feet 6 and females 5 feet 1 inch (Molleson and Cox 1993). Such verification of sex-determination approaches and clarification of problems with age assessments give forensic anthropologists guidance for future work.

The concept of "biological race" was conclusively dismissed by human geneticist Alan Templeton (1998, 647): "Because of the extensive evidence for genetic interchange through population movements and recurrent gene flow going back at least hundreds of thousands of years ago, there is only one evolutionary lineage of humanity and there are no subspecies [races] under either the traditional or phylogenetic definitions. Human evolution and population structure has been and is characterized by many locally differentiated populations coexisting at any given time, but with sufficient genetic contact to make all of humanity a single lineage sharing a common, long-term evolutionary fate." This statement brings together the past, through common evolution, and the present; it suggests strongly that our future is in our own hands.

■ Scientists identify subspecies within certain species only if they form geographically and biologically distinct groups. By this definition, baboons form subspecies. Humans do not form either geographic or biologically distinct groups, because they are geographically intermixed and the traits that identify them do not co-vary. Therefore, "biological races" among humans do not exist.

**page 479**

■ The term "race" is a cultural construct and combines bits of biology, culture, religion, and even language. The term has to do more with ethnicity than with biology.

■ Racism, the belief that one group is superior to others, has no basis in scientific fact. There is no evidence that any group is superior to any other in intelligence, when intelligence is defined as success in problem solving.

■ While all species can be said to be well adapted to their existing environments, human adaptation usually refers to adaptation to temperature extremes and to high altitudes.

■ Applied anthropologists use knowledge gained from research to attempt to solve certain human problems, such as reconstructing prehistoric diets and uncovering the source of HIV.

**page 475**

■ The term *modern humans* refers to hominid populations from the time they evolved to AMH and BMH status, with 50 kyr ago given as a convenient date for this time. Contemporary humans are those alive today.

■ Anthropologists are certain that Native Americans migrated to the New World by walking across the uplifted land bridge between Asia and Alaska while hunting game or perhaps by taking the coastal route using simple boats. When they came and whether they came in one or several waves remain controversial.

■ Humans vary today in many morphological, genetic, and physiological ways, though they are 99.8 percent genetically identical. Some variable traits can be explained: Skin color correlates with sun strength, and body build and length of arms and legs correlate with temperature and humidity. The reasons for the development of other variable traits are not well understood.

■ Population genetics uses complex mathematical models to study microevolution and its causes over a short period of time.

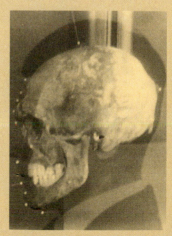

■ Forensic anthropology involves applying knowledge about human variation to help solve legal problems. Forensic anthropologists use DNA fingerprinting and skeletal material to help identify human remains. By examining bones experts can usually determine a person's sex, and can estimate age and ancestry with a fair degree of accuracy.

**page 496**

## KEY WORDS

"biological race", 482
birth control, 470
body build, 475
Buhl Woman, 468
clines, 474
Clovis points, 463
contemporary humans, 461
co-variation of traits, 480
ethnicity, 484

forensic anthropology, 493
founder effect, 470
human variability, 474
intelligence, 485
IQ, 485
Kennewick Man, 468
microevolution, 469
modern humans, 461
Native Americans, 462

non-random mating, 470
nose shape, 477
pre-Clovis artifacts, 463
racism, 485
sickle-cell anemia, 477
skin color, 474
stay-at-home effect, 470

## SUGGESTED READING

*American Anthropologist* 100, no. 3 (1998). This issue is devoted to the anthropological concept of "race," with biological as well as cultural anthropologists writing about aspects of their research. Audrey Smedley's piece on the history of "race" usage is particularly informative.

Bogin, B. *Patterns of Human Growth*, 2nd ed. Cambridge: Cambridge University Press, 2001. Bogin is a demographer who is as interested in how and why humans grow through their lifetimes as he is in the growth of human populations over time.

Brace, C. L. *Race Is a Four-Letter Word*. New York: Oxford University Press, 2005.

Burns, K. R. *Forensic Anthropology Training Manual*. Upper Saddle River, NJ: Prentice Hall, 1999. Although not intended to be read cover to cover, this book is filled with the kind of information forensic anthropologists use to identify skeletal remains. The illustrations are first-rate.

Dillehay, T. D. *The Settlement of the Americas*. New York: Basic Books, 2000. Dillehay is the major excavator at the Monte Verde site in Chile, which may be the oldest settlement in the New World. He discusses this plus other sites and the "settlement" of the Americas.

Eaton, S. B., M. Shostak, and M. Konner. *The Paleolithic Prescription*. New York: Harper and Row, 1988. An interesting recipe for good health by a team of one medical doctor, one biological anthropologist, and one cultural anthropologist, all with cross-cultural experience and ideas about how modern humans can adopt Stone Age habits and live longer and happier lives.

Marks, J. *Human Biodiversity: Genes, Races, and History*. New York: Aldine de Gruyter, 1995. Since the early 1990s biological anthropologists have written many books clarifying why there is no such thing as a "biological race." This is a well-written, balanced approach to the topic.

Power, M. *The Egalitarians—Human and Chimpanzee*. Cambridge: Cambridge University Press, 1991. Primatologists tend to ignore this carefully researched book, which compares (through the published literature) the behavior of chimpanzees before and after banana provisioning in the Gombe Stream Reserve. The author concludes that chimpanzee aggression and other behaviors were direct results of the provisioning.

Steadman, D. W., ed. *Hard Evidence: Case Studies in Forensic Anthropology*. Upper Saddle River, NJ: Prentice Hall, 2003. A modern collection of case studies in forensics, each written by the forensic expert in the case. Some accounts focus on the biological (DNA) aspect, and some combine biology and culture; all describe mystery-solving efforts that usually succeeded.

# Chapter 16  Conclusions: Who Are We?

■ **WHAT MADE HUMANS HUMAN?**

■ **BIOLOGICAL EVOLUTION AND CULTURE CHANGE: PARALLELS OR NOT?**
Biological Evolution: Co-variation? • Cultural Change: Co-variation? • Biological and Cultural Change: Comparing the Records • Conclusion: Different Processes

■ **THE FUTURE OF *HOMO SAPIENS***

▲
**Photo above:** *Homo sapiens*: diverse, yet the same

This concluding chapter sums up the human biological and cultural past by asking and endeavoring to answer several interrelated questions:

1. What is it that made us human? If becoming human was a single phenomenon, what was it, and when did it occur in our evolving past? If the things that make us human are multifaceted, what are those human traits, and did we acquire them all at once or over a long time span?

2. Are biological and cultural change the same thing, or are they very different processes? Did they coevolve?

3. Given that biological and cultural change are ongoing processes, what is the future of the human species? Will our culture continue to change faster than our biology?

# What Made Humans Human?

Can we draw a chronological line between prehuman hominids and humans, with prehumans on the early end of the lineage and true humans on the other? Despite the fact that the two terms (*hominid* and *human*) are not totally comparable, some experts have suggested one or more of the following as "keys to being human":

- *Bipedalism.* Once early hominids became bipedal, their method of food acquisition changed and became more secure on the patchy East African landscape. In addition, with newly freed hands, hominids could have made and used tools and carried food, increasing their survival rate and thus their reproductive success. (See Chapter 6 for details on why experts believe bipedalism evolved.) But birds and kangaroos are bipedal, so that form of locomotion is not unique to the human lineage.

- *Tool manufacturing and use.* Tool making has been viewed as a key trait of humanness. But chimpanzees and, to a lesser extent, bonobos and orangutans (and cebus monkeys) make and use tools, so this characteristic is not unique to hominids or humans.

- *Big-game hunting.* Humanness could have evolved when big-game hunting began. Does hunting and eating large animals make us human? Evidence that hominids' butchery marks preceded carnivores' teeth marks and evidence that hominids butchered the choice meat-bearing parts suggest early access to carcasses, which implies hunting of large animals. Yet it is likely that the majority of early humans' food consisted of small game and nuts, leaves, fruits, and tubers and was obtained by scavenging, possibly some hunting, and gathering by both men and women, not by big-game hunting males.

- *Speech.* Speaking is something humans do a lot of. It is obviously related to the ability to speak (biological traits such as tongue, larynx, and brain) and to what we speak about (cultural traits such as tool manufacturing and big-game hunting). But speech also can be assessed as a potential key to being human, because it appears to have had its beginnings in early hominid days and to have evolved through time.

- *Intelligence.* Intelligence can be evaluated only in species-specific contexts. In the context of the human lineage, that lineage likely became more intelligent through time because hominids/humans evolved larger brains to solve more and more problems. It could be argued that natural selection would favor those individuals who were better at problem solving than other conspecifics, resulting in populations that were even better at problem solving. But what kinds of problems were imperative to solve? Richard Potts, quoted by Michael Balter (2002), suggests that in the evolution of our species it was not the ability to solve specific problems or to adapt to specific environments but general *cognitive ability* to solve problems and adapt to environment that was important. As environments changed—and there is sufficient evidence to suggest that they did, on multiple occasions and over both short and long time periods—an increase in general ability to cope and/or adjust would have been advantageous. An increase in the size of the frontal lobes would have allowed hominids to be able to solve new kinds of problems, such as those requiring creativity, imagination, and intentionality.

In light of the timing and multiplicity of important hominid traits, it is probable that no one key event or trait changed prehuman hominids into humans in any one time period. We can't be human unless we are bipedal, make tools, speak, and are intelligent. But those traits—bipedalism (which is mostly biological) and the others (which are mainly cultural but with biological underpinnings)—did not all arise at the same time. Bipedalism likely evolved just before 6 myr ago; tool manufacturing shows in the artifact record by 2.6 myr ago; and brains increased in size and complexity throughout the last 2 myr of hominid evolution, probably undergirding the development of speech and an increase in cognitive ability. One of the few things all anthropologists agree on is that humanness is a biocultural phenomenon. Without culture, we would not be human; without human biology, we would not be human.

# Biological Evolution and Culture Change: Parallels or Not?

Did human biology and culture—those two parts of what it is to be human—change together? That is, are the changes concordant? For example, when species split in the human lineage, did culture change to a similar degree? In the first half of the twentieth century, anthropologists assumed that biological and cultural change went hand in hand. But new information, more finely tuned dating techniques, and new kinds of analyses have become available over the last 50 years, meaning that assumptions must be reassessed (Foley and Lahr 1997). If new findings suggest that cultural change does parallel biological evolution chronologically, then we can consider the two processes as linked, or at least as a potential single process, while asking whether one generated change in the other. That is, if there is evidence that biological and cultural happenings in the human past occurred together, then such changes are likely linked in a single process. If they do not parallel each other in time and in degree, however, then we have to look at the two processes as separate phenomena.

But before we address the big question of whether biological and cultural change co-occurred, it's important to ask a related set of questions. First, did various aspects of biological evolution—bipedalism, brain size, and dentition, to mention three large complexes of human traits—coevolve during the last 6 myr? Or does the evidence point to a mosaic, with each complex of traits evolving at different times? And second, did the various aspects of human culture change together? For example, did the major steps in tool manufacturing techniques parallel changes in social organization? Did shifts in basic economy (food acquisition) generate social organization changes? And what about speech? The ability to speak is biological, but what humans talk about is cultural. So did the development of language/speech parallel any major changes in biology or culture or both? The answers to these questions should help in answering the bigger question about the possible link between biological change and cultural change.

## Biological Evolution: Co-variation?

Let's look at human biological evolution by reviewing the development of bipedalism, brain size, and dentition:

■ *Bipedalism.* Anatomical evidence of fossils in the human lineage points to the beginnings of bipedalism just before 6 myr ago. Probably hundreds of thousands of years passed between initial and habitual bipedalism. Many experts argue that even as late as 3 myr ago, hominids were walking with bent knees and without a fully modern stride.

By 1.8 myr ago, however, arm and leg proportions were as they are today, and humans had a fully modern stride. So bipedalism took almost 4 myr to develop fully and did not occur in one step.

■ *Brain size.* Based on late Miocene hominoid fossils, and in keeping with the principle of contingency, it is likely that the brain size of early hominids was not much larger than that of early chimpanzees that lived at the same time. Lack of fossils in the early chimpanzee lineage makes this statement somewhat speculative; still, it is unlikely that early chimpanzees had larger brains than late Miocene hominoids, because they lived in similar environments. Brain size and complexity in hominids has grown, if not steadily, since initial hominid times. Australopithecines averaged 500 cc, *Homo habilis* 610 cc, *H. erectus* 1,000 cc, and anatomically modern humans (AMH) 1,350 cc. There was not a steady increase through the lifetime of each grade, however; and recall that Neandertals' cranial capacity was even larger than that of modern humans, averaging 1,520 cc.

■ *Dentition.* Hominid dentition and the shape of the surrounding bone evolved early in the lineage. As discussed (and illustrated) in Chapter 6, the first hominids showed a parabolic-shaped dental arch and only slightly larger canines than modern hominids. The hominid tooth pattern, established early, changed little through time until the last 10 kyr. Then, in areas where domestication of food occurred, molar teeth became reduced in size because people no longer had to chew tough meat.

Thus, these three complexes of traits show differences in timing. Bipedalism and dentition occurred early and did not develop in one stage; in contrast, brain size increased later, and cranial capacity has roughly tripled over the past 6 myr of hominid/human evolution. A similar pattern of inconsistency results when other traits are added. Our conclusion: Human biological evolution is a mosaic of different traits developing at different times and not a single multitrait episode.

## Cultural Change: Co-variation?

Did the cultural complexes of social organization, tool technology, basic economy, and art change at the same time? And did humans in all areas of the Old World change in regard to these four aspects of culture at the same time?

Of the four aspects of culture under discussion here, only one is unique to humans: Primates are generally social and therefore organize themselves in groups, all four great apes and several species of monkeys make and use tools; and all animals must ingest food and thus can be said to have a basic economy. Only humans have art.

■ *Social organization.* As long as the basic economy of early hominids took the form of opportunistic scavenging for plants and/or small animals, individuals could get their own food. Sharing was probably limited to mothers and their offspring. There was no need for pair-bonding between males and females or for families or clans. Since there were dangerous animals in the African savannas, individuals probably formed groups and stayed together for protection. Thus, social organization for hominids was likely not much more complex than that of the last common ancestral group. Most experts believe that when males began to hunt animals larger than themselves, social organization changed, with females continuing to opportunistically scavenge for plant and small animals as the males changed to hunting big game. Pair-bonding likely emerged in populations of *H. erectus*, beginning 1.8 myr ago, so that males would always get enough to eat, given the unreliability of hunting, and so that females and their children would get meat in their diet. This arrangement is likely to have resulted in the two-generation human family with both a male and a female parenting their offspring. Experts do not know when larger social groupings began, but perhaps by 10,000 years ago, when domestication occurred in several parts of the Old World; lineages and clans then formed as well as social classes. Thus, one aspect of social organization does appear to be concordant with one aspect of basic economy: The change to big-game hunting likely is tied to the emergence of pair-bonding and the human family. Additionally, the beginnings of larger social groupings may have begun in the Early Holocene, given the large size and semi-permanent status of some hunter-gatherer sites.

■ *Tool technology.* Tool technology rests on several environmentally grounded variables. Raw materials (such as flint or chert, bamboo, or hard rock such as quartzite and volcanic lava) vary from place to place. The function of the tool also varies: If the tool is for hunting, the size of animal being hunted will govern the nature of the tool; if for gathering, the tool may be for digging, grinding, or pounding; if for fishing, it may have to serve for line or boat fishing. Given all these variables, differences in tool manufacturing are numerous throughout the Old World. It is therefore to be expected that the size, shape, and function of tools varied both geographically and temporally. Africa, for example, has little flint but a large amount of hard volcanic stone suitable for tool manufacturing, whereas Europe has excellent sources of flint. (East Asia has considerable bamboo that is extremely sharp when cut at an angle, but bamboo biodegrades very quickly, so there is no archaeological evidence of bamboo tools. Therefore, we will compare only hard rock and flint/chert tool making here.) The first tools that can be identified as such date to 2.6 myr ago in northeast Africa. Hominids made these flakes and chopper tools from a range of volcanic lava and quartzite by hitting them with another rock, often several times, to form a cutting edge. The end products were unstandardized. Hand axes made of volcanic rock or flint follow, the first dated about 1.8 myr ago in Africa; hand axes occur much later in Europe and were primarily in flint, but also in other rocks when flint was unavailable. Although dates for artifacts between 200 kyr and 40 kyr old are less secure than K-Ar and $^{14}$C dates, flake and core tools emerge as the major tools from about 250 kyr until 22 kyr ago in Africa. The Levallois technique associated with Neandertal/Mousterian people became common around 200 kyr ago, and was used for over 100 kyr. Although blade tools were "invented" in Africa, perhaps 200 kyr ago, they are associated with AMH at European sites dated to somewhat after 40 kyr ago (d'Errico 2003).

Major projectile tool categories were jabbing spears, which appeared in the artifact record by perhaps 400 kyr ago; throwing spears, which probably came somewhat later (d'Errico 2003); spear-throwers associated with the middle Upper Paleolithic; and bows and arrows dated to the late Upper Paleolithic. Thus, tools did vary geographically and temporally as predicted.

■ *Basic economy.* Although the following model is somewhat controversial, most experts suggest that the basic economy of the earliest hominids consisted of opportunistic scavenging and probably some hunting of small animals. Groups collected and hunted as the opportunities arose. This basic economy lasted from 6 myr ago (and before) until it was supplemented by big-game hunting between 1 myr and 500 kyr ago. Gathering wild food probably always continued to be the main food-getting technique, because of its reliability, until the beginning of settled existence and eventual domestication in a few areas of the world between 15 and 10 kyr ago. Fishing at different times occurred in numerous parts of the world: South America, East Africa, Europe, and Japan, among others. In general, scavenging (active, passive, or opportunistic) preceded big-game hunting, and gathering plant foods and small animals was always more reliable than big-game hunting; due to differences in environment and plant/animal populations available to exploit, there was always considerable geographic variability.

■ *Art.* Art, in the form of jewelry, engravings, sculpture, and the famous paintings on cave walls, is usually associated with the Upper Paleolithic. Yet although it is true that art became almost an "explosion" after 32 kyr ago, "inklings" of art show up somewhat earlier in the form of engraved marks on stones and jewelry. If the dating is correct (and it is beyond the possibility of $^{14}$C dating), several chunks of ochre from Blombos Cave in South Africa show early markings that may be art. The same is true of Neandertal markings on bone. These are basically crisscrosses, whereas Upper Paleolithic art is mostly of recognizable animals (see Chapter 9). Even if these earlier marks are "art" in the same sense of the word as used today, the examples are so rare that it cannot be considered systematic (d'Errico 2003). Interestingly, not all art categories show up in the archaeological record at the same time; jewelry and small sculpted animals came first, followed by cave paintings and bone engravings beginning about 32 kyr ago, then by Venus figurines around 25 kyr ago.

As with biology, then, the categories of culture are chronologically disparate. On the other hand, the categories are chronologically logical. First came basic social organization that evolved from mammalian and then primate ancestors; then tool manufacturing, perhaps going back to the LCA but becoming recognizable as human at 2.6 myr ago, with scavenging and the hunting of small animals developing into more intensive big-game hunting when long-distance weapons were invented; religion by 100 kyr ago, if Neandertal burials are indicative of this function; and art by 32 kyr ago. This chronology of cultural changes is logical because it parallels the biological change in the size of the brain's frontal lobes. As the lobes increase in size, as they did through time, the ability to use the imagination and be creative also increased.

We conclude that biological evolution and culture change were not concordant. In addition, a particular culture is not always associated with a particular biological population. For example, in early hominid days in Africa, at least three species of hominids shared the same cultural repertorie. In some parts of the world, similar biological populations have had different cultural repertoires, and in the Middle East, it appears that two different biological groups shared a very similar culture. So "a culture" is not always associated with "a biological population."

■ *Speech.* Speech is easier to assess biologically than culturally, because only rather indirect results of speaking occur in the archaeological record. As we saw in Chapter 7, the different kinds of biological clues to speech ability occur at different times. Some researchers have identified Broca's bumps in the fossil record during australopithecine times; Wernicke's bumps and the beginning of humanlike hypoglossal canals are evident during *Homo erectus* times; and modern hypoglossal canals and hyoid bones appear by *Homo sapiens* times. Thus speech, did not occur as one biocultural event.

## Biological and Cultural Change: Comparing the Records

Figure 16.1 summarizes the major steps in biological and cultural change in the human lineage. Dating problems for the period between 200 and 40 kyr ago mean limited confidence for dates during that period. As you can see in the figure, a comparison of the major changes shows only a limited concordance; most changes are discordant. Even if there are limited concordances, they may be coincidental and not cross-generating. Richard Klein (1989a) has compared the cultural and biological records for possible concordance and concludes that until 50 kyr ago, the two showed some concordance. About 50 kyr ago, he suggests, some biological change resulting from a series of mutations gave humans the full complement of modern behavior (BMH status); since that time, Klein proposes, change has been mostly cultural.

As long as there are some possible concordances, a generating correlation must be investigated. Therefore, let's look at the processes of biological change and cultural change and ask if the processes are the same, similar, or totally different. If the processes are totally different, then any concordance between cultural and biological change is purely coincidental.

### Similarities between Biological and Cultural Change

Populations change biologically through mutations and natural selection (on the individual level) and through gene flow and gene drift (on the population level). Cultures change through invention (on the individual level) and through cultural selection, diffusion, and

*Figure 16.1*

| Years ago | Biological Events | Cranial Capacity | Cultural Events |
|---|---|---|---|
| 10 kyr | Behaviorally modern humans | | Domestication<br>Spear-throwers |
| 50 kyr | Behaviorally modern humans | | Art<br>Blade tools |
| 100 kyr | Anatomically modern humans | | |
| 150 kyr | Neandertal | 1,550 cc | Throwing spears<br>Levallois technique, religion<br>Core/flake tools |
| 200 kyr | *Homo sapiens* (archaic) | 1,450 cc | Jabbing spears |
| 500 kyr | *Homo sapiens* (archaic) | 1,100 cc | |
| 1 myr | | | Big-game hunting |
| | *Homo erectus* | 1,000 cc | Hand axes |
| 2 myr | *Homo habilis* | 610 cc | |
| 3 myr | | | Flakes and<br>chopper tools |
| 4 myr | Australopithecines | 500 cc | Likely simple tools<br>(rocks, sticks) |
| 5 myr | | | |
| 6 myr | (Bipedalism) | | |
| 7 myr | *Preanthropus* | | |

**A COMPARISON OF BIOLOGICAL AND CULTURAL EVENTS.**    Major biological changes appear on the left, major cultural changes on the right. Is there more discordance than concordance?

loss (on the population level). At first glance, these appear to be parallel processes: Each has an individual and a group level; mutations and inventions involve something never seen before in a population; selection operates to weed out that which is advantageous from that which is not; flow or diffusion involves exchange of materials on borders; and drift or loss involves the loss of materials through time.

Both modes of change depend on the principle of contingency: Each mode can work only on what was already in place at any particular time. That is, biological change can affect only what is in a population at a given time; green striped monkeys do not evolve directly out of plaid purple cows. The same is true of cultural change: Manual typewriters can give way to electric typewriters, but they don't morph into cell phones. Additionally, both types of change can be referred to as "inheritance." Humans biologically inherit hair color from their parents, and they also can inherit property. Here, the word *inheritance* merely refers to receiving something from someone else without stipulating the mode.

Some archaeologists see enough similarities between biological and cultural change to consider them the same process, calling both "evolutionary." These archaeologists have coined the term "memes" for the cultural unit, a word that not only rhymes with "genes" but refers to minuscule, gene-like bits of culture that are faithfully replicated during inheritance or transmission (Shennan 2002). But only some features of both change processes are similar—and only superficially. As French archaeologist Jean-Philippe Rigaud (1987), who sees biological and cultural change as separate processes, puts it, "culture can't evolve; it has no sex organs."

## Differences between Biological and Cultural Change

The parallels between cultural and biological change are on the surface only, and there appear to be far more critical differences than similarities. First, let's look more closely at the mechanisms of change. *Mutations* occur spontaneously and randomly, without human decision making; they are not discriminatory in terms of timing (they don't happen when you want them!); and most mutations never go beyond a generation. (We will not address clones here, because they are so new and so rare.) *Inventions*, on the other hand, are very much the conscious choice of humans; they are often timely and may occur under stress conditions, and many stay around for a long time (Shennan 2002). Similarly, although both natural and cultural *selection* involve adaptations, biological adaptation is not in the hands of humans, whereas cultural selection is—we choose to accept Volkswagen Beetles; we choose not to accept new typewriter-key arrangements. Biological selection by definition is never maladaptive, but what about such cultural items as cigarettes, crack cocaine, birth control pills, and condoms? They can cause early death or cause users to have fewer-than-average numbers of offspring. *Gene flow* and cultural diffusion both involve a kind of "borrowing," but one is the result of conscious decision, and the other is not. Finally, though genetic and cultural *drift* may eventually end as the loss of material (such as the loss of curly hair genes or the loss of canoes in the Torres Islands), cultural fixation of a trait is almost never complete, but biofixation often is.

And there are numerous other dissimilaritites in the two processes. Among them:

■ Rates of change differ in the two processes. Although biological traits do not change at a steady rate—much less change together in sets—biological change is always slow relative to the potential change rate of culture; for example, compare the last 50 years of little biological change with the spread of computers and cell phones. Biological change is slow because it adheres to Mendelian genetics; in contrast, culture change is Lamarckian in mode and can be due to large-scale shifts in custom and/or technology in every generation (Alvard 2003).

■ The contributions of individuals differ in the two processes. From the standpoint of a single generation, each individual has biologically inherited about 50 percent of his or her genes from each parent. It is unlikely that the same is true of cultural inheritance. Here, it is more likely that males will inherit a large proportion of their cultural knowledge from their fathers and other males, whereas females will inherit most of their knowledge from their mothers and other females.

■ Biological inheritance in humans comes directly from only two individuals—each person's mother and father. Cultural inheritance, however, involves learning from a myriad of sources: parents, siblings, other adults in the family, peers, teachers, television, and computers, to name only the most obvious sources.

■ The transmission of biological traits is a one-to-one phenomenon, with parental sperm and egg forming a new zygote (potential human) each and every time there is fertilization. Cultural learning is often one-to-many; and the many can be in the hundreds or even millions of individuals, as in teacher–student or television–viewer communications.

■ Natural (biological) selection occurs because individuals differ in their reproductive success relative to conspecifics. Cultural selection often involves groups, rather than individuals, that outproduce others after a single invention. For example, people in New Guinea who adopted domesticated sweet potatoes outproduced those who did not (Shennan 2002) and replaced them by population swamping. The takeover of North America by Europeans in the last 500 years is another example of group cultural selection.

■ Conscious choice is cultural, not biological. Humans may wish they could fly—a biological capability—their entire lives, but they will never grow wings. But when the Lapps, who were snowshoe-wearing reindeer herders, were introduced to snowmobiles in the mid-twentieth century, they discussed the new technology among themselves and consciously decided to add snowmobiles to their cultural repertoire. They chose to make the change (Pelto 1973).

■ Cultural emulation occurs constantly, but biological emulation cannot. Emulation of rock musicians and movie stars is rampant; many young humans successfully attempt to dress and behave like pop celebrities. But there is no way anyone can emulate another person's genetic endowment (Shennan 2002).

■ The amount of biological variability in populations increases through time because of the nature of sexual reproduction and gene exchange. Cultural variability usually decreases in groups, however, because it is easier and socially more profitable for societies to narrow down cultural choices to just a few.

■ Cultural inheritance often includes continuous blending—something that never occurs in Mendelian biological inheritance. For example, American chow mein is a combination or blending of American and Chinese cuisine. But biological traits are not blends, as Mendel convincingly demonstrated. Instead, genetically determined traits are transmitted as discrete units.

■ Whereas biological change occurs between any two generations and within single populations or on borders with neighbors, culture change can occur worldwide when audiences see something on the Internet or on a TV program.

■ Cultural traits can be lost and then can resurface years later; this cannot happen in biological evolution.

■ Natural selection, given enough time, will weed out maladapted traits (i.e., traits no longer suited to the existing environment). Culture seems to involve considerable maladaptive behaviors, such as snake handling, smoking, drinking to excess, and lack of exercise.

■ Individuals are stuck with their biological inheritance all of their lives. Even sex change operations only change morphology, not the genetic endowment that occurred at conception. By contrast, people are constantly changing their culture even if they live their entire lives in the same town. And, of course, many people change their entire cultures by moving from one geographic place to another far away (Mace 2005).

■ Natural selection, as far as we know, operates only on the individual's reproductive differential relative to other individuals in the population. Cultural selection, however, occurs at the group level, with groups deciding which cereal stays on the market or which computer company declares bankruptcy.

## Conclusion: Different Processes

In sum, the modes of inheritance of biology and culture can be boiled down to two very different processes: We inherit our biology through our parents' sexual reproduction. We inherit our cultural traditions by learning them. They are very different processes.

Although there are some parallels between the two processes, those appear to be rather superficial and sometimes must be stretched to fit a model. Down the millennia there have been cases when language, culture, and biology have changed together and at the same rate of speed; but when these cases have occurred, it has been for situational reasons. For example, a group can take its culture, language, and biology elsewhere through migration; but once the group is established, further biological and cultural change over time will involve different processes.

Given that the two modes of change are very different, one occurring through sexual reproduction and the other through learning, we conclude that it is more accurate to speak of "biological evolution" and "cultural change" rather than calling them both "evolutionary." As all language experts know, the words we use have an effect on our cognition and behavior. Using the word "evolutionary" in conjunction with culture implicitly endorses the notion that cultural change, like biological change, is out of humans' conscious control. Nothing could be farther from the truth. Our cultural future is in our own hands.

## The Future of *Homo sapiens*

Paleoanthropology is not by nature a predictive science. Rather, it describes and tries to explain the biological and cultural happenings of the past and present and, when appropriate, uses findings to suggest caution in particular behaviors.

Nevertheless, we wish to offer some thoughts about the future of our species. First, given that our future is firmly contingent on our present, let's look at some facts about our modern world. A decade ago, the world's demography looked like this (Sussman 1999):

■ 57 percent of all people were Asians, 21 percent Europeans, 14 percent North and South Americans, and 8 percent Africans

■ 51 percent were female and 49 percent male

■ 70 percent were "nonwhite" and 30 percent "white"

■ 70 percent were non-Christian and 30 percent Christian

■ 50 percent of the world's wealth was in the hands of six individuals

■ 80 percent of the world's people lived in substandard housing

■ 70 percent were illiterate

■ 50 percent suffered from malnutrition

Because we live in an interrelated world where change in one area will eventually, inevitably, impact all areas, our thinking about our human future must be in concert with these demographic realities.

We probably will never evolve things on our wish list like wings or X-ray vision, although it might be tempting to predict that in the future our legs will atrophy to nubs, that the first finger on the dominant hand will become elongated because of constant button pushing, or that we will evolve nasal filters like built-in gas masks in order to cope with worldwide pollution. In reality, we will change biologically as selection acts on mutations, but biological change is extremely slow and not apt to be observable in even dozens of lifetimes. Because of the nature of transoceanic travel today, it is unlikely that we will speciate by splitting into multiple species. Although catastrophic outbreaks of HIV or other diseases, pollution, and toxic wastes may lower the Earth's human population, reduced population density is not likely to cause sufficient isolation for speciation, but nuclear wars could. Also, many causes of past evolutionary change are no longer effective: Lions and tigers do not carry off the slowest humans, supercold temperatures no longer freeze whole populations, and early warning systems save many groups from hurricanes and tornados. Culture, on the other hand, continues to change rapidly, particularly in the Western world. Technological change seems almost overwhelming at times, but social organization and religion are changing as well. Not so long ago, most marriages in the United States were "for life"; now half end in divorce. A hundred years ago in the United States, cohabitation by members of extended families was the norm; now very few extended families live together or in close proximity. Same-sex marriages are legal in some countries. A generation ago celebration of the Roman Catholic mass had to be in Latin; now it is in the vernacular of individual cultures. Fifty years ago there were very few religious cults in the Western world; now there are hundreds.

Limited biological change and wide-scale cultural change can be expected to continue in the coming generations. Of all the changes ahead, however, the most likely worldwide problem future humans will have to cope with will be overpopulation and its effects. Human populations have been expanding since the origin of the species, with new technology—from advanced spears and spear-throwers to domesticated plants and animals to genetically engineered food (Bray 2001)—endlessly developing to keep up with increasing population numbers. But the Earth is finite in size and carrying capacity, and at the present rate of increase, human consumption will soon outstrip the planet's available resources. Even if extraterrestrial voyages were a viable safety valve for human expansion, the machinery and energy to transport people to outer space would remain earthbound.

A lot of future change will be *due exclusively to human interference*. The world we are accustomed to, with our personal favorite plants and animals, is likely to change, drastically and quickly. Instead of volcanoes, asteroids, or climate change, it will be humans who cause extinctions of species, perhaps our own. One estimate suggests that half of the species in existence today will be gone in 100 years, though many of those species will be microscopic or "bugs." Nonetheless, cutting the Earth's biodiversity in half will likely have dire consequences for the half that is left. Another estimate of the human impact suggests that extinction rates became 100 to 1,000 times greater after humans began manipulating their environment (Zimmer 2005a). Two recent examples will suffice: (1) In central Africa, human laborers are cutting down trees for wood. This in itself is habitat destruction, but humans are also killing the local monkeys for food to feed those laborers. (2) The Galapagos Islands, famous as a natural laboratory to study the forces of evolution, has faced problems from the presence of goats, rats, and pigs, all brought by previous humans. The government of Ecuador has recently said the goat and pig problems are over, and it hopes to have the rat problem taken care of soon. But, at the same time, why is the government allowing huge cruise ships to visit the islands and disembark hundreds of passengers who, for the most part, are not very interested in natural selection and not very good eco-tourists. This is without any sustainable profit to put toward the ecological protection of the islands since there are no tourist shops or restaurants for the passengers to spend money in (Rice 2007).

If we humans are to have a future that involves a continuation of the many species of plants and animals we have come to depend on and enjoy, then we will have to make better decisions that will affect all the species on the planet.

World population has been growing exponentially after a huge surge at the time of domestication. The United Nations estimates that in 2050 there will be roughly

9 billion people, half again more than are currently living on Earth; if family planning does not begin on a global scope now, there will be 12 billion of us at that time. All will have to cope with predicted 1°C to 2°C increase in average temperatures and higher carbon dioxide levels in the atmosphere. Obviously, more food will be needed, but the World Conservation Unit predicts a high percentage of the world's wild birds, mammals, and freshwater fish will be extinct by then (Jenkins 2003). Natural resources will be diminished, air and sea will be polluted, and there will likely be malnutrition and poverty in many areas. The growing gap between rich and poor will result in more terrorism and war.

In addition, as a population, we are aging, primarily due to lower fertility rates in many countries and improved health care. The average life expectancy in some countries is 83 years. Adding years of life is an advantage to individuals, but it may cause problems in the future in terms of an insufficient work force and the need to cope with the physical and mental illnesses of an increasingly older population. The economic cost of a larger older population is also a potential problem.

There is no reason yet to be totally pessimistic about the future of the human species. One note of optimism is the fact that, as a species, *Homo sapiens* is very adaptable and theoretically capable of responding to different circumstances and environments. The Asian tsunami crises of late 2004 and the devastation of New Orleans by Hurricane Katrina in August 2005 are two good examples. Human behavior at all times and places varies as a result of our genes, our environment, and our culture (Richerson and Boyd 2005). Our genes change slowly; we have little control over our external environment. We must call on our internally generated culture to make sure that we have as long a future as we have had a past.

# Glossary

**Acheulian** A tool tradition, originating in Africa but later found in Europe and parts of Asia, in which hand axes are common; named after the St. Acheul site in France, where the first (though not the oldest) hand axes were found.

**acquired characteristics** Lamarck's eighteenth-century theory that traits acquired during the lifetime of parents (in body cells) could be inherited by their offspring.

**adaptation** Successful interaction between a population and an environment resulting in greater behavioral or physiological fitness, which can be short-term and reversible or long-term and permanent.

**Ain Ghazal** Neolithic village site in what is now Jordan that is known for ritual burials of plaster-covered human skulls and large plaster statues of humans.

**Akapana** The largest complex of monumental buildings in Tiwanaku, in the Bolivian altiplano.

**Akkad** Area in the northern part of southern Mesopotamia whose ruler, Sargon, first unified Mesopotamia by conquering the city-states of Sumeria about 4,350 years ago.

**Aksum** Early state that emerged in highland Ethiopia about 2,000 years ago.

**allele** The alternative form of a gene (or DNA sequence) at a given locus.

**altiplano** High plateau of southern Peru and Bolivia.

**Amerind** One of the major language families associated with the early occupation of the Americas.

**amino acid racemization (AAR)** A dating technique that can be used on shells, bones, and teeth and is based on the slow change (racemization) from L amino acids to D amino acids that commences on the death of an organism.

**amniotes** Vertebrates with internal membranes that enclose embryos inside of eggs; reptiles were the first to evolve this kind of egg.

**analogy** Structures that are superficially similar and serve similar functions but have no necessary common evolutionary relationship.

**Anatolia** Region that is now Turkey.

**anatomically modern humans (AMH)** Modern form of the human species that dates back 100 kyr or more.

**Ancestral Pueblo (Anazasi)** Farming groups of the American Southwest known for stone pueblo construction and cliff dwellings.

**ancestral traits** Traits that appear early in the evolution of a lineage; contrast with derived traits that appear after a particular split in that lineage.

**ancient DNA (aDNA)** The nuclear or mitochondrial DNA, usually from bones or teeth, of formerly living organisms.

**angiosperms** Flower-bearing plants, the last plant category to evolve, about 75 myr ago.

**anthropoids** Members of the suborder Anthropoidea, including monkeys, apes, and humans.

**anthropology** The science that investigates human culture and human biology in the past and present and that includes cultural anthropology, archaeology, linguistics, and biological anthropology.

**anthropometry** Measurement of crania or other parts of bodies as a means of comparing populations.

**anthropomorphic** Having human attributes.

**Anyang** Last capital of the Shang dynasty of China.

**ape** Common term that includes small apes (gibbons and siamangs) and large apes (orangutans, gorillas, chimpanzees, and bonobos).

**applied anthropology** A fifth "subfield" of anthropology that uses what basic research has discovered about the human condition to attempt to solve contemporary human problems.

**arboreal** Tree living.

**arboreal hypothesis** The idea that primate traits can be explained as resulting from mammalian ancestors that started living in trees and getting their food there.

**archaeologists** Anthropologists who study past cultures through the analysis of their material culture and its context.

**Archaic** The period from the final stages of the last Ice Age (or the early Holocene), when people lived by hunting and gathering, to the beginning of settled farming in the Americas. *See also* Hoabinian, Jomon, Late Stone Age (LSA), Mesolithic, Natufian.

**archaic *Homo sapiens*** Populations of the genus *Homo* that existed in Africa, Asia, and Europe from about 500 kyr ago and were transitional between *H. erectus* and full *H. sapiens* status.

**artifacts** Portable objects made and used by humans in the past, including pots, spearpoints and arrowheads, and jewelry.

**ascribed status** Status that is inherited rather than achieved through a person's efforts.

**assimilation model** A "compromise" model that explains the origin of anatomically modern humans as evolving in Africa and then spreading out to other Old World continents and interbreeding with native populations of archaic *Homo sapiens*.

**association** A meaningful relationship between objects within the matrix, which may indicate their function.

**Atapuerca sites** A series of sites in northern Spain that date from between 1 myr and 300 kyr ago.

**Aurignacian** The earliest period of the Upper Paleolithic in Europe, which lasted from about 35 kyr to 28 kyr ago and is named after the French site of l'Aurignac.

**australopithecines** Collective name for the members of the genus *Australopithecus*, consisting of hominids that lived in Africa between about 4.2 and 1.2 myr ago and are characterized by bipedal locomotion, small brain size, large faces, and big teeth.

*Australopithecus afarensis* Hominid species that existed in East Africa between 3.9 and 2.9 myr ago and that showed ancestral hominoid features in teeth and skull; Lucy is the most famous example.

*Australopithecus africanus* Hominid species whose fossils have been dated between 3.2 and 2.3 myr old and found mainly in South Africa; may be ancestral to *Homo*.

*Australopithecus anamensis* Hominid species that existed in East Africa between 4.2 and 4.1 myr ago and was bipedal but showed many ancestral hominoid features of skull and teeth.

*Australopithecus boisei* Very robust hominid species that existed between 2.3 and 1.2 myr ago in East Africa.

*Australopithecus garhi* A single hominid fossil, found in East Africa and dated to 2.5 myr ago, with large front and back teeth.

*Australopithecus robustus* Robust species of hominid that existed between 2.6 and 1.5 myr ago in South Africa.

**Aztec** Mesoamerican empire centered in the Valley of Mexico, with its capital at Tenochtitlan; conquered by the Spanish in the sixteenth century.

**ball court** Rectangular court with sloping sides in which a Mesoamerican ritual ball game was played.

**behaviorally modern humans (BMH)** Although modern humans might have been anatomically modern and looked like modern humans before they acted like moderns being capable of the full complement of behavioral traits, this term refers to the whole complement of humanity and dates to perhaps 50 kyr ago.

**Beringia** The landmass between Alaska and Siberia that was exposed during glacial periods, when the levels of the Bering Strait and Chukchi Sea dropped as their waters were taken up in ice.

**bilophodont** Having two ridges of cusps with a low area between them; a diagnostic trait of the molars of monkeys.

**bioarchaeology** The study of human remains in the archaeological record to determine factors such as diet, health, and demographics in past populations.

**bioenergetics/thermoregulation model** The coupling of two ideas to explain the evolution of bipedalism: the energy efficiency of using two legs to walk slowly while looking for food and the reduction of thermal stress that resulted from being upright in the hot savanna (and being able to sweat).

**biological anthropologists** Anthropologists who study humans as animals in the past (their evolution) and in the present (their modern form); also called bioanthropologists.

**"biological race"** A geographically constrained group that shares a set of biological/genetic traits that no other group of the species has in its entirety; nonexistent in humans.

**biological species concept (BSC)** A definition of *species* that focuses on reproductive capabilities: Organisms from different populations are in the same species if they can interbreed and produce fertile offspring.

**biologists** Scientists who study primates the same way they study any group or species of animal and who are interested in the animals' evolution and their modern morphology, genetics, and behavior.

**bio-uniformitarianism** Spin on the geological uniformitarian principle that the evolutionary mechanisms that cause modern species to change are the same as those that caused species to change in the past.

**bipedalism** Movement on two hind legs in a striding motion.

**birth control** Practice that can change gene frequencies between any two generations just because the small number of offspring do not represent the total genome of the parents.

**Black Earth** Archaic site in southern Illinois where differences in burial practices reflect differences in status and age- and sex-related tasks.

**Black Skull** Early australopithecine skull dated at 2.5 myr old and showing super-robust features; also called *A. aethiopicus*.

**blades** Long, narrow, parallel-sided, stone tools that were struck from cores of siliceous stone such as flint; the hallmark of the Upper Paleolithic in Eurasia, although also found in earlier periods.

**Blombos Cave** A Middle Stone Age site in South Africa where engravings on ochre that may indicate use of symbolism were found.

**bloodletting** A ritual practiced in many Mesoamerican cultures in which people deliberately pierced parts of their bodies in order to draw blood.

**body build** The shape of the human body as measured by the ratio between extremities and body core.

**brain evolution** An evolutionary step that followed bipedalism in later hominids and resulted in larger and more complex brains, allowing the development of problem-solving abilities and behavioral changes.

**Buhl Woman** North American female found in Idaho in 1989, dated to 11 kyr ago and reburied under NAGPRA.

**Burgess Shale** The 525-myr-old deposits in the Canadian Rockies that contain all of the earliest phyla of animals including Chordates, the phyla to which humans belong.

**Cahokia** Center of a powerful Mississippian chiefdom in the Mississippi River Valley.

**calibration** A process that uses dendrochronology to correct carbon 14 dates so that they coincide with calendar dates.

**caliche** Plaster of calcium carbonate, or calcite (limestone, marble, or chalk).

**Cambrian explosion** The time (550 to 520 myr ago) when all animal phyla were then on Earth, living in watery environments. All subsequent life forms come from these early phyla.

**camelid** Family of animals that includes domestic llamas, alpacas, and wild vicuñas.

**capacity for culture** The inborn ability to do, to know, and to feel that is subject to the biological laws of inheritance and that allows humans to develop culture—that is, learned behavior, cognition, and emotions.

**carbon 14 ($^{14}$C) dating** A chronometric dating technique that is based on the rate of decay of radioactive carbon 14 ($^{14}$C) into nitrogen 14 ($^{14}$N) that begins at death; it is the most widely used technique in archaeology, has a range of effectiveness over the past 40 kyr or more, and can date any organic material.

**Çatalhöyük (or Çatal Hüyük or Çatal Höyök)** Neolithic farming village in what is now Turkey, known for the inhabitants' emphasis on symbolic representation.

**catastrophism** Idea that the Earth went through a series of violent and sudden catastrophic destructions and subsequent creations with fossils in each layer bounded by these processes.

**cathemeral** Active both at night and during the day.

**causewayed enclosures** Early Neolithic monumental constructions in Britain consisting of a series of discontinuous ditches flanked by small banks of earth and forming a circular enclosure; each ditch and bank were separated from the next set by a causeway.

**cells** The smallest unit able to perform activities called life; all living organisms have one or more cells.

**celt** A type of axe.

**Cerro Baúl** The only Wari settlement located in Tiwanaku territory (present-day southern Peru).

**Cerro Blanco** Largest of the Moche ceremonial, administrative, and residential centers in Peru, dominated by two pyramids.

**Chaco Canyon** Location in present-day New Mexico where, between 1,100 and 850 years ago, several Ancestral Pueblo (Anasazi) pueblos developed and gained wide influence.

**Chatelperronian** The last Middle Paleolithic period associated with Neandertal material culture in France and Spain.

**Chauvet Cave** The earliest Upper Paleolithic painted cave site in France.

**Chavín de Huántar** Early complex site in the highlands of Peru, many of whose distinctive symbolic motifs occur in cultures throughout the Andean region.

**Chengjiang Formation** Earliest Cambrian fossils found in China and dating between 544 and 520 myr ago.

**chicha** Beer made from maize.

**chiefdom** Hierarchical society usually under the control of a hereditary chief.

**chinampas** Raised plots reclaimed from swamps to form fertile blocks of land where year-round cultivation was possible; used by Aztecs at Tenochtitlan.

**chromosomes** Long strands of DNA sequences; the hereditary material in the cells' nuclei.

**chronometric dating** A method of dating fossils and artifacts that specifies ranges of dates at a medium to high level of confidence.

**chronospecies** Ancestral and descendant species in the same lineage, where the former has transformed itself into the latter.

**cladistics** A paradigm, or model, that stresses evolutionary relationships based only on a number of derived and shared traits as opposed to ancestral traits.

**clines** Systematic gradations in some trait (phenotype) over large geographical areas.

**Clovis** Groups associated with a distinctive type of fluted projectile points, which are the first undisputed evidence of widespread occupation of North and Central America.

**Clovis points** The fluted projectile points made between about 13.2 and 12.8 kyr ago in North America.

**codices** Maya or Aztec books of glyphs and pictures usually drawn on bark paper coated with lime but sometimes drawn on animal skins; singular is *codex*.

**common ancestral group** The group from which any two existing sibling groups evolved.

**common ancestry** The principle that states that if two groups evolved from the same earlier group, then they have common ancestry.

**common sense** Based on past experience, common sense is used to solve certain problems.

**communication** The transmission of information from one individual to another by sensory means.

**contemporary humans** Humans that are alive today; contemporary humans are all modern humans, but some modern humans are not contemporary.

**contemporary primates** All primate groups living today, including humans.

**context** The immediate setting where artifacts or fossils are found, comprising matrix, provenience, and association.

**contingency** The principle that states that in general, every population's genetics and morphology exist because the group evolved from a previous group.

**continuity** Change in a lineage that is gradual and accumulative, so that the lineage displays intermediate forms.

**Copan** An important Mesoamerican Maya city located in the lowlands of Honduras.

**core** Stone block from which flakes have been removed.

**co-variation of traits** The fact that certain traits in a group or population always vary together, or are concordant.

**cranial deformation** The practice of changing the shape of a human head through gradual application of force, for example, through head binding.

**cross-dating** Use of several appropriate dating techniques to improve confidence in the dates assigned to objects.

**cultural anthropologists** Anthropologists who study the culture of contemporary humans anywhere in the world.

**cultural historical approach** The traditional descriptive approach to interpretation of archaeological evidence whose main focus was establishing chronological sequences of cultural groups and thus developing culture histories; similarities between cultures (as shown by similarities in artifacts) were seen as arising primarily through migration of peoples or diffusion of ideas.

**cultural transformation processes** Human actions that cause changes in the archaeological record at a site.

**cuneiform** The earliest form of writing developed by the Sumerians, a system of signs produced with a stylus that left wedge-shaped imprints on clay (the term derives from *cuneus*, Latin for "wedge").

**Cuzco** The political, economic, and ritual center of the Inca empire.

**cylinder seal** A cylindrical, bead-like object used in the ancient Near East to produce a type of signature; usually made of stone and incised with designs or scenes that transferred as impressions onto wet clay as the seal was rolled over it.

**deductive reasoning** The scientific process of hypothesizing, gathering data to test the hypothesis, and drawing appropriate conclusions.

**dendrochronology** A chronometric dating technique involving the counting of tree rings, based on the fact that trees in temperate climates accumulate one growth ring a year; can date wood objects back to about 11 kyr ago.

**dental formula (DF)** A shorthand way of indicating how many of each type of tooth—incisors, canines, premolars, and molars—are in a mouth quadrant; for humans the DF is 2.1.2.3.

**derived traits** Traits that have changed from an ancestral state.

**diffusion wave** A hypothesis about how anatomically modern humans arose throughout the Old World, which suggests that an original population evolved in East Africa and expanded as a wave of migrants, interbreeding on its borders with local archaic *Homo sapiens* populations.

**directional selection** A type of natural selection that moves the mean of a trait's variation in a population in a constant direction, with succeeding generations showing short- or long-term directional change in the trait.

**discontinuity** The interruption of one lineage or group by extinction or movement to another location, followed by establishment of a new population.

**diurnal** Active during the day.

**Dmanisi** Lower Palaeolithic site in the Republic of Georgia with the earliest *H. erectus* fossils and artifacts in Europe (1.7 myr old).

**DNA** Deoxyribonucleic acid; the double-stranded molecule that is found in the nuclei of cells and provides the genetic code for organisms.

**domestication** Phenotypic and genetic changes in plants or animals that are the result of human intervention and that make the evolved species unable to live without human aid.

**dominance and recessiveness** The effects of alleles that either mask (dominance) or are masked (recessiveness) by the effects of other alleles in a heterozygous genotype.

**Eastern Woodlands** The region of eastern North America, rich in resources that underpinned a flourishing Archaic lifestyle.

**ecofacts** Culturally relevant nonartifactual finds, such as animal bones, plant remains, charcoal, and soils, that archaeologists can analyze to reconstruct past human diets and environments.

**Ediacara** Disc-shaped blobs of matter dated between 570 and 550 myr ago that are the probable common ancestor of modern multicellular life.

**El Niño** Cyclical climatic event that lowers temperatures in the Pacific ocean along coastal South America, causing a reduction in marine life and heavy rainfall that can lead to extensive flooding.

**El Paraíso** Early complex center in coastal Peru.

**electron spin resonance (ESR) dating** A chronometric dating technique that is based on the accumulation of radioactivity rather than its decay and is used to date tooth enamel and calcite deposits.

**emic perspective** An "insider" perspective on a particular culture, from the point of view of an anthropologist who acts as a member of the group being observed.

**empire** An extensive territory that is under the rule of a single, powerful state.

**enamel hypoplasia** Defects in tooth enamel caused by periods of stress, usually due to shortages of food, during formation of the enamel.

**epigrapher** Someone who studies ancient inscriptions.

**Erligang** An early phase of the Shang state in China.

**Erlitou** An early state in China that preceded the Shang state.

**Eskimo-Aleut** One of the major language families associated with the early occupation of the Americas.

**essentialism** A belief of Greek philosophers that ideal types had been created in perfect form and so did not need to change.

**ethnicity** An individual's cultural affiliation and ancestry.

**ethnoarchaeology** The study of traditional activities in existing societies from an archaeological perspective in order to develop hypotheses about past societies.

**ethnographers** Anthropologists who study people in societies around the world, observing and talking with them in order to understand their cultures.

**ethnographies**  Written descriptions of anthropologists' observations of people's cultures.

**etic perspective**  An "outsider" perspective on a particular culture, for example, how an American anthropologist might view an Australian aboriginal group.

**eukaryotes**  Organisms that have a nucleus containing DNA in their cells.

**evolution**  Transformation of species of organic life over long periods of time.

**evolving species concept (ESC)**  A definition of *species* in evolution as "independently evolving lineages."

**exchange networks**  Mechanisms by which goods are transferred between people, whether between two individuals or by means of a system of redistribution by a central authority or a currency-based market economy.

**experimental archaeology**  The use of experiments to develop hypotheses about or interpret particular human activities or processes in the past.

**facultative bipedalism**  An early form of human bipedalism, probably used from 6 myr to 1.8 myr ago, that likely was accomplished with the knees bent and without a full stride.

**Fayum Depression**  Area of present-day desert west of Cairo, Egypt, where many important early primate fossils were preserved.

**features**  Nonportable artifacts such as walls, pits, postholes, and hearths.

**field studies**  Studies that observe primates or other animals in their natural habitat with a minimum of human interference.

**first life**  A hypothesized set of chemicals, genetics, and behaviors, but at minimum having a cell, living in water, and able to change.

**fission track dating**  A dating technique for volcanic ash deposits that is based on the spontaneous splitting, or fission, of the isotope uranium 238, which leaves microscopic tracks on the mineral structure of the rocks.

**flake tools**  Flakes with one or more edges modified by retouch that were part of the tool kit from the time of *H. erectus* groups 1.6 myr ago in Africa and throughout the Paleolithic/Stone Age.

**flakes**  Fragments of stone that are removed from a block of stone (core) and used as tools.

**fluted points**  Projectile points produced with a stone-working technique that thins the base to assist hafting.

**forensic anthropology**  Application of skeletal and DNA identification techniques to solve legal problems.

**fossils**  Remains of any ancient organism (plant or animal): bone, stains, casts, or molds.

**founder effect**  When a human group leaves its original population, it does not necessarily take a representative sample of that population's overall gene pool with it, so the next generations of the migrating group will have a different gene pool.

**Funnel Beaker culture**  A farming group that orginated in what is now Poland and may have influenced the adoption of farming by southern Scandinavian Mesolithic groups; the name reflects the group's distinctive pottery.

**Gateway God**  An important Tiwanaku diety.

**gene flow**  A mechanism for evolutionary change resulting from movement of genes from one population to another through interbreeding, or exchange of genes between two populations, which introduces new genes and makes the populations more similar to each other.

**generalized**  Adapted to a wide range of conditions or used in a general way.

**genes**  DNA sequences that code for specific proteins and functions.

**genetic drift**  A mechanism for evolutionary change resulting from random changes in gene frequencies from one generation to the next in small populations.

**genotype**  The genetic endowment of an individual.

**genus**  Taxonomic groups of closely related species with similar adaptations.

**Geographic Information Systems (GIS)**  Software that links databases and maps to show relationships relevant to research questions.

**glyph**  A symbol used in Mesoamerican writing that can indicate a concept, a word, a sound, or a mixture of these elements.

**Gona**  Ethiopian site with the earliest evidence of hominid activity (2.6 myr ago).

**Gravettian**  A period of the Upper Paleolithic in France and Spain between 29 and 21 kyr ago.

**Great Houses**  Multi-storied constructions with hundreds of connecting rooms set in a semi-circle around a plaza; an architectural feature of Anasazi groups of the North American Southwest.

**Great Temple**  The religious center of the Aztec world, located in the capital, Tenochtitlan.

**guano**  Bird excrement that provides excellent fertilizer for crops.

**habitual bipedalism**  The modern form of human bipedalism that first appeared in the fossil record about 1.8 myr ago (*Homo erectus* times) and that is accomplished with straight legs and full strides.

**half-life**  The time it takes for half of a radioactive isotope in a sample to decay; varies for different radioactive isotopes.

**hand axe**  A pebble or large flake that hominids worked bifacially, removing flakes from both sides of the stone, to make a tool that is typical of the Lower Paleolithic/Early Stone Age; also called a *biface*.

**Harappa**  A major city of the Indus state of southern Asia.

**hearths**  Ancient campfires.

**Hemudu (or Ho-Mo-Tu)**  Neolithic wetland site in China with excellent preservation of domesticated and wild plants and evidence of sophisticated woodworking skills.

**henges** Late Neolithic monumental constructions in Britain consisting of a circular enclosure formed by banks and ditches with two to four entrances and internal settings of wood or stone.

**heredity (inheritance)** An individual's biological, genetic inheritance from both parents that is governed by principles (or laws) discovered by Gregor Mendel in the late nineteenth century.

**heterodont** Having teeth that differ in type and function.

**heterozygous** Having two different alleles of a particular gene.

**hierarchical settlement pattern** A pattern of differentially sized settlements (large urban center, villages, and hamlets) distributed across a region.

**hieratic** A cursive form of ancient Egyptian writing, written with pen and ink and used for everyday purposes.

**hieroglyphic** The ancient Egyptian pictographic script in which signs could represent objects or sounds; used for inscriptions on monuments and literary texts.

**Hieroglyphic Stairway** Stairway of a temple in Copan that has more than 2,200 glyphs on its steps, which comprise the longest Maya inscription.

**Hoabinian** The period from the final stages of the last Ice Age, when people lived by hunting and gathering, to the beginning of settled farming in Southeast Asia. *See also* Archaic, Jomon, Late Stone Age (LSA), Mesolithic, Natufian.

**Hogup Cave** Archaic site near the Great Salt Lake, in which the dry conditions preserved an extensive range of organic materials.

**Hohokam** Early farming culture of the Sonoran desert of southern Arizona.

**holism** The idea that anthropologists must study the past as well as the present and biology as well as culture in order to fully understand what it means to be human.

**Holocene** The present interglacial geological period, which began 11,500 years ago.

**homeotherms** Organisms that can maintain constant body temperature through physiological means.

**hominid** Humans and their bipedal ancestors since the time of divergence from the LCA of African apes and humans. The term *hominin* is preferred by some.

**hominoid** Superfamily of anthropoids including apes and humans. Traits include no tail and a large brain to body ratio.

*Homo* Genus of hominids having large brains and depending on culture to adapt.

*Homo erectus* A species of *Homo* dated from 1.8 myr to approximately 400 kyr ago, first in Africa and then spreading to Asia and Europe.

*Homo habilis* An early *Homo* species living in Africa 2.3 to 1.5 myr ago, showing brains half the size of moderns and ancestral features in the postcranial skeleton.

*Homo sapiens* A species of *Homo* whose members are both anatomically and behaviorally modern.

**homodont** Having teeth that are all the same in function, though they may differ in size.

**homology** The principle that states that similarity is due to descent from a common ancestor.

**homozygous** Having identical alleles of a particular gene.

**Hopewell** Early farming culture of the central riverine area of eastern North America; known for mound building.

**höyük** A large Neolithic mound in what is now Turkey (known elsewhere as a *tell* or a *tepe*).

**Huaca del Sol and Huaca de la Luna** Monumental mud-brick pyramid complexes at the Moche center of Cerro Blanco.

**human variability** The study of clinal manifestations of those modern human traits that vary.

**hypothesis** An informed explanation of a set of observations that can be tested or falsified.

**ice cores** Samples of ice used to date Earth's environmental changes up to 740 kyr ago.

**ice-free corridor** The possible land route from Alaska southward into Alberta that was exposed when the two major ice sheets in North America (Cordilleran and Laurentide) began to retreat.

**ideology** Belief systems of a group.

**Inca** The empire that controlled much of western South America in the fifteenth century, up to the Spanish conquest.

**independent assortment** A Mendelian principle that states that different traits are independently inherited from each other but that is applicable only to genes on different chromosomes.

**Indian Knoll** Archaic site in Kentucky where grave goods indicate differences associated with status and sex-related tasks.

**inductive reasoning** The branch of scientific discovery that starts by freely gathering data about some phenomenon worth investigating, then allowing the data to generate a hypothesis about that phenomenon.

**Indus (or Harappan)** The first state society in South Asia, which emerged about 4,600 years ago in what is now India and Pakistan.

**intelligence** The ability to solve problems of concern to the species.

**interglacial period** A period between glacial periods, or ice ages, when temperatures rise and the extent of ice sheets decreases.

**Inti** The Inca sun god.

**IQ** Intelligence quotient; the score on a standardized psychological test designed by North American and Western European psychologists to measure problem-solving ability in North American and Western European middle-class and upper-class students.

**irrigation** Supplying water artificially to promote crop growth.

**isotope analyses** Measurements of ratios of stable isotopes of carbon, nitrogen, and strontium to determine past dietary patterns and population movements.

**jacal** Term used in the North American Southwest for wattle-and-daub, a building technique in which mud or clay covers a superstructure of interwoven wooden poles and sticks.

**Jenné-jeno**  Ancient city in West Africa.

**Jericho**  Tell site in the Jordan Valley in what is now Palestine that has evidence of the transition from hunter-gatherer groups to farming groups; known for its monumental stone walls and tower and for the ritual burial of plastered human skulls and plaster statues of humans.

**Jomon**  The period from the final stages of the last Ice Age, when people lived by hunting and gathering, to the beginning of settled farming in Japan. *See also* Archaic, Hoabinian, Late Stone Age (LSA), Mesolithic, Natufian.

**K/T mass extinction**  Extinction of 75 percent of Earth's animal species, including all dinosaurs, about 65 myr ago.

**Kaminaljuyu**  A Maya center in present-day Guatemala, where buildings and artifacts suggest possible Teotihuacan domination.

**K-Ar dating**  A chronometric dating technique that uses the ratio between radioactive potassium (K) and nonradioactive argon (Ar) to date igneous and metamorphic rocks that are 250 kyr old or more, and thus indirectly date fossils and artifacts found in association with such rocks.

**Kennewick Man**  Male found in 1996 in the state of Washington and dated to 7,880 years ago; originally thought to be Native American and thus subject to reburial under NAGPRA but having morphology closer to that of Polynesians than of modern Native Americans.

**kivas**  Subterranean or semi-subterranean ceremonial rooms used by Ancestral Pueblo (Anasazi) and Mogollon groups in the American Southwest.

**knowledge**  That which is probably correct given the data at hand but that may change as new data or new ways to interpret data are found.

**Koster**  A site in Illinois with a long stratigraphic sequence that spans the Archaic period of the North American Eastern Woodlands.

**La Venta**  Large Olmec urban and ceremonial center in present-day Mexico, with monumental architecture that succeeded the earliest Olmec center, San Lorenzo.

**laboratory studies**  Studies of primates or other animals conducted in research facilities and often involving experimentation that must be tightly controlled and requires monitoring.

**labrets**  Lip ornaments used by Northwest Coast people as a sign of status.

**Lake Mungo**  Upper Paleolithic site in southeastern Australia where a cremation was found that dates to 40 kyr ago.

**language**  A type of communication that is complex, symbolic, and structured, but not necessarily oral (speech); examples are sign language, computer language, and bee language.

**large apes**  Common name for the bigger apes: orangutans (Asia) and gorillas, chimpanzees, and bonobos (Africa).

**last common ancestor (LCA)**  The group that evolved into humans in one lineage and evolved into either chimpanzees and bonobos or chimpanzees, bonobos, and gorillas in the other lineage.

**Late Stone Age (LSA)**  The archaeological term for the later part of the Stone Age in sub-Saharan Africa, from about 22 kyr to 2,000 years ago, characterized by the dominance of hunter-gatherers. *See also* Archaic, Hoabinian, Jomon, Mesolithic, Natufian.

**Levallois technique (prepared core technique)**  A stone-working technique in which the knapper (stone worker) prepares a stone block (core) to produce flakes of a predetermined shape and size; characteristic of the Middle Paleolithic/Middle Stone Age.

**Linearbandkeramik (LBK)**  The first farming culture of Europe; its name means Linear Pottery and reflects the distinctive pottery designs of members of the group.

**linguistics**  The subfield of anthropology that studies modern human speech communities, the origins of speech and language, their changes through time, and their structure.

**long barrow**  A long earthen burial mound widely constucted in northwestern Europe during the Neolithic.

**lumper**  A category of scientists who see the same amount of variability in past species as exists in similar modern species and do not add taxonomic names beyond what is necessary.

**Machu Picchu**  Inca town in the Andean mountains above the Urubamba Valley, near Cuzco.

**Magdalenian**  The final period in the Upper Paleolithic in France and Spain from 18 kyr to 10 kyr ago.

**mano**  Term used in the Americas, synonymous with pestle or handstone; used in conjunction with a metate to grind substances, particularly seeds.

**marine cores**  Samples obtained by passing a long tube from a ship down to the ocean floor and bringing up sediments that contain shells and pollen.

**mastaba**  A large, rectangular underground tomb made of mud-brick and stone in ancient Egypt.

**mastodon**  Extinct relative of mammoth and elephant.

**matrix**  The material, such as soil or sediment, surrounding archaeological finds.

**Maya**  Mesoamerican culture that encompassed numerous city-states, known for its pyramidal architecture, stelae, and writing.

**Meadowcroft Rockshelter**  Deeply stratified site in Pennsylvania that may be one of the earliest occupied sites in the Americas.

**megalith**  A large stone set up as a monument.

**meiosis**  The process of replication of sex cells by replication of chromosomes followed by two cycles of cell division so that each ovum or sperm has half of the parent's chromosomes.

**Mesoamerica**  A culture area that included much of present-day Central America, in which different ethnic groups shared similar belief systems and some cultural traits.

**Mesolithic**   The period from the final stages of the last Ice Age, when people lived by hunting and gathering, to the beginning of settled farming in Europe. *See also* Archaic, Hoabinian, Jomon, Late Stone Age (LSA), Natufian.

**Mesopotamia**   The region between the Euphrates and Tigris rivers that today encompasses most of Iraq and parts of Syria; location of the earliest cities and states in the world.

**metate**   Term used in the Americas, synonymous with mortar; the stone slab on which substances are placed for grinding with a mano.

**Mezhirich**   Upper Paleolithic site in the Ukraine with mammoth bone houses dated to between 18 kyr and 15 kyr ago.

**microevolution**   The process of change over only a few generations of a population, which can often be measured and explained.

**microliths**   Small stone flakes or blades, characteristic of the Late Stone Age in South Africa and the early Holocene in Eurasia.

**midden**   Mound formed through the accumulation of people's refuse.

**Middle Paleolithic**   The archaeological term commonly used in Eurasia for part of the Paleolithic period outside sub-Saharan Africa, from about 250 kyr to 35 kyr ago.

**Middle Stone Age (MSA)**   The archaeological term for part of the Stone Age in sub-Saharan Africa, from about 250 kyr to 22 kyr ago.

**Mississippian**   Term for a group of chiefdoms in eastern North America between about 1,150 and 400 years ago, associated with large mound complexes.

**mit'a**   Payment of taxes through labor; characteristic of the Inca, but also used in pre-Inca states.

**mitosis**   The process of replication followed by cell division by which a body cell produces two identical copies.

**mobiliary art**   Artwork that is portable, usually applied to Paleolithic and Stone Age art.

**Moche**   Early state in what is now northern Peru that flourished for about 700 years, from 1,900 to 1,250 years ago; known for its characteristic architecture, symbolic iconography, and skilled craft specialists.

**Mode 1 technology**   The earliest stone-working tradition, used by australopithecines; also known as Oldowan technology.

**Mode 2 technology**   Stone-working technique used by *H. erectus* and later groups of archaic *H. sapiens* to make hand axes.

**Mode 3 technology**   A stone-working technique that includes the Levallois (prepared core) technique and is characteristic of the Middle Paleolithic/Middle Stone Age.

**modern humans**   Humans from between 100 and 50 kyr ago through modern times who are both AMH and BMH.

**modern taxa**   Species that evolved sometime in the past and that have contemporary descendents.

**Mogollon**   Early farming culture in east central Arizona, southern New Mexico, western Texas, and northern Mexico, regions that are mainly mountainous but that also include desert areas.

**Mohenjo-Daro**   The largest of the cities of the Indus state of southern Asia.

**molecular dating**   The application of genetic analysis to estimate the sequence and timing of divergent evolutionary lineages.

**Monte Verde**   Well-dated site in Chile that may be the oldest Paleoindian site in the Americas.

**mound building**   Construction of large earthen structures, often associated with burials, by Archaic and early farming communities in the American Midwest and Southeast.

**multiregional (MR) model**   The hypothesis that after the dispersion of *Homo erectus* anatomically modern humans evolved as a single species throughout the Old World by means of gene flow between populations and/or migration.

**mutation**   A mechanism for evolutionary change acting through random changes in the sex cells; the ultimate source of all genetic variation.

**Nabta Playa**   Series of sites in Egypt with evidence for Neolithic pastoralism and an early megalithic complex.

**Na-Dene Athabaskan**   One of the major language families associated with the early occupation of the Americas.

**Narmer palette**   A carved flat stone that is traditionally believed to depict the unification of Egypt by King Narmer.

**Native Americans**   The descendants of the wave(s) of humans who left Asia via a land bridge at the Bering Strait to inhabit the New World beginning between about 25 and 15 kyr ago.

**Natufian**   The period from the final stages of the last Ice Age, when people lived by hunting and gathering, to the beginning of settled farming in the Middle East; the same period is called the Mesolithic in Europe, the Hoabinian in Southeast Asia, the Jomon in Japan, and the Archaic in the Americas and is part of the Late Stone Age in sub-Saharan Africa.

**natural selection**   A mechanism for evolutionary change that favors survival and reproduction of some organisms over others because of certain biological traits.

**natural transformation processes**   Natural phenomena that cause changes in the archaeological record at a site.

**Neandertal**   A population of late archaic *Homo sapiens* that lived in Europe and the Middle East between about 150 and 28 kyr ago and are characterized by robust bodies and large cranial capacities.

**Neolithic**   The New Stone Age, the period characterized by the emergence of farming cultures.

**New World monkeys**   Species of monkeys, mostly highly arboreal, that are found in Central and South America; their nostrils point straight ahead.

**nocturnal**   Active at night.

**nonhuman primates**   All primates, contemporary or fossil, that are not hominids; includes prosimians, tarsiers, monkeys, and apes.

**non-random mating** The practice whereby humans do not have an equal opportunity to mate with any other human because of incest taboos and cultural restrictions or choices.

**nose shape** The external conformation of the nose, which appears to correlate with climate; populations in cool areas have long, narrow noses, and populations in hot humid areas have short, wide noses.

**obsidian hydration dating** A dating technique based on measurement of the extent of absorption of water into an obsidian artifact through its exposed surfaces.

**ochre** Mineral pigment that has color ranges of reds and yellows.

**Old World monkeys** Species of monkeys, some arboreal and some terrestrial, that are found in Africa and Asia; their nostrils point downward and are separated by a narrow nasal septum.

**Oldowan technology (mode 1 technology)** The earliest stone-working tradition in Africa; named after Olduvai Gorge, Tanzania, where many early—but not the oldest—stone tools have been found.

**Olduvai Gorge** Area in Tanzania that is rich in Early Stone Age sites.

**Olmec** One of the complex societies of Mexico that preceded Mesoamerican states.

**optically stimulated luminescence (OSL) dating** A chronometric dating technique that is based on the accumulation of radioactivity rather than its decay and is used on wind- and water-borne sediments.

**optimal foraging theory** Theoretical model used to assess the efficiency of foraging practices used by hunter-gatherers; it assumes that foragers target resources that give the greatest returns in energy (most calories) for the least amount of effort spent in obtaining them.

**oracle bones** Animal bones (usually scapulae) and turtle shells used in the Shang state in China in divination rituals; when the bone or carapace was heated, cracks appeared that a diviner "read."

**out of Africa–2 (OOA–2)** Another name for the RAO model of the evolution of anatomically modern humans.

**paleoanthropology** The scientific study of fossils and artifacts and the contexts in which they are found.

**Paleoindian** Term denoting the earliest hunter-gatherer groups in the Americas before about 11 kyr ago.

**Paleolithic** The archaeological term used in most of Eurasia for the period between the arrival of the first hominids in the Old World outside Africa, about 1.7 myr ago, and the end of the last Ice Age, about 10 kyr ago.

**paleospecies** Species that are extinct, though their descendant species may still exist.

**paradigm** A way of looking at a broad subject, a world view—for example, science is a paradigm.

**parietal art** Rock wall and cave paintings.

**pastoralism** An economy in which food production is based on animal husbandry.

**Paul Mason** Archaic Northwest Coast village with large rectangular, multi-family houses.

**Permian extinction** A global event probably caused by a comet or asteroid hitting the Earth that caused arboreal ash and dust and halted photosynthesis. Ninety-five percent of land species may have become extinct.

**petrosal bulla** A bone found in the middle ear that is usable as a diagnostic trait of primates.

**phenetics** A paradigm, or model, that stresses the overall similarities among organisms in forming biological classifications.

**phenotype** The observable appearance of organisms influenced by both biology and environment.

**phyletic gradualism** Darwin's idea of the tempo of evolution as being slow and gradual over long periods of time.

**phytoliths** Microscopic silica particles that are present in many plant cells, preserve well, and can be diagnostic of plant types.

**Pikillaqta** The largest provincial center of the Wari state in the Cuzco Valley of Peru.

**placental mammals** A member of the infraclass Eutheria that includes placentals.

**playas** Shallow ponds that result from seasonal rains in arid and semi-arid areas and around which grasses and shrubs grow for a short period each year.

**Pleistocene** A geological period of glacial and interglacial cycles that began 2.3 myr ago.

*Plesiadapis* A primatelike mammal of about 50 myr ago that had a small brain, claws, and a large gap separating molars from incisors.

**Pochteca** Professional merchants who traveled throughout the Aztec empire for the king, simultaneously monitoring political activity.

**pongid** A member of the family Pongidae, which includes gorillas, chimpanzees, and bonobos.

**postdepositional effects** Alterations or movements that affect bones or artifacts after they have been deposited.

**postorbital bars** A trait shown in the skulls of all fossil and modern primates and consisting of bony extensions of both the frontal bone and the zygomatic arch that curve around the outside of each eye and support it.

**postorbital constriction** Narrowness of the skull behind the eye orbits.

**postprocessual archaeology** A theoretical approach to archaeological interpretation that developed as a reaction against the rigid scientific approach of processual archaeology and that stresses the individual and the interactions between humans and their groups, their material culture, their landscape, and their symbolic world.

**Poverty Point** Archaic center in Louisiana that displays many large earthworks and is located in a strategic position on exchange routes.

**pre-Clovis artifacts** Tools found in the Americas that predate Clovis points.

**primate** Any member of an order of mammals called Primates (which includes fossil and modern prosimians, tarsiers, monkeys, apes, and humans) that originally adapted to arboreal life, including the development of binocular vision and grasping hands.

**primate stem group** A hypothesized group of the earliest primates that was reconstructed from more modern primates.

**primatelike mammals** Early mammals that have some primate freatures but not enough to consider them "true primates."

**primatology** The scientific study of any or all of the 250+ species of contemporary primates.

**processual archaeology** A theoretical approach to interpreting archaeological evidence that promoted a problem-oriented, scientific type of archaeological research, seeking explanations rather than just descriptions; it was known as *new archaeology* when it was first developed.

**prokaryotes** Literally, "before nucleated life"; non–sexually reproducing, single-celled, non-nucleated life forms, such as modern blue-green algae.

**prosimians** Members of the suborder Prosimii, which is likely ancestral to later primates and is characterized by small body size and frequently nocturnal adaptations, found today in Africa, Madagascar, and Southeast Asia.

**provenience** The three-dimensional location of artifacts in their matrix; also referred to as provenance.

**psychologists** Scientists who study primate cognition and who are interested in how primates learn and in the similarities and differences between human and primate cognitive abilities.

**Pueblo Bonito** The largest Anasazi Great House in Chaco Canyon.

**pueblos** Villages of adobe or masonry structures with blocks of contiguous rooms set around a plaza; characteristic of early farming communities of the American Southwest.

**punctuated equilibrium** Model of macroevolutionary change in which long periods of little change are followed by short bursts of rapid change.

**quadrupedalism** Movement with four limbs making contact with the ground or tree limbs and usually with the spine parallel to the ground.

**quetzal** A Central American bird whose colored feathers were prized by Mesoamerican artisans.

**quinoa** Grain crop that grows in highland South America.

**quipu** Inca recording system, not yet deciphered, in which information is encoded in strips of colored cotton and wool strings, spun, twisted, and knotted in different ways.

**racism** A policy or attitude that unfairly generalizes real or perceived characteristics of some group to every member of that group.

**raised fields** Artificially raised blocks of land intersected by canals and used for cultivation of crops.

**ranked societies** Hierarchical societies in which people do not have equal access to status and prestige.

**recent African origin (RAO) model** The hypothesis that holds that anatomically modern humans evolved in Africa before 100 kyr ago and then spread out to Asia and Europe after 100 kyr ago, replacing all existing populations; also called OOA-2.

**reconstruction** Pulling together evidence from many sources to facilitate knowledge of what happened in particular lineages, such as the reconstruction of the human lineage.

**regulatory genes** The genes that code for regulation of biological processes such as growth and development.

**relative dating** A comparative method of dating that orders fossils or artifacts in a chronological sequence from older to younger but does not establish calendar dates.

**religion** Framework of beliefs relating to supernatural or superhuman beings or forces that transcend the everyday material world.

**remote sensing techniques** Survey techniques, such as aerial photography, radar mapping, and satellite imagery, used to find archaeological sites buried underground without disturbing the ground surface.

**reproductive differential** An individual's success relative to others of the same species as measured by survival of offspring into adulthood.

**research design** A carefully formulated and systematic plan for executing an archaeological excavation from formulating the research question(s) through publication of the results.

**San Lorenzo** The earliest large Olmec urban and ceremonial center with monumental architecture, located in the Mexican Gulf coast region.

**science** A way of learning about the world through observation and use of TSM.

**segregation** The process in which paired chromosomes separate into different cells during sex cell formation, resulting in sex cells that contain only one of the previously paired chromosomes.

**sexual dimorphism** The existence of differences between males and females of a species in stature, size, and other external morphological features.

**sexual selection** A form of natural selection with an emphasis on the choosing of mating partners, often by some means of identifying "good genes."

**Shang** Early regional state that emerged almost 4,000 years ago in China.

**shell middens** Mounds formed through the accumulation of shells (mainly of mollusks), indicating intensive exploitation of shellfish.

**Shelltown and Hind** Hohokam sites specializing in the manufacture of shell ornaments.

**Shortugai** Indus colony in Afghanistan.

**sickle-cell anemia** A genetic disease that occurs in individuals homozygous for the recessive allele that causes immunity to malaria.

**Sipán** Rich, unlooted tombs of Moche individuals of high status.

**skin color** The human trait often used by non-anthropologists to define and classify "biological races"; does not co-vary with most other traits.

**small apes** Common name for the smaller apes found in Southeast Asia: gibbons and siamangs.

**Snaketown** Large Hohokam settlement in Arizona with several platform mounds and two ball courts.

**social stratification** A characteristic of a society in which people do not have equal access to resources, wealth, prestige, or power.

**Solutrean** A period of the Upper Paleolithic in France and Spain from about 21 kyr to 18 kyr ago, characterized by very finely worked leaf-shaped flint points.

**specialized** Adapted to a narrow range of conditions or used in very specific ways.

**speciation** The origin of new species by change over time or splitting of a lineage.

**species** A group whose members interbreed naturally and produce fertile offspring.

**speech** The vocal, or oral/aural, version of language used by most humans.

**splitter** A category of scientists who believe past species were more variable than similar species today and give new species names to new finds.

**splitting (cladogenesis)** A mechanism of speciation in which an effective isolating barrier (geographic, genetic, or behavioral) keeps two (or more) segments of a species from interbreeding long enough for mutations and natural selection to make the separated populations no longer able to interbreed and thus separate species.

**stabilizing (balancing) selection** A type of natural selection that holds the existing variability of a trait steady in a population generation after generation.

**state** A political structure that is socially and economically stratified under the leadership of a strong central authority whose power is generally legitimized by an army and often strengthened by an ideology; key characteristics include high population density, hierarchical settlement pattern, monumental architecture, and full-time specialists.

**stay-at-home effect** When small groups leave to become "founders" elsewhere, the loss of their genetic material affects the next generations in the population left behind.

**stelae** Inscribed stone slabs or pillars that commemorate important events or serve as territorial markers, tomb markers, or votive markers; the singular form is *stela*.

**Stone Age** The period between the emergence of culture in sub-Saharan Africa, about 2.6 myr ago, and the beginning of farming, about 2,000 years ago.

**Stonehenge** Complex megalithic henge monument in Britain.

**stratigraphy** The charting of the sequence of strata (layers) of deposits that have accumulated over time at a site; can be used to assign relative dates to objects in different layers.

**Street of the Dead** A 5-km (3-mile) long avenue, lined with large pyramidlike structures, that bisected the city of Teotihuacan (in present-day Mexico).

**structural genes** The genes that give instructions that eventually are expressed in observable traits.

**subspecies** Groups within a species whose individuals share certain traits in higher frequencies with each other than with the species as a whole.

**subsurface survey techniques** Survey techniques, such as thumping the ground with a rod, using an auger or bore, or measuring electrical resistivity or magnetism, that can detect a potential archaeological site below ground surface.

**Sumer** Area in southern Mesopotamia where the first states emerged.

**survey** The most common way to locate archaeological sites or finds without excavation.

**symbolism** Use of an object, sign, gesture, or expression to represent something beyond itself.

**taphonomy** Study of the processes affecting the formation of archaeological sites.

**tarsiers** A major subdivision of the order Primates, considered a separate suborder by many experts, found today in Southeast Asia.

**Tawantinsuyu** The name the Inca used for their empire, meaning "The Four Parts Together."

**taxonomy** Scientific classification of groups based on evolutionary relationships.

**Tehuacan caves** Caves in the Tehuacan Valley of Mexico that have long occupation sequences and that together document the gradual adoption of farming.

**tell** An artificial mound formed through repeated occupation of the same site over thousands of years by people who built mud-brick houses on top of earlier structures; called a *tepe* in Iran and a *höyük* in Turkey.

**Tenochtitlan** Capital of the Aztec empire, beneath present-day Mexico City.

**teosinte** Wild ancestor of maize.

**Teotihuacan** One of the largest cities in the world some 1,600 years ago, located near present-day Mexico City; its influence extended into distant areas of Mesoamerica.

**terrestrial** Ground living.

**tetrapod** Technical name for the first lobe-finned fish, meaning four limbs with digits at their ends.

**the scientific method (TSM)** The method of doing science: generating hypotheses, collecting appropriate data, testing, and forming appropriate conclusions.

**theory** A hypothesis or a set of hypotheses that has been tested and retested and not found to be false, so confidence in its value is high.

**therapsids** An early group of mammal-like reptiles, ancestors of later mammals.

**thermoluminescence (TL) dating** A chronometric dating technique that is based on the accumulation of radioactivity rather than its decay and is used on burned materials such as pottery.

**Tikal** One of the largest of the Maya cities, located in the tropical forests of present-day Guatemala.

**Tiwanaku** Pre-Inca state that was contemporaneous with Wari, had its capital in the Lake Titicaca area of the Andean highlands, and was known for its monumental architecture; some experts give it early empire status.

**Tlatelolco** City that was adjacent to Tenochtitlan and in which the largest and most diverse market of the Aztec empire was based.

**transformism (anagenesis)** A mechanism of speciation in which one species changes over time as a whole unit to become a new species.

**true fossil** Ancient bone or tooth that has through time become mineralized.

**tuff** Consolidated volcanic ash.

**Ubaid period** Period that preceded the Uruk period in Mesopotamia and spanned the transition from Neolithic cultures to state societies.

**uniformitarianism** Geological principle that states that the forces that cause the Earth to be the way it is today altered the Earth in the past as well.

**Upper Paleolithic** The archaeological term commonly used for part of the Paleolithic period, from about 40 kyr to 11.5 kyr ago, in the Old World outside of sub-Saharan Africa.

**Ur** A major Mesopotamian city on the Euphrates River famed for its ziggurat, temples, urban neighborhoods, and cemetery.

**Uruk period** Period between 5,500 and 5,000 years ago that saw the emergence of state societies in Mesopotamia.

**Uruk-Warka** Largest city in Mesopotamia and in the world about 5,000 years ago.

**Wari** Pre-Inca Andean state that was contemporaneous with Tiwanaku and developed systems of terracing, irrigation, and roads later adopted by the Inca; possibly an empire.

**wattle-and-daub** A building technique in which clay or mud is used to cover a superstructure of interwoven wooden poles and sticks; known as jacal in the North American Southwest.

**Younger Dryas** Period between 12,900 and 11,500 years ago during which the warming trend at the end of the Ice Age was reversed and a substantial drop in temperatures caused changes in environmental conditions, to which humans had to adapt.

**ziggurat** A temple complex on raised, step-like platforms that dominated most Mesopotamian cities.

**zoo studies** Studies of primates or other animals that reside in captivity in order to supplement findings from the field or observe behavior not seen in the wild.

# References

Abbate, E., A. Albianelli, A. Azzaroli, et al. 1998. A one-million-year-old *Homo* cranium from the Danakil (Afar) Depression of Eritrea. *Nature* 393:458–460.

Abegglen, J-J. 1984. *On socialization in hamadryas baboons: A field study.* Lewisburg, PA: Bucknell University Press.

Abrams, M. 2003. Early humans had tiny brains. *Discover* (January): 47.

Adler, D. S., G. Bar-Oz, A. Belfer-Cohen, and O. Bar-Yosef. 2006. Ahead of the game: Middle and Upper Paleolithic hunting behaviors in the Southern Caucasus. *Current Anthropology* 47 (3): 89–118.

Adler, J. 2006. What can we learn from Neandertal genes? *Newsweek* (July 31).

Adovasio, J. M., D. Pedlar, J. Donahue, and R. Stuckenrath. 1999. No vestige of a beginning nor prospect for an end: Two decades of debate on Meadowcroft Rockshelter. In *Ice Age people of North America: Environments, origins, and adaptations*, eds. R. Bonnichsen and K. L. Turnmire, 416–431. Corvallis: Oregon State University Press.

Aiello, L. 2000. Neandertals in cold weather. Lecture at University College, London, March 23.

Aikens, C. M. 1983. The Far West. In *Ancient Native Americans*, ed. J. D. Jennings, 131–182. San Francisco: W. H. Freeman.

Aikens, C. M., and T. Higuchi. 1982. *Prehistory of Japan*. New York/London: Academic Press.

Aikens, C. M., and D. B. Madsen. 1986. Prehistory of the eastern area. In *Handbook of North American Indians*, vol. 11, *Great Basin*, ed. W. L. D'Azevedo, 149–160. Washington, DC: Smithsonian Institution.

Aitken, M. J. 1990. *Science-based dating in archaeology*. New York: Longman.

Alemseged, Z., F. Spoor, W. H. Kimbel, et al. 2006. A juvenile early hominin skeleton from Dikika, Ethiopia. *Nature* 443:296–301.

Algaze, G. 2001. The prehistory of imperialism: The case of Uruk period Mesopotamia. In *Uruk Mesopotamia and its neighbours*, ed. M. S. Rothman, 27–83. Santa Fe, NM: School of American Research Press.

Allison, A. C., and B. S. Blumberg. 1959. Ability to taste phenylthiocarbamide among Alaska Eskimos and other populations. *Human Biology* 31:352–359.

Alt, K., S. Pichler, W. Vach, et al. 1997. Twenty-five thousand-year-old triple burial from Dolní Vestonice: An Ice-Age family? *American Journal of Physical Anthropology* 102: 123–131.

Alva, W., and C. B. Donnan. 1993. *Royal tombs of Sipán*. Los Angeles: Fowler Museum of Cultural History, University of California.

Alvard, M. S. 2003. The adaptive nature of culture. *Evolutionary Anthropology* 12:136–149.

Ambrose, S. H. 2001. Paleolithic technology and human evolution. *Science* 291:1748–1753.

Ames, K. M. 2003. The Northwest Coast. *Evolutionary Anthropology*, 12:19–33.

———. 2005. Tempo and scale in the evolution of social complexity in western North America: Four case studies. In *North American Archaeology*, eds. T. R. Pauketat and D. DiPaolo Loren, 56–78. Malden, MA: Blackwell Publishing.

Ames, K. M., and H. D. Maschner. 1999. *Peoples of the Northwest Coast: Their archaeology and prehistory*. London: Thames & Hudson.

Andersen, S. H. 1995. Coastal adaption and marine exploitation in late Mesolithic Denmark—with special emphasis on the Limfjord region. In *Man and sea in the Mesolithic: Coastal settlement above and below present sea level*, ed. A. Fischer. Oxford: Oxbow Monograph 53.

Anderson, K. K., N. Azuma, J-M. Barnola, et al. 2004. High-resolution record of Northern Hemisphere climate extending into the last interglacial period. *Nature* 431:147–151.

Andrews, P. 1987. Aspects of hominoid phylogeny. In *Molecules and morphology in evolution: Conflict or compromise*, ed. C. Patterson, 23–33. Cambridge: Cambridge University Press.

———. 1995. Ecological apes and ancestors. *Nature* 376: 555–556.

Andrews, P., and Y. Fernandez-Jalvo. 1997. Surface modifications of the Sima de los Huesos fossil humans. *Journal of Human Evolution* 33:191–217.

Ankel-Simons, F. 2000. *Primate anatomy*. 2nd ed. San Diego: Academic Press.

Anonymous. 2007. *BBC News* (January 25).

Archibald, J. D. 1996. Fossil evidence for a late Cretaceous origin of "hoofed" mammals. *Science* 272: 1150–1153.

Arensburg, B., L. A. Schepartz, A. M. Tillier, et al. 1990. A reappraisal of the anatomical basis for speech in Middle Paleolithic hominids. *American Journal of Physical Anthropology* 83:137–146.

Arsuaga, J. L. 2002. Archaic *Homo sapiens*. In *Encyclopedia of evolution*, ed. M. Pagel, 489–493. Oxford: Oxford University Press.

Arsuaga, J. L., I. Martínez, A. Gracia, et al. 1997. Sima de los Huesos (Sierra de Atapuerca, Spain). The site. *Journal of Human Evolution* 33:109–127.

Ascenzi, A., I. Biddittu, P. F. Cassoli, et al. 1996. A calvarium of late *Homo erectus* from Ceprano, Italy. *Journal of Human Evolution* 31:409–423.

Ascenzi, A., and A. G. Segre. 2000. The fossil calvaria of *Homo erectus* from Ceprano (Central Italy): A new reconstruction. In *The origin of humankind*, eds. M. Aloisi, B.

Attaglia, E. Carafoli, and G. A. Danili. Amsterdam: IOS Press.

Asfaw, B., W. H. Gilbert, Y. Beyene, et al. 2002. Remains of *Homo erectus* from Bouri, middle Awash, Ethiopia. *Nature* 416:317–319.

Asfaw, B., T. White, O. Lovejoy, et al. 1999. *Australopithecus garhi:* A new species of early hominid from Ethiopia. *Science* 284:629–634.

Asouti, E., and A. Fairburn. 2002. Subsistence economy in central Anatolia during the Neolithic: The archaeological evidence. In *The Neolithic of Anatolia: Internal developments and external relations during the 9th–6th millennia Cal. BC.*, eds. F. Gérard and L. Thissen. Istanbul: Yayinlari.

Asquith, P. 2000. Negotiating science: Internationalization and Japanese primatology. In *Primate encounters*, eds. S. Strum and L. Fedigan, 165–183. Chicago: University of Chicago Press.

Attenborough, D. 1981. *Life on Earth.* Glasgow: Fontana Collins.

Audouze, F. 1987. The Paris basin in Magdalenian times. In *The Pleistocene Old World: Regional perspectives*, ed. O. Soffer, 183–199. New York/London: Plenum.

Baba, H., F. Aziz, Y. Karfu, et al. 2003. *Homo erectus* calvarium from the Pleistocene of Java. *Science* 299:1385–1387.

Backwell, L. R., and F. d'Errico. 2001. Evidence of termite foraging by Swartkrans early hominids. *Proceedings of the National Academy of Sciences* 98:1358–1363.

Bada, J. L., and A. Lazcano. 2002. Some like it hot, but not the first biomolecules. *Science* 296:1982–1983.

Bagley, R. 1999. Shang archaeology. In *The Cambridge history of ancient China: From the origins of civilization to 221 BC*, eds. M. Loewe and E. L. Shaughnessy, 124–231. Cambridge: Cambridge University Press.

Bahn, P., and J. Vertut. 1988. *Images of the Ice Age.* Leicester, UK: Winward.

Bailey, W. J. 1993. Hominid trichotomy: A molecular overview. *Evolutionary Anthropology* 2 (3): 100–108.

Baines, J., and N. Yoffee. 1998. Order, legitimacy and wealth in ancient Egypt and Mesopotamia. In *Archaic states*, eds. G. M. Feinman and J. Marcus, 199–260. Santa Fe, NM: School of American Research Press.

Balter, M. 2002. Why get smart? *Science* 295:1225.

Balter, M., and A. Gibbons. 2000. A glimpse of humans' first journey out of Africa. *Science* 288:948–950.

Bard, E. 2001. Extending the calibrated radiocarbon record. *Science* 292:2443–2444.

Bard, K. A. 2000. The emergence of the Egyptian state (c. 3200–2686 BC). In *The Oxford history of ancient Egypt*, ed. I. Shaw, 61–88. New York: Oxford University Press.

Bard, K. A., and R. Fattovich. 2001. Some remarks on the processes of state formation in Egypt and Ethiopia. In *Africa and Africans in antiquity*, ed. E. M. Yamauchi, 276–290. East Lansing: Michigan State University Press.

Barham, L. S. 2000. *The Middle Stone Age of Zambia, south central Africa.* Bristol: Western Academic and Specialist Press.

Barker, P. 1995. *Techniques of archaeological excavation.* New York: Humanities Press.

Barnes, G. L. 1999. *The rise of civilization in east Asia: The archaeology of China, Korea and Japan.* London: Thames & Hudson.

Barton, N. 1997. *Stone Age Britain.* London: B. T. Batsford.

Barton, R. N. E., A. P. Currant, Y. Fernandez-Jalvo, et al. 1999. Gibraltar Neandertals and results of recent excavations in Gorhams, Vanguard and Ibex caves. *Antiquity* 73:13–23.

Bar-Yosef, O. 1986. The walls of Jericho: An alternative interpretation. *Current Anthropology* 27 (2): 157–162.

———. 1994. The Lower Palaeolithic of the Near East. *Journal of World Prehistory* 8 (3): 211–265.

———. 1995. Earliest food producers: Pre-pottery Neolithic (8000–5500). In *The archaeology of society in the Holy Land*, ed. T. Levy, 191–201. New York: Facts on File.

———. 2002. Natufian: A complex society of foragers. In *Beyond foraging and collecting*, eds. B. Fitzhugh and J. Habu, 91–149. New York: Kluwer Academic/Plenum.

Bar-Yosef, O., B. Vandermeersch, B. Arensburg, et al. 1992. The excavations at Kebara Cave, Mt. Carmel. *Current Anthropology*, 33 (5): 497–550.

Basgall, M. 1987. Resource intensification among hunter-gatherers: Acorn economies in prehistoric California. *Research in Economic Anthropology* 9:21–52.

Bauer, B. S., and D. S. Dearborn. 1995. *Astronomy and empire in the ancient Andes.* Austin: University of Texas Press.

Bayman, J. M. 2001. Hohokam of Southwest North America. *Journal of World Prehistory* 15 (3): 257–311.

———. 2002. Hohokam craft economies and the materialization of power. *Journal of Archaeological Method and Theory* 9 (1): 69–95.

Beall, C. M., and T. S. Steegman, Jr. 2000. Human adaptation to climate. In *Human biology*, eds. S. Stinson, B. Bogin, R. Huss-Ashmore, and D. O'Rourke, 163–224. New York: Wiley.

Beard, K. C., Y. Tong, M. R. Dawson, et al. 1996. Earliest complete dentition of an anthropoid primate from the late middle Eocene of Shanxi Province, China. *Science* 272:82–85.

Beard, K. C., and J. Wang. 2004. The eosimiid primates (Anthropoidea) of the Heti Formation, Yuanqu Basin, Shanxi and Henin Proviinces, People's Republic of China. *Journal of Human Evolution* 46:401–432.

Bearder, S. K. 1986. Lorises, bushbabies, and tarsiers: Diverse societies in solitary foragers. In *Primate societies*, ed. B. Smuts, 14–25. Chicago: University of Chicago Press.

Bednarik, R. G. 1992. Palaeoart and archaeological myths. *Cambridge Archaeological Journal* 2:27–57.

Begun, D. R. 2002a. European hominoids. In *The primate fossil record*, ed. W. Hartwig, 339–368. Cambridge: Cambridge University Press.

———. 2002b. Miocene apes. In *Physical anthropology: Original readings in method and practice*, eds. P. N. Peregrine, C. R. Ember, and M. Ember, 68–89. Upper Saddle River, NJ: Prentice Hall.

Bell, M., and M. Walker. 1992. *Late Quaternary environmental change: Physical and human perspectives.* Harlow, UK: Longman.

Benavides, M. C. 1991. Cheqo Wasi, Huari. In *Huari administrative structure: Prehistoric monumental architecture and state government*, eds. W. H. Isbell and G. F. McEwan, 55–69. Washington, DC: Dumbarton Oaks Research Library and Collection.

Benefit, B. R., and M. C. McCrossin. 2002. The *Victoriapithecedae, Cercopithecoidea*. In *The primate fossil record*, ed. W. Hartwig, 241–254. Cambridge: Cambridge University Press.

Berger, L. R. 2002. Early hominid body proportions and energy complexities in human evolution. *Evolutionary Anthropology* 11 (Supplement 1): 32–44.

Berger, L. R., and R. J. Clarke. 1995. Eagle involvement in accumulation of the Taung child fauna. *Journal of Human Evolution* 29 (3): 275–299.

Bermudez de Castro, J. M., J. L. Arsuaga, E. Carbonell, et al. 1997. A hominid from the Lower Pleistocene of Atapuerca, Spain: Possible ancestor to Neandertals and modern humans. *Science* 276:1392–1395.

Bernardini, W. 2004. Hopewell geometric earthworks: A case study in the referential and experiential meaning of monuments. *Journal of Anthropological Archaeology* 23:331–356.

Bettinger, R. L. 2001. Holocene hunter-gatherers. In *Archaeology at the millennium*, eds. G. Feinman and T. D. Price, 137–195. New York: Kluwer Academic/Academic Press/Plenum.

Biasutti, R. 1967. *Razza e popoli della terra*. Turin, Italy: Unione Tipografico.

Billman, B., P. Lambert, and L. Banks. 2000. Cannibalism, warfare, and drought in the Mesa Verde region during the twelfth century A.D. *American Antiquity* 65 (1): 145–178.

Billsborough, A. 1999. Contingency, patterning, and species in hominid solution. In *Structure and contingency*, ed. J. Bintliffe, 43–101. London: Leicester University Press.

Binford, L. R. 1968a. Archaeological perspectives. In *New perspectives in archeology*, eds. S. R. Binford and L. R. Binford, 5–32. Chicago: Aldine de Gruyter.

———. 1968b. Post-pleistocene adaptations. In *New perspectives in archeology*, eds. S. R. Binford and L. R. Binford, 313–341. Chicago: Aldine de Gruyter.

———. 1980. Willow smoke and dog's tails: Hunter-gatherer settlement systems and archaeological site formation. *American Antiquity* 45 (1): 4–20.

———. 1983. *In pursuit of the past*. London: Thames & Hudson.

Binford, L. R., and S. R. Binford. 1966. A preliminary analysis of functional variability in the Mousterian of Levallois facies. *American Anthropologist* 68 (no. 2, part 2): 238–295.

Blanton, R. E. 1996. The Basin of Mexico market system and the growth of empire. In *Aztec imperial strategies*, eds. F. F. Berdan, R. Blanton, E. Hill Boone, et al., 47–84. Washington, DC: Dumbarton Oaks Research Library and Collection.

Blom, D., B. Hallgrímsson, L. Keng, et al. 1998. Tiwanaku "colonization": Bioarchaeological implications for migration in the Moquegua Valley, Peru. *World Archaeology* 30 (2): 238–261.

Blom, D. E. 2005. Embodying borders: Human body modification and diversity in Tiwanaku society. *Journal of Anthropological Archaeology* 24:1–24.

Blomster, J. P., H. Neff, and M.D. Glascock. 2005. Olmec pottery production and export in Ancient Mexico determined through elemental analysis. *Science* 307: 1068–1072.

Blumenschine, R., C. R. Peters, F. T. Matsao, et al. 2003. Late Pleistocene *Homo* and hominid land use from western Olduvai Gorge, Tanzania. *Science* 299:1217–1220.

Boas, N. T., and A. J. Almquist. 2002. *Biological anthropology*. 2nd ed. Upper Saddle River, NJ: Prentice Hall.

Bocquet-Appel, J.-P., and P. Demars. 2000. Neanderthal contraction and modern human colonization of Europe. *Antiquity* 74:544–552.

Boëda, E., J. Connan, D. Dessort, et al. 1996. Bitumen as a hafting material on Middle Palaeolithic artefacts. *Nature* 380 (March 28): 336–338.

Boesch, C. 2003. Is culture a golden barrier between human and chimpanzee? *Evolutionary Anthropology* 12:82–91.

Boesch, C., and H. Boesch. 2000. *Chimpanzees of the Taï forest: Behavioral ecology and evolution*. Oxford: Oxford University Press.

Bogin, B. 1998. The tall and the short of it. *Discover* (February): 40–44.

———. 2001a. *The growth of humanity*. New York: Wiley.

———. 2001b. *Patterns of human growth*. 2nd ed. Cambridge: Cambridge University Press.

———. 2003. Human growth in paleontological perspective. In *Patterns of growth and development in the genus Homo*, eds. J. L. Thompson, G. E. Krovitz, and A. J. Nelson, 15–44. Cambridge: Cambridge University Press.

Bogucki, P. 1996. The spread of early farming in Europe. *American Scientist* 84 (3): 242–253.

———. 2000. How agriculture came to north-central Europe. In *Europe's first farmers*, ed. T. Douglas Price. Cambridge: Cambridge University Press.

———. 2003. Neolithic dispersals in riverine interior central Europe. In *The widening harvest, the Neolithic transition in Europe: Looking back, looking forward*, eds. A. J. Ammerman and P. Biagi, 249–272. Boston: Archaeological Institute of America.

Bonnichsen, R., and A. L. Schneider. 1999. Breaking the impasse on the peopling of the Americas. In *Ice Age people of North America: Environments, origins, and adaptations*, eds. R. Bonnichsen and K. L. Turnmire, 497–519. Corvallis: Oregon State University Press.

Bordes, F. 1961. Mousterian cultures in France. *Science* 134:803–810.

———. 1968. *The Old Stone Age*. New York/Toronto: McGraw-Hill.

Bosinski, G. 1990. *Homo sapiens: Préhistoire des chasseurs du Paléolithique supérieur en Europe*. Paris: Editions Errance.

———. 2006. Les premiers peuplement de l'Europe centrale et de d'Est. *Comptes Rendus Palevol*. 5: 311–317.

Bourget, S. 2001. Rituals of sacrifice: Its practice at Huaca de la Luna and its representation in Moche iconography. In *Moche art and archaeology in ancient Peru*, ed. J. Pillsbury, 89–109. Washington, DC: National Gallery of Art/Yale University Press.

Bowler, J. M., H. Johnston, J. M. Olley, et al. 2003. New ages for human occupation and climatic change at Lake Mungo, Australia. *Nature* 421:837–840.

Boyd, R. 2006. On "sedentism" in the later Epipalaeolithic (Natufian) Levant. *World Archaeology* 38 (2): 167–178.

Boyd, R., and J. Silk. 2006. *How humans evolved*. 4th ed. New York: Norton.

Brace, C. L. 1991. *The stages of human evolution*. 4th ed. Upper Saddle River, NJ: Prentice Hall.

———. 1996. A four letter word called "race." In *Race and other misadventures: Essays in honor of Ashley Montagu in his ninetieth year*, eds. L. T. Reynolds and L. Lieberman. Dix Hills, NY: General Hall Publishers.

———. 2005. *Race is a four letter word*. Oxford: Oxford University Press.

Brace, C. L., and A. R. Nelson. 1999. The peopling of the Americas: Anglo stereotypes and Native American realities. *General Anthropology* 5 (2): 1–6.

Brain, C. K. 1981. *The hunters or the hunted? An introduction to African cave taphonomy*. Chicago: Chicago University Press.

———. 1989. The evidence for bone modification by early hominids in southern Africa. In *Bone modification*, eds. R. I. Bonnichsen and M. H. Sorg, 291–297. Orono, ME: Center for the Study of the First Americans, University of Maine.

Bramble, D. M. 2002. Morphological adaptations. *Encyclopedia of evolution*, ed. M. Pagel, 514–517. Oxford: Oxford University Press.

Brasier, M., and J. Antcliffe. 2004. Decoding the Ediacaran enigma. *Science* 305:115–117.

Brauer, G. 2001. Out of Africa and the question of regional continuity. In *Humanity from African naissance to coming millennia*, ed. P. Tobias, 183–189. Florence: University of Florence Press.

Brauer, G., Y. Yokoyana, C. Falgueres, and E. Mbua. 1997. Modern human origins back dated. *Nature* 386:337–338.

Bray, F. 2001. Are GMOs good for us? What anthropologists can contribute to the debate. *General Anthropology* 8 (1): 1–7.

Brewer, D. J., and E. Teeter. 1999. *Egypt and the Egyptians*. Cambridge: Cambridge University Press.

Broad, W. 2002. Traders from a primordial sea are found in Canada. *New York Times* (June 4): D-3.

Brockman, D. 1999. Reproductive behavior of female *Propithecus verreauxi* at Bezi Mahafaly, Madagascar. *International Journal of Primatology* 20 (3): 375–398.

Brown, D. 1991. *Human universals*. Philadelphia: Temple University Press.

Brown, T. 2001. Ancient DNA. In *Handbook of archaeological science*, eds. D. Brothwell and A. M. Pollard, 301–312. New York: Wiley.

Browne, M. 1995. Animals left the water earlier than thought. *New York Times* (February 21): C 10.

———. 1996. Mass extinction of Permian Era linked to a gas. *New York Times* (July 30): C 1, C 10.

Brunet, M. 2001. Chadian australopithecines: Biochronology and environmental context. In *Humanity from African naissance to coming millennia*, ed. P. Tobias, 103–106. Florence: University of Florence Press.

Brunet, M., A. Beauvilain, Y. Coppens, et al. 1995. The first australopithecine 2,500 kilometers west of the Rift Valley. *Nature* 378:273–275.

Burton, F. 1995. *The multimedia guide to non-human primates*. Scarborough, ON: Prentice Hall Canada.

Butzer, K. 1995. Change in the Near East and human impact on the land. In *Civilizations of the Near East*, ed. J. M. Sasson, 123–151. Peabody, MA: Hendrickson Publishers.

Bynum, N. 2002. Morphological variation within a macaque hybrid zone. *American Journal of Physical Anthropology* 118 (1): 45–49.

Byrne, R. W., and A. Whiten. 1996. Machiavellian intelligence. *Evolutionary Anthropology* 5:172–181.

Campbell, A., and P. C. Rice. 2008. Why do anthropological experts disagree?" In *Thinking anthropologically* (2nd ed.), eds. P. C. Salzman and P. C. Rice, 59–70. Upper Saddle River, NJ: Prentice Hall.

Campbell, C. J., A. Fuentes, K. MacKinnon, et al., eds. 2007. *Primates in perspective*. New York: Oxford University Press.

Cann, R., A. Wilson, and M. Stoneking. 1987. Mitochondrial DNA and human evolution. *Nature* 325:31–36.

Cannon, A. 2002. Sacred power and seasonal settlement on the central Northwest coast. In *Beyond foraging and collecting: Evolutionary change in hunter-gatherer settlement patterns*, eds. B. Fitzhugh and J. Habu, 311–338. New York: Kluwer Academic/Plenum.

Caramelli, D. G., C. Lalueza-Fox, C. Vernesi, et al. 2003. Evidence for a genetic discontinuity between Neandertals and 24,000-year-old anatomically modern Europeans. *Proceedings of the National Academy of Sciences USA* 100 (11): 6593–6957.

Carbonell, E., J. M. Bermudez de Casto, J. L. Arsuaga, et al. 1995. Lower Pleistocene hominids and artifacts from Atapuerca TD6 (Spain). *Science* 269:826–830.

Carbonell, E., M. Mosquera, A. Ollé, et al. 2003. Les premier comportements funéraires auraient-ils pris place à Atapuerca, il ya a 350,000 ans? [Did the earliest mortuary practices take place more than 350,000 years ago at Atapuerca?] *L'anthropologie* 107:1–14.

Carbonell, E., and X. P. Rodríguez. 2006. The first human settlement of Mediterranean Europe. *Comptes Rendus Palevol*. 5:291–298.

Carroll, R. 2002. Early land vertebrates. *Nature* 418:35–36.

Carter, R. 2006. Boat remains and maritime trade in the Persian Gulf during the sixth and fifth millennia BC. *Antiquity* 80:52–63.

Cartmill, M. 1974. Rethinking primate origins. *Science* 184:436–443.

———. 1998a. The gift of gab. *Discover* (November): 57–64.

———. 1998b. The status of the race concept in physical anthropology. *American Anthropologist* 100 (3): 651–660.

Caspari, R. 2002. It's gotta walk the walk: Making sense of the newly reported *Sahelanthropus tchadensis* fossil remains from Chad. *General Anthropology* 9 (1): 1–11.

Cassidy, J., L. M. Raab, and N. A. Kononenko. 2004. Boats, bones, and biface bias: The early Holocene mariners of Eel Point, San Clemente Island, California. *American Antiquity* 69 (1): 109–130.

Cavalli-Sforza, L. 2000. Some conclusions about human evolution. In *Origin of humankind*, eds. M. A. Aloisi et al., 19–20. Amsterdam: IOS Press.

———. 2001. *Genes, peoples, and languages*. Berkeley: University of California Press.

Censky, E. J., K. Hodge, and J. Dudley. 2002. Over-water dispersal of lizards due to hurricanes. *Nature* 395:556.

Chaimanee, Y., D. Jolly, M. Benammi, et al. 2003. A middle Miocene hominoid from Thailand and orangutan origins. *Nature* 422:61–63.

Chang, K. 1980. *Shang civilization*. New Haven, CT: Yale University Press.

———. 1986. *The archaeology of ancient China*. New Haven, CT: Yale University Press.

Chapdelaine, C. 2001. The growing power of a Moche urban class. In *Moche art and archaeology in ancient Peru*, ed. J. Pillsbury, 69–87. Washington, DC: National Gallery of Art/Yale University Press.

———. 2002. Out in the streets of Moche: Urbanism and socio-political organization at a Moche IV urban center. In *Andean art and archaeology I: Variations in sociopolitical organization*, eds. W. H. Isbell and H. Silverman, 53–88. New York: Kluwer Academic/Plenum Publishers.

Chartkoff, J. L. 1998. California culture area. In *Archaeology of prehistoric Native America: An encyclopedia*, ed. G. Gibbon, 104–113. New York/London: Garland.

Chase, P. G., and H. L. Dibble. 1987. Middle Paleolithic symbolism: A review of current evidence and interpretations. *Journal of Anthropological Archaeology* 6:263–296.

Chatterjee, H. J. 2002. Morphology versus molecules: Compatibility or conflict in reconstructing primate evolution. *General Anthropology* 8 (2): 1–5.

Chen, Chun, and J. W. Olsen. 1990. China at the last glacial maximum. In *The world at 18,000 BP: High latitudes*, eds. O. Soffer and C. Gamble, 276–295. New York/London: Plenum.

Childe, V. G. 1950. The urban revolution. *Town Planning Review* 22 (21): 3–17.

———. 1981. *Man makes himself*. Bradford-on-Avon: Moonraker.

Cifelli, R. L., and B. M. Davis. 2003. Marsupial origins. *Science* 302:1890–1899.

Ciochon, R. L., and J. G. Fleagle, eds. 2006. *The human evolution source book*. 2nd ed. Upper Saddle River, NJ: Prentice Hall.

Ciochon, R. L., and G. F. Grinnell. 2002. Chronology of primate discoveries in Myanmar: Influences on the anthropoid origins debate. *Yearbook of Physical Anthropology* 45:2–35.

Ciochon, R. L., J. Olsen, and J. James. 1990. *Other origins: The search for the giant ape in human prehistory*. New York: Bantam.

Clark, A. J. 1990. *Seeing beneath the soil: Prospecting methods in archaeology*. London: B. T. Batsford.

Clark, G. A. 2000. On the questionable practice of invoking the metaphysic. *Current Anthropology* 102 (4): 851–853.

———. 2001. Observations on the epistemology of human origin research. In *Studying human origins*, eds. R. Corbey and W. Roebroeks, 139–146. Amsterdam: Amsterdam University Press.

———. 2002a. Neandertal archaeology: Implications for our origins. *American Anthropologist* 104 (1): 50–67.

———. 2002b. Observation on paradigmatic bias in France and American paleolithic archaeology. In *The role of American archaeology in the study of the European Upper Paleolithic*, ed. L. S. Straus, 19–26. BAR International Series 1048. Oxford: Archaeopress.

Clark, G. A., and J. M. Lindly. 1991. On paradigmatic biases and Paleolithic research traditions. *Current Anthropology* 32 (5): 577–587.

Clark, G. A., and C. Willermet. 1997. *Conceptual issues in modern human origins research*. New York: Aldine de Gruyter.

Clark, J. D., and F. C. Howell. 1966. Recent studies in anthropology. *American Anthropologist* 68 (2).

Clark, J. E., and M. E. Pye. 2000. The Pacific coast and the Olmec question. In *Olmec art and archaeology in Mesoamerica*, eds. J. E. Clark and M. E. Pye, 217–251. Washington, DC: National Gallery of Art/Yale University Press.

Clarke, R., and P. Tobias. 1995. Sterkfontein Member 2 foot bones of the oldest South African hominid. *Science* 269:521–522.

Close, A. E., and F. Wendorf. 1990. North Africa at 18,000 BP. In *The world at 18,000 BP: Low latitudes*, eds. C. Gamble and O. Soffer, 41–57. London: Unwin Hyman.

Clottes, J. 1999. Twenty thousand years of Palaeolithic cave art in southern France. *Proceedings of the British Academy* 99:161–175.

Cobo, B. 1979. *History of the Inca empire: An account of the Indians' customs and their origin together with a treatise on Inca legends, history, and social institutions*. Trans. R. Hamilton. Austin: University of Texas Press.

Coe, M. D. 1993. *The Maya*. 4th ed. London: Thames & Hudson.

Coe, M. D., and J. Kerr. 1997. *The art of the Maya scribe*. London: Thames & Hudson.

Cohen, J. E. 2003. Human population: The next half century. *Science* (November 14): 1172–1175.

Cohen, M. N. 1977. *The food crisis in prehistory: Overpopulation and the origins of agriculture*. New Haven: Yale University Press.

———. 1989. *Health and the rise of civilization*. New Haven, CT: Yale University Press.

Coles, B., and J. Coles. 1986. *Sweet Track to Glastonbury: The Sumerset levels in prehistory*. New York: Thames & Hudson.

———. 1989. *People of the wetlands: Bogs, bodies and lake-dwellers*. New York: Thames & Hudson.

Collard, M. 2002. Grades and transitions in human evolution. In *The speciation of modern Homo sapiens*, ed. J. Crow. *Proceedings of the British Academy* 104:61–100.

Collard, M., and B. Wood. 1999. Grades among the African early hominids. In *African biogeography, climate change, and human evolution*, eds. R. Bromage and F. Schrenk, 316–327. Oxford: Oxford University Press.

Coningham, R. 2005. South Asia: From early villages to Buddhism. In *The human past: World prehistory and the development of human societies*, ed. C. Scarre, 518–551. New York: Thames & Hudson.

Connah, G. 2001. *African civilizations: An archaeological perspective*. Cambridge: Cambridge University Press.

Connolly, P. 1990. *Pompeii*. Oxford: Oxford University Press.

Conroy, G. C. 2002. Speciosity in the early *Homo* lineage: Too many, too few, or just about right? *Journal of Human Evolution* 43 (7): 757–766.

———. 2005. *Reconstructing human origins: A modern synthesis*. New York: Norton.

Conway Morris, S. 1998. *The crucible of creation: The Burgess Shale and the rise of animals*. Oxford: Oxford University Press.

———. 2000. The Cambrian "explosion": Slow fuse or mega-tonnage? *Proceedings of the National Academy of Sciences USA* 97 (9): 4426–4429.

———. 2003. *Life's solutions.* Cambridge: Cambridge University Press.

Cooley, A. E. 2003. *Pompeii.* London: Gerald Duckworth.

Copeland, L., and N. Moloney. 2003. The Mousterian lithic assemblages from Ras el Kelb Cave, Lebanon. In *Lithic analysis at the millennium*, eds. N. Moloney and M. J. Shott, 17–28. London: University College London.

Coppens, Y. 1994. East Side story: The origin of humankind. *Scientific American* 270:88–95.

Corbey, R. 2005. *The metamorphosis of apes.* Cambridge: Cambridge University Press.

Cordell, L. 1997. *Archaeology of the Southwest.* San Diego, CA: Academic Press.

Cordell, L., and B. Smith. 1996. Indigenous farmers. In *The Cambridge history of the native peoples of the Americas*, vol. 1, *North America*, eds. B. Trigger and W. Washburn, 201–267. Cambridge: Cambridge University Press.

Costamago, S., L. Meignen, B. Cédric, et al. 2006. Les Pradelles (Marillac-le-Franc, France): A Mousterian reindeer hunting camp? *Journal of Anthropological Archaeology* 25:466–484.

Coughlan, A. 2000. Land of opportunity. *New Scientist* (November 4): 32.

Coven, H. H. 2002. Earliest primates and the evolution of Prosimians. In *The primate fossil record*, ed. W. C. Hartwig, 13–20. Cambridge: Cambridge University Press.

Cowen, R. 2005. *History of life.* 4th ed. Malden, MA: Blackwell Publishing.

Cowgill, G. L. 1997. State and society at Teotihuacan, Mexico. *Annual Review of Anthropology* 26:129–161.

———. 2003. Teotihuacan and Early Classic interaction: A perspective from outside the Maya region. In *The Maya and Teotihuacan: Reinterpreting Early Classic interaction*, ed. G. Braswell, 317–333. Austin: University of Texas Press.

Crawford, G. W. 2006. East Asian plant domestication. In *Archaeology of Asia*, ed. M. T. Stark, 77–95. Malden, MA: Blackwell Publishing.

Crawford, H. 1992. *Sumer and the Sumerians.* Cambridge: Cambridge University Press.

Crockett, C. M., and J. F. Eisenberg. 1986. Howlers: Variations in group size and demography. In *Primate societies*, ed. B. Smuts, 54–68. Chicago: University of Chicago Press.

Cronin, J. E. 1983. Apes, humans, and molecular clocks. In *New interpretations of ape and human ancestry*, eds. R. L. Ciochon and R. S. Corruccini, 115–137. New York: Plenum.

Cronk, L. 1999. *That complex whole: Culture and the evolution of human behavior.* Boulder, CO: Westview Press.

Culotta, E. 1995. New finds rekindle debate over anthropoid origins. *Science* 268:1851.

———. 1999. A new human ancestor. *Science* 284:572–573.

Cyphers, A. 1996. Reconstructing Olmec life at San Lorenzo. In *Olmec of ancient Mexico*, eds. E. P. Benson and B. de la Fuente, 61–71. Washington, DC: National Gallery of Art/Abrams.

———. 1997. Olmec architecture at San Lorenzo. In *Olmec to Aztec: Settlement patterns in the Ancient Gulf lowlands*, eds. B. L. Stark and P. J. Arnold III, 96–114. Tucson: University of Arizona Press.

Cyranoski, D. 2002. Almost human. *Nature* 418:910–912.

Daeschler, E. B., N. H. Shubin, K. S. Thomson, and W. W. Amaral. 1994. Devonian tetrapod from North America. *Science* 265:639–642.

Dales, F. G. 1991. The phenomenon of the Indus civilization. In *Forgotten cities on the Indus*, eds. M. Jansen, M. Mulloy, and G. Urban, 129–144. Mainz: Verlag Philipp von Zabern.

D'Altroy, T. N. 2002. *The Incas.* Malden, MA: Blackwell.

Dancey, W. S. 2005. The enigmatic Hopewell of the Eastern Woodlands. In *North American archaeology*, eds. T. R. Pauketat and D. DiPaolo Loren, 108–137. Malden, MA: Blackwell Publishing.

Dart, R. 1925. *Australopithecus africanus:* The man-ape of South Africa. *Nature* 115:195–199.

Davies, W., J. Stewart, and T. H. van Andel. 2000. Neandertal landscapes: A preview. In *Neanderthals on the edge*, eds. C. B. Stringer, R. N. E. Barton, and J. C. Finlayson, 1–8. Oxford: Oxbow.

Davis, S. J. 2002. *The archaeology of animals.* London: B. T. Batsford.

Dawkins, R. 1994. *The blind watchmaker.* New York: Norton.

Deacon, H. J. 1989. Late Pleistocene palaeoecology and archaeology in the Southern Cape, South Africa. In *The human revolution*, eds. P. Mellars and C. Stringer, 547–564. Edinburgh: Edinburgh University Press.

Deacon, H. J., and J. Deacon. 1999. *Human beginnings in South Africa.* Walnut Creek, CA: Altamira Press.

Deacon, J. 1990. Changes in the archaeological record in South Africa at 18,000 BP. In *Low latitudes*, eds. C. Gamble and O. Soffer, 170–188. Vol. 2 of *The world at 18,000 BP.* London: Unwin Hyman.

Dean, C., and E. Delson. 1995. *Homo* at the gates of Europe. *Nature* 373:472–473.

Defleur, A., T. White, P. Valensi, et al. 1999. Neanderthal cannibalism at Moula-Guercy, Ardèche, France. *Science* 286 (5437): 128–131.

DeGusta, D. W., W. H. Gilbert, and S. P. Turner. 1999. Hypoglossal canal size and hominid speech. *Proceedings of the National Academy of Sciences USA* 96:1800–1804.

de Heinzelin, J., J. Desmond Clark, T. White, et al. 1999. Environment and behavior of 2.5 million-year-old Bouri hominids. *Science* 284 (5414): 625–629.

de la Torre, I. 2004. Omo revisited. *Current Anthropology* 45:439–466.

Deloukas, P., G. D. Schuler, G. Gyapay, et al. 1998. A physical map of 30,000 human genes. *Science* 282:744–746.

De Lumley, H. 2006. Il y a 400,000 ans: la domestication du feu, un formidable moteur d'hominisation. *Comptes Rendus Palevol.* 5:149–154.

deLumley, M-A., L. Gabunia, A. Vekua, and D. Lordkapanidze. 2006. Human remains from the Upper Pliocene–Early Pleistocene Dmanisi site, Georgia (1991–2000). Part 1:

The fossil skulls (D 2280, D 2282, and D 2200). *L'Anthropologie* 110:1–110.

d'Errico, F. 2003. The invisible frontier: A multiple species model for the origin of behavioral modernity. *Evolutionary Anthropology* 12:188–292.

d'Errico, F., and M. F. S. Goñi. 2003. Neandertal extinction and the millennial scale climatic variability of O1S3. *Quaternary Science Reviews* 22:769–788.

d'Errico, F., C. Henshilwood, G. Lawson, et al. 2003. Archaeological evidence for the emergence of language, symbolism and music—an alternative, multidisciplinary perspective. *Journal of World Prehistory* 17 (1): 1–70.

Desmond, A., and J. Moore. 1991. *Darwin*. New York: Warner Books.

de Waal, F. B. 1997. *Bonobo: The forgotten ape*. Berkeley: University of California Press.

———. ed. 2001. *Tree of origin: What primate behavior can tell us about human social evolution*. Cambridge, MA: Harvard University Press.

Díaz, B. 1963. *The Conquest of New Spain*. Trans. J. M. Cohen. New York: Penguin.

Dibble, H. 1984. Interpreting typological variation of Middle Paleolithic scrapers: Function, style, or sequence of reduction? *Journal of Field Archaeology* 11:431–436.

Dibble, H., and N. Rolland. 1992. On assemblage variability in the Middle Palaeolithic of western Europe: History, perspectives, and a new synthesis. In *The Middle Paleolithic: Adaptation, behavior, and variability*, eds. H. N. Dibble and P. Mellars, 1–28. Philadelphia: University of Pennsylvania, University Museum Monographs No. 72.

Dickinson, A. 1988. Intentionality in animal conditions. In *Thoughts without language*, ed. L. Weiskranz, 305–325. Oxford: Clarendon Press.

Diehl, R. A. 2000. Olmec archaeology after regional perspectives: An assessment of recent research. In *Olmec art and archaeology in Mesoamerica*, eds. J. E. Clark and M. E. Pye, 19–28. New Haven/London: Yale University Press.

Diehl, R. A., and M. D. Coe. 1996. Olmec archaeology. In *The Olmec world: Ritual and rulership*, ed. J. Guthrie, 11–25. Princeton, NJ: The Art Museum, Princeton University.

Dillehay, T. D. 1999. The late Pleistocene cultures of South America. *Evolutionary Anthropology* 7(6): 206–216.

———. 2000. *The settlement of the Americas*. New York: Basic Books.

———. 2003. Tracking the first Americans. *Nature* 425:23–24.

Dillehay, T. D., and J. Rossen. 2002. Plant food and its implications for the peopling of the New World: A view from South America. In *The first Americans: The Pleistocene colonization of the New World*, ed. N. G. Jablonski, 237–253. San Francisco: California Academy of Sciences, No. 27.

Dixson, E. J. 2000. Human colonization of the Americas: Timing, technology and process. *Quaternary Science Reviews* 20:277–299.

Dobres, M-A., and J. Robb. 2000. Agency in archaeology: Paradigm or platitude. In *Agency in archaeology*, eds. M-A. Dobres and J. Robb, 3–17. New York: Routledge.

Dolhinow, P., and A. Fuentes. 2000. A brief history of primate studies: Nationalities, disciplinary origins, and stages in North American field research. In *Primate encounters: Models of science, gender, and society*, eds. L. Fedigen and S. Strum, 258–269. Chicago: University of Chicago Press.

Domínguez-Rodrigo, M., and R. Barba. 2006. New estimates of toothmarks and percussion mark frequencies at the FLK Zinj site: The carnivore-hominid-carnivore hypothesis falsified. *Journal of Human Evolution* 50 (2): 170–194.

Domínguez-Rodrigo, M., and T. R. Pickering. 2003. Early hominid hunting and scavenging: A zooarcheological review. *Evolutionary Anthropology* 12 (6): 275–282.

Donnan, C. B. 2001. Moche ceramic portraits. *Moche art and archaeology in ancient Peru*, ed. J. Pillsbury, 127–139. Washington, DC: National Gallery of Art/Yale University Press.

———. 2004. *Moche portraits from ancient Peru*. Austin: University of Texas Press.

Donoghue, P. C., and Smith, M. P. 2004. *Telling the evolutionary time: Molecular clocks and the fossil record*. Boca Raton, FL: CRC Press.

Doran, D. M., and A. McNeilage. 1998. Gorilla ecology and behavior. *Evolutionary Anthropology* 6 (4): 120–131.

Doyle, A. C. 1891. Scandal in Bohemia. *The Strand Magazine* (July).

Doyle, G. A., and R. Martin. 1974. *Prosimian biology*. Pittsburgh, PA: University of Pittsburgh Press.

Drewett, P. 1999. *Field archaeology: An introduction*. London: UCL Press.

Duarte, C., J. Mauricio, P. B. Pettitt, et al. 1999. The early Upper Paleolithic human skeleton from the Abrigo don Lagar Velho (Portugal) and modern human emergence in Iberia. *Proceedings of the National Academy of Sciences USA* 96 (13): 7604–7609.

Dumont, D. 1987. *The Eskimos and Aleuts*. London: Thames & Hudson.

Dunbar, R. I. M. 1996. On the evolution of language and kinship. In *The archaeology of human ancestry*, eds. J. Steib and S. Shennan, 381–396. London: Routledge.

———. 2005. *The human story: A new history of mankind's evolution*. London: Faber.

Dunsworth, H., and A. Walker. 2002. Early *Homo*. In *Encyclopedia of evolution*, ed. M. Pagel, 485–489. Oxford: Oxford University Press.

Eckhardt, R. 2000. *Human paleobiology*. Cambridge: Cambridge University Press.

Eldredge, N. 2004. The evolution of life. In *The epic of evolution*, ed. J. B. Miller, 53–59. Upper Saddle River, NJ: Prentice Hall.

El Mahdy, C. 2003. *The pyramid building: Cheops, the man behing the Great Pyramid*. London: Headline Book Publishing.

Elston, R. G. 1986. Prehistory of the Western area. In *Handbook of North American Indians*, vol. 11, ed. W. L. D'Azevedo, 135–148. Washington, DC: Smithsonian Institution.

Enard, W., P. Khaitovich, J. Klose, et al. 2002. Intra- and interspecific variation in primate gene expression patterns. *Science* 296:340–344.

Estrada, A., L. Castellanos, Y. Garcia, et al. 2002. Survey of a black howler monkey, *Alouatta pigra*, population in the

Mayan state of Palenque, Chiapas, Mexico. *Primates* 43 (1): 51–58.

Eswaran, V. 2002. A diffusion wave out of Africa. *Current Anthropology* 43:749–774.

Eswaran, V., H. Harpending, and A. R. Rogers. 2005. Genomics refutes an exclusively African origin of humans. *Journal of Human Evolution* 49 (1): 1–18.

Fagan, B. 2005. *Ancient North America: The archaeology of a continent.* 4th ed. New York: Thames & Hudson.

Falk, D. 2000. *Primate diversity.* New York: Norton.

———. 2004. *Brain dance.* Rev. and expanded edition. Tallahassee: University of Florida Press.

Fash, W. L. 1991. *Scribes, warriors and kings: The city of Copán and the ancient Maya.* London: Thames & Hudson.

Fernandez-Jalvo, Y., J. C. Díez, I. Cáceres, and J. Rosell. 1999. Human cannibalism in the early Pleistocene of Europe (Gran Dolina, Sierra de Atapuerca, Burgos, Spain). *Journal of Human Evolution* 37:591–622.

Ferreras, J. 1997. Faces from the past: First views of early humans from Spain's Pit of Bones. *Archaeology* (May/June): 312–333.

Fiedel, S. J. 1992. *Prehistory of the Americas.* Cambridge: Cambridge University Press.

———. 1999a. Older than we thought: Implications of corrected dates for Paleoindians. *American Antiquity* 64 (1): 95–115.

———. 1999b. Monte Verde revisited: Artifact provenience at Monte Verde: Confusion and contradictions. *Scientific American Discovering Archaeology* (November–December): 1–12.

———. 2000. The peopling of the New World: Present evidence, new theories, and future directions. *Journal of Archaeological Research* 8 (1): 39–103.

———. 2002. Human colonization of the Americas. *Radiocarbon* 44 (2): 407–436.

Flannery, K. V. 1969. Origins and ecological effects of early domestication in Iran and the Near East. In *The domestication and exploitation of plants and animals*, eds. P. J. Ucko and G. W. Dimbleby, 73–100. London: Duckworth.

———. 1972. The cultural evolution of civilization. *Annual Review of Ecology and Systematics.* 3:399–426.

———. 1973. The origins of agriculture. *Annual Review of Anthropology* 2:271–310.

———. 1999. Process and agency in early state formation. *Cambridge Archaeological Journal* 9 (1): 3–21.

Fleagle, J. G. 1988. *Primate adaptation and evolution.* San Diego, CA: Academic Press.

———. 1995. The origin and radiation of anthropoid primates. In *Biological anthropology: The state of the science*, eds. N. T. Boas and L. D. Wolfe, 1–21. Bend, OR: International Institute of Human Evolutionary Research.

———. 2002. The primate fossil record. *Evolutionary Anthropology* 11 (Supplement 1): 20–23.

Foley, R., and M. Lahr. 1997. Mode 3 technologies and the evolution of modern humans. *Cambridge Archaeology Journal* 7 (1): 3–36.

Foley, R. A. 1987. *Another unique species: Patterns in human evolutionary ecology.* New York: Wiley.

———. 1991. How many species of hominid should there be? *Journal of Human Evolution* 20 (5): 413–427.

———. 1992. Evolutionary ecology of fossil hominids. In *Evolutionary ecology and human behavior*, eds. E. A. Smith and B. Winterhadter, 131–164. New York: Aldine de Gruyter.

———. 1996. An evolutionary and chronological framework for human social behavior. In *Evolution of social behaviour patterns in primates and man*, eds. W. G. Runciman, J. M. Smith, and R. I. M. Dunbar, 95–117. New York: Oxford University Press.

———. 1999. Hominid behavioral evolution: Missing links in comparative primate sociology. In *Comparative primate socioecology*, ed. P. E. Lee, 363–386. Cambridge: Cambridge University Press.

———. 2001. The evolutionary consequences of increased carnivory in hominids. In *Meat eating and human evolution*, eds. C. Stanford and H. T. Bunn, 305–331. Oxford: Oxford University Press.

Fowler, B. 2000. *Iceman.* New York: Random House.

Franciscus, R. 2002. Neandertals. In *Encyclopedia of evolution*, ed. M. Pagel, 493–497. Oxford: Oxford University Press.

Franciscus, R., and E. Trinkaus. 1995. Determinants of retromolar space presence in Pleistocene *Homo* mandibles. *Journal of Human Evolution* 28:577–595.

Frayer, D. 1992a. Evolution at the European edge: Neandertal and Upper Paleolithic relationships. *European Prehistory* 2:9–49.

———. 1992b. The persistence of Neandertal features in post-Neandertal Europeans. In *Continuity or replacement*, eds. G. Brauer and F. Smith, 179–208. Rotterdam: A. A. Balkema.

Frayer, D. W., M. H. Wolpoff, A. G. Thorne, et al. 1993. Theories of modern human origins: The paleontological test. *American Anthropologist* 95 (1): 14–55.

Fremlin, J. [alias Jehn Fremlen]. 1975. The demese ef the Ne'enderthels: Wes lengege e fecter? *Science* 187:600.

Friedman, I., F. W. Trembour, and R. E. Hughes. 1997. Obsidian hydration dating. In *Chronometric dating in archaeology*, eds. R. E. Taylor and M. J. Aitken, 297–322. New York: Plenum.

Frisancho, A. R. 1993. *Human adaptation and accommodation.* Ann Arbor: University of Michigan Press.

Frison, G. C. 1999. The late Pleistocene prehistory of the northwestern plains, the adjacent mountains, and intermontane basin. In *Ice Age people of North America: Environments, origins, and adaptations*, eds. R. Bonnichsen and K. L. Turnmire, 264–280. Corvallis: Oregon State University Press.

Fujiyama, A., W. Watanabe, A. Toyoda, et al. 2002. Constriction and analysis of a human–chimpanzee comparative clone map. *Science* 295:2002.

Futuyma, D. J. 2005. *Evolution.* Sunderland, MA: Sinauer Associates.

Gabunia, L., and A. Vekua. 1995. A Plio-Pleistocene hominid from Dmanisi, east Georgia, Caucasus. *Nature* 373: 509–512.

———. 2001. Dmanisi and dispersal. *Evolutionary Anthropology* 10 (5): 158–170.

Gabunia, L., A. Vekua, D. Lordkipanidze, et al. 2000. Earliest Pleistocene hominid cranial remains from Dmanisi, Republic of Georgia: Taxonomy, geological setting, and age. *Science* 288:1019–1025.

Gallup, G. G., Jr. 1977. Self-recognition in primates: A comparative approach to the biodirectional properties of consciousness. *American Psychologist* 32:329–338.

Gamble, C. 1999. *The Palaeolithic societies of Europe*. Cambridge: Cambridge University Press.

Garfinkel, Y., M. E. Kislev, and D. Zohary. 1988. Lentils in the pre-pottery Neolithic B at Yiftah'el: Additional evidence of its early domestication. *Israel Journal of Botany* 37:49–51.

Garrard, A. 1999. Charting the emergence of cereal and pulse domestication in south-west Asia. *Environmental Archaeology* 4:67–86.

Gebo, D. L., L. MacLatchy, R. Kityo, et al. 1997. A hominoid genus from the early Miocene of Uganda. *Science* 276: 401–404.

Gee, H. 2000. *In search of deep time: Beyond the fossil record to a new history of life*. New York: Free Press.

Gibbon, G., ed. 1998. *Archaeology of prehistoric Native America: An encyclopedia*. New York/London: Garland.

Gibbons, A. 2001a. The riddle of coexistence. *Science* 291:1725–1729.

———. 2001b. Studying humans—all their cousins and parents. *Science* 292:627–629.

———. 2007. Spear-wielding chimps seen hunting bush babies. *Science* 315:1063.

Gibson, J. 1994. Empirical characterization of exchange systems in Lower Mississippi Valley prehistory. In *Prehistoric exchange systems in North America*, eds. T. G. Baugh and J. E. Ericson, 127–175. New York/London: Plenum.

———. 1996. Poverty Point and greater southeastern prehistory. In *Archaeology of the mid-Holocene Southeast*, eds. K. Sassaman and D. Anderson, 288–305. Gainesville: University of Florida Press.

Gilead, I. 1995. The foragers of the Upper Paleolithic period. In *The archaeology of society in the Holy Land*, ed. T. Levy, 124–140. New York: Facts on File.

Gillespie, R. 2002. Dating the first Australians. *Radiocarbon* 44 (2): 455–472.

Gingerich, P. D. 1984. Punctuated equilibrium—where is the evidence? *Systematic Zoology* 33 (3): 335–338.

Gkiasta, M., T. Russell, S. Shennan, and J. Steele. 2003. Neolithic transition in Europe: The radiocarbon record revisited. *Antiquity* 77 (295): 45–62.

Gladkih, N. L., N. L. Komietz, and O. Soffer. 1984. Mammoth bone dwellings on the Russian plain. *Scientific American* 251 (5): 136–143.

Glassow, M. 2005. Prehistoric dolphin hunting on Santa Cruz Island, California. In *The exploitation and cultural importance of sea mammals*, ed. G. G. Monks, 107–120. Oxford: Oxbow Books.

Goldberg, P., and T. L. Arpin. 1999. Analysis of sediments from Meadowcroft Rockshelter, Pennsylvania: Implications for radiocarbon dating. *Journal of Field Archaeology* 26:325–342.

Gonzalez, D., M. R. Bennett, and A. Gonzalez-Huesca. 2006. Human footprints in central Mexico older than 40 thousand years. *Quaternary Science Reviews* 25:201–222.

González Lauck, R. 1996. La Venta: An Olmec capital. In *Olmec of ancient Mexico*, eds. E. P. Benson and B. de la Fuente, 73–81. Washington, DC: National Gallery of Art/Abrams.

Goodall, J. 1965. Chimpanzees of the Gombe Stream Reserve. In *Primate behavior*, ed. I. DeVore, 425–473. New York: Holt, Rinehart, & Winston.

———. 1988. *In the shadow of man*. Boston: Houghton Mifflin.

———. 1990. *Through a window: My thirty years with the chimpanzees of Gombe*. Boston: Houghton Mifflin.

Goodman, M. 1999. The genomic record of humankind's evolutionary roots. *American Journal of Human Genetics* 64:31–39.

Goodman, M., M. L. Baba, and L. L. Darga. 1983. The bearing of molecular data on the cladogenesis and times of divergence of hominoid lineages. In *New interpretations of ape and human ancestry*, eds. R. L. Ciochon and R. S. Corruccini, 67–86. New York: Plenum.

Goodman, M., J. Czelusniak, S. Page, and C. M. Meireles. 2001. A phylogenetic classification of primates from DNA sequences. In *Humanity from African naissance to coming millennia*, ed. P. Tobias. Florence: University of Florence Press.

Goodman, M., C. A. Porter, J. Czelusniak, et al. 1998. Toward a phylogenetic classification of primates based on DNA evidence complemented by fossil evidence. *Molecular Phylogenetics and Evolution* 9 (3): 585–598.

Goren-Inbar, N., G. Sharon, Y. Melamed, and M. Kislev. 2002. Nuts, nut cracking, and pitted stones at Gesher Benot Ya'aqov, Israel. *Proceedings of the National Academy of Sciences USA* 99 (4): 2455–2460.

Gould, S. J. 1987a. *Evolution and human equality*. Cambridge, MA: Insight Video.

———. 1987b. *Time's arrow, time's cycle*. Cambridge, MA: Harvard University Press.

———. 1989. *Wonderful life: The Burgess Shale and the nature of history*. New York: Norton.

———. 1995. Of it, not above it. *Nature* 377:681–682.

———. 2000. What does the dreaded "e" word mean, anyway? *Natural History* (February): 28–44.

———. 2001. *Rocks of ages*. London: Jonathan Cape.

———. 2002. Macroevolution. In *Encyclopedia of evolution*, ed. M. Pagel, E-23–28. Oxford: Oxford University Press.

Gould, S. J., and N. Eldredge. 1977. Punctuated equilibria: The tempo and mode of evolution reconsidered. *Paleobiology* 3:115–151.

Gowlett, J. A. J. 1992. *Ascent to civilization*. 2nd ed. London: McGraw-Hill.

———. 2006. The early settlement of northern Europe: Fire history in the context of climate change and the social brain. *Comptes Rendus Palevol* 5:299–310.

Graham, E. 1992. The ancient Aztecs. In *Odyssey through the ages*, eds. N. Garfield and C. De Geer, 396–426. Toronto: McGraw-Hill Ryerson.

Graham-Rowe, D. 2004. No bonobos to be seen in the wild. *New Scientist* (December 11): 6–7.

Grant, P. R. 1986. *Ecology and evolution of Darwin's finches*. Princeton, NJ: Princeton University Press.

Grant, P. R., and B. R. Grant. 2002. Adaptive radiation of Darwin's finches. *American Scientist* 90 (2): 130–139.

Grant, V. 1991. *The evolutionary process: A critical study of evolutionary theory*. 2nd ed. New York: Columbia University Press.

Graslund, B. 2005. *Early humans and their world*. New York: Routledge.

Grayson, D. K., and D. J. Meltzer. 2003. A requiem for North American overkill. *Journal of Archaeological Science* 30:585–593.

Greenberg, J. H. 1996. Beringia and New World origins: The linguistic evidence. In *American beginnings: The prehistory and palaeoecology of Beringia*, ed. F. Hadleigh West, 525–536. Chicago: University of Chicago Press.

Grey, J. P., and L. D. Wolfe. 2002. What accounts for population variation in height? In *Physical anthropology: Original readings in method and practice*, eds. P. N. Peregrine, C. A. Ember, and M. Ember, 204–218. Upper Saddle River, NJ: Prentice Hall.

Groves, C. 1997. Species concept in paleoanthropology. In *Perspectives in human biology*, vol. 3, *Human adaptability: Future trends and lessons from the past*, eds. C. Oxnard and L. Freedman. Singapore: World Scientific.

———. 1998. Systematics of tarsiers and lorises. *Primates* 39 (1): 13–27.

———. 2001. Towards a taxonomy of the hominidae. In *Humanity from African naissance to coming millennia*, ed. P. Tobias. Florence: University of Florence Press.

———. 2004. The what, why and how of primate taxonomy. *International Journal of Primatology* 25 (5): 1105–1126.

Gunnell, G. F., and K. D. Rose. 2002. Tarsiiformes: Evolutionary history and adaptation. In *The primate fossil record*, ed. W. Hartwig. Cambridge: Cambridge University Press.

Gursky, S. 2002. The behavioral ecology of the spectral tarsiers, *Tarsius spectrum*. *Evolutionary Anthropology* 11:226–234.

———. 2003. Territoriality in the spectral tarsier, *Tarsius spectrum*. In *Tarsiers*, eds. P. C. Wright, E. L. Simons, and S. Gursky, 221–236. New Brunswick, NJ: Rutgers University Press.

———. 2007. Tarsiers. In *Primates in perspective*, eds. C. J. Campbell, A. Fuentes, K. MacKinnon, et al., 73–85. New York: Oxford University Press.

Gutierrez, G., D. Sanchez, and A. Marin. 2000. A reanalysis of the ancient mtDNA sequences removed from Neandertal bones. *Molecular Biology and Evolution* 19:1359–1366.

Haak, W., P. Forster, B. Bramanti, et al. 2005. First European farmers in 7,500-year-old Neolithic sites. *Science* 310:1016–1018.

Haaland, R. 1995. Sedentism, cultivation, and plant domestication in the Holocene middle Nile region. *Journal of Field Archaeology* 22 (2): 157–173.

Habu, J. 1996. Jomon sedentism and intersite variability: Collectors of the early Jomon Moroiso phase in Japan. *Arctic Anthropology* 33 (2): 38–49.

Habu, J., and M. E. Hall. 1999. Jomon pottery production in central Japan. *Asian Perspectives* 38 (1): 90–110.

Hagelberg, E., S. Quevedo, D. Turbon, and J. B. Clegg. 1994. DNA from ancient Easter Islanders. *Nature* 369:25–26.

Hamilton, G. 2005. Mother superior. *New Scientist* (September 3): 26–27.

Harding, J. 1998. An architecture of meaning: The causewayed enclosures and henges of lowland England. In *Understanding the Neolithic of northwest Europe*, eds. M. Edmonds and C. Richards, 204–230. Glasgow: Cruithne Press.

Hardy, B. L., M. Kay, A. E. Marks, and K. Minigal. 2001. Stone tool function at the Paleolithic sites of Starosele and Buran Kaya III, Crimea: Behavioral implications. *Proceedings of the National Academy of Sciences, USA* 98 (19): 10927–10977.

Hare, P. E., D. W. Von Endt, and J. F. Kokis. 1997. Protein and amino acid diagenesis dating. In *Chronometric dating in Archaeology*, eds. R. E. Taylor and M. J. Aitken, 261–296.

Harlan, J. R. 1993. The tropical African cereals. In *The archaeology of Africa: Metals and towns*, eds. T. Shaw, P. Sinclair, B. Andah, and A. Okpoko. London and New York: Routledge.

Harren, M., and M.-C. King. 2002. The use of DNA in the identification of postmortem remains. In *Advances in forensic taphonomy*, eds. W. D. Waglund and M. H. Sorg, 473–486. Boca Raton, FL: CRC Press.

Harris, C. L. 1981. *Evolution: Genesis and revelations*. Albany: State University of New York Press.

Harris, E. 1979. *Principles of archaeological stratigraphy*. New York: Academic Press.

Harrison, P. T. 1999. *The lords of Tikal: Rulers of an ancient Maya city*. London: Thames & Hudson.

Hartwig, W. 2007. Primate evolution. In *Primates in perspective*, eds. C. J. Campbell, A. Fuentes, K. MacKinnon, et al., 11–22. New York: Oxford University Press.

Hassan, F. A. 1997. Egypt: Emergence of state society. In *Encyclopedia of precolonial Africa*, ed. J. O. Vogel, 473–479. Walnut Creek, CA: Altamira Press.

———. 2000. Climate and cattle in North Africa. In *The origins and development of African livestock: Archaeology, genetics, linguistics and ethnography*, eds. R. M. Blench and K. C. MacDonald. London: UCL Press.

Hawass, Z. 1997. The pyramids. In *Ancient Egypt*, ed. D. Silverman, 168–191. New York: Oxford University Press.

Hayden, B. 1992. Models of domestication. In *Transitions to agriculture in prehistory*, eds. A. B. Gebauer and T. D. Price. Madison, WI: Prehistory Press.

Hecht, J. 2003. Only four ancestral mammals survived the perilous journey to Madagascar. *New Scientist* (February 15): 14.

———. 2006. Why doesn't America believe in evolution? *New Scientist* (August 19): 11.

Hegmon, M. 2005. Beyond the mold: Questions of inequality in southwest villages. In *North American archaeology*, eds. T. R. Pauketat and D. DiPaolo Loren, 212–234. Malden, MA: Blackwell.

Hemphill, B. E., and C. S. Larsen. 1999. Bioarchaeological perspectives on precontact lifeways in the Great Basin wetlands. In *Prehistoric lifeways in the Great Basin wetlands: Bioarchaeological reconstruction and interpretation*, eds. B. E. Hemphill and C. S. Larsen, 1–7. Salt Lake City: University of Utah Press.

Henderson, J. S. 1997. *The world of the ancient Maya*. London: Murray.

Henneberg, M. 1988. Decrease of human skull size in the Holocene. *Human Biology* 60:395–405.

———. 1997. The problem of species. In *Perspectives in human biology*, vol. 3, *Human adaptability: Future trends and lessons from the past*, eds. C. Oxnard and L. Freedman. Singapore: World Scientific.

Henshilwood, C. S., F. d'Errico, R. Yates, et al. 2002. Emergence of modern human behavior: Middle Stone Age engravings from South Africa. *Science* 295 (5558): 1278–1280.

Henshilwood, C. S., and C. W. Marean. 2003. The origin of modern human behavior. *Current Anthropology* 44 (5): 627–651.

Henshilwood, C. S., J. C. Sealy, K. Cruz-Uribe, et al. 2001. Blombos Cave, southern Cape, South Africa: Preliminary report on the 1992–1999 excavations of the Middle Stone Age levels. *Journal of Archaeological Science* 28:421–448.

Hewes, G. W. 1964. Hominid behaviorism: Independent evidence for food carrying theory. *Science* 146:416–418.

Higham, C. 1996. A review of archaeology in mainland Southeast Asia. *Journal of Archaeological Research* 4 (1): 3–49.

Higham, C., and T. Lu. 1998. The origins and dispersal of rice cultivation. *Antiquity* 72:867–877.

Hinde, R. A. 1986. Can nonhuman primates help us understand human behavior? In *Primate societies*, ed. B. Smuts. Chicago: University of Chicago Press.

Hiraguchi, T. 1992. Catching dolphins at the Mawaki site, central Japan, and its contribution to Jomon society. In *Pacific northeast Asia in prehistory*, eds. M. Aikens and S. Rhee. Seattle: Washington State University Press.

Hodder, I. 1991. *Reading the past: Current approaches to interpretation in archaeology*. New York: Cambridge University Press.

———. 2003. *Archaeology beyond dialogue*. Salt Lake City: University of Utah Press.

———. 2005. The spatio-temporal organization of the early "town" at Çatalhöyük. In *(un)settling the Neolithic*, eds. D. Bailey, A. Whittle, and V. Cummings, 126–139. Oxford: Oxbow Books.

———. 2006. *Çatalhöyük the leopard's tale*. London: Thames & Hudson.

Hodder, I., and C. Cessford. 2004. Daily practice and social memory at Çatalhöyük. *American Antiquity* 69 (1): 17–40.

Hodder, I., and R. Matthews. 1998. Çatalhöyük: The 1990s seasons. In *Ancient Anatolia: Fifty years' work by the British Institute of Archaeology at Ankara*, ed. R. Matthews, 43–51. Ankara: British Institute of Archaeology.

Hoffecker, J. F., and S. A. Elias. 2003. Environment and archeology in Beringia. *Evolutionary Anthropology* 12:34–49.

Horodyski, R., and L. P. Knath. 1994. Life on land in the pre-Cambrian. *Science* 263:494–498.

Hovers, E., S. Ilani, O. Bar-Yosef, and B. Vandermeersch. 2003. An early case of symbolism. *Current Anthropology* 44 (4): 491–522.

Howard, A. V. 1993. Marine shell artifacts and production processes at Shelltown and the Hind site. In *Shelltown and the Hind site: A study of two Hohokam craftsman communities in southwestern Arizona*, eds. W. S. Marmaduke and R. J. Martynec, 321–423. Flagstaff, AZ: Northland Research.

Hrdy, S. B., C. Janson, and C. Van Schaik. 1994/1995. Infanticide: Let's not throw out the baby with the bath water. *Evolutionary Anthropology* 3 (5): 151–154.

Hummel, S. 2003. *Ancient DNA typing: Methods, strategies, and applications*. Berlin: Springer.

Hunter, J., C. Roberts, and A. Martin. 1996. *Studies in crime: An introduction to forensic archaeology*. London: B. T. Batsford.

Huxley, L. 1901. *Life and letters of Thomas Henry Huxley*. New York: Appleton.

Imamura, K. 1996. *Prehistoric Japan: New perspectives on insular East Asia*. London: UCL Press.

Ingman, M., H. Kaessmann, S. Pääbo, et al. 2000. Mitochrondrial genome variation and the origin of modern humans. *Nature* 408:708–712.

Ingstad, A. S. 1985. *The Norse discovery of America*. Oslo: Norwegian University Press.

Isaac, G. 1978. The food-sharing behavior of protohuman hominids. *Scientific American* 238 (4): 56–69.

———. 1984. The archaeology of human origins: Studies of the Lower Pleistocene in East Africa 1971–1981. *Advances in World Archaeology* 3:1–87.

Isbell, W. H., and A. Vranich. 2004. The cities of Wari and Tiwanaku. In *Andean archaeology*, ed. H. Silverman, 167–182. Malden, MA: Blackwell Publishing.

Jablonski, N., and G. Chaplin. 2000. The evolution of human skin coloration. *Journal of Human Evolution* 39:57–106.

Jablonski, N. G. 2002. Fossil Old World monkeys: The Late Neogene radiation. In *The primate fossil record*, ed. W. Hartwig, 255–299. Cambridge: Cambridge University Press.

Jacob, F., and J. Monod. 1961. Genetic regularity mechanisms in the synthesis of protein. *Journal of Molecular Biology* 3:316–356.

James, S. R. 1989. Hominid use of fire in the Lower and Middle Pleistocene. *Current Anthropology* 30 (1): 1–26.

Jansen, M. 1991. Mohenjo-Daro—a city on the Indus. In *Forgotten cities on the Indus*, eds. M. Jansen, M. Mulloy, and G. Urban, 145–165. Mainz: Verlag Philipp von Zabern.

Jefferies, R. W., and B. M. Lynch. 1983. Dimensions of middle Archaic cultural adaptation at the Black Earth site, Saline County, Illinois. In *Archaic hunters and gatherers in the American Midwest*, eds. J. L. Phillips and J. A. Brown, 299–322. New York: Academic Press.

Jenkins, M. 2003. Prospects for biodiversity. *Science* 302:1175–1176.

Jennings, J. D. 1957. *Danger Cave*. Salt Lake City: University of Utah Press.

———. 1989. *Prehistory of North America*. 3rd ed. Mountain View, CA: Mayfield.

Jiang, L., and Liu, L. 2006. New evidence for the origins of sedentism and rice domestication in the Lower Yangzi River, China. *Antiquity* 80:355–361.

Jobling, M. A., M. E. Hurles, and C. Tyler Smith. 2004. *Human evolutionary genetics*. New York: Garland Science.

Johanson, D., and M. A. Edey. 1981. *Lucy: The beginnings of humankind*. New York: Simon & Schuster.

Johnson, B. J., & Miller, G. H. 1997. Archaeological applications of amino acid racemization. *Archaeometry* 39 (2): 265–287.

Johnson, M. 2000. *Archaeological theory: An introduction.* Malden, MA: Blackstone.

Jolly, A. 1966. *Lemur behavior: A Madagascar field study.* Urbana, IL: University of Chicago Press.

Jones, C. 1991. Cycles of growth at Tikal. In *Classic Maya political history: Hieroglyphic and archaeological evidence*, ed. T. P. Culbert, 102–127. Cambridge: Cambridge University Press.

Jones, M. 2001. *The molecule hunt.* New York: Penguin.

Jones, P. 1980. Experimental butchery with modern stone tools and its relevance for Palaeolithic archaeology. *World Archaeology* 12 (2): 153–165.

Jones, S. 1994. *The language of genes.* New York: Doubleday.

———. 2000. *The language of the genes: Biology, history, and the evolutionary future.* London: Flamingo.

———. 2003. *Y: The descent of men.* Boston: Houghton Mifflin.

Jones, T. L. 1996. Mortars, pestles, and the division of labor in prehistoric California: A view from Big Sur. *American Antiquity* 61 (2): 243–264.

Jurmain, R., et al. 2003. *Introduction to physical anthropology*, 9th ed. Belmont, CA: Wadsworth.

Kappeler, P. 2000. Lemur origins: Rafting by groups of hibernators? *Folia Primatologica* 71:422–425.

Kardong, K. V. 2005. *An introduction to biological evolution.* New York: McGraw Hill.

Karlin, C. 1992. Analyse d'un processus technique: Le débitage laminaire des Magdaleniens de Pincevent (Seine et Marne). *Tecnologia y cadenas operativas liticas. Reunion internacional U.A.B. 1578 enero 1991*, eds. R. Mora, X. Terradas, A. Parpal, and C. Plana, 125–161. Bellaterra, Spain: Universitat Autonoma de Barcelona.

Kaufman, D. 1999. *Archaeological perspectives on the origin of modern humans: A view from the Levant.* Westport, CT: Bergin & Garvey.

———. 2002. Reevaluating subsistence skills of Levantine Middle and Upper Paleolithic hunters: A comparison of the faunal assemblages. *Oxford Journal of Archaeology* 21 (3): 217–229.

Kay, R. F., M. Cartmill, and M. Barlow. 1998. The hypoglossal canal and the origin of human vocal behavior. *Proceedings of the National Academy of Sciences USA* 95:5417–5419.

Keeley, L. H. 1991. Ethnographic models for Late Glacial hunter-gatherers. In *The Late Glacial in north-west Europe*, eds. N. Barton, A. J. Roberts, and D. A. Roe, 179–190. Council for British Archaeology, Report 77.

Kehoe, A. B. 1992. *North American Indians: A comprehensive account.* 2nd ed. Englewood Cliffs, NJ: Prentice Hall.

Kelly, R. L. 1995. *The foraging spectrum.* Washington, DC: Smithsonian Institution.

Kemp, T. S. 1999. *Fossils and evolution.* Oxford: Oxford University Press.

Kennedy, K. 2001. Middle and late Pleistocene hominids of South Asia. In *Humanity from African naissance to coming millennia*, ed. P. Tobias, 167–173. Florence: University of Florence Press.

———. 2003. Trials in court: The forensic anthropologist takes the stand. In *Hard evidence: Case studies in forensic anthropology*, ed. D. W. Steadman, 77–86. Upper Saddle River, NJ: Prentice Hall.

Kenoyer, J. M. 1998. *Ancient cities of the Indus Valley civilization.* Karachi/New York/Delhi: Oxford University Press.

Kenyon, K. M. 1957. *Digging up Jericho.* London: Ernest Benn Limited.

Kerr, R. A. 2000. Stretching the reign of early animals. *Science* 288:789.

Kessler, D. 1998. The political history of the third to eighth dynasties. In *Egypt: The world of the pharaohs*, eds. R. Schulz and M. Seidel, 40–45. Cologne: Könemann.

Killan, E. W. 1990. *The detection of human remains.* Springfield, IL: Charles Thomas.

Kimbel, W. H., D. Johanson, and Y. Rak. 1994. The first skull and other new discoveries of *Australopithecus afarensis* at Hadar, Ethiopia. *Nature* 368:449–451.

Kimbel, W. H., and L. B. Martin. 1993. Species and speciation: Conceptual issues and their relevance for primate evolutionary biology. In *Species, species concepts, and primate evolution*, eds. W. H. Kimbel and L. B. Martin, 299–330. New York: Plenum.

Kimbel, W. H., Y. Rak, and D. C. Johanson. 2004. *The skull of A. afarensis.* Oxford: Oxford University Press.

King, M. C., and A. C. Wilson. 1975. Evolution at two levels in humans and chimpanzees. *Science* 188:107–116.

Kinzey, W. G. 1997. *New World primates: Ecology, evolution, and behavior.* New York: Aldine de Gruyter.

Klein, J., and N. Takahata. 2002. *Where do we come from: The molecular evidence for human descent.* Berlin: Springer.

Klein, R. G. 1989a. *The human career: Human biological and cultural origins.* Chicago: University of Chicago Press.

———. 1989b. Perspectives on modern human origins in southern Africa. In *The human revolution*, eds. P. Mellars and C. Stringer, 529–546. Edinburgh: Edinburgh University Press.

———. 1999. *The human career: Human biological and cultural origins.* 2nd ed. Chicago: University of Chicago Press.

———. 2000. Archaeology and the evolution of human behavior. *Evolutionary Anthropology* 9 (1): 17–36.

Klima, B. 1988. A triple burial from the Upper Paleolithic of Dolní Vestonice, Czechoslovakia. *Journal of Human Evolution* 16:833–835.

Knoll, A. H., R. K. Bambach, D. E. Canfield, and J. P. Grotzinger. 1996. Comparative earth history and late Permian extinction. *Science* 273:452–457.

Kobayashi, T. 2004. *Jomon reflections: Forager life and culture in the prehistoric Japanese archipelago.* Oxford: Oxbow Books.

Kohn, M., and S. Mithen. 1999. Handaxes: Products of sexual selection? *Antiquity* 73 (281): 518–525.

Kolata, A. L. 1993. *The Tiwanaku: Portrait of an Andean civilization.* Cambridge, MA/Oxford: Blackwell.

———. 1996. Agroecological perspectives on the decline of the Tiwanaku state. In *Tiwanaku and its hinterland: Archaeology and paleoecology of an Andean civilization*, Vol. 1, *Agroecology*, ed. A. L. Kolata, 181–201. Washington/London: Smithsonian Institution.

———. 2001. Economy, ideology, and imperialism in the south-central Andes. In *Ideology and pre-Columbian civilization*, eds. A. A. Demarests and G. W. Conrad, 65–85. Santa Fe, NM: School of American Research Press.

Kottak, C. 2008. *Anthropology: The exploration of human diversity.* 12th ed. New York: McGraw-Hill.

Kowalski, J. K. 1999. Natural order, social order, political legitimacy, and the sacred city: The architecture of Teotihuacan. In *Mesoamerican architecture as a cultural symbol*, ed. J. K. Kowalski, 77–109. New York/Oxford: Oxford University Press.

Kramer, A. 2002. The natural history and evolutionary fate of *Homo erectus*. In *Physical anthropology: Original readings in method and practice*, eds. P. N. Peregrine, C. R. Ember, and M. Ember, 140–154. Upper Saddle River, NJ: Prentice Hall.

Krawczak, M., and J. Schmidke. 1998. *DNA fingerprints*. 2nd ed. New York: Springer.

Kraytsberg, Y., M. Schwartz, T. A. Brown, et al. 2004. Recombination of human mitochondrial DNA. *Science* 304:981.

Krings, M., C. Capelli, F. Tschentscher, et al. 2000. A view of Neandertal genetic diversity. *Nature Genetics* 26:144–147.

Kuhn, T. 1962. *The structure of scientific revolutions*. Chicago: University of Chicago Press.

Kummer, H. 1968. *Social organization of hamadryas baboons: A field study*. New York: Karger.

Kunzig, R. 1999. Learning to love Neandertal. *Discover* (August): 66–75.

Lahr, M. 1996. *The evolution of modern human diversity: A study of cranial variation*. New York: Cambridge University Press.

Laitman, J. 1985. Evolution of the hominid upper respiratory tract: The fossil evidence. In *Hominid evolution, past, present, and future*, ed. P. Tobias, 281–286. New York: Alan R. Liss.

Langdon, J. H. 2005. *The human strategy*. New York: Oxford University Press.

Larsen, C. S. 1984. Health and disease in prehistoric Georgia: The transition to agriculture. In *Paleopathology at the origins of agriculture*, eds. M. N. Cohen and G. J. Armelagos, 367–392. New York: Academic Press.

———. 1997. *Bioarchaeology: Interpreting behaviour from the human skeleton*. New York: Cambridge University Press.

———. 2006. The agricultural revolution as environmental catastrophe: Implications for health and lifestyle in the Holocene. *Quaternary International* 150:12–20.

Larsen, C. S., and D. L. Hutchinson. 1999. Osteopathology of Carson Desert foragers. In *Prehistoric lifeways in the Great Basin wetlands: Bioarchaeological reconstruction and interpretation*, eds. B. E. Hemphill and C. S. Larsen, 184–202. Salt Lake City: University of Utah Press.

Larsen, C. S., and R. L. Kelly. 1995. Summary and conclusion. In *Bioarchaeology of the Stillwater Marsh: Prehistoric human adaptation in the western Great Basin*, Anthropological Papers, No. 77, eds. C. S. Larsen and R. L. Kelly, 134–137. New York: American Museum of Natural History.

Larsson, L. 1990. The Mesolithic of southern Scandinavia. *Journal of World Prehistory* 4 (3): 257–309.

———. 1995. Man and sea in southern Scandinavia during the late Mesolithic: The role of cemeteries in the view of society. In *Man and the sea in the Mesolithic: Coastal settlement above and below present sea level*, ed. A. Fischer. Oxford: Oxbow.

———. 2003. The Mesolithic of Sweden in retrospective and progressive perspectives. In *Mesolithic on the move: Papers presented at the sixth international conference on the Mesolithic in Europe, Stockholm 2000*, eds. L. Larsson, H. Kindgren, K. Knutsson, et al., xxii–xxxii. Oxford: Oxbow.

Leakey, M. D. 1971. *Olduvai Gorge*, vol. 3, *Excavations in beds I and II, 1960–1963*. Cambridge: Cambridge University Press.

Leakey, M. G., C. S. Feibel, I. McDougall, and A. Walker. 1995. New four-million-year-old hominid species from Kanapoi and Allia Bay, Kenya. *Nature* 376:565–571.

Leakey, M. G., C. S. Feibel, I. McDougall, C. Ward, and A. Walker. 1998. New specimens and confirmation of an early age for *Australopithecus anamensis*. *Nature* 393:62–66.

LeBlanc, S. 1989. Cultural dynamics in the southern Mogollon area. In *Dynamics of Southwest prehistory*, eds. L. S. Cordell and G. J. Gumerman, 179–207. Washington, DC: Smithsonian Institution.

Legge, A. J., and P. A. Rowley-Conwy. 2000. The exploitation of animals. In *Village on the Euphrates: From foraging to farming at Abu Hureyra*, eds. A. M. T. Moore, G. C. Hillman, and A. J. Legge, 423–471. New York: Oxford University Press.

Lehner, M. 1997. *The complete pyramids*. London: Thames & Hudson.

Lekson, S. H. 2002. War in the Southwest, war in the world. *American Antiquity* 67 (4): 607–624.

———. 2005. Chaco and Paquimé: Complexity, history, landscape. In *North American Archaeology*, eds. T. R. Pauketat and D. DiPaolo Loren, 235–272. Malden, MA: Blackwell Publishing.

Lemonick, M. D., and A. Dorfman. 2006. Who were the first Americans? *Time* (March 13): 45–52.

Leonard, W. R. 2002. *Human nutritional ecology and evolution*. Boulder, CO: Westview.

Lewin, R. A. 1994. Human origins: The challenge of Java's skull. *New Scientist* 142:36–40.

———. 2001. Why rename things? *Nature* 410: 637.

Lewin, R. A., and R. Foley. 2004. *Principles of human evolution*. London: Blackwell Publishing.

Lewis, R. 2005. *Human genetics*. 6th ed. Upper Saddle River, NJ: Prentice Hall.

Lewis-Williams, J. D. 1997. Harnessing the brain: Vision and shamanism in the Upper Paleolithic western Europe. In *Beyond art: Pleistocene image and symbol*, eds. M. Conkey, O. Soffer, D. Stratman, and N. Jablonski, 321–341. Sacramento: California Academy of Sciences.

———. 2002. *The mind in the cave*. London: Thames & Hudson.

Lidén, K., G. Eriksson, B. Nordqvist, et al. 2004. The wet and wild followed by the dry and the tame—or did they occur at the same time? Diet in Mesolithic-Neolithic southern Sweden. *Antiquity* 78:23–33.

Lieberman, L., and P. Rice. 1997. Races or clines? In *General anthropology division modules in teaching anthropology*. Arlington, VA: American Anthropological Association.

Lindon, E. 2002. The wife beaters of Kibale. *Time* (August 19): 56.

Liu, L. 1996. Settlement patterns, chiefdom variability, and the development of early states in north China. *Journal of Anthropological Archaeology* (15): 237–288.

———. 2004. *The Chinese Neolithic: Trajectories to early states*. New York: Cambridge University Press.

Liu, L., and X. Chen. 2003. *State formation in early China*. London: Duckworth.

———. 2006. Sociopolitical change from Neolithic to Bronze Age China. In *Archaeology of Asia*, ed. M. T. Stark, 148–176. Malden, MA: Blackwell Publishing.

Liu, W., Y. Zhang, and X. Wa. 2005. Middle Pleistocene human cranium from Tangshan (Nanjing), southeast China: A new reconstruction and comparison with *H. erectus* from Eurasia and Africa. *American Journal of Physical Anthropology* 127:253–262.

Livingstone, F. 1964. On the non-existence of human races. In *The concept of race*, ed. A. Montagu, 46–60. New York: Collier.

Lock, G., and T. Harris. 1992. Visualizing spatial data: The importance of Geographic Information Systems. In *Archaeology and the Information Age*, eds. P. Reilly and S. Rahtz, 81–96. New York: Routledge.

Lockwood, C., W. Kimbel, and D. Johanson. 2000. Temporal trends and metric variation in the mandibles and dentition of *A. afarensis*. *Journal of Human Evolution* 39 (1): 23–56.

Lontcho, F. 2000. Georgian *Homo erectus* crania. *Archaeology* (January–February): 2.

Lordkipanidze, D. 1999. Early humans at the gates of Europe. *Evolutionary Anthropology* 8 (1): 4–5.

Lovejoy, C. O., R. S. Meindl, J. C. Ohman, et al. 2002. The Maka femur and its bearing on the antiquity of human walking: Applying contemporary concepts of morphogenesis to the human fossil record. *American Journal of Physical Anthropology* 119:97–133.

Lowe, J. J. 2001. Quaternary geochronological frameworks. In *Handbook of archaeological science*, eds. D. Brothwell and A. M. Pollard, 9–21. New York: Wiley.

Lowe, J. J., and M. J. C. Walker. 1997. *Reconstructing Quaternary environments*. 2nd ed. Harlow, UK: Longman.

Lowenstein, J. M. 1992. Genetic surprises. *Discover* 13 (12): 86.

Ludwig, K. P., and P. R. Renne. 2000. Geochronology on the paleoanthropological time scale. *Evolutionary Anthropology* 9 (2): 101–110.

Lyell, C. 1830. *Principles of geology*. London: Murray.

Macaulay, V., C. Hill, A. Achilli, et al. 2005. Single, rapid coastal settlement of Asia revealed by analysis of complete mitochondrial genomes. *Science* 308:1034–1036.

MacDonald, K. C. 2000. The origins of African livestock: Indigenous or imported? In *The origins and development of African livestock: Archaeology, genetics, linguistics and ethnography*, eds. R. M. Blench and K. C. MacDonald. London: UCL Press.

Mace, R. 2005. Introduction: A phylogenetic approach to the evolution of cultural diversity. In *The evolution of cultural diversity*, eds. R. Mace, C. J. Holden, and S. Shennan. London: UCL Press.

MacKenzie, D. 2006. Matching a face to a skull. *New Scientist* (June 3): 26–27.

MacKinnon, J. R. 1974. *In search of the red ape*. New York: Holt, Rinehart, & Winston.

MacLarnon, A., and G. Hewett. 1999. The evolution of human speech: The role of enhanced breathing control. *American Journal of Physical Anthropology* 109:341–363.

Maisels, C. K. 1999. *Early civilizations of the old world: The formative histories of Egypt, Mesopotamia, India, and China*. London/New York: Routledge.

Malek, J. 2000. The Old Kingdom (c. 2686–2160 BC). In *The Oxford history of ancient Egypt*, ed. T. Shaw, 89–117. New York: Oxford University Press.

Malone, C. 1989. *The English heritage book of Avebury*. London: B. T. Batsford.

Mania, D. 1995. The Elbe–Saale region (Germany). In *The earliest occupation of Europe*, eds. W. Roebroeks and T. Van Kolfschoten, 85–101. Leiden: University of Leiden.

Manley, B. 1996. *The Penguin historical atlas of ancient Egypt*. London: Penguin.

Manzanilla, L. 1999. The first urban developments in the central highlands of Mesoamerica. In *The archaeology of Mesoamerica: Mexican and European perspectives*, eds. W. Bray and L. Manzanilla, 13–31. London: British Museum Press.

———. 2001. Teotihuacan. In *The Oxford encyclopedia of Mesoamerican cultures*, vol. 3, ed. J. K. Kowalski, 201–208. Oxford: Oxford University Press.

———. 2002. Houses and ancestors, altars and relics: Mortuary patterns at Teotihuacan, central Mexico. *Archaeological Papers of the American Anthropological Association* 11:56–65.

Manzi, G. 2001. The earliest diffusion of the genus *Homo* toward Asia and Europe. In *Humanity from African naissance to coming millennium*, ed. P. Tobias. Florence: University of Florence Press.

Maple, T. L. 1980. *Orangutan behavior*. New York: Van Nostrand Reinhold.

Maples, W. 1995. *Dead men do tell tales*. New York: Doubleday.

Marean, C.W., and Z. Assefa. 1999. Zooarcheological evidence for the faunal exploitation of Early Modern Humans. *Evolutionary Anthropology* 8:22–37.

Margulis, L., and D. Sagan. 1997. *Microcosmos: Four billion years of evolution from our microbial ancestors*. Berkeley: University of California Press.

Marks, A. E., H. J. Hietala, and J. K. Williams. 2001. Tool standardization in the Middle East and Upper Paleolithic: A closer look. *Cambridge Archaeology Journal* 11 (1): 17–44.

Marks, J. 1995a. *Human biodiversity: Genes, races, and history*. New York: Aldine de Gruyter.

———. 1995b. Learning to live with a trichotomy. *American Journal of Physical Anthropology* 98:211–213.

———. 2000a. 98% alike? What our similarity to apes tells us about our understanding of genetics. *The Chronicle of Higher Education*, May 12.

———. 2000b. *What it means to be 98% chimpanzee*. Berkeley: University of California Press.

———. 2002. Genes, bodies, and species. In *Physical anthropology: Original readings in method and practice*, eds. P. N. Peregrine, C. R. Ember, and M. Ember, 14–28. Upper Saddle River, NJ: Prentice Hall.

Marks, J., and R. B. Lyles. 1994. Rethinking genes. *Evolutionary Anthropology* 4:139–145.

Marlar, R., L. L. Banks, B. R. Billman, et al. 2000. Biochemical evidence of cannibalism at a prehistoric Puebloan site in southwestern Colorado. *Nature* 407:74–78.

Martin, L. 2000–2001. Hunting, herding, feasting: Animal use at Neolithic Çatalhöyük, Turkey. *Archaeology International* 39–42.

Martin, R. D. 1990. *Primate origins and evolution.* Princeton, NJ: Princeton University Press.

———. 2002. Primatology as an essential basis for biological anthropology. *Evolutionary Anthropology* 11 (Supplement 1): 3–6.

Martin, S., and N. Grube. 2000. *Chronicle of the Maya kings and queens: Deciphering the dynasties of the ancient Maya.* London: Thames & Hudson.

Matos Moctezuma, E. 1988. *The Great Temple of the Aztecs.* New York: Thames & Hudson.

———. 1999. The Great Temple of Tenochtitlan: Cosmic center of the Aztec universe. In *Mesoamerican architecture as a cultural symbol,* ed. J. K. Kowalski, 199–219. New York/London: Oxford University Press.

Matson, R. G., and G. Coupland. 1995. *The prehistory of the Northwest Coast.* San Diego, CA: Academic Press.

Matsui, A. 1996. Archaeological investigations of anadromous salmonid fishing in Japan. *World Archaeology* 27 (3): 444–460.

Matsui, A., and M. Kanehara. 2006. The question of prehistoric plant husbandry during the Jomon period in Japan. *World Archaeology* 38 (2): 259–273.

Matthews, R. 2003. *The archaeology of Mesopotamia.* New York: Routledge.

———. 2005. The rise of civilization in southwest Asia. In *The human past: World prehistory and the development of human societies,* ed. C. Scarre, 432–471. New York: Thames & Hudson.

Mayr, E. 1991. *One long argument: Charles Darwin and the genesis of modern evolutionary thought.* New York: Penguin.

———. 1997. *This is biology.* Cambridge, MA: Harvard University Press.

———. 2000. Darwin's influence on modern thought. *Scientific American* (July): 79–83.

———. 2001. *What evolution is.* New York: Basic Books.

Mays, S. 1998. *The archaeology of human bones.* New York: Routledge.

McBrearty, S., and A. Brooks. 2000. The revolution that wasn't: A new interpretation of the origin of modern human behavior. *Journal of Human Evolution* 39 (5): 453–563.

McBrearty, S., and N. Jablonski. 2005. First fossil chimpanzee. *Nature* 437:105–108.

McClung de Tapia, E. 1992. The origins of agriculture in Mesoamerica and Central America. In *The origins of agriculture: An international perspective,* eds. C. W. Cowan and P. J. Watson, 143–171. Washington/London: Smithsonian Institution.

McEwan, G. E. 1991. Investigations at the Pikillacta site: A provincial Huari center in the valley of Cuzco. In *Huari administrative structure: Prehistoric monumental architecture and state government,* eds. W. H. Isbell and G. F. McEwan, 91–119. Washington, DC: Dumbarton Oaks Research Library and Collection.

McEwan, G. E. (ed.) 2005. *Pikillacta: The Wari empire in Cuzco.* Iowa City: University of Iowa Press.

McGrew, W. C. 1998a. Culture in non-human primates? *Annual Review of Anthropology* 27:301–328.

———. 1998b. Behavioral diversity in populations of free-ranging chimpanzees in Africa: Is it culture? *Human Evolution* 13 (3–4): 209–220.

———. 2001. The nature of culture: Prospects and pitfalls of cultural primatology. In *Tree of origin: What primate behavior can tell us about human social evolution,* ed. F. B. de Waal, 229–254. Cambridge, MA: Harvard University Press.

McHenry, H. 2002. Introduction to the fossil record of human ancestry. In *The fossil primate record,* ed. W. Hartwig, 401–405. Cambridge: Cambridge University Press.

McIntosh, S., and R. McIntosh. 1993. Cities without citadels: Understanding urban origins along the middle Niger. In *The archaeology of Africa: Food, metals, and towns,* eds. T. Shaw, P. Sinclair, B. Andah, and A. Okpoko, 622–641. New York: Routledge.

McKee, J. 1996. Fossil evidence and Sterkfontein Member 2 foot bones of early hominid. *Science* 271:1301–1302.

———. 2000. *The riddled chain: Chance, coincidence, and chaos in human evolution.* New Brunswick, NJ: Rutgers University Press.

McManus, J. F. 2004. A great grand-daddy of ice cores. *Nature* 429:611–612.

McPherron, S. P. 2000. Handaxes as a measure of mental capabilities of early hominids. *Journal of Archaeological Science* 27:655–663.

Mellaart, J. 1967. *Çatal Hüyük: A Neolithic town in Anatolia.* London: Thames & Hudson.

———. 1975. *The Neolithic of the Near East.* London: Thames & Hudson.

Mellars, P. 1994. The Upper Palaeolithic revolution. In *The Oxford illustrated prehistory of Europe,* ed. B. Cunliffe, 42–78. Oxford: Oxford University Press.

———. 1996. *The Neanderthal legacy: An archaeological perspective from western Europe.* Princeton: Princeton University Press.

———. 1999. The Neandertal problem continued. *Current Anthropology* 40:341–350.

———. 2006. Going east: New genetic and archaeological perspectives on the modern human colonization of Eurasia. *Science* 313:796–800.

Meltzer, D. J. 1993. Pleistocene peopling of America. *Evolutionary Anthropology* 1 (5): 157–169.

———. 2002. What do you do when no one's been there before? Thoughts on the exploration and colonization of new lands. In *The first Americans: The Pleistocene colonization of the New World,* ed. N. G. Jablonski, 27–58. San Francisco: California Academy of Sciences, No. 27.

Miller, J. 2000. Cranio-facial variation in *H. habilis:* An analysis of the evidence for multiple species. In *American Journal of Physical Anthropology* 128:103–128.

Miller, L. E., and A. Treves. 2007. Predation on primates. In *Primates in perspective,* eds. C. J. Campbell, A. Fuentes, K. MacKinnon, et al., 525–542. New York: Oxford University Press.

Milner, N., O. E. Craig, G. N. Bailey, et al. 2004. Something fishy in the Neolithic? A re-evaluation of stable isotope analysis of Mesolithic and Neolithic coastal populations. *Antiquity* 78:9–22.

Milo, R. 1998. Evidence for hominid predation at Klasies River mouth, South Africa, and its implications for the behaviour of Early Modern Humans. *Journal of Archaeological Science* 25:99–133.

Milton, K. 1980. *The foraging strategy of howler monkeys: A study in primate economics.* New York: Columbia University Press.

Minagawa, M., and T. Akazawa. 1992. Dietary patterns of Japanese Jomon hunter-gatherers: Stable nitrogen and carbon isotope analyses of human bones. In *Pacific northeast Asia in prehistory*, eds. M. Aikens and S. Rhee. Seattle: Washington State University Press.

Mithen, S. 1994. The Mesolithic age. In *The Oxford illustrated prehistory of Europe*, ed. B. Cunliffe, 79–135. Oxford: Oxford University Press.

Mittermier, R., A. B. Rylands, and W. R. Konstant. 1999. Introduction. In *Walker's primates of the world*, ed. R. M. Nowak, 1–53. Baltimore, MD: Johns Hopkins Press.

Mojzis, S. J., G. Arrcnius, K. D. McKeegan, et al. 1996. Evidence for life on earth before 3,800 million years ago. *Nature* 384:55–59.

Molleson, T., and M. Cox. 1993. *The Spitalfields project: Volume 2. The anthropology.* York: Council for British Archaeology, Report 86.

Moloney, N. 1996. The effect of quartzite pebbles on the technology and typology of Middle Pleistocene lithic assemblages in the Iberian Peninsula. In *Non-flint stone tools and the occupation of the Iberian Peninsula*, eds. N. Moloney, L. Raposo, and M. Santonja, 107–119. Oxford: Tempus Reparatum, British Archaeological Reports International Series.

Morell, C. 2002. Empires across the Andes. *National Geographic* 201 (6): 106–129.

Morell, V. 1998. Genes may link ancient Eurasians, Native Americans. *Science* 280:520.

———. 1999. Forming the robust australopithecine face. *Science* 284:230–231.

Morris, C., and A. von Hagen. 1993. *The Inca empire and its Andean origins.* New York/London/Paris: Abbeville.

Morris, R. 2001. *The evolutionists: The struggle for Darwin's soul.* New York: W. H. Freeman.

Morwood, M. J., F. Aziz, P. O'Sullivan, et al. 1999. Archaeological and palaeontological research in central Flores, east Indonesia: Results of fieldwork 1997–98. *Antiquity* 73:273–286.

Moseley, M., R. Feldman, P. Goldstein, and L. Watanabe. 1991. Colonies and conquest: Tiahuanaco and Huari in Moquegua. In *Huari administrative structure: Prehistoric monumental architecture and state government*, eds. W. H. Isbell and G. F. McEwan, 121–140. Washington, DC: Dumbarton Oaks Research Library and Collection.

Moseley, M. E. 2001. *The Incas and their ancestors: The archaeology of Peru.* London: Thames & Hudson.

Mughal, M. R. 1991. The rise of the Indus civilization. In *Forgotten cities on the Indus*, eds. M. Jansen, M. Mulloy, and G. Urban, 104–110. Mainz: Verlag Philipp von Zabern.

Mulvaney, J., and J. Kamminga. 1999. *Prehistory of Australia.* Washington, DC: Smithsonian Institution.

Munro-Hay, S. 1993. State development and urbanism in northern Ethiopia. In *The archaeology of Africa: Food, metals, and towns*, eds. T. Shaw, P. Sinclair, B. Andah, and A. Okpoko, 609–621. New York: Routledge.

Murray, L. E. 2002. Individual differences in chimpanzee personality and their implications for the evolution of mind. In *New perspectives in primate evolution and behavior*, eds. C. S. Harcourt and B. R. Sherwood. West Yorkshire: Westbury Academic and Scientific Publishing.

Murray, M. A. 2004–2005. Provisions for the pyramid builders: New evidence from the ancient site of Giza. *Archaeology International* 2004–2005:38–42.

Nadel, D., U. Grinberg, E. Boaretto, and E. Werker. 2004. Stone age hut in Israel yields world's oldest evidence of bedding. *Proceedings of the National Academy of Sciences USA* 101:6821–6826.

Nadler, R. D., B. F. M. Galdikas, L. K. Sheeran, and N. Rosen. 1990. Preface. In *The neglected ape.* New York: Wiley-Liss.

Naggioncalda, N., and R. M. Sapolsky. 2002. Disturbing behaviors of the orangutan. *Scientific American* (June): 61–65.

Napier, J. R., and P. H. Napier. 1985. *The natural history of the primates.* Cambridge, MA: MIT Press.

Neff, H., J. Blomster, M. D. Glascock, et al. 2006. Smokescreens in the provenance investigation of Early Formative Mesoamerican ceramics. *Latin American Antiquity* 17 (1): 104–118.

Neiderberger, C. 2000. Ranked societies, iconographic complexity, and economic wealth in the Basin of Mexico toward 1200 BC. In *Olmec art and archaeology in Mesoamerica*, eds. J. E. Clark and M. E. Pye, 169–188. New Haven/London: Yale University Press.

Neumann, K. 2003. New Guinea: A cradle of agriculture. *Science* 301:180–181.

Newman, T. K., C. J. Jolly, and J. Rogers. 2004. Mitochodrial phylogeny and systematics of baboons *(Papio)*. *American Journal of Physical Anthropology* 12 (4): 17–27.

Nissen, H. J. 2001. Cultural and political networks in the ancient Near East during the fourth and third millenium B.C. In *Uruk Mesopotamia and its neighbours*, ed. M. S. Rothman, 149–179. Santa Fe, NM: School of American Research Press.

O'Brien, E. M. 1981. The projectile capabilities of the Acheulean handaxe from Olorgesailie. *Current Anthropology* 22:76–79.

O'Connell, J. F., K. Hawkes, K. D. Lupo, and N. G. Blurton Jones. 2002. Male strategies and Plio-Pleistocene archaeology. *Journal of Human Evolution* 43 (6): 831–872.

Olson, S. 2002a. *Mapping human history.* London: Bloomsbury Press.

———. 2002b. Seeking the signs of selection. *Science* 298:1324–1325.

Oms, O., J. M. Parés, B. Martinez-Navarro, et al. 2000. Early human occupation of western Europe: Paleomagnetic dates for two Paleolithic sites in Spain. *Proceedings of the National Academy of Sciences USA* 97 (19): 10666–10670.

Ortiz, P., and M. C. Rodríguez. 2000. The sacred hill of El Manatí: A preliminary discussion of the site's ritual paraphernalia. In *Olmec art and archaeology in Mesoamerica*, eds. J. E. Clark and M. E. Pye, 75–93. Washington, DC: National Gallery of Art/Yale University Press.

Ovchinnikov, I. V., A. Gotherstron, G. P. Romenova, et al. 2001. Molecular analysis of Neandertal DNA from the northern Caucasus. *Nature* 404:490–493.

Pääbo, S. 2003. The mosaic that is our genome. *Nature* 421: 409–411.

Pace, N. R. 2006. Time for a change. *Nature* 441:289.

Panger, M., A. S. Brooks, B. G. Richmond, and B. Wood. 2003. Older than the Oldowan? Rethinking the emergence of hominid tool use. *Evolutionary Anthropology* 11 (Supplement 1): 235–245.

Parfitt, S. A., R. W. Barendregt, M. Breda, et al. 2005. The earliest record of human activity in northern Europe. *Nature* 438:1008–1012.

Park, M. A. 2003. *Biological anthropology*, 3rd ed. Boston: McGraw-Hill.

Parker, S. T., and M. L. McKinnon. 2005. *Origins of intelligence*. Baltimore: Johns Hopkins University Press.

Parker Pearson, M., and Ramilisonina. 1998. Stonehenge for the ancestors: The stones pass on the message. *Antiquity* 72 (276): 308–326.

Parnell, R. J. 2002. Group size and structure in western lowland gorillas at Mbeli Bai, Republic of Congo. *American Journal of Primatology* 17:304–319.

Patel, A. 1997. The pastoral economy at Dholavira: A first look at animals and the urban life in third millennium Kutch. In *South Asian archaeology, 1995*, Vol. 1, eds. R. Allchin and B. Allchin. Enfield, NH: Science Publishers.

Pearsall, D. M. 2000. *Paleoethnobotany: A handbook of procedures*. San Diego/New York: Academic Press.

Pearson, R. 2006. Jomon hot spot: Increasing sedentism in southwestern Japan in the Incipient Jomon (14,000–9250 cal BC) and the Earliest Jomon (9250–5300 cal BC) period. *World Archaeology* 38 (2): 239–258.

Pelto, P. 1973. *The snowmobile revolution: Technology and social change in the Arctic*. Menlo Park, CA: Cummings.

Pennisi, E. 2002. Gene activity clocks brain fast evolution. *Science* 2 296:234–235.

Peretto, C. 2006. The first peopling of southern Europe: The Italian case. *Comptes Rendus Palevol*. 5:283–290.

Perry, S., and J. H. Manson. 2003. Traditions in monkeys. *Evolutionary Anthropology* 12:17–81.

Peters, H. 2001. Tool use to modify calls by wild orangutans. *Folia Primatologica* 72 (1): 242–244.

Pettitt, P. B. 2002. The Neanderthal dead: Exploring mortuary variability in Middle Palaeolithic Eurasia. *Before Farming* 1 (4): 1–26.

Phillipson, D. W. 1998. *Ancient Ethiopia: Aksum: Its antecedents and successors*. London: British Museum Press.

Pigliucci, M. 2002. *Denying evolution: Creations, scientism, and the nature of science*. Sunderland, MA: Sinauer Associates.

Pilbeam, D. R. 1968. The earliest hominids. *Nature* 219:1335–1330.

———. 2002. Perspectives on the Miocene hominoids. In *The primate fossil record*, ed. W. Hartwig, 303–310. Cambridge: Cambridge University Press.

Pillsbury, J. 2001. Introduction. In *Moche art and archaeology in ancient Peru*, ed. J. Pillsbury, 9–17. Washington, DC: National Gallery of Art/Yale University Press.

Piperno, D. R., and K. V. Flannery. 2001. The earliest archaeological maize (*Zea mays* L.) from highland Mexico: New accelerator mass spectrometry dates and their implications. *Proceedings of the National Academy of Sciences USA* 98 (4): 2101–2103.

Piperno, D. R., and K. E. Stothert. 2003. Phytolith evidence for early Holocene *Cucurbita* domestication in southwest Ecuador. *Science* 299:1054–1057.

Plog, S. 1997. *Ancient peoples of the American Southwest*. London: Thames & Hudson.

Pollock, S. 1999. *Ancient Mesopotamia*. Cambridge: Cambridge University Press.

Pope, K. O., M. E. Pohl, J. G. Jones, et al. 2001. Origin and environmental setting of ancient agriculture in the lowlands of Mesoamerica. *Science* 292 (5520): 1370–1373.

Porcasi, J. F., and H. Fujita. 2000. The dolphin hunters: A specialized prehistoric maritime adaptation in the southern California Channel Islands, and Baja California. *American Antiquity* 65:543–566.

Porcasi, J. F., T. L. Jones, and L. M. Raab. 2000. Trans-Holocene marine mammal exploitation on San Clemente Island, California: A tragedy of the commons revisited. *Journal of Anthropological Research* 19:200–220.

Possehl, G. L. 2002. *The Indus civilization: A contemporary perspective*. Walnut Creek, CA: Altamira Press.

Postgate, N. 1994. *Early Mesopotamia: Society and economy at the dawn of history*. New York: Routledge.

Potts, R. 1987. Reconstructions of early hominid socioecology: A critique of primate models. In *The evolution of human behavior: Primate models*, ed. W. Kinzey. Albany: State University of New York Press.

———. 1996. Evolution and climate variability. *Science* 273:922–923.

Power, M. G. 1991. *The egalitarians—humans and chimpanzees: An anthropological view of social organization*. Cambridge: Cambridge University Press.

———. 1995. Gombe revisited: Are chimpanzees violent and hierarchical in the "free" state? *General Anthropology* 2 (1): 5–9.

Prag, J., and R. Neave. 1997. *Making faces: Using forensic and archaeological evidence*. London: British Museum Press.

Price, T. D. 1991. The Mesolithic of northern Europe. *Annual Review of Anthropology* 20:211–233.

———. 2000. *Europe's first farmers*. Cambridge: Cambridge University Press.

———. 2003. The arrival of agriculture in Europe as seen from the north. In *The widening harvest, the Neolithic transition in Europe: Looking back, looking forward*, eds. A. J. Ammerman and P. Biagi, 273–294. Boston: Archaeological Institute of America.

Price, T. D., R. A. Bentley, J. Luning, D. Gronenborn, and J. Wahl. 2001. Prehistoric human migration in the Linearbandkeramik of central Europe. *Antiquity* 75;593–603.

Price, T. D., A. B. Gebauer, and L. H. Keeley. 1995. The spread of farming into Europe north of the Alps. In *Last hunters, first farmers: New perspectives on the prehistoric transition to agriculture*, eds. T. D. Price and A. B. Gebauer, 95–126. Sante Fe, NM: School of American Research Press.

Prothero, D. R. 2004. Did impacts, volcanic eruptions, or climate change affect mammalian evolution? *Paleogeography, Paleoclimatology, Paleoecology* 214 (3): 283–289.

Pruvost, M., R. Schwarz, V. Bessa-Correlia, et al. 2007. Freshly excavated fossil bones are best for amplification of ancient DNA. *Proceedings of the National Academy of Science USA* 104 (3): 739–744.

Purdy, B. A. 1992. *The art and archaeology of Florida's wetlands*. Boca Raton, FL: CRC Press.

Pusey, A. E. 2001. Of genes and apes: Chimpanzee social organization and reproduction. In *Tree of origin: What primate behavior can tell us about human social evolution*, ed. F. B. de Waal, 11–37. Cambridge, MA: Harvard University Press.

Pye, M. E., and J. E. Clark. 2000. Introducing Olmec archaeology. In *Olmec art and archaeology in Mesoamerica*, eds. J. E. Clark and M. E. Pye, 9–15. Washington, DC: National Gallery of Art/Yale University Press.

Qiang, J. 1999. A Chinese triconodont mammal and mosaic evolution of the mammalian skeleton. *Nature* 398:326–330.

Qiang, J., L. Zhe-Xi, Y. Chong-Xi, et al. 2002. The earliest known Eutherian mammal. *Nature* 416:816–822.

Rak, Y. 1983. *The Australopithecene face*. New York: Academic Press.

———. 2000. Lecture on *A. afarensis* at University College, London, March 24.

Rapp, G., Jr., and C. Hill. 1998. *Geoarchaeology: The earth-science approach to archaeological interpretation*. New Haven: Yale University Press.

Rasmussen, D. T. 2002. The origin of primates. In *The fossil primate record*, ed. W. C. Hartwig, 5–9. Cambridge: Cambridge University Press.

Rawson, J. 1996. *Mysteries of ancient China: New discoveries from the early dynasties*. London: British Museum Press.

Reid, J. J. 1989. A grasshopper perspective on the Mogollon of the Arizona mountains. In *Dynamics of Southwest prehistory*, eds. L. S. Cordell and G. J. Gumerman, 65–97. Washington, DC: Smithsonian Institution.

Reid, J. J., and S. Whittlesey. 1997. *The archaeology of ancient Arizona*. Tucson: University of Arizona Press, 65–95.

Relethford, J. 2001a. *Genetics and the search for modern human origins*. New York: Wiley-Liss.

———. 2001b. New views of Neandertal DNA. *General Anthropology* 8 (1): 9–10.

———. 2002. *The human species*. 5th ed. Boston: McGraw-Hill.

———. 2005. *The human species*. 6th ed. Boston: McGraw-Hill.

Relethford, J., and H. Harpending. 1995. Ancient differences in population size can mimic a recent African origin of modern humans. *Current Anthropology* 36:667–674.

Renfrew, C. 2000. Archaeogenetics: Toward a population prehistory of Europe. In *Archaeogenetics, DNA, and the population prehistory of Europe*, eds. C. Renfrew and K. Boyle, 3–12. Cambridge: Cambridge University Press, McDonald Institute Monographs.

Renfrew, C., and P. Bahn. 2000. *Archaeology: Theories, methods and practice*. 3rd ed. New York: Thames & Hudson.

Rennie, J. 2002. Answers to creationist nonsense. *Scientific American* (July): 79–85.

Reno, P. L., R. S. Meindl, M. A. McCollum, and C. O. Lovejoy. 2003. Sexual dimorphism in *Australopithecus afarensis* was similar to that of modern humans. *Proceedings of the National Academy of Sciences USA* 100 (16): 9404–9409.

Reynolds, V. 1967. *Apes: The gorilla, chimpanzee, orangutan, and gibbon: Their history and their world*. New York: Dutton.

Rice, P. 1981. Prehistoric Venuses: Symbols of motherhood or womanhood? *Journal of Anthropological Research* 37 (4): 402–414.

———. 1998. *Doing archaeology: A hands-on laboratory manual*. Mountain View, CA: Mayfield.

———. 2007. Can the Galapagos survive cruise ship mass tourism? *General Anthropology* 14 (1): 1–10.

Rice, P., and A. Paterson. 1985. Cave art and bones: Exploring the interrelationships. *American Anthropologist* 87:94–100.

———. 1986. Validating the cave art–archaeofaunal relationship in Cantabrian Spain. *American Anthropologist* 88:658–667.

Richard, A. 1978. *Behavioral variation: Case study of a Malagasy lemur*. Lewisburg, PA: Bucknell University Press.

———. 1985. *Primates in nature*. New York: W. H. Freeman.

Richards, M. 2003. The Neolithic invasion of Europe. *Annual Review of Anthropology* 32:135–162.

Richards, M., V. Macauley, and H-J. Baudelt. 2002. Analyzing genetic data in a model-based framework: Inferences about European prehistory. In *Examining the farming/language dispersal hypothesis*, eds. P. Bellwood and C. Renfrew, 459–466. Cambridge: McDonald Institute for Archaeological Research.

Richards, M., V. Macauley, E. Hickey, et al. 2000. Tracing European founder lineages in the Near Eastern mtDNA pool. *American Journal of Human Genetics*.

Richards, M., P. B. Pettitt, E. Trinkaus, et al. 2000. Neanderthal diet at Vindija and Neanderthal predation: The evidence from stable isotopes. *Proceedings of the National Academy of Sciences USA* 97 (13): 7663–7666.

Richards, M. P., T. D. Price, and E. Koch. 2003. Mesolithic and Neolithic subsistence in Denmark: New stable isotope data. *Current Anthropolgy* 44 (2): 288–295.

Richerson, P. J., and R. Boyd. 2005. *Not by genes alone*. Chicago: University of Chicago Press.

Ridley, M. 1999. *Genome*. London: Fourth Estate.

———. 2000. The search for LUCA. *Natural History* 11:82–85.

———. 2004. *Evolution*, 3rd ed. London: Blackwell Science.

———. 2006. *How to read Darwin*. New York: Norton.

Rigaud, J-Ph. 1987. Personal communication.

———. 2000. Late Neandertal in the southwest of France and the emergence of the Upper Paleolithic. In *Neandertals on the edge*, eds. C. B. Stringer, R. N. E. Barton, and J. C. Finlayson, 27–32. Cambridge: Oxbow.

Rightmire, G. P. 1985. The tempo of change in the evolution of the skull size of mid-Pleistocene *Homo*. In *Ancestors, the hard evidence*, ed. E. Delson, 55–64. New York: Alan R. Liss.

Riley, D. N. 1987. *Air photography and archaeology*. Philadelphia: University of Pennsylvania Press.

Rilling, J. K. 2006. Human and nonhuman primate brains: Are they allometrically scaled versions of the same design? *Evolutionary Anthropology* 15:66–77.

Roberts, J. A. G. 1996. *History of China*. Vol. 1, *Prehistory to c. 1800*. Stroud, UK: Alan Sutton.

Roberts, M., and S. Parfitt. 1999. *Boxgrove: A Middle Pleistocene hominid site at Eastham quarry, Boxgrove, West Sussex.* London: English Heritage.

Roberts, M. B. 1994. How old is Boxgrove man? *Nature* 371: 751.

Roberts, M. B., C. B. Stringer, and S. B. Parfitt. 1994. A hominid tibia from middle Pleistocene sediments at Boxgrove, UK. *Nature* 369:311–312.

Roberts, N. 1998. *The Holocene: An environmental history.* Malden, MA: Blackwell.

Roche, H., A. Delanges, J.-P. Brugal, et al. 1999. Early hominid stone tool production and technical skill 2.34 myr ago in west Turkana, Kenya. *Nature* 399:57–60.

Rogers, J. 1994. Levels of the genealogical hierarchy and the problem of hominoid phylogeny. *American Journal of Physical Anthropology* 94:81–88.

Rolland, N. 2004. Fire and home bases. *Asian Perspectives* 43 (2): 248–280.

Rollefson, G., A. Simmons, and Z. Kafafi. 1992. Neolithic cultures at Ain Ghazal, Jordan. *Journal of Field Archaeology* 19:443–470.

Rollefson, G. O. 1997. Changes in architecture and social organization at Ain Ghazal. In *The prehistory of Jordan II: Perspectives from 1997*, eds. H. G. K. Bebel, Z. Kafafi, and G. O. Rollefson, 287–307. Studies in Early Near Eastern Production, Subsistence, and Environment 5. Berlin: *ex oriente*.

Ronin, A. V. 2003. Lecture at University College, London, June 10.

Roosevelt, A. C. 2000. Who's on first? *Natural History* 109 (6): 76–79.

Rose, J. E., X. Ni, and K. Beard. 2006. Cranial remains of an Eocene tarsier. *Proceedings of the National Academy of Sciences USA* 10 (12): 4315–4381.

Rose, K. D., and T. M. Bown. 1993. Species concepts and species recognition in Eocene primates. In *Species concepts and primate evolution*, eds. W. Kimbel and L. R. Martin. New York: Plenum.

Rosenberg, K. R., L. Zune, and C. B. Ruff. 2000. Body size, body proportions, and encephalization in a Middle Pleistocene archaic human from northern China. *Proceedings of the National Academy of Sciences USA* 103 (10): 3552–3556.

Rosenzweig, M. 1997. Tempo and mode of speciation. *Science* 277:1622–1623.

Rostworowski, M., and C. Morris. 1998. Inca power and its social foundations. In *The Cambridge history of the native peoples of the Americas*, vol. 3, *South America*, eds. F. Salomon and S. Schwartz, part 1, 769–863. Cambridge: Cambridge University Press.

Rowley-Conwy, P. 1999. Economic prehistory in southern Scandinavia. In *World prehistory. Studies in memory of Grahame Clark*, eds. J. Coles, R. Bewley, and P. Mellars. *Proceedings of the British Academy* 99:125–159.

Ruff, C. B. 1999. Skeletal structure and behavioral patterns of prehistoric Great Basin populations. In *Prehistoric lifeways in the Great Basin wetlands: Bioarchaeological reconstruction and interpretation*, eds. B. E. Hemphill and C. S. Larsen, 290–320. Salt Lake City: University of Utah Press.

Russo, M. 1996. Southeastern Archaic mounds. In *Archaeology of the mid-Holocene Southeast*, eds. K. Sassaman and D. Anderson, 259–287. Gainesville: University of Florida Press.

Sabloff, J. A. 1997. *The cities of ancient America: Reconstructing a lost world.* London: Thames & Hudson.

Sassaman, K. E. 2005. Structure and practice in the Archaic Southeast. In *North American Archaeology*, eds. T. R. Pauketat and D. DiPaolo Loren, 79–107. Malden, MA: Blackwell Publishing.

Saunders, E. 2004. Kennewick Man decision upheld. *Mammoth Trumpet* 19 (2): 1, 18.

Sauvage, M. 1998. La construction des ziggurats sous la Troisième Dynastie d'Ur. *Iraq* LX:45–63.

Savage-Rumbaugh, S., S. G. Shanker, and J. T. Talbot. 1998. *Apes, language, and the human mind.* New York: Oxford University Press.

Save-Soderberg, T., ed. 1987. *Temples and tombs of ancient Nubia: The international rescue campaign of Abu Simbel, Philae, and other sites.* New York: Thames & Hudson/ UNESCO.

Scarre, C. 2005a. Holocene Europe. In *The human past: World prehistory and the development of human societies*, ed. C. Scarre, 392–431. New York: Thames & Hudson.

———. 2005b. The world transformed: From foragers and farmers to states and empires. In *The human past: World prehistory and the development of human societies*, ed. C. Scarre, 176–199. New York: Thames & Hudson.

———. (ed.) 2005c. *The human past: World prehistory and the development of human societies.* New York: Thames & Hudson.

Scarre, C., and B. Fagan. 2003. *Ancient civilizations.* Upper Saddle River, NJ: Prentice Hall.

Schele, L., and D. Freidel. 1990. *A forest of kings: The untold story of the Ancient Maya.* New York: Morrow.

Schick, K., and N. Toth. 1993. *Making silent stones speak.* London: Weidenfeld & Nicolson.

Schick, K. D., and D. Zhuan. 1993. Early Paleolithic of China and eastern Asia. *Evolutionary Anthropology* 2:22–35.

Schiffer, M. B. 1987. *Formation processes in the archaeological record.* Albuquerque: University of New Mexico Press.

Schmid, P. 2004. Functional interpretation of the Laetoli footprints. In *Laetoli footprints: From biped to strider*, eds. D. J. Meldrun and C. E. Hilton, 48–62. New York: Kluwer Academic/Plenum Publishers.

Schmitz, R. W., D. Serre, G. Bonani, et al. 2002. The Neandertal type site revisited: Interdisciplinary investigations of skeletal remains from the Neander Valley, Germany. *Proceedings of the National Academy of Sciences USA* 99 (20): 13342–13347.

Schoeninger, M. J. 1995. Stable isotope studies in human evolution. *Evolutionary Anthropology* 4:83–98.

———. 1999. Prehistoric subsistence strategies in the Stillwater Marsh region of the Carson Desert. In *Prehistoric lifeways in the Great Basin wetlands: Bioarchaeological reconstruction and interpretation*, eds. B. E. Hemphill and C. S. Larsen, 151–167. Salt Lake City: University of Utah Press.

Schopf, W. 1999. *Cradle of life: The discovery of Earth's earliest fossils.* Princeton, NJ: Princeton University Press.

Schrago, C. G. 2007. On the time scale of New World primate diversification. *American Journal of Physical Anthropology* 132:344–354.

Schreiber, K. J. 1992. *Wari imperialism in middle horizon Peru.* Ann Arbor: University of Michigan, Museum of Anthropology, Anthropological Papers No. 87.

Schulting, R. J. 1998. Creativity's coffin. In *Creativity in human evolution and prehistory,* ed. S. Mithen, 203–226. New York: Routledge.

Schultz, E. 2002. Discourse and politics: Development in linguistic anthropology since the 1970s. *General Anthropology* 8 (2): 1–7.

Schultzhuizen, M. 2001. *Frogs, flies, and dandelions: Speciation— the evolution of new species.* New York: Norton.

Schweingruber, F. H. 1993. *Trees and wood in dendrochronology.* New York: Springer.

Seidlmayer, S. 1998. Egypt's path to advanced civilization. In *Egypt: The world of the pharaohs,* eds. R. Schulz and M. Seidel, 9–23. Cologne: Könemann.

Selim, J. 2004. One small step for fish. *Discover* (July).

Semaw, S., P. Renne, J. W. K. Harris, et al. 1997. 2.5 million-year-old stone tools from Gona, Ethiopia. *Nature* 385:333–336.

Senner, W., ed. 1989. *The origins of writing.* Lincoln: University of Nebraska Press.

Serra Puche, M. C., F. González de la Vara, and K. R. Durand. 1996. Daily life in Olmec times. In *Olmec of ancient Mexico,* eds. E. P. Benson and B. de la Fuente, 35–39. Washington, DC: National Gallery of Art/Abrams.

Shanklin, E. 1994. *Anthropology and race.* Belmont, CA: Wadsworth.

Sharer, R. J. 1994. *The ancient Maya.* 5th ed. Stanford, CA: Stanford University Press.

———. 1996. *Daily life in Maya civilization.* Westport, CT/London: Greenwood.

Sharer, R. J., and W. Ashmore. 2003. *Archaeology: Discovering our past.* 3rd ed. Mountain View, CA: Mayfield.

Sharer, R. J., A. K. Balkansky, J. H. Burton, et al. 2006. On the logic of archaeological inference: Early formative pottery and the evolution of Mesoamerican societies. *Latin American Antiquity* 17 (1): 104–118.

Shea, J. 2003. Neandertals, competition, and the origin of modern human behavior in the Levant. *Evolutionary Anthropology* 12:173–187.

Shennan, S. 2002. *Genes, memes, and human heredity.* London: Thames & Hudson.

Shimada, I. 1999. Evolution of Andean diversity: Regional formations (500 B.C.E.–C.E. 600). In *The Cambridge history of the native peoples of the Americas,* vol. 3, *South America,* eds. F. Salomon and S. Schwartz, part 1, 350–517. Cambridge: Cambridge University Press.

———. 2001. Late Moche urban craft production: A first approximation. In *Moche art and archaeology in ancient Peru,* ed. J. Pillsbury, 177–203. Washington, DC: National Gallery of Art/Yale University Press.

Shimada, I., and J. F. Merkel. 1991. Copper-alloy metallurgy in ancient Peru. *Science* 265 (1): 80–86.

Shipman, P. 2000. Doubting Dmanisi. *American Scientist* (November–December): 491–494.

———. 2002. Hunting the first hominid. *American Scientist* (January–February): 25–27.

Shreeve, J. 1996. New skeleton gives path from trees to ground an odd turn. *Science* 272: 654.

Simons, E. L. 1995. History, anatomy, sub-fossil record and management of *Daubentonia madagascarensis.* In *Creatures of the dark: The nocturnal prosimians,* eds. L. Altermann, G. A. Doyle, and M. K. Izard, 133–140. New York: Plenum Press.

Simons, E. L., and T. Rasmussen. 1994. A whole new world of ancestors: Eocene anthropoids from Africa. *Evolutionary Anthropology* 3:128–129.

Skinner, A. R., B. Blackwell, S. Martin, et al. 2005. ESR dating at Mesmaiskaya Cave, Russia. *Applied Radiation and Isotopes* 62:219–224.

Smedley, A. 1998. "Race" and the construction of human identity. *American Anthropologist* 100 (3): 690–702.

Smith, B. D. 1992. *Rivers of change.* Washington, DC: Smithsonian Institution.

———. 1995. *The emergence of agriculture.* New York: Scientific American Library.

Smith, F. H. 1992. The role of continuity in modern human origins. In *Continuity or replacement,* eds. G. Brauer and F. H. Smith, 145–156. Rotterdam: A. A. Balkema.

———. 1994. Samples, species, and speculations in the study of modern human origins. In *The origins of anatomically modern humans,* eds. M. Nitecki and D. Nitecki, 228–252. New York: Plenum.

Smith, F. H., A. R. Falsetti, and S. M. Donnelly. 1989. Modern human origins. *Yearbook of Physical Anthropology* 32: 35–68.

Smith, F. H., E. Trinkaus, P. B. Pettitt, et al. 1999. Direct radiocarbon dates for Vindija G1 and Velika Pecina late Pleistocene hominid remains. *Proceedings of the National Academy of Sciences USA* 96 (22): 12281–12286.

Smith, M. E. 1996. *The Aztecs.* Malden, MA: Blackwell.

———. 2003. *The Aztecs.* 2nd ed. Malden, MA: Blackwell.

Smith, M. E., and F. F. Berdan. 1996. Introduction. In *Aztec imperial strategies,* eds. F. F. Berdan, et al. 1–9. Washington, DC: Dumbarton Oaks Research Library and Collection.

Smith, M. E., and M. G. Hodge. 1994. An introduction to late classic economies and polities. In *Economies and polities in the Aztec realm,* eds. M. G. Hodge and M. E. Smith, 1–42. Albany, NY: Institute for Mesoamerican Studies, The University at Albany.

Snow, D. R. 1976. *The archaeology of North America.* London: Thames & Hudson.

———. 1996. The first Americans and the differentiation of hunter-gatherer cultures. In *The Cambridge history of the native peoples of the Americas,* vol. 1, *North America,* eds. B. C. Trigger and W. E. Washburn, 125–199. Cambridge: Cambridge University Press.

Soffer, O. 1985. Patterns of intensification as seen from the Upper Paleolithic of the central Russian plain. In *Prehistoric hunter-gatherers,* eds. T. D. Price and J. A. Brown, 235–270. New York: Academic Press.

Sommer, J. D. 1999. The Shanidar IV "flower burial": A re-evaluation of Neanderthal burial ritual. *Cambridge Archaeological Journal* 9 (1): 127–129.

Southwood, T. 2003. *The story of life*. Oxford: Oxford University Press.

Speth, J. D., and E. Tchernov. 1998. The role of hunting and scavenging in Neandertal procurement strategies: New evidence from Kebara Cave (Israel). In *Neandertals and modern humans in western Asia*, eds. T. Akazawa, K. Aoki, and O. Bar-Yosef, 223–239. New York: Plenum.

———. 2001. Neandertal hunting and meat processing in the Near East. In *Meat eating and human evolution*, eds. C. Stanford and H. T. Bunn. Oxford: Oxford University Press.

Spoor, F. 2001. Nachukui formation, west of Lake Turkana. Lecture at University College, London, March 27.

Spoor, F., J-J. Hublin, M. Braun, and F. Zonneveld. 2003. The bony labyrinth of Neanderthals. *Journal of Human Evolution* 44:141–165.

Stadelmann, R. 1998. Royal tombs from the age of the pyramids. In *Egypt: The world of the pharaohs*, eds. R. Schulz and M. Seidel, 47–77. Cologne: Könemann.

Stahl, A. 1984. Hominid dietary selection before fire. *Current Anthropology* 25:151–168.

Stanford, C. B. 1998. Social behavior of chimps and bonobos. *Current Anthropology* 39:399–420.

———. 1999. *The hunting apes: Meat eating and the origins of human behavior*. Princeton, NJ: Princeton University Press.

———. 2001a. The ape's gift: Meat eating, meat sharing, and human evolution. In *Tree of origin: What primate behavior can tell us about human social evolution*, ed. F. B. de Waal, 95–118. Cambridge, MA: Harvard University Press.

———. 2001b. *Significant others*. New York: Basic Books.

Stanford, D. 1999. Paleoindian archaeology and late Pleistocene environments in the Plains and southwestern United States. In *Ice Age people of North America: Environments, origins, and adaptations*, eds. R. Bonnichsen and K. L. Turnmire, 281–338. Corvallis: Oregon State University Press.

Stanford, D., and B. Bradley, 2002. Ocean trails and prairie paths? Thoughts about Clovis origins. In *The first Americans: The Pleistocene colonization of the New World*, Memoirs of the California Academy of Sciences, no. 27, ed. N. Jablonski 255–271. San Francisco: California Academy of Sciences.

Steadman, D. W. 2003. Introducing forensic anthropology. In *Hard evidence: Case studies in forensic anthropology*, ed. D. W. Steadman, 1–22. Upper Saddle River, NJ: Prentice Hall.

Stearns, S. C., and R. F. Hoekstra. 2005. *Evolution: An introduction*. 2nd ed. Oxford: Oxford University Press.

Stein, P., and B. Rowe. 2003. *Physical anthropology*, 8th ed. Boston: McGraw-Hill.

Stiner, M. C. 1994. *Honor among thieves: A zooarchaeological study of Neandertal ecology*. Princeton: Princeton University Press.

Stokstad, E. 2001. Exquisite Chinese fossils add new pages to book of life. *Science* 291:232–236.

———. 2002. Ancient ancestral placental mammals. *Science* 296: 639.

———. 2003. Ancient DNA pulled from soil. *Science* 300:407.

———. 2004. Controversial fossil could shed light on early animals' blueprint. *Science* 304:1425.

Stone, R. 2004. Putting the stone in Stonehenge. *Science* 304:1889–1890.

Stout, D. 2005. Raw material selectivity of the earliest stone toolmakers at Gona, Afar, Ethiopia. *Journal of Human Evolution* 48:365–380.

Straus, L. G. 2000. Solutrean settlement of North America? A review of reality. *American Antiquity* 65 (2): 219–226.

———. 2002. American perspectives on the European Upper Paleolithic. In *The role of American archaeology in the study of the European Upper Paleolithic*, ed. L. G. Straus, 1–5. BAR International Series 1048. Oxford: Archaeopress.

Strauss, E. 1999. Can mitochrondrial clocks keep time? *Science* 283:1435–1438.

Strier, K. B. 2000. *Primate behavioral ecology*. Boston: Allyn & Bacon.

———. 2007. Conservation. In *Primates in perspective*, eds. C. J. Campbell, A. Fuentes, K. MacKinnon, et al., 496–509. New York: Oxford University Press.

Stringer, C. 1984. Fate of the Neanderthals. *Natural History* 93:6–12.

———. 2000. Neandertal and modern humans. Panel discussion, American Anthropological Association meetings, November.

———. 2002a. Modern human origins: Progress and prospects. *Philosophical Transactions of the Royal Society, B* (357): 563–579.

———. 2000b. New perspectives on the Neandertals. *Evolutionary Anthropology* 11 (Supplement 1): 58–59.

Stringer, C., and P. Andrews. 1988. Genetic and fossil evidence for the origin of modern humans. *Science* 239:1263–1268.

———. 2005. *The complete world of human evolution*. London: Thames & Hudson.

Stringer, C., and W. Davies. 2001. Those elusive Neandertals. *Nature* 413:791–792.

Stringer, C., and C. Gamble. 1993. *In search of the Neanderthals*. London: Thames & Hudson.

Stringer, C., and J.-J. Hublin. 1999. New age estimates for the Swanscombe hominid and their significance for human evolution. *Journal of Human Evolution* 37:873–877.

Stringer, C., and R. McKie. 1997. *African exodus: Changing the image of mankind*. New York: Henry Holt.

Struever, S., and F. Holton. 1979. *Koster: Americans in search of their prehistoric past*. New York: Doubleday.

Strum, S., and L. Fedigan. 2000. *Primate encounters: Models of science, gender, and society*. Chicago: University of Chicago Press.

Stumpf, R. 2007. Chimps and bonobos. In *Primates in perspective*, eds. C. J. Campbell, A. Fuentes, K. MacKinnon, et al., 321–344. New York: Oxford University Press.

Sussman, R. W. 1997. Exploring our basic human nature. *Anthro Notes* (Fall): 17–19.

———. 1999. *The biological basis of human behavior: A critical review*. Upper Saddle River, NJ: Prentice Hall.

———. 2000. Piltdown man, the father of American field primatology. In *Primate encounters: Models of science, gender, and society*, eds. S. C. Strum and L. M. Fedigan, 85–103. Chicago: University of Chicago Press.

Suwa, G., B. Asfaw, Y. Beyene, et al. 1997. The first skull of *Australopithecus boisei*. *Nature* 389:489–492.

Svitil, K. A. 1999. Searching for the first animal. *Discover* (January 1999): 52.

———. 2003. A new look for the first Americans. *Discover* (March): 11.

Svoboda, J., V. Lozek, and E. Vlcek. 1996. *Hunters between East and West: The Paleolithic of Moravia*. New York: Plenum.

Swedell, L. 2000. Two takeovers in wild hamadryas baboons. *Folia Primatologica* 71:169–172.

Swisher, C. C., G. H. Curtis, T. Jacob, et al. 1994. Age of the earliest known hominids in Java, Indonesia. *Science* 263:1118–1121.

Swisher, C. C., G. H. Curtis, and R. Lewin. 2000. *Java man*. Chicago: University of Chicago Press.

Swisher, C. C., W. J. Rink, S. C. Anton. 1996. Latest *Homo erectus* of Java: Potential contemporaneity with *Homo sapiens* in Southeast Asia. *Science* 274:1870–1874.

Sykes, B. 2001. *The seven daughters of Eve*. New York: Norton.

Takahashi, R., T. Toizumi, and K. Yasushi. 1997. *Archaeological studies of Japan: Current studies of the Jomon archaeology*, 105–137. Tokyo: Japanese Archaeological Association.

Takasaki, H. 2000. Traditions of the Kyoto school of field primatology in Japan. In *Primate encounters: Models of science, gender, and society*, eds. S. C. Strum and L. M. Fedigan, 151–164. Chicago: University of Chicago Press.

Tappan, M. 2001. Deconstructing the Serengeti. In *Meat eating and human evolution*, eds. C. Stanford and H. T. Brunn. Oxford: Oxford University Press.

Tattersall, I. 1999. *The last Neanderthal*. Boulder, CO: Westview.

———. 2000a. Once we were not alone. *Scientific American* (January): 56–62.

———. 2000b. Paleoanthropology: The last half-century. *Evolutionary Anthropology* 9 (1): 2–16.

———. 2002. *The monkey in the mirror*. Oxford: Oxford University Press.

Tattersall, I., and J. Schwartz. 1999. Hominids and hybrids: The place of Neandertal in human evolution. *Proceedings of the National Academy of Sciences USA* 96:7117–7119.

Taube, K. 2000. Lightning celts and corn fetishes: The formative Olmec and the development of maize symbolism in Mesoamerica and the American Southwest. In *Olmec art and archaeology in Mesoamerica*, eds. J. E. Clark and M. E. Pye, 297–337. Washington, DC: National Gallery of Art/Yale University Press.

Taylor, R. E. 2000. Fifty years of radiocarbon dating. *American Scientist* 88 (January): 60–67.

———. 2002. Radiocarbon dating. In *Handbook of archaeological sciences*, eds. D. R. Brothwell and A. M. Pollard. New York: Wiley.

Taylor, R. E., and M. J. Aitken, eds. 1997. *Chronometric dating in archaeology*. New York: Plenum.

Taylor, R. E., D. G. Smith, and R. Southan. 2001. The Kennewick skeleton: Chronological and biomolecular context. *Radiocarbon* 43 (2): 965–976.

Templeton, A. 1996. Gene lineages and human evolution. *Science* 272:1363–1364.

———. 1997. Testing the Out of Africa replacement hypothesis with mitochondrial DNA data. In *Conceptual issues in modern human origins research*, eds. G. A. Clark and C. M. Willermet, 329–360. New York: Aldine de Gruyter.

———. 1998. Human races: A genetic and evolutionary perspective. *American Anthropologist* 100 (3): 632–650.

———. 2002. Out of Africa again and again. *Nature* 416:45–51.

Thieme, H. 1997. Lower Palaeolithic hunting spears from Germany. *Nature* 385:807–810.

Thomas, D. H. 1985. Integrative synthesis: The lacustrine biome as viewed from Hidden Cave. In *The archaeology of Hidden Cave, Nevada*, ed. D. H. Thomas, 374–391. New York: American Museum of Natural History, Anthropological Papers, vol. 61, part 1.

Thomson, K. 2005. *Fossils*. Oxford: Oxford University Press.

Thorne, A., and D. Curnoe. 2000. Sex and significance of Lake Mungo 3: Reply to Brown, "Australian Pleistocene variation and the sex of Lake Mungo 3." *Journal of Human Evolution* 39:587–600.

Thorne, A., and M. Wolpoff. 1981. Regional continuity in Australasia Pleistocene hominid evolution. *American Journal of Physical Anthropology* 55:337–349.

———. 1992. The multiregional evolution of humans. *Scientific American* 266:76–83.

Thorpe, R. L. 2006. *China in the Early Bronze Age*. Philadelphia: University of Pennsylvania Press.

Tobias, P. V. 1998. Evidence for the early beginnings of spoken language. *Cambridge Archaeological Journal* 1:72–78.

Tomasello, M., and J. Call. 1997. *Private cognition*. Oxford: Oxford University Press.

Tosi, M. 1991. The Indus civilization beyond the Indian subcontinent. In *Forgotten cities on the Indus*, eds. M. Jansen, M. Mulloy, and G. Urban, 111–128. Mainz: Verlag Philipp von Zabern.

Toyama, S. 2002. The origin and spread of rice cultivation as seen from rice remains. In *The origins of pottery and agriculture*, ed. Y. Yasuda, 263–272. New Delhi: Roli Books and Lustre Press.

Trigger, B. G. 1993. *Early civilizations: Ancient Egypt in context*. Cairo: American University at Cairo Press.

———. 2003. *Understanding early civilizations: A comparative study*. New York: Cambridge University Press.

Trinkaus, E. 1992. Cladistics and later Pleistocene human evolution. In *Continuity or replacement?*, eds. G. Brauer and F. H. Smith, 108. Rotterdam: A. A. Balkema.

Trinkaus, E., and P. Shipman. 1992. *The Neandertals: Changing the image of mankind*. New York: Knopf.

Tubb, K. W. 2001–2002. The statues of Ain Ghazal: Discovery, recovery and reconstruction. *Archaeology International* 47–50.

Turner, C. G. 1985. The dental search for native American origins. In *Out of Asia: Peopling the Americas and the Pacific*. eds. R. Kirk and E. Szathmary, 31–78. Canberra: Australian National University.

Turner, C. G., and J. A. Turner. 1999. *Man corn: Cannibalism and violence in the prehistoric American Southwest.* Salt Lake City: University of Utah Press.

Turner, T. R. 2005. *Biological anthropology and ethics.* Albany: SUNY Press.

Underhill, A. P. 1997. Current issues in Chinese Neolithic archaeology. *Journal of World Prehistory* 11 (2): 103–160.

Underhill, A. P., and J. Habu. 2005. Early communities in east Asia: Economic and sociopolitical organization at the local and regional levels. In *Archaeology of Asia*, ed. M. T. Stark, 121–148. Malden, MA: Blackwell Publishing.

Valla, F. 1995. The first settled societies: Natufian (12, 500–10,200 BP). In *The archaeology of society in the Holy Land*, ed. T. Levy, 169–187. New York: Facts on File.

———. 1999. The Natufian: A coherent thought? In *Dorothy Garrod and the progress of the Palaeolithic*, eds. W. Davies and R. Charles, 224–241. Oxford: Oxbow.

van Andel, T. H., and P. C. Tzedakis. 1996. Paleolithic landscapes of Europe and environs, 150,000 to 25,000 years ago: An overview. *Quaternary Science Reviews* 15:481–490.

van Schaik, C. P. 2004. *Among orangutans: Red apes and the rise of human evolution.* Cambridge, MA: Harvard University Press.

van Schaik, C. P., M. Ancrenaz, G. Bogen, et al. 2003. Orangutan cultures and the evolution of material culture. *Science* 299:103–105.

Vandermeersch, B. 2006. Ce que nous apprennent les premières sépultures. *Comptes Rendus Palevol.* 5:161–167.

Vanhaeren, M., and F. d'Errico. 2005. Grave goods from the Saint-Germain-la-Rivière: Evidence for social inequality in the Upper Palaeolithic. *Journal of Anthropological Archaeology* 24:117–134.

Vanhaeren, M., F. d'Errico, C. Stringer, et al. 2006. Middle Paleolithic shell beads in Israel and Algeria. *Science* 312:1785–1788.

Verano, J. W. 2001. War and death in the Moche world: Osteological evidence and visual discourse. *Moche art and archaeology in ancient Peru*, ed. J. Pillsbury, 111–125. Washington, DC: National Gallery of Art/Yale University Press.

Vermeersch, P. M., and E. Paulissen. 1997. Extensive Middle Palaeolithic chert extraction in the Qena area (Egypt). In *Man and flint*, eds. R. Schild and Z. Sulgostowska, 133–142. Warsaw: Institute of Archaeology and Ethnology Polish Academy of Sciences.

Vermeersch, P. M., E. Paulissen, S. Stokes, et al. 1998. A Middle Palaeolithic burial of a modern human at Taramsa Hill, Egypt. *Antiquity* 72:475–484.

Vermeersch, P. M., E. Paulissen, and P. Van Peer. 1990. Paleolithic chert exploitation in the limestone stretch of the Egyptian Nile Valley. *African Archaeological Review* 8:77–122.

Vignaud, P., P. Duringer, H. Tasso, et al. 2002. Geology and palaeontology of the Upper Miocene Toros–Menalla hominid locality, Chad. *Nature* 418:152–155.

Villa, P. 1983. *Terra Amata and the Middle Pleistocene record of southern France.* Berkeley: University of California Press.

Villa, P., E. Soto, M. Santonja, et al. 2005. New data from Ambrona: Closing the hunting *versus* scavenging debate. *Quaternary International* 126–128:223–250.

Vogel, G. 1999. Chimps in the wild show stirrings of culture. *Science* 284:2070–2073.

von Hagen, A., and C. Morris. 1998. *The cities of the ancient Andes.* London: Thames & Hudson.

Vrba, E. 1995. The fossil record of African antelopes (Mammalia, Bovidae) in relation to human evolution and paleoclimate. In *Paleoclimate and evolution, with emphasis on human origins*, eds. E. Vrba, G. H. Denton, T. C. Partridge, and L. H. Burckle, 385–424. New Haven, CT: Yale University Press.

Wade, N. 2001. *Life script: The genome and the new medicine.* New York: Simon & Schuster.

———. 2003a. Once again, scientists say human genome is complete. *New York Times* (April 15).

———. 2003b. Y chromosomes sketch new outline of British history. *New York Times* (May 27).

———. 2005. A gene for romance? *New York Times* (July 19).

———. 2006. *Before the dawn.* New York: Penguin.

Wadley, L., B. Williamson, and M. Lombard. 2004. Ochre hafting in Middle Stone Age southern Africa: A practical role. *Antiquity* 78:661–675.

Wagner, G. A. 1998. *Age determination of young rocks and artifacts: Physical and chemical clocks in quaternary geology and archaeology.* New York: Springer.

Walker, A. 2002. New perspectives on the hominids of the Turkana Basin, Kenya. *Evolutionary Anthropology* 11 (Supplement 1): 38–41.

Walker, A., and P. Shipman. 1996. *The wisdom of the bones: In search of human origins.* New York: Knopf.

———. 2005. *Ape in the tree.* Cambridge, MA: Harvard University Press.

Walker, J., R. A. Cliff, and A. G. Latham. 2006. U-Pb isotopic age of the StW 573 hominid from Sterkfontein, South Africa. *Science* 314:1592–1594.

Walls, D., and J. Mitani. 2002. Hunting behavior of chimpanzees at Ngoro, Kibale National Park, Uganda. *International Journal of Primatology* 23 (1): 1–28.

Walsh, P. D. 2003. Catastrophic ape decline in western equatorial Africa. *Nature* 422:611–613.

Walter, R. C. 1997. Potassium–argon/argon–argon dating methods. In *Chronometric dating in archaeology*, eds. R. E. Taylor and M. J. Aitken, 97–126. New York: Plenum.

Wanpo, H., R. Ciochon, G. Yumin, et al. 1995. Early *Homo* and associated artifacts from Asia. *Nature* 378: 275–278.

Ward, C. 1997. Introduction. In *Function, phylogeny, and fossils: Miocene hominoid evolution and adaptation*, eds. D. R. Begun, C. V. Ward, and M. D. Rose. New York: Plenum.

Ward, C., M. G. Leakey, and A. Walker. 1999. The new hominid species *Australopithecus anamensis. Evolutionary Anthropology:* 197–216.

———. 2001. *A. anamensis. Journal of Human Evolution* (October): 255–368.

Warneken, F., and M. Tomasello. 2006. Altruistic helping in human infants and young chimpanzees. *Science* 311:1301–1304.

Waters, M.R., and T. W. Stafford. 2007. Redefining the age of Clovis: Implications for the peopling of the Americas. *Science* 315:1122–1125.

Webster, D., and Evans, S. T. 2005. Mesoamerican civilization. In *The human past: World prehistory and the development of human societies*, ed. C. Scarre, 594–639. New York: Thames & Hudson.

Weiss, E., M. Kislev, O. Simchoni, et al. 2005. Small-grained wild grasses as staple food at the 23,000 year old site of Ohalo II, Israel. *Economic Botany* 388:125–134.

Weiss, R., and R. Wrangham. 1999. From Pan to pandemic. *Nature* 397:385–386.

Wendorf, F., and R. Schild. 1994. Are the early Holocene cattle in the eastern Sahara domestic or wild? *Evolutionary Anthropology* 3:118–128.

———. 1998. Nabta Playa and its role in Northeastern African prehistory. *Journal of Anthropological Archaeology* 17:97–123.

Wendorf, F., R. Schild, and N. Zedeno. 1996. A late Neolithic complex in the eastern Sahara: A preliminary report. In *Interregional contacts in the later prehistory of northeastern Africa*, eds. L. Krzyaniak, K. Kroeper, and M. Kobusiewicz. Poznañ, Poland: Poznañ Archaeological Museum.

Wenke, R. J. 1991. The evolution of early Egyptian civilization: Issues and evidence. *Journal of World Prehistory* 5 (3): 279–329.

———. 1999. *Patterns in prehistory: Humankind's first three million years.* Oxford: Oxford University Press.

Wessen, K. 2005. *Simulating human origins and evolution.* Cambridge: Cambridge University Press.

Wheeler, P. E. 1991a. The thermoregulatory advantage of hominid bipedalism in open equatorial environments: The contribution of increased convective heat loss and cutaneous evaluative cooling. *Journal of Human Evolution* 21:107–115.

———. 1991b. The influence of bipedalism on the energy and water budgets of early hominids. *Journal of Human Evolution* 21:117–136.

———. 1994. The evolution of bipedality and loss of functional body hair in hominids. *Journal of Human Evolution* 13:91–98.

White, C. D., M. W. Spence, F. J. Longstaffe, et al. 2002. Geographic identities of the sacrificial victims from the Feathered Serpent pyramid, Teotihuacan: Implications for the nature of state power. *Latin American Antiquity* 13 (2): 217–236.

White, C. D., M. W. Spence, F. J. Longstaffe, and K. R. Law. 2004. Demography and ethnic continuity in the Tlailotlacan enclave of Teotihuacan: The evidence from stable oxygen isotopes. *Journal of Anthropological Archaeology* 23:385–403.

White, E., and D. Brown. 1973. *The first men* (Emergence of Man series). New York: Time-Life Books.

White, M. 1994. Raw materials and biface variability in southern Britain: A preliminary examination. *Lithics* 15:1–20.

White, T. D. 1980. Evolutionary implications of Pliocene hominid footprints. *Science* 208:176.

———. 2001. Once were cannibals. *Scientific American* 265 (2): 58–65.

———. 2002. Hominid evolution. In *Encyclopedia of evolution*, ed. M. Pagel, 476–485. Oxford: Oxford University Press.

White, T. D., B. Asfaw, D. DeGusta, et al. 2003. Pleistocene *Homo sapiens* from middle Awash, Ethiopia. *Nature* 423:742–747.

White, T. D., G. WodeGabriel, B. Asfaw, et al. 2006. Asa Issie, Aramis, and the origin of australopithecines. *Nature* 440:883–889.

Whitfield, J. 2004. Born in a watery commune. *Nature* 427:674–676.

Whittle, A. 1997. Remembered and imagined belongings: Stonehenge in its traditions and structures of meaning. *Proceedings of the British Academy* 92:145–166.

———. 1999. The Neolithic period, c. 4000–2500/2200 BC: Changing the world. In *The archaeology of Britain*, eds. J. Hunter and I. Ralston, 58–76. London: Routledge.

Wildman, D. E., M. Uddin, G. Liu, et al. 2003. Implications of natural selection in shaping 99.4% non-synonymous DNA identity between humans and chimpanzees: Enlarging genus *Homo*. *Proceedings of the National Academy of Sciences USA* 100 (12): 7181–7188.

Wilford, J. N. 1994. Early amphibian fossil hints of a trip ashore earlier than thought. *New York Times* (August 2).

———. 2002. Rearranging humanity's family tree. *New York Times* (August 6).

———. 2003. Big teeth in ancient jaw offer clues about our ancestors. *New York Times* (September 30).

Williams, F. L'E., and J. M. Hall. 2005. *Homo ergaster* and *Homo erectus*: Two species or one? *General Anthropology* 11 (2): 1–10.

Williams, P. R., and D. J. Nash. 2002. Imperial interaction in the Andes. Huari and Tiwanaku at Cerro Baúl. In *Andean Archaeology I: Variations in Sociopolitical Organization*, eds. W. H. Isbell and H. Silverman, 243–265. New York: Kluyer Academic/Plenum.

Wilson, D. J. 1999. *Indigenous South Americans of the past and present: An ecological perspective.* Boulder, CO/Oxford: Westview.

Wilson, E. O. 1999. *The diversity of life.* New ed. New York: Norton.

Winston, J. E. 1999. *Describing species.* New York: Columbia University Press.

Wolpoff, M., and R. Caspari. 1997. *Race and human evolution.* New York: Simon & Schuster.

Wolpoff, M. H. 1996. *Human evolution.* New York: McGraw-Hill.

———. 1999. *Paleoanthropology.* 2nd ed. New York: McGraw-Hill.

Wolpoff, M. H., J. Hawks, D. W. Frayer, and K. Hunley. 2001. Modern human ancestry at the peripheries: A test of the replacement theory. *Science* 291:293–307.

Wolpoff, M. H., A. G. Thorne, F. H. Smith, et al. 1994. Multiregional evolution: A world wide source for modern human populations. In *Origins of anatomically modern humans*, eds. M. Nitecki and D. Nitecki, 176–199. New York: Plenum.

Wood, B., and M. Collard. 1999. The changing face of the genus *Homo*. *Evolutionary Anthropology* 8 (6): 195–207.

Wood, B., and A. Turner. 1995. Out of Africa and into Asia. *Nature* 378:239–240.

Woodburn, J. 1980. Hunters and gatherers today and reconstruction of the past. In *Soviet and western anthropolgy*, ed. E. Gellner, 95–117. London: Duckworth.

Wooley, L. 1939. *Ur excavations*. Vol. V. *The ziggurat and its surroundings*. London: Joint Expedition of the British Museum and the Museum of the University of Pennsylvania to Mesopotamia.

Wrangham, R. W. 1996. *Demonic males*. New York: Houghton Mifflin.

———. 1999. The evolution of coalitional killing. *Yearbook of Physical Anthropology* 42:1–30.

Wrangham, R. W., J. H. Jones, G. Laden, et al. 1999. The raw and the stolen: Cooking and the ecology of human origins. *Current Anthropology* 40 (5): 567–595.

Wrangham, R. W., M. L. Wilson, and M. N. Muller. 2006. Comparative rates of violence in chimpanzees and humans. *Primates* 47:14–26.

Wright, S. 1948. On the roles of directed and random changes in gene frequencies in the genetics of populations. *Evolution* 2:279–294.

Wu, X. 2004. Fossil humankind and other anthropoid primates of China. *International Journal of Primatology* 25 (5).

Wynn, T. 1998. Did *Homo erectus* speak? *Cambridge Archaeological Journal* 1:78–81.

Xian-guang, H., et al. 2004. *The Cambrian fossils of Chengjiang, China: The flowering of early animal life*. Malden, MA: Blackwell Publishing.

Xian-guang, H., R. J. Aldridge, D. J. Sivete, et al. 2000. New evidence on the anatomy and phylogeny of the earliest vertebrates. *Proceedings of the Royal Society* (Biological Sciences), 1865–1869.

Yamei, H., R. Potts, Y. Baoyin, et al. 2000. Mid-Pleistocene Acheulean-like stone technology of the Bose Basin, South China. *Science* 287:1622–1626.

Yang, Z., and J. C. Schank. 2006. Women do not synchronize their menstrual cycles. *Human Nature* 17:433–447.

Yoon, C. K. 2003. The evolving peppered moth gains a furry counterpart. *New York Times* (June 17).

Young, D. 1992. *The discovery of evolution*. New York: Cambridge University Press.

Young, E. 2003. Mungo man has his say on Australia's first humans. *New Scientist* (February 22): 15.

Zhenxiang, Z. 1996. The royal consort Fu Hao and her tomb. In *Mysteries of ancient China: New discoveries from the early dynasties*, ed. J. Rawson, 240–247. London: British Museum Press.

Zhu, R. X., K. A. Hoffman, R. Potts, et al. 2001. Earliest presence of humans in northeast Asia. *Nature* 413:413–417.

Zhu, R. X., R. Potts, F. Xie, et al. 2004. New evidence on the earliest human presence at high northern latitudes in northeast Asia. *Nature* 431:559–562.

Zilhao, J., and F. d'Errico. 2000. A case for Neandertal culture. *Scientific American* (April): 98–107.

Zimmer, C. 2005a. Testing Darwin. *Discover* (February).

———. 2005b. *Smithsonian intimate guide to human origins*. Washington, DC: Smithsonian Institution Press.

Zinner, D., F. Perlaez, and F. Torkler. 2001. Distribution and habitat associations of baboons *(Phanadryas hamadryas)* in central Eritrea. *International Journal of Primatology* 22 (3): 397–413.

Zvelebil, M. 1994. Plant use in the Mesolithic and its role in the transition to farming. *Proceedings of the Prehistoric Society* 60:35–74.

———. 2002. Demography and dispersal of early farming populations at the Mesolithic-Neolithic transition: Linguistic and genetic implications. In *Examining the farming/language dispersal hypothesis*, eds. P. Bellwood and C. Renfrew, 379–394. Cambridge: McDonald Institute for Archaeological Research.

———. 2003. Enculturation of Mesolithic landscapes. In *Mesolithic on the move: Papers presented at the sixth international conference on the Mesolithic in Europe, Stockholm 2000*, eds. L. Larsson, H. Kindgren, Kjel Knutsson, et al., 65–73. Oxford: Oxbow.

# Name Index

Abbate, E., 198
Abegglen, J-J., 438
Abrams, M., 179
Addate, T., 95
Adler, D. S., 188, 189
Adovasio, J. M., 352
Aiello, L., 186
Aiken, C. M., 278, 279, 361
Aitken, M. J., 37, 224, 225, 226, 229, 362
Akazawa, T., 275
Alemseged, Z., 150
Algaze, G., 313
Allen, J., 257
Allison, A. C., 48
Almquist, A. J., 185
Alt, K., 261
Altmann, J., 424
Alva, W., 400, 401
Alvard, M. S., 508
Alvarez, L., 94
Alvarez, W., 94
Ambrose, S. H., 236, 241
Ames, K. M., 213, 364, 365, 366, 367, 381
Anaximander, 72
Ancrenaz, M., 446
Andersen, B. G., 271, 272, 276, 279, 350
Anderson, D. G., 363
Anderson, K. K., 32, 33
Andrews, P., 123, 149, 198, 206, 245
Anewalt, P., 413
Ankle-Simons, F., 425
Antcliffe, J., 84
Anton, M., 182, 183
Archibald, J. D., 96
Arensburg, B., 204
Aristotle, 58
Armelagos, G. J., 492
Arpin, T. L., 352
Arsuaga, J. L., 171, 180, 184
Ascenzi, A., 180
Asfaw, B., 154, 198
Ashmore, W., 209
Asouti, E., 303
Asquith, P., 426
Attenborough, D., 90
Audouze, F., 254, 258

Baba, H., 178
Backwell, L. R., 236
Bada, J. L., 82

Bagley, R., 334
Bahn, P., 215, 221, 261, 265, 267, 294
Bailey, W., 123
Bailey, W. J., 139
Baines, J., 311
Balter, M., 80, 467, 502
Bandy, M., 405
Barba, R., 237
Barbujani, G., 294
Bard, E., 225
Bard, K. A., 317, 318, 336
Bareye, P., 405
Barfield, L., 5
Barham, L. S., 248, 249
Barker, P., 217
Barkley, N., 287
Barnes, G. J. K., 492
Barnes, G. L., 279, 329
Barton, N., 243
Barton, R. N. E., 184
Bar-Yosef, O., 240, 248, 270, 275, 278, 281, 282, 288, 289, 290
Basgall, M., 368
Batsford, B. T., 354
Baudelt, H-J., 294
Bauer, B. S., 394, 417
Bayman, J. M., 374, 376
Beall, C. M., 477, 486
Beard, K. C., 116
Bearder, S. K., 430, 431, 456
Beaumont, M., 294,
Bednarik, R. G., 250, 250, 251
Begley, S., 451
Begun, D. R., 120, 121, 123
Bell, M., 233
Bellwood, P., 294
Benavides, M .C., 407
Bender, B., 283
Benefit, B. R., 120
Benson, E. P., 420
Bentley, R. A., 294
Berdan, F. F., 411, 412, 413
Berger, L. R., 160, 240
Berggren, W. A., 119
Bergmann, C., 475
Bermudez de Castro, J. M., 183
Bernardini, W., 373
Bettinger, R. L., 273
Biasutti, R., 475, 481, 482
Billings, P. R., 53

Billman, B., 379
Billsborough, A., 180, 199
Binford, L., 273, 274, 282, 283
Binford, L. R., 221, 236, 247
Binford, S. R., 247
Blakey, M. L., 12, 13
Blanton, R. E., 411
Blinderman, C., 156, 157
Blom, D., 406
Blomster, J. P., 387
Blumberg, B.S., 48
Blumenbach, J., 132
Blumenbach, J. F., 483
Blumenschine, R., 162
Boas, N. T., 185
Bocquet-Apple, J. P., 187
Bodu, P., 254
Boesch, C., 428, 446, 452
Boesch, H., 446, 452
Bogen, G., 446
Bogin, B., 61, 113, 472, 484, 486, 487, 500
Bogucki, P., 290, 291, 295
Boise, C., 158
Bonnichsen, R., 351, 381
Bordes, F., 247, 254
Borns, H. W., Jr., 271, 272, 350
Bortenschlager, S., 5
Bosinski, G., 245, 259, 260, 261
Boule, M., 184
Bourget, S., 400, 401
Bowler, J. M., 195, 257, 261, 462
Bowler, P. J., 45
Bown, T., 118, 119
Boyd, R., 50, 51, 162, 174, 182, 185, 280, 512
Boëda, E., 246
Brace, C. L., 463, 478, 483, 500
Brace, L., 188
Bradley, B., 349
Braidwood, R., 283
Brain, C. K., 161, 236, 237, 240
Bramanti, B., 294
Bramble, D. M., 132, 134, 151
Brasier, M., 84
Brauer, G., 181, 198
Bray, F., 511

Brewer, D. J., 317, 318, 320, 321, 333, 345
Briggs, D. E., 88
Broad, W., 85
Brockman, D., 434
Brooks, A., 246, 248, 249, 250, 252, 253, 461
Broom, R., 158
Brown, D., 178
Brown, P., 464, 467
Brown, T., 28
Brown, T. M., 71
Browne, M., 89, 91
Brunet, M., 146, 154
Burns, K. R., 497, 500
Burton, F., 436, 437
Bustors Galvez, L., 371, 394
Butzer, K., 312, 317
Bynum, N., 68
Byrne, R. W., 428

Caesar, J., 342
Call, J., 428
Campbell, A., 21, 23, 144
Campbell, C. J., 130, 459
Cann, R., 199
Cannon, A., 365, 366
Caramelli, D. G., 189
Carbonell, E., 180, 241, 245
Carpenter, R., 425, 426
Carroll, R., 89
Carter, R., 313
Cartmill, M., 113, 203, 480
Caspari, R., 124, 132, 196, 197
Castle, W., 470
Catherwood, F., 396
Cavalli-Sforza, L., 73, 198, 292, 294, 462, 484
Censky, E. J., 120, 432, 435
Chaimanee, Y., 122
Chang, K., 297, 329, 333, 334, 335, 345
Chapdelaine, C., 399
Chaplin, G., 475
Chartkoff, J. L., 367, 369
Chase, P. G., 250
Chatterjee, H. J., 32, 35
Chen, C., 253
Chen, X., 329
Chikhi, L., 294
Childe, G., 283, 310
Cifelli, R. L., 96
Ciochen, R. L., 32, 117, 122

Rice, P., 21, 23, 24, 64, 144, 220, 263, 265, 478, 481, 511
Richard, A., 105, 106, 107, 434, 435
Richard, A. F., 479
Richards, M., 247, 294, 296
Richards, M. P., 462
Richerson, P. J., 512
Ridley, M., 42, 60, 69, 82, 84, 477
Rigaud, J-Ph., 191
Rightmire, G. P., 174
Riley, D. N., 215
Rilling, J. K., 428
Robb, J., 221, 294
Roberts, J. A., 334, 335
Roberts, M., 243
Roberts, M. B., 180
Roberts, N., 270
Roberts, R. G., 467
Robinson, A., 394
Roche, H., 235
Rodríguez, M. C., 387
Rodríguez, X. P., 241
Rogers, A. R., 200
Rogers, J., 123
Rolland, N., 244, 247
Rollefson, G., 288, 289, 290
Ronin, A., 187
Roosevelt, A. C., 353, 463
Rose, J. E., 116
Rose, K. D., 71, 102, 116
Rosenberg, K. R., 182
Rosenzweig, M., 60
Rossen, J., 352
Rostworowski, M., 416
Rowe, B., 194
Rowley-Conwy, P., 275, 280
Ruff, C. B., 364
Russell, T., 293
Russo, M., 360
Rye, O. S., 287

Sabloff, J. A., 385, 389
Sagan, D., 51
Sapolsky, R. M., 443
Sarich, V., 32
Sassaman, K., 359
Saunders, E., 469
Sauvage, M., 315
Savage-Rumbaugh, S., 424
Save-Soderberge, T., 214
Sawyer, R., 448
Scarre, C., 267, 295, 306, 311, 312, 334, 345, 384, 420
Schele, L., 396

Schick, K., 236, 237, 238, 267, 452
Schiffer, M. B., 209
Schild, R., 299
Schlect, R., 213
Schmid, P., 154
Schmidke, J., 489
Schmitz, R. W., 184
Schneider, A. L., 351
Schoeninger, M. J., 276, 364
Schopf, W., 81
Schrago, C. G., 117
Schreiber, K. J., 407, 408
Schulting, R. J., 281
Schultz, E., 451
Schultzhuitzen, M., 57, 95
Schulz, R., 333
Schwartz, J., 184, 193
Schweingruber, F. H., 225
Scoboda, J., 261
Segre, A. G., 180
Seidel, J., 333
Seidlmayer, S., 318
Selmin, J., 89
Semaw, S., 235, 238
Semino, O., 294
Senner, W., 331
Serra Puche, M. C., 387
Shafer, H. J., 229
Shanklin, E., 41
Sharer, R. J., 209, 386, 387, 391, 394, 395, 397, 420
Shea, J., 195,
Shennan, S., 221, 274, 293, 508, 509
Shick, K. D., 240, 243
Shimada, I., 219, 399, 400
Shipman, P., 37, 130, 142, 143, 175, 177, 180, 187, 206, 476
Shostak, M., 492, 500
Shott, M., 238
Shreeve, J., 153, 155
Silk, J., 50, 51, 162, 174, 182, 185
Simons, E. L., 115, 117, 119, 430
Simpson, G. G., 42, 69, 71, 78, 144
Siner, M., 248
Skinner, A. R., 247
Smeldlev, A., 483
Smith, B., 372, 373, 374, 375, 377, 381
Smith, B. D., 273, 284, 288, 297, 299, 300, 306, 369, 370, 372, 381
Smith, E. A., 446
Smith, F., 170

Smith, F. H., 190, 191, 200
Smith, M. E., 394, 409, 411, 412, 420
Smith, M. P., 32, 33
Snow, D. R., 356, 357, 358, 374, 381
Soejono, M. R. P., 467
Soffer, O., 259, 263, 265
Sommer, J. D., 250
Southwood, T., 82, 83, 89, 93, 95, 99
Speth, J. D., 188
Spielberg, S., 86
Spindler, K., 5
Spoor, F., 184
Stadelmann, R., 321
Stafford, T. W., 463
Stahl, A., 244
Stanford, C., 451, 452, 453
Stanford, D., 349, 356, 447, 449
Stark, M. T., 333
Steadman, D. W., 498, 500
Stearns, S. C., 57, 60, 73, 199
Steegman, T. S., 477, 486
Steele, J., 293
Stein, P., 194
Stern, J., 151
Stiner, M., 247
Stinger, C., 198
Stinnesbeck, W., 95
Stirland, A., 496
Stokstad, E., 83, 85, 91, 93
Stoneking, M., 199
Stothert, K. E., 273, 370
Stout, C., 363
Straus, L., 23, 32
Strauss, E., 349
Strier, K. B., 114, 455
Stringer, C., 32, 33, 178, 182, 183, 184, 189, 197, 198, 199, 200, 206, 248
Struever, S., 358
Strum, S., 424
Stumpf, R., 455
Sussman, R., 113
Sussman, R. L., 457
Sussman, R. W., 425, 488, 510
Sutikna, M. J., 467
Sutton, M. Q., 229
Suwa, G., 158
Svitil, K. A., 82, 83, 463
Svoboda, 262, 265
Swedell, L., 438
Swisher, C., 199
Swisher, C. C., 147, 174, 178, 241

Sykes, B., 28
Sànchez de Lozada, D., 405

Taieb, M., 152
Takahashi, R., 275, 277, 280, 281, 306
Takahata, N., 31, 32, 51, 58, 60, 61, 67, 82, 84, 96
Takassaki, H., 22
Tanner, N., 165
Tappan, M., 137
Tattersall, I., 21, 139, 147, 184, 185, 190, 202, 224
Taube, K., 387
Taylor, R. E., 37, 224, 225, 229, 468, 469
Tchernov, E., 188, 247
Teeter, E., 317, 318, 320, 321, 333, 345
Templeton, A., 197, 199, 200, 473, 480, 499
Thayer, D., 186
Thieme, H., 243
Thomas, D. H., 364
Thomson, K., 25
Thorne, A., 195, 197, 206, 257
Thorne, A. G., 186
Thorpe, R. L., 329
Tobias, P., 146, 155, 203
Toizumi, T., 306
Tomasello, M., 428, 446
Tosi, M., 327
Toth, N., 236, 237, 238, 267
Toyama, S., 296
Treves, A., 432
Trigger, B. G., 310, 313, 319
Trinkaus, E., 142, 186, 187, 190, 193, 206
Tubb, K. W., 290
Turner, C., 351
Turner, C. G., 179, 379
Turner, J. A., 379
Turner, T. R., 10, 11
Turnmire, K. L., 381
Tyers, P., 287
Tzedakis, P. C., 186

Underhill, A. P., 296, 297
Ussher (Bishop), 41

Valla, F., 277, 280, 281
van Andel, T. H., 186
Vandermeersch, B., 250
Vandiver, P., 265
Vanhaeren, M., 250, 236
Van Stone, M., 393
Vekua, A., 179, 180

Clark, A. J., 215
Clark, G. A., 7, 21, 23, 188, 191, 251, 252
Clark, J. D., 7
Clark, J. E., 384, 385
Clarke, R., 155
Clarke, R. J., 240
Close, A. E., 258
Clottes, J., 263, 265
Cobo, B., 416,
Coe, M. D., 385, 386, 389, 391, 392, 393, 394, 395
Cohen, J. E., 472
Cohen, M. N., 283
Coles, B., 210, 288
Coles, J., 210, 288
Collard, M., 141, 163
Collis, J., 343
Coningham, R., 323
Connah, G., 336, 337, 338, 339, 340, 345
Connolly, P., 27, 37
Conroy, G., 141, 148
Conroy, G. C., 123
Conway Morris, S., 80, 83, 84, 88
Cooley, A. E., 27, 37
Coon, C., 483
Cooper, G., 156, 157
Copeland, L., 250
Coppens, Y., 139, 146, 152
Corbey, R., 440
Cordell, L., 372, 373, 374, 375, 377, 378, 379, 381
Costamgo, S., 247
Coughlan, A., 473
Coupland, G., 365, 366, 367
Coven, H. H., 430
Cowen, R., 81, 82, 84, 89, 90, 91, 92, 93, 95, 99
Cowgill, G. L., 387, 389, 390, 391, 420
Cox, M., 498
Crawford, G. W., 296
Crawford, H., 315, 316, 333
Cressford, C., 300, 302
Crick, F., 47, 49, 50
Crockett, C. M., 440
Cronin, J. E., 139
Cronk, L., 18
Crowther, P., 88
Culotta, E., 116, 154, 467
Cummins, T., 394
Cunliffe, B., 291, 294
Curnoe, D., 195
Cyphers, A., 385, 386
Cyranoski, D., 448
Czelusniak, J., 114, 117

Daeschler, E. B., 89
Dales, F. G., 324, 327

Dalton, R., 467
D'Altroy, T. N., 414, 415, 416, 417, 418, 420
Damerow, P., 333
Dancey, W. S., 373
Dart, R., 154, 161, 167, 237, 240
Darwin, C., 19, 32, 33, 39, 42, 45, 54, 55, 56, 57, 58, 60, 61, 62, 63, 64, 65, 72, 137, 156, 486
Daugherty, R., 212, 213
David, R., 333
Davies, W., 189, 233, 251, 294
Davis, B. M., 96
Davis, S. J., 219, 233, 306, 354
Dawkins, R., 60
Dawson, C., 156, 157
Deacon, H. J., 120, 233, 235, 240, 248, 253, 267
Deacon, J., 120, 233, 235, 240, 248, 267
Dean, C., 179
Dearborn, D. S., 394, 417
Defleur, A., 250
DeGusta, D. W., 203
de la Fuente, B., 420
de la Torre, I., 452
Deloukas, B., 50
Delson, E., 179
de Lumley, H., 244
deLumley, M-A., 179
Demars, P., 87
Demel, S. J., 363
d'Errico, F., 191, 236, 250, 263, 505, 506
Desmond, A., 57, 64
DeVore, I., 164
de Vries, H., 42, 58, 72
de Waal, F. B., 128, 130, 449, 455, 456, 457, 459
Diamond, J., 294
Dibble, H., 247, 250
Dickinson, A., 452
Diehl, R. A., 385, 386, 387
Dillehay, T. D., 349, 351, 352, 354, 381, 462, 500
DiPaolo Loren, D., 363
Dixson, F. J., 351
Díaz, B., 409, 411
Dobres, M-A., 221
Dobzhansky, T., 42
Dolhinow, P., 426
Dominguez-Rodrigo, M., 236, 237
Donahue, P. C., 32, 33
Donnan, C. B., 399, 400, 401

Doran, D. M., 447
Dorfman, A., 468
Doyle, A. C., 18, 157
Doyle, G. A., 430, 435
Drewett, P., 209, 210, 217, 229
Duarte, C., 190, 193
Dumont, D., 349
Dunbar, R. I. M., 423, 453
Dunham, K., 448
Dunsworth, H., 163, 178

Earhart, A., 494
Eaton, S. B., 492, 500
Eckhardt, R., 41, 71, 171, 172, 436, 453
Edey, M., 67
Edey, M. A., 91, 149, 153
Eisenberg, J. F., 440
Eldredge, N., 59, 60, 82, 91
Elias, S. A., 349
Elston, R. G., 364
Emerson, T. E., 363, 381
Enard, W., 6, 448
Endler, J. A., 73
Englund, R., 333
Enserink, M., 53
Eswaran, V., 189, 200
Evans, S. T., 409

Fagan, B., 311, 334, 384
Fagan, B. M., 345, 352, 357, 359, 361, 367, 369, 373, 381
Fairburn, A., 303
Falk, D., 148, 163, 431, 464, 466, 467, 472
Fash, W. L., 396, 397
Fattovich, R., 336
Feder, K., 157
Feder, K. L., 37, 229
Fedigan, L., 424,
Fernandez-Jalvo, Y., 244, 245
Ferreras, J., 183
Fiedel, S. J., 351, 352, 353, 356, 358, 359, 371, 463, 469
Fiorelli, G., 27
Fisher, R., 470
Fisher, R. A., 42
Flannery, K., 283
Flannery, K. V., 273, 311, 370
Fleagle, J. G., 32, 102, 105, 106, 115, 119, 120
Foley, R. A., 39, 57, 60, 71, 77, 117, 128, 138, 141, 144, 160, 167, 175, 467, 503

Forster, P., 294
Fossey, D., 424, 426, 440, 447
Fowler, B., 5
Franciscus, R., 185, 186, 190
Frayer, D., 185, 186, 190, 196
Freidel, D., 396
Fremlen, J., 189
Friedman, I., 226
Frisancho, A. R., 486
Frison, G. C., 353, 356
Fuentes, A., 130, 426, 459
Fujita, H., 368
Fujiyama, A., 448
Futuyma, D. J., 80, 83

Gabunia, L., 179, 180, 240
Galdikas, B., 424, 440
Gallup, G., 428
Gamble, C., 206, 241, 243, 245, 248, 257
Garfinkel, Y., 211
Garn, S., 483
Garner, R. L., 425
Garrard, A., 277
Gebauer, A. B., 306
Gebo, D. L., 116, 122
Gee, H., 89, 92
Genomic, C., 52
Gerhard, W., 494
Gibbon, G., 348
Gibbons, A., 178, 180, 189
Gibbson, A., 452
Gibson, J., 359, 360, 374
Gibson, K. R., 451
Gilead, I., 261
Gillespie, R., 462
Gingerich, P. D., 60
Gkiasta, M., 293
Gladkih, N. L., 259
Glasscow, M. A., 368
Goldberg, P., 352
González Lauch, R., 386
Goodall, J., 128, 130, 204, 424, 426, 440, 448, 449, 459, 488
Goodman, M., 31, 32, 96, 103, 111, 114, 116, 117, 122, 124
Goren-Inbar, N., 243, 244
Gould, S. J., 20, 37, 54, 59, 60, 75, 77, 84, 88, 99
Gowlett, J. A. J., 235, 244
Goñi, M. F. S., 191
Graham, E., 409, 411
Graham-Rowe, D., 455,
Grant, B. R., 78
Grant, P., 73
Grant, P. R., 61, 63, 64, 78

Grant, R., 64
Grant, V., 47, 65
Grayson, D. K., 353, 354, 355
Greenberg, J., 351
Grey, J. P., 478
Grinnel, G. F., 117
Groves, C., 51, 71, 102, 431, 433
Grube, N., 397
Guaman Poma de Ayala, F., 371, 394
Gunnell, G. F., 116
Gursky, S., 102, 430, 431
Gutierrez, G., 189

Haak, W., 294
Haaland, R., 299
Habu, J., 275, 279, 296
Hagelberg, E., 462
Hager, L. D., 165
Haldane, J. B. S., 42
Hall, J. M., 173
Hall, M. E., 279
Hall, R. L., 363
Hamilton, G., 82
Harbottle, G., 333
Harding, J., 304
Hardy, B. L., 246, 248
Hardy, G., 470, 471
Hare, P. E., 226
Harlan, J. R., 300
Harlow, H., 427
Harpending, H., 200, 201
Harren, M., 493
Harrington, S. P., 13
Harris, C. L., 40
Harris, D., 294
Harris, T., 215, 216
Harrison, P. T., 391, 395, 396
Hartwig, W., 119, 123, 130
Hassan, F. A., 318
Hawass, Z., 323
Hayden, B., 283
Haynes, G., 354, 355
Hecht, J., 21, 120
Hegmon, M., 376
Helmer, R. P., 495, 496
Hemmings, S., 489
Hempill, B. E., 364
Henderson, J. S., 391, 397
Henneberg, M., 71, 471
Henshilwood, C. S., 249, 252, 461
Hewes, G. W., 137
Hewett, G., 204
Hickey, E., 294
Higham, C., 296, 297
Higuchi, T., 278, 279

Hill, C., 235
Hill Boone, E., 394
Hillier, L. W., 53
Hinde, R. A., 422
Hinton, M., 157
Hiraguchi, T., 276
Hitler, A., 494
Hodder, I., 221, 300, 302, 303
Hodges, M. G., 411
Hoekstra, R. F., 57, 60, 73, 199
Hoffecker, J. F., 349
Holden, C., 293, 294
Holden, E., 190
Holton, F., 358
Hooton, E. A., 483
Horodyski, R., 83
Hovers, E., 249
Howard, A. V., 376
Howell, C., 152
Howell, F. C., 7
Hrdy, S. B., 126
Hublin, J.-J., 182, 183
Hummel, S., 28
Hunter, J. C., 493
Hutchinson, D. L., 364
Huxley, L., 156
Huxley, T., 55

Igman, M., 199
Imamura, K., 273, 281
Ingold, T., 451
Ingstad, H., 214
Isaac, G., 236, 237
Isbell, W. H., 407
Iseminger, W. R., 363
Itani, J., 22

Jablonski, N., 475
Jablonski, N. G., 120, 123, 123
Jacob, F., 54
Jacob, T., 465
Jaiger, J. J., 119
James, S. R., 244
Jansen, M., 324
Janson, C. H., 446
Janusek, J. W., 405
Jefferies, R. W., 360
Jefferson, T., 489
Jenkins, M., 512
Jennings, J. D., 211, 369, 377
Jiang, L., 296
Jobling, M. A., 32
Johanson, D., 91, 131, 146, 149, 150, 152, 153, 167
Johnson, B. J., 226
Johnson, M., 221

Johnston, H., 257
Jolly, A., 434, 435
Jones, C., 395
Jones, M., 32, 51, 69
Jones, P., 242
Jones, S., 53, 58, 80, 449, 472, 485, 488, 489
Jones, T. L., 368
Jurmain, R., 148, 173

Kamminga, J., 233, 257, 267
Kappeler, P., 432
Kardong, K. V., 80
Karlin, C., 254
Kaufman, D., 187, 204
Kawamura, S., 22
Kay, R. F., 119, 203
Keeley, L. H., 273
Kehoe, A. B., 367
Keller, G., 95
Kelly, R. L., 273, 274, 364
Kemp, T. S., 32
Kennedy, K., 199, 498
Kenoyer, J. M., 323, 324, 325, 326, 328, 333, 345
Kenyon, K. M., 288
Kernan, M., 496
Kerr, J., 394
Kerr, R., 83
Kerr, R. A., 88
Kessler, D., 320
Kester, T. R., 229
Killan, E. W., 498
Kimbel, W. H., 69, 143, 151, 153
Kimeu, K., 30, 176
King, M. C., 54, 493
Kirk, R., 213
Klein, J., 31, 32, 51, 58, 60, 61, 67, 82, 84, 96, 108
Klein, R., 248, 255, 258, 267, 355, 506
Klein, R. G., 190, 234
Klima, B., 261, 262, 265
Knath, L. P., 83
Knecht, H., 265
Knoll, A. H., 91, 99
Kobayashi, T., 279, 280, 281
Kohn, M., 242
Kolata, A. L., 402, 403, 404, 405, 406
Konner, M., 492, 500
Kortlandt, A., 118, 139
Kotschnid, E., 134
Kottak, C., 455
Kowalski, J. K., 391
Kramer, A., 172, 198
Kraus, M. J., 119
Krawczak, M., 489

Kraytsberg, Y., 32
Krings, M., 189
Kristiansen, K., 343
Kuhn, T., 21
Kummer, H., 437, 438
Kunzig, R., 190, 193

Lahr, M., 198, 467, 503
Laitman, J., 204
Lamarck, J. B., 19, 41, 58
Langdon, J. H., 97
Laroche, C. J., 13
Larsen, C. S., 276, 283, 285, 364
Larsson, L., 276, 281, 282
Lazcano, A., 82
Leakey, J., 160
Leakey, L., 29, 146, 160, 424
Leakey, M., 29, 146, 149, 150, 158, 160
Leakey, M. D., 236, 237, 244
Leakey, M. G., 150, 149
Leakey, R., 146, 176, 177
LeBlanc, S., 377
Lee, R., 164
Legge, A. J., 275
Lehner, M., 321
Lekson, S. H., 378, 379
Lemonick, M. D., 468
Leonard, W. R., 148
Levy, T. E., 306
Lewin, R. A., 57, 117, 124, 135, 178
Lewis, R. A., 363, 471
Lewis-Williams, D., 263
Lidén, K., 296
Lieberman, L., 478, 481
Lin, J., 492
Lindly, J. M., 21
Lindon, E., 449
Linnaeus, 41
Lipe, W., 377
Liu, L., 179, 296, 328, 329
Livingstone, F., 483
Lock, G., 215
Lockwood, C., 150
Lontcho, F., 180
Lopinot, N. H., 363
Lordkipanidze, D., 179
Lovejoy, O., 91, 151
Lowe, J. J., 32, 33, 34, 233, 235
Lowenstein, J. M., 59
Loy, T. H., 238
Lu, T., 296
Lubell, D., 285
Lucey, R. F., 405
Ludwig, K. P., 224
Lyell, C., 54

Lyles, R. B., 51
Lynch, B. M., 360

Macaulay, V., 201, 294, 462
MacDonald, K. C., 299
Mace, R., 509
Mackenzie, D., 493
MacKinnon, J. R., 442, 459
MacKinnon, K., 130
MacLarnon, A., 204
Madsen, D. B., 361
Magle, J. W., 195
Maisels, C. K., 325
Malek, J., 321
Malone, C., 303
Malthus, C., 54, 55
Malthus, T., 472
Mania, D., 245
Manley, B., 317, 320, 321
Manson, J. H., 439
Manzanilla, L., 389, 390
Manzi, G., 170
Marean, C. W., 247, 252, 461
Margulis, L., 51
Marivaux, L., 119
Marks, J., 40, 50, 51, 57, 73, 123, 124, 184, 188, 484, 500
Marlar, R., 379
Martin, J., 302
Martin, L. B., 69
Martin, P., 355
Martin, R., 430, 435
Martin, R. D., 108, 110, 114, 117, 130, 144
Martin, S., 397
Maschner, H. D., 213, 365, 366, 367, 381
Matos Moctezuma, E., 214, 409, 412, 414
Matson, R. G., 365, 366, 367
Matsui, A., 275, 278
Matsuzawa, T., 459
Matthews, R., 302, 312, 313, 316
Mauricio, J., 193
Mayr, E., 42, 57, 58, 68, 69, 80, 82, 84, 144
Mays, S., 488, 498
McBreaty, S., 123, 246, 248, 249, 250, 252, 253, 461
McClung de Tapia, E., 370
McCrossin, M. C., 120
McEwan, G. E., 408
McGrew, W., 130, 459
McGrew, W. C., 423, 446, 447, 449

McHenry, H., 143
McIntosh, R., 339, 340
McIntosh, S., 339, 340
McKee, J., 58, 60, 71, 155, 158
McKie, R., 184, 200
McKinney, M. L., 449, 452
McLelland, D., 401
McManus, J. F., 32, 33, 34
McNeilage, A., 447
McPherron, S. P., 241
Mellaart, J., 300, 301, 302
Mellars, P., 191, 196, 201, 247, 249, 250, 251, 262, 263, 265
Meltzer, D. J., 349, 352, 353, 355, 356
Meltzer, K., 355
Mendel, G., 19, 39, 41, 42, 43, 44, 45, 46, 47, 48, 49, 72
Mengele, J., 494, 495, 496
Menozzi, P., 73
Merkel, J. F., 219
Mignolo, W. D., 394
Miller, G. H., 226
Miller, J., 20, 160
Miller, L. E., 432
Miller, S., 80
Millon, R., 388
Milner, N., 296
Milo, R., 248
Milton, K., 439, 440
Minagawa, M., 275
Mitani, J., 452
Mithen, S., 242, 280, 306
Mittermier, R., 104, 105
Mojzis, S. J., 81
Molleson, T., 498
Moloney, N., 238, 241, 250
Monod, J., 54
Moore, A. M. T., 285
Moore, J., 57, 64
Morell, V., 158, 407, 469
Morgan, T. H., 57
Morris, C., 398, 399, 402, 403, 407, 415, 416, 418, 420
Morris, R., 56, 59
Morwood, M., 464, 465, 467
Morwood, M. J., 241
Moseley, M., 407, 408
Moseley, M. E., 398, 399
Mughal, M .R., 323
Mulvaney, J., 233, 257
Munro-Hay, S., 336, 339
Murrary, M. A., 321, 323
Murray, L. E., 429

Nadel, D., 258
Nadler, R. D. 443
Naggioncalda, N., 443
Napier, J., 134, 424
Napier, J. R., 102, 116, 431
Napier, P., 424
Napier, P. H., 102, 116, 431
Nash, D. J., 408
Neave, R., 489, 493
Neff, H., 387
Neiderberger, C., 387
Nelson, A. R., 463
Neuman, K., 284
Newman, T. K., 437
Nichols, T., 294
Nissen, H., 333
Nissen, H. J., 313, 316
Norris, S., 193

Oakley, K., 157
O'Brien, E. M., 242
Ockham, W., 144
O'Connell, J. F., 175, 257
Oefner, P., 294
Oeggl, K., 5
Olby, R., 45
Olley, J. M., 257
Olsen, J. W., 253
Olson, S., 65, 480, 484, 485
Oms, O., 241
Orbitz, P., 387
Orel, V., 44, 45
Orton, C., 287
Ovchinnikov, I. V., 189

Pääbo, S., 6, 28, 32, 123, 198, 473
Pace, N. R., 82
Panger, M., 128, 138, 459, 472
Parfitt, S., 241, 243
Parfitt, S. A., 180
Park, M. A., 43
Parker, M., 213
Parker, S. T., 442, 449, 452
Parker Pearson, M., 304
Pascua, M. P., 213
Passarino, G., 294
Patel, A., 326
Patterson, A., 263
Patterson, B., 149
Pauketat, T. R., 363, 381
Paulissen, E., 246
Pearsall, D. M., 276
Pearson, R., 280, 305
Pelto, P., 509
Pennisi, E., 54
Peretto, C., 241
Perry, S., 439

Perry, W., 13
Peters, H., 443
Pettitt, P. B., 193, 250, 265
Phillipson, D. W., 294, 336, 337, 338, 339
Piazza, A., 73
Pickering, T. R., 236
Pigliucci, M., 19
Pike-Tay, A., 265
Pilbeam, D. R., 120, 132
Pillsbury, J., 399, 420
Piperno, D. R., 273, 370
Plato, 40
Plog, S., 374, 376, 377, 379
Pollock, S., 314, 315, 333
Polo, M., 483
Pope, K. O., 370
Porcasi, J. F., 368
Porter, C. A., 114, 117
Possehl, G., 323, 324, 325, 326, 328
Postgate, J. N., 345
Postgate, N., 312, 316
Potts, R., 127, 160, 422
Power, M., 488, 500
Prag, J., 489, 493
Price, D., 296
Price, T., 294, 295
Price, T. D., 280, 306
Pringle, H., 165
Prothero, D. R., 32, 33, 119
Pruvost, M., 28
Pryce-Jones, R., 64
Purdy, B. A., 210, 358
Pusey, A. E., 449
Pye, M. E., 384, 385

Qiang, J., 96

Rak, Y., 151, 153, 159
Ramilisonina, 304
Rapp, G., Jr., 235
Rasmussen, D. T., 119
Rasmussen, T., 115, 116, 117
Rawson, J., 335
Ray, J., 68
Raymond, R., 257
Reader, J., 167
Reid, J. J., 374, 375, 377, 378
Relethford, J., 7, 28, 50, 61, 67, 85, 91, 93, 120, 122, 183, 189, 191, 201, 206, 486
Renfrew, C., 215, 221, 294, 462
Renne, P. R., 224
Rennie, J., 68, 71
Reno, P. L., 151
Reynolds, V., 441

Verano, J. W., 400
Vermeersch, P. M., 246, 255
Vertut, J., 261, 265, 267
Vignaud, P., 138, 139
Villa, P., 245, 248
Vince, A., 287
Vogel, G., 427
von Hagen, A., 399, 402, 403, 407, 415, 416, 418, 420
von Linne, C., 41
Vranich, A., 407
Vrba, E., 138, 160

Wade, N., 9, 51, 53, 82, 126, 462
Wadley, L., 249
Wagner, G. A., 225
Walcott, C., 86, 87, 88
Walker, A., 30, 37, 130, 143, 146, 162, 163, 175, 176, 177, 178, 206, 476
Walker, J., 155
Walker, M., 233
Walker, M. J. C., 233, 235
Wallace, A. R., 57
Walls, D., 452
Walsh, P. D., 455
Walter, R. C., 224

Wang, C., 333
Wang, J., 116
Wanpo, H., 179
Ward, C., 122, 149, 150, 151
Warneken, F., 428
Washburn, S., 3, 137
Waters, M. R., 463
Watson, J., 47, 49, 50
Watson, N., 496
Webster, D., 409
Weinberg, W., 470, 471
Weiner, J. S., 157
Weisman, A., 47
Weiss, E., 258
Weiss, K., 45
Weiss, R., 489
Wells, P. S., 343
Wendorf, F., 258, 299
Wenke, R. J., 317, 318
Wessen, K., 143
Wheeler, M., 216, 325, 326
Wheeler, P. E., 138
White, C. D., 391
White, E., 178
White, M., 241
White, P., 496
White, R., 265
White, T., 149, 195

White, T. D., 25, 145, 160, 180, 250, 379
Whitfield, J., 82
Whittle, A., 285, 291, 303, 304
Whittlesey, S., 374, 375, 378
Wildman, D. E., 102, 123, 440, 441, 447
Wilford, J. N., 90, 180
Williams, F. L., 173
Williams, P. R., 408
Wilson, D. J., 399, 400, 414, 415
Wilson, A., 32, 199
Wilson, A. C., 54
Wilson, E. O., 71
Wing, S. L., 119
Winston, J. E., 68
Woese, C., 80, 82
Wolfe, L. D., 478
Wolpoff, M. H., 170, 186, 190, 195, 196, 197, 206
Wong, K., 193, 467
Wood, B., 141, 163, 179
Woodburn, J., 273, 274, 282
Woodward, A. S., 156
Wooley, L., 315
Wrangham, R., 128, 441, 449, 455, 459, 489

Wright, S., 42, 65, 66, 470, 471
Wu, X., 179
Wynn, T., 203

Xian-guang, H., 84
Xueqin, L., 333

Yamei, H., 241
Yassushi, K., 306
Yerkes, R., 22
Yoffee, N., 311
Yohe, R. M., 229
Yoon, C. K., 64, 65, 66
Young, D., 68, 196
Yunis, J. J., 448

Zhang, J., 333
Zhenxiang, Z., 334
Zhu, R. X., 178, 241
Zhuan, D., 240, 243
Zihlman, A., 165
Zilhao, J., 191, 193
Zimmer, C., 511
Zinner, D., 437
Zuckerman, S., 425
Zvelebil, M., 279, 282, 293, 294

# Subject Index

AAA (American Anthropological Association) Code of Ethics, 10–11
AAR (amino acid racemization), 31, 226, 227
Abu Hureyra (Syria), 275, 285
Abu Simbel, temple of (Egypt), 214
Abydos (Egypt), 318, 331
Accelerator mass spectrometry (AMS), 4, 222, 225, 227
Acheulian period, 232, 241
Acid racemization. *See* Amino acid racemization (AAR)
Acorn processing, 368
Acquired characteristics, theory of, 19, 41–42
Acquired immunodeficiency syndrome (AIDS), 489
Adapids, 116
Adaptation, 56–57, 486–487
aDNA (ancient DNA), 26, 28
Adulis (Africa), 337
*Aegyptopithecus*, 116, 117
Afar triangle (Ethiopia), 150, 152
Africa. *See also specific sites*
    AMH in, 195
    archaics in, 181–182
    australopithecines in, 145–160
    baboons in, 479
    *Homo habilis* in, 160–163
    pastoralism/cultivation in, 298–300
    prosimians in, 432–433
    states in East and West, 336–340
African Burial Ground, 11, 12–13, 29
Age of Exploration, 41
Agriculture. *See* Farming
AIDS (acquired immunodeficiency syndrome), 489
Ain Ghazal (Jordan), 288–290
Ain Mallaha (Israel), 275, 280
Akapana (Bolivia), 402
Akkad (Mesopotamia), 312
Akrotiri (Greece), 211
Aksum state, 336, 337–339
Allele, 43, 47, 48, 50–51
Allen's Rule, 476
Allia Bay (Kenya), 149
Altiplano, 402
American Anthropological Association (AAA) Code of Ethics, 10–11
American Board of Forensic Anthropology, 498
Amerind migration, 351
AMH. *See* Anatomically modern humans
Amino acid racemization (AAR), 31, 226, 227
Amino acids, 49, 50
Amniotes, 91
Amphibians, 85, 89–91. *See also specific types*

AMS (accelerator mass spectroscopy), 4, 222, 225, 227
Amud (Israel), 187
Anagenesis, 70
Analogy, principle of, 75
Anasazi, 377–379
Anatolia (Turkey), 290, 292, 300
Anatomically modern humans (AMH), 77, 191–201, 461
    derived traits of, 194
    evolutionary models of, 196–201
    Neandertals and, 189–191, 192–193, 251–253
Ancestor ideology, 282, 289–290
Ancestral Pueblo, 377–379
Ancestral traits, 76–77
    of australopithecines, 147
    of contemporary tarsiers, 430
    of Neandertals, 185
Ancient DNA (aDNA), 26, 28
Andean farming, 403, 404–405, 407–408
Anemia, sickle-cell, 477, 478
Angiosperms, 96, 101
Animal Welfare Act of 1985, 11
*Anomalocaris*, 87
Ant dipping, 445
*Anthropoidea*, 78, 117–120
Anthropoids, 102, 117–120
Anthropologists, 7–8, 424. *See also specific types*
Anthropology, 2–3. *See also* Archaeology; Biological anthropology
    ethics and, 2, 10–13
    forensic, 493–498
    holism and, 8–10
    subfields of, 2–3, 6–7
Anthropometry, 25
Anthropomorphic representations, 399
Anu temple complex (Mesopotamia), 313
Anyang (China), 329, 334, 335
Anzick (Montana), 356
Apes, 120. *See also individual species*
    contemporary, 440–455
    evolution of, 123
    large, 442–455
    small, 441–442
    social systems of, 107
Applied anthropology, 7
Applied cultural anthropologists, 7
Aramis (Ethiopia), 149
Arboreal, 107
Arboreal hypothesis, 113
Arboreal quadrupedalism, 105, 108, 119
Archaeae, 82
Archaeobotany, 219
Archaeological evidence, 208–221
Archaeologists, 2, 6–7, 8
Archaeology, 208

dating techniques of, 221–227
prehistory and, 3
subfields of, 6–7
Archaic *Homo sapiens*
    in Africa, 181–182
    early, 181–183
    late (Neandertals), 183–191
    religion and, 359–360, 366–367
    structure building and, 280–281, 376–377
    technology of, 367
    trade and, 358–359, 373–374, 376–379
*Ardipithecus ramidus*, 125, 145
Arnhem Land (Australia), 257
Art, 263, 264–265. *See also* Symbolism
Arthropods, 87
Artifacts, 171, 208
    analysis of, 217–221
    dating of, 30, 221–227
Arunachal macaque, 436
Asana (Peru), 370
Ascribed status, 369
Asia
    AMH in, 195
    archaics in, 182
As-Sabiyah (Kuwait), 313
Assimilation model, of AMH evolution, 200, 201
Association, in archaeology, 209
Atapuerca (Spain), 241
Atlatl, 255
Atoms, 49
Auger technique, 215
Aurignacian period, 251, 252, 254
Australia
    AMH in, 195–196
    human occupation of, 256–257
Australopithecines (*Australopithecus*), 28, 145–160
    anatomy of, 148–149
    capacity for culture of, 9
    comparative data on species of, 150
    grade scheme for, 141
    sites of, 145, 146, 147
    taxonomy of, 145
    as tool makers, 236
    traits of, 146–149, 194
*Australopithecus aethiopicus*, 148, 159–160
*Australopithecus afarensis*, 145, 148, 150–154
*Australopithecus africanus*, 145, 148, 150, 154–157, 160
*Australopithecus anamensis*, 145, 149–150
*Australopithecus boisei*, 145, 148, 150, 158–159
*Australopithecus garhi*, 145, 154
*Australopithecus robustus*, 145, 148, 150, 158–159, 161

Avebury (England), 285
Awkaypata plaza (Inca), 414
Axes
  groundstone, 279
  hand, 241–242, 243, 288, 505
Aye-ayes, 432, 433
Aztec empire, 393, 408–414
Aztlan (Aztec), 409

Baboons
  co-variation of traits in, 480
  cognitive abilities of, 428
  distribution of, in Africa, 479
  hamadryas, 425, 437–438
  interbreeding of, 68–69
  as model for human evolution, 422
Bacteria, 82
Balancing selection, 65
Ball games, ritual, 375–376, 387
Bantu languages, 293
Barranco León (Spain), 241
Basalt columns (Olmec), 386
Bashidang (China), 296
Basiocranium, and speech, 194, 203–204
Bauplan, 84
Bear Village (Arizona, 377
Beeches Pit (England), 244
Behavior(s)
  culture and, 444
  evolution of, in primates, 125–128
  of large apes, 444–446
  of modern humans, 461
Behaviorally modern humans (BMH), 77,
  461
Belmont Report, 10
Bennett stela, 402
Bergmann's Rule, 475–476
Beringia, 233, 349–351
Bias, 21–24, 71, 444
Bifaces. See Hand axes
Big Bang, 78
Bilateral symmetry, 108–109, 177
Bilophodont teeth, 117, 120, 435
Bilzinsleben (Germany), 244, 245
Bioanthropologists. See Biological anthro-
  pologists
Bioarchaeology, 364
Bioenergetics/thermoregulation model,
  138
Biological anthropologists, 2, 3, 7–8, 422,
  424
Biological anthropology, 488–493
Biological evidence, 24–28. See also Fossils
  analysis of, 34–35
  dating of, 30–34
"Biological race," 3, 6, 480–481, 482–486
Biological species concept (BSC), 68–69
Biologists, 423–424
Biomineralization, 84
Biosignatures, 81
Biostratigraphy, 222
Bio-uniformitarianism, principle of, 78
Bipedalism, 105, 106, 108, 110, 124,
  132–133, 134–139, 151, 154, 169,
  502, 503–504
Birth control, 470

Black Earth (Illinois), 359
Black Land (Egypt), 317
Black Skull, 148, 159–160
Blades, 253
Blombos Cave (South Africa), 247, 249,
  505
Blood types, human, 48, 51, 477
Bloodletting, 387, 395, 396, 412
Bluefish Caves (Alaska), 352
BMH. See Behaviorally modern
  humans
Bocksteinschmiede (Germany), 250
Bodo, 181
Body build, 475–476
Body cells, mutations in, 60–61
Bog bodies, 4, 28, 29
Bone(s). See also Forensic anthropology
  fossilization of, 25, 26
  male vs. female, 497, 498
  oracle, 332, 334, 335
  tools made of, 236, 247
Bone camp, and LCA, 123–124
Bonobos, 453–455
  language acquisition by, 450–451, 452
  as model for human evolution, 422,
    424
  sex and, 456–457
Border Cave (South Africa), 195
Borer technique, 215
Bose Basin (China), 241
Bouri (Ethiopia), 235
Boxgrove (England), 243
Brachiating, 105, 106, 108, 133, 441
Brachycephalic head shape, 495
Brain
  evolution of, 203
  of primates, 110
  size of, 139–140, 186, 487, 504, 506
Broca's area, 203
Broken Hill (Zambia), 181, 182
Bronze technology, 335
BSC (biological species concept), 68–69
Buddhism, and observer bias, 444
Buhl Woman, 468
Bulgaria, 190
Bulla, 330
Burakumin, 484
Burgess Shale, 84, 85, 86–88
Burial pools, 24
Burials
  in Archaic communities, 358, 359–360,
    366, 369, 375
  in late glacial/early Holocene, 281,
    295–296
  in Lower Paleolithic/ESA, 245
  in Mesoamerica, 389–390
  in Mesopotamia, 316–317
  in Middle Paleolithic/MSA, 250–251
  in Old World, 334
  in South America, 401
  in Upper Paleolithic/LSA, 261
Burnishing, of pottery, 286
Bush babies, 433
Buto (Egypt), 318

Cactus Hill (Virginia), 352

Cahokia (Mississippi), 360, 362–363
Calendar round, 392
Calendars, 226
  in Maya culture, 392
  in Mesoamerica and South America,
    392–393
Calibration, 32, 224
Caliche, 375
California, Southern, 367–369
Callithricidae (family of monkeys), 439
Calpolli, 411
Cambrian explosion, 83–85
Camelids, 370, 416
Cannibalism, 243–244, 250
Capacity for culture, 9
Capuchin monkeys, 428, 439
Caracol (Guatemala), 396
Carbon 14 ($^{14}$C) dating, 31, 222, 224–225,
  227, 287, 290
Carbon isotopes, 276
Carrying hypothesis, 136, 137
Casts, as fossils, 25, 26, 27
Çatalhöyük (Turkey), 300–303
Catastrophism, 42
Cathedra, 86
Cathemeral activity patterns, 106
Catholic Church, view of evolution of,
  40–41
Catopithecus, 118
Cattle herding. See Pastoralism
Causewayed enclosures, 303–304
Cave sites, preservation in, 361, 364
Cebidae (family of monkeys), 439
Cells, 49
Celtic society, 342–343
Celts (axes), 385
Cenozoic era, 114
Centers for Disease Control, 492
Central America. See Mesoamerica
Central Plaza (Aztec), 409
Ceprano (Italy), 180
Cercopithecines, 436
Cerro Baúl (Peru), 408
Cerro Blanco (Peru), 399–400
Chaco Canyon (New Mexico), 378–379
Chad, 139, 146, 154
Channel Islands (California), 367–368
Chatelperronian period, 251–252, 254
Chauvet Cave (France), 261–262, 264,
  265
Chavín de Huántar (Peru), 398
Chengjiang Formation, 84
Cheops, 321
Chesowanja (Kenya), 244
Chicha, 400
Chicxulub crater, 94–95
Chiefdom societies, 360, 362–363
Chimpanzees, 123, 447–453, 454
  cognitive abilities of, 428
  culture of, 444–446
  laboratory studies of, 427
  language acquisition by, 450–451, 452,
    453
  as model for human evolution, 422, 424
  sex and, 456
  social organization of, 448–449

China
Erlitou state of, 328–329
farming in, 296–298
*Homo erectus* in, 178–179
Shang state of, 328–329, 332, 334–335
*Chinampas* (Aztec), 409, 411
Chordates, 84–85
Christianity, in Aksum state, 338
Chromosomes, 46, 47, 49, 50, 448
Chronometric dating, 222–227
Chronospecies, 70
Circular symbolism, 282, 303–304
Citadel complex, 387, 388
Ciudadela (Teotihuacan), 387, 388
Clacton (England), 243
Cladistics, 141, 142, 423
Cladogenesis, 66, 70–71
Classification of species. *See* Taxonomy
Clavicles, primate, 108
Clean Air Acts (England), 65
Climate changes, 233–235
Clines, 474–475, 483
Clovis groups, 351–352, 353–354, 356
Clovis points, 463
Co-variation of traits, 480–482
Coa Valley (Portugal), 265
Codices, 393, 408, 413
Coelacanth, 89
Cognition
in contemporary primates, 427–428
culture and, 444
as human trait, 502–503
Coins, dating and, 226
Colby (Wyoming), 356
Collectors/foragers
health of, 490–492
model of, 273, 274
Colobines, 436
Colobus, 437
Common ancestral groups, principle of, 75, 76–77
Common ancestry, principle of, 75
Common sense, 19–21
Communication, 202
Comparative method of reconstruction, 126–127, 422
Contemporary apes, 440–455. *See also individual species*
Contemporary humans, 461, 471–473
adaptations of, 486–487
biological variability in, 473–482
diets of, 491–492
disease in, 487–488, 490–492
growth in, 487–488
microevolution in, 469–471
race and, 482–486
traits of, 474–479, 502–503
violence and, 488
Contemporary nonhuman primates, 422. *See also individual species*
case studies of, 429
cognitive abilities of, 427–428
personalities of, 429
traits of, 435
Context, in archaeology, 208

Continental drift, 113
Contingency, principle of, 75, 76–77
Continuity, 23
Copan (Honduras), 209, 396–397
Cordilleran ice sheet, 349, 350
Cores
ice, 30, 33–34, 223
marine, 30, 33–34, 234
stone, 235
Cradle of chordate evolution, 84
Cradle of civilization, 312
Cradle of humanity, 312
Cranial deformation, 378, 406
Creationism, 21
Cretaceous/Tertiary boundary, 94. *See also* K/T mass extinction
Cro-Magnon, 156, 196
Cross-dating, 222
Cultural anthropologists, 6, 7–8, 20
Cultural anthropology, 3
Cultural development
biological evolution and, 503–510
environment and, 233, 236–237, 240
evidence for, 233–235
in Lower Paleolithic/ESA, 232, 235–245
Cultural drift, 508
Cultural historical approach, 221
Cultural transformation processes, 209
Cuneiform, 316, 330
Cuzco (Inca), 414
Cylinder seals, 313, 330

Daamat, kingdom of (Ethiopia), 336
Danger Cave (Utah), 211
Dating, 221–222. *See also specific techniques*
Datum point, 29
Deductive reasoning, 18–19
"Deep time," 77, 80
Demotic script, 331
Dendrochronology, 225, 227
Dental formula (DF), 109–110
Dentition, pattern of
in humans, 504
in primates, 109–110
Derived traits, 76–77
of AMH, 194
of australopithecines, 147–148
of contemporary apes, 440
of contemporary tarsiers, 430
of *Homo erectus*, 173–174, 194
of *Homo* genus, 169
of *Homo sapiens*, 181, 194
of Neandertals, 185
of Old World monkeys, 436
Desert baboons. *See* Hamadryas baboons
Desert kites, 275
DF (dental formula), 109–110
Dholavira (Indus), 326, 332
Diet
of contemporary humans, 491–492
of Fayum primates, 119
of modern primates, 106, 110
Diffusion wave, and AMH evolution, 200, 201
Dik Dik Hill (Tanzania), 153

DIK-1 (Lucy's baby), 150, 151
Dikika (Ethiopia), 150
Dinosaurs, 91
Directional selection, 61–66
Dirty War (Argentina), 489
Discontinuity, 23
Diseases, human, 487–488, 490–492
Diurnal activity patterns, 106
Dmanisi (Georgia), 179–180, 240
DNA, 49–54
analysis of, 488–489, 496
ancient, 26, 28
of eukaryotes, 82
of Iceman, 2, 5
mitochondrial, 31, 32, 199, 292
nuclear, 31, 32
Watson-Crick model of, 50, 51
Dogs, species of, 70, 71
Dolichocephalic head shape, 495
Dolné Vestonice (Czech Republic), 261, 262, 264
Domestication, 284–285, 290, 369. *See also* Pastoralism
Dominance, 45, 46, 49
Douara Cave (Syria), 248
Double helix, 50, 51
"Dreamtime," 257
Druids, 343
Dry sieving, 217
Dryopithecines, 121
Dutch East India Company, 12

Eanna complex (Mesopotamia), 313, 330
Early Stone Age (ESA), 232, 235–245
"East Side Story" hypothesis, 139
Easter Island, 462
Eastern Woodlands Archaic, 357–360
Ecofacts, 208
Ediacara, 83, 84, 88
Eel Point (California), 368
Egypt
Early Dynastic and Old Kingdom periods in, 318–319, 330–332, 333–334
early state in, 317–323
predynastic, 318
trade in, 318–320
Eighteen (18) Rabbit (Maya), 397
El Manatí (Mexico), 386–387
El Mirador (Guatemala), 395
El Niño, 367, 399
El-Omari (Egypt), 318
El Paraíso (Peru), 398
El Pindo (Spain), 191
Electrical resistivity meter, 215
Electron spin resonance (ESR), 31, 178, 225–226, 227
Emic perspective, 6
Enamel hypoplasia, 364
Encephalization, 169
Encephalization quotient (EQ), 148
Environment
cultural development and, 233, 236–237, 240
evolutionary selection and, 19, 54–58, 61–67

Clark, A. J., 215
Clark, G. A., 7, 21, 23, 188, 191, 251, 252
Clark, J. D., 7
Clark, J. E., 384, 385
Clarke, R., 155
Clarke, R. J., 240
Close, A. E., 258
Clottes, J., 263, 265
Cobo, B., 416,
Coe, M. D., 385, 386, 389, 391, 392, 393, 394, 395
Cohen, J. E., 472
Cohen, M. N., 283
Coles, B., 210, 288
Coles, J., 210, 288
Collard, M., 141, 163
Collis, J., 343
Coningham, R., 323
Connah, G., 336, 337, 338, 339, 340, 345
Connolly, P., 27, 37
Conroy, G., 141 148
Conroy, G. C., 123
Conway Morris, S., 80, 83, 84, 88
Cooley, A. E., 27, 37
Coon, C., 483
Copeland, L., 250
Coppens, Y., 139, 146, 152
Corbey, R., 440,
Cordell, L., 372, 373, 374, 375, 377, 378, 379, 381
Costamgo, S., 247
Coughlan, A., 473
Coupland, G., 365, 366, 367
Coven, H. H., 430
Cowen, R., 81, 82, 84, 89, 90, 91, 92, 93, 95, 99
Cowgill, G. L., 387, 389, 390, 391, 420
Cox, M., 498
Crawford, G. W., 296
Crawford, H., 315, 316, 333
Cressford, C., 300, 302
Crick, F., 47, 49, 50
Crockett, C. M., 440
Cronin, J. E., 139
Cronk, L., 18
Crowther, P., 88
Culotta, E., 116, 154, 467
Cummins, T., 394
Cunliffe, B., 291, 294
Curnoe, D., 195
Cyphers, A., 385, 386
Cyranoski, D., 448
Czelusniak, J., 114, 117

Daeschler, E. B., 89
Dales, F. G., 324, 327

Dalton, R., 467
D'Altroy, T. N., 414, 415, 416, 417, 418, 420
Damerow, P., 333
Dancey, W. S., 373
Dart, R., 154, 161, 167, 237, 240
Darwin, C., 19, 32, 33, 39, 42, 45, 54, 55, 56, 57, 58, 60, 61, 62, 63, 64, 65, 72, 137, 156, 486
Daugherty, R., 212, 213
David, R., 333
Davies, W., 189, 233, 251, 294
Davis, B. M., 96
Davis, S. J., 219, 233, 306, 354
Dawkins, R., 60
Dawson, C., 156, 157
Deacon, H. J., 120, 233, 235, 240, 248, 253, 267
Deacon, J., 120, 233, 235, 240, 248, 267
Dean, C., 179
Dearborn, D. S., 394, 417
Defleur, A., 250
DeGusta, D. W., 203
de la Fuente, B., 420
de la Torre, I., 452
Deloukas, B., 50
Delson, E., 179
de Lumley, H., 244
deLumley, M-A., 179
Demars, P., 87
Demel, S. J., 363
d'Errico, F., 191, 236, 250, 263, 505, 506
Desmond, A., 57, 64
DeVore, I., 164
de Vries, H., 42, 58, 72
de Waal, F. B., 128, 130, 449, 455, 456, 457, 459
Diamond, J., 294
Dibble, H., 247, 250
Dickinson, A., 452
Diehl, R. A., 385, 386, 387
Dillehay, T. D., 349, 351, 352, 354, 381, 462, 500
DiPaolo Loren, D., 363
Dixson, F. J., 351
Díaz, B., 409, 411
Dobres, M-A., 221
Dobzhansky, T., 42
Dolhinow, P., 426
Dominguez-Rodrigo, M., 236, 237
Donahue, P. C., 32, 33
Donnan, C. B., 399, 400, 401

Doran, D. M., 447
Dorfman, A., 468
Doyle, A. C., 18, 157
Doyle, G. A., 430, 435
Drewett, P., 209, 210, 217, 229
Duarte, C., 190, 193
Dumont, D., 349
Dunbar, R. I. M., 423, 453
Dunham, K., 448
Dunsworth, H., 163, 178

Earhart, A., 494
Eaton, S. B., 492, 500
Eckhardt, R., 41, 71, 171, 172, 436, 453
Edey, M., 67
Edey, M. A., 91, 149, 153
Eisenberg, J. F., 440
Eldredge, N., 59, 60, 82, 91
Elias, S. A., 349
El Mahdy, C., 323
Elston, R. G., 364
Emerson, T. E., 363, 381
Enard, W., 6, 448
Endler, J. A., 73
Englund, R., 333
Enserink, M., 53
Estrada, A., 440
Eswaran, V., 189, 200
Evans, S. T., 409

Fagan, B., 311, 334, 384
Fagan, B. M., 345, 352, 357, 359, 361, 367, 369, 373, 381
Fairburn, A., 303
Falk, D., 148, 163, 431, 464, 466, 467, 472
Fash, W. L., 396, 397
Fattovich, R., 336
Feder, K., 157
Feder, K. L., 37, 229
Fedigan, L., 424,
Fernandez-Jalvo, Y., 244, 245
Ferreras, J., 183
Fiedel, S. J., 351, 352, 353, 356, 358, 359, 371, 463, 469
Fiorelli, G., 27
Fisher, R., 470
Fisher, R. A., 42
Flannery, K., 283
Flannery, K. V., 273, 311, 370
Fleagle, J. G., 32, 102, 105, 106, 115, 119, 120
Foley, R. A., 39, 57, 60, 71, 77, 117, 128, 138, 141, 144, 160, 167, 175, 467, 503

Forster, P., 294
Fossey, D., 424, 426, 440, 447
Fowler, B., 5
Franciscus, R., 185, 186, 190
Frayer, D., 185, 186, 190, 196
Freidel, D., 396
Fremlen, J., 189
Friedman, I., 226
Frisancho, A. R., 486
Frison, G. C., 353, 356
Fuentes, A., 130, 426, 459
Fujita, H., 368
Fujiyama, A., 448
Futuyma, D. J., 80, 83

Gabunia, L., 179, 180, 240
Galdikas, B., 424, 440
Gallup, G., 428
Gamble, C., 206, 241, 243, 245, 248, 257
Garfinkel, Y., 211
Garn, S., 483
Garner, R. L., 425
Garrard, A., 277
Gebauer, A. B., 306
Gebo, D. L., 116, 122
Gee, H., 89, 92
Genomic, C., 52
Gerhard, W., 494
Gibbon, G., 348
Gibbons, A., 178, 180, 189
Gibbson, A., 452
Gibson, J., 359, 360, 374
Gibson, K. R., 451
Gilead, I., 261
Gillespie, R., 462
Gingerich, P. D., 60
Gkiasta, M., 293
Gladkih, N. L., 259
Glassow, M. A., 368
Goldberg, P., 352
González Lauch, R., 386
Goodall, J., 128, 130, 204, 424, 426, 440, 448, 449, 459, 488
Goodman, M., 31, 32, 96, 103, 111, 114, 116, 117, 122, 124
Goren-Inbar, N., 243, 244
Gould, S. J., 20, 37, 54, 59, 60, 75, 77, 84, 88, 99
Gowlett, J. A. J., 235, 244
Goñi, M. F. S., 191
Graham, E., 409, 411
Graham-Rowe, D., 455,
Grant, B. R., 78
Grant, P., 73
Grant, P. R., 61, 63, 64, 78

Grant, R., 64
Grant, V., 47, 65
Grayson, D. K., 353, 354, 355
Greenberg, J., 351
Grey, J. P., 478
Grinnel, G. F., 117
Groves, C., 51, 71, 102, 431, 433
Grube, N., 397
Guaman Poma de Ayala, F., 371, 394
Gunnell, G. F., 116
Gursky, S., 102, 430, 431
Gutierrez, G., 189

Haak, W., 294
Haaland, R., 299
Habu, J., 275, 279, 296
Hagelberg, E., 462
Hager, L. D., 165
Haldane, J. B. S., 42
Hall, J. M., 173
Hall, M. E., 279
Hall, R. L., 363
Hamilton, G., 82
Harbottle, G., 333
Harding, J., 304
Hardy, B. L., 246, 248
Hardy, G., 470, 471
Hare, P. E., 226
Harlan, J. R., 300
Harlow, H., 427
Harpending, H., 200, 201
Harren, M., 493
Harrington, S. P., 13
Harris, C. L., 40
Harris, D., 294
Harris, T., 215, 216
Harrison, P. T., 391, 395, 396
Hartwig, W., 119, 123, 130
Hassan, F. A., 318
Hawass, Z., 323
Hayden, B., 283
Haynes, G., 354, 355
Hecht, J., 21, 120
Hegmon, M., 376
Helmer, R. P., 495, 496
Hemmings, S., 489
Hempill, B. E., 364
Henderson, J. S., 391, 397
Henneberg, M., 71, 471
Henshilwood, C. S., 249, 252, 461
Hewes, G. W., 137
Hewett, G., 204
Hickey, E., 294
Higham, C., 296, 297
Higuchi, T., 278, 279

Hill, C., 235
Hill Boone, E., 394
Hillier, L. W., 53
Hinde, R. A., 422
Hinton, M., 157
Hiraguchi, T., 276
Hitler, A., 494
Hodder, I., 221, 300, 302, 303
Hodges, M. G., 411
Hoekstra, R. F., 57, 60, 73, 199
Hoffecker, J. F., 349
Holden, C., 293, 294
Holden, E., 190
Holton, F., 358
Hooton, E. A., 483
Horodyski, R., 83
Hovers, E., 249
Howard, A. V., 376
Howell, C., 152
Howell, F. C., 7
Hrdy, S. B., 126
Hublin, J-J., 182, 183
Hummel, S., 28
Hunter, J. C., 493
Hutchinson, D. L., 364
Huxley, L., 156
Huxley, T., 55

Igman, M., 199
Imamura, K., 273, 281
Ingold, T., 451
Ingstad, H., 214
Isaac, G., 236, 237
Isbell, W. H., 407
Iseminger, W. R., 363
Itani, J., 22

Jablonski, N., 475
Jablonski, N. G., 120, 123, 123
Jacob, F., 54
Jacob, T., 465
Jaiger, J. J., 119
James, S. R., 244
Jansen, M., 324
Janson, C. H., 446
Janusek, J. W., 405
Jefferies, R. W., 360
Jefferson, T., 489
Jenkins, M., 512
Jennings, J. D., 211, 369, 377
Jiang, L., 296
Jobling, M. A., 32
Johanson, D., 91, 131, 146, 149, 150, 152, 153, 167
Johnson, B. J., 226
Johnson, M., 221

Johnston, H., 257
Jolly, A., 434, 435
Jones, C., 395
Jones, M., 32, 51, 69
Jones, P., 242
Jones, S., 53, 58, 80, 449, 472, 485, 488, 489
Jones, T. L., 368
Jurmain, R., 148, 173

Kamminga, J., 233, 257, 267
Kappeler, P., 432
Kardong, K. V., 80
Karlin, C., 254
Kaufman, D., 187, 204
Kawamura, S., 22
Kay, R. F., 119, 203
Keeley, L. H., 273
Kehoe, A. B., 367
Keller, G., 95
Kelly, R. L., 273, 274, 364
Kemp, T. S., 32
Kennedy, K., 199, 498
Kenoyer, J. M., 323, 324, 325, 326, 328, 333, 345
Kenyon, K. M., 288
Kernan, M., 496
Kerr, J., 394
Kerr, R., 83
Kerr, R. A., 88
Kessler, D., 320
Kester, T. R., 229
Killan, E. W., 498
Kimbel, W. H., 69, 143, 151, 153
Kimeu, K., 30, 176
King, M. C., 54, 493
Kirk, R., 213
Klein, J., 31, 32, 51, 58, 60, 61, 67, 82, 84, 96, 108
Klein, R., 248, 255, 258, 267, 355, 506
Klein, R. G., 190, 234
Klima, B., 261, 262, 265
Knath, L. P., 83
Knecht, H., 265
Knoll, A. H., 91, 99
Kobayashi, T., 279, 280, 281
Kohn, M., 242
Kolata, A. L., 402, 403, 404, 405, 406
Konner, M., 492, 500
Kortlandt, A., 118, 139
Kotschnid, E., 134
Kottak, C., 455
Kowalski, J. K., 391
Kramer, A., 172, 198
Kraus, M. J., 119
Krawczak, M., 489

Kraytsberg, Y., 32
Krings, M., 189
Kristiansen, K., 343
Kuhn, T., 21
Kummer, H., 437, 438
Kunzig, R., 190, 193

Lahr, M., 198, 467, 503
Laitman, J., 204
Lamarck, J. B., 19, 41, 58
Langdon, J. H., 97
Laroche, C. J., 13
Larsen, C. S., 276, 283, 285, 364
Larsson, L., 276, 281, 282
Lazcano, A., 82
Leakey, J., 160
Leakey, L., 29, 146, 160, 424
Leakey, M., 29, 146, 149, 150, 158, 160
Leakey, M. D., 236, 237, 244
Leakey, M. G., 150, 149
Leakey, R., 146, 176, 177
LeBlanc, S., 377
Lee, R., 164
Legge, A. J., 275
Lehner, M., 321
Lekson, S. H., 378, 379
Lemonick, M. D., 468
Leonard, W. R., 148
Levy, T. E., 306
Lewin, R. A., 57, 117, 124, 135, 178
Lewis, R. A., 363, 471
Lewis-Williams, D., 263
Lidén, K., 296
Lieberman, L., 478, 481
Lin, J., 492
Lindly, J. M., 21
Lindon, E., 449
Linnaeus, 41
Lipe, W., 377
Liu, L., 179, 296, 328, 329
Livingstone, F., 483
Lock, G., 215
Lockwood, C., 150
Lontcho,F., 180
Lopinot, N. H., 363
Lordkipanidze, D., 179
Lovejoy, O., 91, 151
Lowe, J. J., 32, 33, 34, 233, 235
Lowenstein, J. M., 59
Loy, T. H., 238
Lu, T., 296
Lubell, D., 285
Lucey, R. F., 405
Ludwig, K. P., 224
Lyell, C., 54

Lyles, R. B., 51
Lynch, B. M., 360

Macaulay, V., 201, 294, 462
MacDonald, K. C., 299
Mace, R., 509
Mackenzie, D., 493
MacKinnon, J. R., 442, 459
MacKinnon, K., 130
MacLarnon, A., 204
Madsen, D. B., 361
Magle, J. W., 195
Maisels, C. K., 325
Malek, J., 321
Malone, C., 303
Malthus, C., 54, 55
Malthus, T., 472
Mania, D., 245
Manley, B., 317, 320, 321
Manson, J. H., 439
Manzanilla, L., 389, 390
Manzi, G., 170
Maple, T. L., 443
Maples, W., 493
Marean, C. W., 247, 252, 461
Margulis, L., 51
Marivaux, L., 119
Marks, J., 40, 50, 51, 57, 73, 123, 124, 184, 188, 484, 500
Marlar, R., 379
Martin, L., 302
Martin, L. B., 69
Martin, P., 355
Martin, R., 430, 435
Martin, R. D., 108, 110, 114, 117, 130, 144
Martin, S., 397
Maschner, H. D., 213, 365, 366, 367, 381
Matos Moctezume, E., 214, 409, 412, 414
Matson, R. G., 365, 366, 367
Matsui, A., 275, 278
Matsuzawa, T., 459
Matthews, R., 302, 312, 313, 316
Mauricio, J., 193
Mayr, E., 42, 57, 58, 68, 69, 80, 82, 84, 144
Mays, S., 488, 498
McBrearty, S., 123, 216, 248, 249, 250, 252, 253, 461
McClung de Tapia, E., 370
McCrossin, M. C., 120
McEwan, G. E., 408
McGrew, W., 130, 459
McGrew, W. C., 423, 446, 447, 449

McHenry, H., 143
McIntosh, R., 339, 340
McIntosh, S., 339, 340
McKee, J., 58, 60, 71, 155, 158
McKie, R., 184, 200
McKinney, M. L., 449, 452
McLelland, D., 401
McManus, J. F., 32, 33, 34
McNeilage, A., 447
McPherron, S. P., 241
Mellaart, J., 300, 301, 302
Mellars, P., 191, 196, 201, 247, 249, 250, 251, 262, 263, 265
Meltzer, D. J., 349, 352, 353, 355, 356
Meltzer, K., 355
Mendel, G., 19, 39, 41, 42, 43, 44, 45, 46, 47, 48, 49, 72
Mengele, J., 494, 495, 496
Menozzi, P., 73
Merkel, J. F., 219
Mignolo, W. D., 394
Miller, G. H., 226
Miller, J., 20, 160
Miller, L. E., 432
Miller, S., 80
Millon, R., 388
Milner, N., 296
Milo, R., 248
Milton, K., 439, 440
Minagawa, M., 275
Mitani, J., 452
Mithen, S., 242, 280, 306
Mittermier, R., 104, 105
Mojzis, S. J., 81
Molleson, T., 498
Moloney, N., 238, 241, 250
Monod, J., 54
Moore, A. M. T., 285
Moore, J., 57, 64
Morell, V., 158, 407, 469
Morgan, T. H., 57
Morris, C., 398, 399, 402, 403, 407, 415, 416, 418, 420
Morris, R., 56, 59
Morwood, M., 464, 465, 467
Morwood, M. J., 241
Moseley, M., 407, 408
Moseley, M. E., 398, 399
Mughal, M .R., 323
Mulvaney, J., 233, 257
Munro-Hay, S., 336, 339
Murrary, M. A., 321, 323
Murray, L. E., 429

Nadel, D., 258
Nadler, R. D. 443
Naggioncalda, N., 443
Napier, J., 134, 424,
Napier, J. R., 102, 116, 431
Napier, P., 424
Napier, P. H., 102, 116, 431
Nash, D. J., 408
Neave, R., 489, 493
Neff, H., 387
Neiderberger, C., 387
Nelson, A. R., 463
Neuman, K., 284
Newman, T. K., 437
Nichols, T., 294
Nissen, H., 333
Nissen, H. J., 313, 316
Norris, S., 193

Oakley, K., 157
O'Brien, E. M., 242
Ockham, W., 144
O'Connell, J. F., 175, 257
Oefner, P., 294
Oeggl, K., 5
Olby, R., 45
Olley, J. M., 257
Olsen, J. W., 253
Olson, S., 65, 480, 484, 485
Oms, O., 241
Orbitz, P., 387
Orel, V., 44, 45
Orton, C., 287
Ovchinnikov, I. V., 189

Pääbo, S., 6, 28, 32, 123, 198, 473
Pace, N. R., 82
Panger, M., 128, 138, 459, 472
Parfitt, S., 241, 243
Parfitt, S. A., 180
Park, M. A., 43
Parker, M., 213,
Parker, S. T., 442, 449, 452
Parker Pearson, M., 304
Pascua, M. P., 213
Passarino, G., 294
Patel, A., 326
Patterson, A., 263
Patterson, B., 149
Pauketat, T. R., 363, 381
Paulissen, E., 246
Pearsall, D. M., 276
Pearson, R., 280, 305
Pelto, P., 509
Pennisi, E., 54
Peretto, C., 241
Perry, S., 439

Perry, W., 13
Peters, H., 443
Pettitt, P. B., 193, 250, 265
Phillipson, D. W., 294, 336, 337, 338, 339
Piazza, A., 73
Pickering, T. R., 236
Pigliucci, M., 19
Pike-Tay, A., 265
Pilbeam, D. R., 120, 132
Pillsbury, J., 399, 420
Piperno, D. R., 273, 370
Plato, 40
Plog, S., 374, 376, 377, 379
Pollock, S., 314, 315, 333
Polo, M., 483
Pope, K. O., 370
Porcasi, J. F., 368
Porter, C. A., 114, 117
Possehl, G., 323, 324, 325, 326, 328
Postgate, J. N., 345
Postgate, N., 312, 316
Potts, R., 127, 160, 422
Power, M., 488, 500
Prag, J., 489, 493
Price, D., 296
Price, T., 294, 295
Price, T. D., 280, 306
Pringle, H., 165
Prothero, D. R., 32, 33, 119
Pruvost, M., 28
Pryce-Jones, R., 64
Purdy, B. A., 210, 358
Pusey, A. E., 449
Pye, M. E., 384, 385

Qiang, J., 96

Rak, Y., 151, 153, 159
Ramilisonina, 304
Rapp, G., Jr., 235
Rasmussen, D. T., 119
Rasmussen, T., 115, 116, 117
Rawson, J., 335
Ray, J., 68
Raymond, R., 257
Reader, J., 167
Reid, J. J., 374, 375, 377, 378
Relethford, J., 7, 28, 50, 61, 67, 85, 91, 93, 120, 122, 183, 189, 191, 201, 206, 486
Renfrew, C., 215, 221, 294, 462
Renne, P. R., 224
Rennie, J., 68, 71
Reno, P. L., 151
Reynolds, V., 441

Rice, P., 21, 23, 24, 64, 144, 220, 263, 265, 478, 481, 511
Richard, A., 105, 106, 107, 434, 435
Richard, A. F., 479
Richards, M., 247, 294, 296
Richards, M. P., 462
Richerson, P. J., 512
Ridley, M., 42, 60, 69, 82, 84, 477
Rigaud, J-Ph., 191
Rightmire, G. P., 174
Riley, D. N., 215
Rilling, J. K., 428
Robb, J., 221, 294
Roberts, J. A., 334, 335
Roberts, M., 243
Roberts, M. B., 180
Roberts, N., 270
Roberts, R. G., 467
Robinson, A., 394
Roche, H., 235
Rodrìguez, M. C., 387
Rodríguez, X. P., 241
Rogers, A. R., 200
Rogers, J., 123
Rolland, N., 244, 247
Rollefson, G., 288, 289, 290
Ronin, A., 187
Roosevelt, A. C., 353, 463
Rose, J. E., 116
Rose, K. D., 71, 102, 116
Rosenberg, K. R., 182
Rosenzweig, M., 60
Rossen, J., 352
Rostworowski, M., 416
Rowe, B., 194
Rowley-Conwy, P., 275, 280
Ruff, C. B., 364
Russell, T., 293
Russo, M., 360
Rye, O. S., 287

Sabloff, J. A., 385, 389
Sagan, D., 51
Sapolsky, R. M., 443
Sarich, V., 32
Sassaman, K., 359
Saunders, E., 469
Sauvage, M., 315
Savage-Rumbaugh, S., 424
Save-Soderberge, T., 214
Sawyer, R., 448
Scarre, C., 267, 295, 306, 311, 312, 334, 345, 384, 420
Schele, L., 396

Schick, K., 236, 237, 238, 267, 452
Schiffer, M. B., 209
Schild, R., 299
Schlect, R., 213
Schmid, P., 154
Schmidke, J., 489
Schmitz, R. W., 184
Schneider, A. L., 351
Schoeninger, M. J., 276, 364
Schopf, W., 81
Schrago, C. G., 117
Schreiber, K. J., 407, 408
Schulting, R. J., 281
Schultz, E., 451
Schultzhuitzen, M., 57, 95
Schulz, R., 333
Schwartz, J., 184, 193
Schweingruber, F. H., 225
Scoboda, J., 261
Segre, A. G., 180
Seidel, M., 333
Seidlmayer, S., 318
Selmin, J., 89
Semaw, S., 235, 238
Semino, O., 294
Senner, W., 331
Serra Puche, M. C., 387
Shafer, H. J., 229
Shanklin, E., 41
Sharer, R. J., 209, 386, 387, 391, 394, 395, 397, 420, 
Shea, J., 195, 
Shennan, S., 221, 274, 293, 508, 509
Shick, K. D., 240, 243
Shimada, I., 219, 399, 400
Shipman, P., 37, 130, 142, 143, 175, 177, 180, 187, 206, 476
Shostak, M., 492, 500
Shott, M., 238
Shreeve, J., 153, 155
Silk, J., 50, 51, 162, 174, 182, 185
Simons, E. L., 115, 117, 119, 430
Simpson, G. G., 42, 69, 71, 78, 144
Siner, M., 248
Skinner, A. R., 247
Smeldley, A., 483
Smith, B., 372, 373, 374, 375, 377, 381
Smith, B. D., 273, 284, 288, 297, 299, 300, 306, 369, 370, 372, 381
Smith, E. A., 446
Smith, F., 170

Smith, F. H., 190, 191, 200
Smith, M. E., 394, 409, 411, 412, 420
Smith, M. P., 32, 33
Snow, D. R., 356, 357, 358, 374, 381
Soejono, M. R. P., 467
Soffer, O., 259, 263, 265
Sommer, J. D., 250
Southwood, T., 82, 83, 89, 93, 95, 99
Speth, J. D., 188
Spielberg, S., 86
Spindler, K., 5
Spoor, F., 184
Stadelmann, R., 321
Stafford, T. W., 463
Stahl, A., 244
Stanford, C., 451, 452, 453
Stanford, D., 349, 356, 447, 449
Stark, M. T., 333
Steadman, D. W., 498, 500
Stearns, S. C., 57, 60, 73, 199
Steegman, T. S., 477, 486
Steele, J., 293
Stein, P., 194
Stern, J., 151
Stiner, M., 247
Stinger, C., 198
Stinnesbeck, W., 95
Stirland, A., 496
Stokstad, E., 83, 85, 91, 93
Stoneking, M., 199
Stothert, K. E., 273, 370
Stout, C., 363
Straus, L., 23, 32
Strauss, E., 349
Strier, K. B., 114, 455
Stringer, C., 32, 33, 178, 182, 183, 184, 189, 197, 198, 199, 200, 206, 248
Struever, S., 358
Strum, S., 424
Stumpf, R., 455
Sussman, R., 113
Sussman, R. L., 457
Sussman, R. W., 425, 488, 510
Sutikna, M. J., 467
Sutton, M. Q., 229
Suwa, G., 158
Svitil, K. A., 82, 83, 463
Svoboda, J., 262, 265
Swedell, L., 438
Swisher, C., 199
Swisher, C. C., 147, 174, 178, 241

Sykes, B., 28
Sànchez de Lozada, D., 405

Taieb, M., 152
Takahashi, R., 275, 277, 280, 281, 306
Takahata, N., 31, 32, 51, 58, 60, 61, 67, 82, 84, 96
Takassaki, H., 22
Tanner, N., 165
Tappan, M., 137
Tattersall, I., 21, 139, 147, 184, 185, 190, 202, 224
Taube, K., 387
Taylor, R. E., 37, 224, 225, 229, 468, 469
Tchernov, E., 188, 247
Teeter, E., 317, 318, 320, 321, 333, 345
Templeton, A., 197, 199, 200, 473, 480, 499
Thayer, D., 186
Thieme, H., 243
Thomas, D. H., 364
Thomson, K., 25
Thorne, A., 195, 197, 206, 257
Thorne, A. G., 186
Thorpe, R. L., 329
Tobias, P., 146, 155, 203
Toizumi, T., 306
Tomasello, M., 428, 446
Tosi, M., 327
Toth, N., 236, 237, 238, 267
Toyama, S., 296
Treves, A., 432
Trigger, B. G., 310, 313, 319
Trinkaus, E., 142, 186, 187, 190, 193, 206
Tubb, K. W., 290
Turner, C., 351
Turner, C. G., 179, 379
Turner, J. A., 379
Turner, T. R., 10, 11
Turnmire, K. L., 381
Tyers, P., 287
Tzedakis, P. C., 186

Underhill, A. P., 296, 297
Ussher (Bishop), 41

Valla, F., 277, 280, 281
van Andel, T. H., 186
Vandermeersch, B., 250
Vandiver, P., 265
Vanhaeren, M., 250, 236
van Schaik, C., 442, 443, 446
Van Stone, M., 393
Vekua, A., 179, 180

fossilization and, 24, 25–26
in late glacial/early Holocene, 270, 272
major biological events and, 33–34
Maya culture and, 391, 395
of Northwest Coast, 365
Enzymes, 49
*Eoanthropus dawsonii*, 156–157
Eocene primates, 115–116
Eosimiids, 116
Epifauna, 86
Epigraphers, 396
Epipaleolithic period, 277
Erligang phase, of Shang state (China), 329
Erlitou state (China), 328–329
Ertebölle groups, 295
EQ (encephalization quotient), 148
ESA. *See* Early Stone Age
ESC (evolving species concept), 69, 71
Eskimo-Aleut migration, 351
ESR (electron spin resonance), 31, 178, 225–226, 227
Essentialism, 40
Ethics
    anthropology and, 2, 10–11, 12–13
    Human Genome Project and, 53
Ethnicity, 484
Ethnoarchaeology, 219
Ethnographers, 6, 7–8
Ethnology, 3
Etic perspective, 6
Eubacteria, 82
Eukaryotes, 82
Europe
    agriculture in, 290–295
    AMH in, 196
    archaics in, 182–183, 187–191
    Celtic society in, 342–343
    *Homo erectus* in, 179–180
    Neandertals in, 187
"Eve" hypothesis, 197
Events, dating of, 31–33. *See also* Dating
    techniques; Molecular dating
Evolution, 19, 20–21
    biological, and cultural change, 503–510
    causes of, 60–67
    cultural anthropologists on, 20
    of *Homo sapiens*, 77–96, 180–181
    of human brain, 139–140
    models of, 59–60, 422, 424
    modern synthesis and, 42–59
    of plants, 97
    of species, 68–71
    of speech, 202–204
Evolving species concept (ESC), 69, 71
Excarnation, 303
Exchange networks, 358–359
Experimental archaeology, 219
"Experiments in Plant Hybridization," 44
Extinction(s), 354, 356
    K/T mass, 94–95, 96
    Permian, 91

Face/jaw reduction, 140
Facial reconstruction, 489, 493

Facultative bipedalism, 136
Farming. *See also* Pastoralism
    in Americas, 369–379
    in Andes, 403, 404–405, 407–408
    at Çatalhöyük (Turkey), 302–303
    in China, 296–298
    in Europe, 290–295
    in Inca empire, 416
    in Middle East, 288–290, 292
    in Old World Neolithic societies, 282–288
    in Scandinavia, 295–296
    social complexity and, 300–304
Fayum Depression, 116–120
Features, 208
Fertile Crescent, 288–289
Field studies, 426
Filler, in pottery, 286
Finch beaks, and directional selection, 61–65
Fire, control of, 244
"First family," 183
Fish
    lobe-finned, 85, 89
    ray-finned, 85
"Fishapod," 89
Fission track dating, 226, 227
Flake tools, 241
Flakes, 235, 246
Flesh-and-skin fossil, 24
Flomborn (Germany), 295
Flores Island (Indonesia), 241
Flotation, 217
Fluorine dating, 31
Fluted points, 351
Foragers/collectors
    health of, 490–492
    in late glacial/early Holocene, 273–282
    model of, 273, 274
Foramen magnum, 108, 135
Foraminifera, 234
Forensic anthropology, 493–498
Fossils, 24–26
    dating of, 30–34
    from Eocene, 115–116
    from Fayum Depression, 117
    finding of, 28–30
    from Oligocene, 117–120
    from Paleocene, 114–116
    of primate events, 111–112
Founder effect, 470
Fruit flies, and evolution, 40
Fu Hao, 334
Fuente Nueva 3 (Spain), 241
FUN dating, 222
Functional analysis, of artifacts, 219
Fungi, 82
Funnel Beaker culture, 296

Galapagos Islands, 61–65
Gateway God, 403, 406
Gene(s), 19, 46, 47, 50, 51
    master color, 481
    nontaster, 67
    primate behavior and, 125–126

regulatory, 54
structural, 54
Gene flow, 60, 66, 508
Generalized animals, 107, 133
Genetic drift, 60, 66–67, 474, 508
Genetic theory of natural selection, 45
Genome, human, 52–53
Genotype, 48
Genus, 69
Geographic Information Systems (GIS), 215
Geology, 219
Geomorphology, 219
Gesher Benot Ya'aqov (Israel), 243, 244
Gibbons, 122, 425, 441–442
Gibraltar monkeys, 436–437
Gibraltar sites, 184, 190
Gibraltar skull, 28
*Gigantopithecus*, 122
Giraffe's neck, evolution of, 41–42
GIS (Geographic Information Systems), 215
Giza Plateau Mapping Project (GPMP), 321–323
Glacial periods, 233, 235
Gloger's Rule, 475
Glyphs, 393, 395
Golden Temple, or Qorikancha (Inca), 414
Gombe Stream Reserve, 445, 448, 449, 452, 453, 488
Gona (Ethiopia), 235, 236
Gondwanaland, 84
Gönnersdorf (Germany), 260
Gorillas, 443, 447, 454
Gorillidae (family of apes), 440
Government
    in Aztec empire, 411–413
    in early Egypt, 320
    in Inca empire, 415–416
    in Mesoamerica, 391
    of Shang state, 334–335
    in South America, 403, 406
GPMP (Giza Plateau Mapping Project), 321–323
Gracile australopithecines, 148–149, 155
Grade scheme
    for *Homo erectus*, 140
    for *Homo habilis*, 140, 170–171
    for *Homo sapiens*, 141
    for Neandertals, 140
Gradualism, 59–60
Gran Dolina (Spain), 180, 243–244
GRASP (Great Apes Survival Project), 455
Gravettian period, 254
Gray langur, 436
Great Basin, 360–361, 364
Great Bath (Indus), 324, 328
Great Chain of Being, 40, 41
Great Houses (Anasazi), 378
Great Mound (La Venta), 386
Great Plaza (Tikal), 395
Great Rift Valley, 139
Great Temple (Aztec), 214, 409, 412, 414
Groove and splinter technique, 255
Grotta Breuil (Italy), 247

Grotta dei Moscerini (Italy), 247
Grotta di San Agostino (Italy), 247
Grotta Guattari (Italy), 247
Ground-penetrating radar, 215
Ground survey, 214
Groundstone axes, 279
Growth, human, 487–488
Guano, 399
Guilá Naquitz Cave (Mexico), 369

Habitual bipedalism, 136
Habuba Kabira (Syria), 315
Hadar (Ethiopia), 146, 150, 152–153
Hafting, 246, 249
Hair form in humans, 480–481, 482
Hairlessness, 140
Half-life, 224
*Hallucigenia*, 87
Hamadryas baboons, 425, 437–438
Hand axes, 241–242, 243, 288, 505
Hanging/suspensory primates, 105
Hanuman langur, 436
Haplorhini, 102, 431
HapMap, 53
Harappa (Indus), 323, 324–325, 328, 332
Harappan state. *See* Indus state
Hardy-Weinberg law, 470–471
Hastinapura (India), 216
Hearths, 208
Hemudu (China), 297
Henges, 303–304
Herculaneum, 27
Heredity, 19, 39, 43–49, 57. *See also*
    Chromosomes; Gene(s)
Herto (Ethiopia), 195
Heterodont teeth, 92, 110
Heterozygous, 48
HGP (Human Genome Project), 52–53
Hidden Cave (Nevada), 364
Hierakonpolis (Egypt), 318
Hierarchical settlement pattern, 312
Hieratic writing, 319, 331
Hieroglyphic Stairway (Maya), 397
Hieroglyphics, 318, 331, 332
Historic archeologists, 7
Hitchhiker's thumb, 48
HIV (human immunodeficiency virus),
    489
H-O (horizontal-oval) mandibular fora-
    men, 186, 187, 190
Hoabinian period, 273
Hobbit. *See Homo floresiensis*
Hogup Cave (Utah), 361
Hohokam culture, 374–376
Holism, 8–10
Holocene period, 232, 235, 270–272,
    273–282, 356–360, 505
Homeotherms, 92
Hominid gang, 176–177
Hominids, 78, 124, 132–133
    anatomy of, 134, 135
    candidates for first, 124–125
    early habitats of, 137
    early society of, 235–245
    as hunter/gatherers, 164–165, 237
    species of, 141–144

taxonomy of, 140–144
    traits of, 107–108, 133–140, 169,
        502–503
Hominins, 124
Hominoids, 78, 114
    of Miocene, 120–123
    traits of, 120–122
*Homo* (genus), 103, 160, 162–165, 169
*Homo antecessor*, 171, 180
*Homo erectus*, 169–175, 176–183
    Archaic, 181–183
    cultural development of, 240–245
    in Europe, 179–180
    grade scheme for, 140
    traits of, 173–174, 194
*Homo ergaster*, 171
*Homo floresiensis*, 462, 464–467
*Homo habilis*, 140, 150–151, 160, 162–163,
    165, 169, 170–171
*Homo heidelbergensis*, 171, 179, 180
*Homo neandertalensis. See* Neandertals
*Homo rudolfensis*, 160
*Homo sapiens*, 77. *See also* Anatomically
    modern humans; Behaviorally mod-
    ern humans; Contemporary humans
    early Archaic, 181–183, 242–244
    evolution of, 77–96, 180–181
    future of, 510–512
    grade scheme for, 141
    late Archaic, 183–191
    traits of, 180–181, 194, 480–482
*Homo sapiens idaltu*, 195
*Homo sapiens sapiens*, 191
Homodont teeth, 92
Homology, principle of, 75, 76–77
Ho-Mo-Tu (China), 297
Homozygous, 48
Hopewell culture, 372–374
Horizontal-oval (H-O) mandibular fora-
    men, 186, 187, 190
Hormones, 49
Howler monkeys, 439–440
Höyük, 288, 300
Huaca de la Luna (Moche), 399, 401
Huaca del Sol (Moche), 399
Huitzilopochtli (Aztec), 412, 414
Human evolution, 3. *See also* Adaptation;
    Evolution; Natural selection
Human Genome Project (HGP), 52–53
Human immunodeficiency virus (HIV),
    489
Human molecular genetics, 35
Human sacrifice, 395–396, 400–401, 412
Human variability, 3, 473–482
Hunter-gatherers, 502, 505
    chimpanzees as, 452–453
    hominids as, 164–165, 237
    of late glacial/early Holocene, 273–282
Hybridization
    of pea plants, 43–49
    of species, 68–69
Hydroxyapatite, 28
Hylobatidae (family of apes), 440. *See also*
    Gibbons; Siamangs
Hyoid bone, 204
Hyperdexterity, 48

Hypoglossal canal, 203
Hypothesis, 16–19
Hypoxia, 486

Ice cores, 30, 33–34, 223
Ice-free corridor, 349
Ice sheets, 349, 350
Iceman, 2, 4–5, 28
Ideology, 289–290
    ancestor, 282
    of Celts, 343
    Middle Eastern, 289–290
    Olmec, 386
    South American, 406, 416
Imhotep, 321
Imprint fossils, 25, 26
Inca empire, 371, 393–394, 399, 414–418
Independent assortment, 46
Indian Knoll (Kentucky), 360
Indian rhesus macaque, 436
Indris, 432
Inductive reasoning, 18–19
Indus state, 323–328, 332
Industrial Revolution, and directional se-
    lection, 65–66
Infant care, by primates, 110
Infauna, 86
Inheritance, 19, 39, 43–49, 508. *See also*
    Heredity
Institute of Human Origins, 152
Institutional Review Boards (IRBs), 10
Intelligence, 485–486, 502–503
Intelligence quotient (IQ), 485
Intelligent design, 21
Interglacial periods, 232, 235, 270
International Afar Research Expedition,
    152
International Code of Zoological
    Nomenclature, 68
International Society of Ethicists, 10
Interstadials, 233
Intertidal zones, excavation in, 218
Inti (Inca Sun God), 416–417
Inventions, 508
IQ (intelligence quotient), 485
Iraq sites, 187
IRBs (Institutional Review Boards), 10
Irrigation, 374, 403, 404–405, 407, 408
Island rule, 466
Isotope analysis, 276, 390
Israel sites, 187

Jacal, 375
Japanese macaques, 436, 444–445
Japanese Monkey Center, 425–426
Jenné-jeno (Africa), 300, 339–341
Jericho (Jordan Valley), 288–289, 290,
    304
Jinniushan (China), 182
Jomon period (Japan), 273, 275–276, 277,
    279, 280, 281

Kabwe (Zambia), 181, 182
Kaminaljuyu (Guatemala), 390
Kanapoi (Kenya), 149
Kanzi, 450, 451, 452

K-Ar (potassium-argon) dating, 31, 145, 146, 222, 223–224, 227
Kebara Cave (Israel), 204, 247, 248, 250
Kennewick Man, 468
Keros (Inca), 394
Khufu, great pyramid of, 321
Kibale National Park (Uganda), 449, 452
King Djoser, 321
King Narmer, 318
Kingdoms of life, 82–83
Kivas, 377, 378
Klasies River Mouth (South Africa), 195
KNM-ER 1470, 162
KNM-WT 15000 (Nariokotome), 29, 30, 176–177, 476
Knowledge, 18
Knuckle walking, 105
Konso (Ehtiopia), 158
Koonalda Cave (Australia), 255
Koster (Illinois), 358
Krapina (Croatia), 187, 250
K/T mass extinction, 94–95, 96

La Brea tar pits, 25
La Piage (France), 191
La Venta (Olmec), 386, 387
Laboratory studies, 427
Labrets, 366
Lactose tolerance, 9–10
Laetoli (Africa), 150
Laetoli footprints, 25
Lake Junin Basin caves (Peru), 370
Lake Mungo (Australia), 195–196, 256, 261
Lake Turkana (Kenya), 159, 175, 176–177, 181
Lamarckian principles, 19, 41–42
Language, 202
    in bonobos, 450–451, 452
    in chimpanzees, 450–451, 452, 453
    farmers and, 292–294
    proto-Indo-European, 292–293
Langur, 436, 437
L'Anse Amour (Labrador), 359
Lantien (China), 179
Laoguantai (China), 297
Lapedo Valley (Spain), 192
Lapita ware, 256
Large apes, 442–455. See also Bonobos; Chimpanzees; Gorillas; Orangutans
Lascaux Cave (France), 264
Last common ancestor (LCA), 78, 123–124, 128, 199
Last universal common ancestor (LUCA), 81–82
Late glacial period, 272–282
Late Stone Age (LSA), 232, 235, 251–265
Laurentia, 86
Laurentide ice sheet, 349, 350
Laws of inheritance, 19
LBK (Linearbandkeramik) culture, 291–295
LCA (last common ancestor), 78, 123–124, 128, 199
Leaping primates, 105

Lemurs, 116, 123, 431, 432, 433
Les Eyzies (France), 196
Lesser apes. See Gibbons; Siamangs; Small apes
Levallois technique, 246, 505
Levant region, 274–275, 277
Liang Bua (Indonesia), 464–467
Life system, three-domain, 82
Lineage X marker, 469
Linearbandkeramik (LBK, or Linear Pottery) culture, 291–295
"Lingua franca," 292
Linguistics, 6
Linguists, 8
Little Foot, 155
Lobe-finned fish, 85, 89
Locomotion. See also Bipedalism; Brachiating; Quadrupedalism; Saltatory locomotion
    of amphibians, 90
    of mammals, 93
    of modern primates, 105–106
    of reptiles, 90
Lokalalei (Kenya), 235, 236
London Geological Society, 156
Long barrow tombs, 295–296
Longgupo (China), 179
Longhouses, 212
Looking hypothesis, 136–137
Lorises, 123, 431, 433
Lovelock Cave (Nevada), 361, 364
Lower Paleolithic, 232, 235–245
Lowland gorillas, 447
LSA. See Late Stone Age
Lucy, 150–151, 153, 162
Lucy's baby, 150, 151
Lumpers, 101, 101, 141–144, 171
Lungfenpithecus, 122

Maadi (Egypt), 318
Macaques, 436, 444–445
Machu Picchu, 417–418
Macroevolution, 77–97
    microevolution and, 78
    model of, 78, 79
    principles of reconstructing, 75–77
Madagascar, prosimians in, 432
Magdalenian period, 254
Magnetometers, 215
Majuangou (China), 240–241
Makah tribe, 212–213
Makapansgat (South Africa), 237
Malaria, 477, 478
Mammals
    evolution of, 92–96
    placental, 92, 96
    primatelike, 101, 114–116
    shrewlike, 93
Mammoths, 356
Man the Hunter, 164
Manching (Germany), 343
Manos, 357
Mantas, 413
Marine cores, 30, 33–34, 234
Marmosets, 439
Marrella, 87

Marsupial mammals, 96
Mastaba, 320
Master color genes, 481
Mastodons, 352
Matara (Eritrea), 337
Mating
    of bonobos, 456–457
    non-random, 470
Matrix, 208–209
Mauer mandible, 180
Mawaki (Japan), 275
Max Planck Institute, 189
Maximum parsimony analysis, 293
Maya culture, 391–393, 395–397
Meadowcroft Rockshelter (Pennsylvania), 352
Meat sharing, 453
Megaliths, 299, 303–304
Meiosis, 54, 55
Mellaart's shrines, 302
Memes, 508
Memphis (Egypt), 318
Mendelian inheritance, 39, 43–49
Menes, 318
Menex-Dregan (France), 244
Mesoamerica, 384–397, 400–401
Mesolithic period, 273, 276–277, 280, 281, 295–296
Mesopotamia, 312–317, 330, 332–333
Messenger RNA (mRNA), 49
Metal detectors, 215
Metalworking, 319, 320
Metates, 357
Mezhirich (Ukraine), 258–260
Mezin (Ukraine), 264
Mezmaiskaya Cave (Russia), 247
Microevolution
    in contemporary humans, 469–471
    macroevolution and, 78
Microliths, 253, 277
Midden deposits, 299
Middle East
    AMH in, 195
    archaics in, 187–191
    farming in, 288–290, 292
    Neandertals in, 187
Middle Paleolithic, 232, 235, 245–251, 252
Middle Stone Age (MSA), 232, 235, 245–251, 252
Miocene hominoids, 120–123
Missing link, 122–123, 154, 175. See also Piltdown Man
Mit'a, 399, 415
Mitmaqkuna, 415
Mitochondrial DNA, 31, 32, 199, 292
Mitosis, 54, 55
Mobiliary art, 263, 264
Moche state, 398–401
Mode 1 technology, 236
Mode 2 technology, 241
Mode 3 technology, 246
Models, 23–24
Modern synthesis, and evolution, 19, 42–59
Modern taxa, 142
"Modes of Immediate Change," 471

Mogollon groups, 376–378
Mohenjo-Daro (Indus), 324–326, 328, 332
Molecular camp, and LCA, 123–124
Molecular comparison technique, 31–32
Molecular dating, 30, 31–33, 111–112
Molecules, 49
Molodova (Ukraine), 248
Monkeys
    arboreal, 436, 439
    Callithricidae family of, 439
    Cebidae family of, 439
    Gibraltar, 436–437
    howler, 439–440
    New World, 102, 436–440
    Old World, 102, 120, 123, 436–438
    social systems of, 107
    squirrel, 439
    terrestrial, 436
    traits of, 435
    vervet, 428, 445
Monks Mound (Mississippi), 362
Monte Poggiolo (Italy), 241
Monte Verde (Chile), 352–353
*Morotopithecus*, 122
Moula-Guercy (France), 250
Mound building, 360, 362–363, 373, 375–376
Mount Vesuvius, 26, 27
MR (multiregional) model, of AMH evolution, 196–197, 197–198, 201
mRNA (messenger RNA), 49
MSA. *See* Middle Stone Age
Multiregional (MR) model, of AMH evolution, 196–197, 198–199, 201
Mumbwa Cave (Zambia), 248
Mutations, 32–33, 58–59, 60–61, 508

Nabataeans, 209
Nabke (Guatemala), 395
Nabta Playa (Egypt), 299, 304
Na-Dene Athabaskan migration, 351
NAGPRA. *See* Native American Grave Protection and Repatriation Act of 1990
Namu (Canada), 365, 366
Naqada (Egypt), 318
Nariokotome, 29, 30, 176–177, 476
Narmer palette, 318, 319
National Geographic Society, 176
National Science Foundation, 425
Native American Grave Protection and Repatriation Act of 1990 (NAGPRA), 10, 468–469
Native Americans, 462–463, 468–469, 484
Natufian period, 275, 277, 280, 281, 282
Natural History Museum (British), 156, 157
Natural selection, 19, 54–58, 61–67
Natural transformation processes, 209
Nazlet Khater 4 (Egypt), 255
Neander Valley (Germany), 184
Neanderthal Genome Project, 189
Neandertals, 145, 183–191
    demise/evolution of, 187–191, 192–193, 251–253

in Europe, 187
grade scheme for, 140
stature of, 471–472
subsistence strategies of, 247–248
traits of, 184, 185–186
Nekton, 86
Neolithic period, 273, 282–288, 290–295, 302
Neolithic Revolution, 283
Nevado Ampato (Peru), 417
"New Physical Anthropology," 3
New World monkeys, 102, 436–440
New World tradition, 23
Niah cave (Borneo), 195
Nile River, 317
Nitrogen isotopes, 276
Nocturnal activity patterns, 106
Nonhuman primates, 422. *See also* Contemporary nonhuman primates
Non-random mating, 470
Nontaster gene, and genetic drift, 67
North America, peopling of, 349–356
Northwest Coast groups, 364–367
Nose shape, of humans, 477
Notochords, 84

Observer effect, 71, 444
Obsidian hydration dating, 226, 227
Ochre, 249, 250, 257, 356, 505
Ockham's razor, 23
Ohalo II (Israel), 258
OIS (Oxygen Isotope Stages), 33
Old World monkeys, 102, 120, 123, 436–438
Old World tradition, 23
Oldowan technology, 232, 236
Olduvai Gorge (Kenya), 29, 146, 153, 158, 160, 175, 236, 237, 240, 244–245
Olduvai picks, 176
Oligocene anthropoids, 117–120
*Oligopithecus*, 118
Olmec societies, 384–387
Omo (Ethiopia), 29, 146, 152, 195
Omomyids, 116
OOA-2 (Out of Africa–2), 197
Open area excavation, 217
Oppida, 341, 342–343
Optically stimulated luminescence (OSL), 31, 225, 227
Optimal foraging theory, 274
Oracle bones, 332, 334, 335
Orangutans, 122, 123, 442–443, 454
    cooperation among, 428
    culture of, 444–446
    violence among, 441
*Oreopithecus bamboli*, 122
*Origin of Species, The*, 58
*Orrorin tugenensis*, 125
OSL (optically stimulated luminescence), 31, 225, 227
Osteodontokeratic tool kit, 161, 237
Ötzi. *See* Iceman
Out of Africa–2 (OOA-2) model, 197
Overpopulation, 472–473
Oxygen isotope analysis, 24

Oxygen Isotope Stages (OIS), 33
Ozette Village (Washington), 211, 212–213, 365

Pacific islands, human occupation of, 256–257
Pakefield (England) 241
Paleoanthropologists, 8
Paleoanthropology, 7, 23
Paleocene primatelike mammals, 114–116
Paleoindian groups, 351–352
Paleolithic
    Lower, 232, 235–245
    Middle, 232, 235, 245–251, 252
    tools of, 239
    Upper, 232, 235, 251–265, 351
Paleomagnetism, 31, 234
Paleospecies, and ESC, 71
Palmigrade animals, 120
Palynologists, 219
Pampa Grande (Peru), 371, 399–400
*Pan paniscus*. *See* Bonobos
*Pan troglodytes*. *See* Chimpanzees
Pangea, 84, 90
Panidae (family of apes), 440. *See also* Bonobos; Chimpanzees
*Papio papio*, 68
*Papio papio hamadryas*, 437–438
Paradigms, 23–24
*Paranthropus*, 145, 158
*Paranthropus aethiopicus*, 145
Parietal art, 263, 264–265
Pastoralism, 298–300, 416
    in Africa, 298–300
    in Inca empire, 416
Paul Mason (Canada), 366
Paviland Cave (Wales), 264
Pavlov (Czech Republic), 264
Pea plants, traits of, 43–49
Peiligang (China), 297
Pengtoushan (China), 296
Peppered moth, and directional selection, 65–66
Permafrost, 233
Permian extinction, 91
Persian jird, 250
Petra (Jordan), 209
Petralona (Greece), 182
Petrographic analysis, 286
Petrosal bulla, 108
Phenetics, 141, 142
Phenotype, 48
Phenylthiocarbamide (PTC), 48
Phyla, 84
Phyletic gradualism, 59–60
Physical anthropologists. *See* Biological anthropologists
Phytoliths, 296, 302, 370
Pictographic writing, 330, 331
*Pikaia*, 84
Pikillaqta (Peru), 407–408
Piltdown Man, 154, 156–157
Pincevent (France), 254–255, 258
Pit dwellings, 377
Pit of Bones (Atapuerca, Spain), 183, 245

*Pithecanthropus erectus*, 154. *See also* Homo erectus
Placental mammals, 92, 96
Plankton, 86
Plants
  evolution of major types of, 97
  first, 82, 83
Platyrrhini, 102, 436–440
Playas, 299
Plaza des Armas, 414
Pleistocene, 235–245, 354
*Plesiadapis*, 114–115
Pliocene hominoids, 140
Pochteca (Aztec), 411, 412
Pollen analysis, 219, 220, 272, 285, 370
Pomo Indians, 368
Pompeii (Italy), 27, 211, 212
Pongids (Pongidae), 124, 134, 135, 440
*Pongo pygmaeus. See* Orangutans
Population genetics, 470–471
Portuguese Kid, 190–191, 192–193
Postdepositional effects, 30
Postorbital bars, 108, 109
Postorbital constriction, 147
Postorbital septum, 108, 109
Postprocessual archaeology, 221
Potassium-argon (K-Ar) dating, 31, 145, 146, 222, 223–224, 227
Pottery making, 279–280, 285, 286–287
Poverty Point (Louisiana), 359
Pre-Clovis artifacts, 463
Prehistory, 3, 7
Prepared core technique. *See* Levallois technique
Preservation, in archaeology, 210–213
Priest king, of Indus state, 328
Primate cows. *See* Lowland gorillas
Primate stem group, 114–115
Primatelike mammals, 101, 114–116
*Primates*, 424, 425
Primates, 107–108, 422. *See also*
    Contemporary nonhuman primates;
    Nonhuman primates
  activity patterns of, 106
  angiosperms and, 101
  behavior of, 125–128, 444–446
  cladogram of, 423
  diet of, 106, 110
  distribution of, 104–105
  endangered, 455
  evolution of, 110–122, 123–128
  locomotion of, 105–106, 108, 110, 133, 441
  social systems of, 106–107
  taxonomy of, 101–103, 427
  traits of, 108–110
Primatology, 423–424
  history of, 425–426
  Japanese vs. Western, 21–22
*Principles of Geology*, 54
Processual archaeology, 221
*Proconsul*, 121–122
Prokaryotes, 82
*Propithecus verreauxi*, 432, 433–435
Prosimians, 102, 116, 123, 431–433

Protein synthesis, 49, 50
Protists, 82
Proto-Indo-European language, 292–293
Provenience (or provenance), 29–30, 209
PTC (phenylthiocarbamide), 48
Pueblo Bonito (New Mexico), 378
Pueblos, 377
Pumapunku (Bolivia), 402
Punctuated equilibrium, 59–60
Puppets, 328
Pyramids, 320–323

Qafzeh (Israel), 195, 250
Qollqa (Inca), 416
Qorikancha, or Golden Temple (Inca), 414
Quadrupedalism, 105, 108, 134–135
Quetzal feathers, 387
Quinoa, 370
Quipu system (Inca), 311, 393–394, 408, 414
Quipumayocs, 393–394
Quirigua (Honduras), 397

Race(s), 3, 6, 480–481, 482–486
Racemization, amino acid, 31, 226, 227
Racism, 485–486
Radar mapping, 215
Rafting, 435
Raised fields, 374, 403, 404–405, 407, 408
Ranked societies, 366
RAO model. *See* Recent African origin (RAO) model
Rapid gradualism, 60
Ray-finned fish, 85
Reasoning, 18–19
Rebus principle, 330, 331
Recent African origin (RAO) model, of AMH evolution, 197–198, 199–200, 201
Recessiveness, 45, 46, 49
Reconstruction, comparative method of, 126–127, 422
Red apes. *See* Orangutans
Red Land (Egypt), 317
Red Palace (Olmec), 385
Reed stylus, 330
Regulatory genes, 54
Relative dating, 222
Religion and ritual
  in Aksum state, 338
  as approach to questions, 19–21
  in Archaic communities, 359–360, 366–367
  in Aztec empire, 412, 414
  cultural anthropologists on, 20
  in early Egypt, 320
  in Inca empire, 416–417
  in Indus state, 327–328
  in Mesoamerica, 389–390, 400–401
  in South America, 403, 406
  in Upper Paleolithic/LSA, 262–263
Remote sensing techniques, 214–215
Replacement model, 197
Reproductive differential, 56
Reptiles, 90–92, 93

Research design, for excavation, 215
Retromolar space, 186, 190
Rhine Valley sites (Germany), 295
Rhodesian Man, 181, 182
Ribonucleic acid (RNA), 50, 51
Rift Valley (Africa), 146, 236
Ringkloster (Scandinavia), 280
Ritual. *See* Religion and ritual
Ritual calendar (Maya), 392
RNA (ribonucleic acid), 50, 51
Road system
  in Chaco Canyon, 378–379
  in Inca empire, 415
  in Wari state, 407–408
Robust australopithecines, 148–149
Roc-de-Combe (France), 191
Rocky Mountains, 87
Rosetta Stone, 332

Sahel region (Africa), 300
*Sahelanthropus tchadensis*, 124–125, 139, 146
Saint-Germaine-la-Rivière (France), 263
Saltation, 59–60
Saltatory locomotion, 431
San Andrés (Mexico), 369
San Lorenzo (Mexico), 385–386, 387
San Marcos Cave (Mexico), 369
Saqqara (Egypt), 321
Saqsawaman fortress, 414
Sargon of Akkad, 313, 314
Sarsen stones, 304
Satellite imagery, 215
*Scala Naturae*, 41, 483
"Scandal in Bohemia, A," 18
Scandinavia, farming in, 295–296
Scent marking, 433, 434, 435
Schöningen (Germany), 243, 244
Schwetzinger (Germany), 295
Science, 16
  as approach to questions, 19–21
  bias in, 21–24
Scientific laws, 19
Scientific method, the (TSM), 16–19
Scribes, in Old World, 332–333
Segregation, principle of, 46, 47
Selection, directional, 61–66
Selection, natural, 19, 54–58, 61–67
Self-recognition, 428
Senescence, 487
Seriation, 287
Sex
  bonobos and, 456–457
  chimpanzees and, 456
Sex cells, mutations in, 60–61
Sexual dimorphism, 147
Sexual selection, 57
Shamans, 263
Shang state (China), 328–329, 332, 334–335
Shangshan (China), 296
Shanidar (Iraq), 187, 250
Shell middens, 270
Shell preservation, 84
Shelltown and Hind (Arizona), 376

Shrewlike mammals, 93
Siamangs, 122, 441, 442
Sickle-cell anemia, 477, 478
Sifakas, 432, 433–435
Sign language, 451
Sima de los Huesos (Atapuerca, Spain), 183, 245
*Sinanthropus pekinensis*, 178
Sipán (Peru), 400, 401
Sites
    excavating of, 215–217
    finding of, 28–34, 214–215
    maps of, 231, 269, 308–309, 347, 383
*Sivapithecus*, 122
Skateholm (Sweden), 281, 282
Skeletization, 84
Skhul (Israel), 195, 250
Skin color, 474–475
Slip, in pottery, 286
Small apes, 441–442. *See also* Gibbons; Siamangs
Smell, sense of, 109
Smoke Imix (Maya), 397
Snaketown (Arizona), 376
Social gossip function, 204
Social stratification, 366, 411. *See also* Social system(s)
Social system(s), 504–505
    of Aksum state, 337–339
    of Aztec empire, 411
    of Chacoans/Anasazi, 379
    of chimpanzees, 448–449
    of early hominids, 235–245, 504–505
    farming communities and, 300–304
    of Indus state, 327
    of Jenné-jeno, 340, 341
    in late glacial/early Holocene, 281–282, 505
    of Mesopotamia, 316–317
    of modern primates, 106–107
    Olmec, 384–387
Solar calendar (Maya), 392
Solutrean period, 254
South America
    early states in, 398–408
    peopling of, 349–356
Southern California, 367–369
Spears, 243, 244, 255, 505
Specialized animals, 107
Speciation, 70–71
Species, 68–71
Speech, 9, 202
    evolution of, 202–204
    as human trait, 502, 506
    in Upper Paleolithic/LSA, 251
Spirit Cave (Nevada), 469
Spitalfields (England), 498
Splitters, 101, 141–144, 171
Splitting, 66, 70–71
Spy skull, 156
Squirrel monkeys, 439
Stabilizing selection, 65
Stadials, 233
State(s), 310–312
    early Egyptian, 317–323

in East and West Africa, 336–340
Indus, 323–328, 332
Mesopotamian, 312–317, 330, 332–333
Shang, 328–336
systems model of, 311–312
trade among, 311
Stature variability, of humans, 477–478, 481
Stay-at-home effect, 470
Steinheim (Gemany), 182, 183
Stelae, 311, 337, 338, 395, 402
Stem group, primate, 114–115
Sterkfontein (South Africa), 154–155, 237
Stillwater Marsh (Nevada), 364
Stone Age. *See* Early Stone Age; Late Stone Age; Middle Stone Age
Stone tools, 235, 238–239
    of Clovis groups, 353, 356
    of Eastern Woodlands Archaic, 357
    in Lower Paleolithic/ESA, 239, 241–242
    in Mesoamerica, 386
    in Middle Paleolithic/MSA, 246–247
    in Old World Neolithic societies, 285, 288
    in Upper Paleolithic/LSA, 253–255
Stonehenge, 9, 282, 303–304
Stratigraphy, 216, 222, 227
Street of the Dead, 387
Strepsirhini, 102, 431
Strollers, 86
Stromatolites, 81, 82
Strontium analysis, 295
Strontium isotopes, 276
Structural genes, 54
Structures
    in Hohokam culture, 375
    in late glacial/early Holocene, 280–281, 376–377
    in Lower Paleolithic/ESA, 244–245
    in Middle Paleolithic/MSA, 248
    in Old World Neolithic, 288–289, 302
    in Upper Paleolithic/LSA, 258–260
Stylistic analysis, of artifacts, 219
Suaq swamp (Sumatra), 443
Subsurface survey techniques, 215
Sumer (Mesopotamia), 312, 330
Super-lumpers, 171
Suprainiac fossa, 190
Survey, archaeological, 214
Swamp orangutans, 442, 443
Swanscombe (England), 182
Swartkrans Cave (South Africa), 158, 161, 236, 240, 244
Sweating, of hominids, 138
Sweet potato washing, 444–445
Sweet Track (England), 288
Symbolic speech, 204
Symbolism, 505–506
    in late glacial/early Holocene, 281
    in Lower Paleolithic/ESA, 245
    in Middle Paleolithic/MSA, 249–251
    in Neolithic period, 301–304
    in Upper Paleolithic/LSA, 260–263, 264–265
Symphereal retreat, 192

*Symphylangus. See* Siamangs
Synthetic theory of evolution, 19
Systems model, of states, 311–312

Tabun (Israel), 250
Taï forest, 445, 452
Taima Taima (Venezuela), 352
Talheim (Germany), 295
Tamarins, 439
*Tampu* (Inca), 415
Taphonomy, 161, 236–237
Taramsa Hill (Egypt), 246
Tarsiers, 102, 116
    contemporary, 429–431
    Eocene omomyids and, 116
Tasmania, human occupation of, 256–257
Tassili n'Ajjer (Algeria), 298
Taster allele, 48
Taung (South Africa), 154, 155, 161, 240
Taurodont teeth, 185
Tawantinsuyu. *See* Inca empire
Taxonomy, 41
    of hominids, 140–144
    of primates, 101–103, 427
Technology. *See also* Bone(s), tools made of; Stone tools; Tools
    of Archaic communities, 367
    bronze, 335
    irrigation, 374, 407, 408
    in late glacial/early Holocene, 277–279
    Levallois, 246, 505
    in Mesoamerica, 390, 400
    metalworking, 319, 320
    Oldowan, 176, 232, 236
    in South America, 403, 407
Teeth
    bilophodont, 117, 120, 435
    heterodont, 92, 110
    of hominids, 140
    homodont, 92
    of pongids, 140
    taurodont, 185
Tehuacan caves (Mexico), 370
Tell, 288
Tell es-Sultan (Jordan Valley), 288
Temper, in pottery, 286
Tenotchtitlan (Aztec), 391, 393, 409–410
*Teosinte*, 370
Tepe, 288
Termiting, 449
Terra Amata (France), 244, 245
Terracing, 407, 408, 416
Terrestrial, 107
Terrestrial bipedalism, 105, 106, 108, 124
Terrestrial quadrupedalism, 105, 108
Teshik-Tash (Uzbekistan), 250
Test pits, 217
Tetrapods, 89
Textile production, Neolithic, 302
Theory, 19
Therapsids, 93
Thermoluminescence (TL), 31, 225, 227, 287
Thompson's Rule, 477
Tikal (Guatemala), 395–396

Tiwanaku state, 402–406, 408
TL (thermoluminescence), 31, 225, 227, 287
Tlaloc (Aztec), 412
Tlanecuilo (Aztec), 411
Tlatelolco market (Aztec), 411
Tolland Man (Denmark), 29, 210
Tools, 136, 137, 235–243, 502, 505. *See also* Bone(s), tools made of; Stone tools
Torcs, 342
Trade, 311
    in Aksum state, 337
    in Archaic communities, 358–359, 373–374, 376, 379
    in Aztec empire, 411
    in early Egypt, 318–320
    in Fertile Crescent, 290
    in Indus state, 327
    in Jenné-jeno, 340
    language for, 292
    in Mesoamerica, 386, 390–391
    in Mesopotamian states, 313, 315
    in Shang state, 335
    in South America, 406
Traits. *See also specific traits*
    ancestral vs. derived, 75–77
    body build, 475–476
    of bones of males/females, 497, 498
    co-variation of, 480–482
    of contemporary prosimians, 431–433
    dominant and recessive, 45
    of Eocene primates, 115–116
    of hominids, 107–108, 133–140, 169, 502–503
    of hominoids, 120–122
    of *Homo erectus*, 173–174, 194
    of *Homo sapiens*, 180–181, 194, 480–482
    of Neandertals, 184, 185–186
    of Oligocene anthropoids, 117
    of LCA, 128
    of primate stem group, 114–115

variable, in humans, 474–479
Transformism, 70
Trenches, in archaeology, 217
Trilobites, 84, 86
Trinil (Java), 175_176
Troy (Turkey), 214
True fossil, 25
*T'se* (books), 332
TSM (the scientific method), 16–19
Tuberculosis, 489
Tuff, 396
Turkana Boy. *See* Nariokotome
Turner Farm (Maine), 357
Twin Rivers (Zambia), 246
Typological sequencing, 222

Ubaid period, 312–313
Ubeidiya (Israel), 240
Umm el Tlel (Syria), 246
Uniformitarianism, 42
United Nations' Great Apes Survival Project (GRASP), 455
Upper Paleolithic, 232, 235, 251–265, 351
Ur (Mesopotamia), 315
Ur III dynasty, 314, 316
Uranium (U-series) dating, 31, 178
Uruk period, 312
Uruk-Warka (Mesopotamia), 313–314, 330
U-series (uranium) dating, 31, 178

Variable traits, 474–479
Venus figurines, 17–18, 263, 264
Vértesszöllös (Hungary), 244
Vervet monkeys, 428, 445
*Victoriapithecus*, 117
Viking settlements (Newfoundland), 214
Vilas Ruivas (Portugal), 248
Vindija (Croatia), 190, 191, 193, 250
Violence, 400–401, 488
Visier, 318
Vision, primate, 108
Vix (France), 342

Vocal grooming function, 204
Vogelherd (Germany), 190

Wadi Kubbaniya (Egypt), 258
Wadjak (Java), 195
Wakamba tribe, 176
Warehouses, in Inca state, 416
Wari state, 407–408
Watson-Crick model of DNA, 51
Wattle and daub, 375
Wernicke's area, 203
Wet sieving, 217
Willendorf (Austria), 18
Windmill Hill (England), 303
Windover (Florida), 210, 358
Wiraqocha (Inca Creator God), 416
Woodhenges, 362
World Conservation Unit, 512
Writing
    in early states, 318, 330–333, 340, 341
    hieratic, 319, 331
    in Mesoamerica and South America, 393–394
    Old World, 332–333
    pictographic, 330, 331

Yeha (Ethiopia), 336
Yiftah'el (Israel), 211
Younger Dryas, 270, 282

Zambia sites, 181, 182
Zebra finch, and sexual selection, 57
Zhengzhou (China), 329
Zhoukoudian (China), 195, 242–243, 469
Ziggurat of Ur (Mesopotamia), 314, 315
*Zinjanthropus boisei*, 158
Zoo studies, 425, 426–427
Zooarchaeologists, 219
Zygomatic arch, 108

# Credits

p. v, Sygma/Corbis; p. vi, Robert Frerck/Odyssey Productions; p. vii, Tui De Roy/Minden Pictures; p. viii, Robin Smith/Photolibrary.com; p. ix, Stephen J. Krasemann/Photo Researchers; p. x, The Natural History Museum, London; p. xi, Courtesy of Paris Paulakis; p. xii, Norah Moloney; p. xiii, AP Wide World Photos; p. xiv, Erich Lessing/Art Resource, N.Y.; p. xv, Barney Burstein/Corbis; p. xvi, Courtesy of the Granger Collection; p. xvii, Dannielle Hayes/Omni-Photo Communications; p. xviii, Norbert Wu/Minden Pictures; p. xix, Elaine Thompson/AP Wide World Photos; p. xx, Reuters/Corbis; p. 1, Sygma/Corbis; p. 4, Sygma/Corbis; p. 15, Robert Frerck/Odyssey Productions; p. 18, Danita Delimont Photography/Ancient Art & Architecture; p. 26 (top left), Scott Nielsen/Bruce Coleman, Inc.; p. 26 (top right) Lynton Gardiner/Dorling Kindersley Media Library; p. 26 (bottom left), Sean Sexton Collection/Corbis; p. 26 (bottom right) Explorer/Photo Researchers; p. 27 (top and bottom right), Courtesy of Peter Connolly/AKG Images; p. 29, Chris Lisle/Corbis; p. 30, Courtesy of Alan Walker; p. 34 (left), British Antarctic Survey/Science Photo Library/Photo Researchers; p. 34 (right), D. A. Peel/Photo Researchers; p. 36 (bottom left), Danita Delimont Photography/Ancient Art & Architecture; p. 36 (top right), Courtesy of Alan Walker; p. 38, Tui De Roy/Minden Pictures; p. 62 (top), Frans Lanting/Minden Pictures; p. 62 (middle), Tui De Roy/Minden Pictures; p. 62 (bottom), Rob Reichenfeld/Dorling Kindersley Media Library; p. 63 (left), Heather Angel/Natural Visions; p. 63 (right), Heather Angel/Natural Visions; p. 64, Patricia Rice; p. 65, Michael Tweedie/Photo Researchers; p. 69 (left), Hans Thomashoff/Das Fotoarchiv/Peter Arnold; p. 69 (right), Frans Lanting/Minden Pictures; p. 72, Patricia Rice; p. 74, Robin Smith/Photolibrary.com; p. 81, Robin Smith/Photolibrary.com; p. 94, Dr. Robert Spicer/Photo Researchers; p. 100, Stephen J. Krasemann/Photo Researchers; p. 116, Harry Taylor/Dorling Kindersley Media Library; p. 121, Harry Taylor/Dorling Kindersley Media Library; p. 129, Harry Taylor/Dorling Kindersley Media Library; p. 131, The Natural History Museum, London; p. 151, The Natural History Museum, London; p. 157, Popperfoto/Petrofile.com; p. 159, Pat Shipman/Alan Walker/National Museums of Kenya; p. 161, Philippe Plailly/Eurelios Photographic Press Agency; p. 163, David L. Brill Photography; p. 168, Courtesy of Paris Pavlakis; p. 182, Courtesy of Paris Pavlakis; p. 183, Mauncio Anton/Madrid Scientific Films; p. 205, Mauncio Anton/Madrid Scientific Films; p. 207, Norah Moloney; p. 209, Norah Moloney; p. 210, Chris Lisle/Corbis; p. 211, Roger Ressmeyer/Corbis; p. 213, Richard Schlecht/National Geographic Image Collection; p. 228, Norah Moloney; p. 230: AP Wide World Photos; p. 240, John Reader/Photo Researchers; p. 242, Norah Moloney; p. 243, Courtesy of Simon Parfitt/Institute of Archaeology, London; p. 244, Kenneth Garrett/Kenneth Garrett Photography; p. 246, Norah Moloney; p. 249, Centre for Development Studies; p. 260, Kenneth Garrett/Kenneth Garrett Photography; p. 265, AP Wide World Photos; p. 266 (left), John Reader/Photo Researchers; p. 266 (middle right) Centre for Development Studies; p. 268, Erich Lessing/Art Resource, N.Y.; p. 277, Norah Moloney; p. 279, Norah Moloney; p. 287, Norah Moloney; p. 288, Courtesy of Stuart Laidlaw; p. 289, Prof. Nasser D. Khalili; p. 298, Erich Lessing/Art Resource, N.Y.; p. 304, Lawrence Migdale/Photo Researchers; p. 305, Prof. Nasser D. Khalili; p. 307, Barney Burstein/Corbis; p. 313, Gianni Dagli Orti/Bettmann/Corbis; p. 314, The British Museum Images; p. 321, Marilyn Bridges; p. 324, Paulo Koch/Photo Researchers; p. 333, Richard Swiecki/Royal Ontario Museum/Corbis; p. 335, Barney Burstein/Corbis; p. 344 (top left), Gianni Dagli Orti/Bettmann/Corbis; p. 344 (right), Richard Swiecki/Royal Ontario Museum/Corbis; p. 346, Courtesy of the Granger Collection; p. 353, Helga Teiwes/University of Arizona, Arizona State Museum; p. 358, Photograph by Del Baston/Center for American Archaeology; p. 359, Richard A. Cooke/Corbis; p. 361, L. L. Loud/Phoebe Hearst Museum of Anthropology; p. 365, Special Collections/University of Washington Libraries; p. 368, Edward S. Curtis/Library of Congress; p. 370, Norah Moloney; p. 371, Courtesy of the Granger Collection; p. 373, Werner Forman Archive/Art Resource, N.Y.; p. 375 (left), George H. H. Huey/George H. H. Huey Photography; p. 375 (right), The Cleveland Museum of Natural History; p. 376, Richard A. Cooke/Corbis; p. 378, David Hiser/David Hiser Photography; p. 380 (left), Helga Teiwes/University of Arizona; p. 380 (right), Richard A. Cooke/Corbis; p. 382, Dannielle Hayes/Omni-Photo Communications; p. 385, Patricia Rice; p. 389, Dannielle Hayes/Omni-Photo Communications; p. 394, The Granger Collection; p. 396, Courtesy of Dr. Elizabeth Graham, Institute of Archaeology, London; p. 397, Frederick Catherwood/The Beinecke Rare Book and Manuscript Library; p. 403, Courtesy of Dr. William Sillar, Institute of Archaeology, London; p. 415, Norah Moloney; p. 416, Courtesy of Stuart Laidlaw, Institute of Archaeology, London; p. 417, Courtesy of Stuart Laidlaw, Institute of Archaeology, London; p. 419 (top left), Patricia Rice; p. 419 (bottom right), Courtesy of Stuart Laidlaw, Institute of Archaeology, London; p. 421, Norbert Wu/Minden Pictures; p. 426, Peter Veit/DRK Photo; p. 430, Frans Lanting/Minden Pictures; p. 433 (left), Frans Lanting/Minden Pictures; p. 433 (right), Art Wolfe/Stone Allstock/Getty Images; p. 437 (left), National Geographic Image Collection; p. 437 (right), Stephen J. Krasemann/Photo Researchers; p. 439 (top), Michael & Patricia Fogden/Minden Pictures; p. 439 (bottom), Norbert Wu/Minden Pictures; p. 441, Frans Lanting/Minden Pictures; p. 450, Michael K. Nichols/National Geographic Image Collection; p. 454 (top left), B. G. Thomson/Photo Researchers; p. 454 (top right), George Holtman/Photo Researchers; p. 454 (bottom left), National Geographic Image Collection; p. 454 (bottom right), Connie Bransilver/Photo Researchers; p. 458 (left), Frans Lanting/Minden Pictures; p. 458 (right), National Geographic Image Collection; p. 460, Elaine Thompson/AP Wide World Photos; p. 465, Stringer/Indonesia/Reuters/Corbis; p. 466, Dr. Peter Brown; p. 468, Elaine Thompson/AP Wide World Photos; p. 496, Courtesy of Richard P. Helmer; p. 499, Courtesy of Richard P. Helmer; p. 501, Reuters/Corbis.